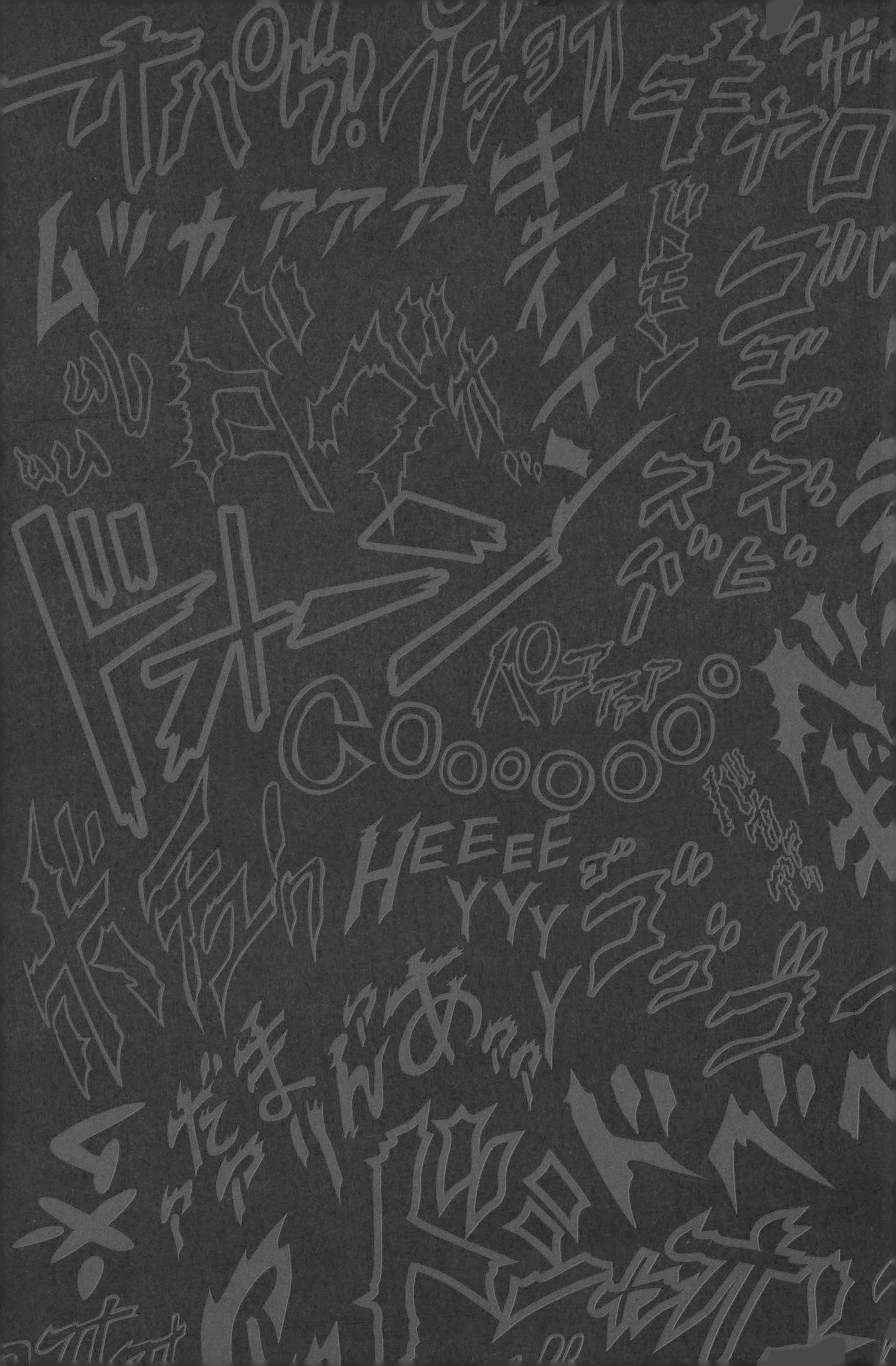
GOOOOOOOO
HEEEEYYYY

THIS IS THE LAST PAGE

ドドド

JoJo's Bizarre Adventure
has been printed in the original Japanese format in order to preserve the orientation of the original artwork.

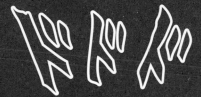

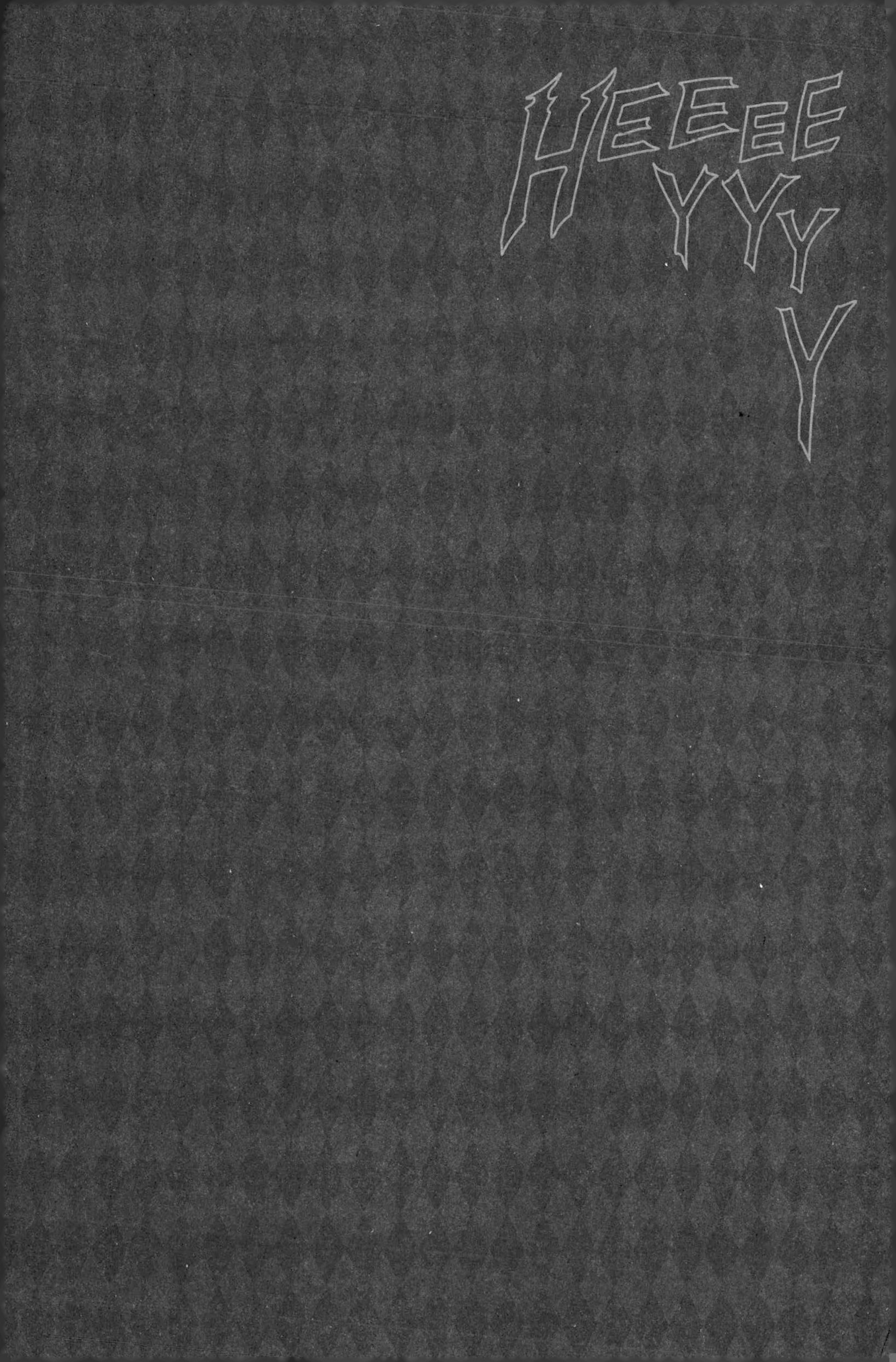
HEEEEYYYY

Jo

01

JoJo's BIZARRE ADVENTURE

PART 2 BATTLE TENDENCY

BY

HIROHIKO ARAKI

Translation ☆ Evan Galloway
Touch-Up Art & Lettering ☆ Mark McMurray
Design ☆ Fawn Lau
Editor ☆ Urian Brown

Original Japanese cover design by
MITSURU KOBAYASHI (GENI A LÒIDE)

Printed in the U.S.A.

Published by VIZ Media, LLC
P.O. Box 77010
San Francisco, CA 94107

10 9 8 7 6 5 4 3 2
First printing, November 2015
Second printing, November 2016

RATED T+ FOR OLDER TEEN ratings.viz.com

PARENTAL ADVISORY
JOJO'S BIZARRE ADVENTURE PART TWO BATTLE TENDENCY
is rated T+ for Older Teen and is recommended for ages 16 and up.
This volume contains graphic violence and some mature themes.

VIZ media
www.viz.com

SHONEN JUMP ADVANCED
www.shonenjump.com

Jo
Joseph

Joseph Joestar was the one who took up the torch from the original JoJo, Jonathan Joestar, to become the main character of the second generation. Looking back on it, it seems that a lot of fans feel as if the two of them look rather identical. The thing is, when this was originally being serialized, it was unprecedented to have a main character die in a *Weekly Shonen Jump* story. "The manga has the same title, but it now has a different main character"–it was difficult to think of a way to overcome the reader's perception that it had turned into an entirely different manga altogether! That's why I decided to keep Joseph's appearance the same as Jonathan's but change his personality. Now that the series is up to Part 8, though, I wish I had differentiated the appearances of the protagonists of Parts 1 and 2 a bit more (laughs).

As I mentioned when discussing Jonathan, Dio is the black to Jonathan's white--rather passive and perhaps a bit uninteresting as a main character. Joseph, on the other hand, is easier to perceive as being proactive, and I felt like that worked. As I wrote Joseph's tale, it was more as if he was in control of how the story progressed, so I think he ended up being more of an "adventurer," if you will. In comparison to the gentlemanly Jonathan, Joseph is constantly looking to win in confrontations or games and will do insane things without hesitation. In more crude terms, he has the personality of a swindler. This isn't only to create a contrast between him and Jonathan, but also because I wanted the focus to shift from the physical battles of Part 1 to more cerebral confrontations.

Back then, as an extension of my other work, *Cool Shock B.T.*, I wanted to make Joseph a *shonen* manga character that bends the rules as he fights. Essentially, have him use the playbook of a swindler to win using cunning and logic. I also didn't want him to be the type of character who wins with bravery and perseverance, so it was easier to flesh out his personality with lines like "Your next line is…" where he ends up reading the actions of his opponent ahead of time. To put it simply, Joseph is more of a muscle-bound B.T. I put some Stallone into B.T. and added some cheerfulness for good measure to make him more of a jolly fellow.

Joseph is the character that connects the Joestar bloodline to Parts 3 and 4. I made Jonathan die for the storyline in Part 1, but I didn't even consider killing off Joseph. If I had known JoJo would go on until Part 8, I think I might have changed his visual design a little bit.

The story behind the new illustration for JoJo Part 2 01!

Q. Why does Joseph have a hat and goggles?

A. To help differentiate him from Jonathan.

Part 2 takes place when airplanes were first becoming prevalent.
That's why I gave him a pilot's hat with goggles--sort of a steampunk or biker look.

Hirohiko Araki

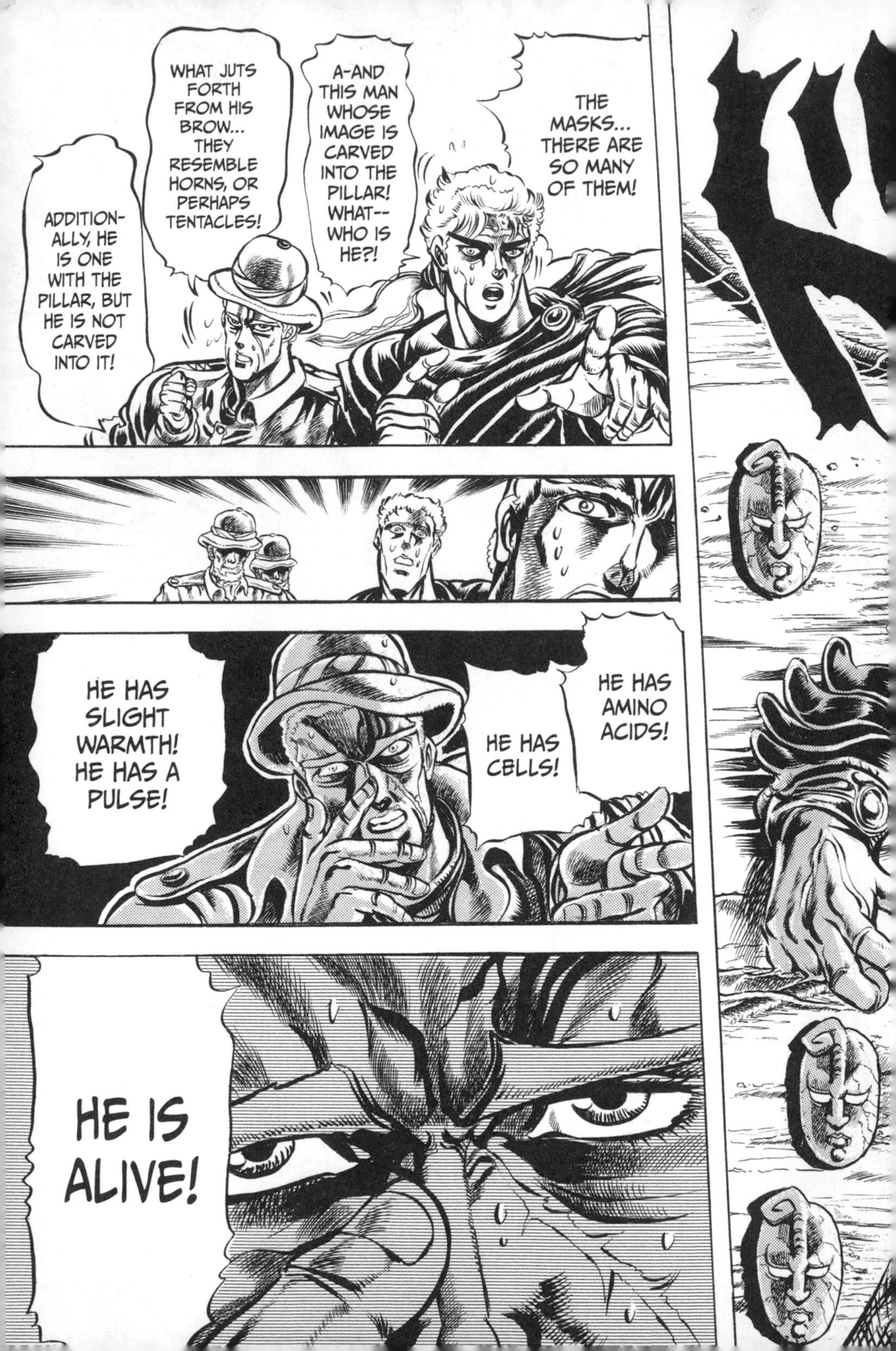
THE MASKS... THERE ARE SO MANY OF THEM!
A-AND THIS MAN WHOSE IMAGE IS CARVED INTO THE PILLAR! WHAT-- WHO IS HE?!
WHAT JUTS FORTH FROM HIS BROW... THEY RESEMBLE HORNS, OR PERHAPS TENTACLES!
ADDITION-ALLY, HE IS ONE WITH THE PILLAR, BUT HE IS NOT CARVED INTO IT!
HE HAS AMINO ACIDS!
HE HAS CELLS!
HE HAS SLIGHT WARMTH! HE HAS A PULSE!
HE IS ALIVE!

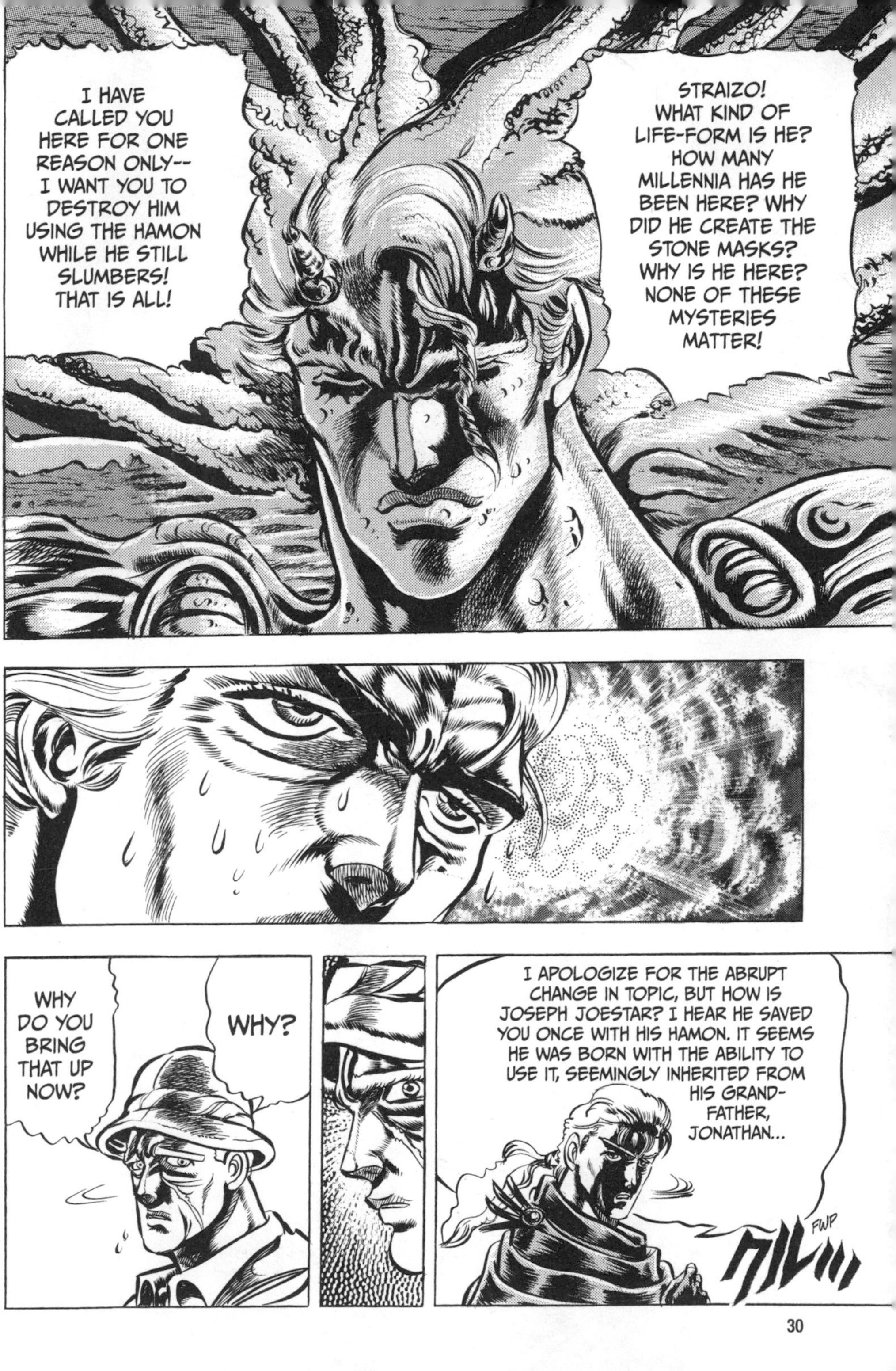
STRAIZO! WHAT KIND OF LIFE-FORM IS HE? HOW MANY MILLENNIA HAS HE BEEN HERE? WHY DID HE CREATE THE STONE MASKS? WHY IS HE HERE? NONE OF THESE MYSTERIES MATTER!
I HAVE CALLED YOU HERE FOR ONE REASON ONLY-- I WANT YOU TO DESTROY HIM USING THE HAMON WHILE HE STILL SLUMBERS! THAT IS ALL!
I APOLOGIZE FOR THE ABRUPT CHANGE IN TOPIC, BUT HOW IS JOSEPH JOESTAR? I HEAR HE SAVED YOU ONCE WITH HIS HAMON. IT SEEMS HE WAS BORN WITH THE ABILITY TO USE IT, SEEMINGLY INHERITED FROM HIS GRAND-FATHER, JONATHAN...
FWP
WHY?
WHY DO YOU BRING THAT UP NOW?

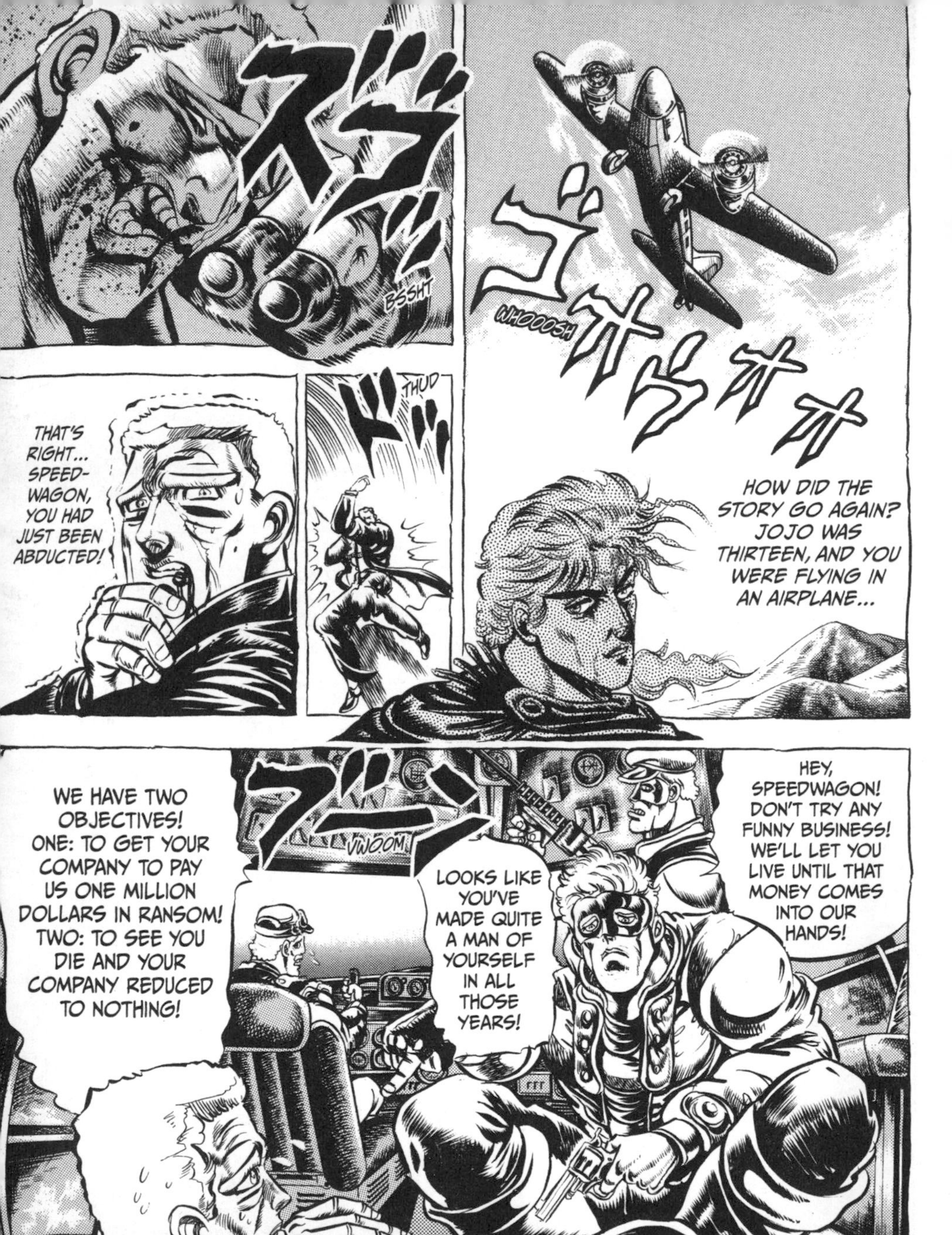
WHOOOSH
HOW DID THE STORY GO AGAIN? JOJO WAS THIRTEEN, AND YOU WERE FLYING IN AN AIRPLANE...
BSSHT
THUD
THAT'S RIGHT... SPEED-WAGON, YOU HAD JUST BEEN ABDUCTED!
VWOOM
HEY, SPEEDWAGON! DON'T TRY ANY FUNNY BUSINESS! WE'LL LET YOU LIVE UNTIL THAT MONEY COMES INTO OUR HANDS!
LOOKS LIKE YOU'VE MADE QUITE A MAN OF YOURSELF IN ALL THOSE YEARS!
WE HAVE TWO OBJECTIVES! ONE: TO GET YOUR COMPANY TO PAY US ONE MILLION DOLLARS IN RANSOM! TWO: TO SEE YOU DIE AND YOUR COMPANY REDUCED TO NOTHING!

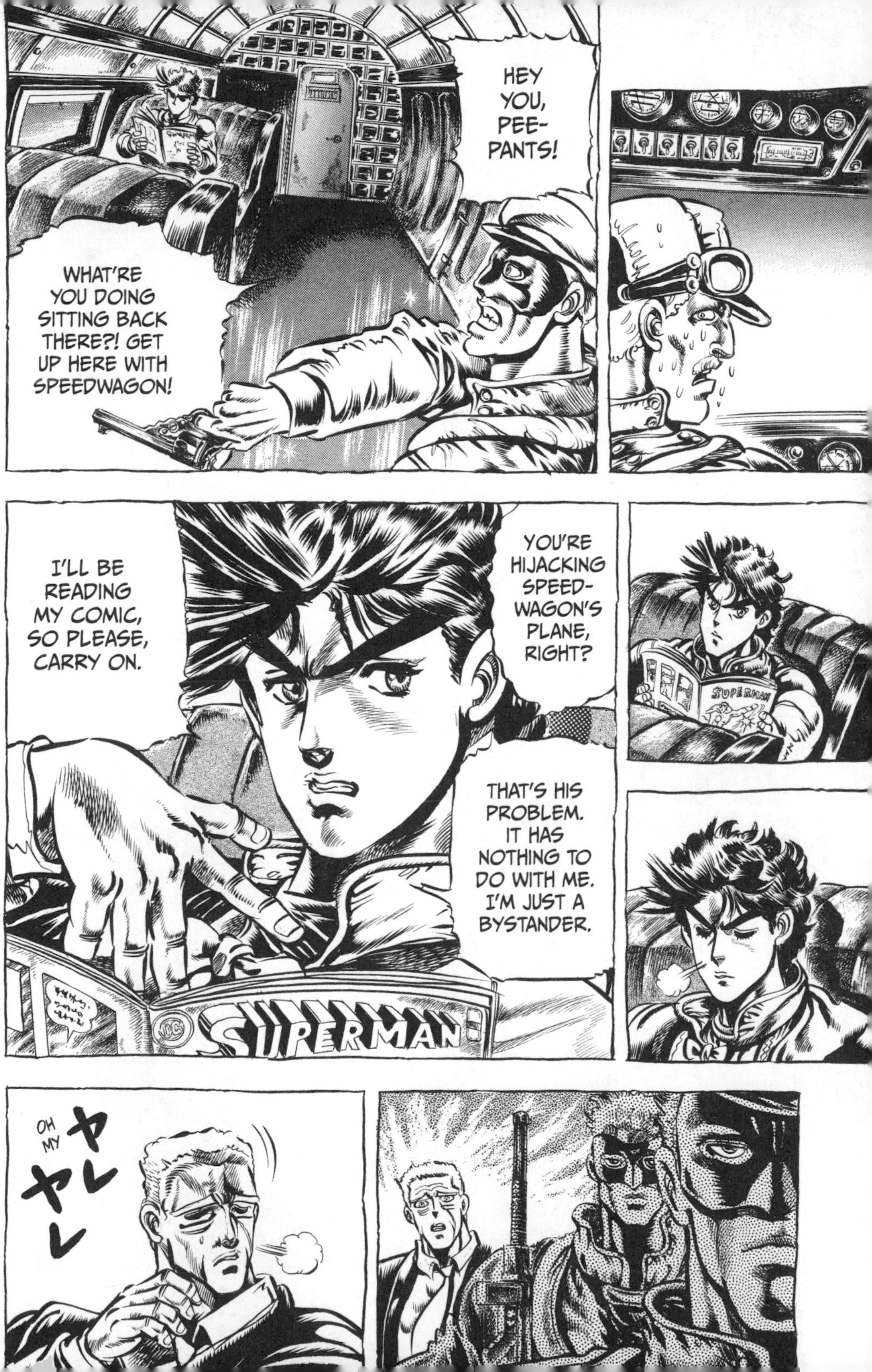
HEY YOU, PEE-PANTS!
WHAT'RE YOU DOING SITTING BACK THERE?! GET UP HERE WITH SPEEDWAGON!
YOU'RE HIJACKING SPEED-WAGON'S PLANE, RIGHT?
THAT'S HIS PROBLEM. IT HAS NOTHING TO DO WITH ME. I'M JUST A BYSTANDER.
I'LL BE READING MY COMIC, SO PLEASE, CARRY ON.
SUPERMAN
OH MY
ヤレヤレ

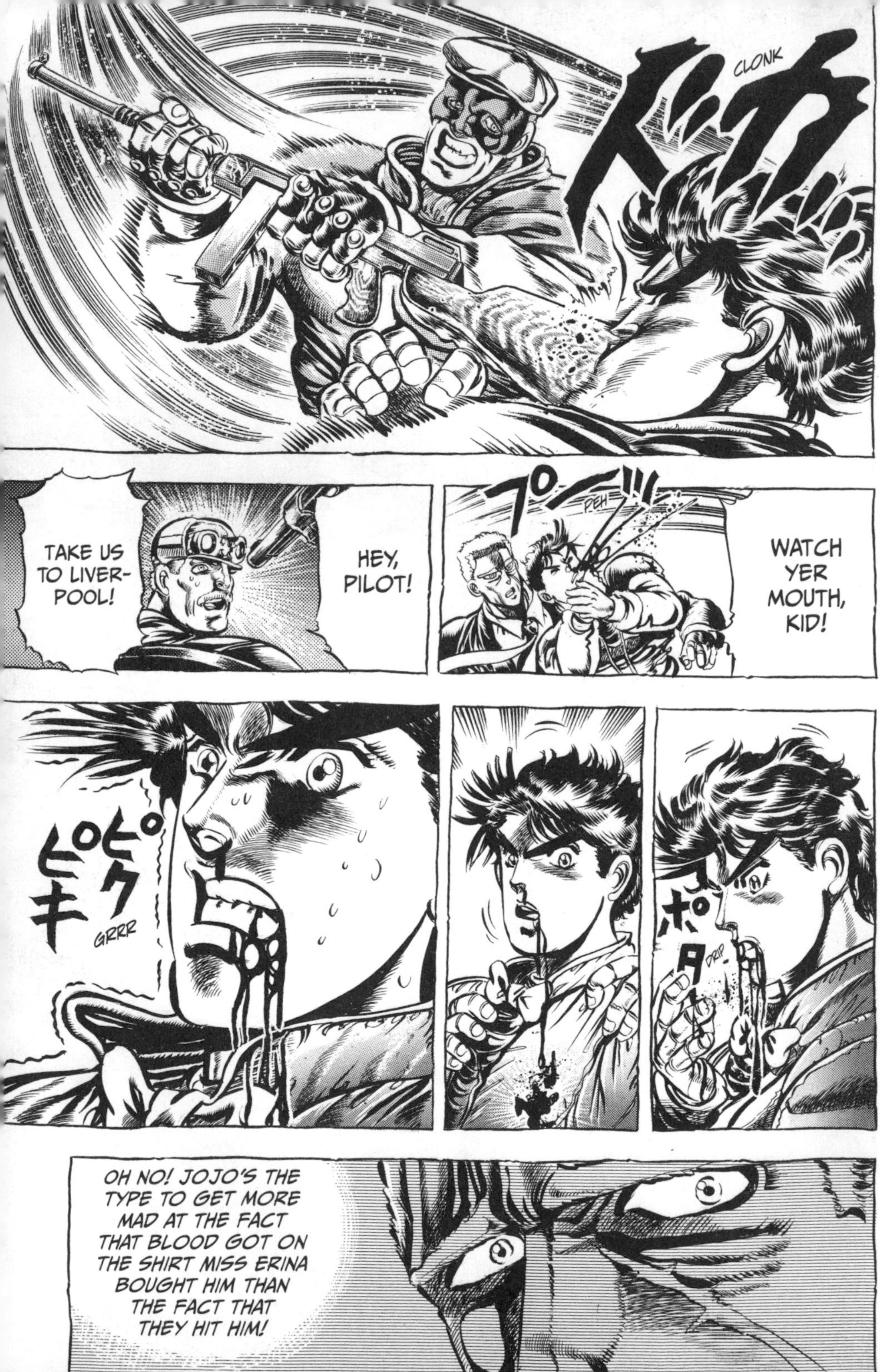

ドカ
CLONK
プー
PEH
WATCH YER MOUTH, KID!
HEY, PILOT!
TAKE US TO LIVER-POOL!
ポタ
DRIP
ピクピキ
GRRR
OH NO! JOJO'S THE TYPE TO GET MORE MAD AT THE FACT THAT BLOOD GOT ON THE SHIRT MISS ERINA BOUGHT HIM THAN THE FACT THAT THEY HIT HIM!

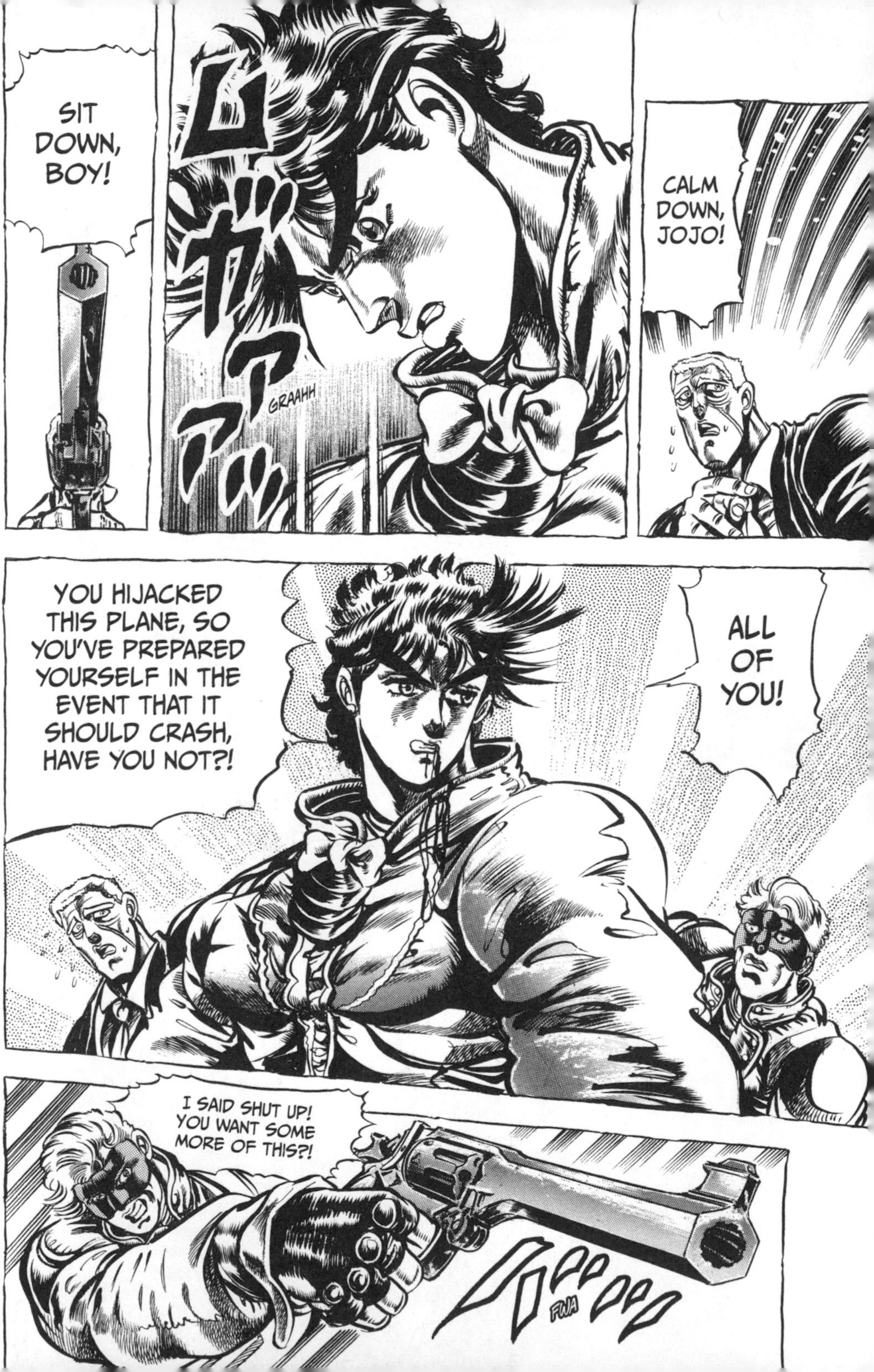
CALM DOWN, JOJO!
GRAAHH
SIT DOWN, BOY!
ALL OF YOU!
YOU HIJACKED THIS PLANE, SO YOU'VE PREPARED YOURSELF IN THE EVENT THAT IT SHOULD CRASH, HAVE YOU NOT?!
I SAID SHUT UP! YOU WANT SOME MORE OF THIS?!
FWA

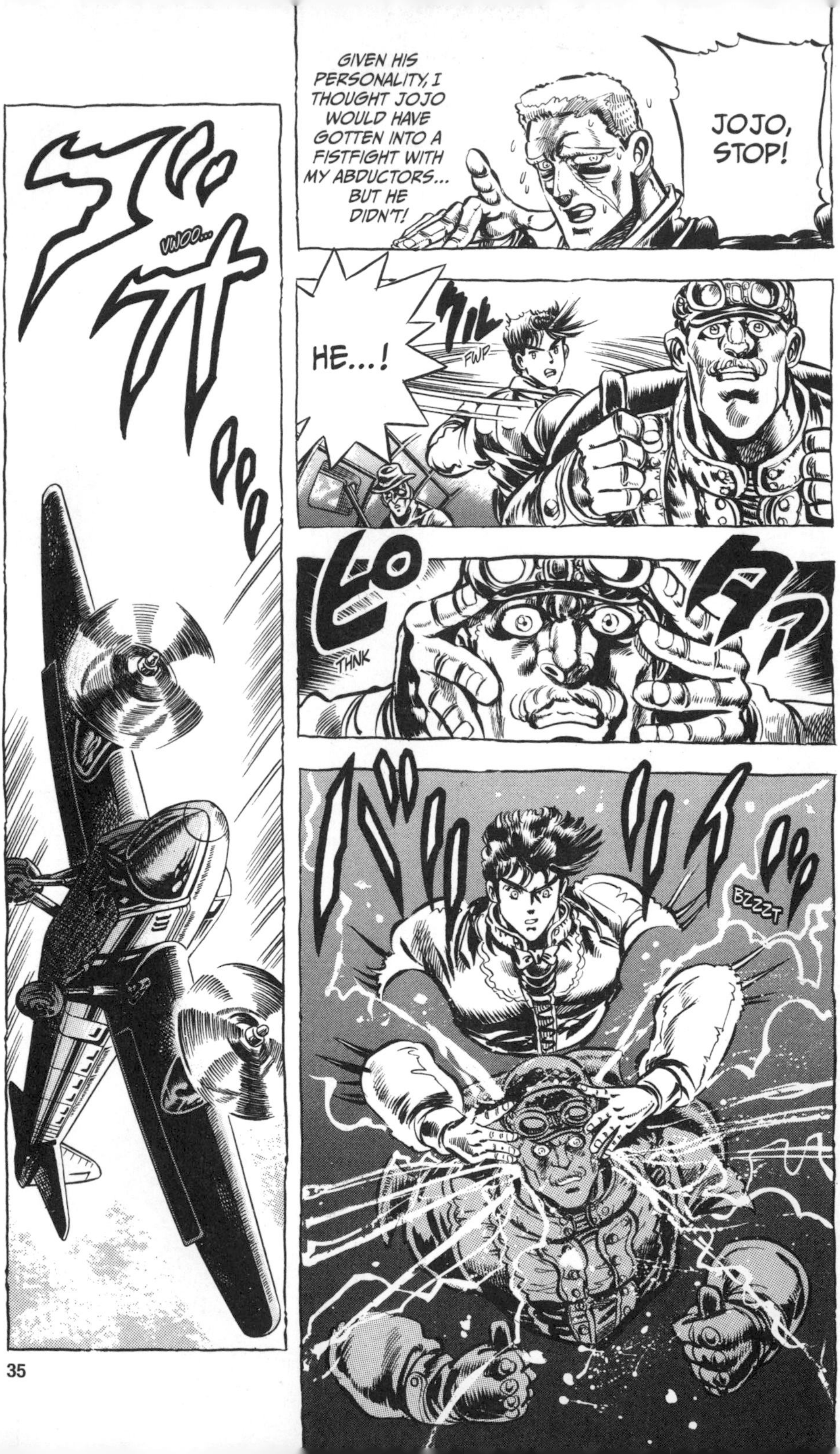
JOJO, STOP!
GIVEN HIS PERSONALITY, I THOUGHT JOJO WOULD HAVE GOTTEN INTO A FISTFIGHT WITH MY ABDUCTORS... BUT HE DIDN'T!
HE...!
FWP
THNK
BZZZT
VWOO...

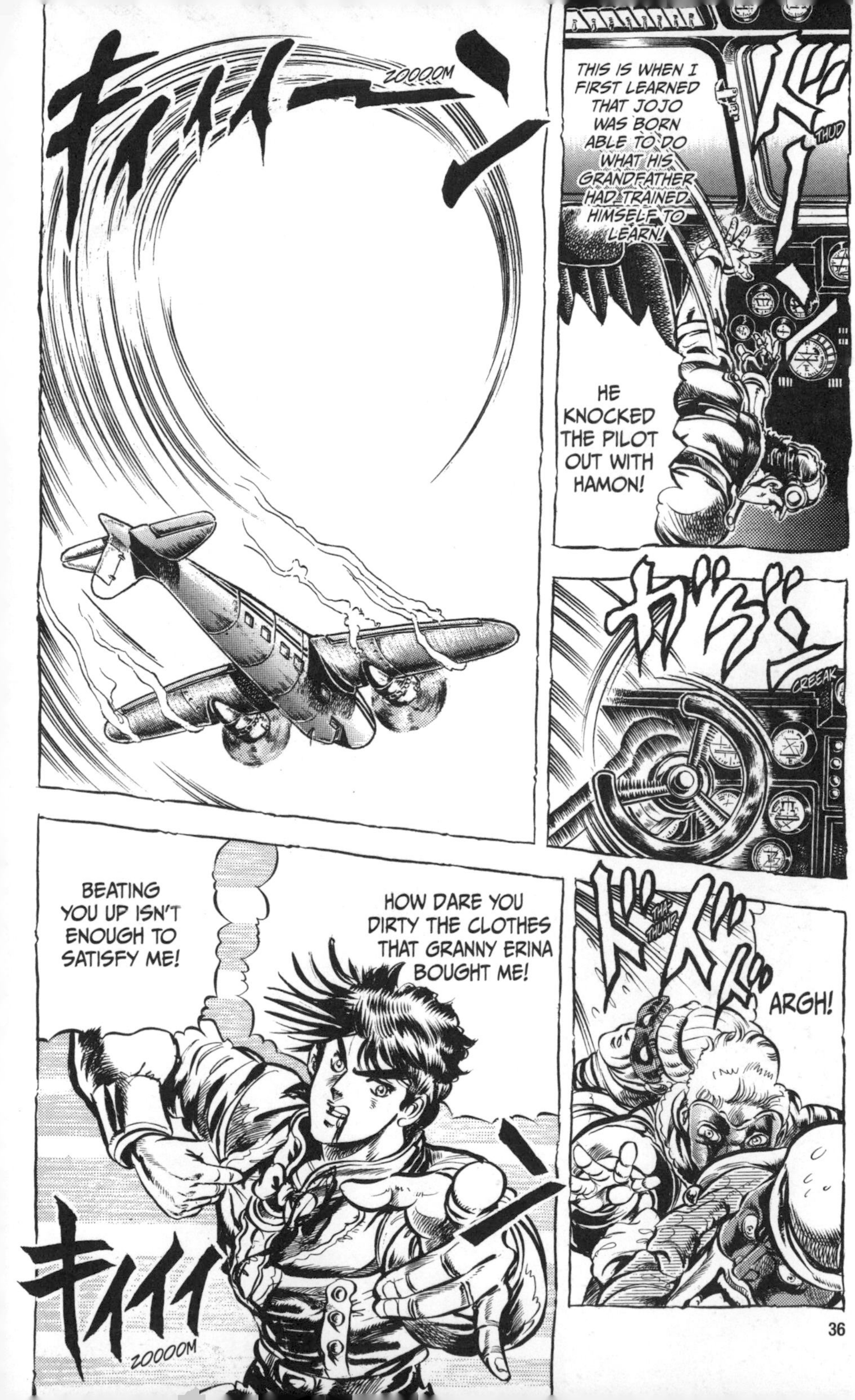

THUD
THIS IS WHEN I FIRST LEARNED THAT JOJO WAS BORN ABLE TO DO WHAT HIS GRANDFATHER HAD TRAINED HIMSELF TO LEARN!
HE KNOCKED THE PILOT OUT WITH HAMON!
CREEAK
キィィーン
ZOOOOM
THA-THUMP
ARGH!
HOW DARE YOU DIRTY THE CLOTHES THAT GRANNY ERINA BOUGHT ME!
BEATING YOU UP ISN'T ENOUGH TO SATISFY ME!
キィィ
ZOOOOM

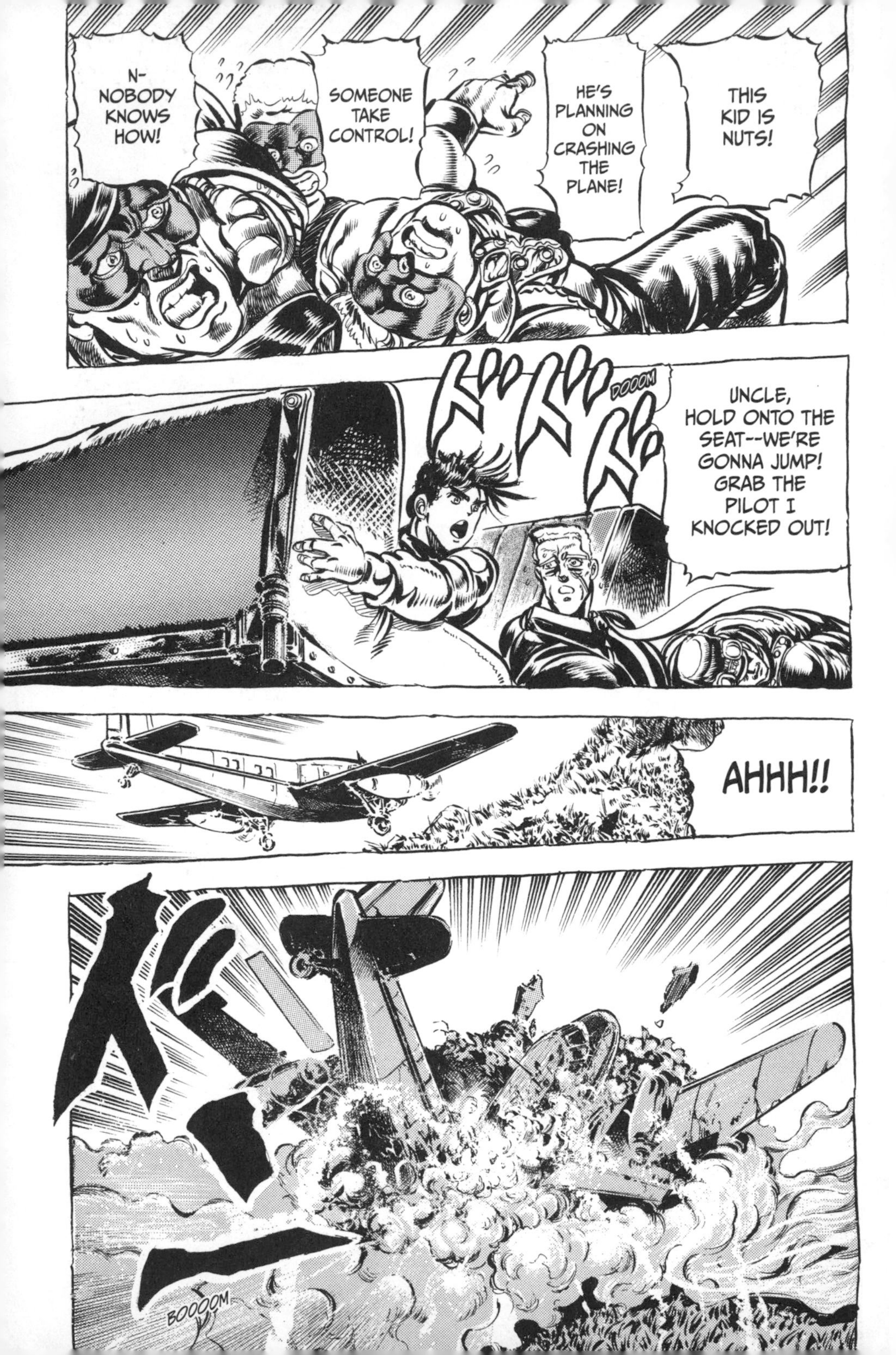
THIS KID IS NUTS!
HE'S PLANNING ON CRASHING THE PLANE!
SOMEONE TAKE CONTROL!
N- NOBODY KNOWS HOW!
UNCLE, HOLD ONTO THE SEAT--WE'RE GONNA JUMP! GRAB THE PILOT I KNOCKED OUT!
DOOOM
AHHH!!
BOOOOM

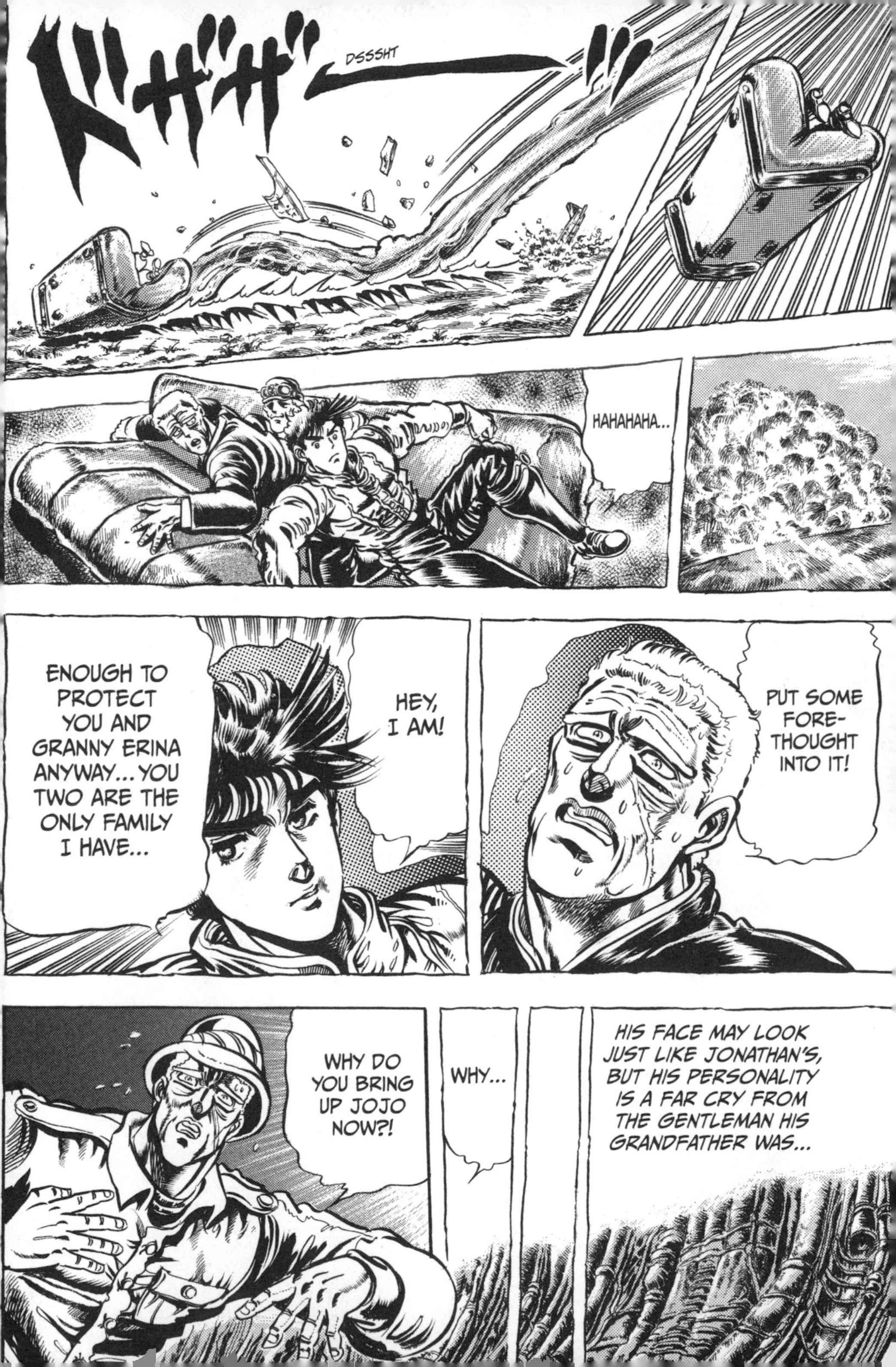
DSSSHT
HAHAHAHA...
PUT SOME FORE-THOUGHT INTO IT!
HEY, I AM!
ENOUGH TO PROTECT YOU AND GRANNY ERINA ANYWAY... YOU TWO ARE THE ONLY FAMILY I HAVE...
HIS FACE MAY LOOK JUST LIKE JONATHAN'S, BUT HIS PERSONALITY IS A FAR CRY FROM THE GENTLEMAN HIS GRANDFATHER WAS...
WHY...
WHY DO YOU BRING UP JOJO NOW?!

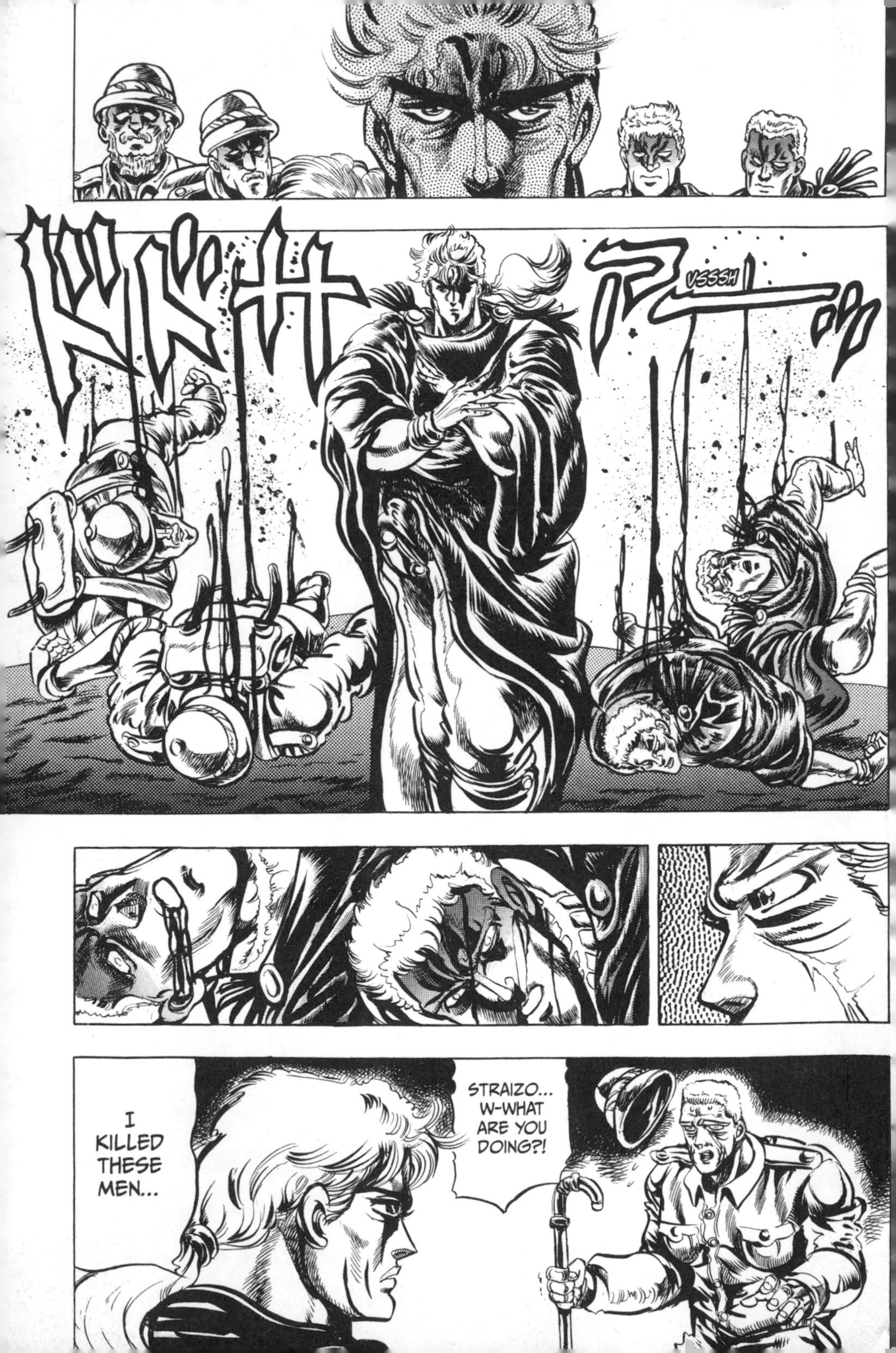
VSSSH
STRAIZO... W-WHAT ARE YOU DOING?!
I KILLED THESE MEN...

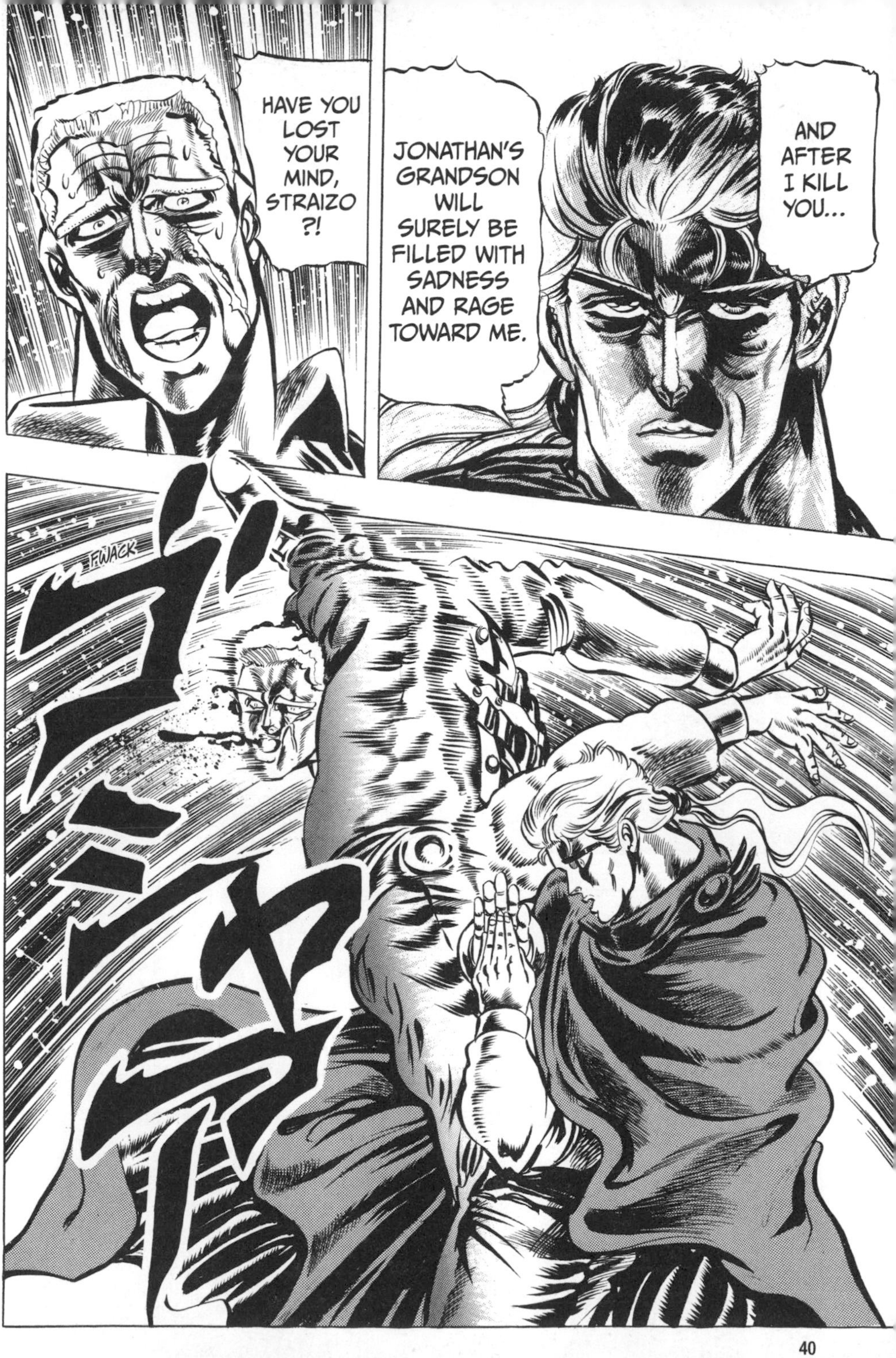
AND AFTER I KILL YOU...
JONATHAN'S GRANDSON WILL SURELY BE FILLED WITH SADNESS AND RAGE TOWARD ME.
HAVE YOU LOST YOUR MIND, STRAIZO?!
FWACK

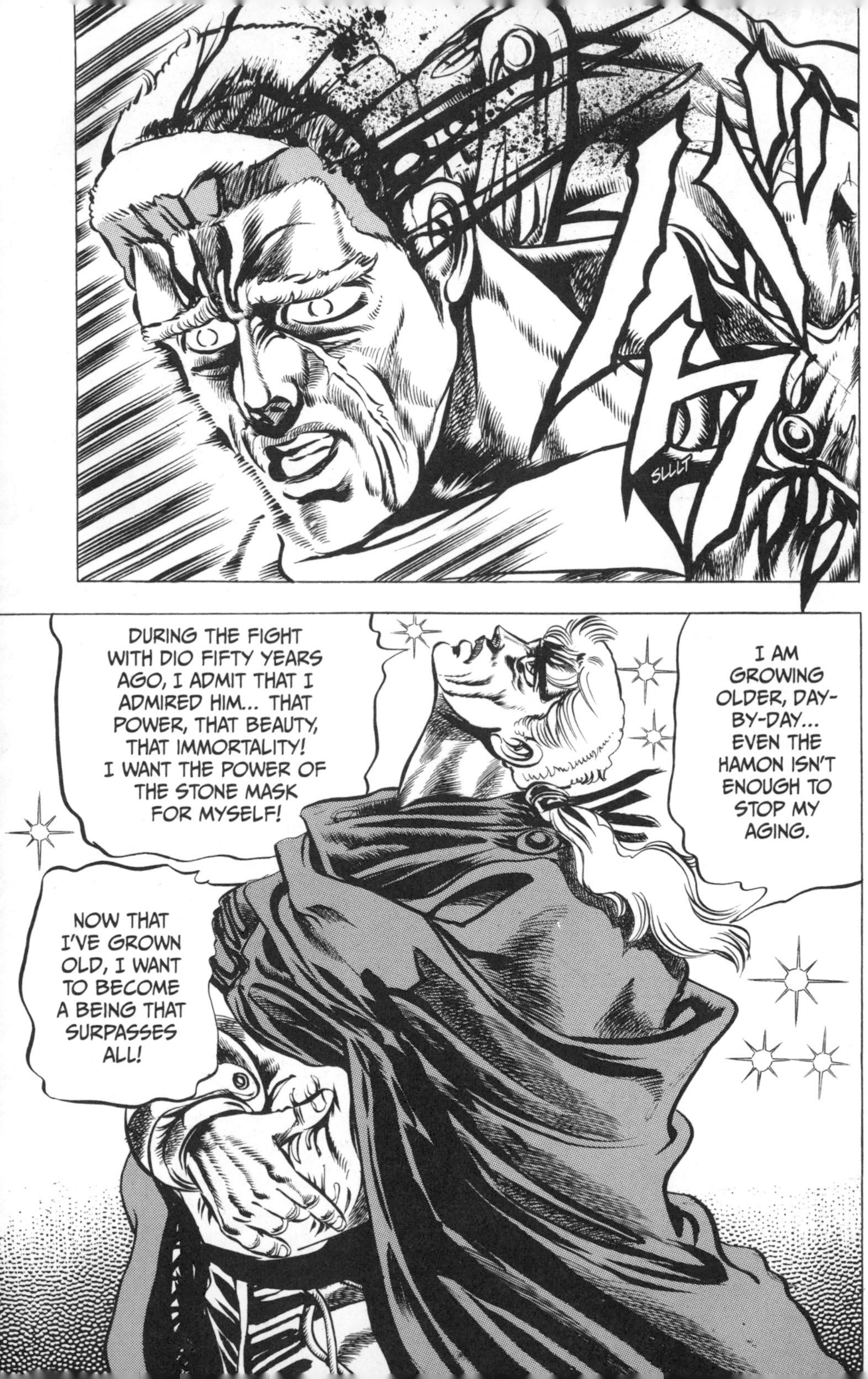
SLLLT
I AM GROWING OLDER, DAY-BY-DAY... EVEN THE HAMON ISN'T ENOUGH TO STOP MY AGING.
DURING THE FIGHT WITH DIO FIFTY YEARS AGO, I ADMIT THAT I ADMIRED HIM... THAT POWER, THAT BEAUTY, THAT IMMORTALITY! I WANT THE POWER OF THE STONE MASK FOR MYSELF!
NOW THAT I'VE GROWN OLD, I WANT TO BECOME A BEING THAT SURPASSES ALL!

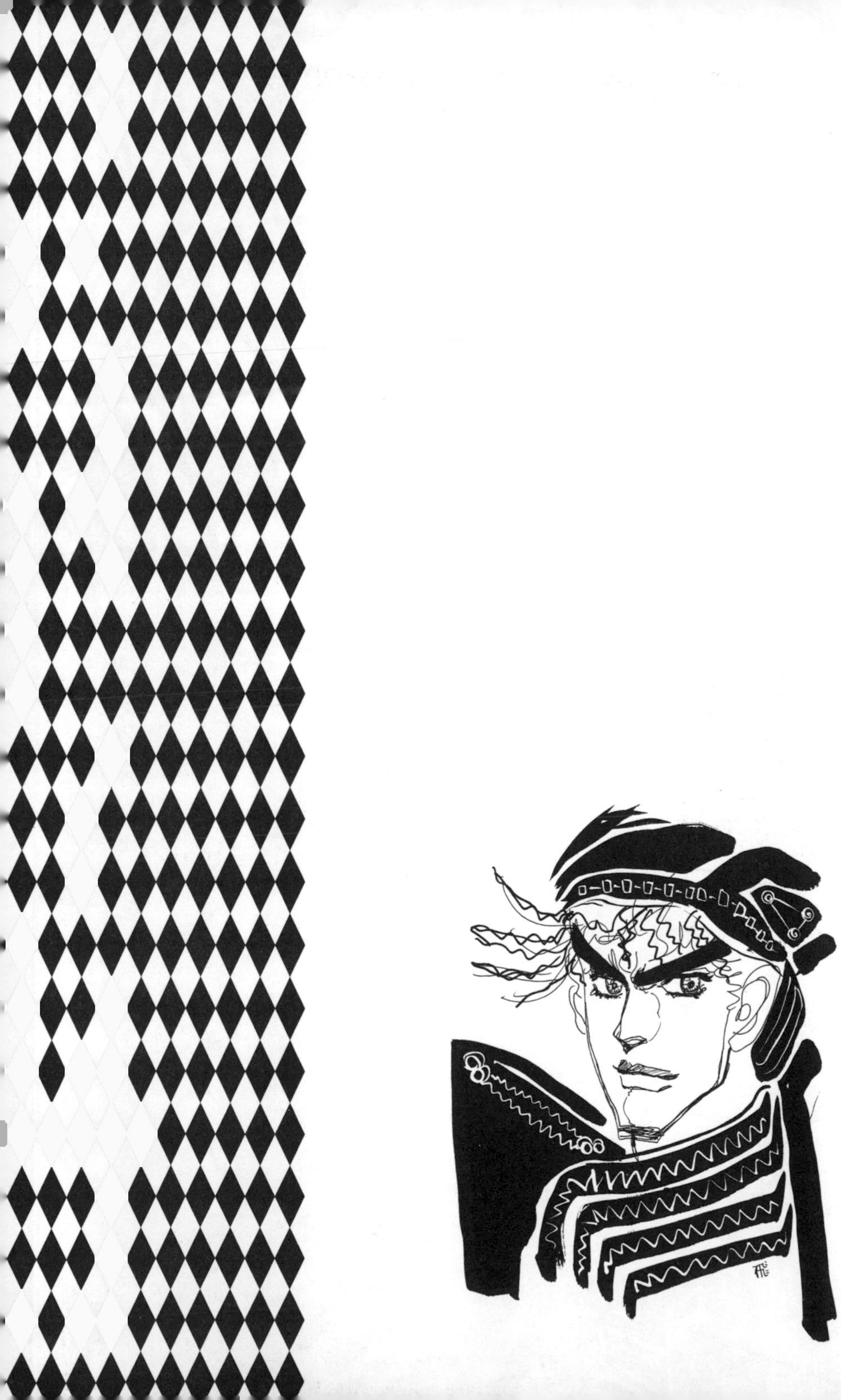

CHAPTER 3: Joseph Joestar of New York PART 3

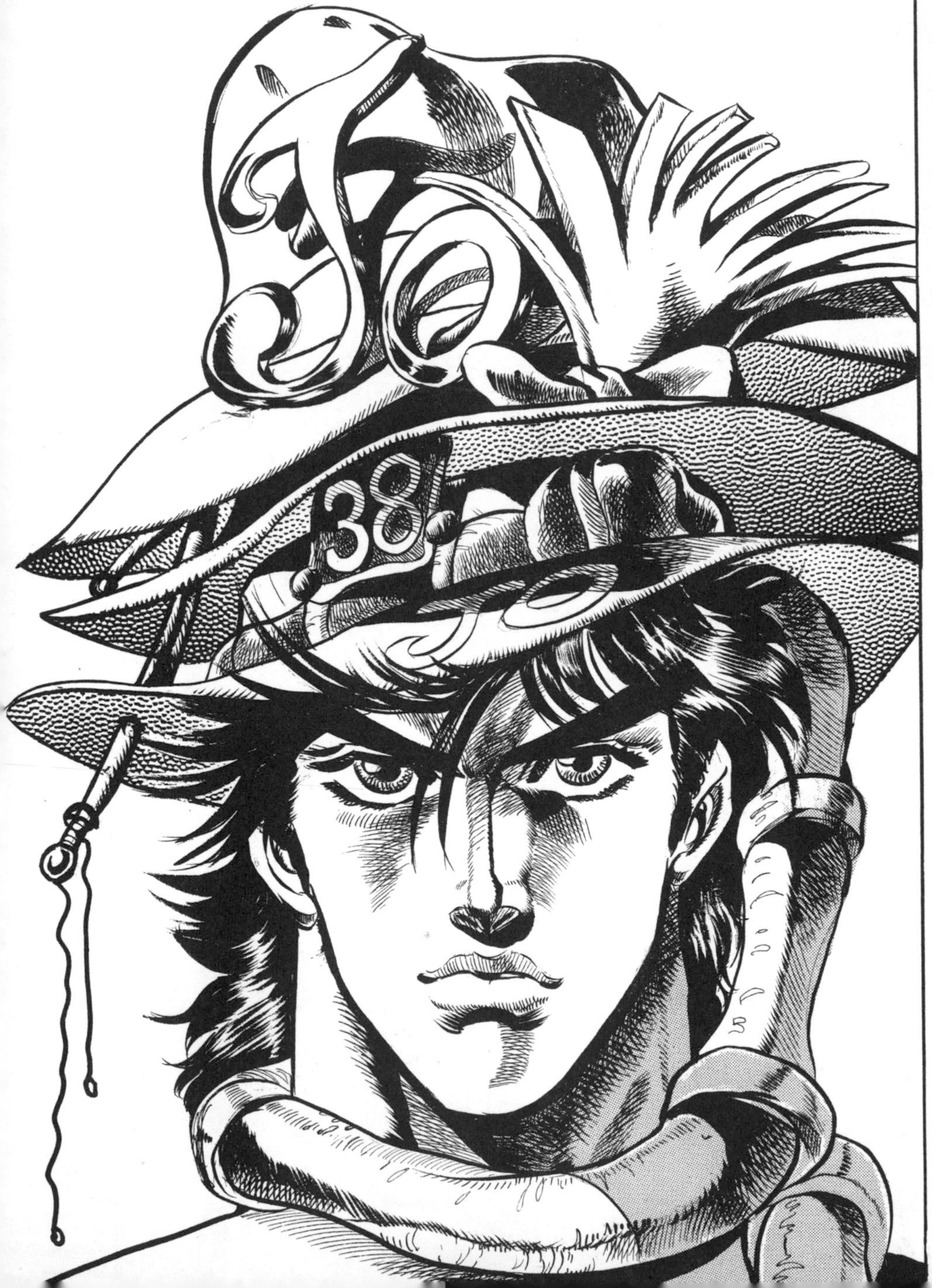
38

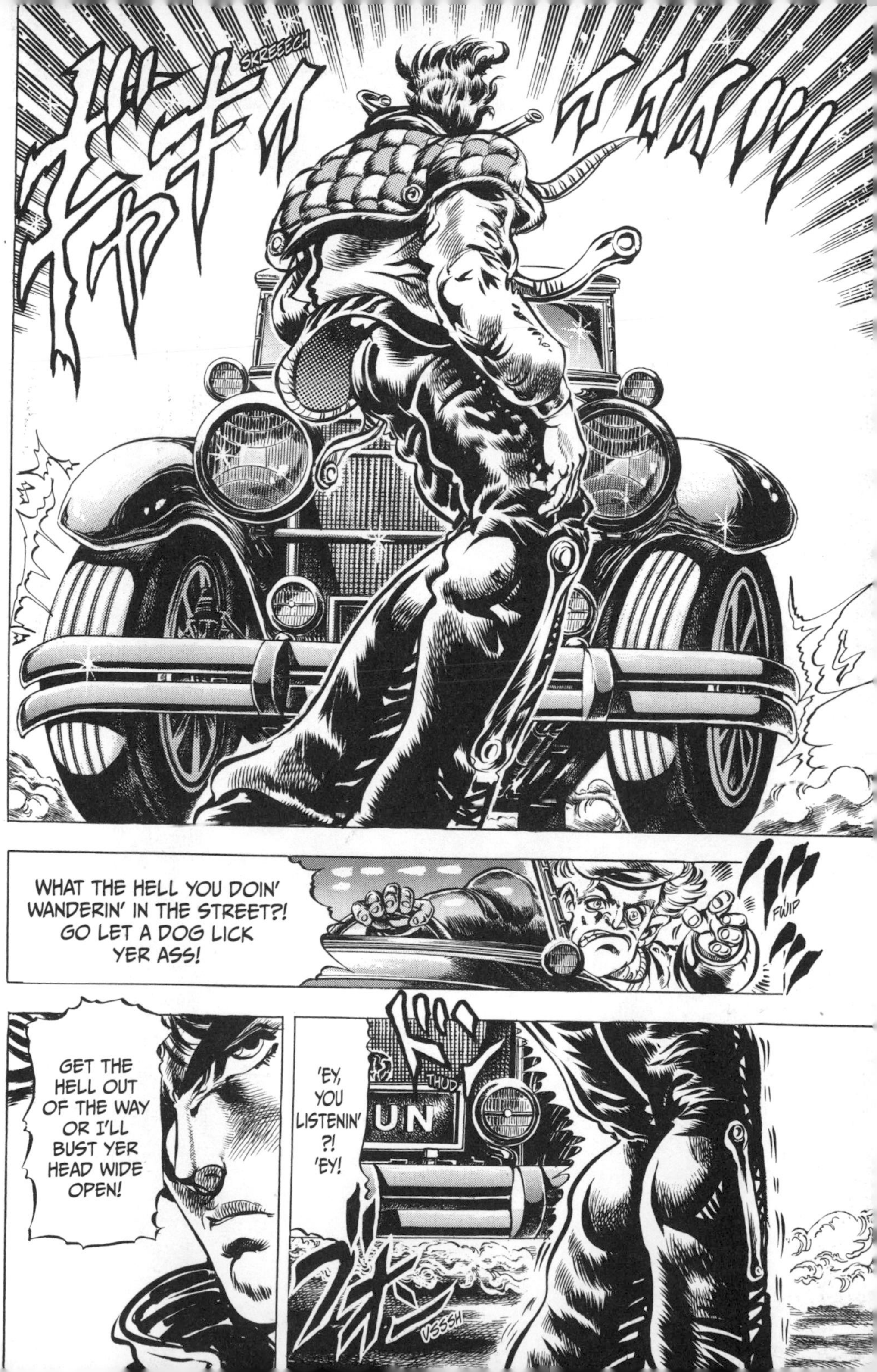
SKREEECH
WHAT THE HELL YOU DOIN' WANDERIN' IN THE STREET?! GO LET A DOG LICK YER ASS!
FWIP
THUD
'EY, YOU LISTENIN' ?! 'EY!
VSSSH
GET THE HELL OUT OF THE WAY OR I'LL BUST YER HEAD WIDE OPEN!

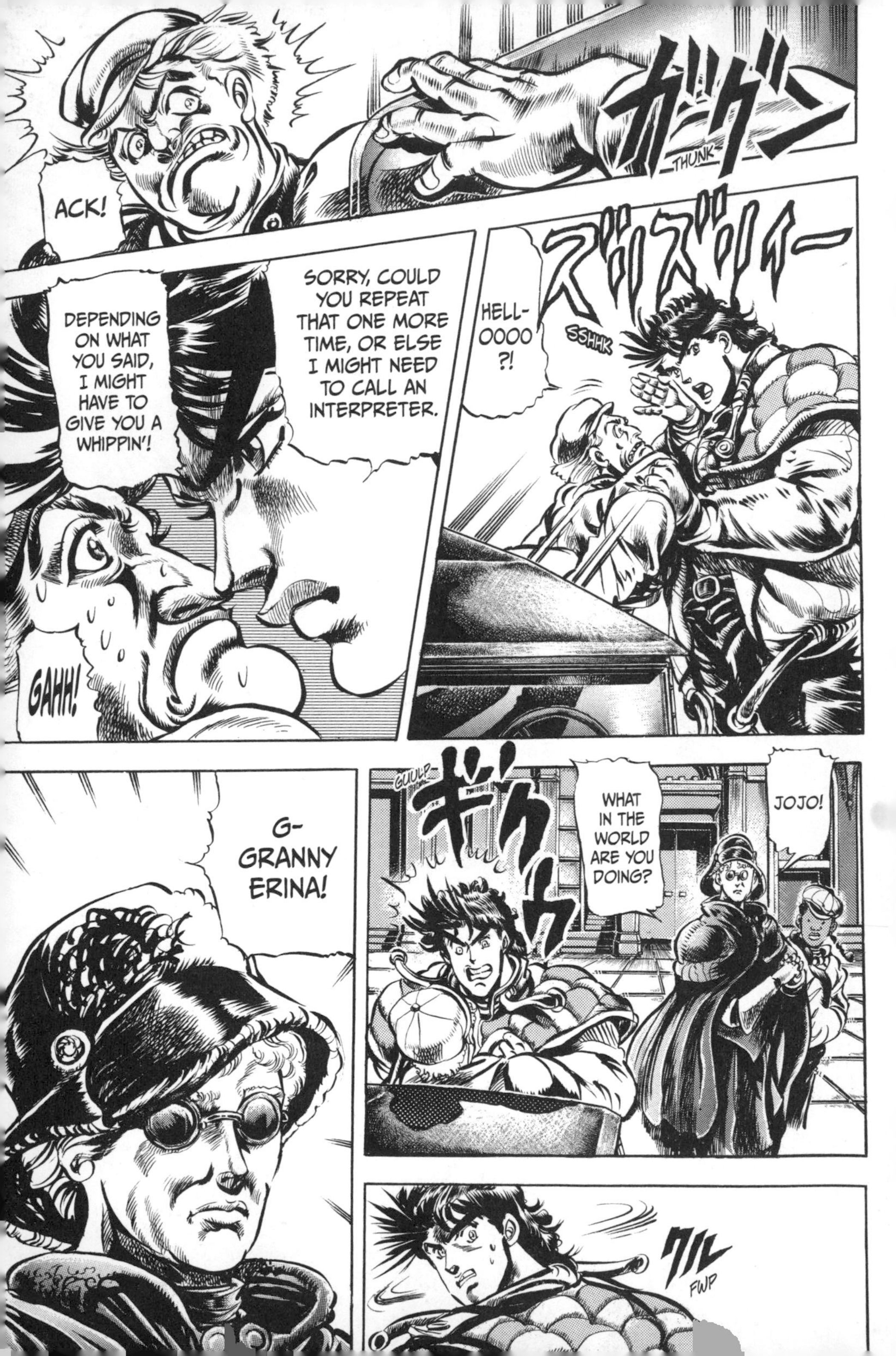
THUNK
ACK!
HELL-OOOO?!
SSHHK
SORRY, COULD YOU REPEAT THAT ONE MORE TIME, OR ELSE I MIGHT NEED TO CALL AN INTERPRETER.
DEPENDING ON WHAT YOU SAID, I MIGHT HAVE TO GIVE YOU A WHIPPIN'!
GAHH!
JOJO!
WHAT IN THE WORLD ARE YOU DOING?
GUULP
FWP
G-GRANNY ERINA!

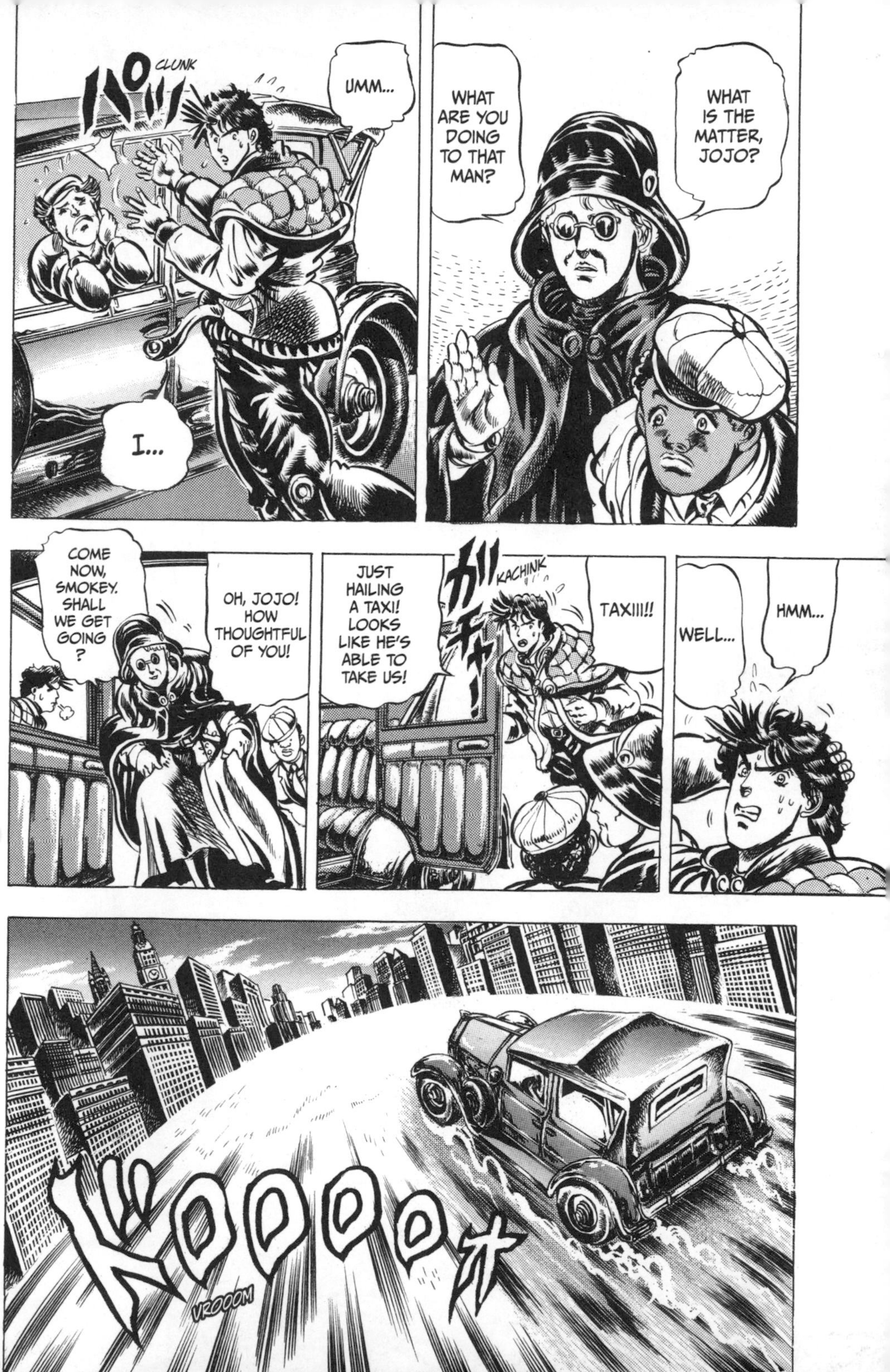
WHAT IS THE MATTER, JOJO?
WHAT ARE YOU DOING TO THAT MAN?
CLUNK
UMM...
I...
HMM...
WELL...
TAXIII!!
KACHINK
JUST HAILING A TAXI! LOOKS LIKE HE'S ABLE TO TAKE US!
OH, JOJO! HOW THOUGHTFUL OF YOU!
COME NOW, SMOKEY. SHALL WE GET GOING?
VROOOM

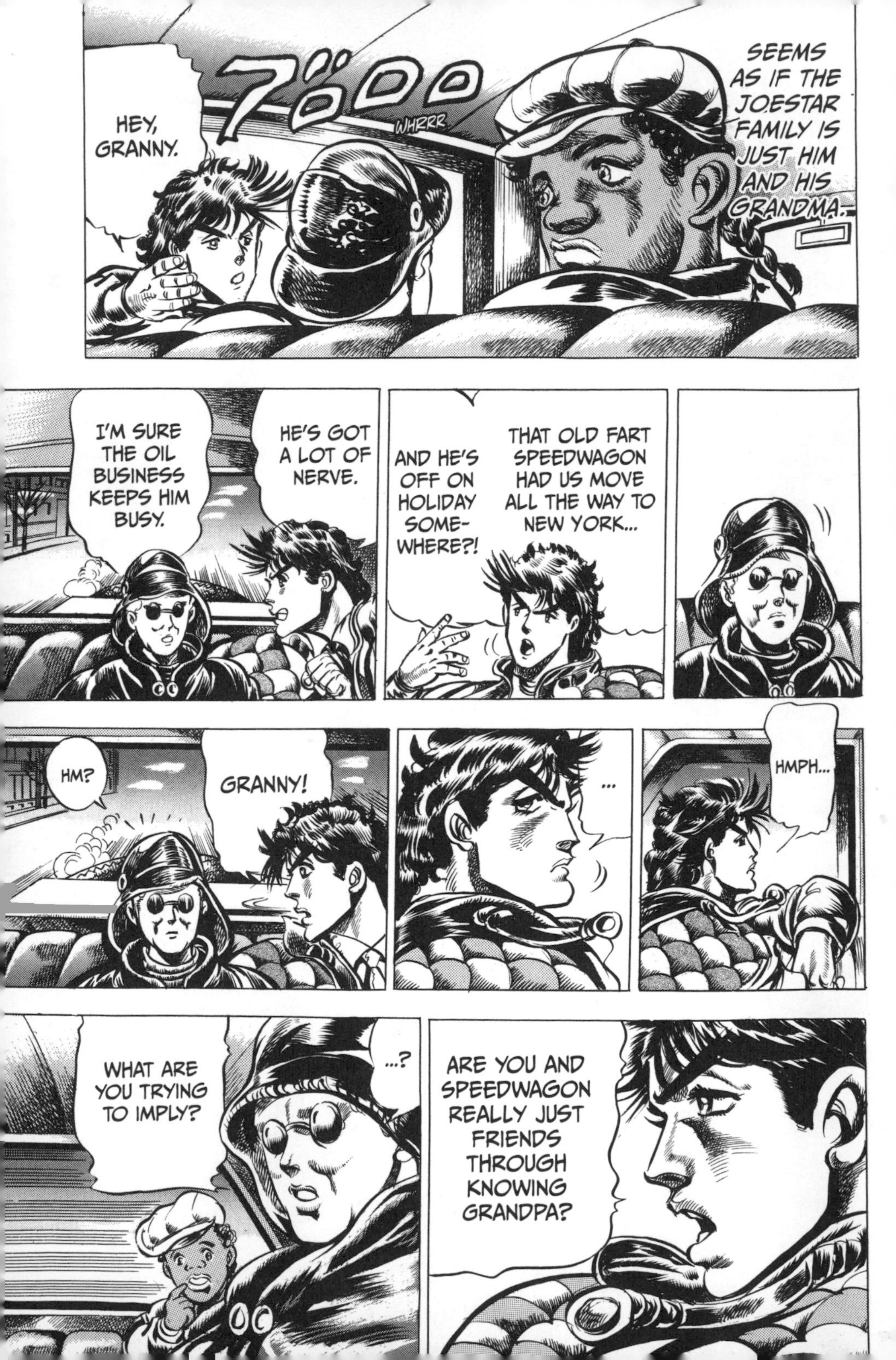
SEEMS AS IF THE JOESTAR FAMILY IS JUST HIM AND HIS GRANDMA.
WHRRR
HEY, GRANNY.
THAT OLD FART SPEEDWAGON HAD US MOVE ALL THE WAY TO NEW YORK...
AND HE'S OFF ON HOLIDAY SOME-WHERE?!
HE'S GOT A LOT OF NERVE.
I'M SURE THE OIL BUSINESS KEEPS HIM BUSY.
HMPH...
...
GRANNY!
HM?
ARE YOU AND SPEEDWAGON REALLY JUST FRIENDS THROUGH KNOWING GRANDPA?
...?
WHAT ARE YOU TRYING TO IMPLY?

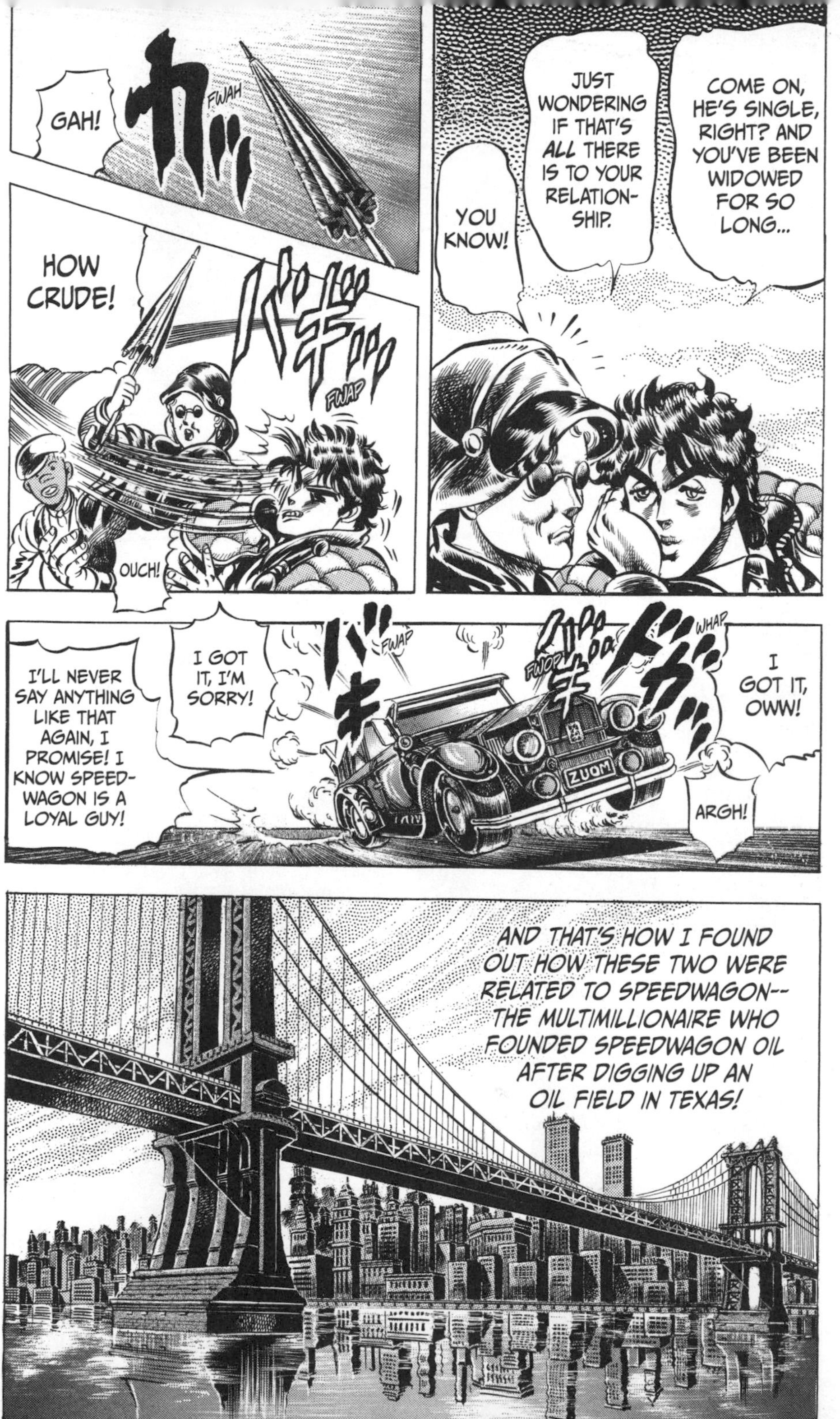
COME ON, HE'S SINGLE, RIGHT? AND YOU'VE BEEN WIDOWED FOR SO LONG...
JUST WONDERING IF THAT'S *ALL* THERE IS TO YOUR RELATION-SHIP.
YOU KNOW!
GAH!
FWAH
HOW CRUDE!
FWAP
OUCH!
I GOT IT, OWW!
WHAP
FWOP
ARGH!
ZUOM
FWAP
I GOT IT, I'M SORRY!
I'LL NEVER SAY ANYTHING LIKE THAT AGAIN, I PROMISE! I KNOW SPEED-WAGON IS A LOYAL GUY!
AND THAT'S HOW I FOUND OUT HOW THESE TWO WERE RELATED TO SPEEDWAGON-- THE MULTIMILLIONAIRE WHO FOUNDED SPEEDWAGON OIL AFTER DIGGING UP AN OIL FIELD IN TEXAS!

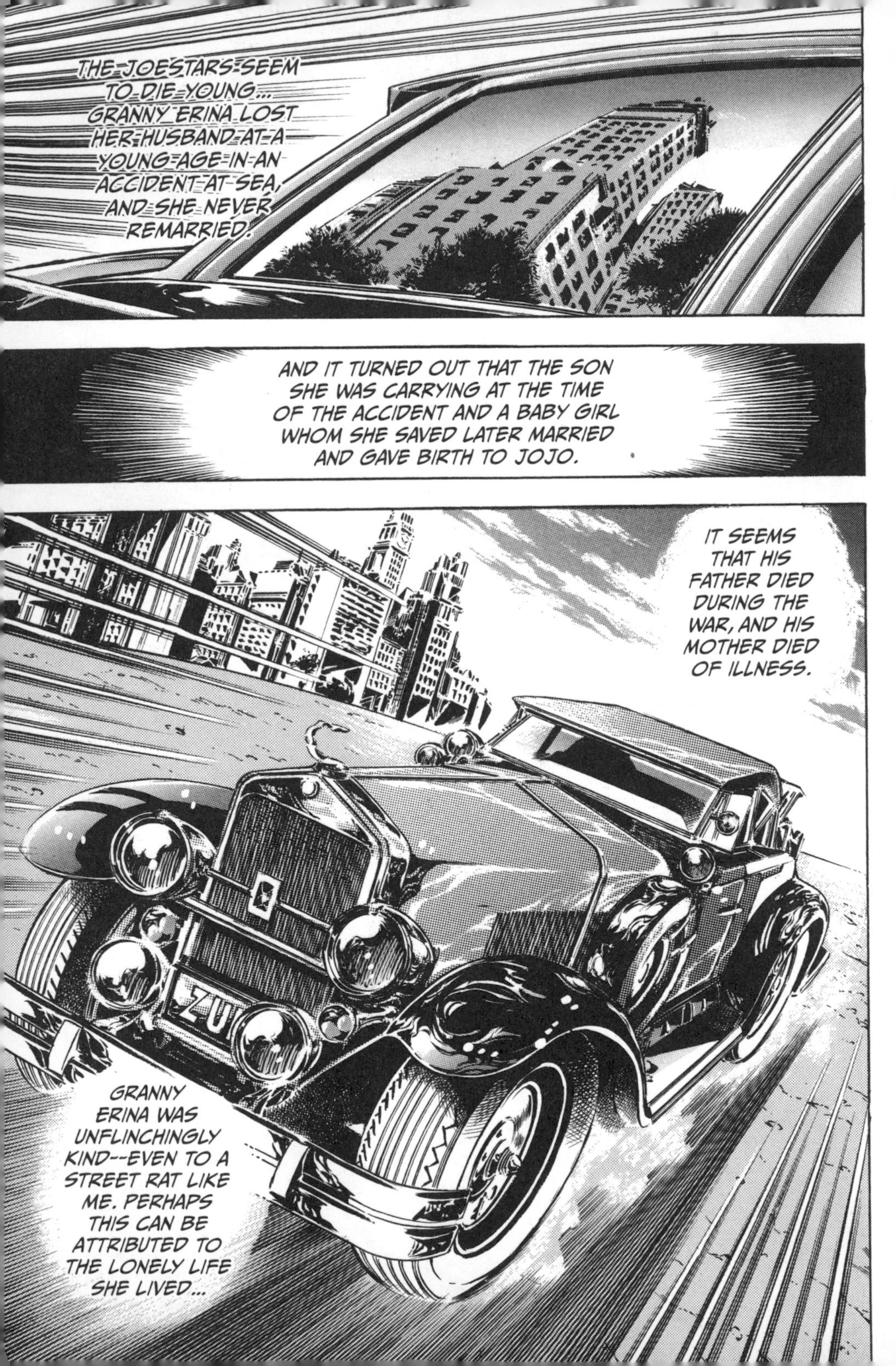
THE JOESTARS SEEM TO DIE YOUNG... GRANNY ERINA LOST HER HUSBAND AT A YOUNG AGE IN AN ACCIDENT AT SEA, AND SHE NEVER REMARRIED.
AND IT TURNED OUT THAT THE SON SHE WAS CARRYING AT THE TIME OF THE ACCIDENT AND A BABY GIRL WHOM SHE SAVED LATER MARRIED AND GAVE BIRTH TO JOJO.
IT SEEMS THAT HIS FATHER DIED DURING THE WAR, AND HIS MOTHER DIED OF ILLNESS.
ZU
GRANNY ERINA WAS UNFLINCHINGLY KIND--EVEN TO A STREET RAT LIKE ME. PERHAPS THIS CAN BE ATTRIBUTED TO THE LONELY LIFE SHE LIVED...

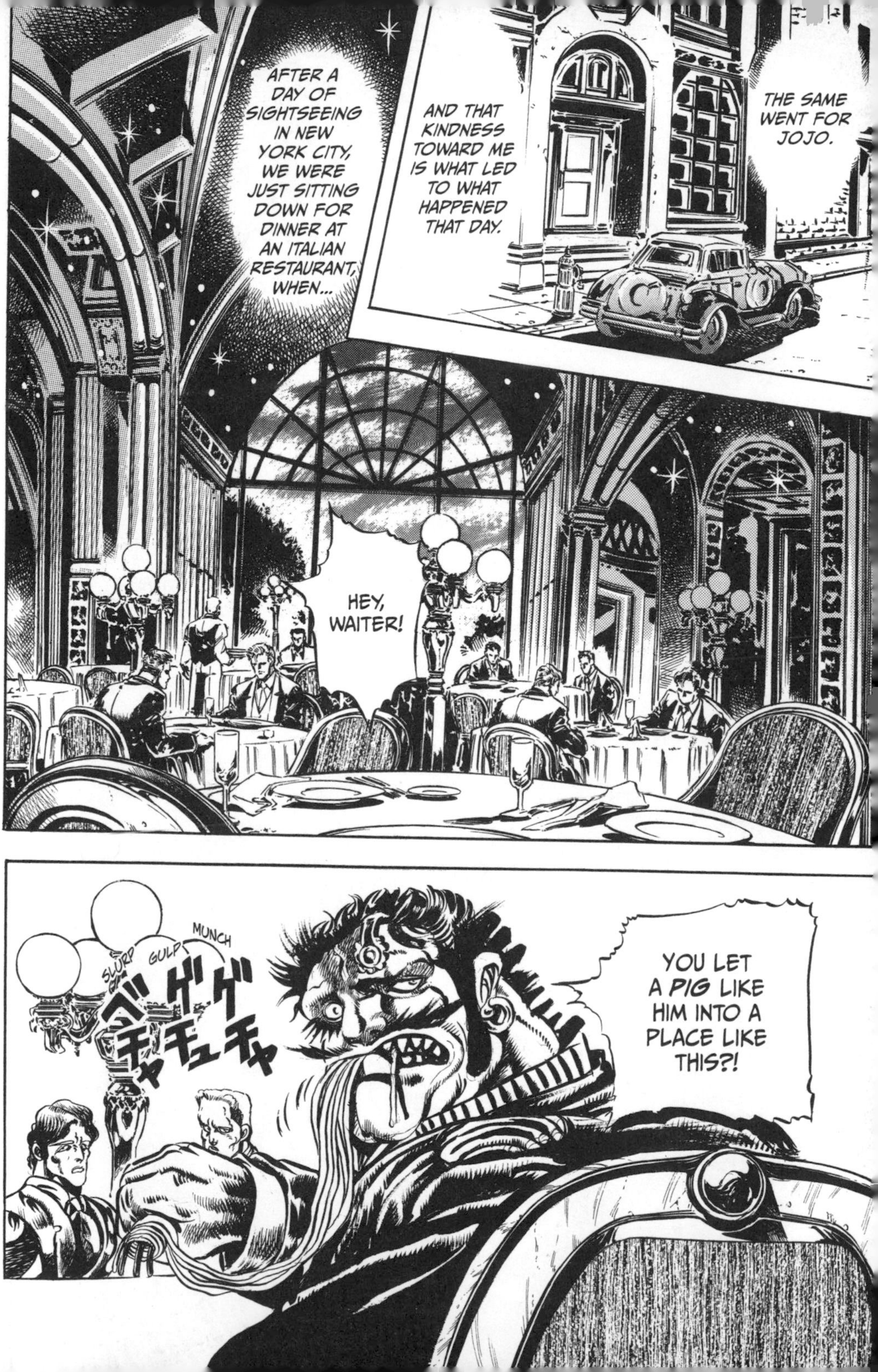
AND THAT KINDNESS TOWARD ME IS WHAT LED TO WHAT HAPPENED THAT DAY.
THE SAME WENT FOR JOJO.
AFTER A DAY OF SIGHTSEEING IN NEW YORK CITY, WE WERE JUST SITTING DOWN FOR DINNER AT AN ITALIAN RESTAURANT, WHEN...
HEY, WAITER!
YOU LET A *PIG* LIKE HIM INTO A PLACE LIKE THIS?!
MUNCH
GULP
SLURP
ゲチャ
ゲチュ
ベチャ

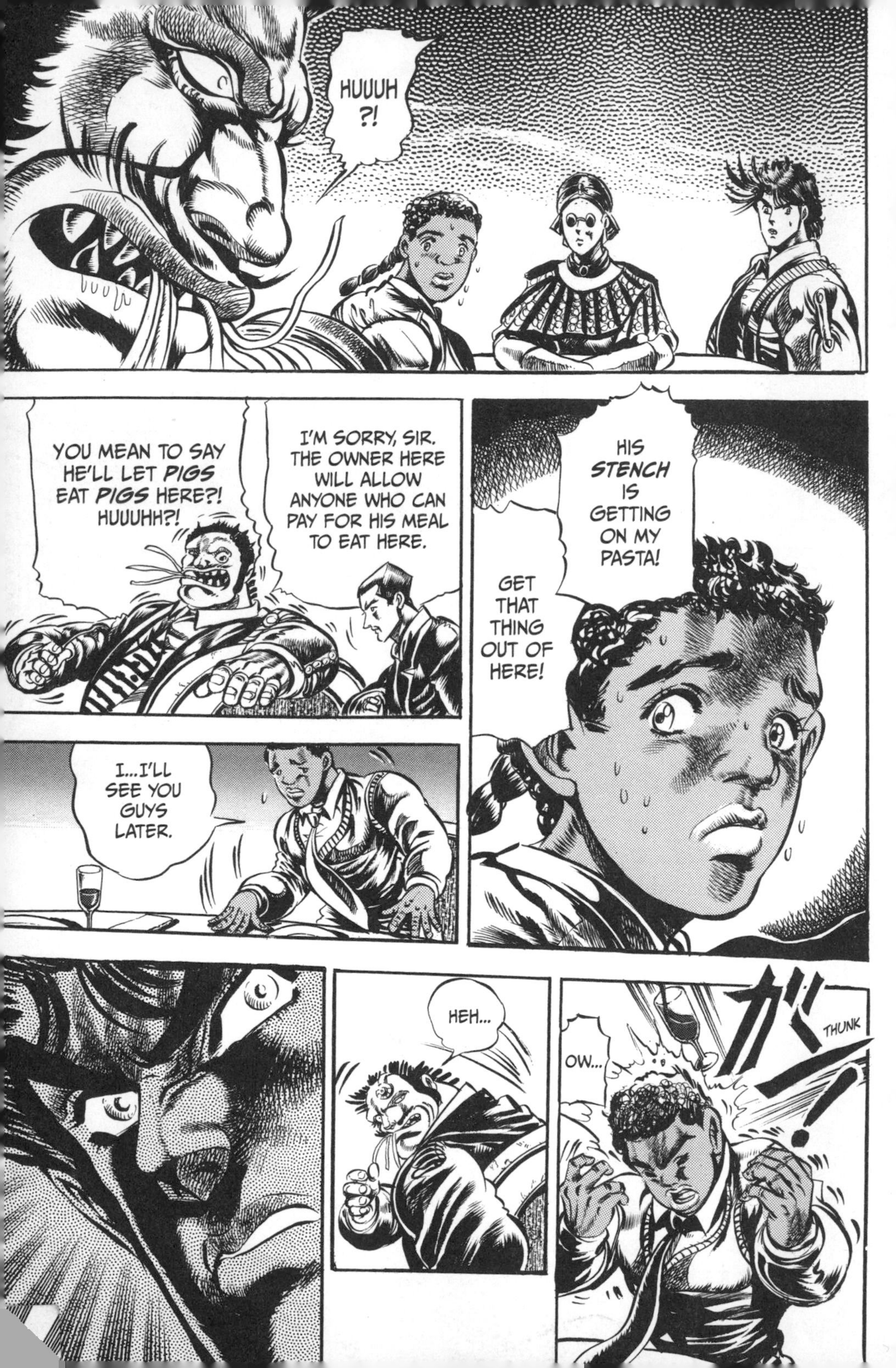
HUUUH ?!
HIS STENCH IS GETTING ON MY PASTA!
GET THAT THING OUT OF HERE!
I'M SORRY, SIR. THE OWNER HERE WILL ALLOW ANYONE WHO CAN PAY FOR HIS MEAL TO EAT HERE.
YOU MEAN TO SAY HE'LL LET PIGS EAT PIGS HERE?! HUUUHH?!
I...I'LL SEE YOU GUYS LATER.
THUNK
OW...
HEH...

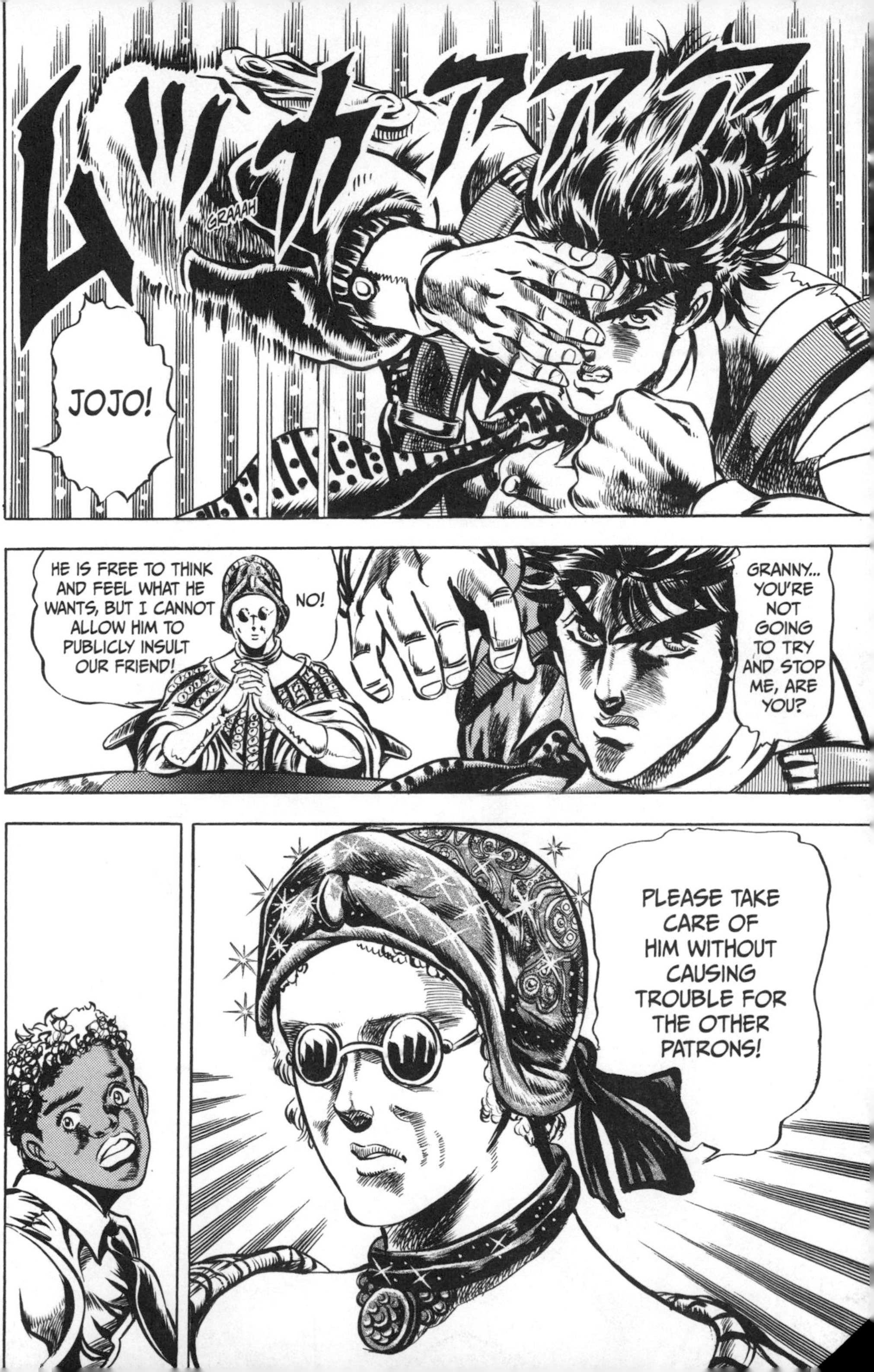
GRAAAH
JOJO!
GRANNY... YOU'RE NOT GOING TO TRY AND STOP ME, ARE YOU?
NO!
HE IS FREE TO THINK AND FEEL WHAT HE WANTS, BUT I CANNOT ALLOW HIM TO PUBLICLY INSULT OUR FRIEND!
PLEASE TAKE CARE OF HIM WITHOUT CAUSING TROUBLE FOR THE OTHER PATRONS!

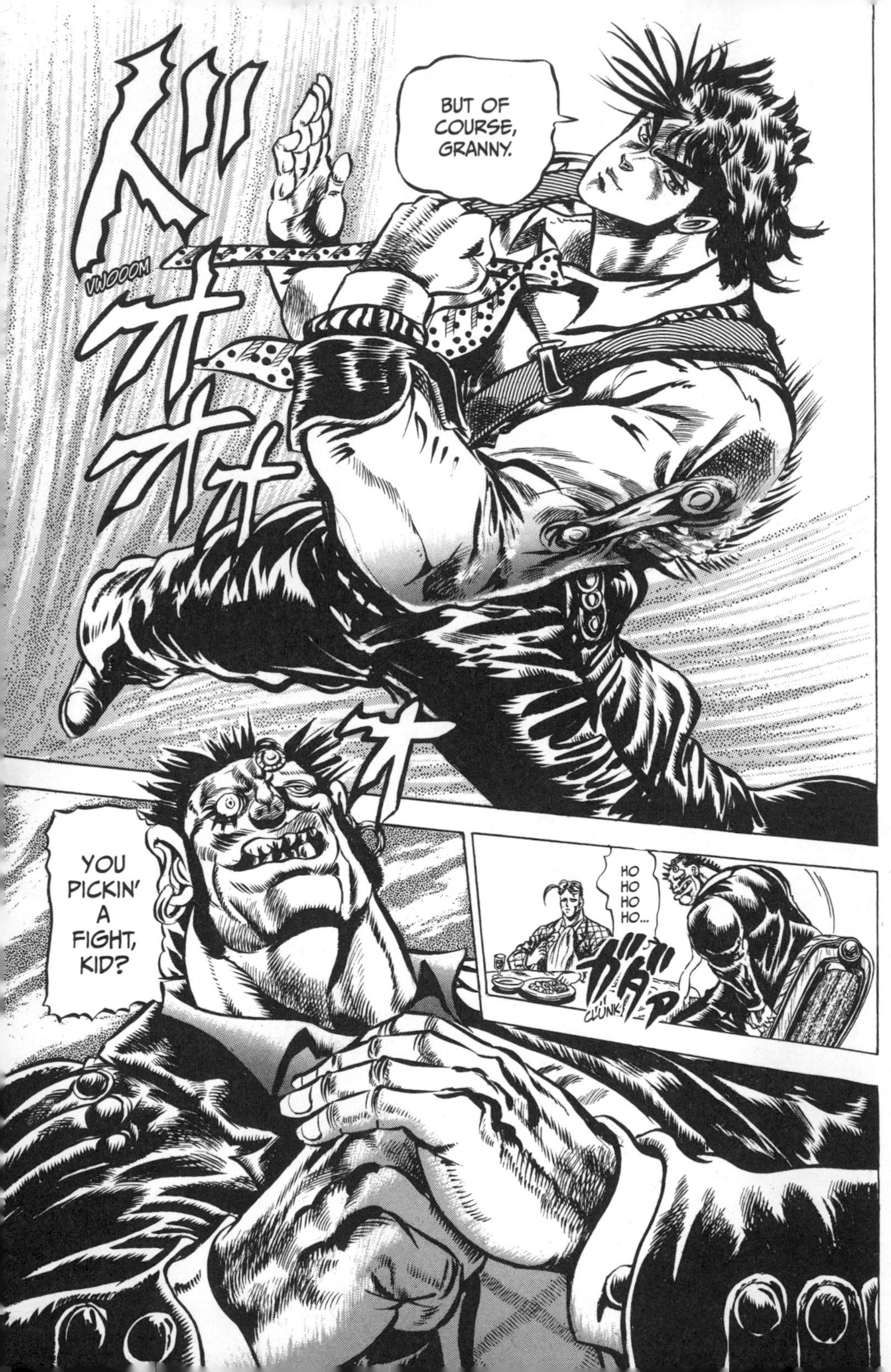
BUT OF COURSE, GRANNY.
VWOOOM
HO HO HO HO HO...
CLUNK!
YOU PICKIN' A FIGHT, KID?

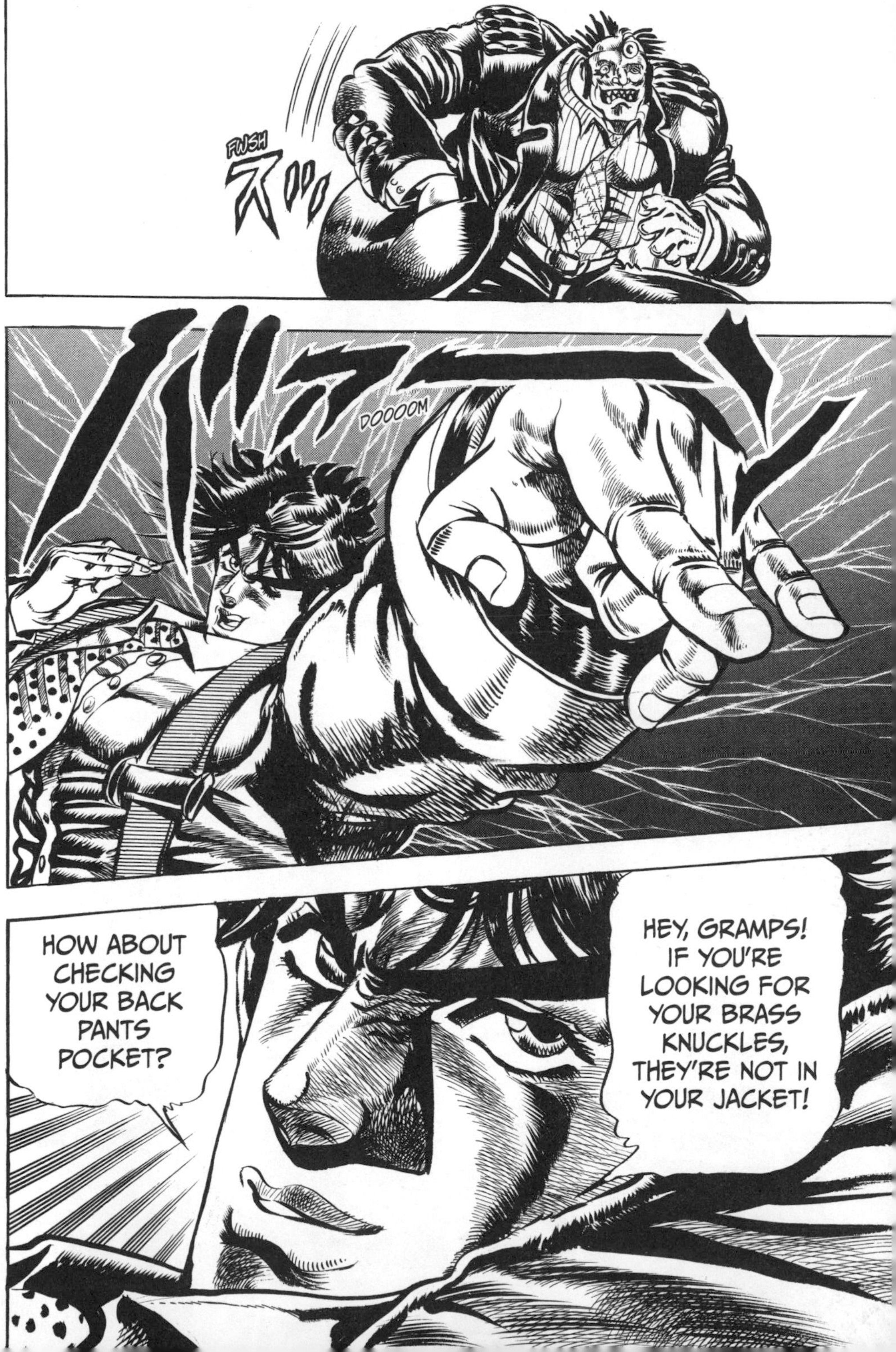
FWSH
DOOOOM
HEY, GRAMPS! IF YOU'RE LOOKING FOR YOUR BRASS KNUCKLES, THEY'RE NOT IN YOUR JACKET!
HOW ABOUT CHECKING YOUR BACK PANTS POCKET?

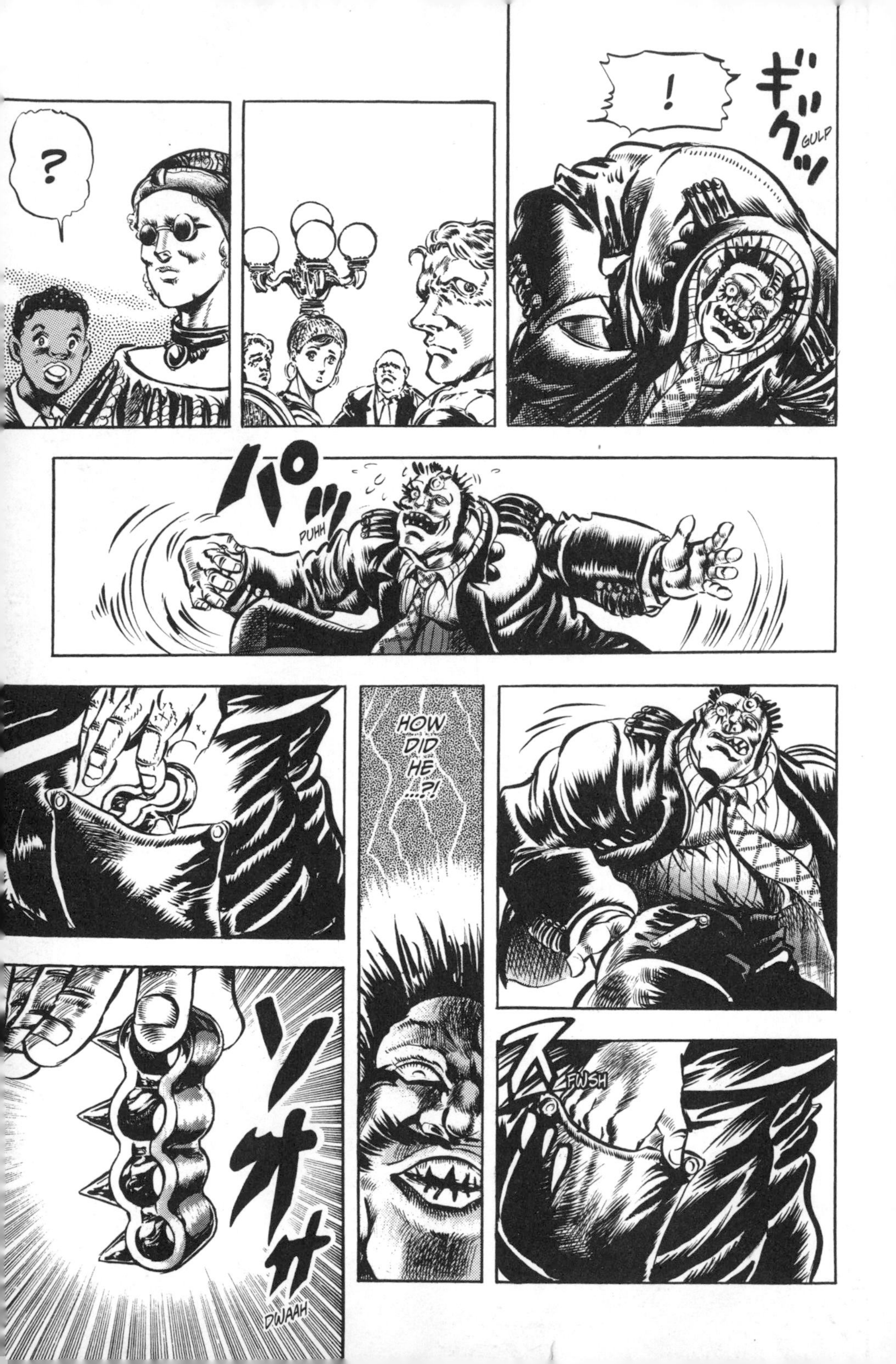
!
ギクッ
GULP
?
パッ
PUHH
ス
FWSH
HOW DID HE ...?!
DWAAH

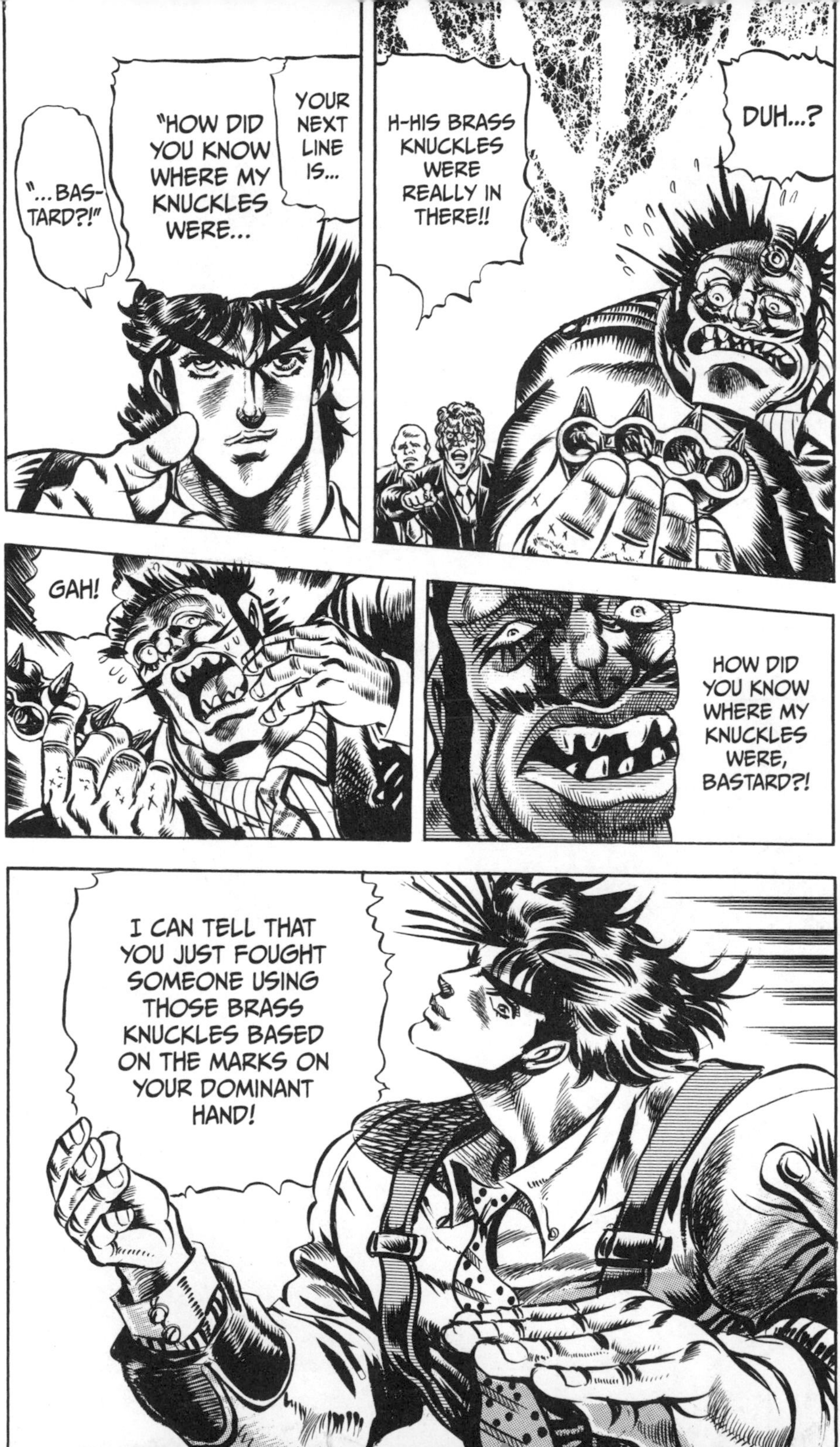
DUH...?
H-HIS BRASS KNUCKLES WERE REALLY IN THERE!!
YOUR NEXT LINE IS...
"HOW DID YOU KNOW WHERE MY KNUCKLES WERE...
"...BAS-TARD?!"
HOW DID YOU KNOW WHERE MY KNUCKLES WERE, BASTARD?!
GAH!
I CAN TELL THAT YOU JUST FOUGHT SOMEONE USING THOSE BRASS KNUCKLES BASED ON THE MARKS ON YOUR DOMINANT HAND!

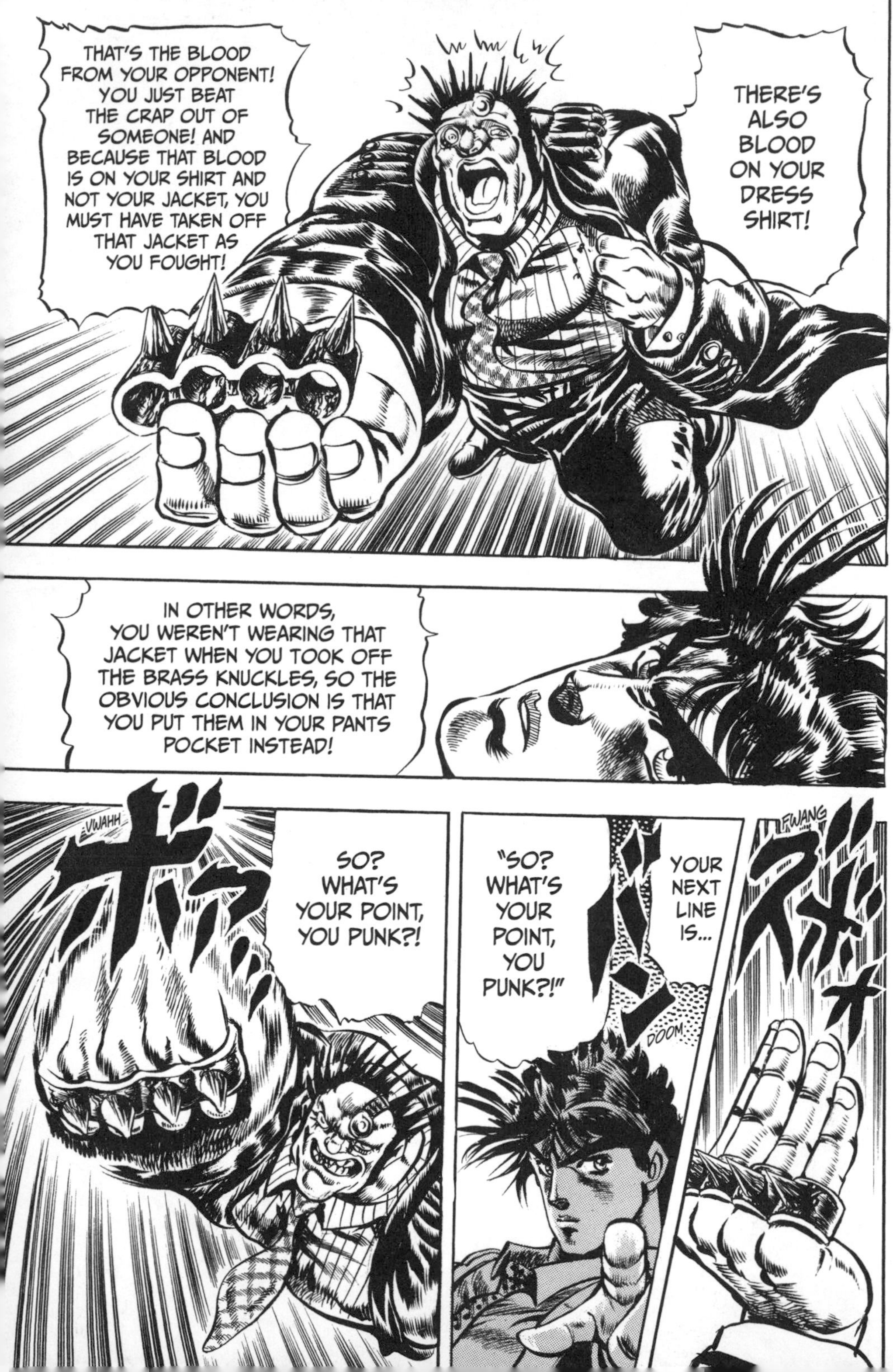
THERE'S ALSO BLOOD ON YOUR DRESS SHIRT!
THAT'S THE BLOOD FROM YOUR OPPONENT! YOU JUST BEAT THE CRAP OUT OF SOMEONE! AND BECAUSE THAT BLOOD IS ON YOUR SHIRT AND NOT YOUR JACKET, YOU MUST HAVE TAKEN OFF THAT JACKET AS YOU FOUGHT!
IN OTHER WORDS, YOU WEREN'T WEARING THAT JACKET WHEN YOU TOOK OFF THE BRASS KNUCKLES, SO THE OBVIOUS CONCLUSION IS THAT YOU PUT THEM IN YOUR PANTS POCKET INSTEAD!
FWANG
YOUR NEXT LINE IS...
"SO? WHAT'S YOUR POINT, YOU PUNK?!"
DOOM
VWAHH
SO? WHAT'S YOUR POINT, YOU PUNK?!

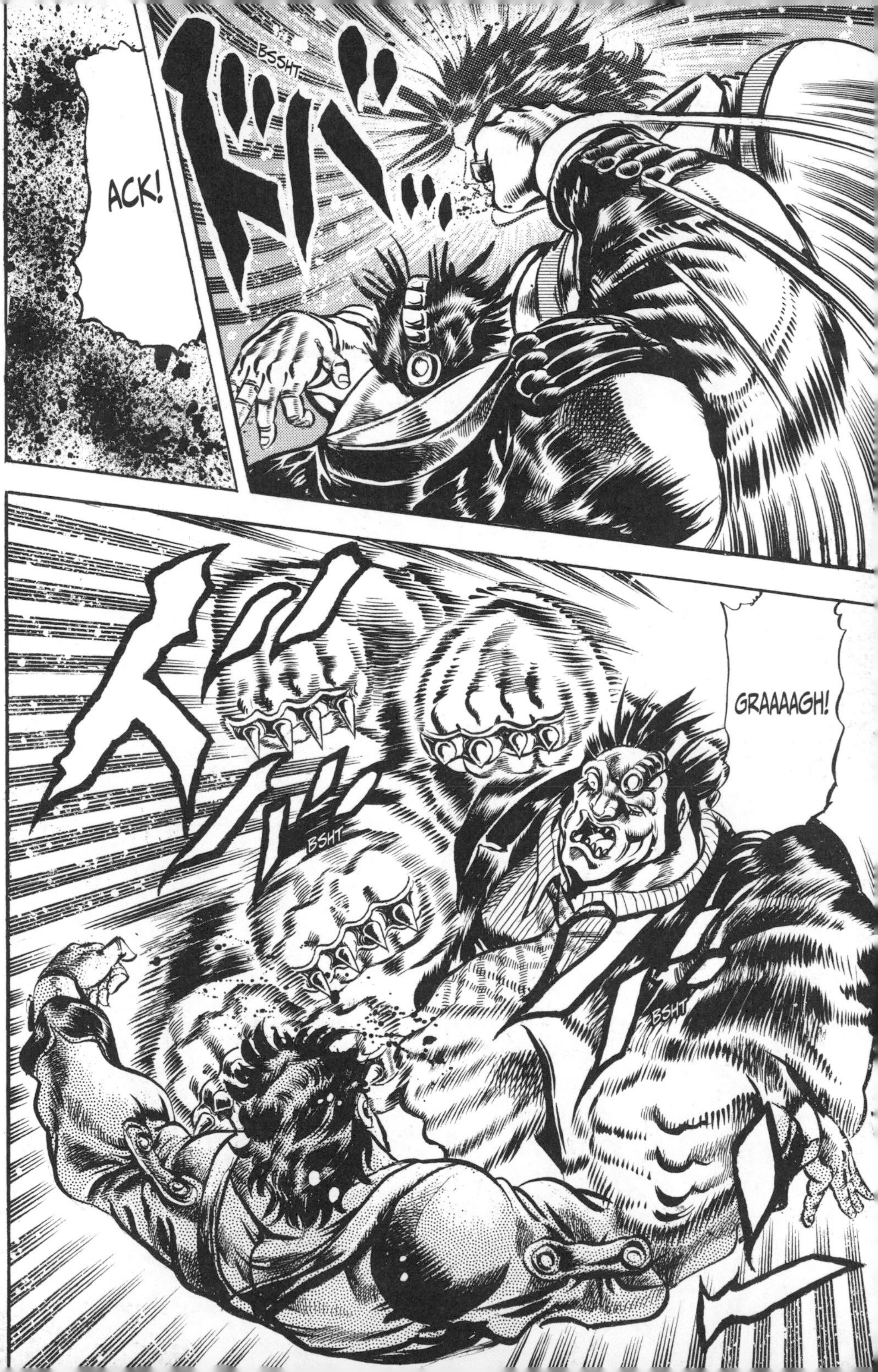
BSSHT
ACK!
GRAAAAGH!
BSHT
BSHT

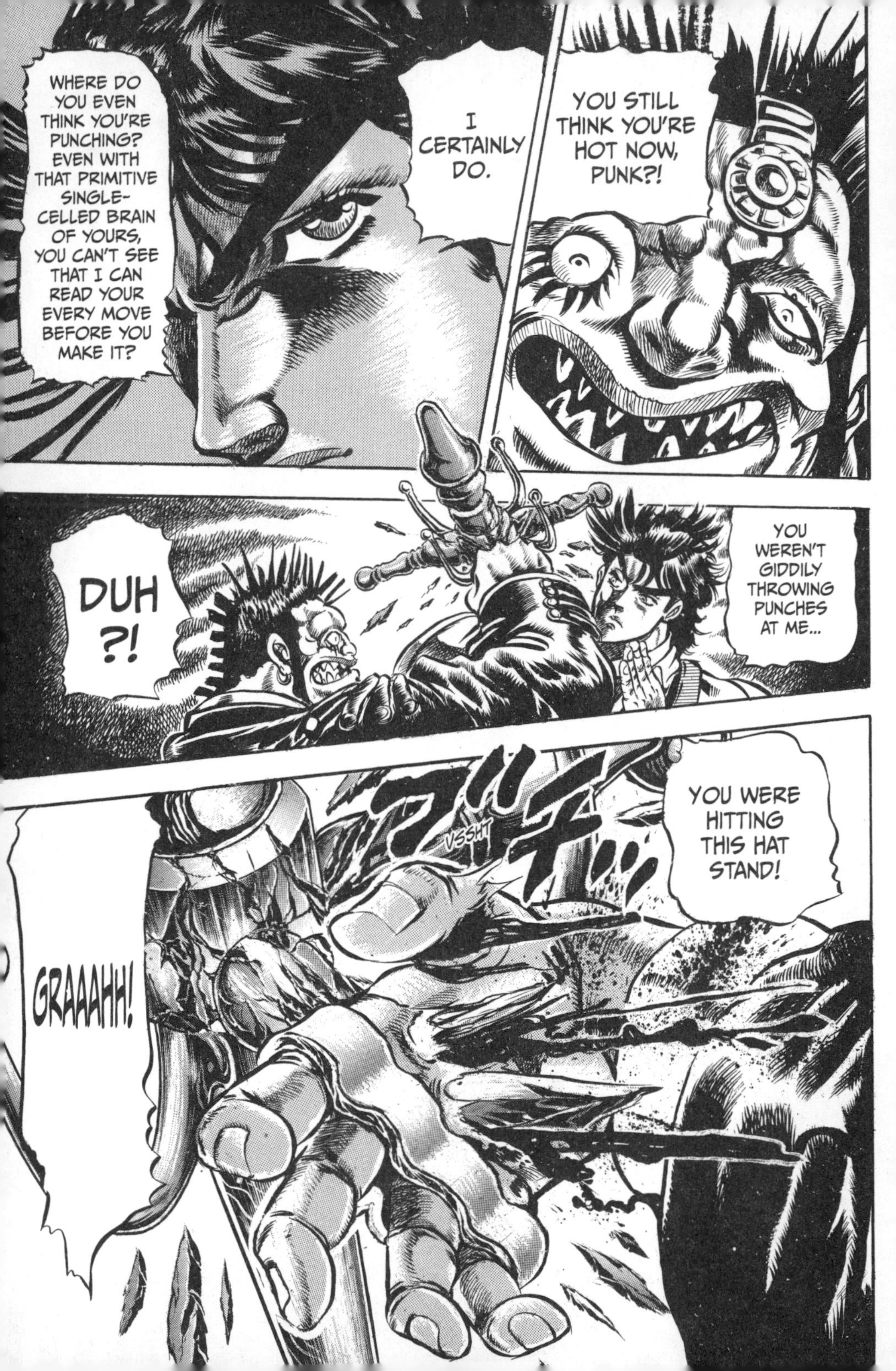
YOU STILL THINK YOU'RE HOT NOW, PUNK?!
I CERTAINLY DO.
WHERE DO YOU EVEN THINK YOU'RE PUNCHING? EVEN WITH THAT PRIMITIVE SINGLE-CELLED BRAIN OF YOURS, YOU CAN'T SEE THAT I CAN READ YOUR EVERY MOVE BEFORE YOU MAKE IT?
YOU WEREN'T GIDDILY THROWING PUNCHES AT ME...
DUH ?!
YOU WERE HITTING THIS HAT STAND!
VSSHT
GRAAAHH!

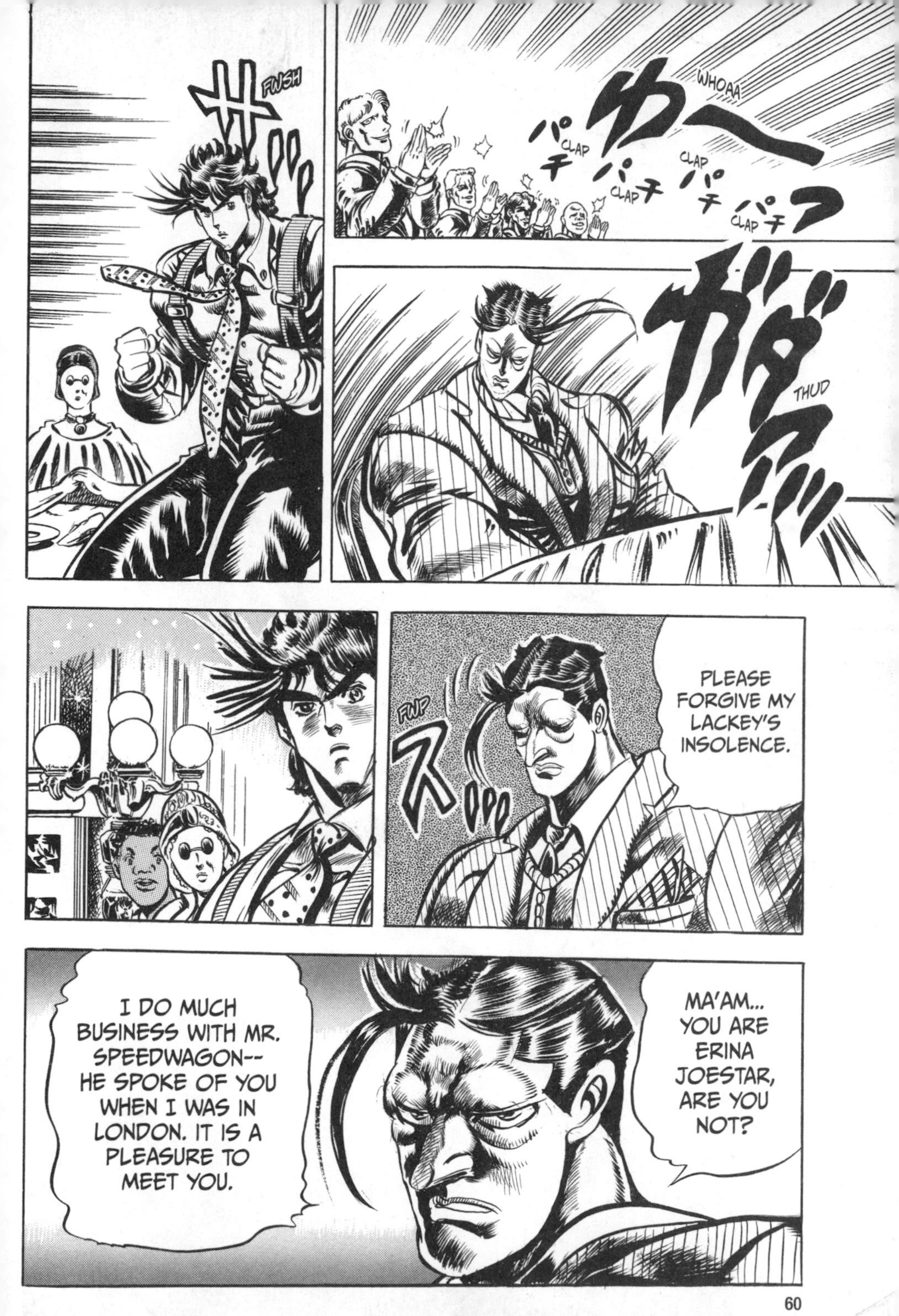
WHOAA
CLAP
CLAP
CLAP
CLAP
THUD
FWSH
FWP
PLEASE FORGIVE MY LACKEY'S INSOLENCE.
MA'AM... YOU ARE ERINA JOESTAR, ARE YOU NOT?
I DO MUCH BUSINESS WITH MR. SPEEDWAGON-- HE SPOKE OF YOU WHEN I WAS IN LONDON. IT IS A PLEASURE TO MEET YOU.

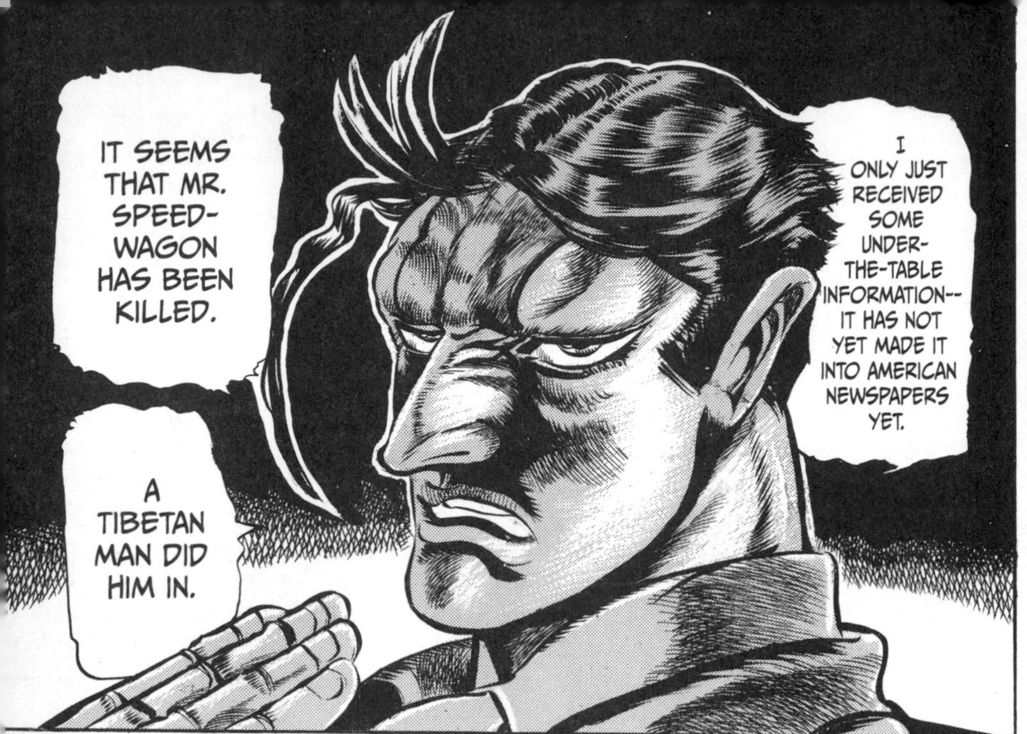
I ONLY JUST RECEIVED SOME UNDER-THE-TABLE INFORMATION-- IT HAS NOT YET MADE IT INTO AMERICAN NEWSPAPERS YET.
IT SEEMS THAT MR. SPEED-WAGON HAS BEEN KILLED.
A TIBETAN MAN DID HIM IN.
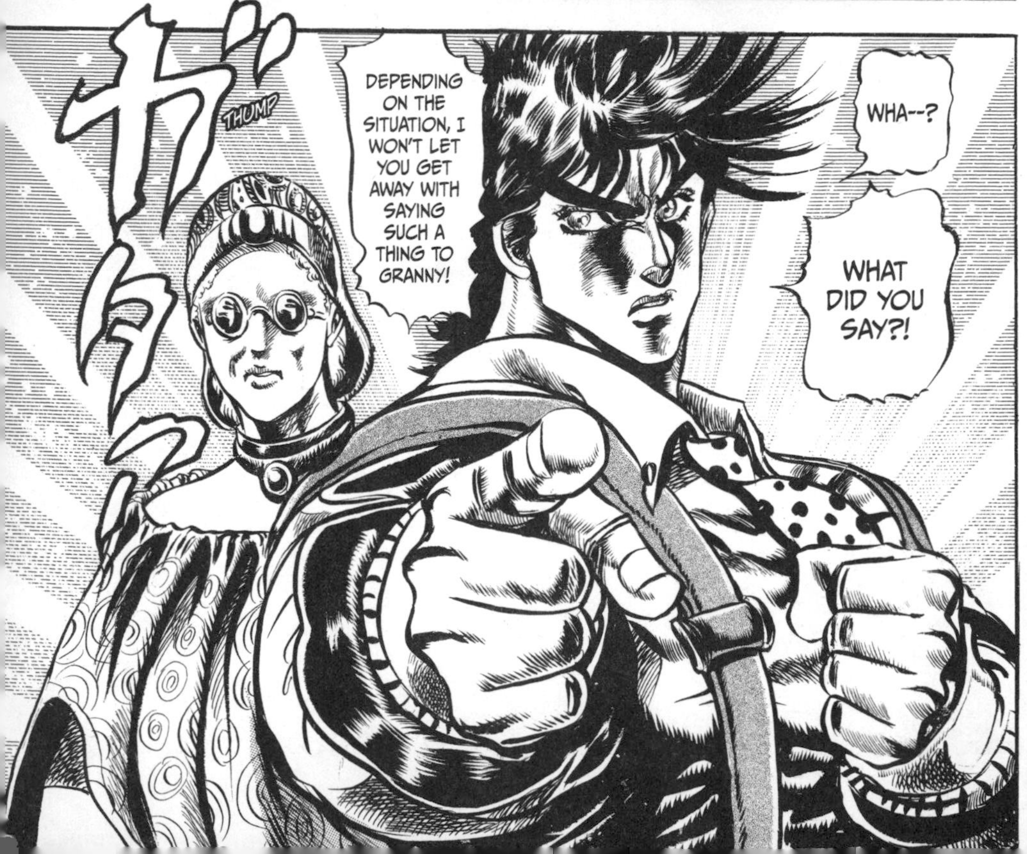
WHA--?
WHAT DID YOU SAY?!
DEPENDING ON THE SITUATION, I WON'T LET YOU GET AWAY WITH SAYING SUCH A THING TO GRANNY!
ガタッ
THUMP

CHAPTER 4: Straizo vs. Joseph PART 1

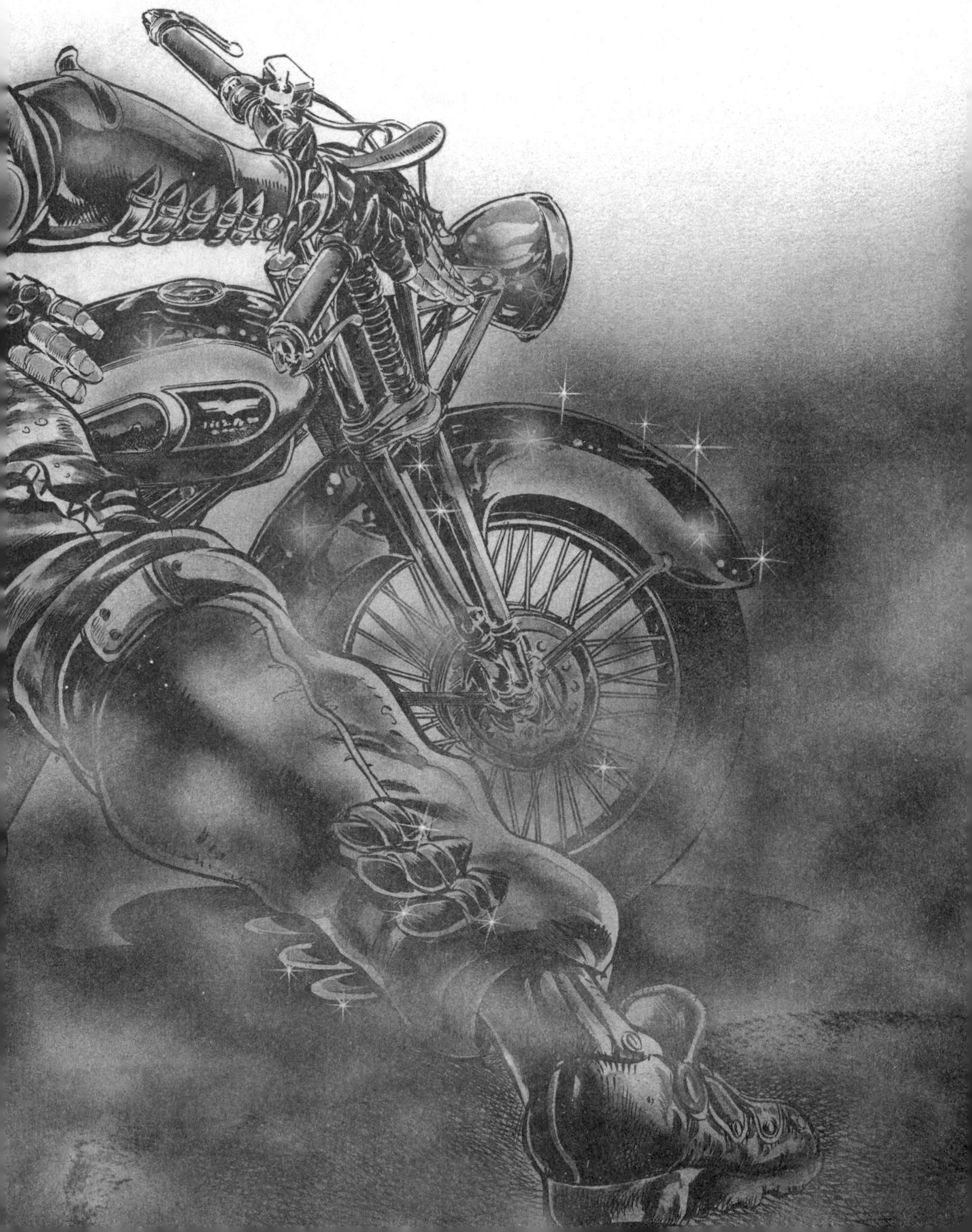

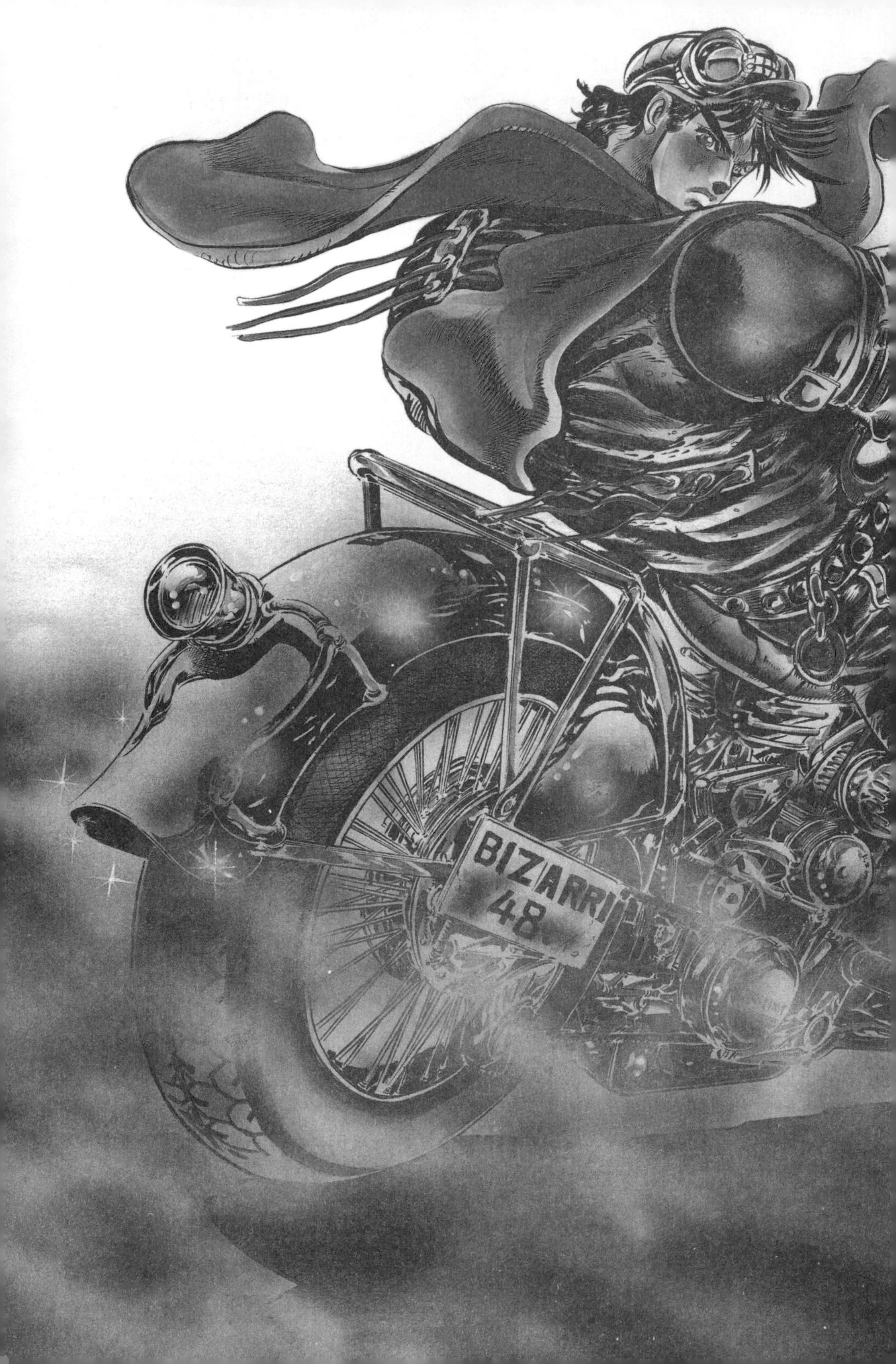
BIZARRI
48

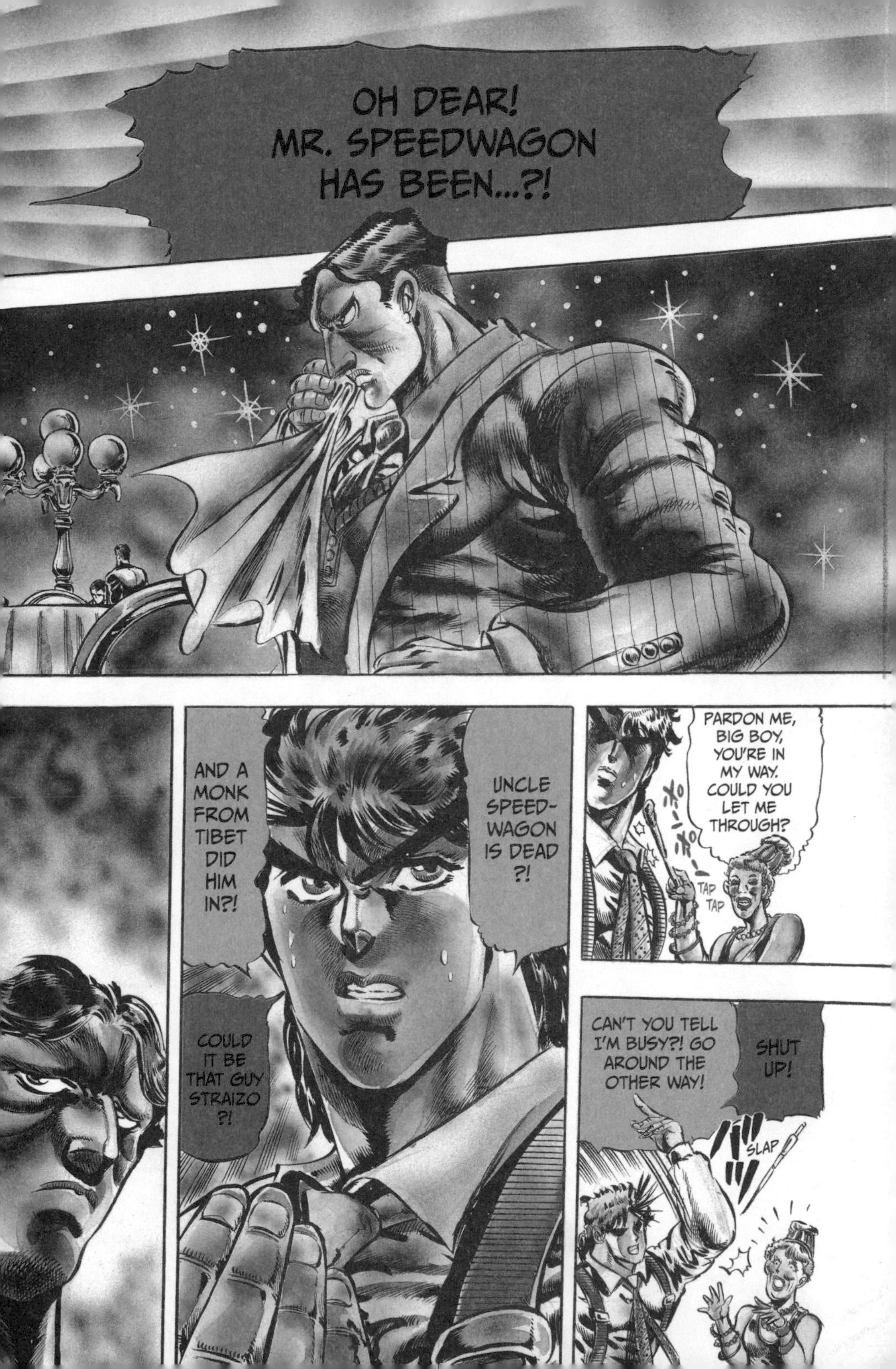
OH DEAR! MR. SPEEDWAGON HAS BEEN...?!
PARDON ME, BIG BOY, YOU'RE IN MY WAY. COULD YOU LET ME THROUGH?
TAP TAP
SHUT UP!
CAN'T YOU TELL I'M BUSY?! GO AROUND THE OTHER WAY!
SLAP
UNCLE SPEEDWAGON IS DEAD?!
AND A MONK FROM TIBET DID HIM IN?!
COULD IT BE THAT GUY STRAIZO?!

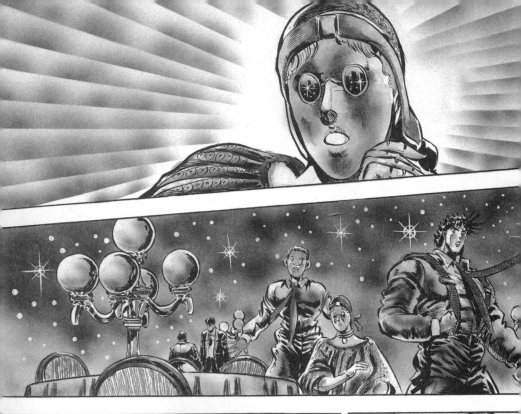

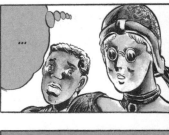

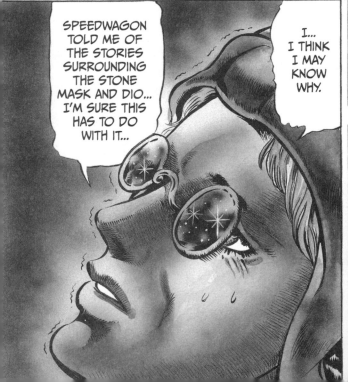

...
IT SEEMS AS IF THE BODIES OF SPEEDWAGON AND TWO OTHERS WERE DISCOVERED DOWN THE RIVER, DEEP IN TH MEXICAN WILDERNESS. NO ONE KNOWS WHERE THE MON WENT OR WHY HE DID IT.
I... I THINK I MAY KNOW WHY.
SPEEDWAGON TOLD ME OF THE STORIES SURROUNDING THE STONE MASK AND DIO... I'M SURE THIS HAS TO DO WITH IT...

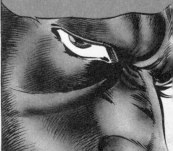

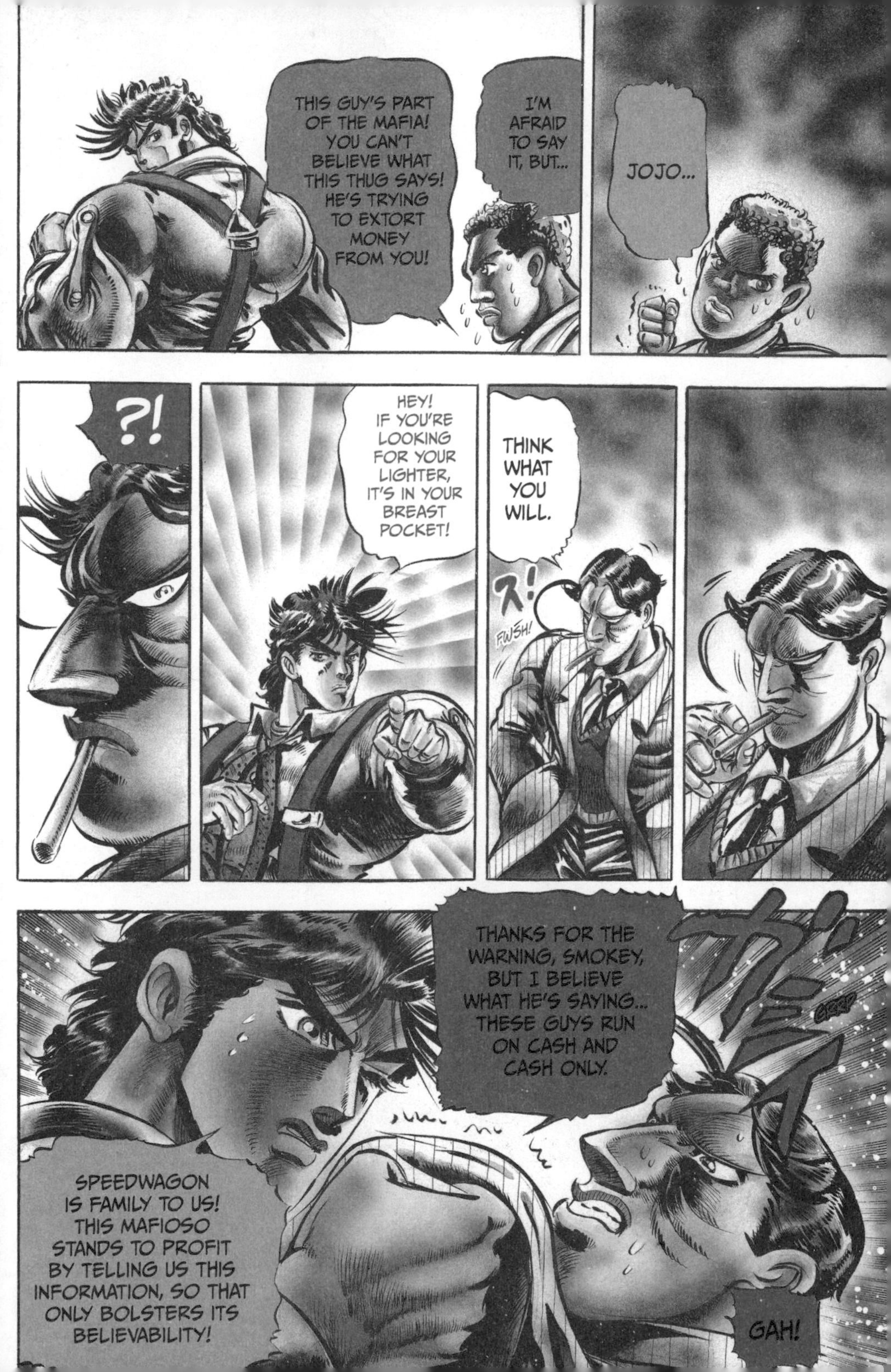
JOJO...
I'M AFRAID TO SAY IT, BUT...
THIS GUY'S PART OF THE MAFIA! YOU CAN'T BELIEVE WHAT THIS THUG SAYS! HE'S TRYING TO EXTORT MONEY FROM YOU!
THINK WHAT YOU WILL.
FWSH!
HEY! IF YOU'RE LOOKING FOR YOUR LIGHTER, IT'S IN YOUR BREAST POCKET!
?!
THANKS FOR THE WARNING, SMOKEY, BUT I BELIEVE WHAT HE'S SAYING... THESE GUYS RUN ON CASH AND CASH ONLY.
GAH!
SPEEDWAGON IS FAMILY TO US! THIS MAFIOSO STANDS TO PROFIT BY TELLING US THIS INFORMATION, SO THAT ONLY BOLSTERS ITS BELIEVABILITY!

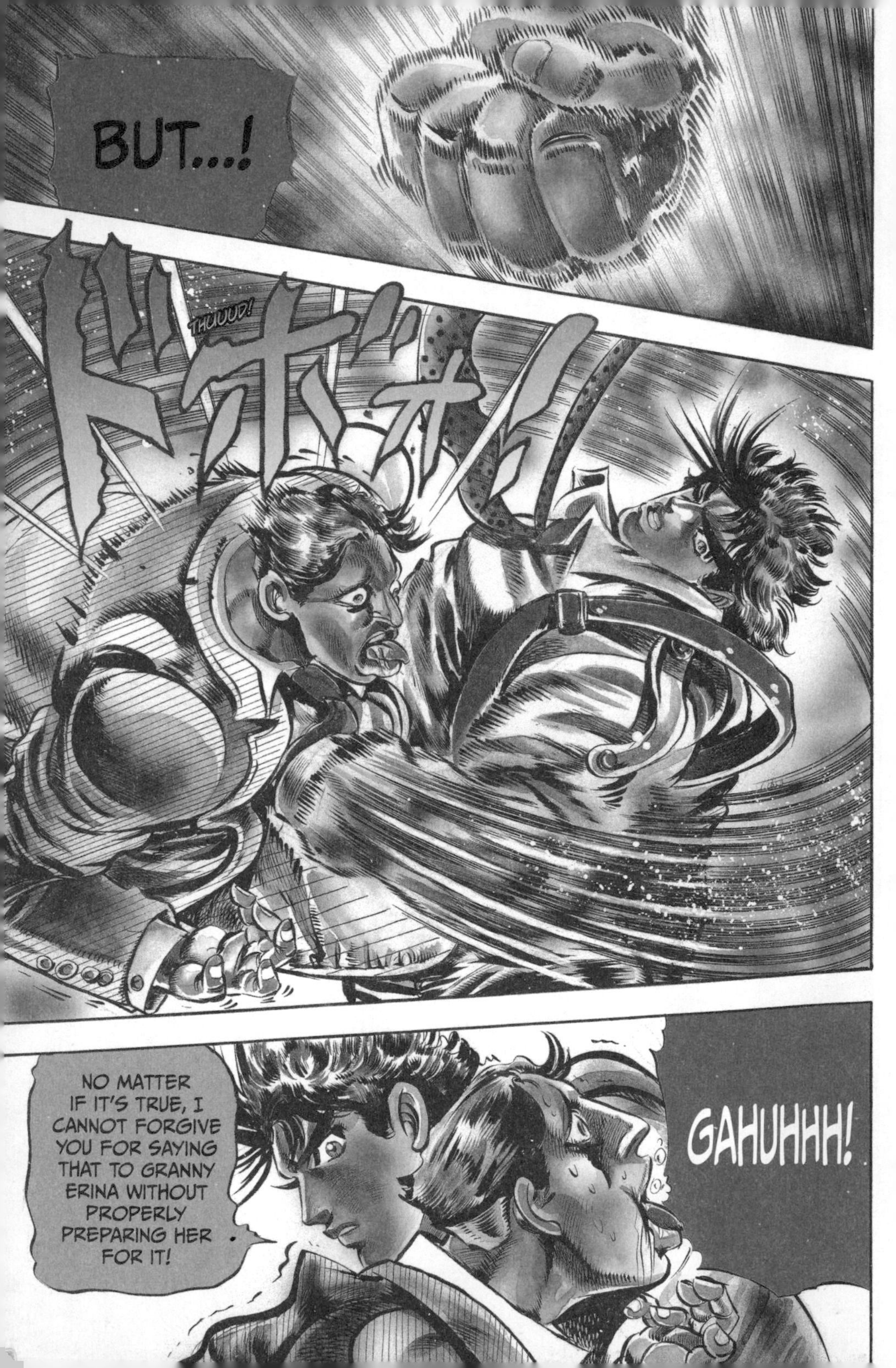
BUT...!
ドゴォ
THUUUD!
GAHUHHH!
NO MATTER IF IT'S TRUE, I CANNOT FORGIVE YOU FOR SAYING THAT TO GRANNY ERINA WITHOUT PROPERLY PREPARING HER FOR IT!

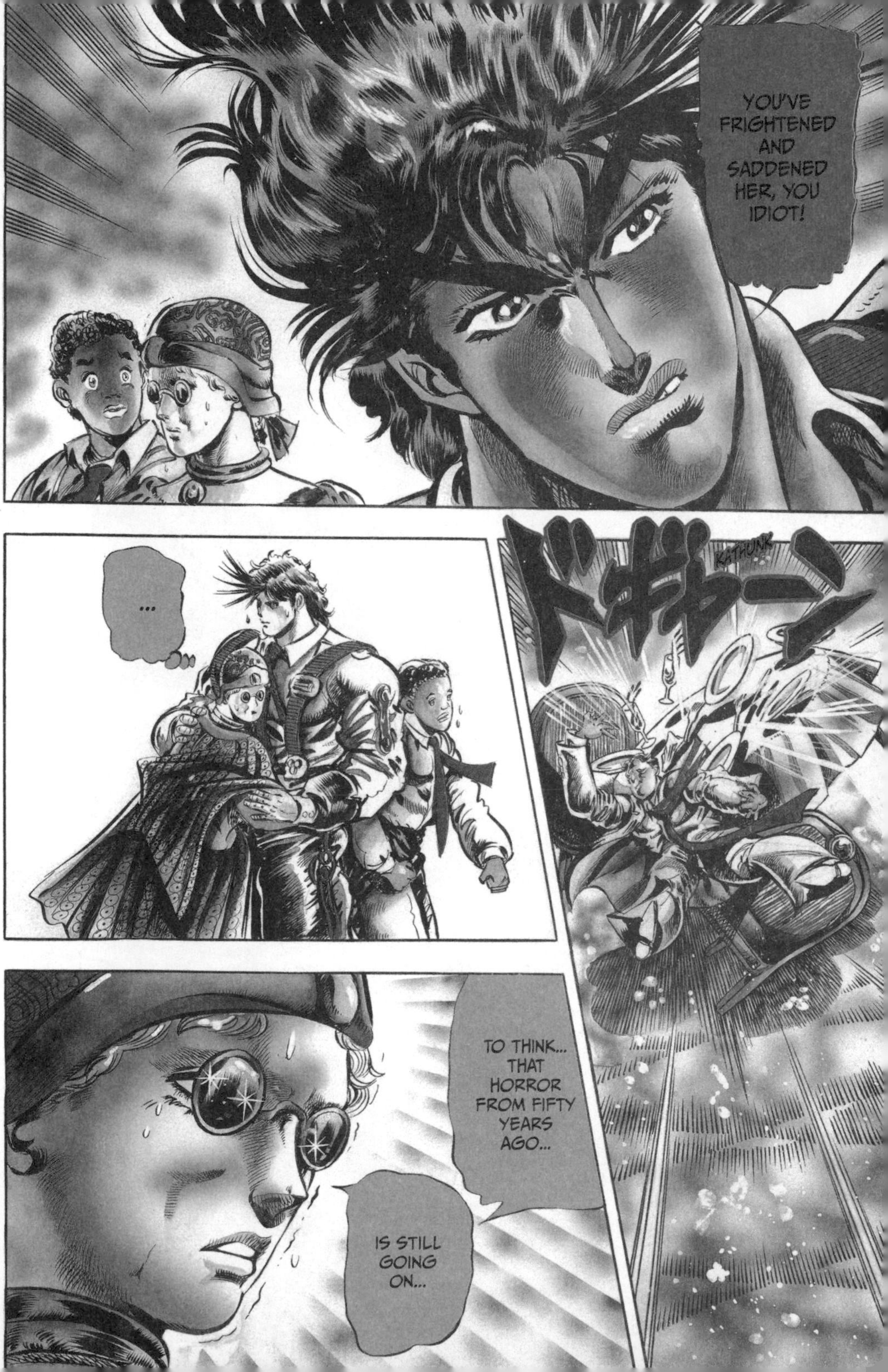

YOU'VE FRIGHTENED AND SADDENED HER, YOU IDIOT!
KATHUNK
...
TO THINK... THAT HORROR FROM FIFTY YEARS AGO...
IS STILL GOING ON...

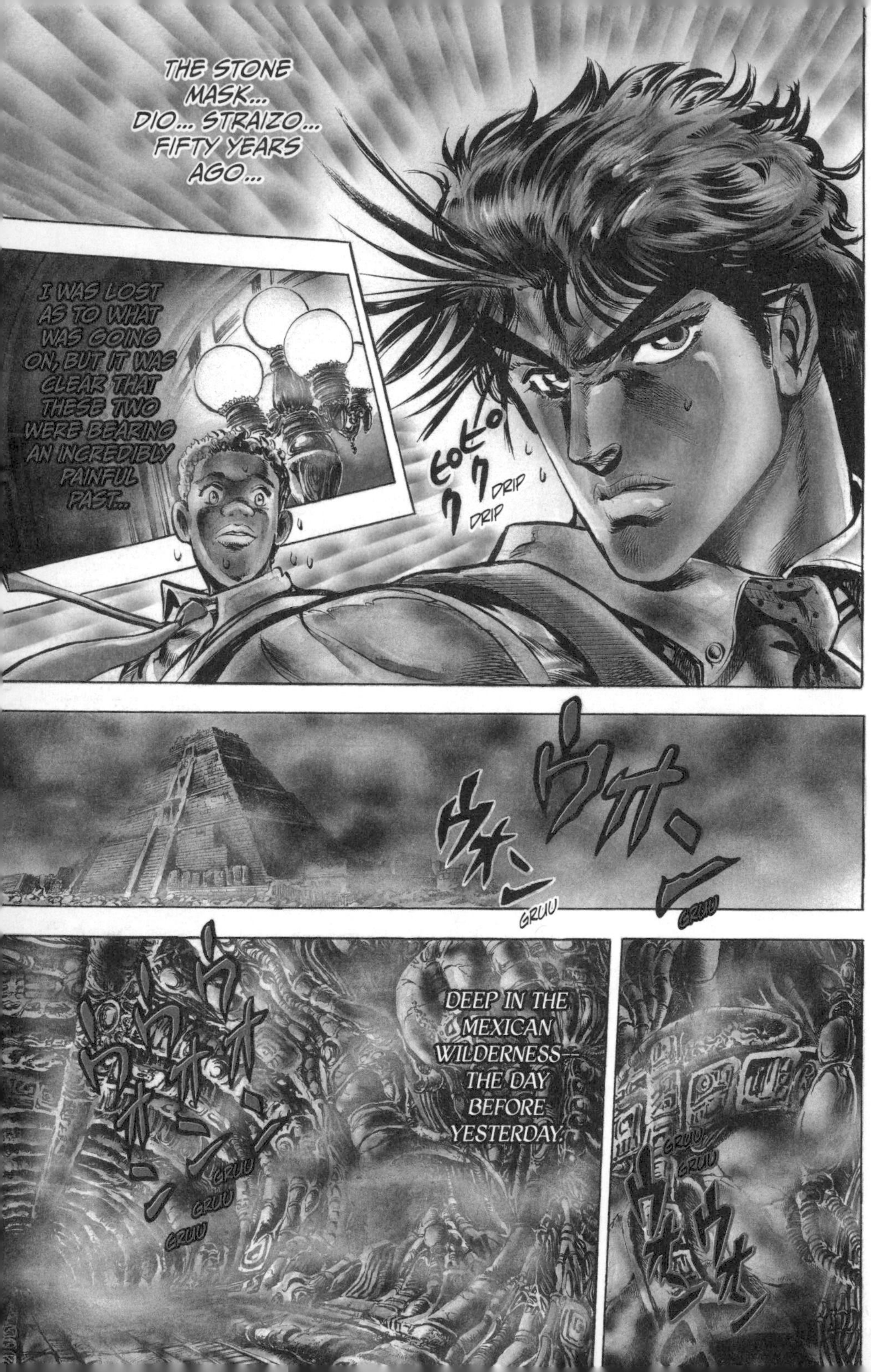
THE STONE MASK... DIO... STRAIZO... FIFTY YEARS AGO...
I WAS LOST AS TO WHAT WAS GOING ON, BUT IT WAS CLEAR THAT THESE TWO WERE BEARING AN INCREDIBLY PAINFUL PAST...
DRIP
DRIP
GRUU
GRUU
GRUU
GRUU
DEEP IN THE MEXICAN WILDERNESS-- THE DAY BEFORE YESTERDAY.
GRUU
GRUU
GRUU

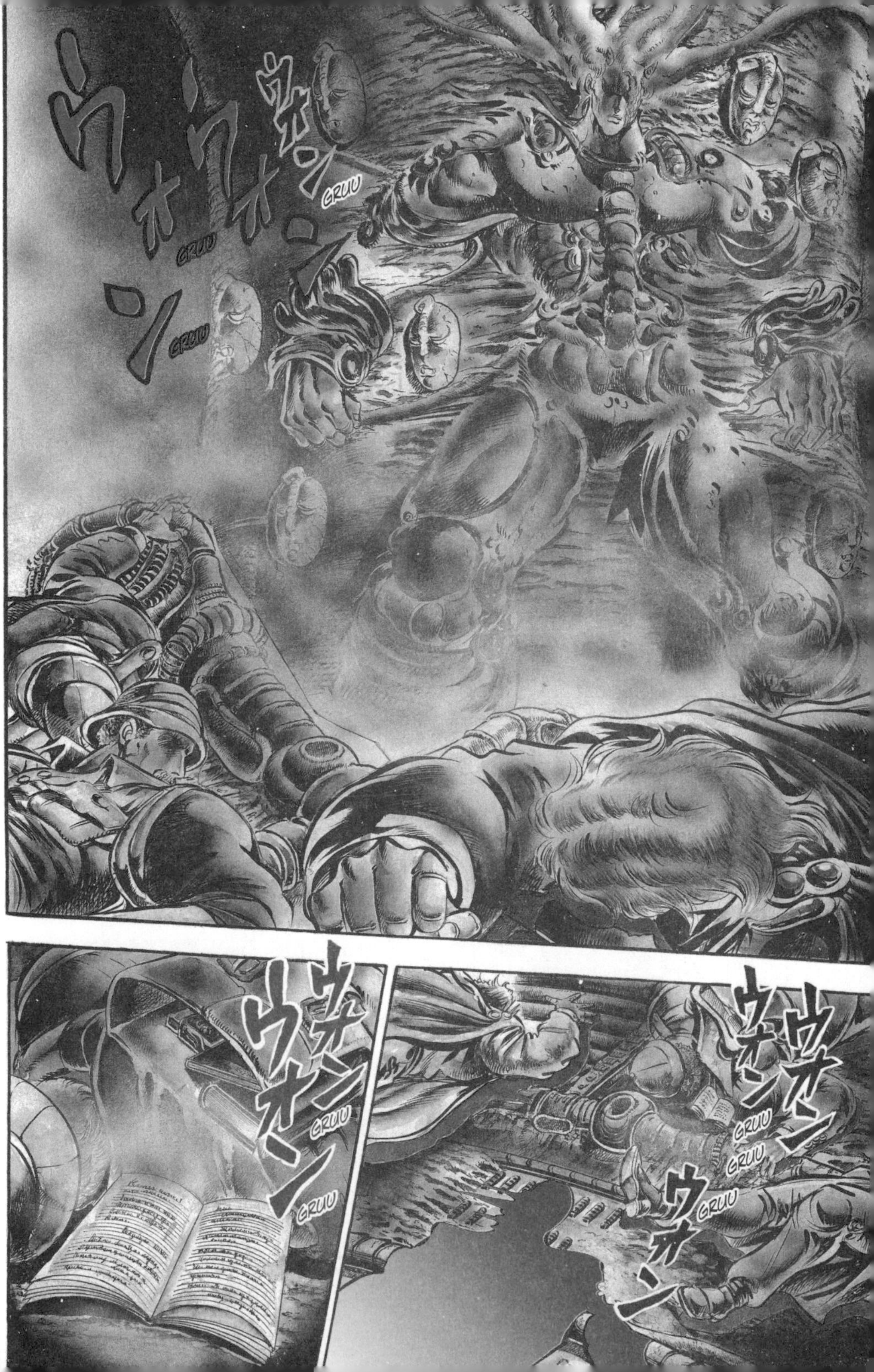

GRUU
GRUU
GRUU
ウォンウォン
GRUU
GRUU
GRUU
ウォン
GRUU
ウォンウォン
GRUU
GRUU

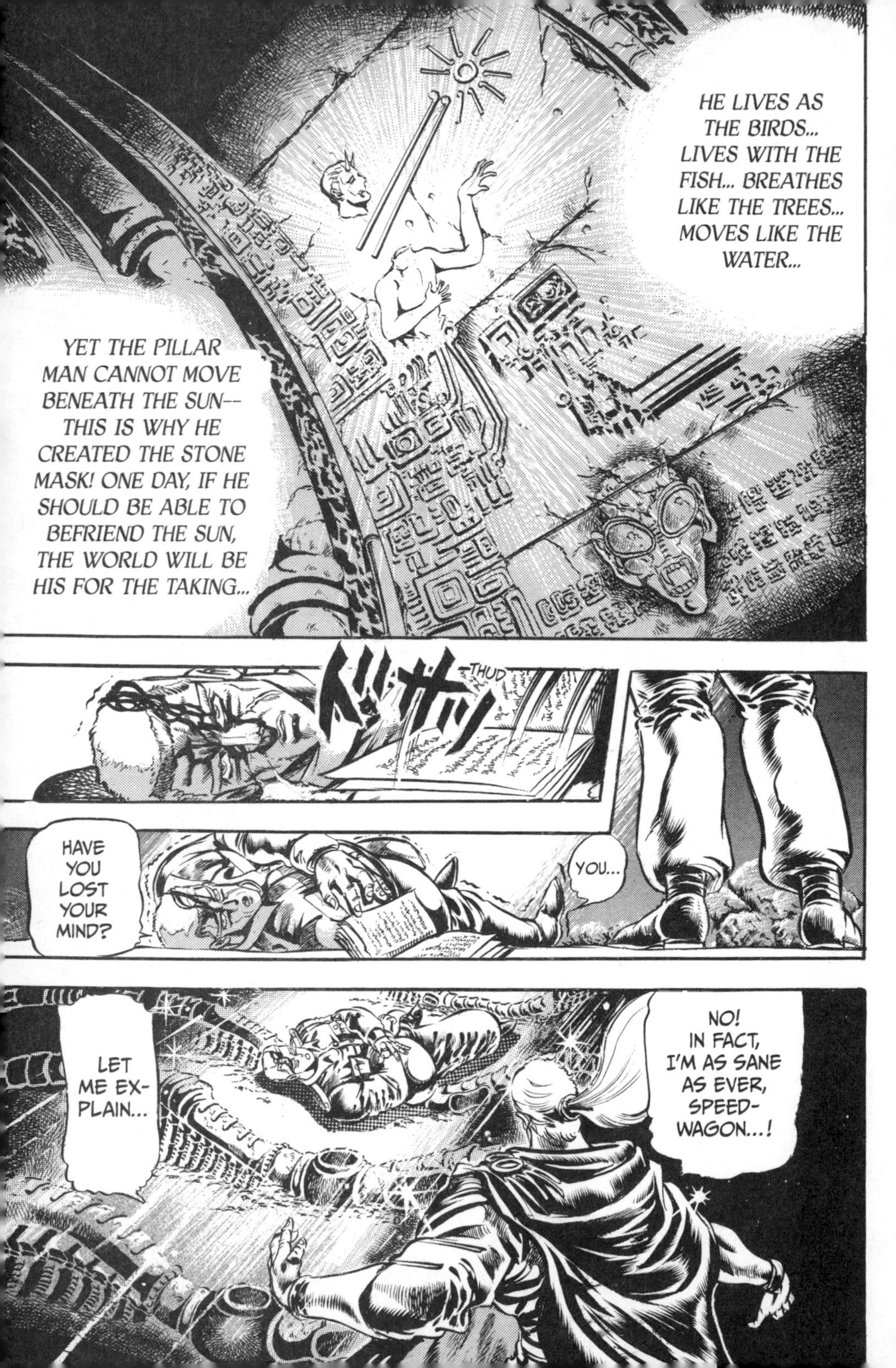
HE LIVES AS THE BIRDS... LIVES WITH THE FISH... BREATHES LIKE THE TREES... MOVES LIKE THE WATER...
YET THE PILLAR MAN CANNOT MOVE BENEATH THE SUN-- THIS IS WHY HE CREATED THE STONE MASK! ONE DAY, IF HE SHOULD BE ABLE TO BEFRIEND THE SUN, THE WORLD WILL BE HIS FOR THE TAKING...
THUD
YOU...
HAVE YOU LOST YOUR MIND?
NO! IN FACT, I'M AS SANE AS EVER, SPEED-WAGON...!
LET ME EX-PLAIN...

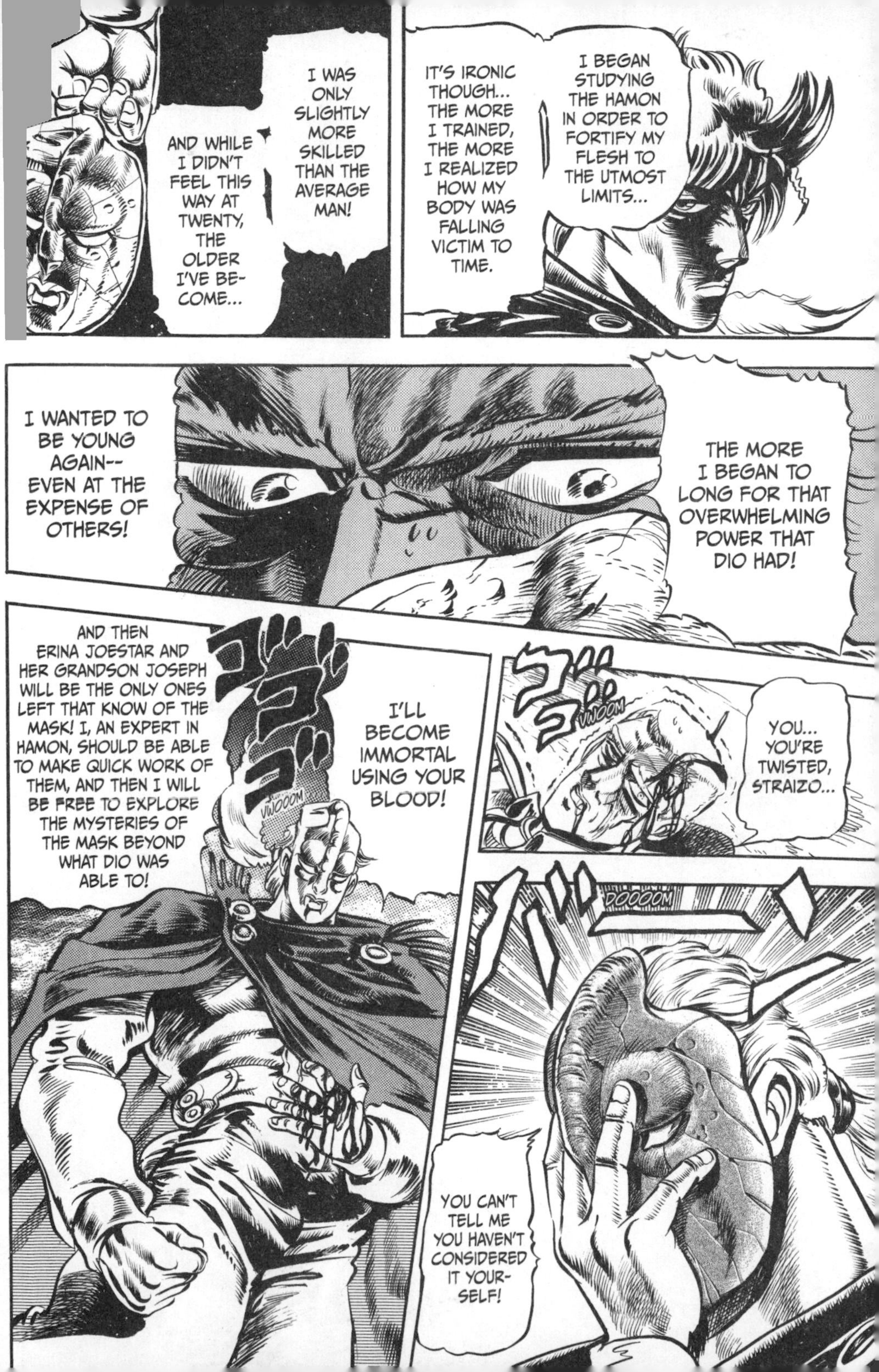

I BEGAN STUDYING THE HAMON IN ORDER TO FORTIFY MY FLESH TO THE UTMOST LIMITS...
IT'S IRONIC THOUGH... THE MORE I TRAINED, THE MORE I REALIZED HOW MY BODY WAS FALLING VICTIM TO TIME.
I WAS ONLY SLIGHTLY MORE SKILLED THAN THE AVERAGE MAN!
AND WHILE I DIDN'T FEEL THIS WAY AT TWENTY, THE OLDER I'VE BE-COME...
THE MORE I BEGAN TO LONG FOR THAT OVERWHELMING POWER THAT DIO HAD!
I WANTED TO BE YOUNG AGAIN-- EVEN AT THE EXPENSE OF OTHERS!
VWOOM
YOU... YOU'RE TWISTED, STRAIZO...
DOOOOM
YOU CAN'T TELL ME YOU HAVEN'T CONSIDERED IT YOUR-SELF!
VWOOOM
I'LL BECOME IMMORTAL USING YOUR BLOOD!
AND THEN ERINA JOESTAR AND HER GRANDSON JOSEPH WILL BE THE ONLY ONES LEFT THAT KNOW OF THE MASK! I, AN EXPERT IN HAMON, SHOULD BE ABLE TO MAKE QUICK WORK OF THEM, AND THEN I WILL BE FREE TO EXPLORE THE MYSTERIES OF THE MASK BEYOND WHAT DIO WAS ABLE TO!

VWOOM

THERE ARE TERRIBLE THINGS ABOUT THE MASK WE STILL DON'T KNOW...

NO, STOP...

SPLCH

NO...

MISS... ERINA...

JO... JO...

GASHIING

CHING

CHING CHING

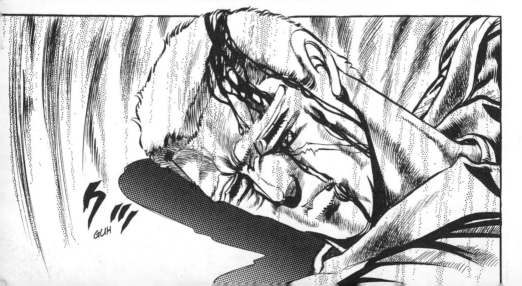

GUH

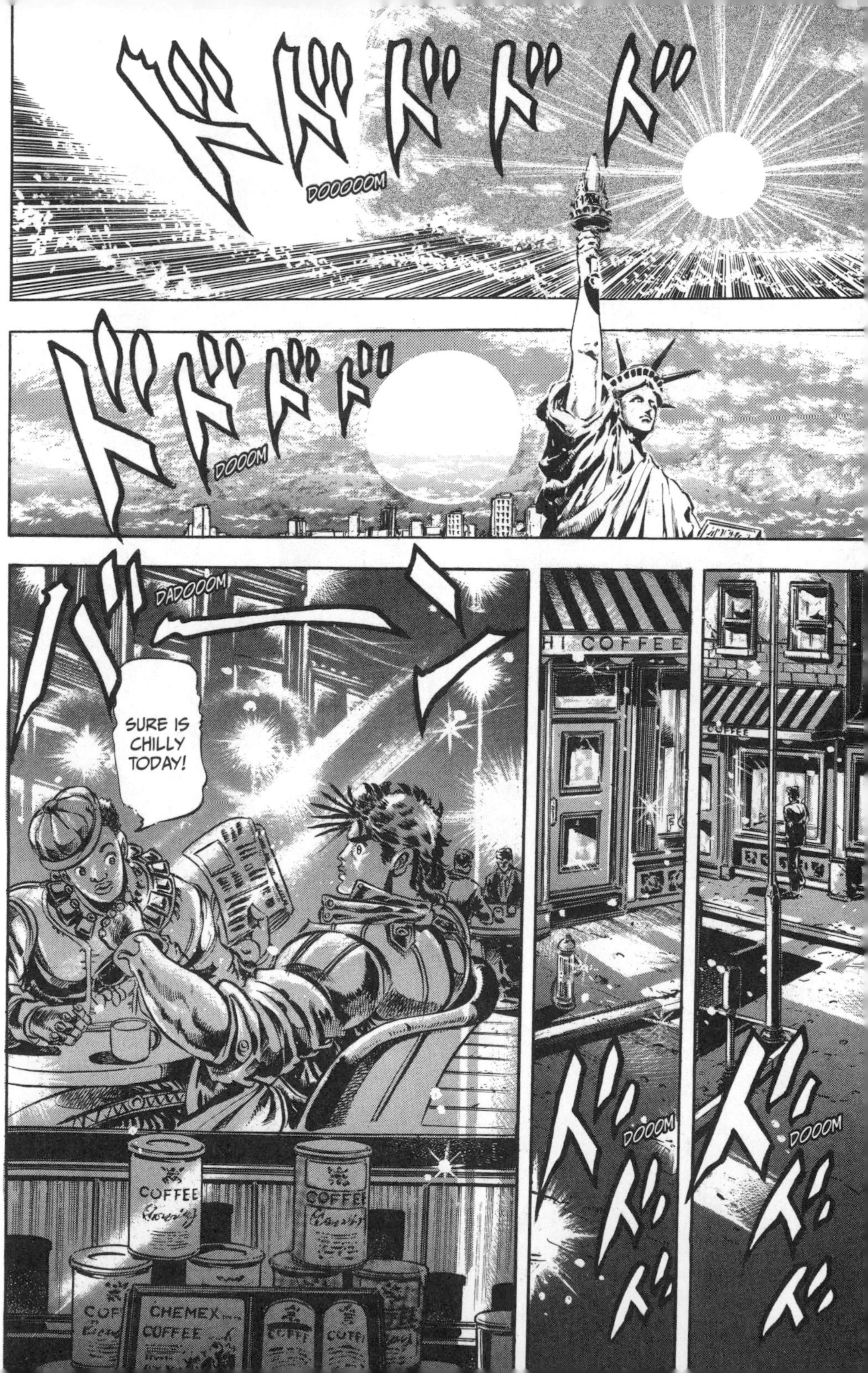
DOOOOOM
DOOOM
COFFEE
DOOOM
HI COFFEE
DOOOM
DADOOOM
SURE IS CHILLY TODAY!
COFFEE
COFFEE
CHEMEX
COFFEE

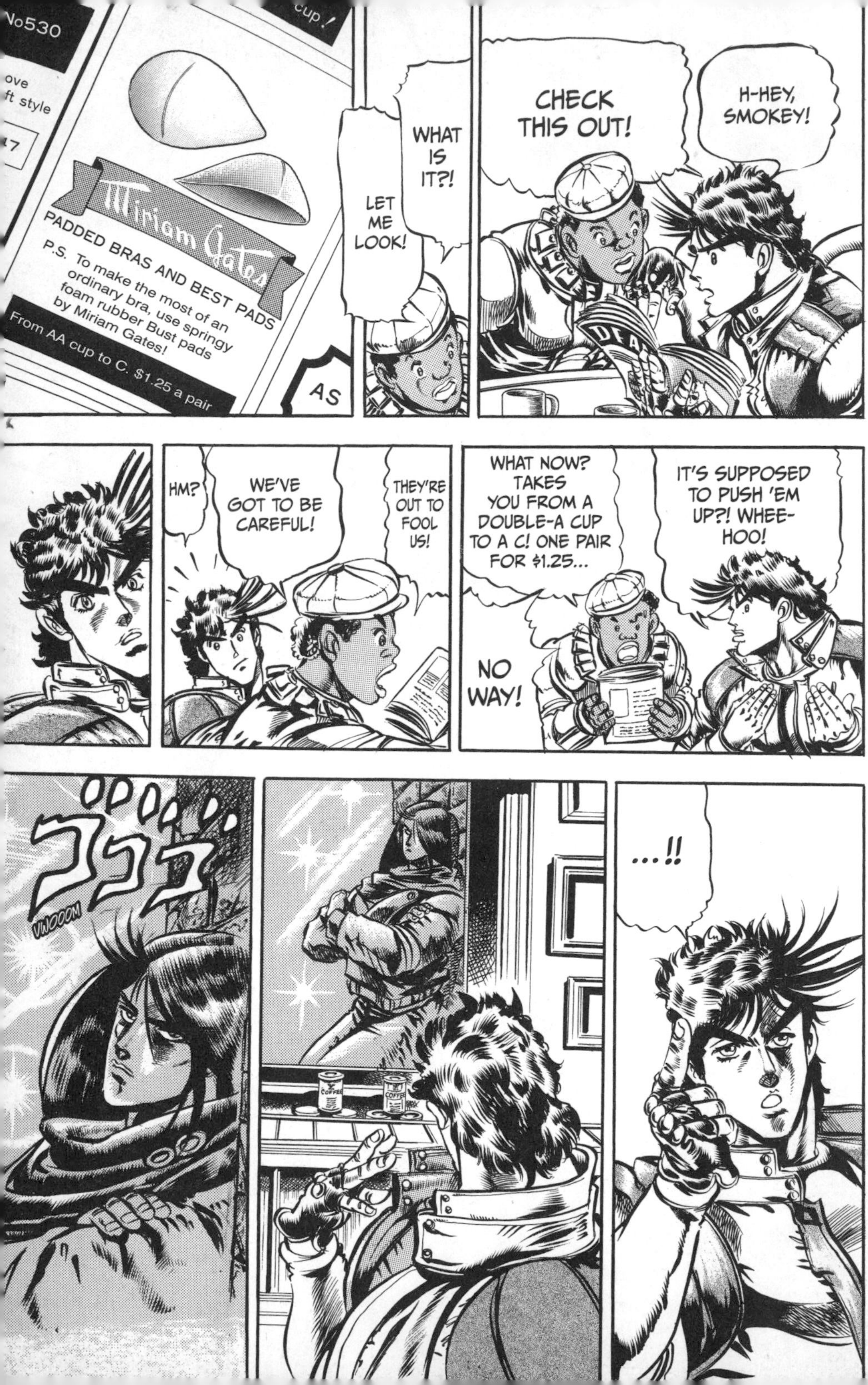

H-HEY, SMOKEY!
CHECK THIS OUT!
WHAT IS IT?!
LET ME LOOK!
cup!
No530
ove
ft style
Miriam Gates
PADDED BRAS AND BEST PADS
P.S. To make the most of an ordinary bra, use springy foam rubber Bust pads by Miriam Gates!
From AA cup to C. $1.25 a pair
AS
IT'S SUPPOSED TO PUSH 'EM UP?! WHEE-HOO!
WHAT NOW? TAKES YOU FROM A DOUBLE-A CUP TO A C! ONE PAIR FOR $1.25...
NO WAY!
THEY'RE OUT TO FOOL US!
WE'VE GOT TO BE CAREFUL!
HM?
...!!
COFFEE
COFFEE
ゴゴゴ
VWOOOM

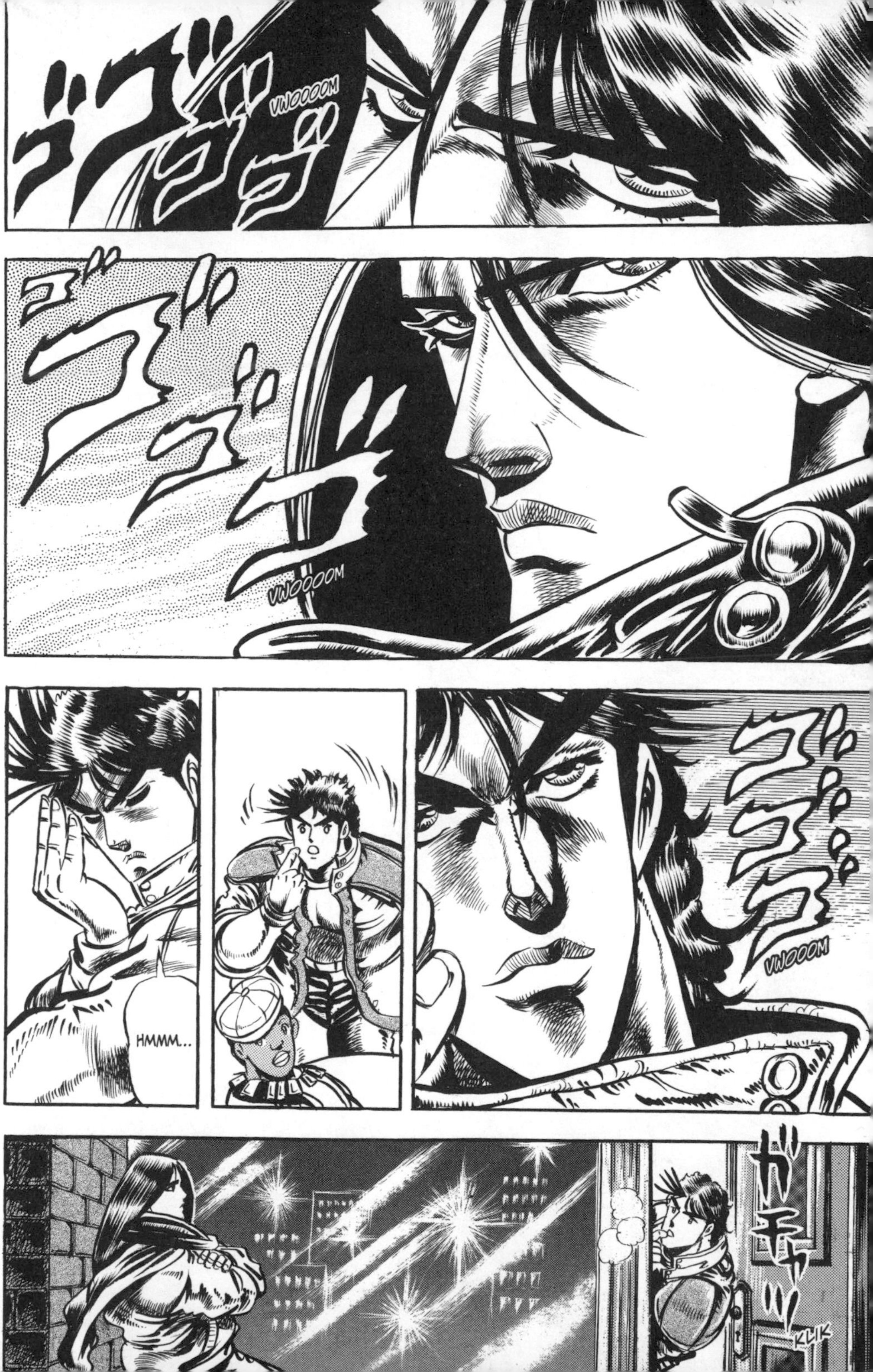
VWOOOOM
VWOOOOM
VWOOOM
HMMM...
KLIK

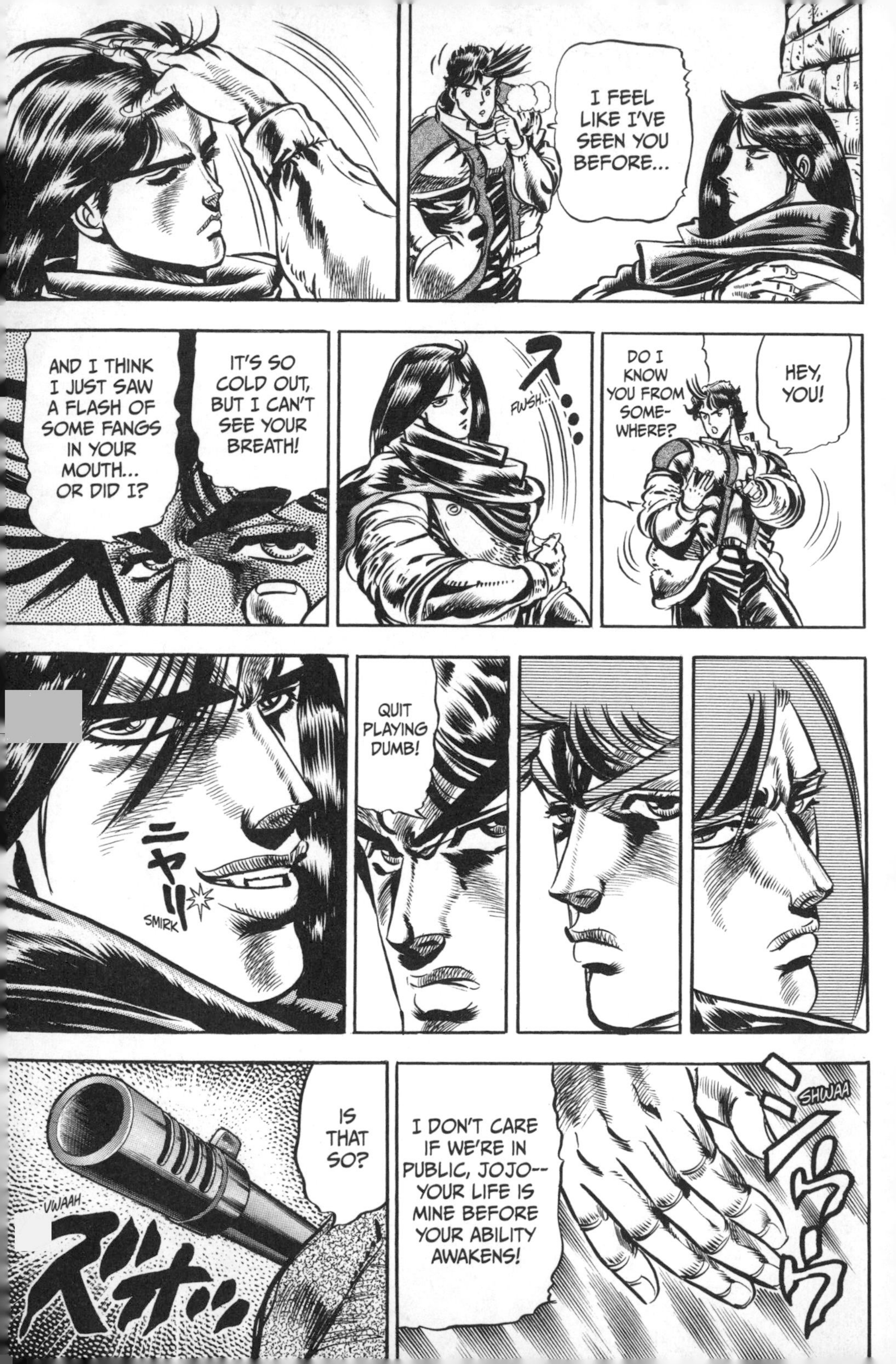
I FEEL LIKE I'VE SEEN YOU BEFORE...
HEY, YOU!
DO I KNOW YOU FROM SOME-WHERE?
FWSH...
IT'S SO COLD OUT, BUT I CAN'T SEE YOUR BREATH!
AND I THINK I JUST SAW A FLASH OF SOME FANGS IN YOUR MOUTH... OR DID I?
QUIT PLAYING DUMB!
SMIRK
SHWAA
I DON'T CARE IF WE'RE IN PUBLIC, JOJO-- YOUR LIFE IS MINE BEFORE YOUR ABILITY AWAKENS!
IS THAT SO?
VWAAH

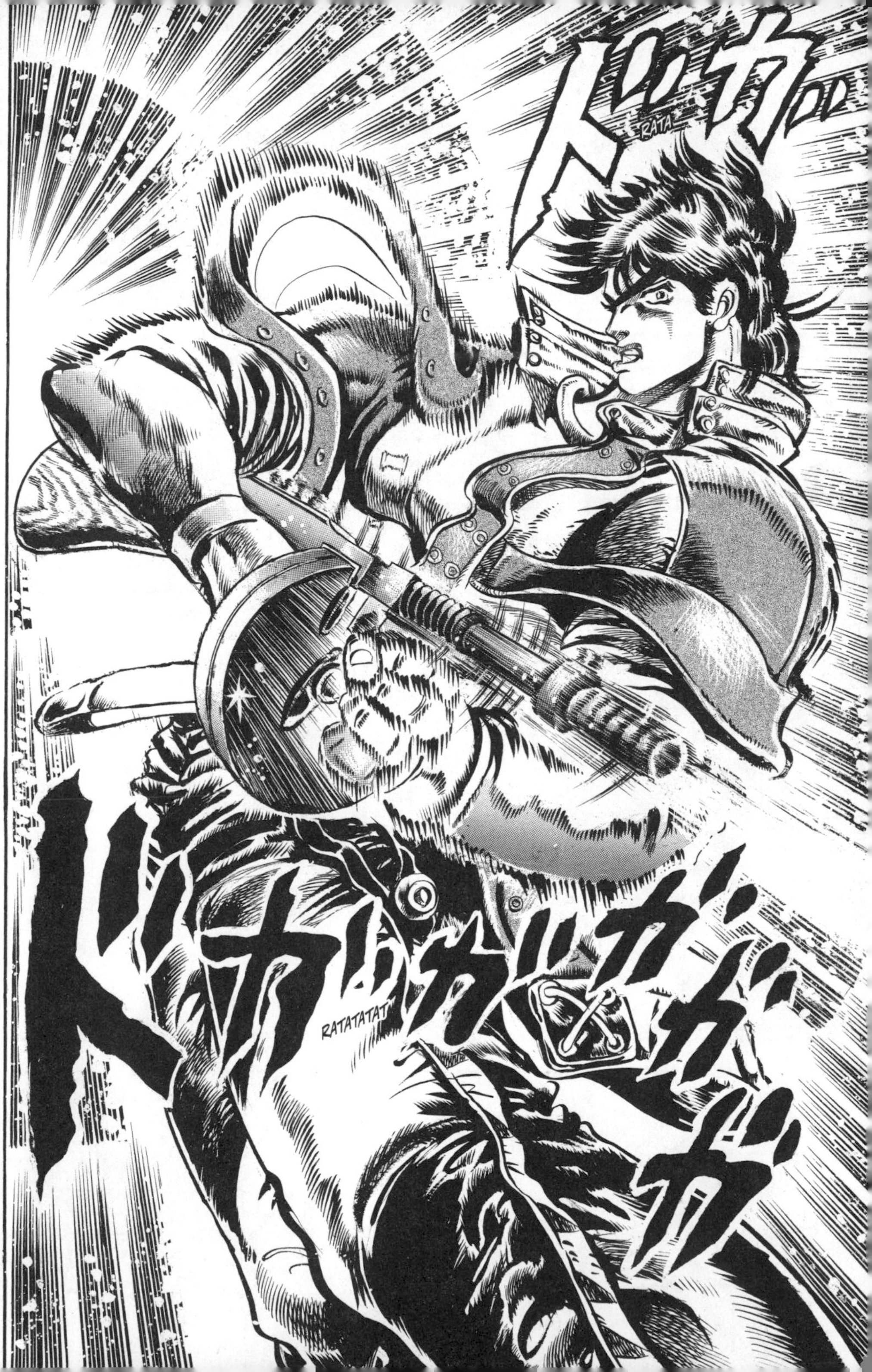
RATA
RATATATAT

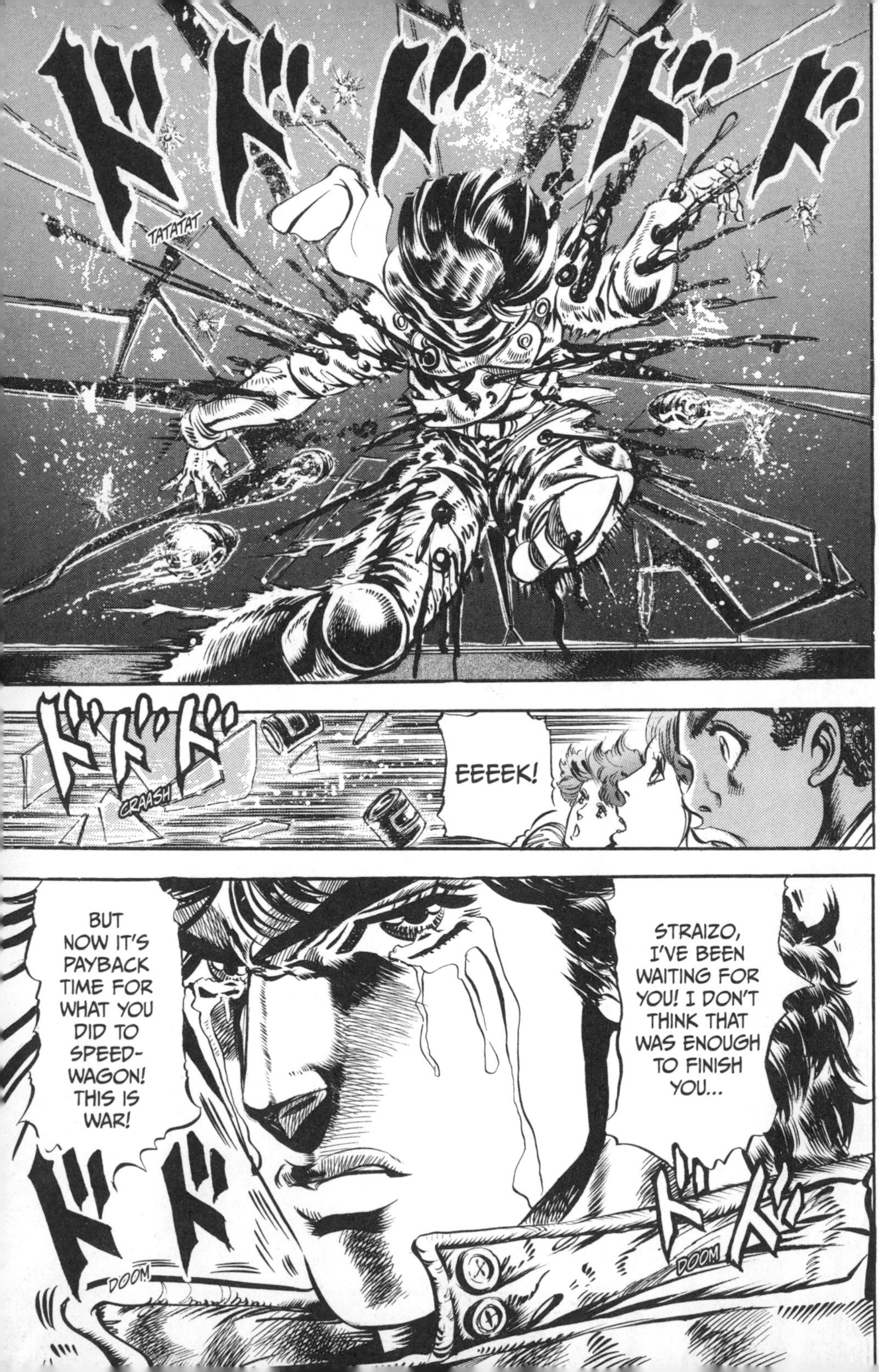
TATATAT
EEEEK!
CRAASH
STRAIZO, I'VE BEEN WAITING FOR YOU! I DON'T THINK THAT WAS ENOUGH TO FINISH YOU...
BUT NOW IT'S PAYBACK TIME FOR WHAT YOU DID TO SPEED-WAGON! THIS IS WAR!
DOOM
DOOM

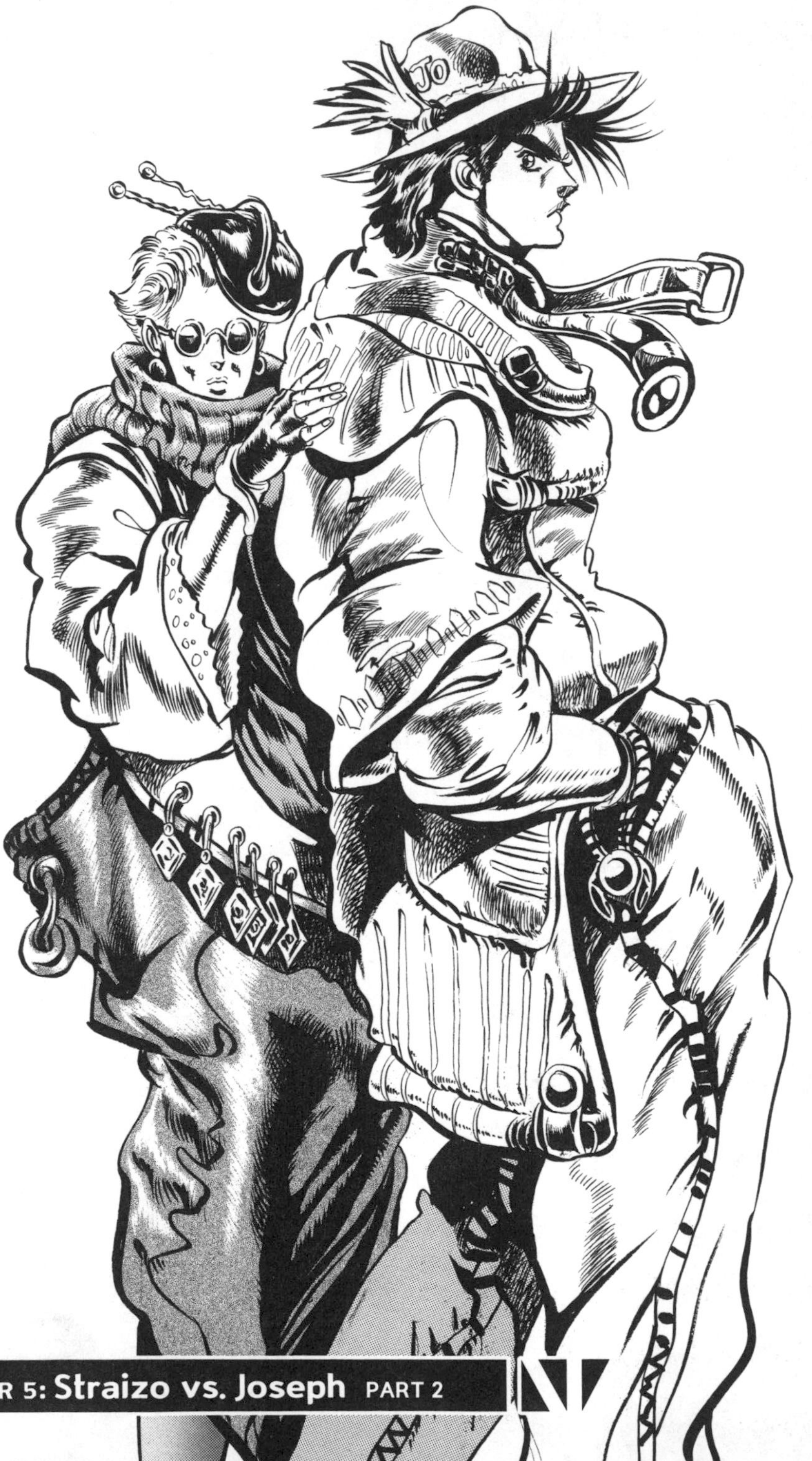
JO

CHAPTER 5: Straizo vs. Joseph PART 2

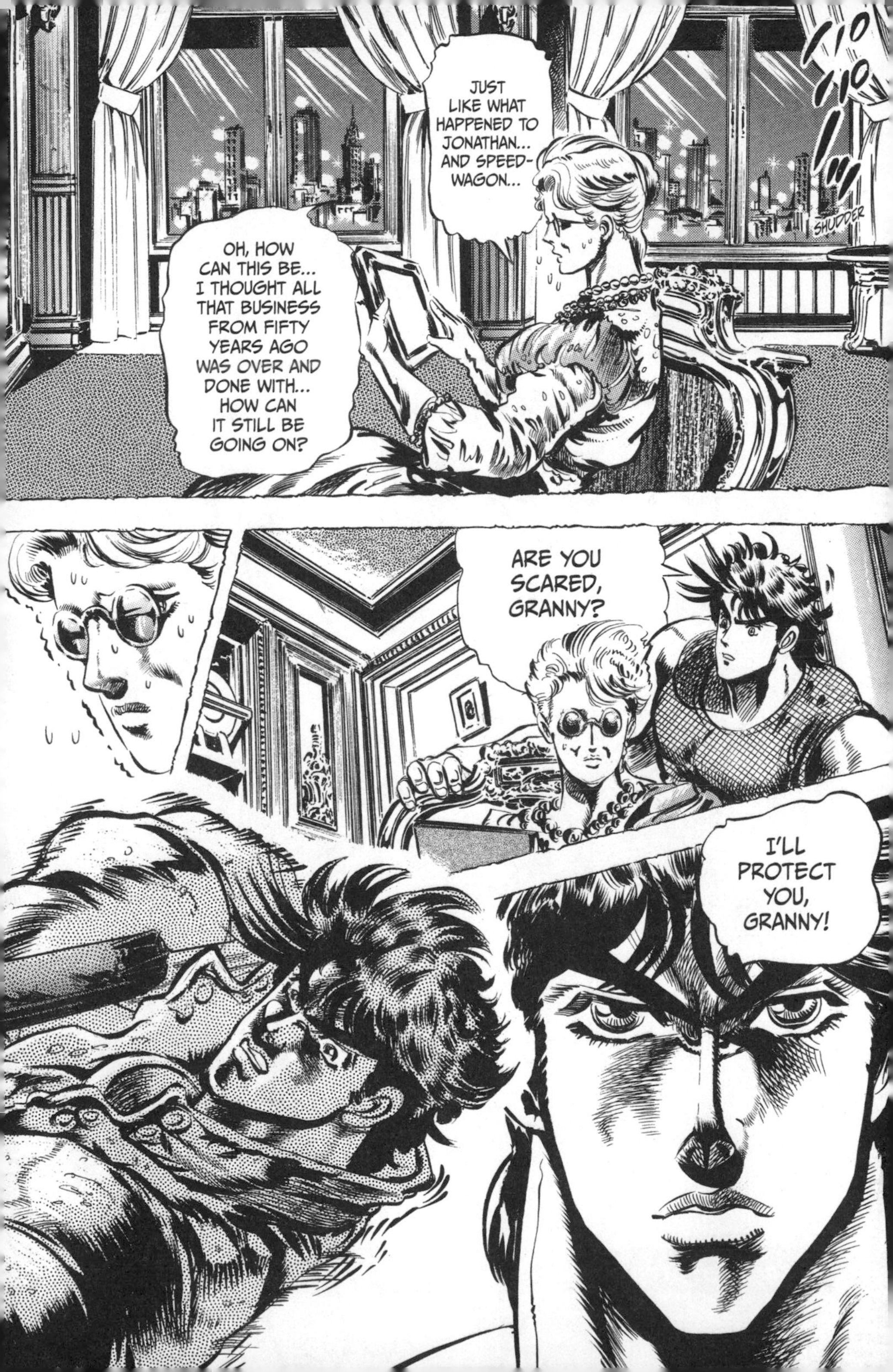
JUST LIKE WHAT HAPPENED TO JONATHAN... AND SPEED-WAGON...
SHUDDER
OH, HOW CAN THIS BE... I THOUGHT ALL THAT BUSINESS FROM FIFTY YEARS AGO WAS OVER AND DONE WITH... HOW CAN IT STILL BE GOING ON?
ARE YOU SCARED, GRANNY?
I'LL PROTECT YOU, GRANNY!

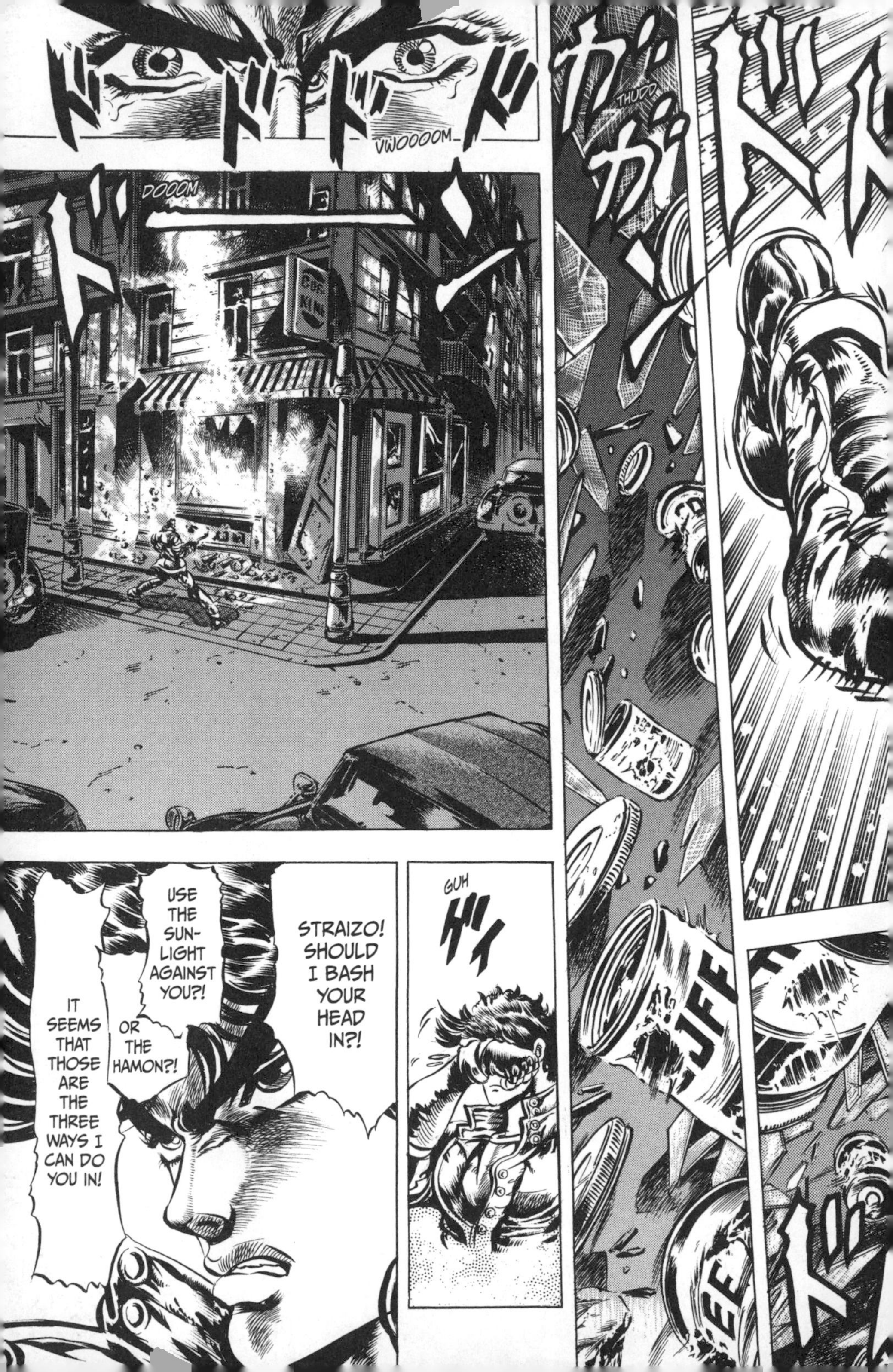
THUDD
VWOOOOM
DOOOM
GUH
STRAIZO! SHOULD I BASH YOUR HEAD IN?!
USE THE SUN-LIGHT AGAINST YOU?!
OR THE HAMON?!
IT SEEMS THAT THOSE ARE THE THREE WAYS I CAN DO YOU IN!

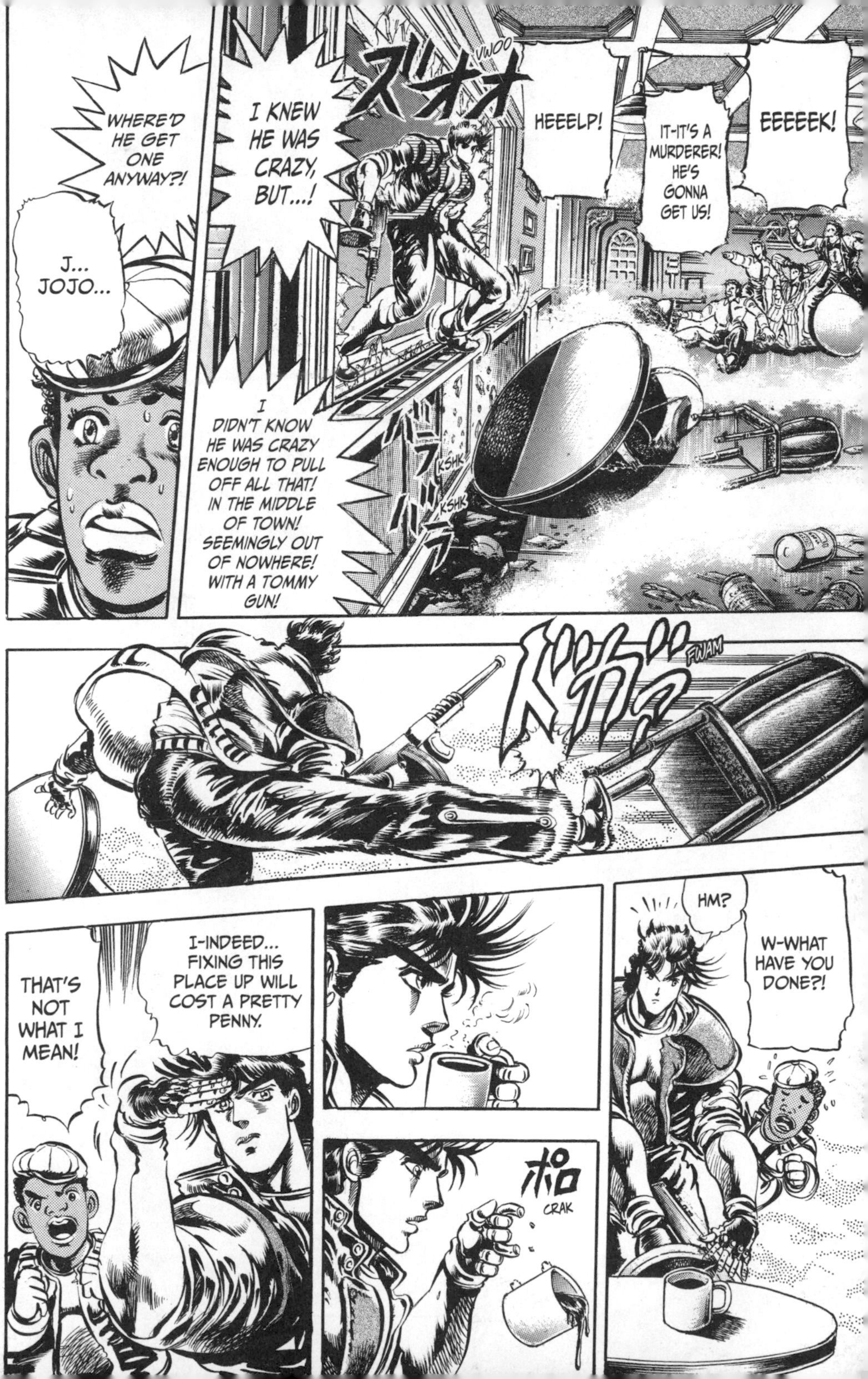
EEEEEK!
IT-IT'S A MURDERER! HE'S GONNA GET US!
HEEELP!
VWOO
I KNEW HE WAS CRAZY, BUT...!
I DIDN'T KNOW HE WAS CRAZY ENOUGH TO PULL OFF ALL THAT! IN THE MIDDLE OF TOWN! SEEMINGLY OUT OF NOWHERE! WITH A TOMMY GUN!
KSHK
KSHK
WHERE'D HE GET ONE ANYWAY?!
J... JOJO...
FWAM
HM?
W-WHAT HAVE YOU DONE?!
CRAK
I-INDEED... FIXING THIS PLACE UP WILL COST A PRETTY PENNY.
THAT'S NOT WHAT I MEAN!

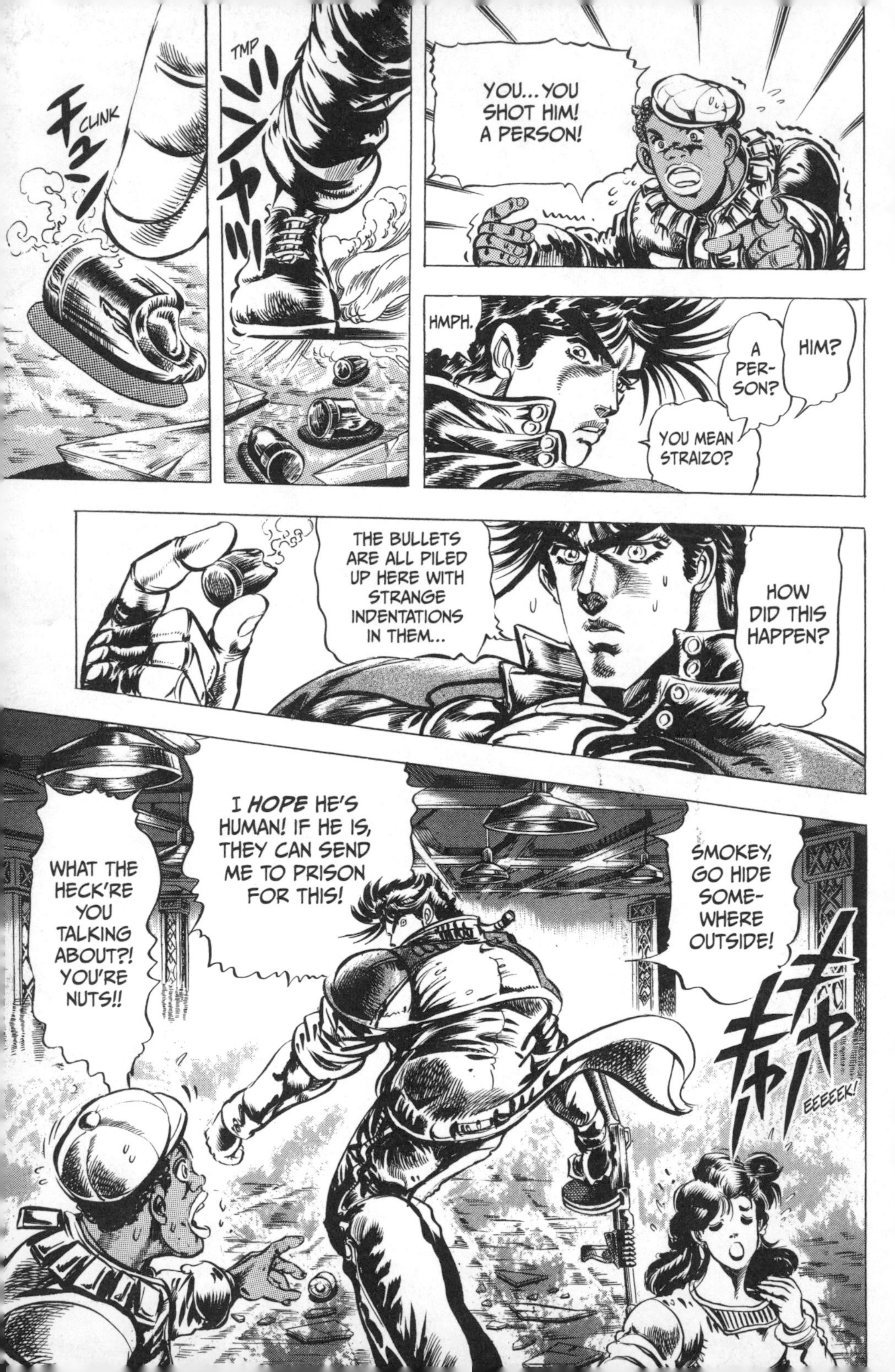
YOU... YOU SHOT HIM! A PERSON!
HIM?
A PER-SON?
YOU MEAN STRAIZO?
HMPH.
TMP
CLINK
HOW DID THIS HAPPEN?
THE BULLETS ARE ALL PILED UP HERE WITH STRANGE INDENTATIONS IN THEM...
SMOKEY, GO HIDE SOME-WHERE OUTSIDE!
EEEEEK!
I *HOPE* HE'S HUMAN! IF HE IS, THEY CAN SEND ME TO PRISON FOR THIS!
WHAT THE HECK'RE YOU TALKING ABOUT?! YOU'RE NUTS!!

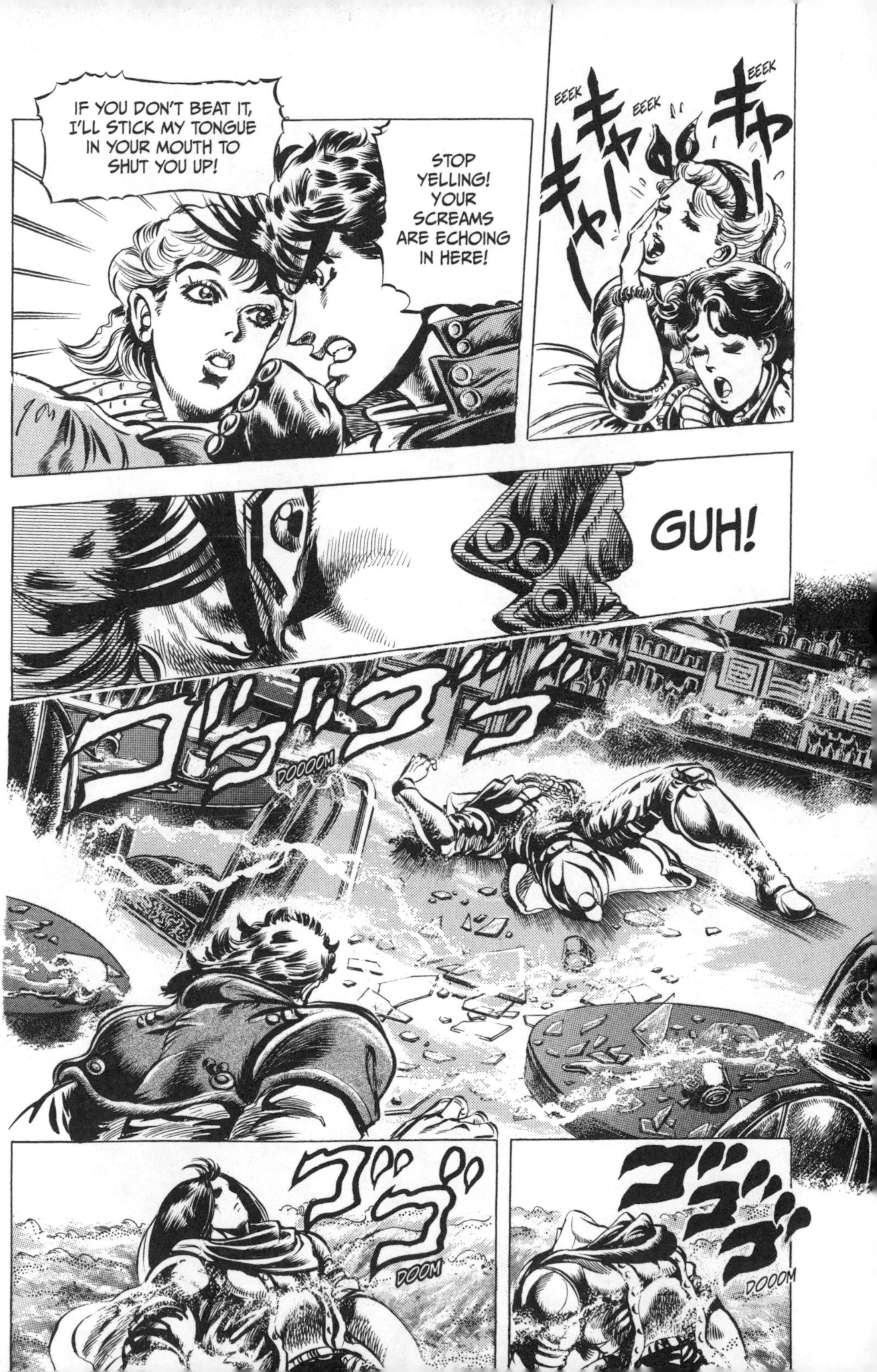
EEEK
EEEK
EEEK
STOP YELLING! YOUR SCREAMS ARE ECHOING IN HERE!
IF YOU DON'T BEAT IT, I'LL STICK MY TONGUE IN YOUR MOUTH TO SHUT YOU UP!
GUH!
DOOOOM
DOOOM
DOOM

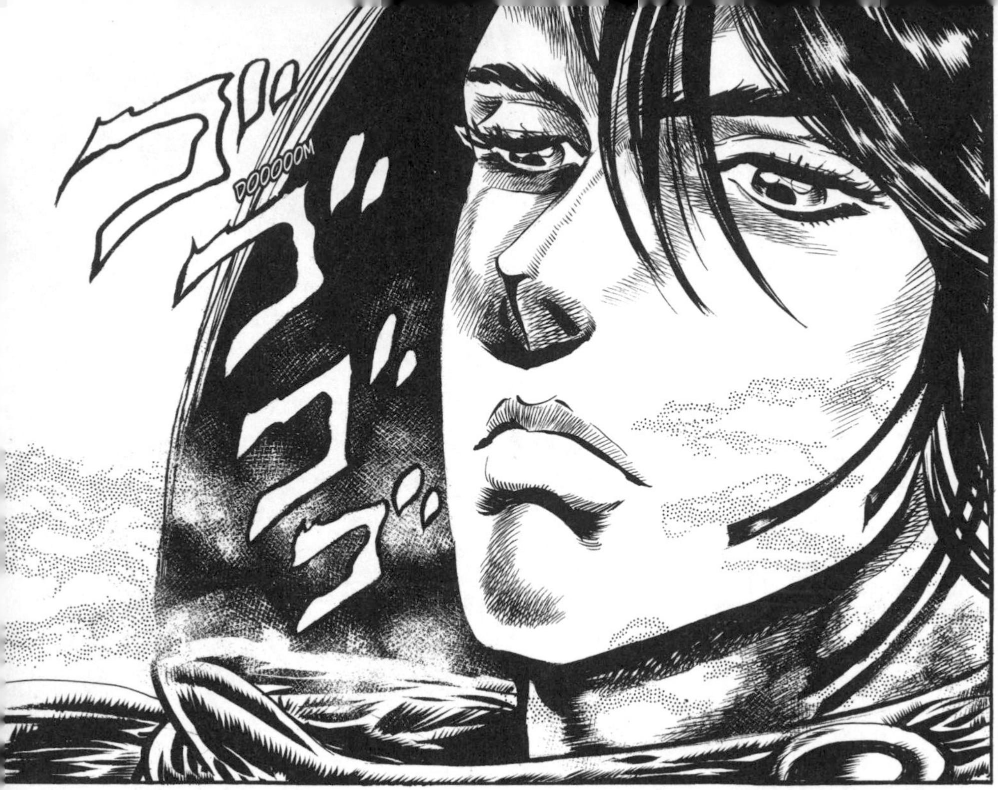
DOOOOOM
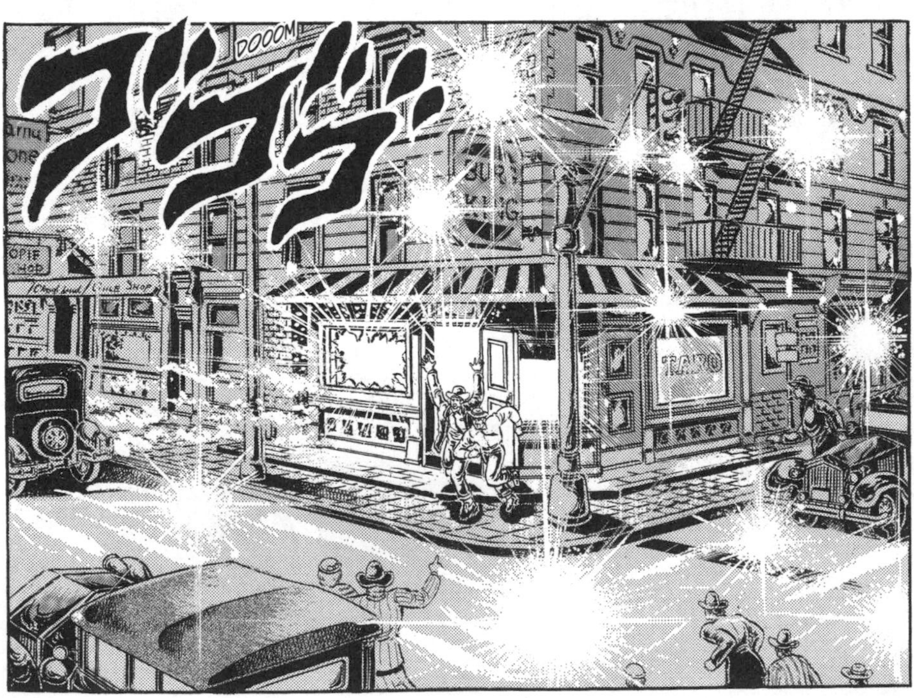
DOOOM

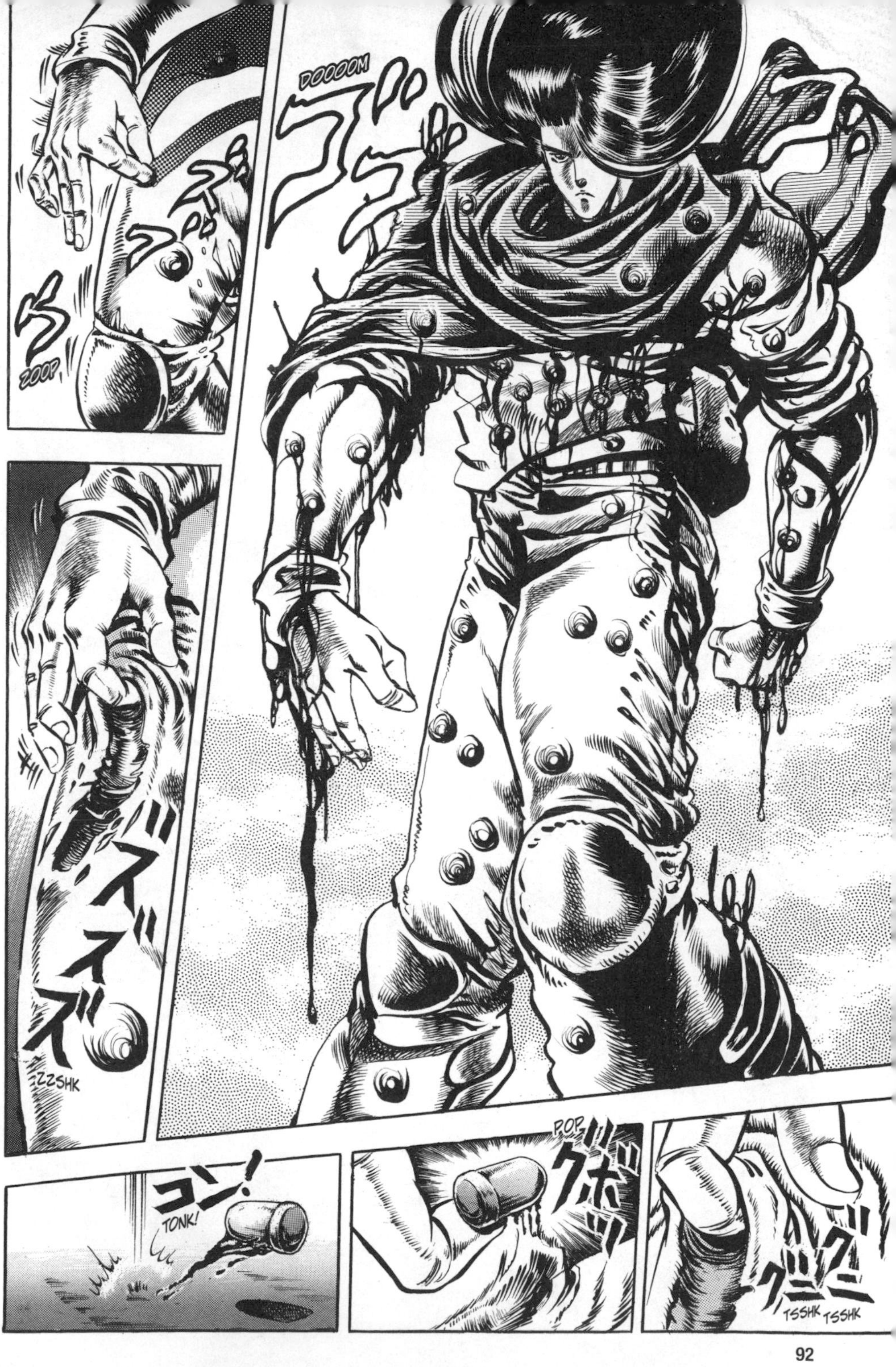
DOOOOM
ZOOP
ZZSHK
TSSHK TSSHK
POP
コン!
TONK!

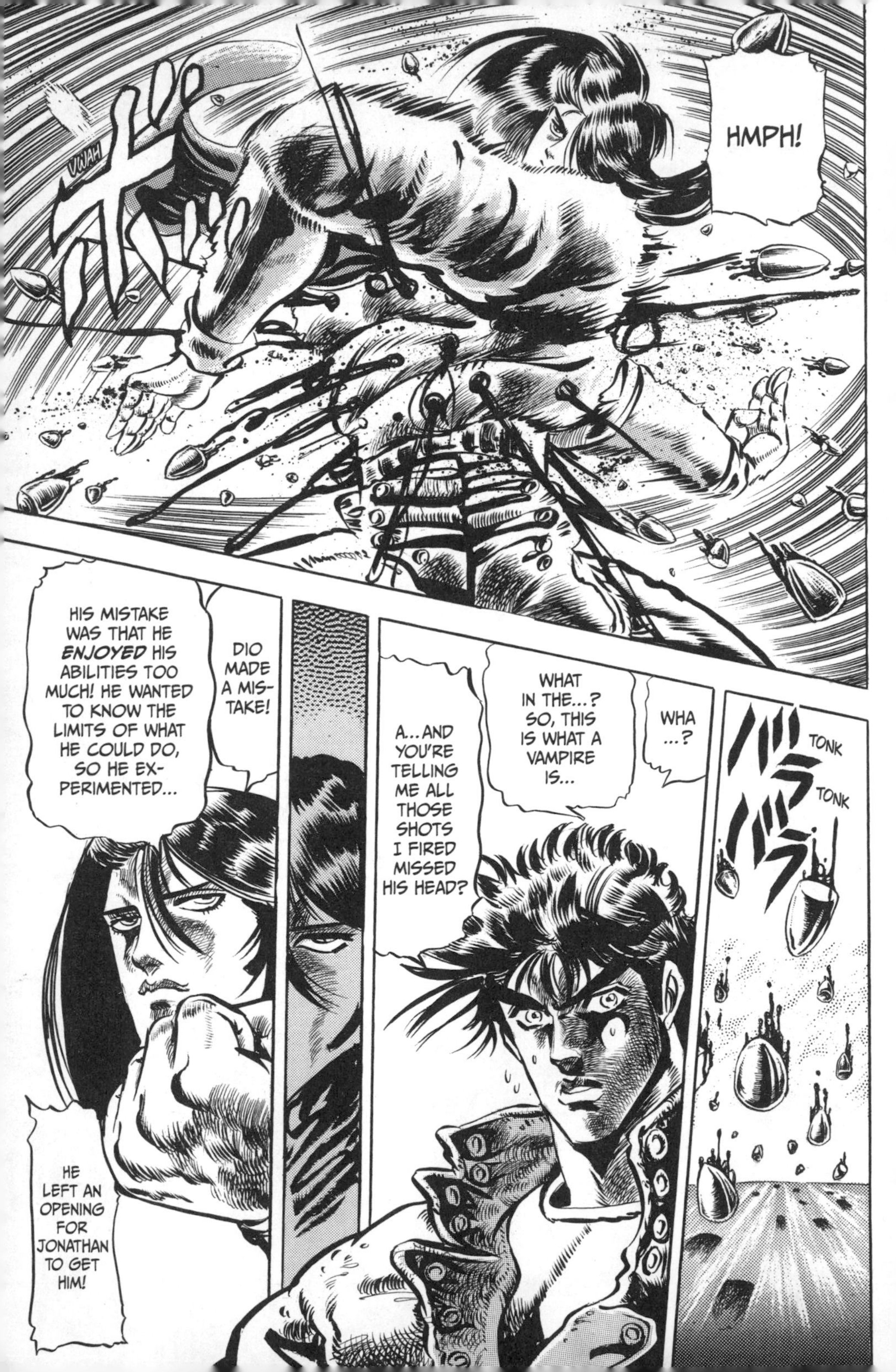

HMPH!
VWAH
バラ
バラ
TONK
TONK
WHA ...?
WHAT IN THE...? SO, THIS IS WHAT A VAMPIRE IS...
A...AND YOU'RE TELLING ME ALL THOSE SHOTS I FIRED MISSED HIS HEAD?
DIO MADE A MIS-TAKE!
HIS MISTAKE WAS THAT HE *ENJOYED* HIS ABILITIES TOO MUCH! HE WANTED TO KNOW THE LIMITS OF WHAT HE COULD DO, SO HE EX-PERIMENTED...
HE LEFT AN OPENING FOR JONATHAN TO GET HIM!

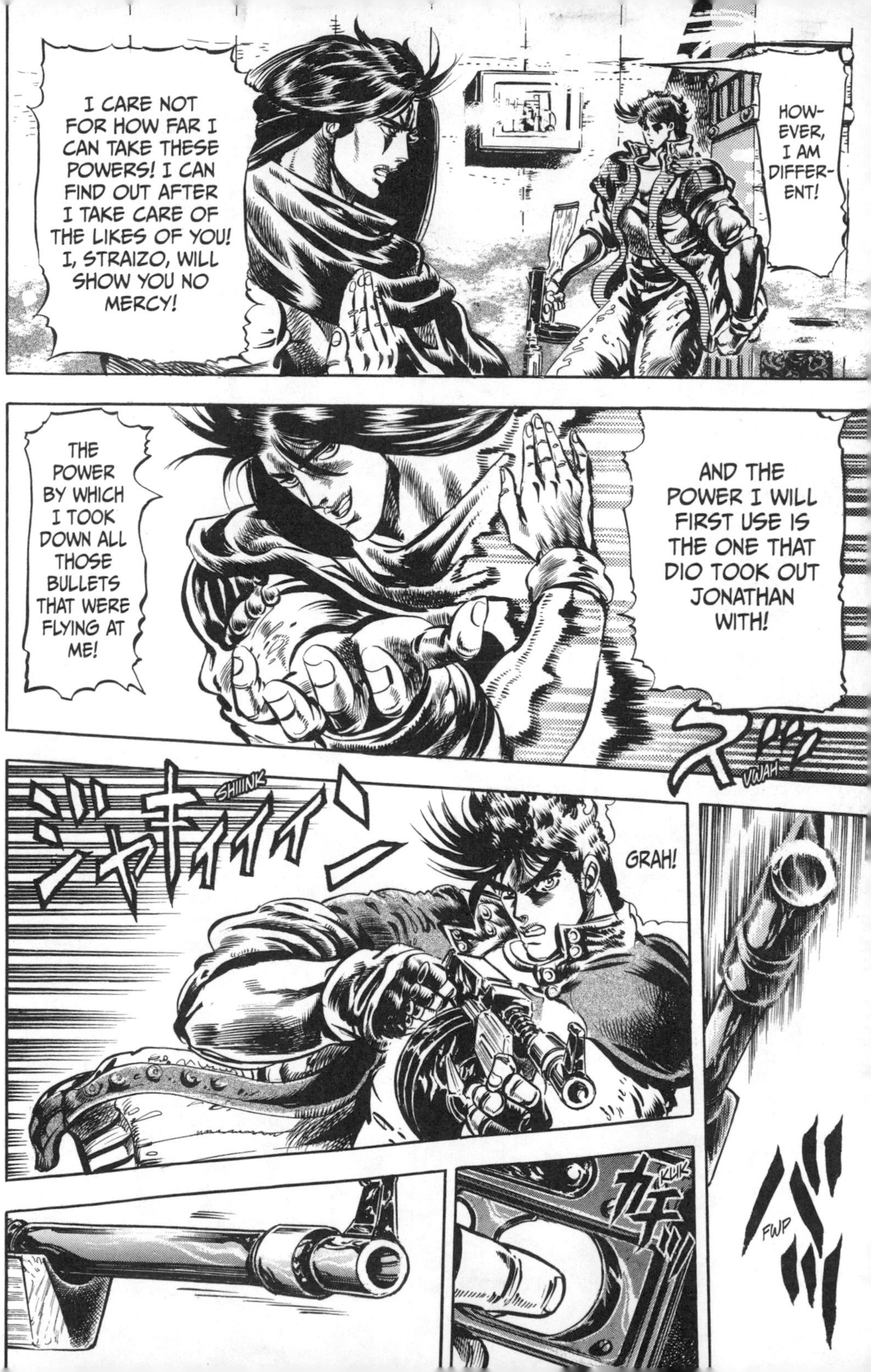
I CARE NOT FOR HOW FAR I CAN TAKE THESE POWERS! I CAN FIND OUT AFTER I TAKE CARE OF THE LIKES OF YOU! I, STRAIZO, WILL SHOW YOU NO MERCY!
HOW-EVER, I AM DIFFER-ENT!
THE POWER BY WHICH I TOOK DOWN ALL THOSE BULLETS THAT WERE FLYING AT ME!
AND THE POWER I WILL FIRST USE IS THE ONE THAT DIO TOOK OUT JONATHAN WITH!
VWAH
SHIIINK
GRAH!
KLIK
FWP

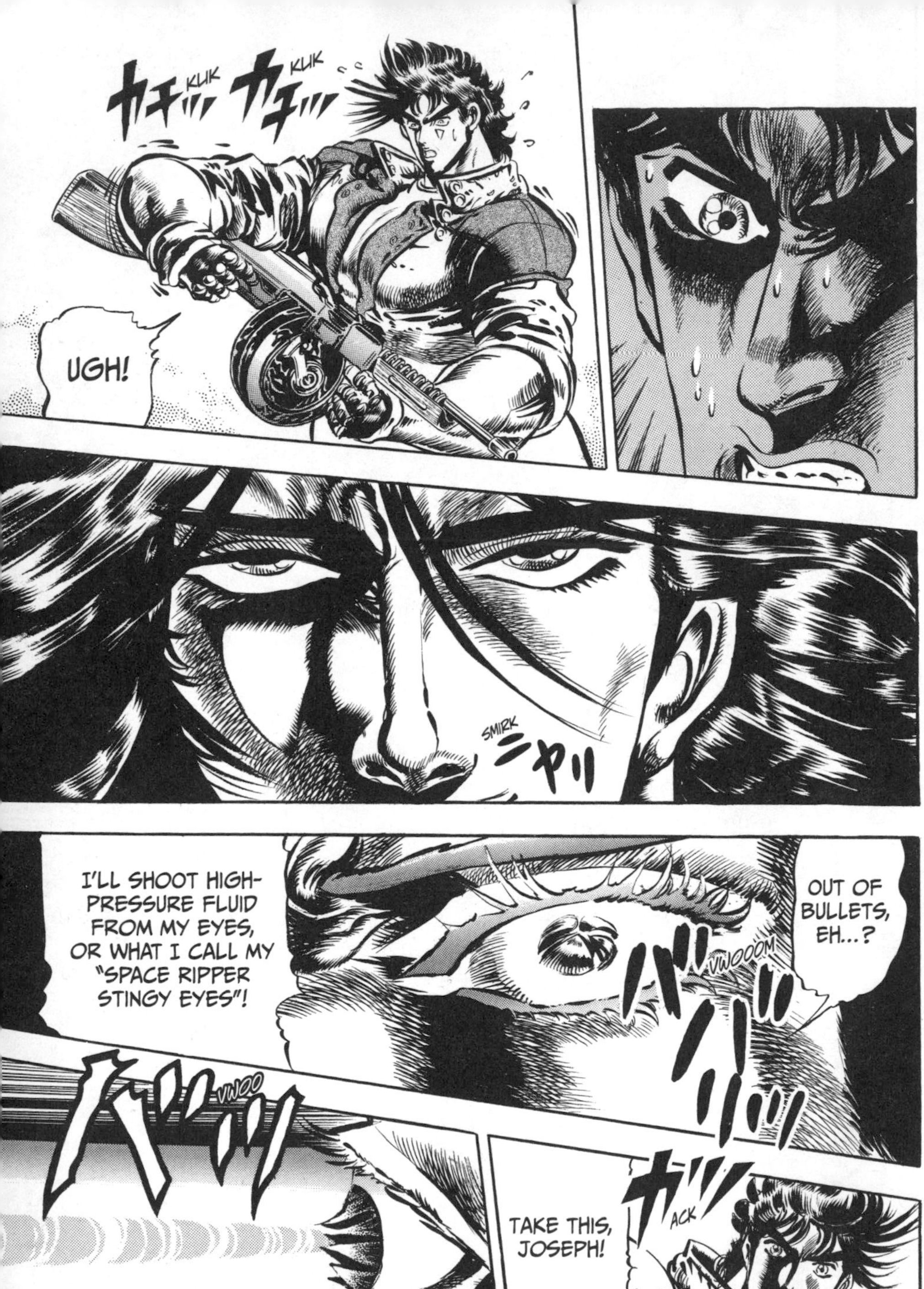
KUK
KUK
UGH!
SMIRK
OUT OF BULLETS, EH...?
I'LL SHOOT HIGH-PRESSURE FLUID FROM MY EYES, OR WHAT I CALL MY "SPACE RIPPER STINGY EYES"!
VWOOOM
TAKE THIS, JOSEPH!
ACK
VWOO

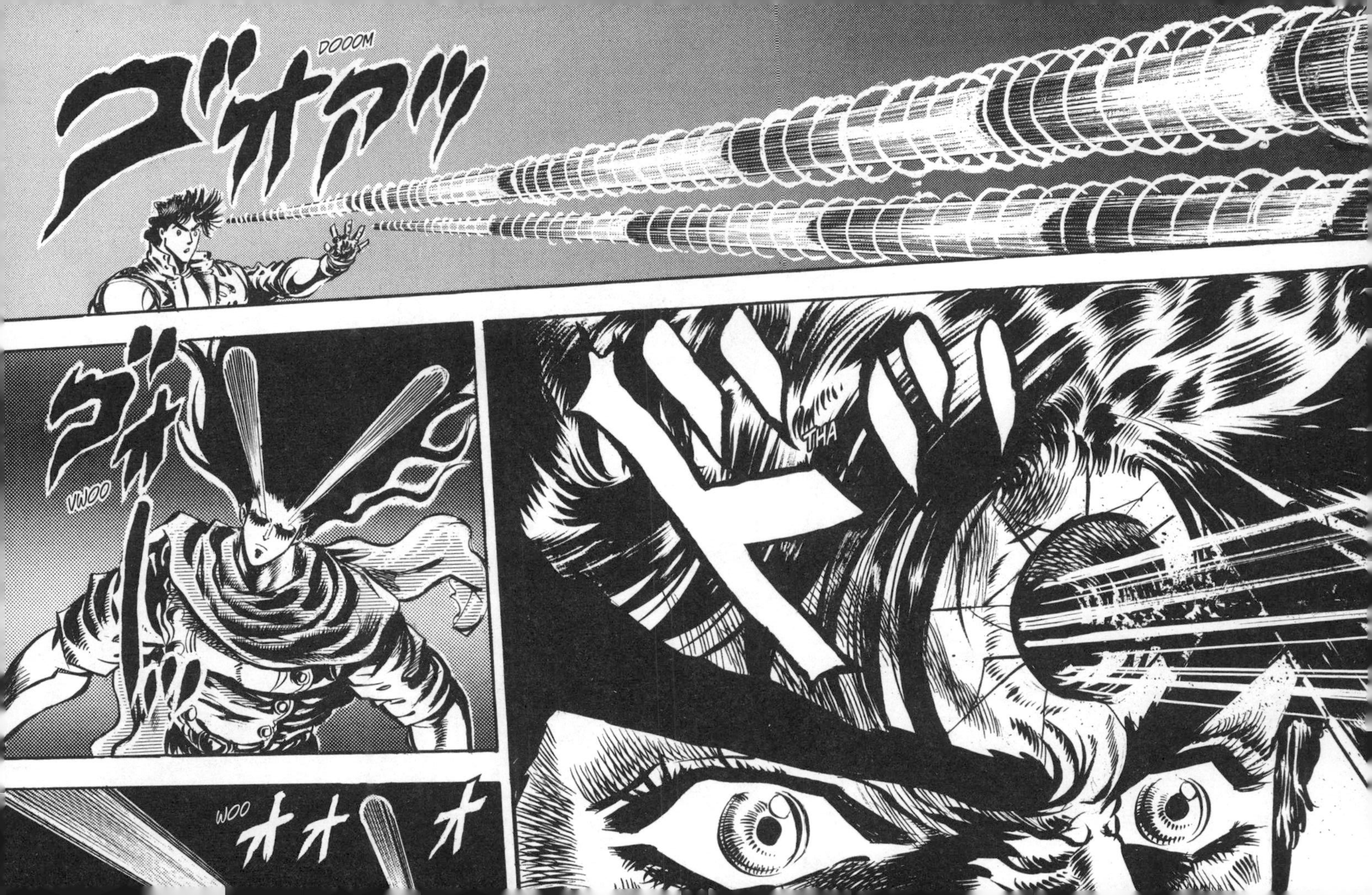
ゴオアッ
DOOOM
ドン
THA
ウオ
VWOO
オオオ
WOO

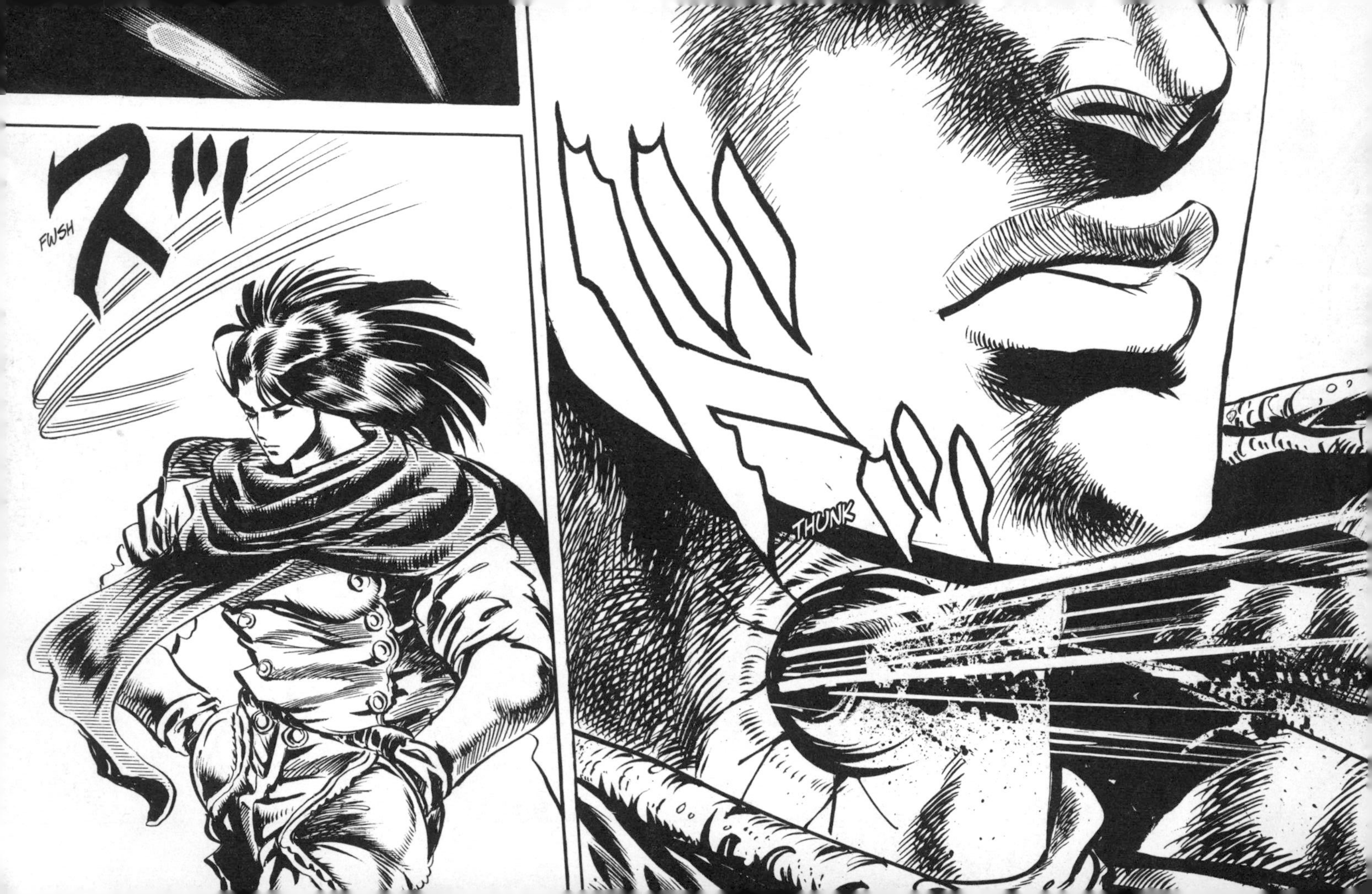
THUNK
FWSH

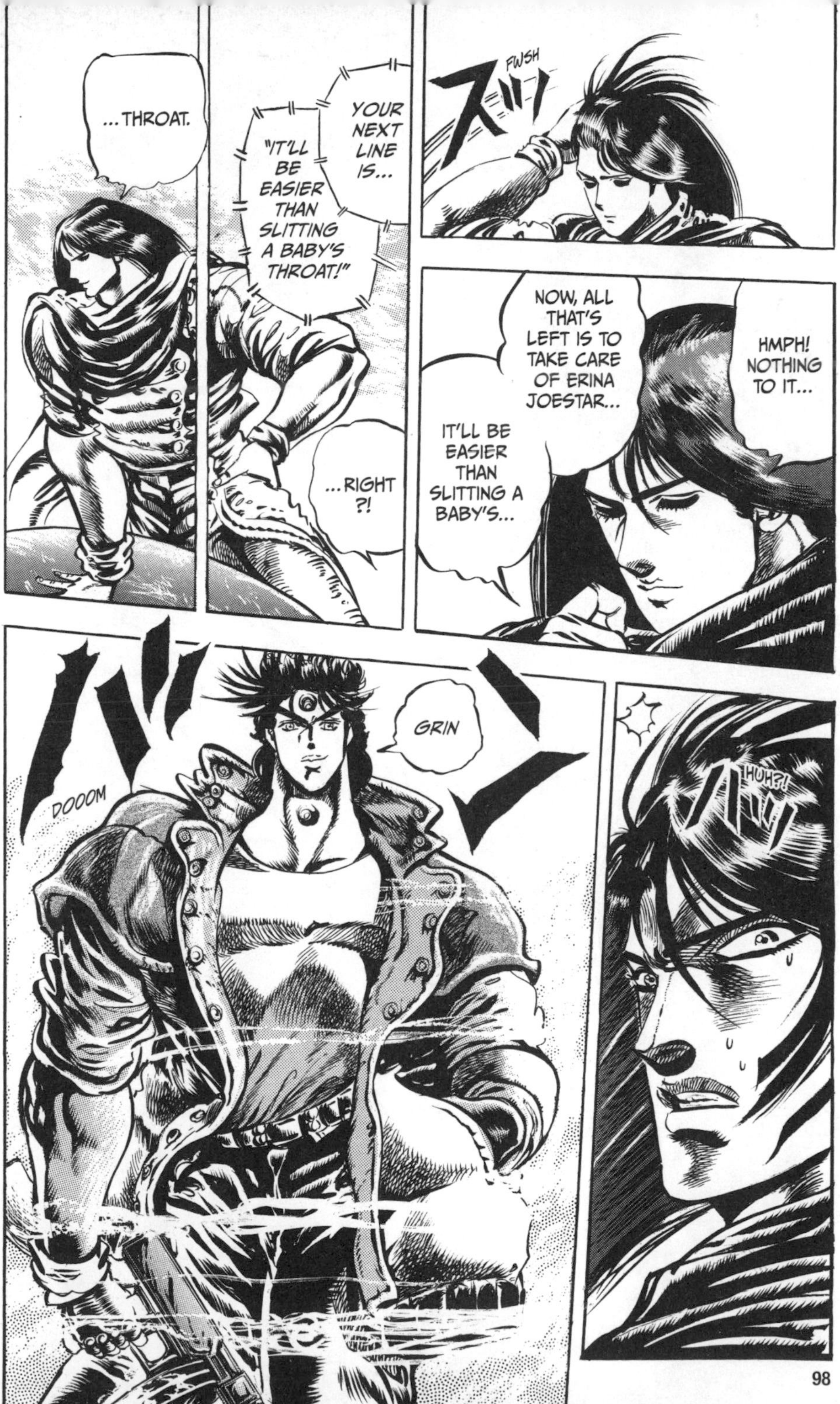
FWSH
HMPH! NOTHING TO IT...
NOW, ALL THAT'S LEFT IS TO TAKE CARE OF ERINA JOESTAR...
IT'LL BE EASIER THAN SLITTING A BABY'S...
YOUR NEXT LINE IS...
"IT'LL BE EASIER THAN SLITTING A BABY'S THROAT!"
...RIGHT?!
...THROAT.
HUH?!
GRIN
DOOOM

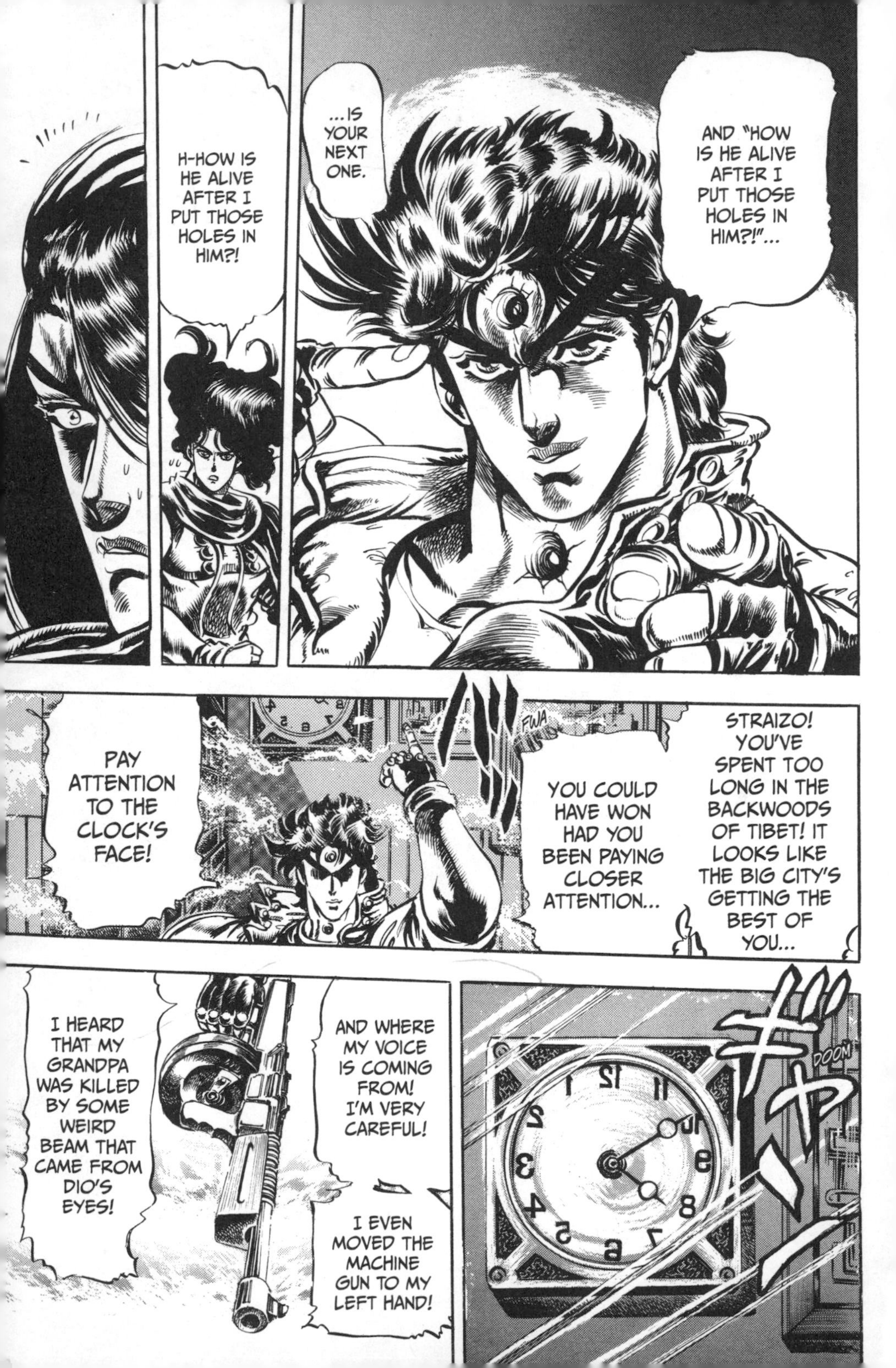
AND "HOW IS HE ALIVE AFTER I PUT THOSE HOLES IN HIM?!"...
...IS YOUR NEXT ONE.
H-HOW IS HE ALIVE AFTER I PUT THOSE HOLES IN HIM?!
STRAIZO! YOU'VE SPENT TOO LONG IN THE BACKWOODS OF TIBET! IT LOOKS LIKE THE BIG CITY'S GETTING THE BEST OF YOU...
YOU COULD HAVE WON HAD YOU BEEN PAYING CLOSER ATTENTION...
FWA
PAY ATTENTION TO THE CLOCK'S FACE!
DOOM
AND WHERE MY VOICE IS COMING FROM! I'M VERY CAREFUL!
I HEARD THAT MY GRANDPA WAS KILLED BY SOME WEIRD BEAM THAT CAME FROM DIO'S EYES!
I EVEN MOVED THE MACHINE GUN TO MY LEFT HAND!

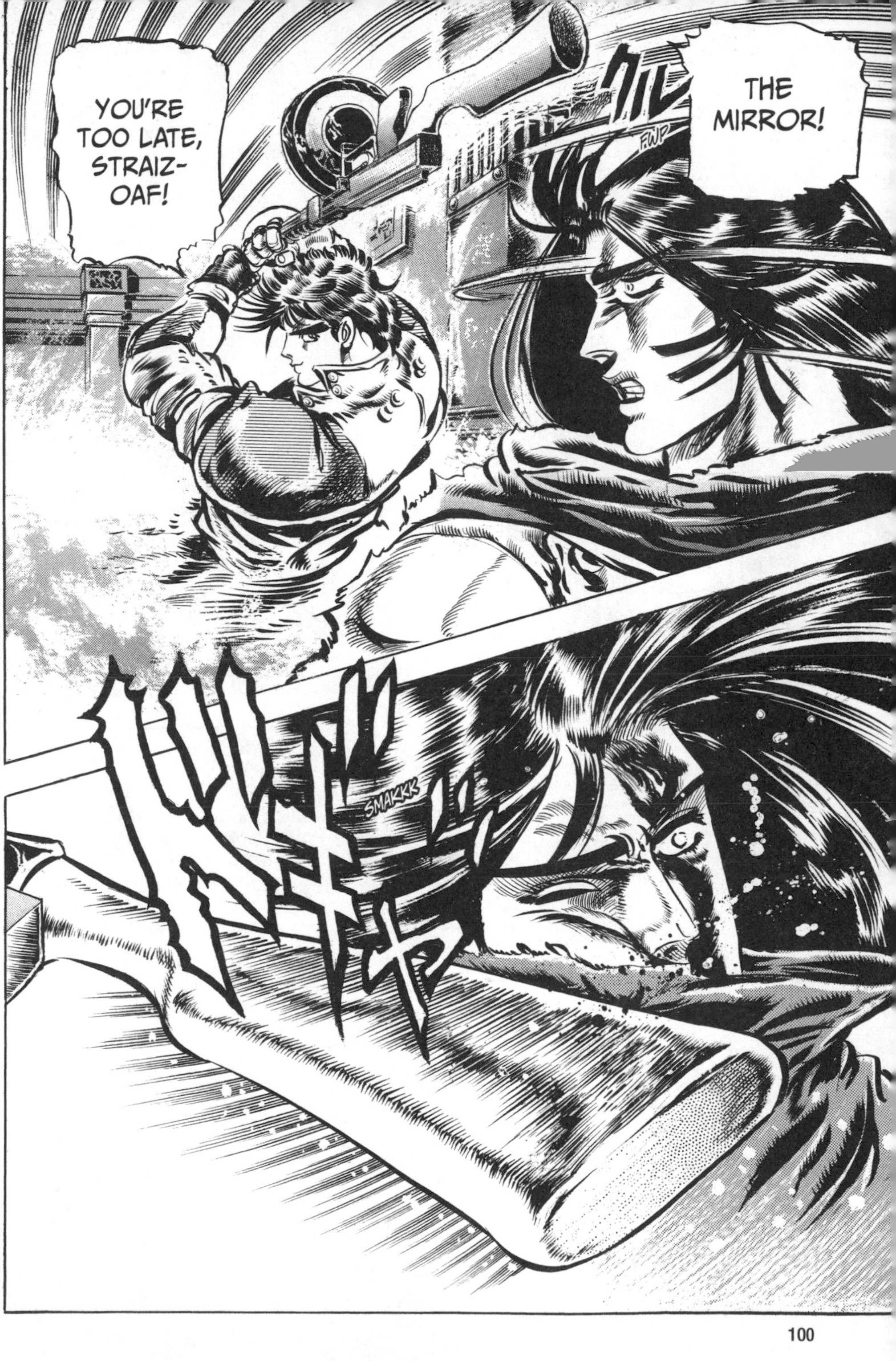
THE MIRROR!
FWP
YOU'RE TOO LATE, STRAIZ-OAF!
SMAKKK

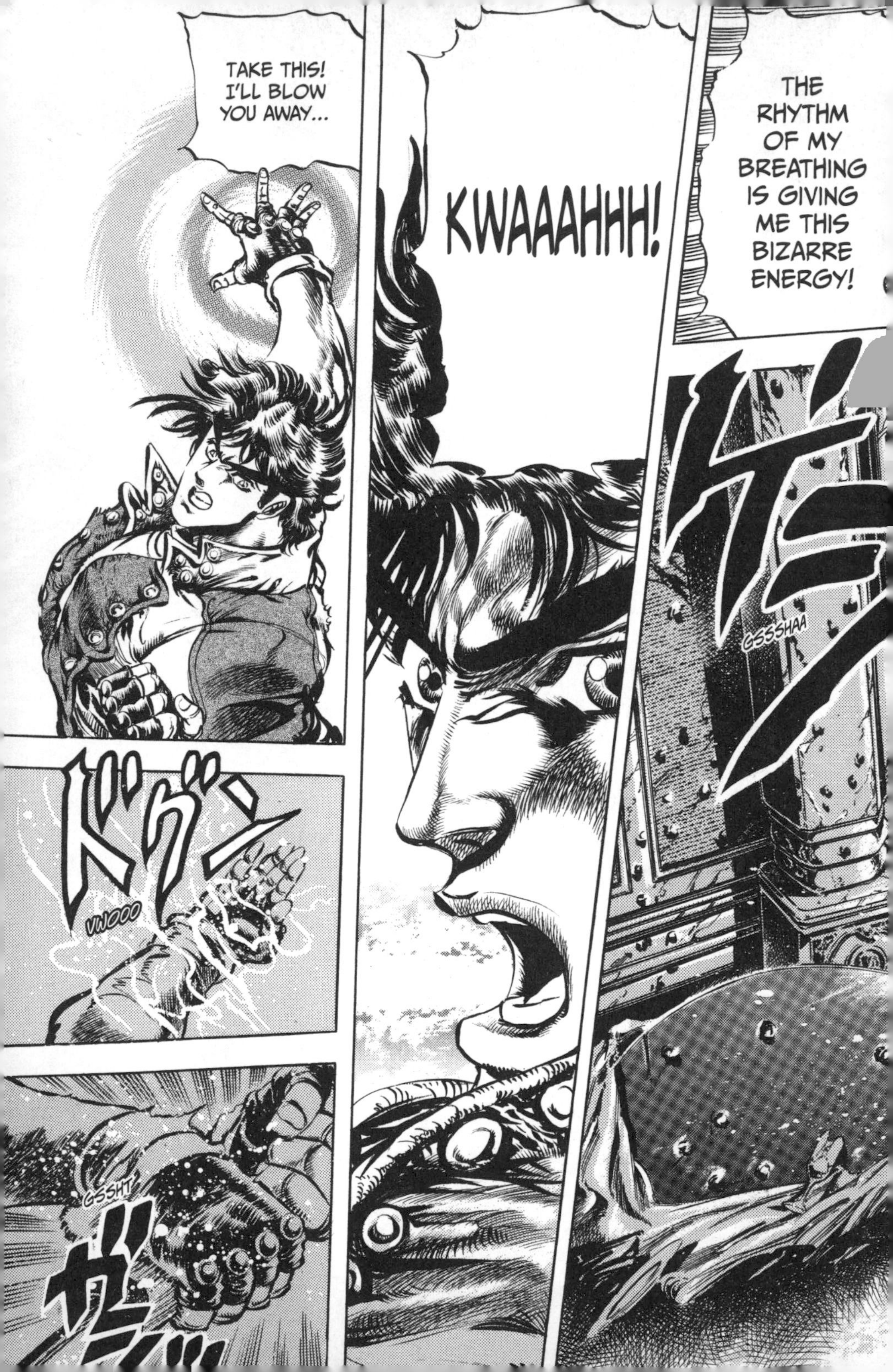
THE RHYTHM OF MY BREATHING IS GIVING ME THIS BIZARRE ENERGY!
GSSSHAA
KWAAAHHH!
TAKE THIS! I'LL BLOW YOU AWAY...
VWOOO
GSSHT

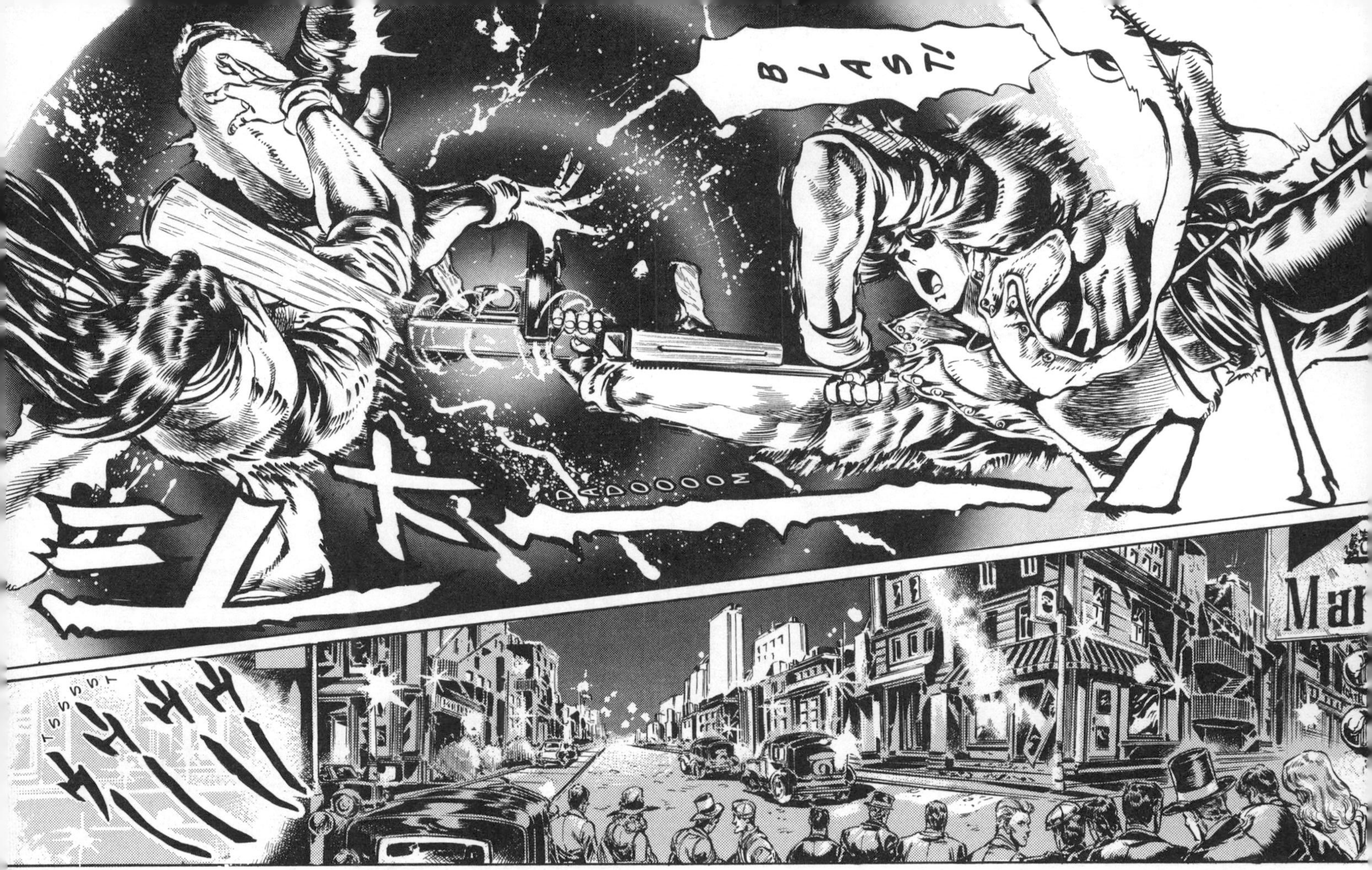
BLAST!
DADOOOOOM
TSSSST

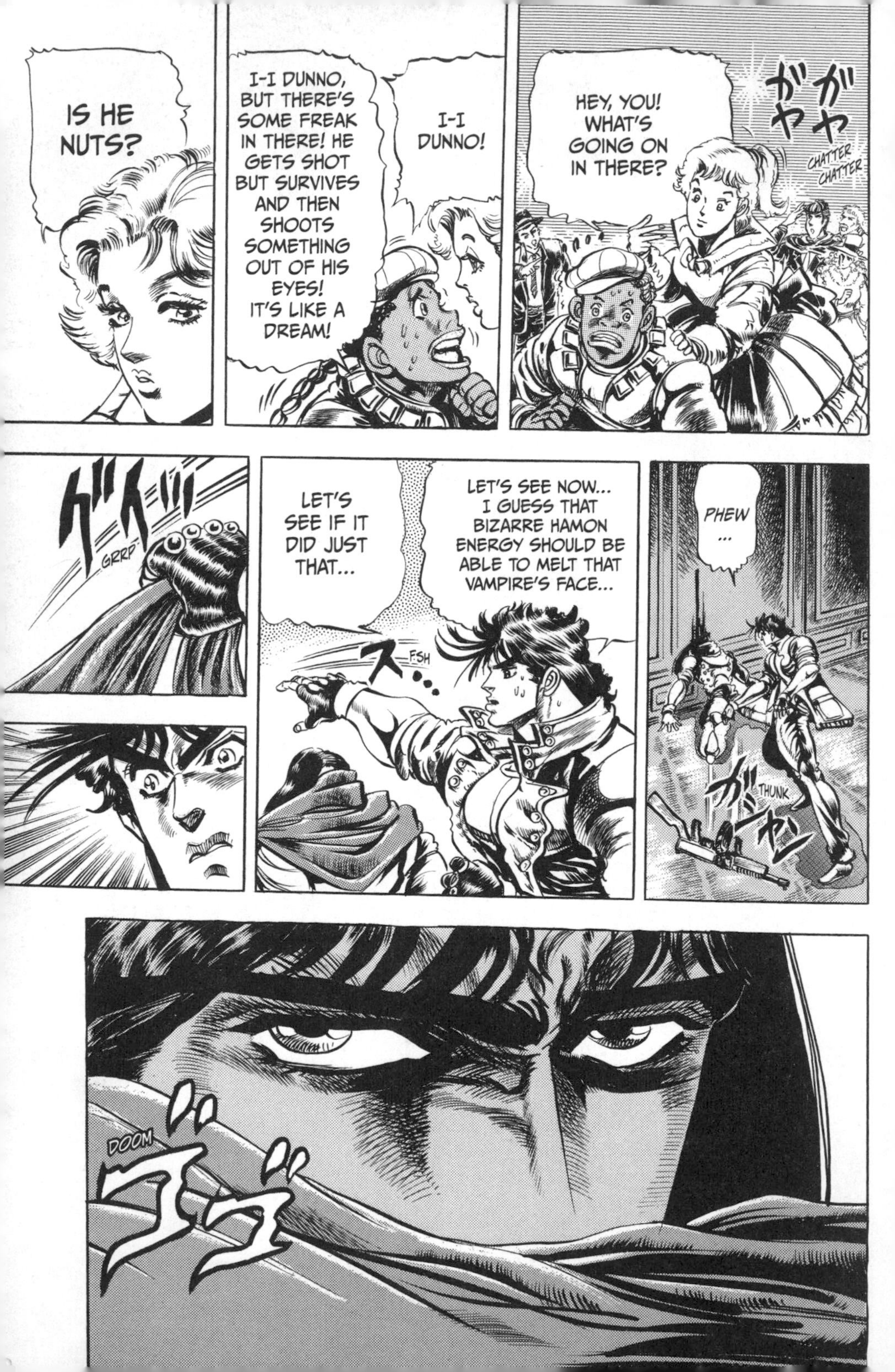

HEY, YOU! WHAT'S GOING ON IN THERE?
がやがや
CHATTER CHATTER
I-I DUNNO!
I-I DUNNO, BUT THERE'S SOME FREAK IN THERE! HE GETS SHOT BUT SURVIVES AND THEN SHOOTS SOMETHING OUT OF HIS EYES! IT'S LIKE A DREAM!
IS HE NUTS?
PHEW...
THUNK
LET'S SEE NOW... I GUESS THAT BIZARRE HAMON ENERGY SHOULD BE ABLE TO MELT THAT VAMPIRE'S FACE...
LET'S SEE IF IT DID JUST THAT...
F-SH
GRRP
DOOM

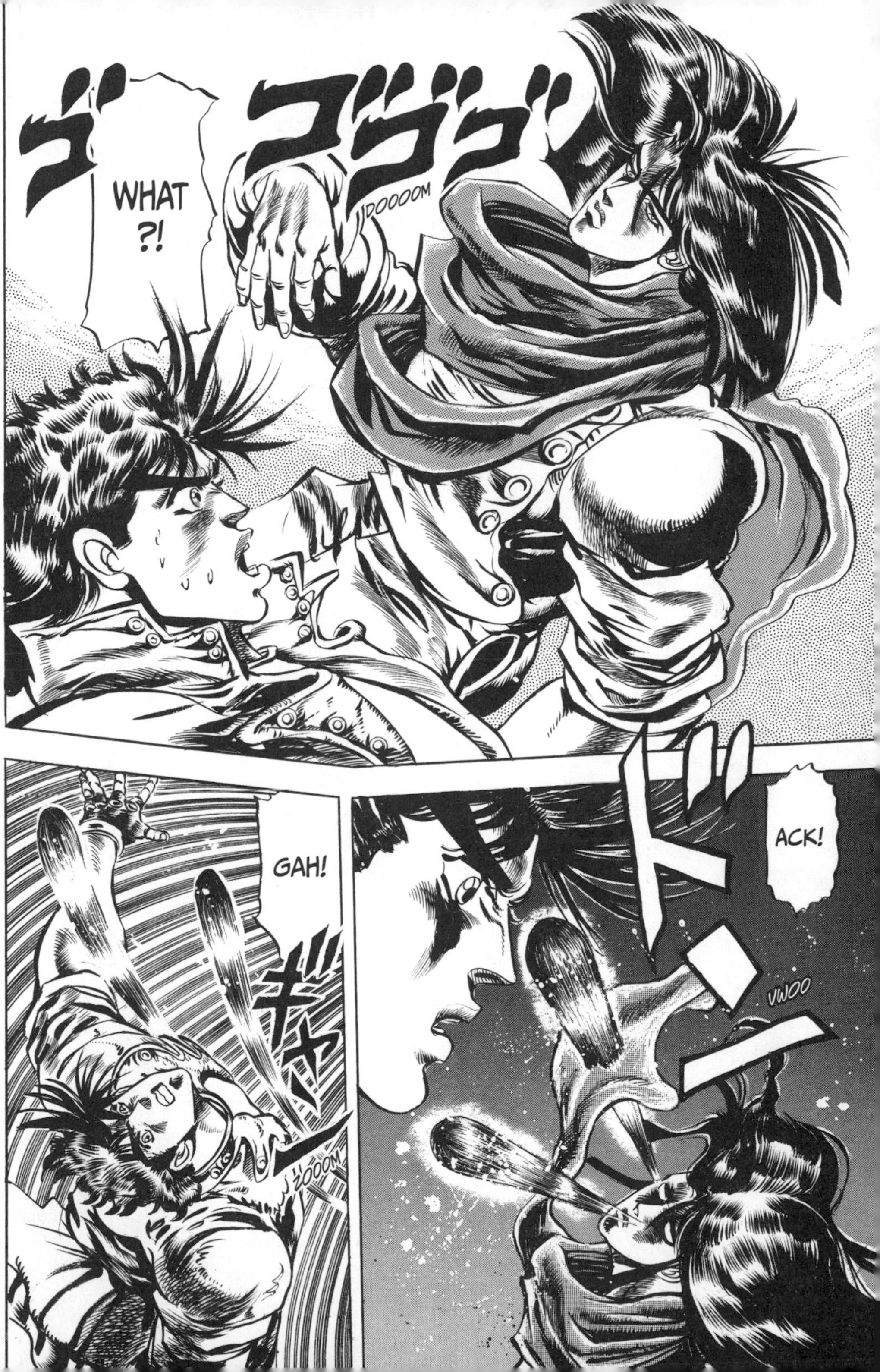
WHAT ?!
DOOOOM
ACK!
VWOO
GAH!
ZOOOM

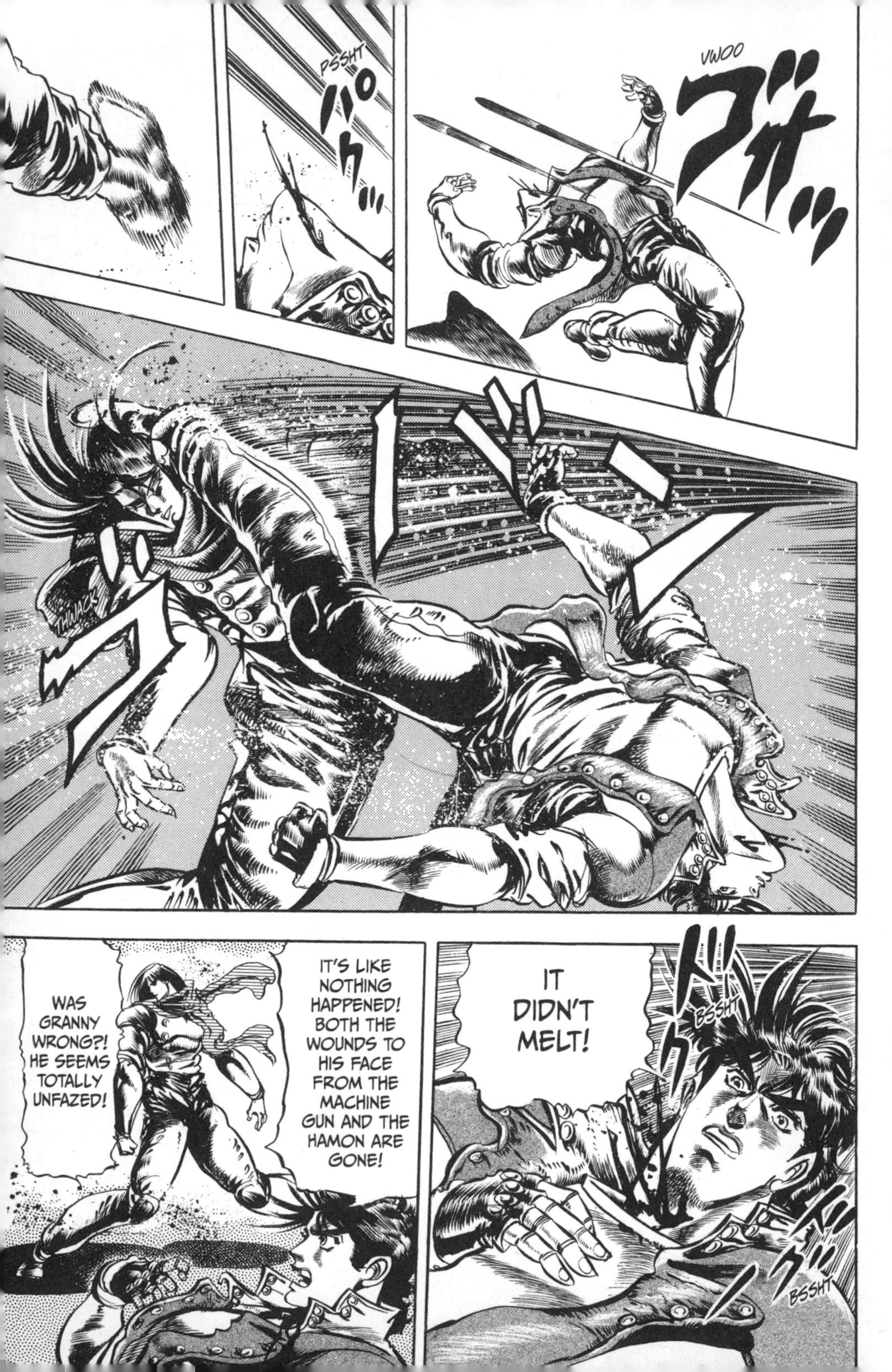
VWOO
PSSHT
THWACK
IT DIDN'T MELT!
BSSHT
BSSHT
IT'S LIKE NOTHING HAPPENED! BOTH THE WOUNDS TO HIS FACE FROM THE MACHINE GUN AND THE HAMON ARE GONE!
WAS GRANNY WRONG?! HE SEEMS TOTALLY UNFAZED!

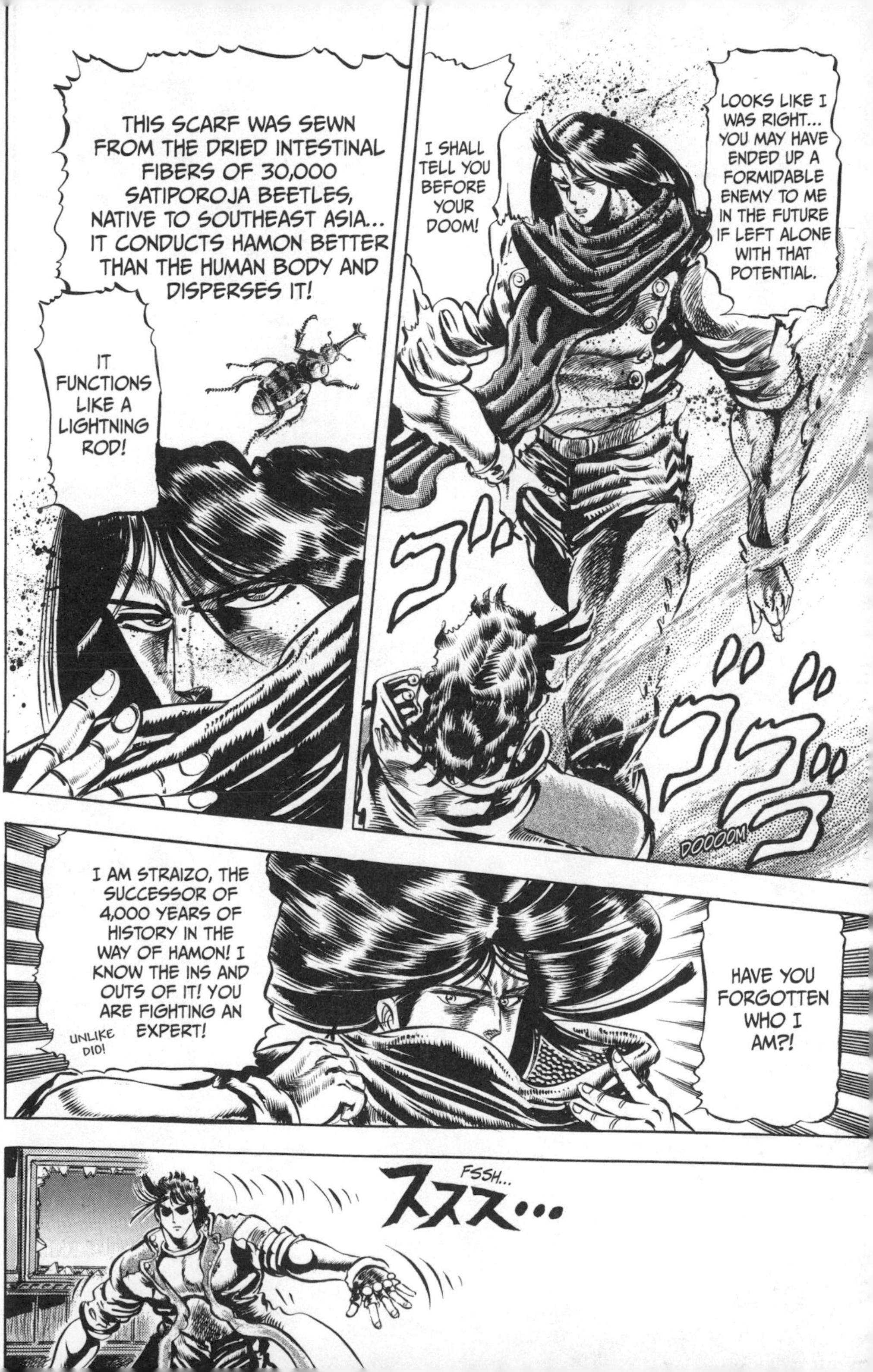

LOOKS LIKE I WAS RIGHT... YOU MAY HAVE ENDED UP A FORMIDABLE ENEMY TO ME IN THE FUTURE IF LEFT ALONE WITH THAT POTENTIAL.
I SHALL TELL YOU BEFORE YOUR DOOM!
ゴゴゴ
DOOOOM
THIS SCARF WAS SEWN FROM THE DRIED INTESTINAL FIBERS OF 30,000 SATIPOROJA BEETLES, NATIVE TO SOUTHEAST ASIA... IT CONDUCTS HAMON BETTER THAN THE HUMAN BODY AND DISPERSES IT!
IT FUNCTIONS LIKE A LIGHTNING ROD!
HAVE YOU FORGOTTEN WHO I AM?!
I AM STRAIZO, THE SUCCESSOR OF 4,000 YEARS OF HISTORY IN THE WAY OF HAMON! I KNOW THE INS AND OUTS OF IT! YOU ARE FIGHTING AN EXPERT!
UNLIKE DIO!
スス ス...
FSSH...

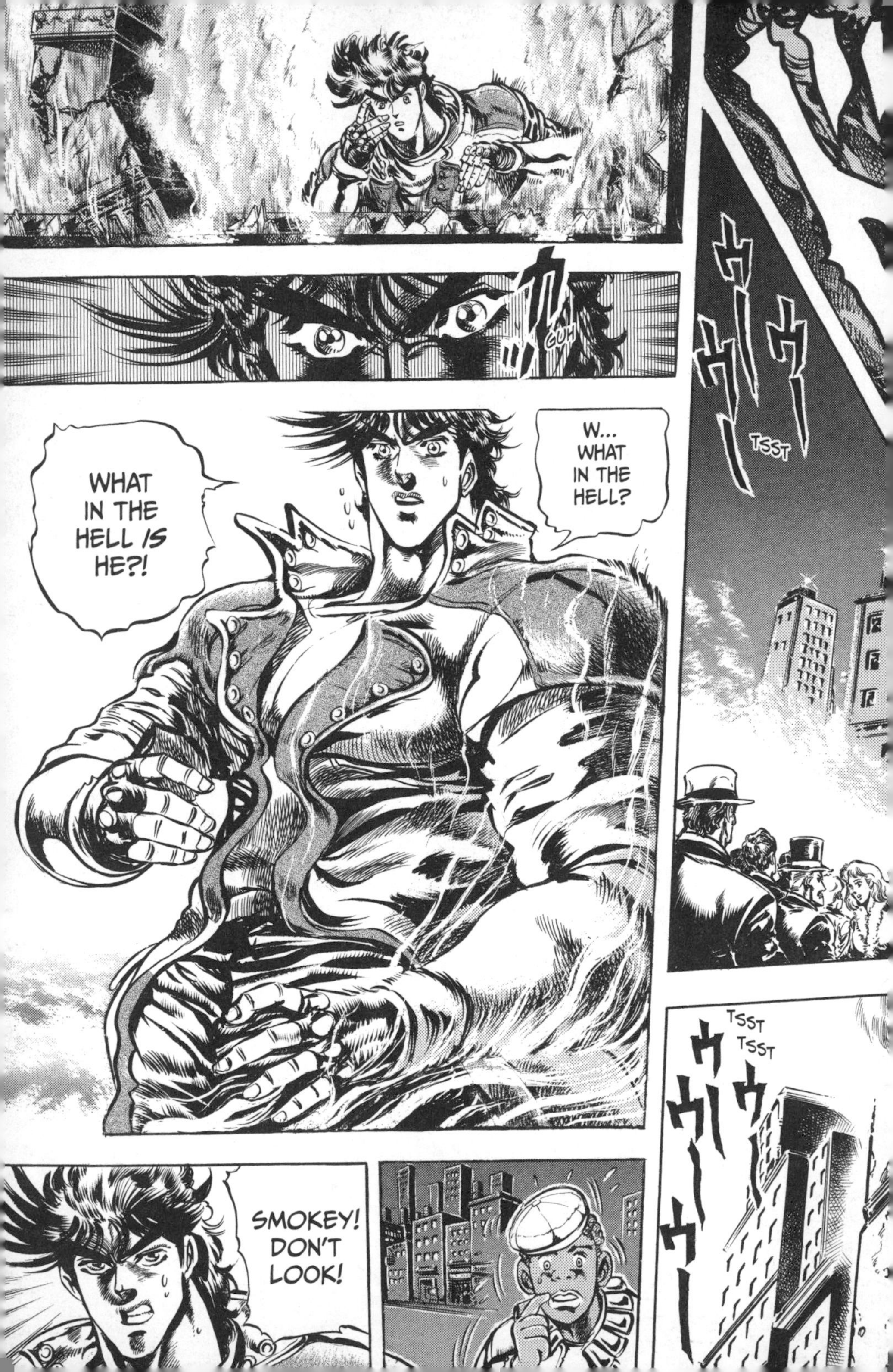

ウーウーウーウー
TSST
カッ
GUH
W... WHAT IN THE HELL?
WHAT IN THE HELL IS HE?!
TSST
TSST
ウーウーウーウー
SMOKEY! DON'T LOOK!

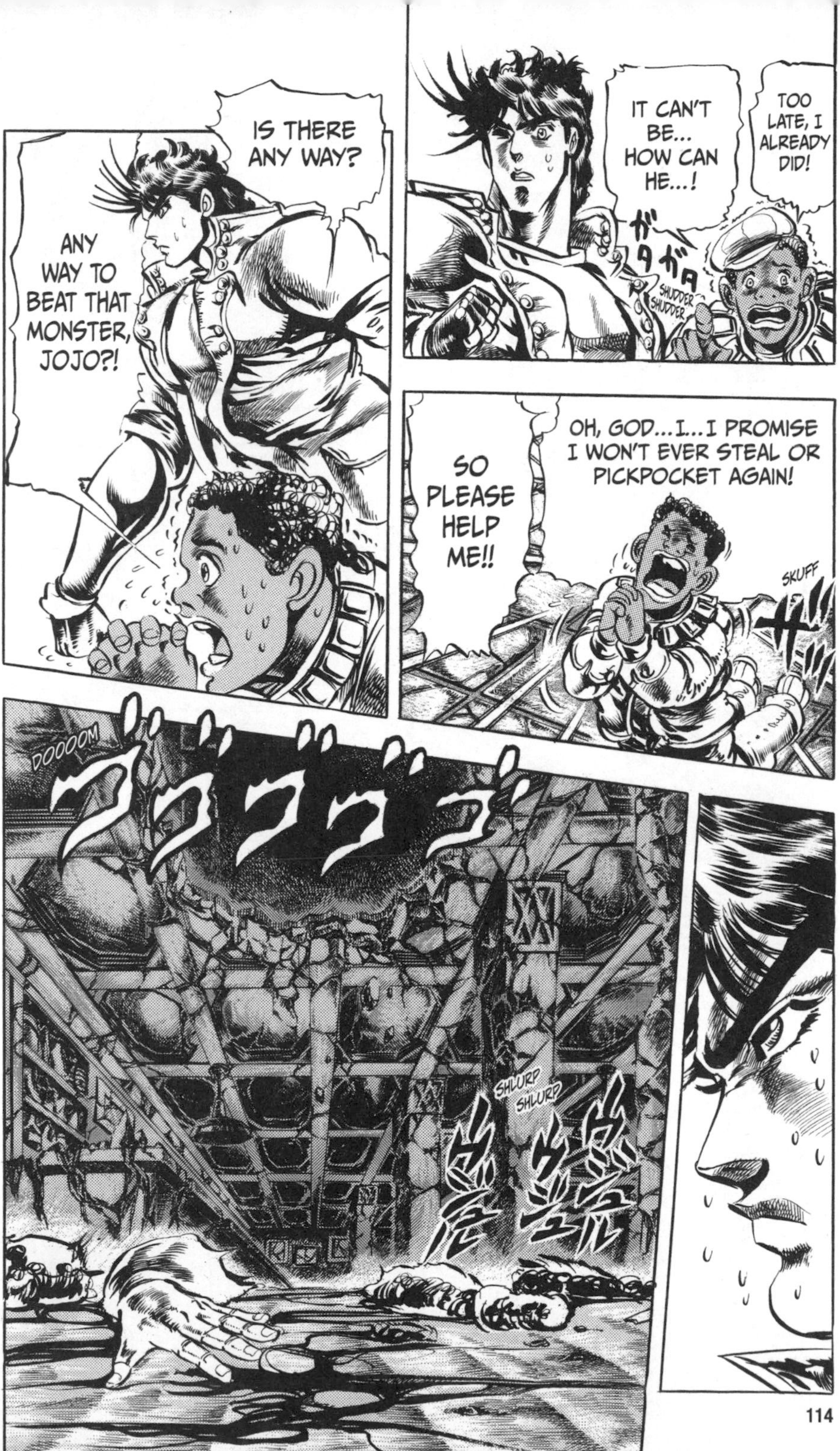
TOO LATE, I ALREADY DID!
IT CAN'T BE... HOW CAN HE...!
SHUDDER SHUDDER
OH, GOD...I...I PROMISE I WON'T EVER STEAL OR PICKPOCKET AGAIN!
SO PLEASE HELP ME!!
SKUFF
IS THERE ANY WAY?
ANY WAY TO BEAT THAT MONSTER, JOJO?!
DOOOOM
SHLURP
SHLURP

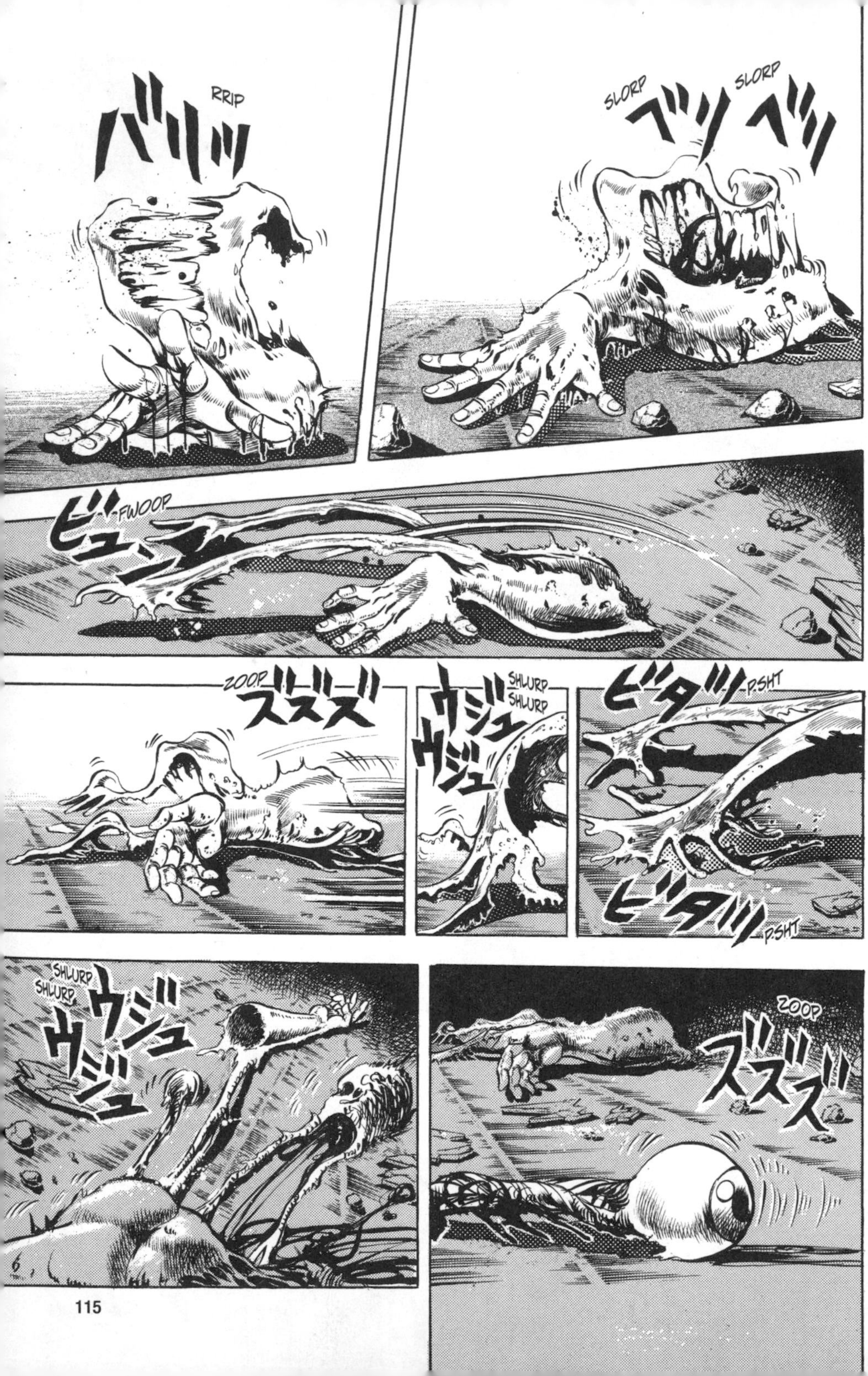
SLORP SLORP
RRIP
FWOOP
P.SHT
P.SHT
SHLURP SHLURP
ZOOP
ZOOP
SHLURP SHLURP

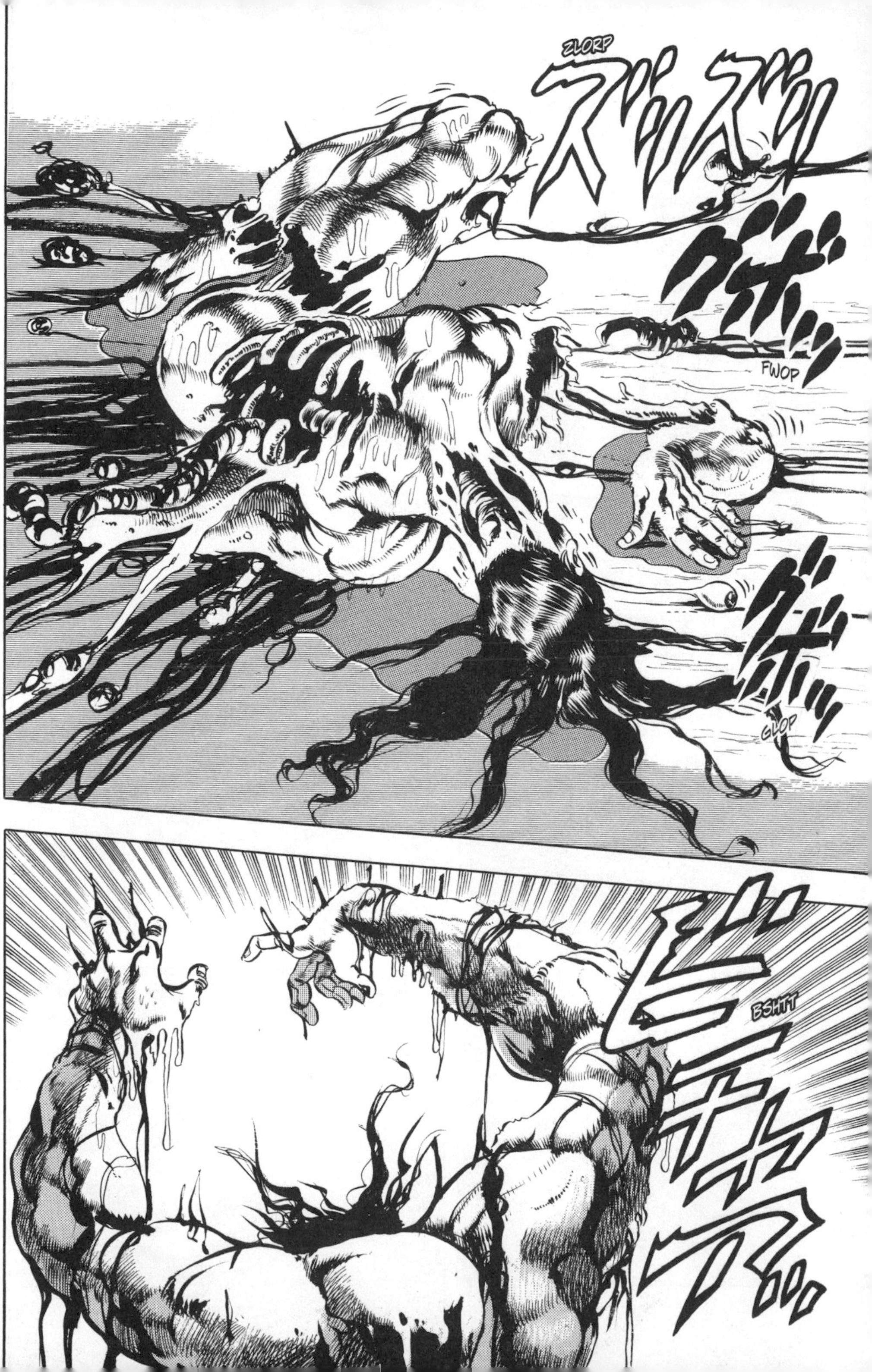
ZLORP
FWOP
GLOP
BSHTT

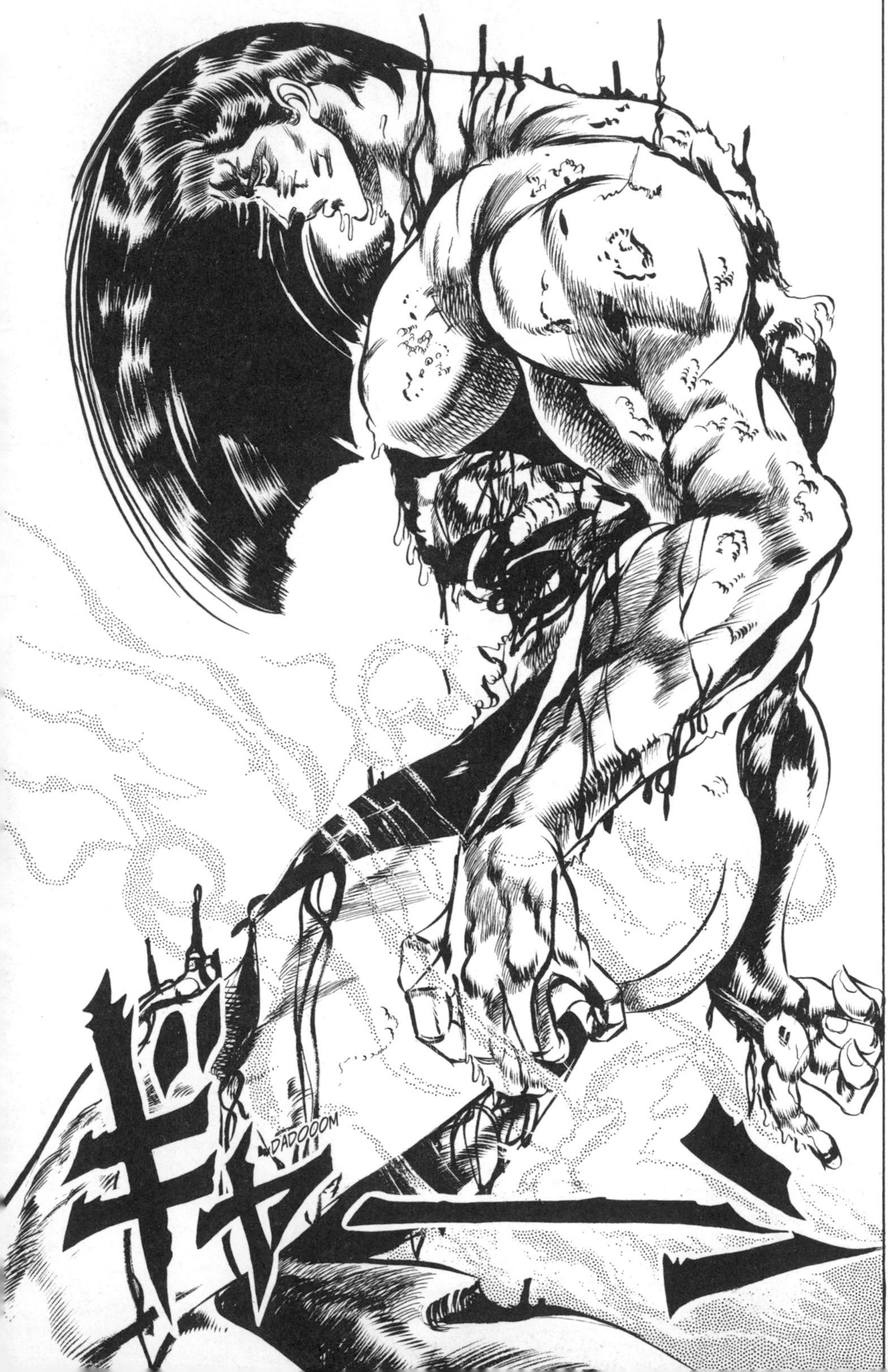
DADOOOM

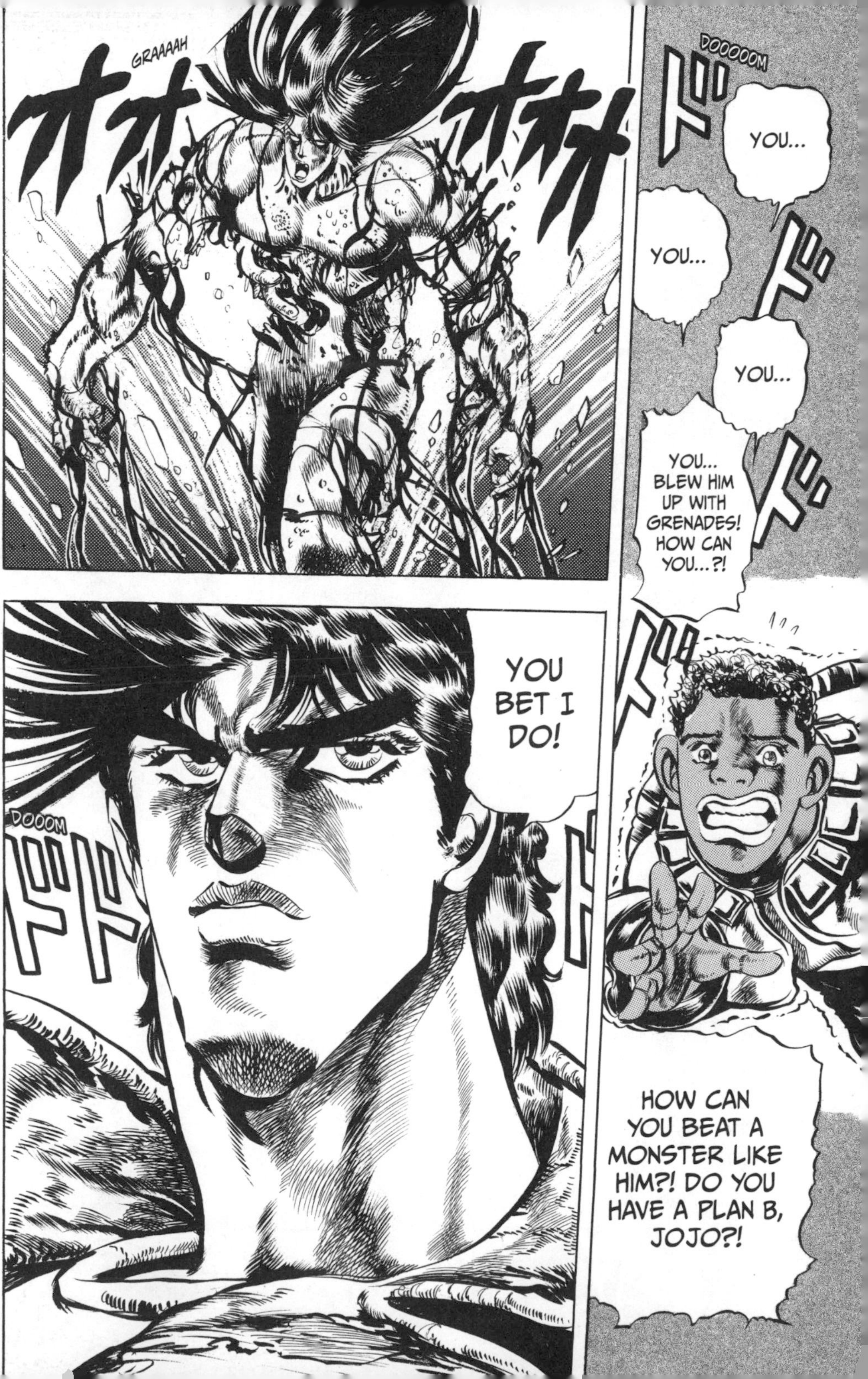
DOOOOOM
YOU...
YOU...
YOU...
YOU... BLEW HIM UP WITH GRENADES! HOW CAN YOU...?!
GRAAAAH
HOW CAN YOU BEAT A MONSTER LIKE HIM?! DO YOU HAVE A PLAN B, JOJO?!
YOU BET I DO!
DOOOM

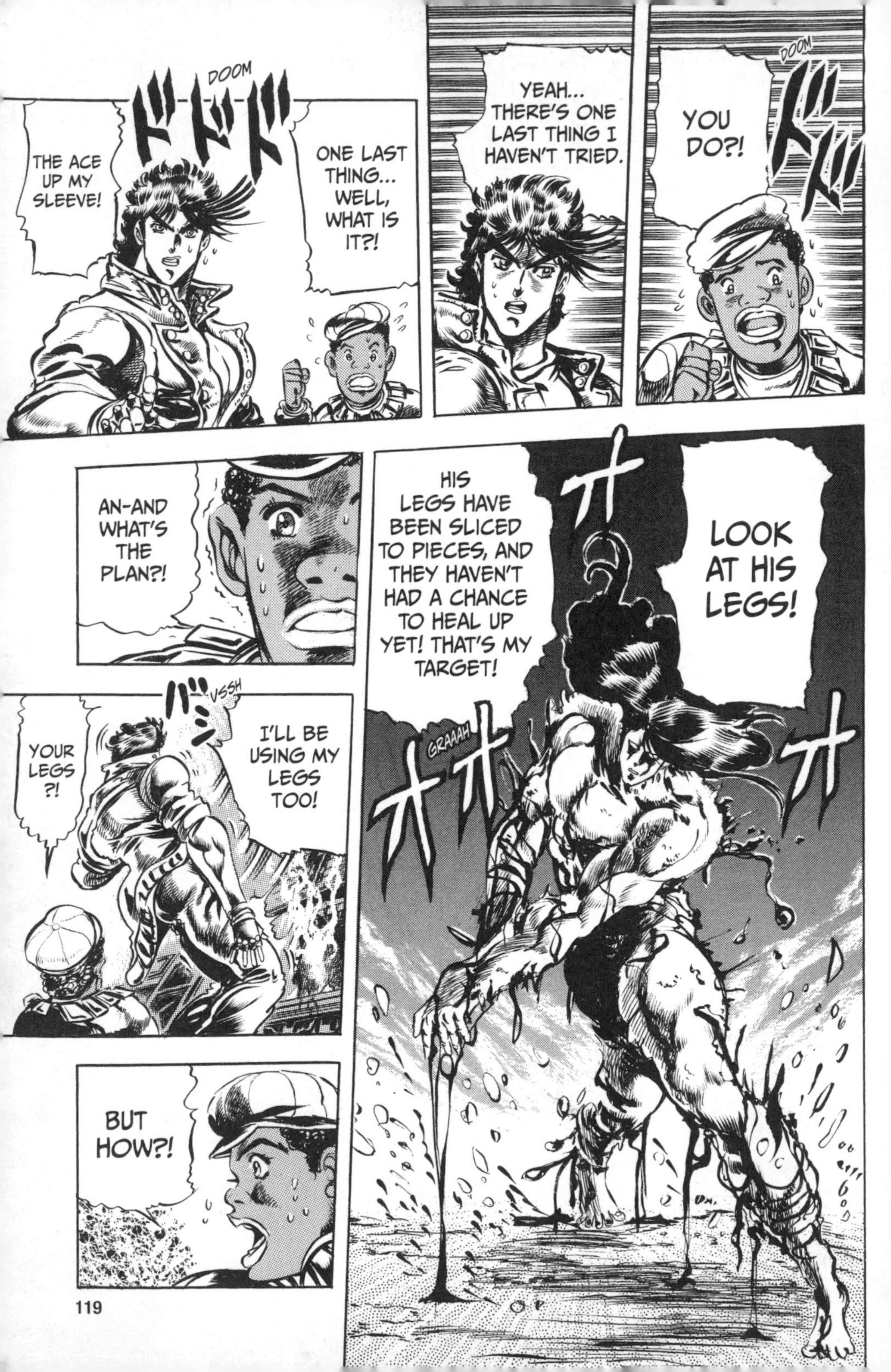
DOOM
YOU DO?!
YEAH... THERE'S ONE LAST THING I HAVEN'T TRIED.
DOOM
ONE LAST THING... WELL, WHAT IS IT?!
THE ACE UP MY SLEEVE!
LOOK AT HIS LEGS!
HIS LEGS HAVE BEEN SLICED TO PIECES, AND THEY HAVEN'T HAD A CHANCE TO HEAL UP YET! THAT'S MY TARGET!
GRAAAH
AN-AND WHAT'S THE PLAN?!
VSSH
I'LL BE USING MY LEGS TOO!
YOUR LEGS ?!
BUT HOW?!

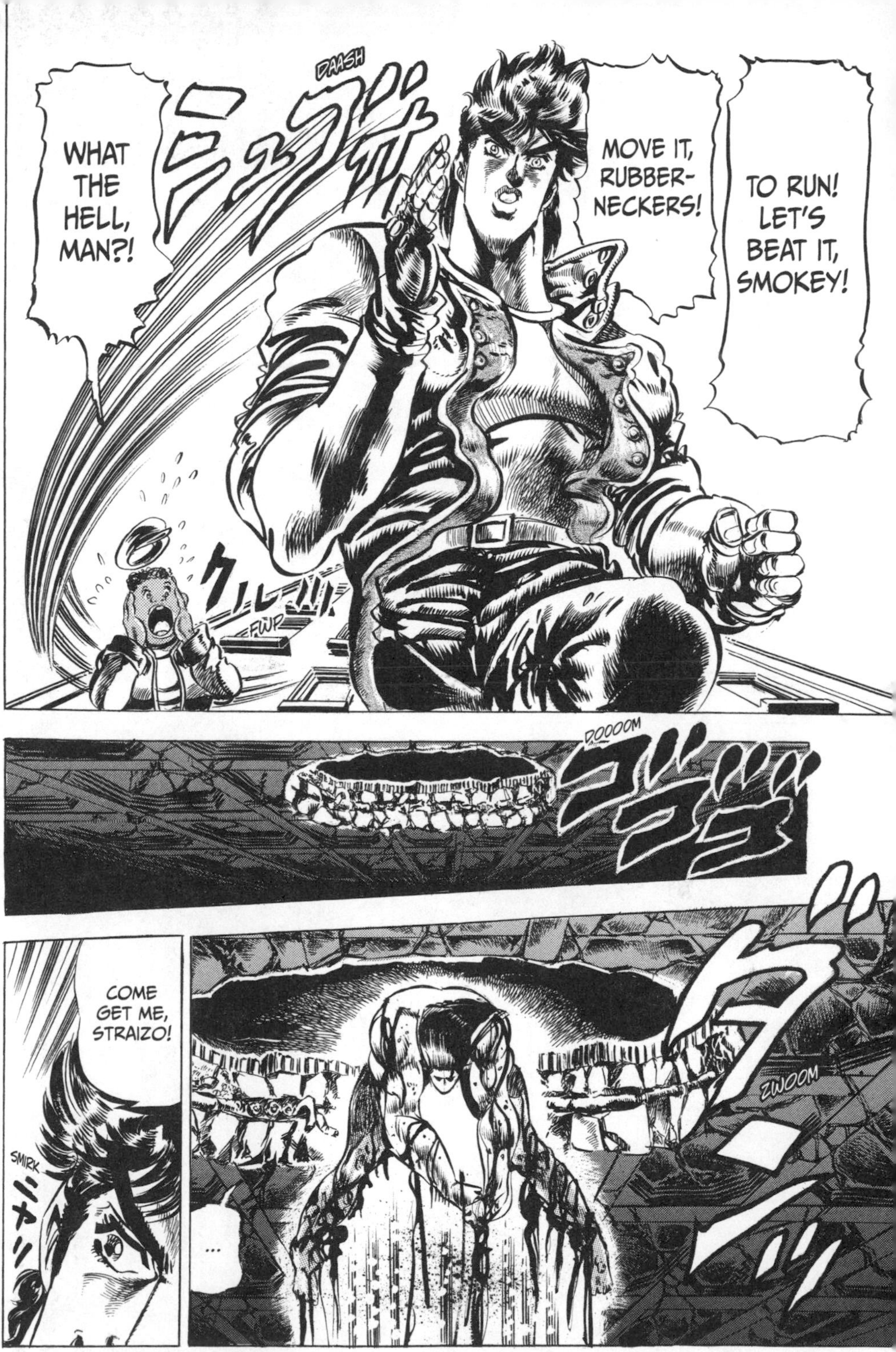
TO RUN! LET'S BEAT IT, SMOKEY!
MOVE IT, RUBBER-NECKERS!
DAASH
WHAT THE HELL, MAN?!
FWIP
DOOOOM
ZWOOM
...
COME GET ME, STRAIZO!
SMIRK

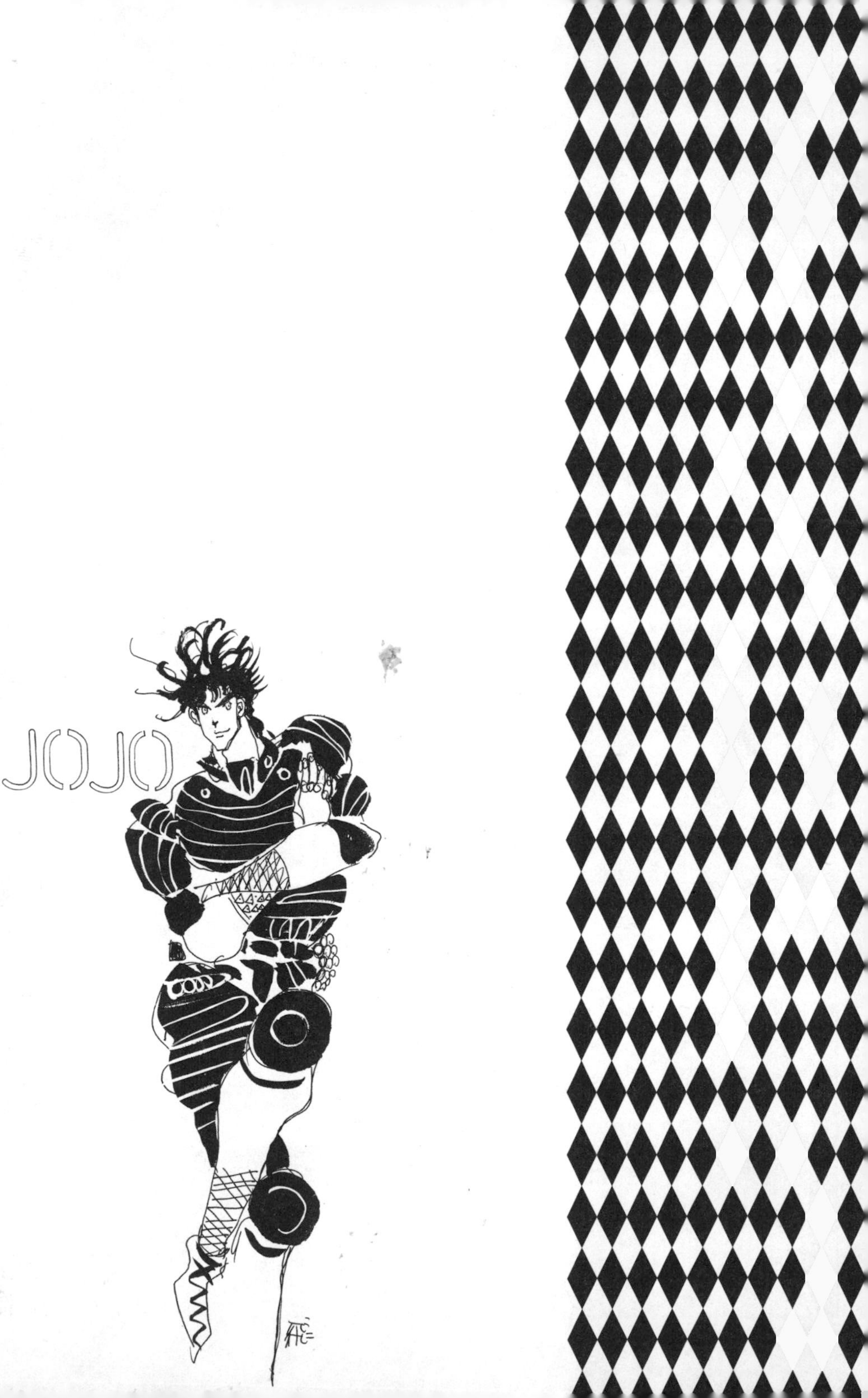
JOJO

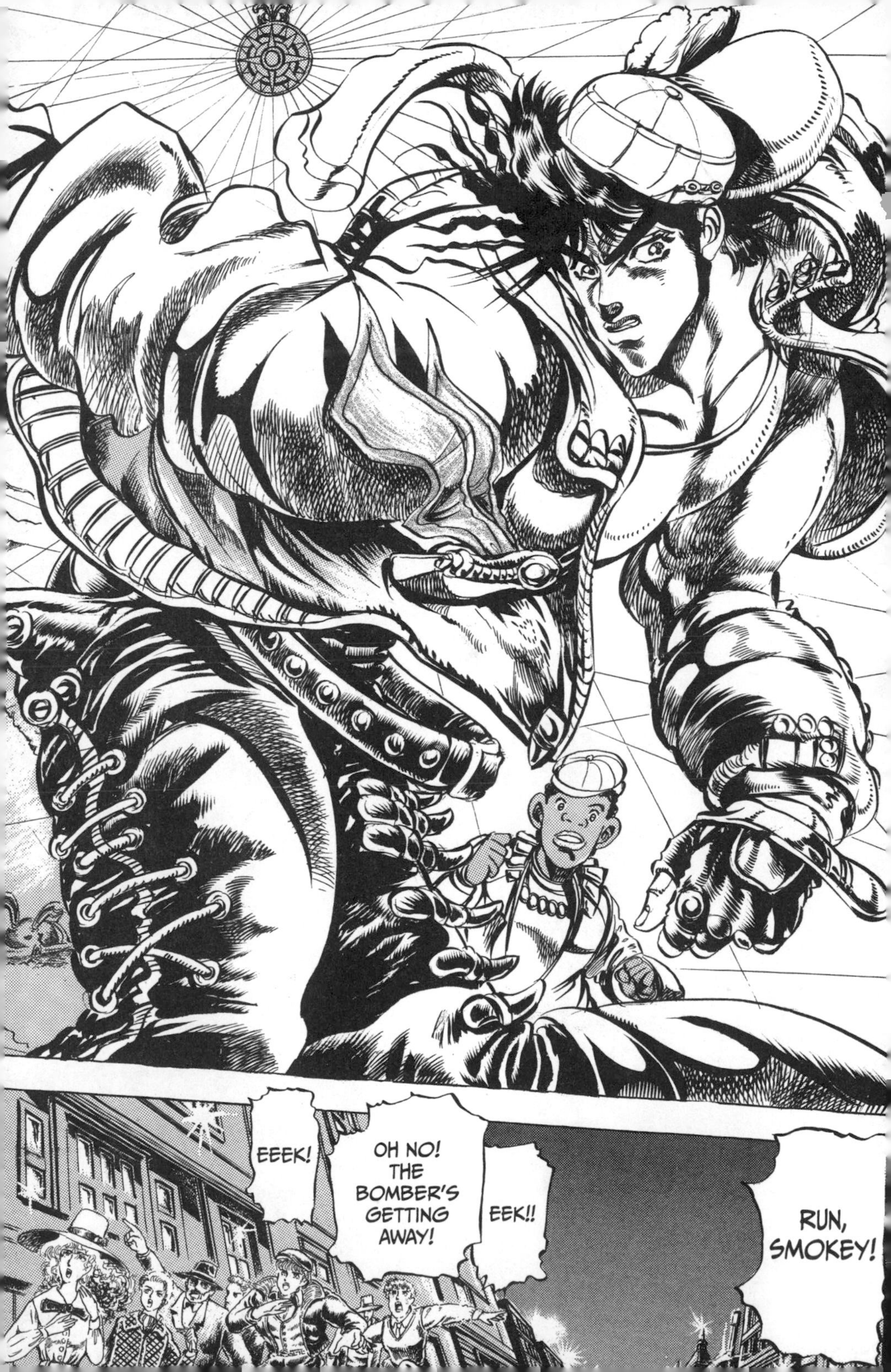
RUN, SMOKEY!
EEK!!
OH NO! THE BOMBER'S GETTING AWAY!
EEEK!

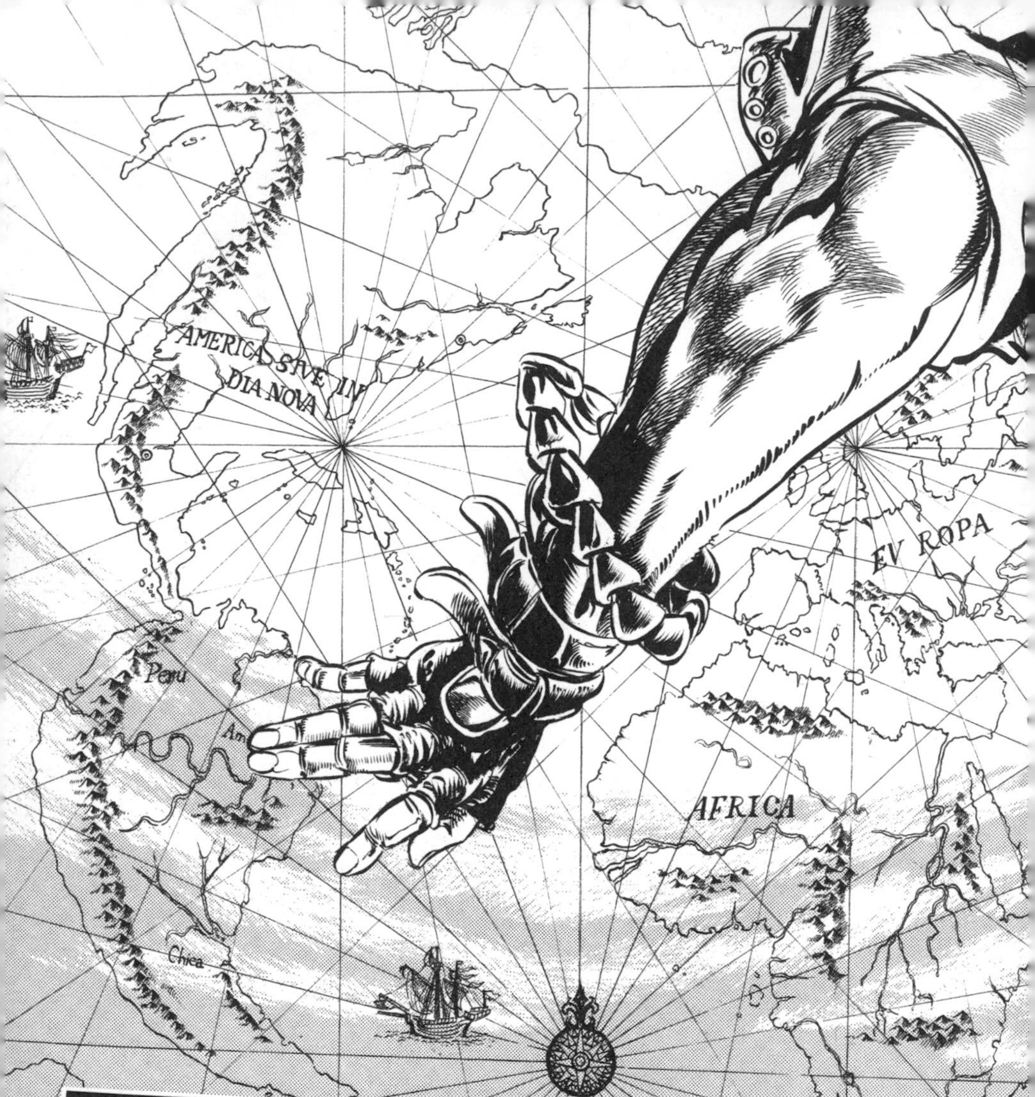
AMERICA SIVE IN DIA NOVA
EV ROPA
Peru
AFRICA
Chica

CHAPTER 7: Straizo vs. Joseph PART 4

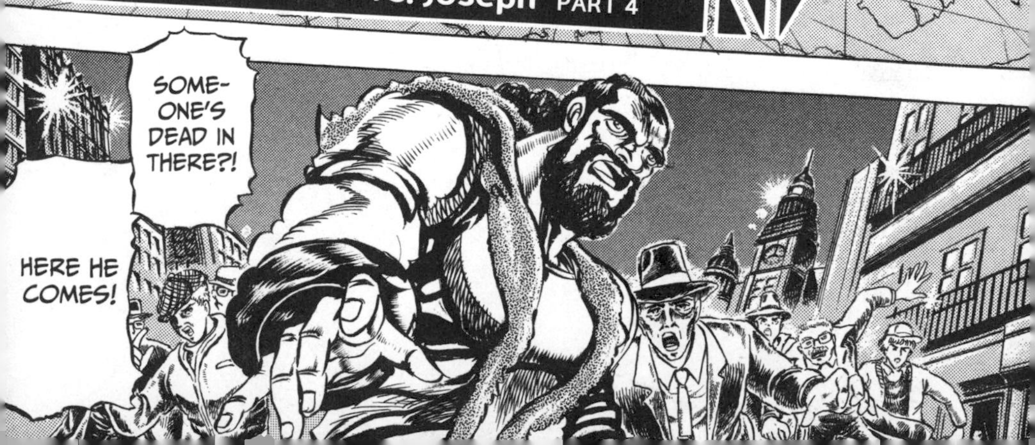
SOME-ONE'S DEAD IN THERE?!
HERE HE COMES!

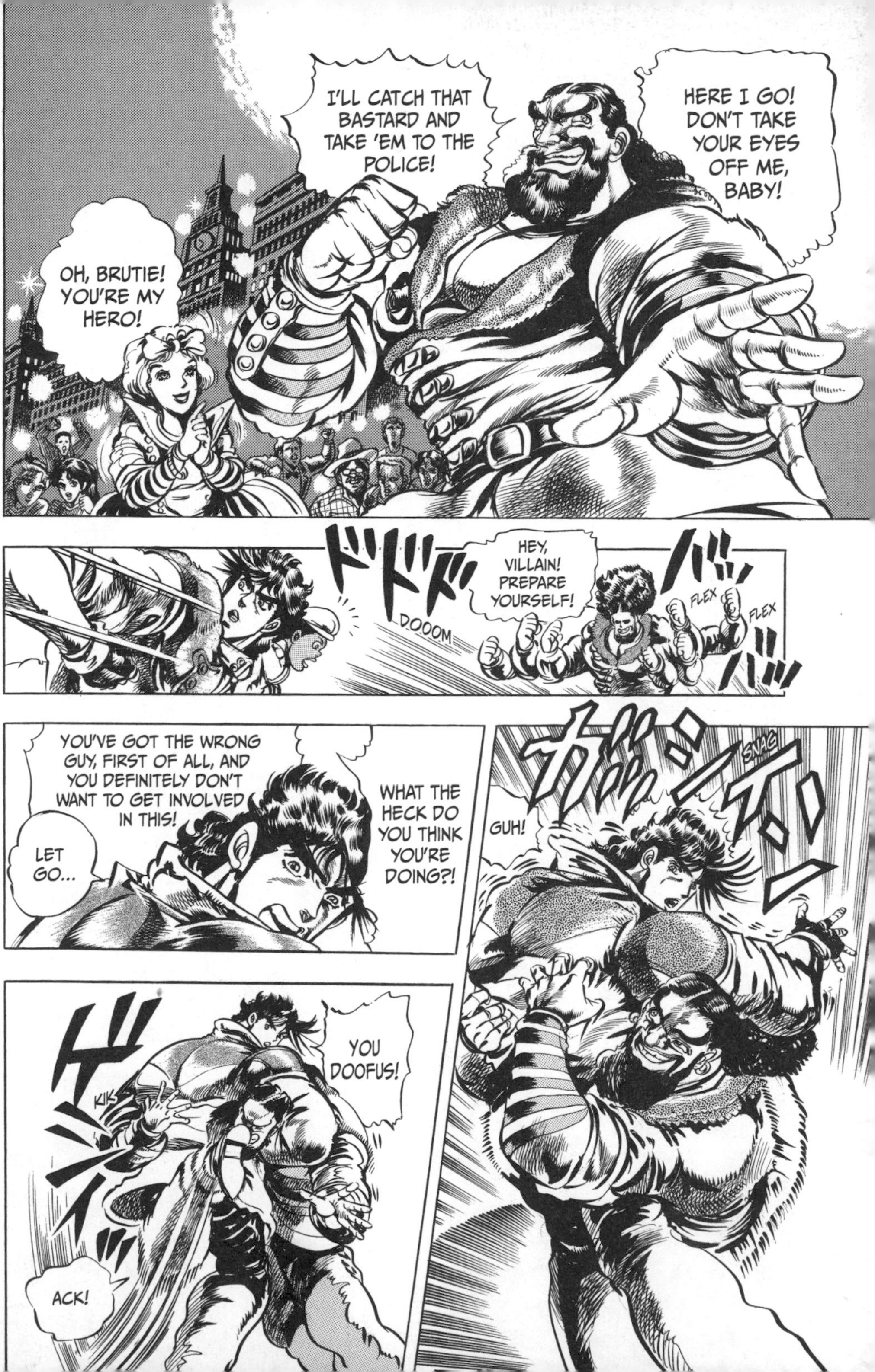
HERE I GO! DON'T TAKE YOUR EYES OFF ME, BABY!
I'LL CATCH THAT BASTARD AND TAKE 'EM TO THE POLICE!
OH, BRUTIE! YOU'RE MY HERO!
FLEX
FLEX
HEY, VILLAIN! PREPARE YOURSELF!
DOOOM
SNAG
GUH!
WHAT THE HECK DO YOU THINK YOU'RE DOING?!
YOU'VE GOT THE WRONG GUY, FIRST OF ALL, AND YOU DEFINITELY DON'T WANT TO GET INVOLVED IN THIS!
LET GO...
YOU DOOFUS!
KIK
ACK!

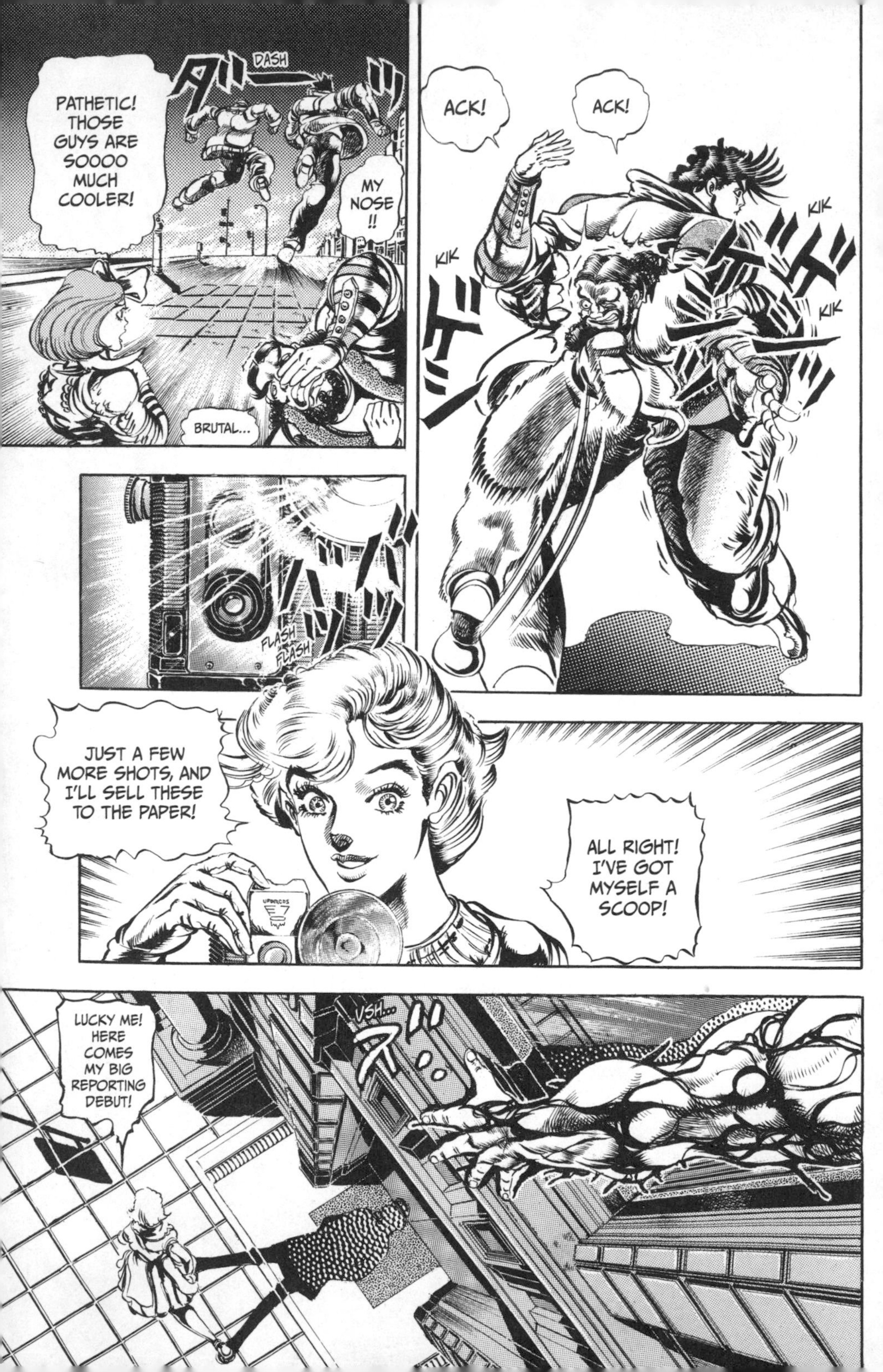
ACK!
ACK!
KIK
KIK
KIK
DASH
PATHETIC! THOSE GUYS ARE SOOOO MUCH COOLER!
MY NOSE !!
BRUTAL...
FLASH FLASH
ALL RIGHT! I'VE GOT MYSELF A SCOOP!
JUST A FEW MORE SHOTS, AND I'LL SELL THESE TO THE PAPER!
VSH...
LUCKY ME! HERE COMES MY BIG REPORTING DEBUT!

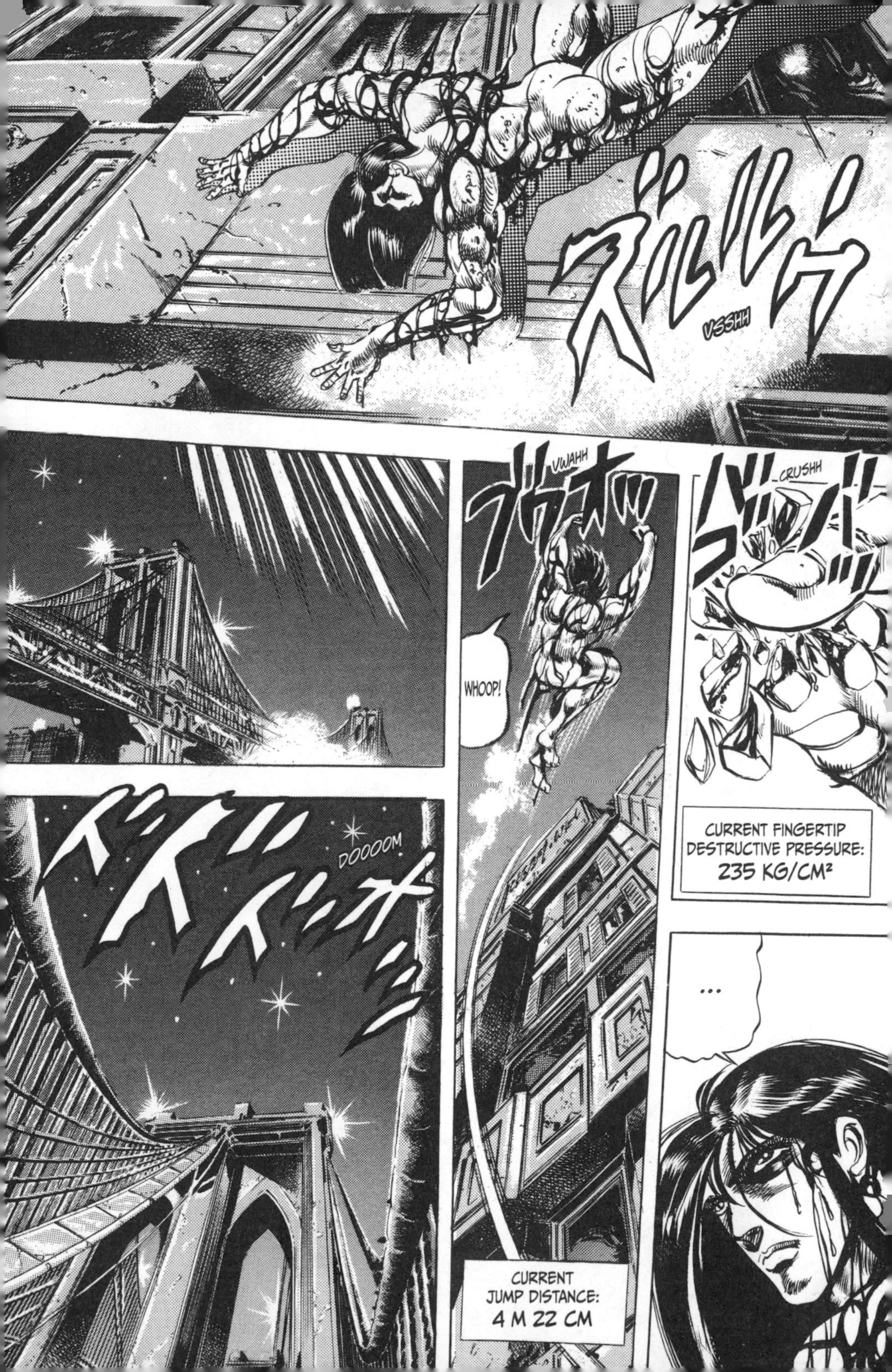
VSSHH
CRUSHH
CURRENT FINGERTIP DESTRUCTIVE PRESSURE: 235 KG/CM^2
...
VWAHH
WHOOP!
CURRENT JUMP DISTANCE: 4 M 22 CM
DOOOOM

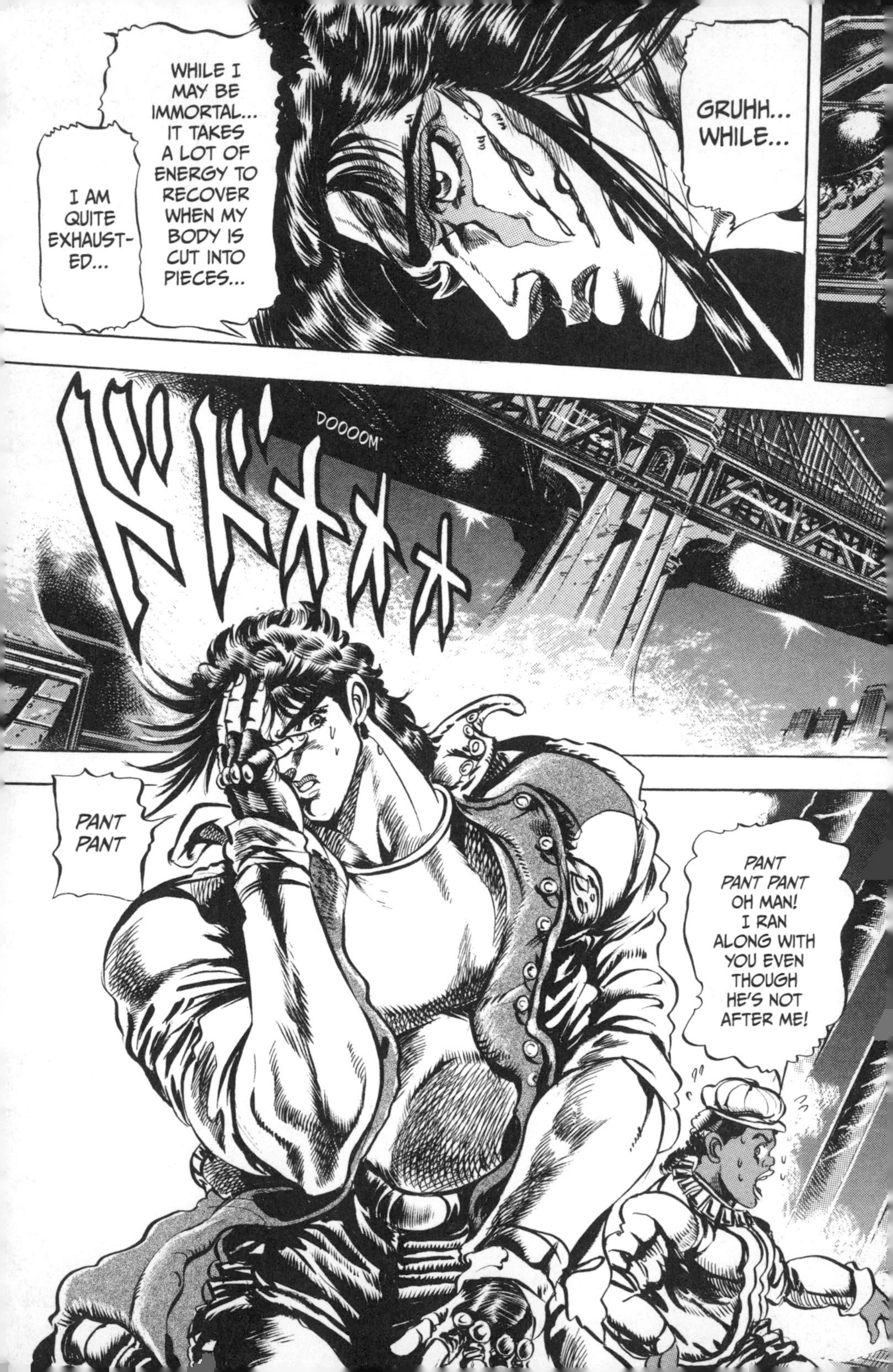
GRUHH... WHILE...
WHILE I MAY BE IMMORTAL... IT TAKES A LOT OF ENERGY TO RECOVER WHEN MY BODY IS CUT INTO PIECES...
I AM QUITE EXHAUST-ED...
DOOOOM
PANT PANT PANT OH MAN! I RAN ALONG WITH YOU EVEN THOUGH HE'S NOT AFTER ME!
PANT PANT

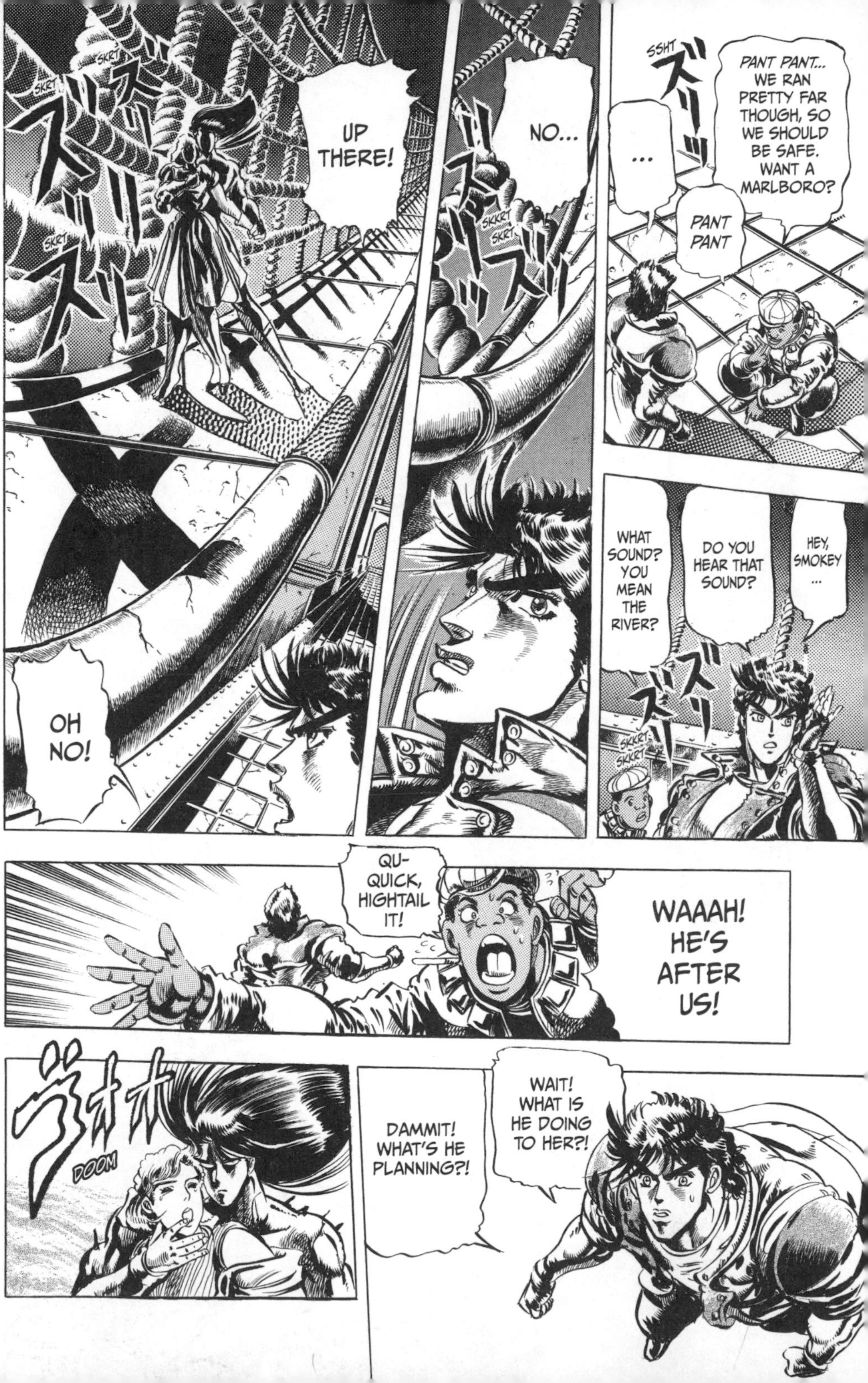
SSHT
PANT PANT... WE RAN PRETTY FAR THOUGH, SO WE SHOULD BE SAFE. WANT A MARLBORO?
...
PANT PANT
HEY, SMOKEY ...
DO YOU HEAR THAT SOUND?
WHAT SOUND? YOU MEAN THE RIVER?
SKKRT SKKRT
NO...
SKKRT SKRT
SKRT SKRT SKRT
UP THERE!
OH NO!
WAAAH! HE'S AFTER US!
QU-QUICK, HIGHTAIL IT!
WAIT! WHAT IS HE DOING TO HER?!
DAMMIT! WHAT'S HE PLANNING?!
DOOM

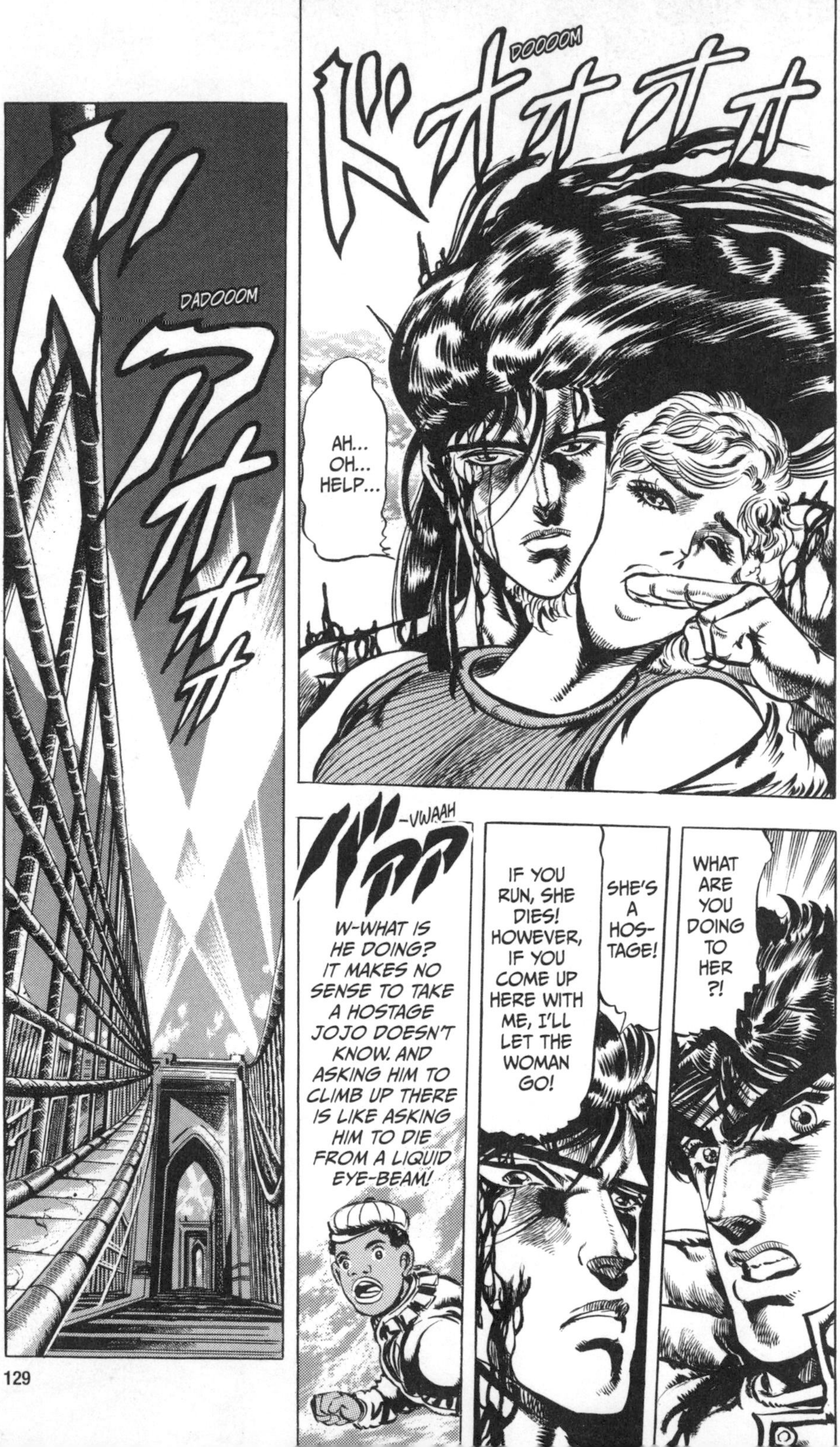
DOOOOM
AH... OH... HELP...
WHAT ARE YOU DOING TO HER ?!
SHE'S A HOS-TAGE!
IF YOU RUN, SHE DIES! HOWEVER, IF YOU COME UP HERE WITH ME, I'LL LET THE WOMAN GO!
-VWAAH
W-WHAT IS HE DOING? IT MAKES NO SENSE TO TAKE A HOSTAGE JOJO DOESN'T KNOW. AND ASKING HIM TO CLIMB UP THERE IS LIKE ASKING HIM TO DIE FROM A LIQUID EYE-BEAM!
DADOOOM

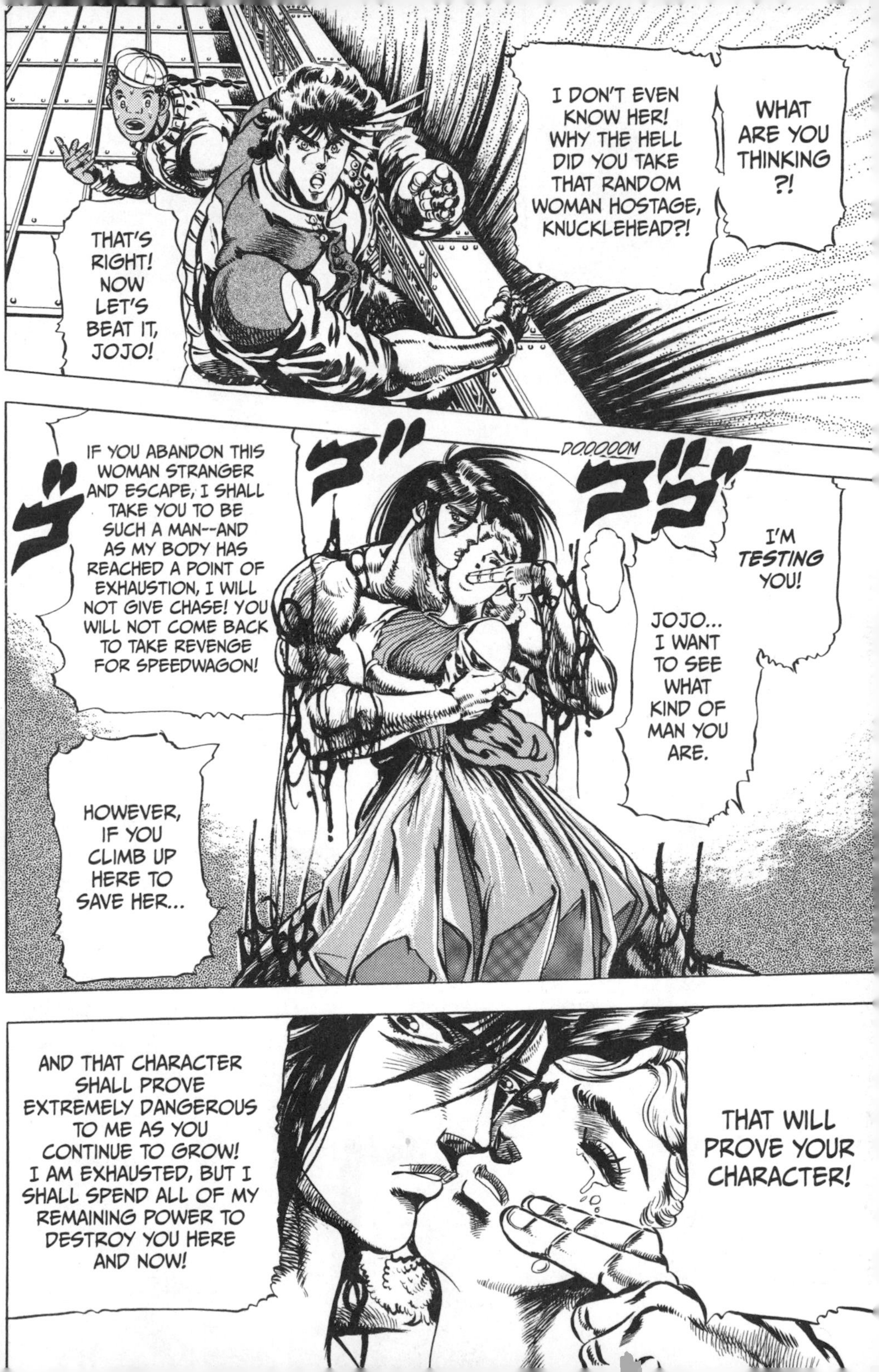
WHAT ARE YOU THINKING?!
I DON'T EVEN KNOW HER! WHY THE HELL DID YOU TAKE THAT RANDOM WOMAN HOSTAGE, KNUCKLEHEAD?!
THAT'S RIGHT! NOW LET'S BEAT IT, JOJO!
DOOOOOOM
I'M *TESTING* YOU!
JOJO... I WANT TO SEE WHAT KIND OF MAN YOU ARE.
IF YOU ABANDON THIS WOMAN STRANGER AND ESCAPE, I SHALL TAKE YOU TO BE SUCH A MAN--AND AS MY BODY HAS REACHED A POINT OF EXHAUSTION, I WILL NOT GIVE CHASE! YOU WILL NOT COME BACK TO TAKE REVENGE FOR SPEEDWAGON!
HOWEVER, IF YOU CLIMB UP HERE TO SAVE HER...
THAT WILL PROVE YOUR CHARACTER!
AND THAT CHARACTER SHALL PROVE EXTREMELY DANGEROUS TO ME AS YOU CONTINUE TO GROW! I AM EXHAUSTED, BUT I SHALL SPEND ALL OF MY REMAINING POWER TO DESTROY YOU HERE AND NOW!

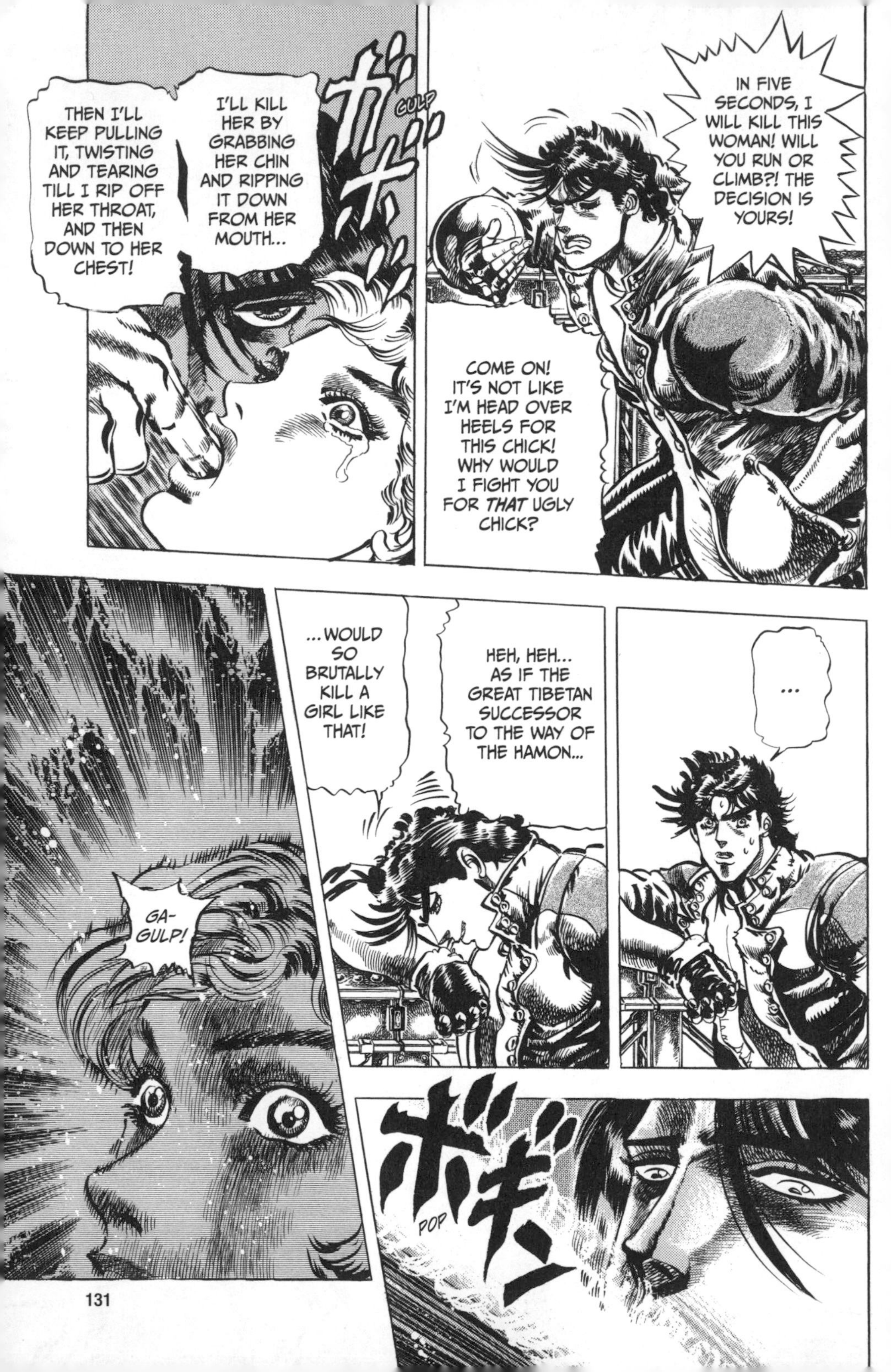

IN FIVE SECONDS, I WILL KILL THIS WOMAN! WILL YOU RUN OR CLIMB?! THE DECISION IS YOURS!
COME ON! IT'S NOT LIKE I'M HEAD OVER HEELS FOR THIS CHICK! WHY WOULD I FIGHT YOU FOR *THAT* UGLY CHICK?
GULP
I'LL KILL HER BY GRABBING HER CHIN AND RIPPING IT DOWN FROM HER MOUTH...
THEN I'LL KEEP PULLING IT, TWISTING AND TEARING TILL I RIP OFF HER THROAT, AND THEN DOWN TO HER CHEST!
...
HEH, HEH... AS IF THE GREAT TIBETAN SUCCESSOR TO THE WAY OF THE HAMON...
...WOULD SO BRUTALLY KILL A GIRL LIKE THAT!
POP
GA-GULP!

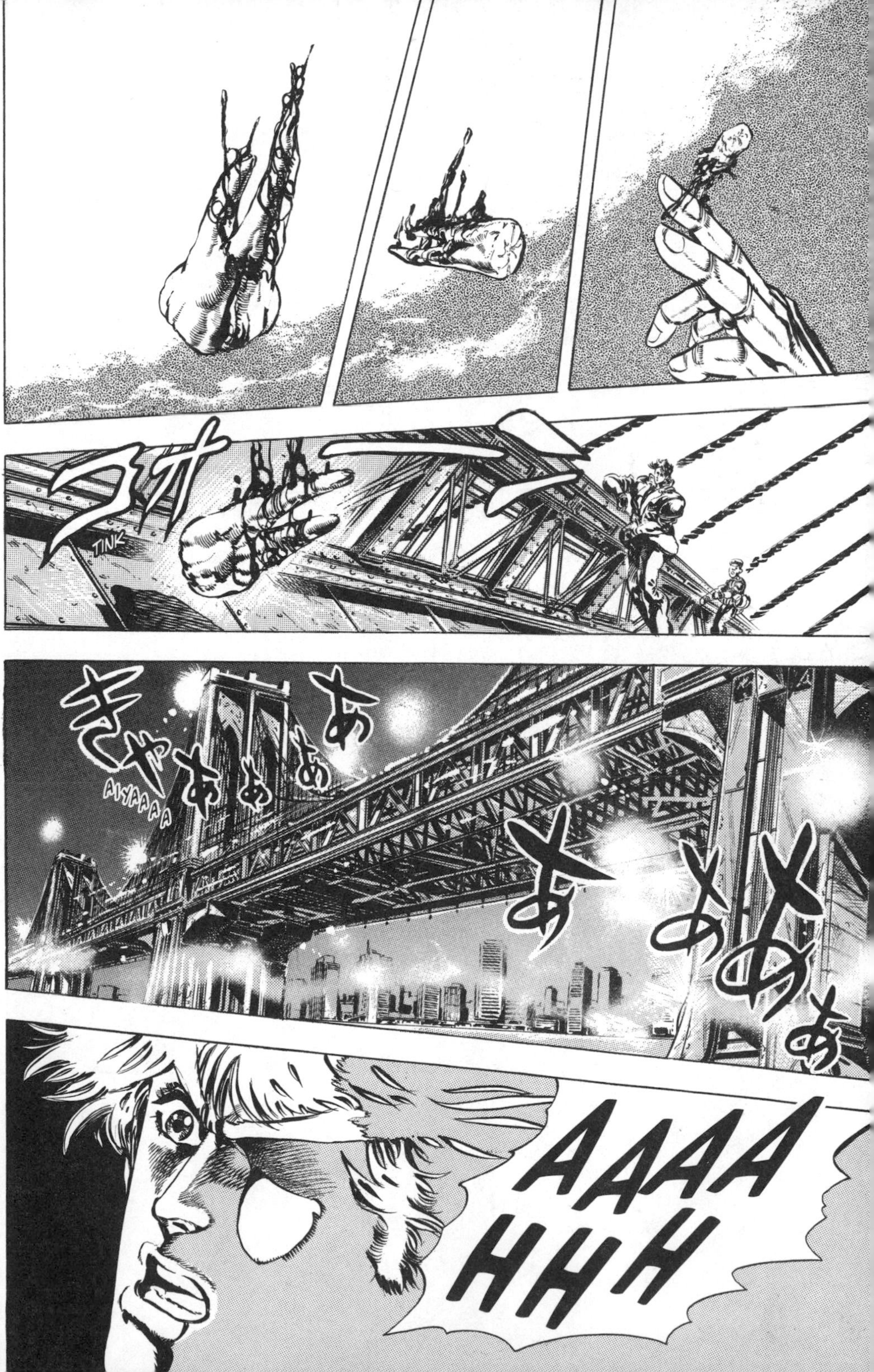
ゴオー
TINK
AIYAAAA
AAAAHHH

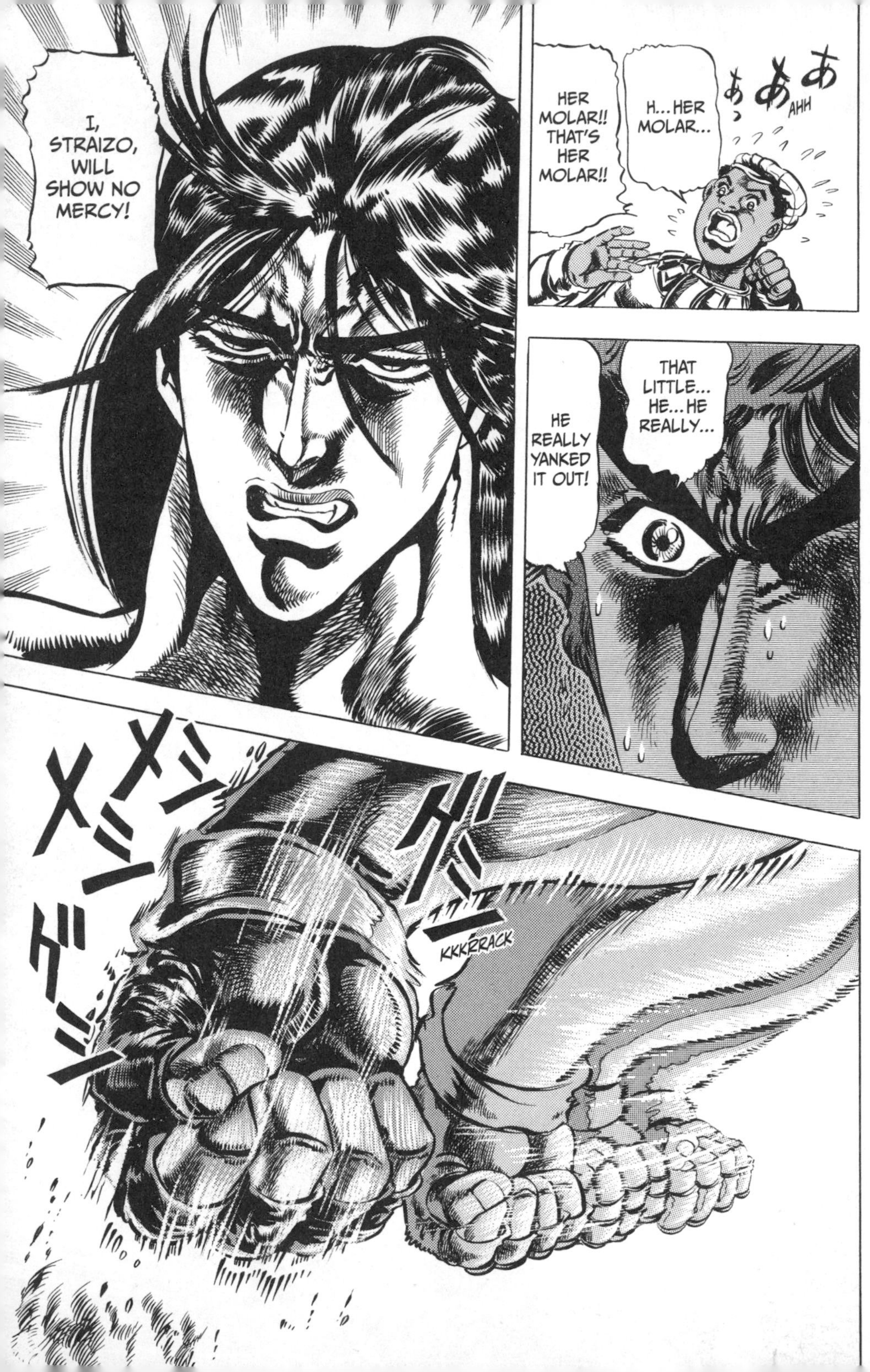
AHH
H... HER MOLAR...
HER MOLAR!! THAT'S HER MOLAR!!
THAT LITTLE... HE... HE REALLY...
HE REALLY YANKED IT OUT!
I, STRAIZO, WILL SHOW NO MERCY!
KKKRRACK

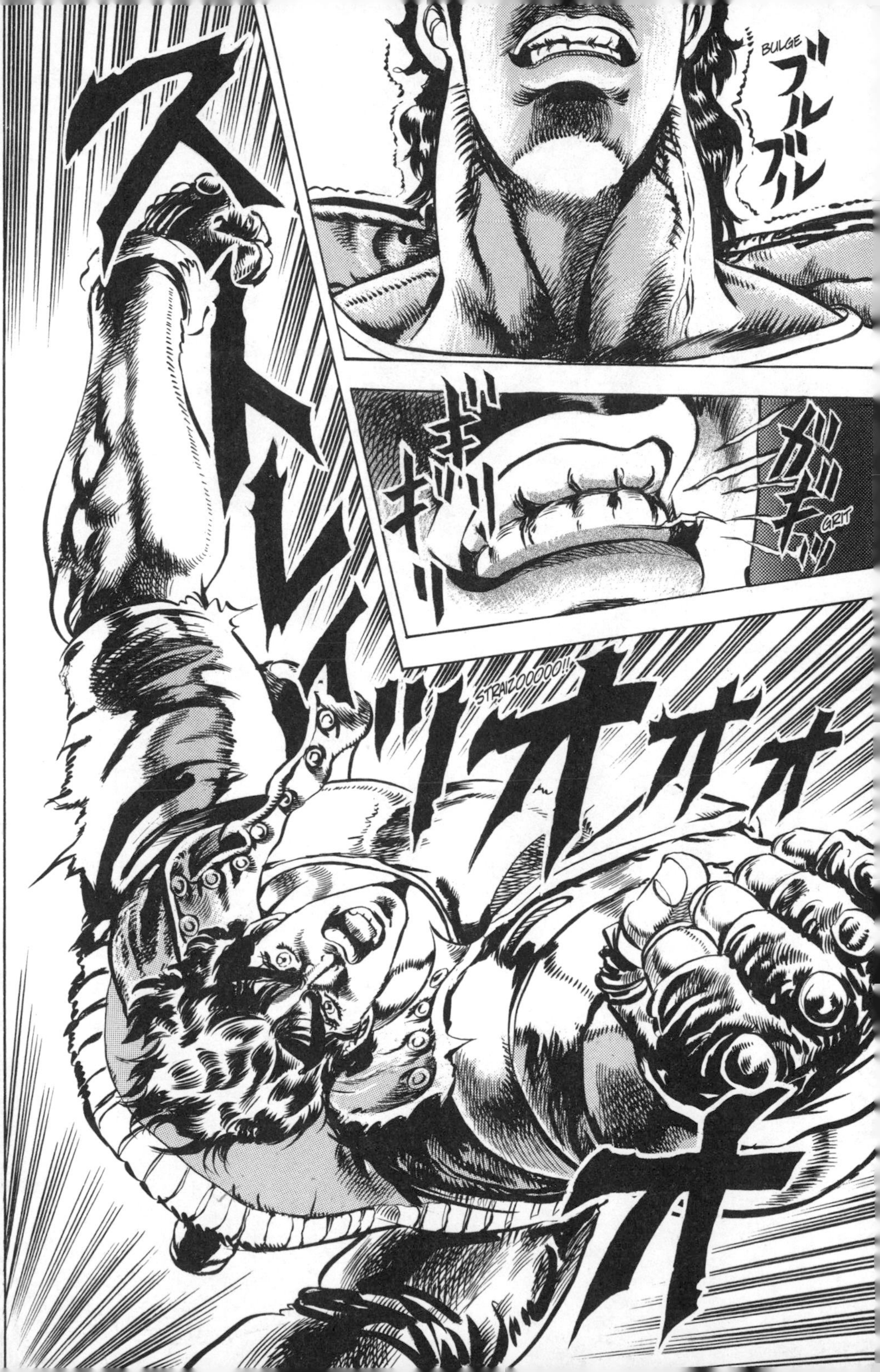
BULGE
GRIT
STRAIZOOOOO!!

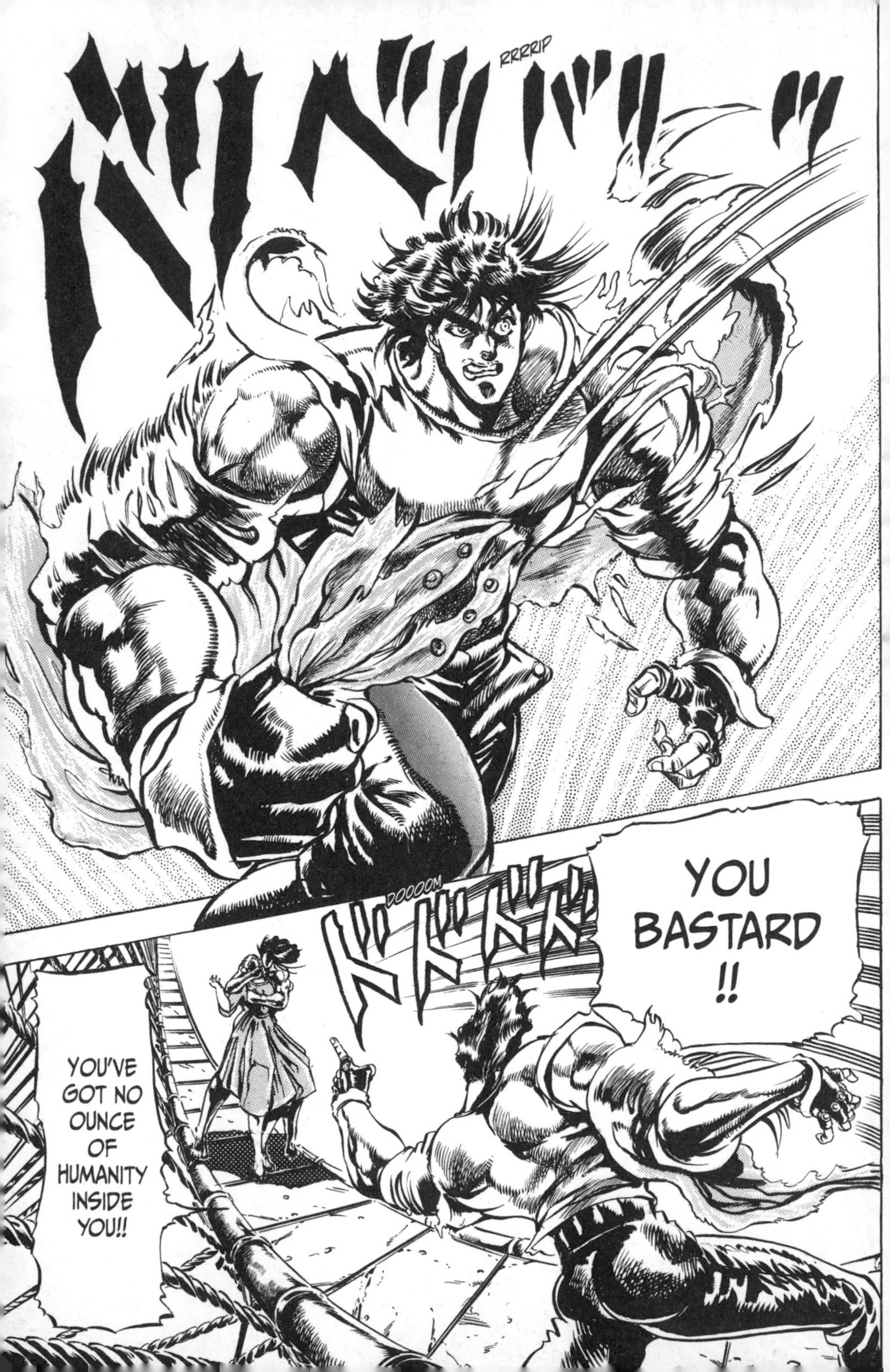

バリベリバリーッ
RRRRIP
YOU BASTARD!!
ドドドド
DOOOOM
YOU'VE GOT NO OUNCE OF HUMANITY INSIDE YOU!!

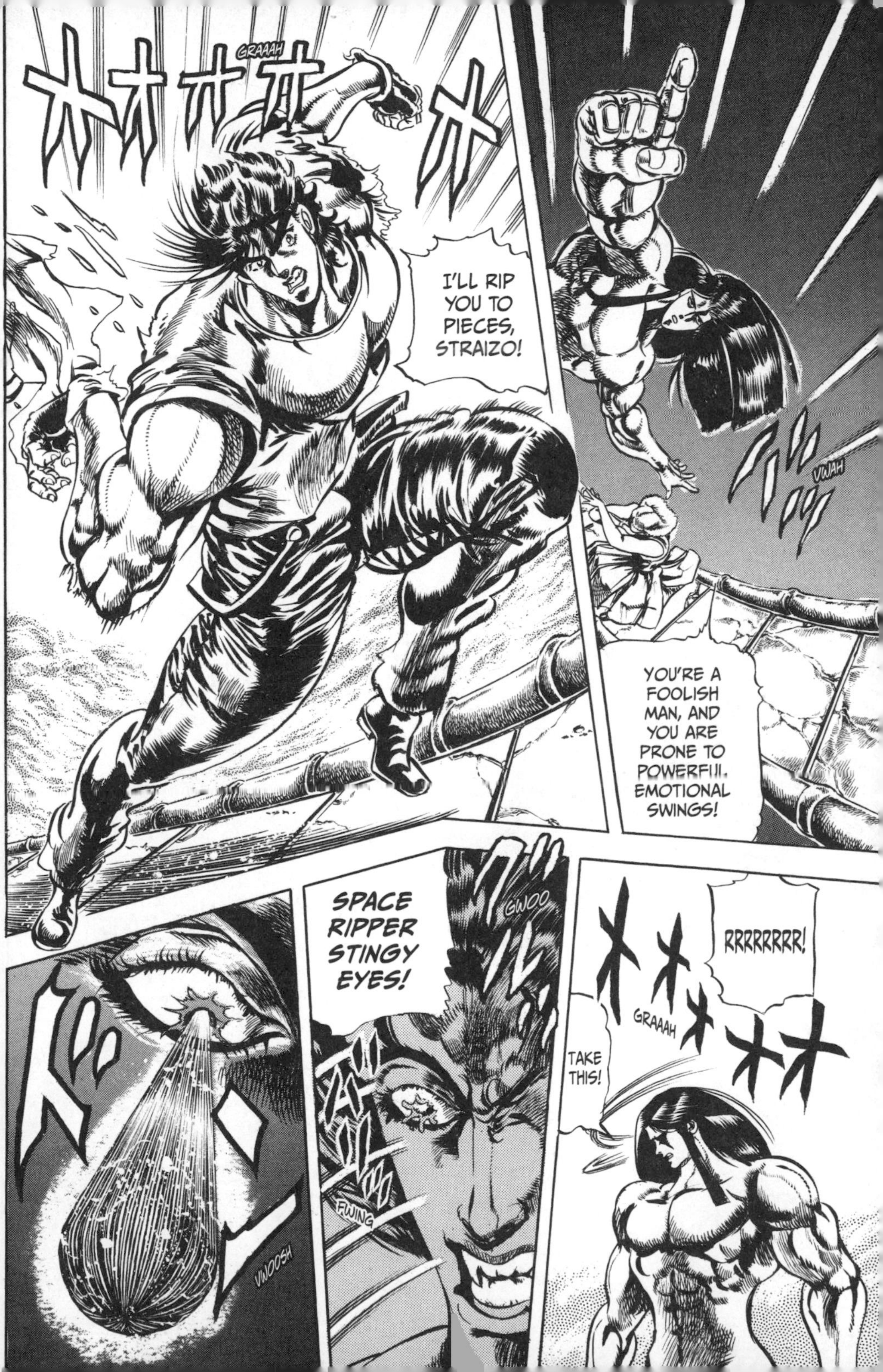
VWAH
YOU'RE A FOOLISH MAN, AND YOU ARE PRONE TO POWERFUL EMOTIONAL SWINGS!
GRAAAH
I'LL RIP YOU TO PIECES, STRAIZO!
RRRRRRRR!
GRAAAH
TAKE THIS!
SPACE RIPPER STINGY EYES!
GWOO
FWING
VWOOSH

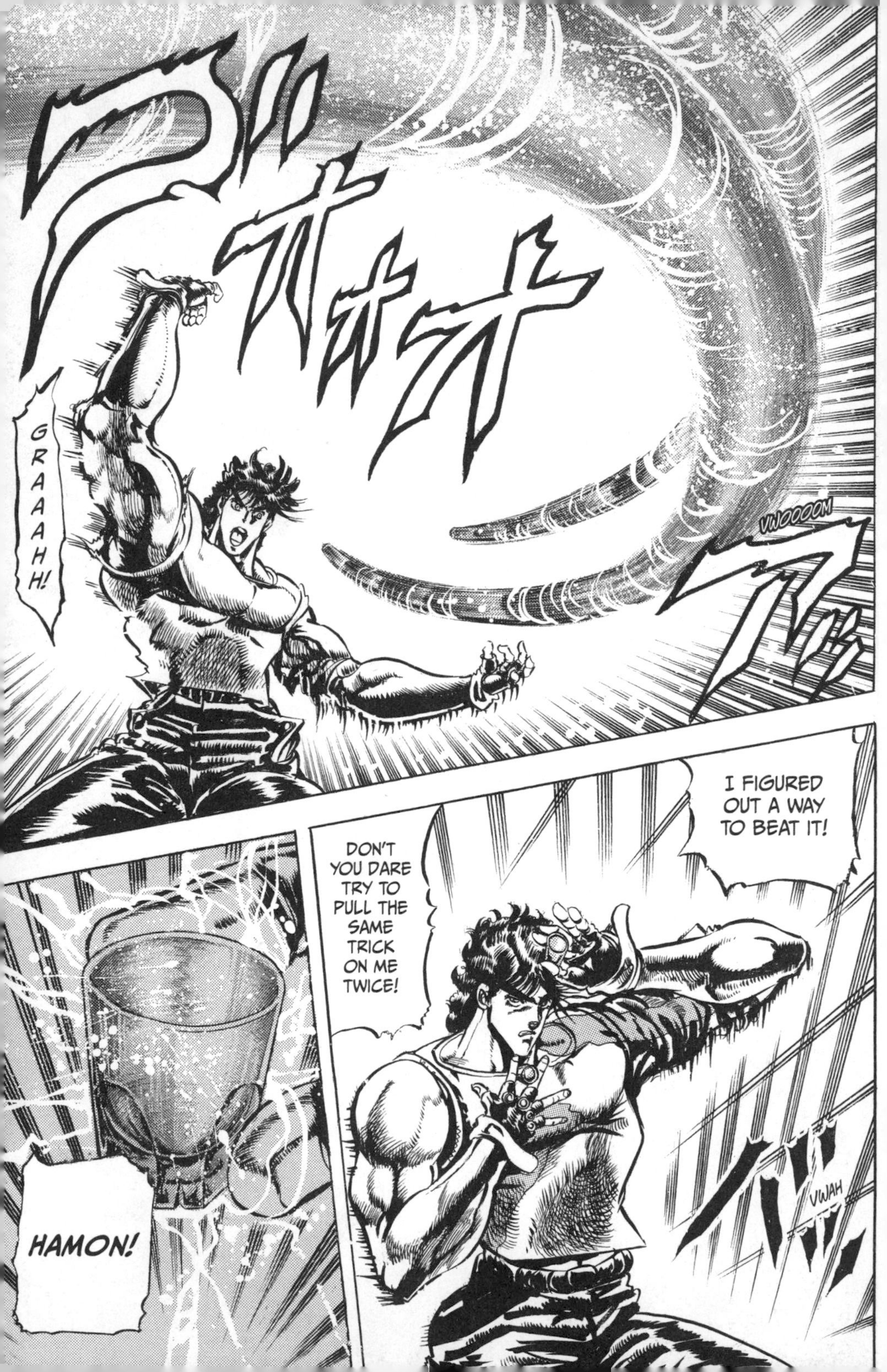
VWOOOOM
GRAAAAH!
I FIGURED OUT A WAY TO BEAT IT!
DON'T YOU DARE TRY TO PULL THE SAME TRICK ON ME TWICE!
VWAH
HAMON!

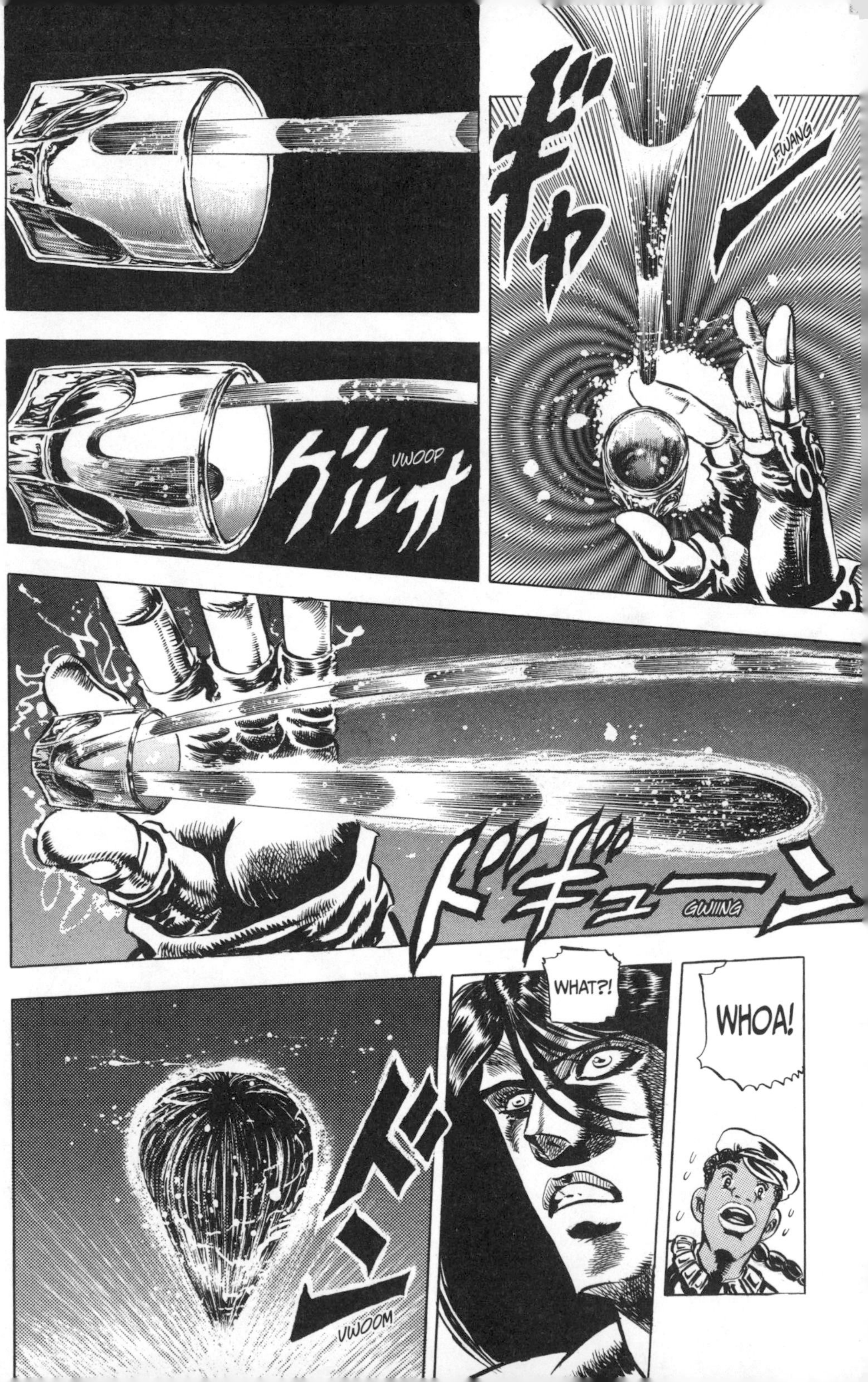
FWANG
VWOOP
GWIING
WHOA!
WHAT?!
VWOOM

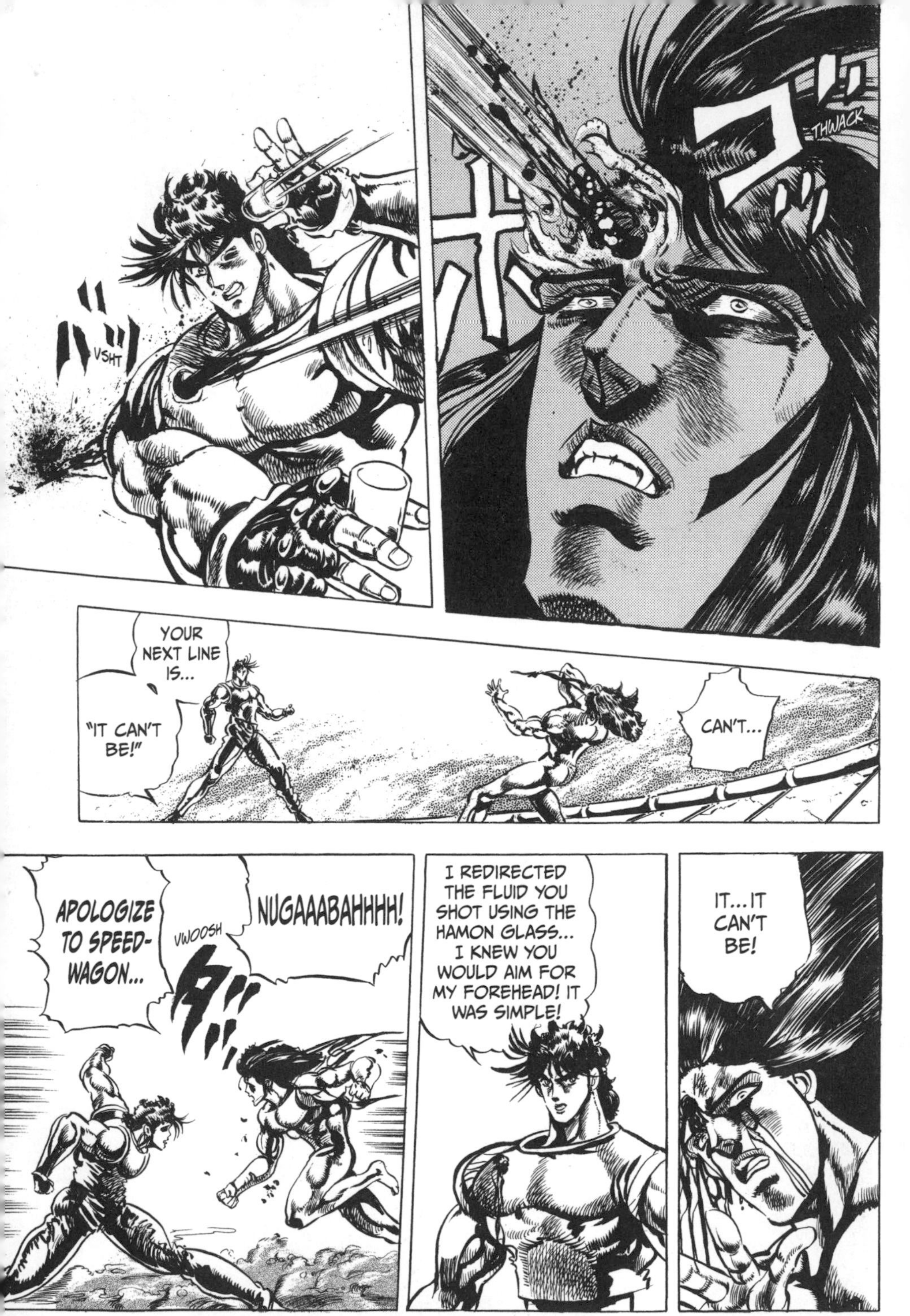
THWACK
VSHT
CAN'T...
YOUR NEXT LINE IS...
"IT CAN'T BE!"
IT... IT CAN'T BE!
I REDIRECTED THE FLUID YOU SHOT USING THE HAMON GLASS... I KNEW YOU WOULD AIM FOR MY FOREHEAD! IT WAS SIMPLE!
NUGAAABAHHHH!
APOLOGIZE TO SPEED-WAGON...
VWOOSH

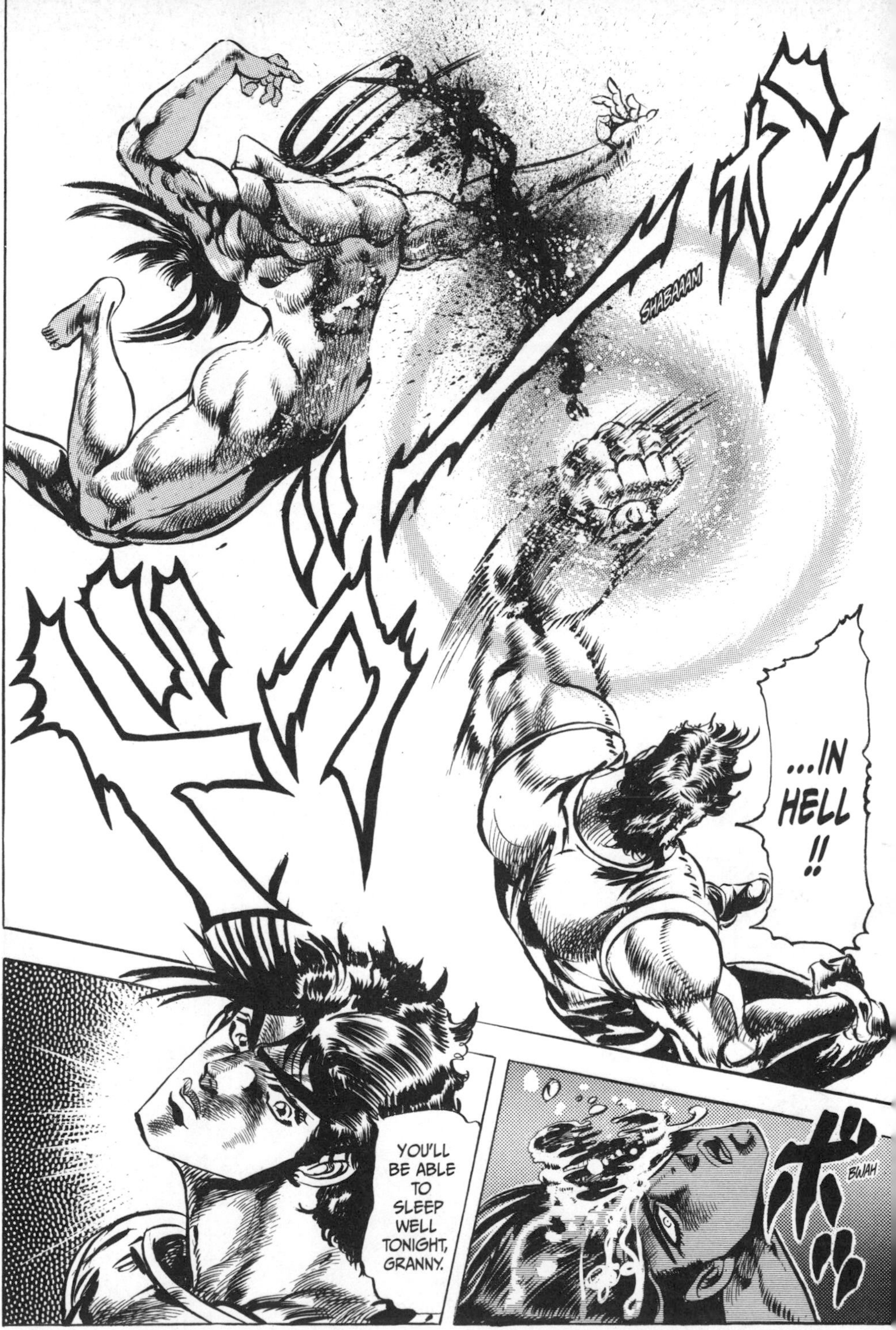
SHABAAAM
...IN HELL!!
BWAH
YOU'LL BE ABLE TO SLEEP WELL TONIGHT, GRANNY.

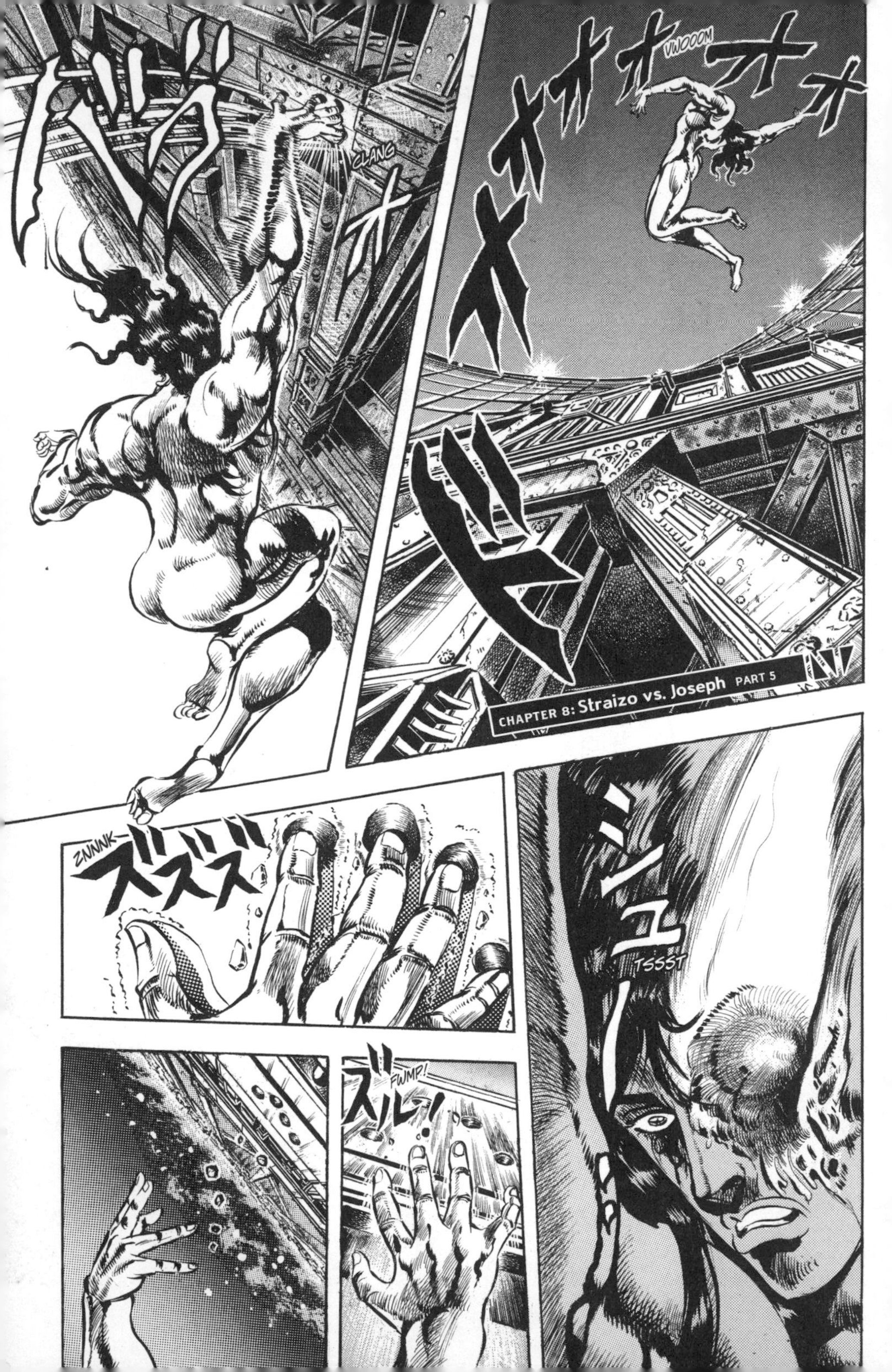
VWOOOM
CHAPTER 8: Straizo vs. Joseph PART 5
CLANG
TSSST
ZNNNK
FWMP!

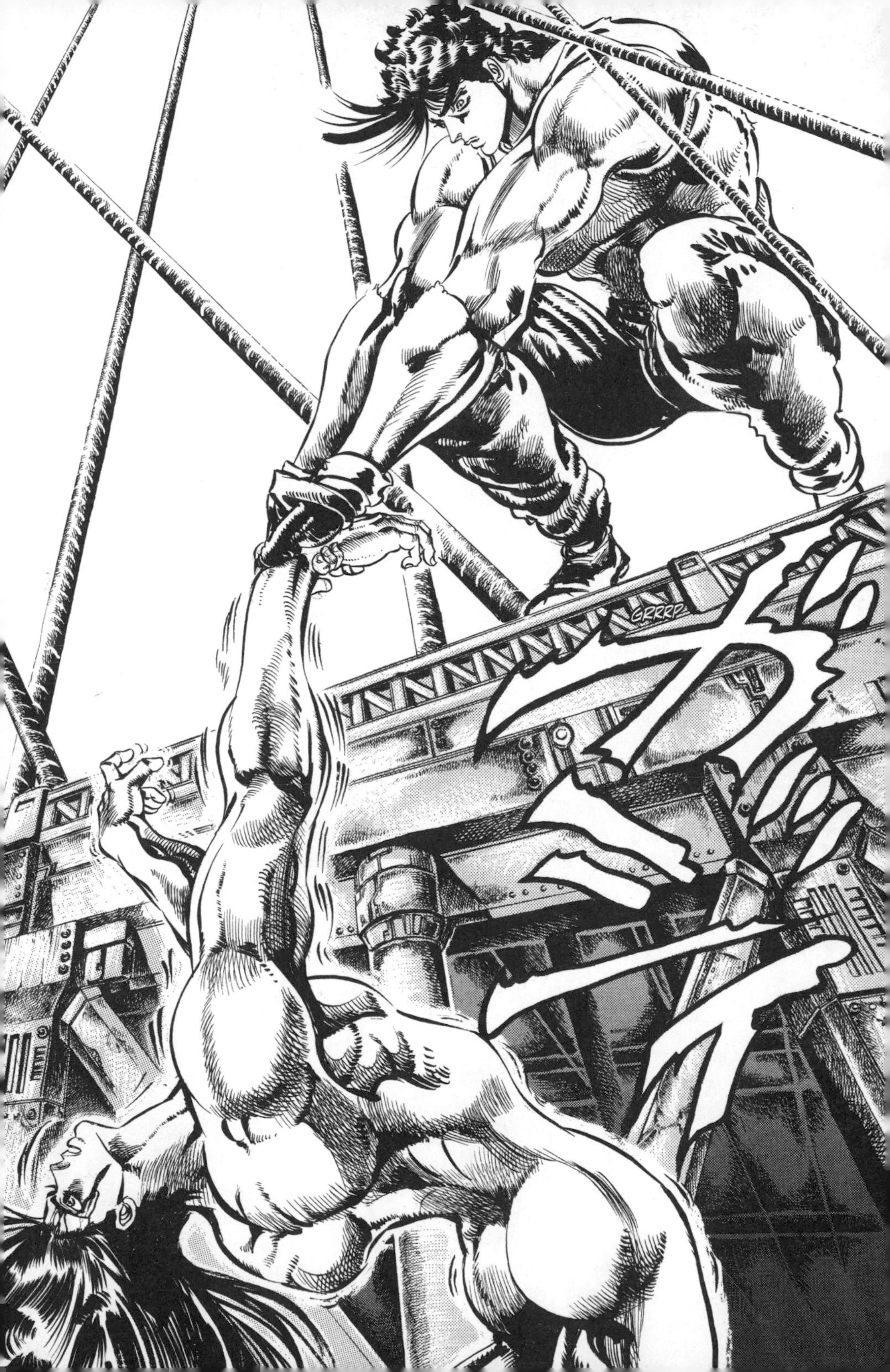
GRRRP

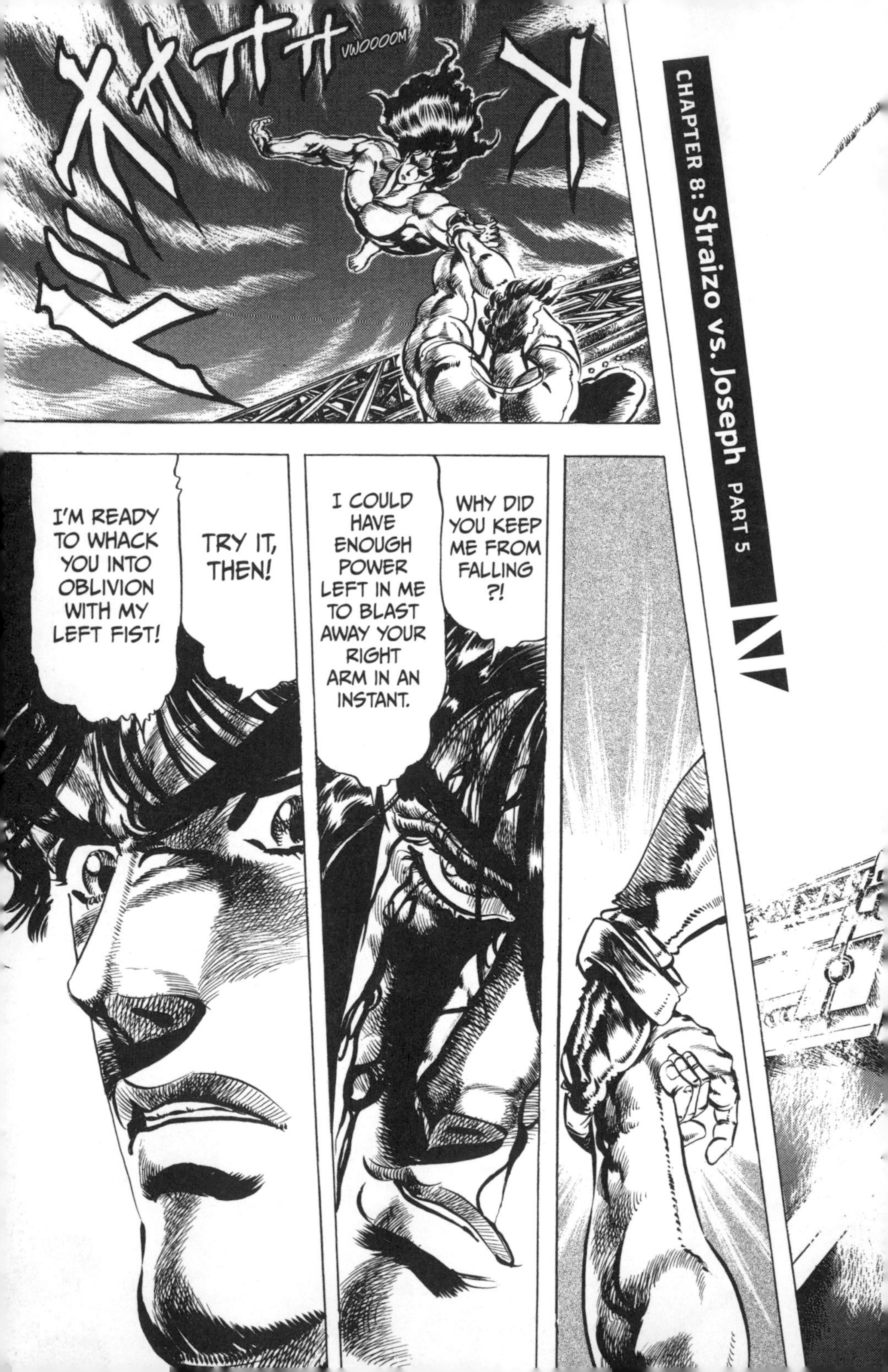
CHAPTER 8: Straizo vs. Joseph PART 5
VWOOOOM!
WHY DID YOU KEEP ME FROM FALLING ?!
I COULD HAVE ENOUGH POWER LEFT IN ME TO BLAST AWAY YOUR RIGHT ARM IN AN INSTANT.
TRY IT, THEN!
I'M READY TO WHACK YOU INTO OBLIVION WITH MY LEFT FIST!

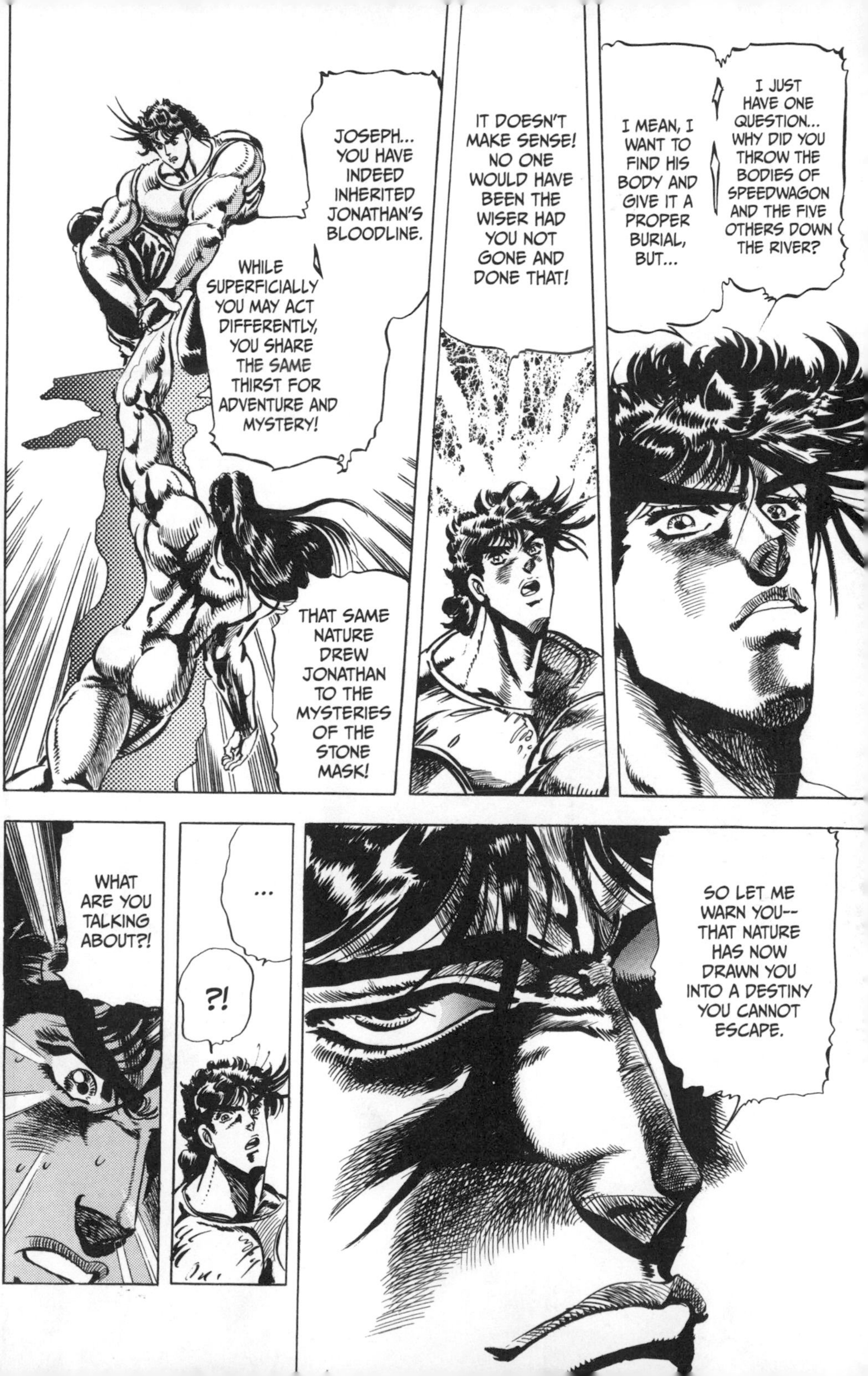
I JUST HAVE ONE QUESTION... WHY DID YOU THROW THE BODIES OF SPEEDWAGON AND THE FIVE OTHERS DOWN THE RIVER?
I MEAN, I WANT TO FIND HIS BODY AND GIVE IT A PROPER BURIAL, BUT...
IT DOESN'T MAKE SENSE! NO ONE WOULD HAVE BEEN THE WISER HAD YOU NOT GONE AND DONE THAT!
JOSEPH... YOU HAVE INDEED INHERITED JONATHAN'S BLOODLINE.
WHILE SUPERFICIALLY YOU MAY ACT DIFFERENTLY, YOU SHARE THE SAME THIRST FOR ADVENTURE AND MYSTERY!
THAT SAME NATURE DREW JONATHAN TO THE MYSTERIES OF THE STONE MASK!
SO LET ME WARN YOU-- THAT NATURE HAS NOW DRAWN YOU INTO A DESTINY YOU CANNOT ESCAPE.
...
?!
WHAT ARE YOU TALKING ABOUT?!

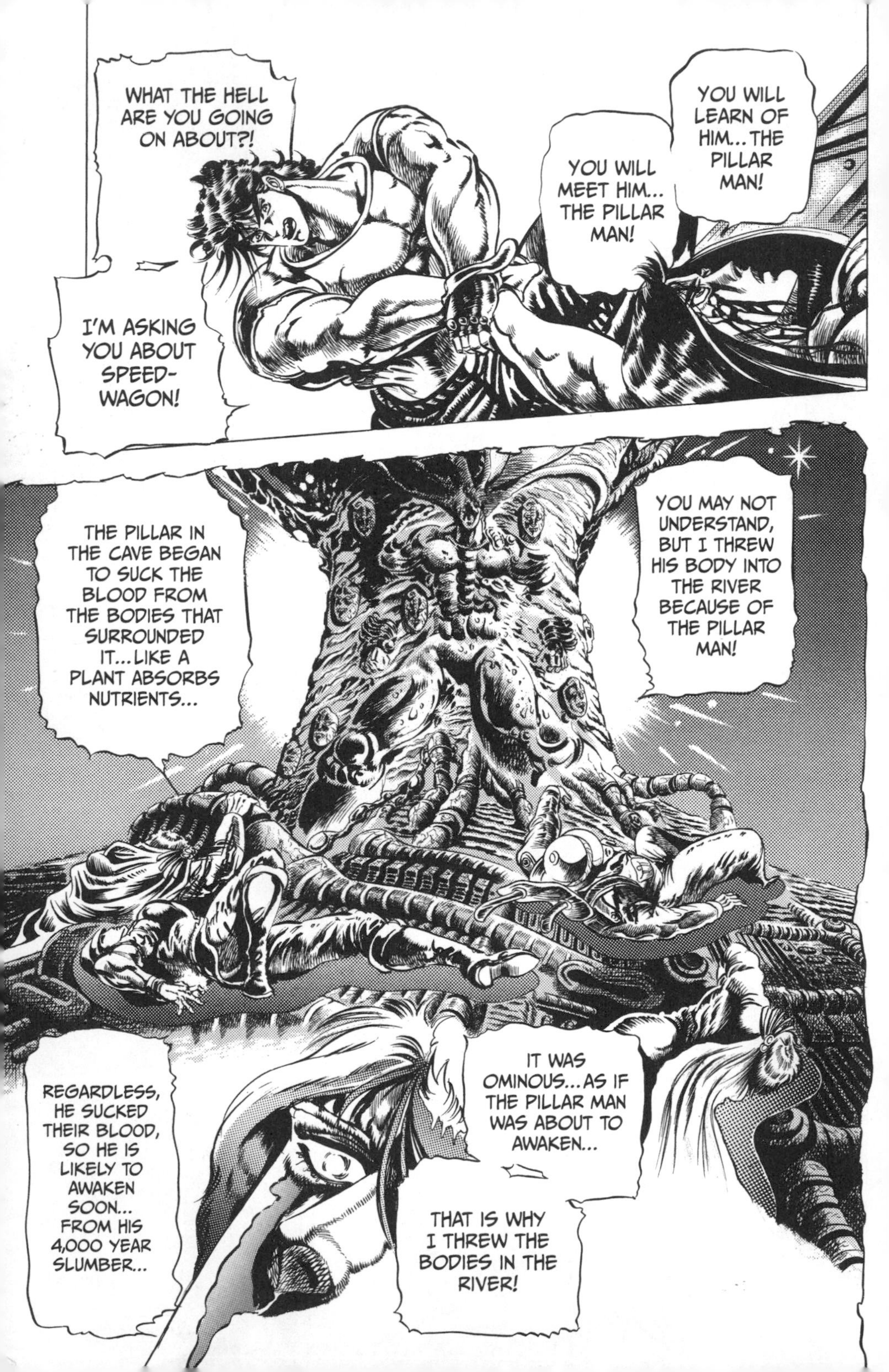
YOU WILL LEARN OF HIM...THE PILLAR MAN!
YOU WILL MEET HIM... THE PILLAR MAN!
WHAT THE HELL ARE YOU GOING ON ABOUT?!
I'M ASKING YOU ABOUT SPEED-WAGON!
YOU MAY NOT UNDERSTAND, BUT I THREW HIS BODY INTO THE RIVER BECAUSE OF THE PILLAR MAN!
THE PILLAR IN THE CAVE BEGAN TO SUCK THE BLOOD FROM THE BODIES THAT SURROUNDED IT...LIKE A PLANT ABSORBS NUTRIENTS...
IT WAS OMINOUS...AS IF THE PILLAR MAN WAS ABOUT TO AWAKEN...
THAT IS WHY I THREW THE BODIES IN THE RIVER!
REGARDLESS, HE SUCKED THEIR BLOOD, SO HE IS LIKELY TO AWAKEN SOON... FROM HIS 4,000 YEAR SLUMBER...

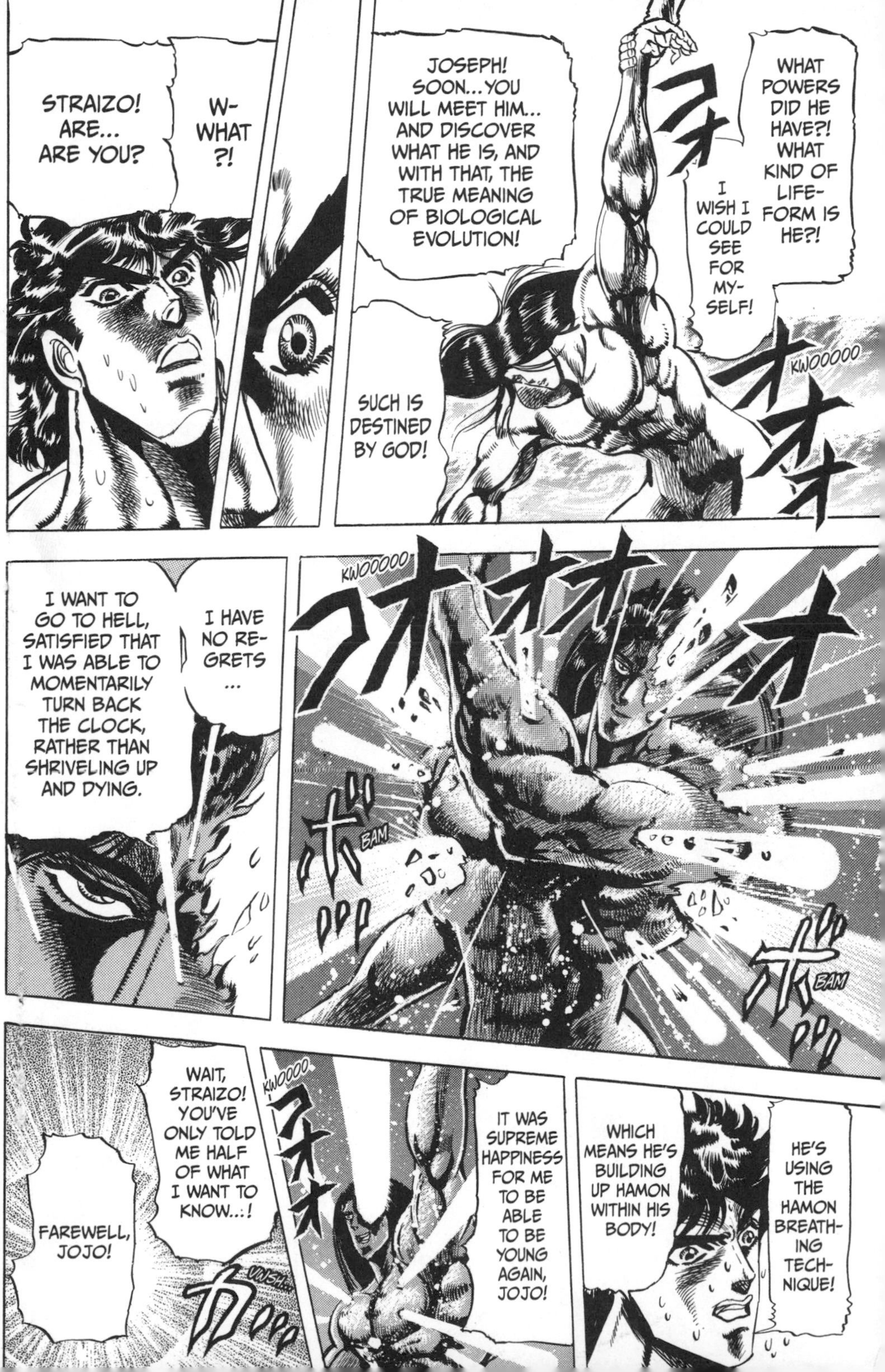
WHAT POWERS DID HE HAVE?! WHAT KIND OF LIFE-FORM IS HE?!
I WISH I COULD SEE FOR MY-SELF!
KWOOOOO
JOSEPH! SOON...YOU WILL MEET HIM... AND DISCOVER WHAT HE IS, AND WITH THAT, THE TRUE MEANING OF BIOLOGICAL EVOLUTION!
SUCH IS DESTINED BY GOD!
W-WHAT?!
STRAIZO! ARE... ARE YOU?
KWOOOOO
BAM
BAM
I HAVE NO RE-GRETS...
I WANT TO GO TO HELL, SATISFIED THAT I WAS ABLE TO MOMENTARILY TURN BACK THE CLOCK, RATHER THAN SHRIVELING UP AND DYING.
HE'S USING THE HAMON BREATH-ING TECH-NIQUE!
WHICH MEANS HE'S BUILDING UP HAMON WITHIN HIS BODY!
IT WAS SUPREME HAPPINESS FOR ME TO BE ABLE TO BE YOUNG AGAIN, JOJO!
KWOOOO
VWSH...
WAIT, STRAIZO! YOU'VE ONLY TOLD ME HALF OF WHAT I WANT TO KNOW...!
FAREWELL, JOJO!

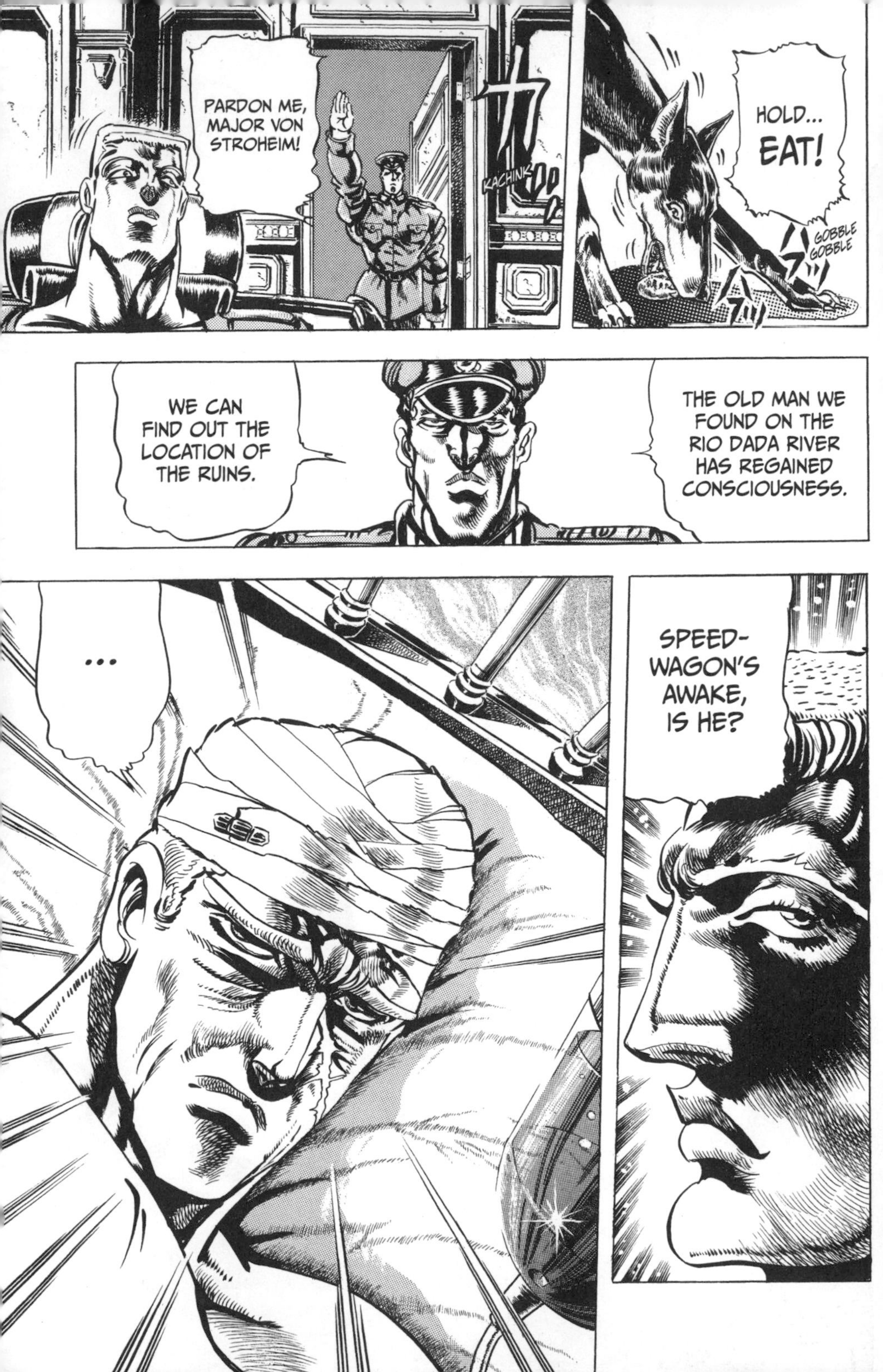
HOLD... EAT!
GOBBLE GOBBLE
KACHINK
PARDON ME, MAJOR VON STROHEIM!
THE OLD MAN WE FOUND ON THE RIO DADA RIVER HAS REGAINED CONSCIOUSNESS.
WE CAN FIND OUT THE LOCATION OF THE RUINS.
SPEED-WAGON'S AWAKE, IS HE?
...

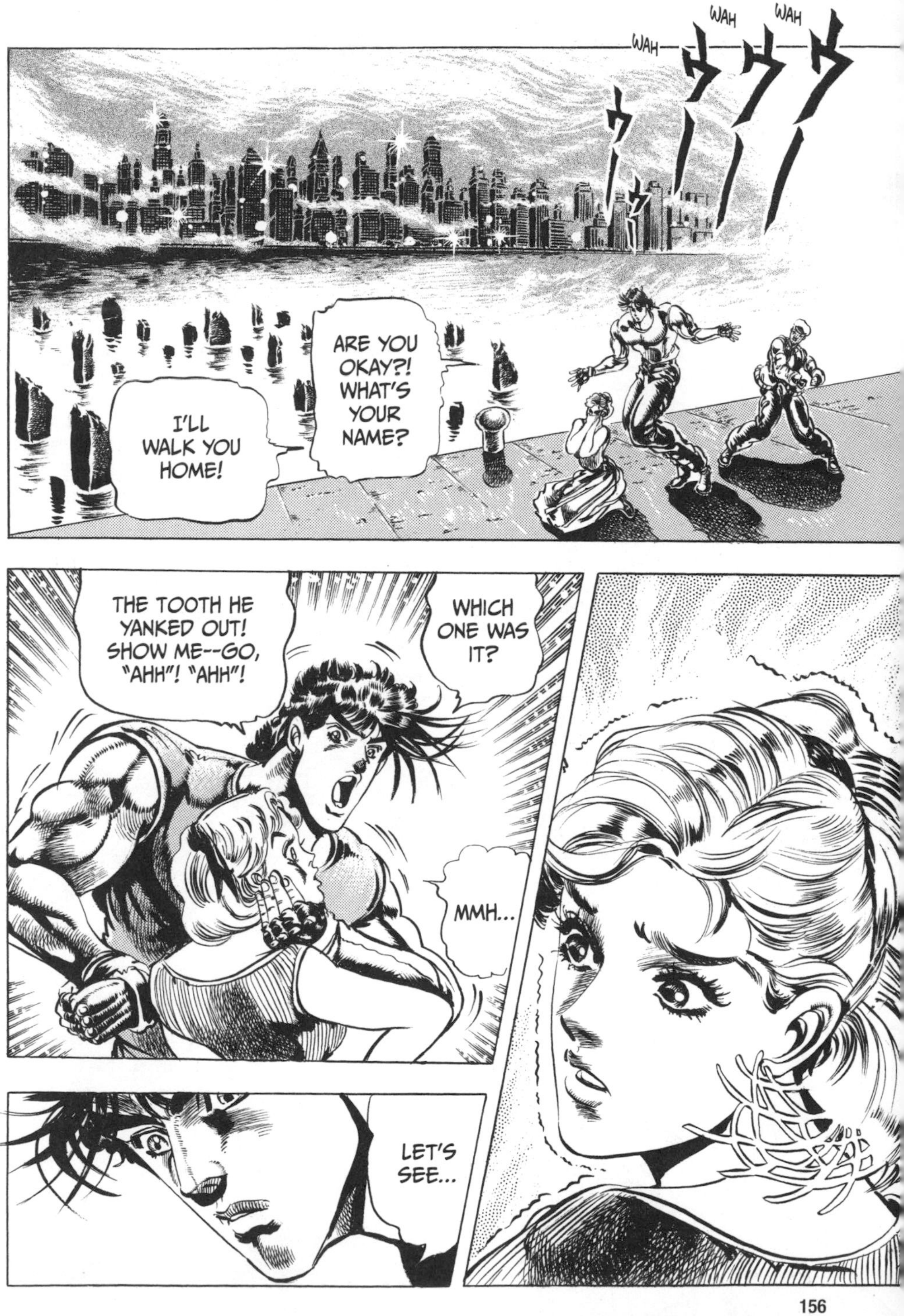
WAH
WAH
WAH
ARE YOU OKAY?! WHAT'S YOUR NAME?
I'LL WALK YOU HOME!
WHICH ONE WAS IT?
THE TOOTH HE YANKED OUT! SHOW ME--GO, "AHH"! "AHH"!
MMH...
LET'S SEE...

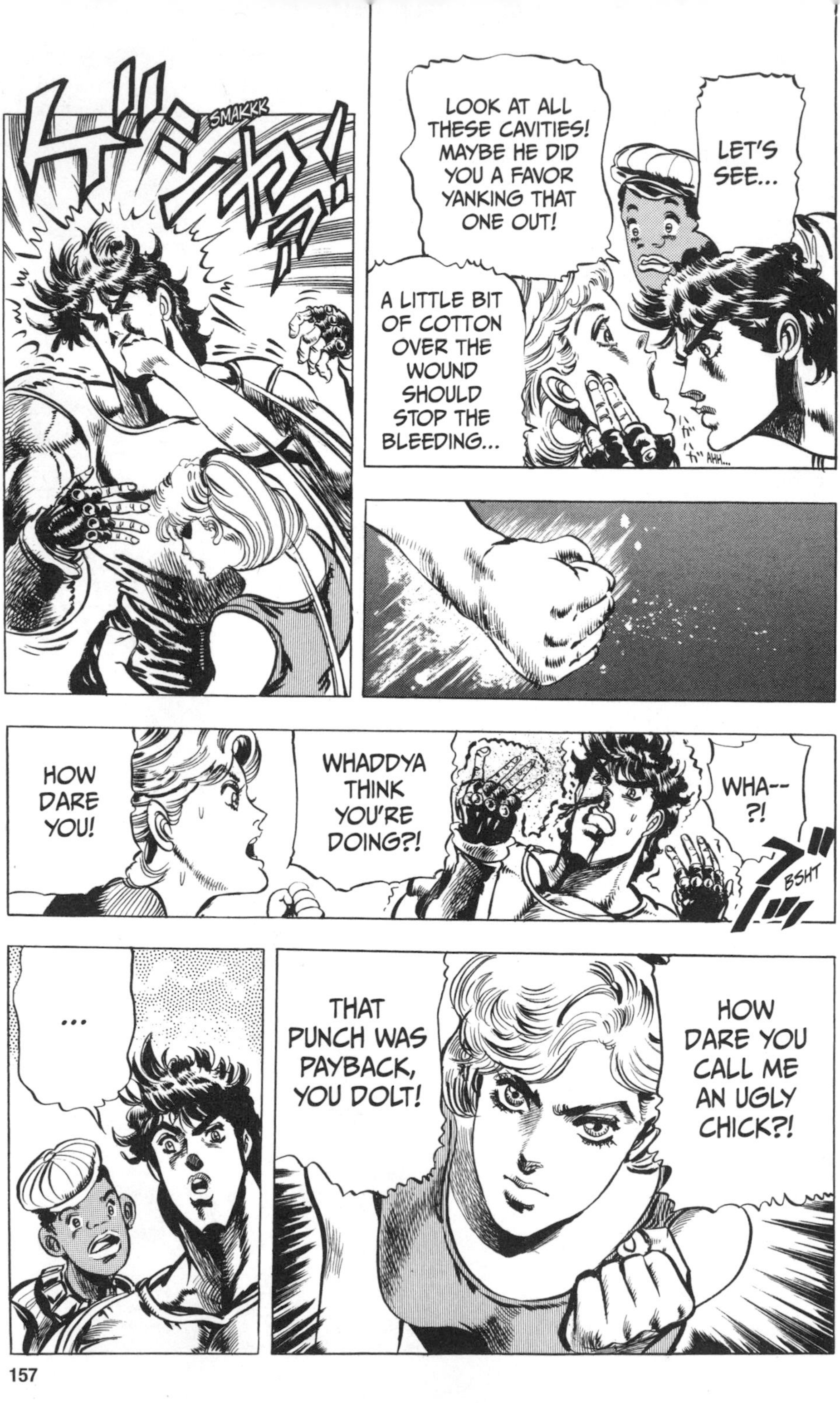
LET'S SEE...
LOOK AT ALL THESE CAVITIES! MAYBE HE DID YOU A FAVOR YANKING THAT ONE OUT!
A LITTLE BIT OF COTTON OVER THE WOUND SHOULD STOP THE BLEEDING...
AHH...
SMAKKK
WHA-- ?!
BSHT
WHADDYA THINK YOU'RE DOING?!
HOW DARE YOU!
HOW DARE YOU CALL ME AN UGLY CHICK?!
THAT PUNCH WAS PAYBACK, YOU DOLT!
...

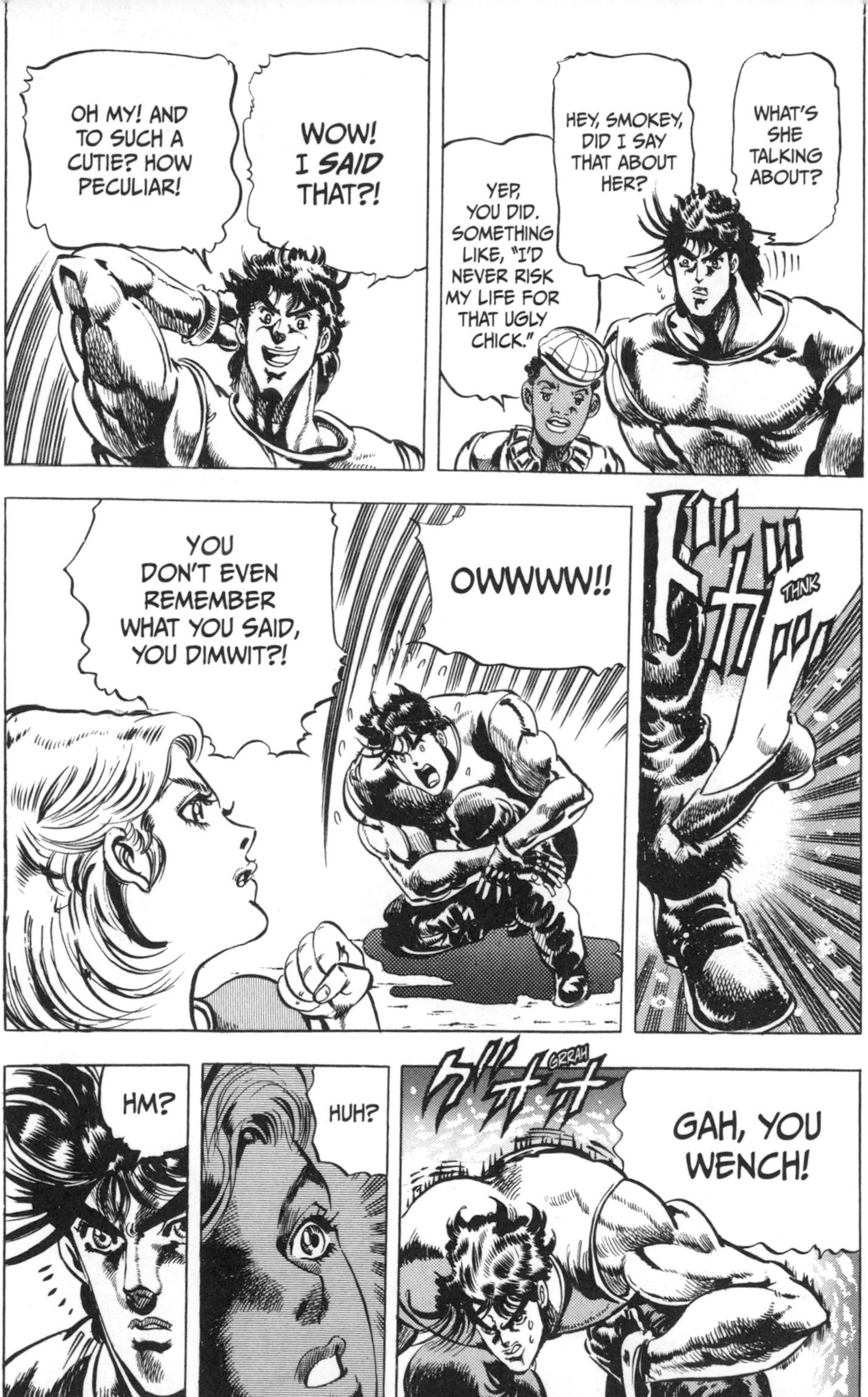
WHAT'S SHE TALKING ABOUT?
HEY, SMOKEY, DID I SAY THAT ABOUT HER?
YEP, YOU DID. SOMETHING LIKE, "I'D NEVER RISK MY LIFE FOR THAT UGLY CHICK."
WOW! I *SAID* THAT?!
OH MY! AND TO SUCH A CUTIE? HOW PECULIAR!
THNK
OWWWW!!
YOU DON'T EVEN REMEMBER WHAT YOU SAID, YOU DIMWIT?!
GRRAH
GAH, YOU WENCH!
HUH?
HM?

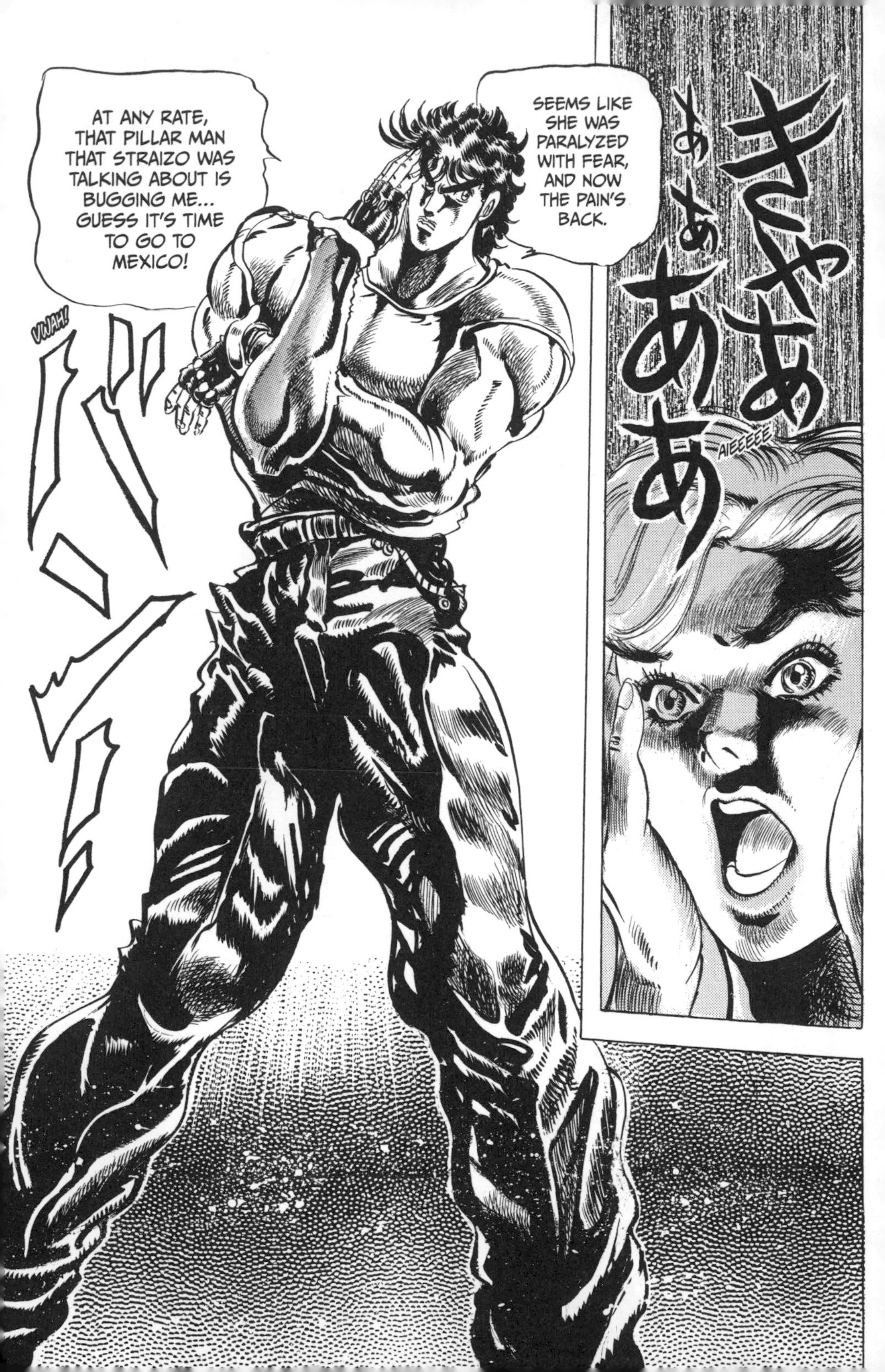
きゃあああ
ぁぁぁ
AIEEEEE
SEEMS LIKE SHE WAS PARALYZED WITH FEAR, AND NOW THE PAIN'S BACK.
AT ANY RATE, THAT PILLAR MAN THAT STRAIZO WAS TALKING ABOUT IS BUGGING ME... GUESS IT'S TIME TO GO TO MEXICO!
VWAH!
バーン

JoJo's
BIZARRE ADVENTURE

CHAPTER 9: The Pillar Man

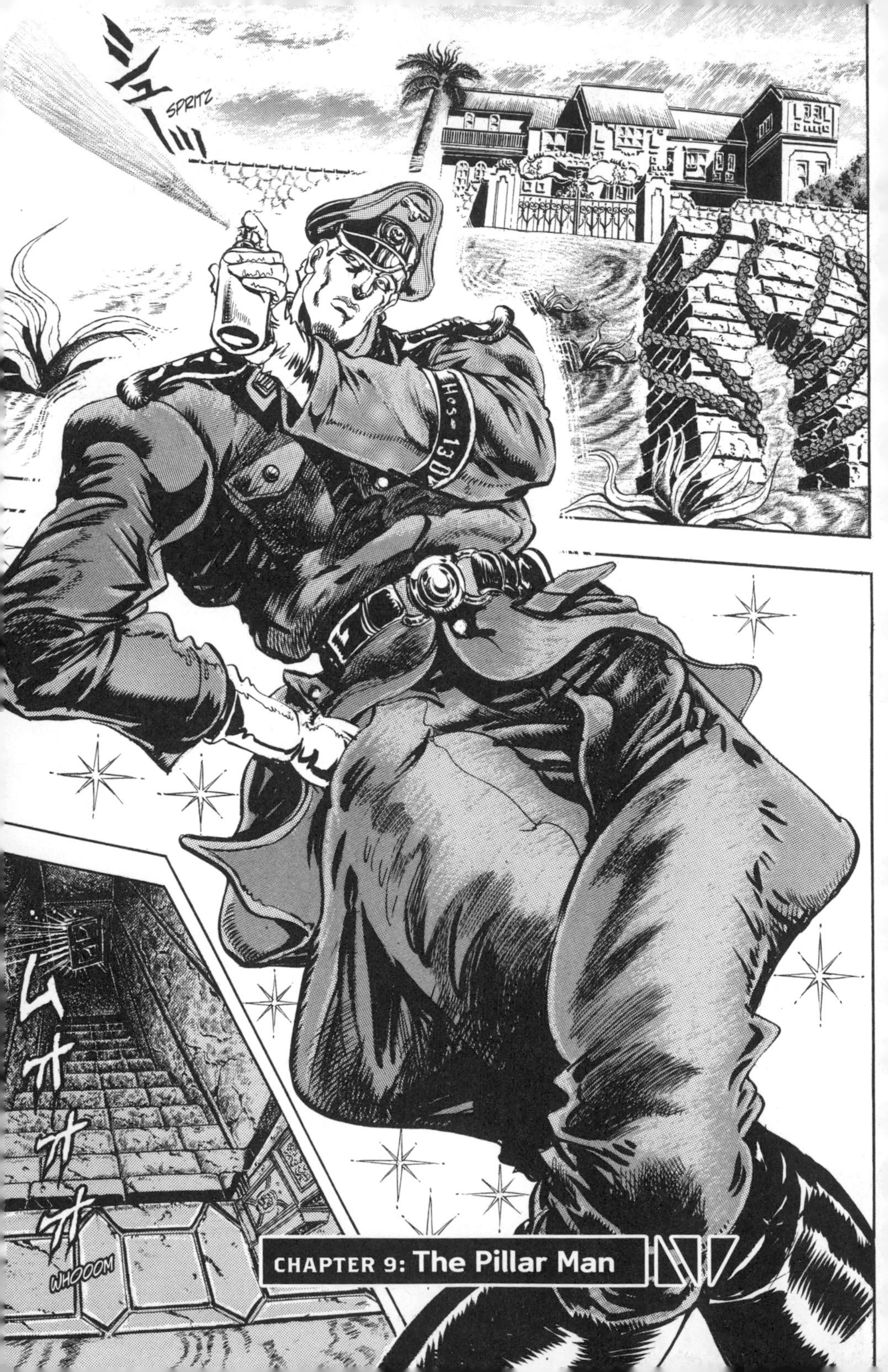
SPRITZ
WHOOOM

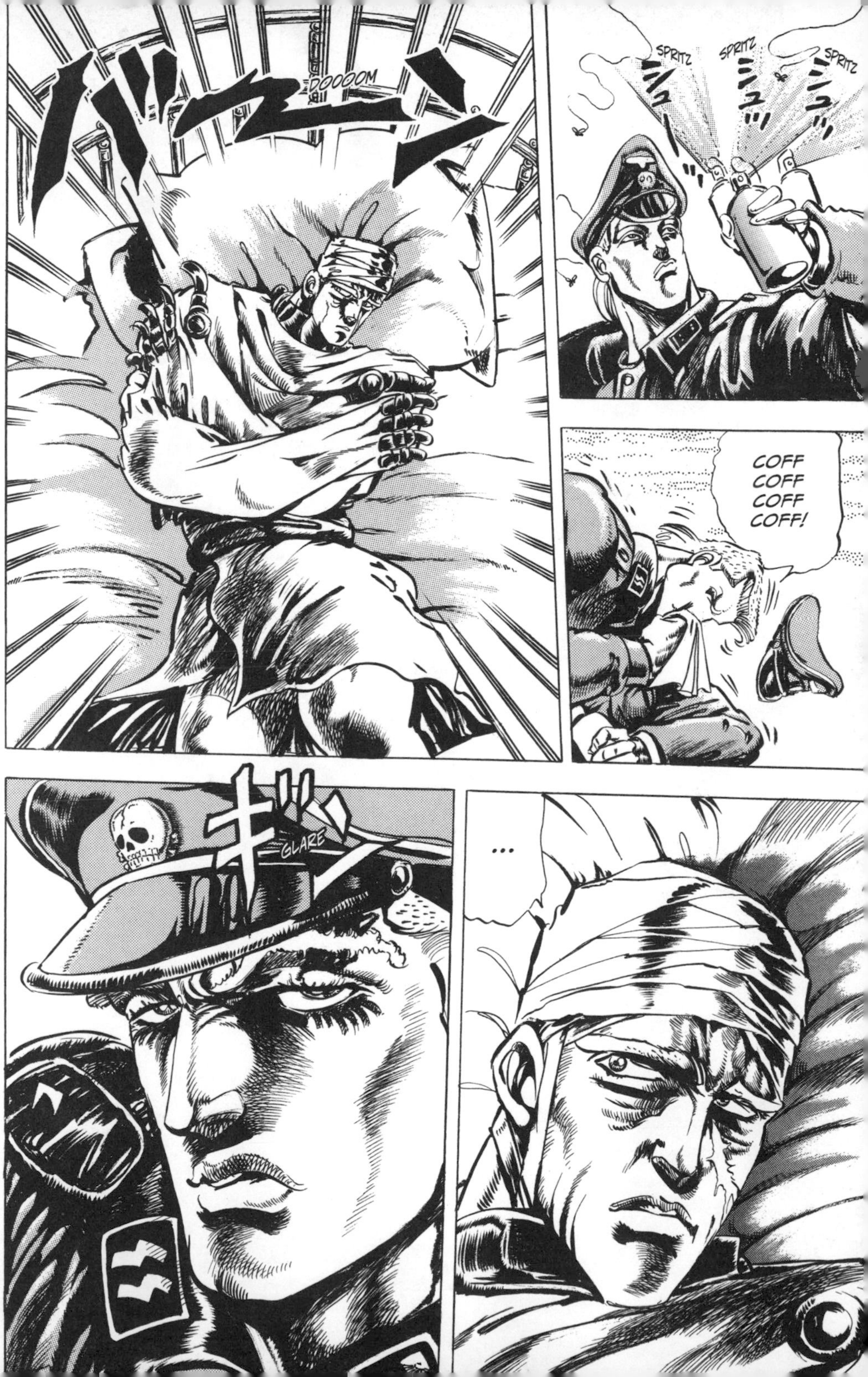
SPRITZ
SPRITZ
SPRITZ
COFF COFF COFF COFF!
バーン
DOOOOM
...
ギッ
GLARE

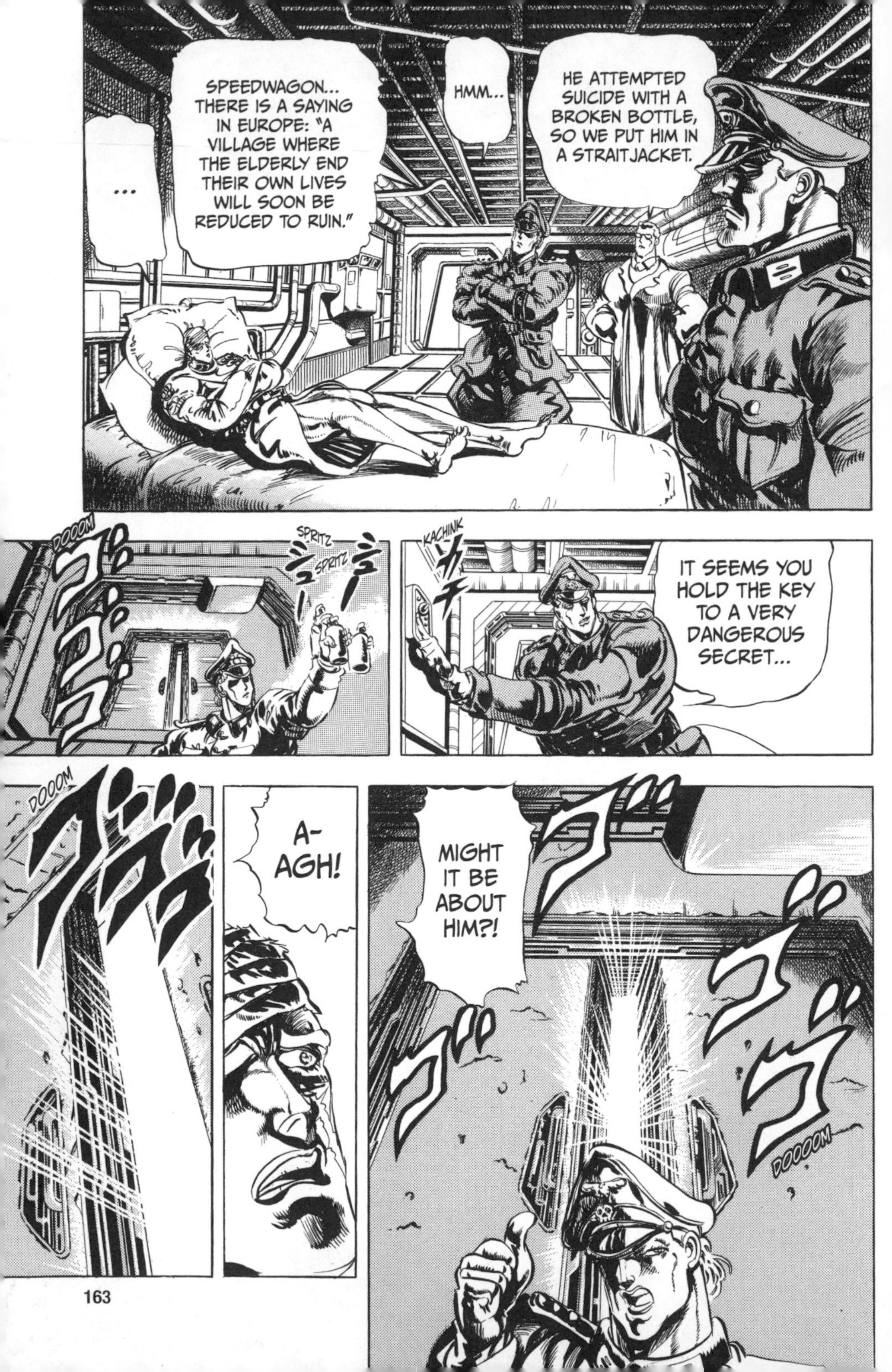
HE ATTEMPTED SUICIDE WITH A BROKEN BOTTLE, SO WE PUT HIM IN A STRAITJACKET.
HMM...
SPEEDWAGON... THERE IS A SAYING IN EUROPE: "A VILLAGE WHERE THE ELDERLY END THEIR OWN LIVES WILL SOON BE REDUCED TO RUIN."
...
KACHINK
IT SEEMS YOU HOLD THE KEY TO A VERY DANGEROUS SECRET...
SPRITZ SPRITZ
DOOOM
MIGHT IT BE ABOUT HIM?!
DOOOOM
A- AGH!
DOOOM

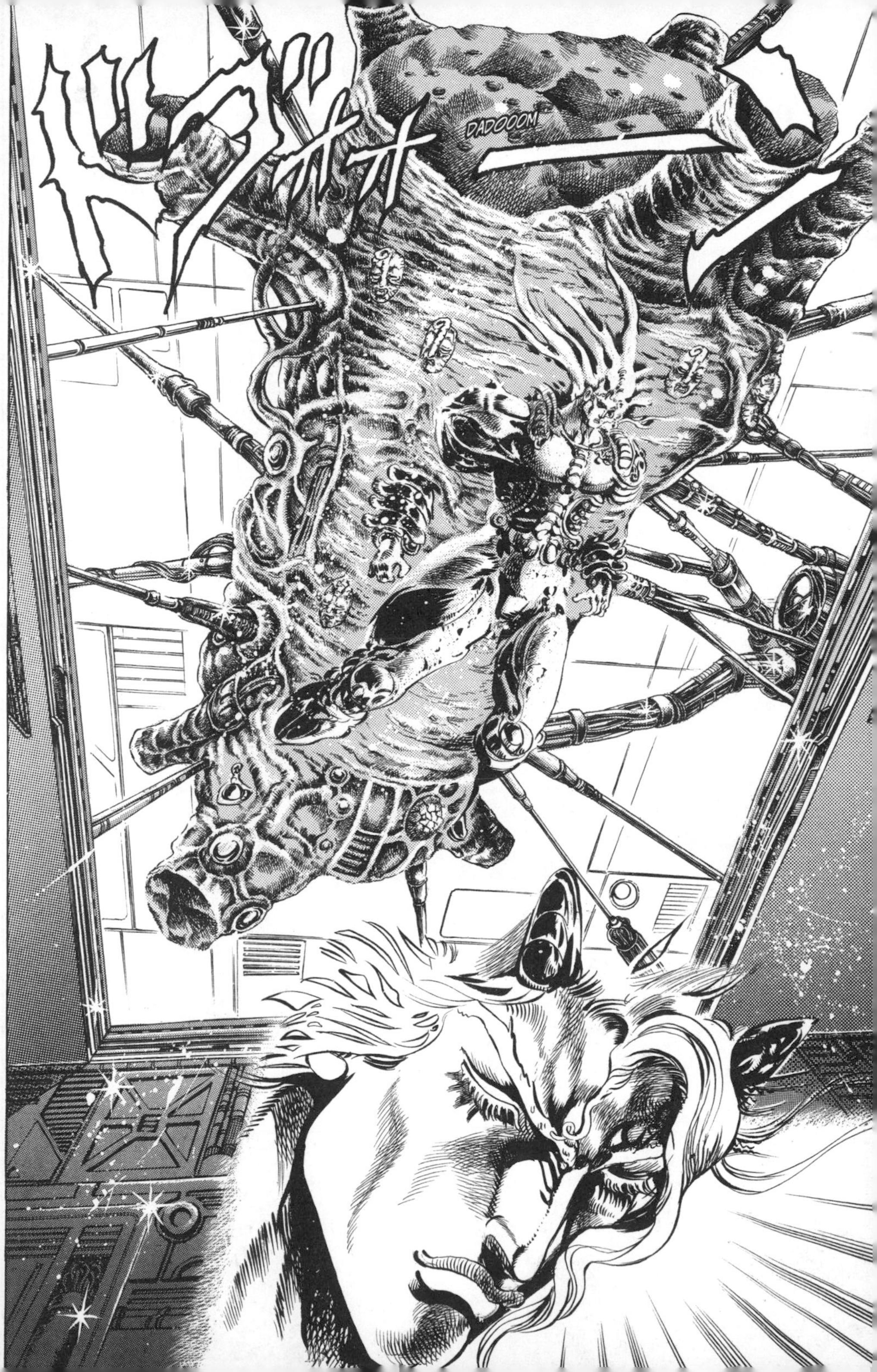
DADOOOM

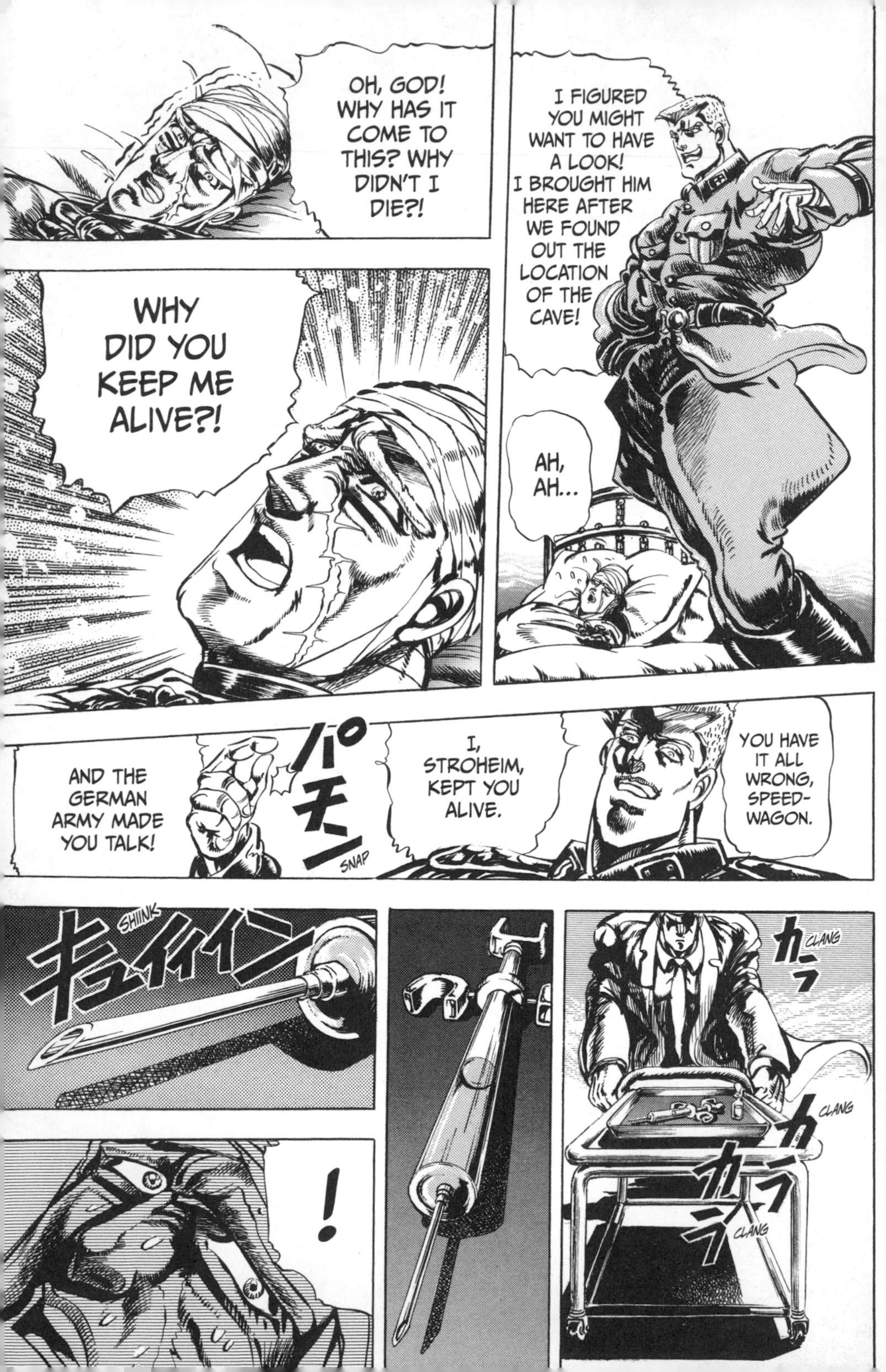
I FIGURED YOU MIGHT WANT TO HAVE A LOOK! I BROUGHT HIM HERE AFTER WE FOUND OUT THE LOCATION OF THE CAVE!
AH, AH...
OH, GOD! WHY HAS IT COME TO THIS? WHY DIDN'T I DIE?!
WHY DID YOU KEEP ME ALIVE?!
YOU HAVE IT ALL WRONG, SPEED-WAGON.
I, STROHEIM, KEPT YOU ALIVE.
SNAP
AND THE GERMAN ARMY MADE YOU TALK!
CLANG
CLANG
CLANG
SHIINK
!

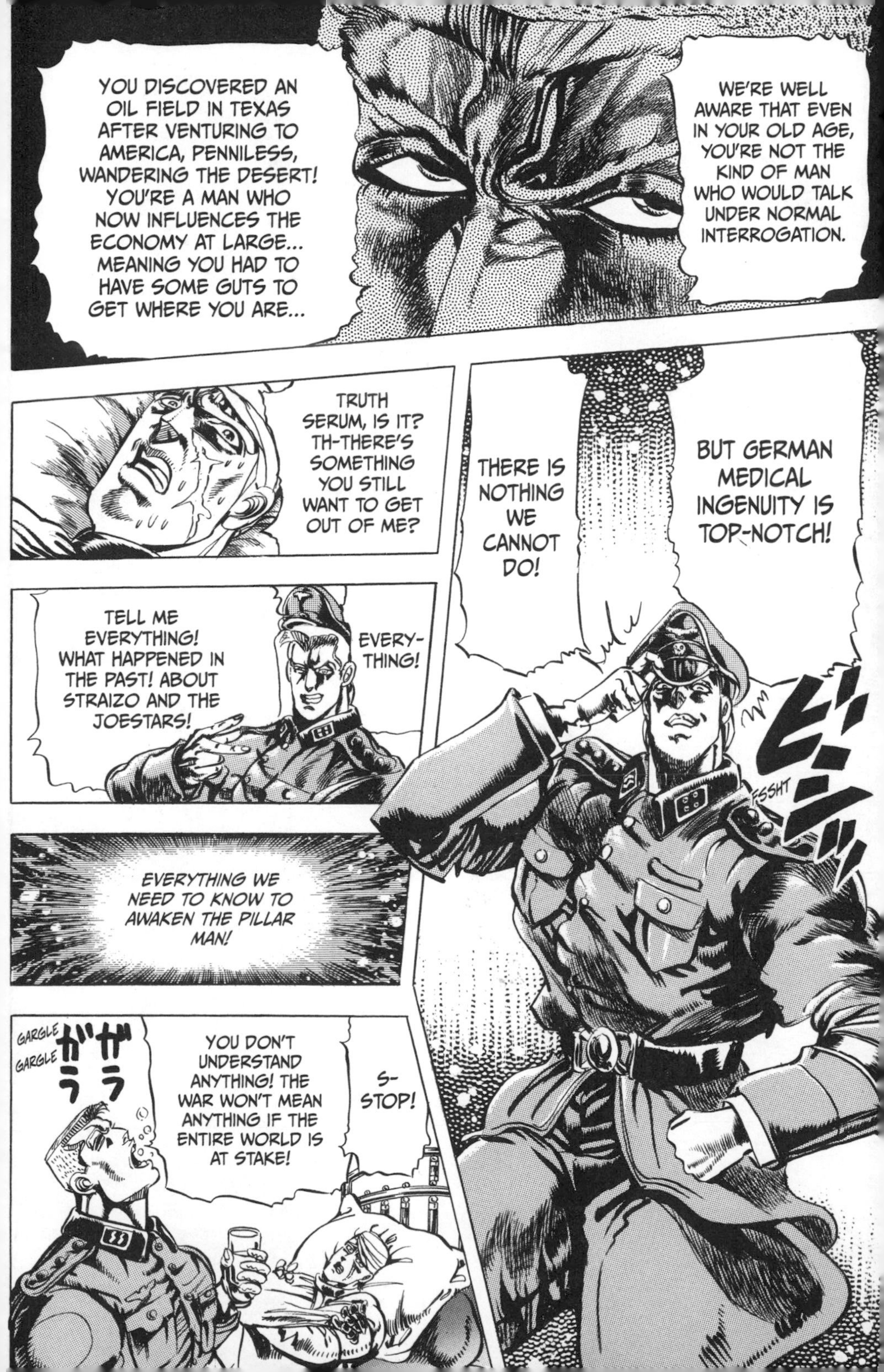
WE'RE WELL AWARE THAT EVEN IN YOUR OLD AGE, YOU'RE NOT THE KIND OF MAN WHO WOULD TALK UNDER NORMAL INTERROGATION.
YOU DISCOVERED AN OIL FIELD IN TEXAS AFTER VENTURING TO AMERICA, PENNILESS, WANDERING THE DESERT! YOU'RE A MAN WHO NOW INFLUENCES THE ECONOMY AT LARGE... MEANING YOU HAD TO HAVE SOME GUTS TO GET WHERE YOU ARE...
BUT GERMAN MEDICAL INGENUITY IS TOP-NOTCH!
THERE IS NOTHING WE CANNOT DO!
FSSHT
TRUTH SERUM, IS IT? TH-THERE'S SOMETHING YOU STILL WANT TO GET OUT OF ME?
EVERY-THING!
TELL ME EVERYTHING! WHAT HAPPENED IN THE PAST! ABOUT STRAIZO AND THE JOESTARS!
EVERYTHING WE NEED TO KNOW TO AWAKEN THE PILLAR MAN!
S-STOP!
YOU DON'T UNDERSTAND ANYTHING! THE WAR WON'T MEAN ANYTHING IF THE ENTIRE WORLD IS AT STAKE!
ガラ
GARGLE
ガラ
GARGLE

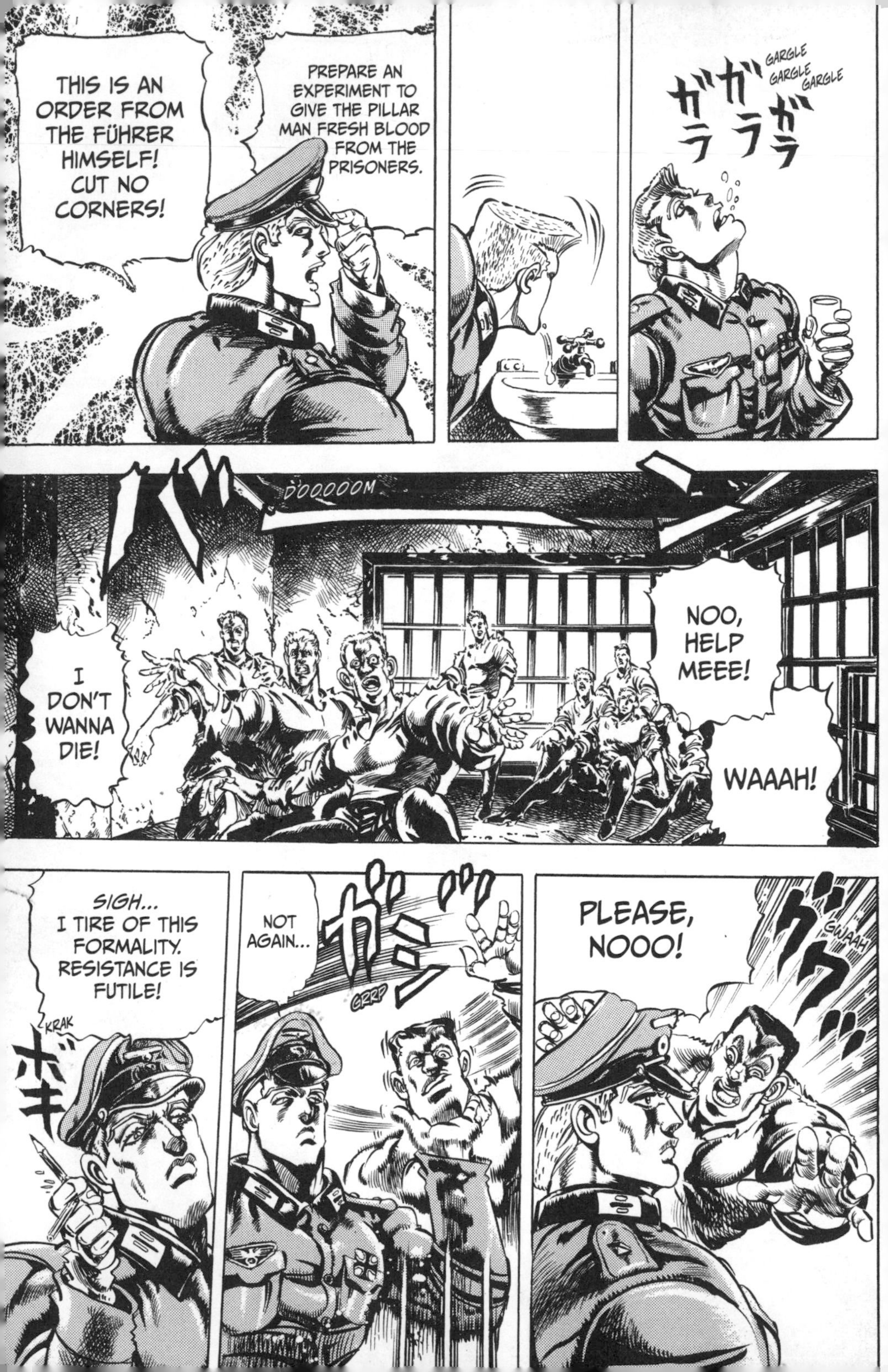
ガラガラガラ
GARGLE GARGLE GARGLE
PREPARE AN EXPERIMENT TO GIVE THE PILLAR MAN FRESH BLOOD FROM THE PRISONERS.
THIS IS AN ORDER FROM THE FÜHRER HIMSELF! CUT NO CORNERS!
DOOOOOOM
NOO, HELP MEEE!
WAAAH!
I DON'T WANNA DIE!
PLEASE, NOOO!
GWAAH
NOT AGAIN...
GRRP
SIGH... I TIRE OF THIS FORMALITY. RESISTANCE IS FUTILE!
KRAK

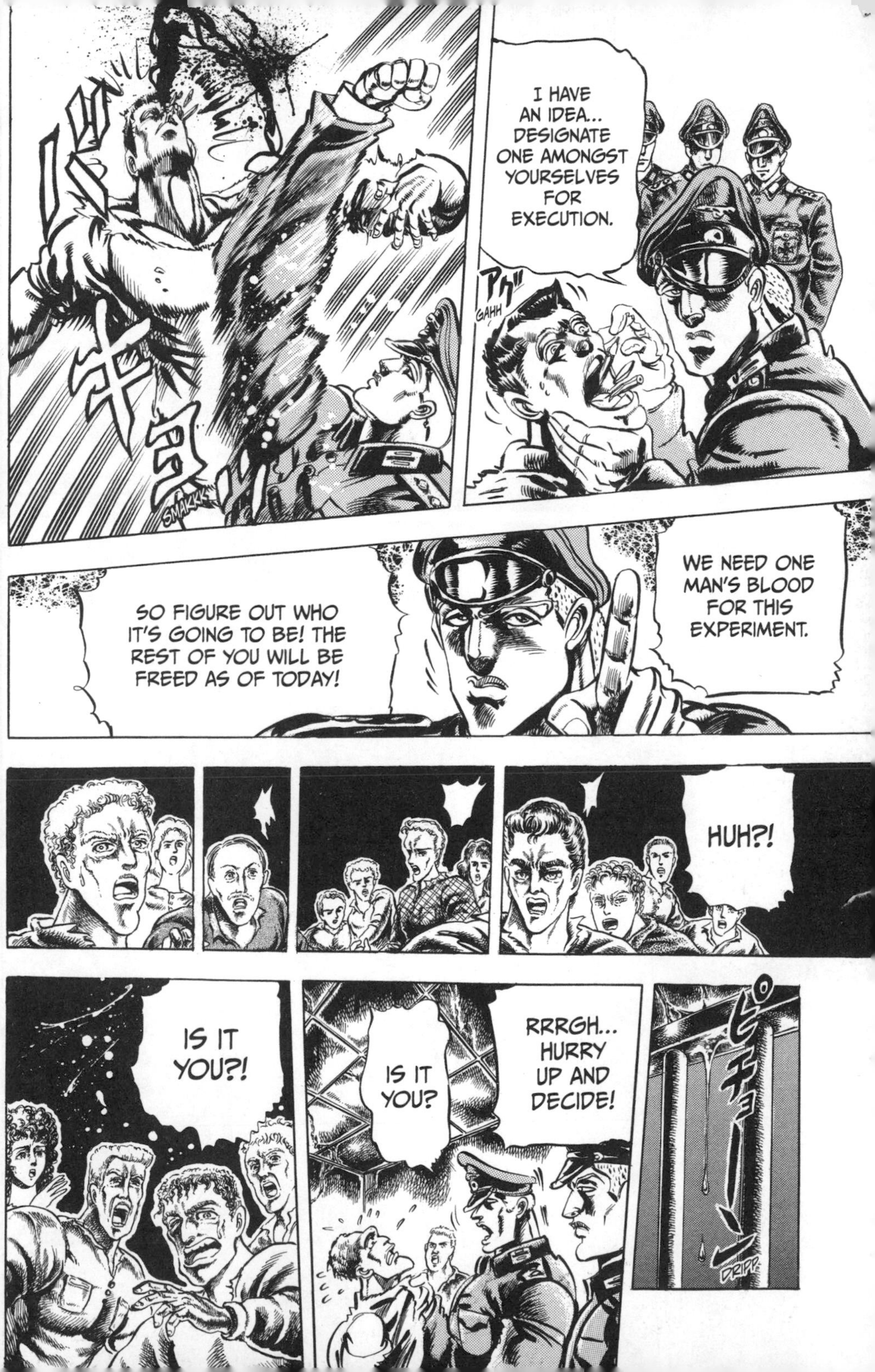
I HAVE AN IDEA... DESIGNATE ONE AMONGST YOURSELVES FOR EXECUTION.
アク
GAHH
SMAKKK
WE NEED ONE MAN'S BLOOD FOR THIS EXPERIMENT.
SO FIGURE OUT WHO IT'S GOING TO BE! THE REST OF YOU WILL BE FREED AS OF TODAY!
HUH?!
ピチョーン
DRIPP
RRRGH... HURRY UP AND DECIDE!
IS IT YOU?
IS IT YOU?!

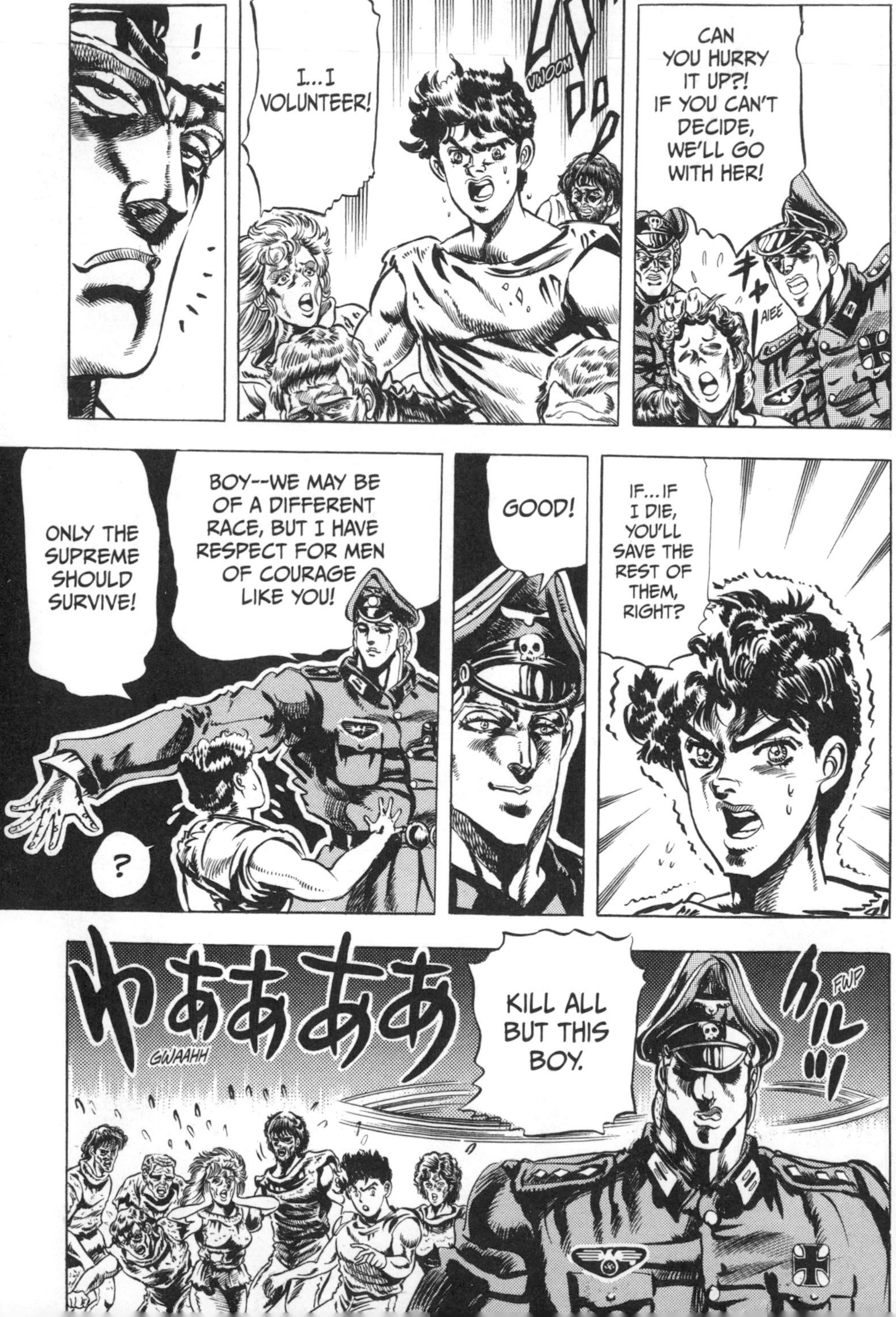
CAN YOU HURRY IT UP?! IF YOU CAN'T DECIDE, WE'LL GO WITH HER!
AIEE
VWOOM
I...I VOLUNTEER!
!
IF...IF I DIE, YOU'LL SAVE THE REST OF THEM, RIGHT?
GOOD!
BOY--WE MAY BE OF A DIFFERENT RACE, BUT I HAVE RESPECT FOR MEN OF COURAGE LIKE YOU!
ONLY THE SUPREME SHOULD SURVIVE!
?
クル
FWP
KILL ALL BUT THIS BOY.
ゆああああ
GWAAHH

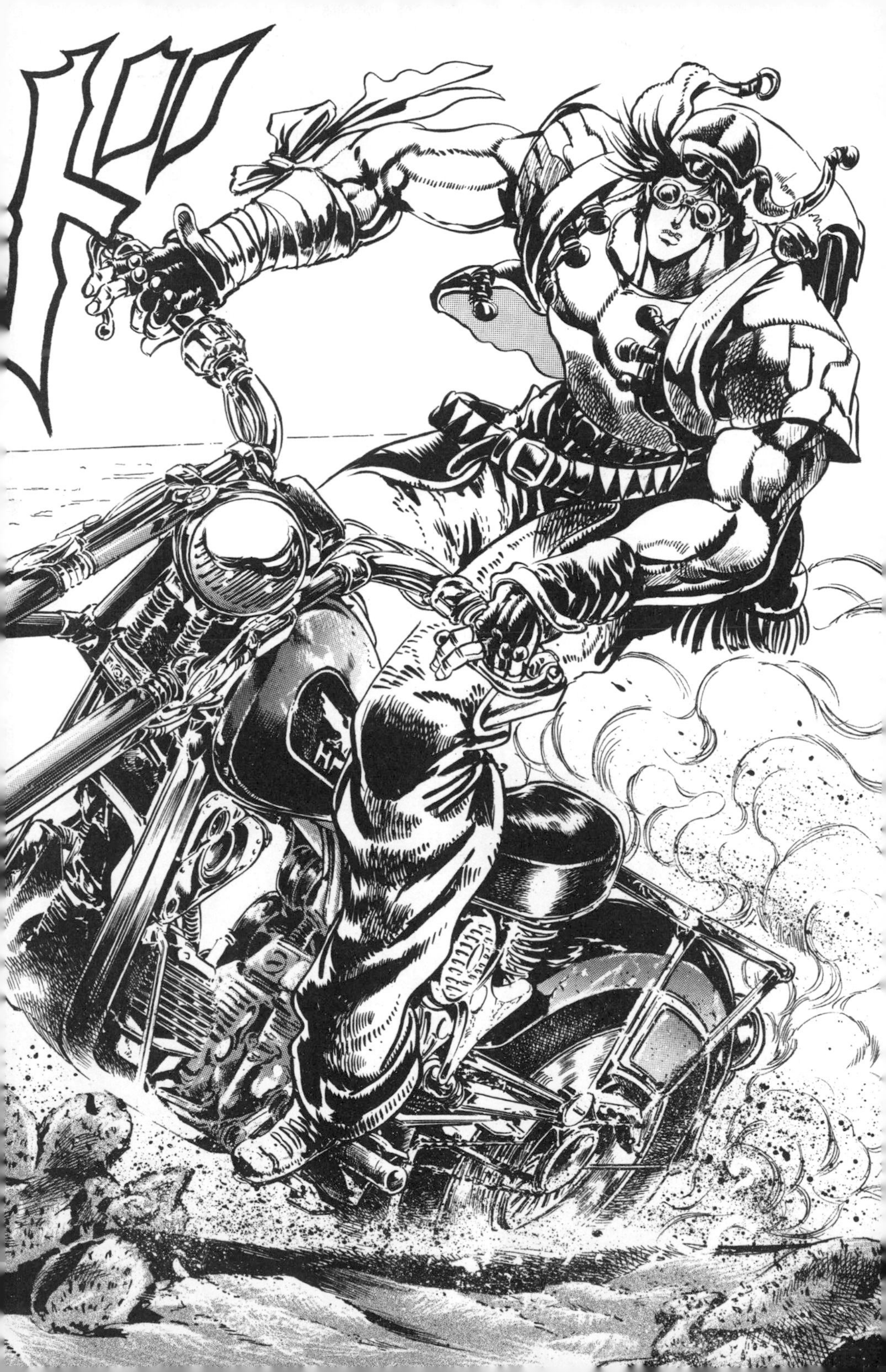

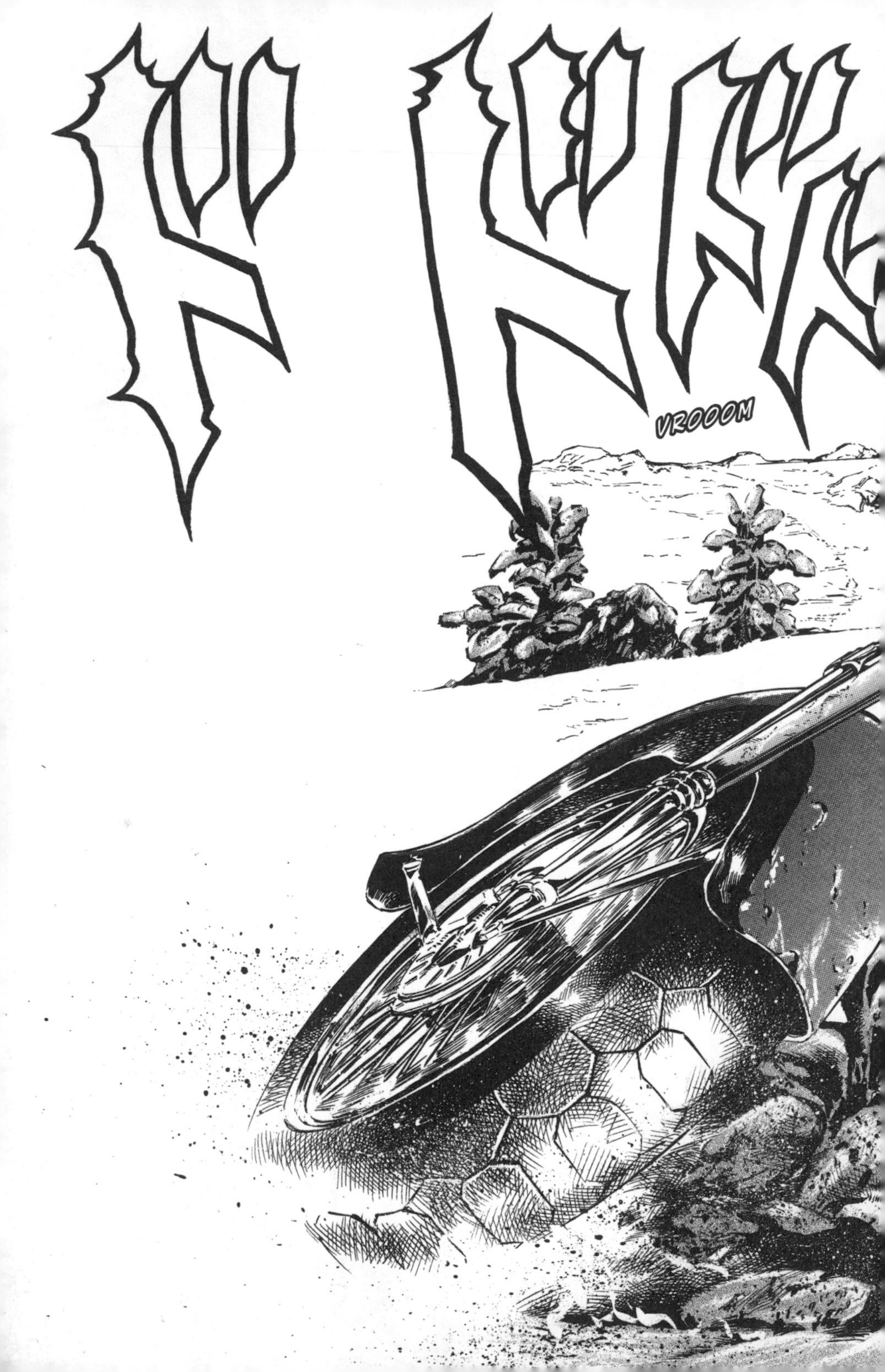
VROOOM

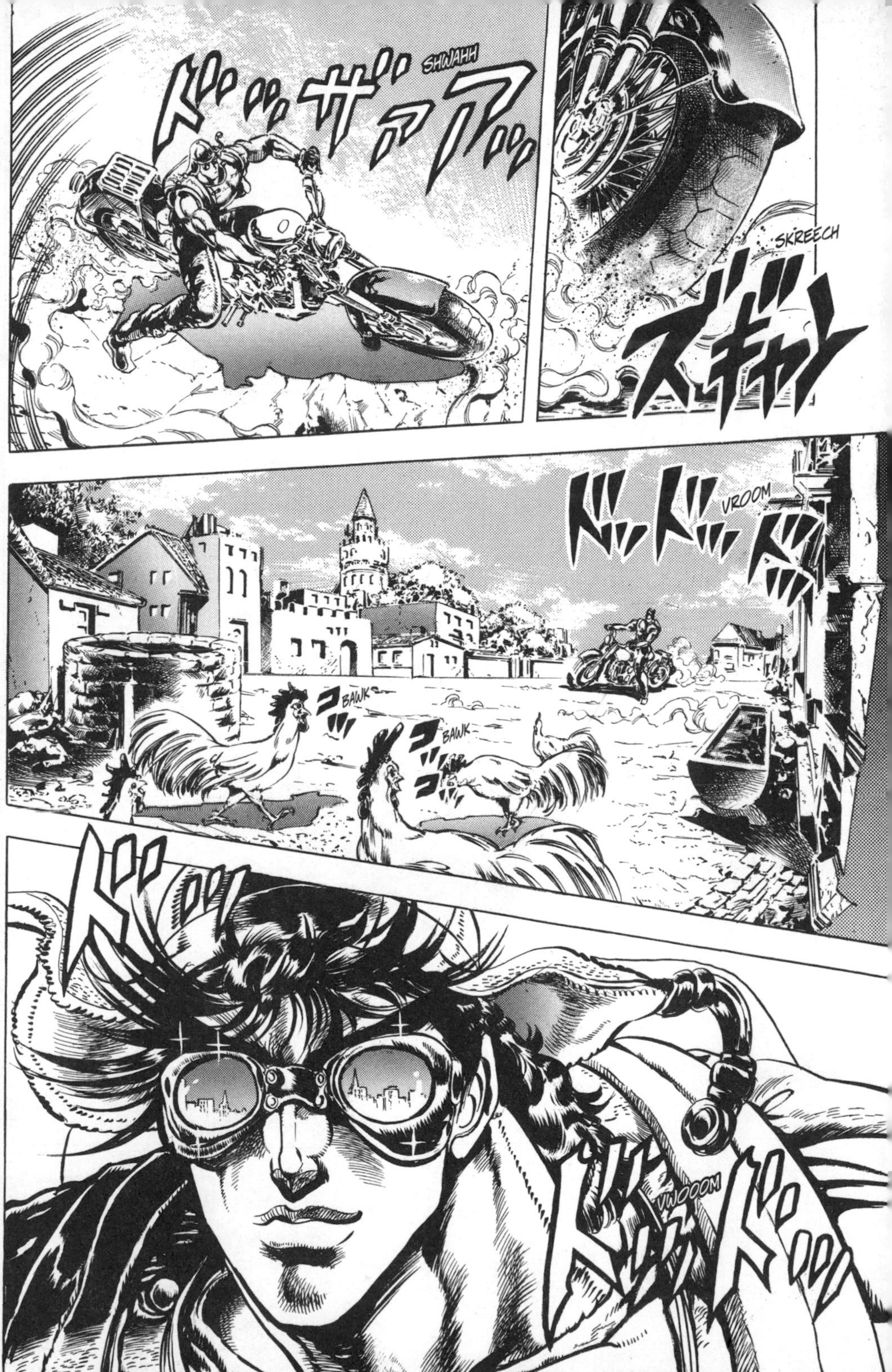
SKREECH
SHWAHH
VROOM
BAWK
BAWK
VWOOOM

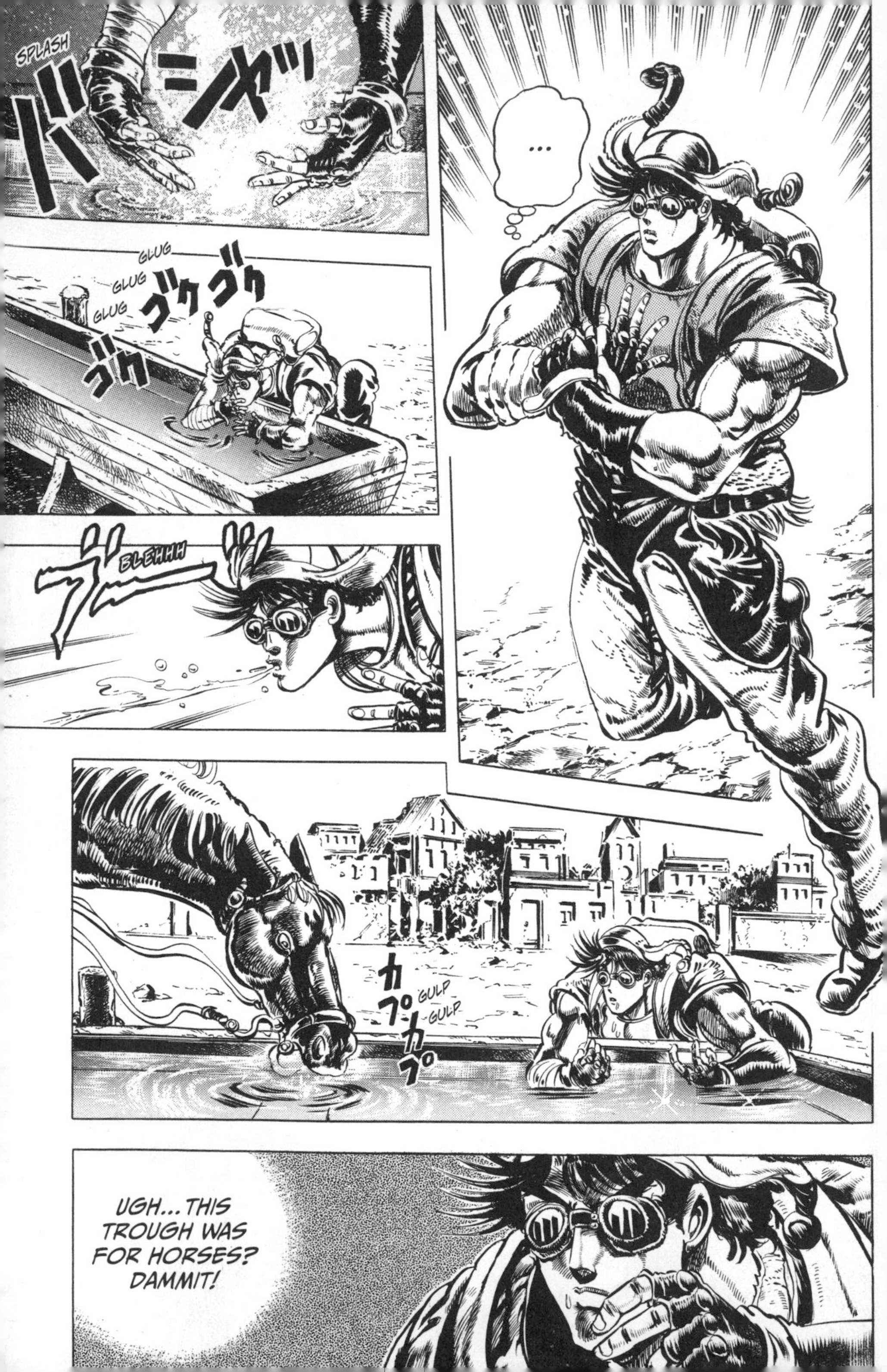
...
SPLASH
バシャッ
GLUG GLUG GLUG
ゴクゴク
ゴク
BLEHHH
ブーーッ
カプカプ
GULP GULP
UGH...THIS TROUGH WAS FOR HORSES? DAMMIT!

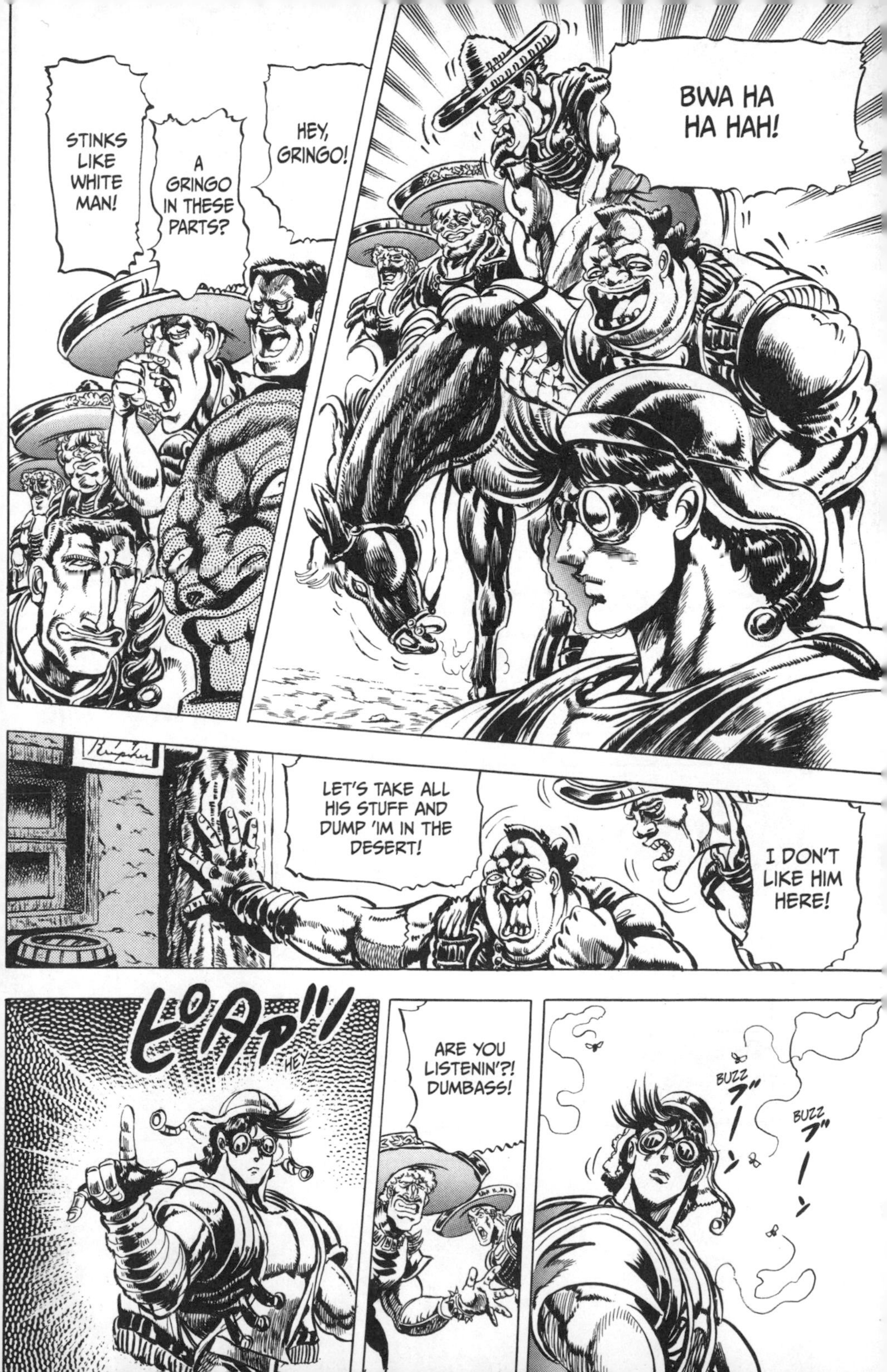
BWA HA HA HAH!
HEY, GRINGO!
A GRINGO IN THESE PARTS?
STINKS LIKE WHITE MAN!
I DON'T LIKE HIM HERE!
LET'S TAKE ALL HIS STUFF AND DUMP 'IM IN THE DESERT!
BUZZ
BUZZ
ARE YOU LISTENIN'?! DUMBASS!
HEY

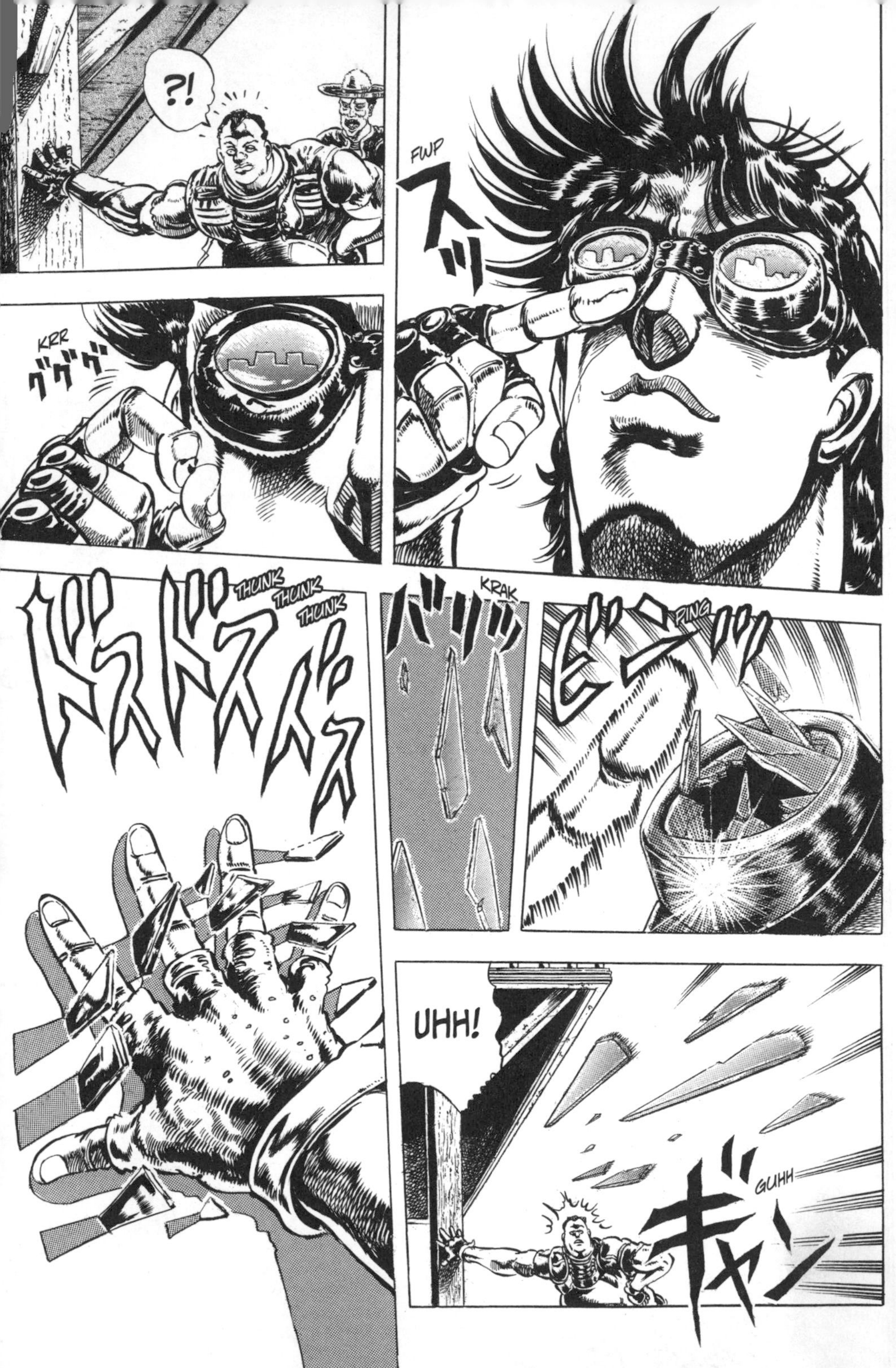
FWP
スッ
?!
KRR
ググ
KRAK
バリッ
PING
ピシ
THUNK
THUNK
THUNK
ドスドスッ
UHH!
GUHH
ギャン

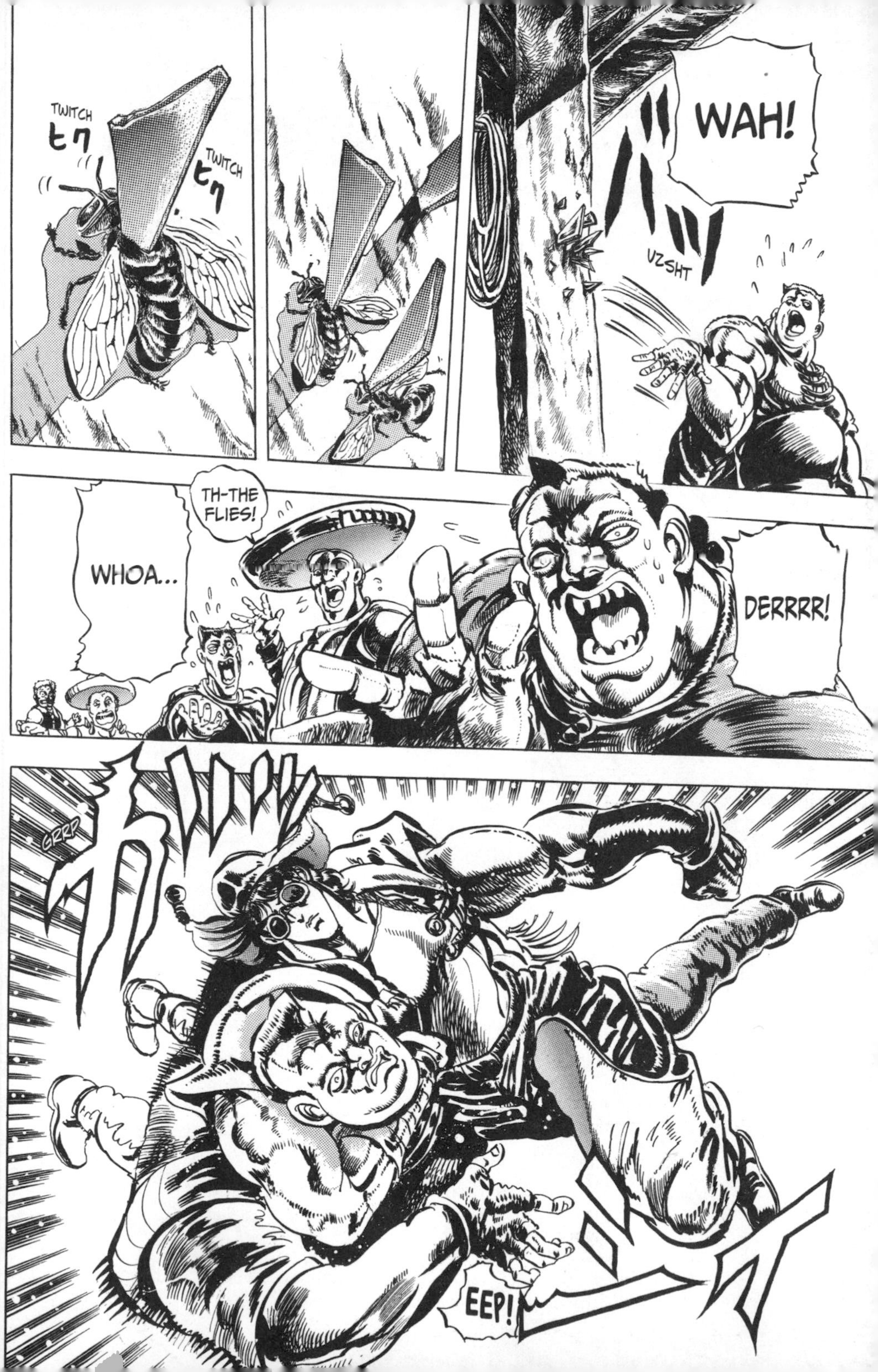
WAH!
VZSHT
TWITCH
ヒク
TWITCH
ヒク
DERRRR!
TH-THE FLIES!
WHOA...
GRRP
EEP!

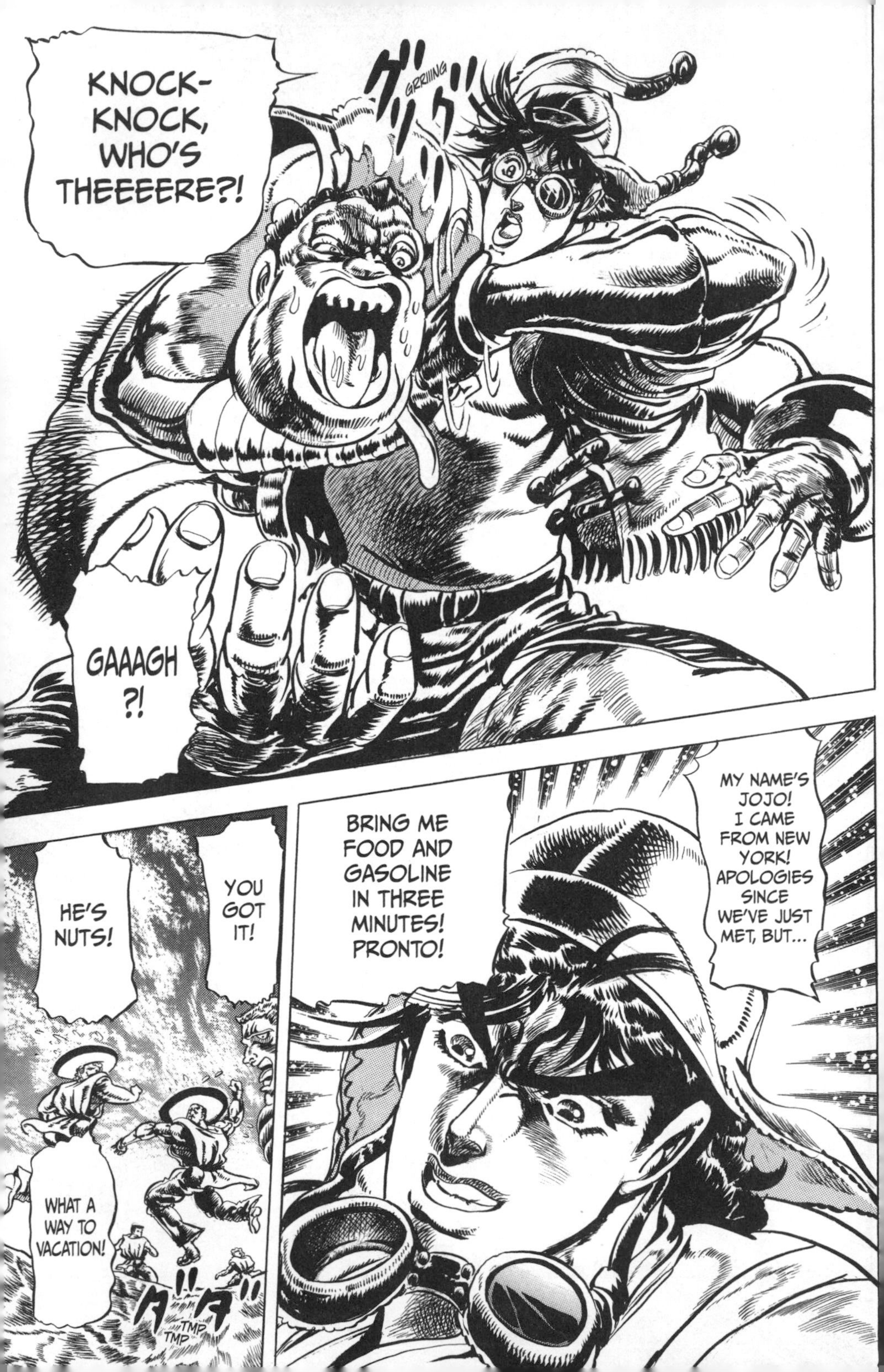
KNOCK-KNOCK, WHO'S THEEEEERE?!
GRRIING
GAAAGH ?!
MY NAME'S JOJO! I CAME FROM NEW YORK! APOLOGIES SINCE WE'VE JUST MET, BUT...
BRING ME FOOD AND GASOLINE IN THREE MINUTES! PRONTO!
YOU GOT IT!
HE'S NUTS!
WHAT A WAY TO VACATION!
TMP TMP

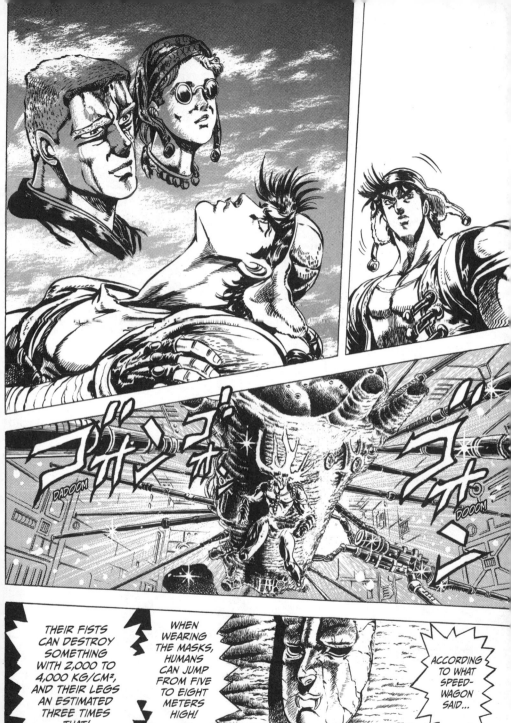

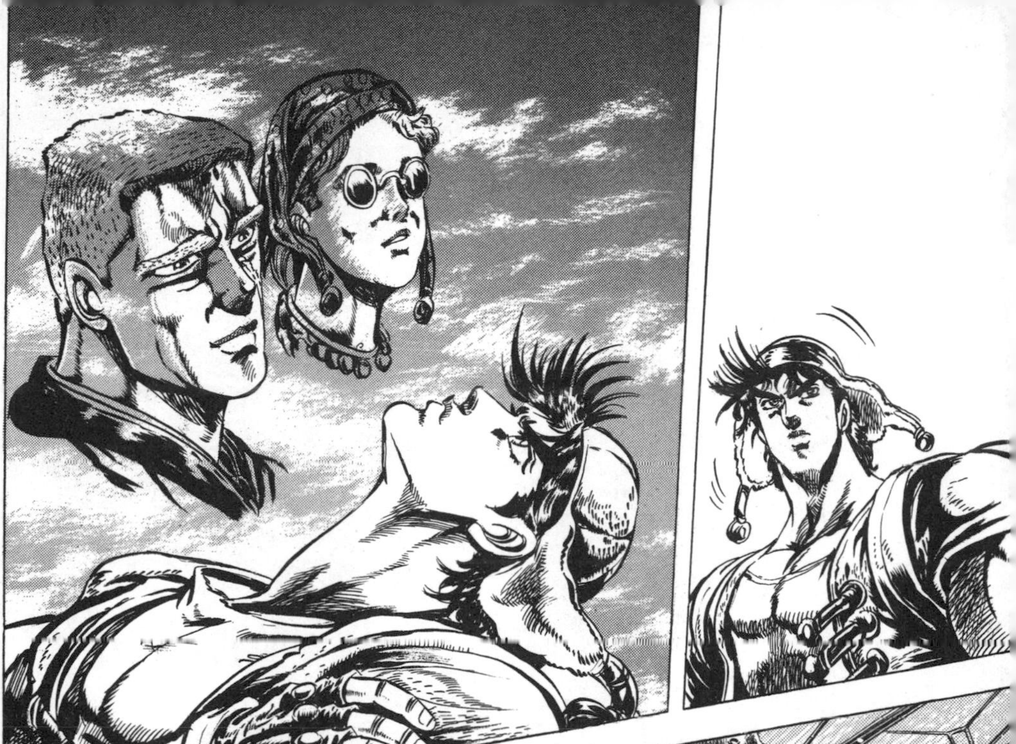
DOOOM
DADOOM
ACCORDING TO WHAT SPEED-WAGON SAID...
WHEN WEARING THE MASKS, HUMANS CAN JUMP FROM FIVE TO EIGHT METERS HIGH!
THEIR FISTS CAN DESTROY SOMETHING WITH 2,000 TO 4,000 KG/CM², AND THEIR LEGS AN ESTIMATED THREE TIMES THAT!

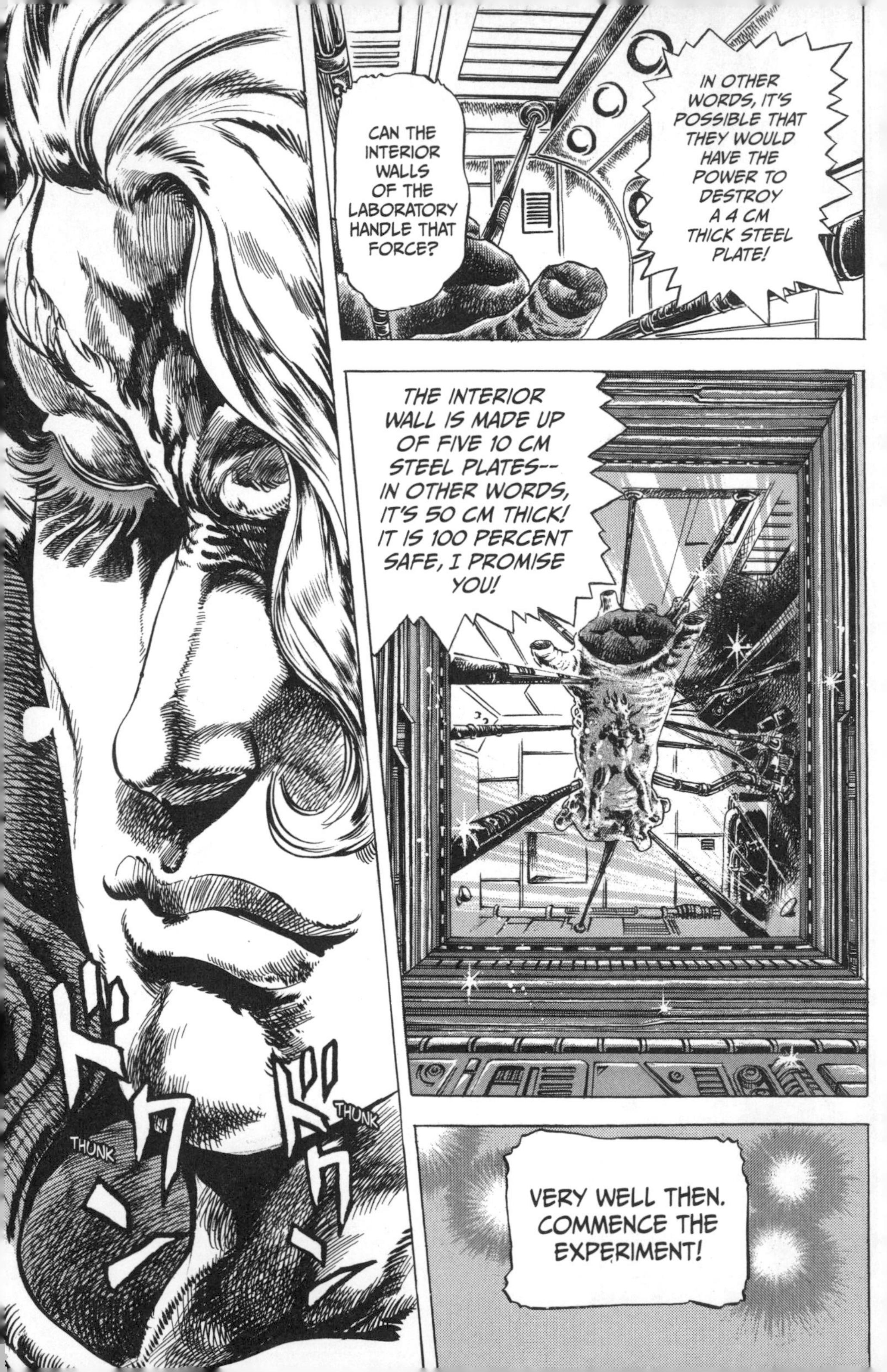
IN OTHER WORDS, IT'S POSSIBLE THAT THEY WOULD HAVE THE POWER TO DESTROY A 4 CM THICK STEEL PLATE!
CAN THE INTERIOR WALLS OF THE LABORATORY HANDLE THAT FORCE?
THE INTERIOR WALL IS MADE UP OF FIVE 10 CM STEEL PLATES-- IN OTHER WORDS, IT'S 50 CM THICK! IT IS 100 PERCENT SAFE, I PROMISE YOU!
VERY WELL THEN. COMMENCE THE EXPERIMENT!
THUNK
THUNK

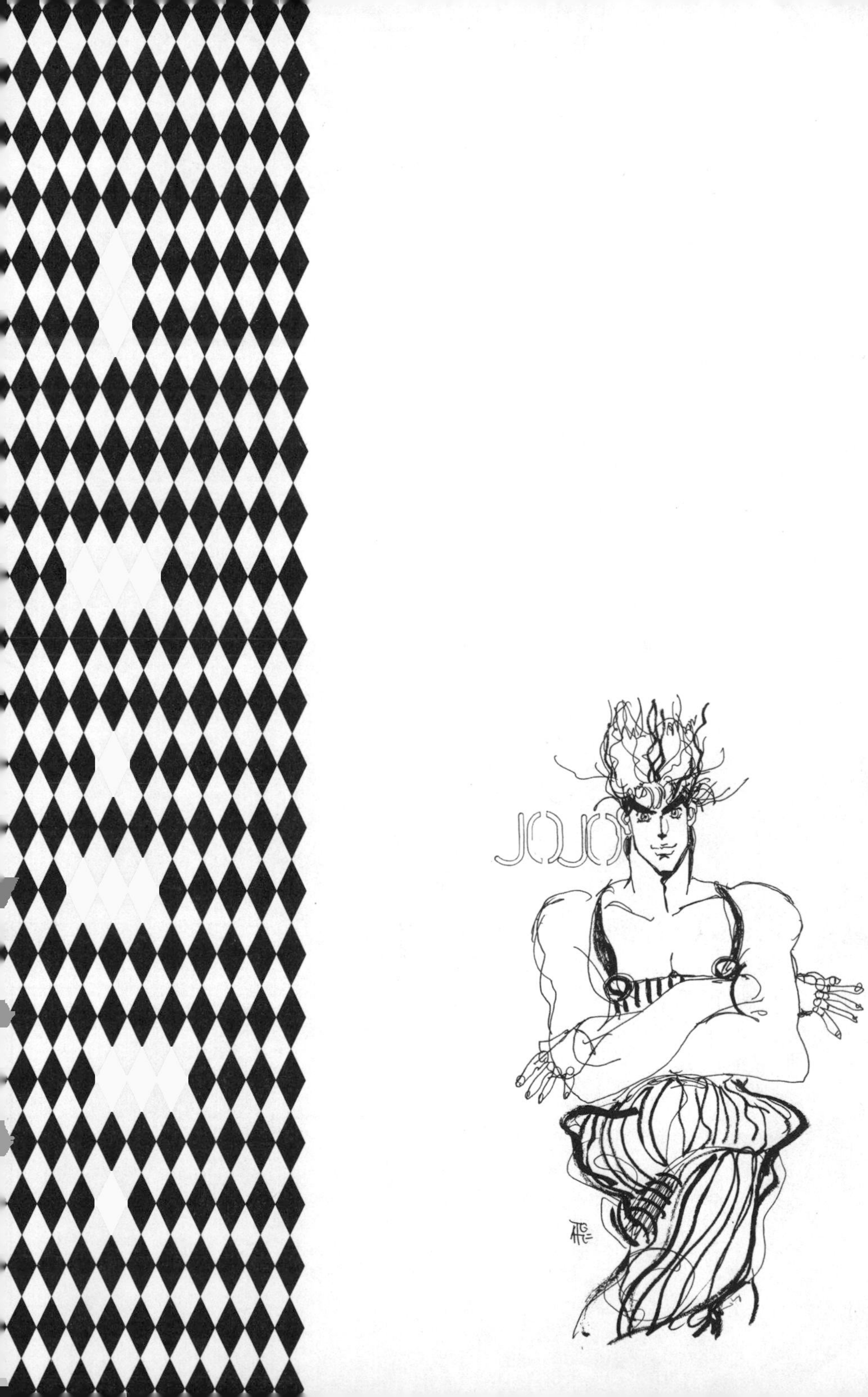
JOJO

CHAPTER 10: The Pillar Man, Santviento PART 1

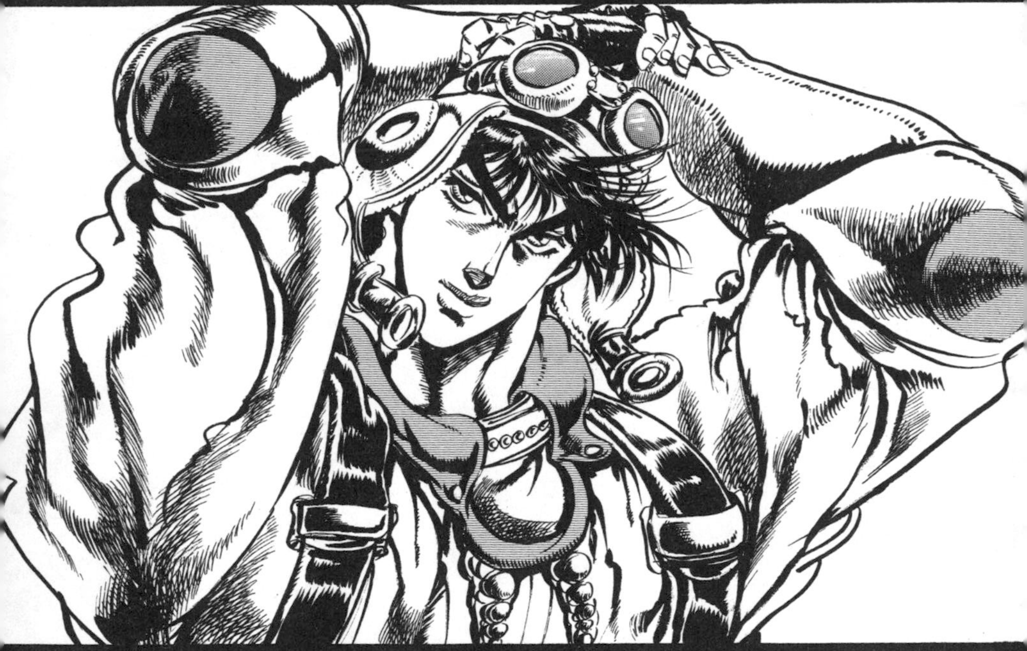

Joseph Joestar

★ September 27, 1920 Born in London, England (18 years old)
★ **Height** 195 cm **Weight** 97 kg **Blood Type** B
★ **Family** Parents dead, raised by his grandmother (Erina Joestar)
★ **Schooling** Graduated high school (English)
★ **Record** Imprisoned seven times for fighting, expelled once
★ **Hobby** Comic collecting
★ **Girlfriend** Not at the moment, but very picky (her smarts don't matter if she's cute)
★ **Favorite Food** Fried chicken, chewing gum
★ **Favorite Color** Marine blue ★**Favorite Animal** Dog
★ **Least Favorite Animal** Cow (because they slobber)
★ **Aspiration** To become a pilot ★**Favorite Actor** Jean Gabin

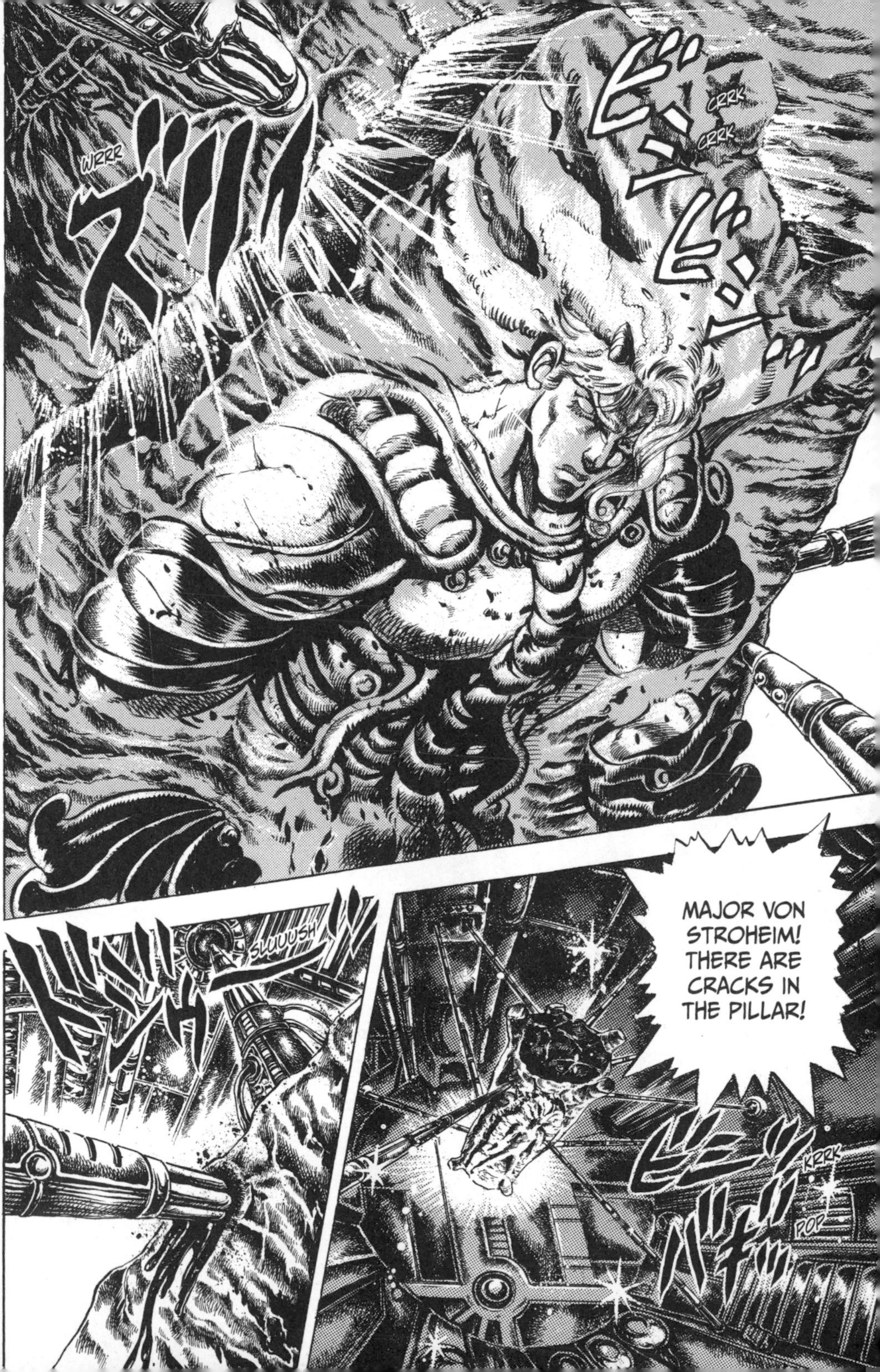
CRRK
CRRK
WRRR
MAJOR VON STROHEIM! THERE ARE CRACKS IN THE PILLAR!
KRRK
POP
SLUUUSH

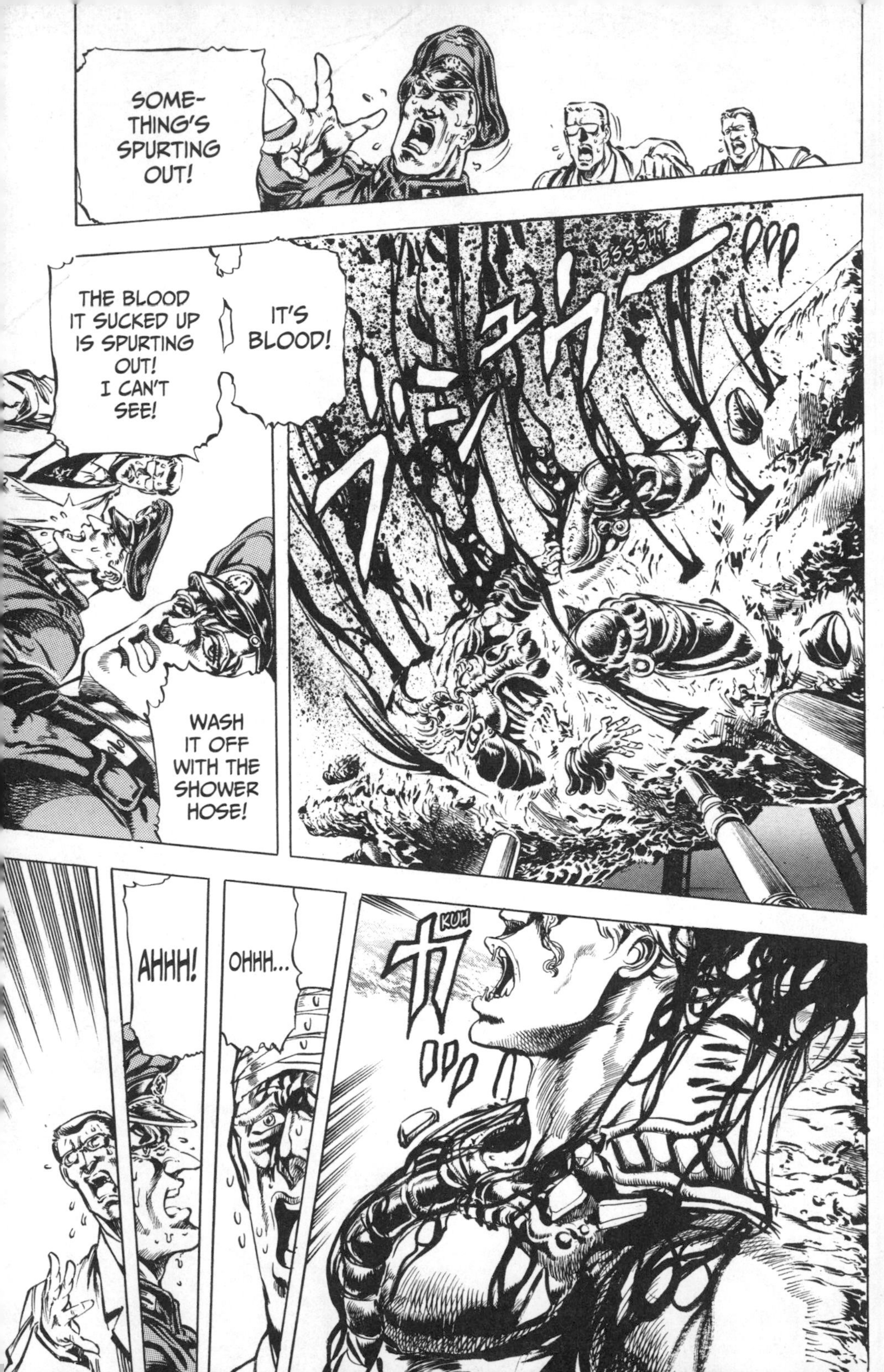
SOME-THING'S SPURTING OUT!
BSSSHT
IT'S BLOOD!
THE BLOOD IT SUCKED UP IS SPURTING OUT! I CAN'T SEE!
WASH IT OFF WITH THE SHOWER HOSE!
KUH
OHHH...
AHHH!

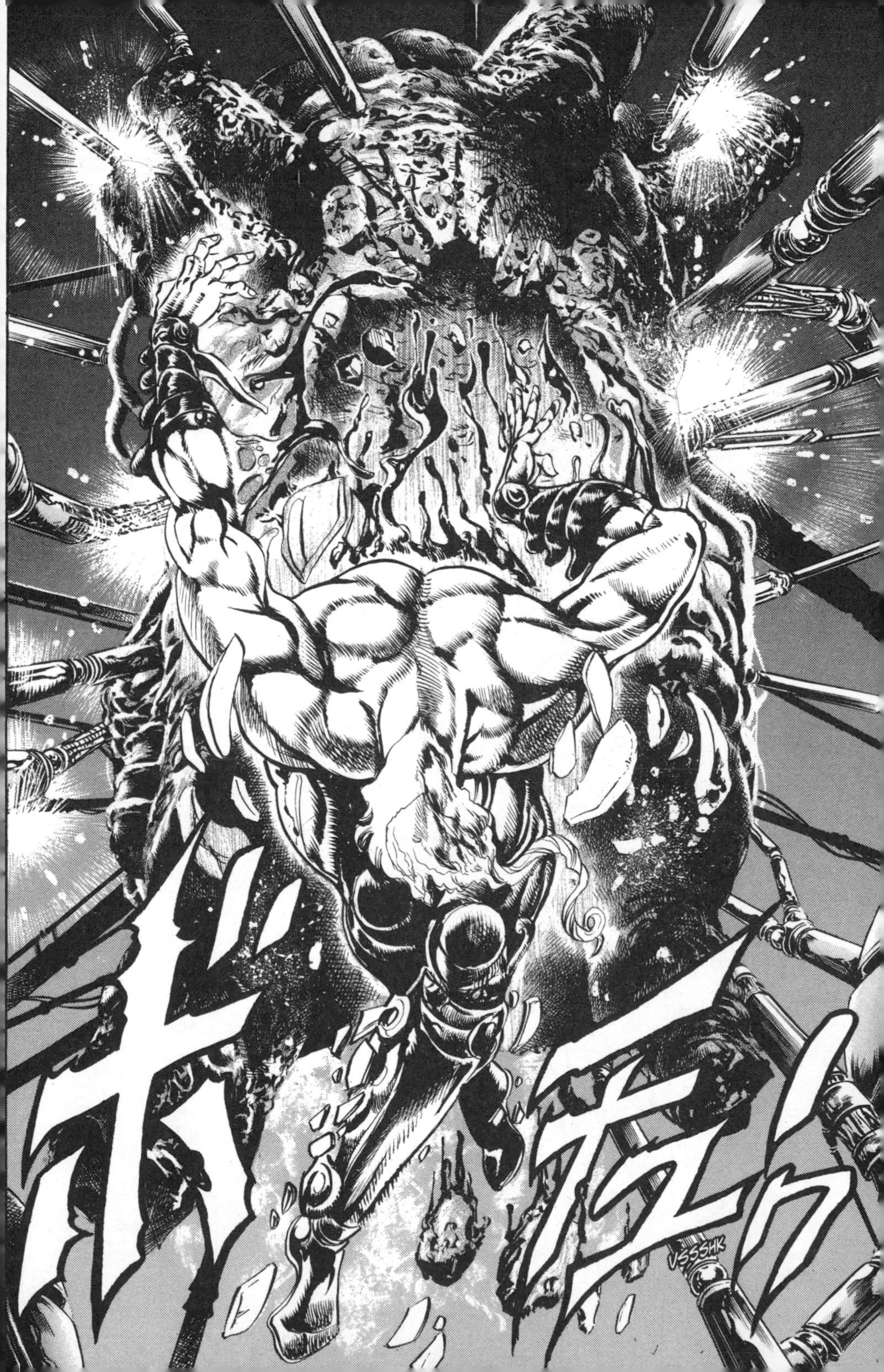
VSSSHK

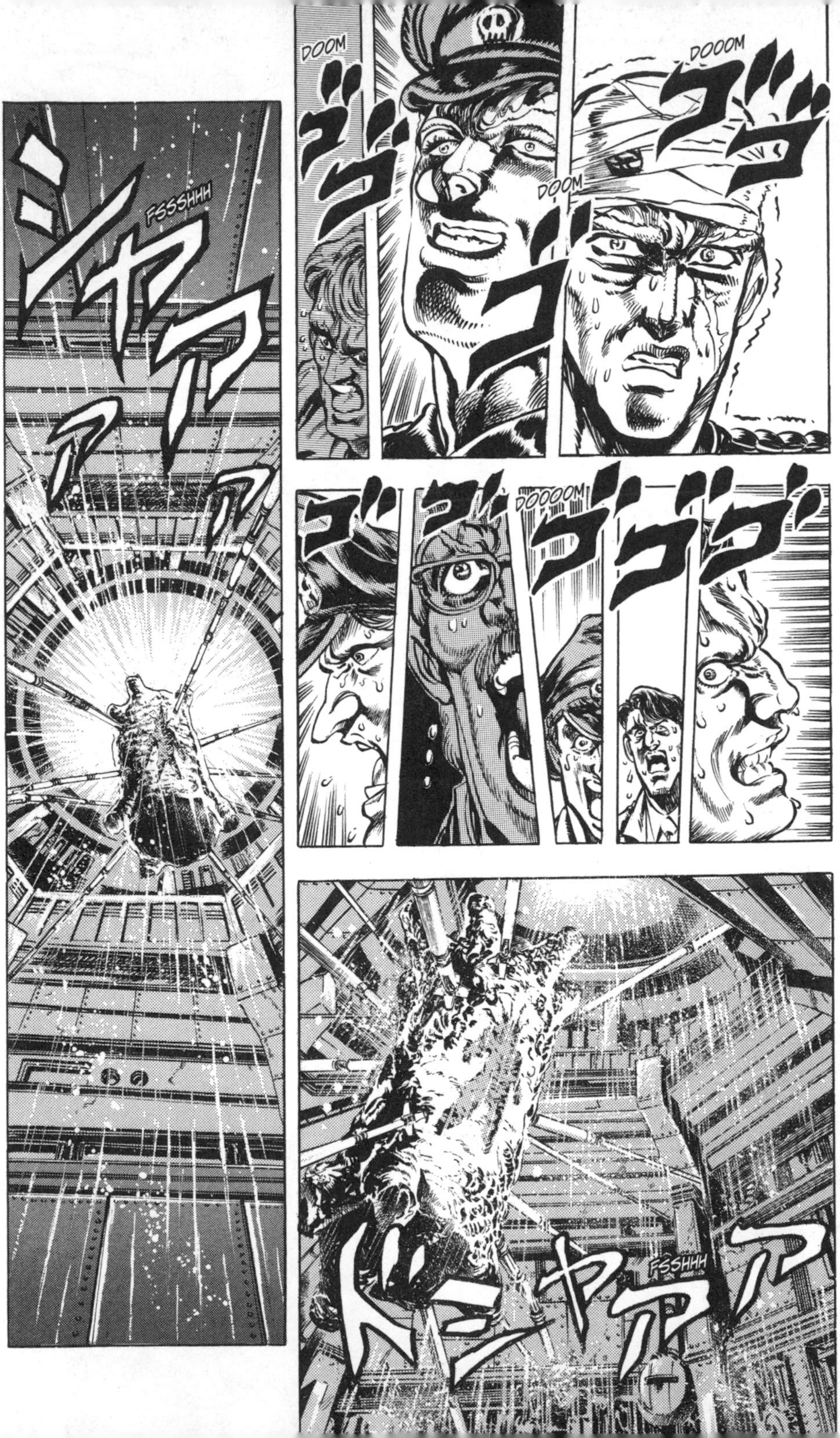
DOOOM
DOOM
DOOM
DOOOOM
FSSHHH
FSSSHHH

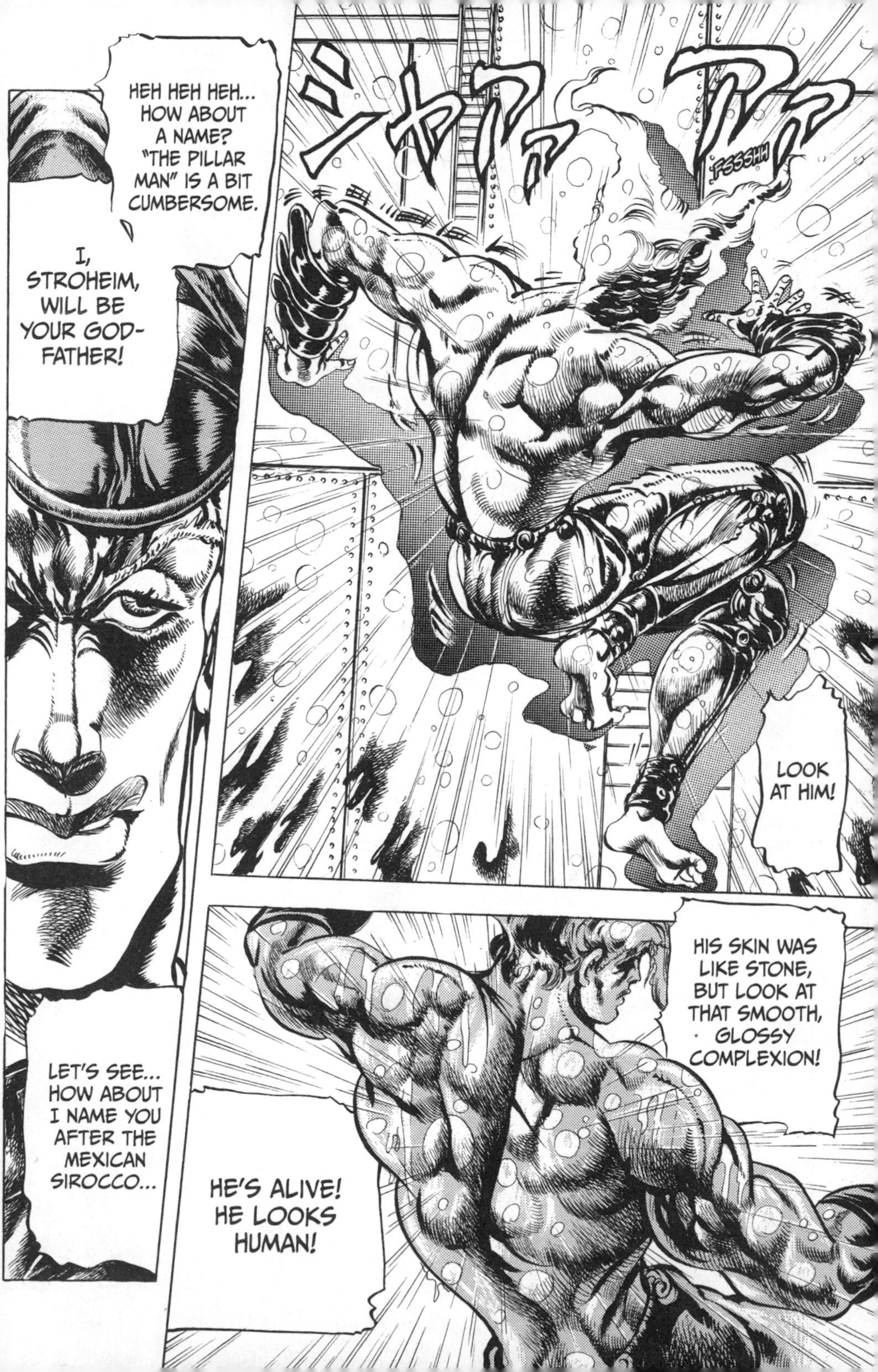
FSSSHH
LOOK AT HIM!
HIS SKIN WAS LIKE STONE, BUT LOOK AT THAT SMOOTH, GLOSSY COMPLEXION!
HE'S ALIVE! HE LOOKS HUMAN!
HEH HEH HEH... HOW ABOUT A NAME? "THE PILLAR MAN" IS A BIT CUMBERSOME.
I, STROHEIM, WILL BE YOUR GOD-FATHER!
LET'S SEE... HOW ABOUT I NAME YOU AFTER THE MEXICAN SIROCCO...

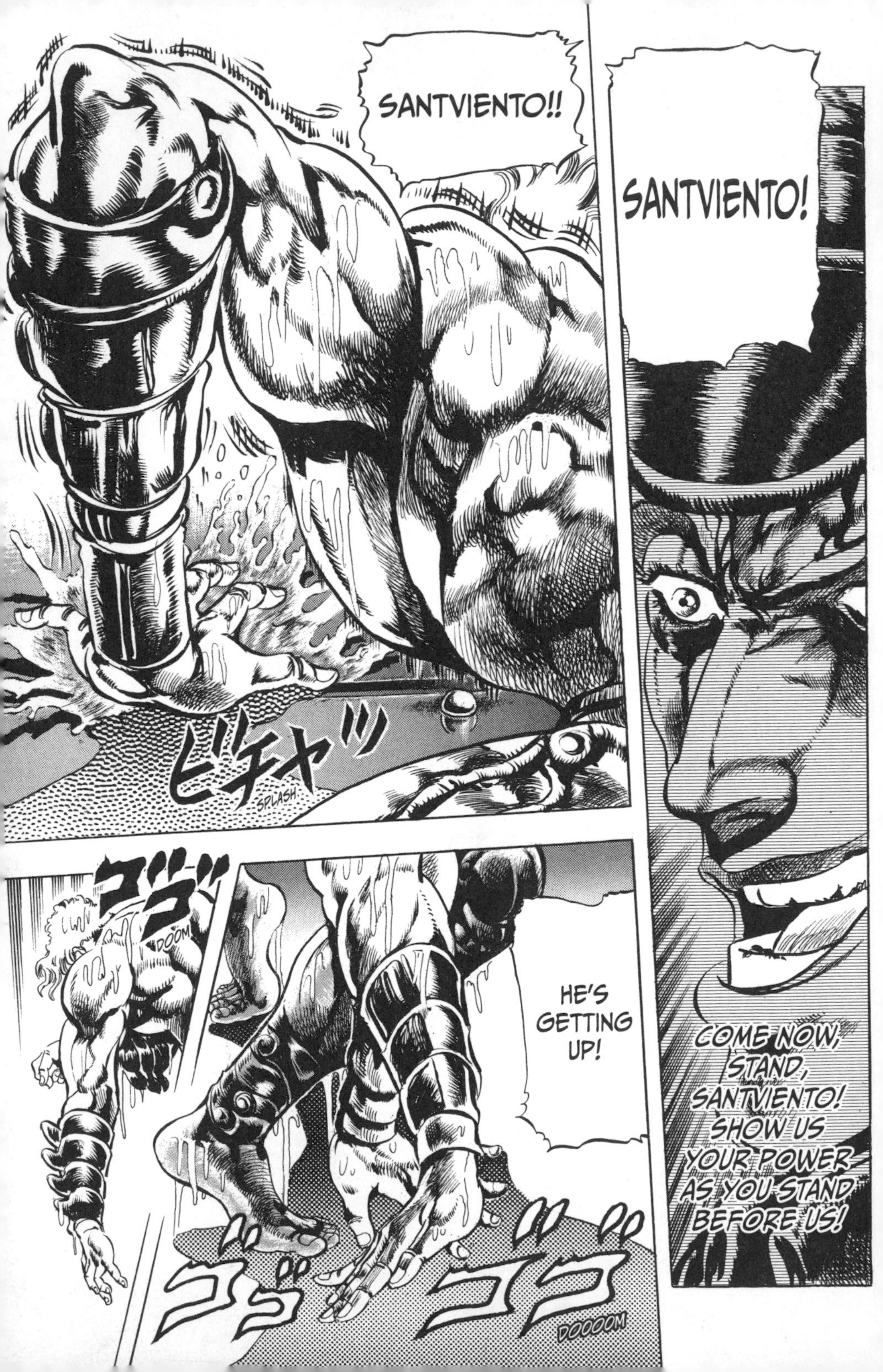
SANTVIENTO!
COME NOW, STAND, SANTVIENTO! SHOW US YOUR POWER AS YOU STAND BEFORE US!
SANTVIENTO!!
ビチャッ
SPLASH
HE'S GETTING UP!
DOOM
DOOOOM

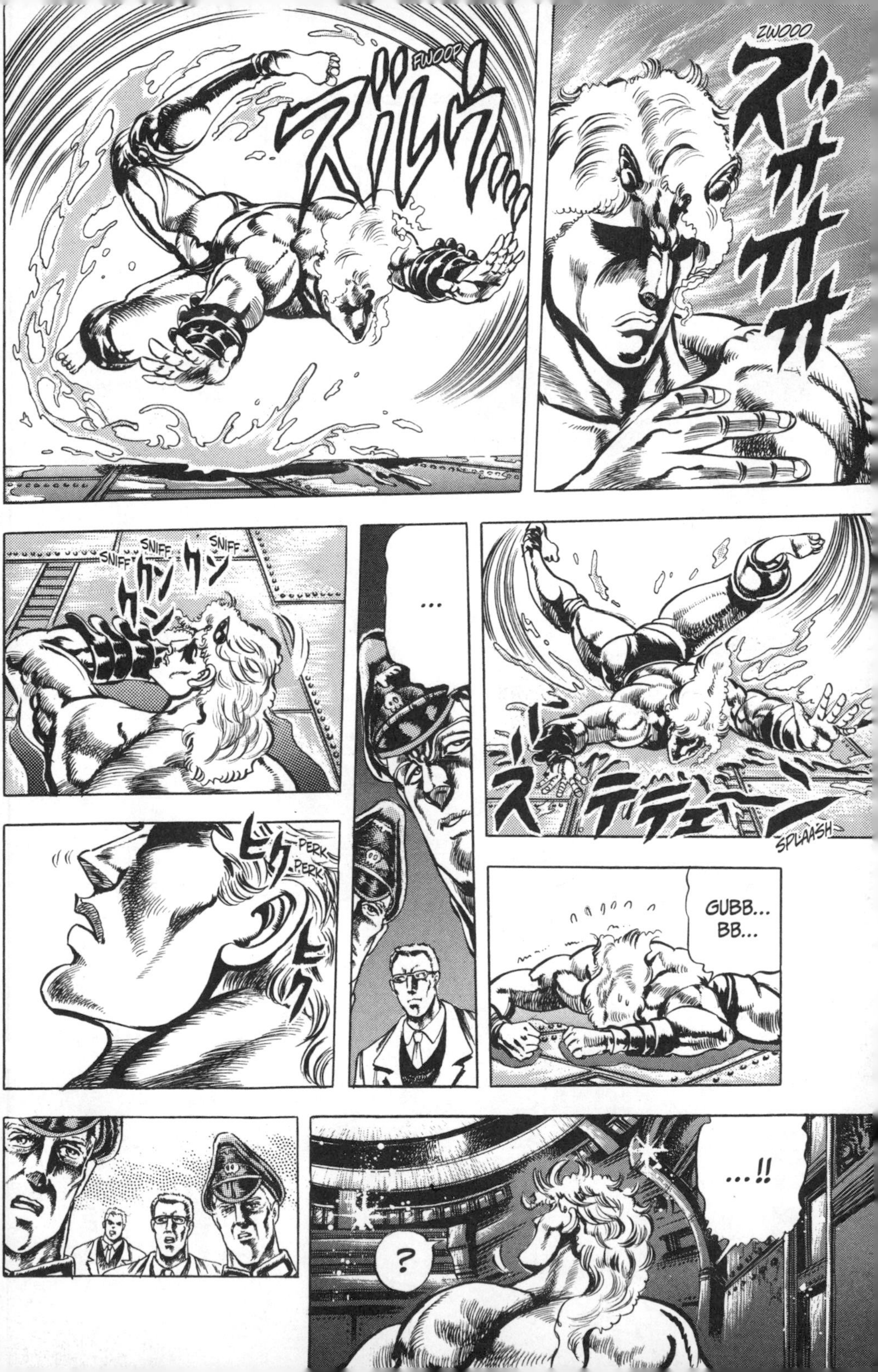
ZWOOO
FWOOP
SPLAASH
GUBB... BB...
...
SNIFF
SNIFF
SNIFF
PERK
PERK
...!!
?

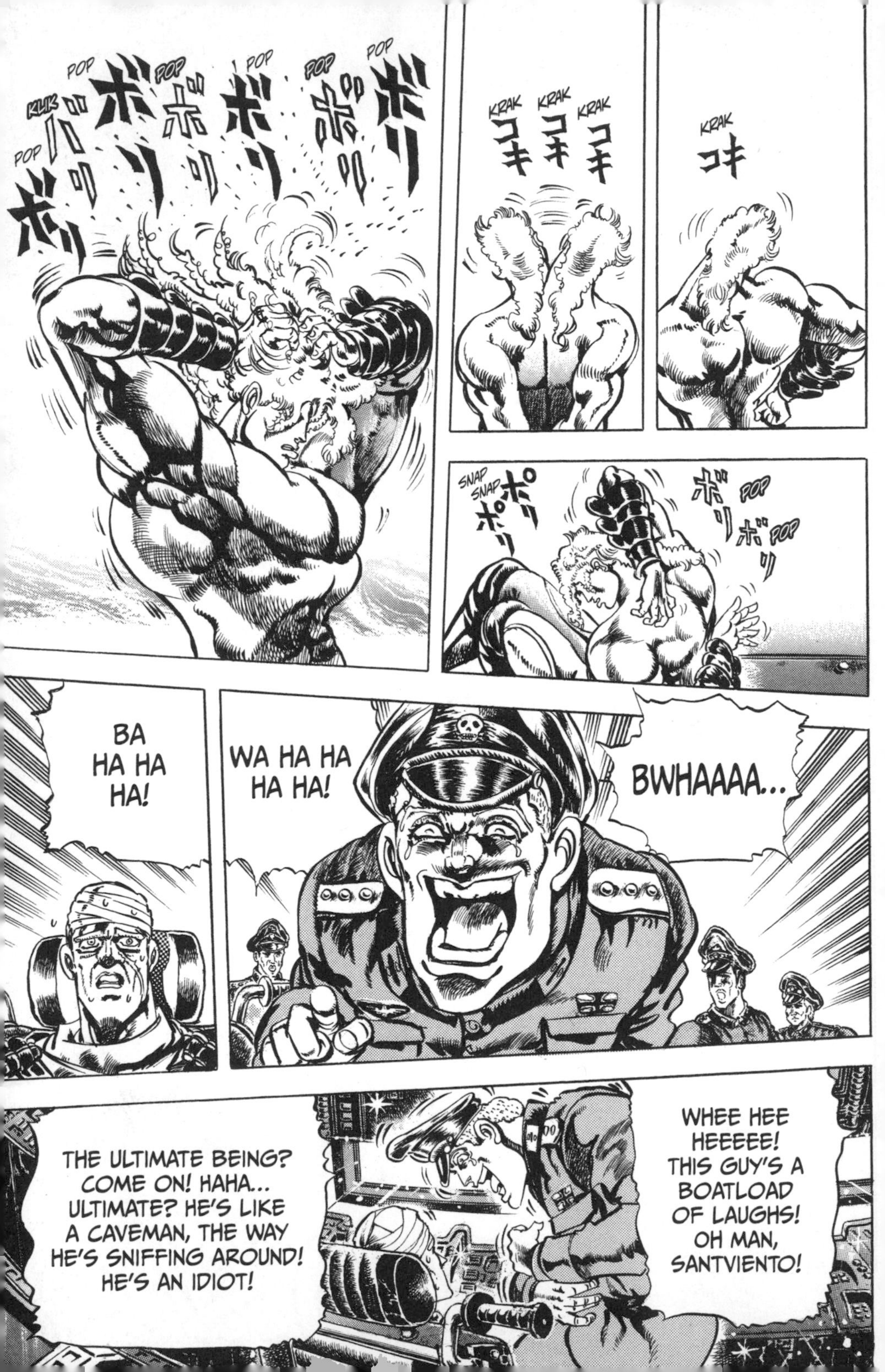

KRAK
コキ
KRAK KRAK KRAK
コキ コキ コキ
SNAP SNAP
POP POP
POP POP POP
KUK POP POP POP
BWHAAAA...
WA HA HA HA HA!
BA HA HA HA!
WHEE HEE HEEEEE! THIS GUY'S A BOATLOAD OF LAUGHS! OH MAN, SANTVIENTO!
THE ULTIMATE BEING? COME ON! HAHA... ULTIMATE? HE'S LIKE A CAVEMAN, THE WAY HE'S SNIFFING AROUND! HE'S AN IDIOT!

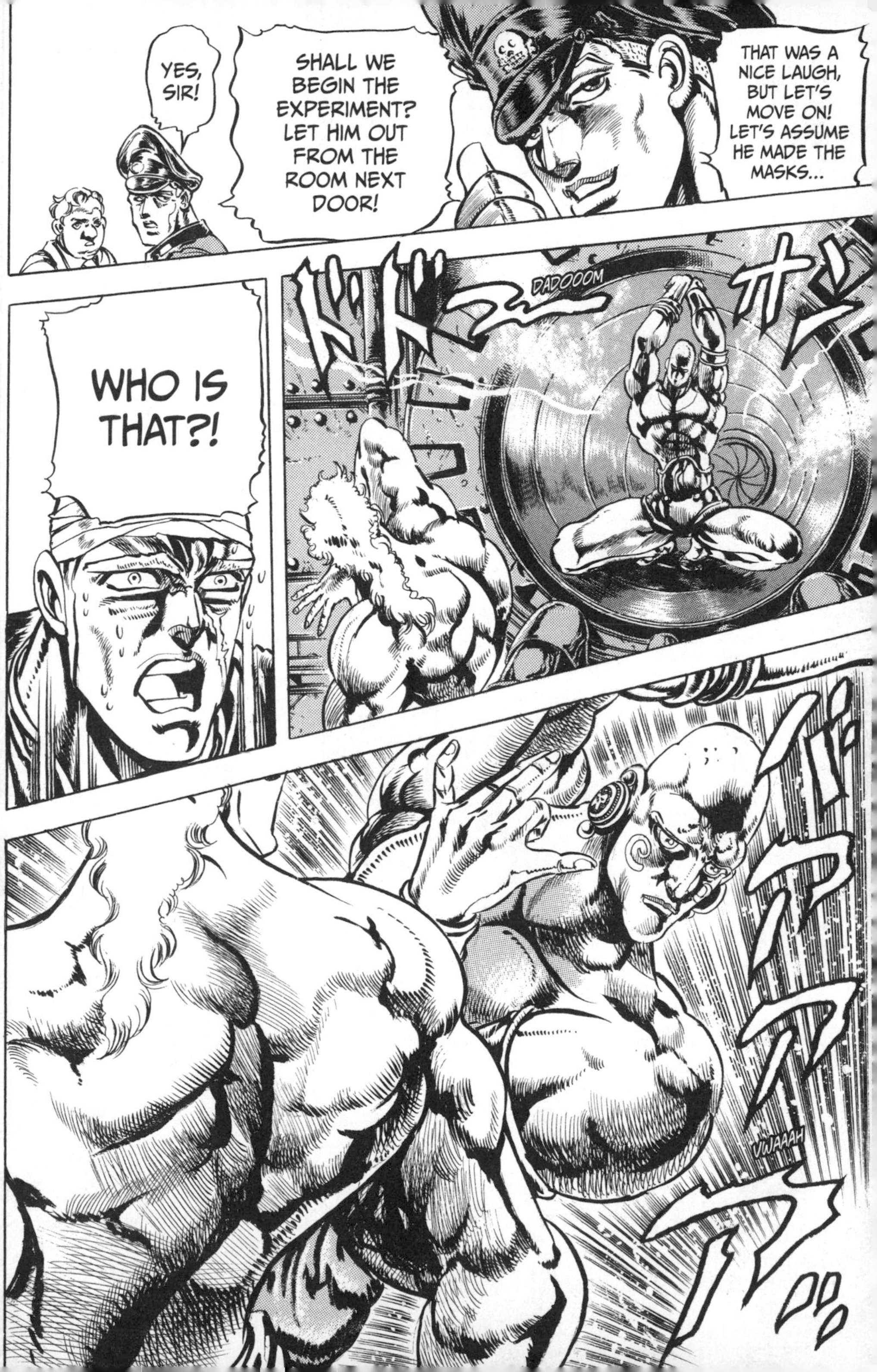
THAT WAS A NICE LAUGH, BUT LET'S MOVE ON! LET'S ASSUME HE MADE THE MASKS...
SHALL WE BEGIN THE EXPERIMENT? LET HIM OUT FROM THE ROOM NEXT DOOR!
YES, SIR!
DADOOOM
WHO IS THAT?!
VWAAAH

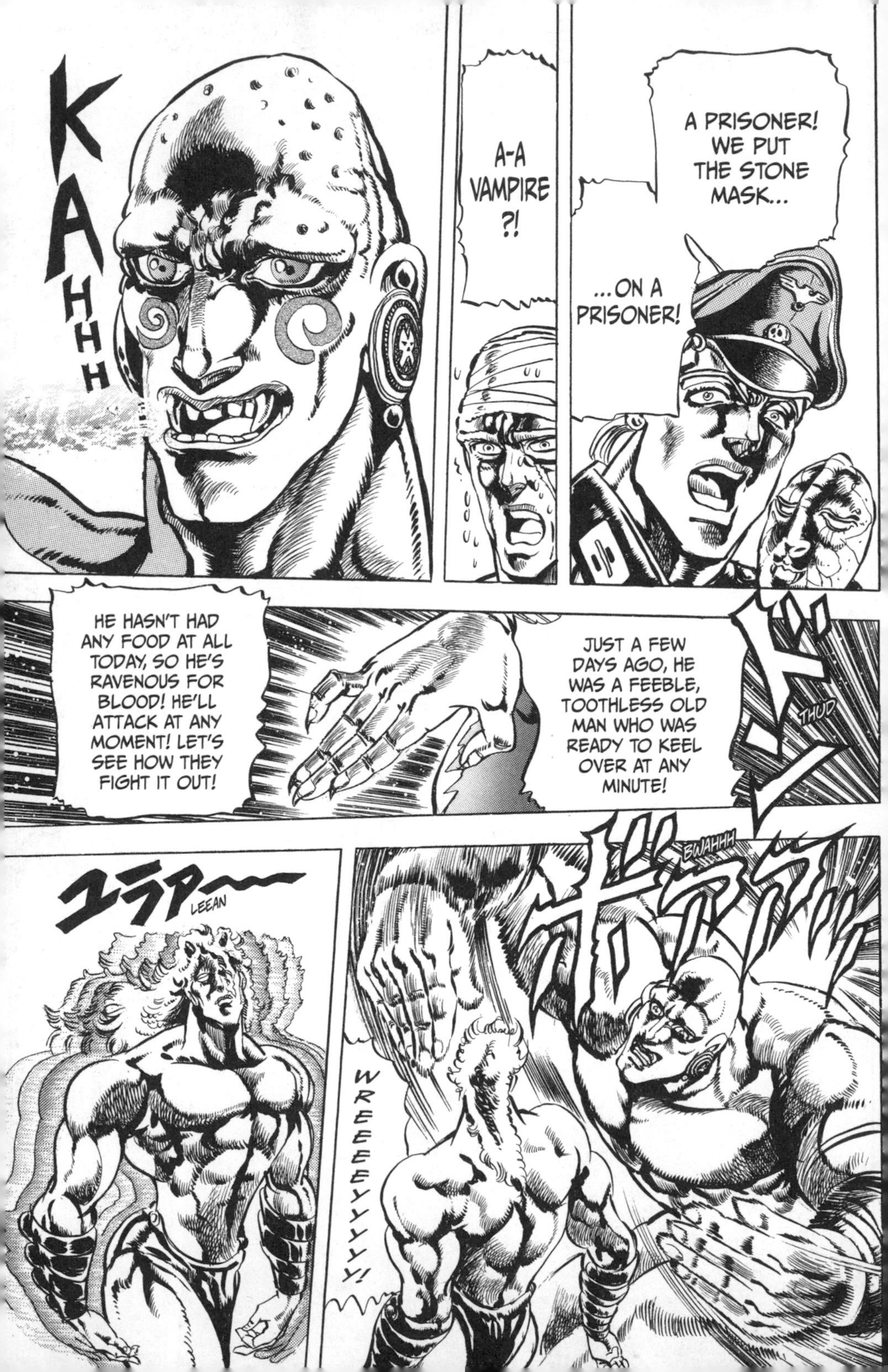
A PRISONER! WE PUT THE STONE MASK...
...ON A PRISONER!
A-A VAMPIRE ?!
KAHHH
THUD
JUST A FEW DAYS AGO, HE WAS A FEEBLE, TOOTHLESS OLD MAN WHO WAS READY TO KEEL OVER AT ANY MINUTE!
HE HASN'T HAD ANY FOOD AT ALL TODAY, SO HE'S RAVENOUS FOR BLOOD! HE'LL ATTACK AT ANY MOMENT! LET'S SEE HOW THEY FIGHT IT OUT!
BWAHHH
WREEEEYYYY!
LEEAN

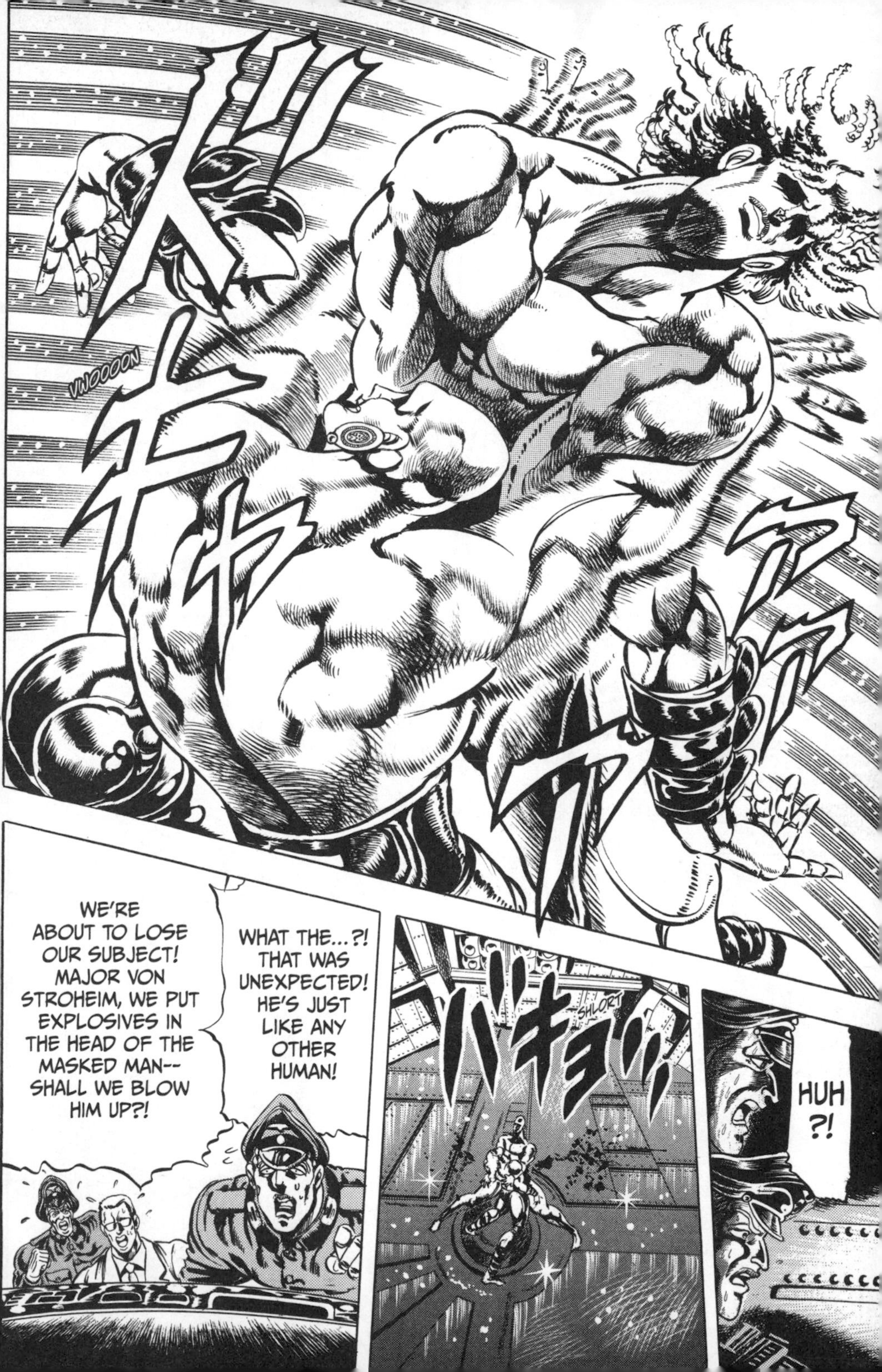
VWOOOON
HUH ?!
SHLORT
WHAT THE...?! THAT WAS UNEXPECTED! HE'S JUST LIKE ANY OTHER HUMAN!
WE'RE ABOUT TO LOSE OUR SUBJECT! MAJOR VON STROHEIM, WE PUT EXPLOSIVES IN THE HEAD OF THE MASKED MAN-- SHALL WE BLOW HIM UP?!

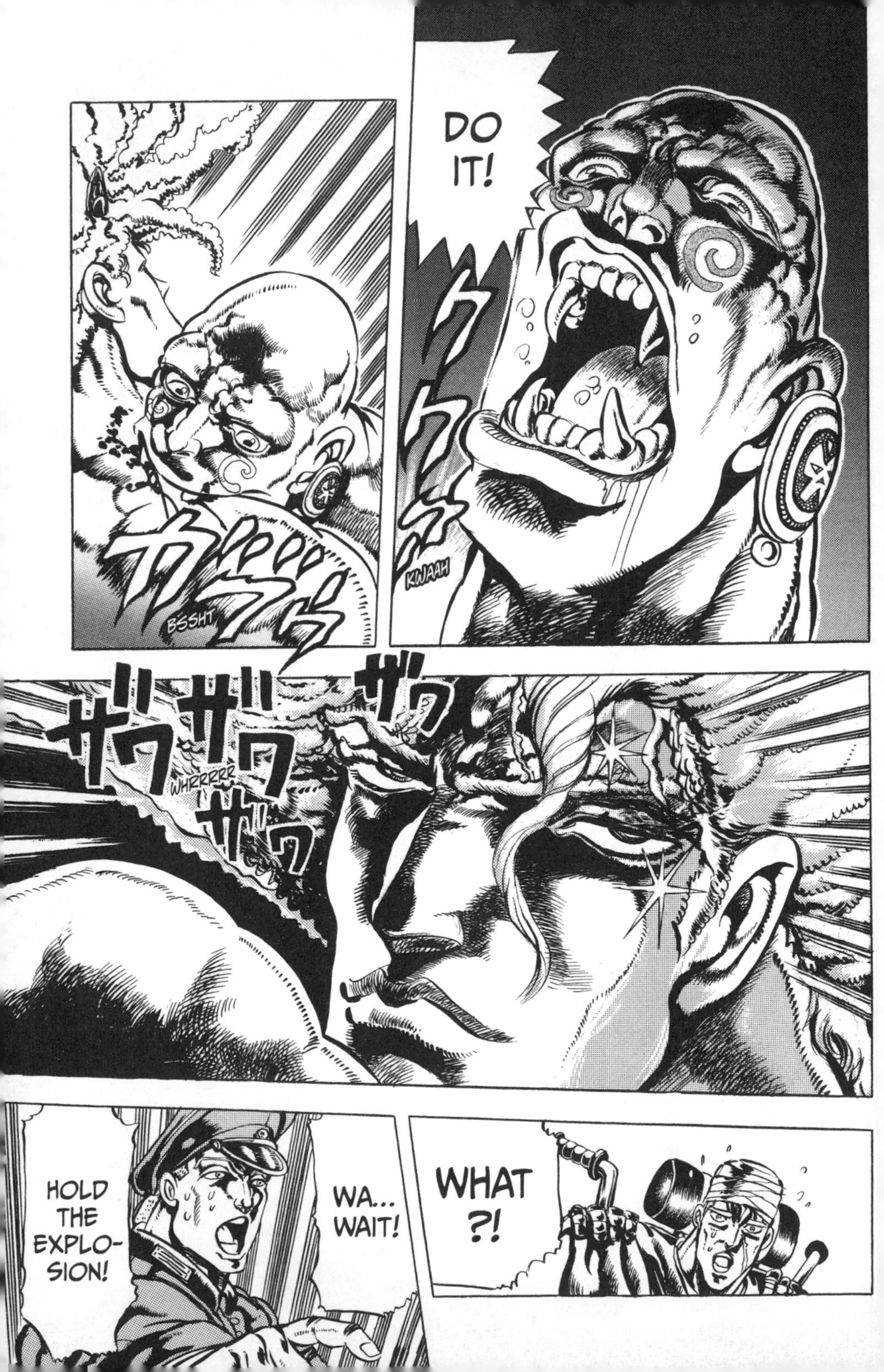
DO IT!
KWAAH
BSSHT
WHRRRRR
WHAT?!
WA... WAIT!
HOLD THE EXPLOSION!

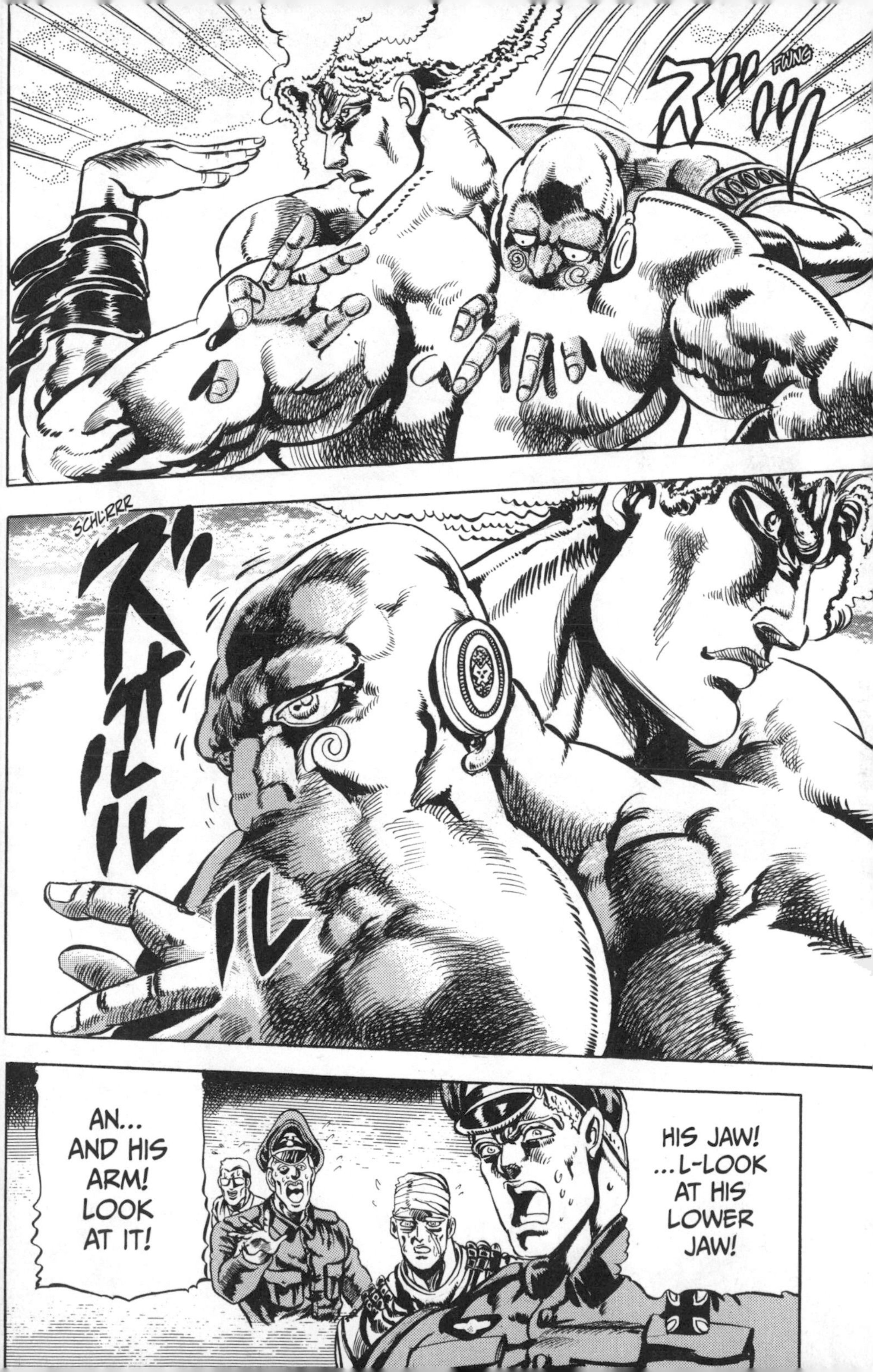
FWNG
SCHLRRR
HIS JAW! ...L-LOOK AT HIS LOWER JAW!
AN... AND HIS ARM! LOOK AT IT!

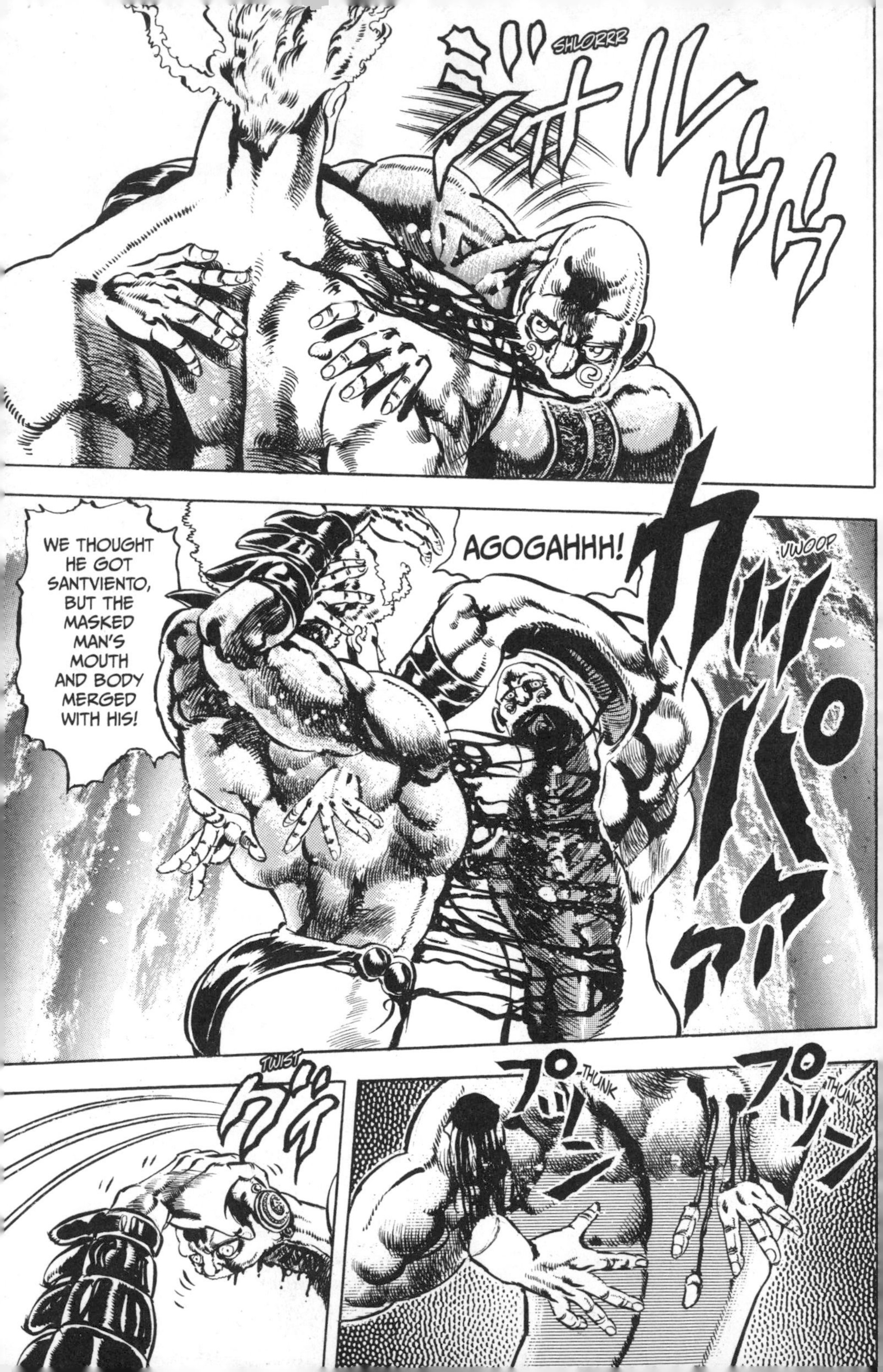
SHLORRR
VWOOP
AGOGAHHH!
WE THOUGHT HE GOT SANTVIENTO, BUT THE MASKED MAN'S MOUTH AND BODY MERGED WITH HIS!
THUNK
-THUNK
TWIST

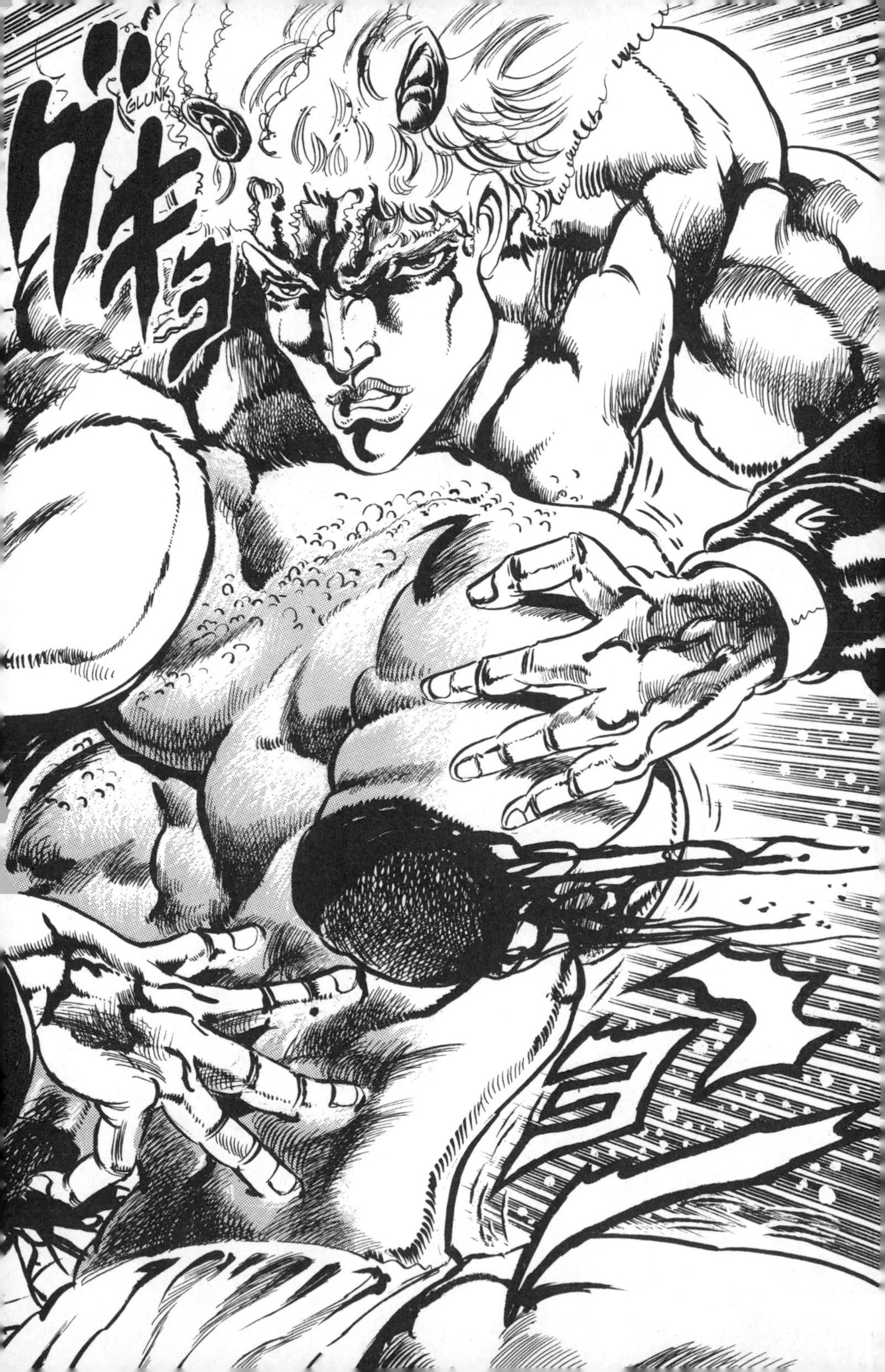
GLUNK

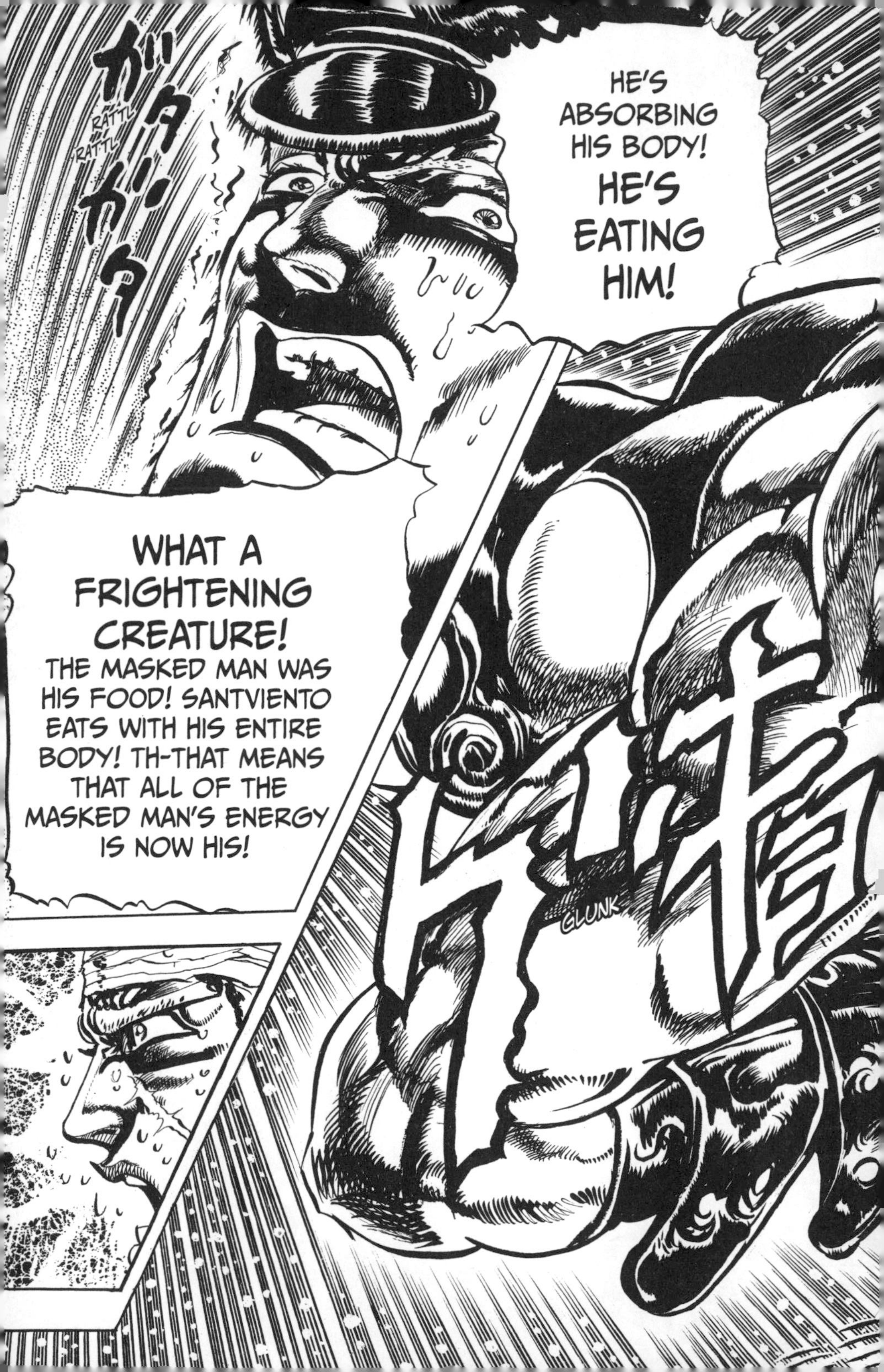
HE'S ABSORBING HIS BODY! HE'S EATING HIM!
RATTL RATTL
GLUNK
WHAT A FRIGHTENING CREATURE! THE MASKED MAN WAS HIS FOOD! SANTVIENTO EATS WITH HIS ENTIRE BODY! TH-THAT MEANS THAT ALL OF THE MASKED MAN'S ENERGY IS NOW HIS!

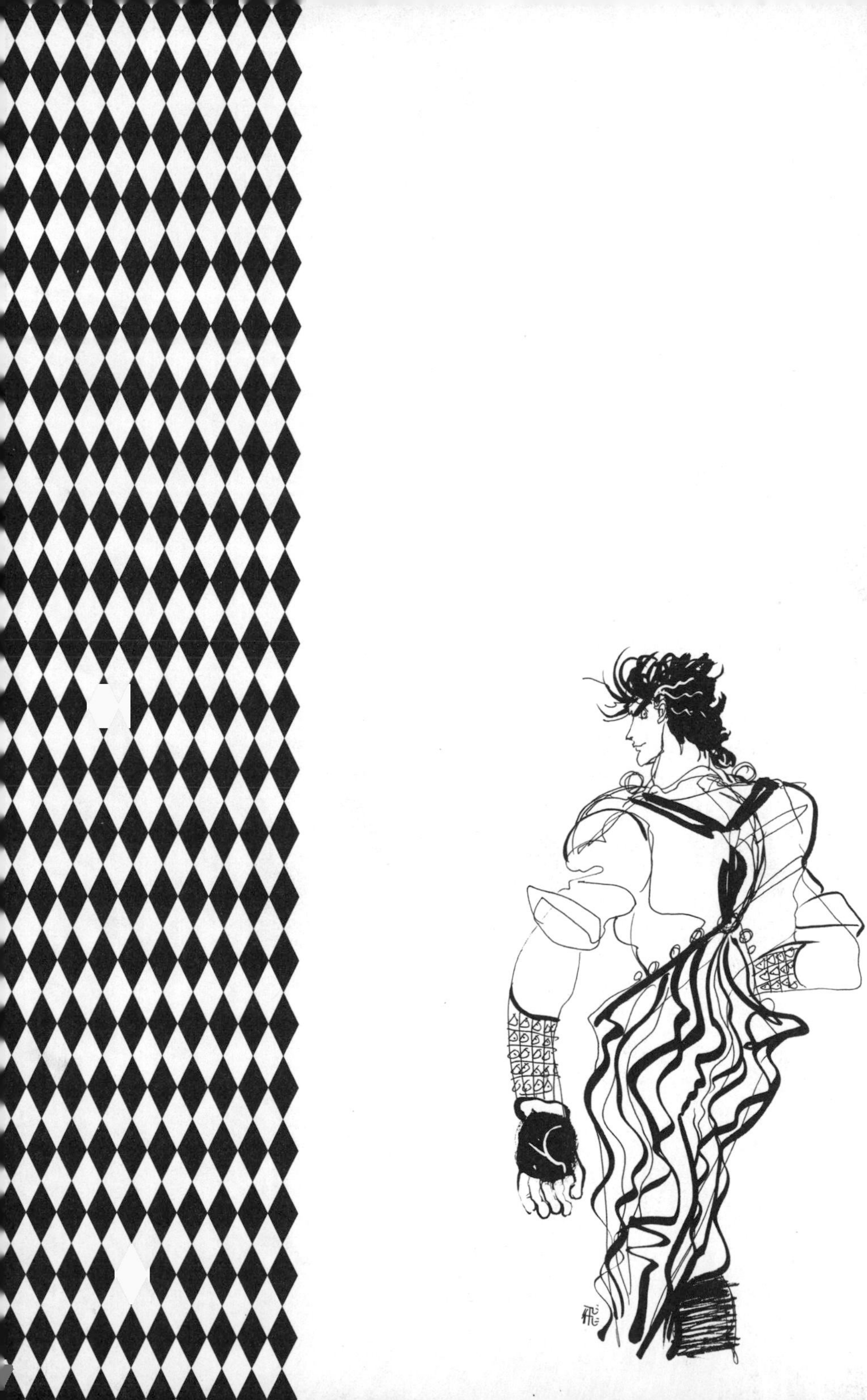

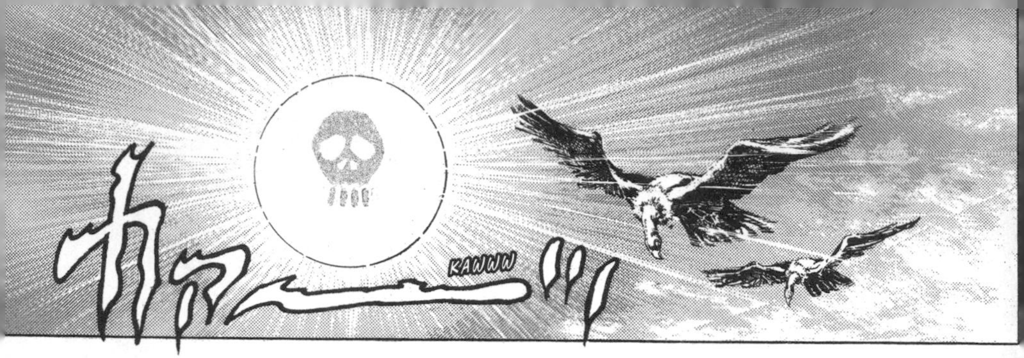
KAWWW

CHAPTER 11: The Pillar Man, Santviento PART 2

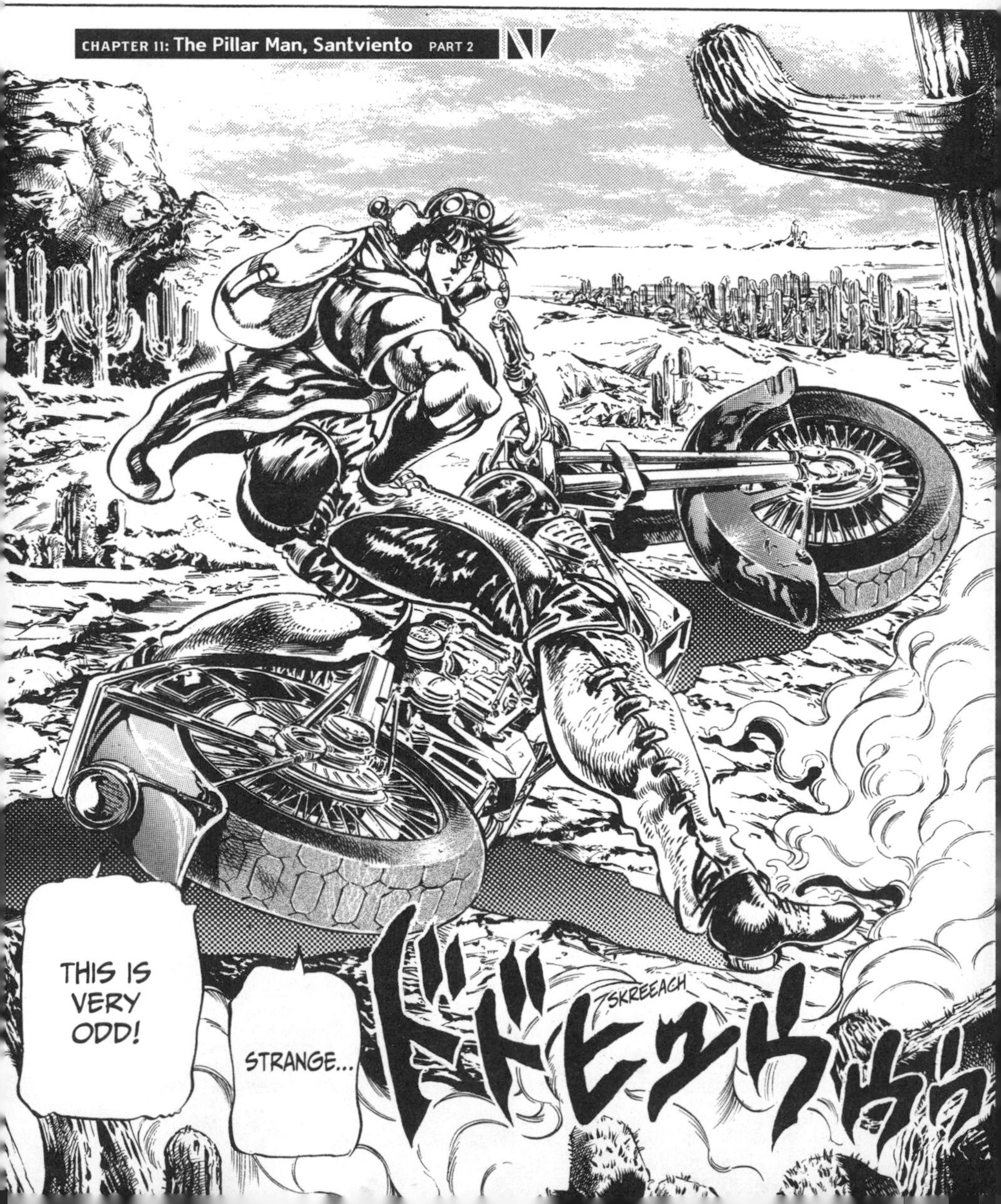
SKREEACH
STRANGE...
THIS IS VERY ODD!

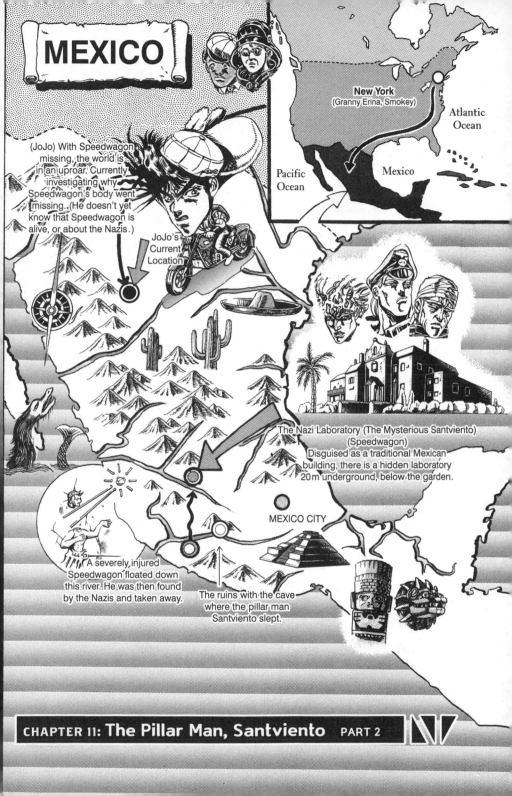

MEXICO

New York
(Granny Erina, Smokey)

Atlantic
Ocean

Pacific
Ocean

Mexico

(JoJo) With Speedwagon missing, the world is in an uproar. Currently investigating why Speedwagon's body went missing. (He doesn't yet know that Speedwagon is alive, or about the Nazis.)

JoJo's Current Location

The Nazi Laboratory (The Mysterious Santviento) (Speedwagon) Disguised as a traditional Mexican building, there is a hidden laboratory 20m underground, below the garden.

MEXICO CITY

A severely injured Speedwagon floated down this river. He was then found by the Nazis and taken away.

The ruins with the cave where the pillar man Santviento slept.

CHAPTER 11: The Pillar Man, Santviento PART 2

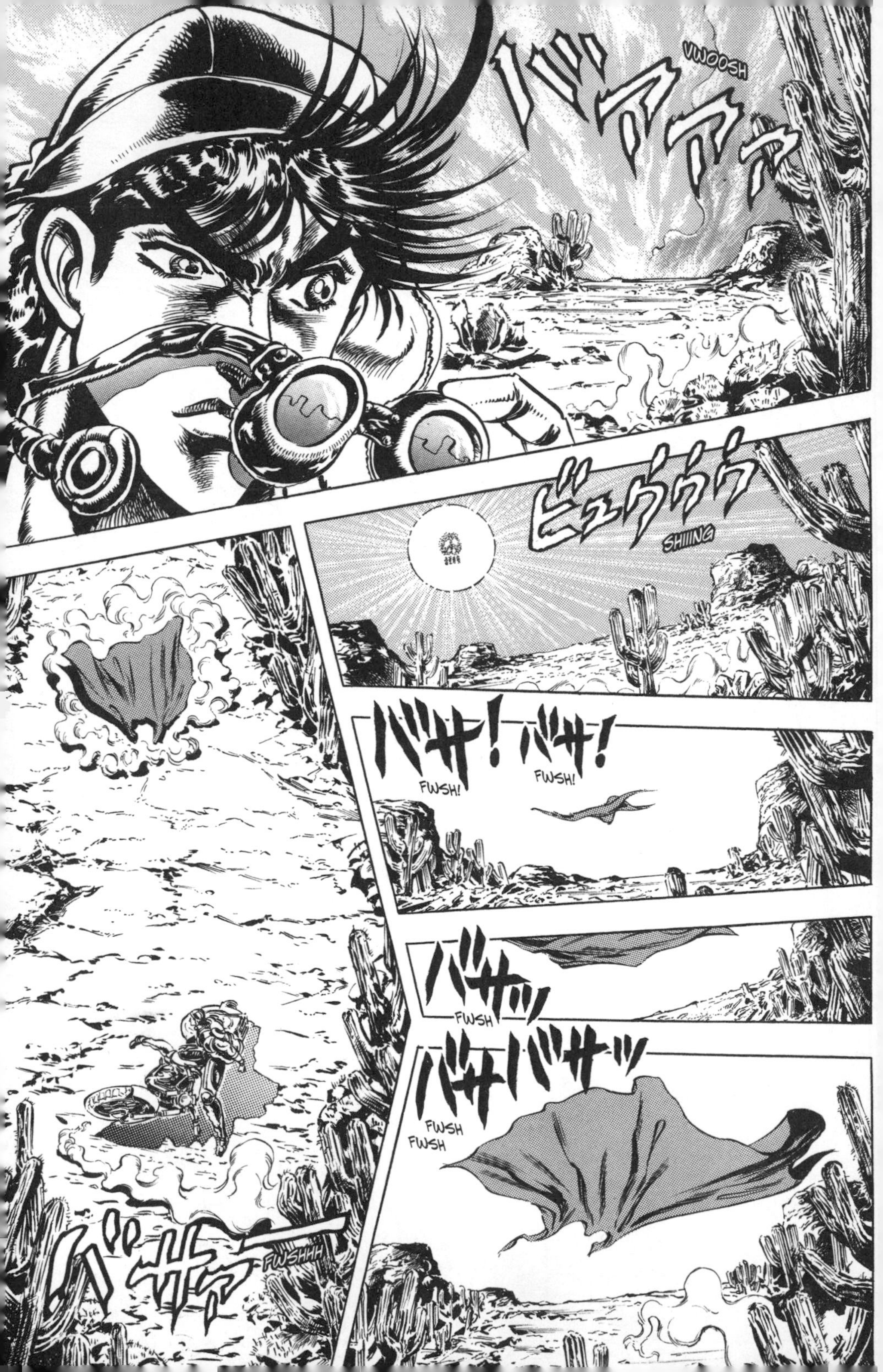
バッアアァ
VWOOSH
ビュウウウ
SHIING
バサ！バサ！
FWSH! FWSH!
バサッ
FWSH
バサバサッ
FWSH FWSH
パサァ
FWSHHH

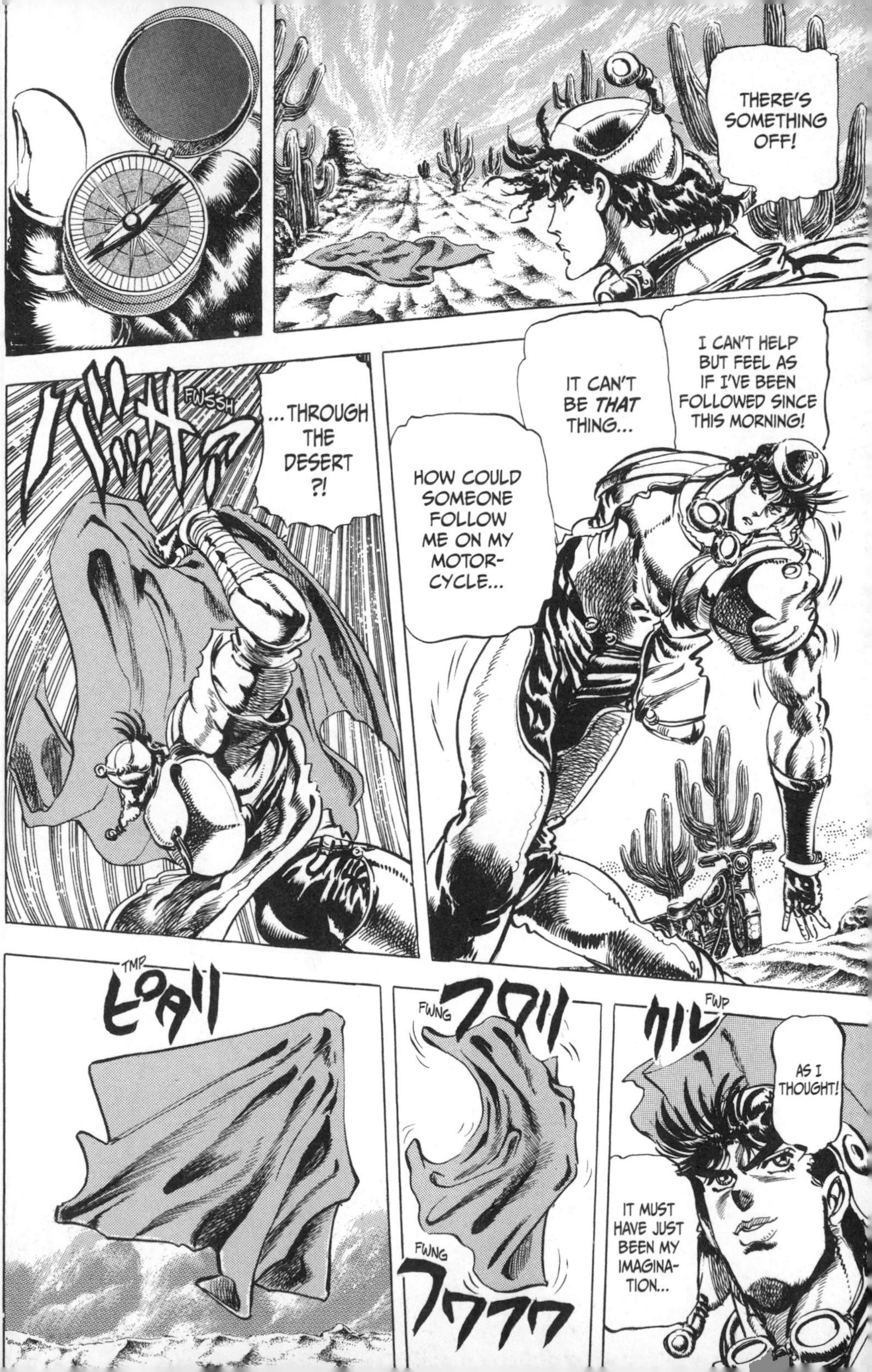
THERE'S SOMETHING OFF!
I CAN'T HELP BUT FEEL AS IF I'VE BEEN FOLLOWED SINCE THIS MORNING!
IT CAN'T BE *THAT* THING...
HOW COULD SOMEONE FOLLOW ME ON MY MOTOR-CYCLE...
FWSSH
...THROUGH THE DESERT ?!
FWP
AS I THOUGHT!
IT MUST HAVE JUST BEEN MY IMAGINA-TION...
FWNG
FWNG
TMP

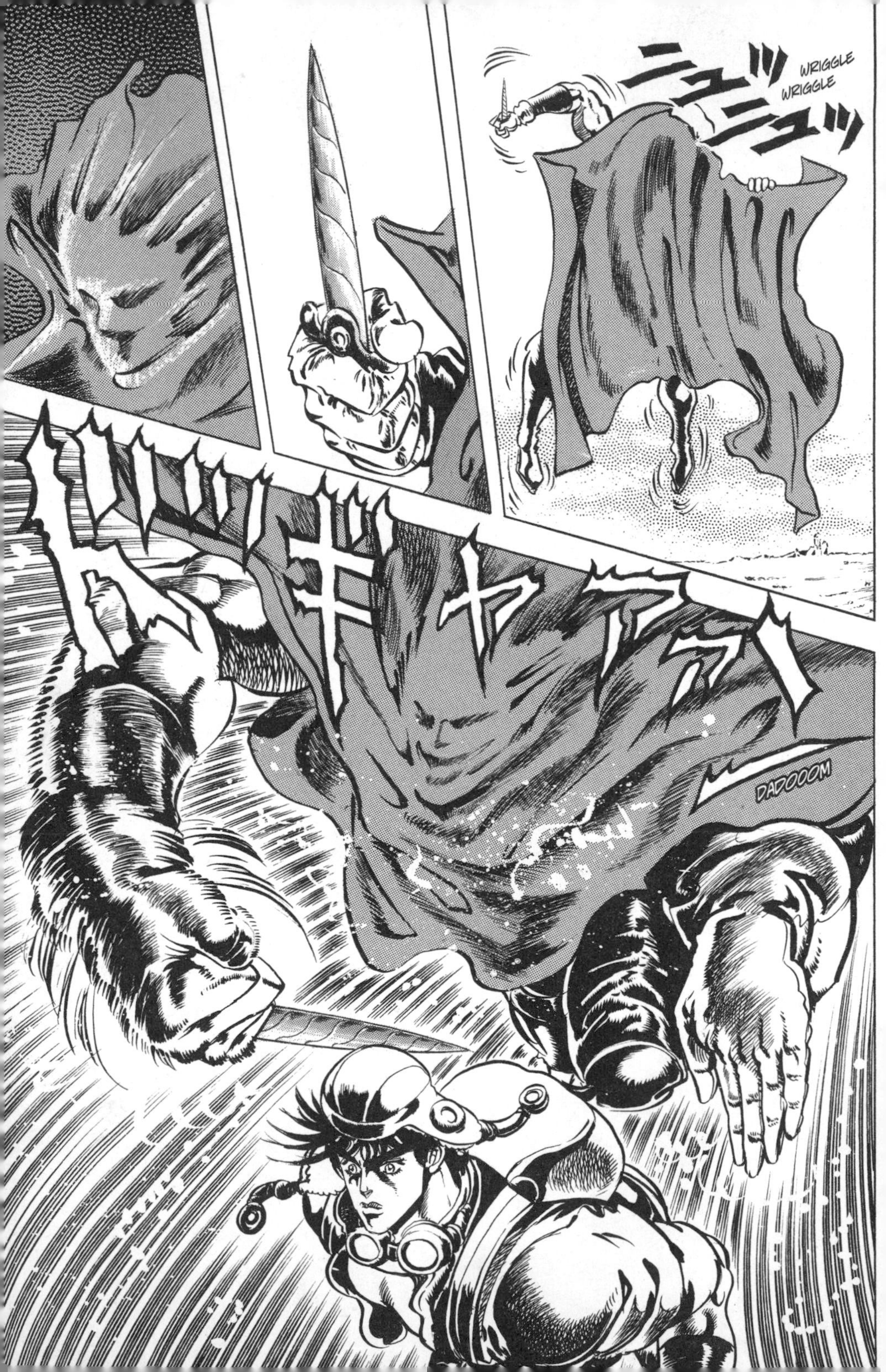
ニュッ
ニュッ
WRIGGLE
WRIGGLE
DADOOOM

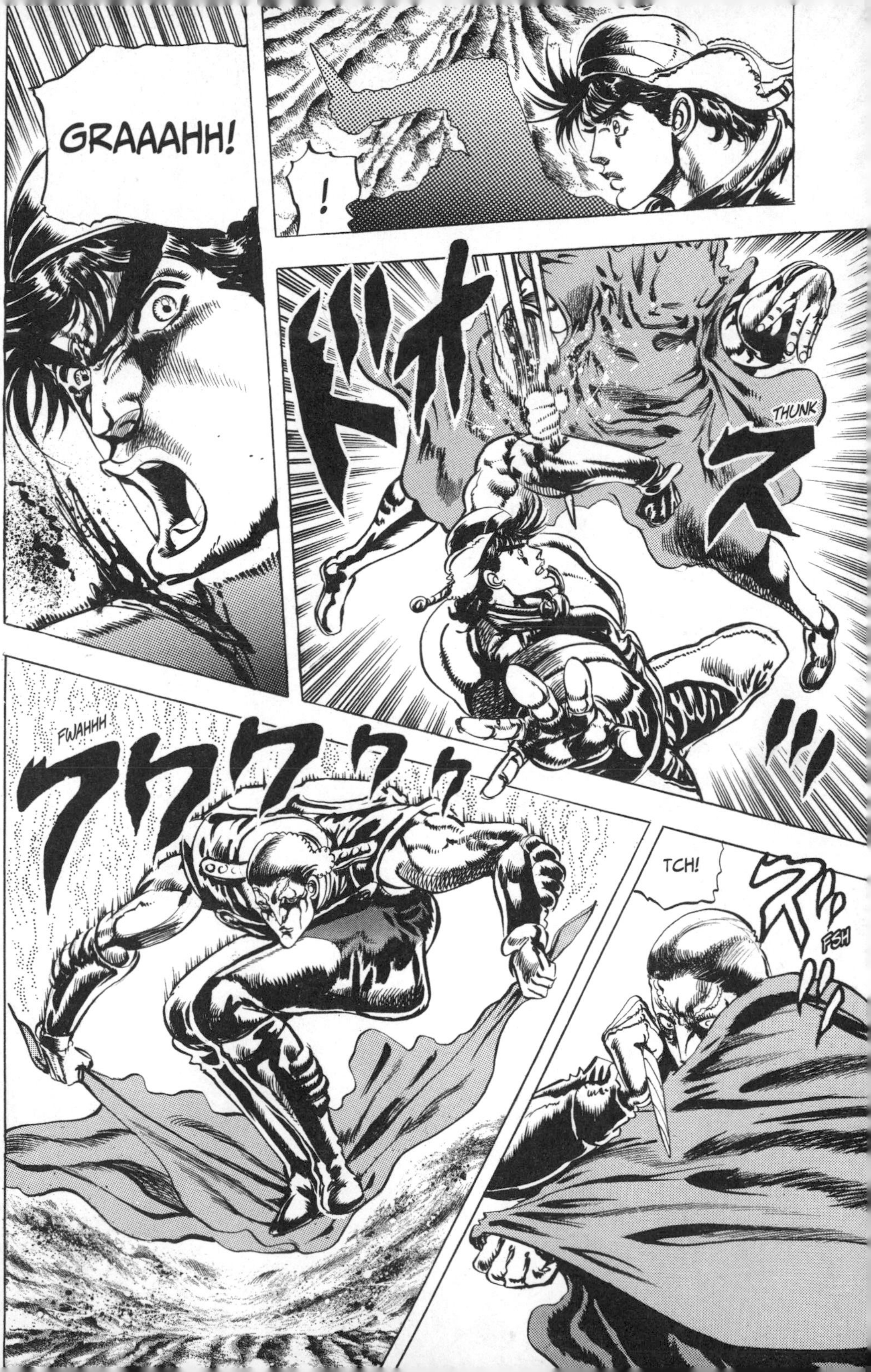
!
THUNK
GRAAAHH!
TCH!
FSH
FWAHHH

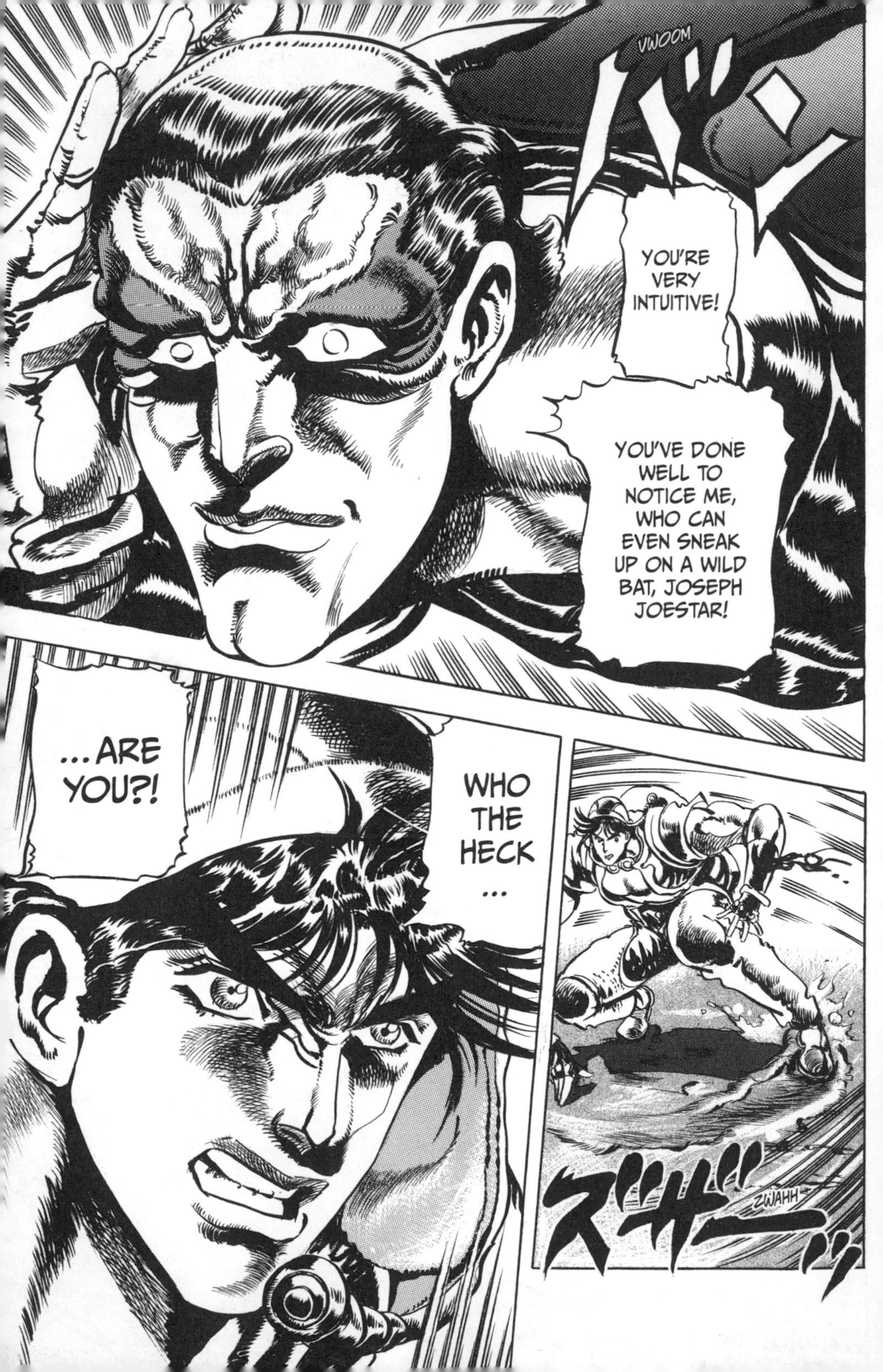
VWOOM
YOU'RE VERY INTUITIVE!
YOU'VE DONE WELL TO NOTICE ME, WHO CAN EVEN SNEAK UP ON A WILD BAT, JOSEPH JOESTAR!
ZWAHH
WHO THE HECK ...
...ARE YOU?!

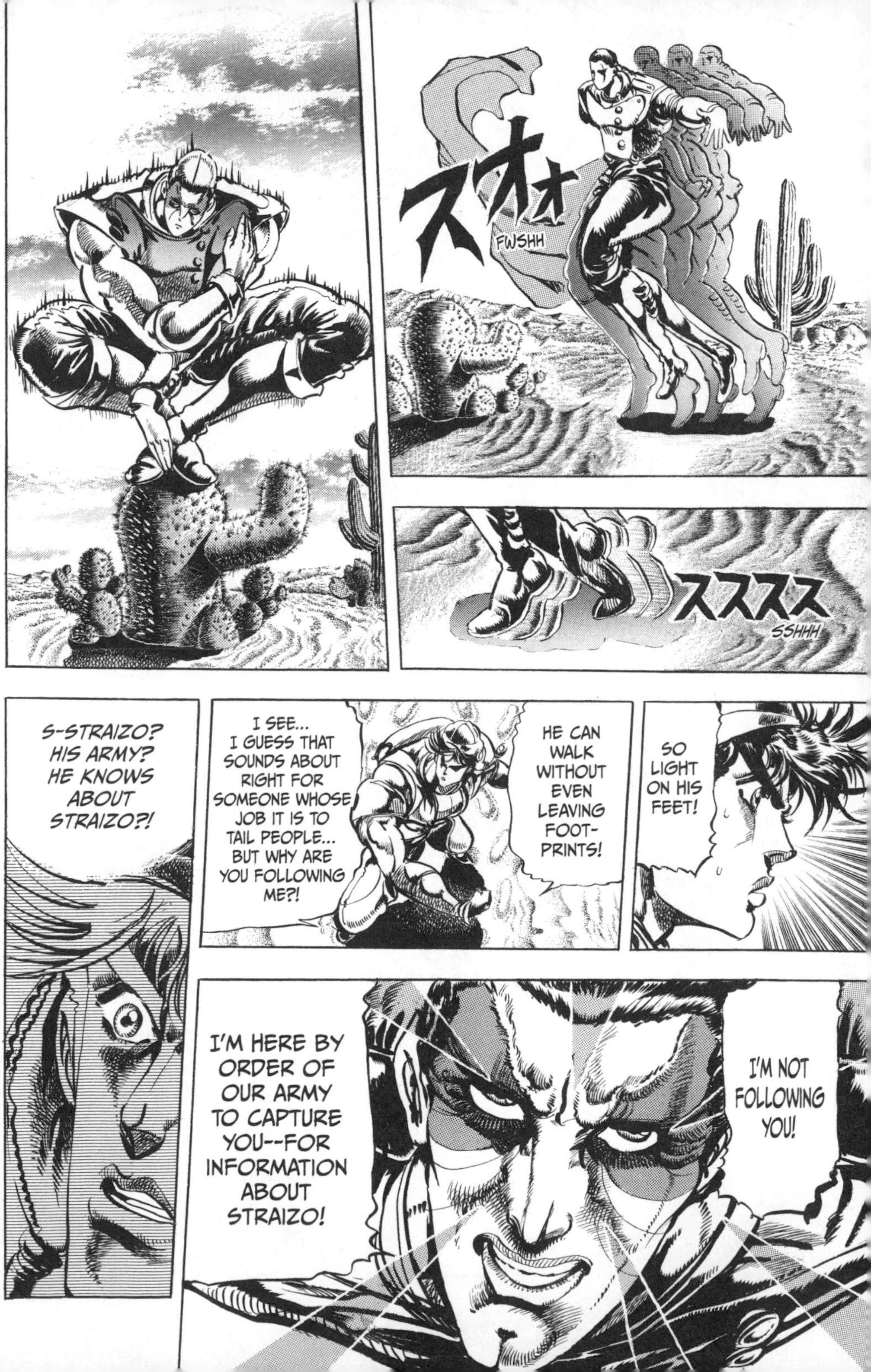
スオォ
FWSHH
スススス
SSHHH
SO LIGHT ON HIS FEET!
HE CAN WALK WITHOUT EVEN LEAVING FOOT-PRINTS!
I SEE... I GUESS THAT SOUNDS ABOUT RIGHT FOR SOMEONE WHOSE JOB IT IS TO TAIL PEOPLE... BUT WHY ARE YOU FOLLOWING ME?!
I'M NOT FOLLOWING YOU!
I'M HERE BY ORDER OF OUR ARMY TO CAPTURE YOU--FOR INFORMATION ABOUT STRAIZO!
S-STRAIZO? HIS ARMY? HE KNOWS ABOUT STRAIZO?!

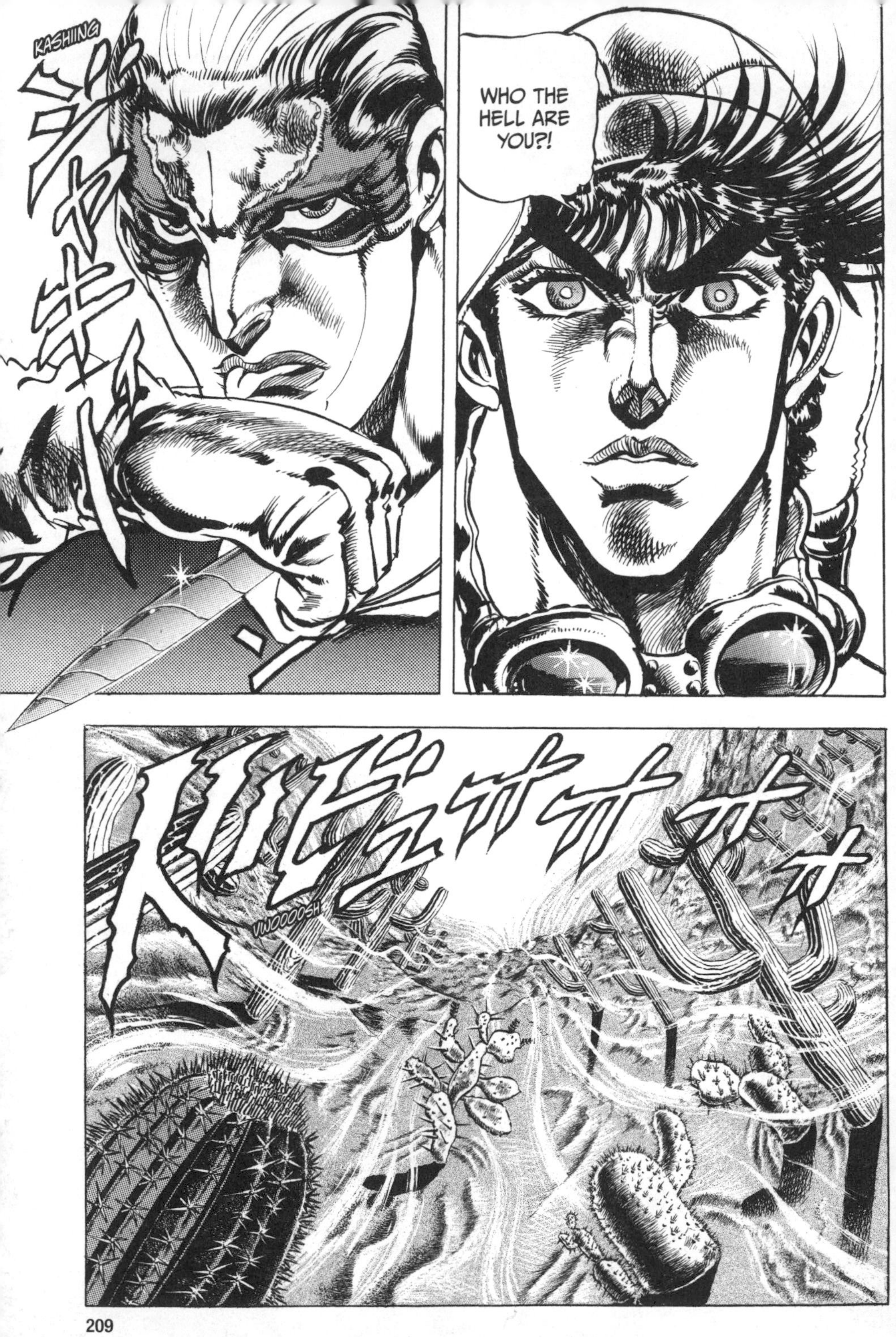
WHO THE HELL ARE YOU?!
KASHIING
VWOOOOSH

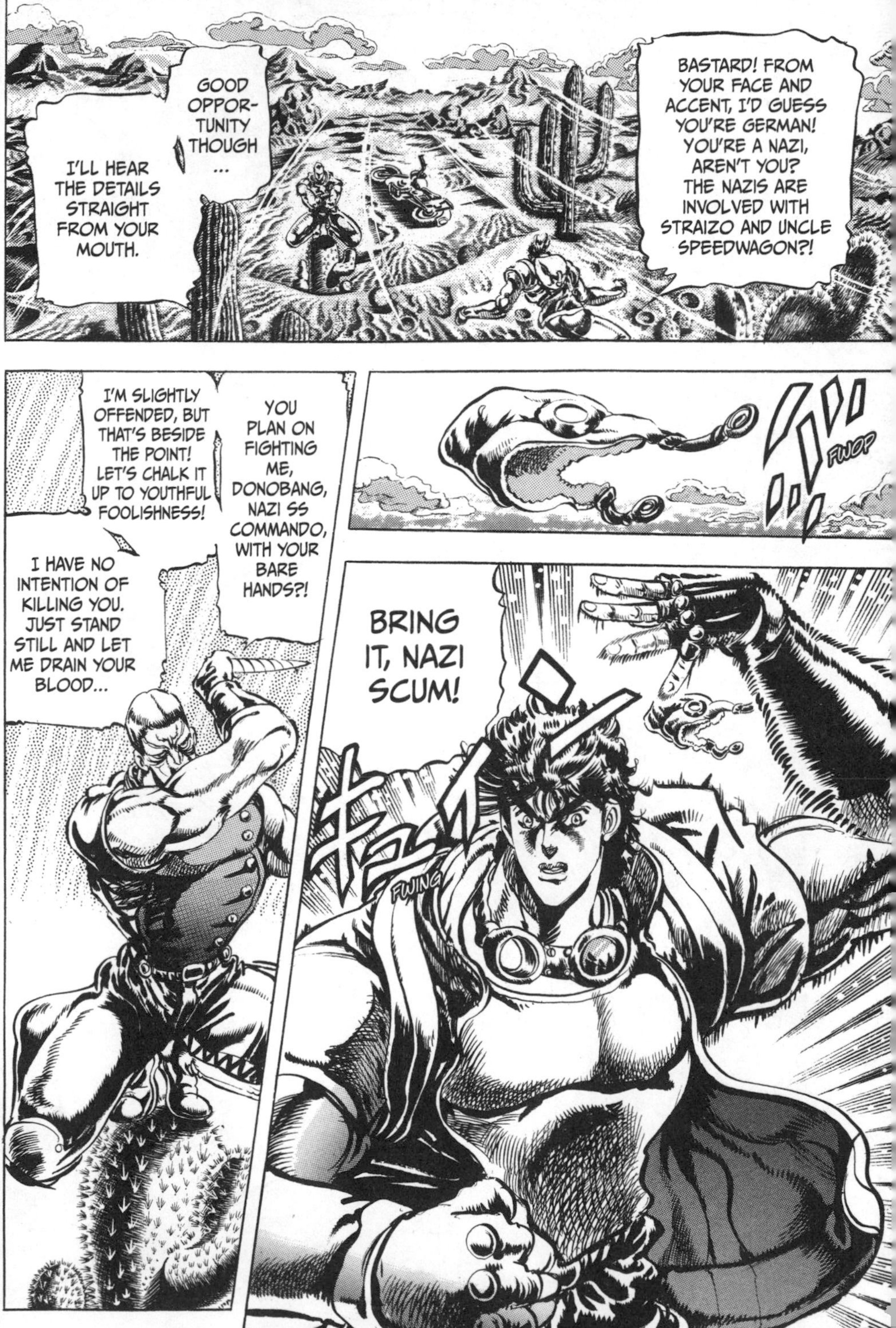

BASTARD! FROM YOUR FACE AND ACCENT, I'D GUESS YOU'RE GERMAN! YOU'RE A NAZI, AREN'T YOU? THE NAZIS ARE INVOLVED WITH STRAIZO AND UNCLE SPEEDWAGON?!
GOOD OPPORTUNITY THOUGH ...
I'LL HEAR THE DETAILS STRAIGHT FROM YOUR MOUTH.
FWOP
BRING IT, NAZI SCUM!
FWING
YOU PLAN ON FIGHTING ME, DONOBANG, NAZI SS COMMANDO, WITH YOUR BARE HANDS?!
I'M SLIGHTLY OFFENDED, BUT THAT'S BESIDE THE POINT! LET'S CHALK IT UP TO YOUTHFUL FOOLISHNESS!
I HAVE NO INTENTION OF KILLING YOU. JUST STAND STILL AND LET ME DRAIN YOUR BLOOD...

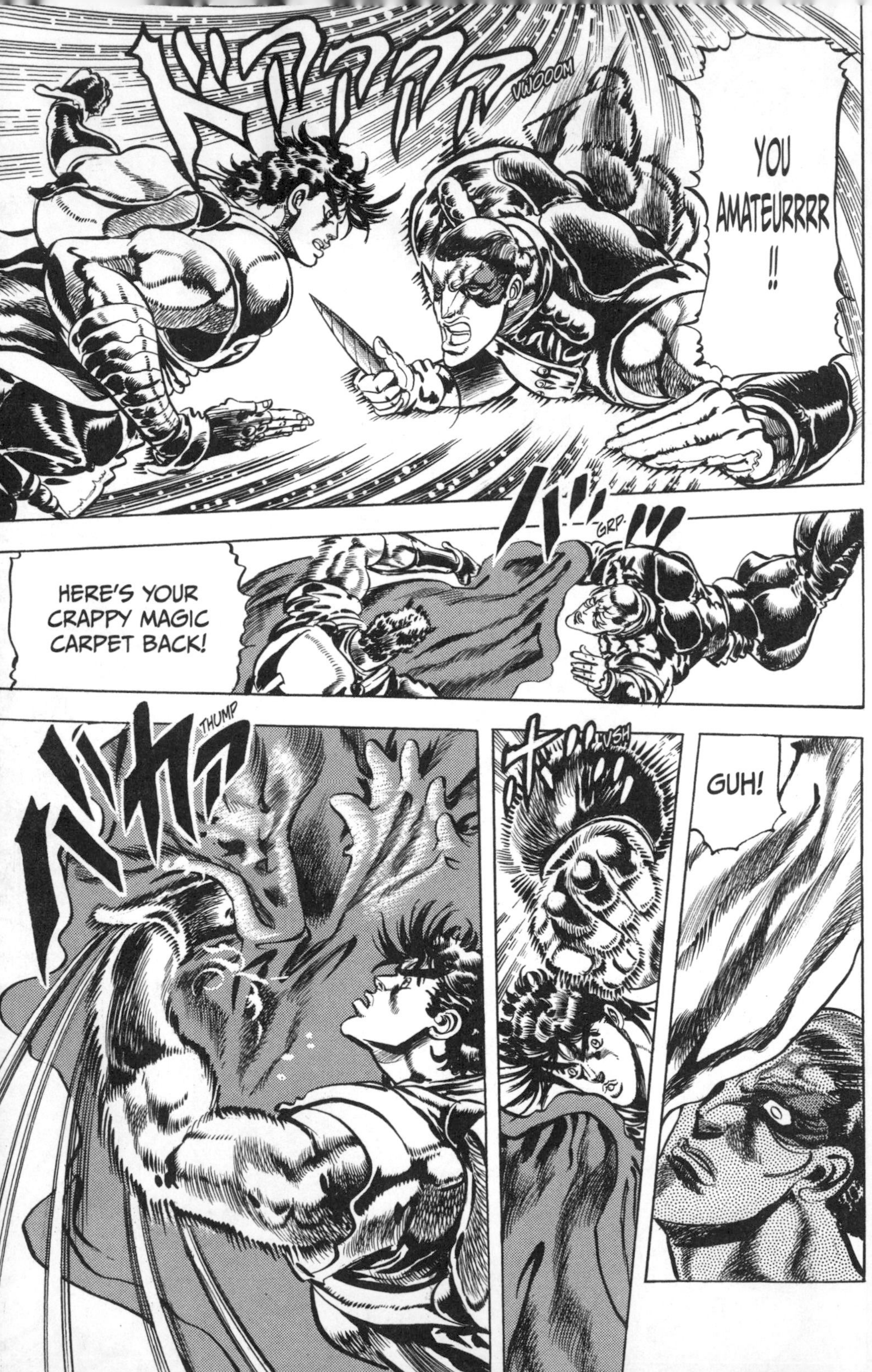
VWOOOM
YOU AMATEURRRR !!
GRP
HERE'S YOUR CRAPPY MAGIC CARPET BACK!
GUH!
VSH
THUMP

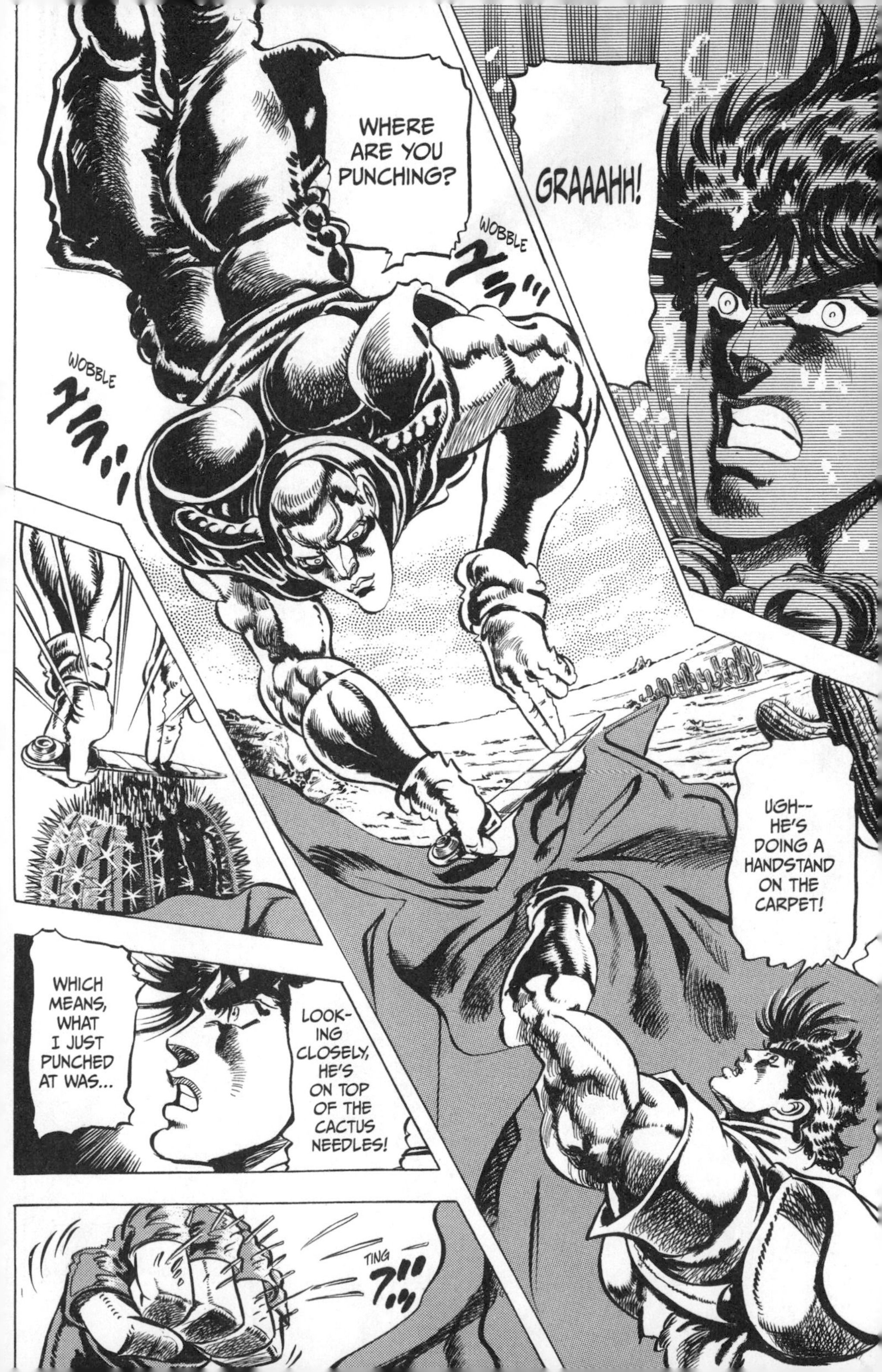
GRAAAHH!
WHERE ARE YOU PUNCHING?
WOBBLE
WOBBLE
UGH-- HE'S DOING A HANDSTAND ON THE CARPET!
LOOK-ING CLOSELY, HE'S ON TOP OF THE CACTUS NEEDLES!
WHICH MEANS, WHAT I JUST PUNCHED AT WAS...
TING

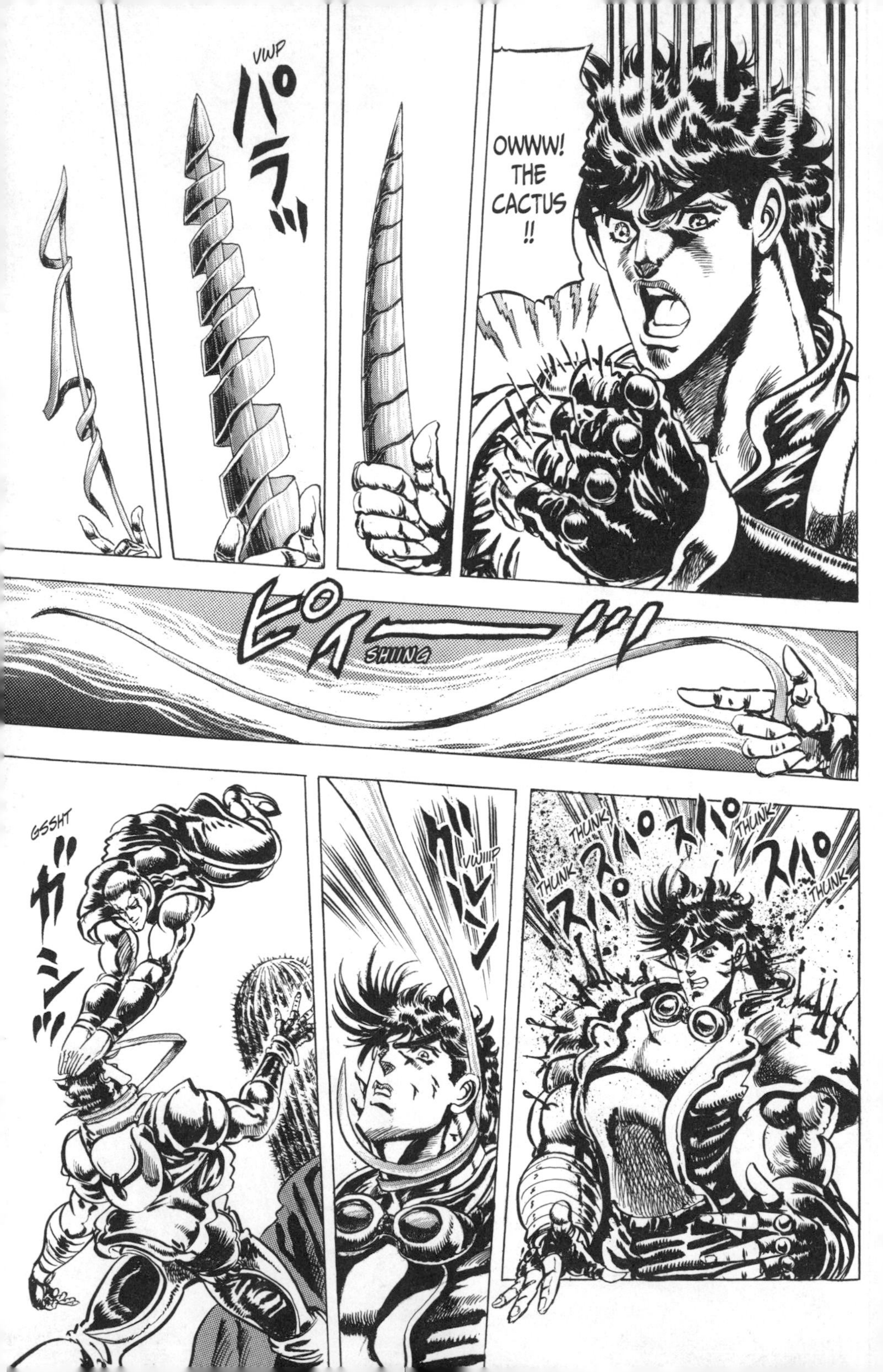
OWWW! THE CACTUS !!
VWP
パラッ
ピイーーッ
SHING
THUNK
THUNK
THUNK
THUNK
VWIIP
GSSHT

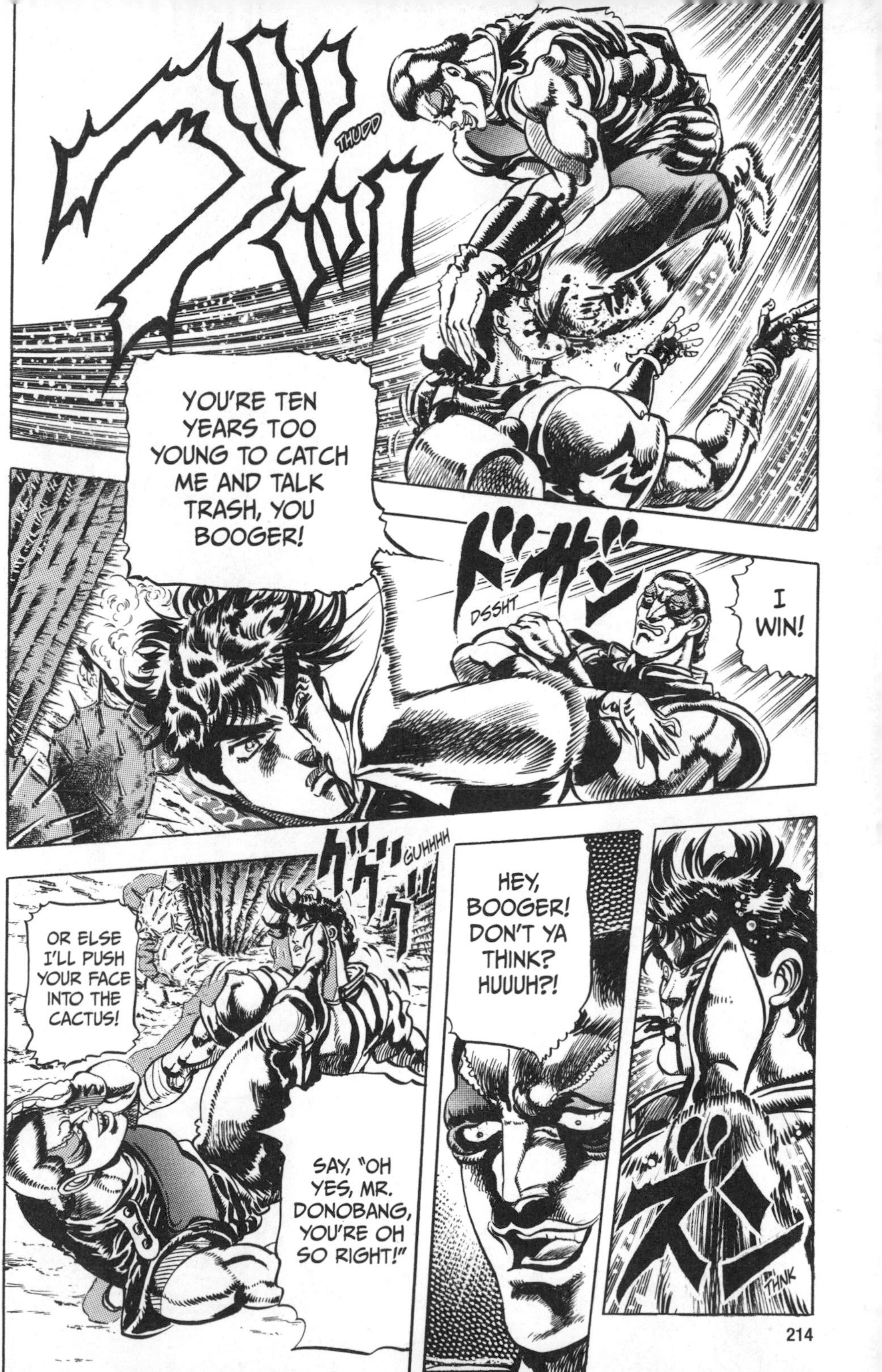
THUDD
YOU'RE TEN YEARS TOO YOUNG TO CATCH ME AND TALK TRASH, YOU BOOGER!
DSSHT
I WIN!
THNK
HEY, BOOGER! DON'T YA THINK? HUUUH?!
GUHHHH
SAY, "OH YES, MR. DONOBANG, YOU'RE OH SO RIGHT!"
OR ELSE I'LL PUSH YOUR FACE INTO THE CACTUS!

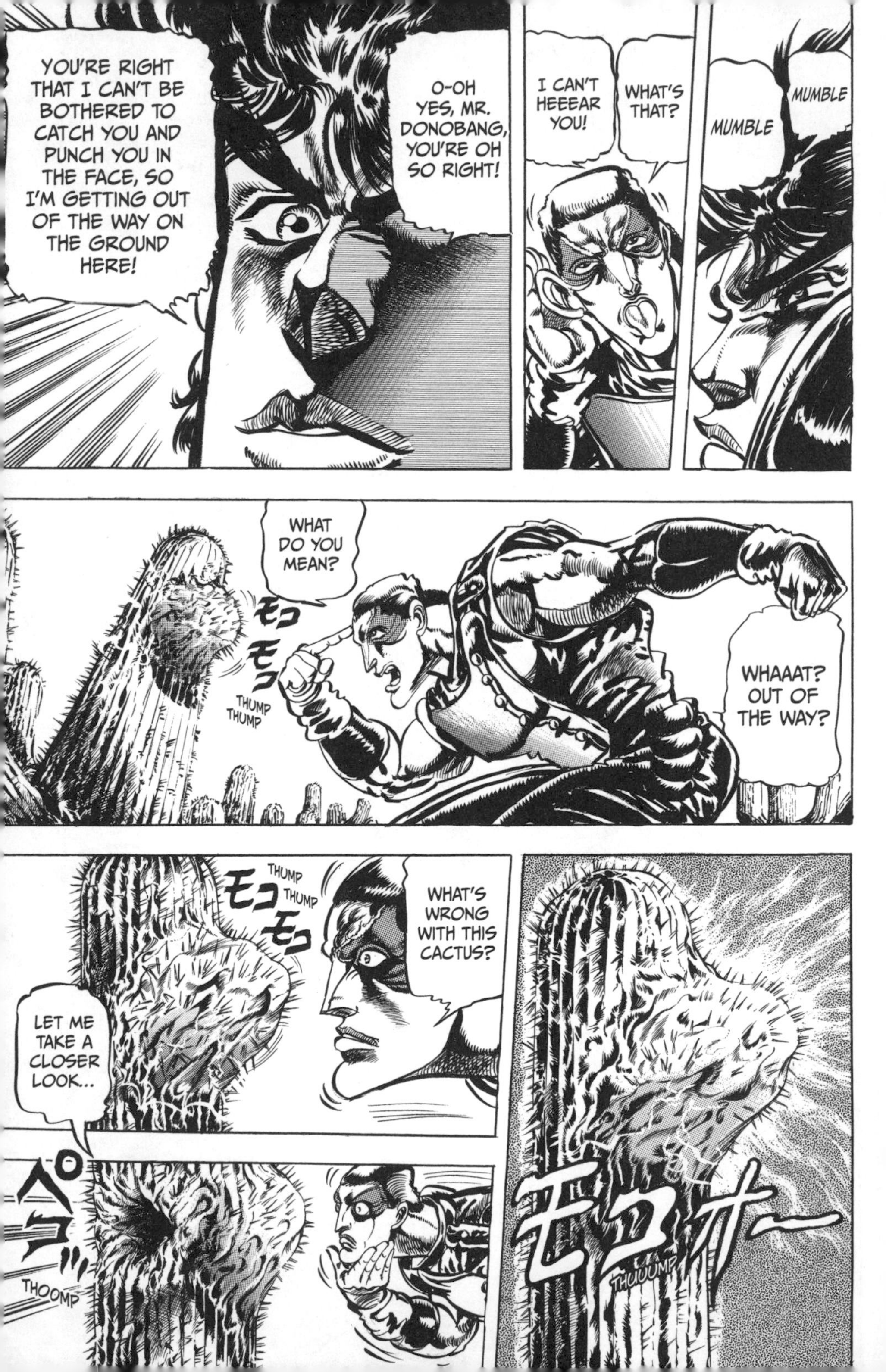

MUMBLE
MUMBLE
WHAT'S THAT?
I CAN'T HEEEAR YOU!
O-OH YES, MR. DONOBANG, YOU'RE OH SO RIGHT!
YOU'RE RIGHT THAT I CAN'T BE BOTHERED TO CATCH YOU AND PUNCH YOU IN THE FACE, SO I'M GETTING OUT OF THE WAY ON THE GROUND HERE!
WHAAAT? OUT OF THE WAY?
WHAT DO YOU MEAN?
モコ モコ
THUMP THUMP
モコォー
THUUUMP
WHAT'S WRONG WITH THIS CACTUS?
モコ モコ
THUMP THUMP
LET ME TAKE A CLOSER LOOK...
ペコッ
THOOMP

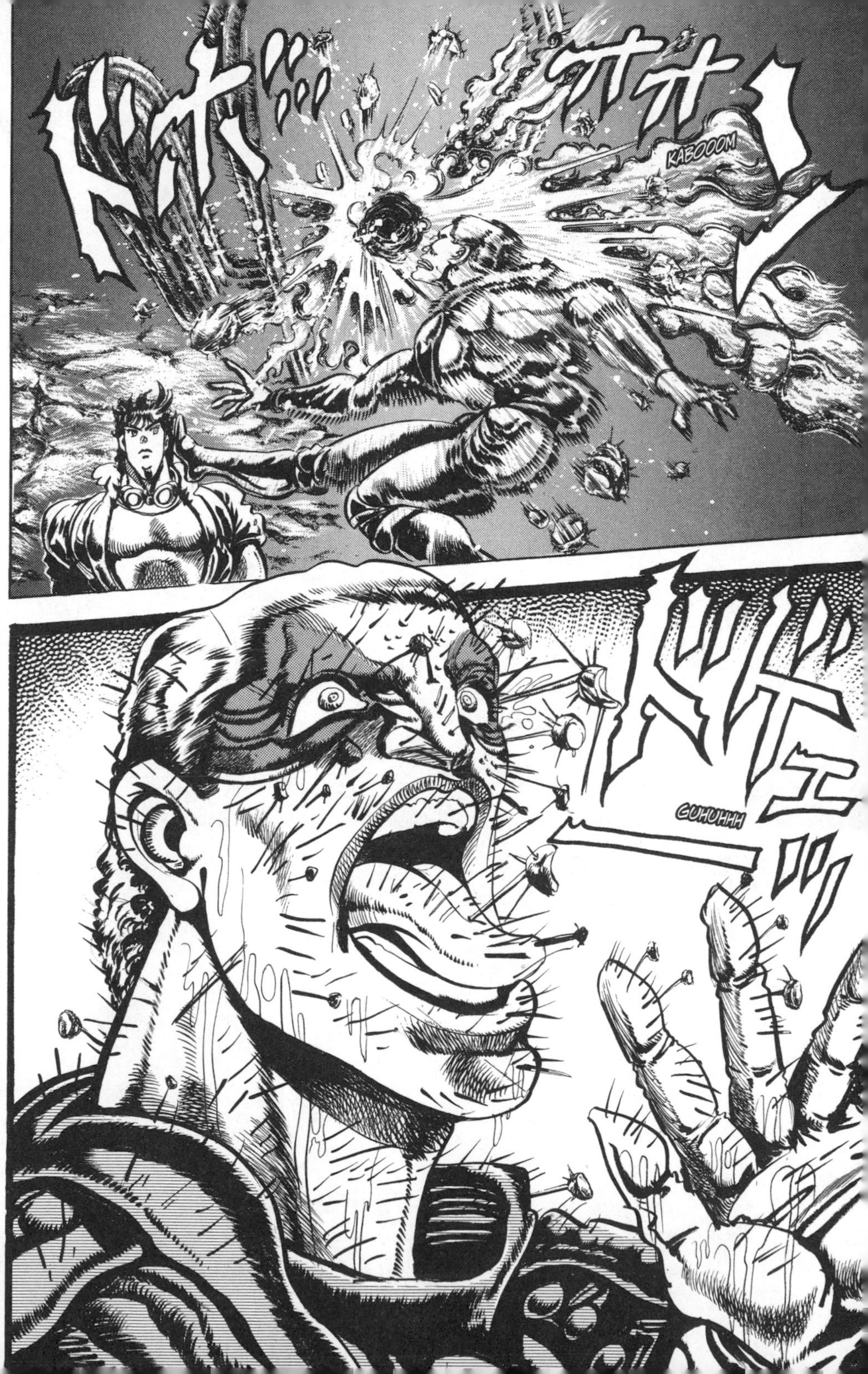
KABOOOM
GUHUHHH

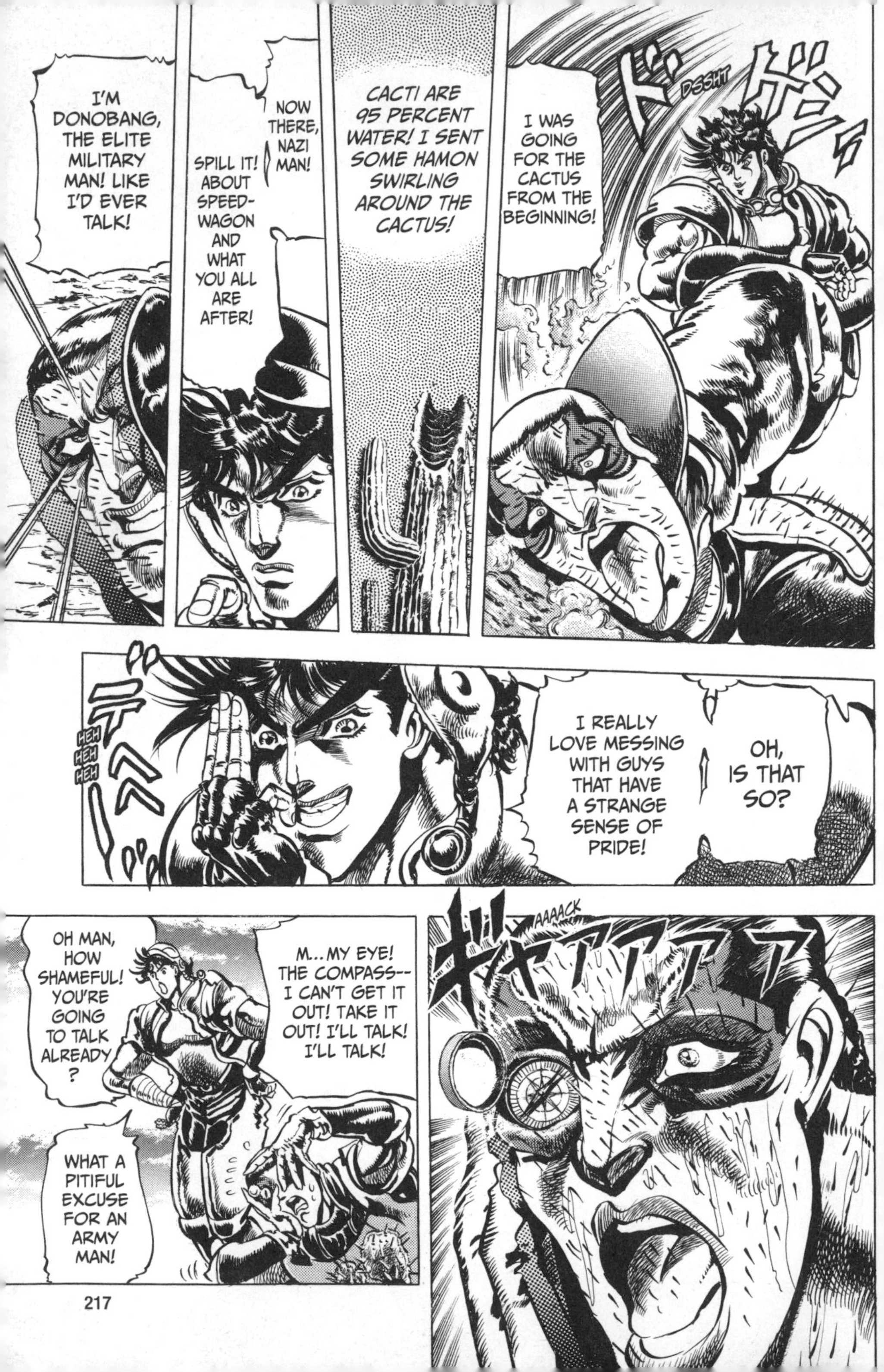
DSGHT
I WAS GOING FOR THE CACTUS FROM THE BEGINNING!
CACTI ARE 95 PERCENT WATER! I SENT SOME HAMON SWIRLING AROUND THE CACTUS!
NOW THERE, NAZI MAN!
SPILL IT! ABOUT SPEED-WAGON AND WHAT YOU ALL ARE AFTER!
I'M DONOBANG, THE ELITE MILITARY MAN! LIKE I'D EVER TALK!
OH, IS THAT SO?
I REALLY LOVE MESSING WITH GUYS THAT HAVE A STRANGE SENSE OF PRIDE!
HEH HEH HEH
AAAACK
M...MY EYE! THE COMPASS-- I CAN'T GET IT OUT! TAKE IT OUT! I'LL TALK! I'LL TALK!
OH MAN, HOW SHAMEFUL! YOU'RE GOING TO TALK ALREADY?
WHAT A PITIFUL EXCUSE FOR AN ARMY MAN!

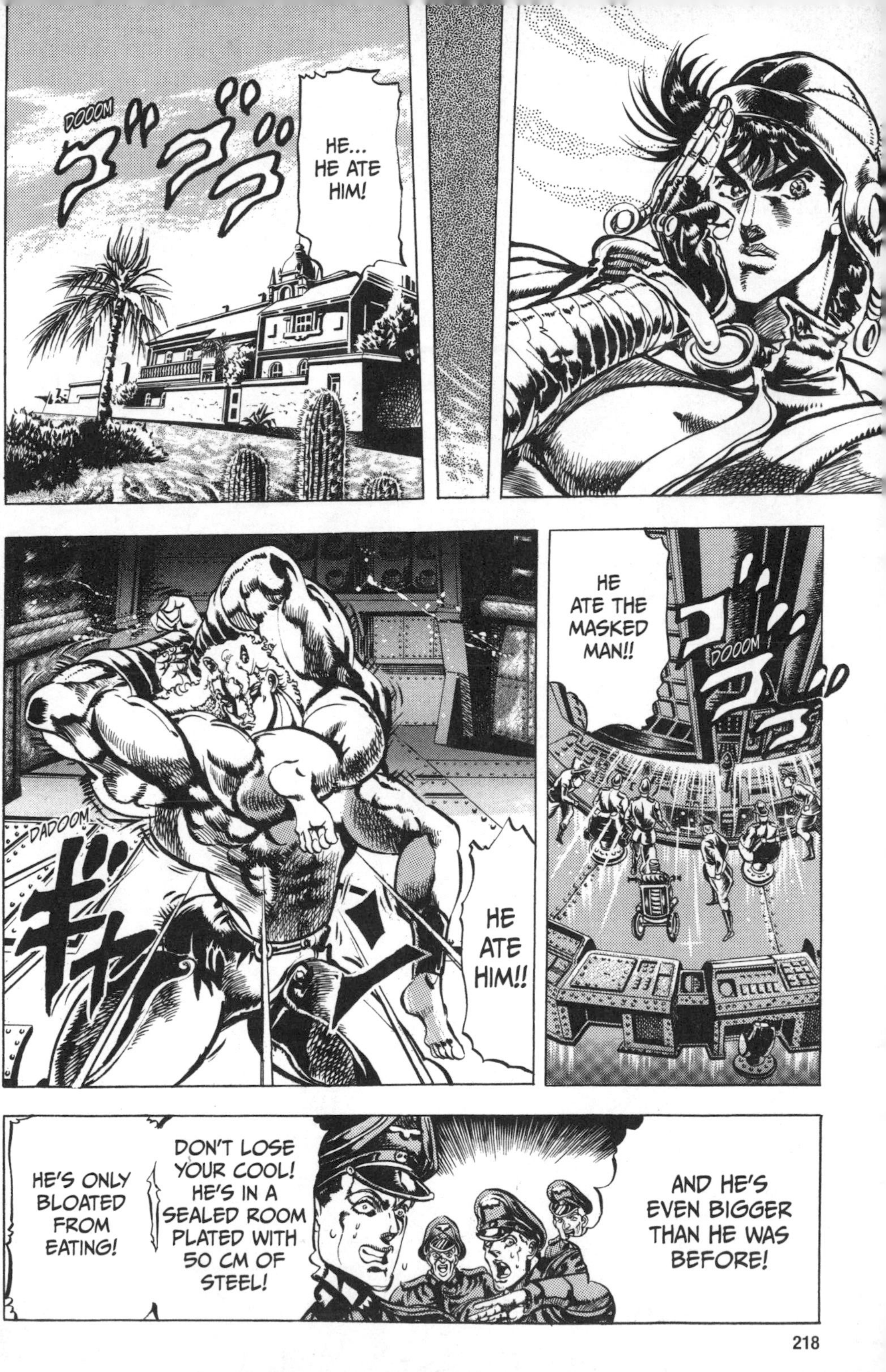
DOOOM
HE... HE ATE HIM!
HE ATE THE MASKED MAN!!
DOOOM
DADOOM
HE ATE HIM!!
AND HE'S EVEN BIGGER THAN HE WAS BEFORE!
DON'T LOSE YOUR COOL! HE'S IN A SEALED ROOM PLATED WITH 50 CM OF STEEL!
HE'S ONLY BLOATED FROM EATING!

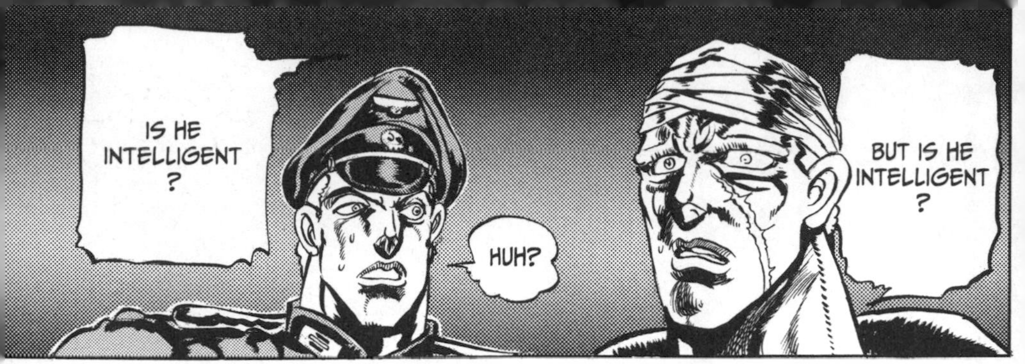
BUT IS HE INTELLIGENT ?
HUH?
IS HE INTELLIGENT ?

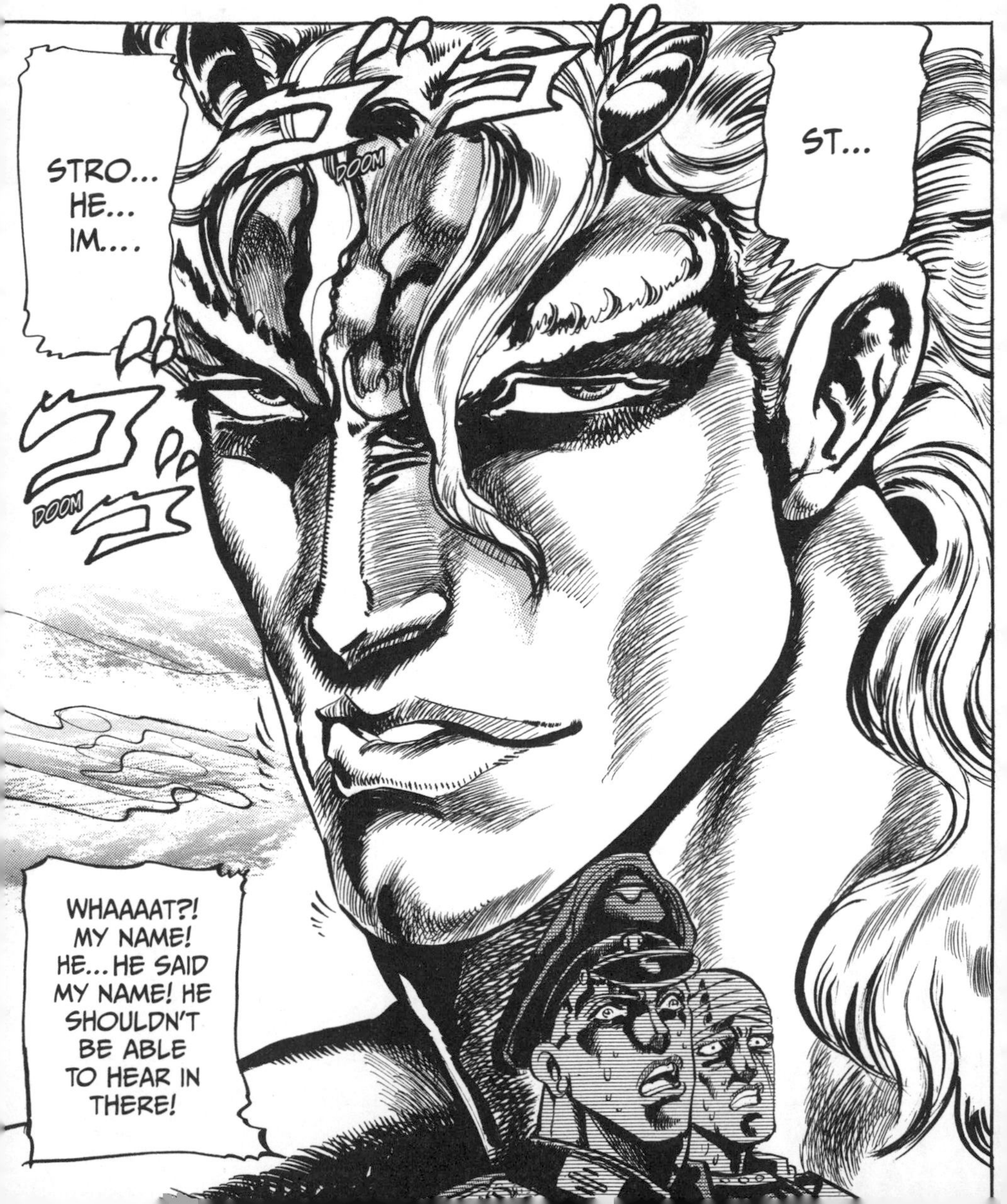
ST...
STRO... HE... IM....
DOOM
DOOM
WHAAAAT?! MY NAME! HE...HE SAID MY NAME! HE SHOULDN'T BE ABLE TO HEAR IN THERE!

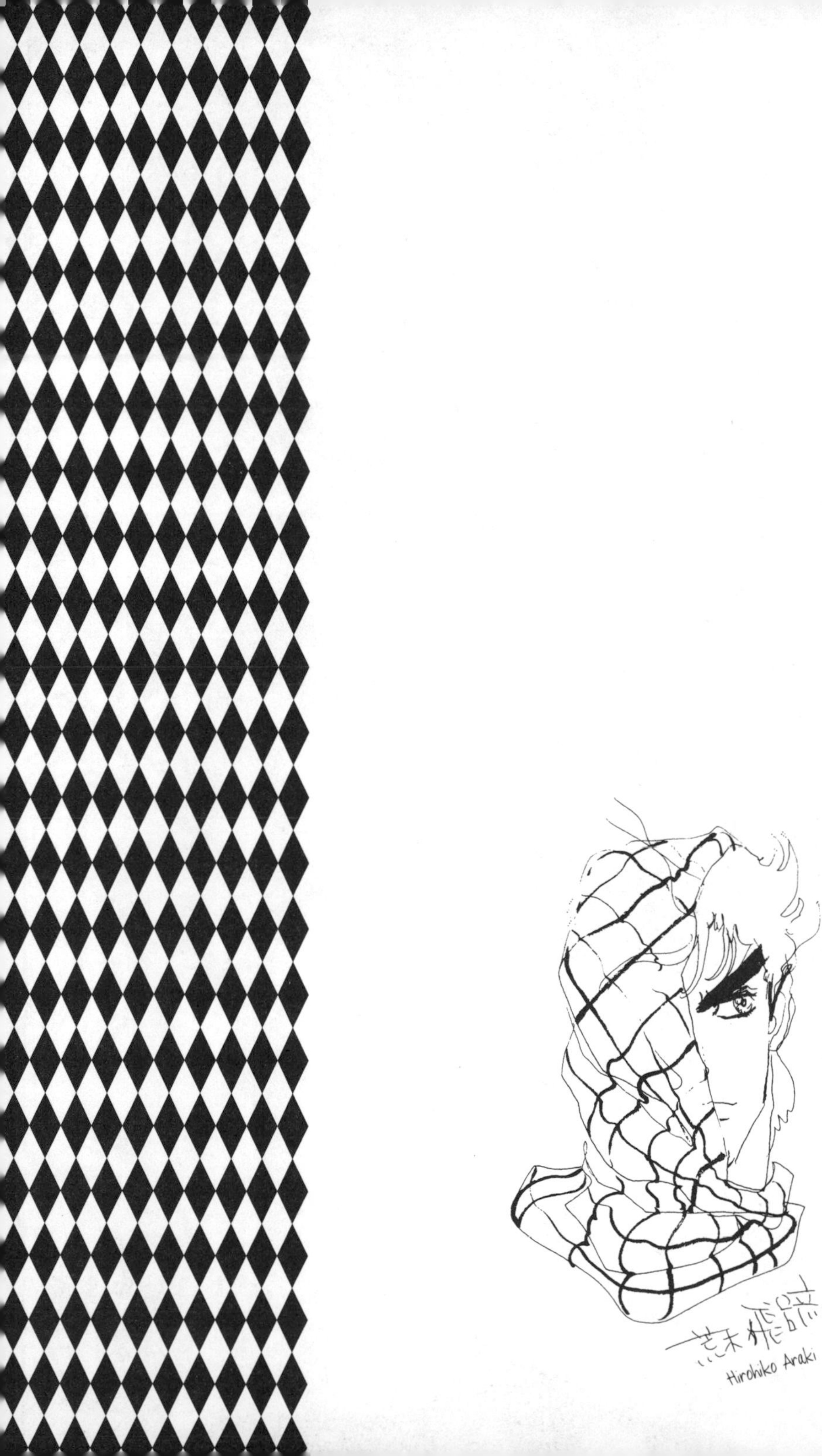
荒木飛呂彦
Hirohiko Araki

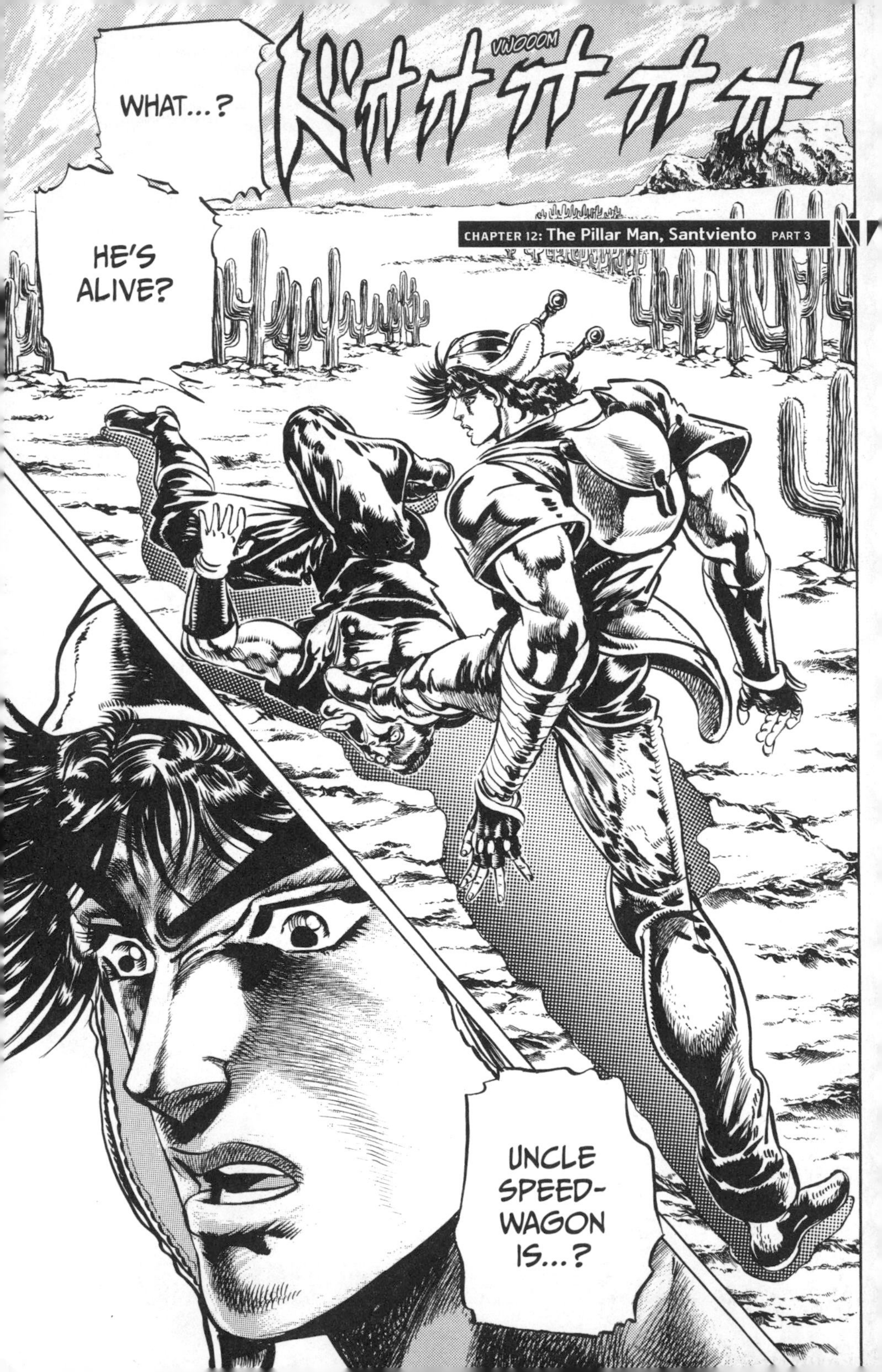
VWOOOM
CHAPTER 12: The Pillar Man, Santviento PART 3
WHAT...?
HE'S ALIVE?
UNCLE SPEED-WAGON IS...?

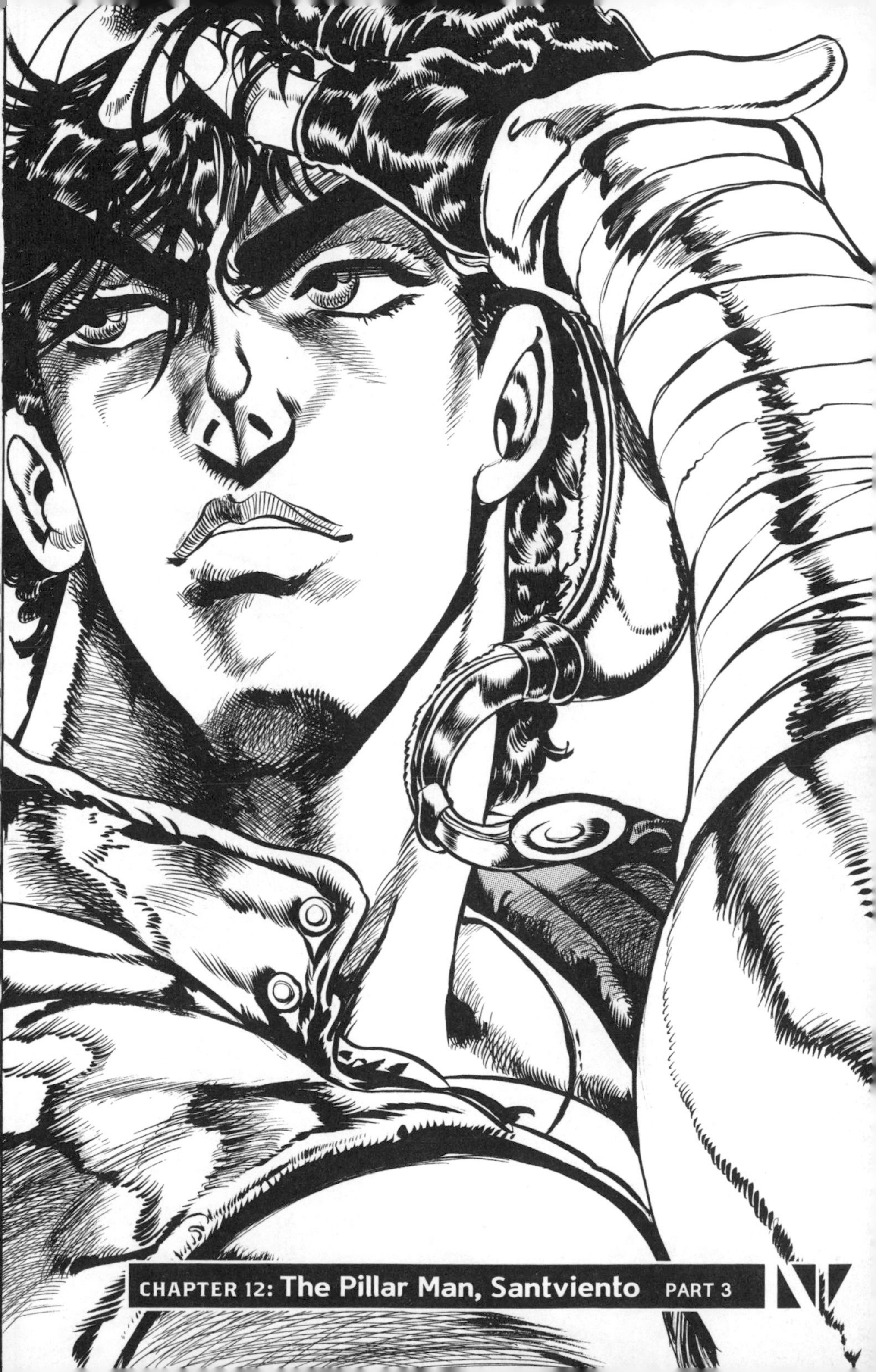

CHAPTER 12: The Pillar Man, Santviento PART 3

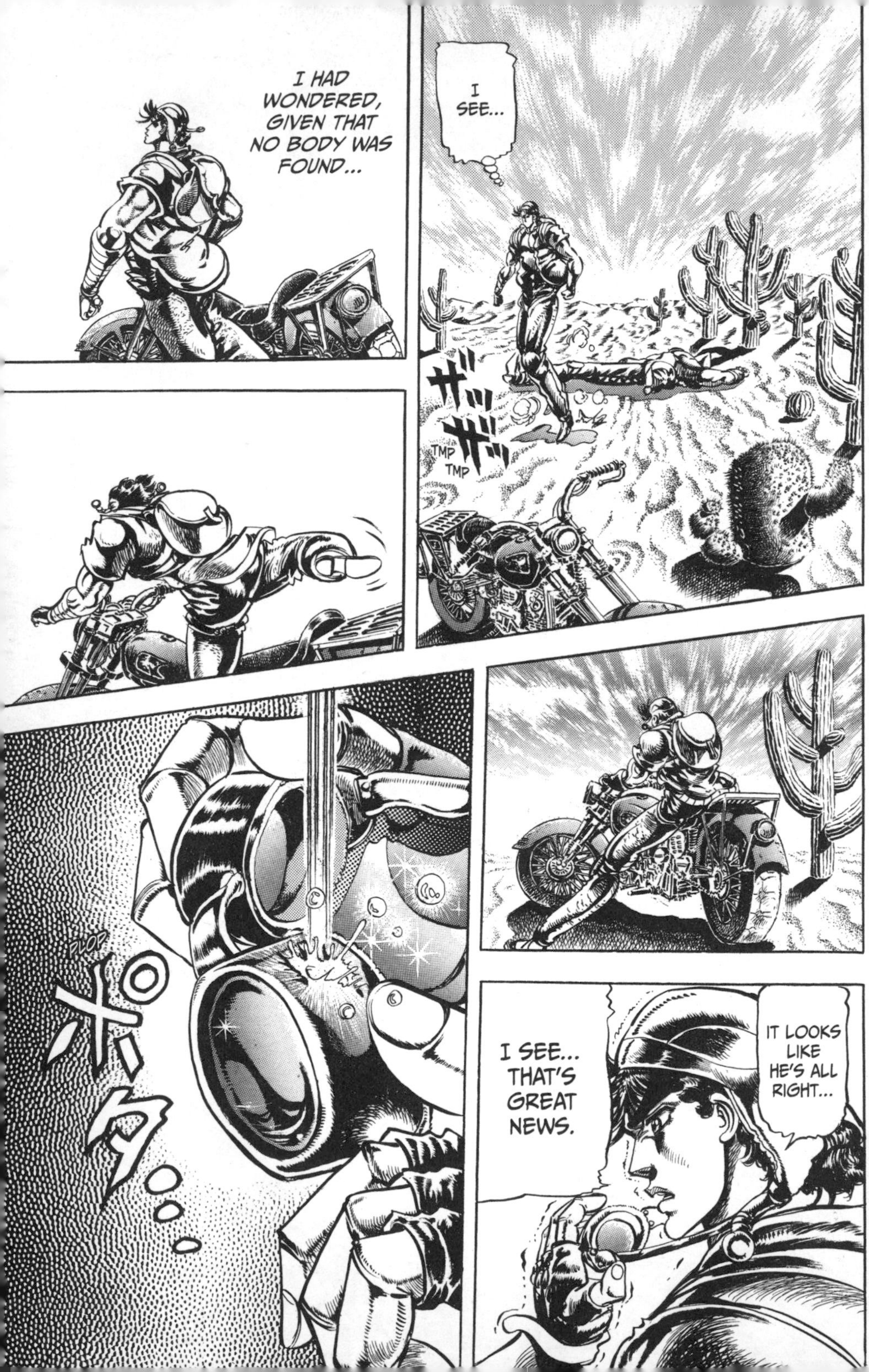
I SEE...
TMP TMP
I HAD WONDERED, GIVEN THAT NO BODY WAS FOUND...
IT LOOKS LIKE HE'S ALL RIGHT...
I SEE... THAT'S GREAT NEWS.
DROP

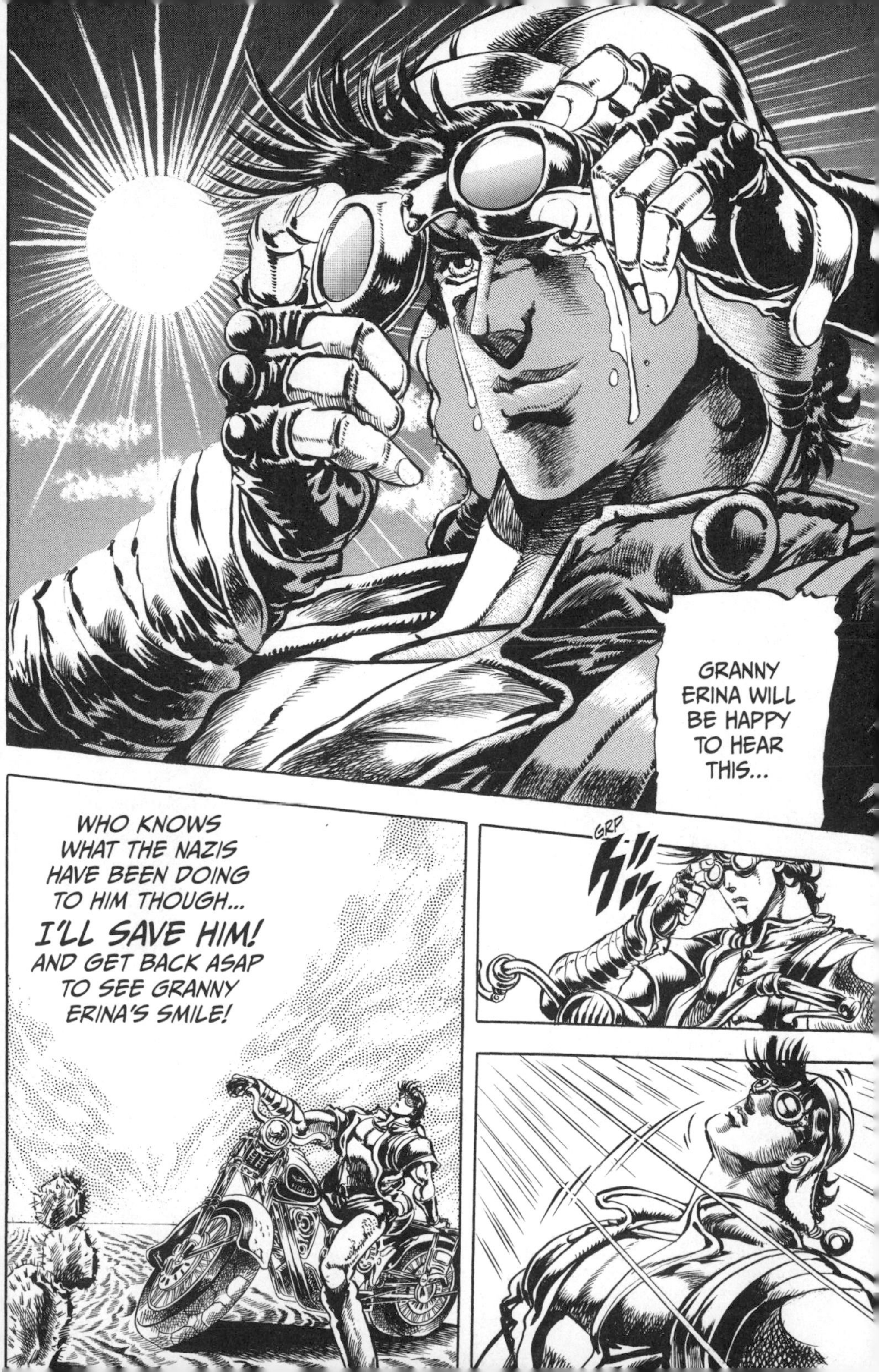
GRANNY ERINA WILL BE HAPPY TO HEAR THIS...
GRP
WHO KNOWS WHAT THE NAZIS HAVE BEEN DOING TO HIM THOUGH... I'LL SAVE HIM! AND GET BACK ASAP TO SEE GRANNY ERINA'S SMILE!

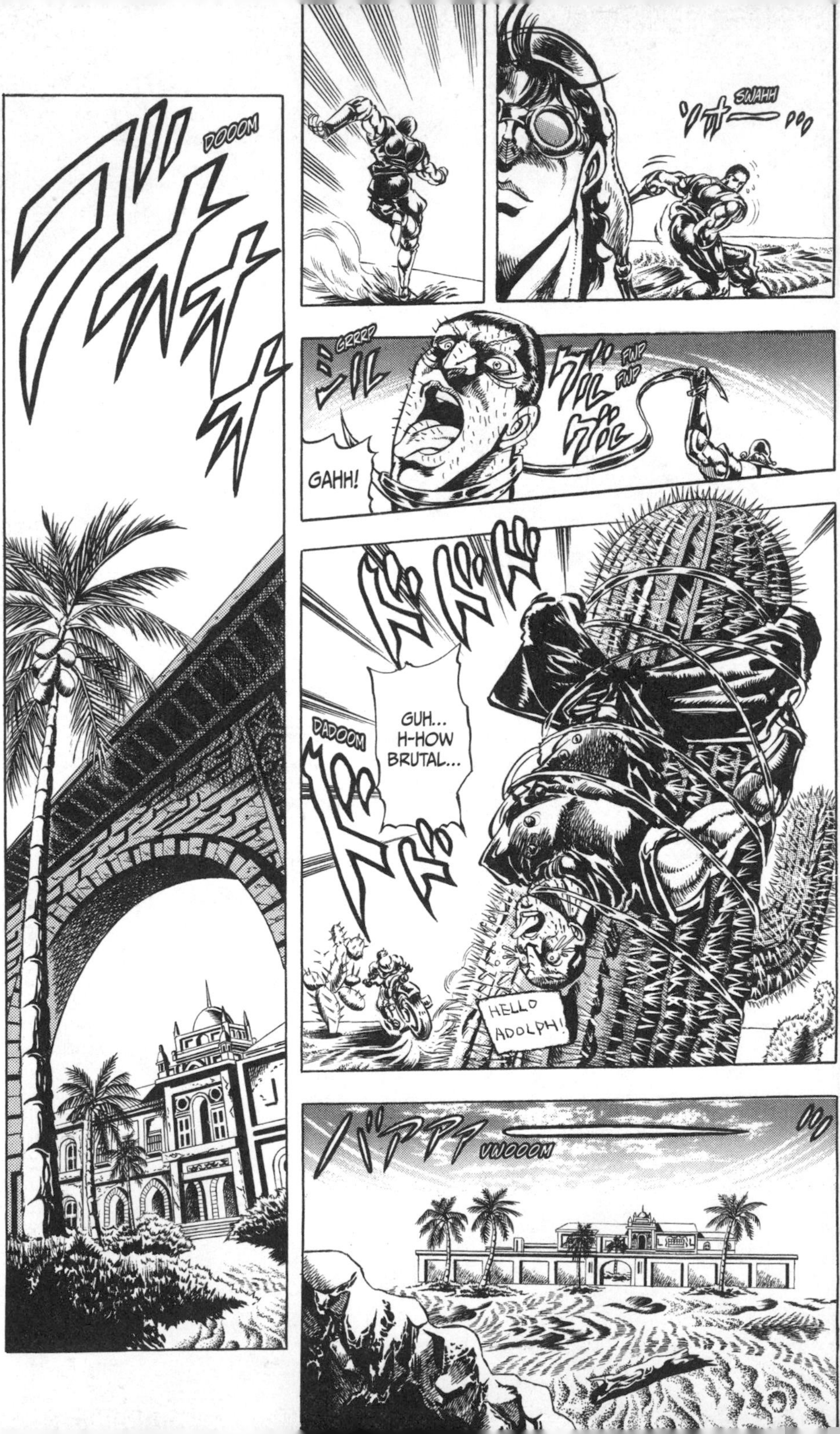

SWAHH
GRRRP
GAHH!
FWP FWP
DADOOM
GUH... H-HOW BRUTAL...
HELLO ADOLPH!
VWOOOM
DOOOM

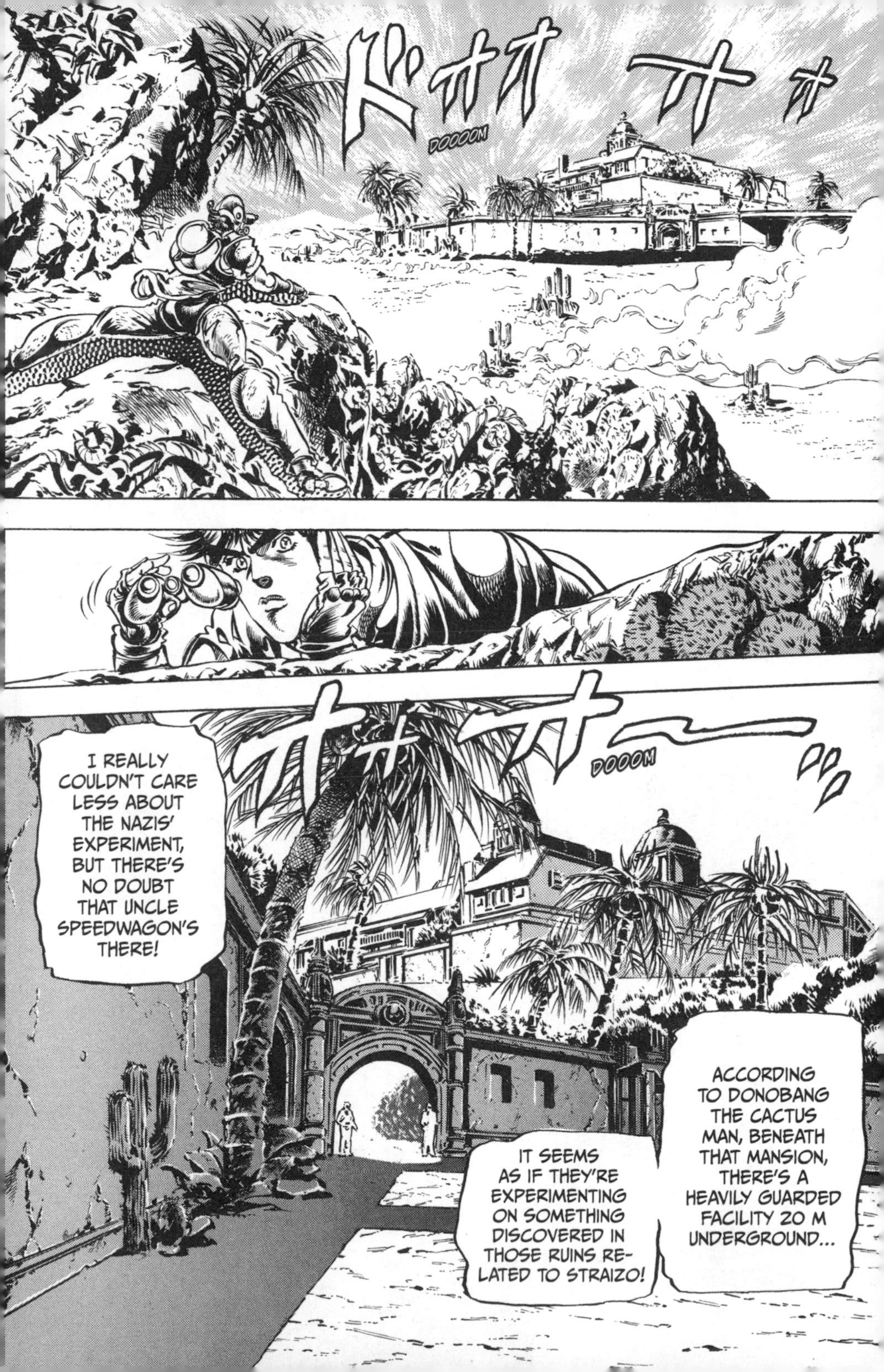
DOOOOM
DOOOM
ACCORDING TO DONOBANG THE CACTUS MAN, BENEATH THAT MANSION, THERE'S A HEAVILY GUARDED FACILITY 20 M UNDERGROUND...
IT SEEMS AS IF THEY'RE EXPERIMENTING ON SOMETHING DISCOVERED IN THOSE RUINS RE-LATED TO STRAIZO!
I REALLY COULDN'T CARE LESS ABOUT THE NAZIS' EXPERIMENT, BUT THERE'S NO DOUBT THAT UNCLE SPEEDWAGON'S THERE!

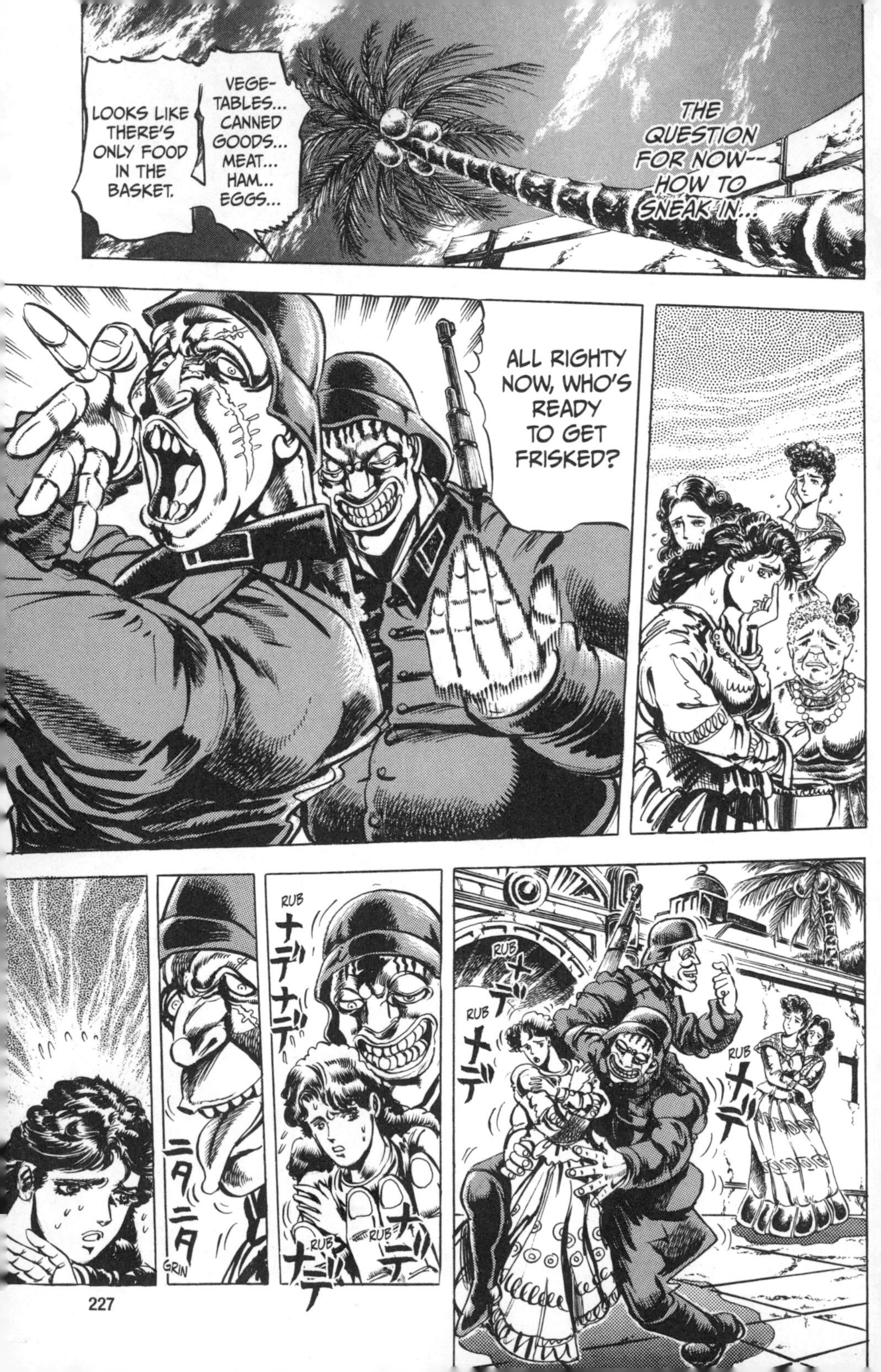

THE QUESTION FOR NOW-- HOW TO SNEAK IN...
VEGE-TABLES... CANNED GOODS... MEAT... HAM... EGGS...
LOOKS LIKE THERE'S ONLY FOOD IN THE BASKET.
ALL RIGHTY NOW, WHO'S READY TO GET FRISKED?
RUB ナデ
RUB ナデ
RUB ナデ
RUB ナデナデ
RUB ナデ
RUB ナデ
ニタニタ GRIN

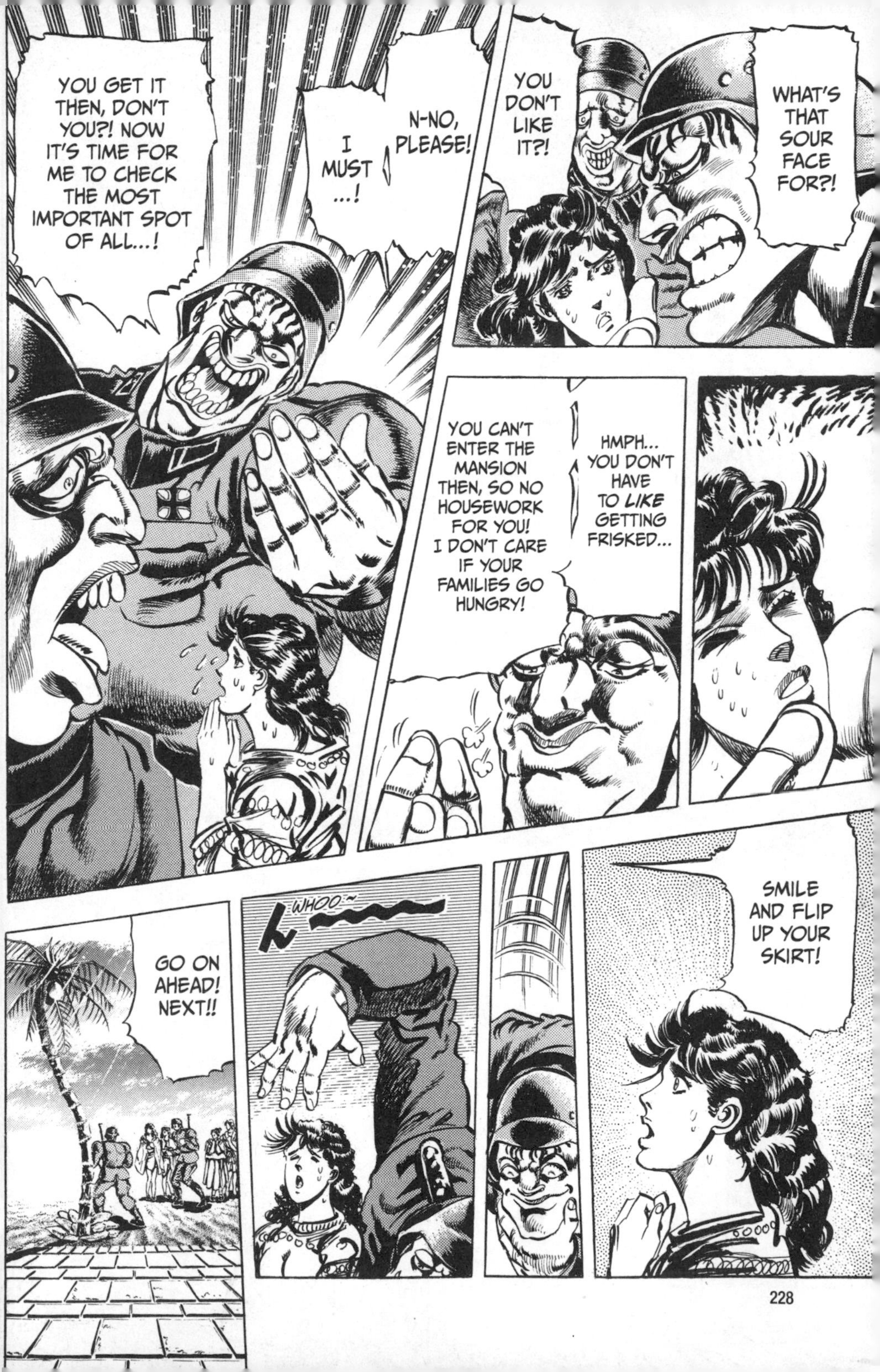
WHAT'S THAT SOUR FACE FOR?!
YOU DON'T LIKE IT?!
HMPH... YOU DON'T HAVE TO *LIKE* GETTING FRISKED...
YOU CAN'T ENTER THE MANSION THEN, SO NO HOUSEWORK FOR YOU! I DON'T CARE IF YOUR FAMILIES GO HUNGRY!
N-NO, PLEASE!
I MUST ...!
YOU GET IT THEN, DON'T YOU?! NOW IT'S TIME FOR ME TO CHECK THE MOST IMPORTANT SPOT OF ALL...!
SMILE AND FLIP UP YOUR SKIRT!
WHOO~
GO ON AHEAD! NEXT!!

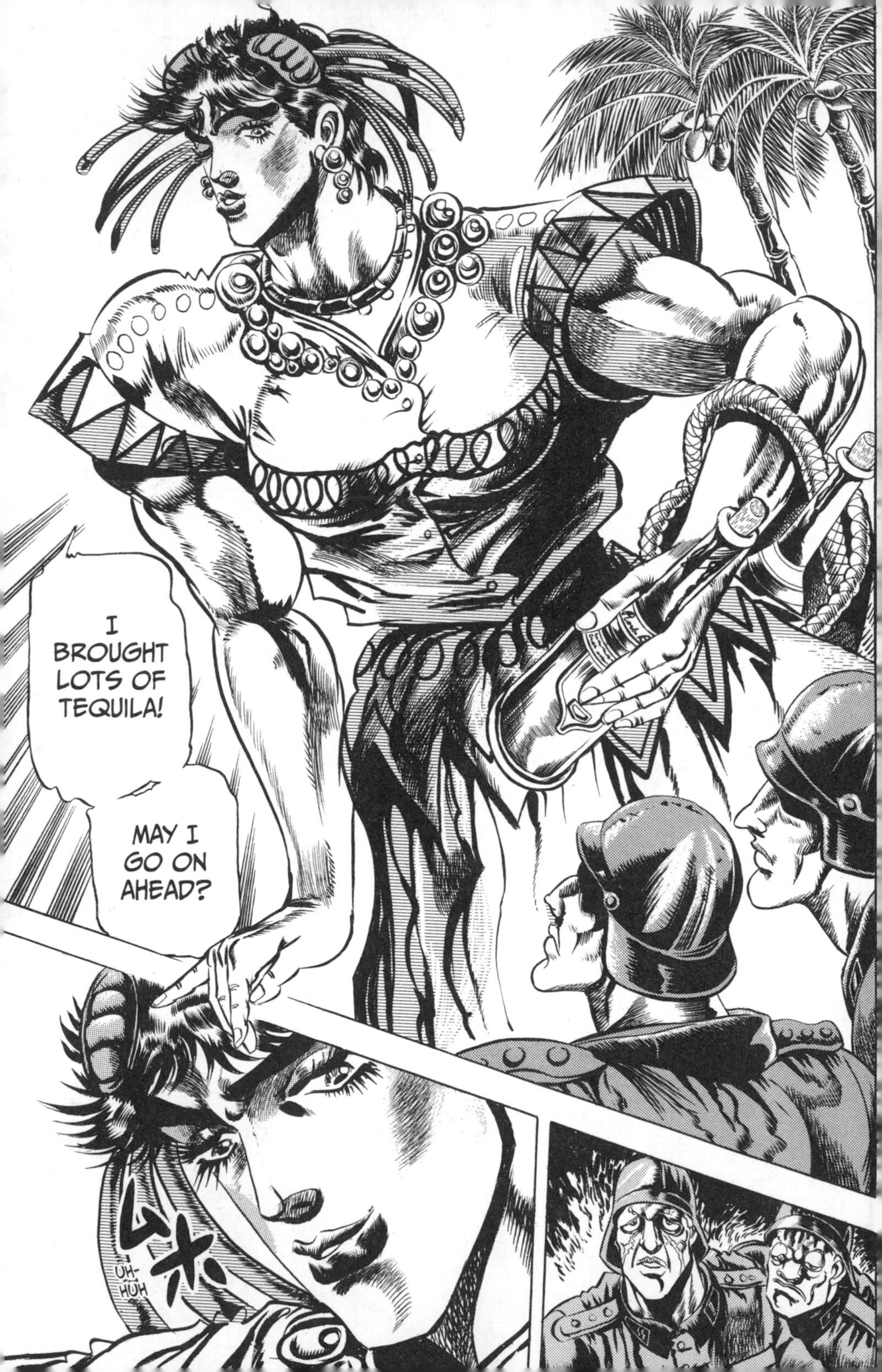
I BROUGHT LOTS OF TEQUILA!
MAY I GO ON AHEAD?
UH-HUH

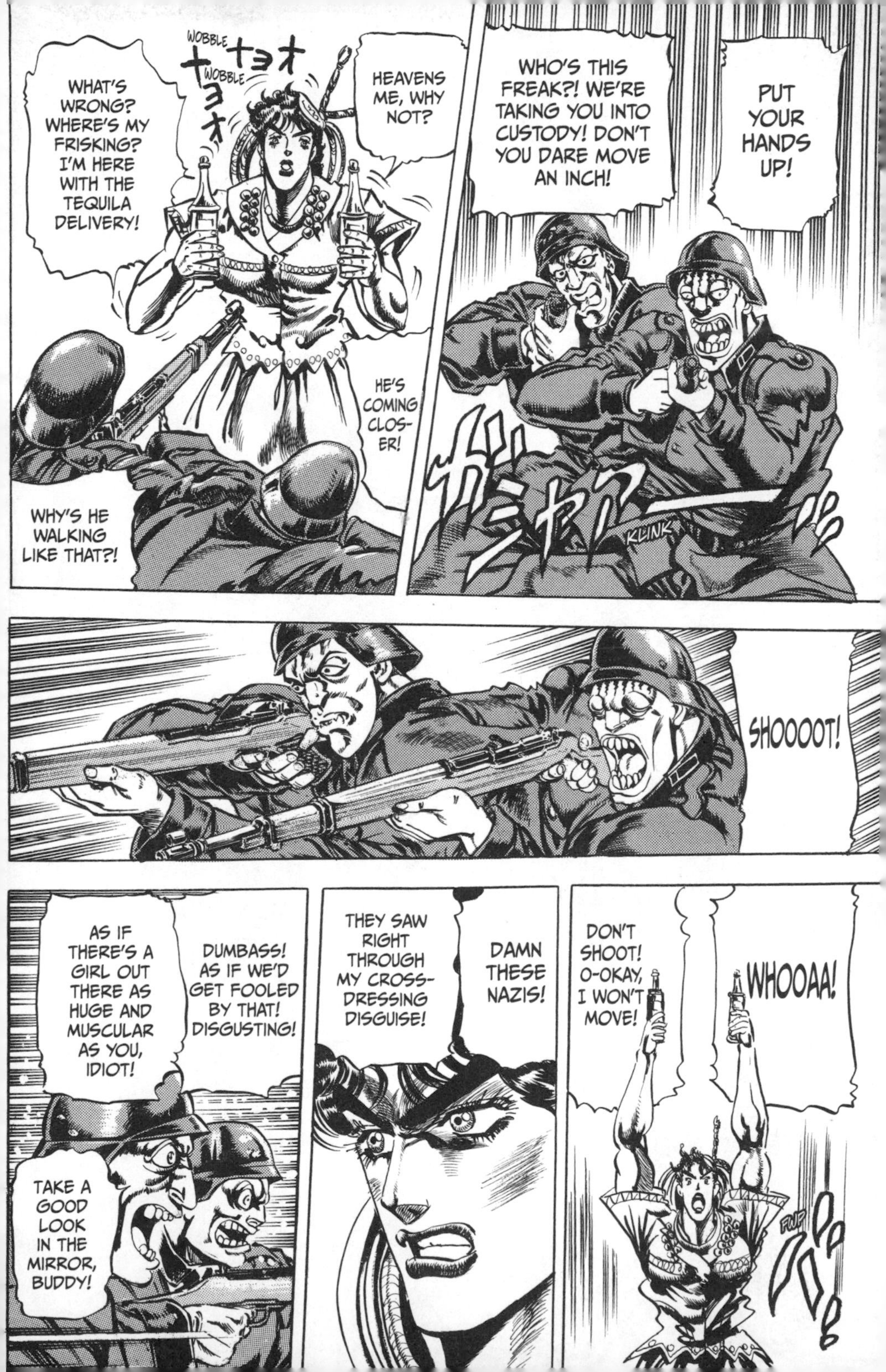
PUT YOUR HANDS UP!
WHO'S THIS FREAK?! WE'RE TAKING YOU INTO CUSTODY! DON'T YOU DARE MOVE AN INCH!
KLINK
HEAVENS ME, WHY NOT?
WOBBLE
ナヨオ
WOBBLE
ナヨオ
WHAT'S WRONG? WHERE'S MY FRISKING? I'M HERE WITH THE TEQUILA DELIVERY!
HE'S COMING CLOSER!
WHY'S HE WALKING LIKE THAT?!
SHOOOOT!
WHOOAA!
DON'T SHOOT! O-OKAY, I WON'T MOVE!
FWP
DAMN THESE NAZIS!
THEY SAW RIGHT THROUGH MY CROSS-DRESSING DISGUISE!
DUMBASS! AS IF WE'D GET FOOLED BY THAT! DISGUSTING!
AS IF THERE'S A GIRL OUT THERE AS HUGE AND MUSCULAR AS YOU, IDIOT!
TAKE A GOOD LOOK IN THE MIRROR, BUDDY!

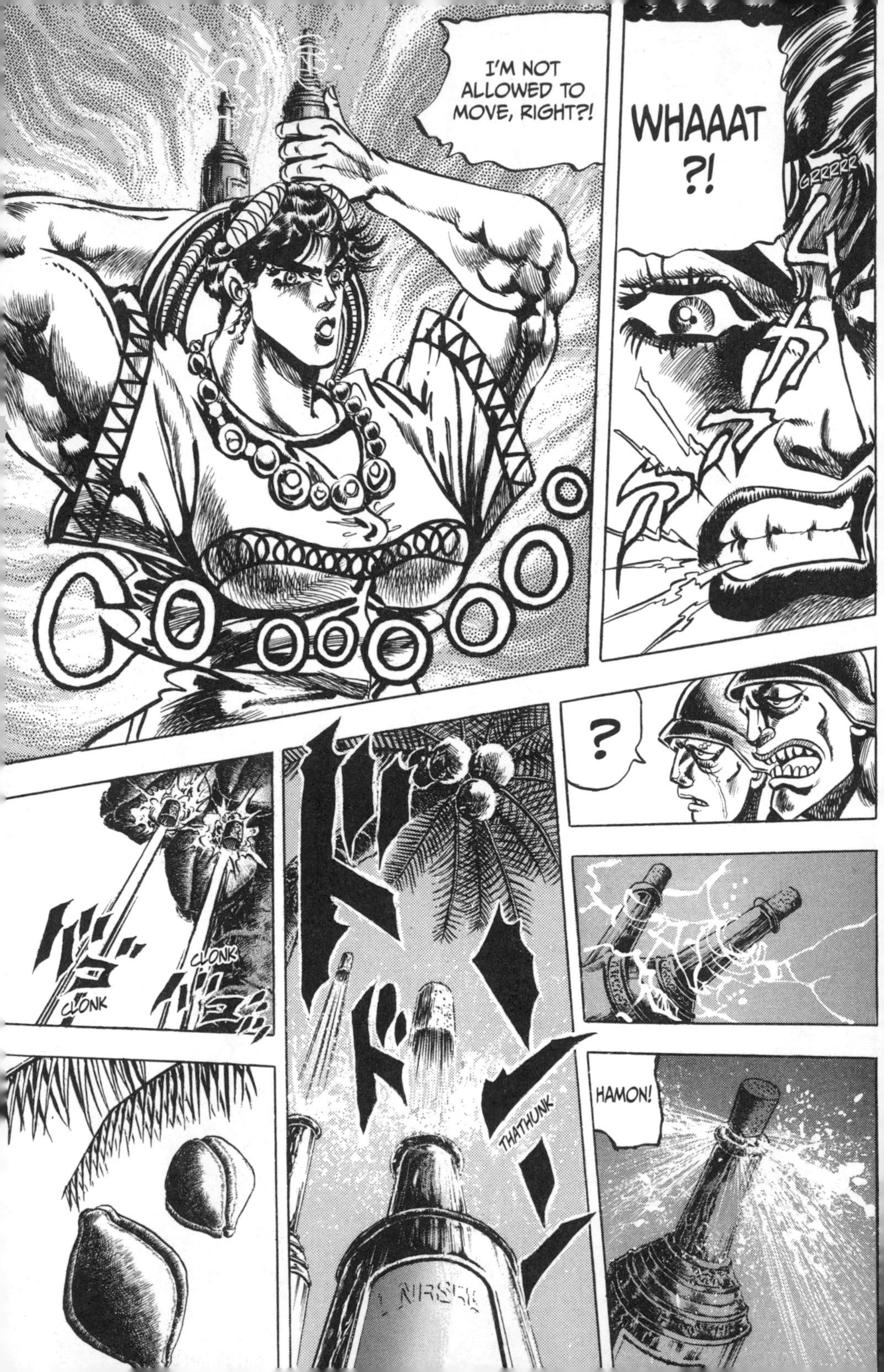
WHAAAT ?!
GRRRRR
I'M NOT ALLOWED TO MOVE, RIGHT?!
?
HAMON!
THATHUNK
CLONK
CLONK

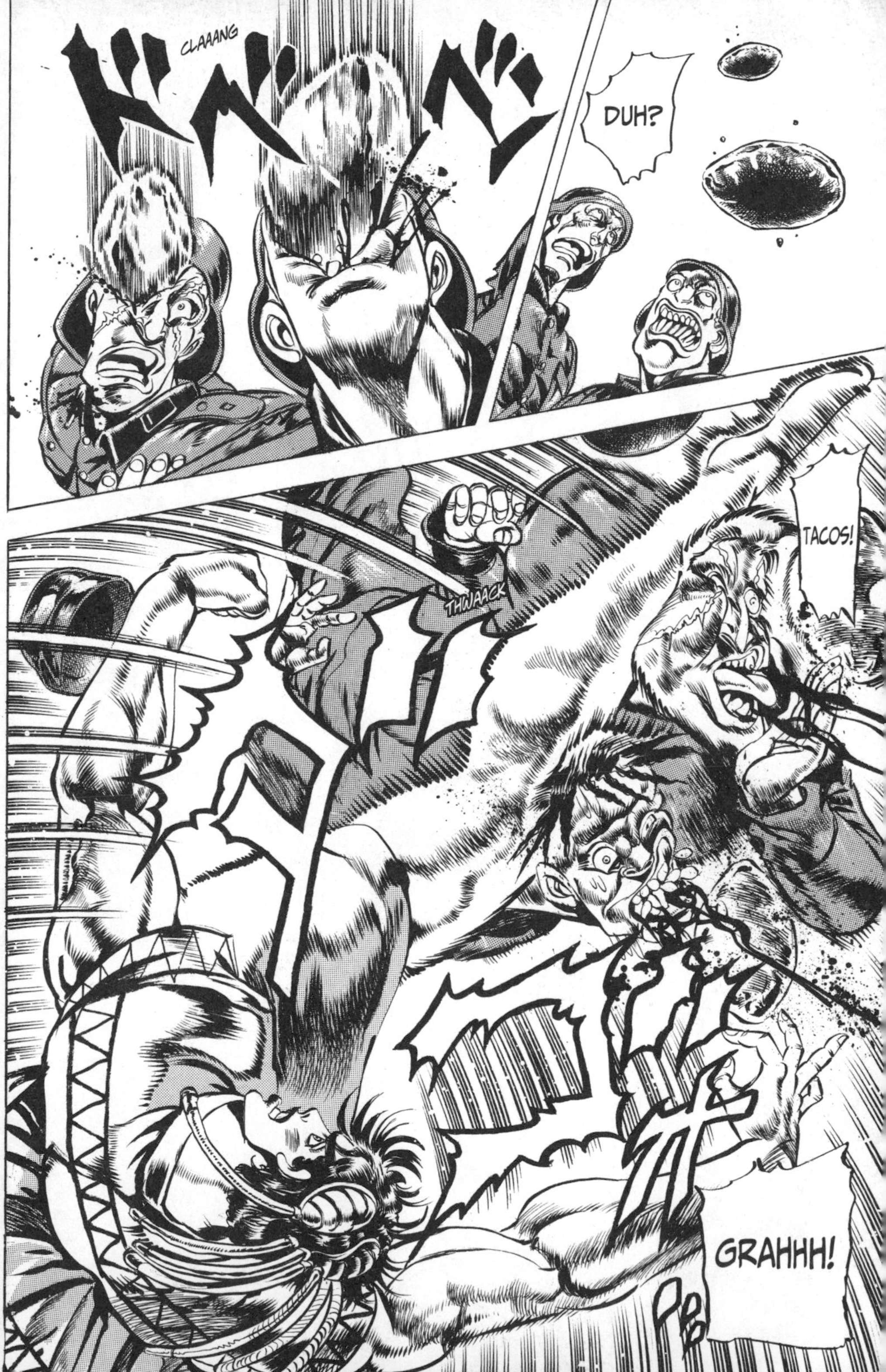
DUH?
CLAAANG
TACOS!
THWAACK
GRAHHH!

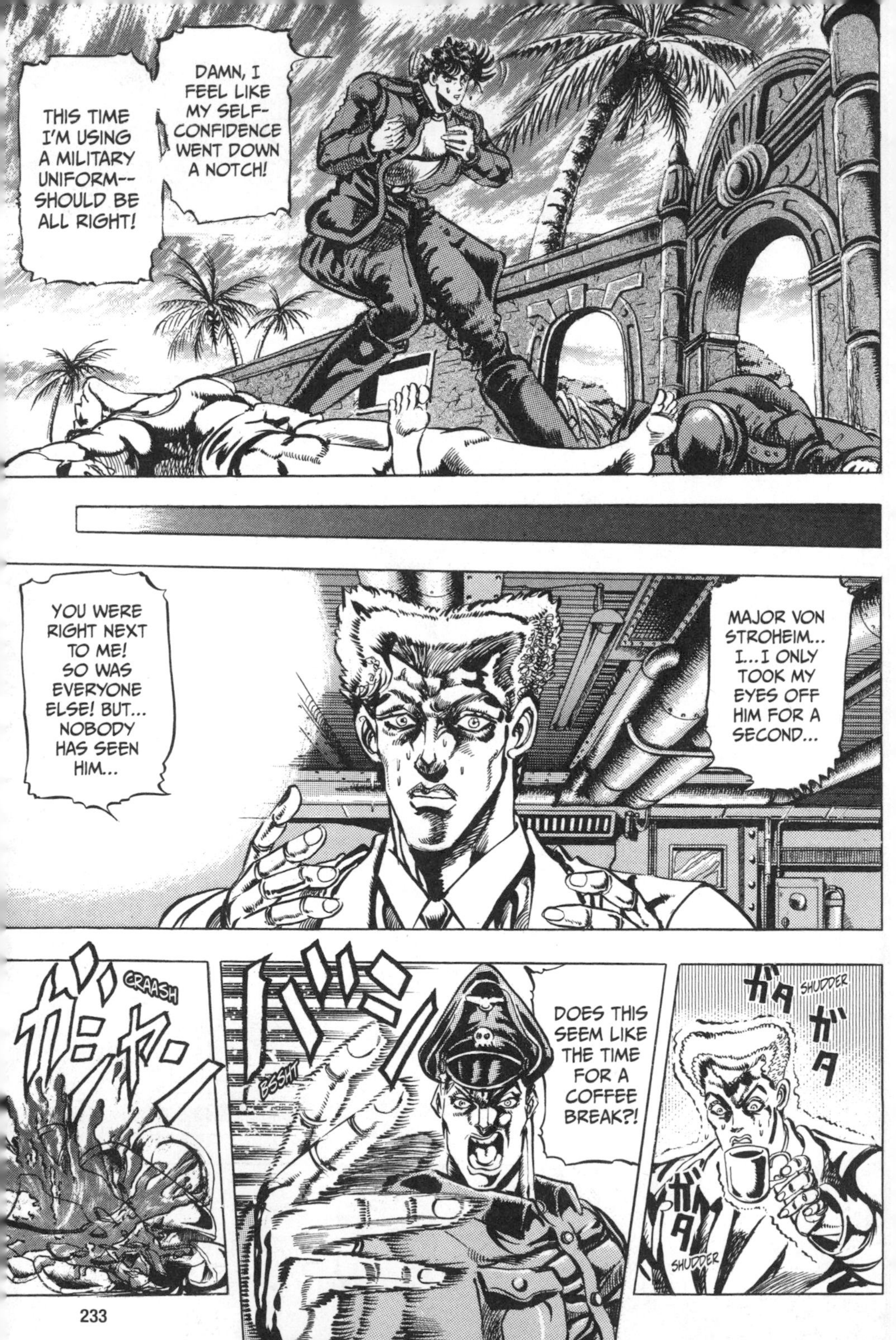
DAMN, I FEEL LIKE MY SELF-CONFIDENCE WENT DOWN A NOTCH!
THIS TIME I'M USING A MILITARY UNIFORM--SHOULD BE ALL RIGHT!
MAJOR VON STROHEIM... I...I ONLY TOOK MY EYES OFF HIM FOR A SECOND...
YOU WERE RIGHT NEXT TO ME! SO WAS EVERYONE ELSE! BUT... NOBODY HAS SEEN HIM...
ガタ
SHUDDER
ガタ
ガタ
SHUDDER
DOES THIS SEEM LIKE THE TIME FOR A COFFEE BREAK?!
BSSHT
CRAASH

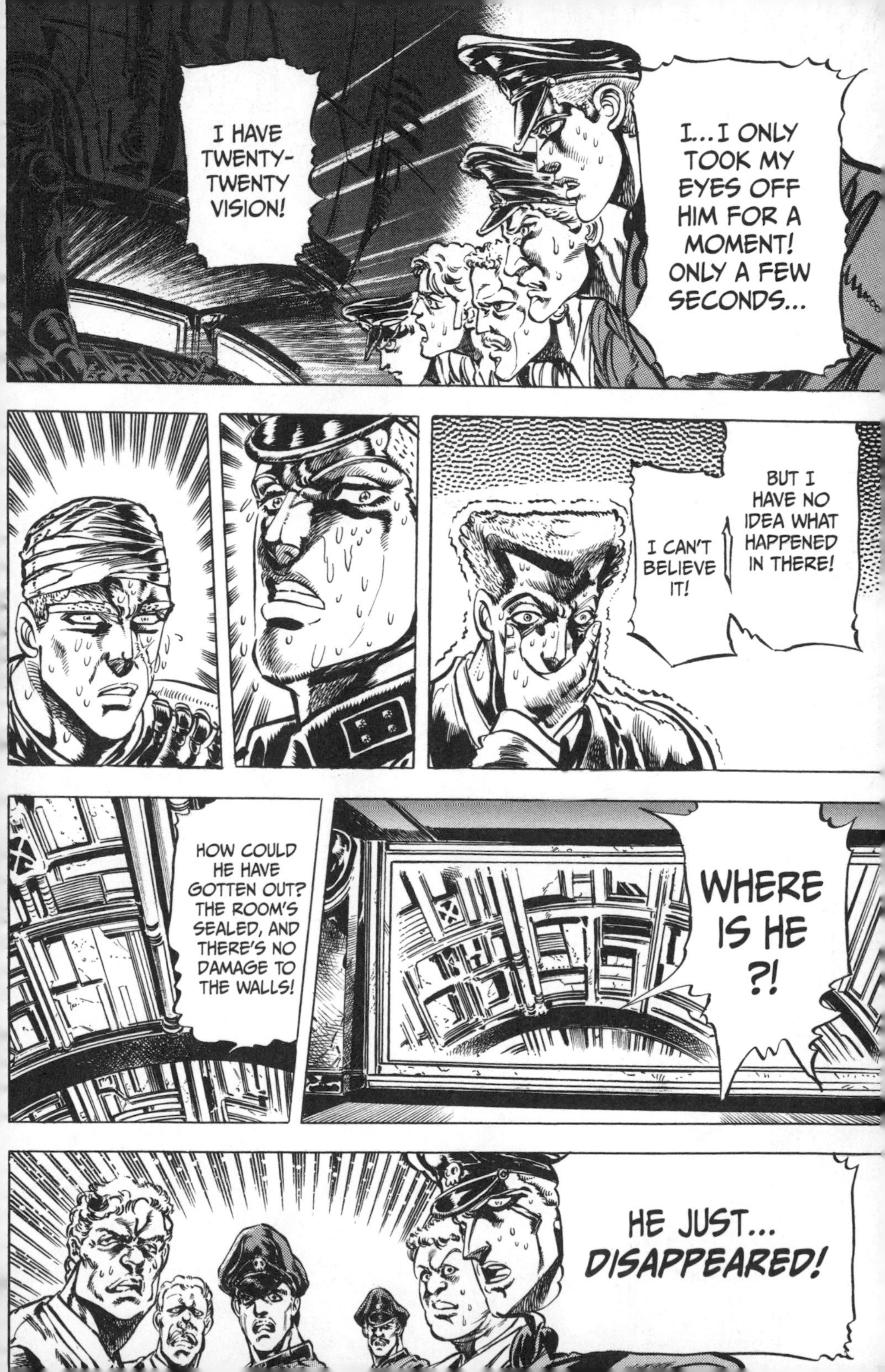
I...I ONLY TOOK MY EYES OFF HIM FOR A MOMENT! ONLY A FEW SECONDS...
I HAVE TWENTY-TWENTY VISION!
BUT I HAVE NO IDEA WHAT HAPPENED IN THERE!
I CAN'T BELIEVE IT!
WHERE IS HE ?!
HOW COULD HE HAVE GOTTEN OUT? THE ROOM'S SEALED, AND THERE'S NO DAMAGE TO THE WALLS!
HE JUST... *DISAPPEARED!*

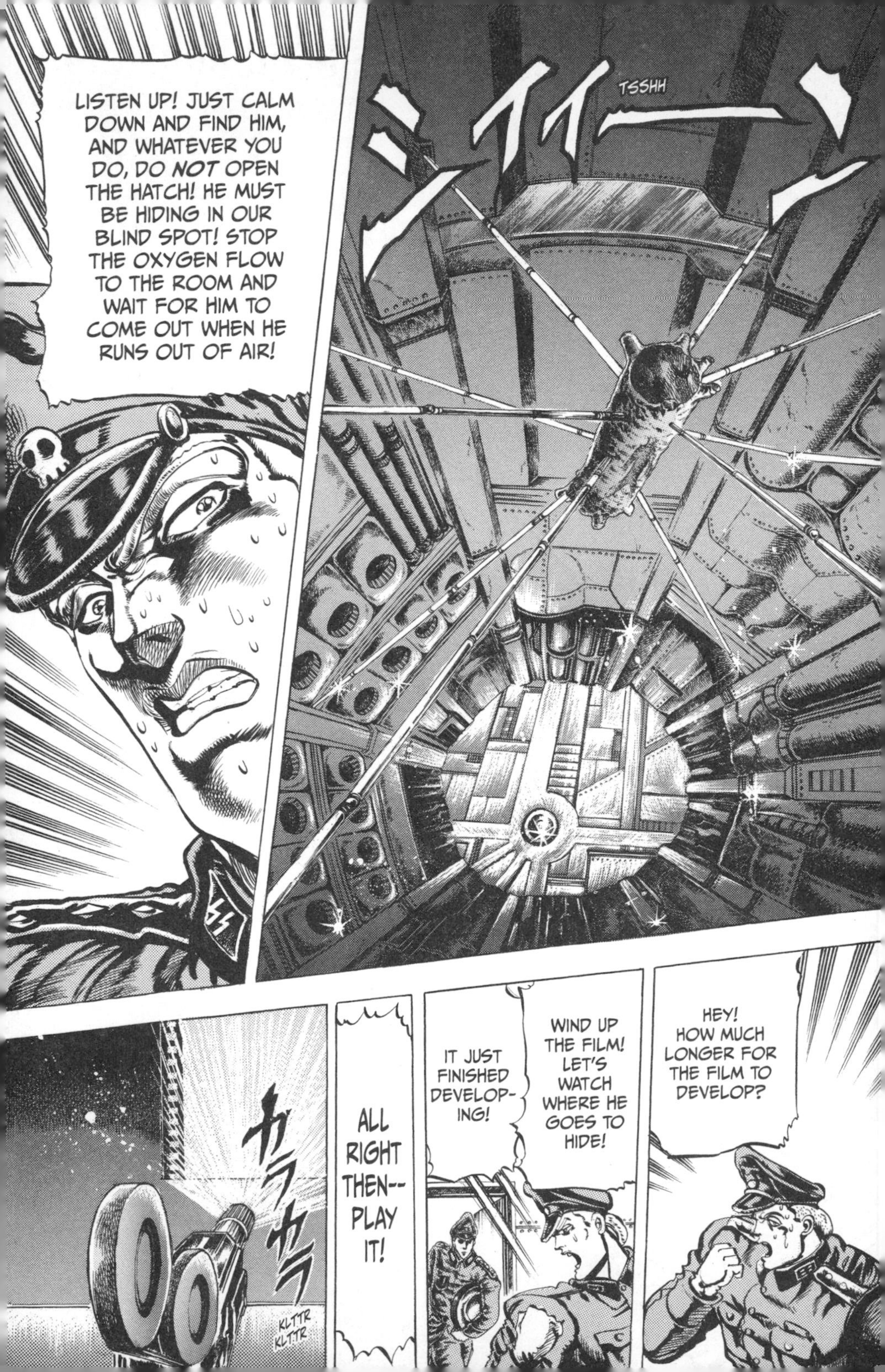
シイイーン
TSSHH
LISTEN UP! JUST CALM DOWN AND FIND HIM, AND WHATEVER YOU DO, DO *NOT* OPEN THE HATCH! HE MUST BE HIDING IN OUR BLIND SPOT! STOP THE OXYGEN FLOW TO THE ROOM AND WAIT FOR HIM TO COME OUT WHEN HE RUNS OUT OF AIR!
HEY! HOW MUCH LONGER FOR THE FILM TO DEVELOP?
WIND UP THE FILM! LET'S WATCH WHERE HE GOES TO HIDE!
IT JUST FINISHED DEVELOP-ING!
ALL RIGHT THEN-- PLAY IT!
カラカラ
KLTTR KLTTR

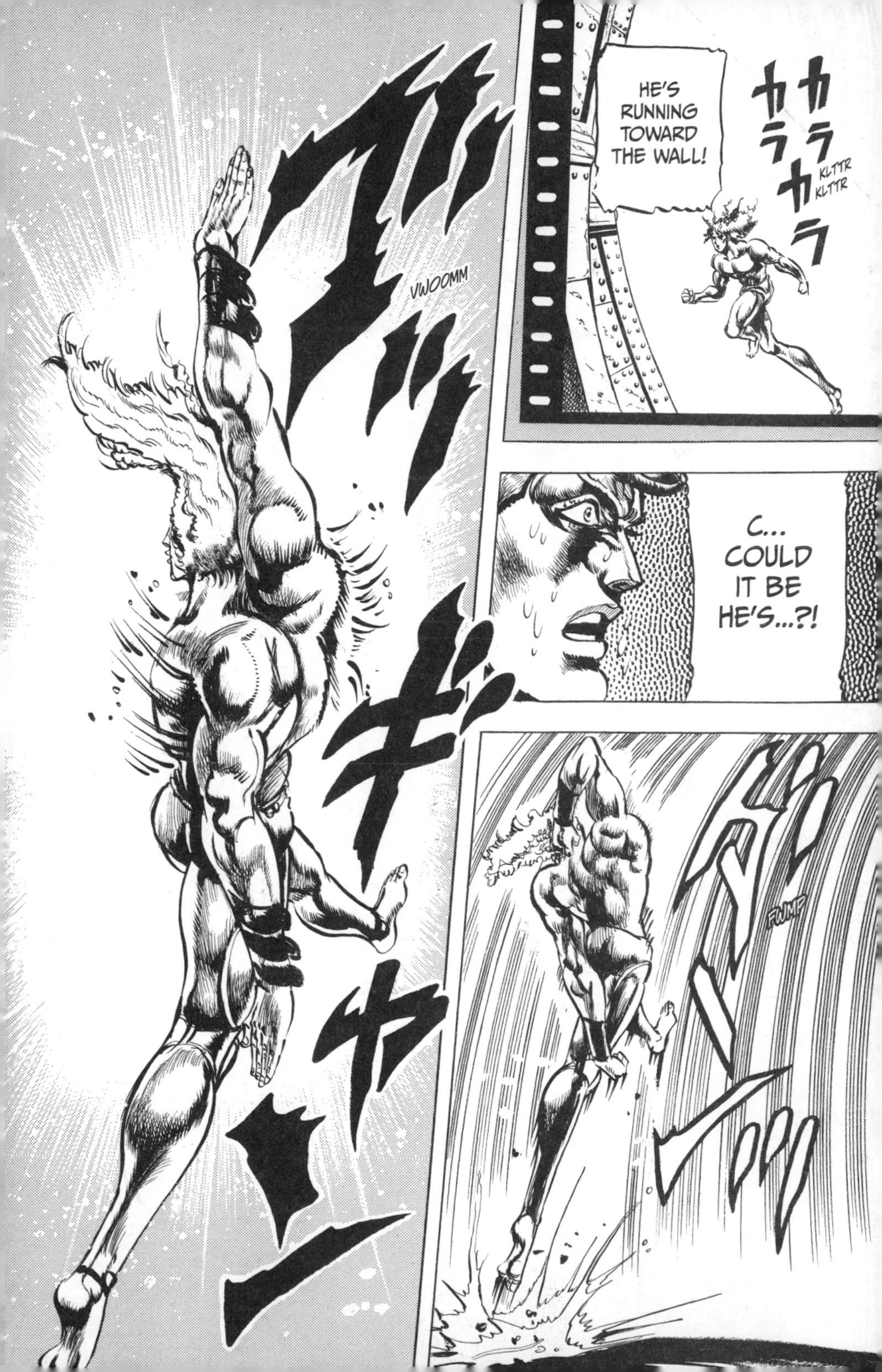
HE'S RUNNING TOWARD THE WALL!
カラカラカラ
KLTTR KLTTR
C... COULD IT BE HE'S...?!
FWUMP
VWOOMM

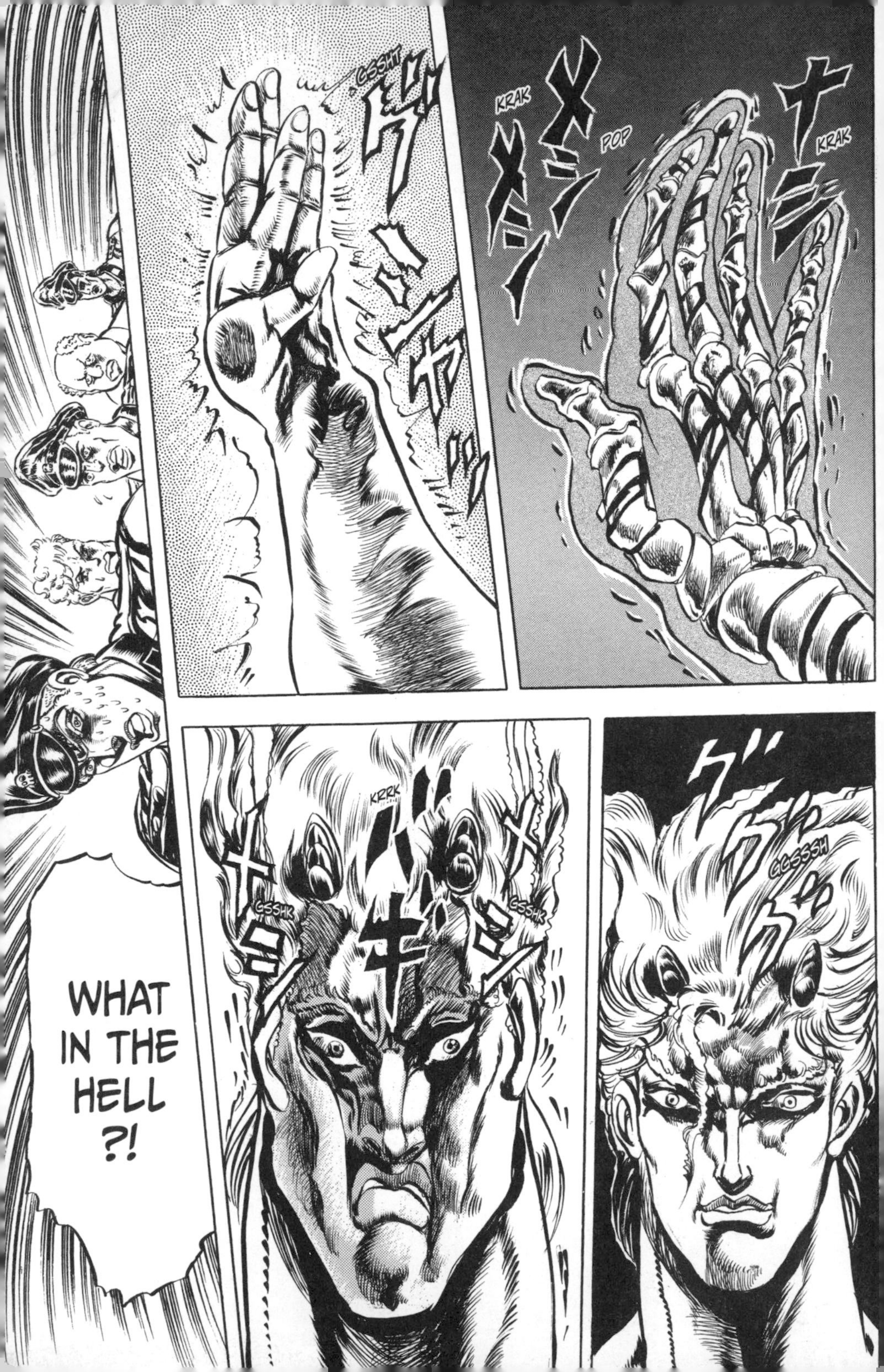
KRAK
POP
KRAK
GSSHT
GSSSSH
KRRK
GSSHK
GSSHK
WHAT IN THE HELL ?!

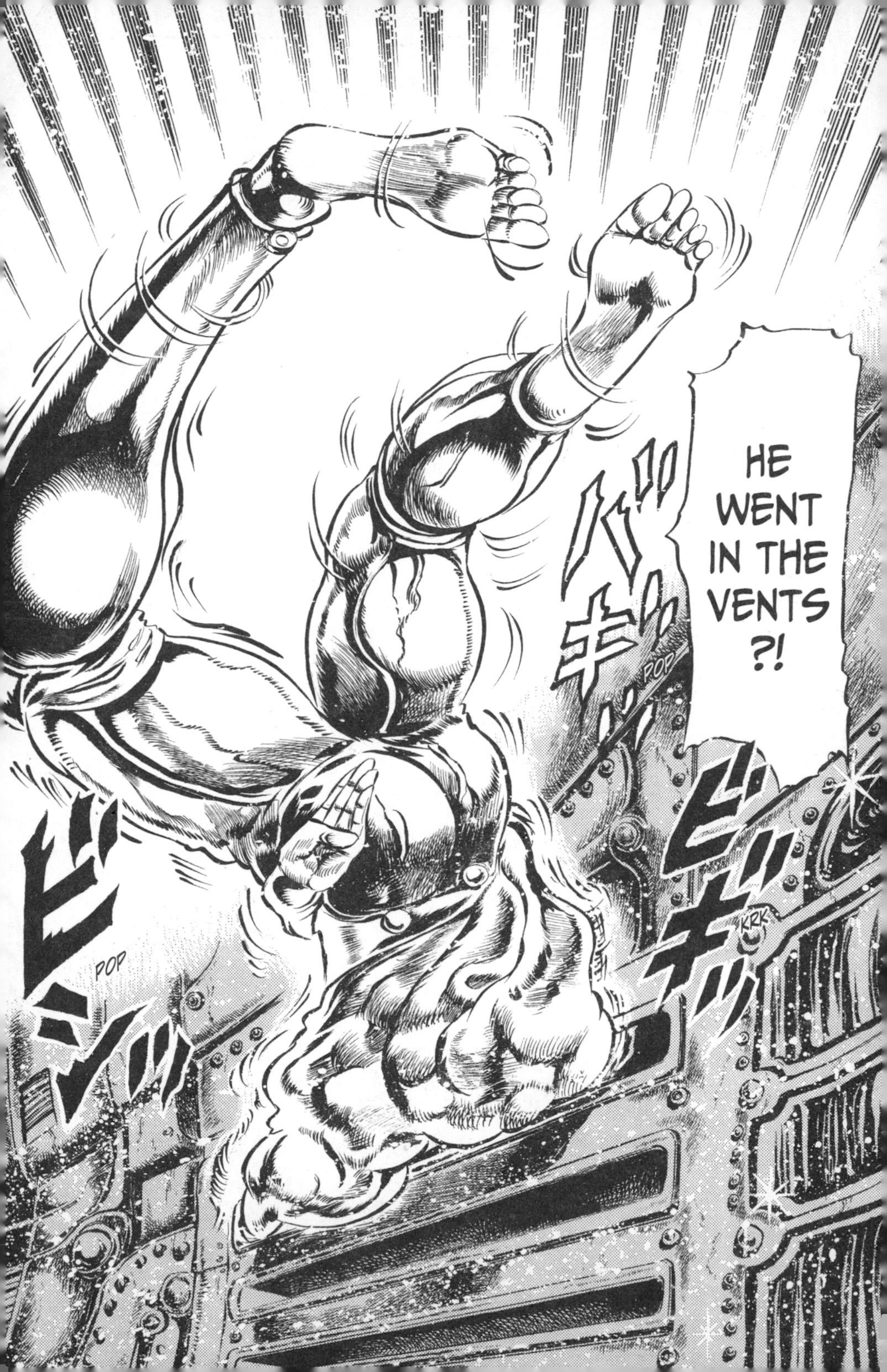
HE WENT IN THE VENTS ?!
POP
KRK
POP

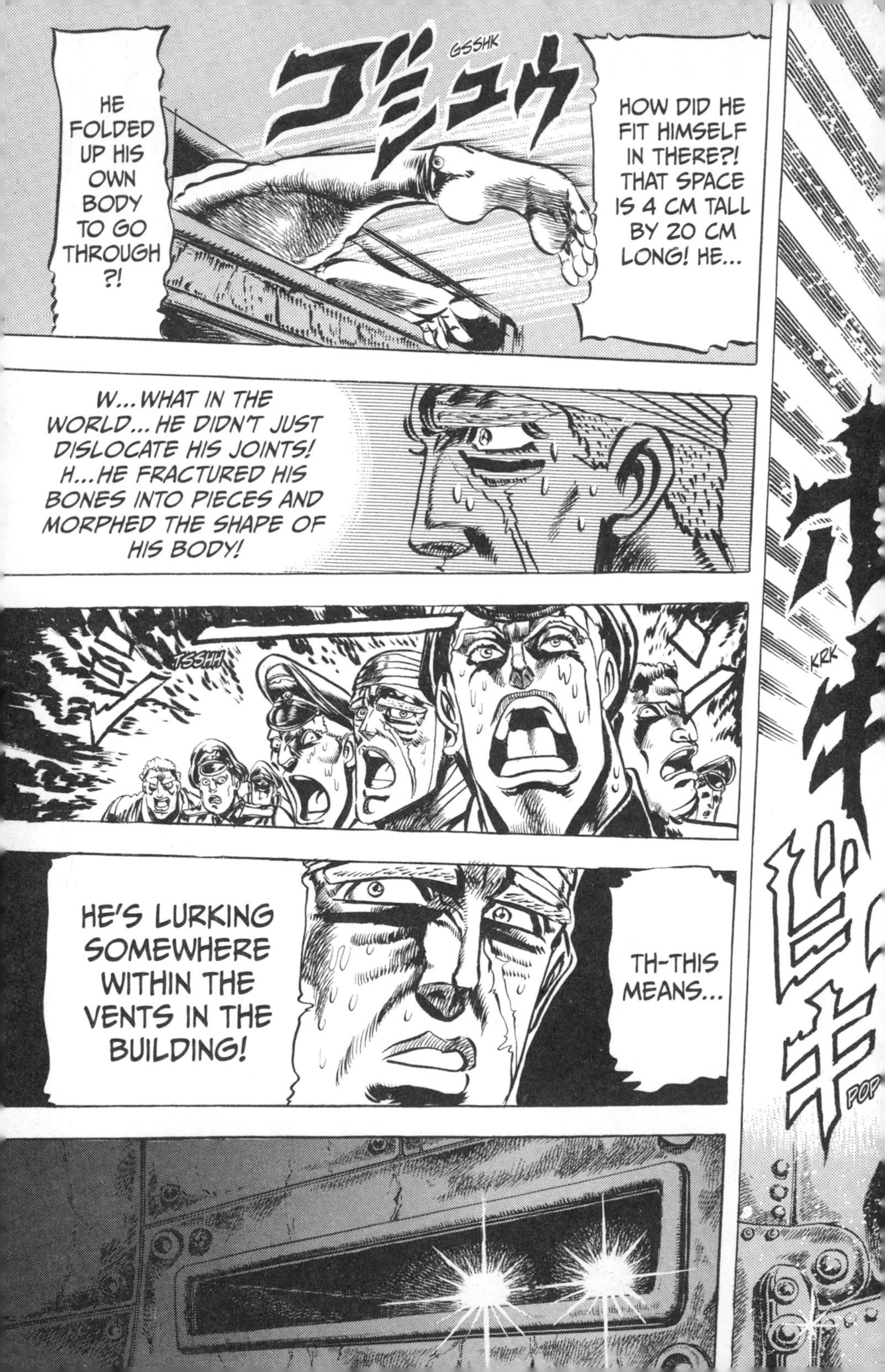
KRK
POP
HOW DID HE FIT HIMSELF IN THERE?! THAT SPACE IS 4 CM TALL BY 20 CM LONG! HE...
GSSHK
HE FOLDED UP HIS OWN BODY TO GO THROUGH ?!
W...WHAT IN THE WORLD... HE DIDN'T JUST DISLOCATE HIS JOINTS! H...HE FRACTURED HIS BONES INTO PIECES AND MORPHED THE SHAPE OF HIS BODY!
TSSHH
TH-THIS MEANS...
HE'S LURKING SOMEWHERE WITHIN THE VENTS IN THE BUILDING!

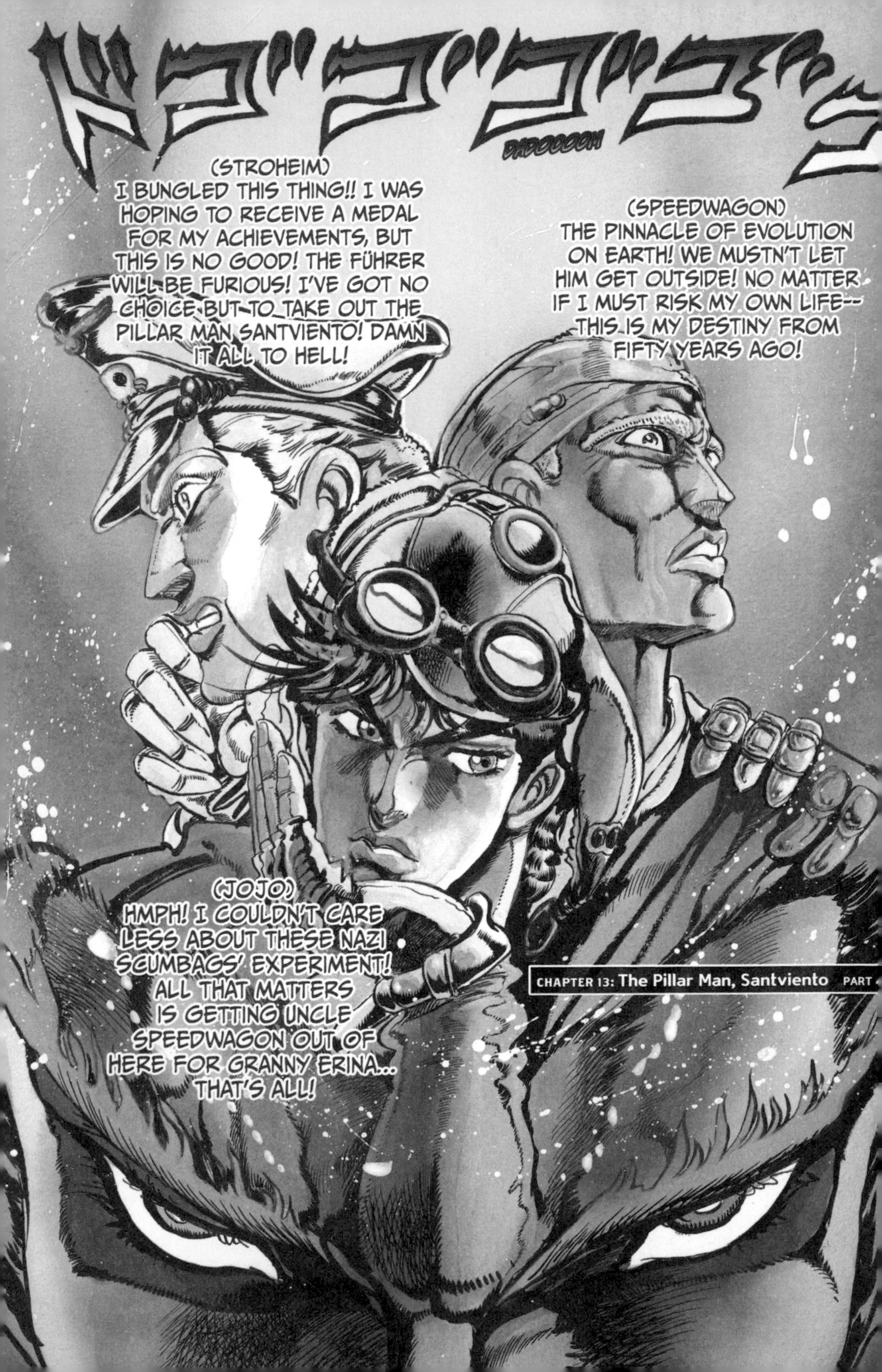
DADOOOOOM
(SPEEDWAGON) THE PINNACLE OF EVOLUTION ON EARTH! WE MUSTN'T LET HIM GET OUTSIDE! NO MATTER IF I MUST RISK MY OWN LIFE-- THIS IS MY DESTINY FROM FIFTY YEARS AGO!
(STROHEIM) I BUNGLED THIS THING!! I WAS HOPING TO RECEIVE A MEDAL FOR MY ACHIEVEMENTS, BUT THIS IS NO GOOD! THE FÜHRER WILL BE FURIOUS! I'VE GOT NO CHOICE BUT TO TAKE OUT THE PILLAR MAN SANTVIENTO! DAMN IT ALL TO HELL!
(JOJO) HMPH! I COULDN'T CARE LESS ABOUT THESE NAZI SCUMBAGS' EXPERIMENT! ALL THAT MATTERS IS GETTING UNCLE SPEEDWAGON OUT OF HERE FOR GRANNY ERINA... THAT'S ALL!
CHAPTER 13: The Pillar Man, Santviento PART

CHAPTER 13: The Pillar Man, Santviento PART 4

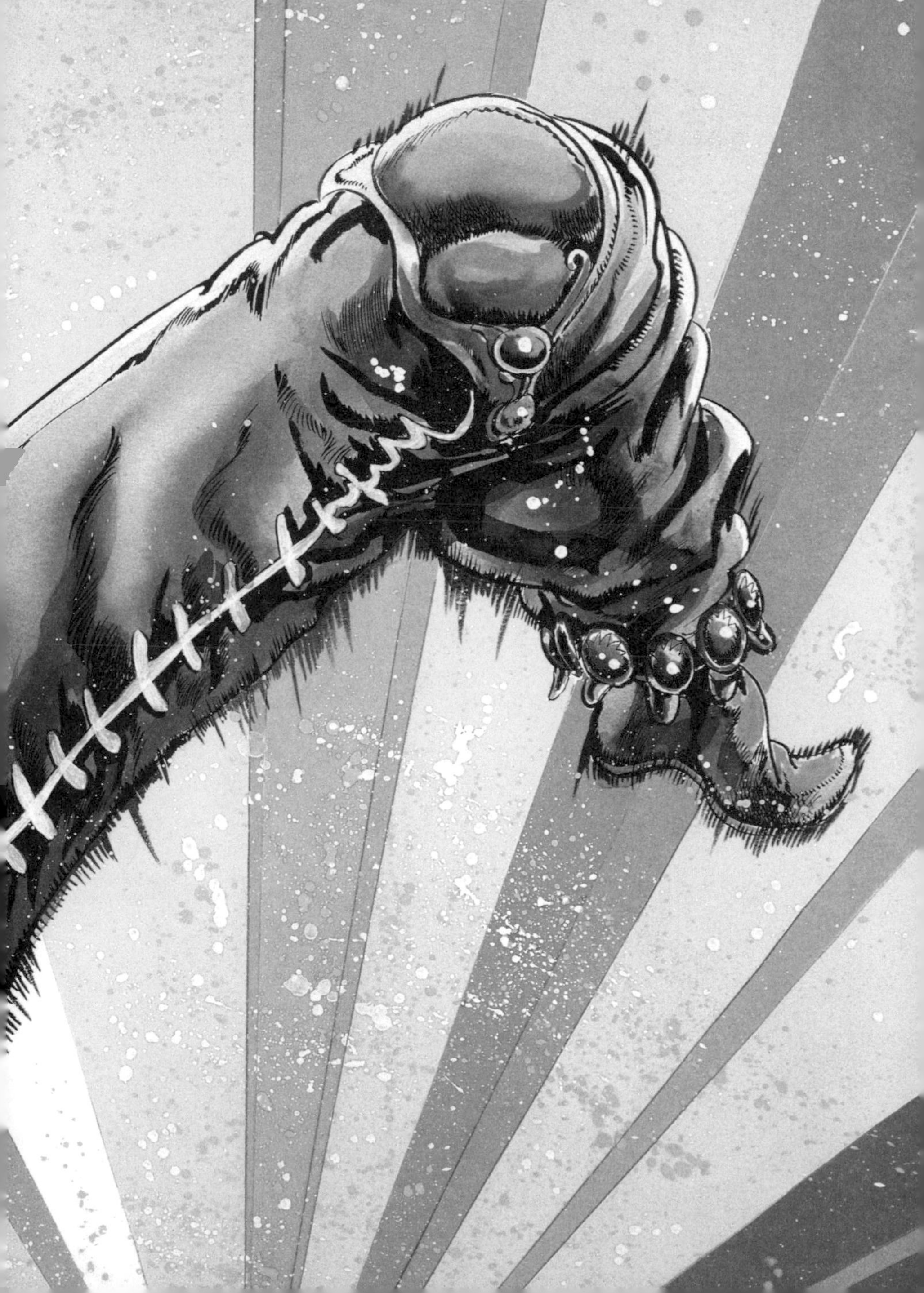

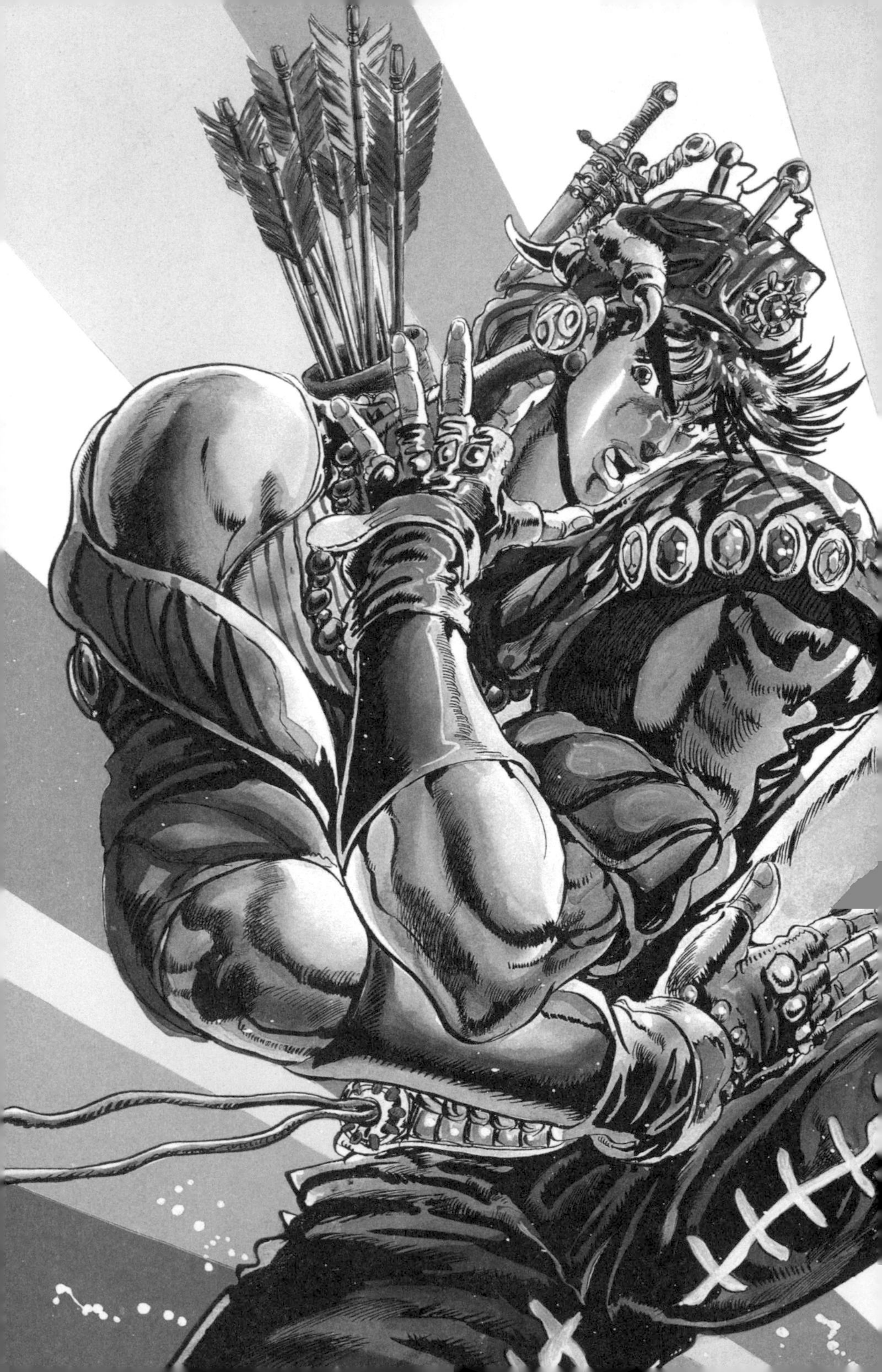

JoJo's

BIZARRE ADVENTURE

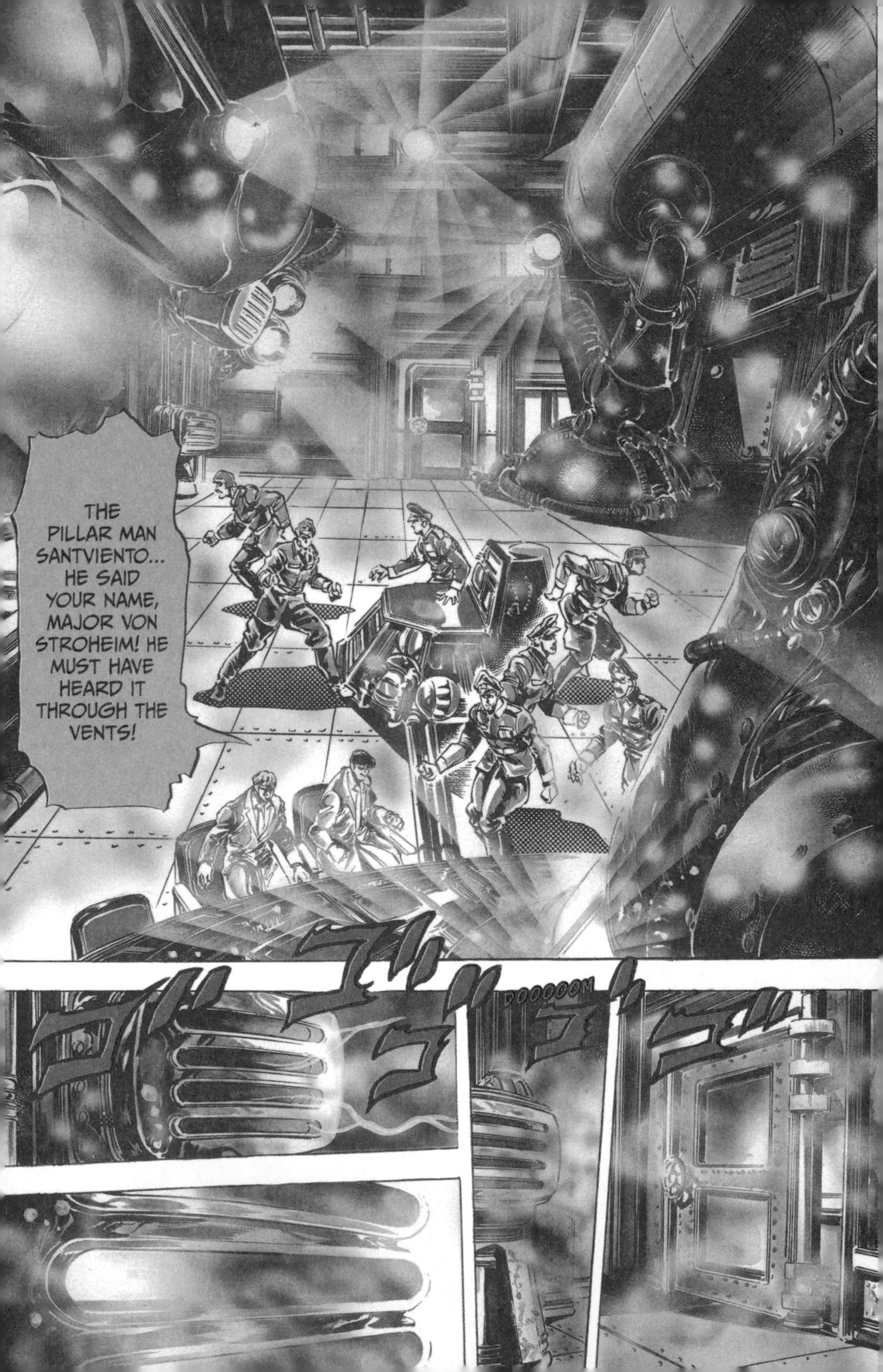
THE PILLAR MAN SANTVIENTO... HE SAID YOUR NAME, MAJOR VON STROHEIM! HE MUST HAVE HEARD IT THROUGH THE VENTS!
DOOOOOM

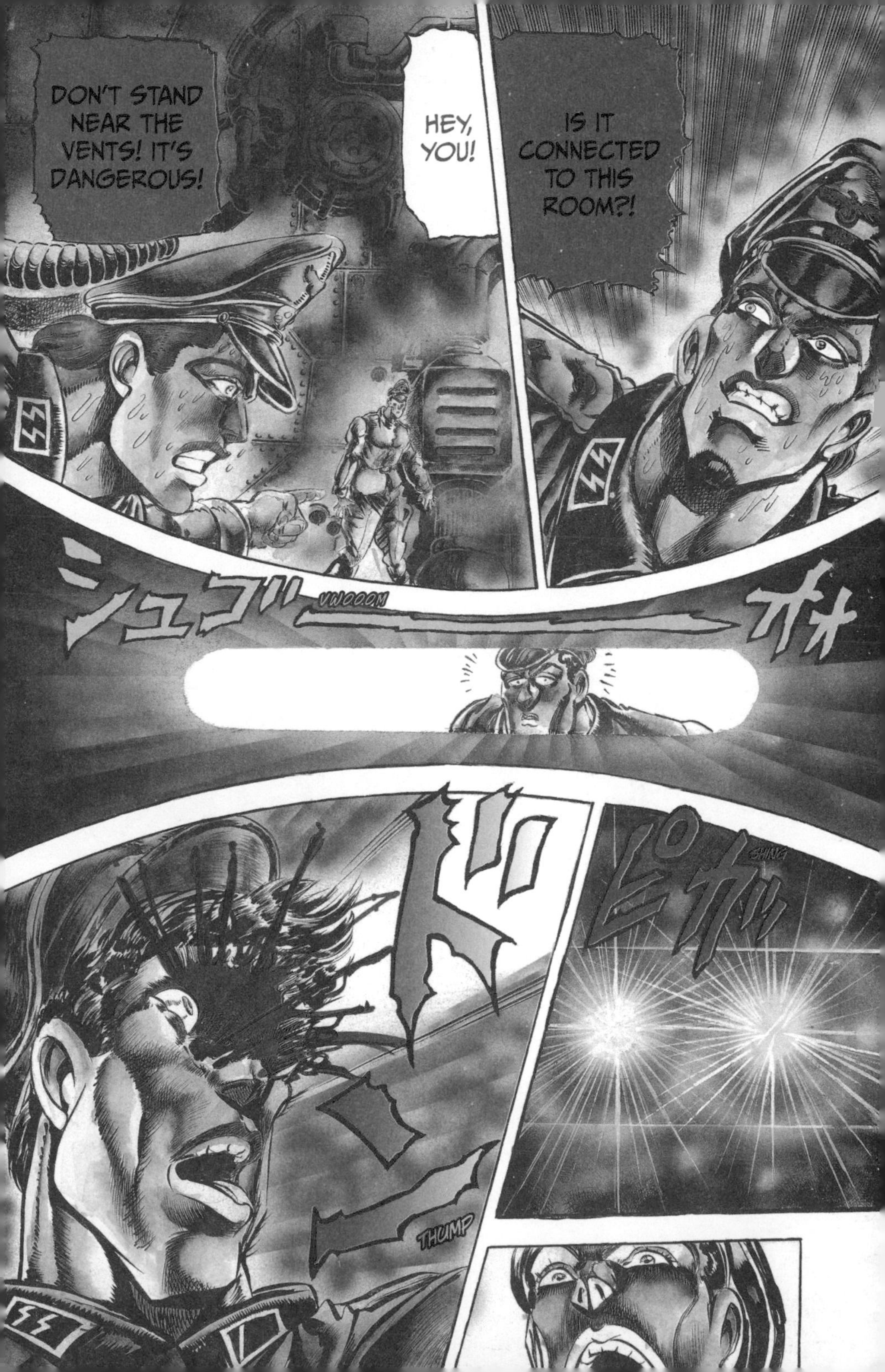
IS IT CONNECTED TO THIS ROOM?!
HEY, YOU!
DON'T STAND NEAR THE VENTS! IT'S DANGEROUS!
シュゴォーーーオオ
VWOOOM
ピカッ
SHING
ドン
THUMP

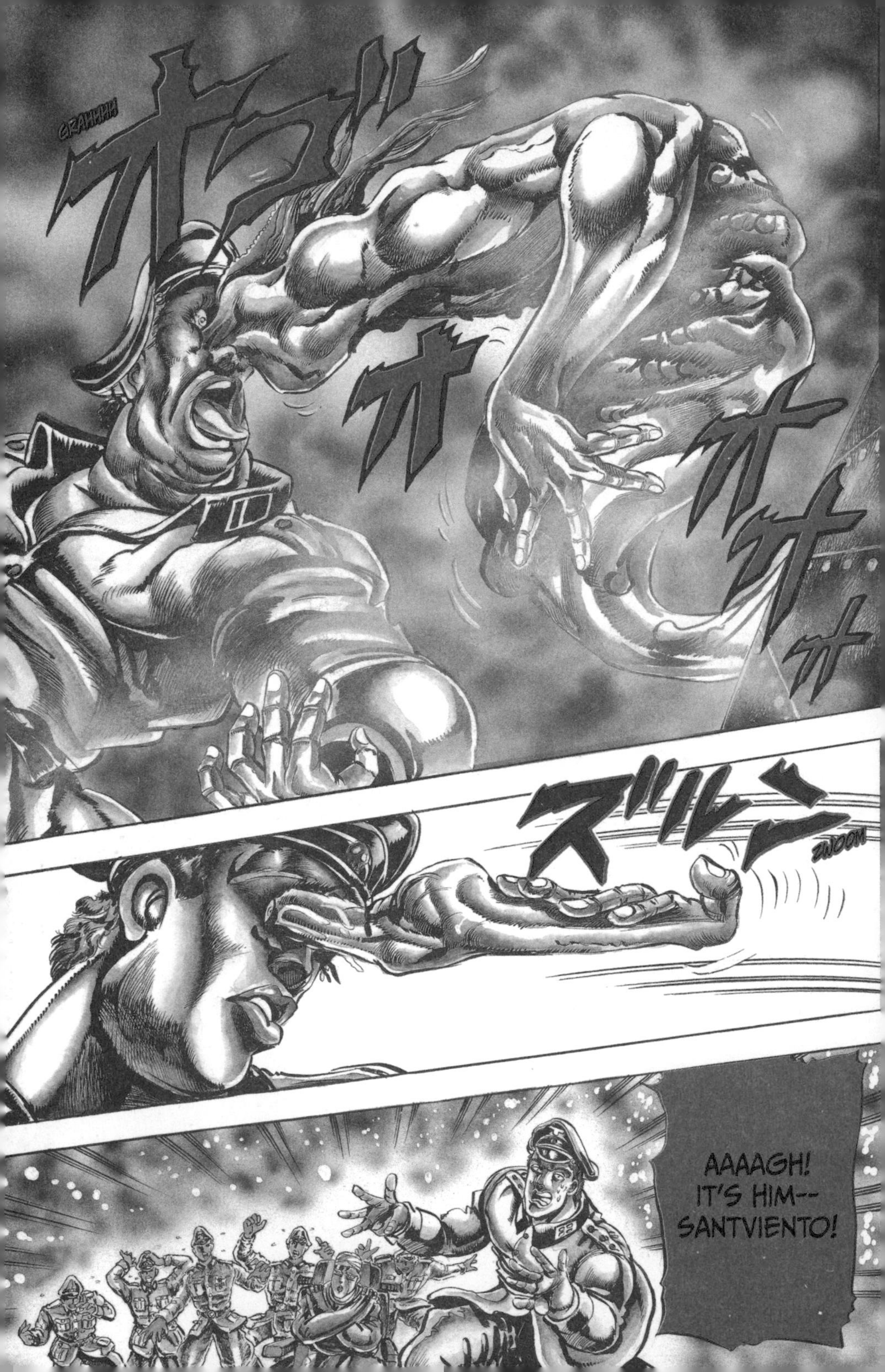
GRAHHHH
ZWOOM
AAAAGH!
IT'S HIM--
SANTVIENTO!

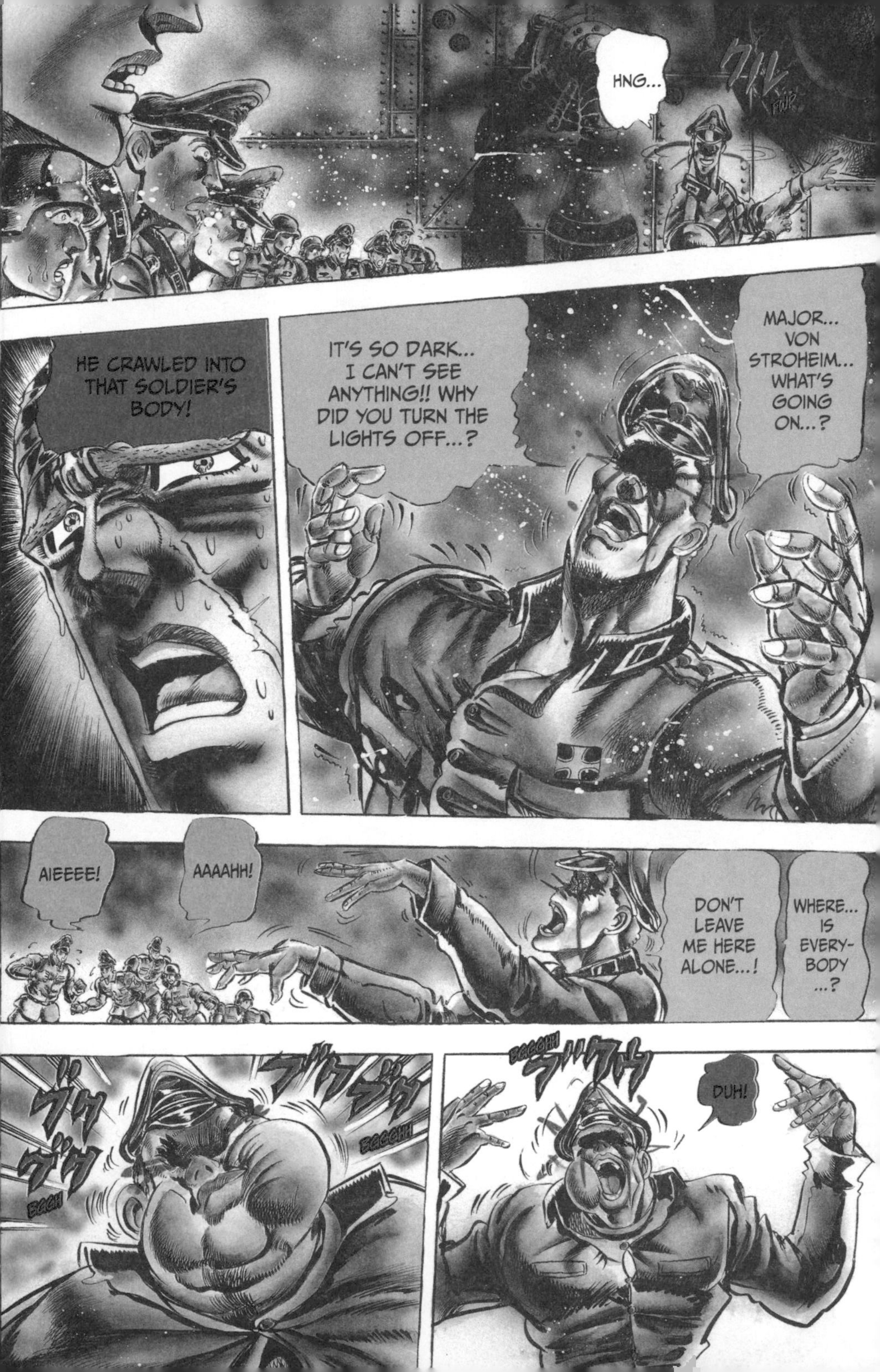
HNG...
FWP
MAJOR... VON STROHEIM... WHAT'S GOING ON...?
IT'S SO DARK... I CAN'T SEE ANYTHING!! WHY DID YOU TURN THE LIGHTS OFF...?
HE CRAWLED INTO THAT SOLDIER'S BODY!
WHERE... IS EVERY-BODY ...?
DON'T LEAVE ME HERE ALONE...!
AAAAHH!
AIEEEE!
BGGGHH
DUH!
BGGGHH
BGGH

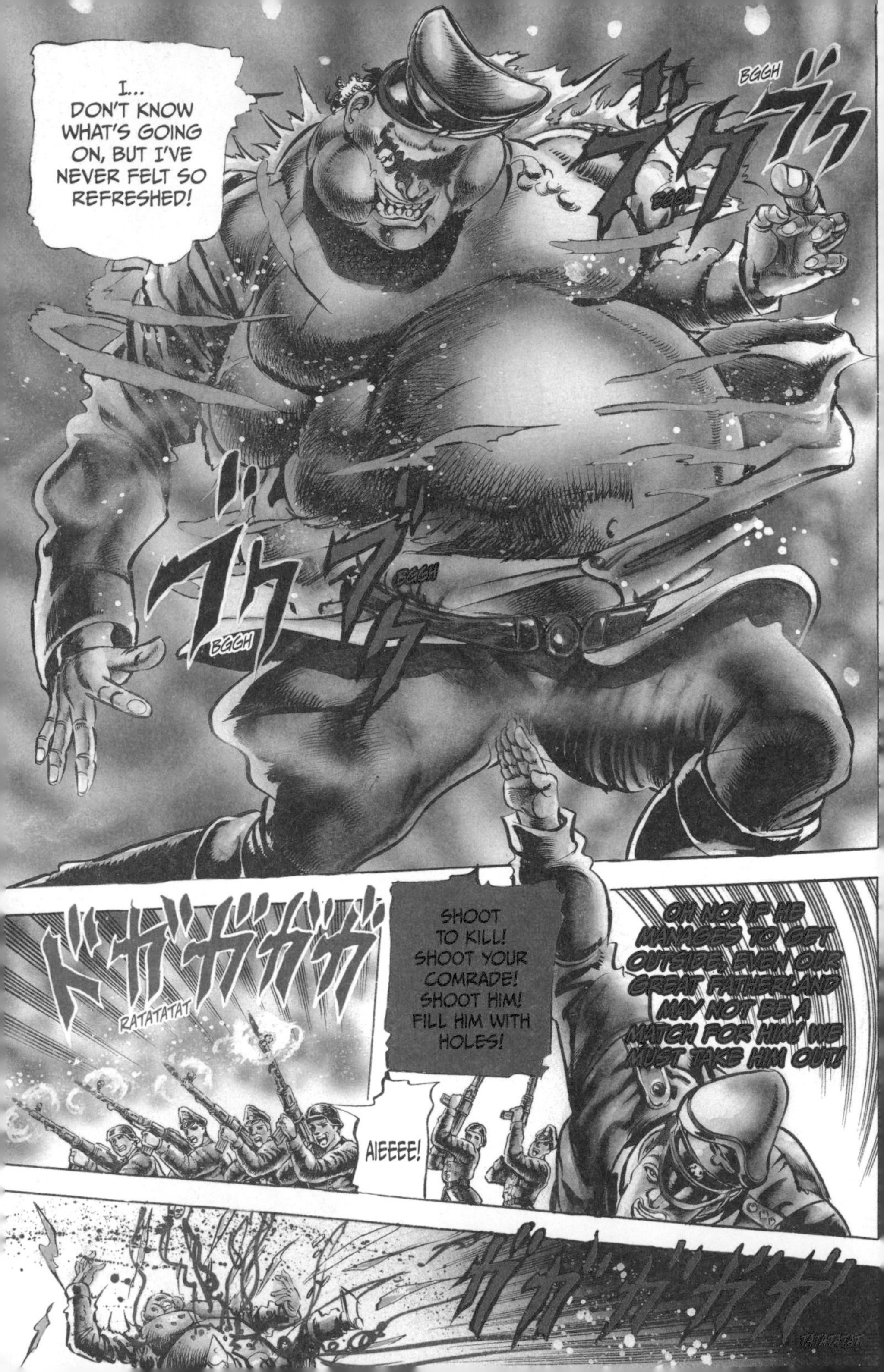
I... DON'T KNOW WHAT'S GOING ON, BUT I'VE NEVER FELT SO REFRESHED!
BGGH
BGGH
BGGH
BGGH
OH NO! IF HE MANAGES TO GET OUTSIDE, EVEN OUR GREAT FATHERLAND MAY NOT BE A MATCH FOR HIM! WE MUST TAKE HIM OUT!
SHOOT TO KILL! SHOOT YOUR COMRADE! SHOOT HIM! FILL HIM WITH HOLES!
AIEEEE!
RATATATAT

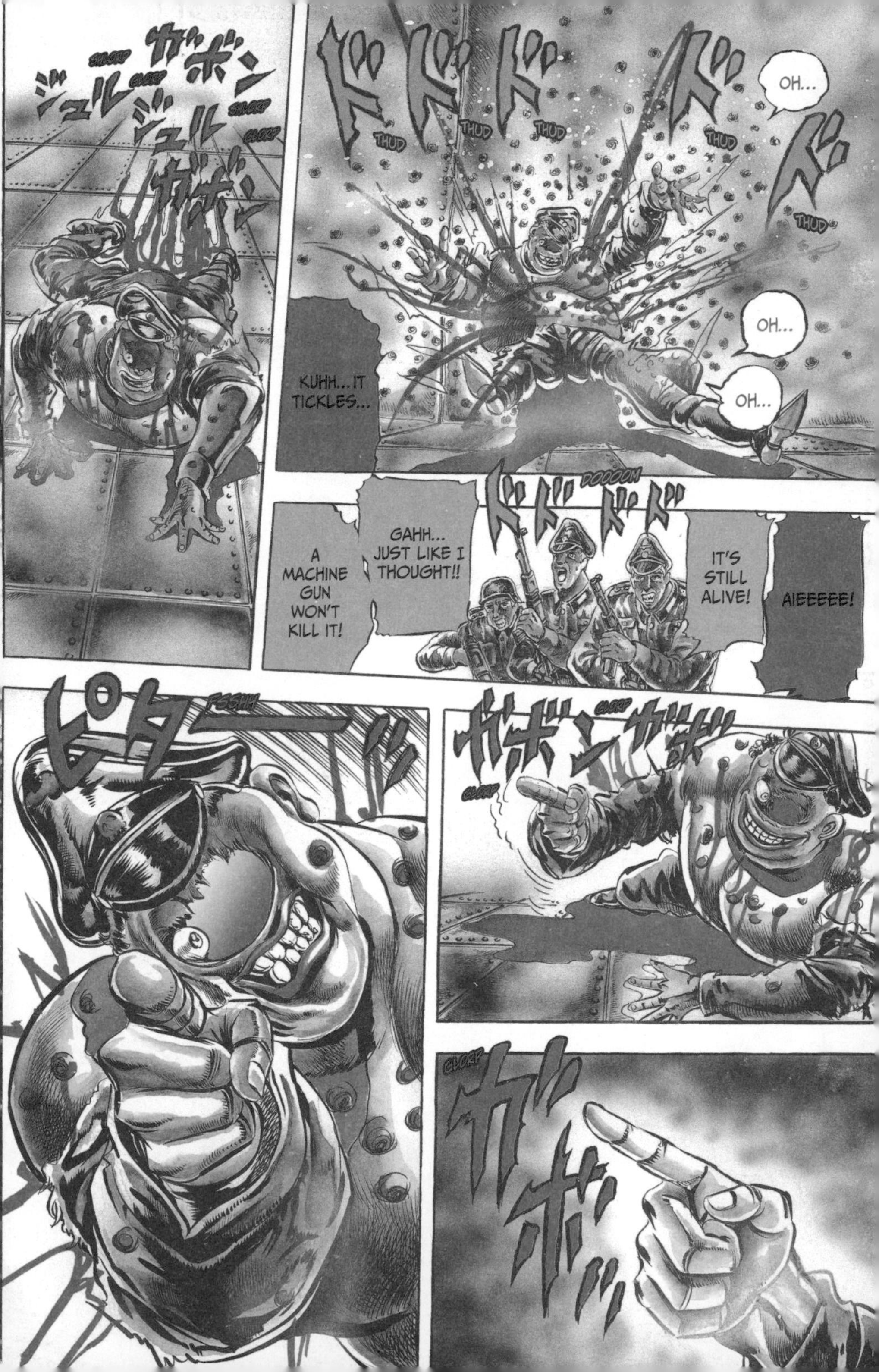
ドドドドド
THUD
THUD
THUD
THUD
THUD
OH...
OH...
OH...
KUHH...IT TICKLES...
ドドドド
DOOOOM
AIEEEEE!
IT'S STILL ALIVE!
GAHH... JUST LIKE I THOUGHT!!
A MACHINE GUN WON'T KILL IT!
ガボンジュルジュルガボッ
SLORP
GLORP
SLORP
GLORP
ガボンガボッ
GLORP
GLORP
ガボッ
GLORP
ピターッ
FSSH

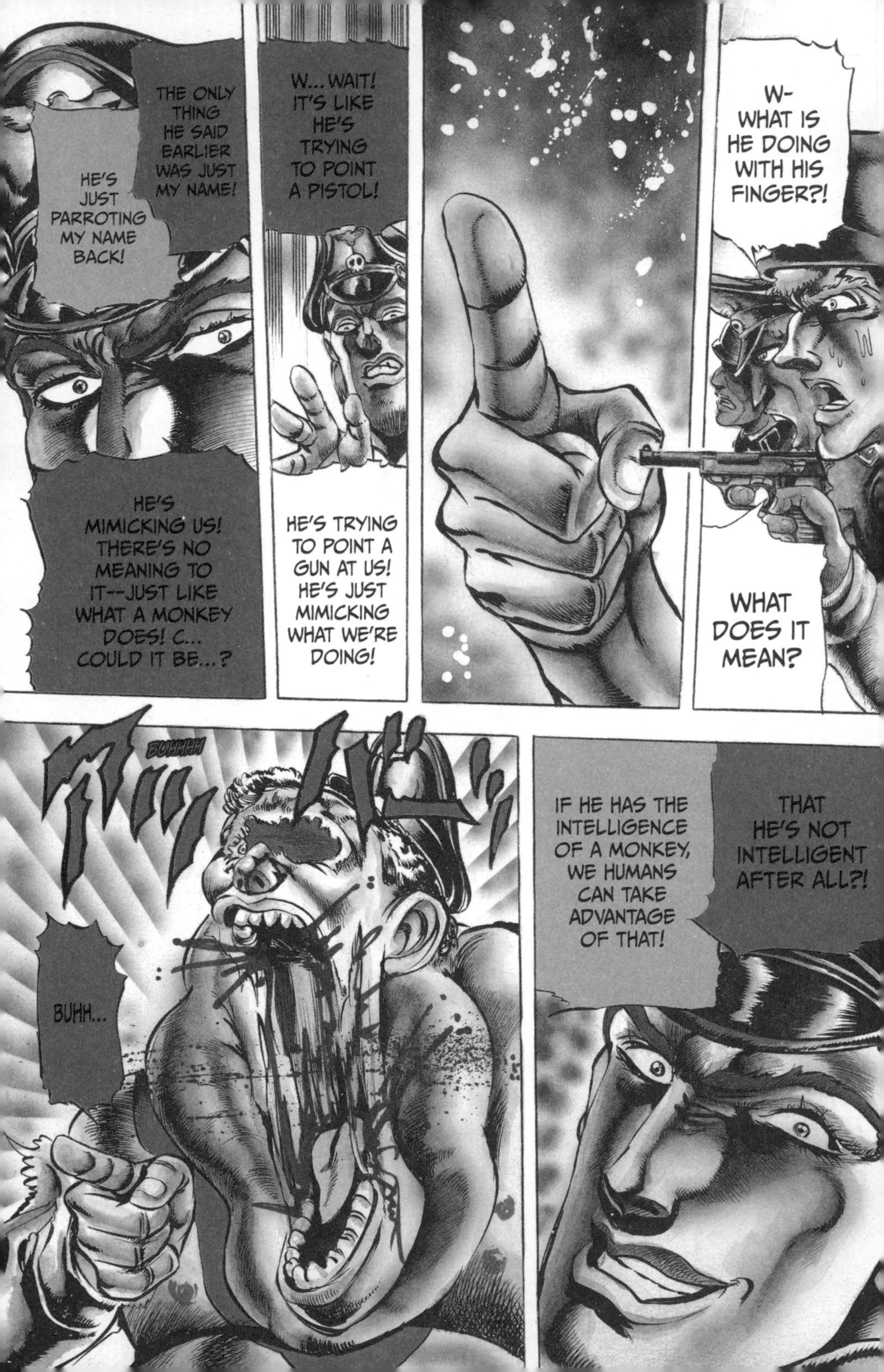
W-WHAT IS HE DOING WITH HIS FINGER?!
WHAT DOES IT MEAN?
W...WAIT! IT'S LIKE HE'S TRYING TO POINT A PISTOL!
HE'S TRYING TO POINT A GUN AT US! HE'S JUST MIMICKING WHAT WE'RE DOING!
THE ONLY THING HE SAID EARLIER WAS JUST MY NAME!
HE'S JUST PARROTING MY NAME BACK!
HE'S MIMICKING US! THERE'S NO MEANING TO IT--JUST LIKE WHAT A MONKEY DOES! C... COULD IT BE...?
THAT HE'S NOT INTELLIGENT AFTER ALL?!
IF HE HAS THE INTELLIGENCE OF A MONKEY, WE HUMANS CAN TAKE ADVANTAGE OF THAT!
BUHHHH
BUHH...

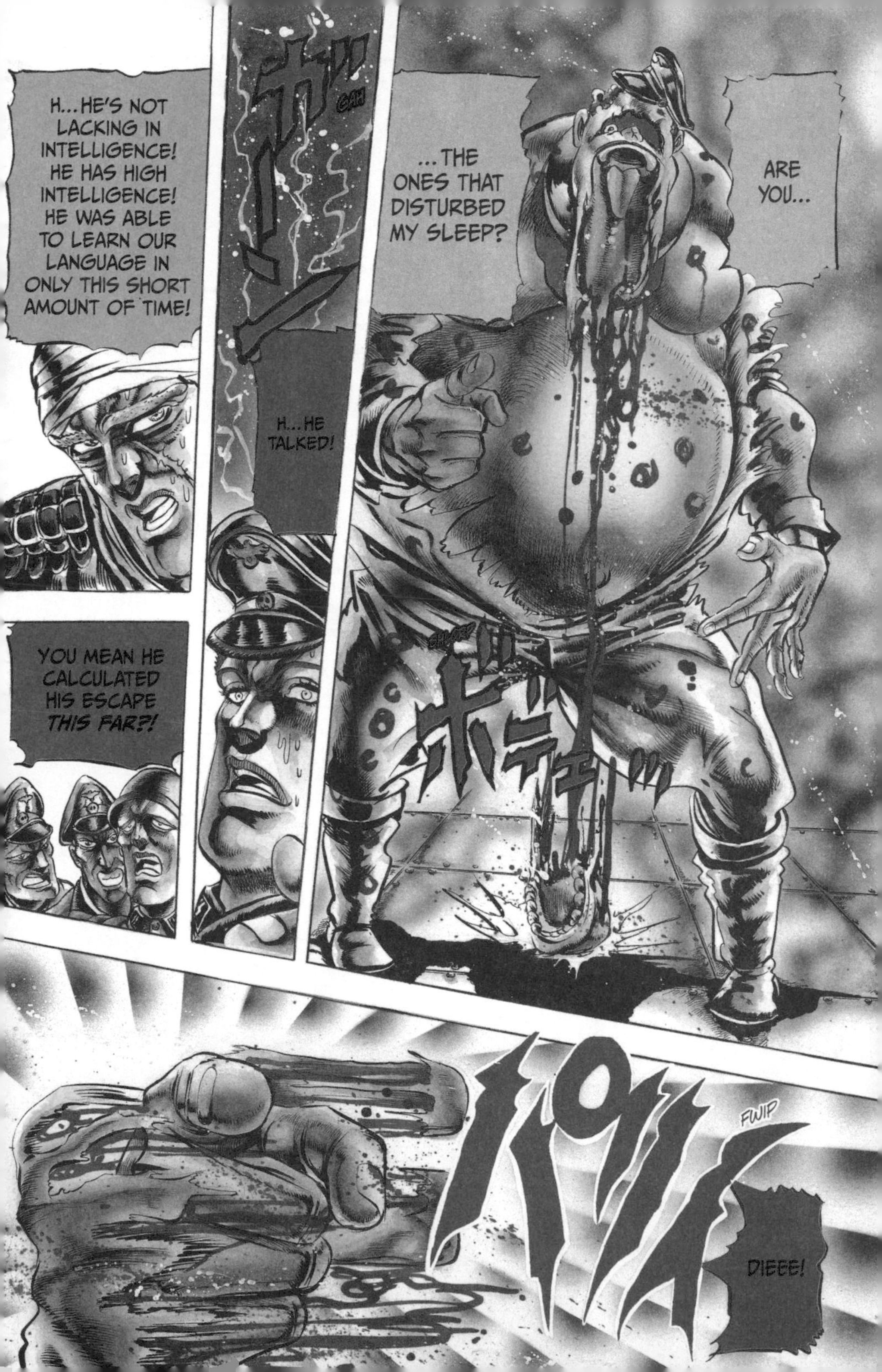
ARE YOU...
...THE ONES THAT DISTURBED MY SLEEP?
GAH
H...HE TALKED!
H...HE'S NOT LACKING IN INTELLIGENCE! HE HAS HIGH INTELLIGENCE! HE WAS ABLE TO LEARN OUR LANGUAGE IN ONLY THIS SHORT AMOUNT OF TIME!
YOU MEAN HE CALCULATED HIS ESCAPE *THIS FAR?!*
FWIP
DIEEE!

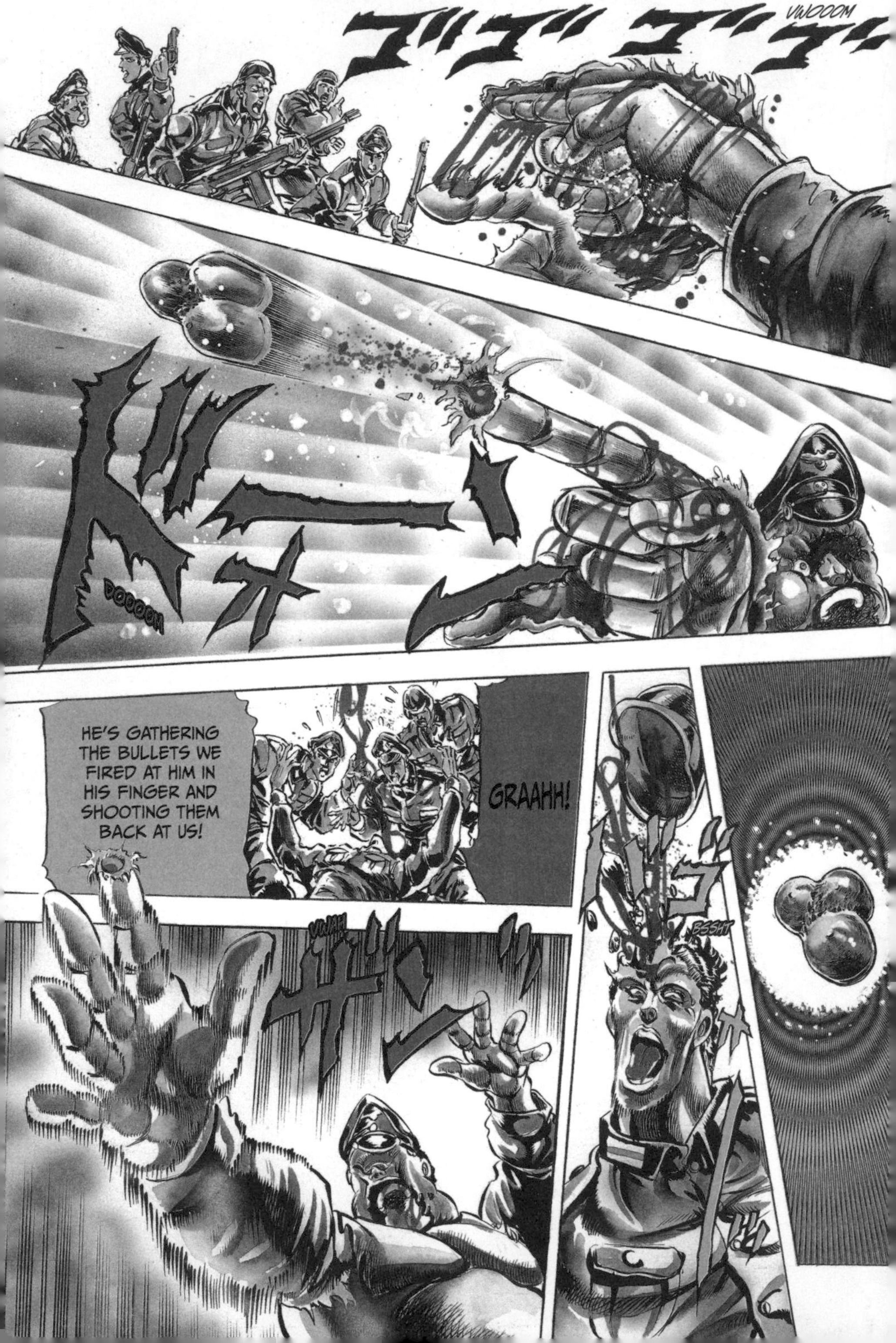
VWOOOM
DOOOOM
BSSHT
HE'S GATHERING THE BULLETS WE FIRED AT HIM IN HIS FINGER AND SHOOTING THEM BACK AT US!
GRAAHH!
VWAH

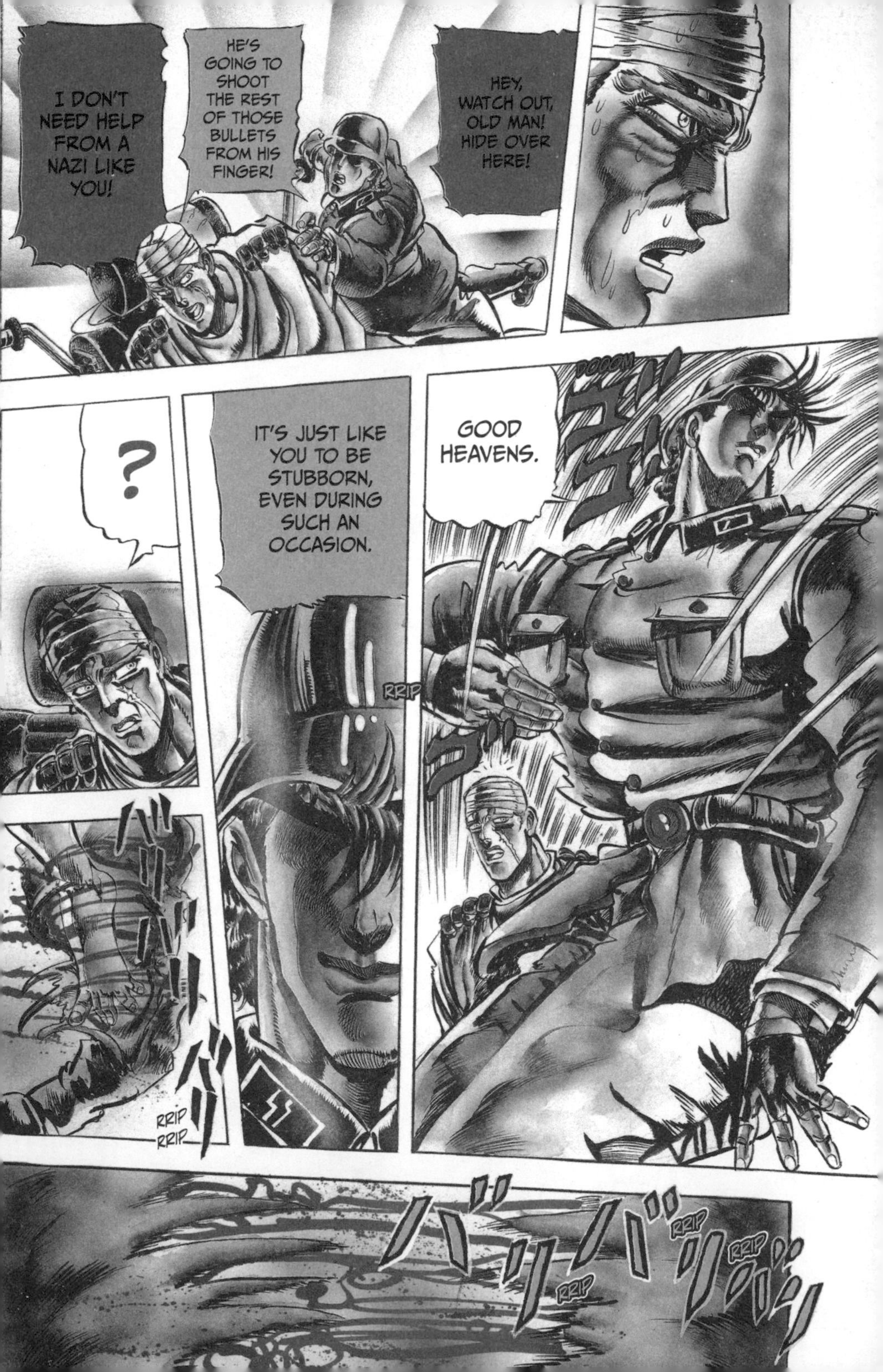
HEY, WATCH OUT, OLD MAN! HIDE OVER HERE!
HE'S GOING TO SHOOT THE REST OF THOSE BULLETS FROM HIS FINGER!
I DON'T NEED HELP FROM A NAZI LIKE YOU!
DOOOM
GOOD HEAVENS.
IT'S JUST LIKE YOU TO BE STUBBORN, EVEN DURING SUCH AN OCCASION.
RRIP
?
RRIP
RRIP
RRIP
RRIP
RRIP

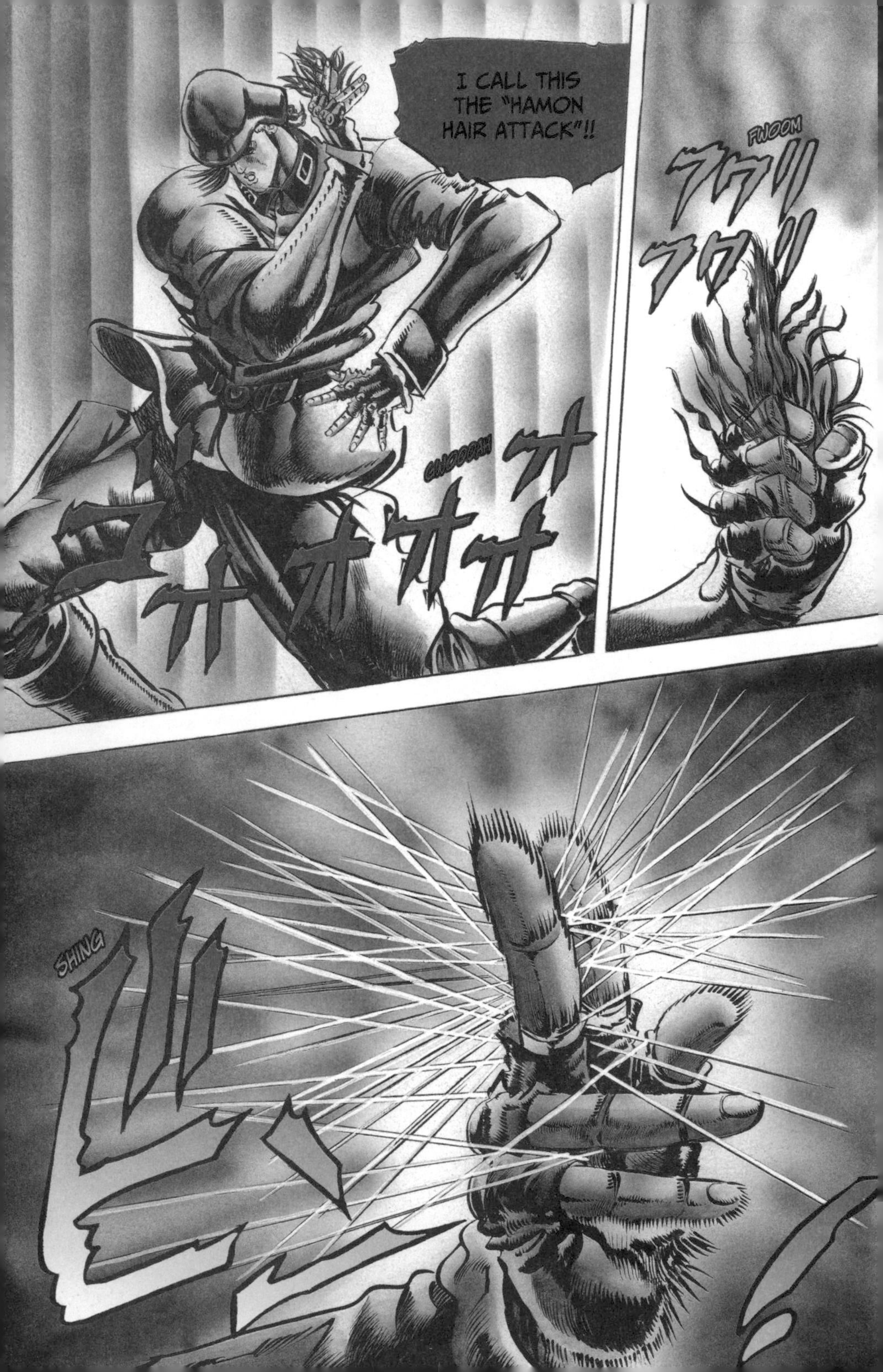
FWOOM
I CALL THIS THE "HAMON HAIR ATTACK"!!
SHING

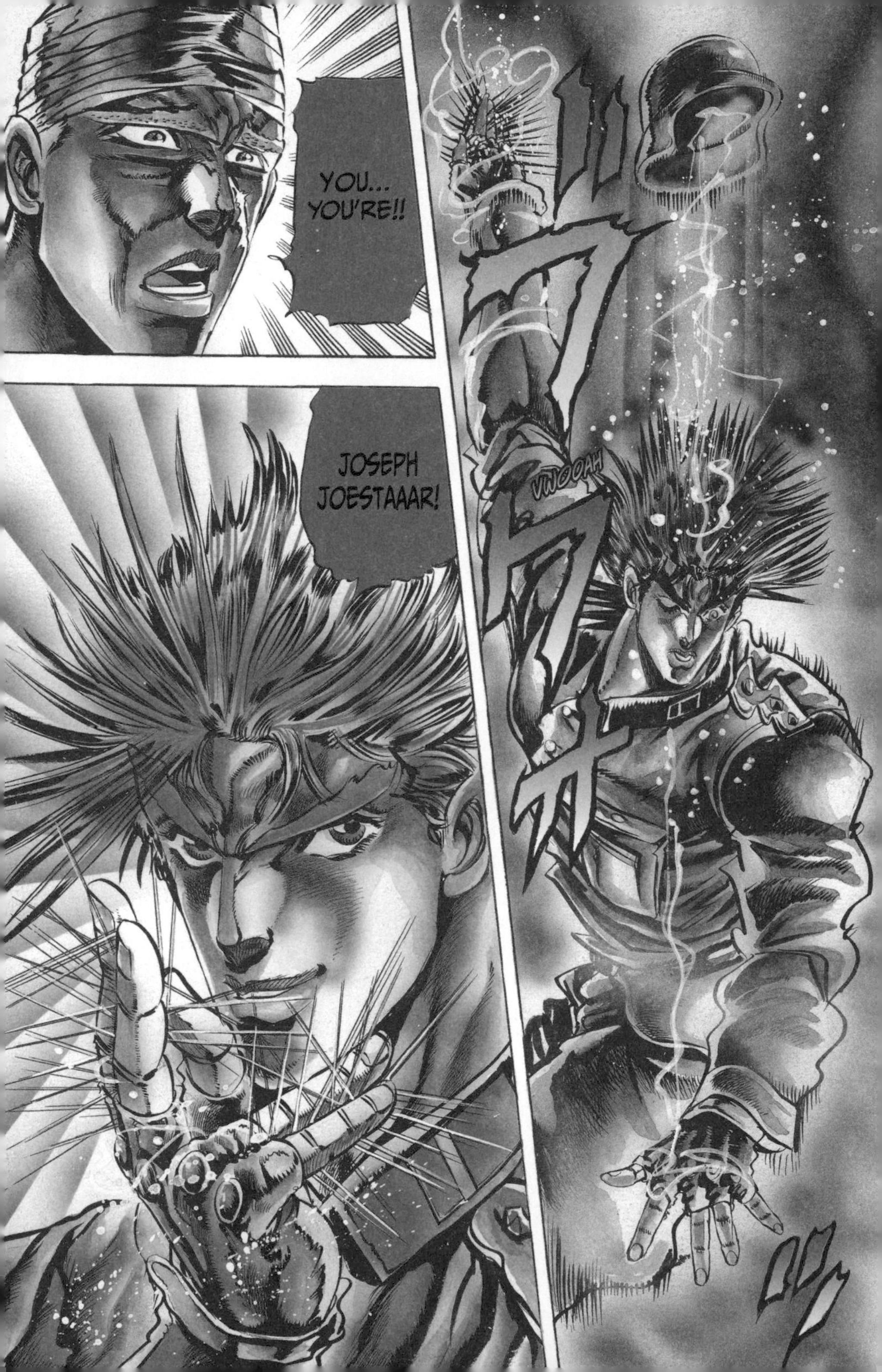
VWOOAH
YOU... YOU'RE!!
JOSEPH JOESTAAAR!

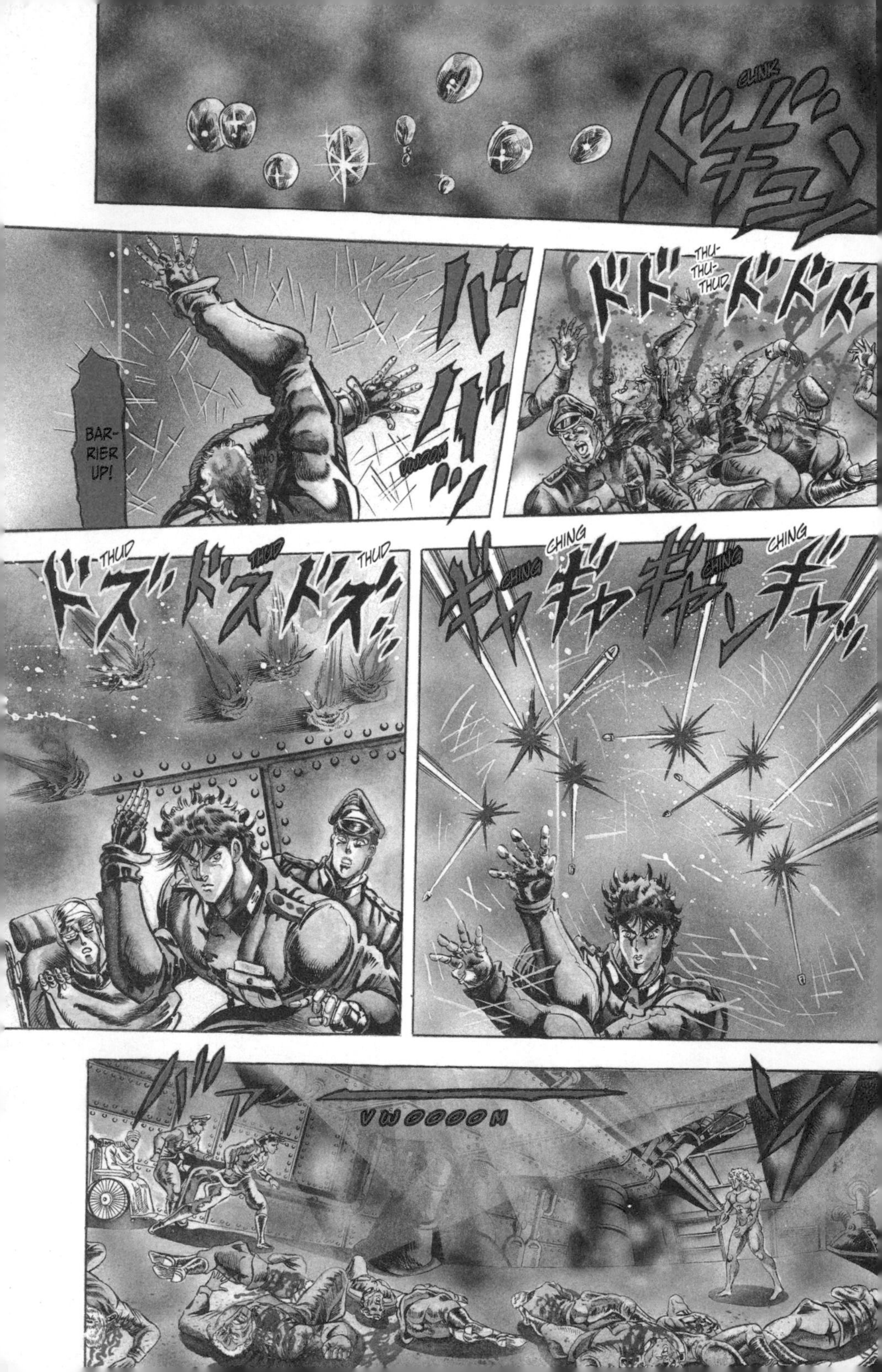
CLINK
THU-
THU-
THUD
VWOOM
BAR-
RIER
UP!
CHING
CHING
CHING
CHING
THUD
THUD
THUD
VWOOOOOM

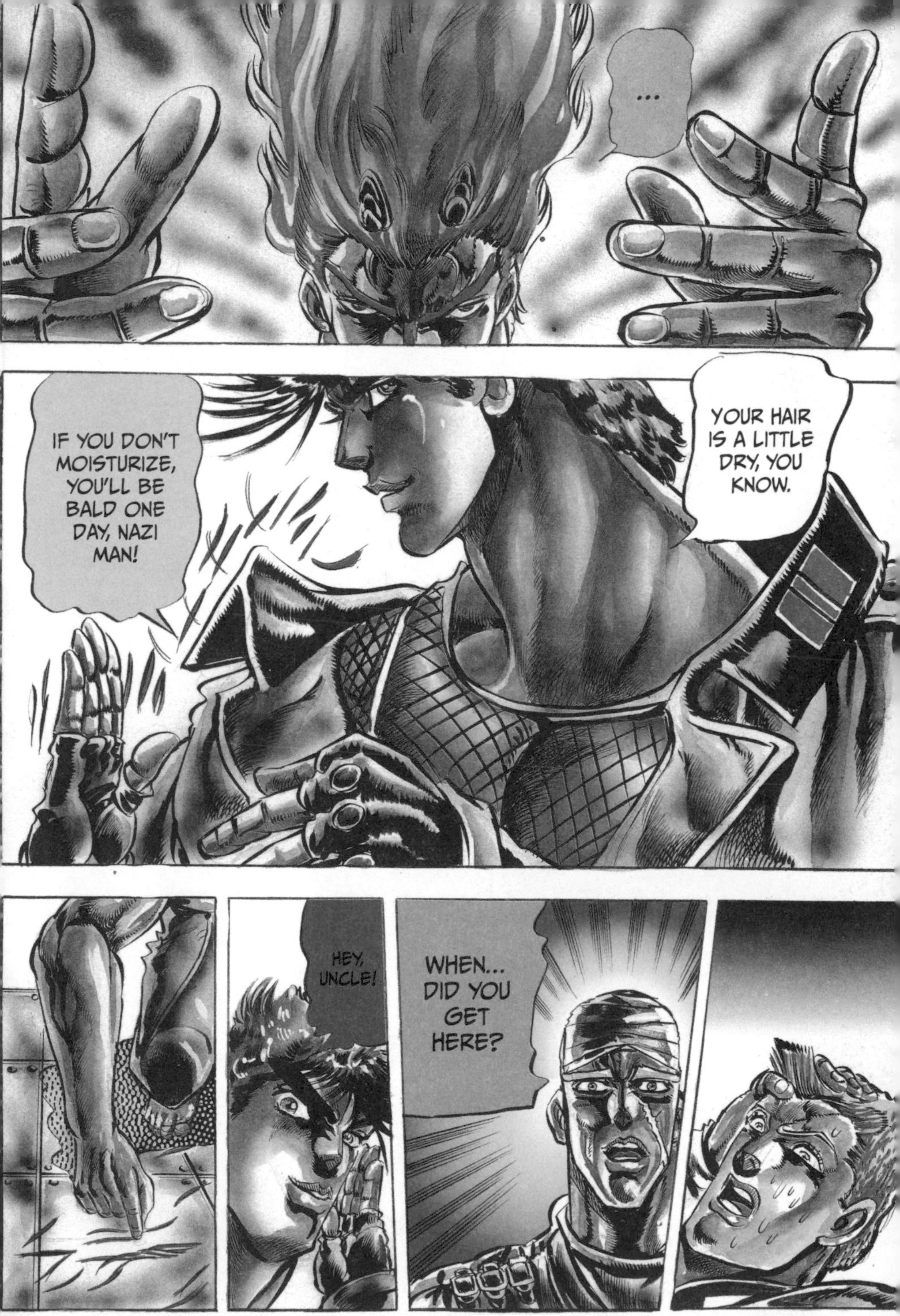
...
YOUR HAIR IS A LITTLE DRY, YOU KNOW.
IF YOU DON'T MOISTURIZE, YOU'LL BE BALD ONE DAY, NAZI MAN!
WHEN... DID YOU GET HERE?
HEY, UNCLE!

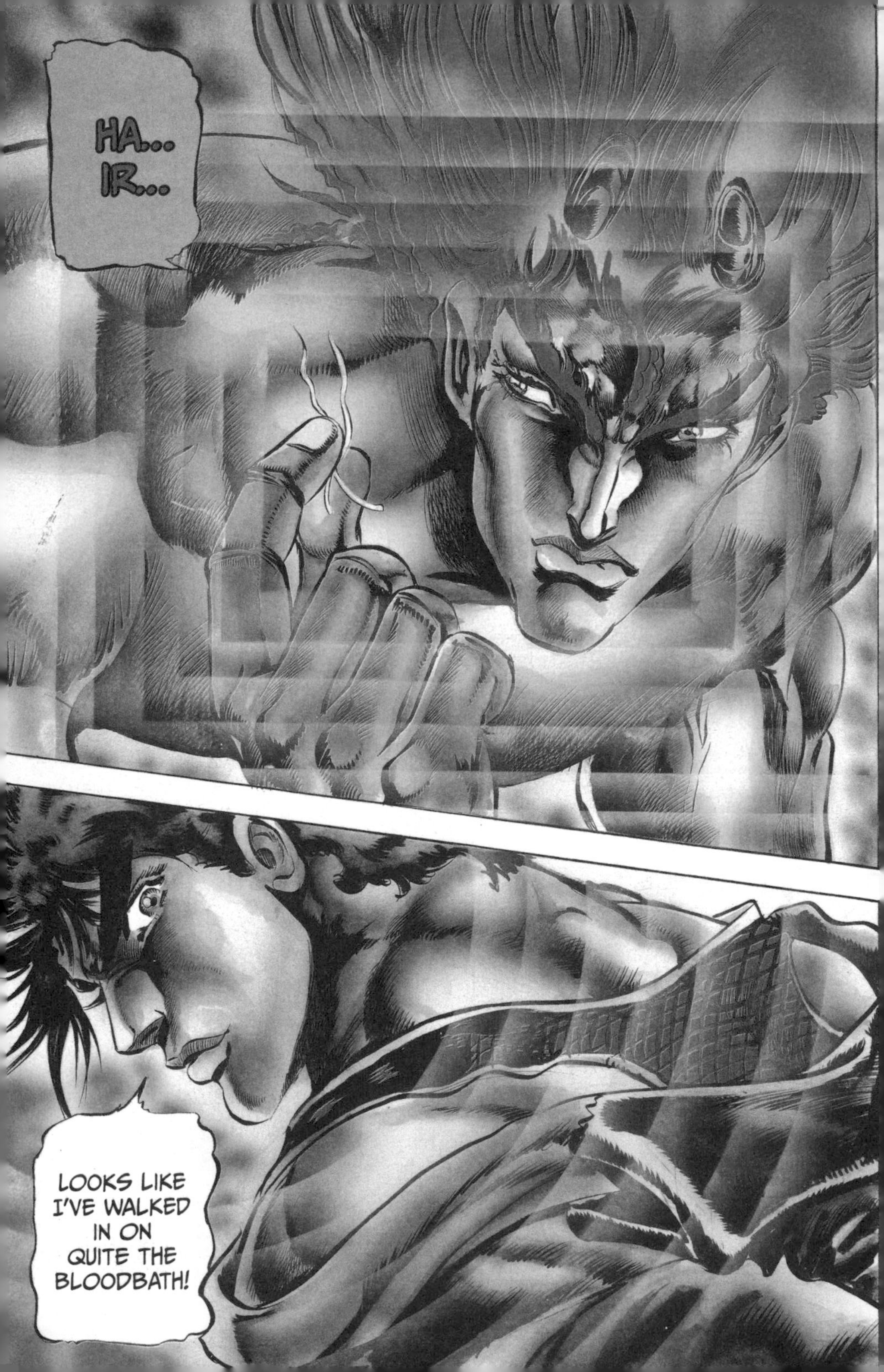
HA...
IR...
LOOKS LIKE I'VE WALKED IN ON QUITE THE BLOODBATH!

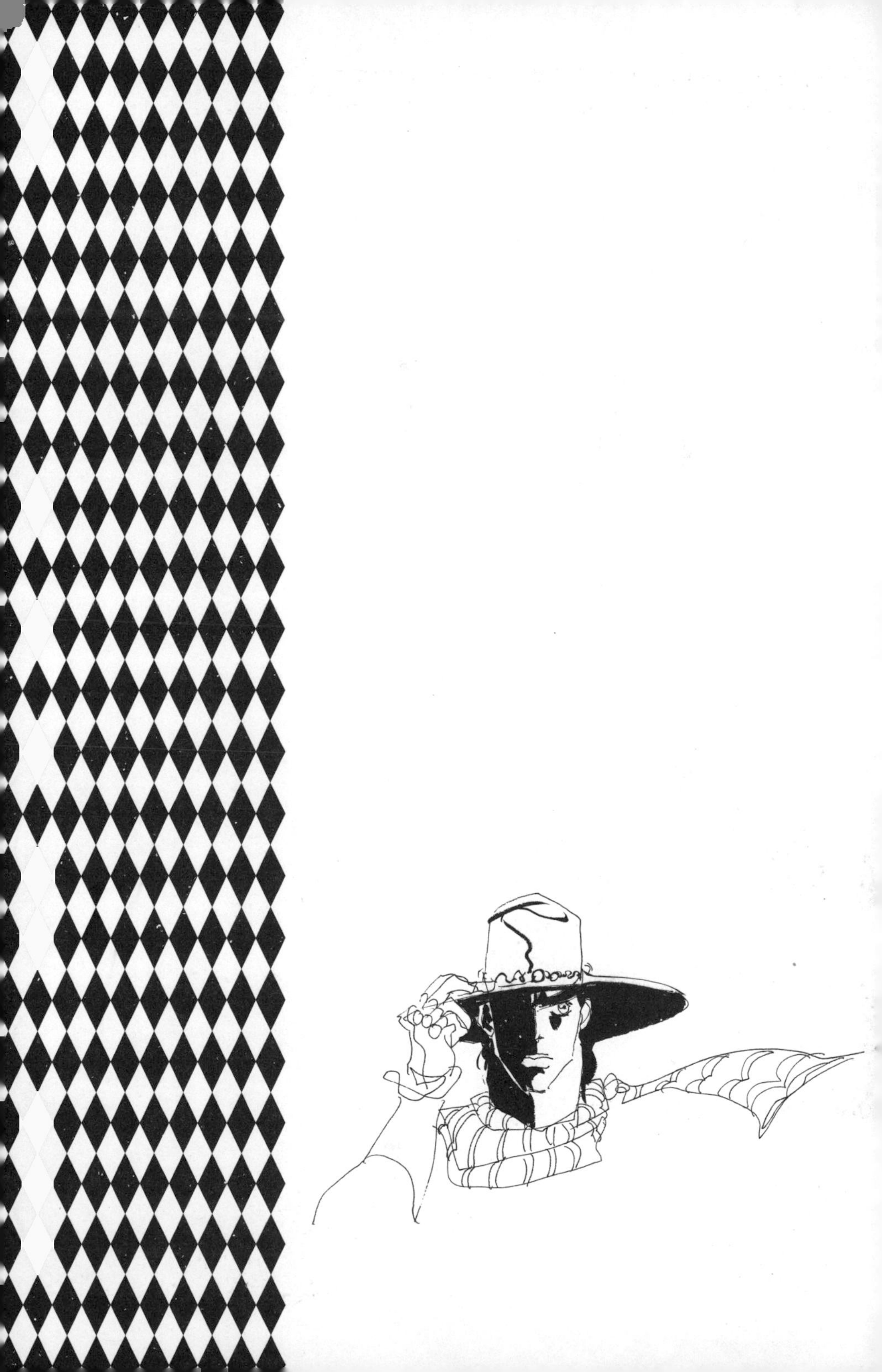

CHAPTER 14: The Pillar Man, Santviento PART 5

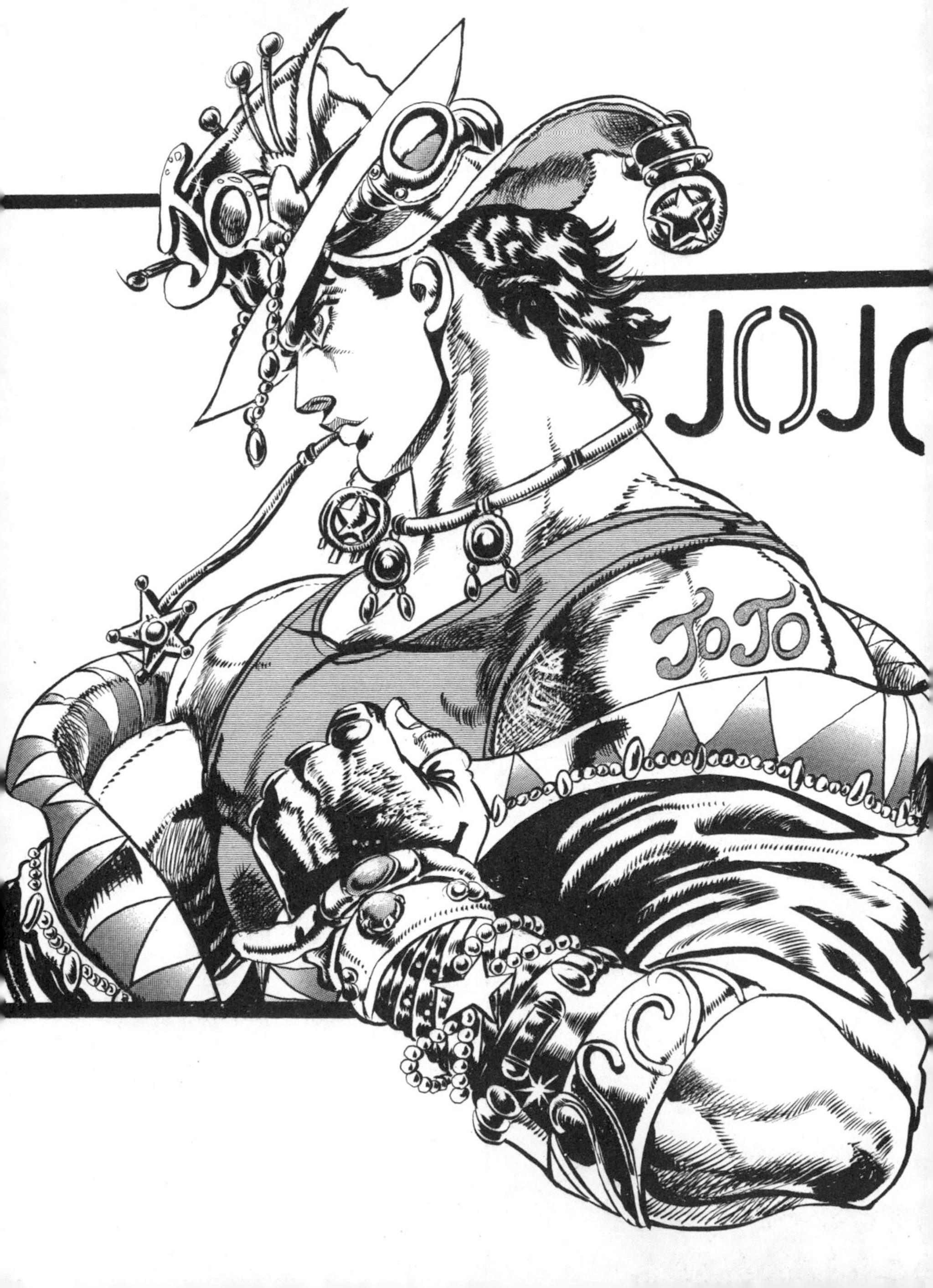
JOJO
JoJo

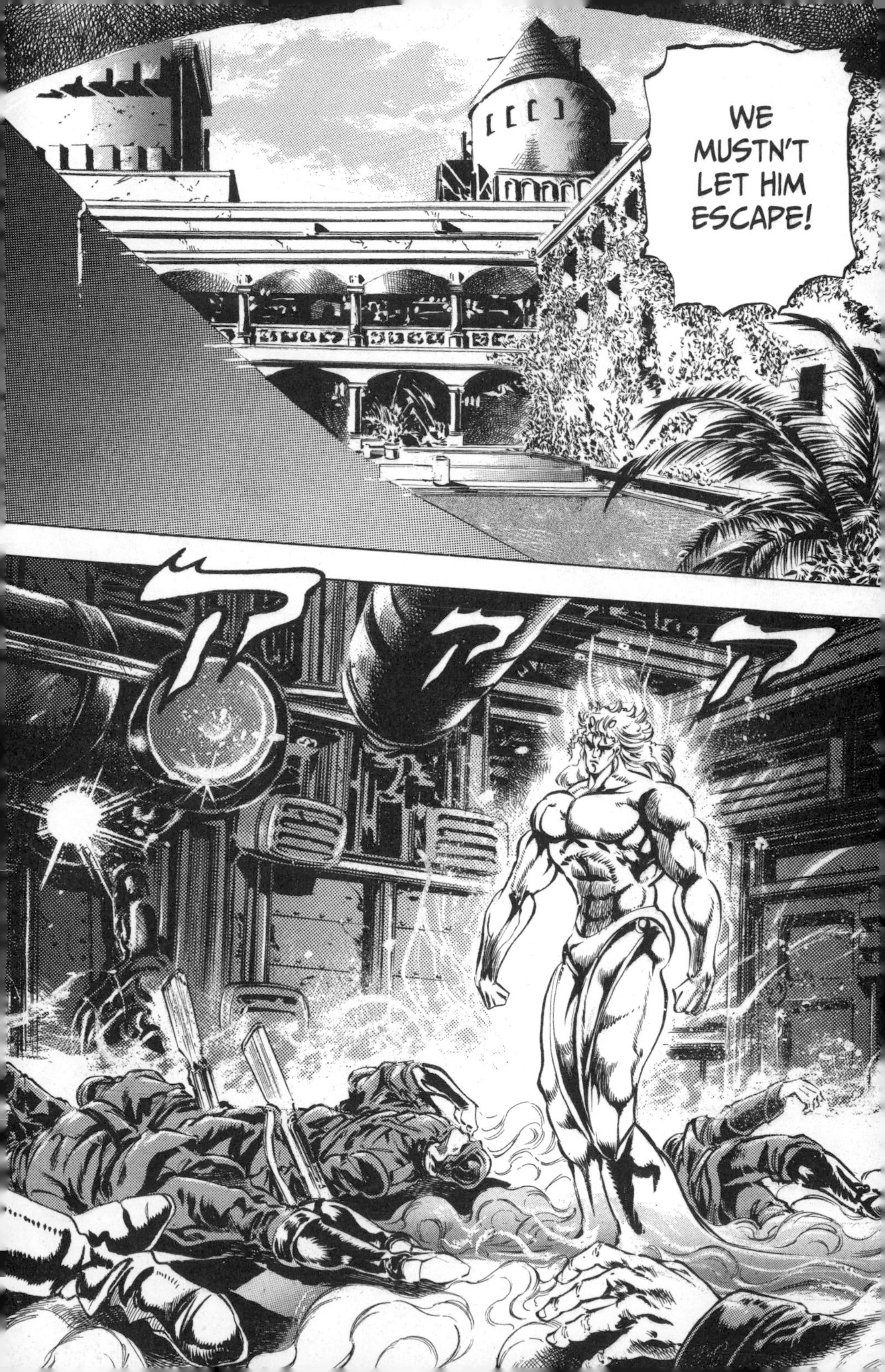
WE MUSTN'T LET HIM ESCAPE!

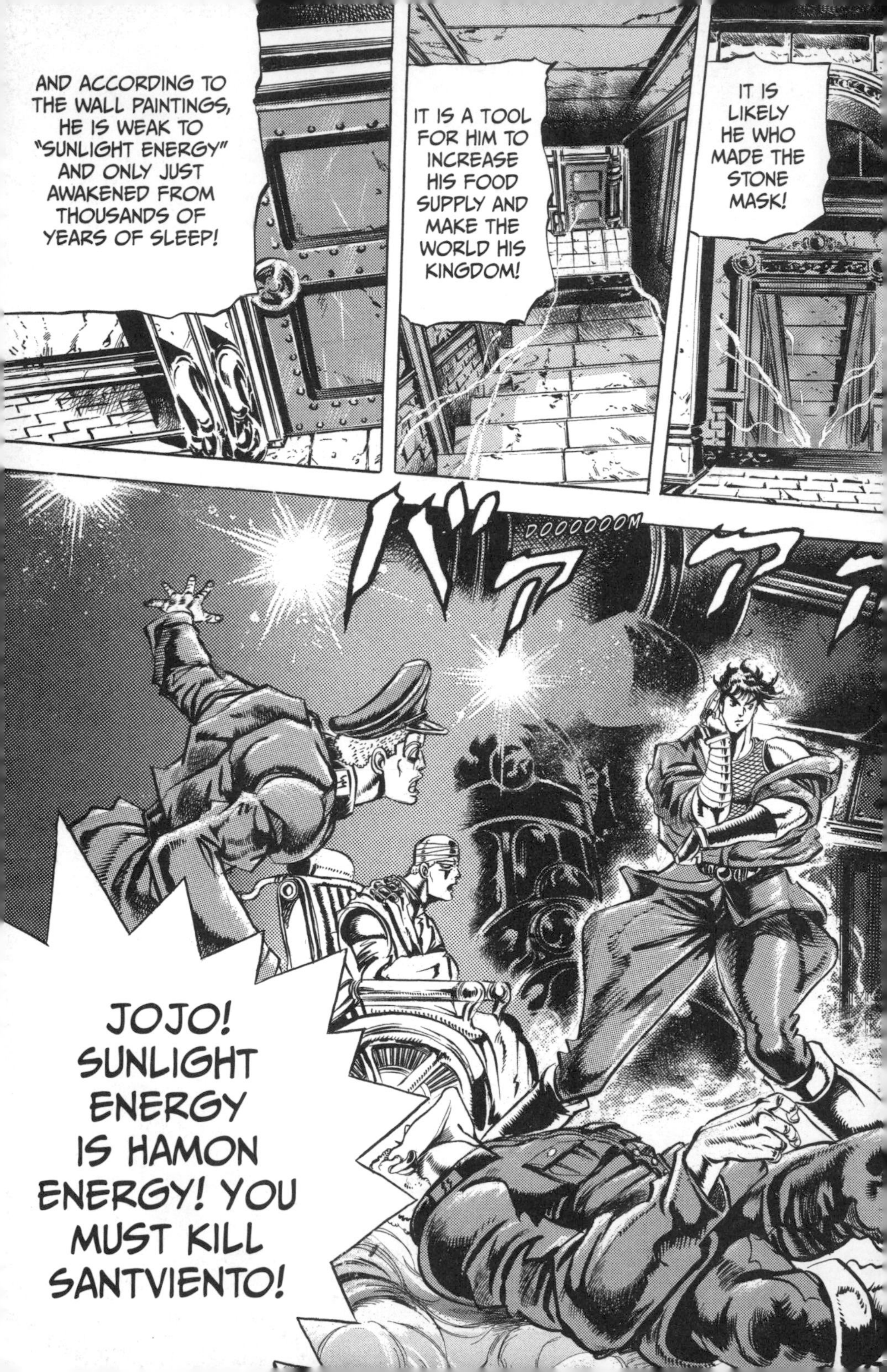
IT IS LIKELY HE WHO MADE THE STONE MASK!
IT IS A TOOL FOR HIM TO INCREASE HIS FOOD SUPPLY AND MAKE THE WORLD HIS KINGDOM!
AND ACCORDING TO THE WALL PAINTINGS, HE IS WEAK TO "SUNLIGHT ENERGY" AND ONLY JUST AWAKENED FROM THOUSANDS OF YEARS OF SLEEP!
DOOOOOOOM
JOJO! SUNLIGHT ENERGY IS HAMON ENERGY! YOU MUST KILL SANTVIENTO!

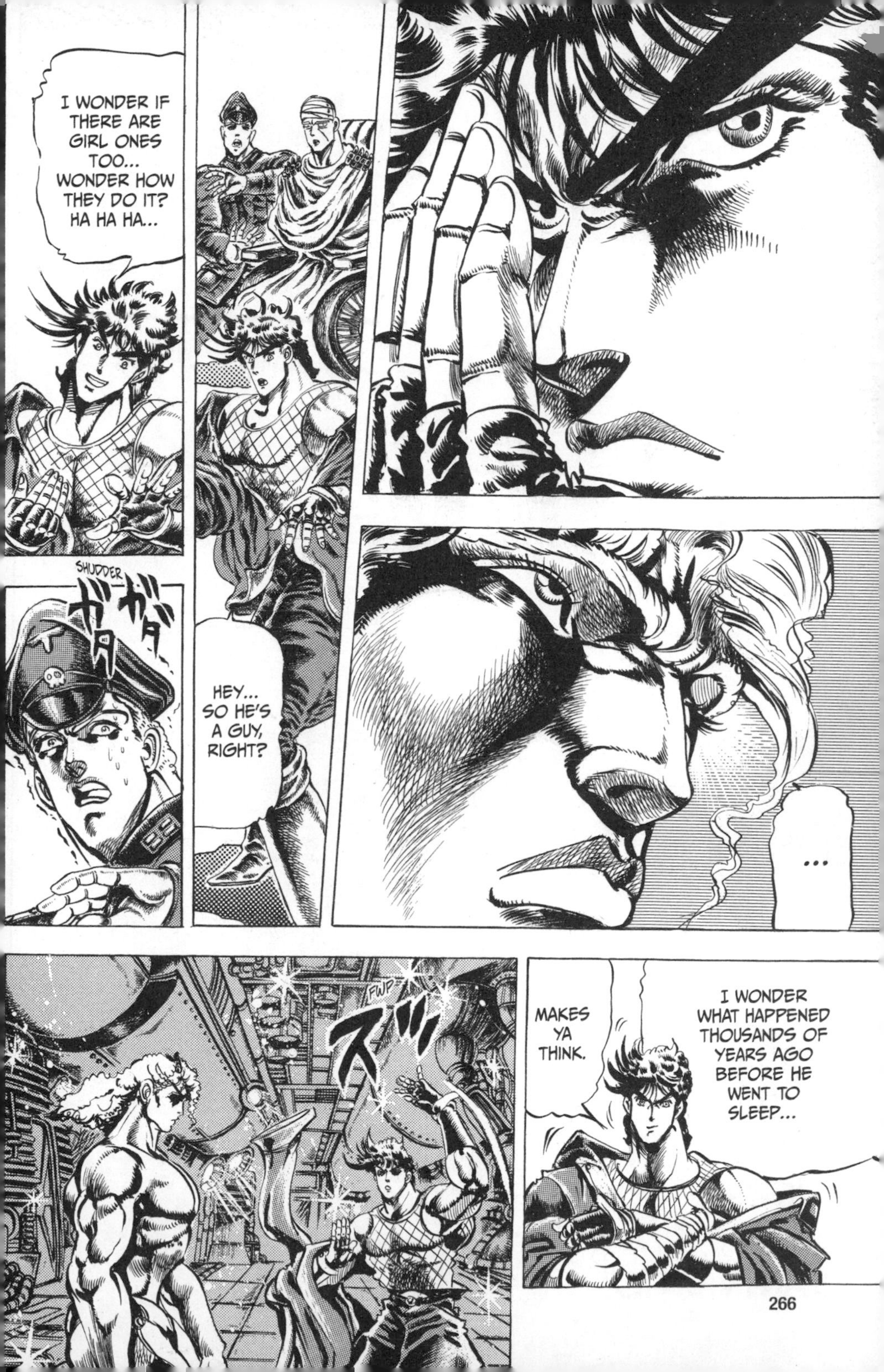
...
HEY... SO HE'S A GUY, RIGHT?
I WONDER IF THERE ARE GIRL ONES TOO... WONDER HOW THEY DO IT? HA HA HA...
SHUDDER
I WONDER WHAT HAPPENED THOUSANDS OF YEARS AGO BEFORE HE WENT TO SLEEP...
MAKES YA THINK.
FWP

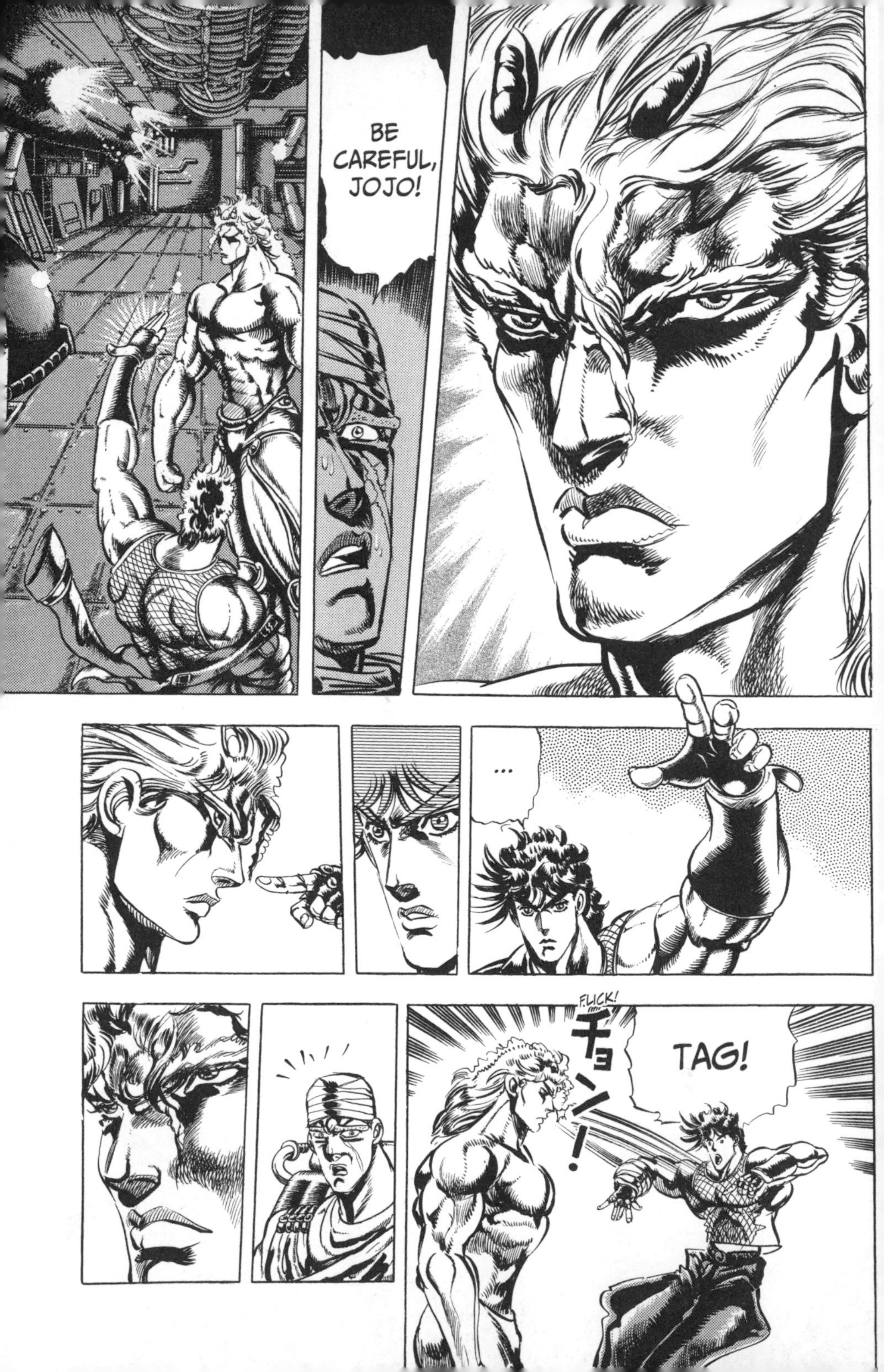
BE CAREFUL, JOJO!
...
FLICK!
チョン!
TAG!

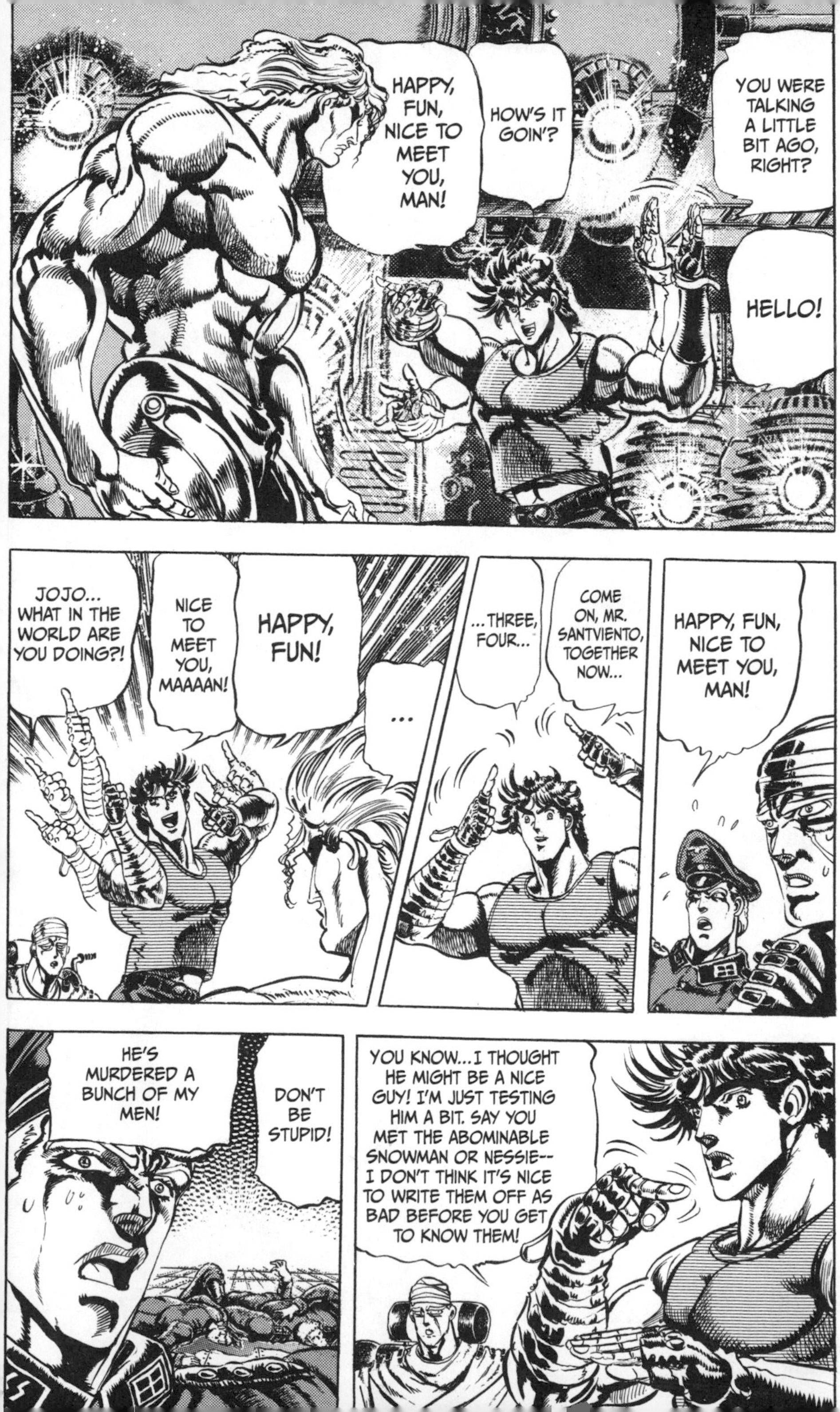

YOU WERE TALKING A LITTLE BIT AGO, RIGHT?
HELLO!
HOW'S IT GOIN'?
HAPPY, FUN, NICE TO MEET YOU, MAN!
HAPPY, FUN, NICE TO MEET YOU, MAN!
COME ON, MR. SANTVIENTO, TOGETHER NOW...
...THREE, FOUR...
HAPPY, FUN!
NICE TO MEET YOU, MAAAAN!
...
JOJO... WHAT IN THE WORLD ARE YOU DOING?!
YOU KNOW...I THOUGHT HE MIGHT BE A NICE GUY! I'M JUST TESTING HIM A BIT. SAY YOU MET THE ABOMINABLE SNOWMAN OR NESSIE-- I DON'T THINK IT'S NICE TO WRITE THEM OFF AS BAD BEFORE YOU GET TO KNOW THEM!
DON'T BE STUPID!
HE'S MURDERED A BUNCH OF MY MEN!

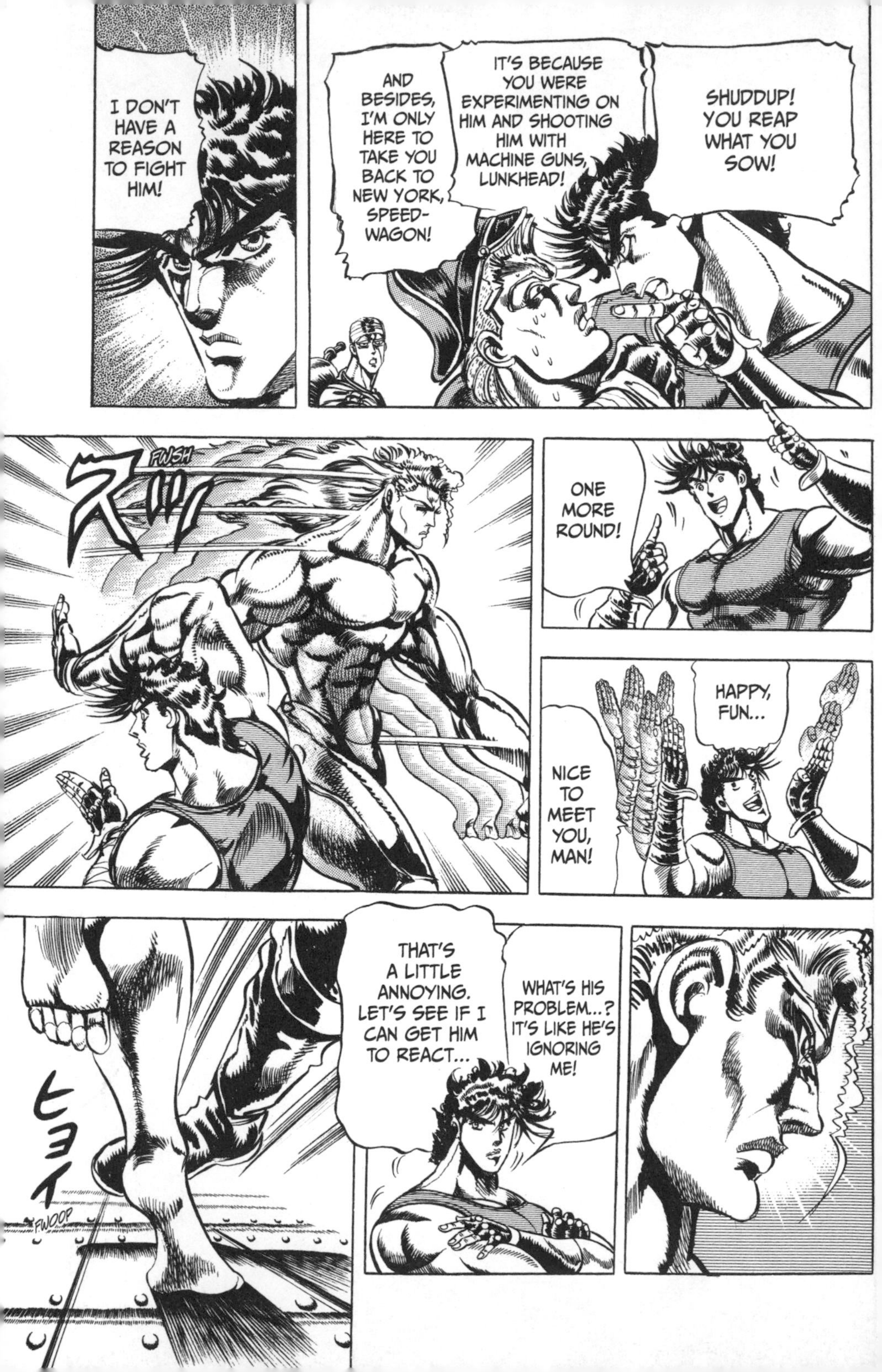
SHUDDUP! YOU REAP WHAT YOU SOW!
IT'S BECAUSE YOU WERE EXPERIMENTING ON HIM AND SHOOTING HIM WITH MACHINE GUNS, LUNKHEAD!
AND BESIDES, I'M ONLY HERE TO TAKE YOU BACK TO NEW YORK, SPEED-WAGON!
I DON'T HAVE A REASON TO FIGHT HIM!
ONE MORE ROUND!
HAPPY, FUN...
NICE TO MEET YOU, MAN!
FWSH
WHAT'S HIS PROBLEM...? IT'S LIKE HE'S IGNORING ME!
THAT'S A LITTLE ANNOYING. LET'S SEE IF I CAN GET HIM TO REACT...
ヒョイ
FWOOP

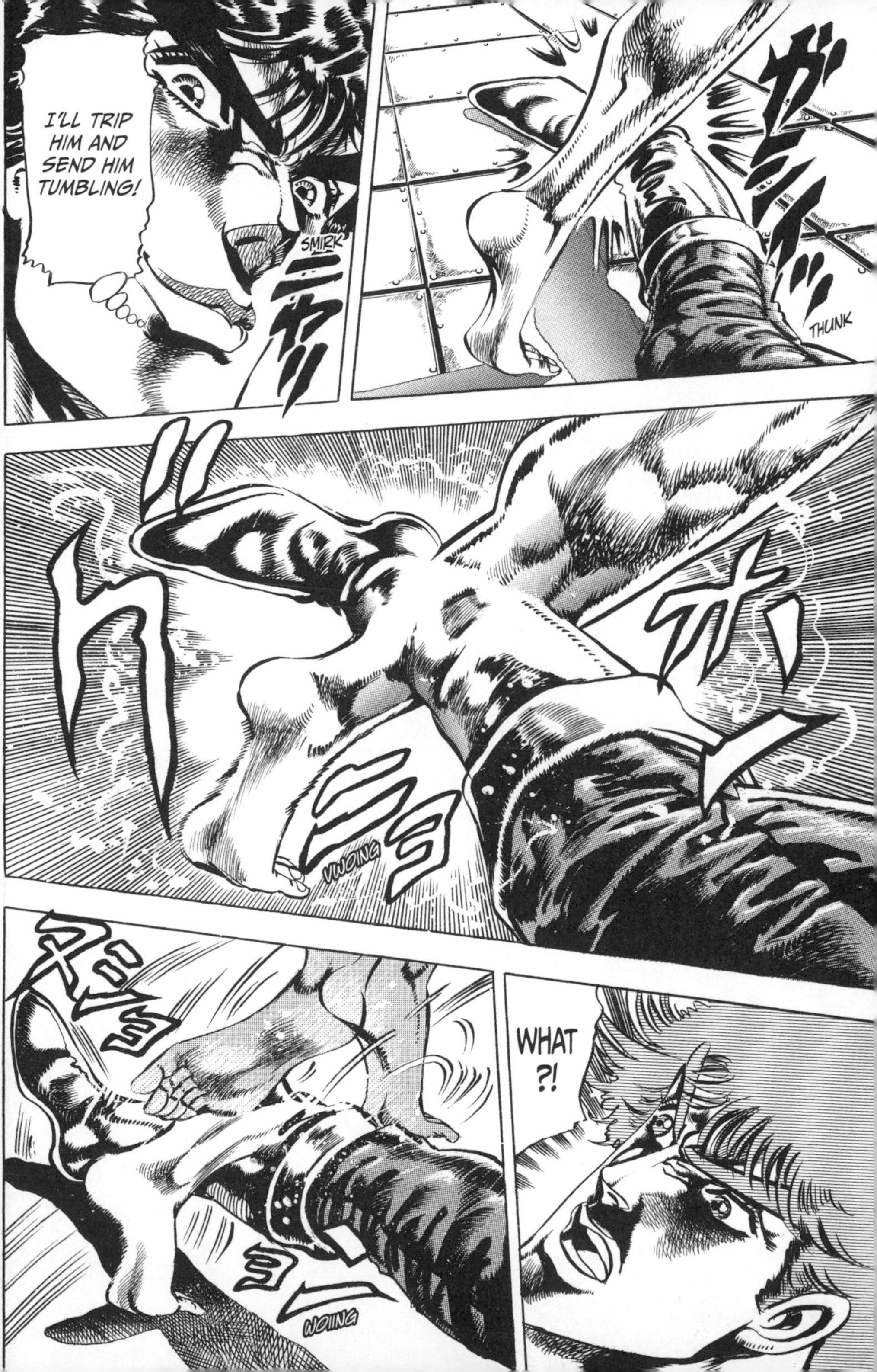
THUNK
I'LL TRIP HIM AND SEND HIM TUMBLING!
SMIRK
VWOING
WHAT?!
WOING

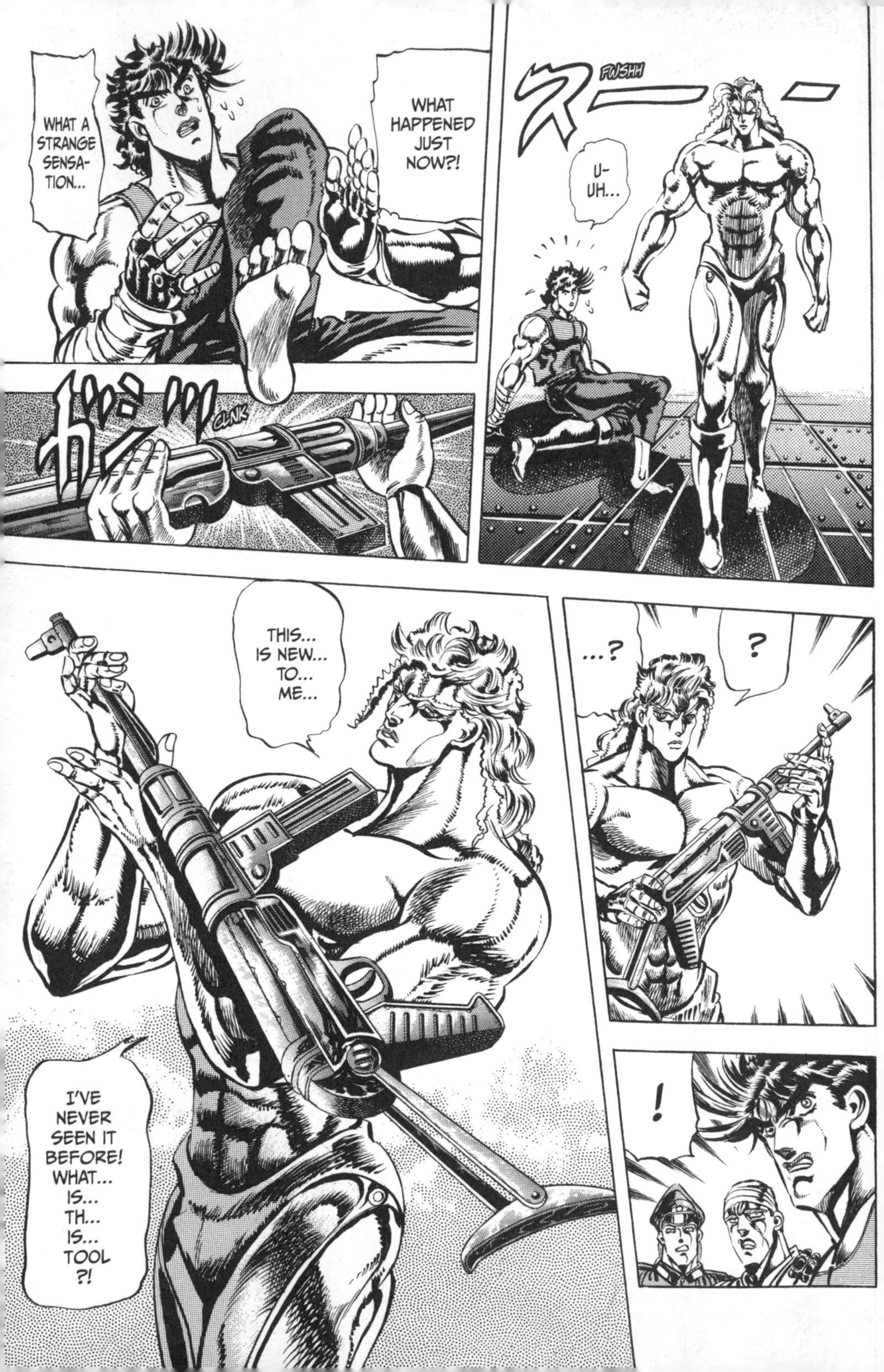
FWSHH
U-UH...
WHAT HAPPENED JUST NOW?!
WHAT A STRANGE SENSATION...
CLNK
?
...?
!
THIS... IS NEW... TO... ME...
I'VE NEVER SEEN IT BEFORE! WHAT... IS... TH... IS... TOOL?!

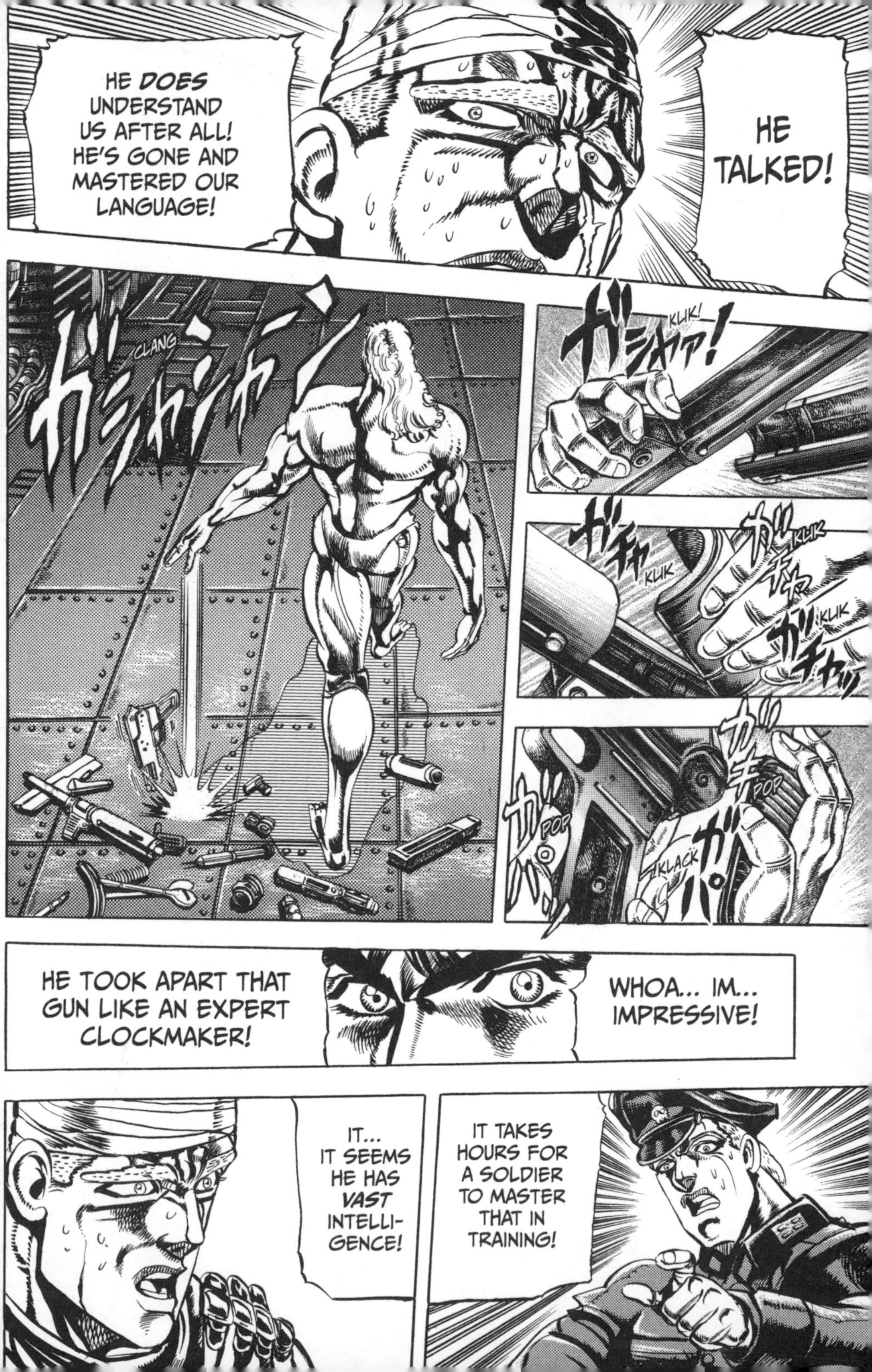

HE TALKED!
HE DOES UNDERSTAND US AFTER ALL! HE'S GONE AND MASTERED OUR LANGUAGE!
KLIK!
KLIK
KLIK
KLIK
POP
POP
KLACK
CLANG
WHOA... IM... IMPRESSIVE!
HE TOOK APART THAT GUN LIKE AN EXPERT CLOCKMAKER!
IT TAKES HOURS FOR A SOLDIER TO MASTER THAT IN TRAINING!
IT... IT SEEMS HE HAS VAST INTELLI-GENCE!

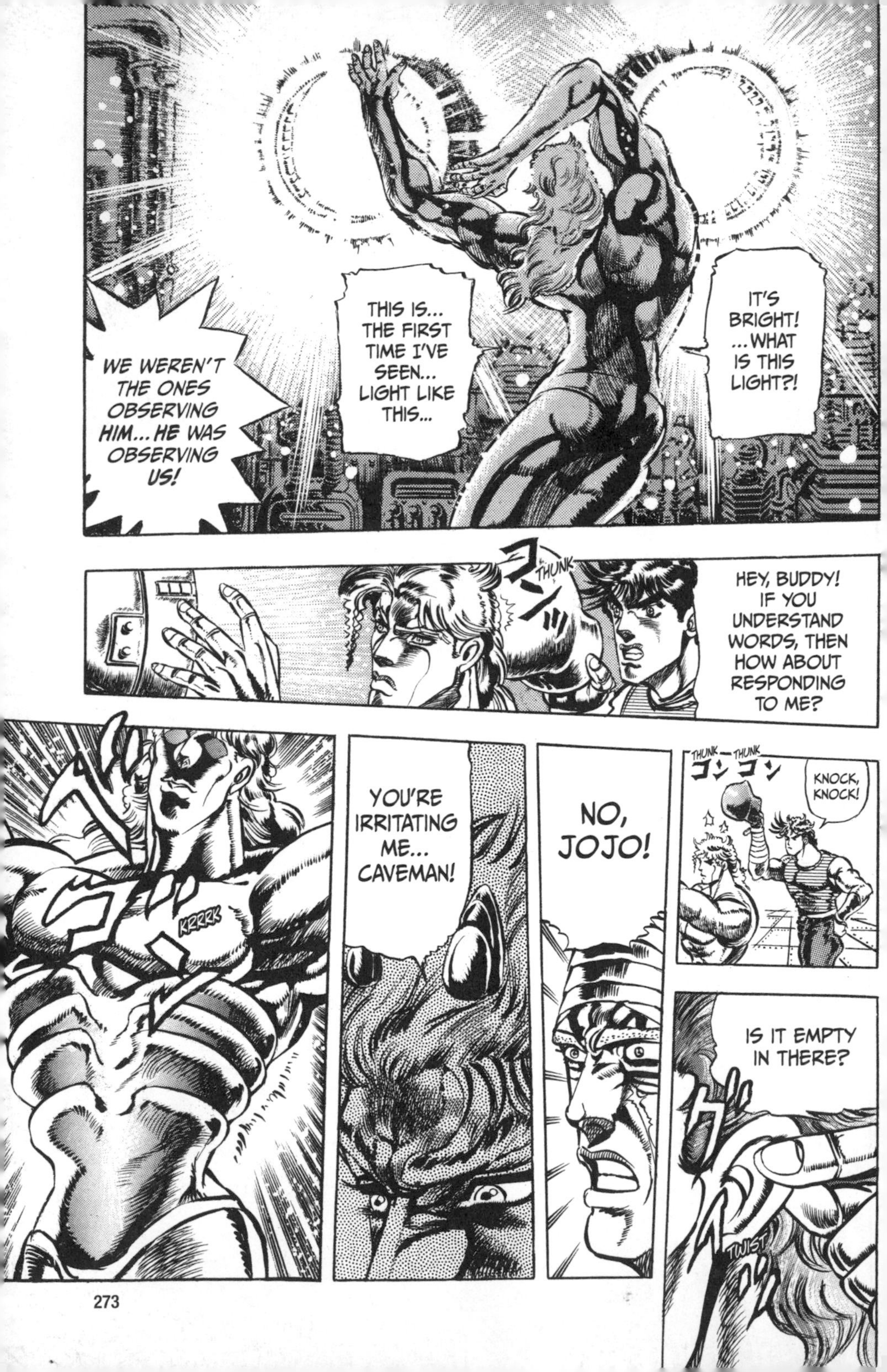
IT'S BRIGHT! ...WHAT IS THIS LIGHT?!
THIS IS... THE FIRST TIME I'VE SEEN... LIGHT LIKE THIS...
WE WEREN'T THE ONES OBSERVING HIM... HE WAS OBSERVING US!
HEY, BUDDY! IF YOU UNDERSTAND WORDS, THEN HOW ABOUT RESPONDING TO ME?
THUNK
THUNK THUNK
KNOCK, KNOCK!
IS IT EMPTY IN THERE?
TWIST
NO, JOJO!
YOU'RE IRRITATING ME... CAVEMAN!
KRRRK

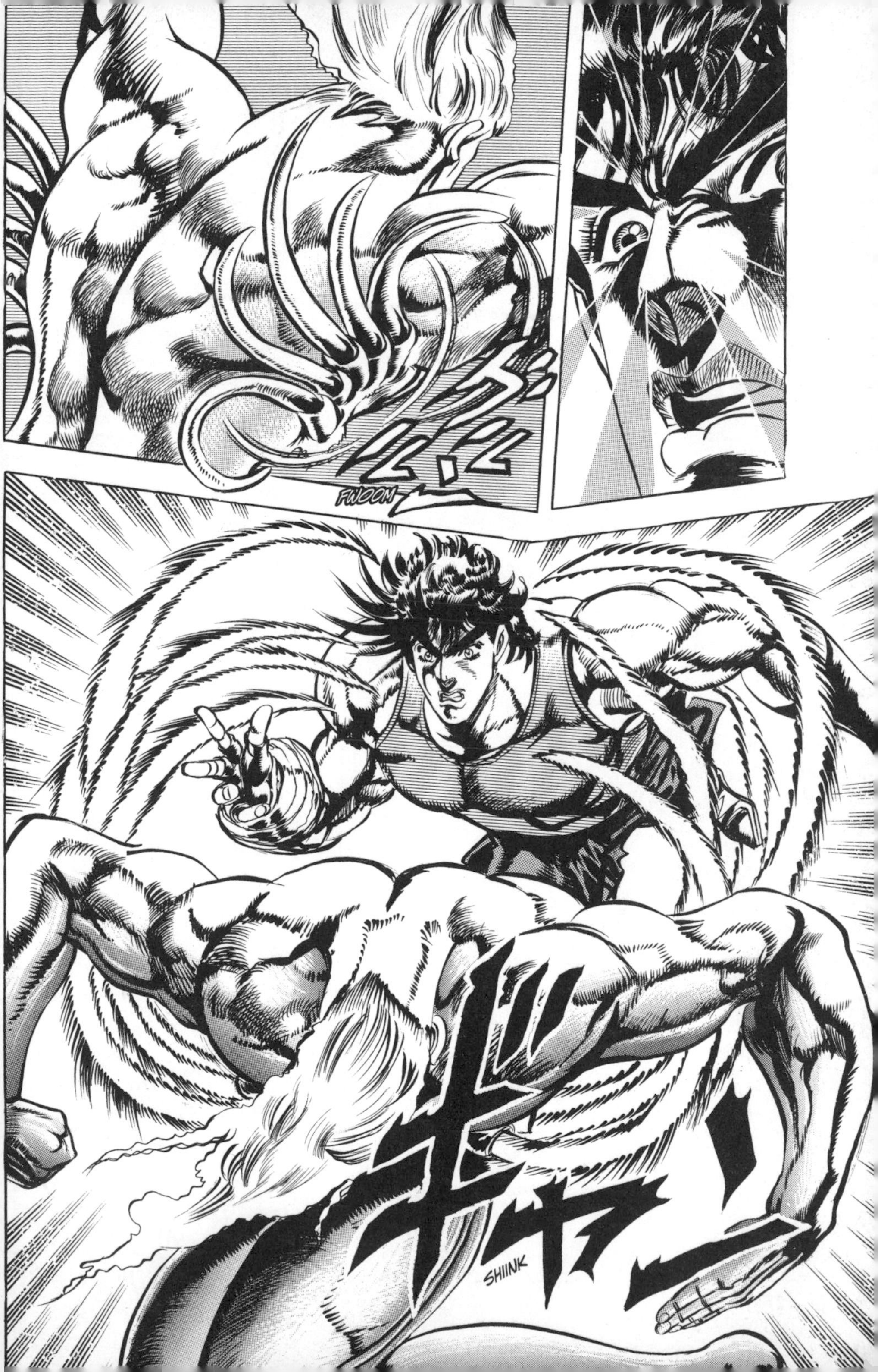
FWOOM
SHIINK

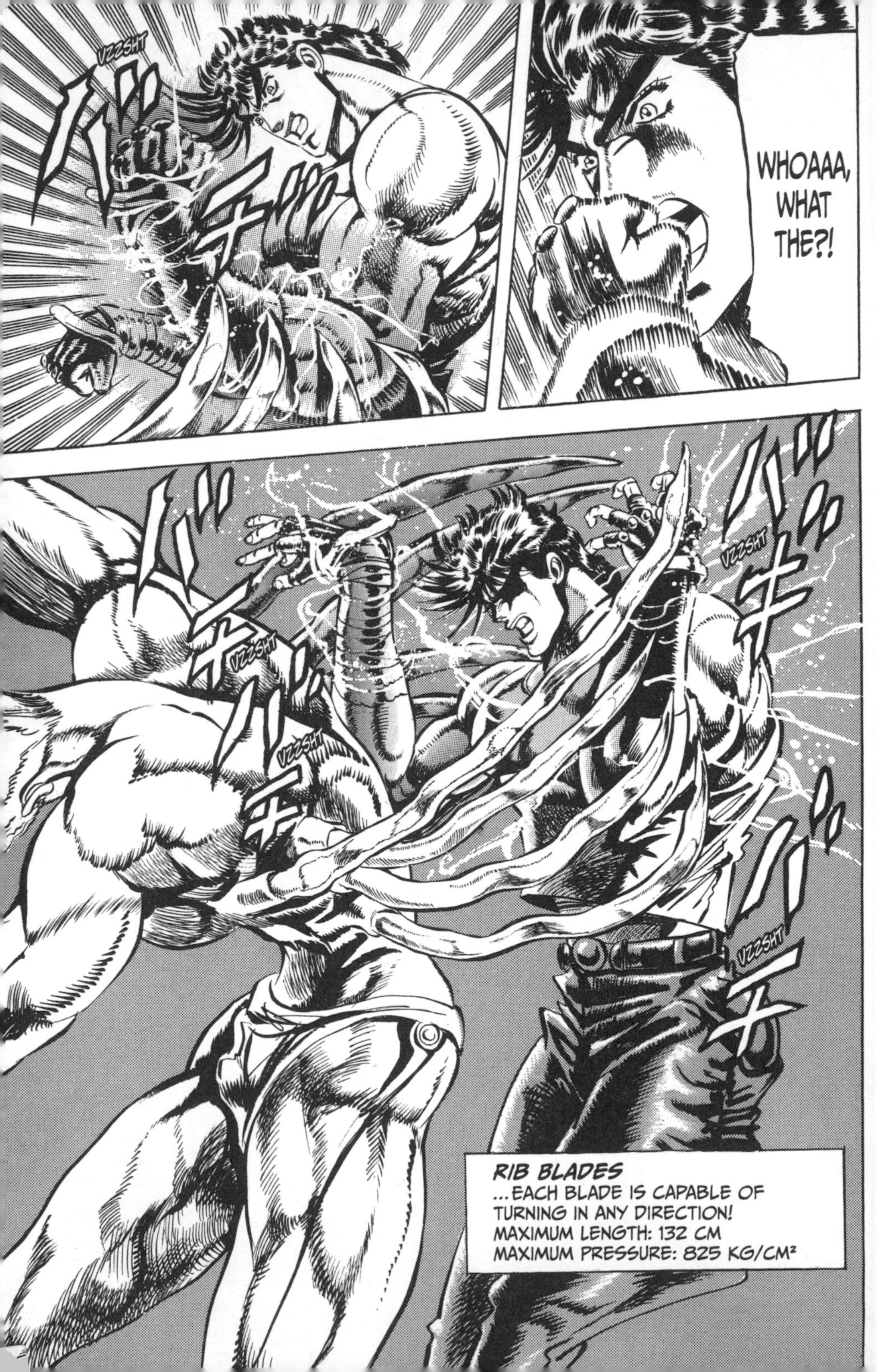
WHOAAA, WHAT THE?!
VZZSHT
VZZSHT
VZZSHT
VZZSHT
VZZSHT
RIB BLADES
...EACH BLADE IS CAPABLE OF TURNING IN ANY DIRECTION!
MAXIMUM LENGTH: 132 CM
MAXIMUM PRESSURE: 825 KG/CM²

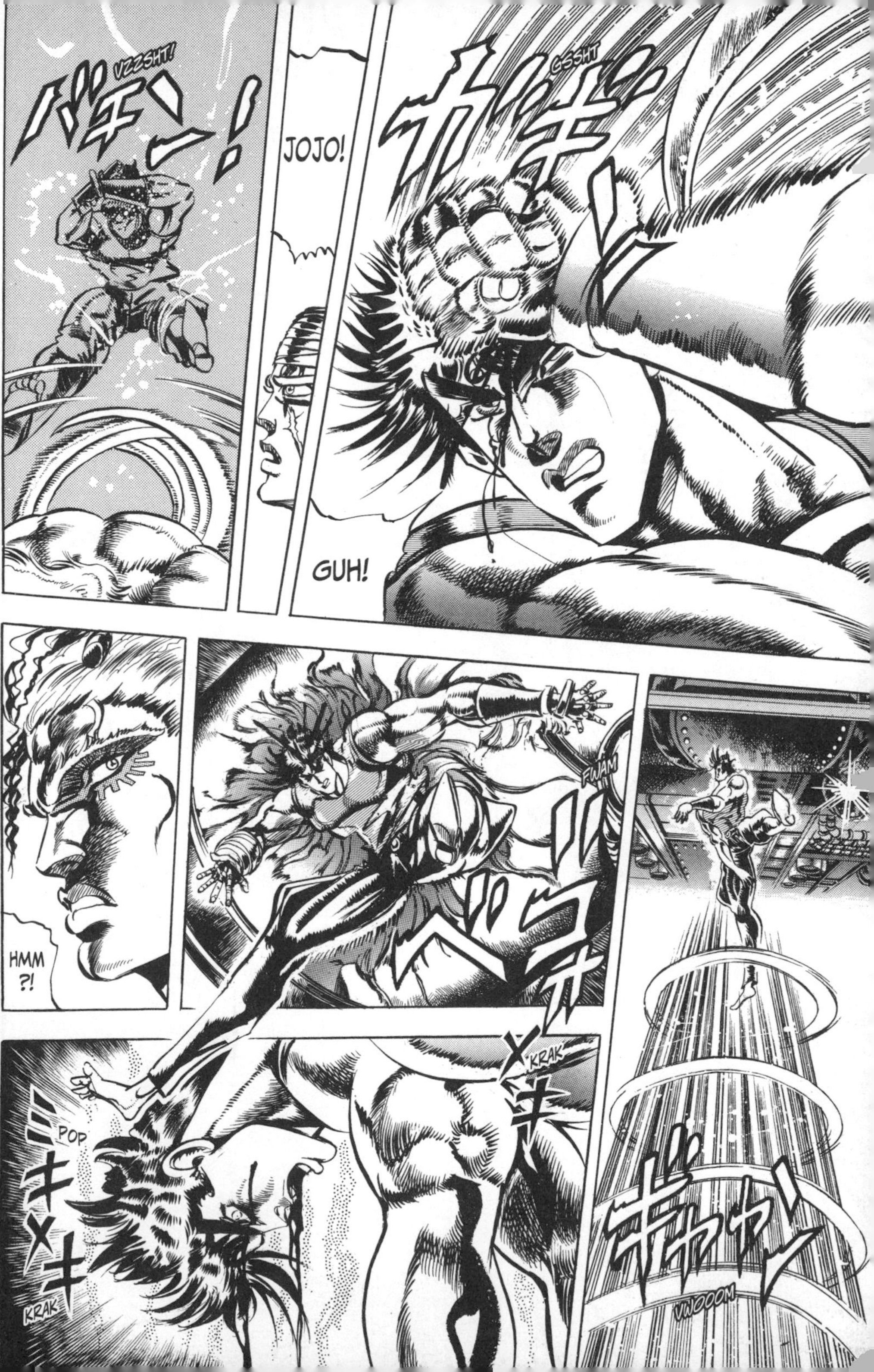
GSSHT
GUH!
JOJO!
VZZSHT!
VNOOOM
FWAM
KRAK
HMM ?!
POP
KRAK

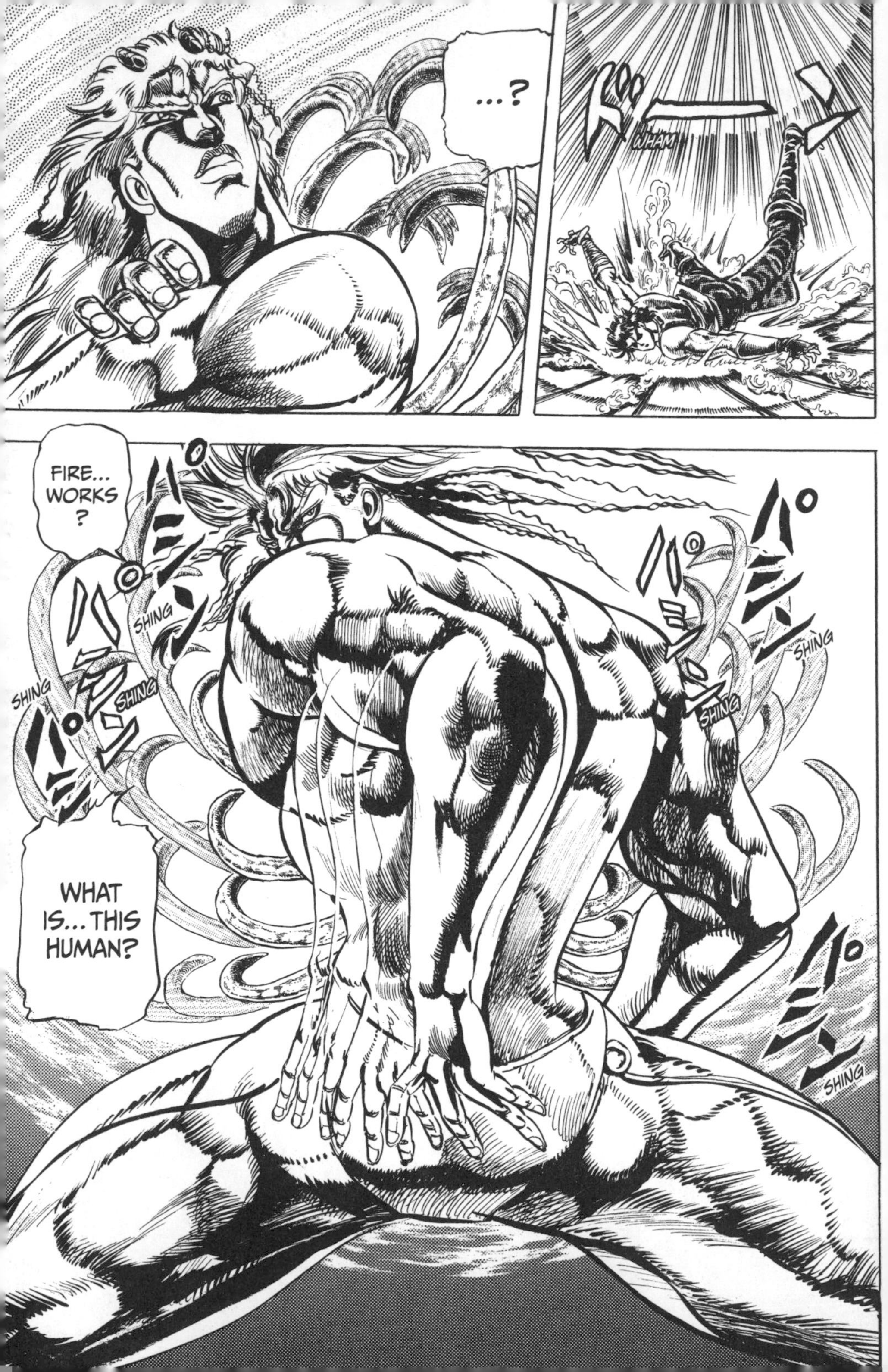
WHAM
...?
SHING
SHING
SHING
FIRE... WORKS?
SHING
SHING
SHING
WHAT IS... THIS HUMAN?

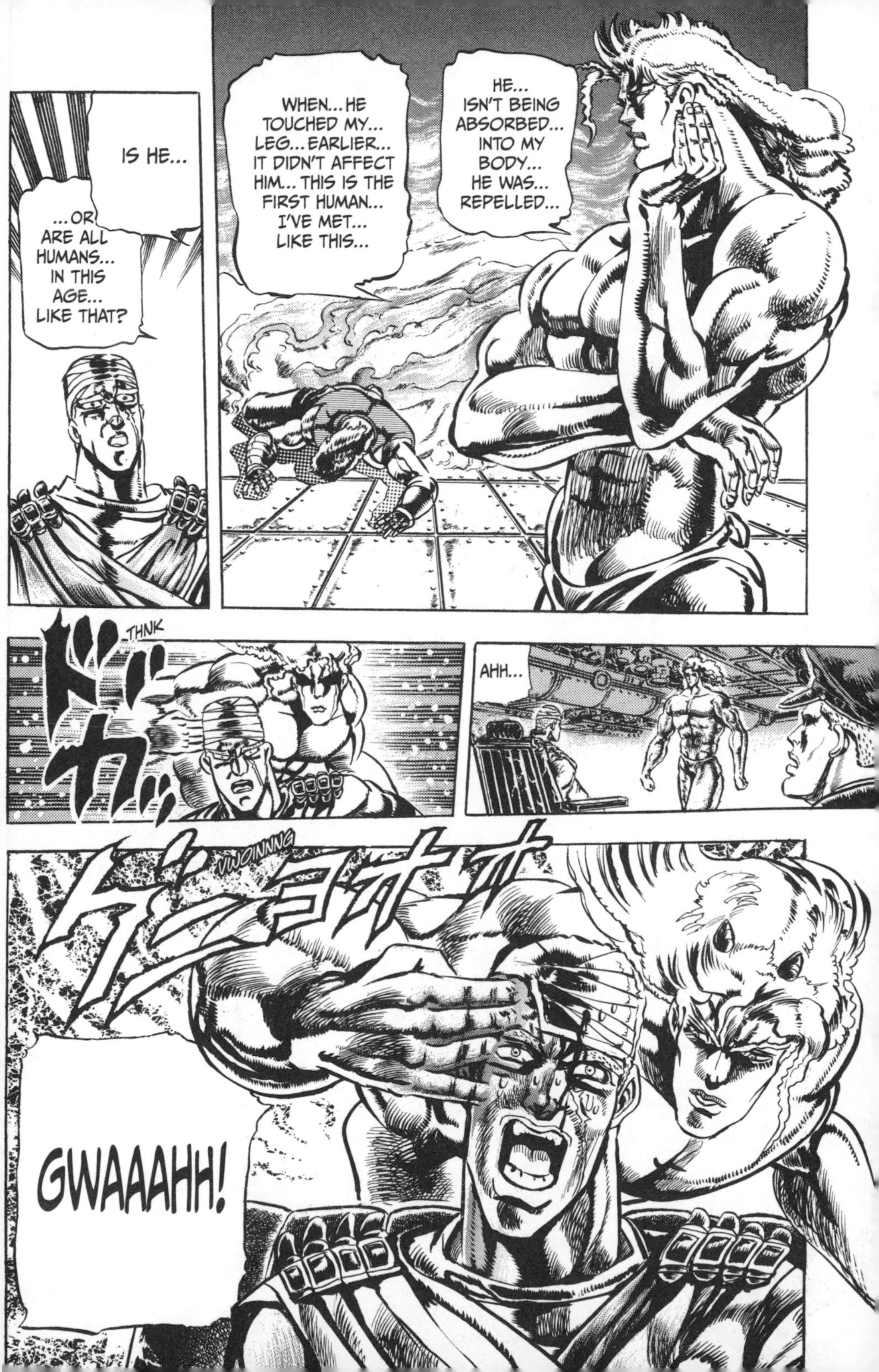
HE... ISN'T BEING ABSORBED... INTO MY BODY... HE WAS... REPELLED...
WHEN... HE TOUCHED MY... LEG... EARLIER... IT DIDN'T AFFECT HIM... THIS IS THE FIRST HUMAN... I'VE MET... LIKE THIS...
IS HE...
...OR ARE ALL HUMANS... IN THIS AGE... LIKE THAT?
AHH...
THNK
NWOINNNG
GWAAAHH!

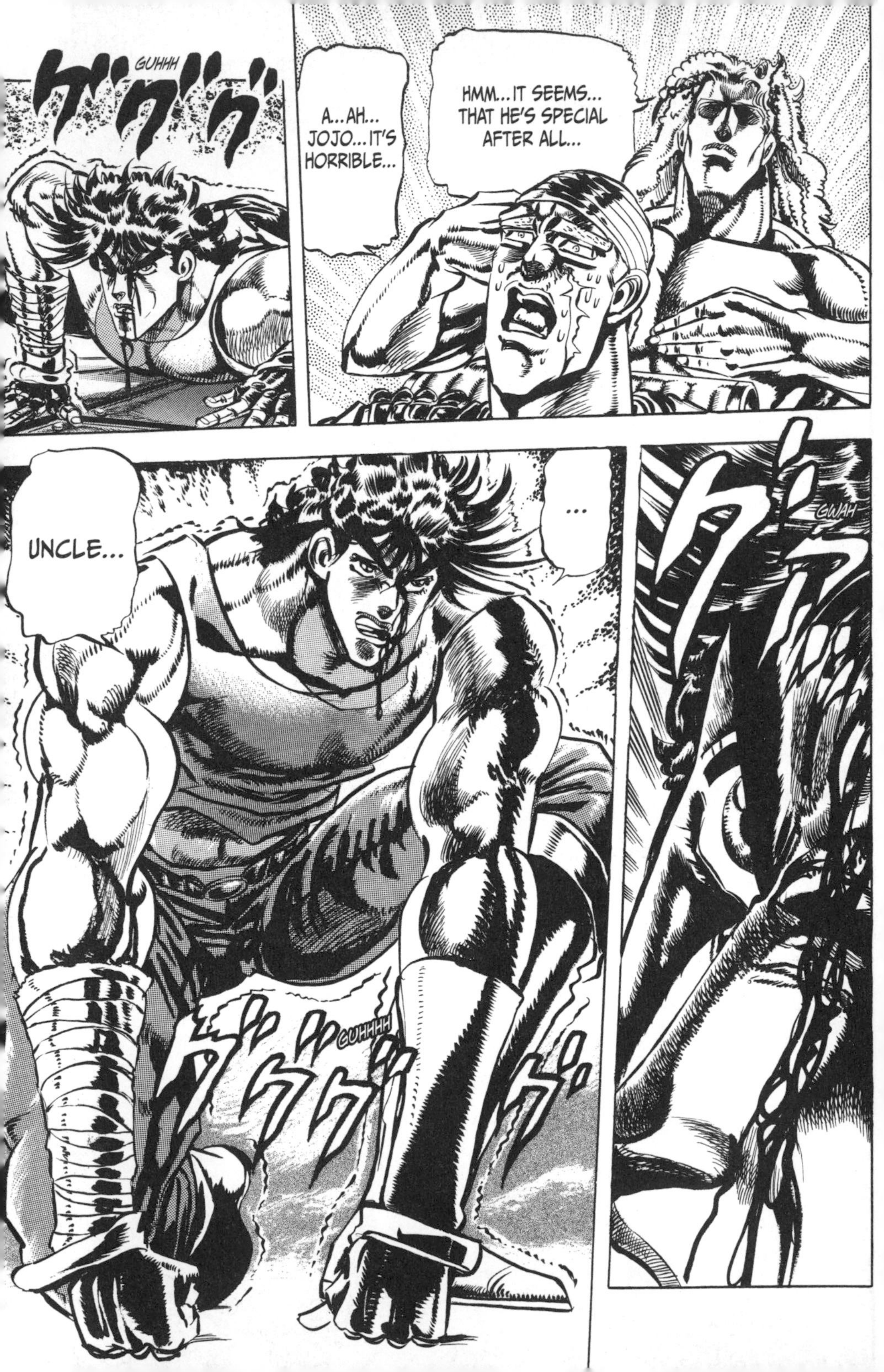
HMM...IT SEEMS... THAT HE'S SPECIAL AFTER ALL...
A...AH... JOJO...IT'S HORRIBLE...
GUHHH
GWAH
...
UNCLE...
GUHHHH

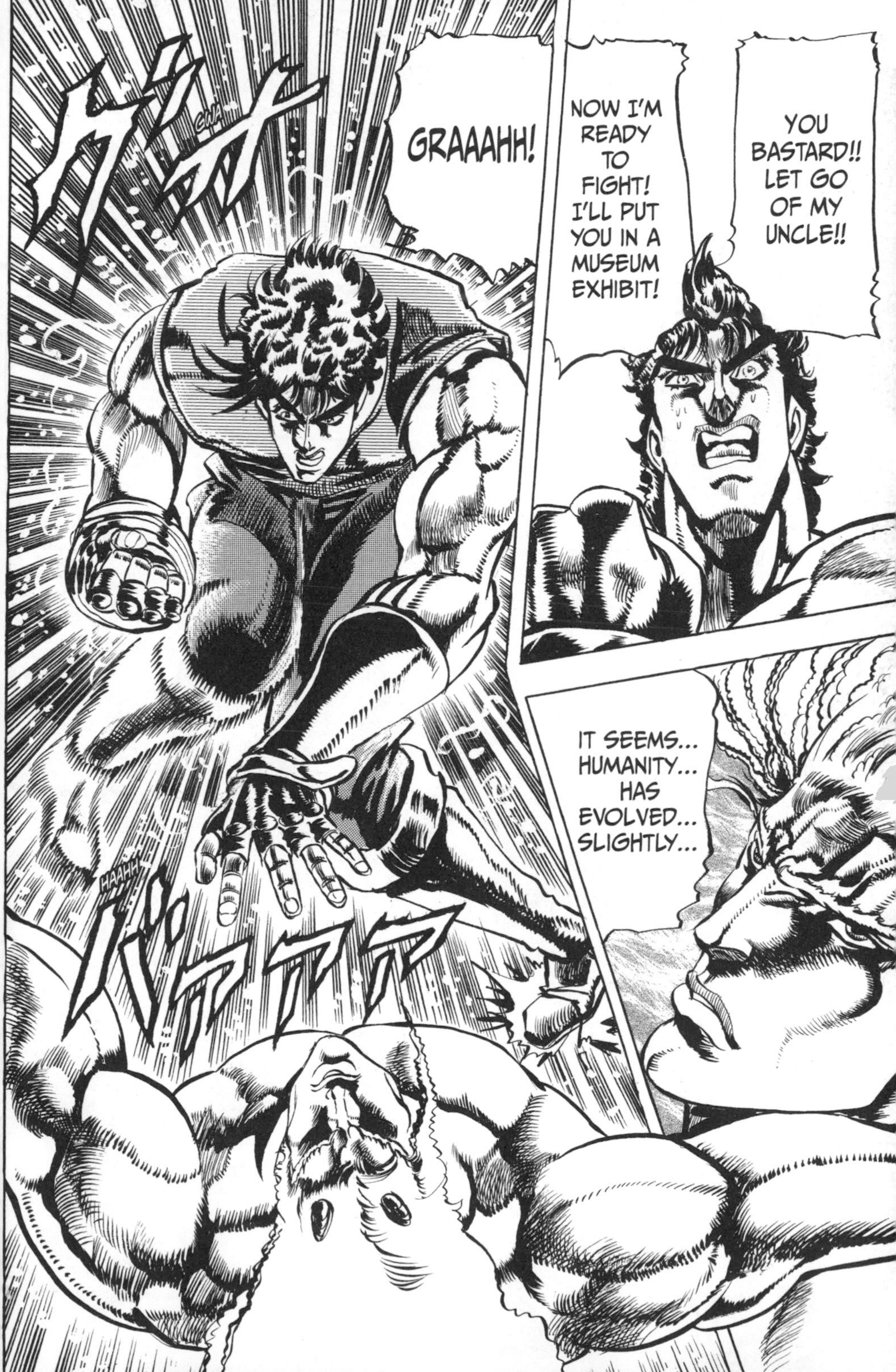
YOU BASTARD!! LET GO OF MY UNCLE!!
NOW I'M READY TO FIGHT! I'LL PUT YOU IN A MUSEUM EXHIBIT!
IT SEEMS... HUMANITY... HAS EVOLVED... SLIGHTLY...
GRAAAHH!
GWA
HAAHH

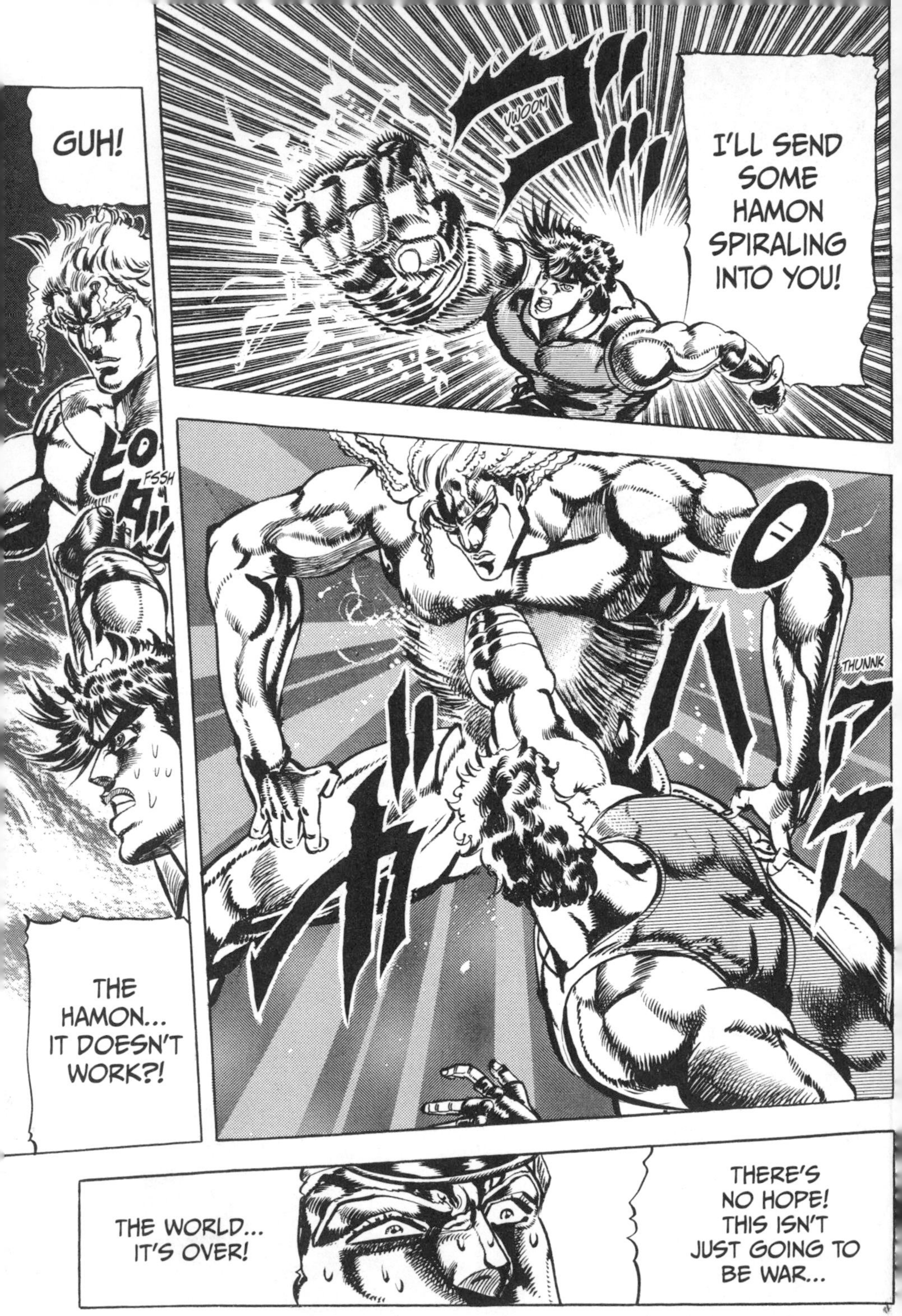
I'LL SEND SOME HAMON SPIRALING INTO YOU!
VWOOM
THUNNK
GUH!
FSSH
THE HAMON... IT DOESN'T WORK?!
THERE'S NO HOPE! THIS ISN'T JUST GOING TO BE WAR...
THE WORLD... IT'S OVER!

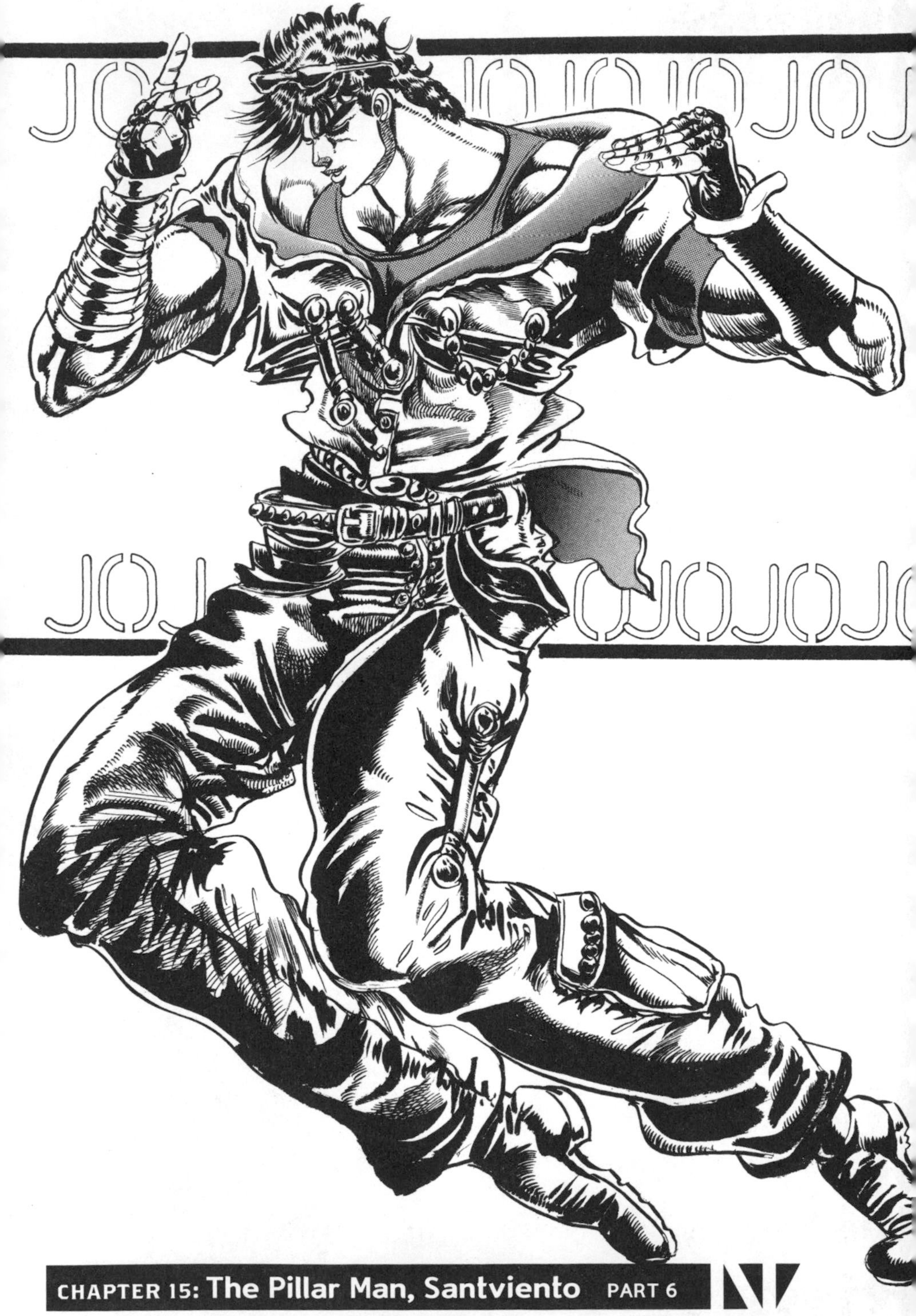

CHAPTER 15: The Pillar Man, Santviento PART 6

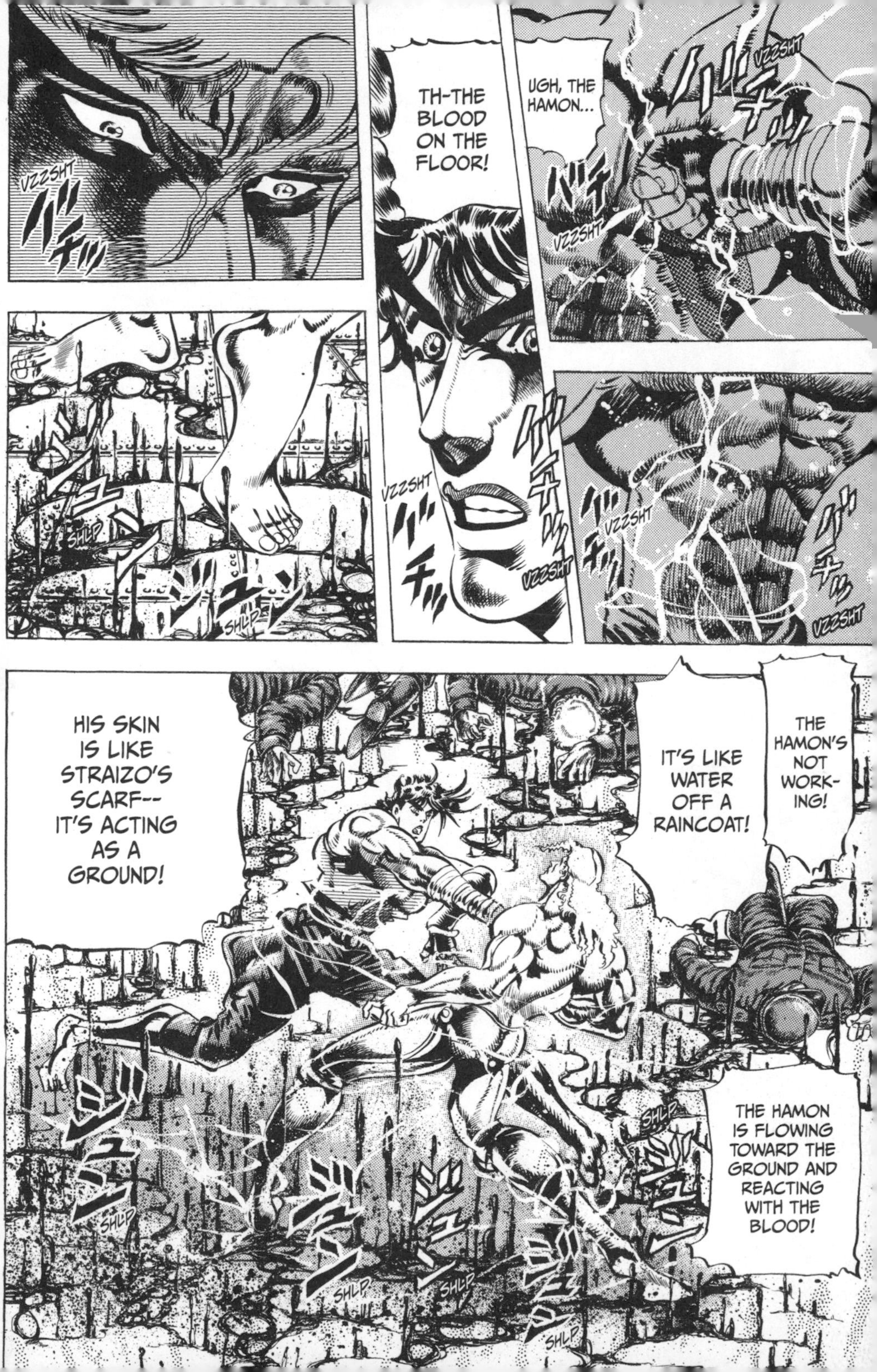
UGH, THE HAMON...
VZZSHT
VZZSHT
VZZSHT
VZZSHT
VZZSHT
TH-THE BLOOD ON THE FLOOR!
VZZSHT
VZZSHT
SHLP
SHLP
THE HAMON'S NOT WORK-ING!
IT'S LIKE WATER OFF A RAINCOAT!
HIS SKIN IS LIKE STRAIZO'S SCARF-- IT'S ACTING AS A GROUND!
THE HAMON IS FLOWING TOWARD THE GROUND AND REACTING WITH THE BLOOD!
SHLP
SHLP
SHLP
SHLP
SHLP

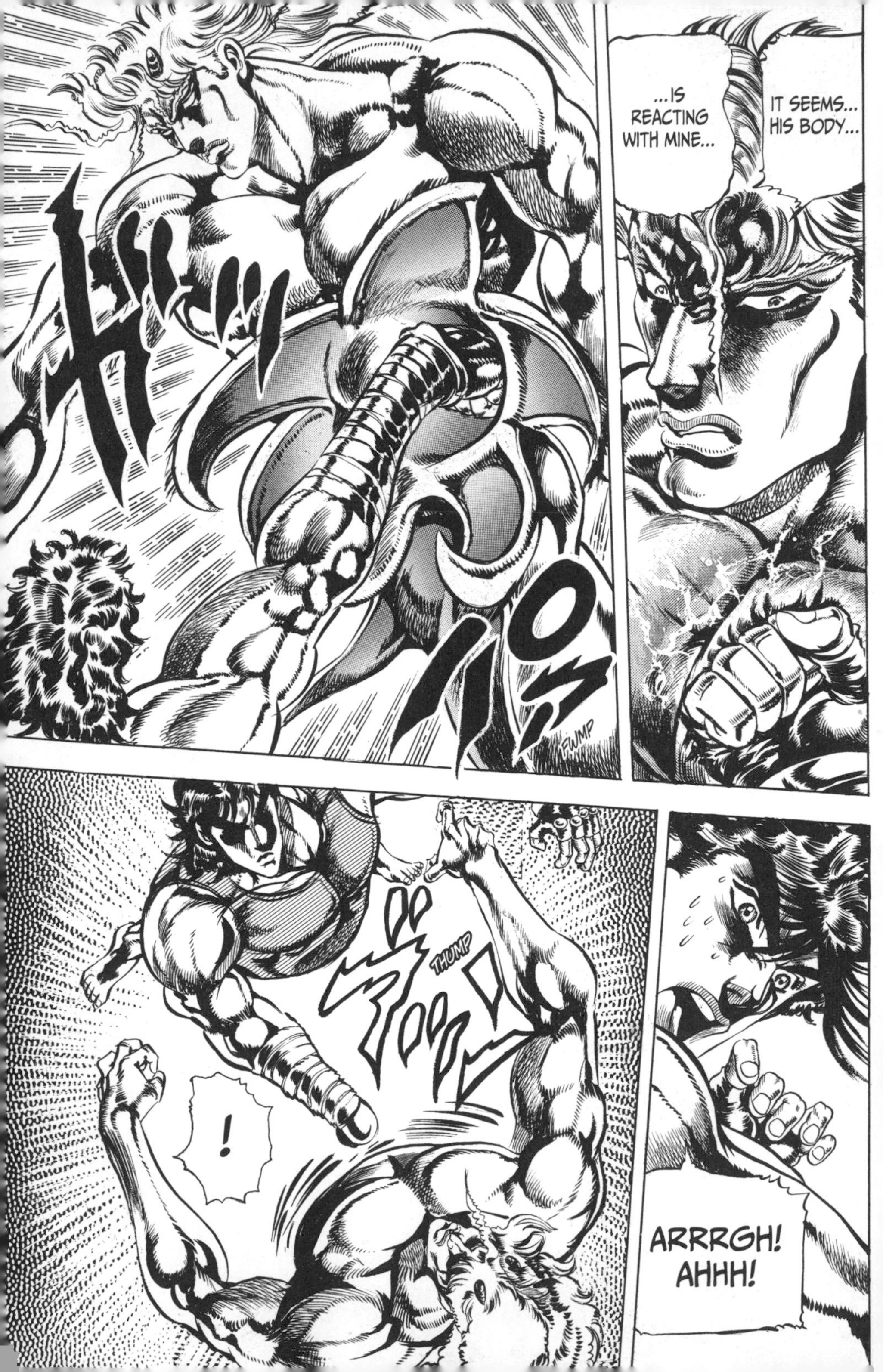
IT SEEMS... HIS BODY...
...IS REACTING WITH MINE...
FWUMP
ARRRGH! AHHH!
THUMP
!

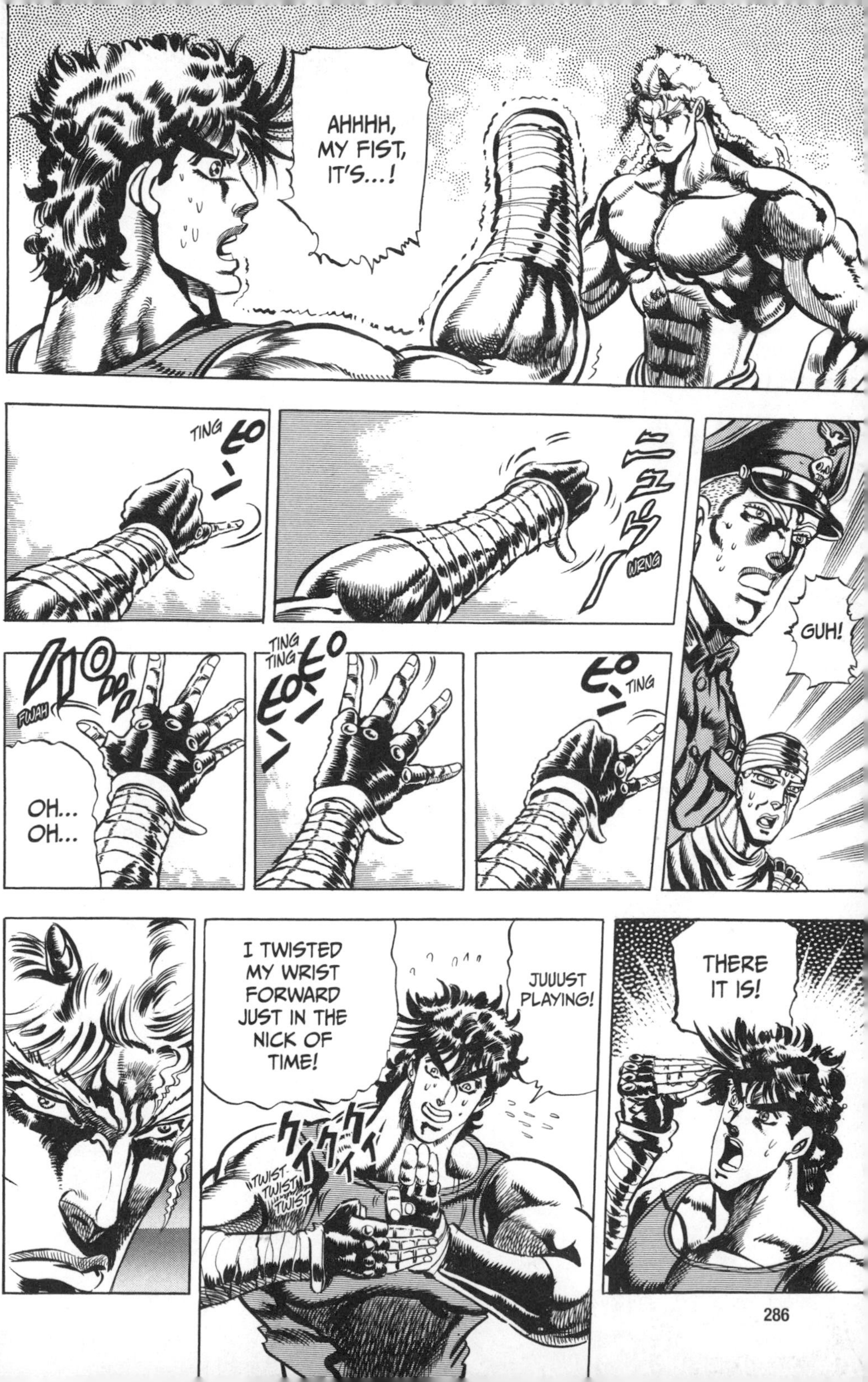

AHHHH, MY FIST, IT'S...!
GUH!
WRNG
TING
TING
TING TING
FWAH
OH... OH...
THERE IT IS!
JUUUST PLAYING!
I TWISTED MY WRIST FORWARD JUST IN THE NICK OF TIME!
TWIST TWIST TWIST

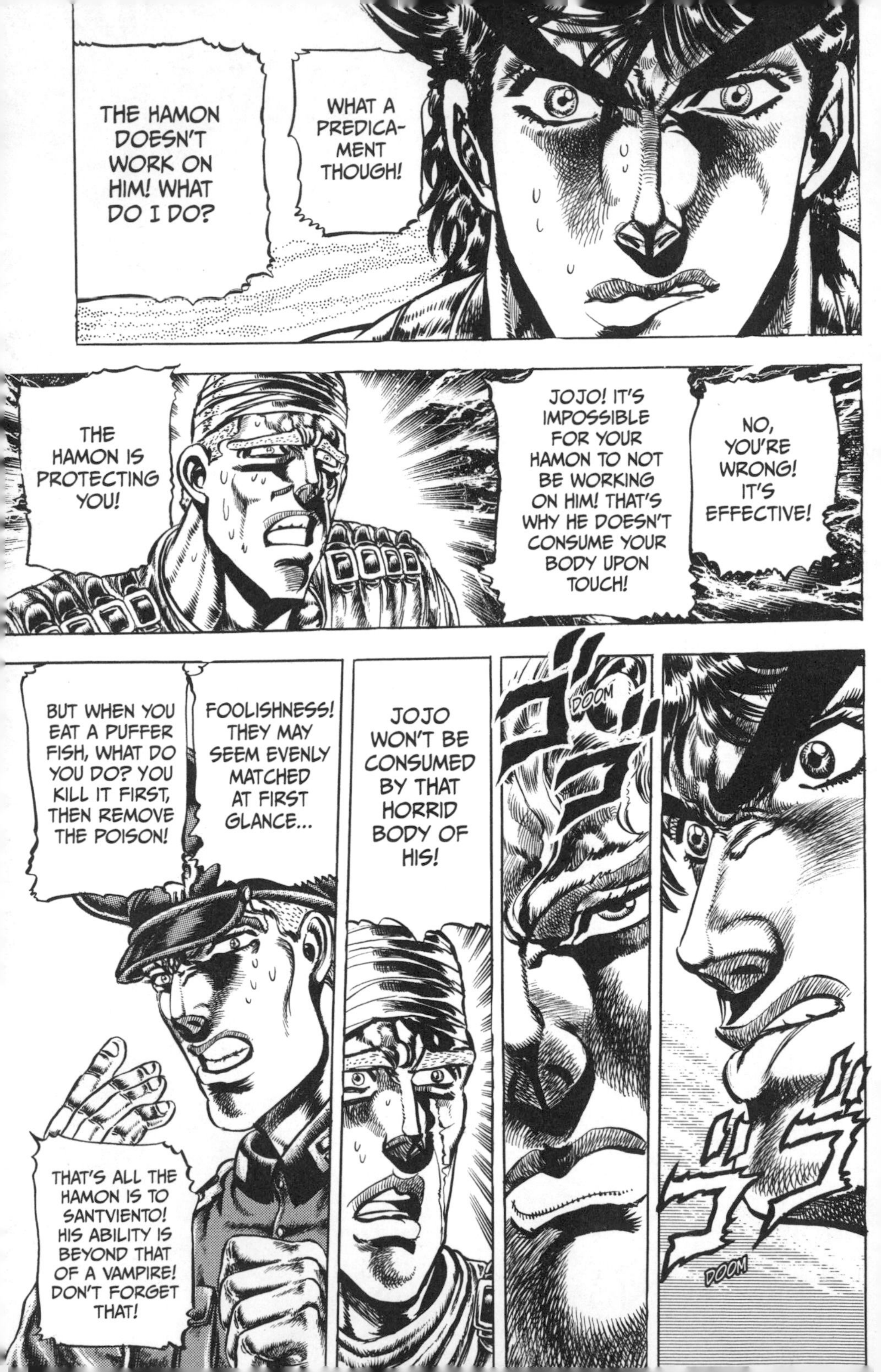
WHAT A PREDICAMENT THOUGH!
THE HAMON DOESN'T WORK ON HIM! WHAT DO I DO?
NO, YOU'RE WRONG! IT'S EFFECTIVE!
JOJO! IT'S IMPOSSIBLE FOR YOUR HAMON TO NOT BE WORKING ON HIM! THAT'S WHY HE DOESN'T CONSUME YOUR BODY UPON TOUCH!
THE HAMON IS PROTECTING YOU!
DOOM
DOOM
JOJO WON'T BE CONSUMED BY THAT HORRID BODY OF HIS!
FOOLISHNESS! THEY MAY SEEM EVENLY MATCHED AT FIRST GLANCE...
BUT WHEN YOU EAT A PUFFER FISH, WHAT DO YOU DO? YOU KILL IT FIRST, THEN REMOVE THE POISON!
THAT'S ALL THE HAMON IS TO SANTVIENTO! HIS ABILITY IS BEYOND THAT OF A VAMPIRE! DON'T FORGET THAT!

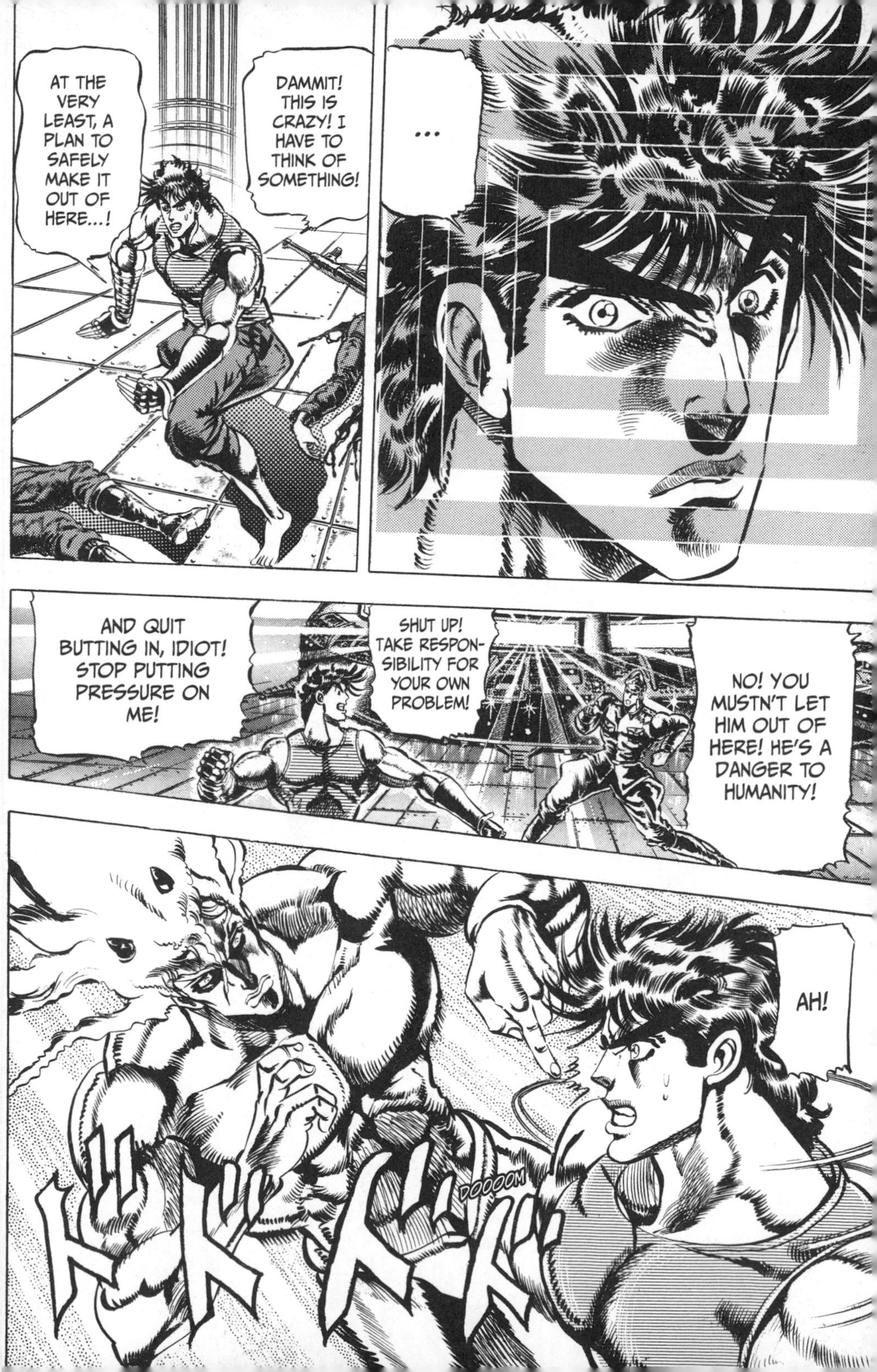
...
DAMMIT! THIS IS CRAZY! I HAVE TO THINK OF SOMETHING!
AT THE VERY LEAST, A PLAN TO SAFELY MAKE IT OUT OF HERE...!
NO! YOU MUSTN'T LET HIM OUT OF HERE! HE'S A DANGER TO HUMANITY!
SHUT UP! TAKE RESPON-SIBILITY FOR YOUR OWN PROBLEM!
AND QUIT BUTTING IN, IDIOT! STOP PUTTING PRESSURE ON ME!
AH!
DOOOOM

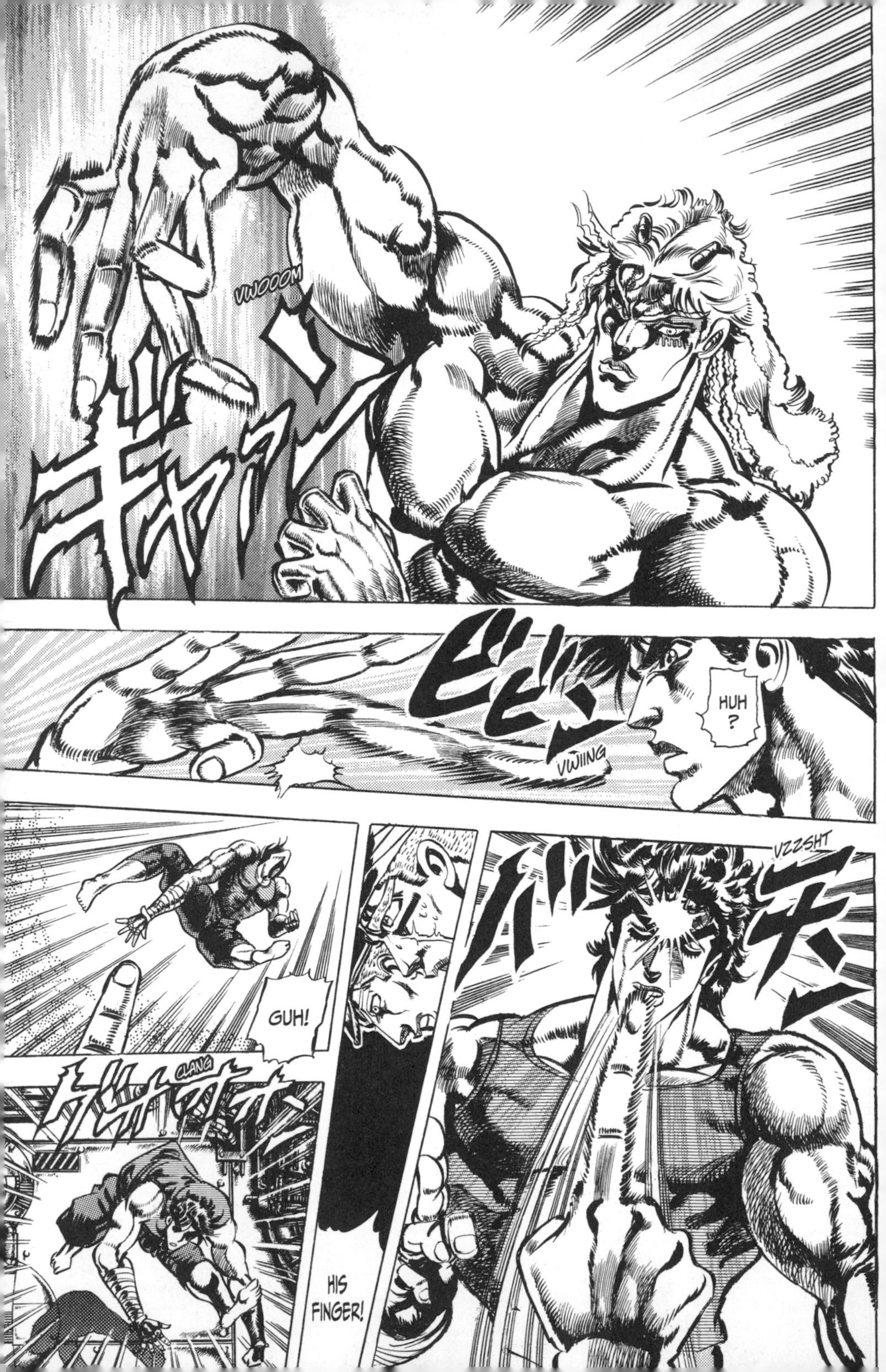
VWOOOM
HUH ?
VWIING
VZZSHT
HIS FINGER!
GUH!
CLANG

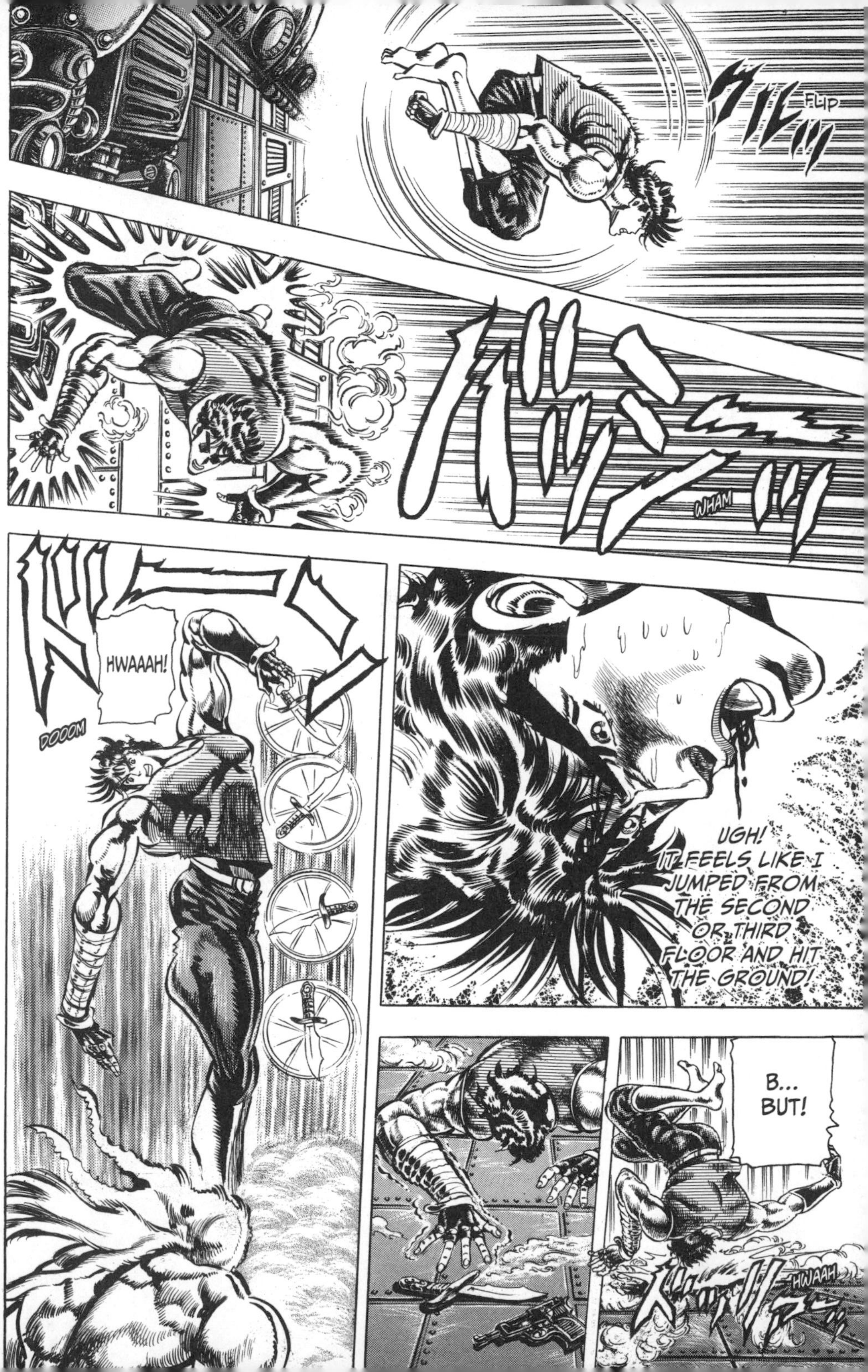
FLIP
WHAM
UGH! IT FEELS LIKE I JUMPED FROM THE SECOND OR THIRD FLOOR AND HIT THE GROUND!
B... BUT!
HWAAH
HWAAAH!
DOOOM

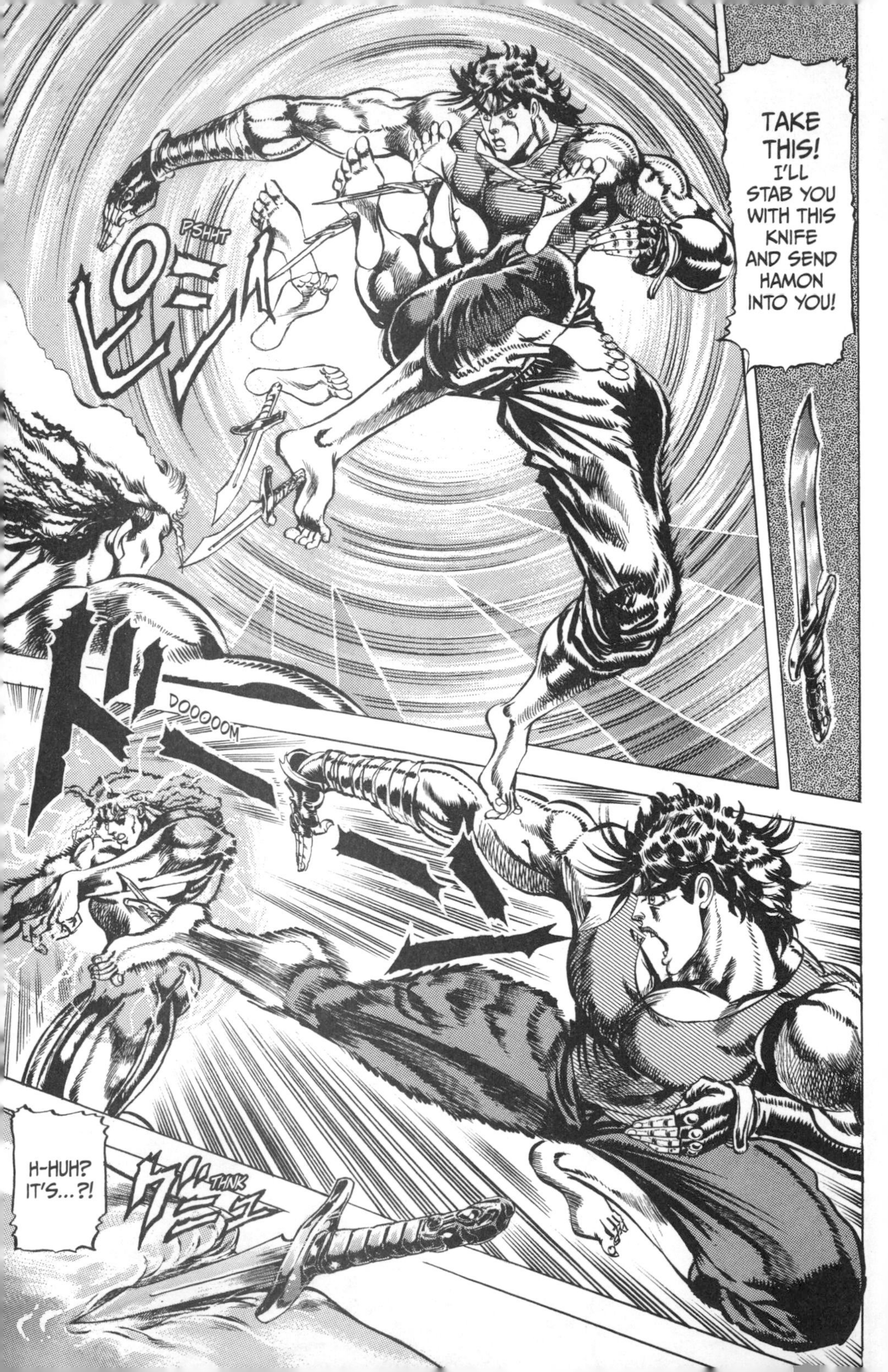
TAKE THIS! I'LL STAB YOU WITH THIS KNIFE AND SEND HAMON INTO YOU!
PSHHT
DOOOOOM
H-HUH? IT'S...?!
THNK

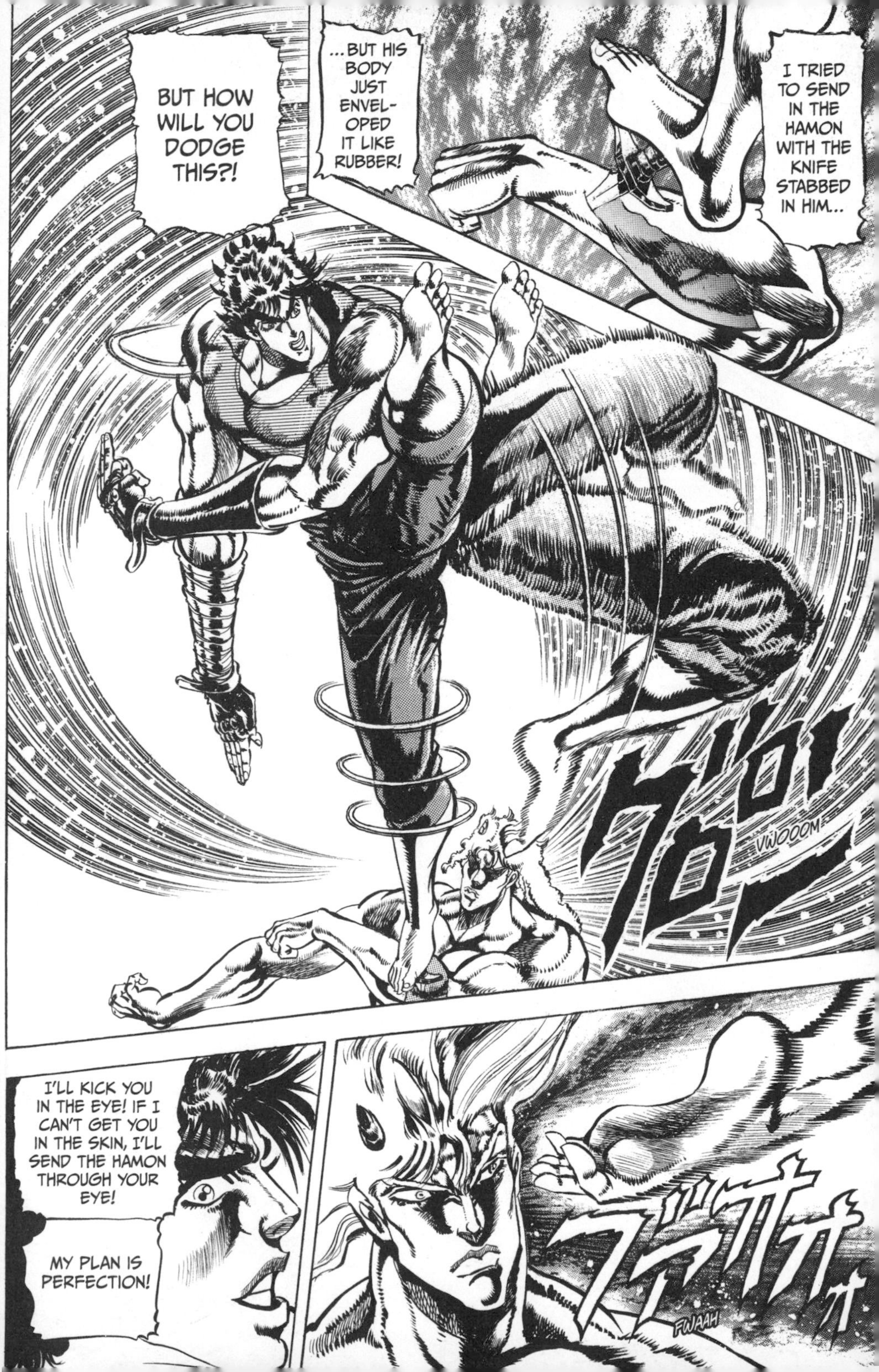
I TRIED TO SEND IN THE HAMON WITH THE KNIFE STABBED IN HIM...
...BUT HIS BODY JUST ENVELOPED IT LIKE RUBBER!
BUT HOW WILL YOU DODGE THIS?!
VWOOOM
FWAAH
I'LL KICK YOU IN THE EYE! IF I CAN'T GET YOU IN THE SKIN, I'LL SEND THE HAMON THROUGH YOUR EYE!
MY PLAN IS PERFECTION!

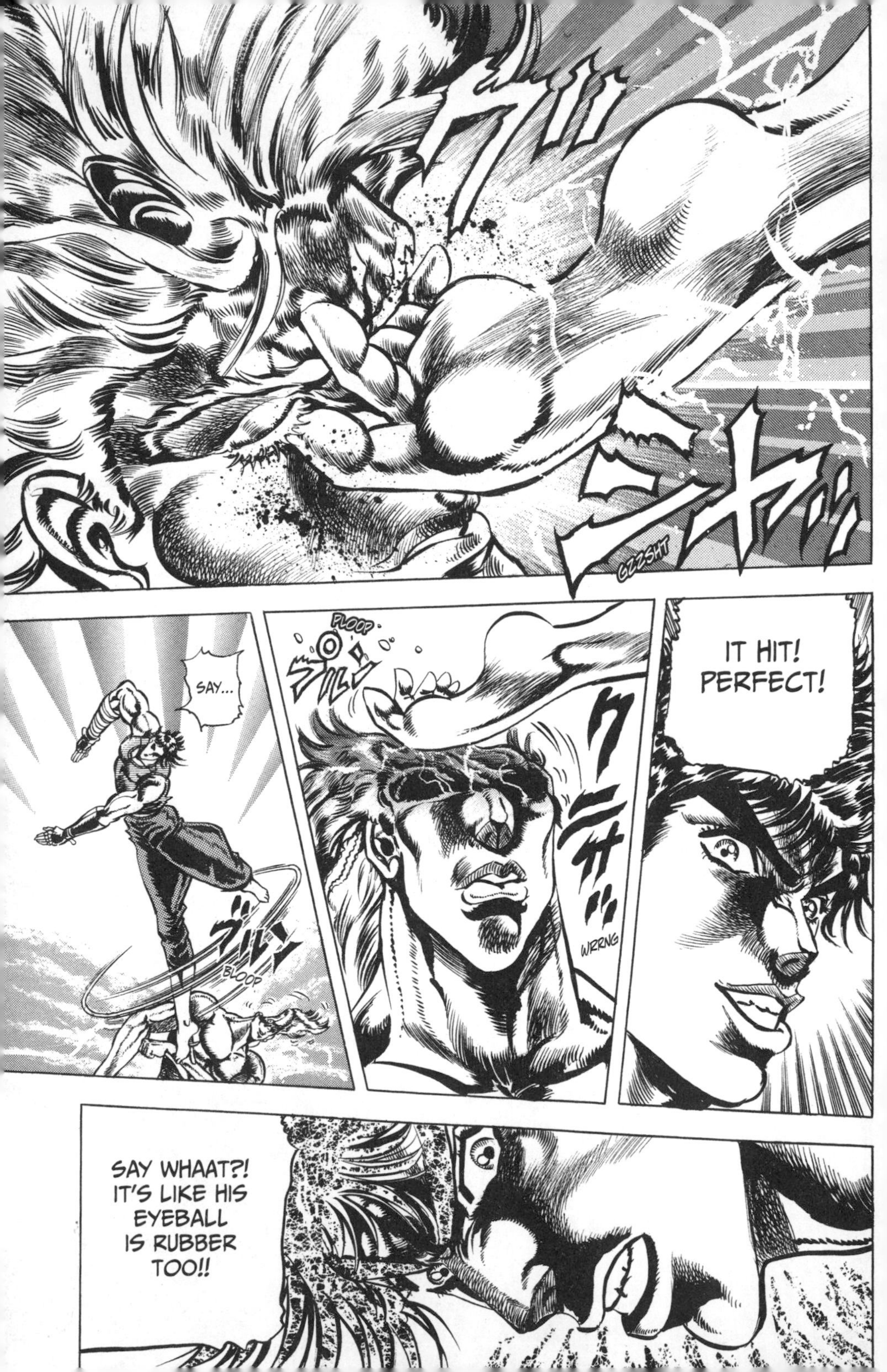
CZZSHT
IT HIT! PERFECT!
PLOOP
WRRNG
SAY...
BLOOP
SAY WHAAT?! IT'S LIKE HIS EYEBALL IS RUBBER TOO!!

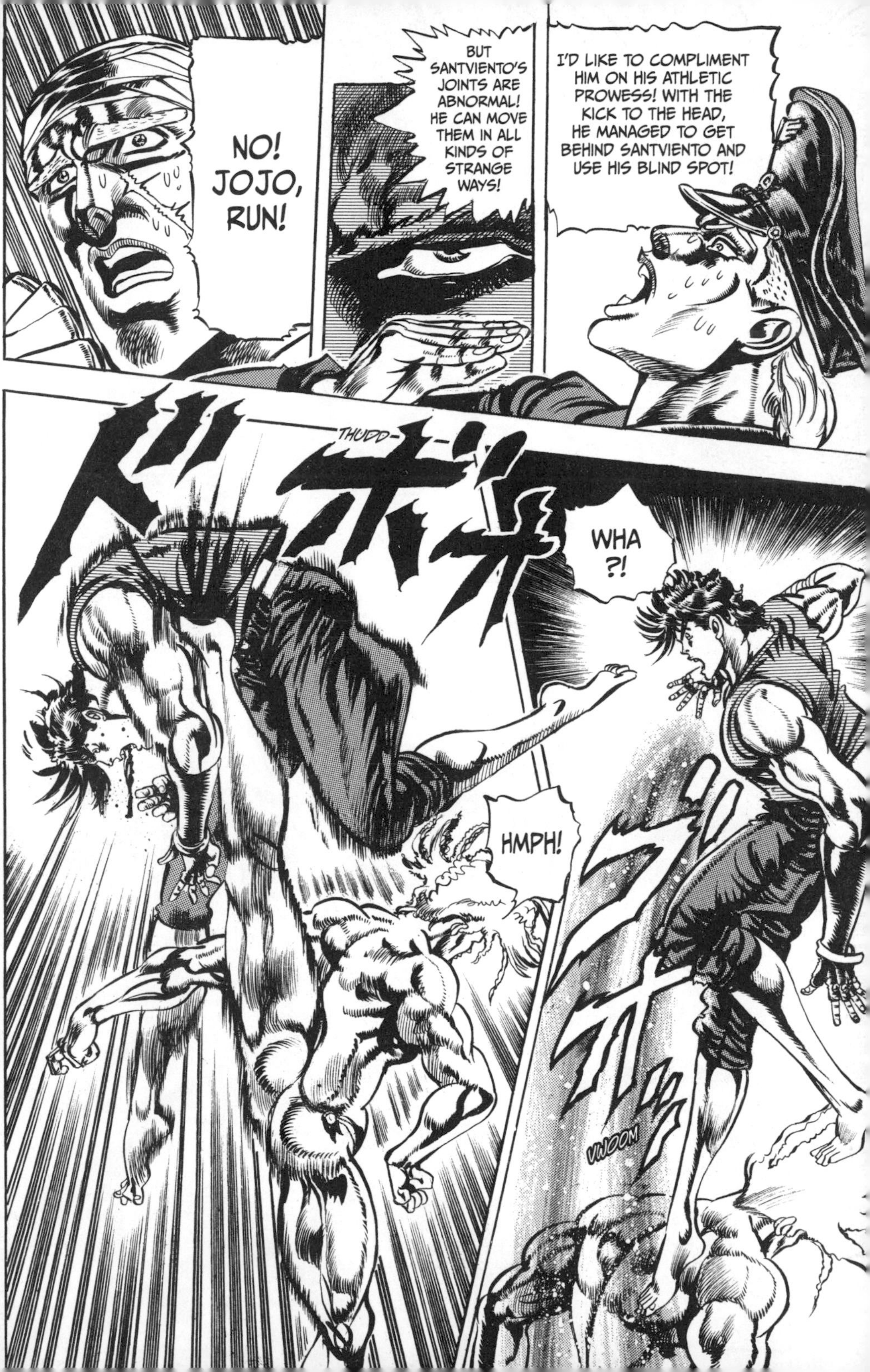
I'D LIKE TO COMPLIMENT HIM ON HIS ATHLETIC PROWESS! WITH THE KICK TO THE HEAD, HE MANAGED TO GET BEHIND SANTVIENTO AND USE HIS BLIND SPOT!
BUT SANTVIENTO'S JOINTS ARE ABNORMAL! HE CAN MOVE THEM IN ALL KINDS OF STRANGE WAYS!
NO! JOJO, RUN!
THUDD
WHA ?!
HMPH!
VWOOM

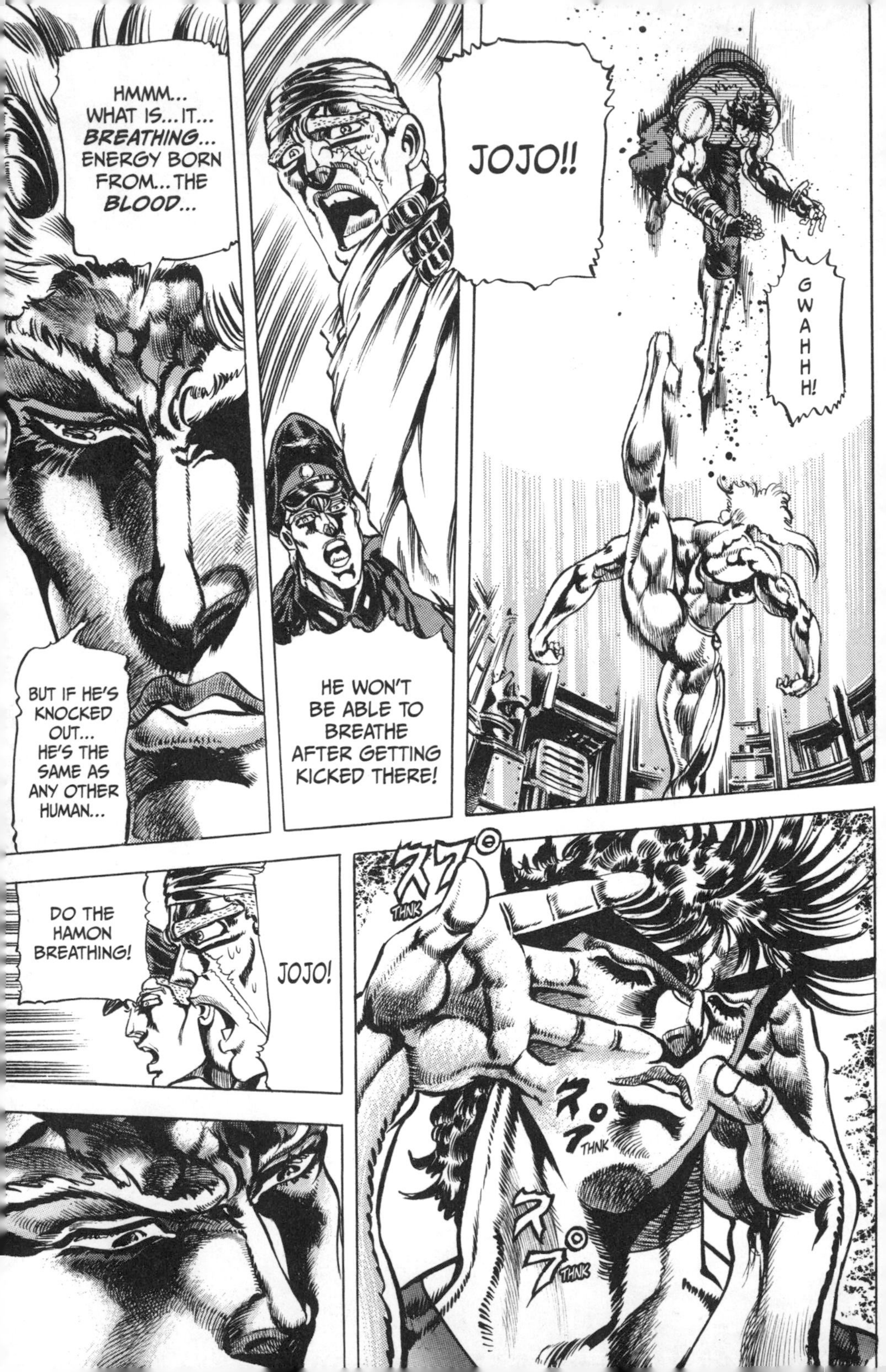
GWAHHH!
JOJO!!
HE WON'T BE ABLE TO BREATHE AFTER GETTING KICKED THERE!
HMMM... WHAT IS... IT... BREATHING... ENERGY BORN FROM... THE BLOOD...
BUT IF HE'S KNOCKED OUT... HE'S THE SAME AS ANY OTHER HUMAN...
THNK
THNK
THNK
JOJO!
DO THE HAMON BREATHING!

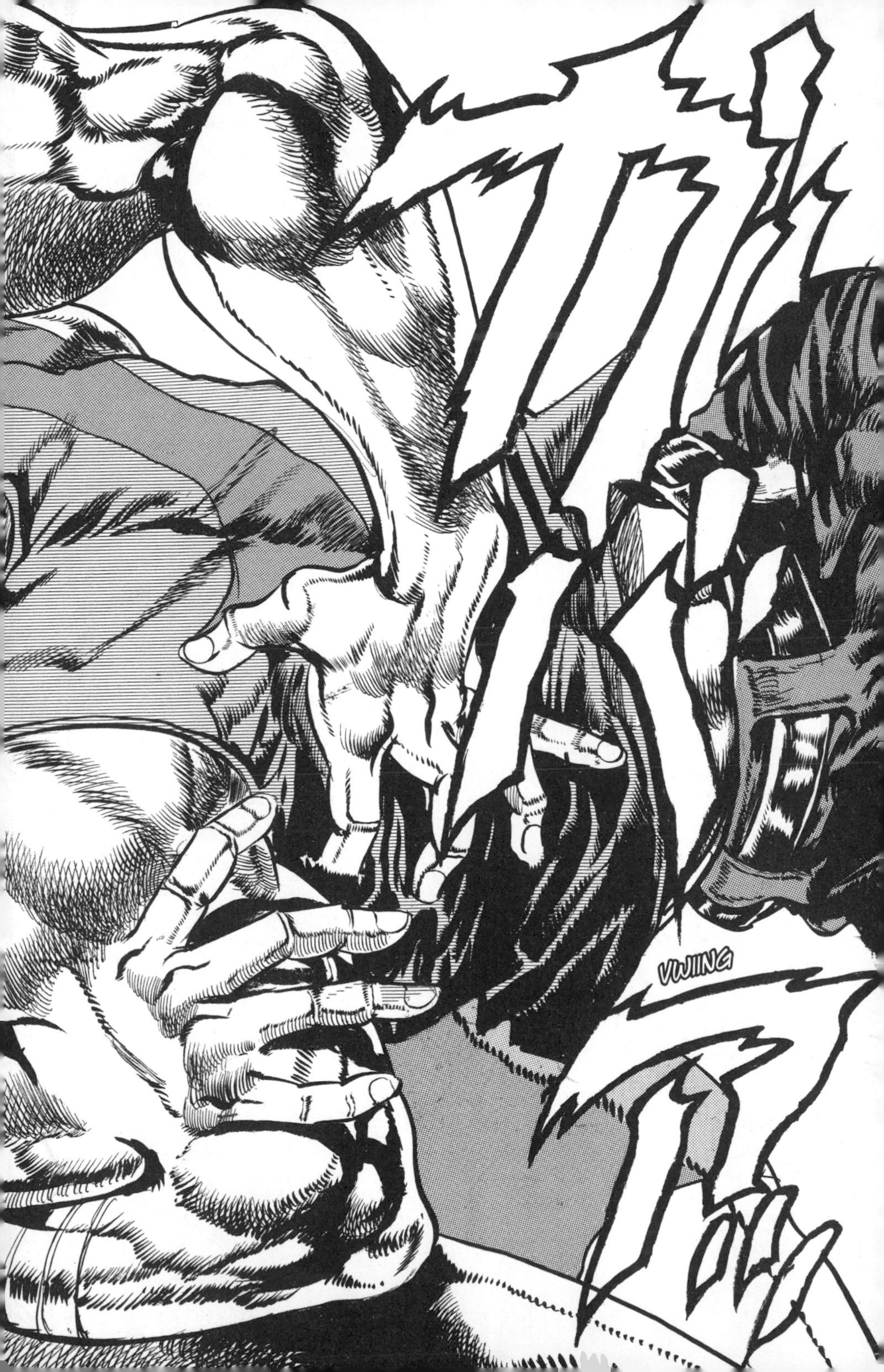
VWIING

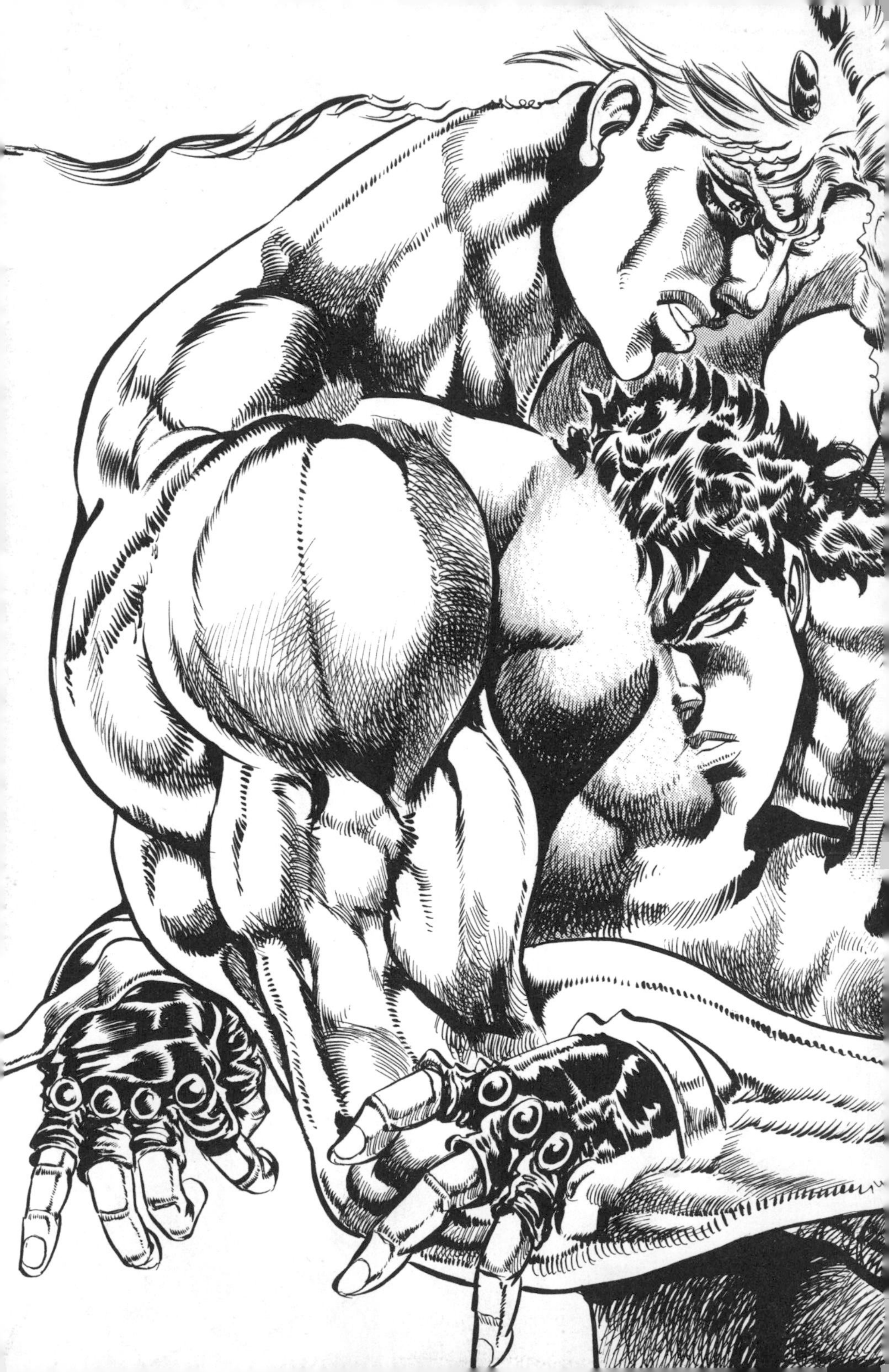

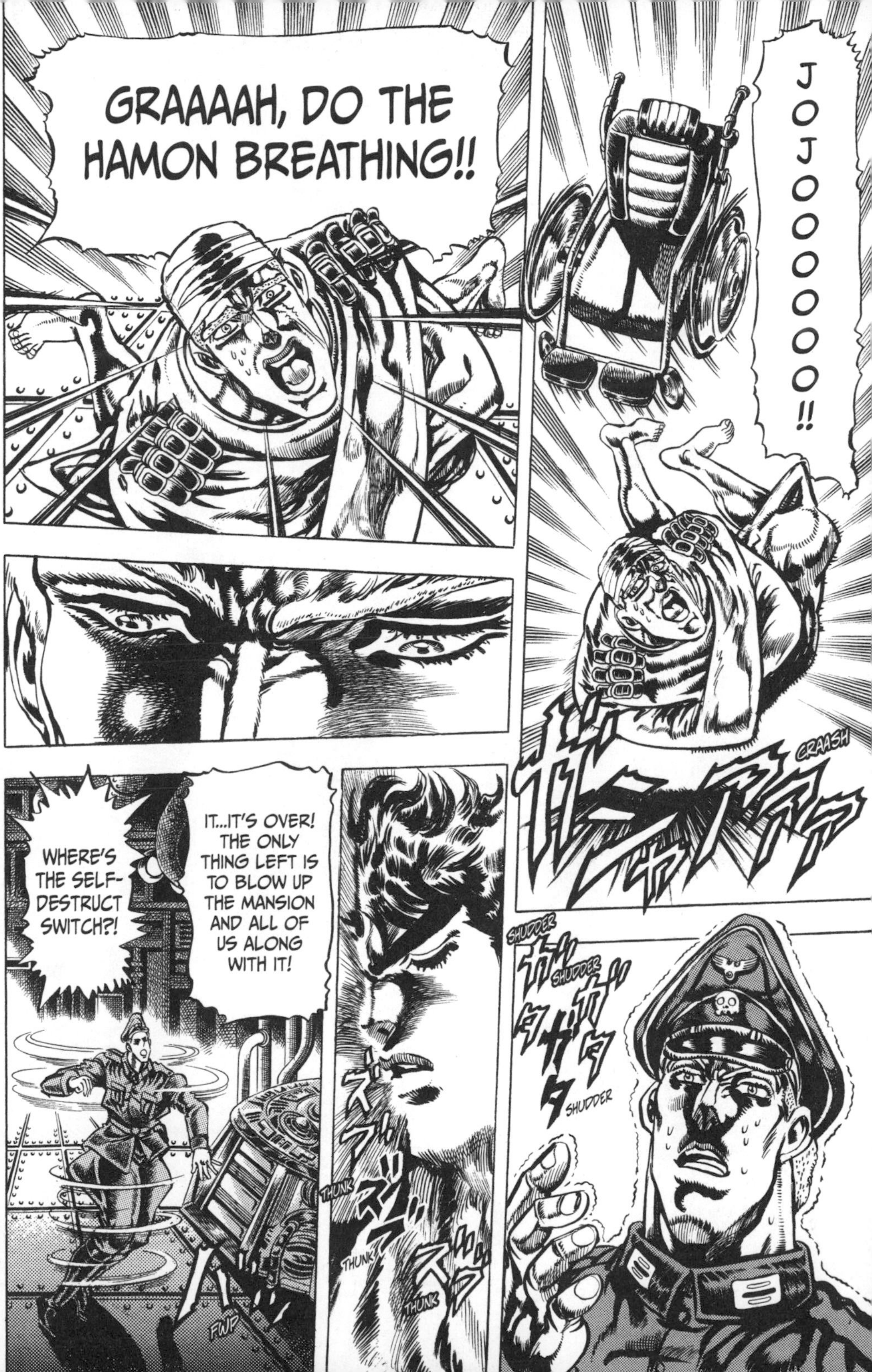
JOJOOOOOOOO!!
CRAASH
GRAAAAH, DO THE HAMON BREATHING!!
SHUDDER
SHUDDER
SHUDDER
THUNK
THUNK
THUNK
IT...IT'S OVER! THE ONLY THING LEFT IS TO BLOW UP THE MANSION AND ALL OF US ALONG WITH IT!
WHERE'S THE SELF-DESTRUCT SWITCH?!
FWP

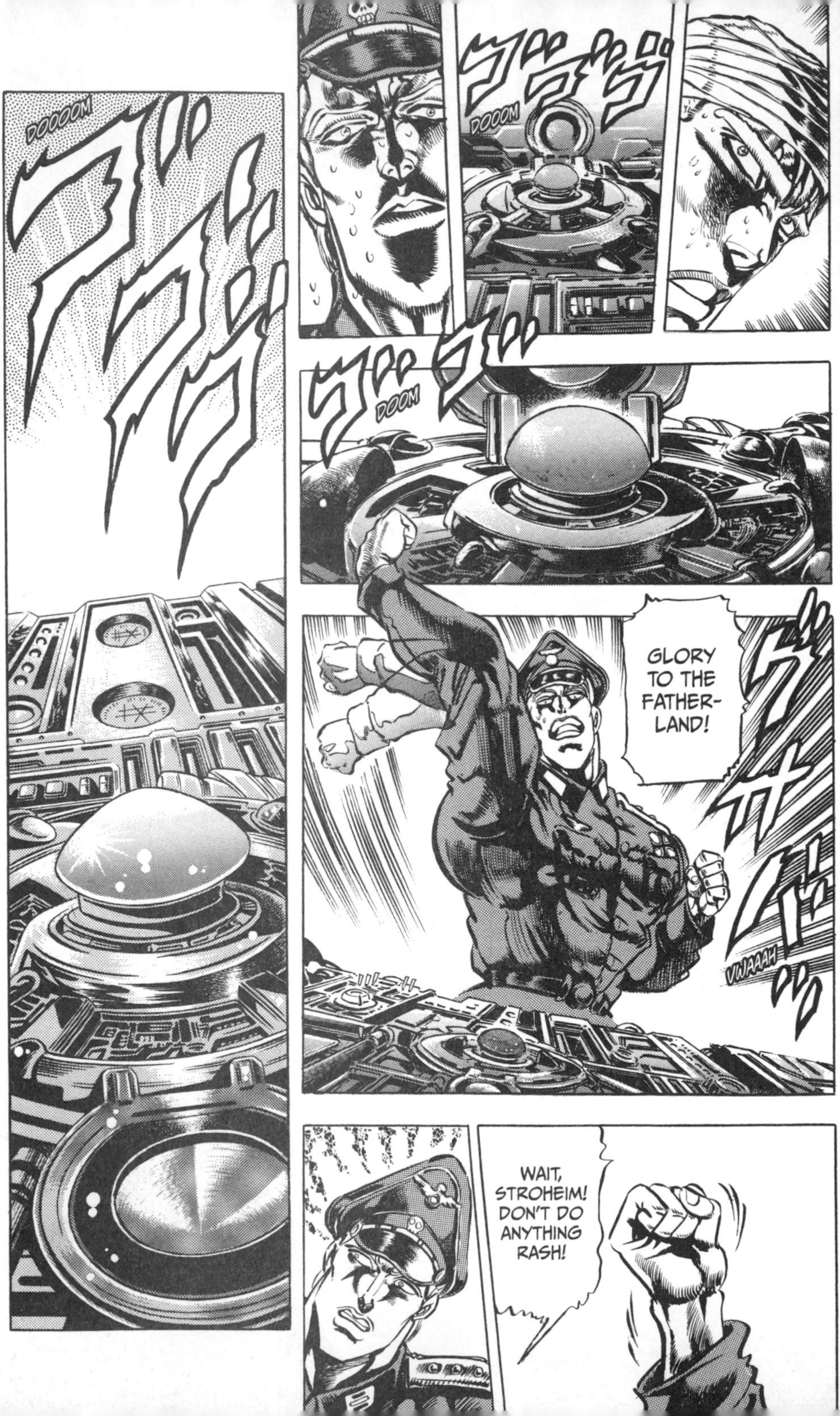
DOOOM
DOOM
GLORY TO THE FATHER-LAND!
VWAAAH
WAIT, STROHEIM! DON'T DO ANYTHING RASH!
DOOOOM

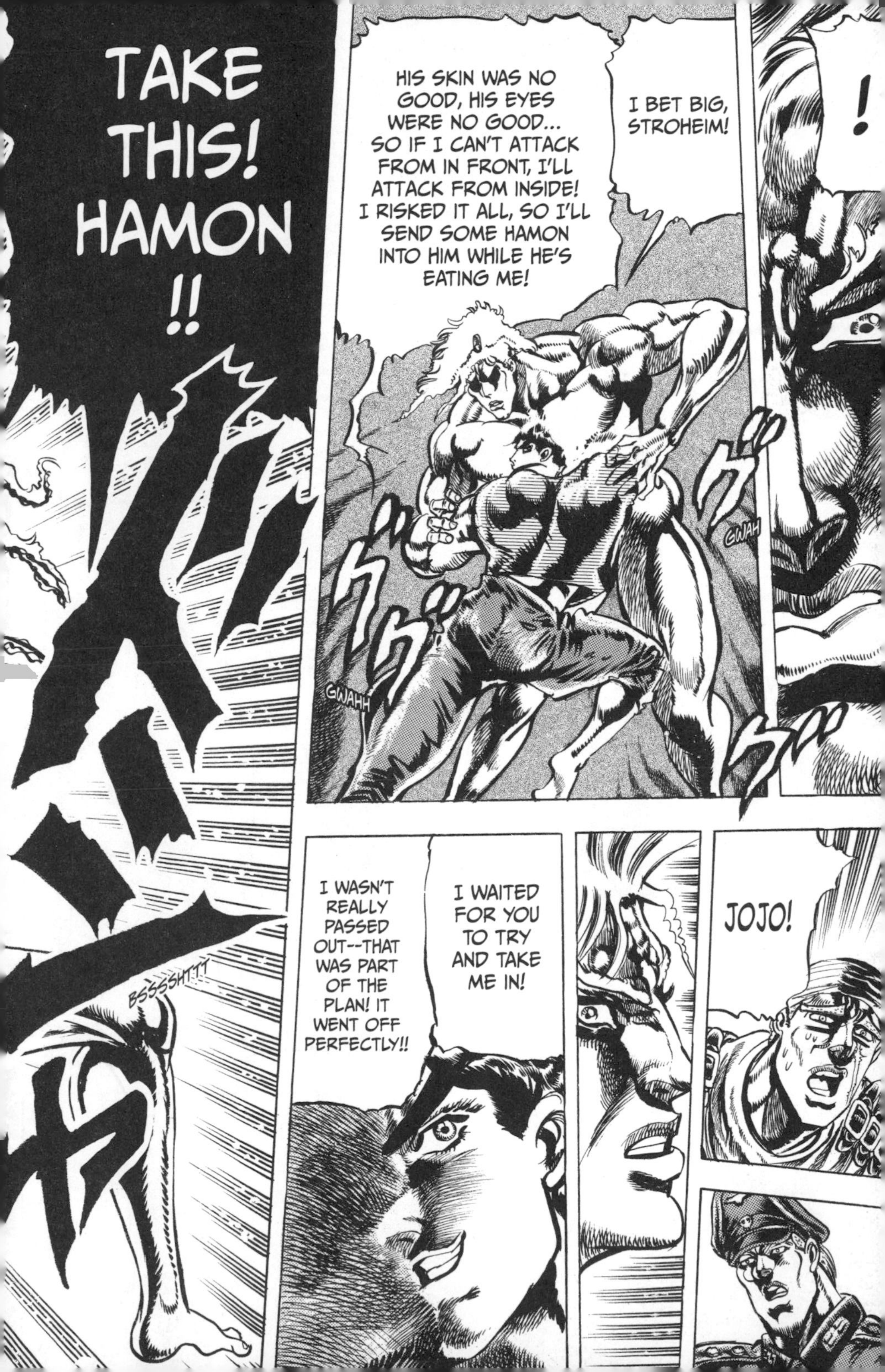
!
I BET BIG, STROHEIM!
HIS SKIN WAS NO GOOD, HIS EYES WERE NO GOOD... SO IF I CAN'T ATTACK FROM IN FRONT, I'LL ATTACK FROM INSIDE! I RISKED IT ALL, SO I'LL SEND SOME HAMON INTO HIM WHILE HE'S EATING ME!
GWAH
GWAHH
JOJO!
I WAITED FOR YOU TO TRY AND TAKE ME IN!
I WASN'T REALLY PASSED OUT--THAT WAS PART OF THE PLAN! IT WENT OFF PERFECTLY!!
TAKE THIS! HAMON !!
BSSSSHT!!!

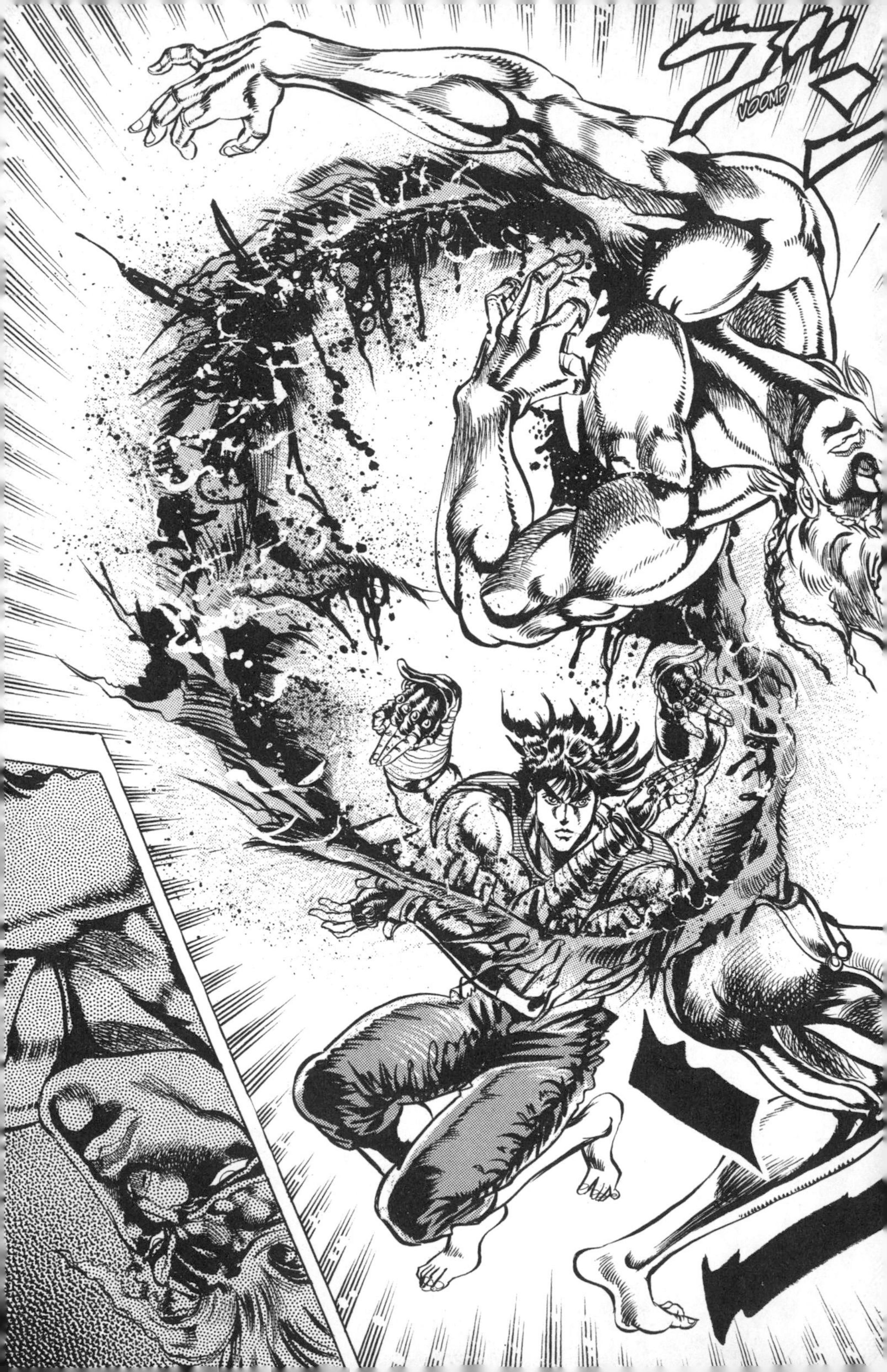
VOOMP

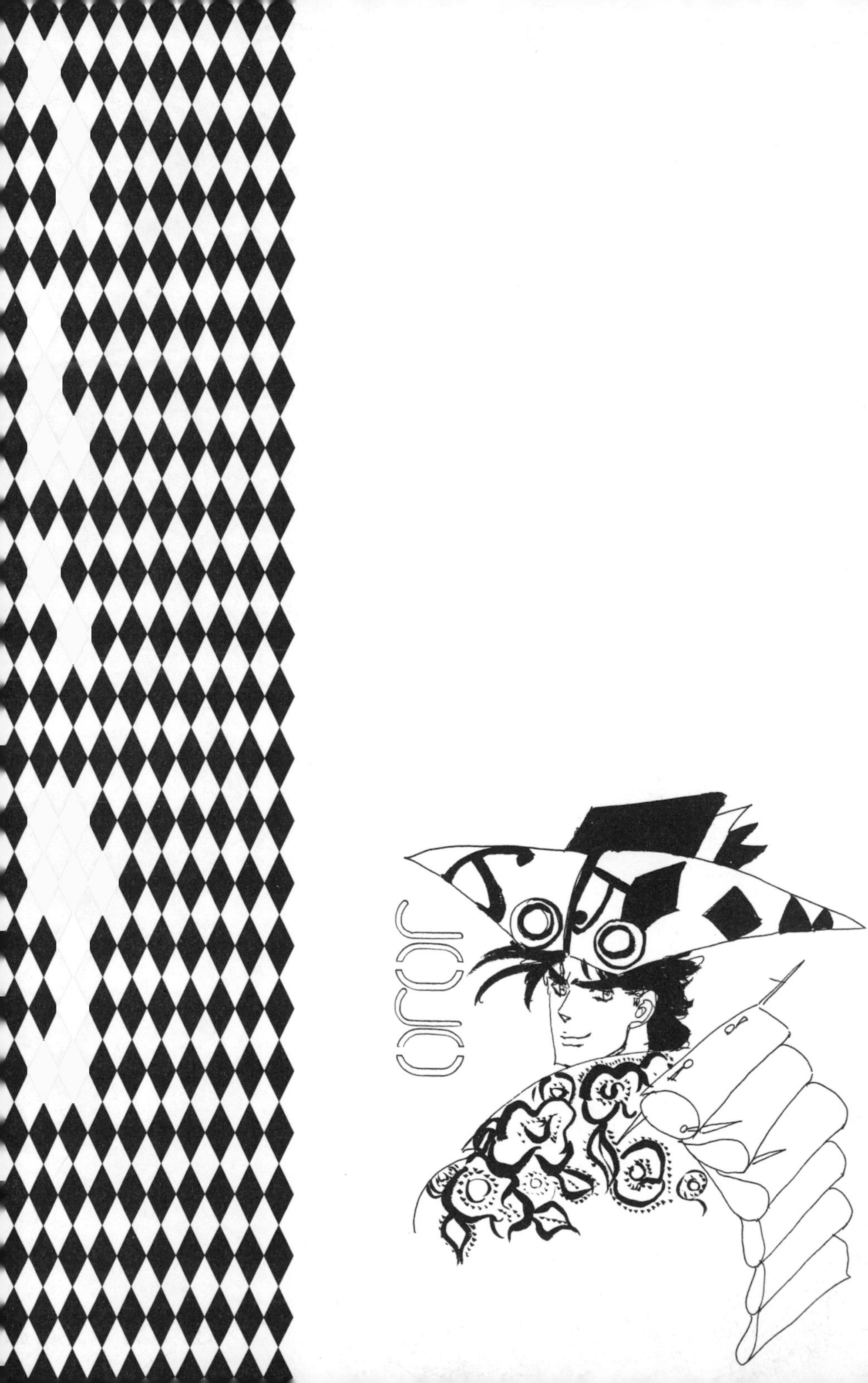
JOJO

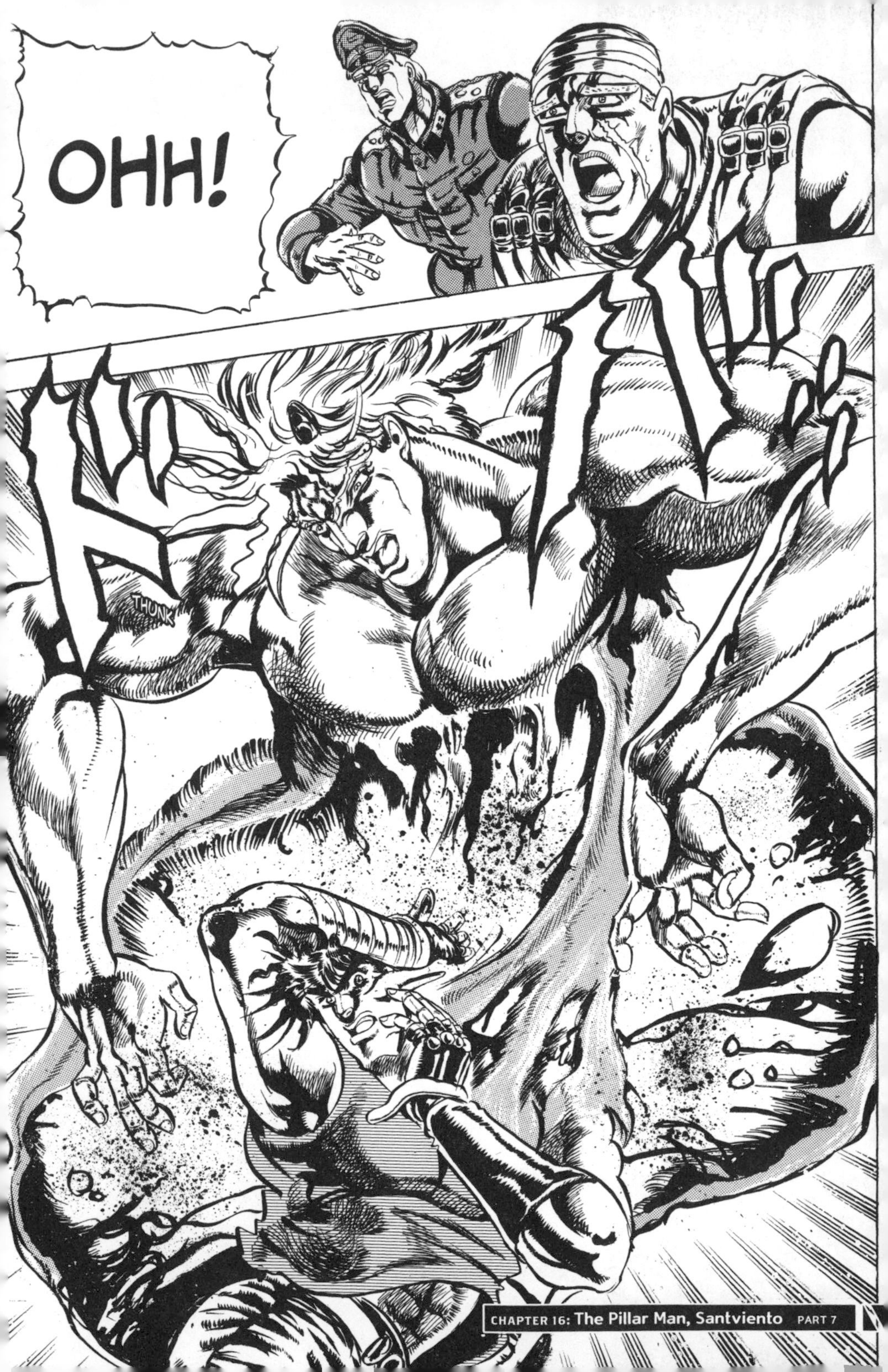
OHH!
THUNK
CHAPTER 16: The Pillar Man, Santviento PART 7

CHAPTER 16: The Pillar Man, Santviento PART 7

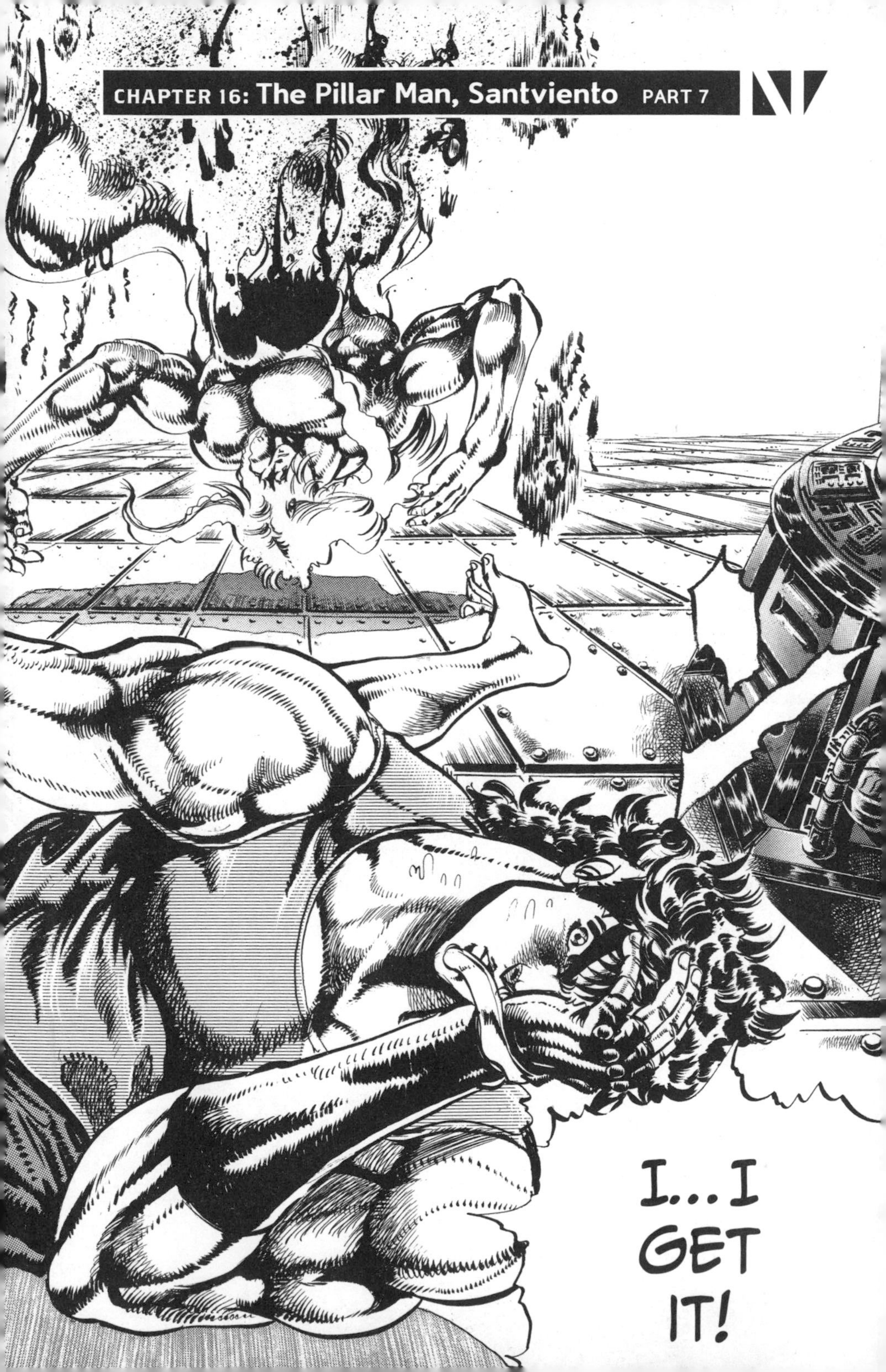
I...I GET IT!

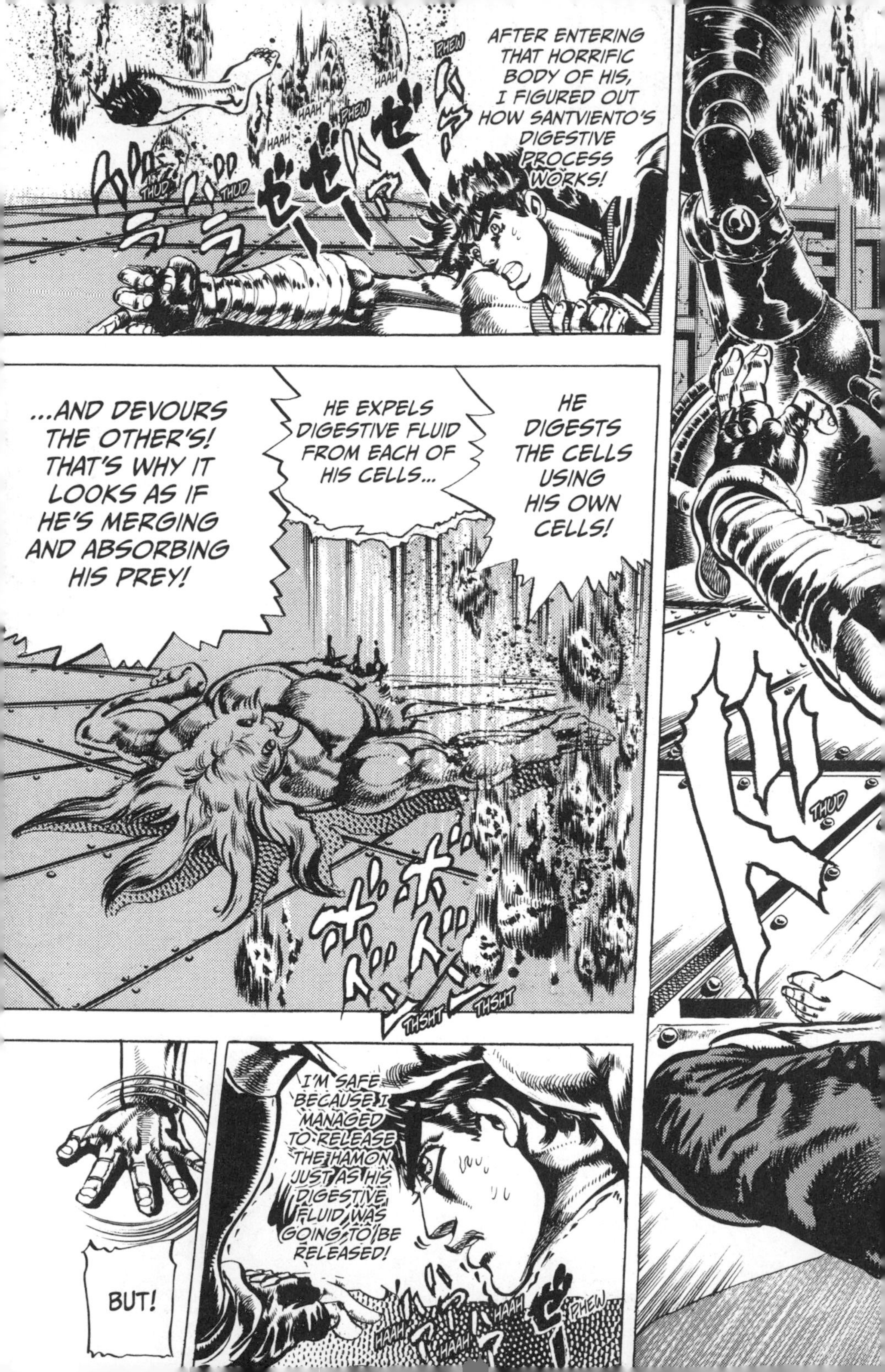
THUD
AFTER ENTERING THAT HORRIFIC BODY OF HIS, I FIGURED OUT HOW SANTVIENTO'S DIGESTIVE PROCESS WORKS!
PHEW
HAAH
HAAH
PHEW
HAAH
THUD
THUD
HE DIGESTS THE CELLS USING HIS OWN CELLS!
HE EXPELS DIGESTIVE FLUID FROM EACH OF HIS CELLS...
...AND DEVOURS THE OTHER'S! THAT'S WHY IT LOOKS AS IF HE'S MERGING AND ABSORBING HIS PREY!
THSHT
THSHT
I'M SAFE BECAUSE I MANAGED TO RELEASE THE HAMON JUST AS HIS DIGESTIVE FLUID WAS GOING TO BE RELEASED!
PHEW
HAAH
HAAH
HAAH
BUT!

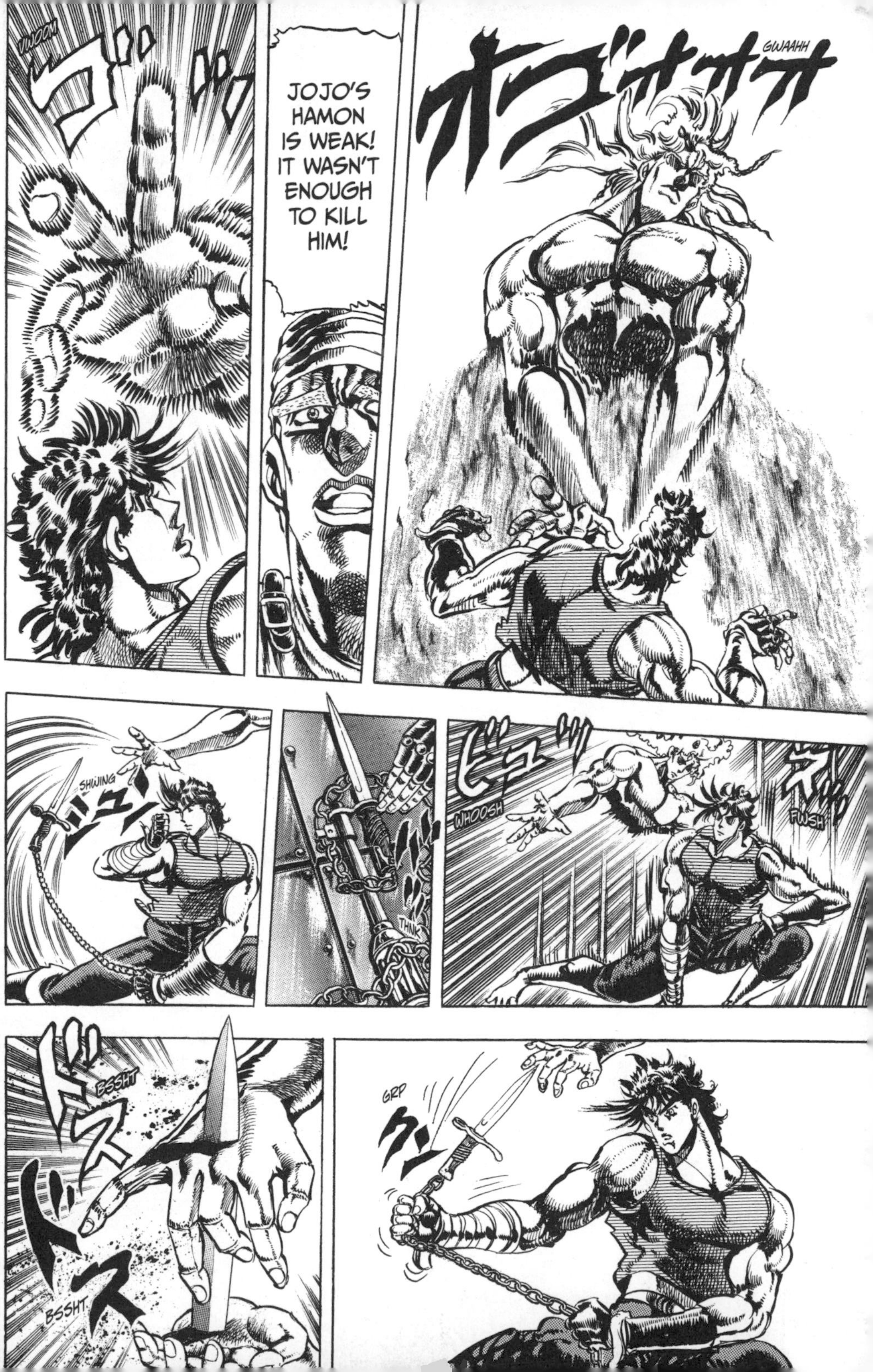
GWAAHH
JOJO'S HAMON IS WEAK! IT WASN'T ENOUGH TO KILL HIM!
VWOOM
WHOOSH
FWSH
THNK
SHWING
GRP
BSSHT
BSSHT

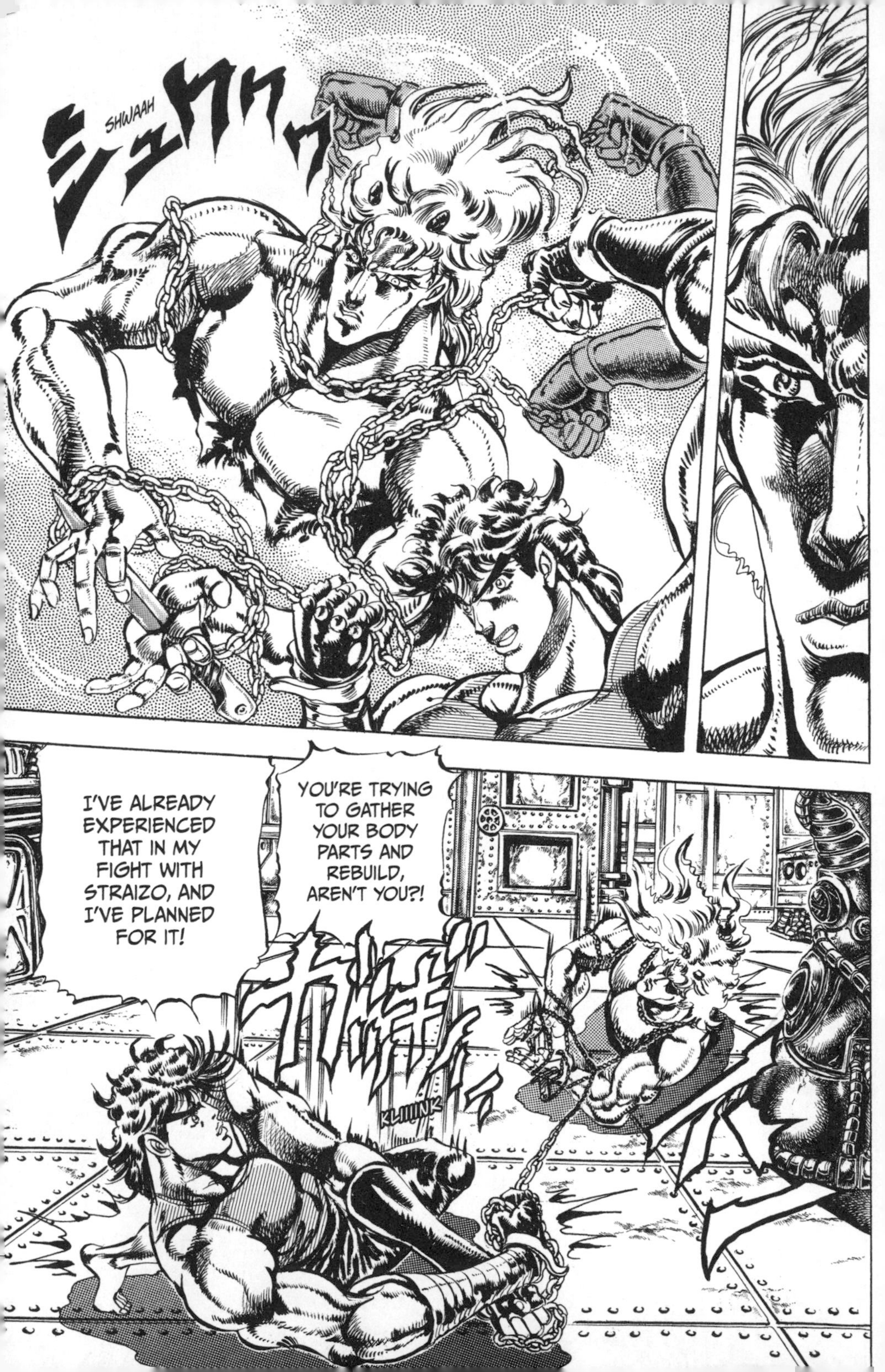
SHWAAH
YOU'RE TRYING TO GATHER YOUR BODY PARTS AND REBUILD, AREN'T YOU?!
I'VE ALREADY EXPERIENCED THAT IN MY FIGHT WITH STRAIZO, AND I'VE PLANNED FOR IT!
KLIIIINK

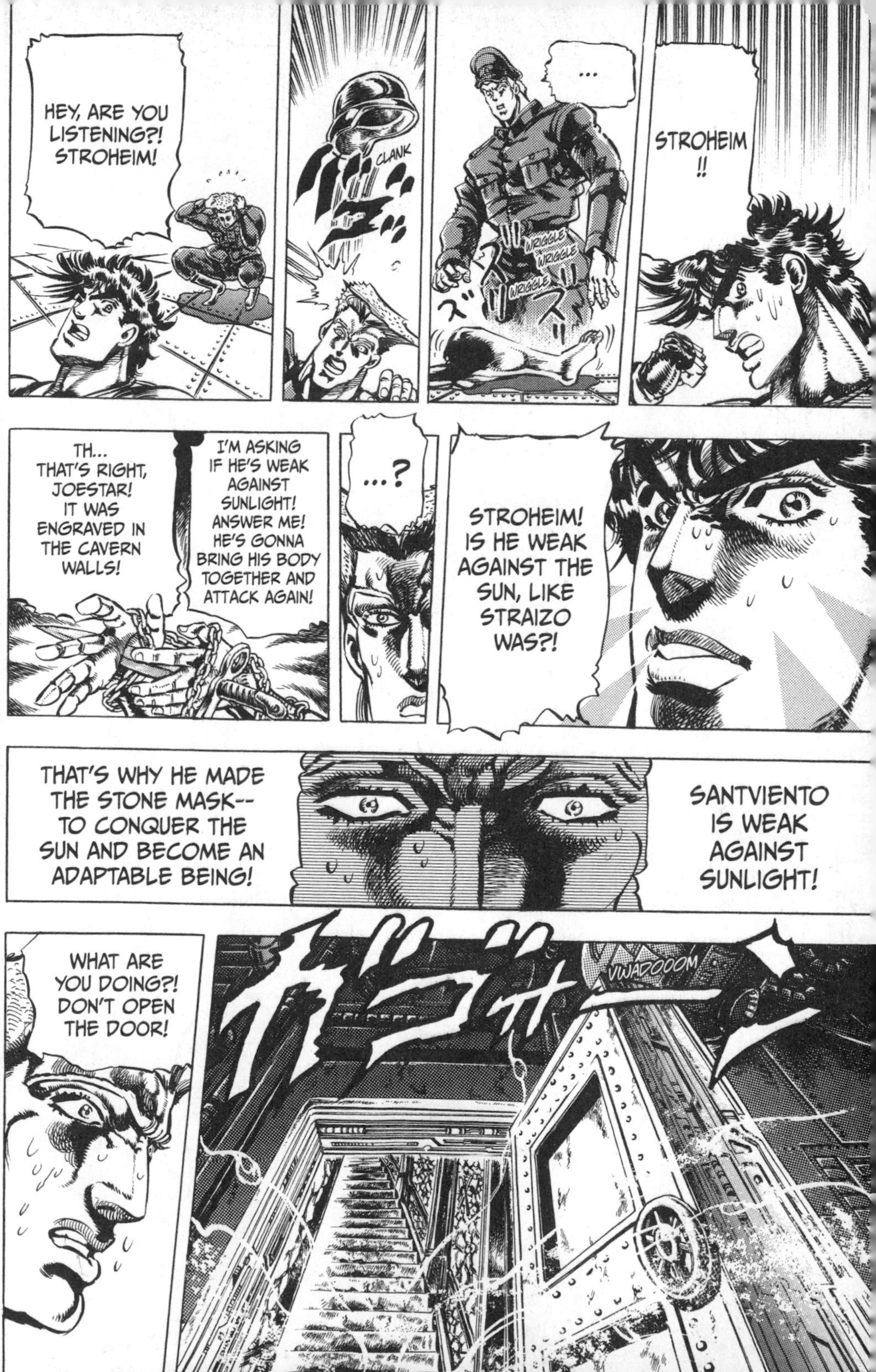
STROHEIM !!
...
WRIGGLE WRIGGLE WRIGGLE
CLANK
HEY, ARE YOU LISTENING?! STROHEIM!
STROHEIM! IS HE WEAK AGAINST THE SUN, LIKE STRAIZO WAS?!
...?
I'M ASKING IF HE'S WEAK AGAINST SUNLIGHT! ANSWER ME! HE'S GONNA BRING HIS BODY TOGETHER AND ATTACK AGAIN!
TH... THAT'S RIGHT, JOESTAR! IT WAS ENGRAVED IN THE CAVERN WALLS!
SANTVIENTO IS WEAK AGAINST SUNLIGHT!
THAT'S WHY HE MADE THE STONE MASK-- TO CONQUER THE SUN AND BECOME AN ADAPTABLE BEING!
VWADOOOM
WHAT ARE YOU DOING?! DON'T OPEN THE DOOR!

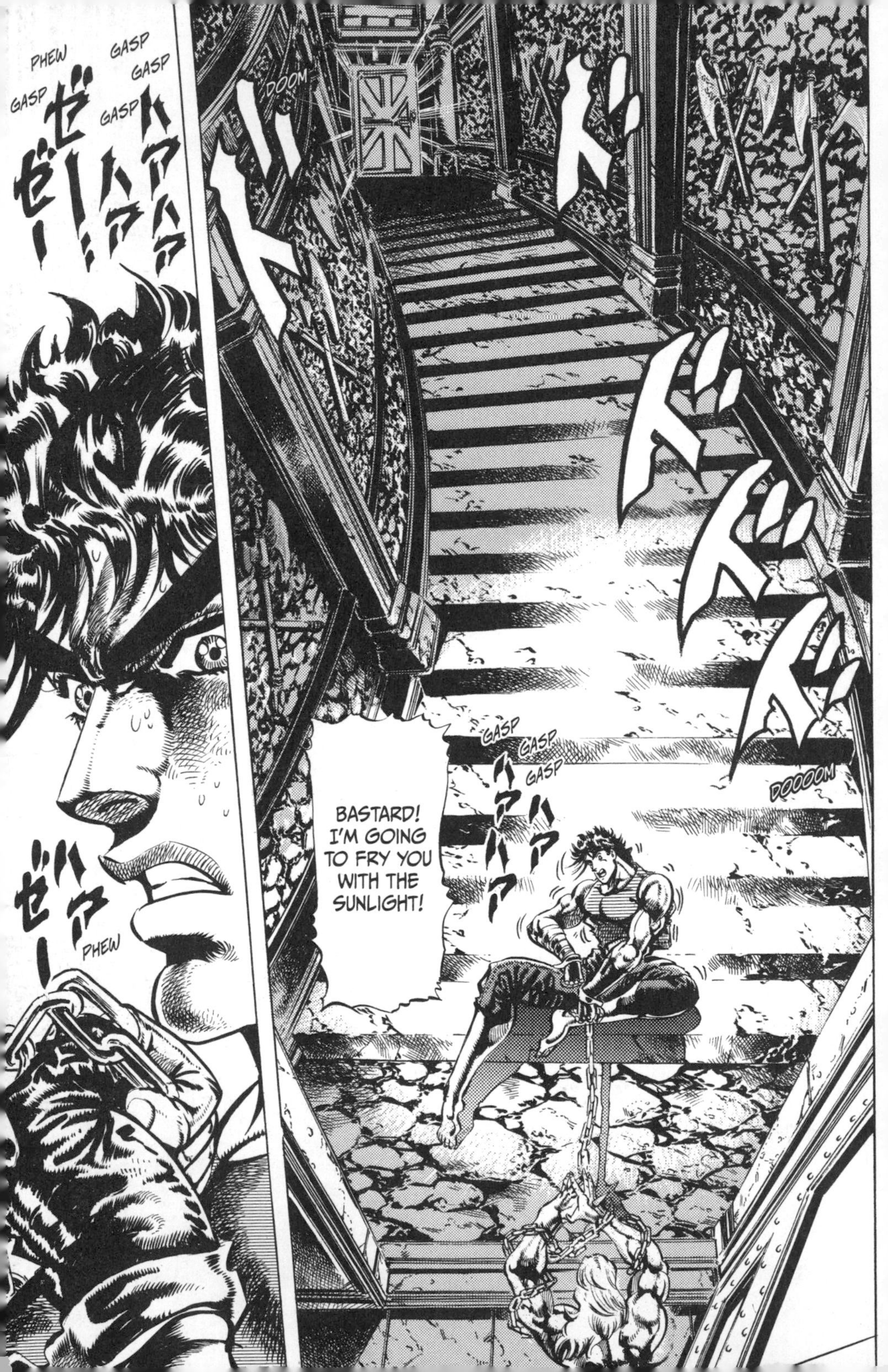
ドドド
DOOM
ドドドド
DOOOOM
GASP
GASP
GASP
ハァハァ
ハァ
BASTARD! I'M GOING TO FRY YOU WITH THE SUNLIGHT!
PHEW
GASP
GASP
GASP
GASP
ゼーゼー!!
ハァハァハァハァ
ハァ
ゼー
PHEW

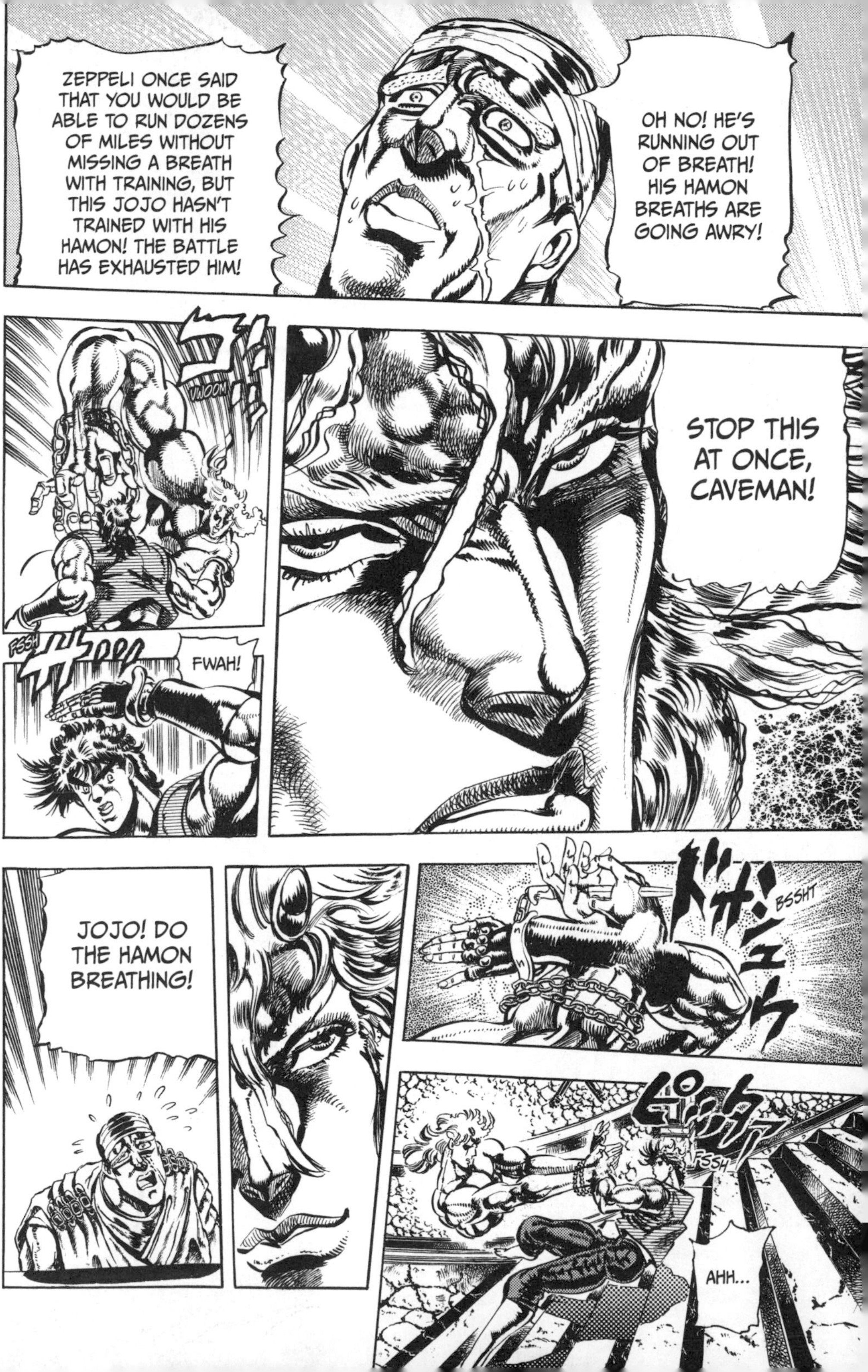
OH NO! HE'S RUNNING OUT OF BREATH! HIS HAMON BREATHS ARE GOING AWRY!
ZEPPELI ONCE SAID THAT YOU WOULD BE ABLE TO RUN DOZENS OF MILES WITHOUT MISSING A BREATH WITH TRAINING, BUT THIS JOJO HASN'T TRAINED WITH HIS HAMON! THE BATTLE HAS EXHAUSTED HIM!
STOP THIS AT ONCE, CAVEMAN!
VWOOM
FSSH
FWAH!
BSSHT
FSSH
AHH...
JOJO! DO THE HAMON BREATHING!

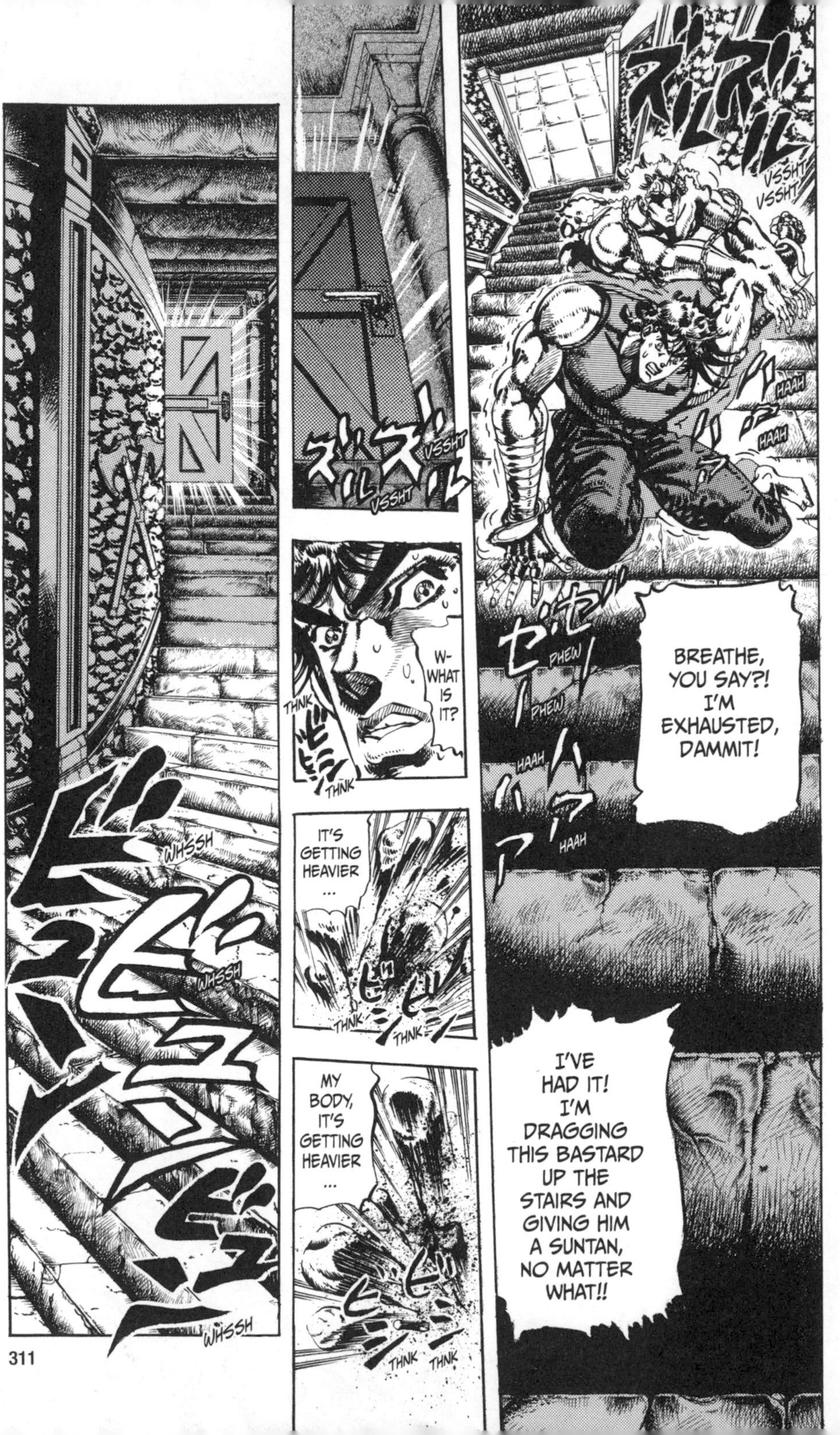
VSSHT
VSSHT
HAAH
HAAH
PHEW
PHEW
BREATHE, YOU SAY?! I'M EXHAUSTED, DAMMIT!
HAAH
HAAH
I'VE HAD IT! I'M DRAGGING THIS BASTARD UP THE STAIRS AND GIVING HIM A SUNTAN, NO MATTER WHAT!!
VSSHT
VSSHT
W-WHAT IS IT?
THNK
THNK
IT'S GETTING HEAVIER ...
THNK
THNK
MY BODY, IT'S GETTING HEAVIER ...
THNK
THNK
WHSSH
WHSSH
WHSSH

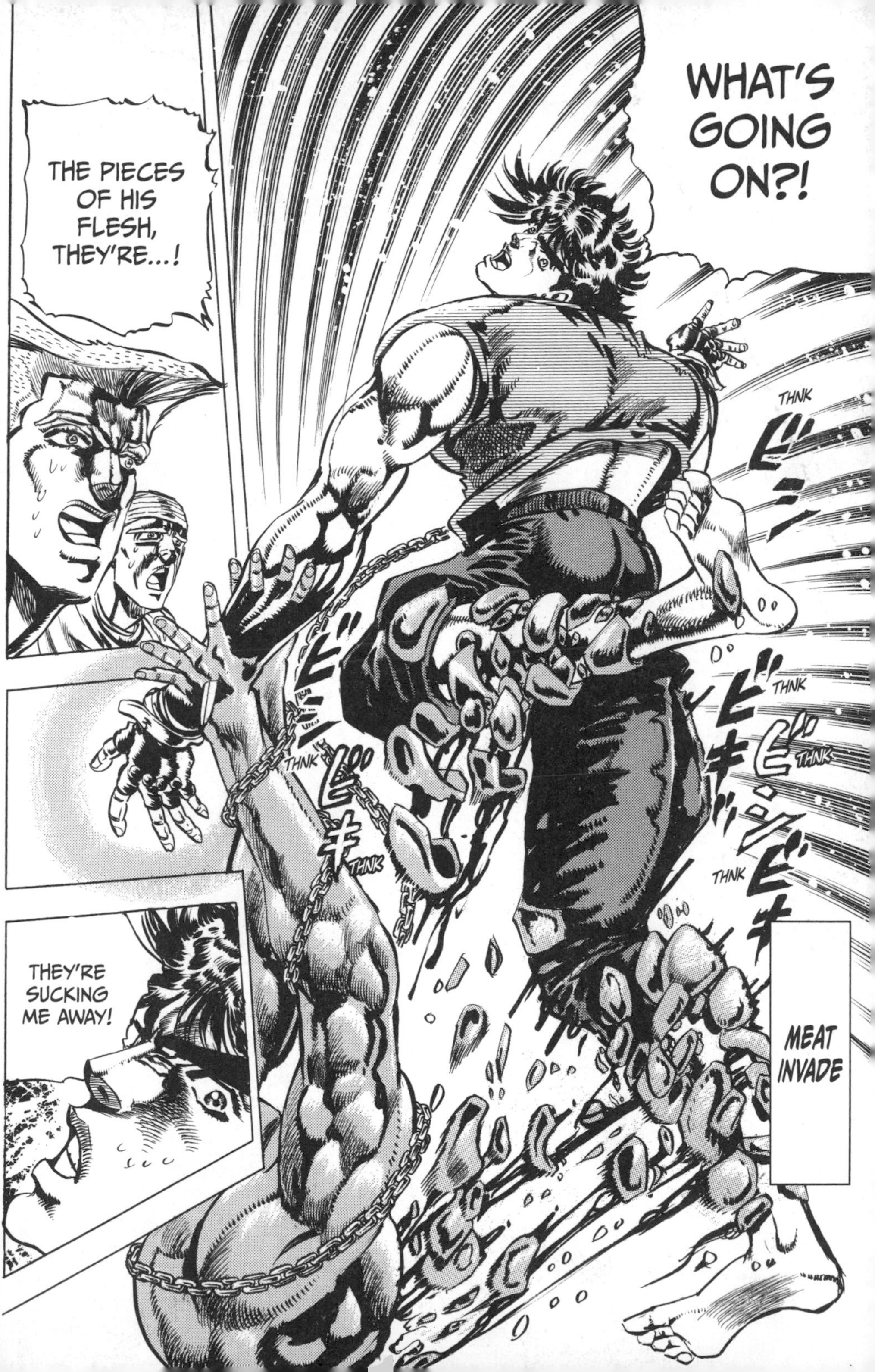
WHAT'S GOING ON?!
THNK
THNK
THNK
THNK
MEAT INVADE
THNK
THNK
THE PIECES OF HIS FLESH, THEY'RE...!
THEY'RE SUCKING ME AWAY!

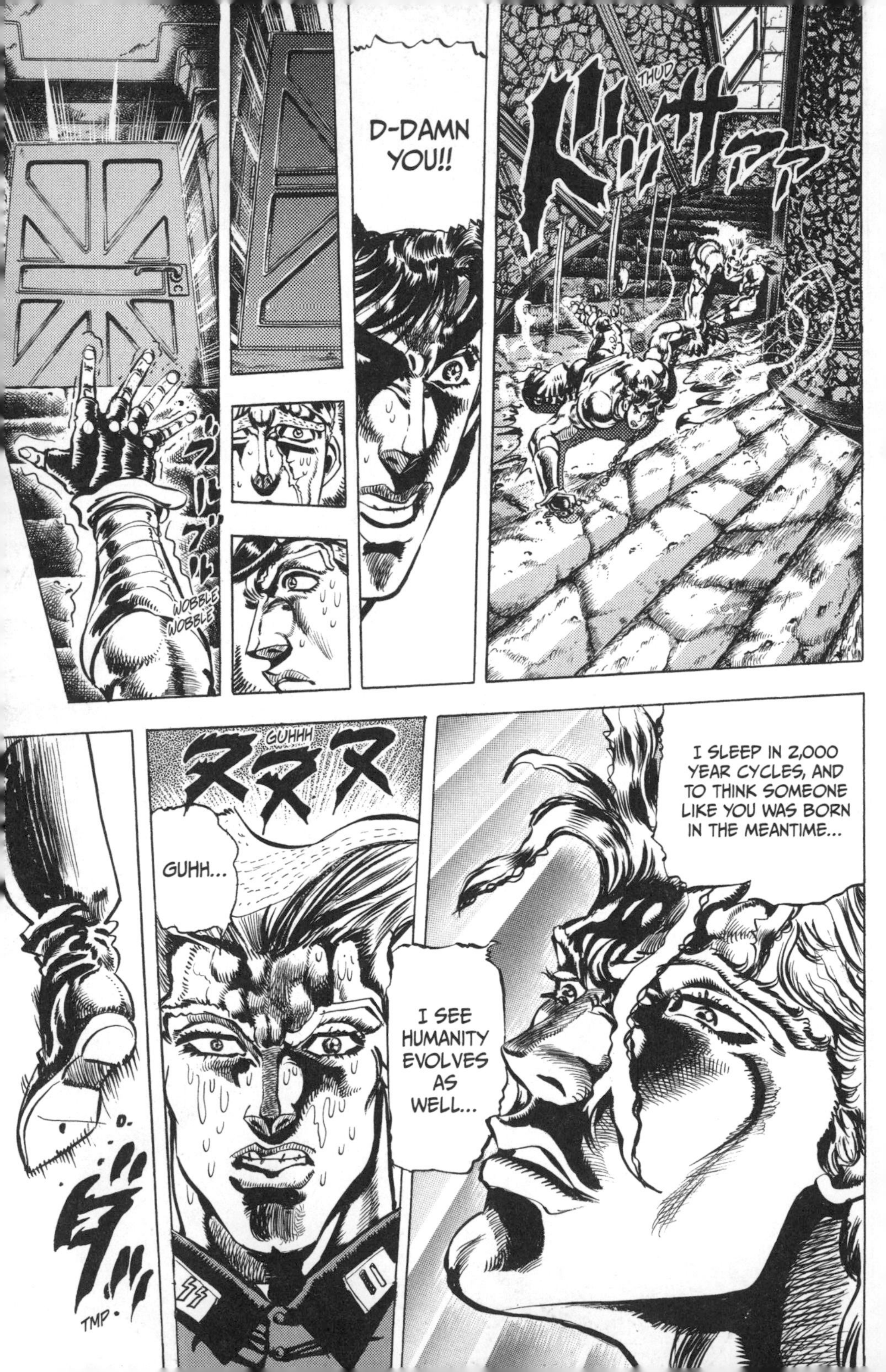
THUD
D-DAMN YOU!!
WOBBLE WOBBLE
I SLEEP IN 2,000 YEAR CYCLES, AND TO THINK SOMEONE LIKE YOU WAS BORN IN THE MEANTIME...
I SEE HUMANITY EVOLVES AS WELL...
GUHHH
GUHH...
TMP

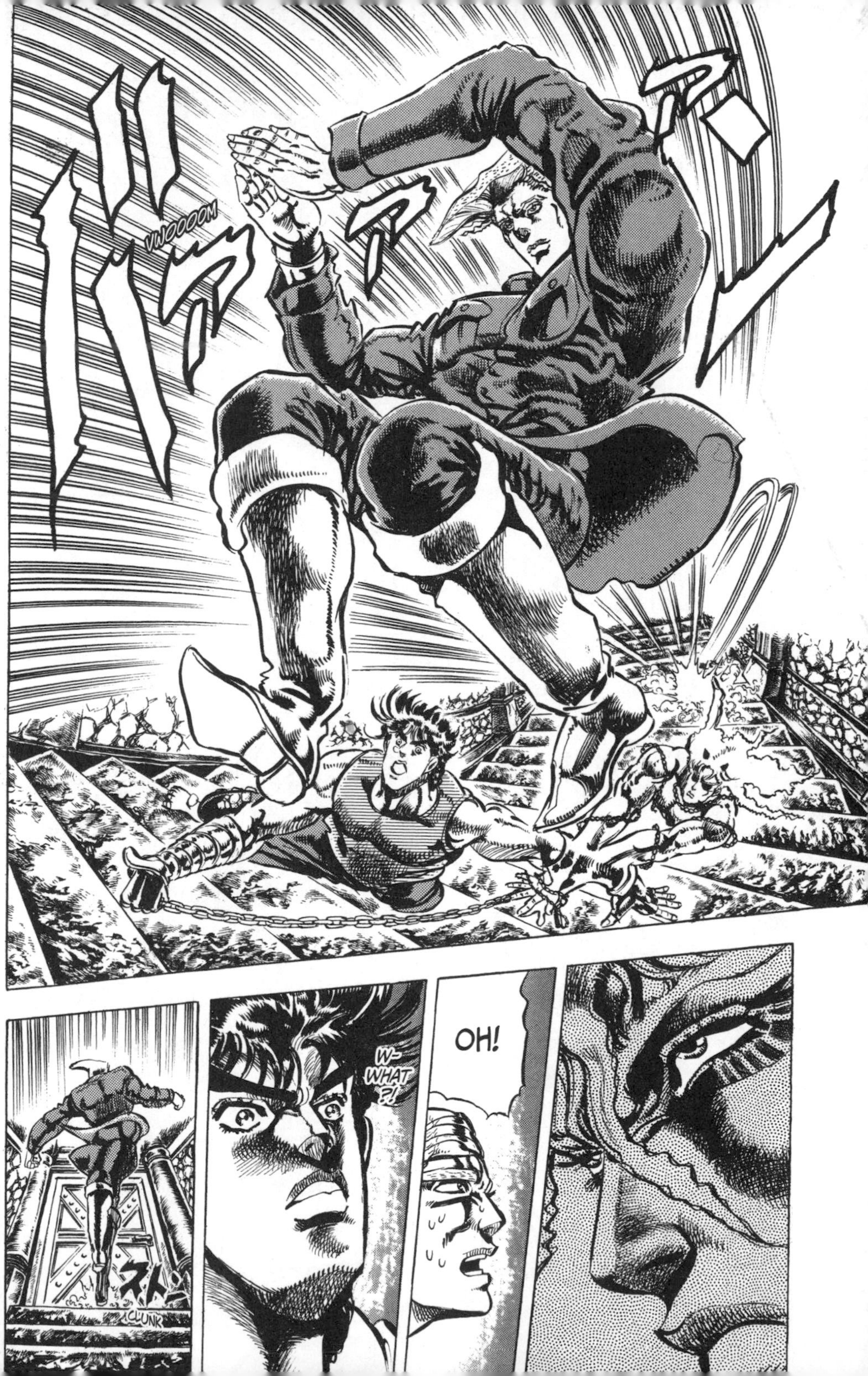
VWOOOOM
OH!
W-WHAT?!
CLUNK

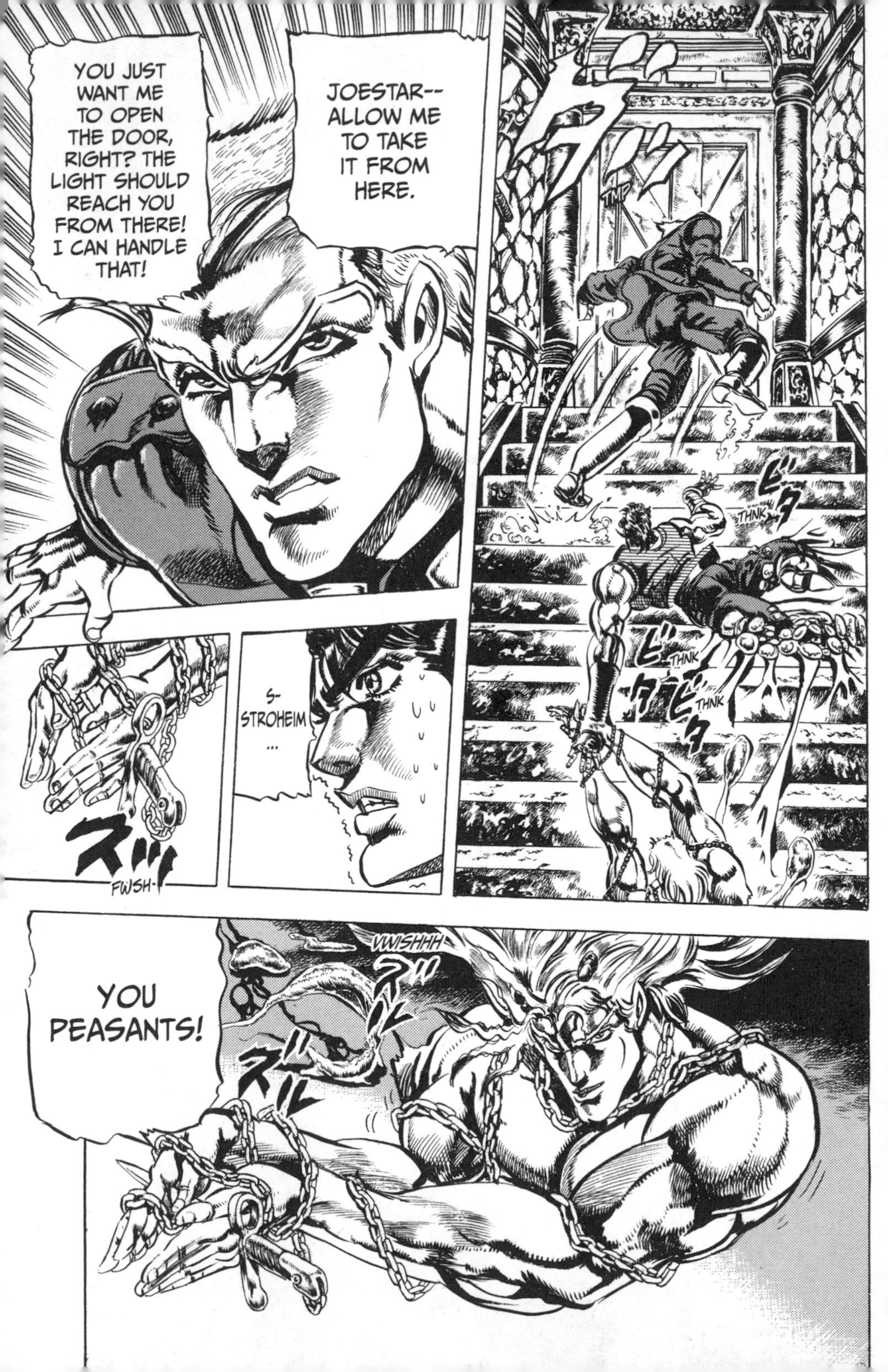
TMP
THNK
THNK
THNK
JOESTAR-- ALLOW ME TO TAKE IT FROM HERE.
YOU JUST WANT ME TO OPEN THE DOOR, RIGHT? THE LIGHT SHOULD REACH YOU FROM THERE! I CAN HANDLE THAT!
S-STROHEIM ...
FWSH
VWISHHH
YOU PEASANTS!

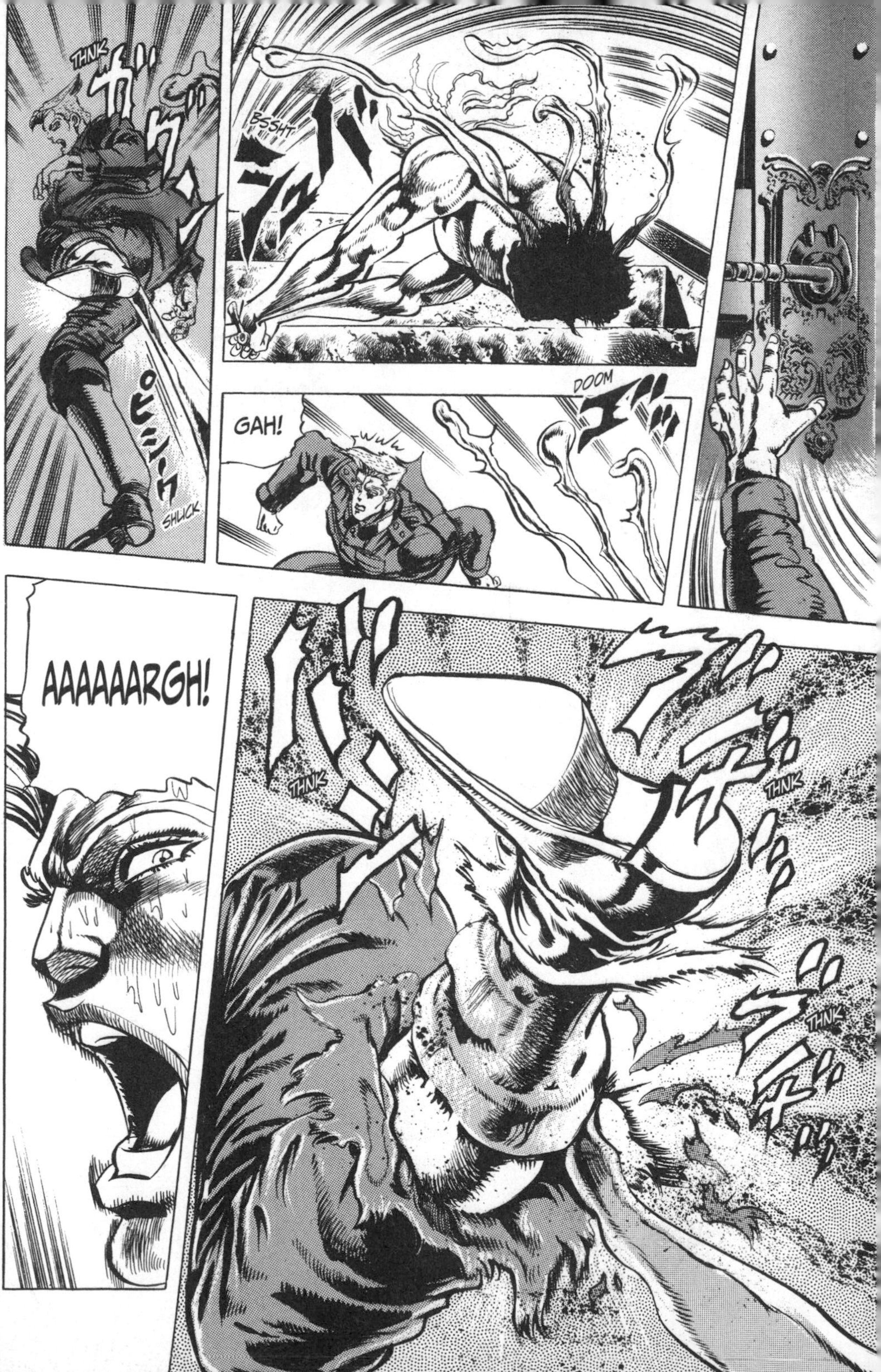

BSSHT
DOOM
GAH!
THNK
SHLICK
THNK
THNK
THNK
AAAAAARGH!

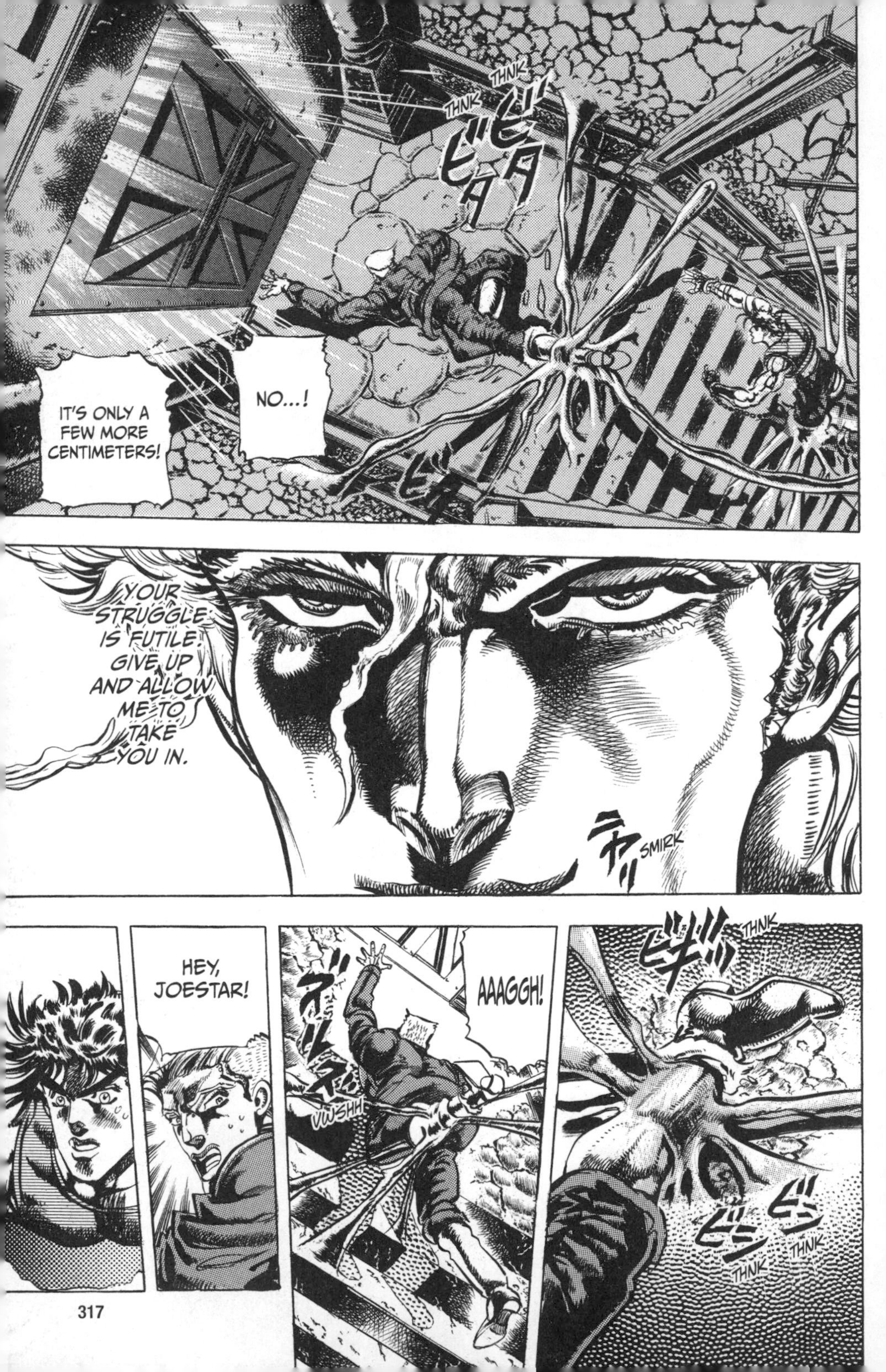
THNK
THNK
NO...!
IT'S ONLY A FEW MORE CENTIMETERS!
YOUR STRUGGLE IS FUTILE. GIVE UP AND ALLOW ME TO TAKE YOU IN.
SMIRK
THNK
THNK
THNK
AAAGGH!
VWSHH
HEY, JOESTAR!

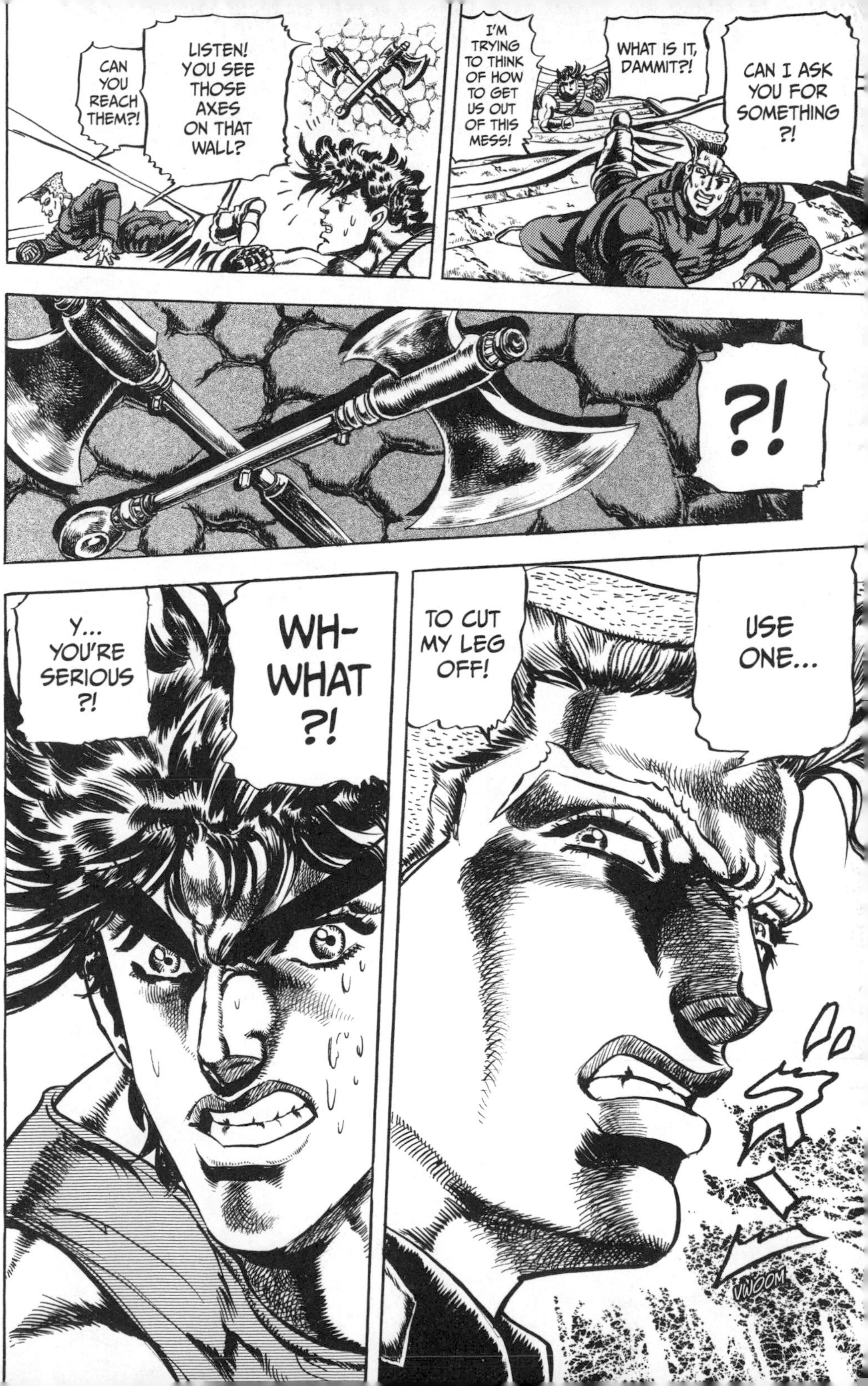
CAN I ASK YOU FOR SOMETHING ?!
WHAT IS IT, DAMMIT?!
I'M TRYING TO THINK OF HOW TO GET US OUT OF THIS MESS!
LISTEN! YOU SEE THOSE AXES ON THAT WALL?
CAN YOU REACH THEM?!
?!
USE ONE...
TO CUT MY LEG OFF!
VWOOM
WH- WHAT ?!
Y... YOU'RE SERIOUS ?!

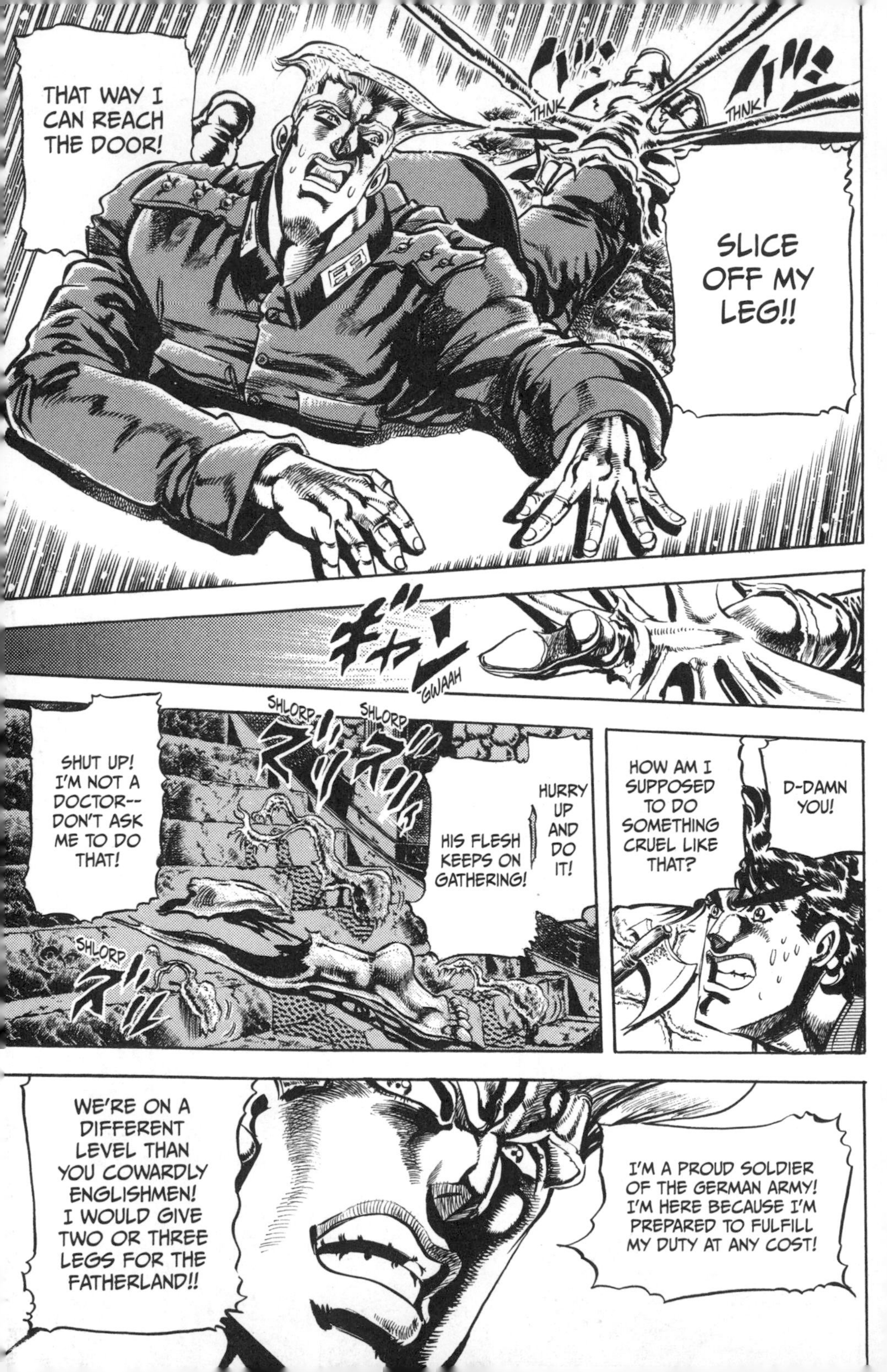
THNK
THNK
SLICE OFF MY LEG!!
THAT WAY I CAN REACH THE DOOR!
GWAAH
D-DAMN YOU!
HOW AM I SUPPOSED TO DO SOMETHING CRUEL LIKE THAT?
HURRY UP AND DO IT!
HIS FLESH KEEPS ON GATHERING!
SHLORP
SHLORP
SHUT UP! I'M NOT A DOCTOR-- DON'T ASK ME TO DO THAT!
SHLORP
I'M A PROUD SOLDIER OF THE GERMAN ARMY! I'M HERE BECAUSE I'M PREPARED TO FULFILL MY DUTY AT ANY COST!
WE'RE ON A DIFFERENT LEVEL THAN YOU COWARDLY ENGLISHMEN! I WOULD GIVE TWO OR THREE LEGS FOR THE FATHERLAND!!

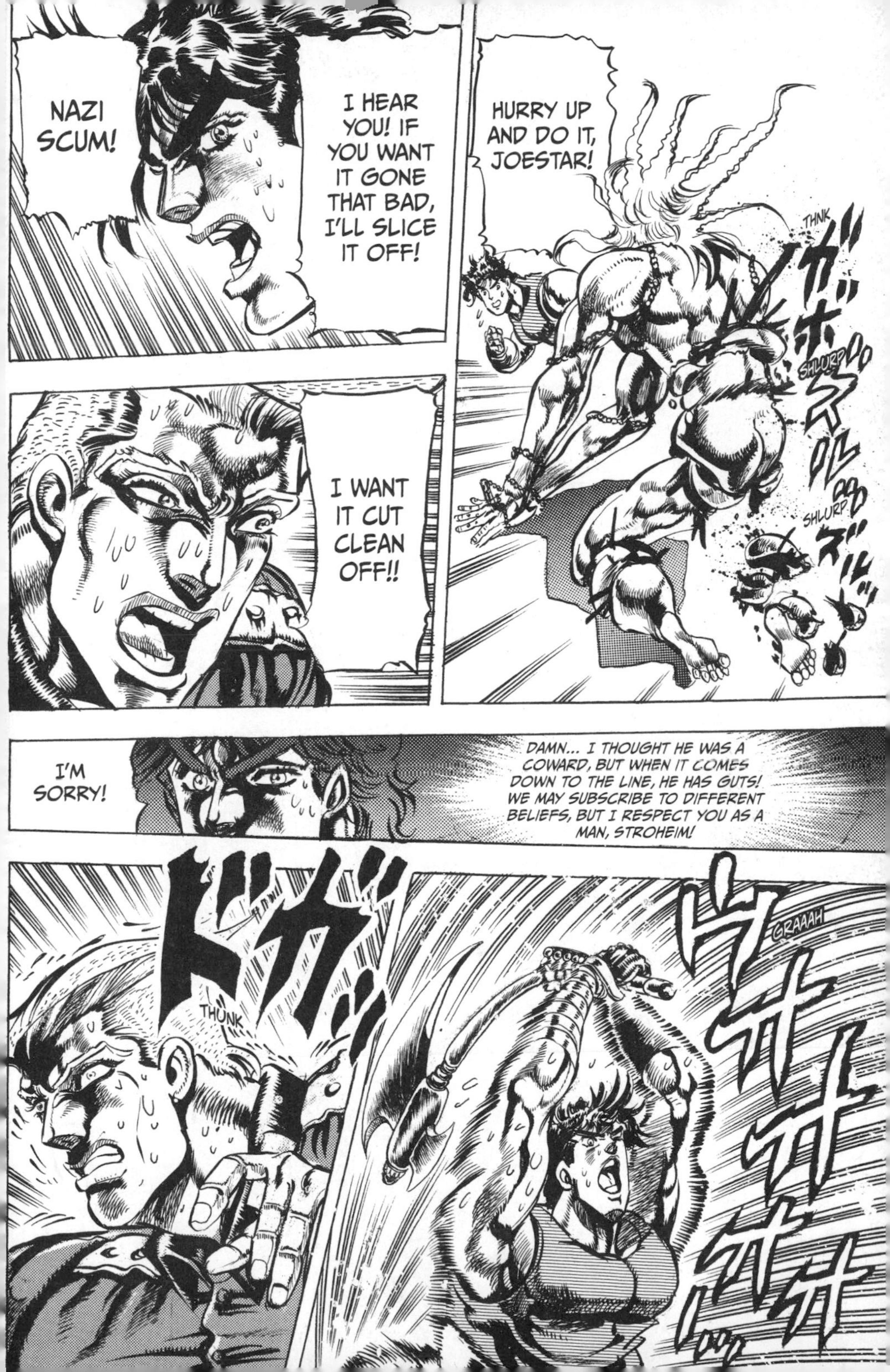

HURRY UP AND DO IT, JOESTAR!
THNK
SHLURP
SHLURP
I HEAR YOU! IF YOU WANT IT GONE THAT BAD, I'LL SLICE IT OFF!
NAZI SCUM!
I WANT IT CUT CLEAN OFF!!
DAMN... I THOUGHT HE WAS A COWARD, BUT WHEN IT COMES DOWN TO THE LINE, HE HAS GUTS! WE MAY SUBSCRIBE TO DIFFERENT BELIEFS, BUT I RESPECT YOU AS A MAN, STROHEIM!
I'M SORRY!
GRAAAH
THUNK

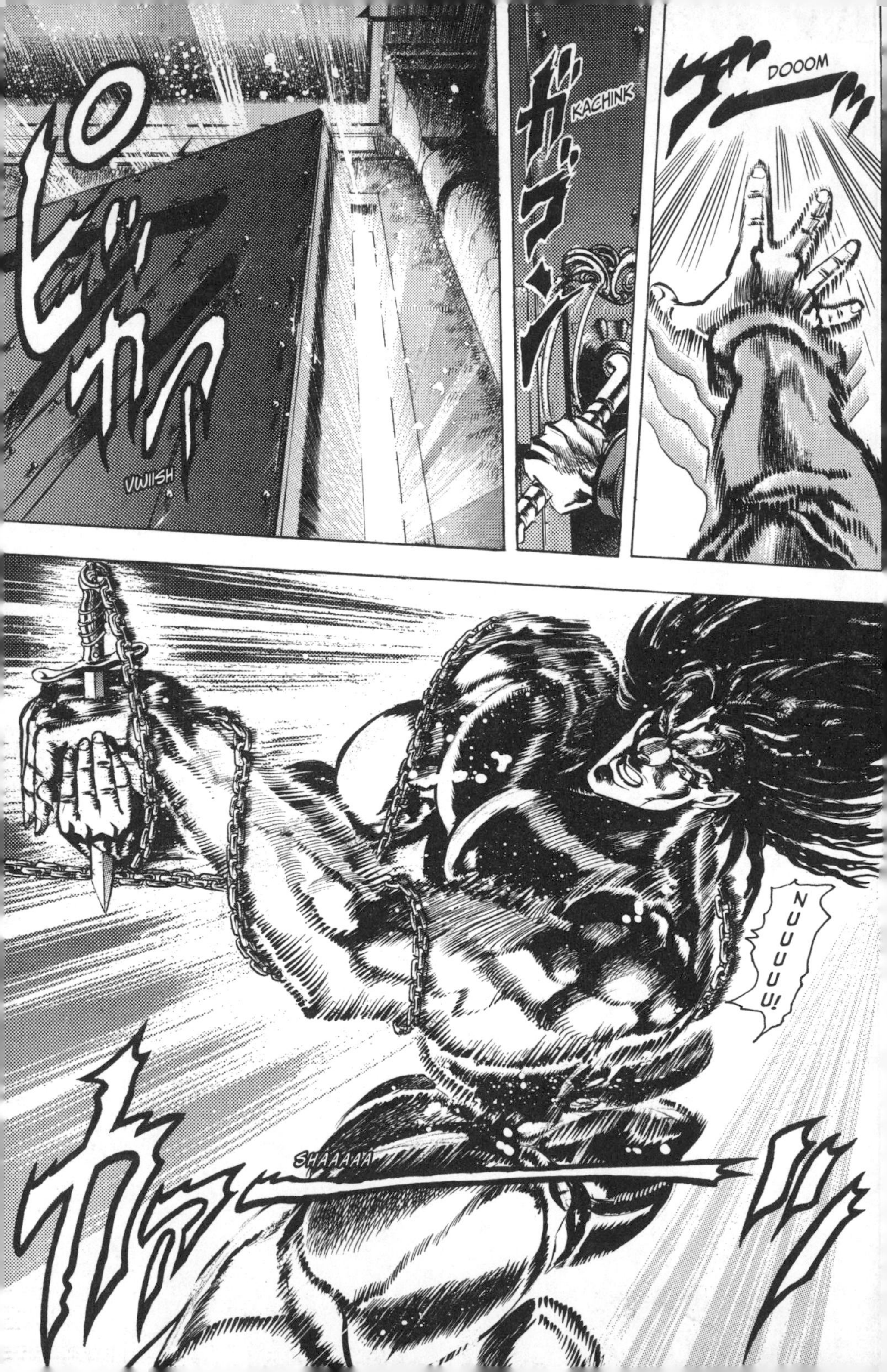
DOOOM
KACHINK
VWIISH
NUUUUUU!
SHAAAAA

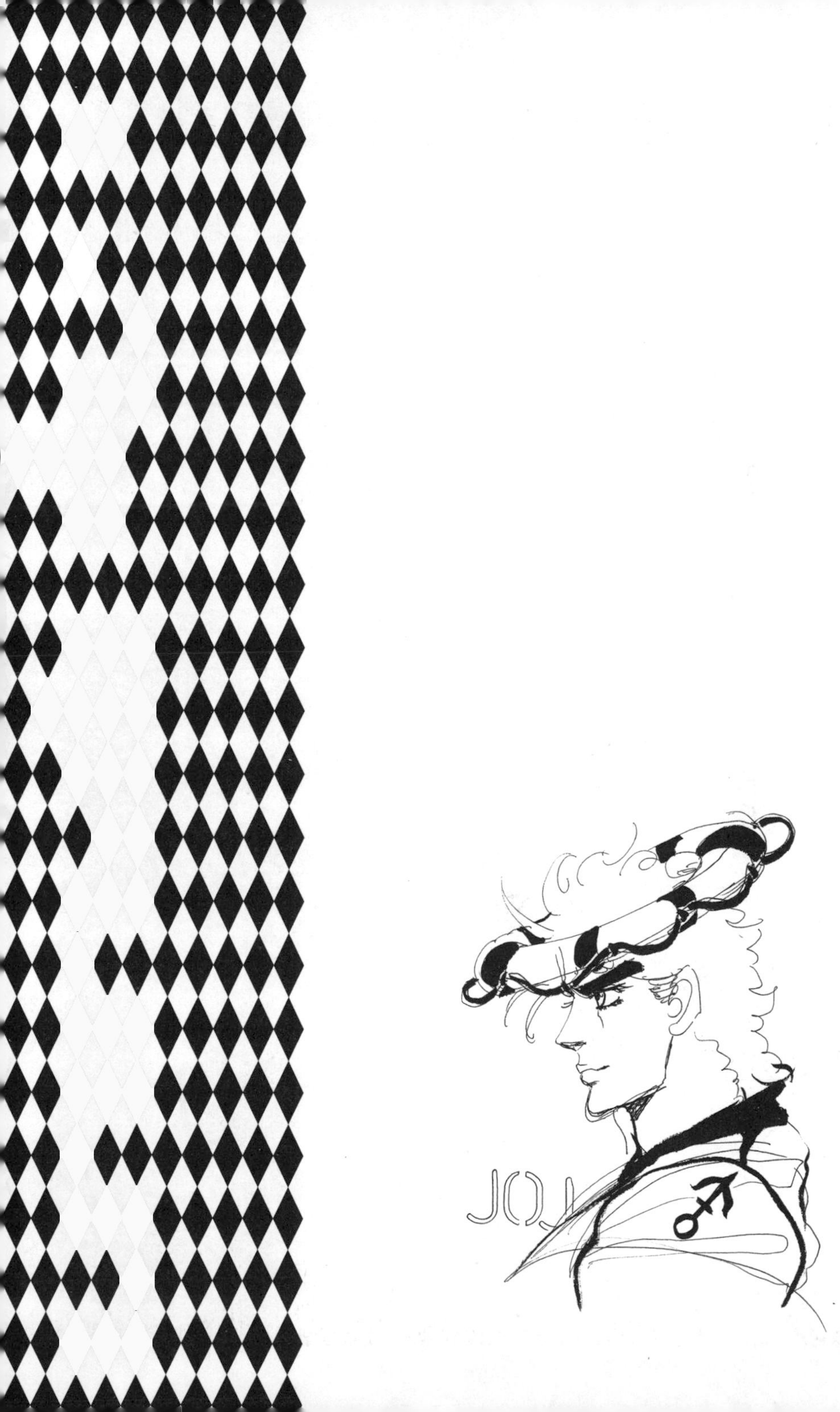
JOJ

CHAPTER 17: The Pillar Man, Santviento PART 8

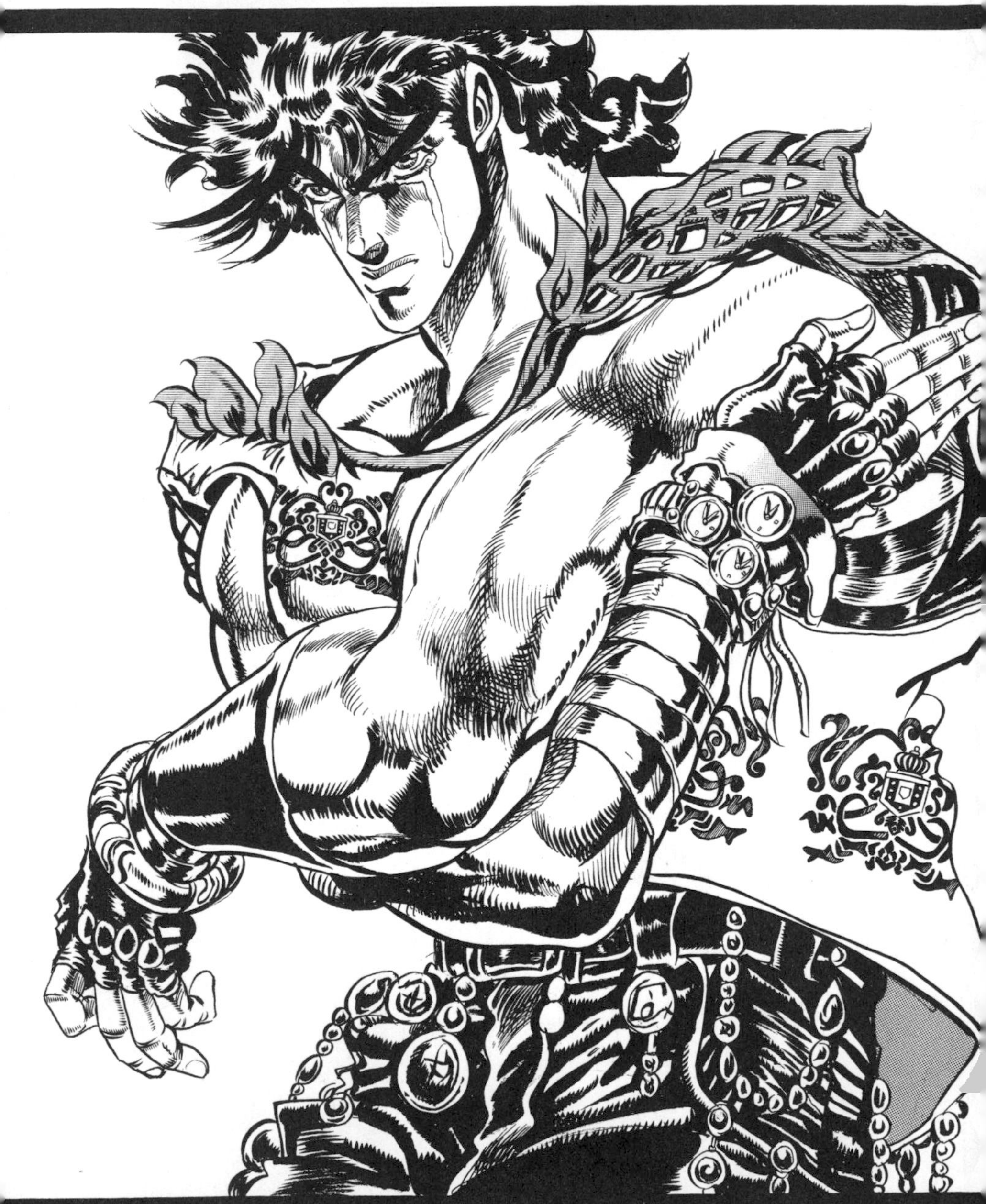

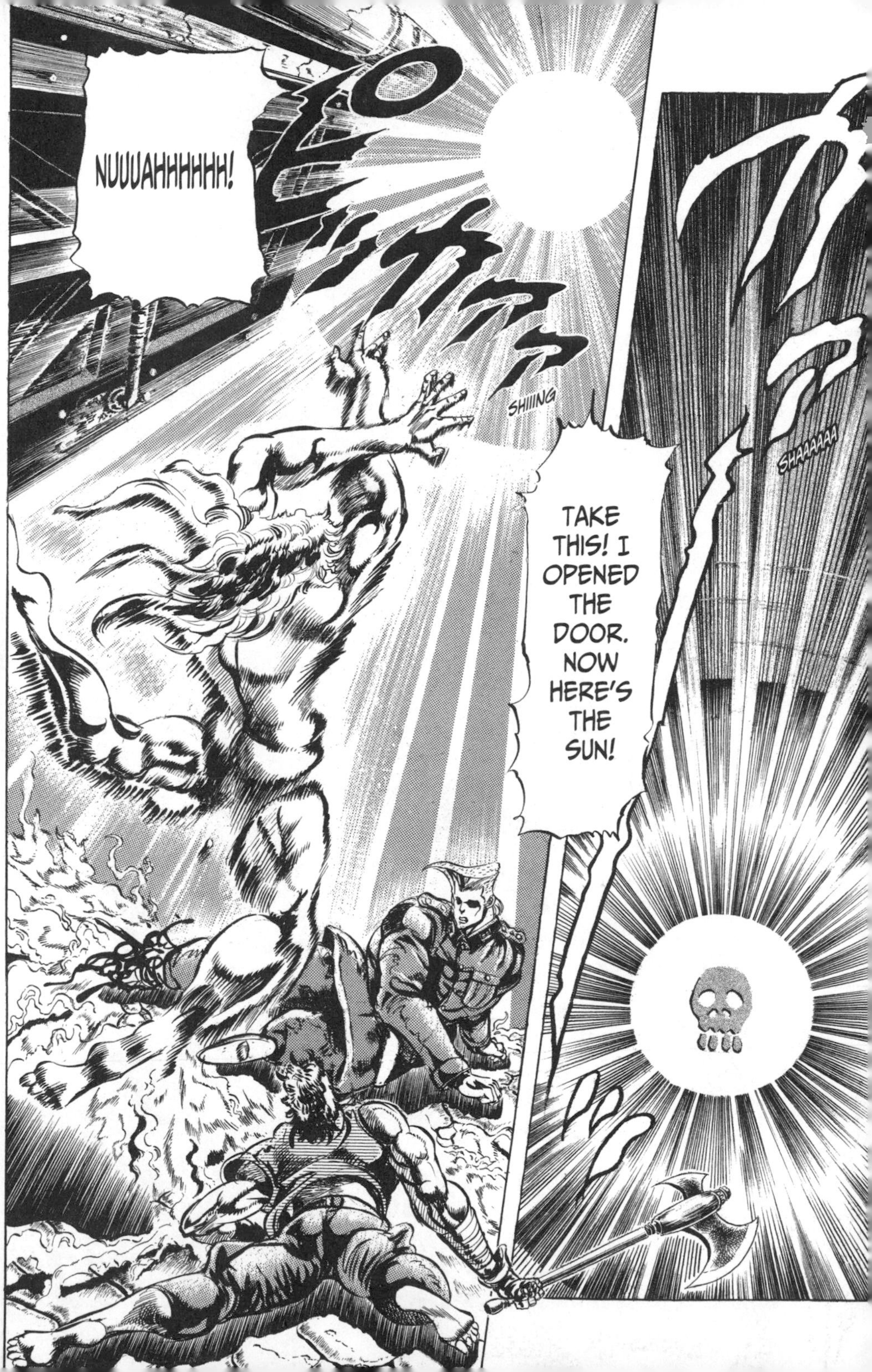
SHAAAAAA
TAKE THIS! I OPENED THE DOOR. NOW HERE'S THE SUN!
SHIIING
NUUUAHHHHHH!

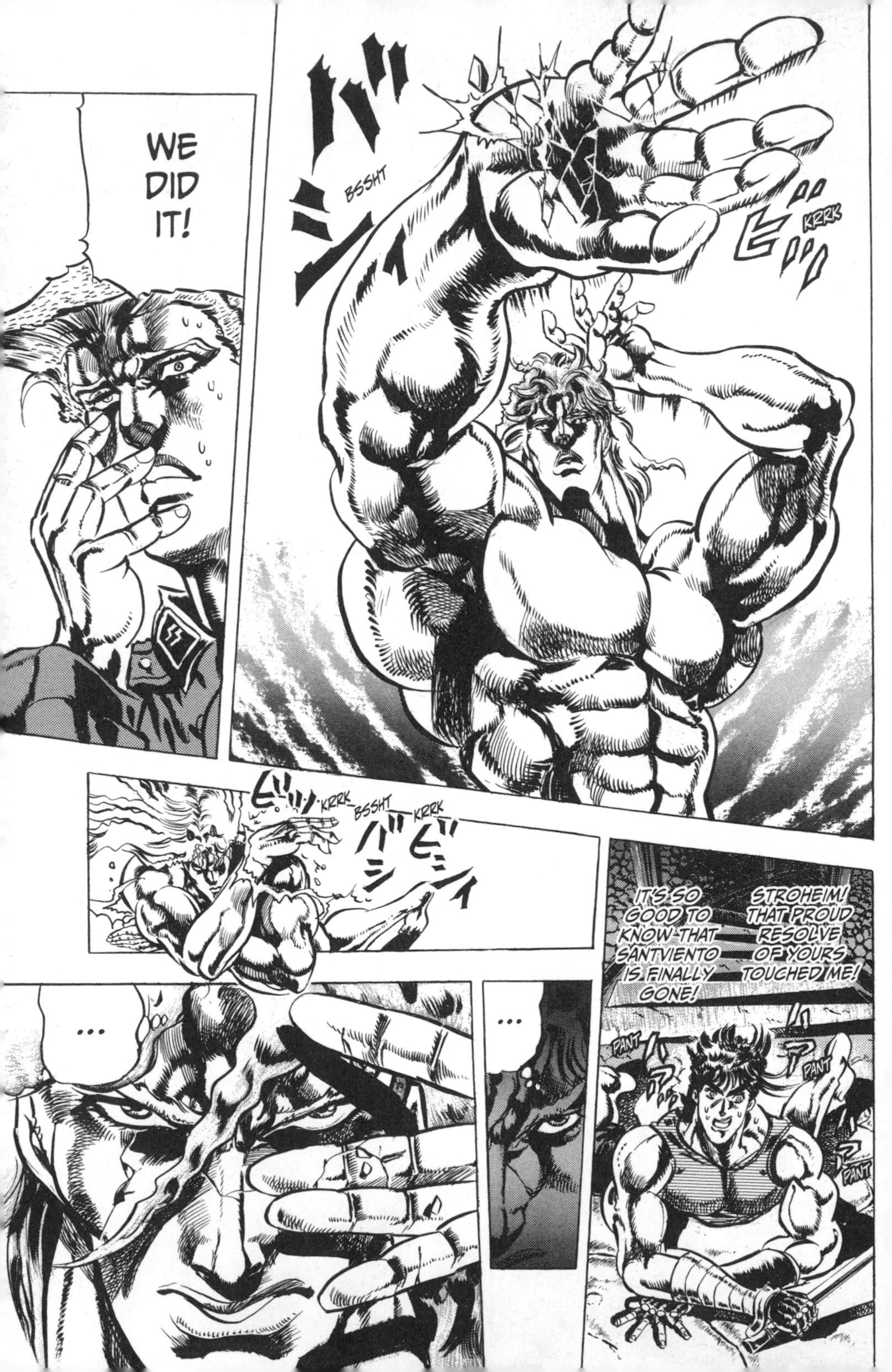
BSSHT
KRRK
WE DID IT!
STROHEIM! THAT PROUD RESOLVE OF YOURS TOUCHED ME!
IT'S SO GOOD TO KNOW THAT SANTVIENTO IS FINALLY GONE!
PANT
PANT
PANT
PANT
KRRK
BSSHT
KRRK
...
...

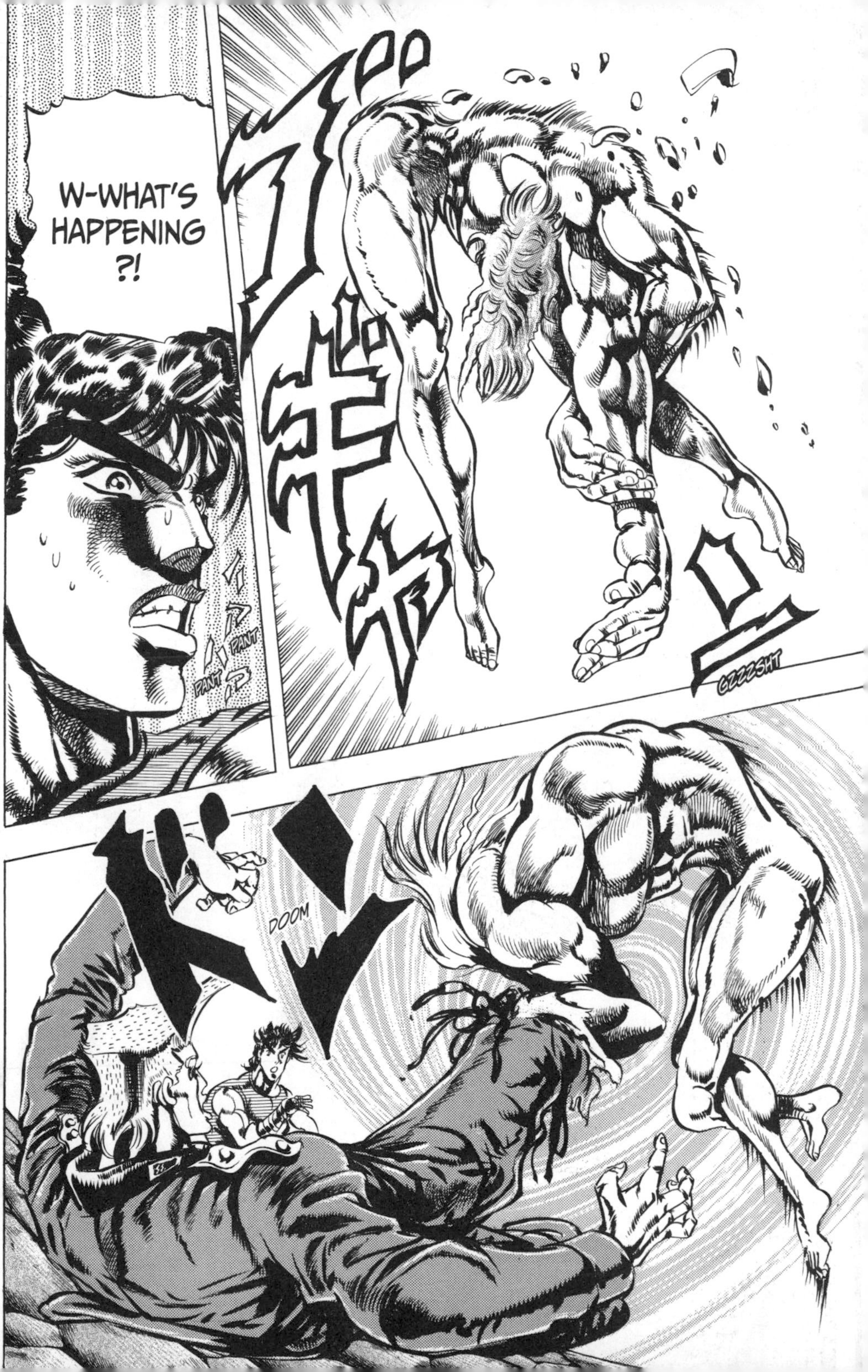
GZZZSHT
W-WHAT'S HAPPENING ?!
PANT PANT
DOOM

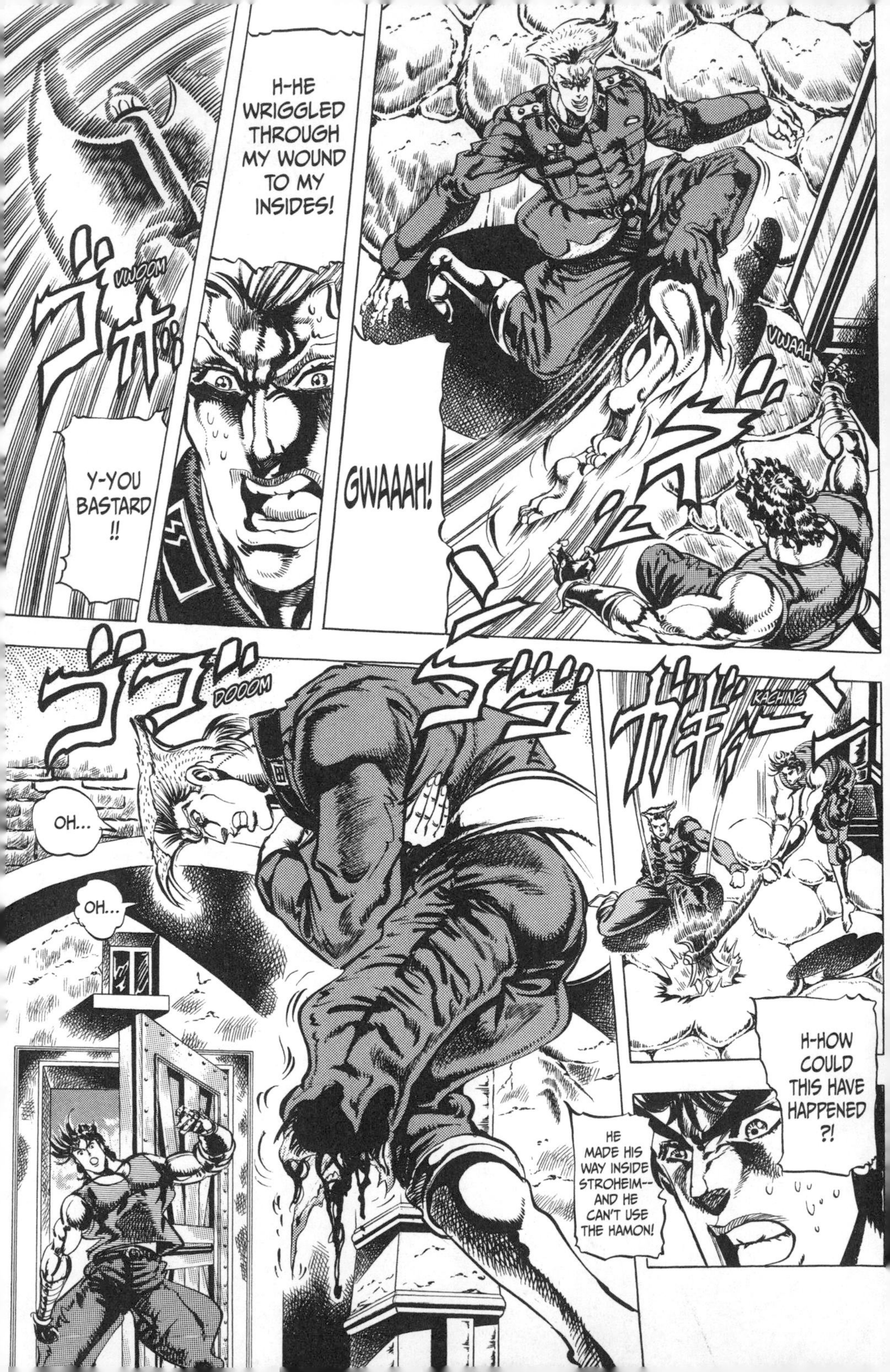
VWAAH
GWAAAH!
H-HE WRIGGLED THROUGH MY WOUND TO MY INSIDES!
VWOOM
Y-YOU BASTARD !!
KACHING
H-HOW COULD THIS HAVE HAPPENED ?!
HE MADE HIS WAY INSIDE STROHEIM-- AND HE CAN'T USE THE HAMON!
DOOOM
OH...
OH...

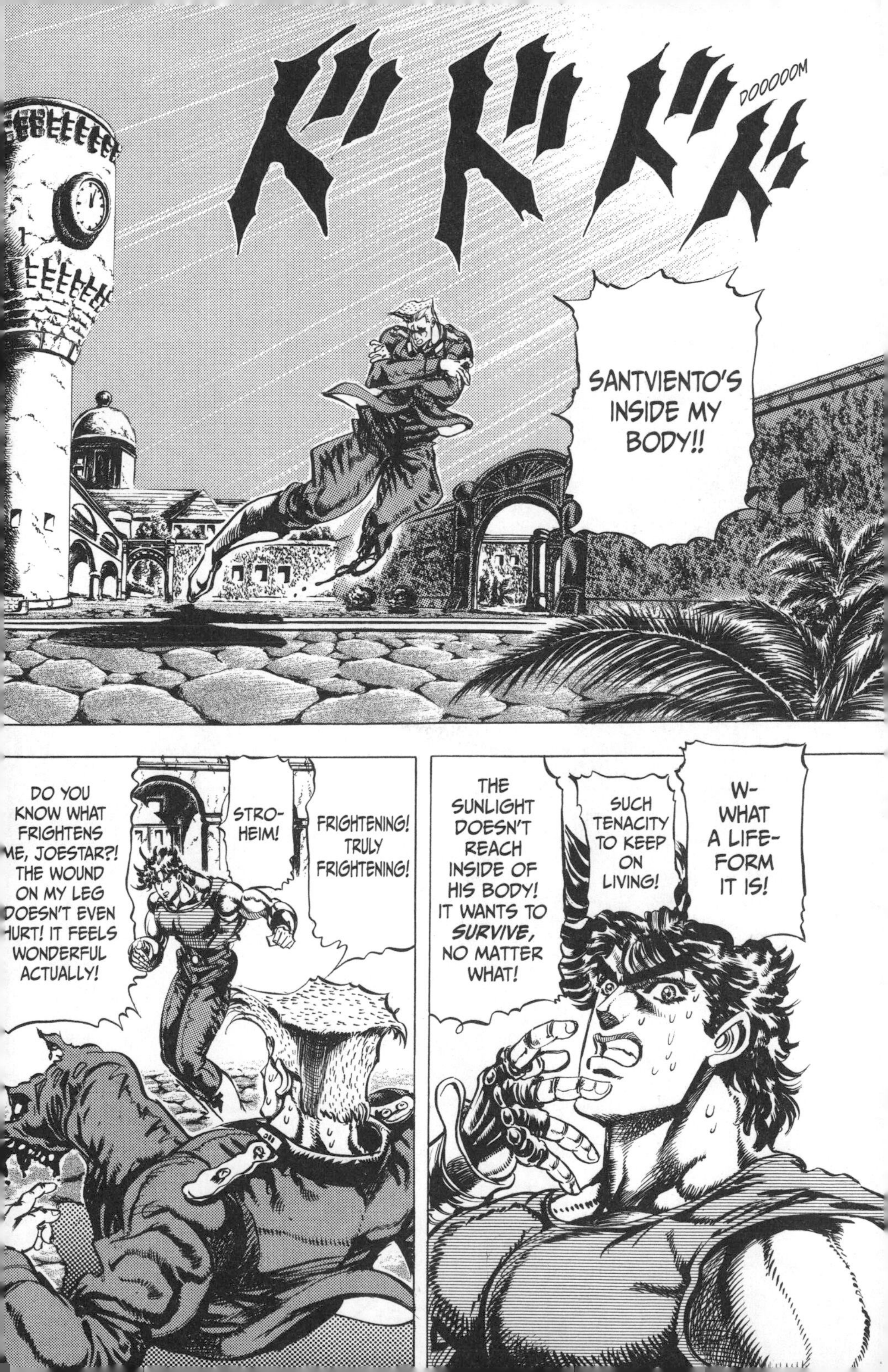
DOOOOOM
SANTVIENTO'S INSIDE MY BODY!!
W- WHAT A LIFE-FORM IT IS!
SUCH TENACITY TO KEEP ON LIVING!
THE SUNLIGHT DOESN'T REACH INSIDE OF HIS BODY! IT WANTS TO *SURVIVE*, NO MATTER WHAT!
FRIGHTENING! TRULY FRIGHTENING!
STRO-HEIM!
DO YOU KNOW WHAT FRIGHTENS ME, JOESTAR?! THE WOUND ON MY LEG DOESN'T EVEN HURT! IT FEELS WONDERFUL ACTUALLY!

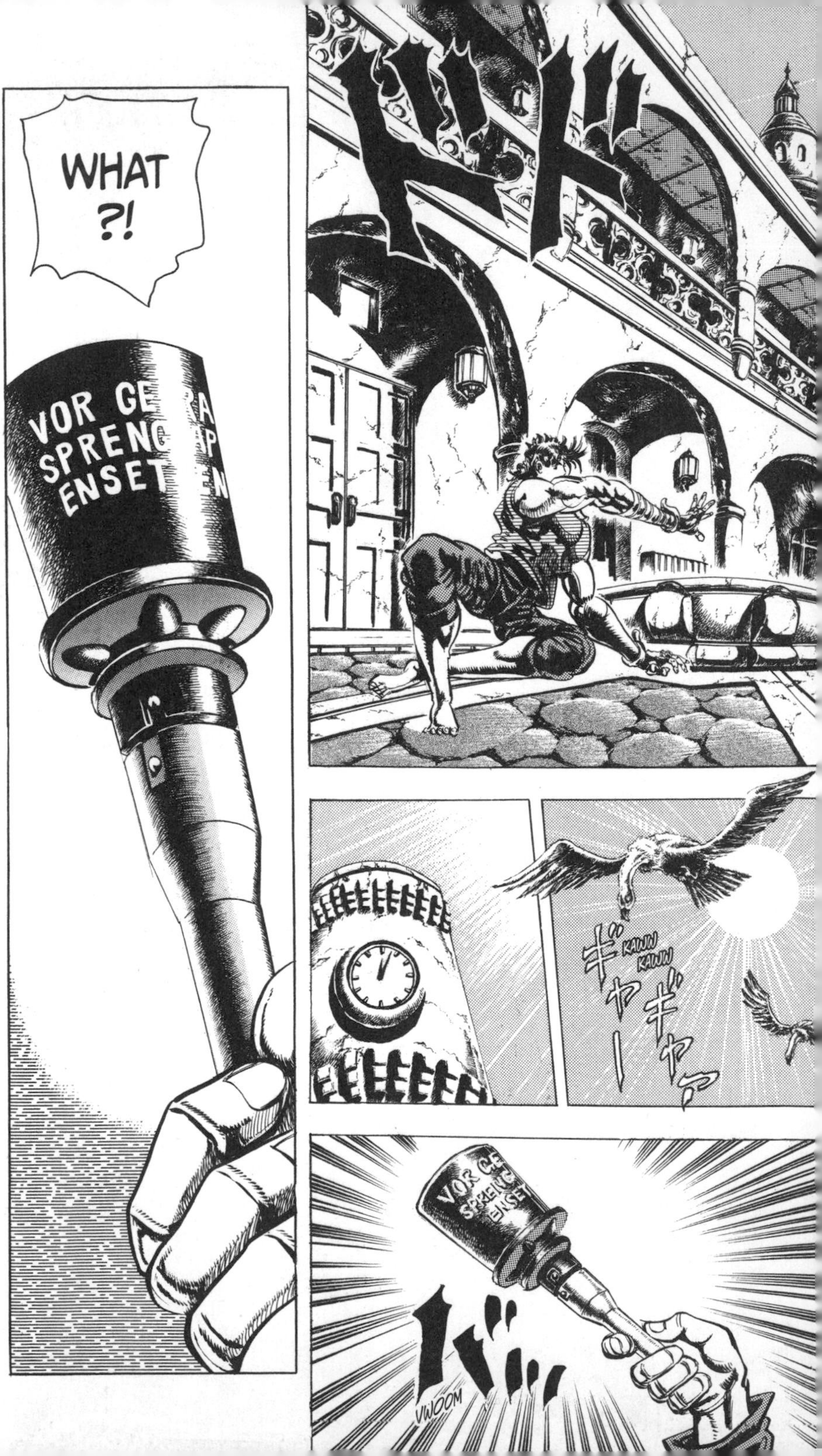
KAWW KAWW
ギャー ギャァ
VWOOM
WHAT ?!
VOR GE RA
SPRENG P
ENSET EN

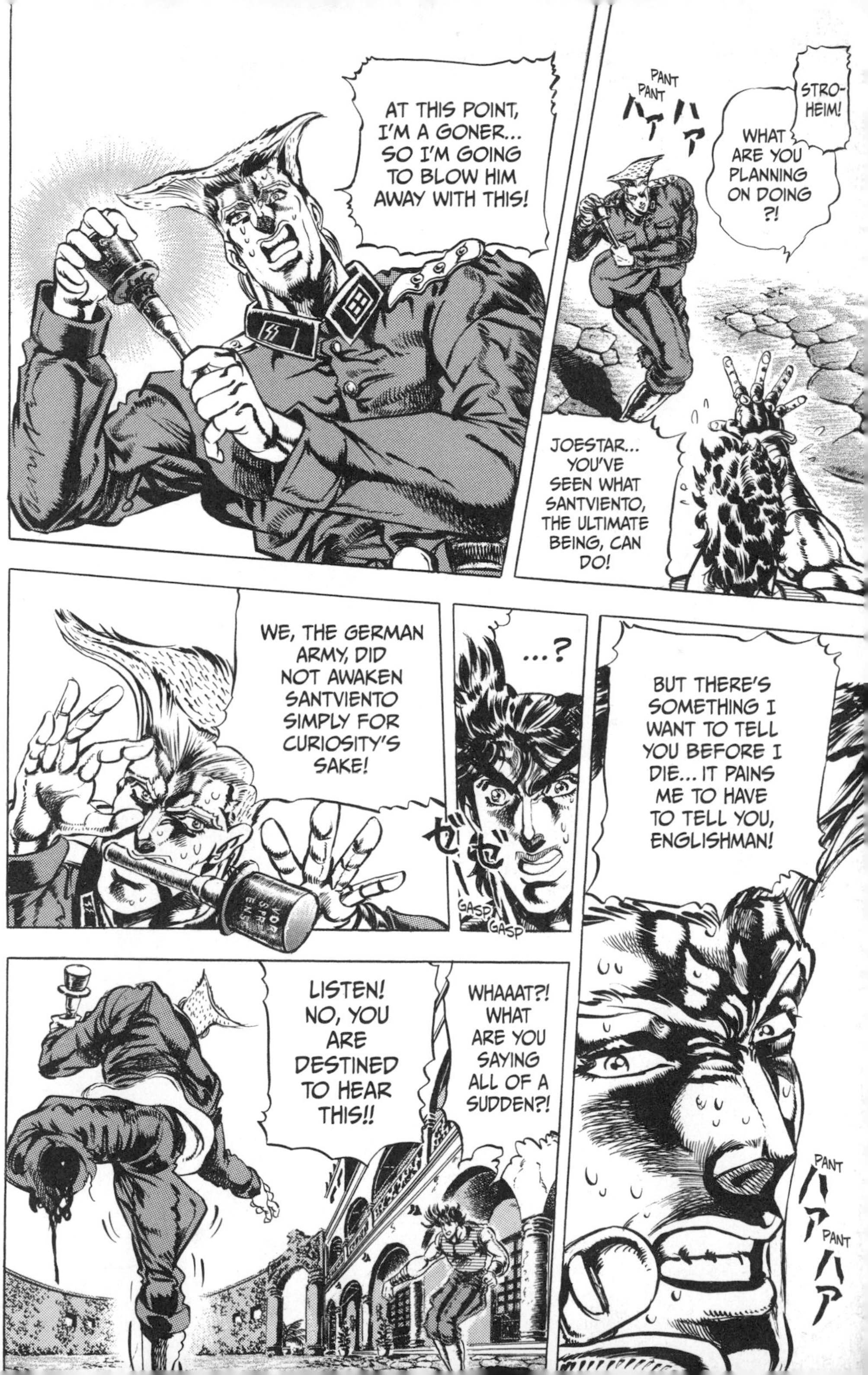
STRO-HEIM!
WHAT ARE YOU PLANNING ON DOING?!
PANT PANT
ハァ ハァ
JOESTAR... YOU'VE SEEN WHAT SANTVIENTO, THE ULTIMATE BEING, CAN DO!
AT THIS POINT, I'M A GONER... SO I'M GOING TO BLOW HIM AWAY WITH THIS!
BUT THERE'S SOMETHING I WANT TO TELL YOU BEFORE I DIE... IT PAINS ME TO HAVE TO TELL YOU, ENGLISHMAN!
PANT PANT
ハァ ハァ
...?
GASP GASP
WE, THE GERMAN ARMY, DID NOT AWAKEN SANTVIENTO SIMPLY FOR CURIOSITY'S SAKE!
WHAAAT?! WHAT ARE YOU SAYING ALL OF A SUDDEN?!
LISTEN! NO, YOU ARE DESTINED TO HEAR THIS!!

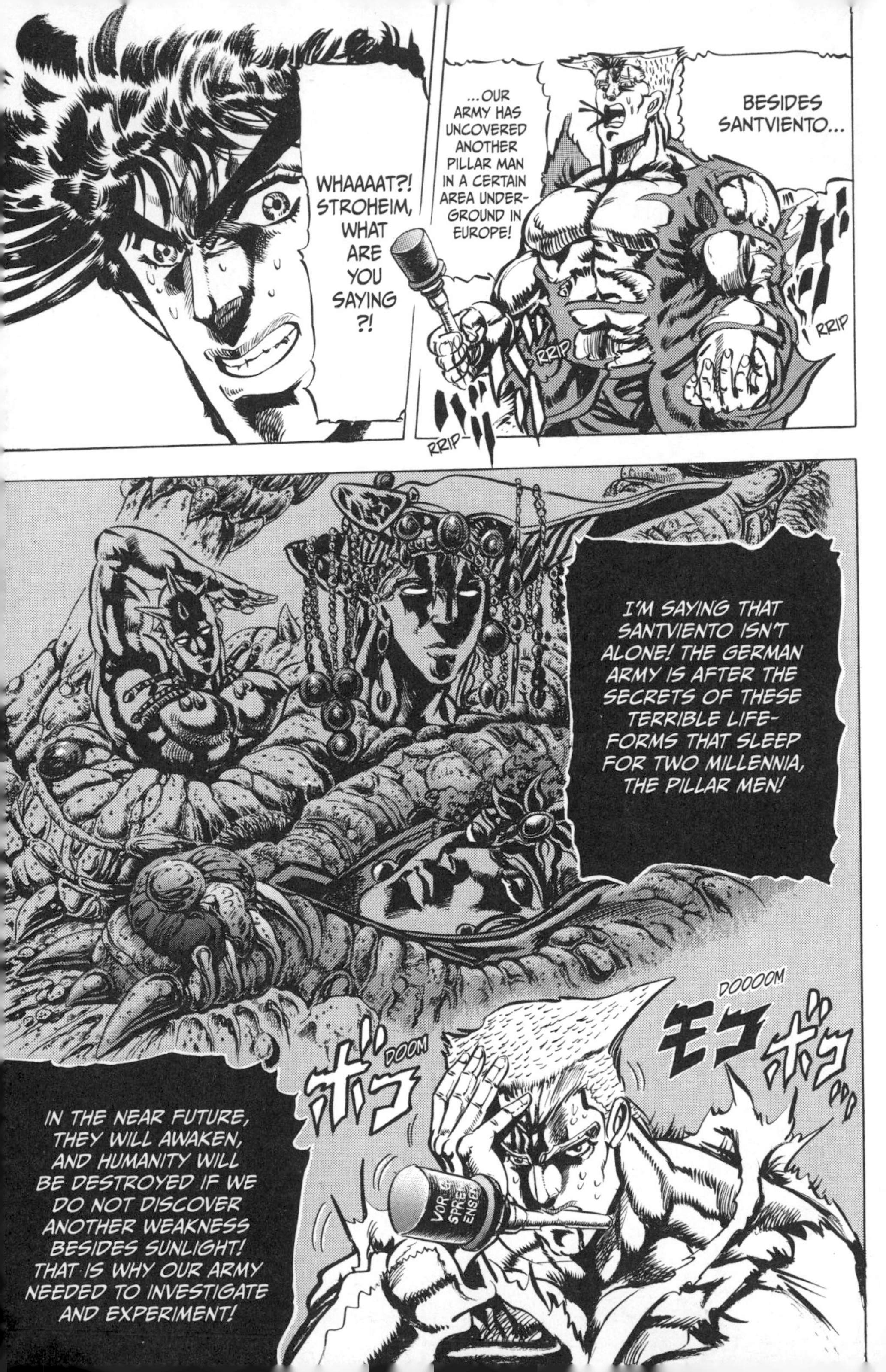
BESIDES SANTVIENTO...
...OUR ARMY HAS UNCOVERED ANOTHER PILLAR MAN IN A CERTAIN AREA UNDER-GROUND IN EUROPE!
RRIP
RRIP
RRIP
WHAAAAT?! STROHEIM, WHAT ARE YOU SAYING ?!
I'M SAYING THAT SANTVIENTO ISN'T ALONE! THE GERMAN ARMY IS AFTER THE SECRETS OF THESE TERRIBLE LIFE-FORMS THAT SLEEP FOR TWO MILLENNIA, THE PILLAR MEN!
DOOOOM
DOOM
IN THE NEAR FUTURE, THEY WILL AWAKEN, AND HUMANITY WILL BE DESTROYED IF WE DO NOT DISCOVER ANOTHER WEAKNESS BESIDES SUNLIGHT! THAT IS WHY OUR ARMY NEEDED TO INVESTIGATE AND EXPERIMENT!

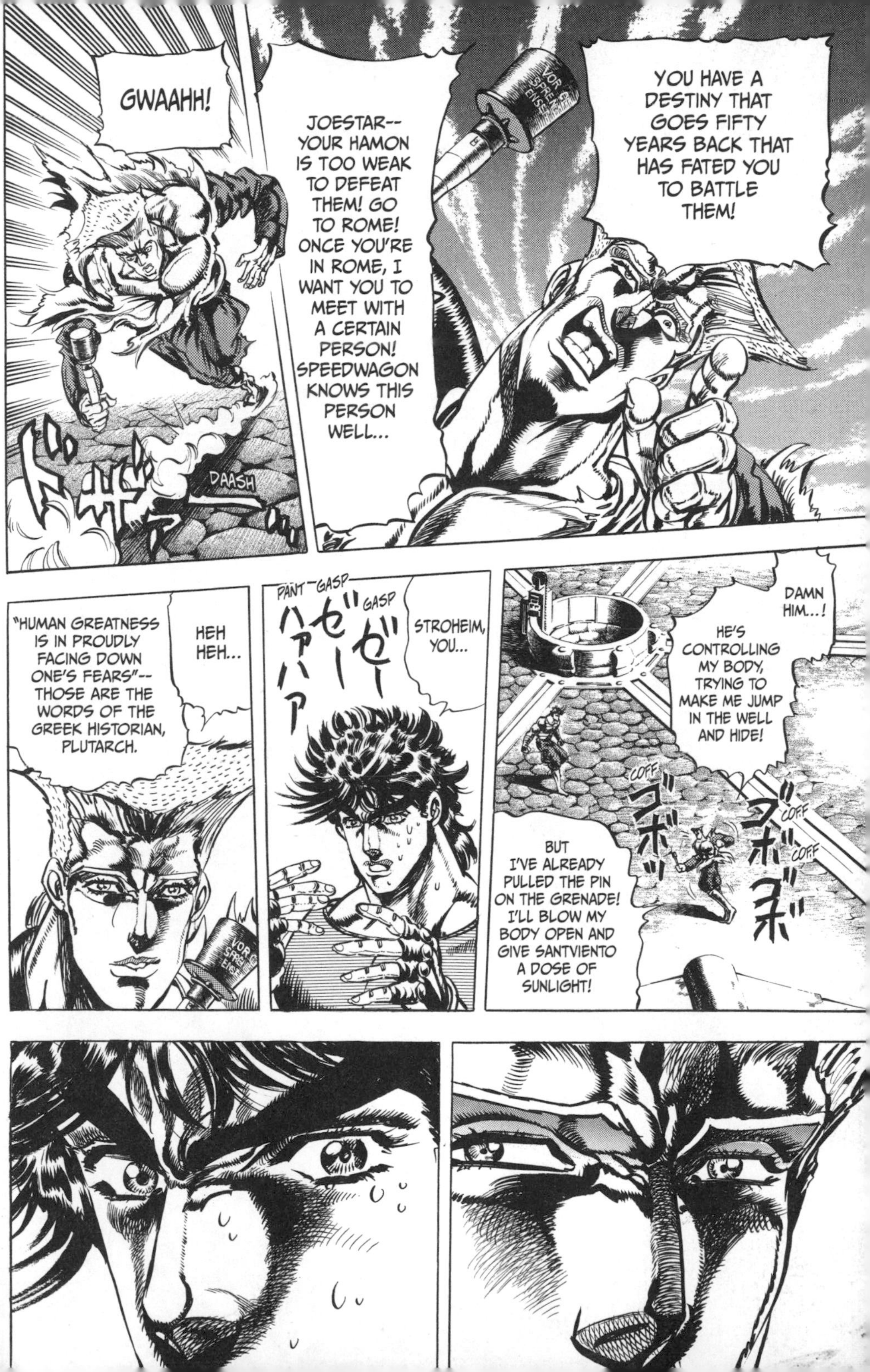
YOU HAVE A DESTINY THAT GOES FIFTY YEARS BACK THAT HAS FATED YOU TO BATTLE THEM!
JOESTAR-- YOUR HAMON IS TOO WEAK TO DEFEAT THEM! GO TO ROME! ONCE YOU'RE IN ROME, I WANT YOU TO MEET WITH A CERTAIN PERSON! SPEEDWAGON KNOWS THIS PERSON WELL...
GWAAHH!
DAASH
DAMN HIM...!
HE'S CONTROLLING MY BODY, TRYING TO MAKE ME JUMP IN THE WELL AND HIDE!
COFF
COFF
COFF
BUT I'VE ALREADY PULLED THE PIN ON THE GRENADE! I'LL BLOW MY BODY OPEN AND GIVE SANTVIENTO A DOSE OF SUNLIGHT!
PANT GASP
GASP
ゼーゼー
ハァハァ
STROHEIM, YOU...
HEH HEH...
"HUMAN GREATNESS IS IN PROUDLY FACING DOWN ONE'S FEARS"-- THOSE ARE THE WORDS OF THE GREEK HISTORIAN, PLUTARCH.

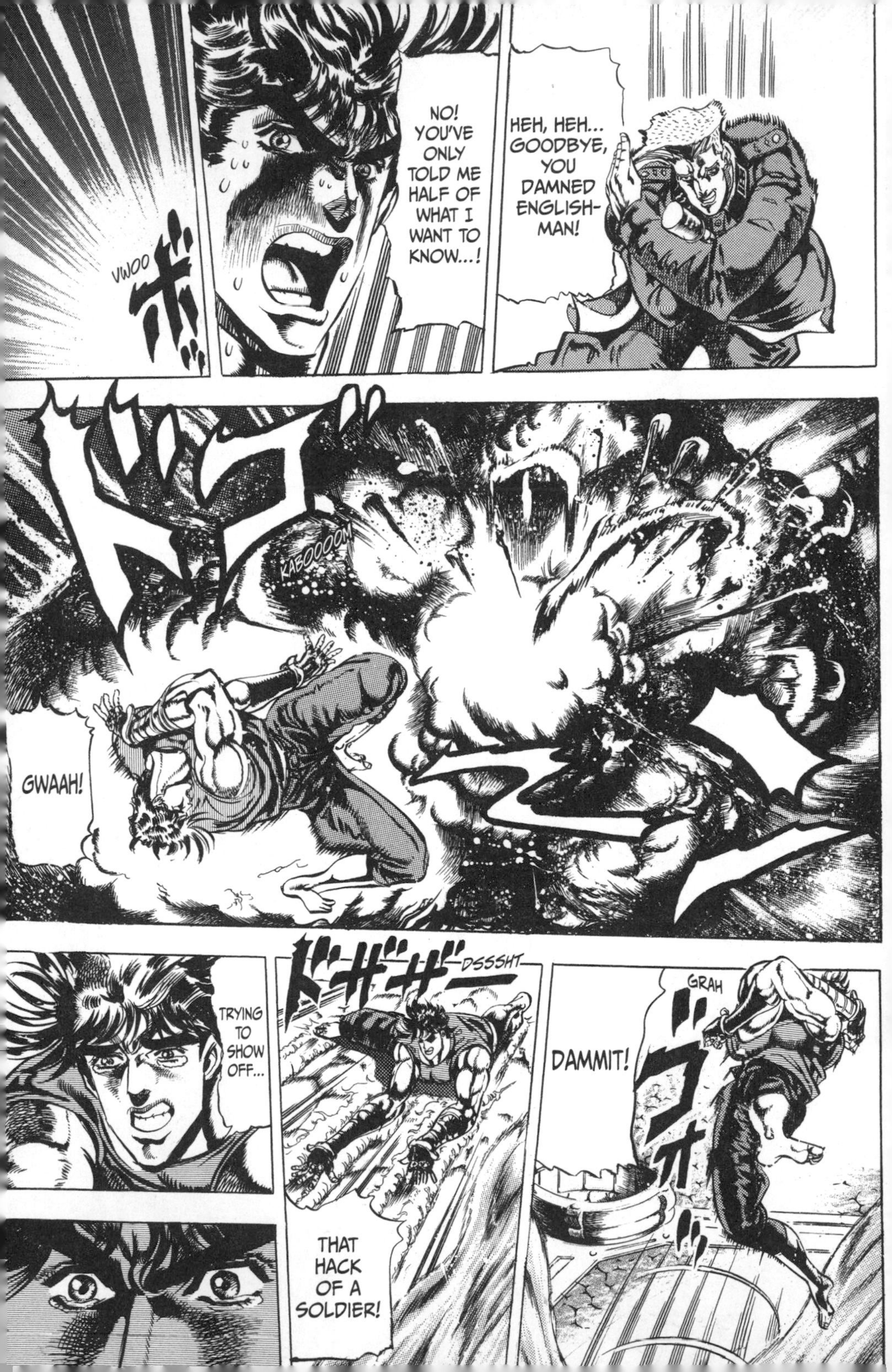
HEH, HEH... GOODBYE, YOU DAMNED ENGLISH-MAN!
NO! YOU'VE ONLY TOLD ME HALF OF WHAT I WANT TO KNOW...!
VWOO
KABOOOOM
GWAAH!
GRAH
DAMMIT!
DSSSHT
THAT HACK OF A SOLDIER!
TRYING TO SHOW OFF...

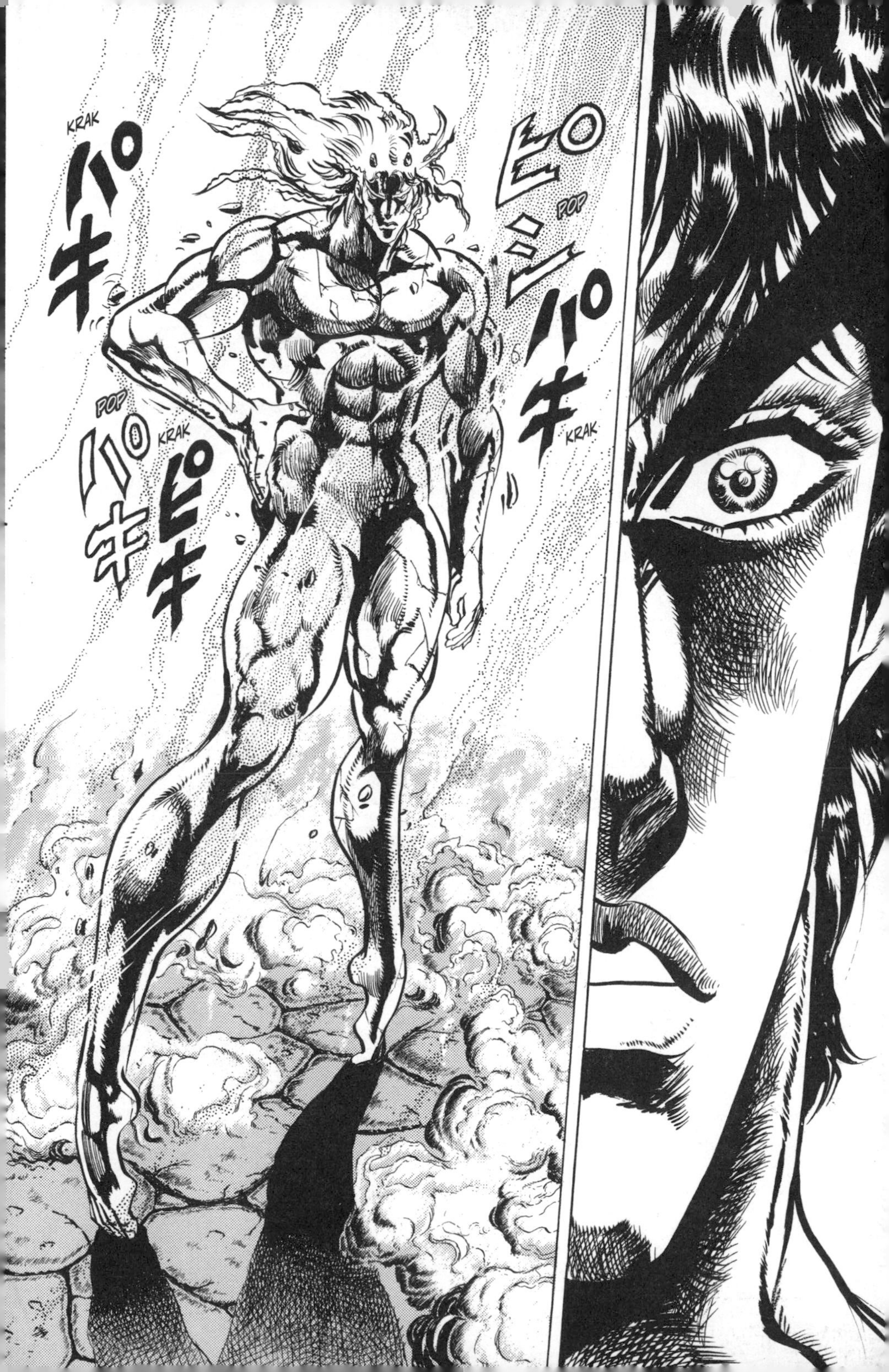
ピシ
POP
パキ
KRAK
ピキ
KRAK
パキ
POP
パキ
KRAK

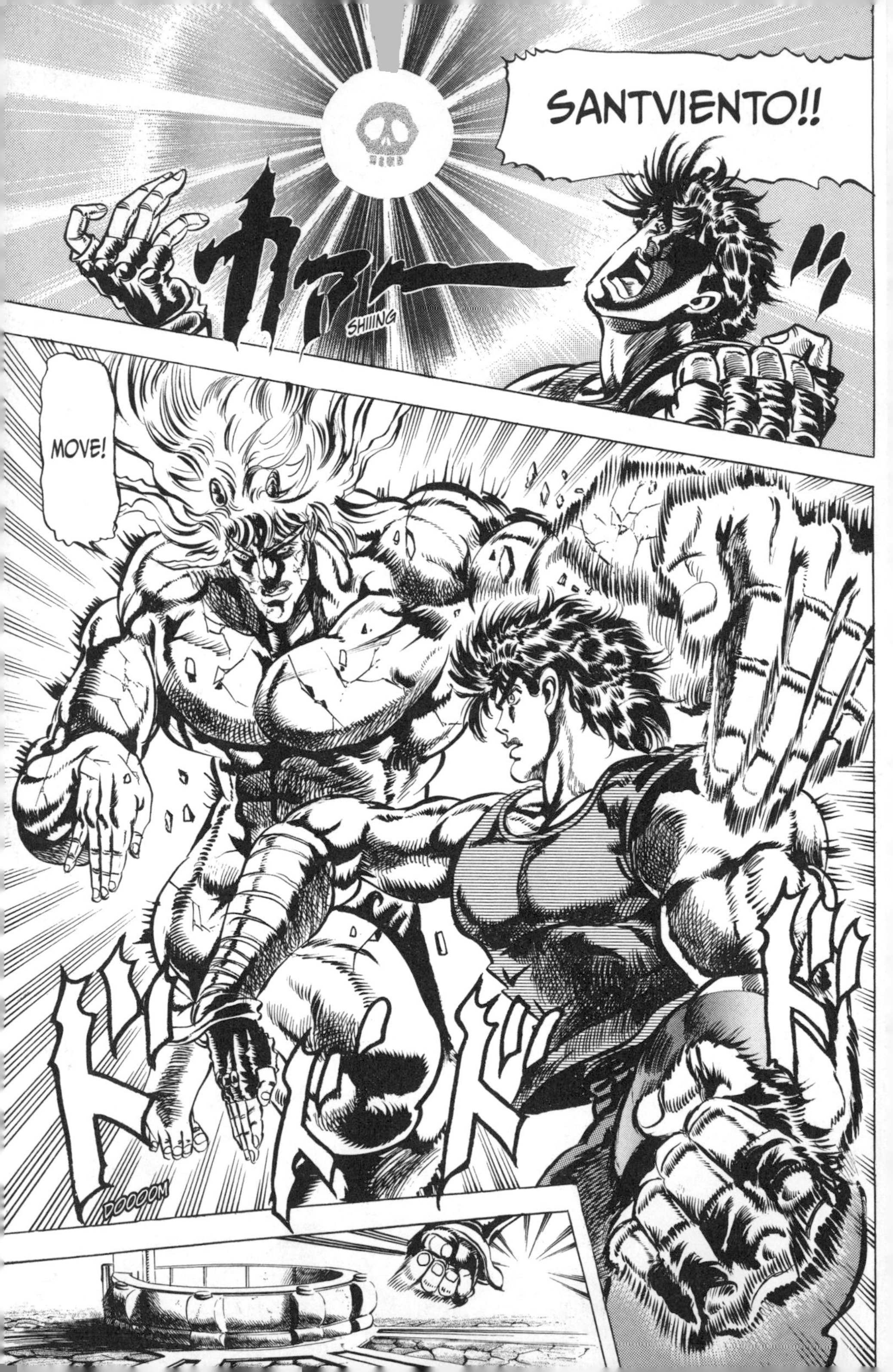
SANTVIENTO!!
SHIING
MOVE!
DOOOOM

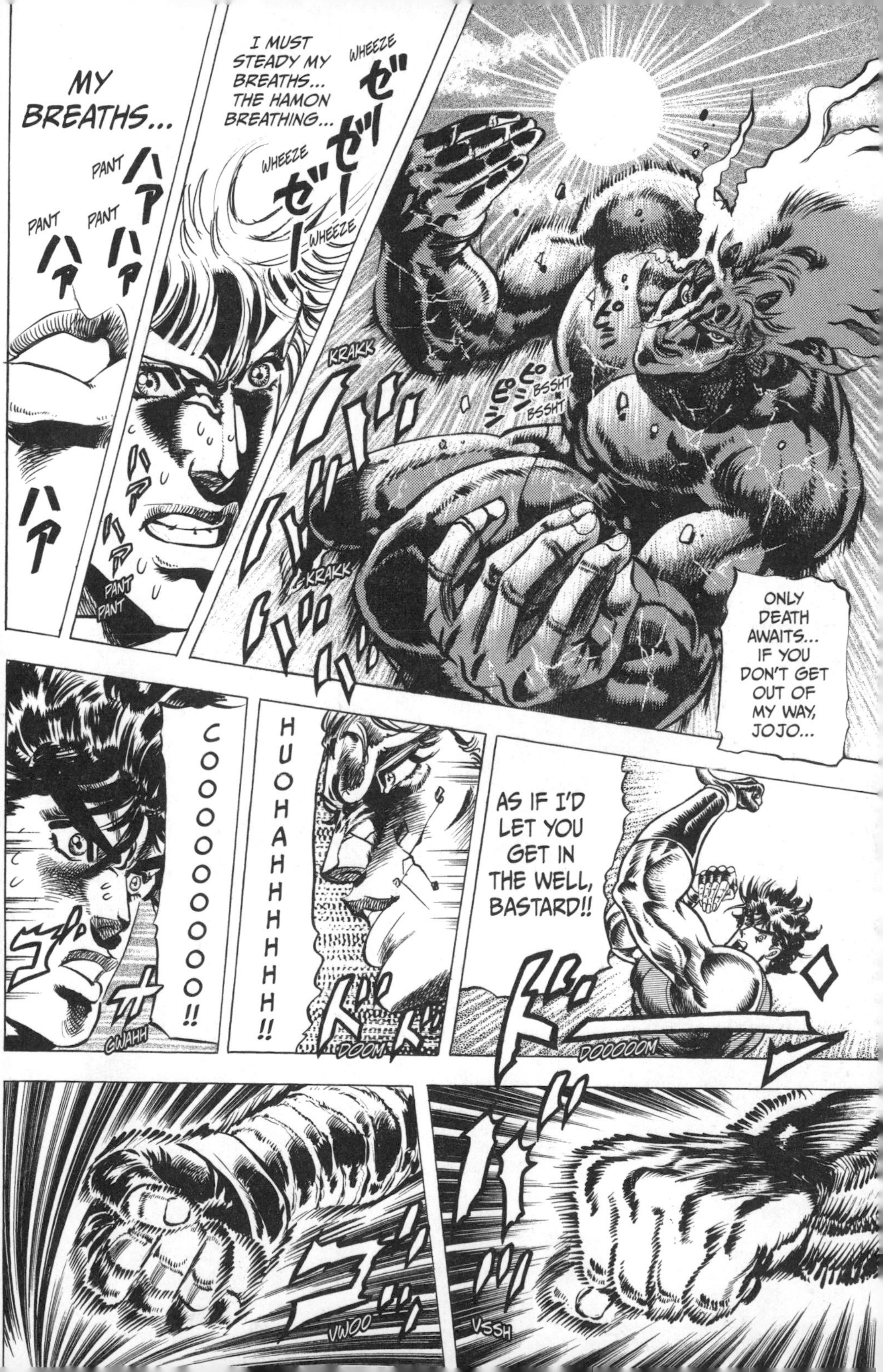
KRAKK
BSSHT
BSSHT
KRAKK
ONLY DEATH AWAITS... IF YOU DON'T GET OUT OF MY WAY, JOJO...
I MUST STEADY MY BREATHS... THE HAMON BREATHING...
WHEEZE
WHEEZE
WHEEZE
PANT
PANT
MY BREATHS...
PANT
PANT
PANT
AS IF I'D LET YOU GET IN THE WELL, BASTARD!!
DOOOOOM
HUOHAHHHHHHHH!!
DOOM
COOOOOOOOOOO!!
GWAHH
VSSH
VWOO

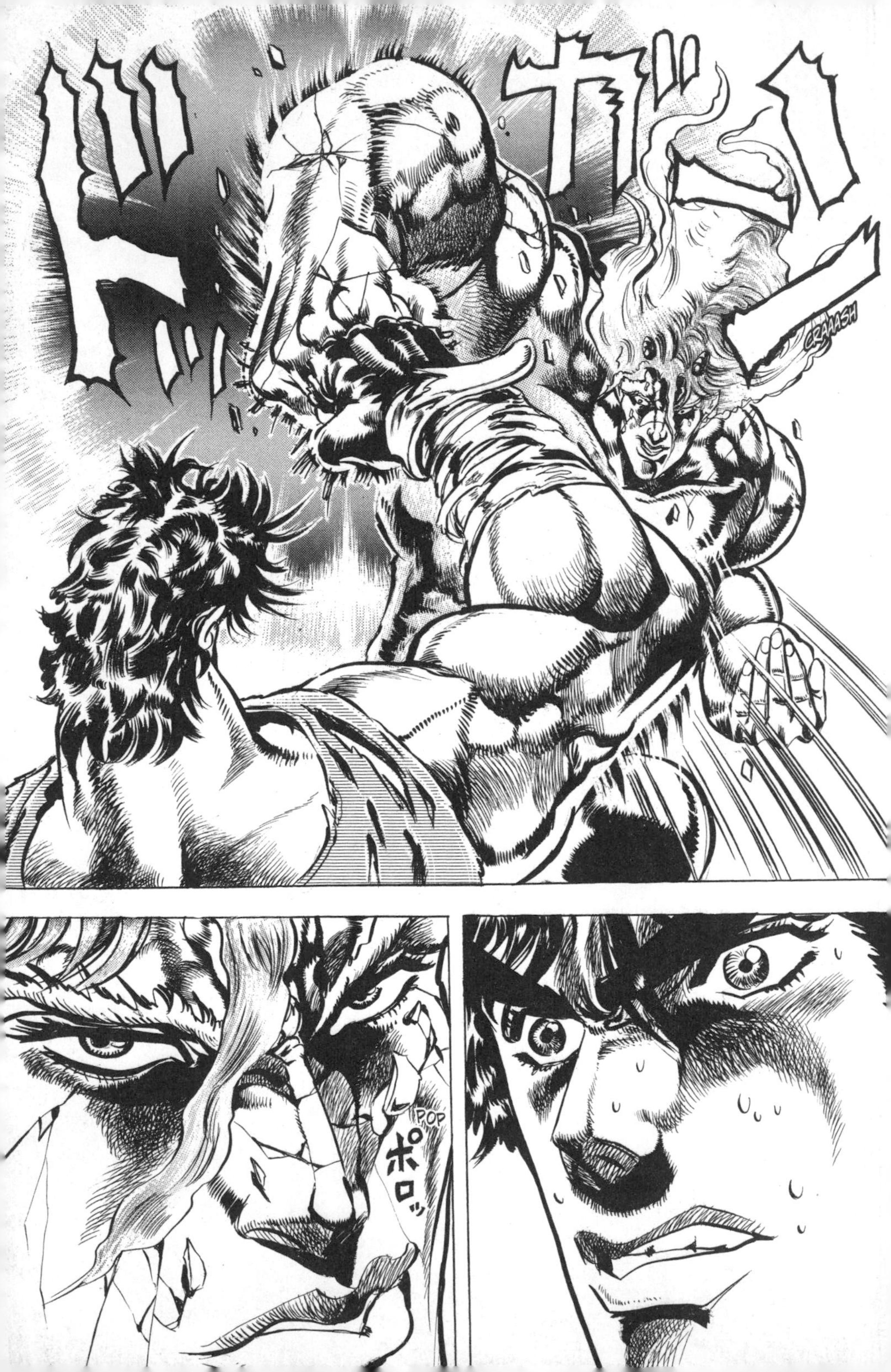
CRAAASH
POP
ポロッ

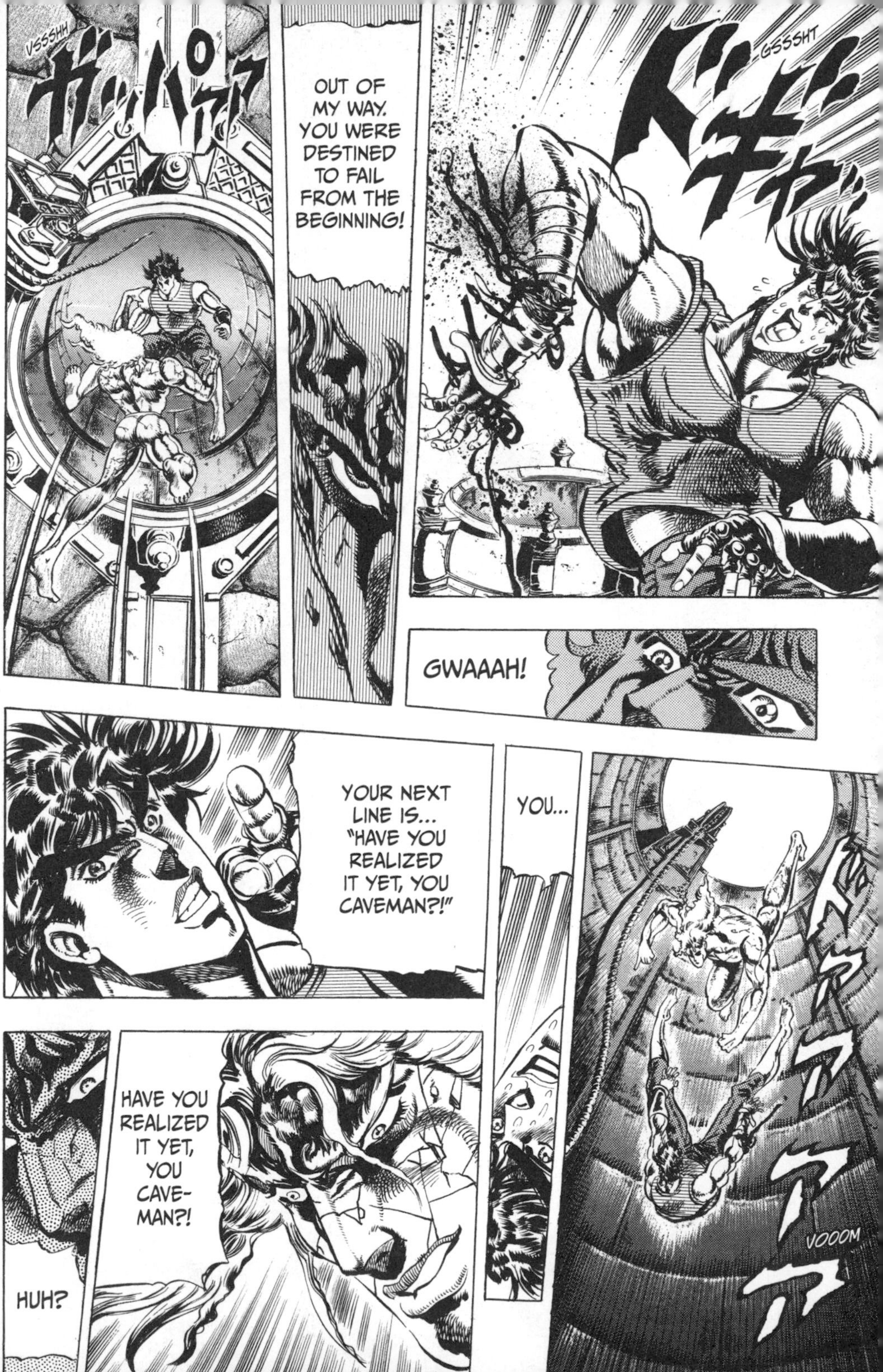
GSSSHT
GWAAAH!
OUT OF MY WAY. YOU WERE DESTINED TO FAIL FROM THE BEGINNING!
VSSSHH
VOOOM
YOU...
YOUR NEXT LINE IS... "HAVE YOU REALIZED IT YET, YOU CAVEMAN?!"
HAVE YOU REALIZED IT YET, YOU CAVE-MAN?!
HUH?

SHIIING

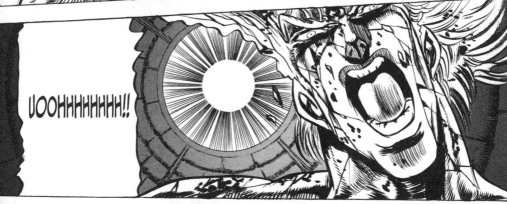

UOOHHHHHHHH!!

IT'S EXACTLY NOON! THE SUN IS RIGHT ABOVE AND REFLECTING OFF THE WATER BELOW, FRYING YOU UP LIKE BACON AND EGGS IN THE MORNING! YOU MIGHT WANT TO THINK BEFORE DIVING INTO THE WELL, BIRDBRAIN! I GUESS YOU DIDN'T KNOW ANY BETTER SINCE THIS IS YOUR FIRST TIME IN THE SUN, HUH?! FOOL!

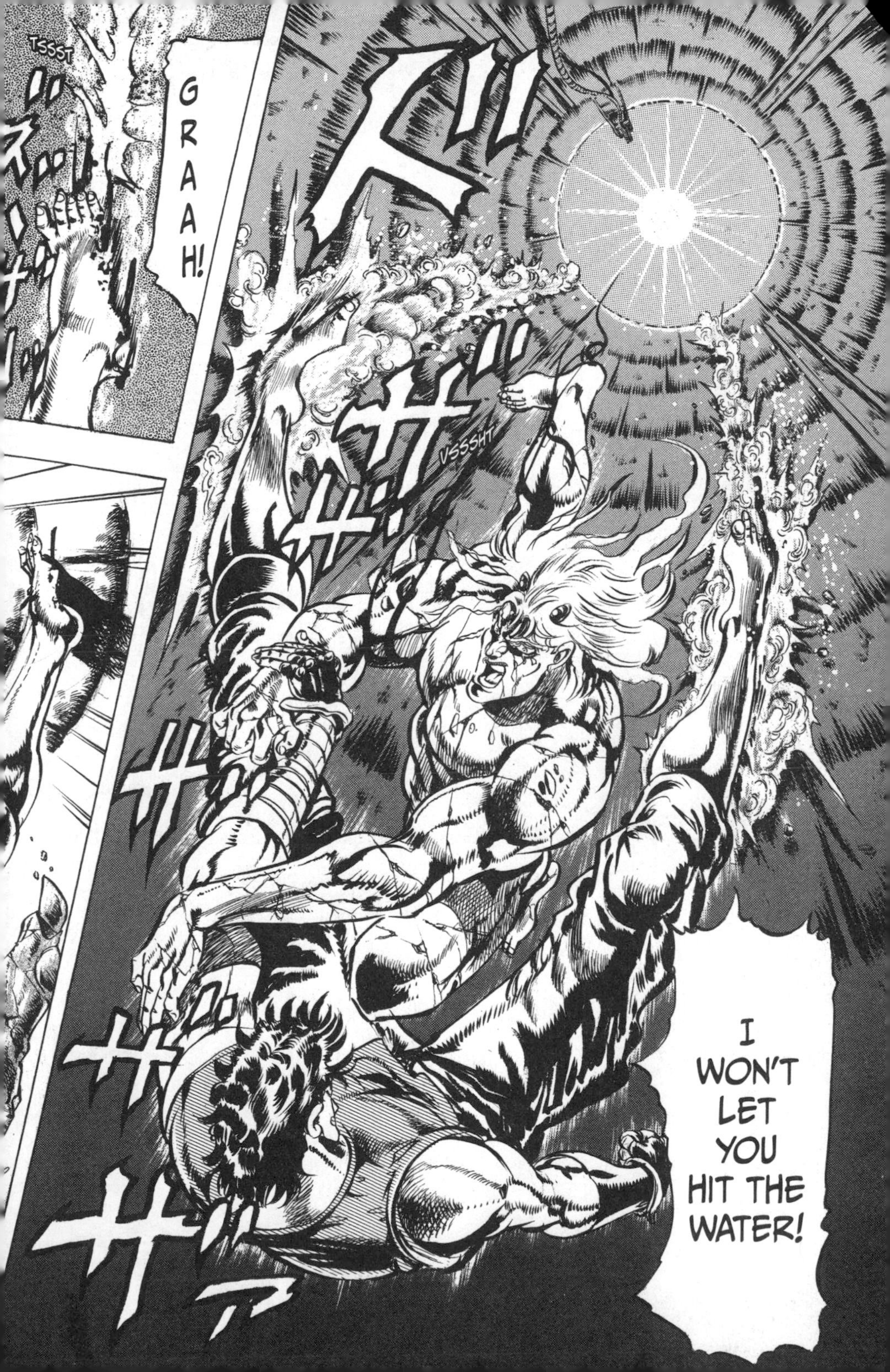
VSSSHT
I WON'T LET YOU HIT THE WATER!
TSSST
GRAAH!

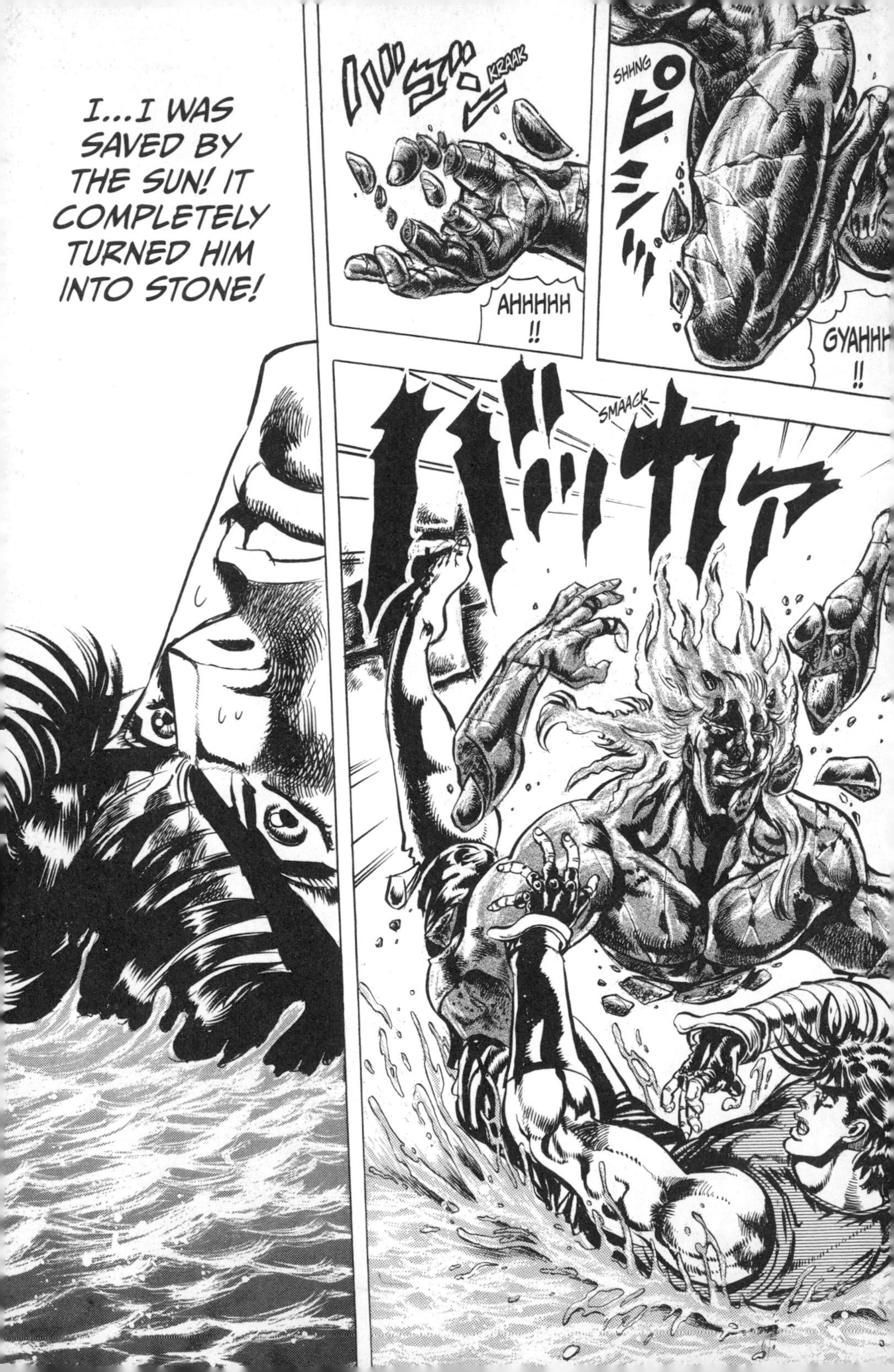
SHHNG
GYAHHH !!
KRAAK
AHHHHH !!
SMAACK !!
I...I WAS SAVED BY THE SUN! IT COMPLETELY TURNED HIM INTO STONE!

JOJO

CHAPTER 18: The Pillar Man, Santviento PART 9

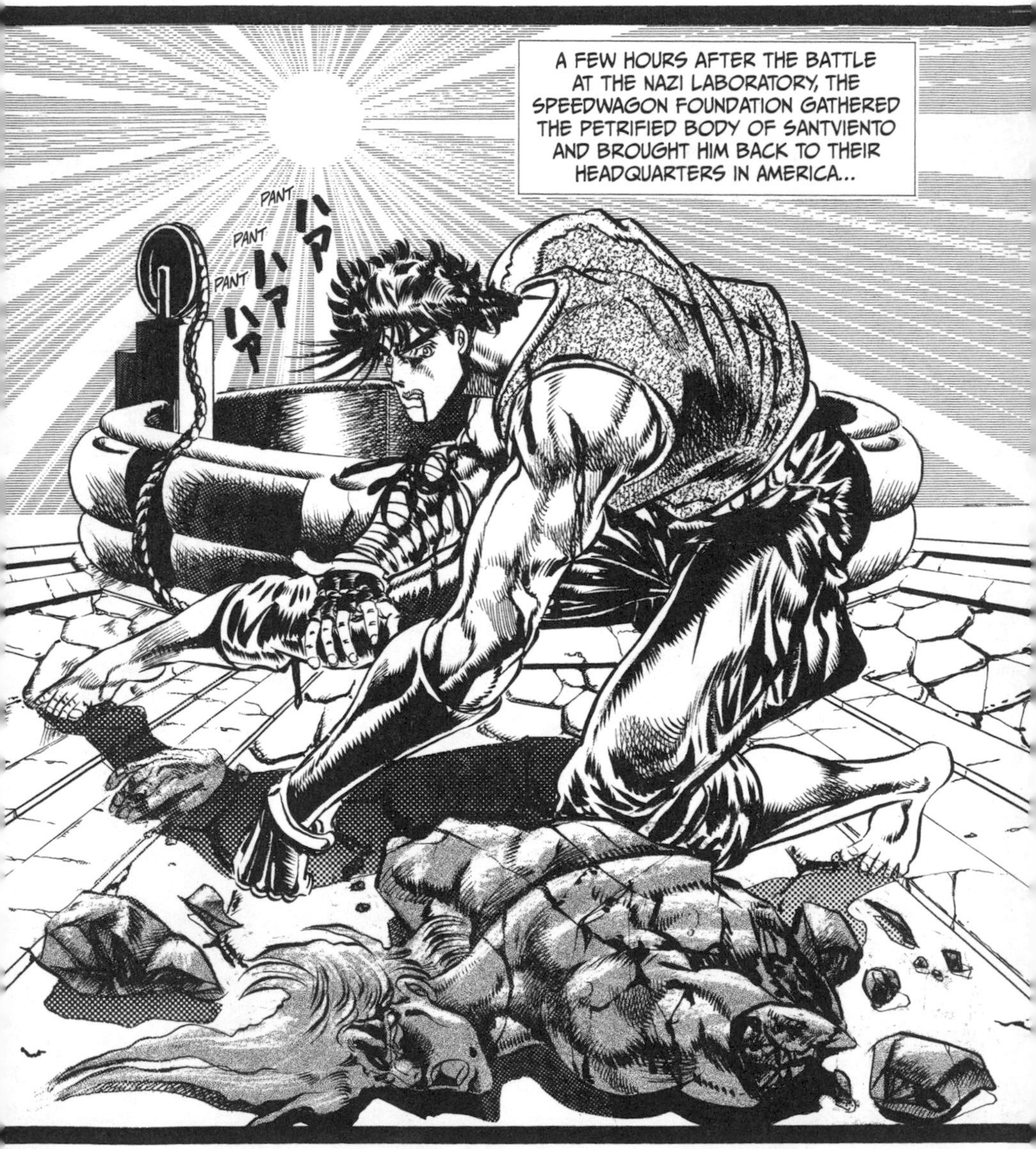
A FEW HOURS AFTER THE BATTLE AT THE NAZI LABORATORY, THE SPEEDWAGON FOUNDATION GATHERED THE PETRIFIED BODY OF SANTVIENTO AND BROUGHT HIM BACK TO THEIR HEADQUARTERS IN AMERICA...
PANT ハァ
PANT ハァ
PANT ハァ

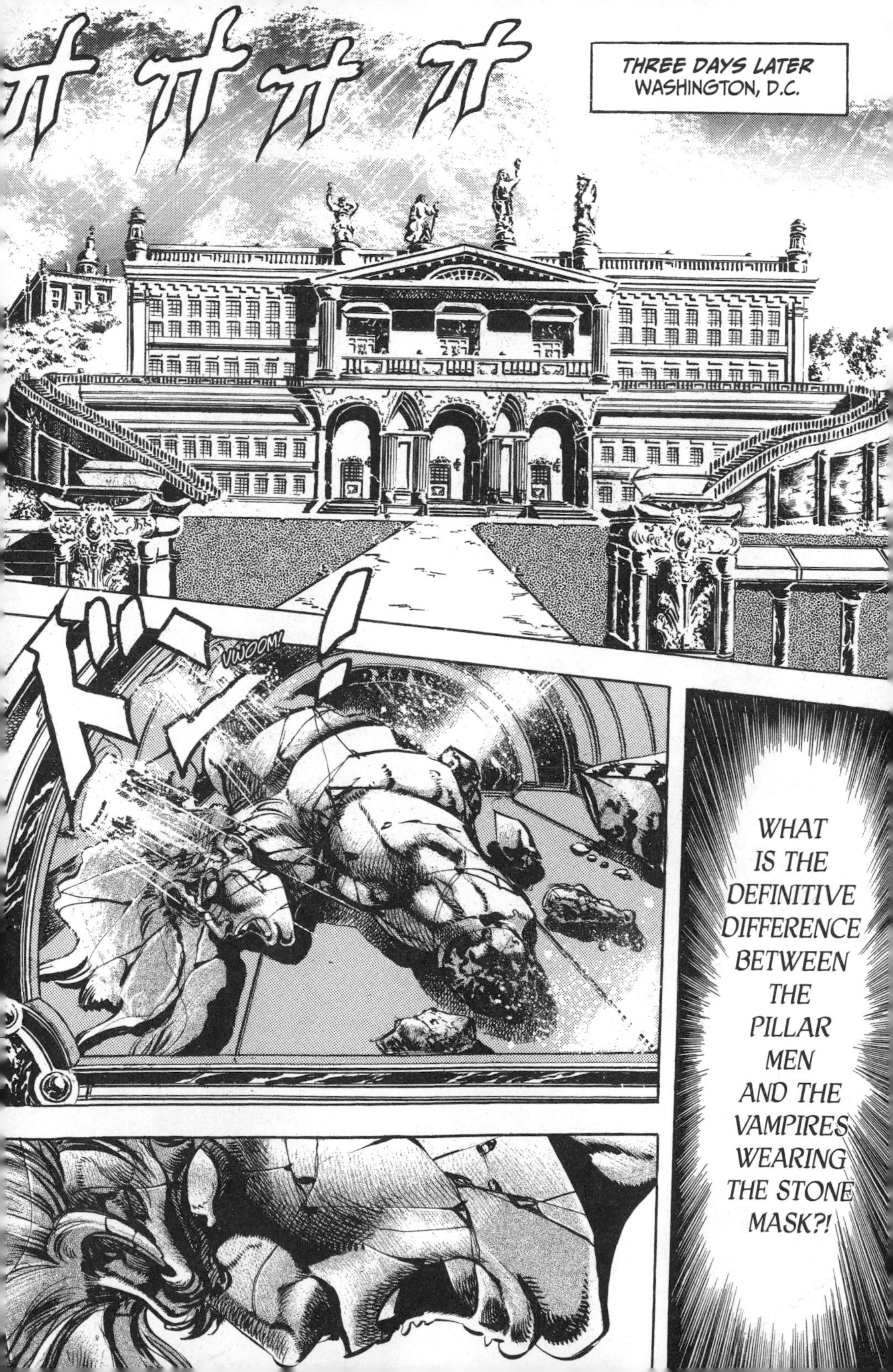
THREE DAYS LATER
WASHINGTON, D.C.
WHAT IS THE DEFINITIVE DIFFERENCE BETWEEN THE PILLAR MEN AND THE VAMPIRES WEARING THE STONE MASK?!
VWOOM!

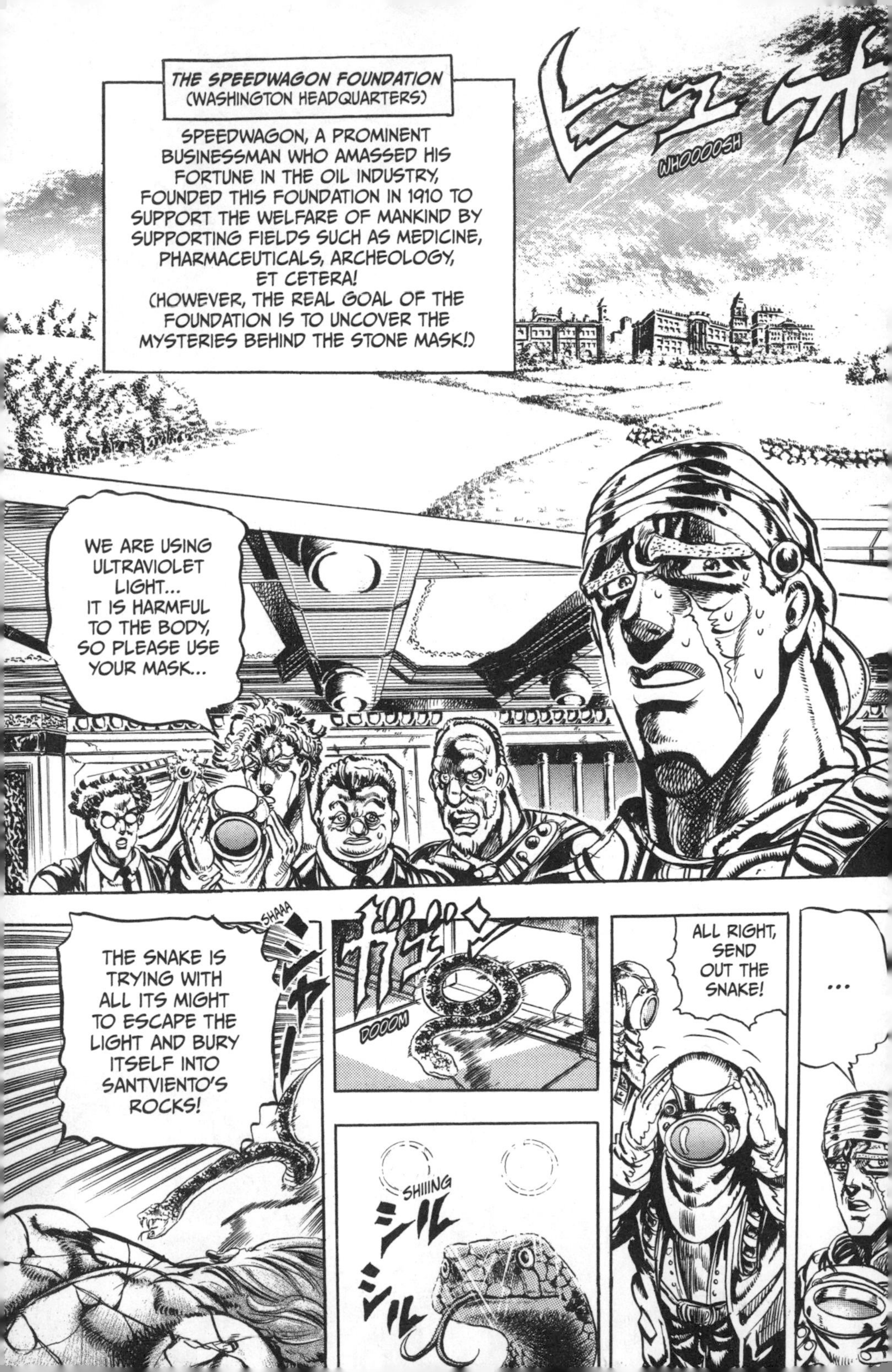
THE SPEEDWAGON FOUNDATION
(WASHINGTON HEADQUARTERS)
SPEEDWAGON, A PROMINENT BUSINESSMAN WHO AMASSED HIS FORTUNE IN THE OIL INDUSTRY, FOUNDED THIS FOUNDATION IN 1910 TO SUPPORT THE WELFARE OF MANKIND BY SUPPORTING FIELDS SUCH AS MEDICINE, PHARMACEUTICALS, ARCHEOLOGY, ET CETERA! (HOWEVER, THE REAL GOAL OF THE FOUNDATION IS TO UNCOVER THE MYSTERIES BEHIND THE STONE MASK!)
WHOOOOSH
WE ARE USING ULTRAVIOLET LIGHT... IT IS HARMFUL TO THE BODY, SO PLEASE USE YOUR MASK...
...
ALL RIGHT, SEND OUT THE SNAKE!
DOOOM
SHIIING
シル
シル
SHAAA
THE SNAKE IS TRYING WITH ALL ITS MIGHT TO ESCAPE THE LIGHT AND BURY ITSELF INTO SANTVIENTO'S ROCKS!

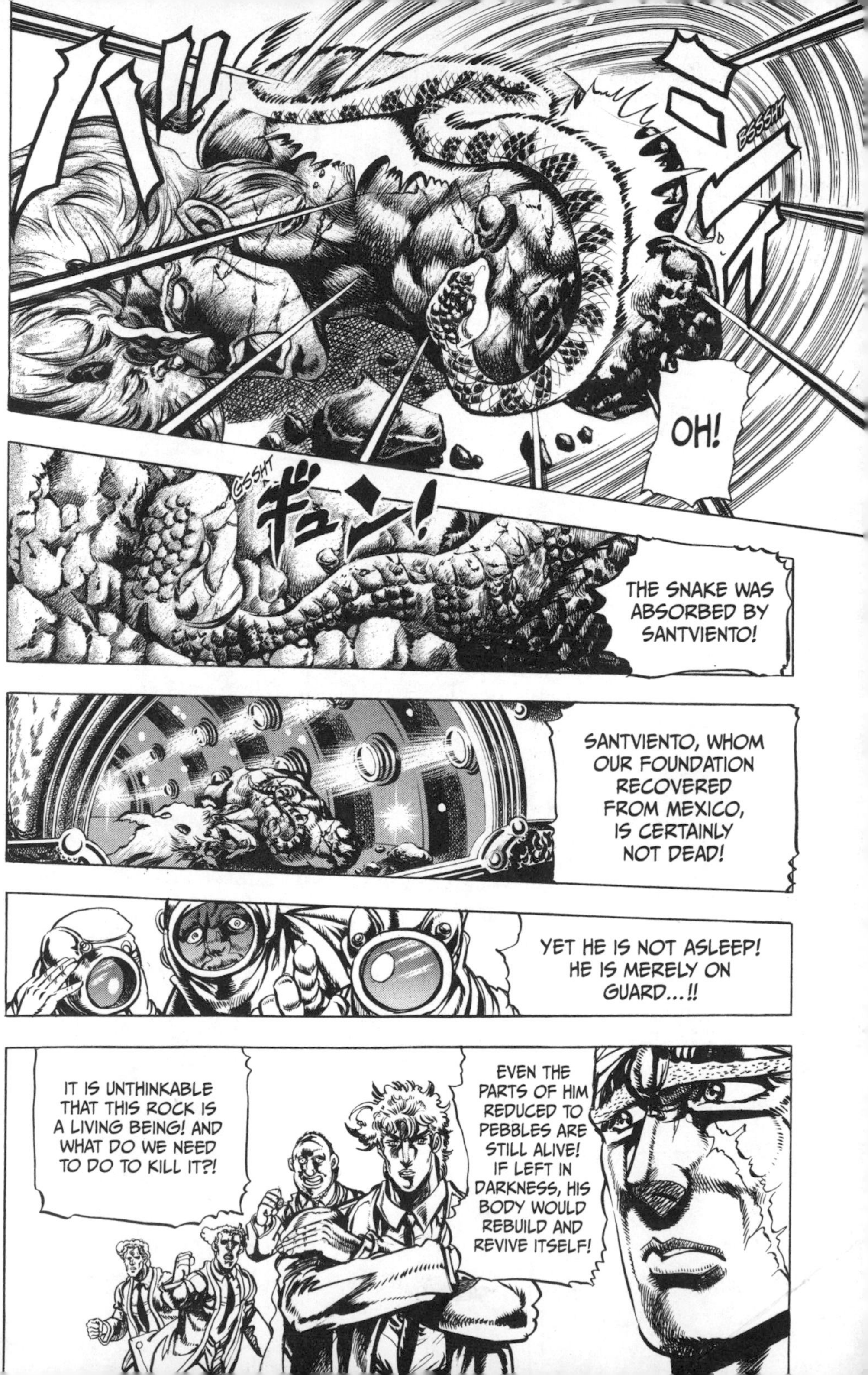

BSSSHT
OH!
SSSHT
ギュン!
THE SNAKE WAS ABSORBED BY SANTVIENTO!
SANTVIENTO, WHOM OUR FOUNDATION RECOVERED FROM MEXICO, IS CERTAINLY NOT DEAD!
YET HE IS NOT ASLEEP! HE IS MERELY ON GUARD...!!
EVEN THE PARTS OF HIM REDUCED TO PEBBLES ARE STILL ALIVE! IF LEFT IN DARKNESS, HIS BODY WOULD REBUILD AND REVIVE ITSELF!
IT IS UNTHINKABLE THAT THIS ROCK IS A LIVING BEING! AND WHAT DO WE NEED TO DO TO KILL IT?!

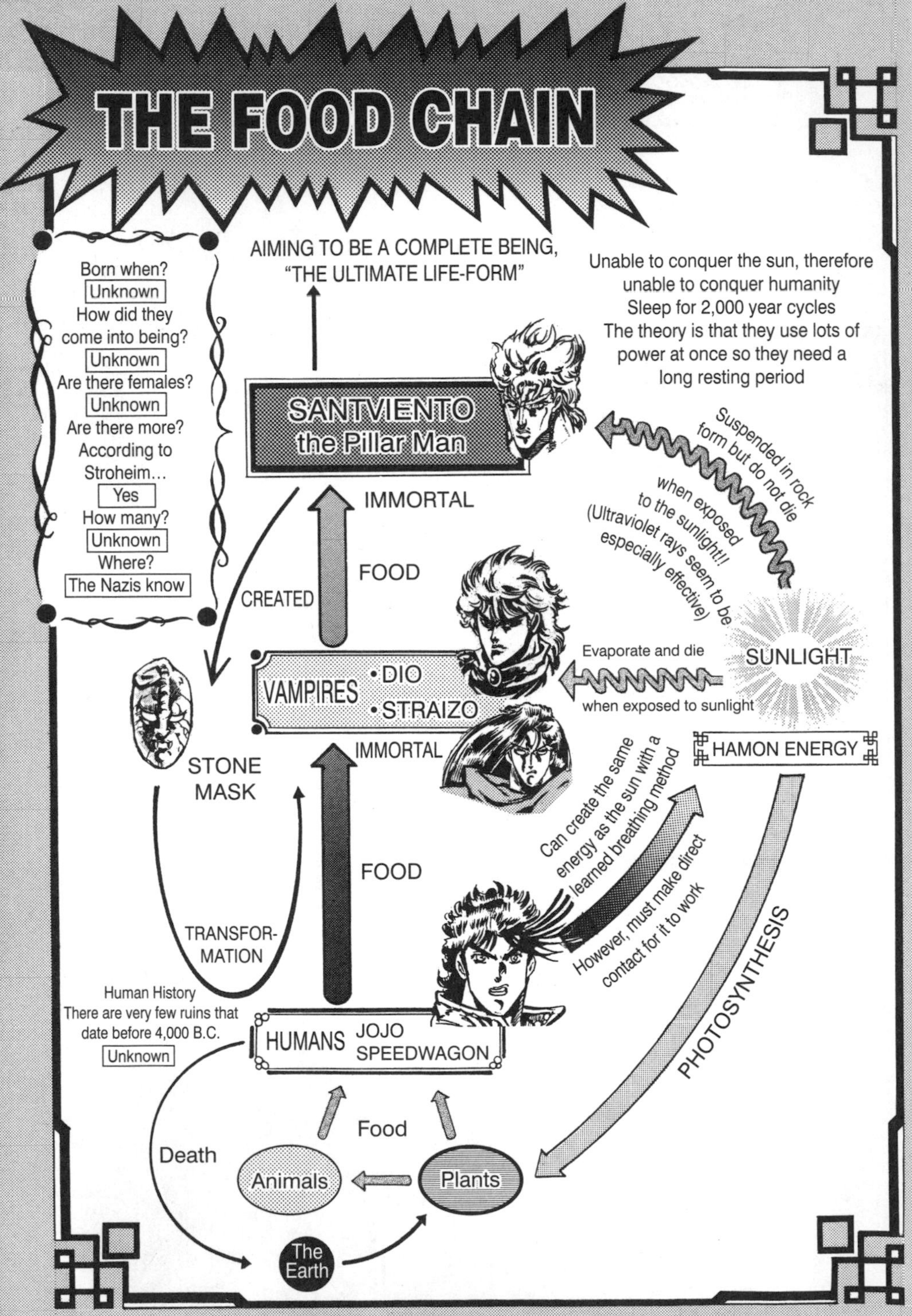
THE FOOD CHAIN
Born when?
Unknown
How did they come into being?
Unknown
Are there females?
Unknown
Are there more?
According to Stroheim…
Yes
How many?
Unknown
Where?
The Nazis know
AIMING TO BE A COMPLETE BEING, "THE ULTIMATE LIFE-FORM"
Unable to conquer the sun, therefore unable to conquer humanity
Sleep for 2,000 year cycles
The theory is that they use lots of power at once so they need a long resting period
SANTVIENTO the Pillar Man
Suspended in rock form but do not die
when exposed to the sunlight!! (Ultraviolet rays seem to be especially effective)
IMMORTAL
FOOD
CREATED
SUNLIGHT
Evaporate and die
when exposed to sunlight
VAMPIRES
•DIO
•STRAIZO
STONE MASK
IMMORTAL
HAMON ENERGY
Can create the same energy as the sun with a learned breathing method
However, must make direct contact for it to work
FOOD
TRANSFOR-MATION
PHOTOSYNTHESIS
Human History
There are very few ruins that date before 4,000 B.C.
Unknown
HUMANS
JOJO
SPEEDWAGON
Food
Death
Animals
Plants
The Earth

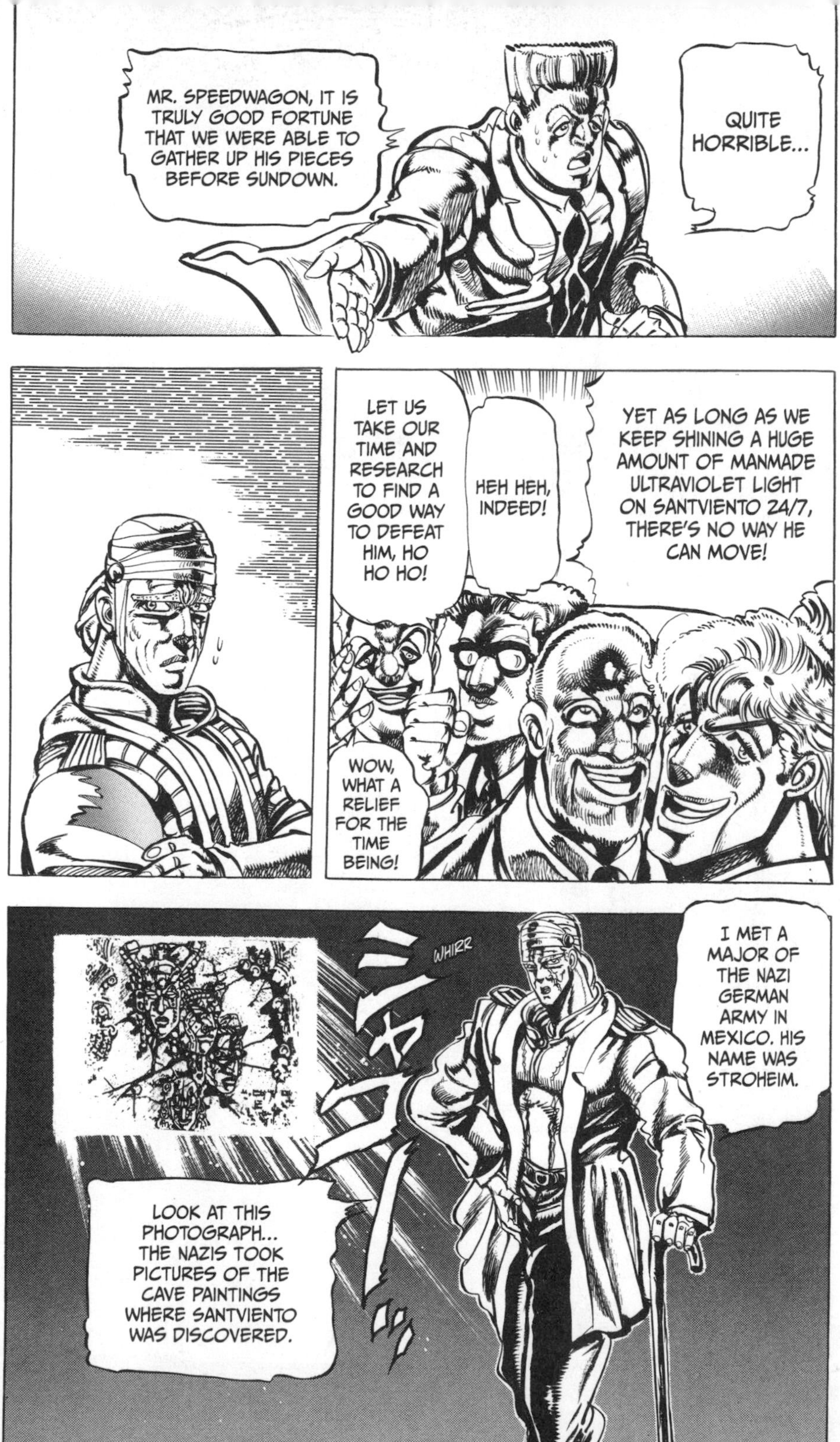
QUITE HORRIBLE...
MR. SPEEDWAGON, IT IS TRULY GOOD FORTUNE THAT WE WERE ABLE TO GATHER UP HIS PIECES BEFORE SUNDOWN.
YET AS LONG AS WE KEEP SHINING A HUGE AMOUNT OF MANMADE ULTRAVIOLET LIGHT ON SANTVIENTO 24/7, THERE'S NO WAY HE CAN MOVE!
HEH HEH, INDEED!
LET US TAKE OUR TIME AND RESEARCH TO FIND A GOOD WAY TO DEFEAT HIM, HO HO HO!
WOW, WHAT A RELIEF FOR THE TIME BEING!
I MET A MAJOR OF THE NAZI GERMAN ARMY IN MEXICO. HIS NAME WAS STROHEIM.
WHIRR
LOOK AT THIS PHOTOGRAPH... THE NAZIS TOOK PICTURES OF THE CAVE PAINTINGS WHERE SANTVIENTO WAS DISCOVERED.

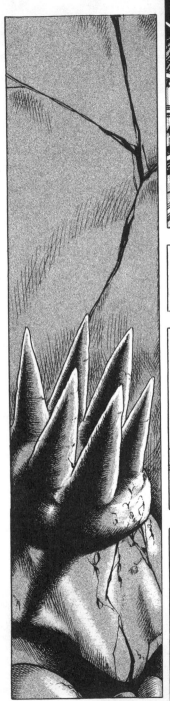

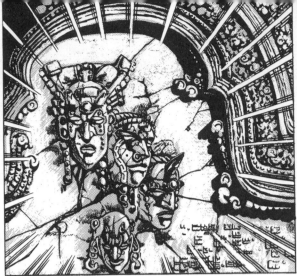

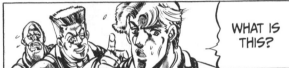

WHAT IS THIS?
LOOK *VERY* CLOSELY AT THEIR FACES! WE HADN'T NOTICED THIS UNTIL NOW!
AT FIRST GLANCE, IT LOOKS LIKE SIMPLE FACE CARVINGS ...
BUT EXAMINE THEM INDIVIDU-ALLY!
ONE BY ONE!
THEIR *HORNS* ARE SHAPED DIFFER-ENTLY!
LET'S SAY THAT THE VERY BOTTOM ONE IS SHAPED THE SAME AS SANTVIENTO'S... THEN WHAT OF THE REST ?!

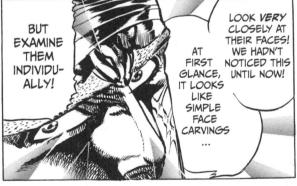

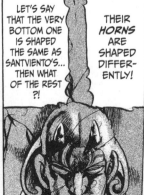

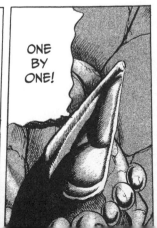

DOOOOOM
WHO EXACT-LY...
...ARE THEY ?!

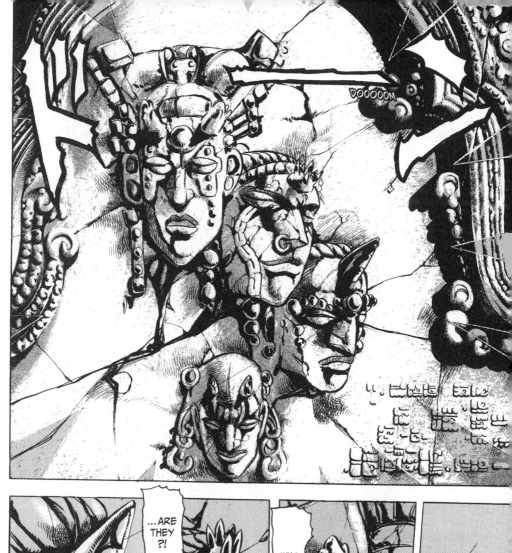

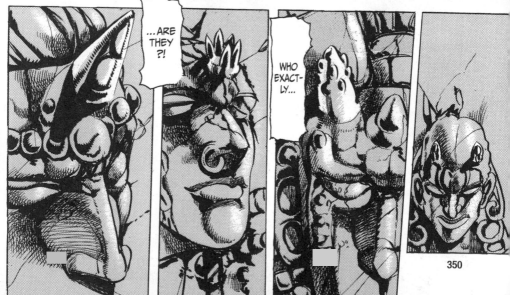

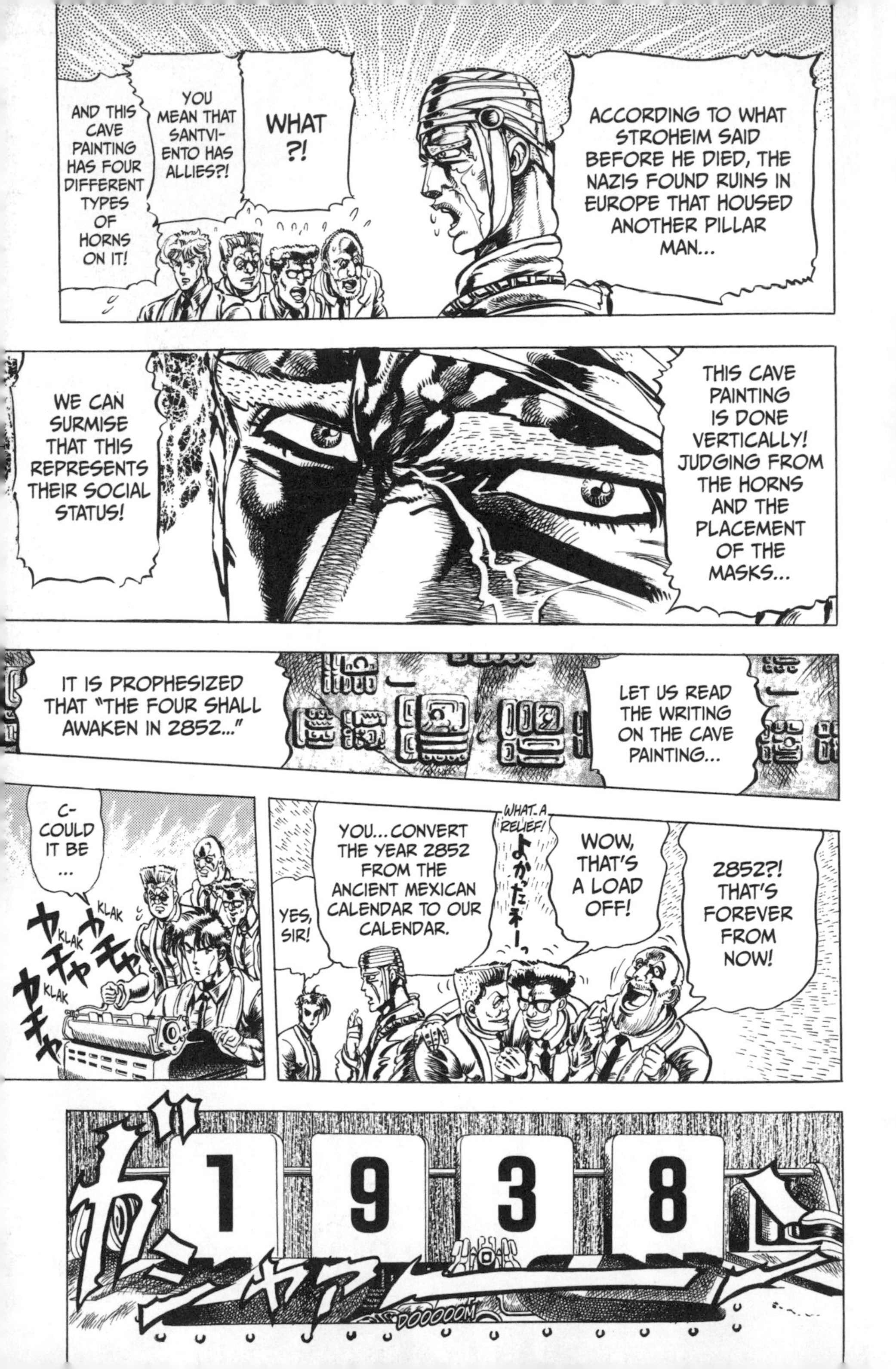

ACCORDING TO WHAT STROHEIM SAID BEFORE HE DIED, THE NAZIS FOUND RUINS IN EUROPE THAT HOUSED ANOTHER PILLAR MAN...
WHAT ?!
YOU MEAN THAT SANTVI-ENTO HAS ALLIES?!
AND THIS CAVE PAINTING HAS FOUR DIFFERENT TYPES OF HORNS ON IT!
THIS CAVE PAINTING IS DONE VERTICALLY! JUDGING FROM THE HORNS AND THE PLACEMENT OF THE MASKS...
WE CAN SURMISE THAT THIS REPRESENTS THEIR SOCIAL STATUS!
LET US READ THE WRITING ON THE CAVE PAINTING...
IT IS PROPHESIZED THAT "THE FOUR SHALL AWAKEN IN 2852..."
2852?! THAT'S FOREVER FROM NOW!
WOW, THAT'S A LOAD OFF!
WHAT A RELIEF!
よかったねー
YOU... CONVERT THE YEAR 2852 FROM THE ANCIENT MEXICAN CALENDAR TO OUR CALENDAR.
YES, SIR!
C-COULD IT BE ...
KLAK
KLAK
KLAK
1938
DOOOOOM

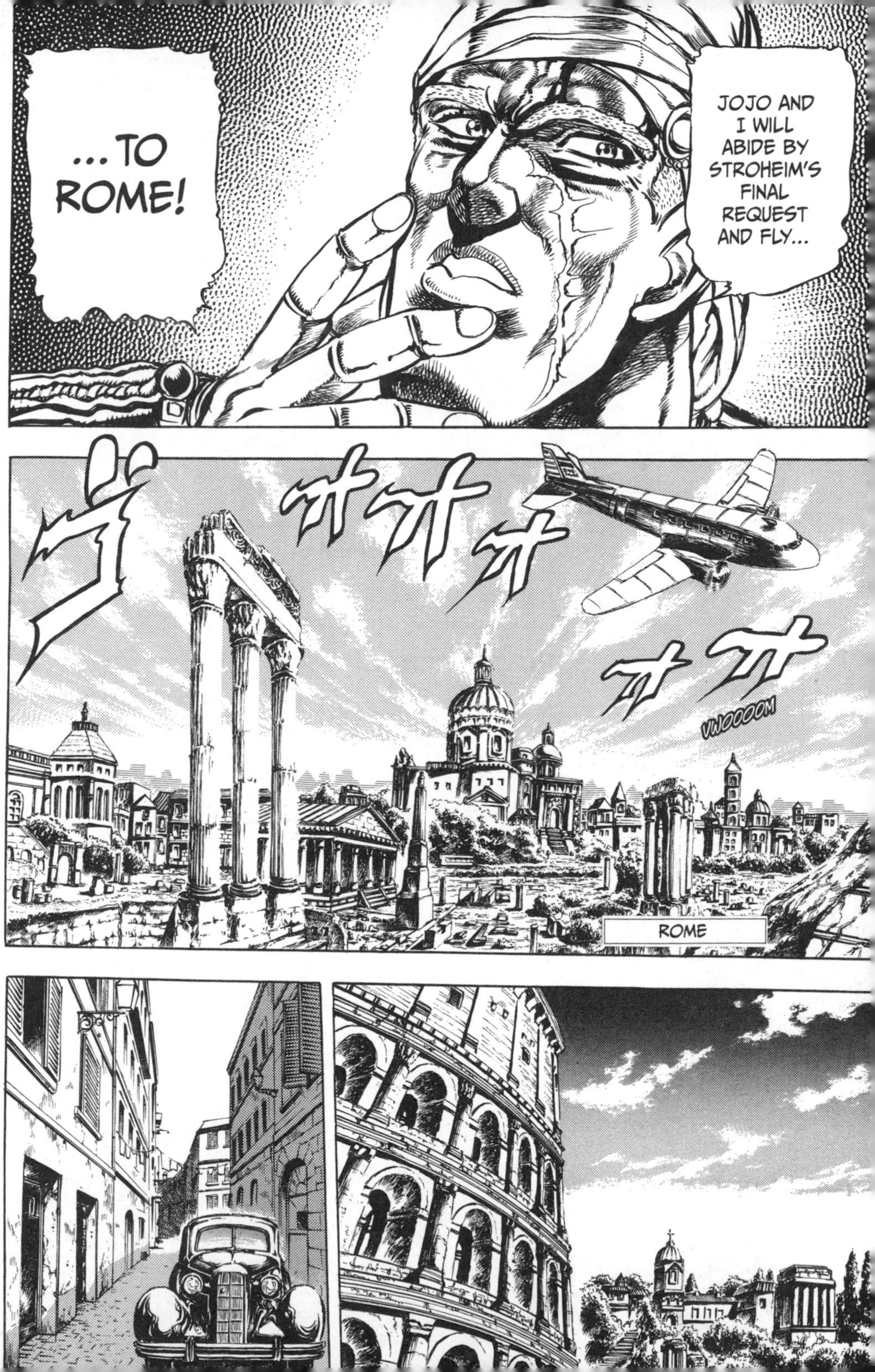
JOJO AND I WILL ABIDE BY STROHEIM'S FINAL REQUEST AND FLY...
...TO ROME!
VWOOOOM
ROME

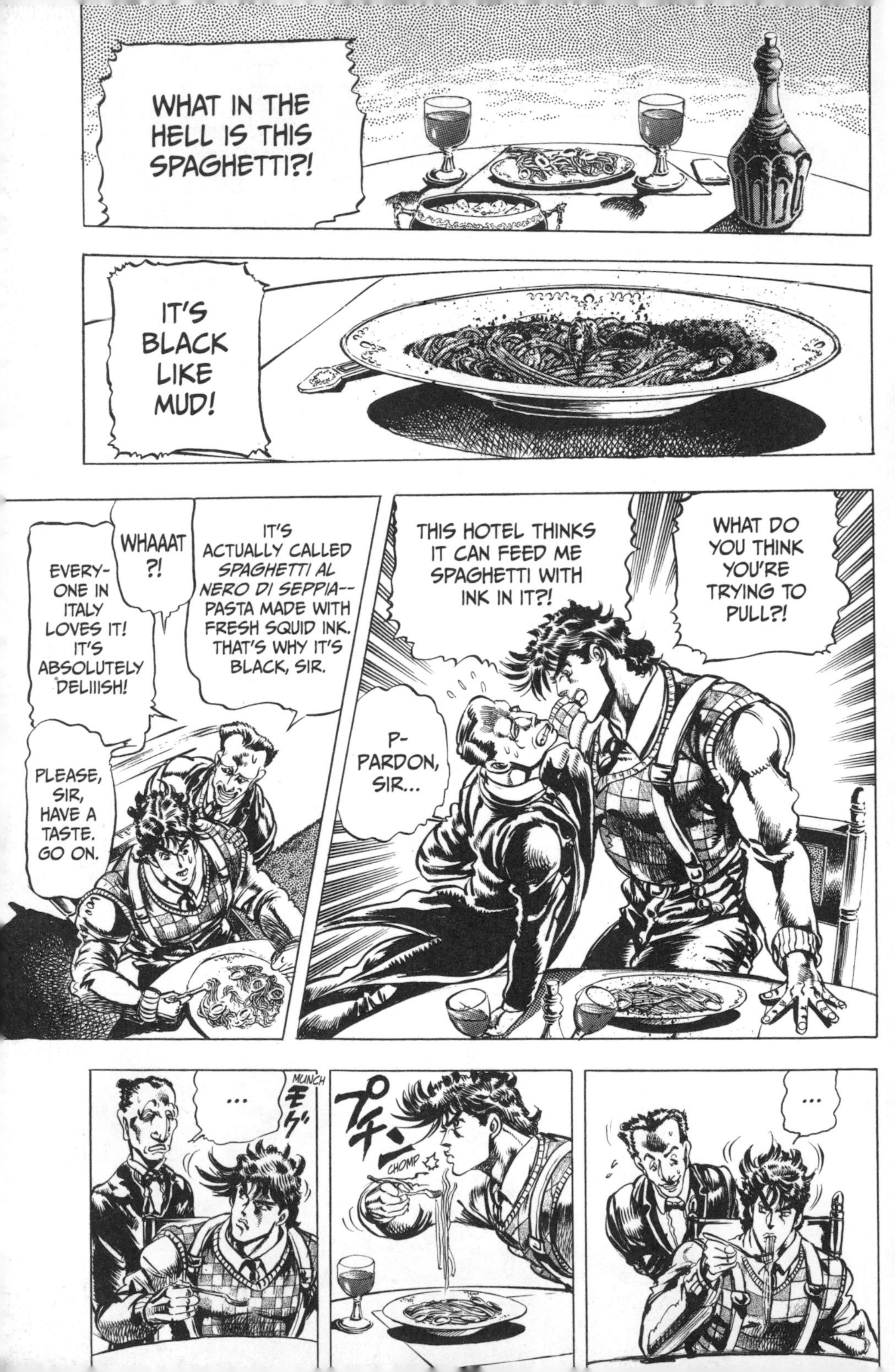
WHAT IN THE HELL IS THIS SPAGHETTI?!
IT'S BLACK LIKE MUD!
WHAT DO YOU THINK YOU'RE TRYING TO PULL?!
THIS HOTEL THINKS IT CAN FEED ME SPAGHETTI WITH INK IN IT?!
P-PARDON, SIR...
IT'S ACTUALLY CALLED *SPAGHETTI AL NERO DI SEPPIA*--PASTA MADE WITH FRESH SQUID INK. THAT'S WHY IT'S BLACK, SIR.
WHAAAT?!
EVERY-ONE IN ITALY LOVES IT! IT'S ABSOLUTELY DELIIISH!
PLEASE, SIR, HAVE A TASTE. GO ON.
...
プチン
CHOMP
モグ
MUNCH
...

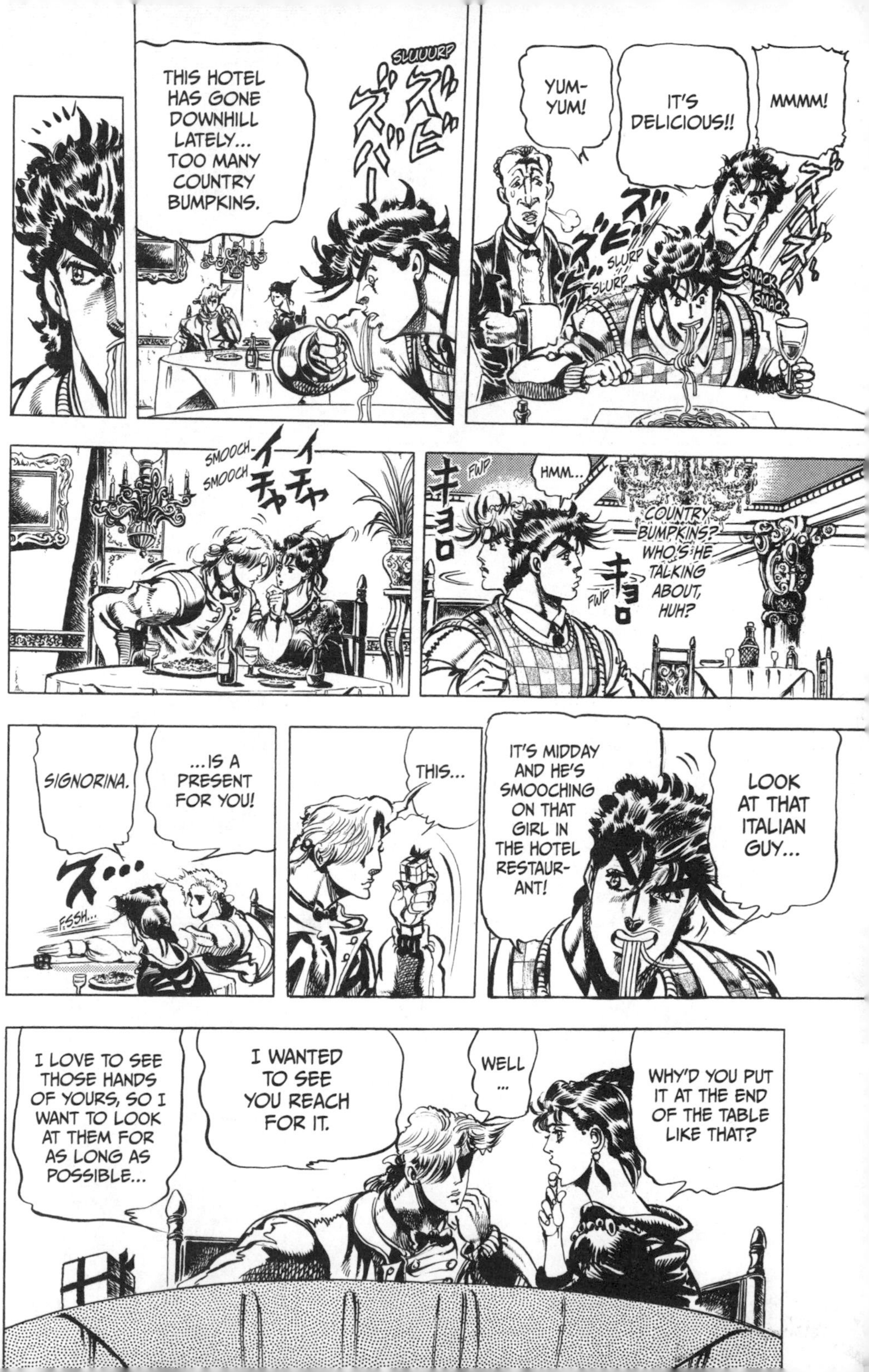
MMMM!
IT'S DELICIOUS!!
YUM-YUM!
SMACK SMACK
SLURP SLURP
SLUUURP
THIS HOTEL HAS GONE DOWNHILL LATELY... TOO MANY COUNTRY BUMPKINS.
HMM...
COUNTRY BUMPKINS? WHO'S HE TALKING ABOUT, HUH?
FWP
FWP
SMOOCH-SMOOCH
LOOK AT THAT ITALIAN GUY...
IT'S MIDDAY AND HE'S SMOOCHING ON THAT GIRL IN THE HOTEL RESTAURANT!
THIS...
...IS A PRESENT FOR YOU!
SIGNORINA.
FSSH...
WHY'D YOU PUT IT AT THE END OF THE TABLE LIKE THAT?
WELL...
I WANTED TO SEE YOU REACH FOR IT.
I LOVE TO SEE THOSE HANDS OF YOURS, SO I WANT TO LOOK AT THEM FOR AS LONG AS POSSIBLE...

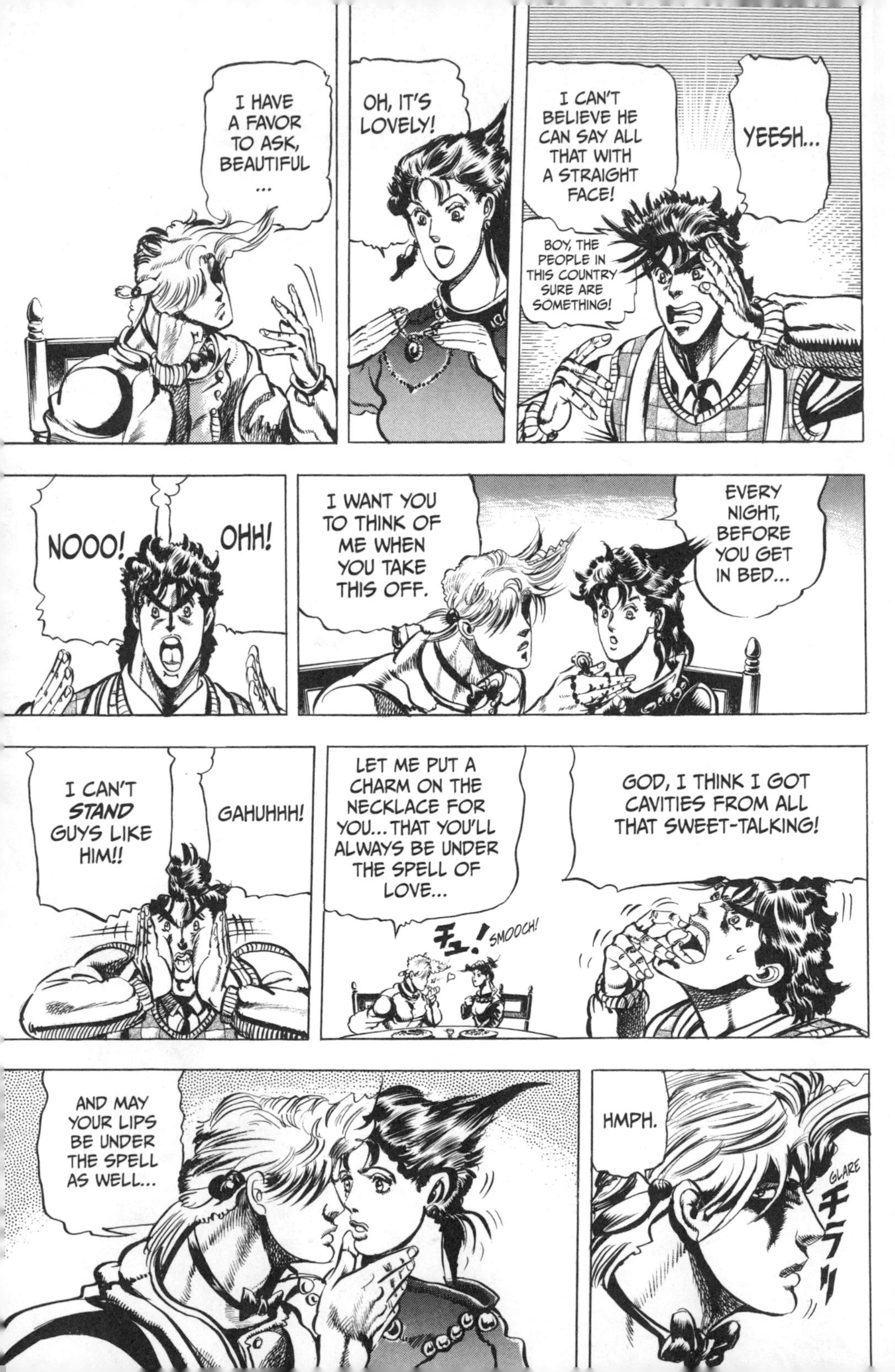
YEESH...
I CAN'T BELIEVE HE CAN SAY ALL THAT WITH A STRAIGHT FACE!
BOY, THE PEOPLE IN THIS COUNTRY SURE ARE SOMETHING!
OH, IT'S LOVELY!
I HAVE A FAVOR TO ASK, BEAUTIFUL ...
EVERY NIGHT, BEFORE YOU GET IN BED...
I WANT YOU TO THINK OF ME WHEN YOU TAKE THIS OFF.
OHH!
NOOO!
GOD, I THINK I GOT CAVITIES FROM ALL THAT SWEET-TALKING!
LET ME PUT A CHARM ON THE NECKLACE FOR YOU... THAT YOU'LL ALWAYS BE UNDER THE SPELL OF LOVE...
チュ! SMOOCH!
GAHUHHH!
I CAN'T *STAND* GUYS LIKE HIM!!
HMPH.
GLARE
AND MAY YOUR LIPS BE UNDER THE SPELL AS WELL...

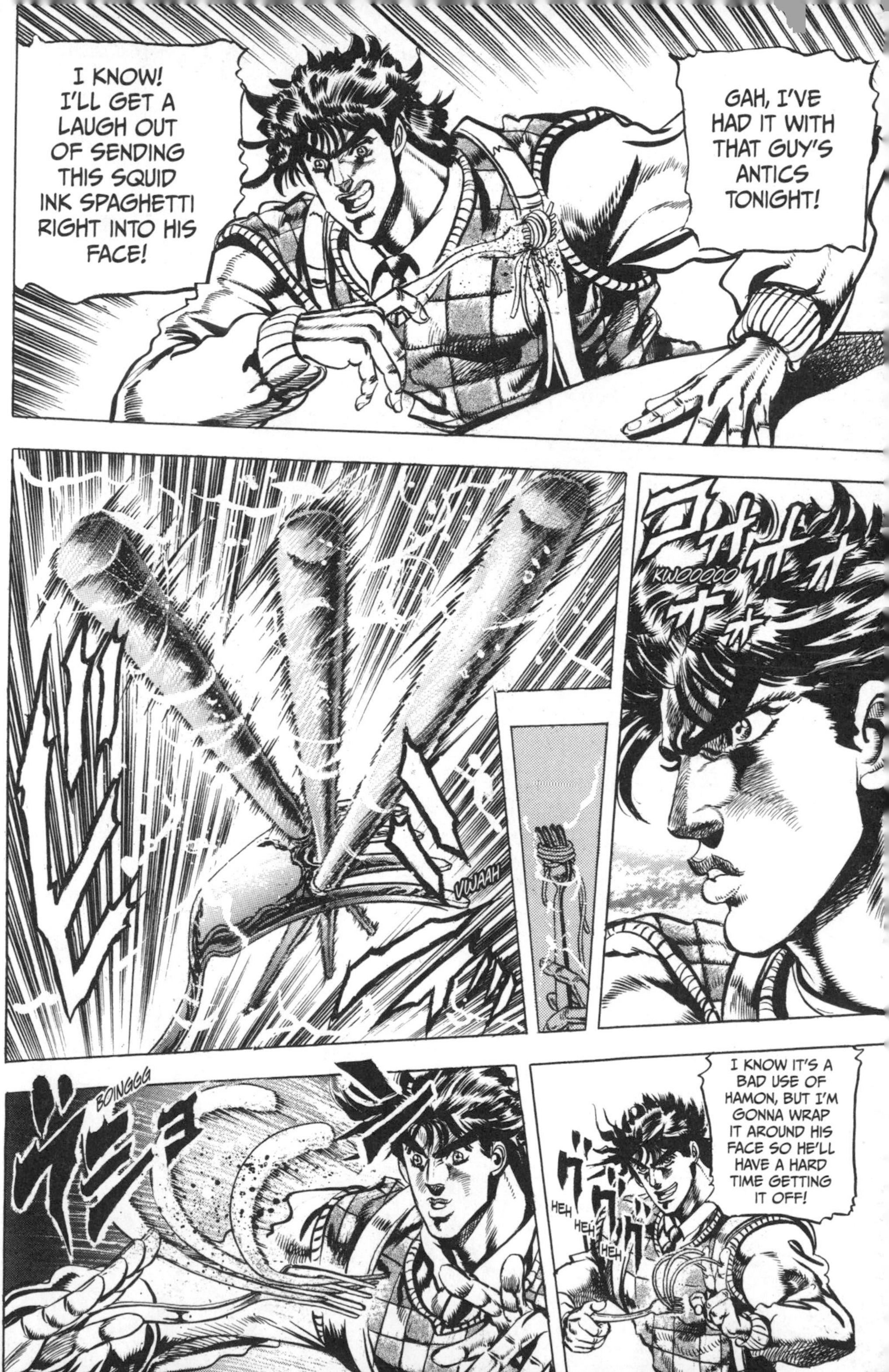
GAH, I'VE HAD IT WITH THAT GUY'S ANTICS TONIGHT!
I KNOW! I'LL GET A LAUGH OUT OF SENDING THIS SQUID INK SPAGHETTI RIGHT INTO HIS FACE!
KWOOOOO
VWAAH
I KNOW IT'S A BAD USE OF HAMON, BUT I'M GONNA WRAP IT AROUND HIS FACE SO HE'LL HAVE A HARD TIME GETTING IT OFF!
HEH HEH HEH
BOINGGG

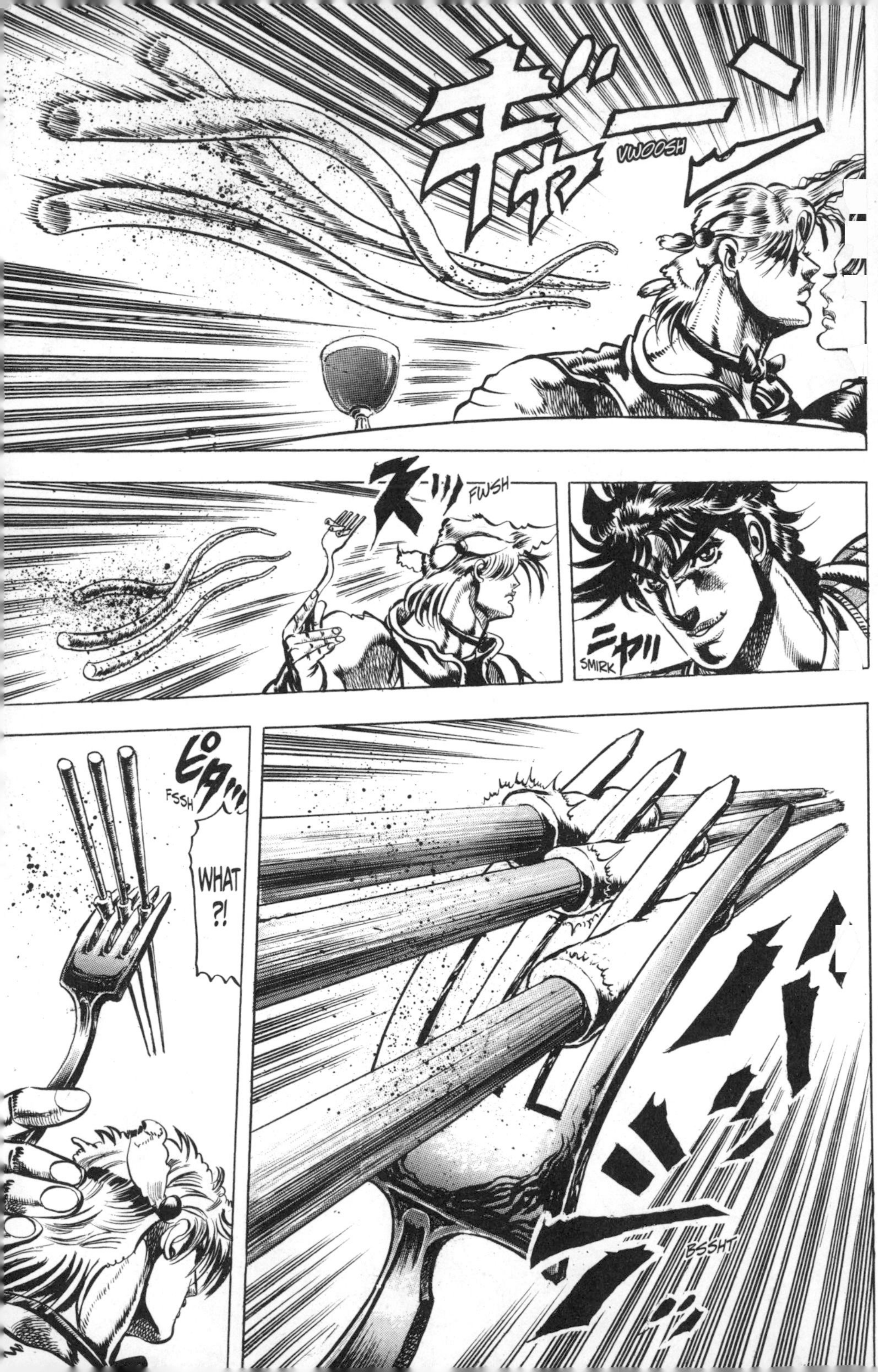
VWOOSH
SMIRK
FWSH
BSSHT
FSSH
WHAT ?!

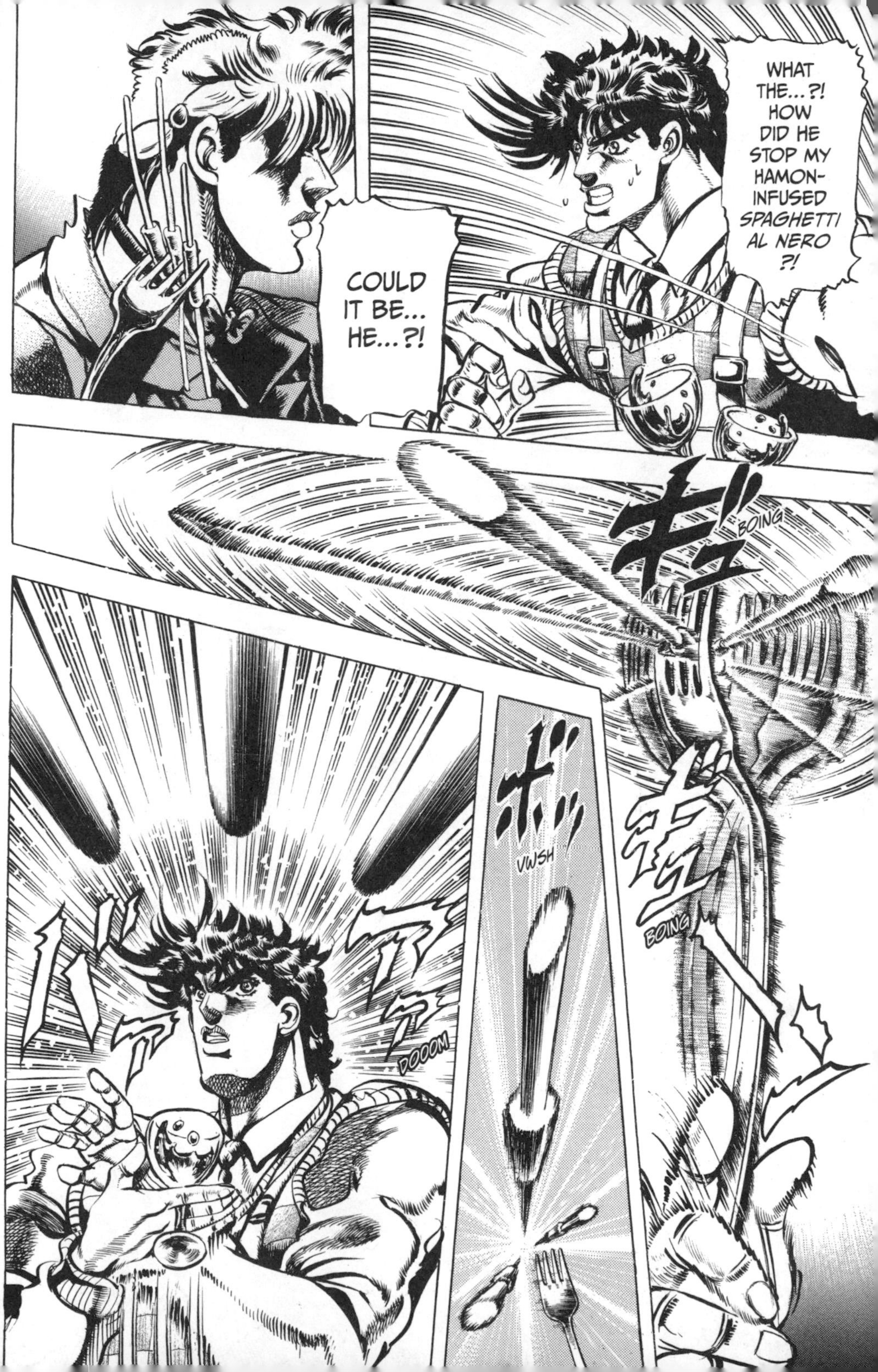
WHAT THE...?! HOW DID HE STOP MY HAMON-INFUSED SPAGHETTI AL NERO ?!
COULD IT BE... HE...?!
BOING
BOING
VWSH
DOOOM

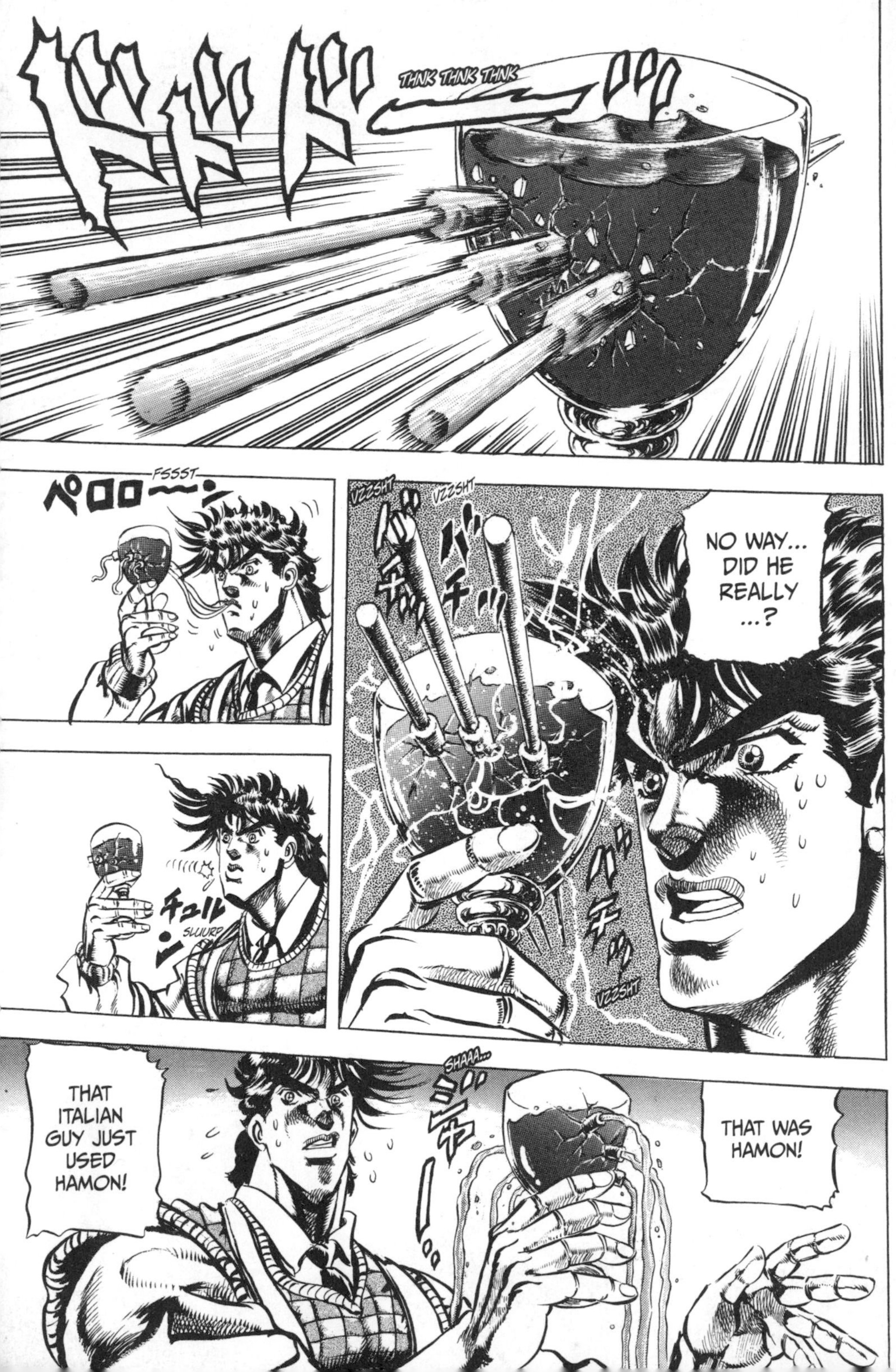

THNK THNK THNK
VZZSHT
VZZSHT
NO WAY... DID HE REALLY ...?
VZZSHT
ペロローン
FSSST
チュルン
SLUURP
THAT WAS HAMON!
SHAAA...
THAT ITALIAN GUY JUST USED HAMON!

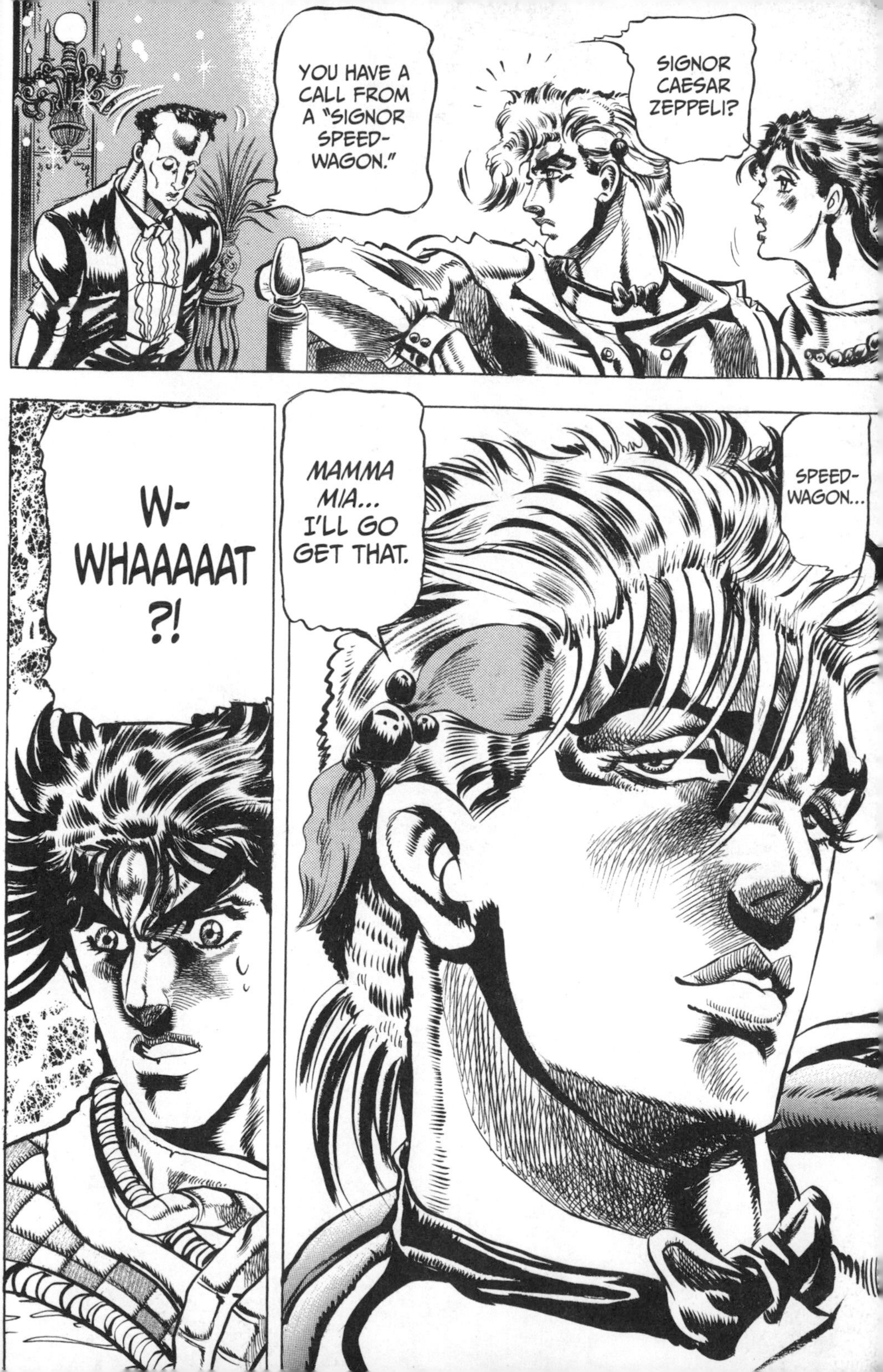
SIGNOR CAESAR ZEPPELI?
YOU HAVE A CALL FROM A "SIGNOR SPEED-WAGON."
SPEED-WAGON...
MAMMA MIA... I'LL GO GET THAT.
W-WHAAAAAT?!

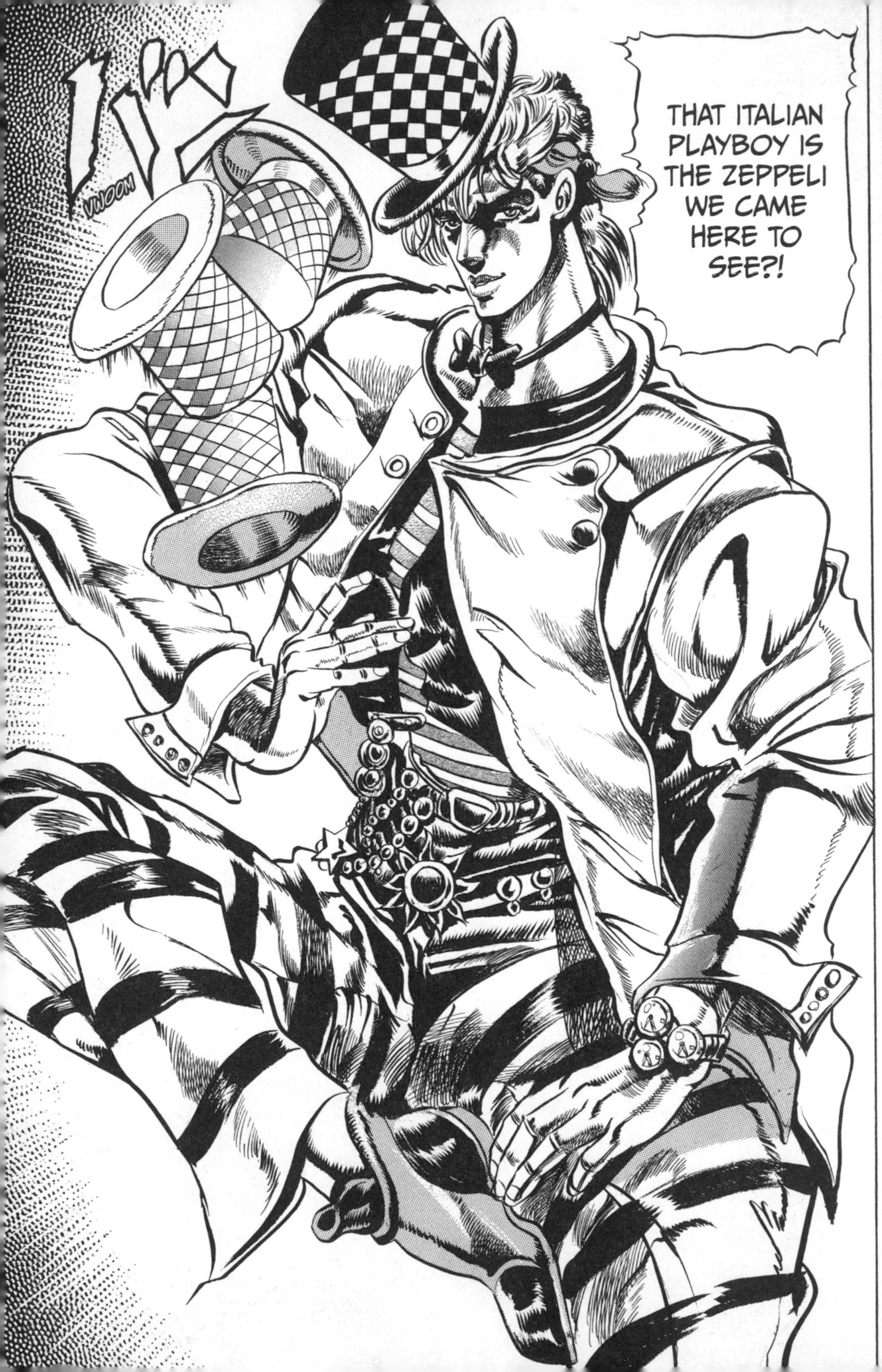
THAT ITALIAN PLAYBOY IS THE ZEPPELI WE CAME HERE TO SEE?!
VWOOM

JoJo's

BIZARRE ADVENTURE

01

END

 To Be Continued

JoJo's BIZARRE ADVENTURE

01

JO

荒木飛呂彦が語るキャラクター誕生秘話

Hirohiko Araki talks about character creation!

JoJo's BIZARRE ADVENTURE
PART 2
BATTLE TENDENCY

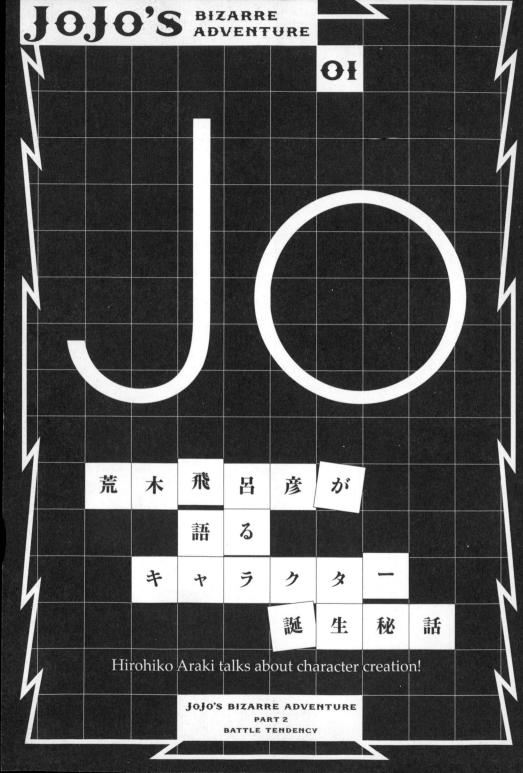

Joestar

01

DATA

Birthday: **September 27, 1920**
Height: **195 cm**
Weight: **97 kg**
Sign: **Libra**
Blood Type: **B**
Nationality: **British**

"JOSEPH'S CHARACTER IS LIKE B.T. PLUS STALLONE"

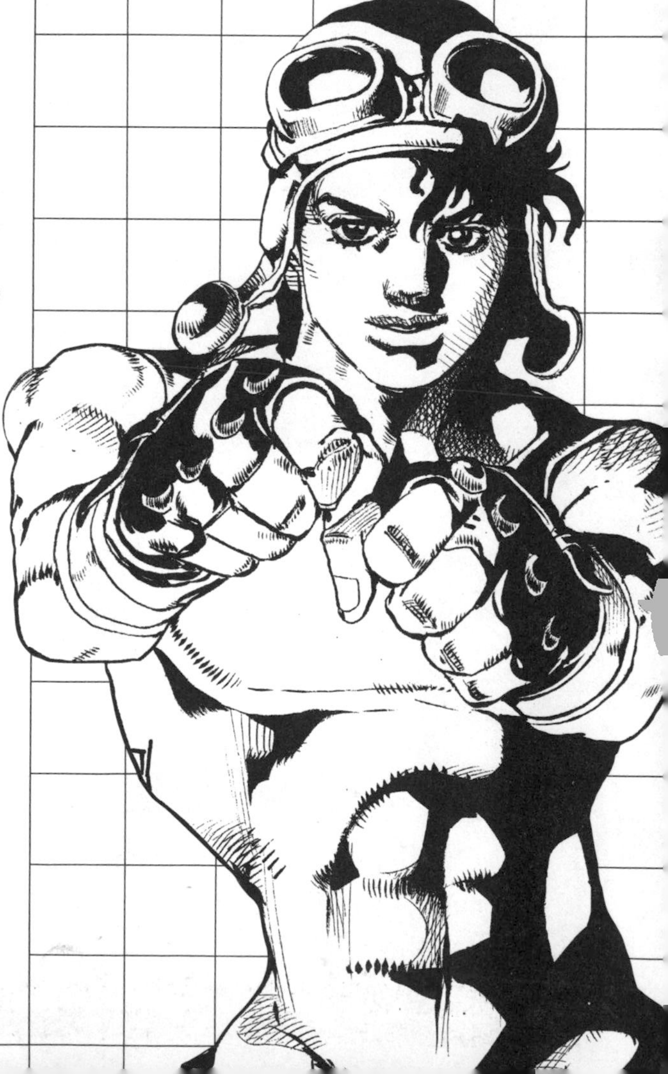

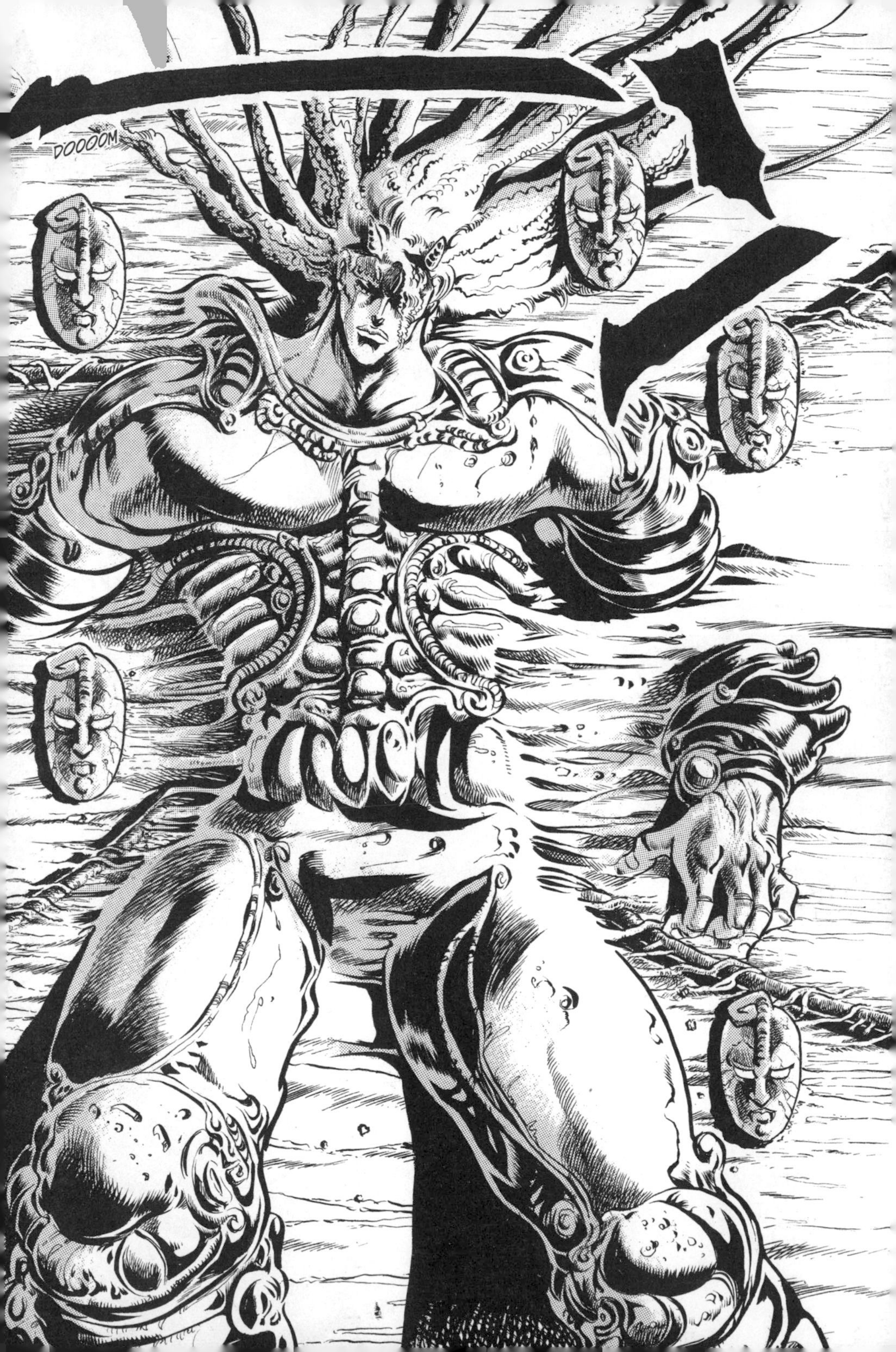
DOOOOM

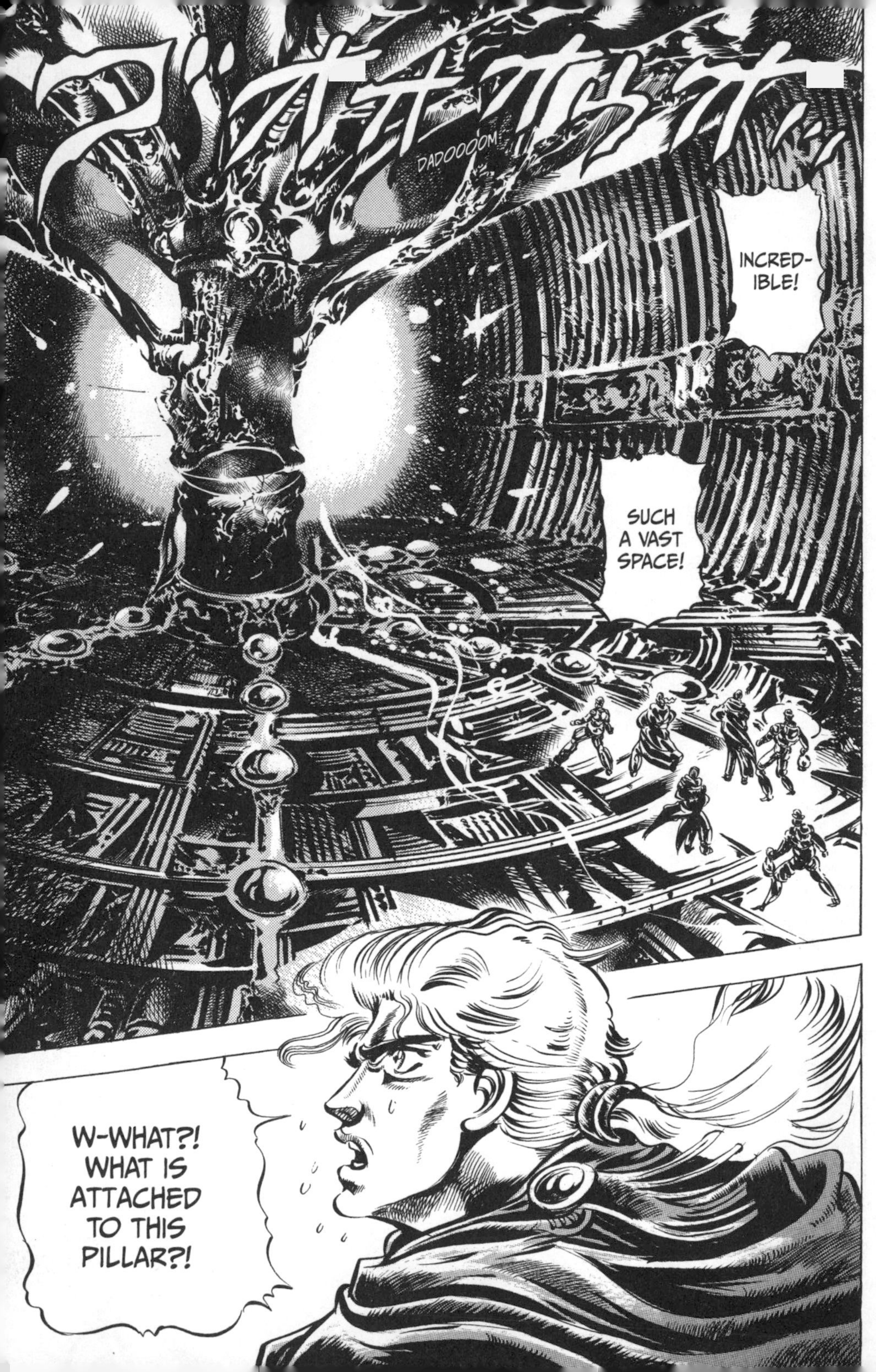
DADOOOOM
INCRED-IBLE!
SUCH A VAST SPACE!
W-WHAT?! WHAT IS ATTACHED TO THIS PILLAR?!

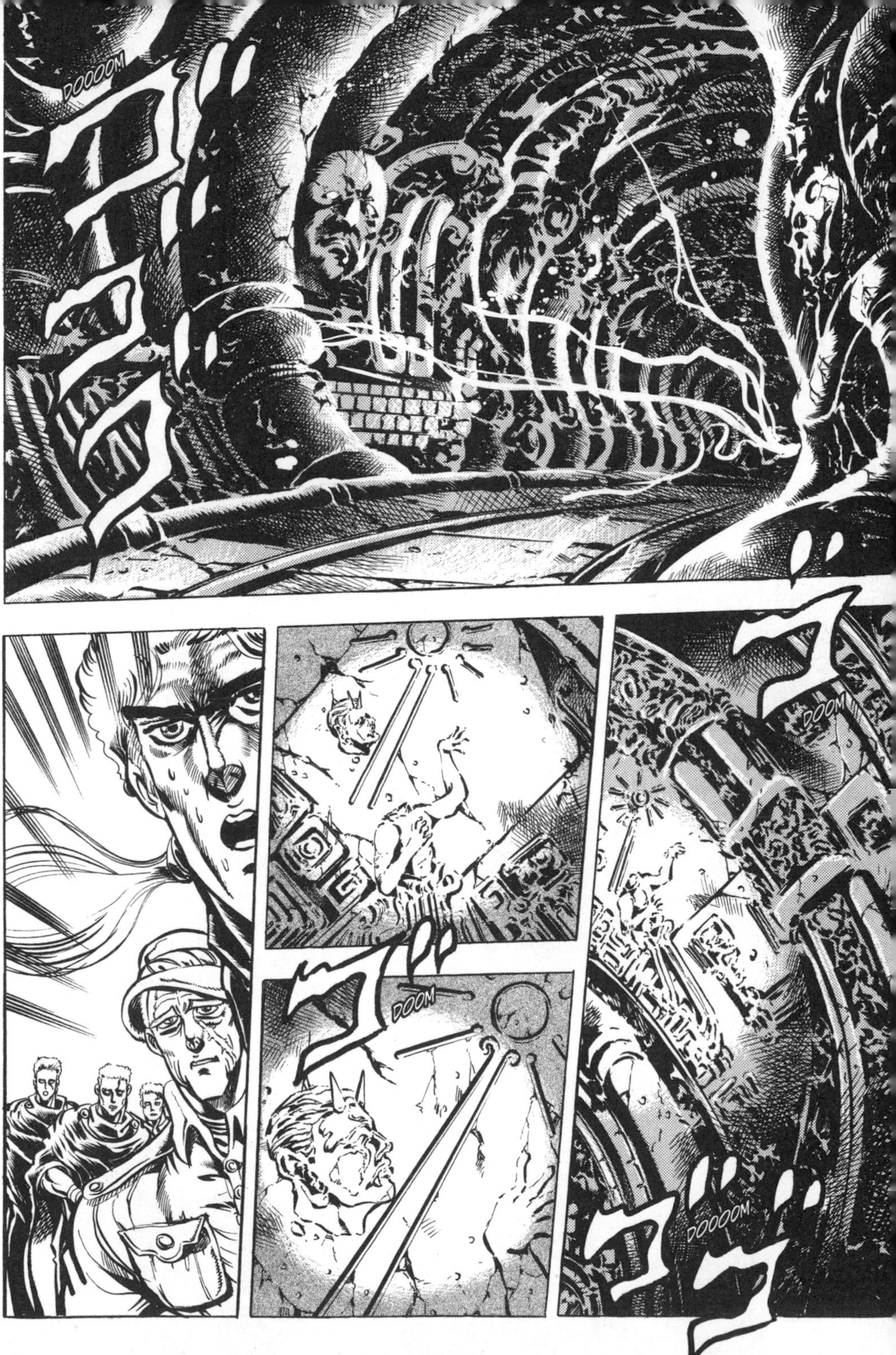
DOOOOM
DOOM
DOOOOM
DOOM

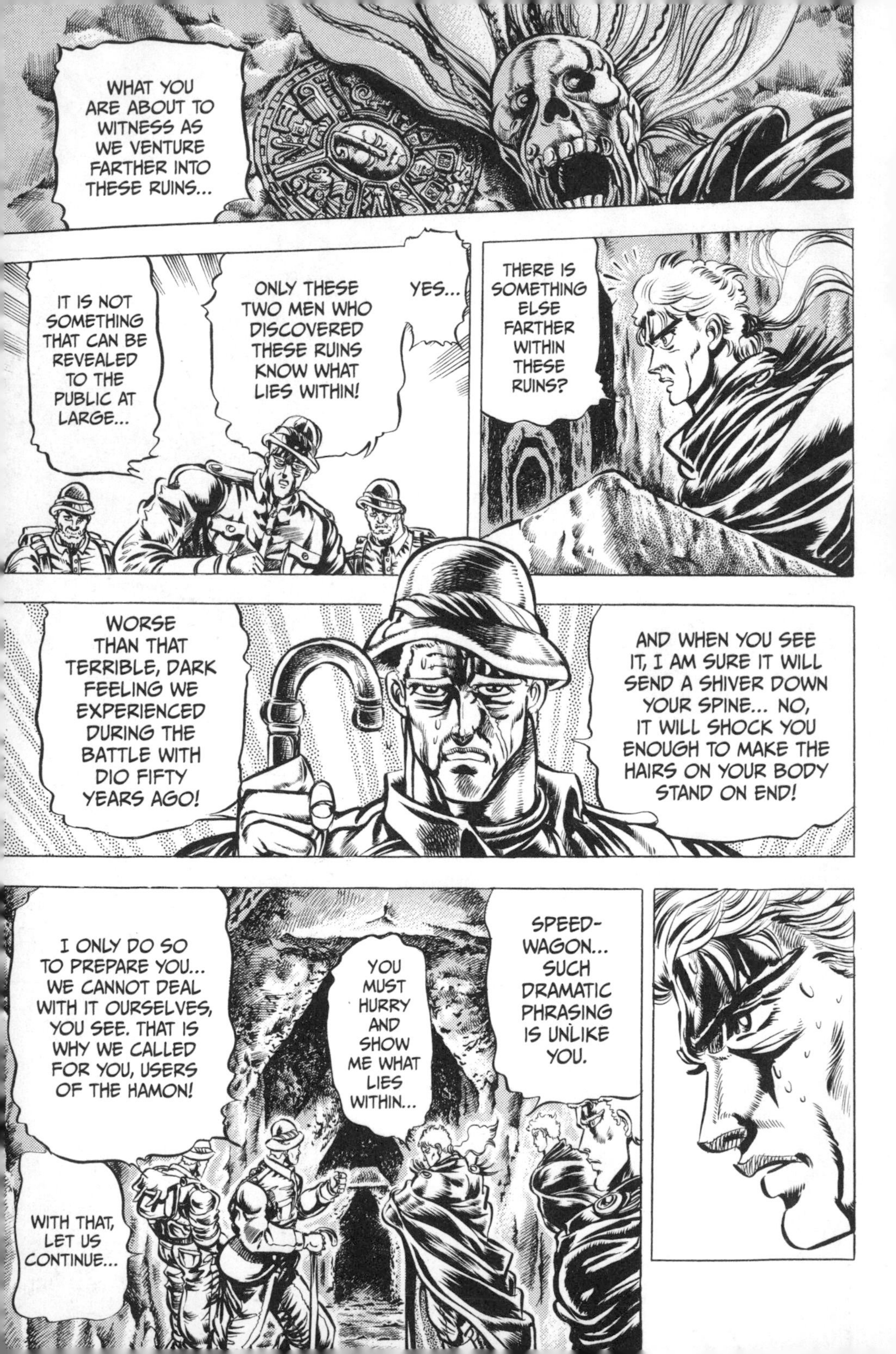

WHAT YOU ARE ABOUT TO WITNESS AS WE VENTURE FARTHER INTO THESE RUINS...
THERE IS SOMETHING ELSE FARTHER WITHIN THESE RUINS?
YES...
ONLY THESE TWO MEN WHO DISCOVERED THESE RUINS KNOW WHAT LIES WITHIN!
IT IS NOT SOMETHING THAT CAN BE REVEALED TO THE PUBLIC AT LARGE...
AND WHEN YOU SEE IT, I AM SURE IT WILL SEND A SHIVER DOWN YOUR SPINE... NO, IT WILL SHOCK YOU ENOUGH TO MAKE THE HAIRS ON YOUR BODY STAND ON END!
WORSE THAN THAT TERRIBLE, DARK FEELING WE EXPERIENCED DURING THE BATTLE WITH DIO FIFTY YEARS AGO!
SPEED-WAGON... SUCH DRAMATIC PHRASING IS UNLIKE YOU.
YOU MUST HURRY AND SHOW ME WHAT LIES WITHIN...
I ONLY DO SO TO PREPARE YOU... WE CANNOT DEAL WITH IT OURSELVES, YOU SEE. THAT IS WHY WE CALLED FOR YOU, USERS OF THE HAMON!
WITH THAT, LET US CONTINUE...

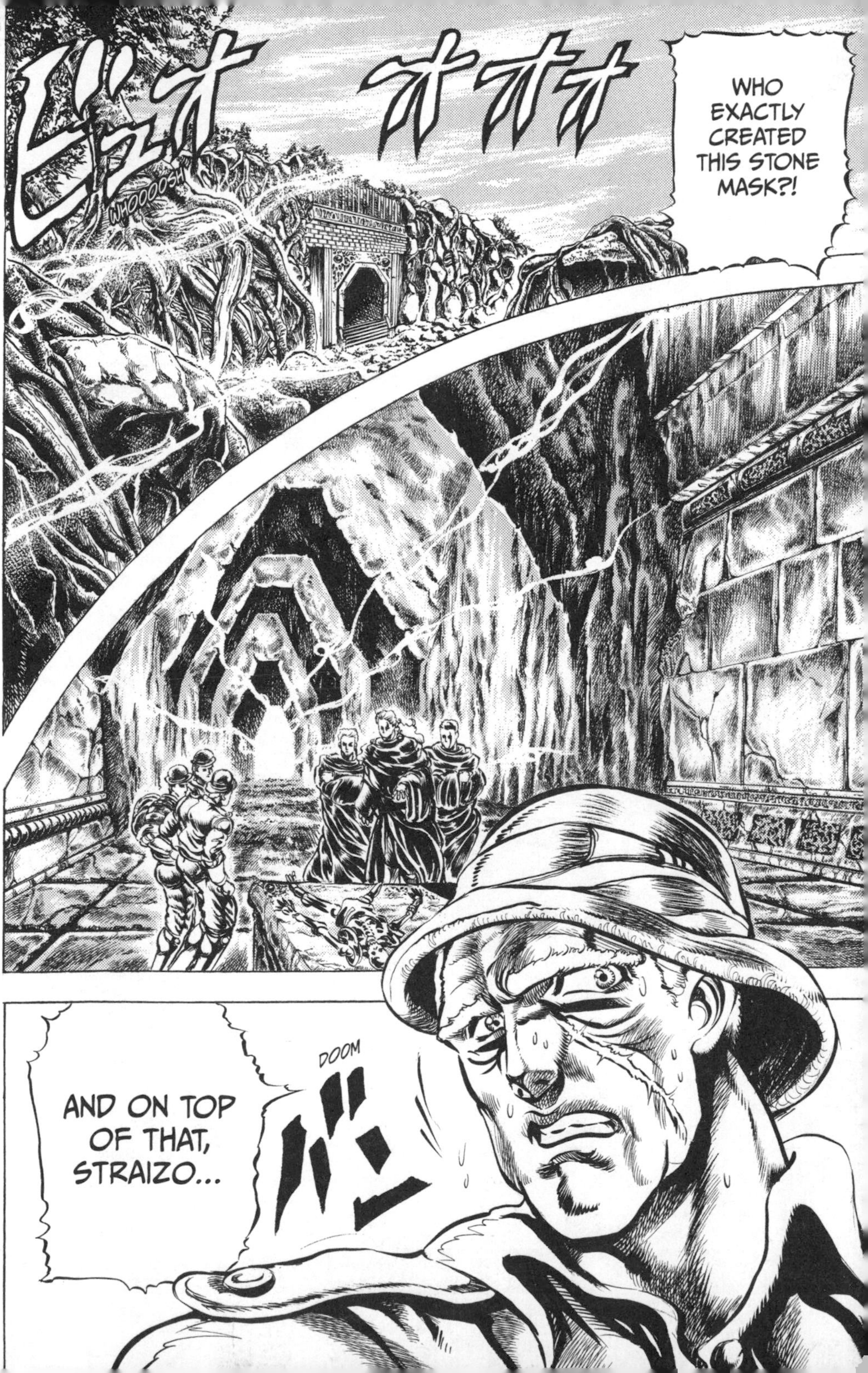
WHO EXACTLY CREATED THIS STONE MASK?!
WHOOOOSH
DOOM
AND ON TOP OF THAT, STRAIZO...

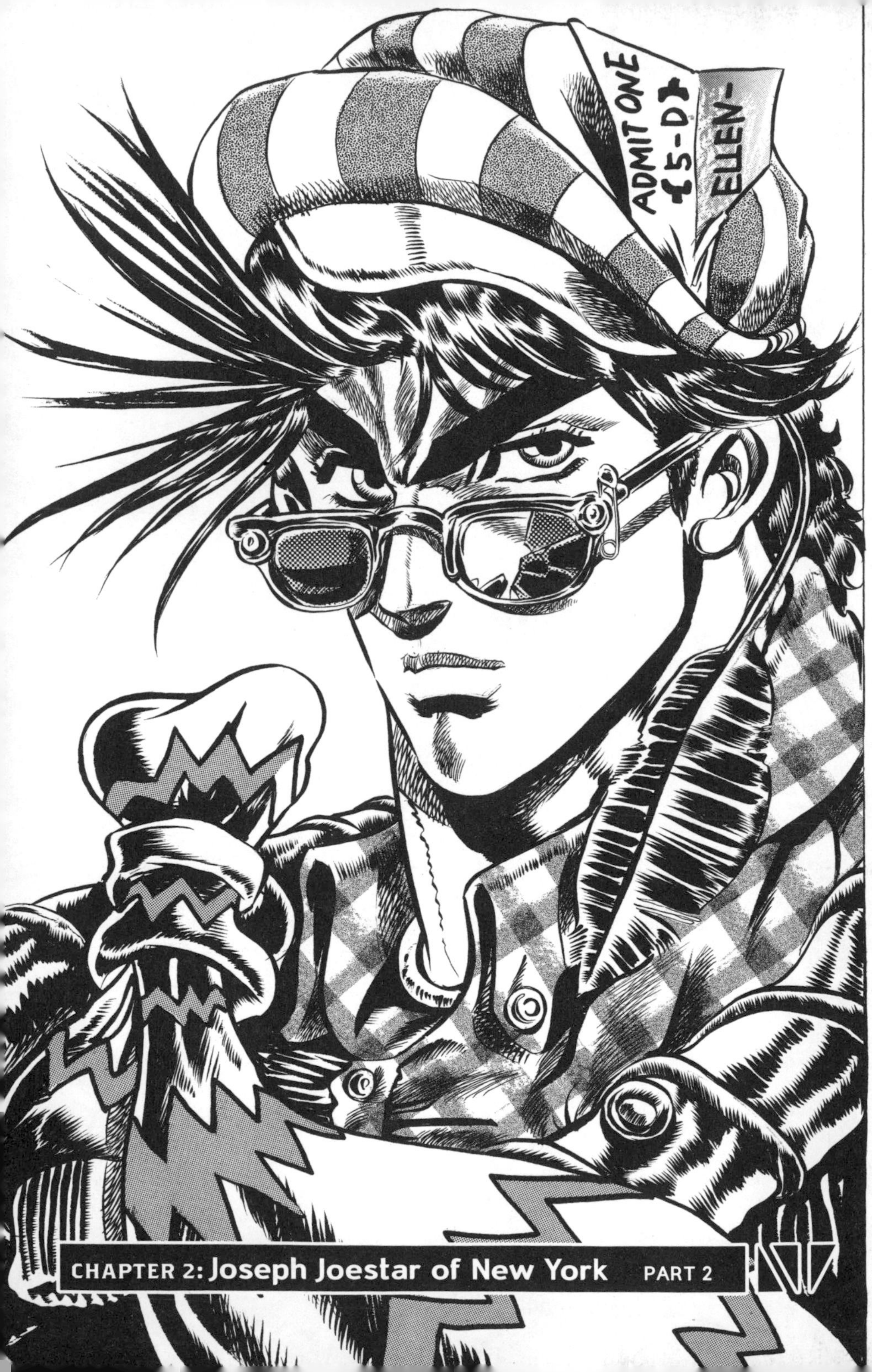
ADMIT ONE
5-D
ELLEN

CHAPTER 2: Joseph Joestar of New York PART 2

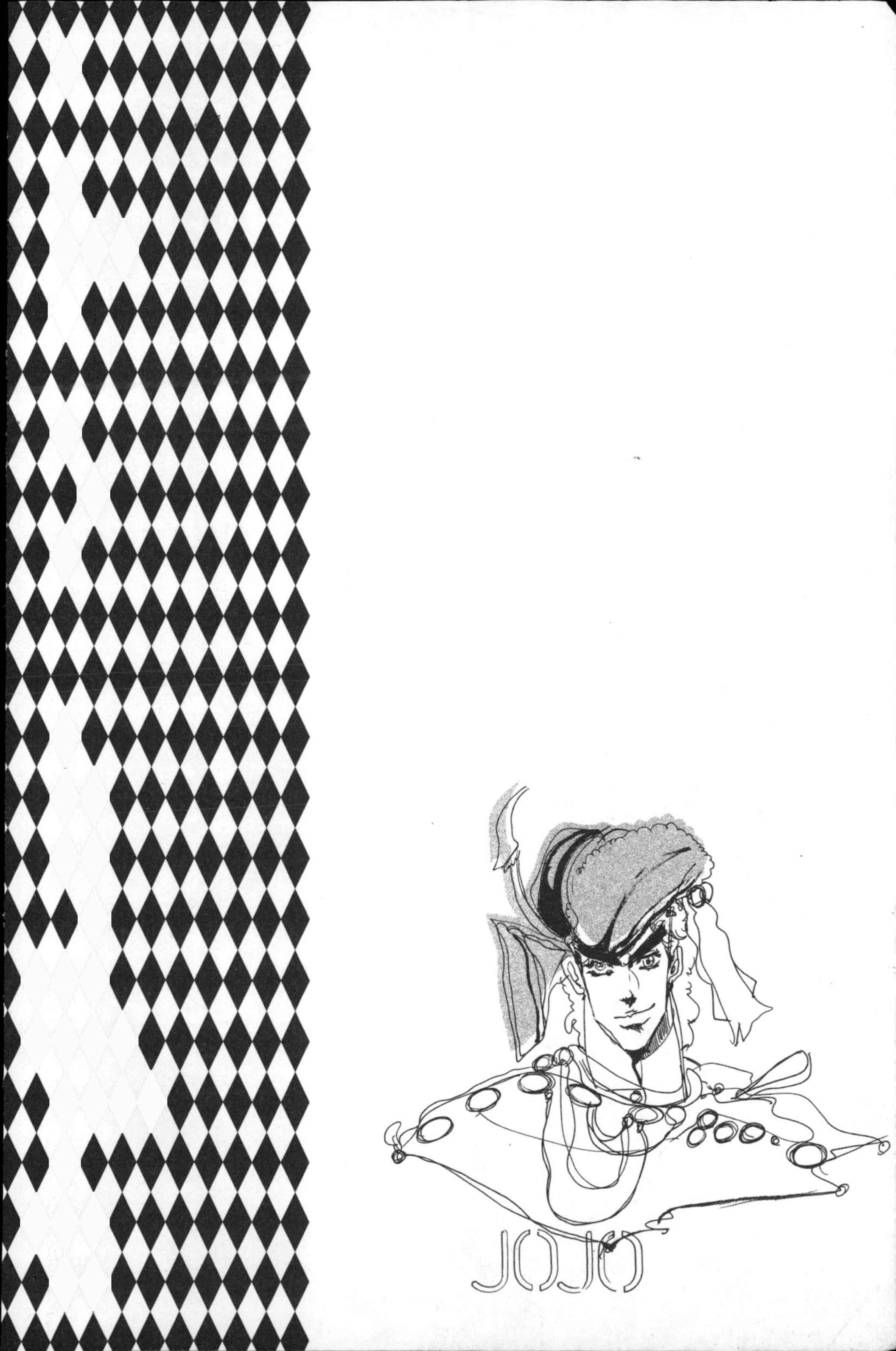
JOJO

PART 2

BATTLE TENDENCY

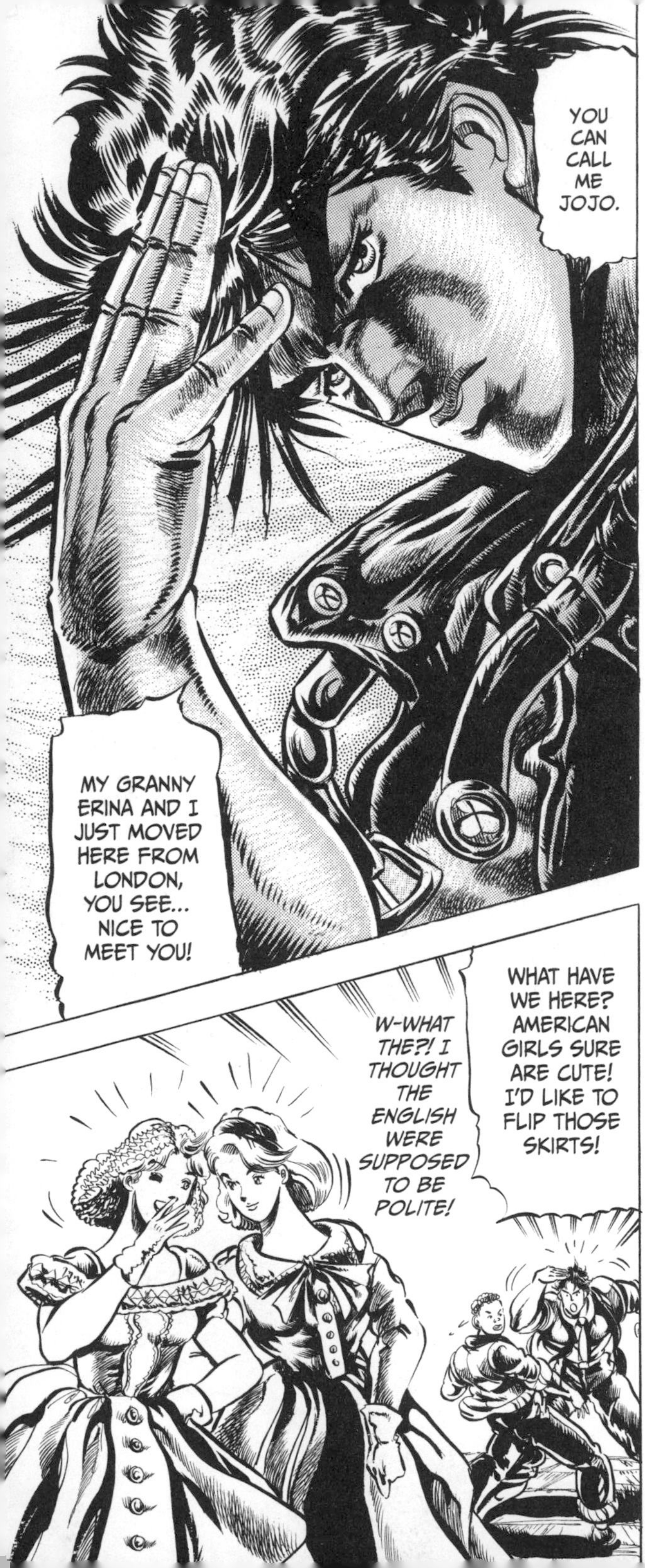
YOU CAN CALL ME JOJO.
MY GRANNY ERINA AND I JUST MOVED HERE FROM LONDON, YOU SEE... NICE TO MEET YOU!
WHAT HAVE WE HERE? AMERICAN GIRLS SURE ARE CUTE! I'D LIKE TO FLIP THOSE SKIRTS!
W-WHAT THE?! I THOUGHT THE ENGLISH WERE SUPPOSED TO BE POLITE!

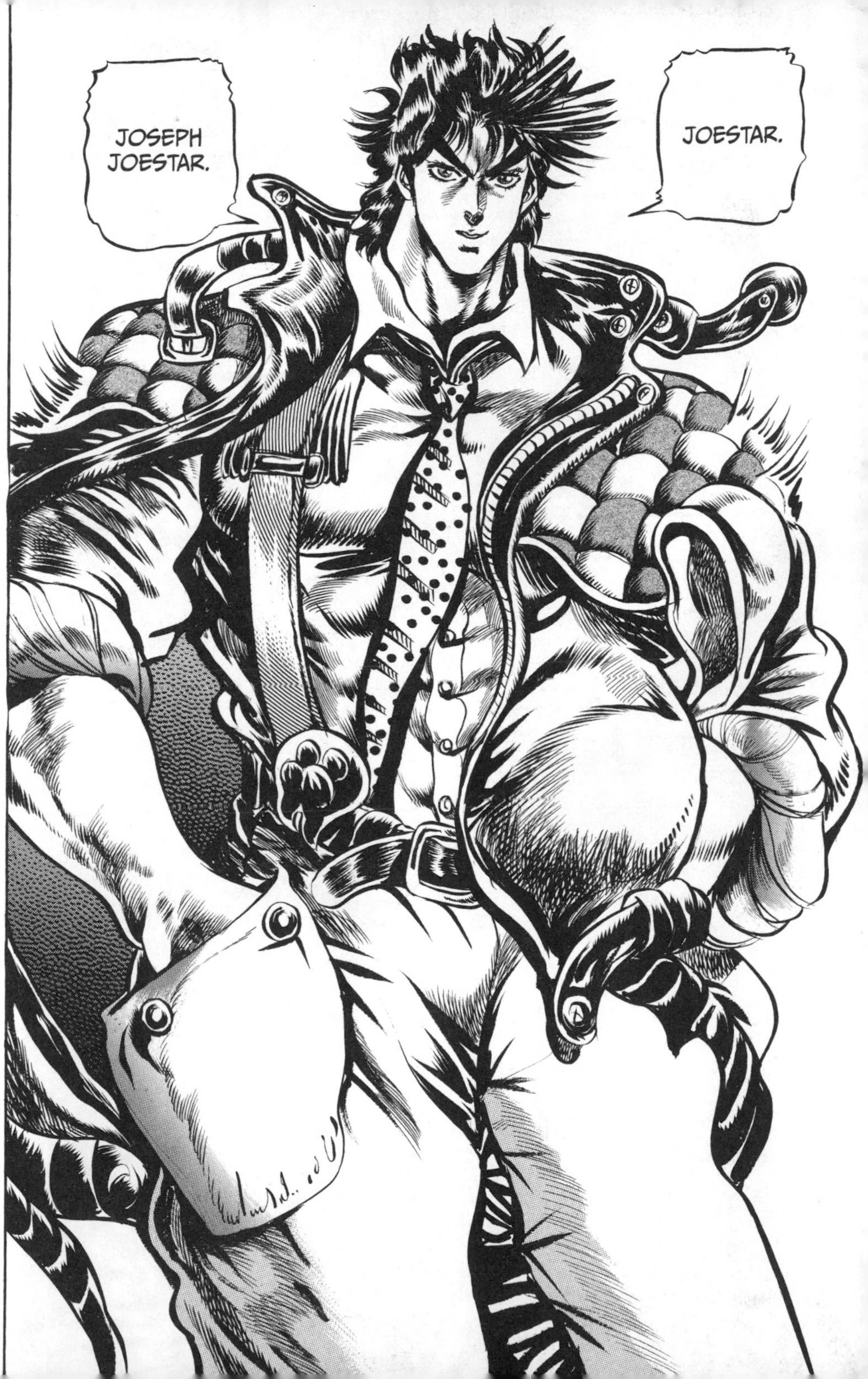
JOESTAR.
JOSEPH JOESTAR.

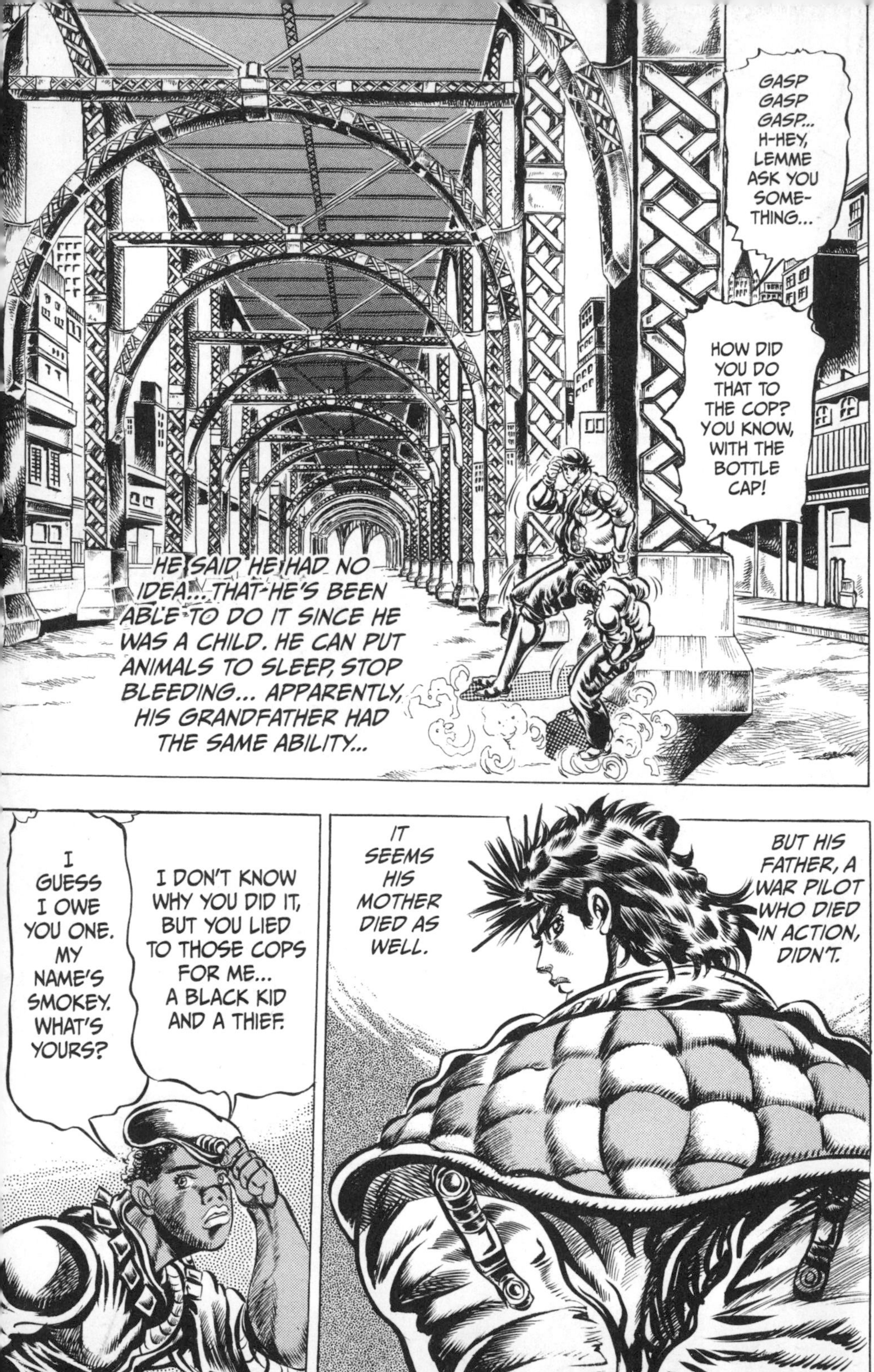
GASP GASP GASP... H-HEY, LEMME ASK YOU SOME-THING...
HOW DID YOU DO THAT TO THE COP? YOU KNOW, WITH THE BOTTLE CAP!
HE SAID HE HAD NO IDEA... THAT HE'S BEEN ABLE TO DO IT SINCE HE WAS A CHILD. HE CAN PUT ANIMALS TO SLEEP, STOP BLEEDING... APPARENTLY, HIS GRANDFATHER HAD THE SAME ABILITY...
IT SEEMS HIS MOTHER DIED AS WELL.
BUT HIS FATHER, A WAR PILOT WHO DIED IN ACTION, DIDN'T.
I DON'T KNOW WHY YOU DID IT, BUT YOU LIED TO THOSE COPS FOR ME... A BLACK KID AND A THIEF.
I GUESS I OWE YOU ONE. MY NAME'S SMOKEY. WHAT'S YOURS?

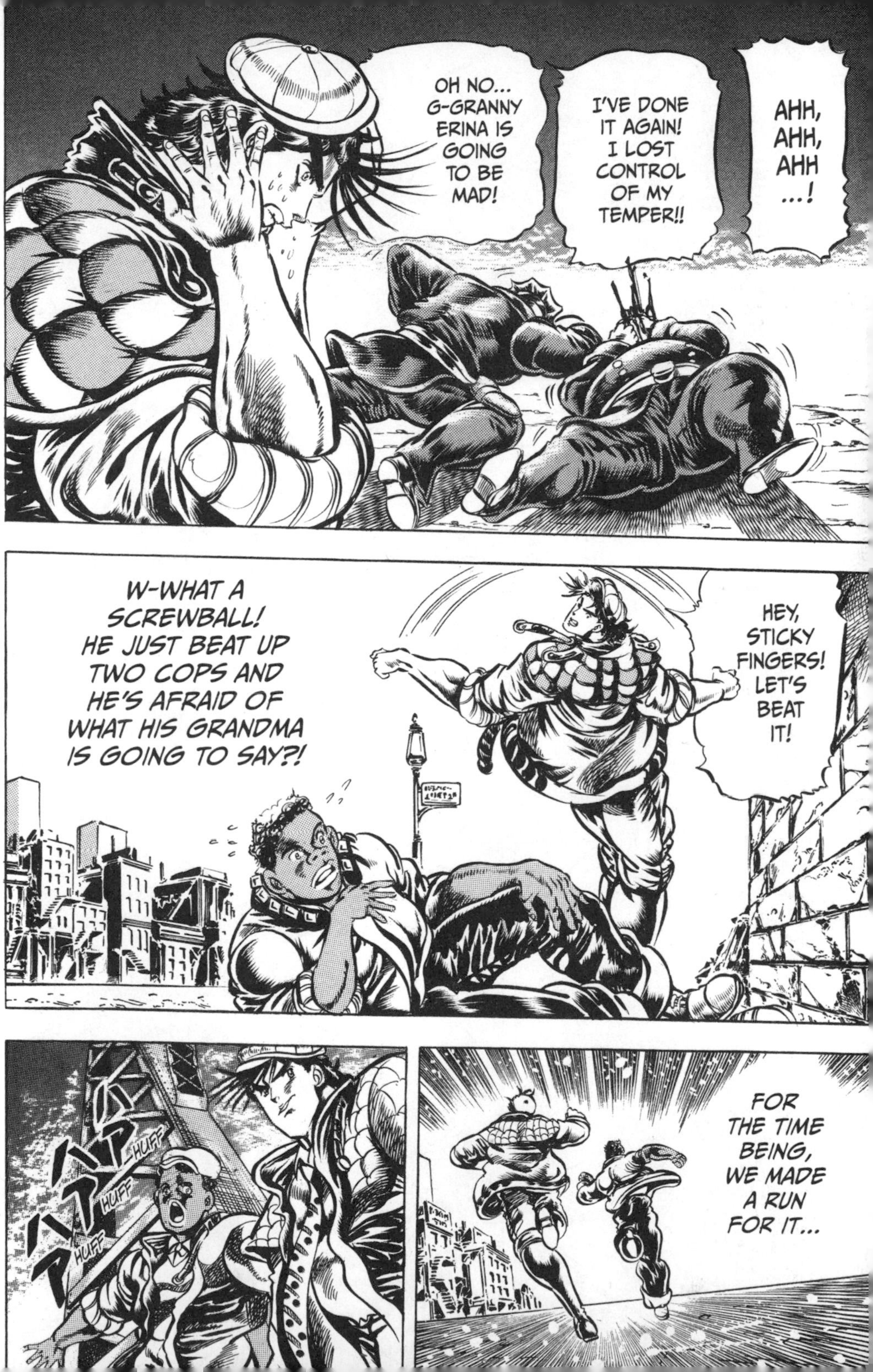
AHH, AHH, AHH ...!
I'VE DONE IT AGAIN! I LOST CONTROL OF MY TEMPER!!
OH NO... G-GRANNY ERINA IS GOING TO BE MAD!
HEY, STICKY FINGERS! LET'S BEAT IT!
W-WHAT A SCREWBALL! HE JUST BEAT UP TWO COPS AND HE'S AFRAID OF WHAT HIS GRANDMA IS GOING TO SAY?!
FOR THE TIME BEING, WE MADE A RUN FOR IT...
HUFF
HUFF
HUFF

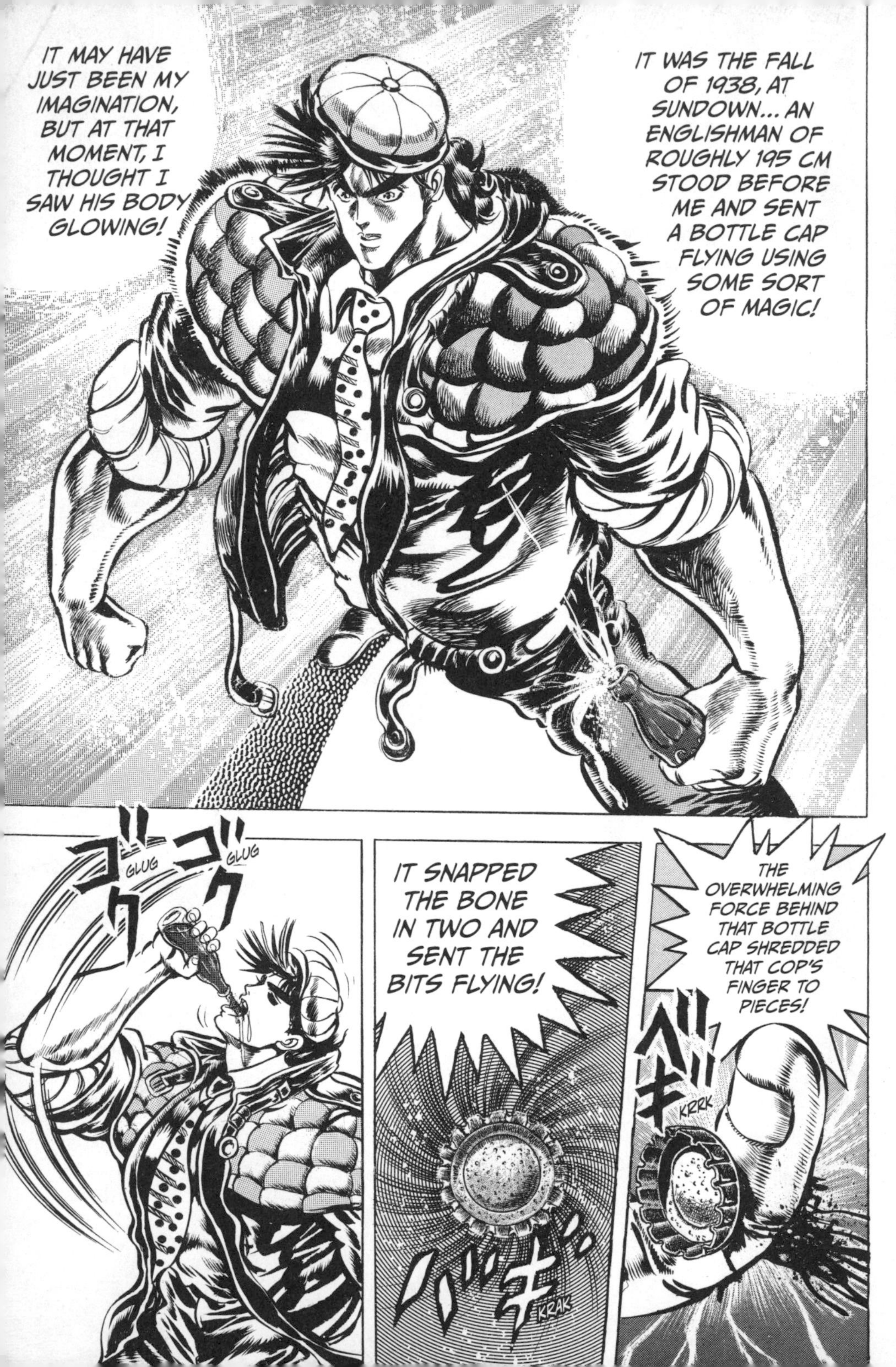

IT WAS THE FALL OF 1938, AT SUNDOWN... AN ENGLISHMAN OF ROUGHLY 195 CM STOOD BEFORE ME AND SENT A BOTTLE CAP FLYING USING SOME SORT OF MAGIC!
IT MAY HAVE JUST BEEN MY IMAGINATION, BUT AT THAT MOMENT, I THOUGHT I SAW HIS BODY GLOWING!
THE OVERWHELMING FORCE BEHIND THAT BOTTLE CAP SHREDDED THAT COP'S FINGER TO PIECES!
KRRK
IT SNAPPED THE BONE IN TWO AND SENT THE BITS FLYING!
KRAK
GLUG
GLUG

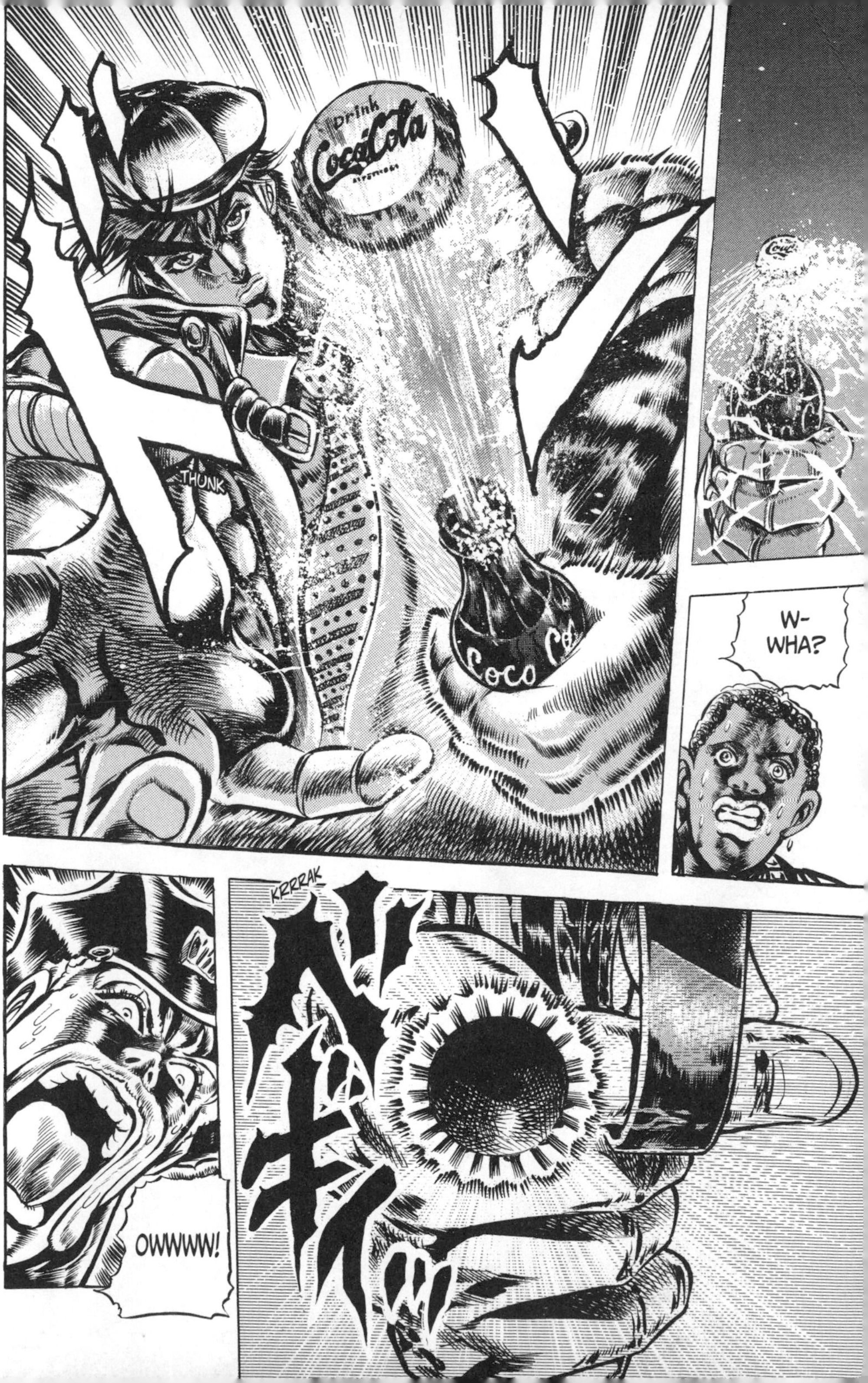
W-WHA?
THUNK
KRRRAK
OWWWW!

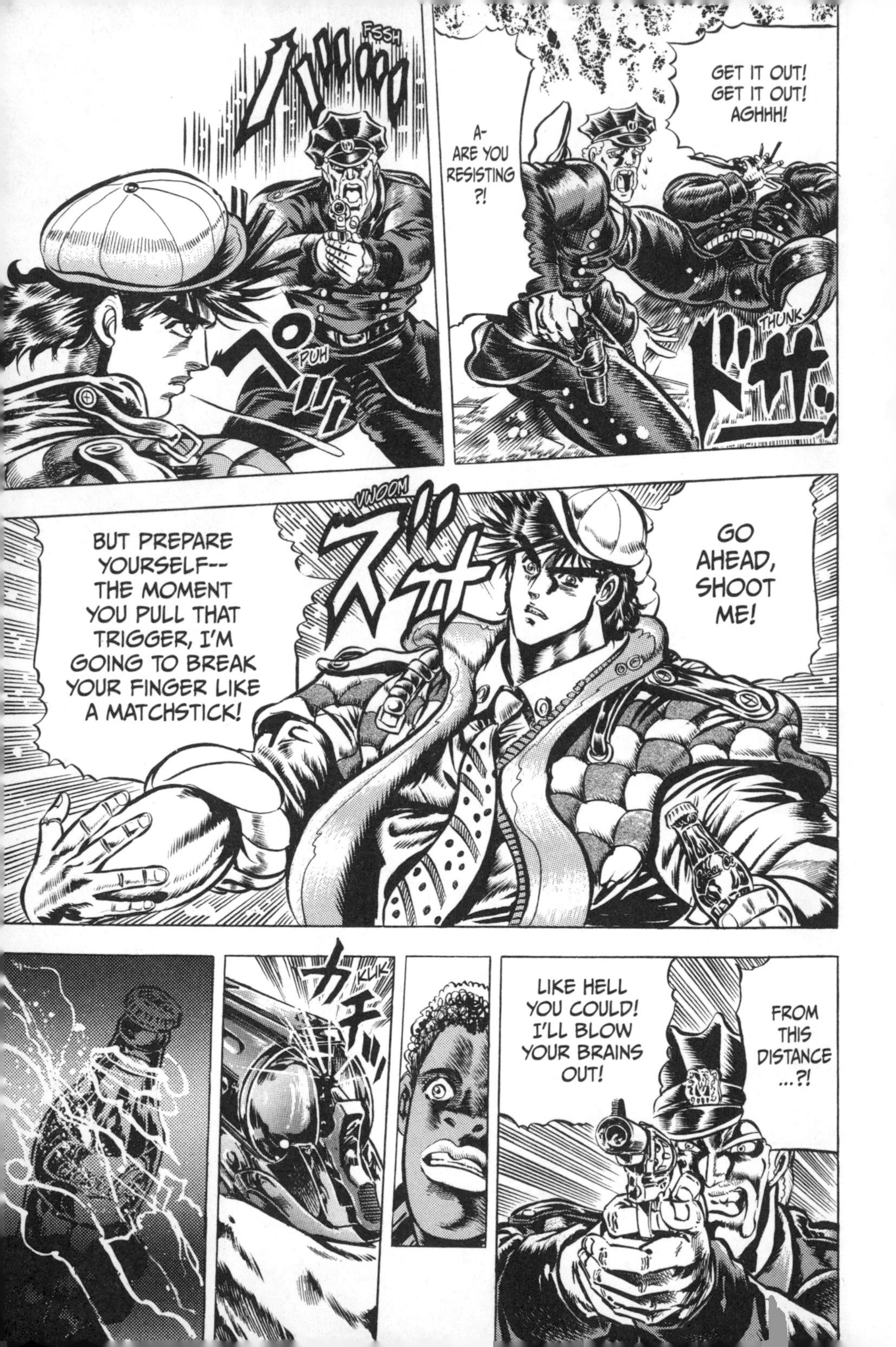
GET IT OUT! GET IT OUT! AGHHH!
A- ARE YOU RESISTING ?!
THUNK
FSSH
PUH
GO AHEAD, SHOOT ME!
VWOOM
BUT PREPARE YOURSELF-- THE MOMENT YOU PULL THAT TRIGGER, I'M GOING TO BREAK YOUR FINGER LIKE A MATCHSTICK!
FROM THIS DISTANCE ...?!
LIKE HELL YOU COULD! I'LL BLOW YOUR BRAINS OUT!
KLIK

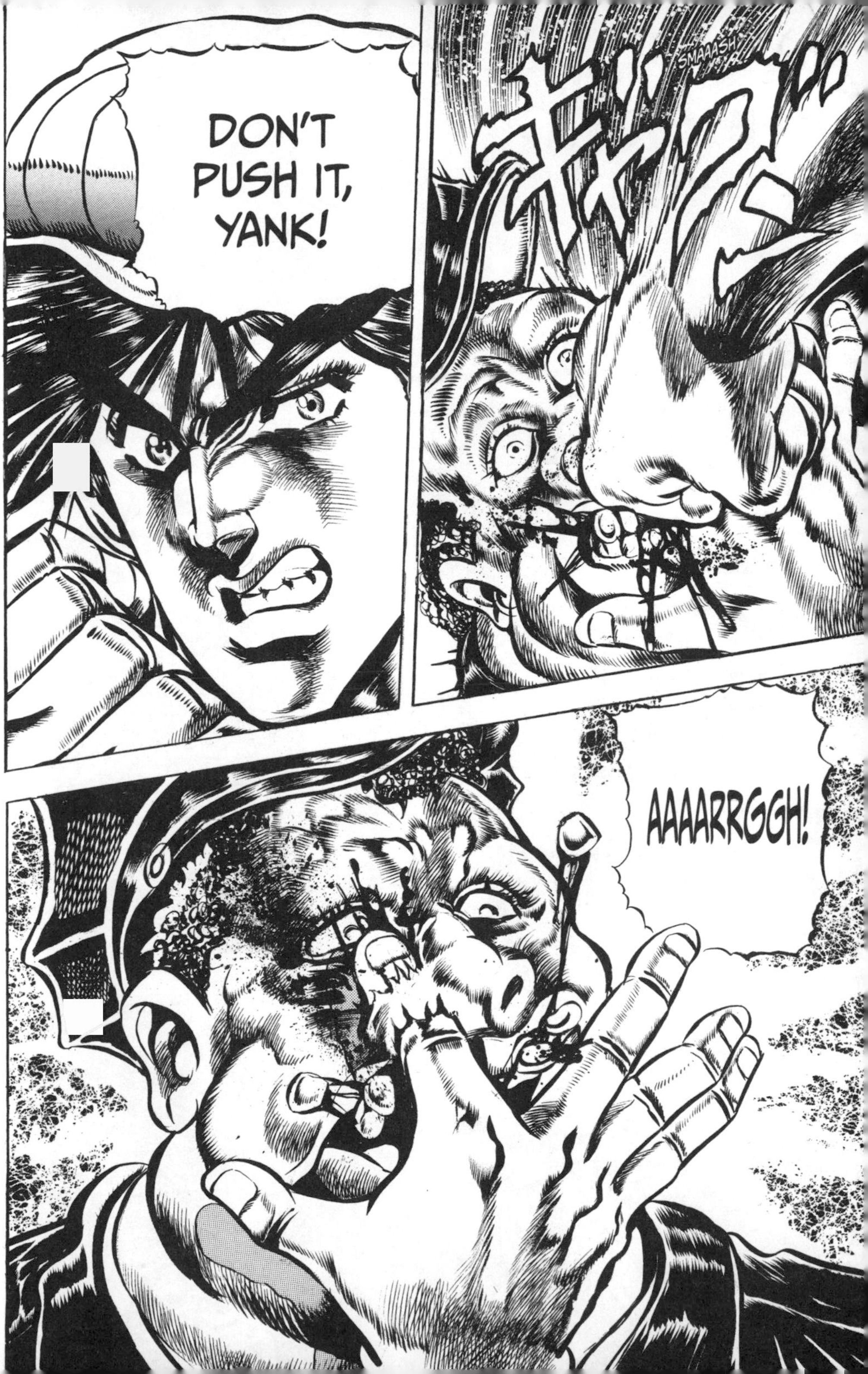
SMAAASH
DON'T PUSH IT, YANK!
AAAARRGGH!

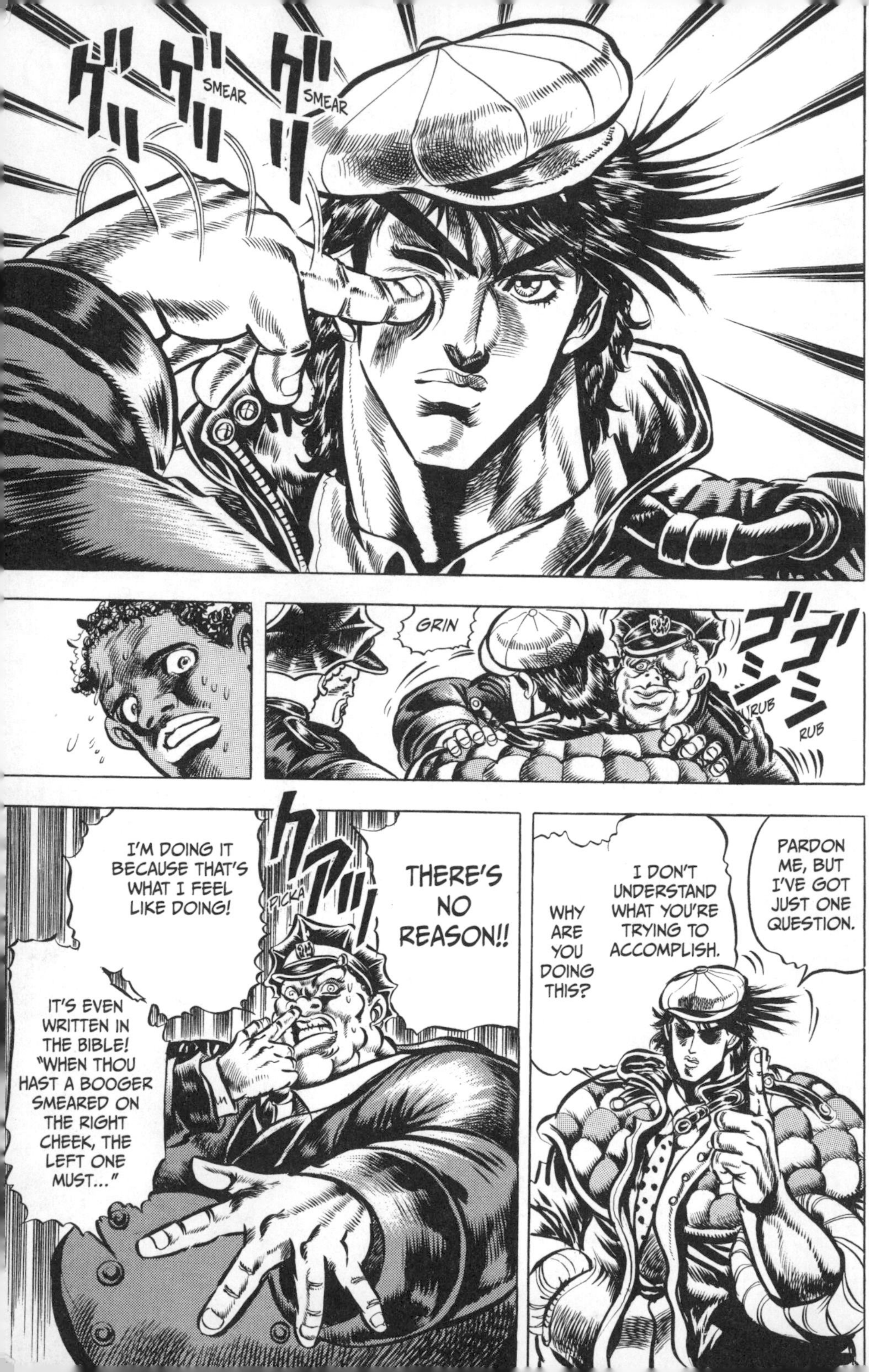

SMEAR
SMEAR
GRIN
RUB
RUB
PARDON ME, BUT I'VE GOT JUST ONE QUESTION.
I DON'T UNDERSTAND WHAT YOU'RE TRYING TO ACCOMPLISH.
WHY ARE YOU DOING THIS?
PICKA
THERE'S NO REASON!!
I'M DOING IT BECAUSE THAT'S WHAT I FEEL LIKE DOING!
IT'S EVEN WRITTEN IN THE BIBLE! "WHEN THOU HAST A BOOGER SMEARED ON THE RIGHT CHEEK, THE LEFT ONE MUST..."

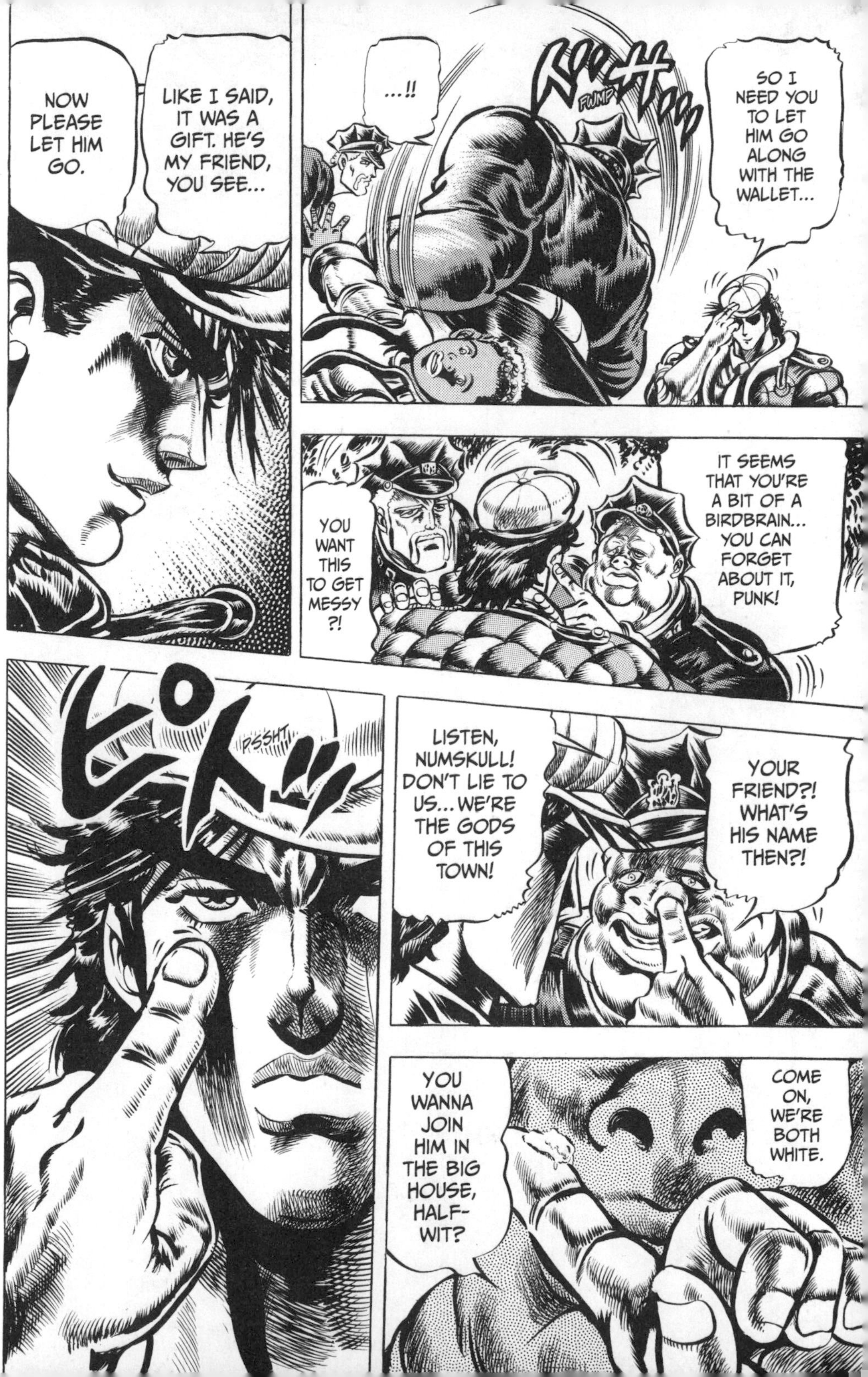

SO I NEED YOU TO LET HIM GO ALONG WITH THE WALLET...
FWUMP
...!!
IT SEEMS THAT YOU'RE A BIT OF A BIRDBRAIN... YOU CAN FORGET ABOUT IT, PUNK!
YOU WANT THIS TO GET MESSY ?!
LIKE I SAID, IT WAS A GIFT. HE'S MY FRIEND, YOU SEE...
NOW PLEASE LET HIM GO.
YOUR FRIEND?! WHAT'S HIS NAME THEN?!
LISTEN, NUMSKULL! DON'T LIE TO US... WE'RE THE GODS OF THIS TOWN!
COME ON, WE'RE BOTH WHITE.
YOU WANNA JOIN HIM IN THE BIG HOUSE, HALF-WIT?
PSSHT

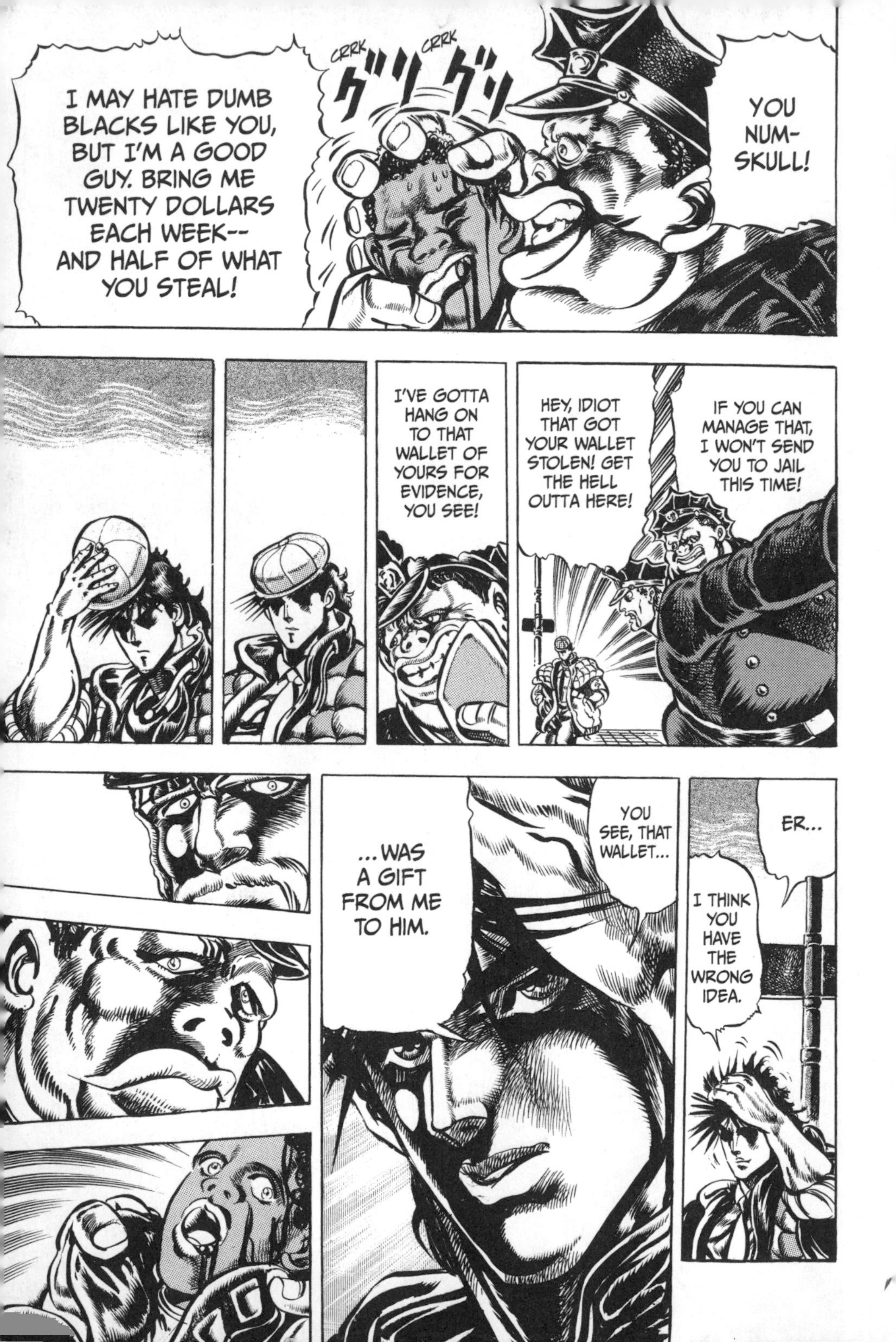
YOU NUM-SKULL!
CRRK CRRK
I MAY HATE DUMB BLACKS LIKE YOU, BUT I'M A GOOD GUY. BRING ME TWENTY DOLLARS EACH WEEK-- AND HALF OF WHAT YOU STEAL!
HEY, IDIOT THAT GOT YOUR WALLET STOLEN! GET THE HELL OUTTA HERE!
IF YOU CAN MANAGE THAT, I WON'T SEND YOU TO JAIL THIS TIME!
I'VE GOTTA HANG ON TO THAT WALLET OF YOURS FOR EVIDENCE, YOU SEE!
ER...
I THINK YOU HAVE THE WRONG IDEA.
YOU SEE, THAT WALLET...
...WAS A GIFT FROM ME TO HIM.

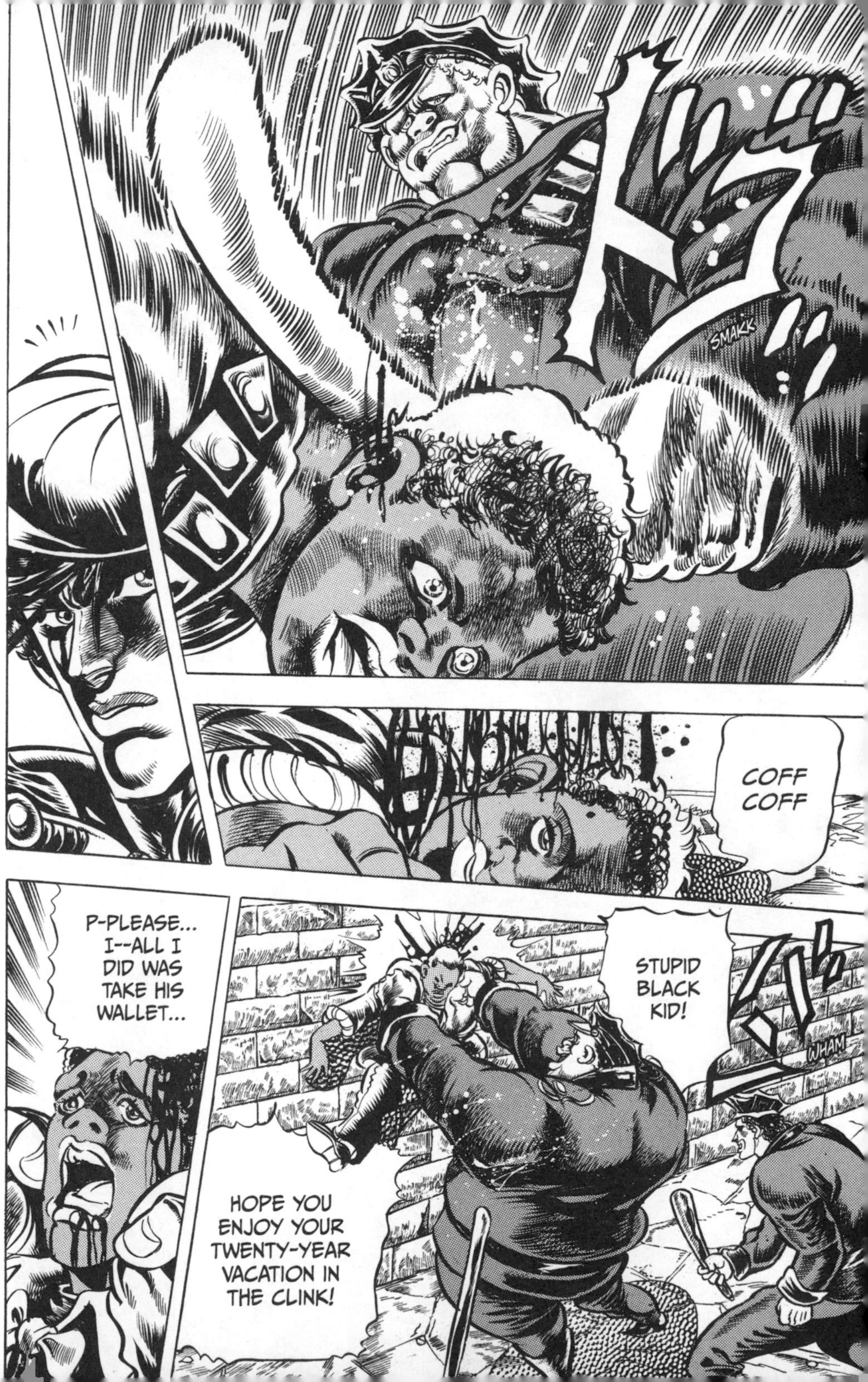
SMAKK
COFF COFF
STUPID BLACK KID!
WHAM
HOPE YOU ENJOY YOUR TWENTY-YEAR VACATION IN THE CLINK!
P-PLEASE... I--ALL I DID WAS TAKE HIS WALLET...

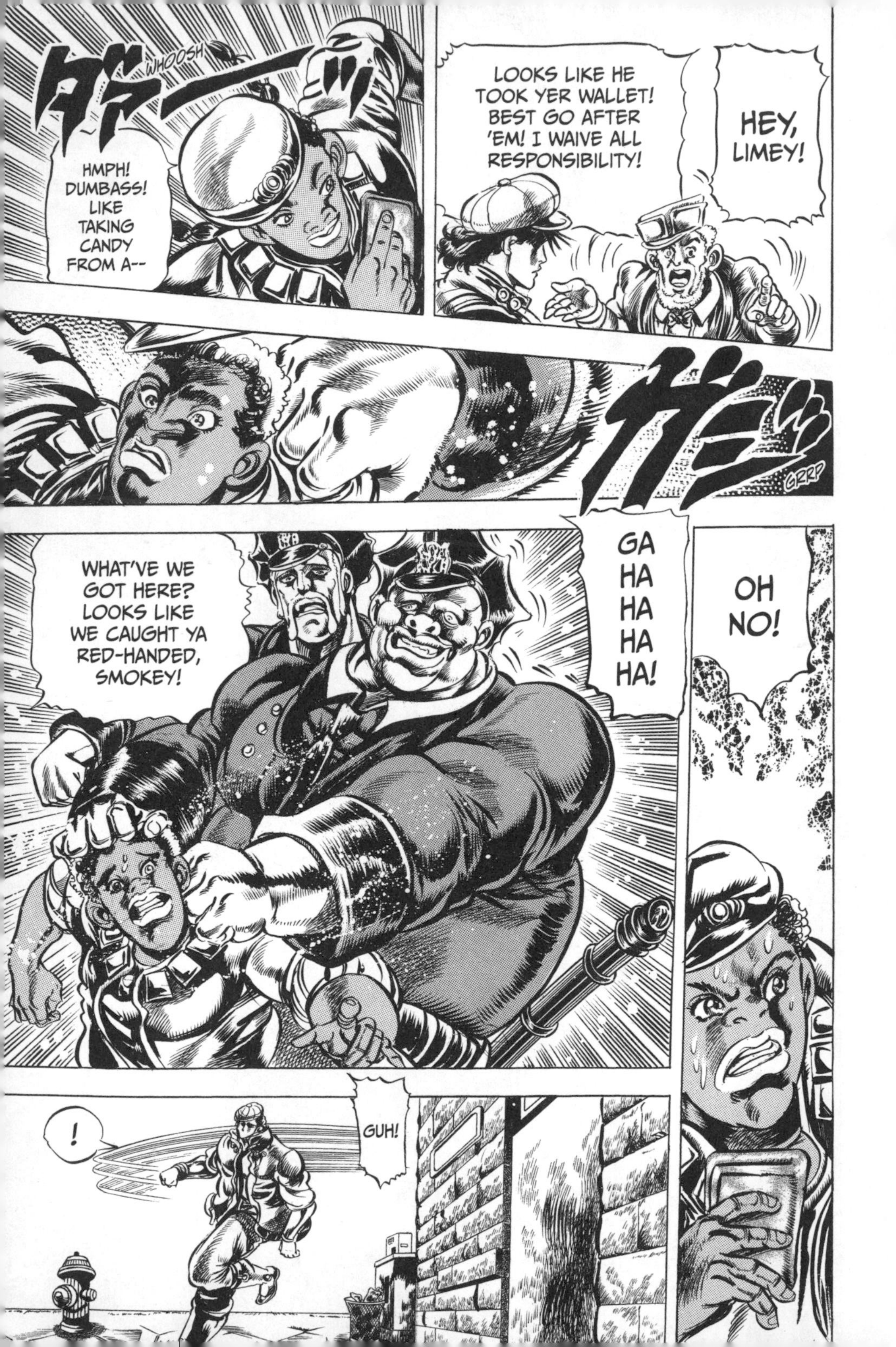
HEY, LIMEY!
LOOKS LIKE HE TOOK YER WALLET! BEST GO AFTER 'EM! I WAIVE ALL RESPONSIBILITY!
WHOOSH
HMPH! DUMBASS! LIKE TAKING CANDY FROM A--
GRRP
OH NO!
GA HA HA HA HA!
WHAT'VE WE GOT HERE? LOOKS LIKE WE CAUGHT YA RED-HANDED, SMOKEY!
GUH!
!

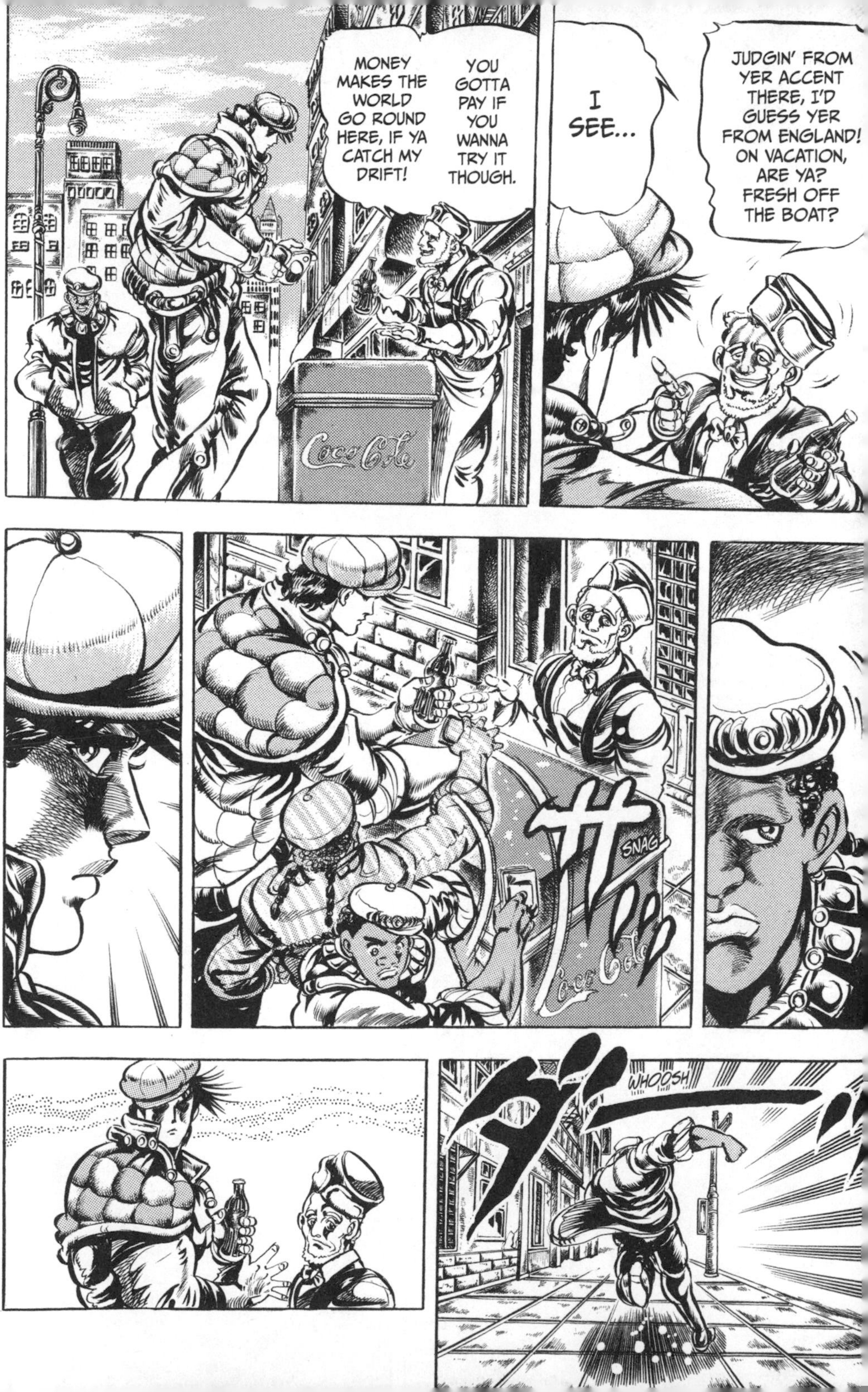
JUDGIN' FROM YER ACCENT THERE, I'D GUESS YER FROM ENGLAND! ON VACATION, ARE YA? FRESH OFF THE BOAT?
I SEE...
YOU GOTTA PAY IF YOU WANNA TRY IT THOUGH.
MONEY MAKES THE WORLD GO ROUND HERE, IF YA CATCH MY DRIFT!
Coca-Cola
SNAG
Coca-Cola
WHOOSH

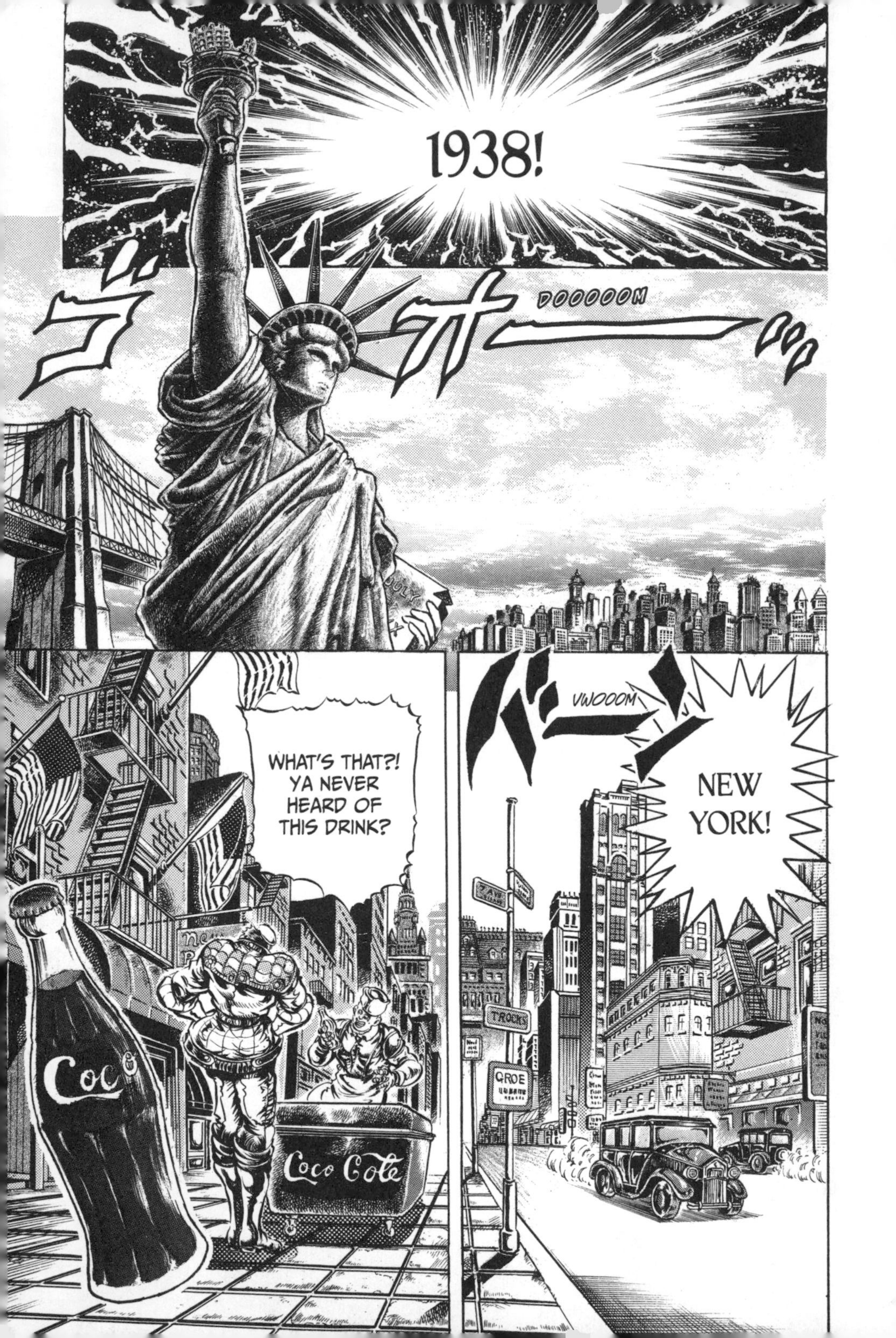
1938!
DOOOOOM
VWOOOM
NEW YORK!
WHAT'S THAT?! YA NEVER HEARD OF THIS DRINK?
Coco Cole

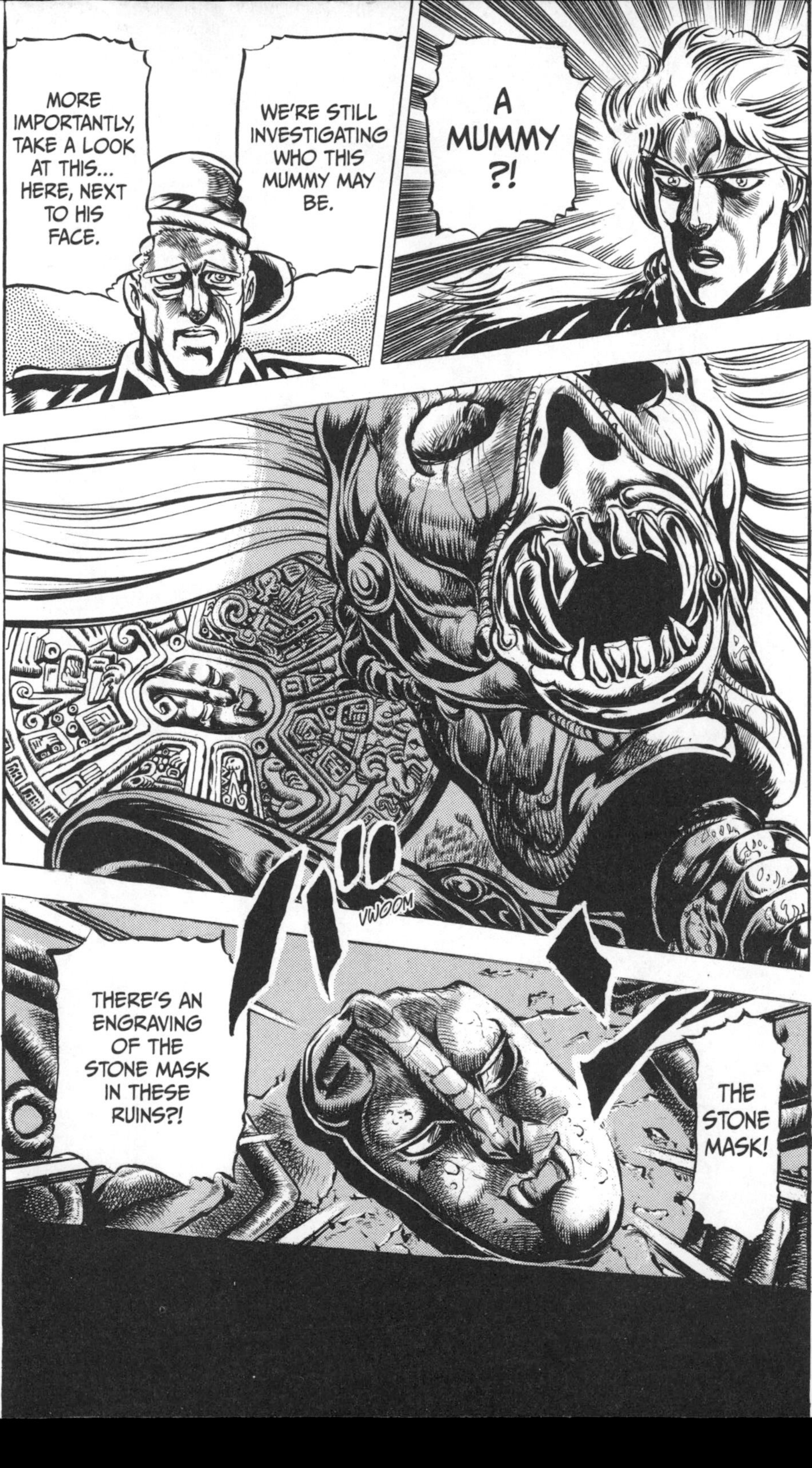
A MUMMY?!
WE'RE STILL INVESTIGATING WHO THIS MUMMY MAY BE.
MORE IMPORTANTLY, TAKE A LOOK AT THIS... HERE, NEXT TO HIS FACE.
VWOOM
THE STONE MASK!
THERE'S AN ENGRAVING OF THE STONE MASK IN THESE RUINS?!

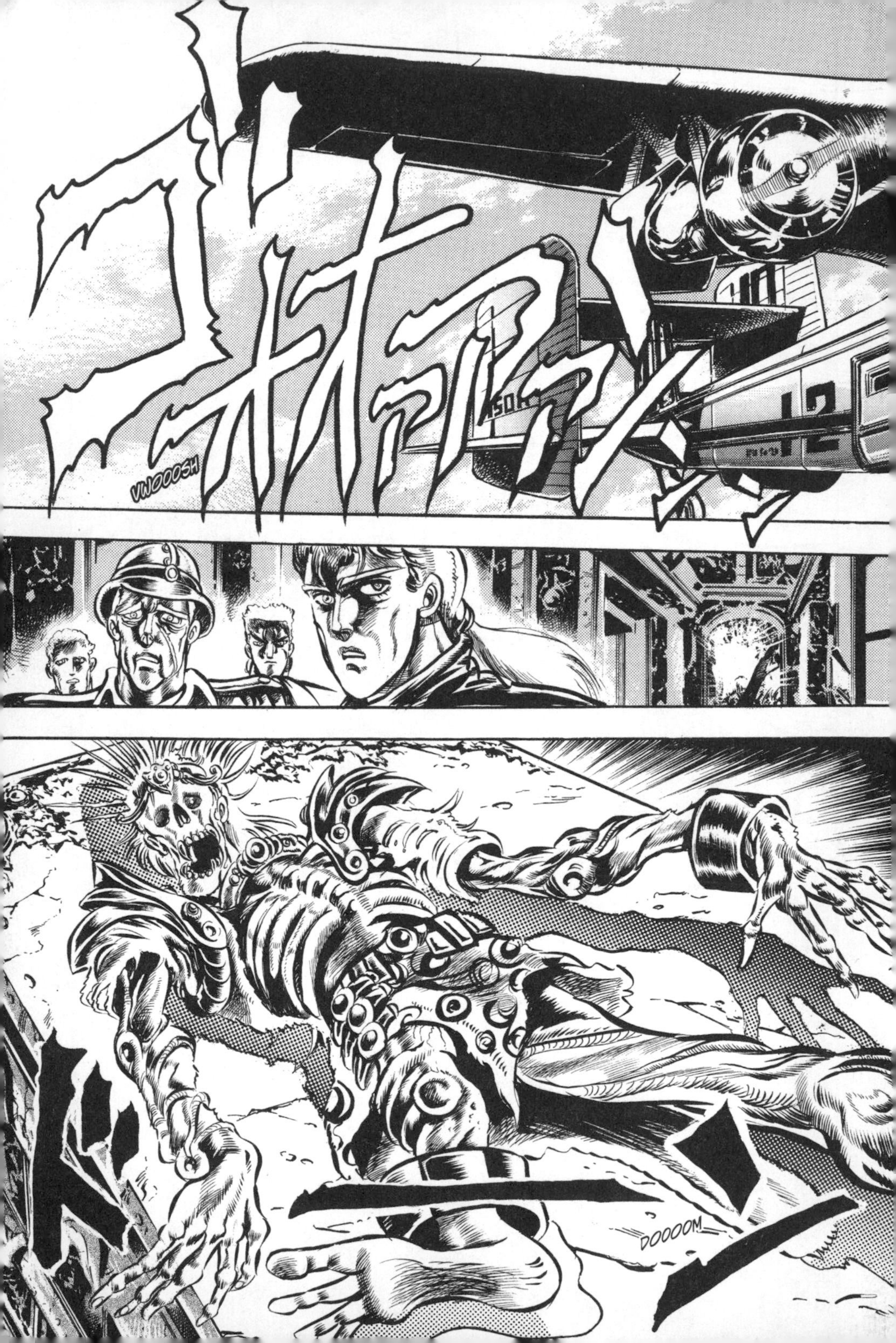
VWOOOSH
DOOOOM

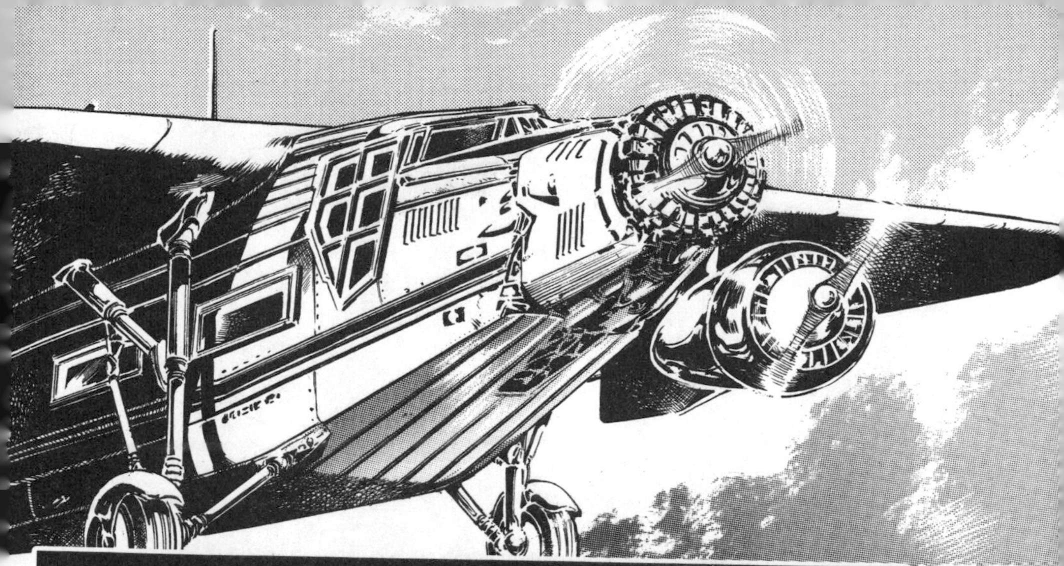

CHAPTER 1: Joseph Joestar of New York PART 1

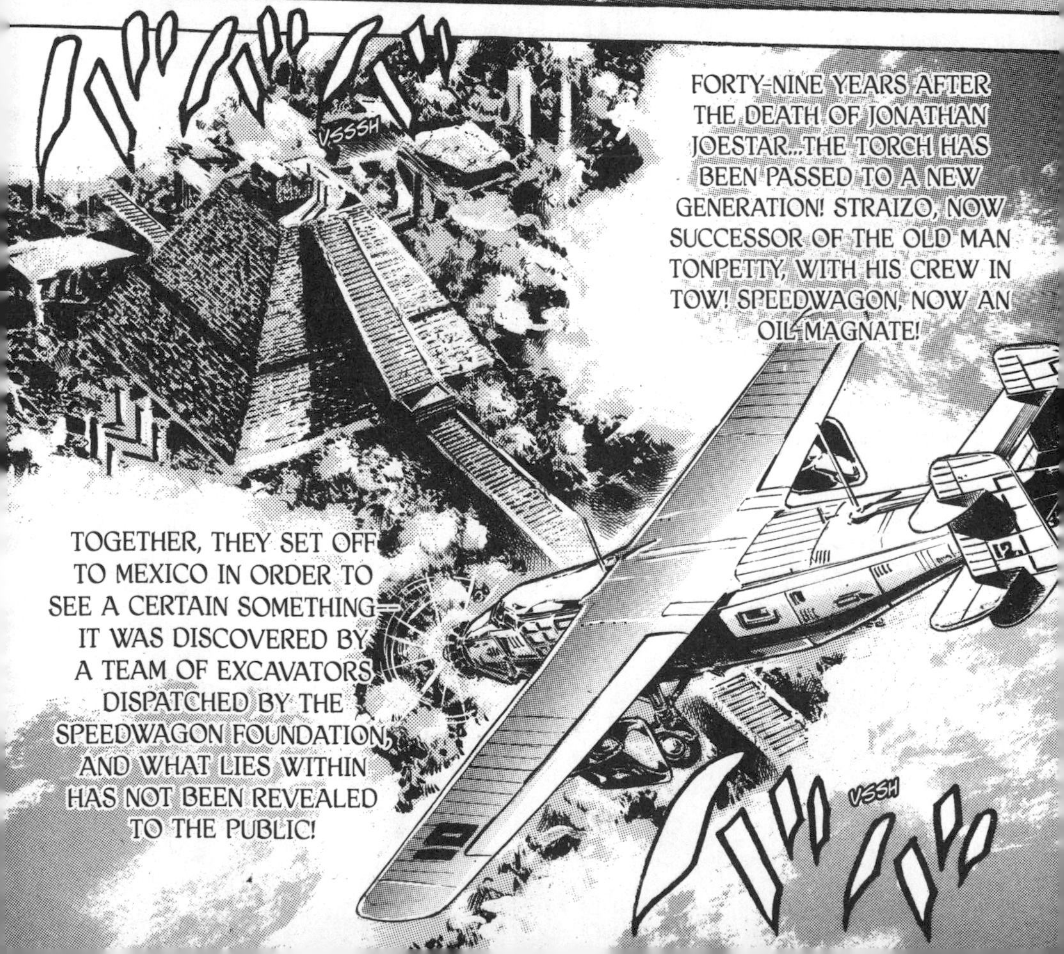
FORTY-NINE YEARS AFTER THE DEATH OF JONATHAN JOESTAR...THE TORCH HAS BEEN PASSED TO A NEW GENERATION! STRAIZO, NOW SUCCESSOR OF THE OLD MAN TONPETTY, WITH HIS CREW IN TOW! SPEEDWAGON, NOW AN OIL MAGNATE!
VSSSH
TOGETHER, THEY SET OFF TO MEXICO IN ORDER TO SEE A CERTAIN SOMETHING— IT WAS DISCOVERED BY A TEAM OF EXCAVATORS DISPATCHED BY THE SPEEDWAGON FOUNDATION, AND WHAT LIES WITHIN HAS NOT BEEN REVEALED TO THE PUBLIC!
VSSH

CHAPTER 1: Joseph Joestar of New York PART 1

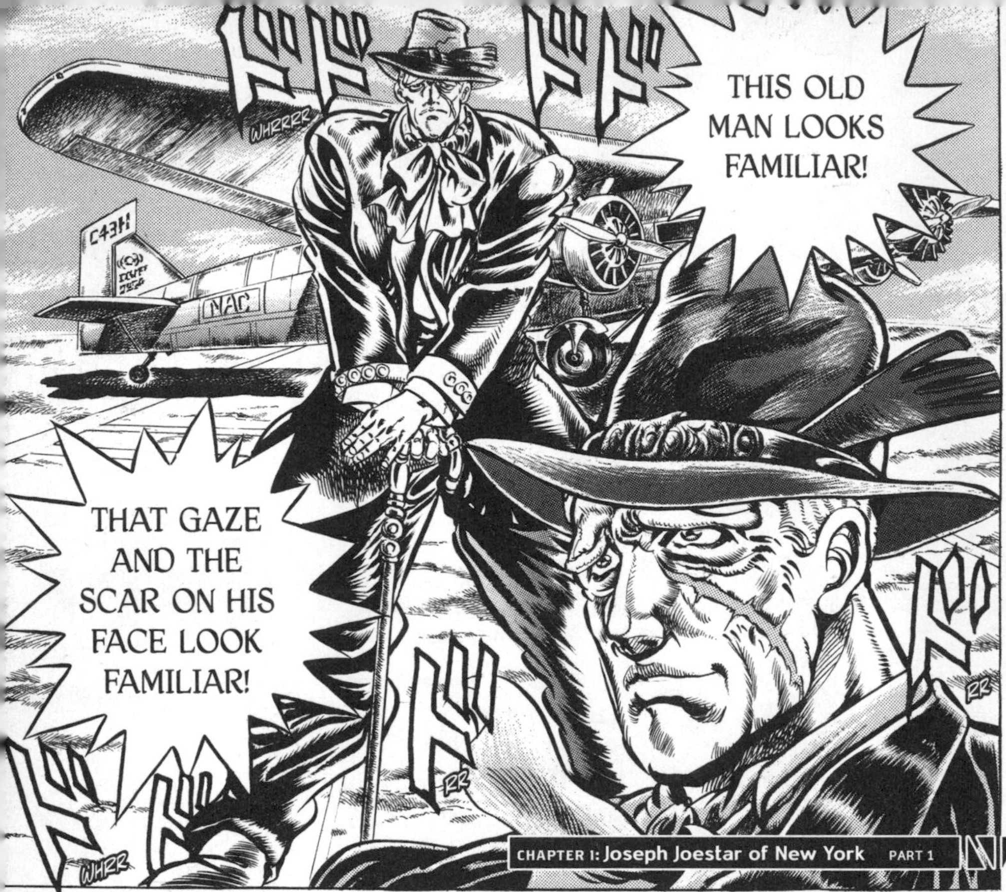
THIS OLD MAN LOOKS FAMILIAR!
WHRRRR
RR
THAT GAZE AND THE SCAR ON HIS FACE LOOK FAMILIAR!
RR
WHRR

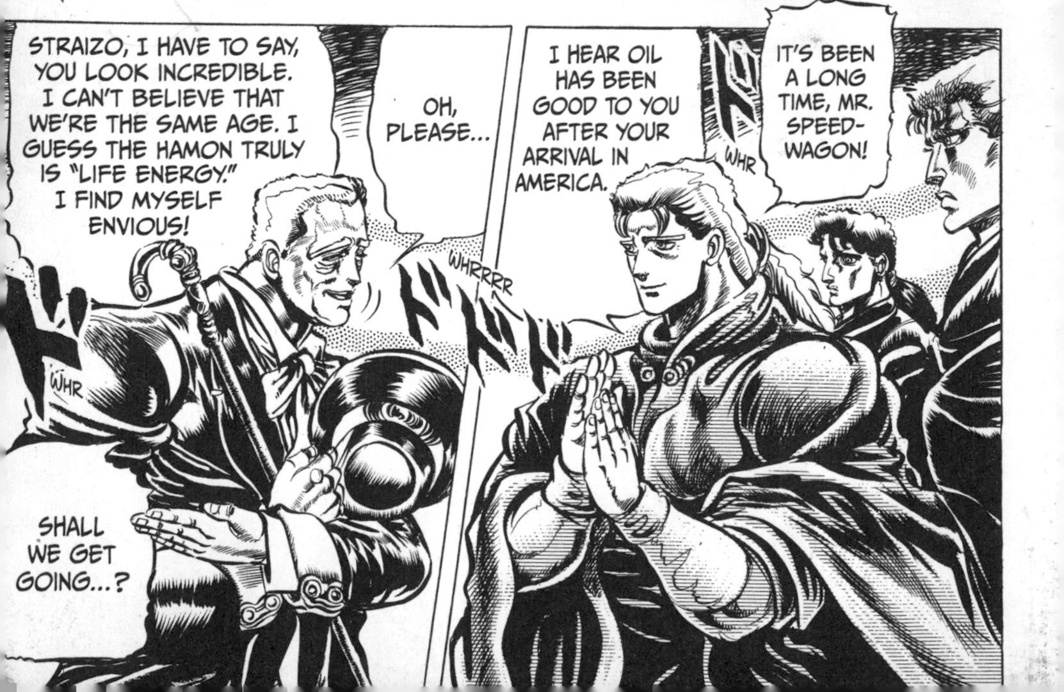
IT'S BEEN A LONG TIME, MR. SPEED-WAGON!
WHR
I HEAR OIL HAS BEEN GOOD TO YOU AFTER YOUR ARRIVAL IN AMERICA.
WHRRRR
OH, PLEASE...
STRAIZO, I HAVE TO SAY, YOU LOOK INCREDIBLE. I CAN'T BELIEVE THAT WE'RE THE SAME AGE. I GUESS THE HAMON TRULY IS "LIFE ENERGY." I FIND MYSELF ENVIOUS!
WHR
SHALL WE GET GOING...?

TF
140
.J64
S6

Spence, Vernon G
Colonel Morgan
Jones.

COLONEL
MORGAN
JONES

GRAND OLD MAN OF TEXAS RAILROADING

UNIVERSITY OF OKLAHOMA PRESS : NORMAN

COLONEL MORGAN JONES

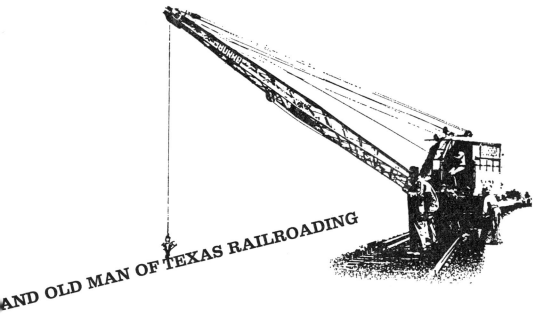

AND OLD MAN OF TEXAS RAILROADING

by Vernon Gladden Spence

The paper on which this book is printed bears the watermark of the University of Oklahoma Press and has an effective life of at least three hundred years.

INTERNATIONAL STANDARD BOOK NUMBER: 0–8061–0977–7

LIBRARY OF CONGRESS CATALOG CARD NUMBER: 73–160505

 Composed and printed at Norman, Oklahoma, U.S.A., by the University of Oklahoma Press. First edition.

To the Memory of
GRENVILLE DODGE JONES

PREFACE

THE Republic of Texas in 1839 did not have a single mile of railroad track. By 1926, however, the state of Texas contained approximately fifty railroad properties, including 16,071 miles of rails, and led all other states of the Union in railroad mileage. Within one life span, therefore, the railroad builders constructed one-fortieth of the world's total rails within the boundaries of a single state.

Morgan Jones, who was born on a Welsh farm in 1839 and died in Abilene, Texas, in 1926, built and operated many of those Texas lines, and he built them with a singleness of purpose unmatched by any other individual in the state's railroad history.

Included among his friends and business associates were such railroad builders as General Grenville M. Dodge, Jay Gould, and Collis P. Huntington; but, unlike those and other railroad "tycoons" of his age, he was not a "promoter," a "manipulator," or a "politician." Throughout his lifetime Morgan Jones worked diligently to avoid the limelight of publicity. He was a "builder," and he was never happy at any other task.

While few people knew him well, his accomplishments were obvious to those who benefited from them. At his death, the *Abilene Daily Reporter* editorialized, "Of the thousands who toiled and wrought in the building of Texas railroads, none achieved greater things than Morgan Jones." And in Fort Worth, a thriving city perhaps as indebted to the Welshman as to anyone else, the local editor reminded his readers, "Fort Worth and West Texas will never be able to estimate its obligation to Morgan Jones."

But while the Southwest continued to thrive through its use of the Morgan Jones railroads—a form of transportation essential to the development of any region without navigable rivers—its people soon forgot the man who built them. Indeed, so successfully did he avoid public recognition during his lifetime that, for more than four decades following his death, historians have failed to recognize the significance of his contributions to Texas railroading.

This biography is an attempt to correct that oversight. Through the years fires have destroyed valuable records, many of his friends and business associates have died, and newspapers have vanished. Most appalling of all, the modest Welshman refused to grant a single newspaper interview until his eighty-third year.

Morgan Jones was unable, however, to cover his tracks completely. He left only traces of his numerous business activities outside of the railroad industry. I have inserted such evidence of his interests in mining, ranching, banking, farming, and public utilities as I was able to locate, but this book is essentially the story of the railroad builder.

When Jones arrived in the United States shortly after the end of the Civil War, he was twenty-six years old and an experienced construction crewman with the Cambrian Railway Company in Wales. General Grenville M. Dodge promoted him to construction foreman for the Union Pacific as that railroad advanced westward to link with the Central Pacific as the nation's first transcontinental line.

Upon its completion in 1869, young Jones contracted with General John C. Frémont to build sections of the Southern Transcontinental (predecessor to the Southern Pacific) in East Texas, just as that state's postwar boom commenced. From that beginning, Jones spent the next half-century in railroad construction, and when he died in 1926, he had built lengthy sections of the Southern Pacific, the Texas and Pacific, the Gulf, Colorado and Santa Fe, and the Fort Worth and Denver City. He campaigned successfully to complete the latter railroad after the Texas legislature nullified its railroad land-grant laws, and after subsequent antitrust legislation discouraged and threatened to halt other significant railroad construction in the state. Upon that road's completion, the young railroad builder served the Gulf-to-Rockies system's southern section as vice-president, president, and receiver. During the Fort Worth and Denver City's critical first decade, he played a vital and distinguished role in its development.

The Welshman, despite his proven administrative abilities, preferred to *build* railroads. He persistently advocated new branch lines into potentially prosperous agricultural regions near the company's main route. Eventually, he built the Pan Handle Railway Company road, from the Fort Worth and Denver City's main line at Washburn, to Panhandle City, and the Wichita Valley Railway Company road from Wichita Falls to Seymour. Each little company was a financial success, and each was a valuable feeder line to the main road.

By the beginning of the twentieth century, Texas railroad construction followed an intricate pattern of short-line rails. Their purposes were twofold: they connected the trans-Texas main lines at strategic points, and they created and served agricultural communities far removed from distribution centers. During the short-line boom, Jones resigned from the Fort Worth and Denver City and built the Wichita Falls and Oklahoma railroad into ranch and oil lands near the Red River; he extended the Wichita Valley line to Stamford and other farming communities in the valley; he built the Abilene and Northern from Abilene's Texas and Pacific tracks to Stamford's Wichita Valley rails; he built the Abilene and Southern into Taylor and Runnels counties' prosperous cattle, sheep, and farming areas and, concurrently, he connected the Texas and Pacific to the Gulf, Colorado and Santa Fe rails at Ballinger; and, finally, he extended the Abilene and Southern northward from Anson to Hamlin, thereby connecting the Texas and Pacific, the

Kansas City, Mexico and Orient, the Wichita Valley, and the Fort Worth and Denver City. Jones was the major stockholder in each short-line company.

He planned to build other railroads into central-west Texas and into southwest Texas. Stronger railroad organizations—the Gulf, Colorado and Santa Fe and the Texas Central—successfully stopped him. His proposed projects, however, forced the larger companies to extend their roads deeper into the Texas railroad frontier.

Almost all of Morgan Jones's railroads penetrated Texas' treeless "semi-deserts" that later developed into some of the state's richest farming and stock-raising areas. This was his challenge and he devoted his life to it. A bachelor to the end, he explained that women were "too impractical to marry." The truth was, of course, that they knew nothing about railroading, and he could communicate only with persons who did. His achievements testify to his success in an industry—and during an era—dominated by a very few men. This, then, in the words of historian Rupert N. Richardson, is the story of "the ingenuity of a capable and determined man."

VERNON GLADDEN SPENCE

George Mason College
of the University of Virginia
April 7, 1971

ACKNOWLEDGMENTS

EVERY historian begins his research with the built-in assumption that certain traumatic discoveries await him: perhaps disastrous fires have destroyed needed records; perhaps newspaper publishers have neglected to preserve early editions; perhaps a lowly mouse has digested the carefully wrapped contents of a shoebox depository of cherished letters; or perhaps inexpensive ink has lost its battle to survive against time and the elements.

But the researcher also anticipates moments of exhilaration: he may discover a letter of major significance, dropped many years ago, between the pages of an old and dusty hymnal.

These experiences are typical of the trade. My efforts to piece together the life and accomplishments of Colonel Morgan Jones produced such moments of trauma and exhilaration. A Fort Worth fire in March, 1898, caused no greater panic at that time than in November, 1967, when I first learned about it. That catastrophe destroyed almost all of the records of the Fort Worth and Denver City Railway Company. Colonel Jones, with his own hands, helped to build that railroad, he invested a relatively large fortune in it, and he served it at various and critical times as vice-president, president, and receiver.

Happily, then, I discovered that the railroad company and its official historian, Richard C. Overton, had pieced together a remarkably complete history of the Fort Worth and Denver City entitled *Gulf to Rockies*. Disappointment returned once again when I realized that Jones's personal papers were not available when Overton reconstructed that railroad's story.

Shortly thereafter Mrs. Percy Jones, the Colonel's niece by marriage, granted my request to read the Jones papers, which she had carefully preserved and left untouched since his death in 1926. More than that, Mrs. Jones allowed me to use those papers without restrictions of any sort. A researcher's natural greediness led me to hope for even greater good fortune: perhaps the Colonel was a stickler for orderliness; perhaps he had filed neatly in logical sequence every letter or bill of sale.

Such, of course, was not the case. On the contrary, Jones was a man totally dedicated to the present, unconcerned about his significant role in the economic history of the Lone-Star State. Whatever private or public records he left for posterity resulted from oversight. This railroad builder, unlike many builders of his day, was noted for his honesty and integrity; but his friends, business associates, and even casual acquaintances marveled at the lengths to which he went to protect his privacy.

Small wonder, then, that Morgan Jones was better known on Wall Street than in his own home town; small wonder, too, that, in spite of his significant role in Texas history, his name rarely appears in the history books. My efforts, therefore, to rescue from almost total oblivion Texas' leading individual railroad builder forced me to rely on the assistance of an unusually long list of individuals and groups, to all of whom I am enormously indebted.

In that special group with Mrs. Percy Jones and Richard C. Overton, mentioned above, I must include more than a score of persons whom I have never met but who, some years ago, recorded their personal reminiscences for the Fort Worth and Denver Railway Company. Morgan Jones built railroads for "people to use" and I tried, consequently, to emphasize Jones's influence on their lives as they told it. Without the assistance of this group, I could not have reconstructed the Jones story.

Piecing the biography together required many long hours of

labor by still another flock of history buffs. Katharyn Duff, associate editor of the *Abilene Reporter-News*, west Texas historian and author, and affectionately known as "the voice of west Texas," first interested me—a new acquaintance at the time—in Morgan Jones. Having inspired me with her contagious enthusiasm, she then pointed me in the right direction toward the Jones papers. She read every chapter of the resulting manuscript (and improved each of them).

Vernie E. Newman, professor of history in McMurry College, was another faithful counselor. Her knowledge of historical fact equals her abhorrence of history written in the passive voice, and thus she saved me from factual errors and grammatical absurdities.

Mrs. Morgan Jones, Sr., another niece by marriage of the Colonel's, and Mr. Roland Jones, the Colonel's nephew, graciously invited me into their homes, reminisced for many fascinating hours about life during the "Old Mahn's" day, and, in many instances, rescued me from hopeless chronological chaos.

Mr. and Mrs. Morgan Jones, Jr., and Mr. and Mrs. Grant Jones opened many doors for me during the early stages of research. With Mrs. C. E. Fulgham and Mrs. Lockett Shelton, their assistance and encouragement continued to the date of publication. Mrs. Morgan Jones, Jr., in addition, wrote numerous letters of inquiry to other family members scattered around the world who, in turn, responded with much valuable information.

Mrs. Curry Longstaff of Pyrford, Surrey County, England, the Colonel's only surviving niece, was particularly helpful. She located and sent to Mrs. Morgan Jones, Jr., many facts about the Colonel's early life as a Welsh farm boy.

Rupert N. Richardson, professor of history in Hardin-Simmons University, read every chapter and, with his experienced and professional eye, prevented embarrassing inaccuracies and omissions.

Giles Bradford, former professor of history in McMurry College, acted as a sounding board for my ideas during the early drafts of the manuscript and more than once boosted my morale.

One of the rewards of historical research is making new friends and renewing old acquaintances among that special breed of people who have in their custody the contents of public depositories, libraries, and private collections. In the offices of the Percy Jones Estate, I was helped in ways too numerous to mention by Walter W. Ford, Melvin W. Holt, Eugene M. Allen, and Mrs. E. D. Fomby. Their assistance in locating and sifting through every scrap of the Morgan Jones papers, their patience in having me underfoot for long months and years, and their genuine enthusiasm for this project made even the most unproductive day seem worth while. Others who made me feel as if they had nothing to do but assist me were Miss Thelma Andrews of the Abilene Public Library; Joe Easterly and Mrs. Ruth Hodges of the Jay-Rollins Library, McMurry College; Mrs. Julia Jones of the Hardin-Simmons University library; Claude Cook and Mrs. Aloys Gilman of the Iowa State Department of History and Archives, Des Moines; Mrs. Alys Freeze and Mrs. Opal M. Harber of the Western History Department, Denver Public Library; Mrs. Enid Thompson, Mrs. Kathleen Pierson, and Mrs. Laura Ekstrom of the State Historical Society of Colorado, Denver; E. L. Simmons and C. Lee Morris of the Fort Worth and Denver Railway Company, Fort Worth; and R. A. Malone of the Texas and Pacific Railway Company, Dallas.

Numerous little bits and, sometimes, great chunks of significant information were provided by Mrs. Robert Roy Duncan of Fort Worth, Miss Sarah Hardy and Mrs. Lucia M. Wilson of Abilene, and Mrs. Bill Calhoun of Denton. Their family histories, all directly related to the Morgan Jones story, helped to fill blank spots in the narrative.

Personal interviews with Jones's surviving friends and business associates made possible a more accurate description of the reticent railroad builder's personality and habits. Particularly helpful in that respect were Harry Benge Crozier of Austin; Jack Scott and S. F. Bond of Cross Plains; and W. G. Swenson, Judge Walter S. Pope, the Reverend Dr. Willis P. Gerhart, Mrs. Ruth Bradfield Gay, Judge and Mrs. R. M. Wagstaff, Mrs. Julia Legett Pickard, Mr. and Mrs. C. A. Creagh, and Mrs. C. L. Hailey, all of Abilene.

During a long period of study, research, and writing, an author is fortunate indeed if he has a mentor who, in word and action, rejects any effort which he considers less than the author's very best. My academic "godfather" on this project was Robert G. Athearn of the University of Colorado. The standards he set were always just beyond my reach; but, more importantly, his example never failed to inspire.

Also at the University of Colorado, Lee Scamehorn's familiarity with Morgan Jones's activities in the Colorado mines proved invaluable to that chapter in the Jones story.

To Mrs. Volney Farnsworth of Abilene, and to Mrs. Barbara Kirtland of Boulder, I owe special thanks. Their abilities to master that temperamental demon, the typewriter, and to decode my original manuscript make me both envious and grateful.

When my research led me, as it often did, to the various depositories in Colorado, I was fortunate indeed to have not one but five good friends who made it their business that I did not live on research alone. Mrs. Louise Taborsky and Mr. and Mrs. Phil Cohen provided both mental and physical sustenance; and, as if their good deeds were not enough, Mr. and Mrs. Foy Langford of Greeley, Colorado, drove, literally, through snowstorms to provide encouragement when I needed it most.

At home, my gratitude to other friends and to my family cannot be measured. To my close friends, Mr. and Mrs. Kirk McKinnon, and Miss Beth Duff, and especially to my parents, Mr. and Mrs. Vernon L. Spence, I shall always remain indebted.

My children, John Randolph Gladden, Deborah Anne, and Kevin Douglas, who have heard more about Colonel Morgan Jones than about their own ancestors, contributed far more than they realize to make this book a reality.

And, finally, my wife, Wanda Smith Spence, who, alone, knows the full story, gave me the confidence I needed to undertake this project in the first place.

VERNON GLADDEN SPENCE

CONTENTS

ILLUSTRATIONS

xix

COLONEL
MORGAN
JONES

GRAND OLD MAN OF TEXAS RAILROADING

1. APPRENTICE TO JOURNEYMAN

THE ruggedly beautiful Cambrian Mountains which occupy two-thirds of Wales are the particular pride of every Welshman. These majestic peaks, rather than the serene river valleys below, symbolize the unyielding tenacity with which many a Welsh farmer ignores the stormy winds and steep pastures of his environment. In spite of the adverse elements, he produces, year after year, considerable quantities of wheat, oats, and barley.

At mid-nineteenth century, the average farmer there, though courageous and independent, was ignorant of the outside world. The social, political, and economic changes which swept across Great Britain as a result of the Industrial Revolution did not touch all Welshmen equally. As late as the middle decades of the nineteenth century, the Welsh farmer's life was influenced by the Industrial Revolution only through increased demands for his crops in the growing cities along the coast and near the coal mines. Like his ancestors, he accepted his lot as he accepted the mountains around him, without question.

Younger men near him, however—sons, brothers, cousins—felt no challenge from raising crops north of the fiftieth degree of latitude. Their energies and ambitions could not be fulfilled by tilling the soil. As sporadic bits of news from the industrial areas reached the agricultural regions, men of all ages, and in increasing

3

numbers, left their farms. Thousands of them sought employment in the expanding coal fields and the bustling coastal cities of Wales. Tens of thousands emigrated to the United States, the country which the Industrial Revolution was to make a new leader among nations.

Morgan Jones, one such Welshman, was nineteen when he succumbed to the pull of this rising industrial order. In 1858 he rode away from "Vachwen," the family farm. He wanted to see the one man with whom he was acquainted who was already a part of the new life he sought for himself. He passed through the familiar little village of Tregynon in Montgomery County and followed the road two miles to the southeast toward a slightly larger town, Newtown, on a branch of the Severn River. As he approached, he shifted his direction southwestward toward his destination—a town named Llandinam—about five miles distant. These villages had existed for centuries, almost untouched by developments of the Industrial Revolution.[1] They offered little indeed to a young man caught up in the spirit of a new age. He passed them now, undisturbed by the thought that they would never again be a meaningful part of his world.

Young Jones was the first child of Morgan and Mary Charles Jones. According to a family custom of the past six generations, Morgan was the name given to the first son of each new generation. The proud parents continued the tradition at the hour of his birth, about two o'clock on the morning of October 7, 1839.[2] His childhood years passed in a manner as traditional as his name. The oldest son of a relatively prosperous, God-fearing, sober-minded farmer, he performed without complaint the duties assigned to him. Each day must be "productive."

In 1849 his father died. At the age of ten young Morgan inherited, with his mother, the responsibilities of tending the farm and caring for his younger brothers and sister. From this early

[1] Letter from E. G. S. Tomley, superintendent registrar, Registration District of Newtown, Montgomeryshire, Wales, to Walter W. Ford, Abilene, Texas (November 7, 1967).

[2] Great Britain, Office of the Registrar General, Registration District of Newtown, Sub-district of Tregynon, County of Montgomery, Wales. Certified Copy of an Entry of Birth (CF 759622), No. 225.

4

beginning, and for the next three-quarters of a century, Jones assumed a stern but compassionate concern for all members of his family.

Mary Jones was not, however, a weak or helpless widow. She was "a big, fine woman and a marvelous horseback rider."[3] With the assistance of her small children,[4] she continued to operate the "rather large" farm and to raise Shetland ponies, which, because of their small size, were in great demand by operators of the Welsh coal mines. Most of her neighbors were Methodists, but the Joneses belonged to the Church of England. Mrs. Jones continued her husband's efforts to provide the children with a religious education, and she read to them each day from the family Bible. She paid the village schoolmaster for instructing the children in writing, arithmetic, and reading and did not discourage his use of the stick.[5]

Morgan was primarily responsible for the care of the ponies and, as he grew to young manhood, he arranged for their sale. Usually the purchasers came to Vachwen; at other times Morgan delivered small herds of Shetlands to their new owners at the mines. On these short trips he gradually became familiar with the coal-mining industry. He developed a greater interest, however, in the railroads which transported the coal to the industrial centers.

Thus it was that just before his twentieth birthday the young man journeyed the few miles down to Llandinam to apply for a job with the only railroad man he knew. Lord David Davies visited his home town after having made a name for himself in Wales as a builder of the Cambrian Railway Company.[6] He hired young Jones at once and assigned him to a construction crew in South Wales.[7] Morgan Jones's apprenticeship in railroading had begun.

For seven years Jones worked at various positions with the

[3] Letter from Mrs. Edith Longstaff, Surrey, England, niece of Morgan Jones (November 21, 1967).

[4] *Ibid.* Other children born to Morgan and Mary Charles Jones were Thomas Charles, 1840; Henry, 1844; and Mary, 1846.

[5] *Ibid.*

[6] Letter from Mrs. Longstaff to Mrs. Morgan Jones, Jr., Abilene, Texas (July 14, 1967).

[7] Harry Benge Crozier, *Dallas News* (March 25, 1923), Sec. 2, 8.

5

Cambrian Railway Company. It was a valuable apprenticeship, but as he matured and gained experience in his new profession, he realized that opportunities for advancement were increasingly limited. Railroad construction in all of Great Britain reached its peak in the 1840's, and most of the main lines were complete. More than fifteen thousand miles of track were in operation. Any additional construction required enormous amounts of capital which Jones did not have. Safety precautions, insisted upon by parliamentary decree, plus almost endless tunnels, viaducts, and bridges, prohibited all but the most affluent railroad men from building more railroads. Jones knew, therefore, that he could continue working on railroads in his own country only as a salaried employee.

Frustrated in his work at home, the ambitious young Welchman dreamed about railroad opportunities in America. The rapid development of the railroad industry in that country was familiar to him. A map of the United States demonstrated clearly enough that no other country in the world had greater need for an immense railroad system. He assumed correctly that the Civil War, then raging in that country, had postponed only temporarily the construction of a vast transcontinental railroad across the United States.

In 1865, Morgan Jones, twenty-six years of age, decided to join the mass exodus from Europe to America. Three recent incidents, two of them family tragedies, influenced his decision. In 1862 his only sister, Mary, died unexpectedly at the age of seventeen. Three years later his mother died. Also, in 1865, the American Civil War ended. Meanwhile, Jones read that the Congress of the United States had chartered the first transcontinental railroad. In July, 1865, construction of the road commenced at Omaha, Nebraska.

Still without an interest in farming and no longer responsible for the care of his immediate family,[8] Jones investigated the opportunities for passage across the Atlantic. He learned that a Mr. Cook, owner of an explosives factory in Wales, had sold an order of dynamite to the Union Pacific Railroad Company. It happened

---

[8] Interview with Roland Jones, Carrollton, Texas (November 8, 1967). Jones's brother Thomas left home about the same time and went to Durham City, Newcastle, in northern England. Henry, the youngest brother, remained at Vachwen.

that Mr. Cook was seeking a responsible person to accompany this shipment to New York. Jones applied for and received the assignment to deliver the dynamite to General Grenville M. Dodge, chief engineer of the eastern end of the transcontinental road.[9]

On May 15, 1866, Morgan Jones arrived in New York City from Liverpool.[10] Although his wealth was "not significant"[11] at that time, he was not the typical emigrant from Wales, nor was he typical of the hordes of immigrants pouring into the United States from continental Europe. His financial resources were sufficient to supply his personal needs for an indefinite period; he had no European relatives dependent on him for support; and, unlike most other immigrants, he had a valuable apprenticeship in railroad construction. His peculiar skill was in great demand in the United States. Aware of this, he entered the country with confidence, eager to accept greater responsibilities.

Physically and mentally Jones was well equipped to win a place of distinction for himself in a land which prided itself on the number of its rugged individuals. There was no mistaking his origin: "You could tell the man was British as far as you could see him."[12] His talk, his manners, and even his physical features were distinctively representative of his native land. He spoke slowly and deliberately and his deep voice was heavy with a pronounced Welsh accent.[13] Standing six feet tall, with broad shoulders, a powerful neck, a "massive, placid face, with the ruddy complexion of his native Wales,"[14] and keen, alert blue eyes, Morgan Jones was an impressive young man. His early family responsibilities had matured him beyond his years. His calm, almost stolid, demeanor masked a restless, incessant energy which enabled him to do both mental and physical labor for twelve to sixteen hours every day.

On his arrival in New York City, he carried all his worldly

9 Letter from Longstaff to Jones (July 14, 1967).
10 Letter from John P. Creveling, prothonotary of Lehigh County, Allentown, Pennsylvania (January 2, 1968).
11 Interview with Morgan Jones, Jr., Abilene, Texas (November 7, 1967).
12 Interview with Mrs. Percy Jones, Abilene, Texas (July 11, 1967).
13 *Ibid.*
14 Frank Grimes, "Pioneers Laid to Rest," *West Texas Historical Association Year Book*, Vol. II (June, 1926), 85.

possessions in one medium-sized, leather-bound trunk. The manufacturer's description, printed on a label inside the lid, described not only the qualities of the trunk, but the qualities of its owner as well: "durable and tough . . . being practically indestructible."[15]

In the trunk were two newspapers which the immigrant kept in his possession to the day of his death. One, the Saturday edition of *The London Sun*, July 7, 1838, carried a full description of the coronation of Queen Victoria. The other, *The New York Herald*, dated April 15, 1865, described the assassination of President Lincoln.[16] They were odd souvenirs indeed for a man who rarely took time to look back, and yet they were symbolic of the loyalty Jones always felt toward his native and his adopted lands.

The mood of the new country vacillated between a state of emotional exhaustion and physical vigor. Morgan Jones was instantly conscious of the two minds—the two attitudes—in America. One group was deeply enmeshed in the political and philosophical residue of the Civil War. The other group regarded the recent conflict as a tragic disruption of the nation's industrial development. These "builders," eager to resume or to intensify their economic interests, left political recrimination to those of lesser vision. Jones, unfamiliar with the economic, social, or political causes of the sectional struggle, was, and continued to be, free of the self-destructive passions of the time. His interests and his talents drew him, as a magnet, toward the builders. He could not have arrived among them at a more opportune time.

Records do not reveal precisely Jones's activities during his first three years in the United States, but a few specific facts are known. He delivered his lading of explosives to General Dodge and, presumably, presented his credentials as an experienced railroader to him. This meeting proved tremendously significant to both men. During the next half-century, the energetic "builder" and the shrewd "promoter," both astute judges of human character, were intimate friends and business associates.[17] Dodge hired the im-

15 Morgan Jones Papers, in custody of Mrs. Percy Jones, 508 First National Ely Building, Abilene, Texas.
16 *Ibid.*
17 Interview with Mrs. Morgan Jones, Sr., Abilene, Texas (November 28, 1967).

pressive young immigrant and immediately placed him on the line as the foreman of one of the construction crews.[18]

Although they shared a mutual interest in railroading and worked together on one of the most significant construction projects ever attempted in American railroad history, the celebrated chief engineer and the unknown construction foreman had backgrounds as diverse as their responsibilities. General Dodge was a nationally famous war hero who had entered the Union Army as a colonel with his own Iowa regiment. Subsequently, President Lincoln promoted him to major general and made him responsible for keeping northern railroads repaired and open.

A native of Danvers, Massachusetts, Dodge worked his way through Norwich University, in Vermont. He graduated in 1851 near the head of his class with a degree in science. Later, at Partridge's private school, he received a diploma in civil and military engineering. During the 1850's, while Jones performed his duties at Vachwen and dreamed of employment with the Cambrian Railway Company, Dodge surveyed land and used his other engineering skills for the Illinois Central and the Rock Island railroads. During his boyhood days in New England, he, too, had caught "railroad fever" and, by the time he prepared himself for that profession, opportunities were greater in the states immediately adjacent to the Mississippi River.[19]

For three decades before Jones's arrival, American railroad construction developed spectacularly. The depression of 1857 and the holocaust of the Civil War years slowed the pace of new construction, but, at the end of the war, the reunited nation still boasted of more than thirty-five thousand miles of usable track. Less than one-tenth of the roads lay in that expanse of territory west of the Mississippi River. In the older and more densely

Mrs. Jones commented, "The Colonel was more devoted to General Dodge than to any other living person."

[18] Interview with W. G. Swenson, Abilene, Texas (November 9, 1967). Mr. Swenson recalls a conversation with Jones concerning this first assignment. Also, he saw a letter from one of Jones's Union Pacific friends (identity unknown) which referred to the same subject.

[19] For contrasting accounts of Grenville M. Dodge's career, compare Jacob Randolph Perkins, *Trails, Rails and War: The Life of General G. M. Dodge*, and Stanley P. Hirshson, *Grenville M. Dodge: Soldier, Politician, Railroad Pioneer*.

9

populated East, where construction began, railroads almost invariably pointed in a westerly direction. By the 1850's, the rails connected the Atlantic seaports with the Mississippi River towns.

During that decade also, locomotives operated west of the Mississippi. The first one completed its initial run on December 9, 1852. "The Pacific," falling short of its ambitious name, operated from St. Louis to Cheltenham, Missouri, a distance of five miles. The "General Sherman" in Texas (1853) and the "Albany" in Kansas (1860) traveled short distances on local lines.

Since the earliest years of the new industry, many proposals advanced the idea of a transcontinental railroad from the Atlantic to the Pacific seacoasts. From the mid-forties, members of Congress discussed the possibilities and debated location of routes. The discovery of gold in California in 1848 and the admission of that state into the Union in 1850 instigated greater action. Congress, anticipating the possibility of a southern route, purchased a strip of territory in northern Mexico for $10,000,000. This "Gadsden Purchase" included two passes through the mountains, the Messila Valley and the Río Grande Valley, through which the southern transcontinental could be built at a minimum elevation.

Also anticipating a southern route to the Pacific, the Texas legislature granted nearly seventy-five railroad charters during the years from 1852 to 1856. Southern optimism increased again when Secretary of War Jefferson Davis recommended, after extensive surveys, the thirty-second parallel of latitude as the most logical route for a transcontinental railroad.

Others, however, advocated a northern or a middle route across the trans-Mississippi West and, as sectional jealousies multiplied during the late 1850's, possibilities for an unbiased decision lessened. Congressional debate on the issue less frequently centered around distance or cost.

The outbreak of the Civil War eliminated the southern route from further consideration. President Lincoln, following the advice of such knowledgeable men as General Dodge, recommended to Congress that the nation's first transcontinental railroad be located so as to compromise the demands of those who proposed the middle or northern routes. Consequently, Congress passed the Pacific Railroad Acts of 1862 and 1864 which provided financial assistance for the construction of the road. The acts designated Council Bluffs, Iowa, as the eastern terminus, with connecting lines from the east serving both middle and northern states.

Westward from Omaha, Nebraska, the Union Pacific Railroad built toward the Rocky Mountains. The Central Pacific Railroad, meanwhile, built eastward from Sacramento, California. In May, 1866, General Dodge began his duties as chief engineer of the Union Pacific, which, at that time, reached a point only a few miles west of Omaha. Before the end of that month, Morgan Jones, having safely delivered the shipment of dynamite to the General, joined the company's construction crew.

Jones and Dodge had few opportunities to become well acquainted during these years of joint effort. Jones, with his small crew, worked close to the rails, while Dodge's responsibilities kept him constantly afield. Jones soon learned that American railroad construction was quite unlike anything in his past experience. Building the Union Pacific involved two elements—time and distance—which had little to do with his work on the Cambrian railroad. "It was entirely different from my railroad experience in South Wales," he reflected many years later, "but I knuckled to the job and pretty soon was able to hold my own."[20] By the time the rails of the Union Pacific and the Central Pacific met, Jones was justly proud of his contribution.

The construction company completed the project several months earlier than predicted—an accomplishment which amazed the young Welshman. Almost exactly three years from the date he had arrived in New York, he observed, from an appropriate distance, the celebrated "joining of the rails" at Promontory Summit, Utah.[21] On several occasions more than seven miles of track had been laid in one day. Jones never forgot this exercise in rapid construction. In later years, his ability to meet seemingly impossible construction deadlines became legend in the Southwest.

20 Crozier, *Dallas News*, 8.
21 Interview with W. G. Swenson (November 9, 1967).

11

Long before his first American employment ended at Promontory Summit in 1869, Jones knew that he wanted to remain in the United States and build more railroads. He filed a declaration of intention to become an American citizen[22] and familiarized himself with other building projects around the country. Finally, when the transcontinental line was complete, Morgan Jones, now more experienced in his trade, eager for larger responsibilities, and approaching his thirtieth birthday, went to Washington, D.C. There was in that city, he learned, another famous man who wanted to build a railroad to the Pacific. General John C. Frémont, soldier, explorer, and former aspirant to the American Presidency, had caught "railroad fever."

The General and other men of wealth and influence in the East still held to the conviction that a southern railroad should be built across Texas and the far Southwest. The old survey made in the 1850's had emphasized three advantages of this route: it was the shortest overland route,[23] it had the most favorable climate, and it had the lowest elevation. Had the Civil War not intervened, these important factors likely would have dictated a southern location of the first transcontinental. The exact location of the rails across Texas would have been determined at a later date.

Of all the many railroad charters granted by the Texas legislature in the 1850's, only two produced any reasonable hope of laying rail across the entire state: the Southern Pacific Railroad Company[24] (formerly The Texas Western Railroad Company) and the Memphis, El Paso and Pacific Railroad Company. The latter road, with its eastern terminus at Memphis, was to have connected with the Southern Pacific, out of New Orleans, somewhere in the vicinity of Dallas. It was hoped that from there they could form a common trunk line across Texas.

Frémont and his associates invested in the Memphis, El Paso

---

[22] Creveling letter (January 2, 1968).

[23] Actually, the comparative distances from coast to coast were not significant. From New York to San Francisco, the distance was 3,323 miles. From New York to San Diego, by the southern route, would be 3,133 miles. Of greater importance was the fact that New York freight could be shipped by boat to New Orleans and thence to San Diego by rail. This would involve only 1,800 miles of overland travel.

[24] No connection with the present company of that name.

12

and Pacific[25] in 1867 and had financial difficulties from the beginning. In an effort to secure stronger financial support, the ME & P reorganized in 1870 as the Southern Trans-Continental Railroad Company. It was at this point in the reorganization that General Frémont and Morgan Jones met in Washington. Jones received a contract to build a section of the line, called the Jefferson Branch, between Texarkana and Jefferson, Texas.[26] The young contractor hurried to his new assignment and gathered his construction crew along the way.

Financial problems continued to plague the struggling company. Jones was never sure when, or if, he would be paid for his work. He managed to keep his crew's loyalty, and together they stayed on the job until, finally, the Southern Trans-Continental Railroad Company, like its predecessor, failed and all work along the line stopped.

There were rumors, however, that a new company would soon resume the project. In spite of the debts he had incurred, Jones was anxious to resume the project as soon as the new company could be reorganized. To keep his construction crew together, he contracted to work on a short line being built from Fort Smith, Arkansas, to Little Rock. Some of his associates, meanwhile, urged him to sue his former employers for the money due him. He shrewdly rejected the suggestion. "I couldn't see the advantages of a lawsuit," he explained later. "If my claim had been paid I would have had an efficient organization and no work to do, because I couldn't get any more contracts."[27]

Instead, he explained the situation to his men, saw to it that they had plenty to eat, found them temporary work in Arkansas, and they, in turn, stuck by him. He had followed a wise course. Within a year eastern financiers reorganized the company and Jones received a new contract. The new company paid Jones's claims against the old.

25 John A. Wright, *A Paper on the Character and Promise of the Country on the Southern Border*, 46; see Virginia H. Taylor, *The Franco-Texan Land Company*, Chap. 1, for an excellent summary of Frémont's association with the Memphis, El Paso and Pacific Railroad.

26 *The Texas Almanac for 1872*, 60.

27 Crozier, *Dallas News*, 8.

13

Congress incorporated the Texas and Pacific Railroad Company[28] on March 3, 1871. The charter authorized the construction of a railroad along the thirty-second parallel of latitude from Marshall, Texas, to the Pacific Coast. The new company, under the authority of Congress and the state of Texas, acquired some of the properties of the defunct Southern Pacific and the Southern Trans-Continental railroads. The new company's history, consequently, through the old Texas Western Railroad Company, dated back to 1852.

The Texas and Pacific was directed by bold, vigorous men familiar with the intricacies of the railroad industry. Its president was Thomas A. Scott, former vice-president and general manager of the Pennsylvania line, who during the war years had been superintendent of all Union railroads. General Grenville M. Dodge became chief engineer. He had resigned a similar position with the Union Pacific six months after that road was completed.[29] Since then he had spent most of his time surveying western lands for the Union Pacific and building a permanent home for his family in Council Bluffs, Iowa.[30] Dodge, lured into the new project, accepted T & P's offer of a $20,000 annual salary.[31] He set up his office at Marshall, Texas, the initial part of the road.

The California and Texas Construction Company was organized on August 6, 1872, to build west from Marshall. According to the terms of the company's charter, at least one hundred miles of track had to be in operation within two years, and the entire line completed to the Pacific within ten years.[32]

Dodge, on his arrival in Texas, granted Jones a new contract. At that time he made arrangements to pay—both principal and interest—the old debts from the Southern Trans-Continental.[33]

28 The name was later changed to the Texas and Pacific Railway Company.
29 Richard C. Overton, *Gulf to Rockies: The Heritage of the Fort Worth and Denver–Colorado and Southern Railways, 1861–1898*, 66.
30 Hirshson, *Grenville M. Dodge: Soldier, Politician, Railroad Pioneer*, 178.
31 J. B. Shores, *From Ox-Teams to Eagles: A History of the Texas and Pacific Railway*, 13. (Publishers, place of publication, and date are unknown. The book was apparently prepared by the company. This copy was loaned to the author by Mr. R. A. Malone, assistant director of Public Relations, The Texas and Pacific Offices, Dallas, Texas.)
32 *Ibid.*, 14.
33 Crozier, *Dallas News*, 8.

Some of the masterminds of the nation were at work on the T & P. Spirits were high. President Scott, with the enthusiasm of an evangelist, preached the glories of the untapped wealth of Texas. Chief engineer Dodge organized surveying parties and awarded construction contracts. Marshall, Texas, was a beehive of activity. Jones, with his crew, was busily at work grubbing the old grade just west of Sulphur Creek.[34] Five thousand men and three thousand teams pushed the project along at a rapid pace. The Texas winter was mild, and from Marshall to Dallas, elevation above the sea increased only 104 feet.[35] By late spring the crew graded four hundred miles along the main line and its branches, tracklayers followed them, and bridge-building crews spanned the rivers along the route.

Warmer weather brought problems. First, epizootic broke out among the mules, and Jones reported that his work was seriously hampered.[36] Then almost all the working force fell victim to yellow fever.[37] The men used barrels of redeye whisky, however reluctantly, as an insect repellent.[38] Oxen and teams hauled supplies of all kinds forty to sixty miles because the water level in the Red River fell so low.[39]

Minor problems interspersed the major ones. Men still able to work, and who worked without pay on many occasions, almost went berserk every payday when storekeepers were unable to provide exact change for their checks. The situation grew serious enough that Dodge was forced to instruct the company officials not to send checks in dollars and cents. "There are no pennies in Marshall," he explained.[40]

The Panic of 1873 brought progress on the road almost to a standstill. Jay Cooke's collapse on September 2 went virtually unnoticed in local Texas papers, but the effects of the depression

[34] Dodge to Jones (January 8, 1873), Grenville M. Dodge Papers, Iowa State Department of History and Archives, Des Moines, Iowa, VIII (No. 597).

[35] Wright, *The Country on the Southern Border*, 62.

[36] Crozier, *Dallas News*, 8.

[37] Dodge to Nathan Dodge (December 22, 1873), Grenville M. Dodge Letters (No. 423), Box No. 2, Denver Public Library.

[38] Interview with R. A. Malone, Dallas, Texas (November 8, 1967).

[39] Wright, *The Country on the Southern Border*, 62.

[40] Interview with R. A. Malone (November 8, 1967).

eventually spread throughout the country. Unpaid railroad laborers abandoned the T & P and roadbeds began to deteriorate. The company faced obligations totaling $4,500,000 which must be paid within the year. President Scott, unable to sell more of the T & P bonds in the United States, made a hurried trip to Europe where he had even less success. Once again Morgan Jones was not paid on schedule. For the first time since his arrival in the United States he was forced to borrow money from his Welsh relatives so that he could feed his workmen.[41]

President Scott finally managed to persuade the banks and financial houses in the East to extend their credit. Gradually conditions improved and the company's work resumed. The new year brought increased activity, and by March 1, 1874, one could travel by rail from St. Louis to Dallas, Texas. On the T & P branch lines, however, major gaps were unfilled. Connections had not been made between Brookston and Nash in northeast Texas nor from Sherman south to Fort Worth. Construction at the western end of the road reached Eagle Ford, just west of Dallas. With the T & P in debt and unable to continue with its original plans to build into West Texas, the railroad company and the construction company agreed to cancel their contract.[42]

"There wasn't much doing in Texas during 1875 in the way of railroad building," according to Jones.[43] After his recent experiences in East Texas, he looked around for more profitable work. Various reports about West Texas made him curious to see that country through which the T & P had hoped to build. According to President Scott, West Texas had inexhaustible quantities of gold, silver, and copper. He heard, also, of the fabulous riches of northern Mexico; but for the indolence of its people, it was said, that nation could be one of the richest in the world. Another report written by R. W. Raymond in 1869 described the silver and gold deposits "lying along the east base of the Sierras, and stretching southward into Mexico."[44]

41 Interview with Mrs. Percy Jones (July 11, 1967).
42 Wright, *The Country on the Southern Border*, 49–52.
43 Crozier, *Dallas News*, 8.
44 Wright, *The Country on the Southern Border*, 20, 21.

16

Intrigued by these stories, Morgan Jones eagerly accepted when Judge Bell of Austin invited him to accompany him on a prospecting trip in the Davis Mountains of southwest Texas. They rode the stage to Fort Davis and from there made prospecting trips into the mountains. The two located silver ore in the area and with the assistance of the United States consul at Presidio del Norte transported some of the ore to Chihuahua with a team of oxen. The journey was so difficult, however, and the location of the ore so remote from railroad transportation that they decided silver mining in the area could not be done profitably.

Returning to Fort Davis, Jones decided to see more of Mexico and to visit some of the working mines in that country. He bought an old army ambulance from the troops stationed at the fort and for several months toured many isolated regions south of the border. The mining industry interested him, but his thoughts turned back inevitably to railroading. He read reports which proposed a railroad to Mexico City via the trends of the mountain ranges and valleys, but as he traveled the country, he dreamed instead of a great railroad line across northern Mexico to the Pacific.[45] He needed immediate employment, however, so he returned to East Texas to check on recent railroad developments there.

He found the little town of Fort Worth, population 1,600, in a state of extreme agitation; only sixteen miles separated its city limits from the T & P tracks at Eagle Ford. Determined to bring the railroad into town, the citizens organized the Tarrant County Construction Company. The Texas and Pacific Railway Company was equally eager to reach Fort Worth. The company's charter would be revoked if its rails did not reach Fort Worth by the end of the present session of the Texas legislature.

Governor Brown of Tennessee, receiver of the T & P at the time, appealed to Morgan Jones to complete the line into Fort Worth. Short of money and aware of the almost impossible task facing the railroad, Jones hesitated to accept the offer.[46] It was a chance to

[45] Jones never lost this dream. Even in the 1920's, Jones hoped to build a railroad to Topolobampo, Mexico.
[46] Grimes, "Pioneers Laid to Rest," *loc. cit.*, 87.

17

return to railroading, however, and he took the assignment. Within weeks he directed one of the most dramatic accomplishments in the annals of Texas railroading. As a result of this brief race against time, his abilities as a builder of railroads became legend throughout the Southwest.

2. EMERGENCE OF A MASTER

CONDITIONS in East Texas in the 1870's resembled those in the deep South. The Civil War brought the same economic, social, and political disorder to its people, but to a slightly less traumatic degree.[1] The three most thickly settled eastern regions of the state, the pine woods, the Gulf Coast plain, and the post oak belt, suffered the same loss of slave labor. Similarly, many free white laborers did not return from the battlefields. On the other hand, the war did not destroy Texas railroads as thoroughly as it did those east of the Mississippi River. Since Union armies did not gain control of the state until 1865, there was no need to carry out wholesale destruction of railroad property. By the end of the conflict, only two roads had been destroyed and two abandoned of the eleven in operation in 1861.[2] The remaining seven, their roadbeds neglected and their rolling stock generally deteriorated, managed to serve farmers and ranchers as before.

Landowners generally refused to employ free Negro labor. Texans did whatever they could to encourage white men from any state or any European nation to settle among them. As the nation's economic conditions improved, immigrants from northwestern

[1] S. S. McKay, "Economic Conditions in Texas in the 1870s," *West Texas Historical Association Year Book*, Vol. XV (October, 1939), 84.

[2] Charles S. Potts, "Railroad Transportation in Texas," *Bulletin of the University of Texas*, No. 119 of the Humanistic Series, No. 7 (1909), 36.

Europe and the Iberian Peninsula, as well as displaced Southerners, infiltrated the unclaimed land.[3]

Earlier settlers in the East Texas regions had come largely from the states of the deep South—Louisiana, Mississippi, Alabama, Tennessee, the Carolinas, and Virginia—and were primarily of Scottish, Irish, and English descent.[4] They settled Texas in the 1840's and 1850's for the same reason that their ancestors had pushed across the Alleghenies almost a century before, to get good free or cheap land.

Wherever possible, these immigrants settled along watercourses in a manner not unlike the early settlers along the Atlantic Coast. Small agricultural communities dotted the banks of the Sabine, Neches, Trinity, Brazos, and Colorado rivers. Unlike the eastern rivers, all were navigable only for comparatively short distances from the coast. Texas pioneers, therefore, pushed the Indian tribes westward to where the water levels prohibited transportation. Having come from wooded regions in the East, they believed that running water proved the fertility of the soil. Prairie lands, left vacant except for the Indian tribes, remained that way until the later development of the cattle industry.

By the end of the Civil War, the grand prairie region, just west of the blackland prairie, was called "West Texas" and beyond it lay the frontier. The westward movement of the Texas frontier stopped, and then receded, during the years of the war. In 1865 the frontier line lay roughly along the dividing line of the Gulf coastal plains and the interior plains of north-central Texas. New immigrants moved into this area of West Texas in response to current literature.

The *Texas Rural Almanac* invited even the penniless to the Lone Star State, promising that "in two years [one could] be independent." A man could get provisions advanced, dry goods "on credit," and land which he could pay for later. After one year he

3 John S. Spratt, *The Road to Spindletop: Economic Change in Texas, 1875–1901*, viii.
4 "Early Settlement of Northeast Texas," *Frontier Times*, Vol. V (November, 1927), quoted in Bulletin No. 327 (College Station, Texas Agricultural Experiment Station [n.d.]), 57.

could become a rancher "without using the means resulting from the farm."[5]

To those young men going west, Horace Greeley recommended the sparsely settled areas of Texas. In *The New York Tribune*, in 1872, he described to his readers "the rich level prairie, covered with horses and cattle." He emphasized the welcome they could expect from a legislature eager to "encourage the transfer of lands from the non-residents to the cultivators."[6] One hundred million fertile acres were held by absentee owners who must sell them or lose them to tax collectors. Most of the land, he believed, sold for one dollar an acre. In terms which undoubtedly pleased the most patriotic Texan, Greeley wrote:

arth by railroads into squares ten
ve thousand square miles of coal
as gypsum enough to plaster the
She has more land good for wheat
s of excellent timber. . . . [There
ises now impatiently awaiting the

migrant's Hand Book praised
"With her bright skies, genial
] to the poor and homeless 'as

s approached one million. New
at the state's increase consider-
ge. In that year approximately
e land—a figure roughly similar
ier. The average Texan owned
e state then unoccupied by the
rmers produced only for home
espread practice of the barter
orn, wheat, chickens, eggs, and

s, Vol. I, No. 3 (December, 1923), 7.
and Book for 1876, 78–79.

pecans for purchases in town. There they received in return such household items as sugar, coffee, salt, and calico. Their selection was limited. The local storekeeper had few if any competitors, and the next town was beyond the reach of his customers. Galveston, the largest city in the state, had fourteen thousand people, and the only other towns with populations large enough to be more than "villages" were San Antonio, Austin, and Houston. Waco, Dallas, and Fort Worth struggled to survive.

When Morgan Jones returned from his mining expedition in far West Texas and Mexico in early 1876, Dallas was considerably larger than Fort Worth and, each month, grew more rapidly. The arrival of the Texas and Pacific Railroad in Dallas in 1874 accounted for her recent rapid growth. Dallas was the distributing point for farmers and ranchers of old "West Texas," just east of the frontier line. Local jealousies between Dallas and Fort Worth had developed as early as 1856. In November of that year, a spirited contest erupted between Birdville and Fort Worth, on opposite sides of the Trinity River. Each sought the county seat of Tarrant County. Dallas supported the claims of Birdville and contributed several barrels of whisky for voters who supported her cause. Although Fort Worth won the election by thirteen votes, her citizens never forgot Dallas' interference.[10]

The feud intensified during the next two decades. When, in 1874, construction of the Texas and Pacific Railroad stopped at Eagle Ford, businessmen in Fort Worth mourned the consequences. Without a railroad, they could not continue their dream to build their little town into a metropolitan gateway to the West. From its earliest days as a trading post, however, the town struggled to survive.

Fort Worth began as an army camp on June 6, 1849. Shortly after the Republic of Texas joined the United States, Major General William Jenkins Worth commanded the Texas station along the Texas frontier. It was his duty to protect the Indians and the settlers from each other. With less than one thousand troops—

10 "Fort Worth, 1849–1949," *Fort Worth Chamber of Commerce Magazine*, Vol. XXIII (June, 1949), 24–25.

which nevertheless made up approximately one-tenth of the United States Army—he guarded the territory along the Río Grande to the south, the territory along the Red River to the north, and five hundred miles of the Texas frontier between the two rivers. General Worth directed Major Ripley Arnold to erect a fort along the north-south frontier line in order to protect the northern section of the state.[11] Major Arnold selected a site just below the juncture of the West and Clear forks of the Trinity River. He named the station Camp Worth in memory of the General, who had died one month before on May 7, 1849. The army occupied Camp Worth until 1853 and then abandoned it. A few settlers in the area moved into the unoccupied buildings and established a trading post. They called it "Fort" Worth although it had no aspects of a fort. Slowly other buildings began to shape up a town square. The first lawyer arrived before the town was a year old, and the first physician, Dr. Carroll M. Peak, opened his office there in 1853.[12]

By the outbreak of the Civil War, Tarrant County citizens were almost as western as southern. Approximately one thousand men in the county voted on the issue of secession, and the Secessionists won by a majority of fifty-three.[13] The largest slaveowner in the area owned only twenty-six slaves. The frontier was still so near that one could stand at the town square and see tipis of the Caddo Indians scattered along Marine Creek.[14] Fort Worth in 1861 was relatively prosperous and the Indians were relatively peaceful, but in that year Texas went to war.

When the conflict ended, the little village was destitute. It shared with the state the uncertainties and turmoil of Reconstruction. Indians pillaged near by. In town, houses and former businesses stood unclaimed. Fort Worth seemed destined to become a ghost town, and only the arrival of Major K. M. Van Zandt, coincidental with "a bunch of well-heeled Yankees" eager to develop the cattle industry, saved it from such a fate.[15]

Major Van Zandt was a lawyer without a practice when he

11 Oliver Knight, *Fort Worth: Outpost on the Trinity*, 8–9.
12 "Fort Worth, 1849–1949," *loc. cit.*, 20.
13 James Farber, *Fort Worth in the Civil War*, 11.
14 *Ibid.*
15 *Ibid.*, 52.

arrived with his family in late 1865. He was the son of a former minister to the United States during the years of the Texas Republic. During the war he commanded the Seventh Texas Infantry.[16] Van Zandt and other new arrivals believed that Fort Worth was destined to become an important "cow town." He opened a dry-goods store, helped to erect a courthouse, and supported efforts to build a new high school. Slowly the village revived. For several years in succession crops were good, and, as Van Zandt anticipated, Fort Worth was soon the major stop on the cattle trail to the North. Once again citizens spread the old rumor that a railroad would soon reach the town.

When the outbreak of the Civil War ended any possibility that the first transcontinental railroad would follow a southern route, it ended, also, Fort Worth's dream. After the war, hope arose and then descended as repeated attempts to build railroads in East Texas failed. When the Texas and Pacific Railroad Company received a new charter, the old confidence of local citizens returned. News in 1874 that the T & P would cease construction at Eagle Ford, just sixteen miles short of Fort Worth, brought cries of outrage in Fort Worth.

Unable, or unwilling, to understand another delay, the citizens bitterly denounced all railroad officials. The townsmen refused to accept President Thomas A. Scott's statement that he was "embarrassed" by the delay.[17] They knew that the company suffered from the epidemics of 1873; they knew that President Scott held controlling interest in the Texas and Pacific; and they knew that the New York financial house of Jay Cooke & Company held most of the liens on the railroad. But when Cooke's financial empire collapsed on September 2, 1873, they refused to acknowledge the correlative relationship of these facts. Cooke's failure went unobserved in the *Fort Worth Democrat*'s September 7 weekly edition. Local sacrifices during the past few years overshadowed all of the company's problems.

Two years earlier, Fort Worth had invited Mr. Scott to the town.

16 Knight, *Fort Worth: Outpost on the Trinity*, 54.
17 Third Annual Report of the Board of Directors of the Texas and Pacific Railway Company to the Stockholders, 7.

24

He asked the city fathers for a railroad right-of-way and a few acres for terminal buildings and yards. Major Van Zandt and others, eager to show their willingness to make personal sacrifices for the road, donated, in the name of the town, 360 acres of the town's most valuable real estate. This assured the road to Fort Worth and the number of new arrivals sharply increased. Twenty-five hundred immigrants created a boom town. City lots doubled in value overnight.

The bubble burst with the disappointing news from Eagle Ford that construction had stopped once again. Property sold for half its worth, if it sold at all. City funds disappeared, and officers of the city government served without salary. Campfires of immigrants who hurriedly departed for Dallas and other points east "made a flickering string of light from the edge of town to Dallas."[18] Whether or not these persons recognized what was happening, Fort Worth was in the midst of a national panic. The Texas and Pacific released its construction crews, and it was at this time that Morgan Jones, accompanied by Judge Bell, sought greener pastures in Mexico.

There was no place for others to go. Such men as B. B. Paddock, the editor of the local newspaper, preferred to stay. He had arrived in Fort Worth during the prosperous days of 1872 from his home in Mississippi. He was a veteran of the late war and a recent law student, but when Major Van Zandt offered him a job as editor of the *Fort Worth Democrat*, he accepted.[19] The young man quickly became the town's most loyal promoter. From the beginning he devoted more space to Texas and Pacific activities than to any other subject. His readers learned to expect lengthy items concerning the company's plans in every issue of the paper. He minutely dissected and sometimes editorialized upon the most improbable railroad rumor. Paddock's editorials rose and fell with the town's spirits. At times they expressed hope, optimism, enthusiasm, and confidence. Just as often they reflected pessimism, despondency, cynicism, and disappointment.

18 "Fort Worth, 1849–1949," *loc. cit.*, 28.
19 Knight, *Fort Worth: Outpost on the Trinity*, 64–65.

25

He condemned the railroad's inactivity but denounced with equal vehemence any effort in the state legislature to revoke the company's charter. He opposed extension of the charter as long as he believed the road could be built into Fort Worth within the allotted time, but supported without reservation an additional period of time when it was evident that the deadline could not possibly be met.

On January 3, 1874, Paddock asked the representatives in Austin to refuse to delay the deadline. "They have not shown even ordinary interest in securing by the sale of lands or bonds the necessary funds to complete the road according to contract."[20] When, later that month, R. E. Montgomery came to Fort Worth and informed the residents that General Grenville M. Dodge, chief engineer of the T & P, required more aid from the town in order to complete the line, Paddock supported the effort to raise subscriptions "under the condition that the Texas and Pacific resume construction by February 15."[21] He also supported the company's request that Congress lend its aid by a guaranty on the interest on the T & P's 5 per cent bonds,[22] but within two weeks he accused the company of "making no sacrifices, no inconveniences."[23] He insisted that the line to Fort Worth required only six months' work and, consequently, opposed in March the railroad's request for another extension of time to December 15.[24]

When, in May, the California and Texas Construction Company resumed construction, Paddock chided the "doubting Thomases'" for their drooping spirits.[25] He described in exhilarating detail the progress of the work on the first section west of Dallas, and refused to believe rumors that the company planned construction only to Eagle Ford.[26] It was, he said, only a vicious *Dallas Herald* rumor. The editor supported T & P's request that Fort

---

20 *Fort Worth Democrat* (January 3, 1874), 2.
21 *Ibid.* (January 31, 1874), 1.
22 *Ibid.* (February 21, 1874), 1.
23 *Ibid.* (March 7, 1874), 1.
24 *Ibid.* (March 14, 1874), 2.
25 *Ibid.* (May 23, 1874), 2.
26 *Ibid.* (June 20, 1874), 2.

26

Worth citizens buy $30,000 of 7 per cent bonds, and reminded his "generous, patriotic, liberal, self-sacrificing" readers that "the world was not built in a day."[27]

In January, 1875, a group of "railroad magnates" visited Fort Worth. The tireless promoter reported every move and every casual statement from the time of their arrival on the 2:40 P.M. stage. With an overly eager editorial finger, he pointed to the Fort Worth Cornet Band and reminded the visitors that the "stirring pieces" were in their honor. Almost desperate for a word of encouragement from them, he said, ". . . we hope this visit means something."[28]

Two months later Paddock was outraged when the Fourteenth Legislature granted the gentlemen's request for another time extension to January 1, 1876, "against the wishes of ninety-nine per cent of the people."[29] Yet he published a letter from President Scott to Samuel B. Maxey of Paris, Texas, which convinced him that the company planned "something constructive" to renew work on the road. In the letter Scott explained the reorganization of the company and the reason it canceled the California and Texas Construction Company's contract. The railroad company itself planned to complete the line to Fort Worth in time to handle the fall crops.[30]

By late summer, however, Paddock lamented the fact that construction had not resumed. Still optimistic, he cautioned his readers not to ignore, "with a shrug of the shoulders," the latest rumor that the project would begin in September. He assured them that the Texas and Pacific did not intend to forfeit its land subsidy. He reminded the businessmen that, upon completion of the railroad to Fort Worth, their town would take away seven-tenths of the business then enjoyed in Dallas.[31]

Harvest time passed, still without further construction. The indomitable promoter, finally convinced that the railroad company would lose its charter and, thereby, abandon the project, began a

27 *Ibid.* (September 26, 1874), 2.
28 *Ibid.* (January 23, 1875), 2.
29 *Ibid.* (March 20, 1875), 3.
30 *Ibid.* (June 5, 1875), 2.
31 *Ibid.* (September 25, 1875), 2.

new crusade. "If the Texas and Pacific cannot build . . . we must look elsewhere; . . . railroad transportation must be had."[32]

Responding to the call, a group of Fort Worth businessmen agreed upon a plan unique at the time in Texas railroad construction. They pooled their resources and organized the Tarrant County Construction Company. Its permanent officers included Major Van Zandt, president; John S. Hirshfield, vice-president; Jesse Zane-Cetti, secretary; and W. A. Huffman, treasurer. The local company agreed to a contract with the Texas and Pacific, and Editor Paddock shook "every bush for capital and brains to carry out the undertaking ahead."[33] Finally, the construction company let a contract to Roche Brothers and Tierney to build the tracks into the city.

Again, Fort Worth business improved. All vacant houses rented or sold, stages brought in more people, who overcrowded, for the first time in two years, every hotel in town. In November, the Tarrant County Construction Company increased its capital stock to $100,000 and subscriptions poured in.[34] Hopes soared when Major D. W. Washburn, an engineer for the Texas and Pacific, arrived on November 11 and closed a contract the following day to grade the first eleven sections of the road east of Fort Worth. These sections comprised about three-fourths of the distance to Eagle Ford.[35]

The editor of the *Fort Worth Democrat*, once again supremely confident, informed his readers that work would begin within a few days and would be "prosecuted vigorously until completed." Each issue of the paper reported "a bouyancy of spirits and a renewal of energy" unlike anything since the "palmy days of 1873." The surrounding area had been "steady [*sic*] filling up with sturdy enterprising farmers, whose enterprise will react on the town."[36] Fort Worth's future indeed looked bright.

The Texas legislature provided additional reason to rejoice

32 *Ibid.* (October 2, 1875), 2.
33 "Fort Worth, 1849–1949," *loc. cit.*, 32.
34 *Fort Worth Democrat* (November 6, 1875), 1.
35 *Ibid.* (November 13, 1875), 1.
36 *Ibid.*

when, once again and for the final time, it extended T & P's deadline into Fort Worth. The last ordinance instructed the company to reach the city with its rails, and a locomotive, by June 6, the intended adjournment date of the next session of the legislature. Editor Paddock, sure of his successful crusade but acutely aware of past disappointments, warned the company that "they will not be shown any more favors."[37] Hence his "warning" was consistent with his conviction that the rails could be completed within a six-month period.

As the railroad inched its way westward, a dizzying wave of excitement swept through Fort Worth. Exhilaration turned to pride and pride quickly turned to bombast. Old resentments and jealousies toward Dallas developed into a swaggering braggadocio. The Dallas *Commercial*, conversely, revealed that city's anxiety over the effects of the railroad's westward extension. Its November 19 issue suggested to Dallasites that the Texas and Pacific "might possibly be . . . an enemy instead of a friend."[38] It boasted, without conviction, that Dallas, at least, was "not owned by a railroad" and apparently attempted to convince itself, as well as its local readers, that Fort Worth and the Texas and Pacific were "both too impecunious" to do Dallas any injury.

Paddock reprinted such articles in the *Fort Worth Democrat* and assured his readers that they proved Dallas' impending economic decline. "Examine the map of Texas, and measure the relative distances from the counties west to the two places," he exhorted. Farmers from Wise, Parker, Hood, and Johnson counties and from even greater distances to the north and west no longer would need to make the long ox-wagon journey to Dallas with their wheat. Fort Worth mills would replace those in Dallas. They would exchange their flour for household goods in the Fort Worth stores. Fort Worth would surely become "the trading center for all farmers and ranchers in the western counties."

The exuberant editor, eager to continue the debate, then reminded Dallasites that Fort Worth enjoyed other natural advantages:

37 *Ibid.* (November 27, 1875), 1.
38 *Ibid.*, quoted in the Dallas *Commercial*.

We ask them to consult the map and the topography of northern Texas, and they will find Fort Worth situated on a high commanding, limestone bluff at the intersection of the Clear and West forks of the Trinity River, one hundred and ten feet above the level of these streams, where it is fanned by the passing breezes, and where it is above all the malarial influences that may be found in the river bottoms, and which insures it undisputed health, year in and year out. It is surrounded for a hundred miles in either direction with a country whose fertility is unexcelled on the Continent. . . . Here may be found prairie and forest, woodland and stream, all suited and adapted to the diversified tastes and inclinations of men.[39]

Promotion turned into prognostication. He forecast such an extensive railway development for Fort Worth that even his loyal readers good-naturedly derided him.[40] He published a map with Fort Worth represented by a central black dot. From it he drew nine black lines, radiating in every direction, which represented future railroads. Local citizens called it the "tarantula."[41] Dallasites called him a "slightly teched dreamer."[42] Undaunted, Paddock predicted that Fort Worth would become the converging point for the Red River and Río Grande branch of the Missouri, Kansas and Texas Railway Company; the Waco and Fort Worth extension of the Houston and Texas Central; the Fort Worth and Denver Railway Company; and the Beaumont, Corsicana and Fort Worth Railroad.

His predictions were not without foundation. The Missouri, Kansas and Texas already enjoyed a profitable cattle trade and, to keep it, the company needed to construct its Red River and Río Grande branch.[43] To compete for that trade, the Texas and Pacific needed to complete its Trans-Continental branch to give it greater control of the northern-bound cattle and other products from

39 *Ibid.* (November 27, 1875), 1.

40 *Fort Worth Star-Telegram* (April 26, 1931), magazine section, 12.

41 *Ibid.* Editor Paddock's predictions proved to be amazingly accurate. Eventually, nine lines originated or passed through Fort Worth and, appropriately enough, Paddock was president of the last road built into the city. Dates of the first trains completed to Fort Worth: Texas and Pacific, July 19, 1876; Santa Fe, January 1, 1882; Fort Worth and Denver City, April 30, 1882; Southern Pacific, December 6, 1886; Frisco Lines, October 1, 1887; Cotton Belt, April 14, 1888; Missouri, Kansas and Texas, November 1, 1888; Rock Island, July 30, 1893; Missouri Pacific, May 1, 1903. (Fort Worth and Denver City Files, 1230A.)

42 "Fort Worth, 1849–1949," *loc. cit.*, 28.

30

Texas.[44] With the completion of those lines, Paddock expected St. Louis to offer greater inducements and better facilities to secure the Texas trade.[45] To meet that competition, therefore, the coastal cities must build additional railroad lines. The Houston and Texas Central had no choice, as Paddock explained it, but to build its Waco and Fort Worth branch leading directly to Fort Worth.

As a result of these railroad communications, Paddock prophesied that "beef packeries," tanneries, mills, machine shops, and foundries would make Fort Worth "the richest and most prosperous city in the interior of Texas."[46] Maliciously, he asked his Dallas antagonists "not to tear up the rails, destroy the grade, burn the bridges, or do anything else that might make them ridiculous to we [sic] frontier people."[47]

Through the winter months, the *Fort Worth Democrat* published extensive reports about Texas and Pacific construction. Each week the editor counted and reported the exact number of "teams" and "hands" at work. Every new bridge and every additional mile of grading represented another milestone. The city's growth competed for attention. New houses to satisfy the needs of the incoming crowds, new hotels to accommodate the "drummers" and other businessmen, new restaurants to feed them, and new saloons to keep them happy—all reflected the activities of a prosperous town. The announcement that the railroad depot would be located between, and at the end of, Houston and Main streets instigated a brisk trade among real-estate men.

On May 20, 1876, Paddock announced "to the world" that sufficient iron had been purchased to grade, bridge, and iron the road all the way to Fort Worth. In the same issue, he reported that the railroad company had relieved the Tarrant County Construction Company of its labors and that the railroad company itself

43 *Texas Rural Almanac for 1873*, 36.

44 Paddock apparently based his predictions on information from the *Texas Almanac*.

45 Again Paddock's reasoning was sound. Texas freight helped to make St. Louis one of the major marketing centers for the Southwest. The "St. Louis drummer" became a familiar sight in Fort Worth.

46 *Fort Worth Democrat* (November 26, 1875), 1.

47 *Ibid.*

planned to complete the work.[48] Both announcements assured the editor that the Texas and Pacific rails would soon reach the city.

The railroad company meanwhile wrestled with the more serious problem of saving its land subsidy. The new session of the state legislature had opened on the second Tuesday of January, 1876. The Texas and Pacific immediately had requested another deadline extension to complete its construction into Fort Worth. The railroad's friends had managed by a narrow margin to gain more time through the new agreement which provided that the rails must reach Fort Worth before that session of the legislature adjourned.

The company had made every effort to speed construction, but the realization that certain legislators were determined to adjourn on June 6, as previously announced, almost destroyed hope that the Texas and Pacific could save its charter and claim its land subsidy from the state. The company's desire to bring in the rails was not entirely selfish. Fort Worth's fervent effort to help the Texas and Pacific save its land—as demonstrated by the organization of the Tarrant County Construction Company—had challenged every railroad official to reciprocate. Aware that their railroad-building experience could provide more rapid construction, they had released the Tarrant County Construction Company from its commitment and had resumed their own responsibilities to complete the project. Desperately they looked for a man capable enough to complete the road in time. Finally, on June 3, 1876, the company awarded the contract to Morgan Jones. The *Fort Worth Democrat* headlined the announcement: "The Year of Jubilee is Come." Paddock informed his readers that Jones's acceptance of the construction contract insured "speedy and good work."[49]

Jones, of course, could not perform the miracle in three days. The T & P, therefore, began "the most strenuous parliamentary battle recorded in the history of this or any other state"[50] to prevent

48 *Ibid.* (May 20, 1876), 1.
49 *Ibid.* (June 3, 1876), 3.
50 "Fort Worth, July 19, 1876," *Fort Worth Chamber of Commerce Magazine*, Vol. XXIII (July, 1949), 8.

adjournment of the legislature. It required all the legal strategy at the command of the railroad's friends. Regular duties kept the legislators at work beyond their June 6 deadline, and Jones and his crews worked feverishly to take advantage of the delayed adjournment.

By early July, however, the legislature completed its labors; the Senate passed a concurrent resolution of adjournment and sent it to the House. Jones's crews were still several miles east of Fort Worth. The vote in the House was so close that the absence of a single member could mean disaster for the company.

General Nicholas H. Darnell represented Tarrant County in the House. A friend of the Texas and Pacific, he worked diligently to avoid adjournment. But at this critical time, General Darnell fell ill, and the railroad's efforts seemed in vain. Representatives unfriendly to the railroad called hurriedly for another vote to adjourn. The dauntless representative from Tarrant county would not surrender so easily. As the roll call began, Darnell entered the hall on a stretcher supported by his friends. Day after day, the same drama was re-enacted as they carried him to the House, where, to the cheers of the packed gallery, he voted against the resolution to adjourn sine die and voted for the motion to adjourn only until the next day.[51]

Meanwhile the herculean task performed east of Fort Worth held local citizens entranced. After the long, exasperating wait for the railroad, it rushed toward them in July, 1876, in a most dramatic manner. Suddenly Morgan Jones, the unostentatious contractor, was the local hero. As he rushed back and forth along the line, he tested every bridge crossing, supervised every rail-tying, and checked every weakness in the roadbed. Businessmen, farmers, and ranchers, enraptured by the amazing Welshman's ability to work under such massive pressure, grabbed picks and shovels and rallied to his side. The project developed into a patriotic crusade to "bring the railroad home."[52] No able-bodied man

[51] *Fort Worth Press* (July 13, 1949), 28.
[52] "Fort Worth, July 19, 1876," *loc. cit.,* 9.

33

dared to stand on the streets at the end of his working day. Clerks, salesmen, bartenders, doctors, lawyers, janitors, dentists, and printers joined the "crusade" with Jones.[53]

While the townsmen joined the laborers at work under the blistering Texas sun, their wives, mothers, and daughters loaded buggies with coffee and sandwiches and raced to the construction site. While the men rested or grabbed a few minutes' sleep, housewives and children fed the mules and prepared more food. Whenever Jones rushed by, a rebel yell arose from the crowd. The challenge to beat the legislative clock, and the cheers from the crowd, drove the reticent young man to superhuman efforts. Paddock's reporters observed that Jones did not change his clothes or go regularly to bed during the final two weeks' construction.[54] Admiring citizens marveled that he never seemed weary or sleepy-eyed throughout the ordeal.

They reached Sycamore Creek just one mile east of the city on July 17 when news spread through Fort Worth that the legislature could not be kept in session much longer. General Darnell and his allies had played out, to the end, every hand. The news electrified the T & P builders. There was no time to build a conventional bridge across the creek. Jones, desperate to save every possible hour, tried a bold innovation. He took the bridge timbers and ties, converted them into a crib, attached the rails to it, stretched the contraption across the creek, and hurried forward.

The crews were still short of their goal at daybreak on July 19, when the rail-laying crew caught up with the workers on the roadbed. Painfully aware that the bed could not be set down as fast as the workers could stretch the steel, Jones directed that the track take to the dirt road which ran nearly parallel to the right-of-way. They laid ties on the ground and spiked the rails with stones picked up along the way.

Local citizens—those who had managed to sleep at home—awoke that morning aware that the day they had awaited so long had arrived. A holiday spirit engulfed the town. Crowds gathered

---

53 *Ibid.*
54 *Fort Worth Press* (July 13, 1949); *Dallas News* (June 30, 1936); *Fort Worth Star* (July 19, 1906).

at the edge of town as Jones's rails pushed relentlessly forward along the dusty road. Men, women, and children, all in Sunday dress, with picnic baskets filled for the celebration, prepared to give the first train a jubilant welcome. Lined along both sides of the road, they predicted the exact moment the first locomotive would touch the city limits. The men made bets to back up their predictions, and all the while they inquired nervously about news from Austin. The women tried to keep their eyes on their frenzied children while they strained their ears to hear the Fort Worth Cornet Band, which was on hand once again to serenade the railroad builders. Many in the gathering had never seen an "iron horse."

Engineer Kelly, "a big, red-faced Irishman," kept his engine and two flatcars just a few feet behind the construction gang. A sudden yell, followed by a roar from the crowd, signaled the first sighting of a great cloud of black smoke from Kelly's iron horse. Shortly, they saw the construction gang, and, close behind them, the dark outline of "engine no. 20." Someone remarked that such great occasions deserved cannon fire, and some of the younger men scattered across town looking for a cannon. Unable to locate one, they rushed back with various substitutes just as Engineer Kelly inched the first locomotive into Fort Worth's city limits.[55]

It was exactly 11:23 A.M., July 19, 1876. Without cannons, the noisemakers pounded anvils, beat drums, sounded horns, fired guns, and cried their welcome to the Texas and Pacific Railway Company. City officials, hoarse from their own cheers, made their speeches and proudly declared a holiday. The legislature was still in session.

For Fort Worth it marked the beginning of a new era. Editor Paddock, convinced now that all his predictions would come true, made the *Fort Worth Democrat* a daily newspaper. On July 20 he filled his front page with railroad information. It was, in fact, local news of such magnitude that it crowded national news to the back pages. General Custer's defeat at the Battle of Little Big Horn was

[55] *Fort Worth Press* (July 13, 1949); *Dallas News* (June 30, 1936); *Fort Worth Star* (July 19, 1906); B. B. Paddock (ed.), *History of Texas*, Vol. II: *Fort Worth and The Texas Northwest*, 611–12.

not mentioned for the first time since July 7. Apparently too much was happening at home. Paddock did find space to announce, however, that the state legislature finally adjourned on that date.

Fort Worth was the westernmost railhead, and it exploded into the "wildest town in western Texas."[56] Adventurers of every description, cowboys, professional gunmen, buffalo hunters, and dance-hall girls joined the more legitimate and permanent settlers. Within a year the booming town overflowed into the hills. One thousand persons living in tents and wagons encircled the bustling community.[57]

Having successfully completed a railroad project which attracted attention throughout the Southwest, Morgan Jones joined the ranks of established railroad authorities. Fort Worth citizens looked upon him as one of their own, and, whether he liked it or not, their esteem made him a local celebrity. During that hectic morning of July 19, a *Fort Worth Democrat* reporter overheard an admiring spectator comment, "He looks like a furriner, and he talks like a furriner, but danged if he don't work like a Texan."

City fathers, recognizing his abilities, eagerly invited him to join them in numerous business ventures. Fort Worth offered the ambitious young Welshman all the opportunities unavailable to him in Tregynon, Newtown, and Llandinam, Wales. When Major Van Zandt invited him to join a local business enterprise then under consideration, he accepted.

[56] Knight, *Fort Worth: Outpost on the Trinity*, 87.
[57] *Ibid.*

3. LOOKING AROUND FOR SOMETHING TO DO

ON the evening of August 1, 1876, Fort Worth citizens formally expressed their appreciation to the railroad builders. Under a large pavilion erected for the purpose they "wined and dined until the wee hours" officers of the Texas and Pacific operating department, the engineering corps, and the contractors. The *Fort Worth Democrat* listed Morgan Jones among the special guests at the complimentary banquet.

At ten o'clock, beneath a "brilliantly illuminated" tent, the guests and their hosts sat at a table, arranged in the form of a cross, and enjoyed the services of "that prince of caterers, Colonel Ross." Meats of all kinds, salads, pickles, breads, "side dishes in endless variety," grapes, cakes, "toothsome confections," and sparkling wines made the festive occasion the most "pleasurable and joyous" celebration booming Fort Worth had ever sponsored.

It was a cool, calm summer night, and, with the reliable Fort Worth Cornet Band providing more "sweet strains of music" under a bright moon, toasts to Fort Worth and the Texas and Pacific Railway Company continued until two o'clock in the morning. Appropriately, Editor Paddock responded with an address entitled "Our City and its Future." Other speeches followed. Amidst popping corks from the champagne bottles, the guests and hosts listened, also, to a glowing forecast of the future of the T & P and

37

of northwest Texas, and to a recital of the past history of Fort Worth. With the others, Jones received numerous toasts for "service rendered under the most trying and adverse circumstances."[1]

Morgan Jones was not at ease at such celebrations. It was not his nature to mingle in large crowds, and looking back at past accomplishments bored him. Undoubtedly he was relieved when one of his hosts, Major Van Zandt, approached him that night about another project for Fort Worth. The Major invited Jones to join a group who wanted to build a street railway in the city.

Galveston, Texas' largest city, had built a street railway in 1869 on Market Street, and whatever Galveston could build Fort Worth could surely duplicate. Van Zandt reasoned with Jones that their city's eight thousand busy citizens would make the project a financial success. Jones had seen some of these "streetcars" in the northeastern states. He liked Van Zandt's proposal better than any other suggestions he had heard during the two weeks since he had completed the Texas and Pacific. He accepted the offer.

Since New York City had built the original street railway on Fourth Avenue, from Prince Street to Harlem, the "horse railway" had become an accepted institution. The original streetcar resembled a stagecoach. A mule team pulled it on tracks made from strips of flat iron laid on granite blocks. Boston soon followed New York's example, and in 1873, San Francisco built the nation's first cable car. This rapidly expanding industry interested Jones, and he agreed with Van Zandt that Fort Worth would support the enterprise. He knew, also, that no streets could be dustier in dry weather nor muddier in rainy weather than those in Fort Worth. At that time prisoners and delinquent taxpayers provided the town's only street work.[2]

Van Zandt informed his new business associate that work must begin as soon as possible since another group of local men planned a similar project.[3] Paddock's editorial a few weeks later directed public attention to Fort Worth's transportation needs and, consequently, added pressure for an early beginning:

1 *Fort Worth Democrat* (August 2, 1876), 4.
2 Knight, *Fort Worth: Outpost on the Trinity*, 81.

This morning the *Democrat* calls the attention of parties interested to the necessity, daily more apparent and pressing, of a Street Railway. . . . Today it would pay a handsome dividend upon the money invested . . . for its construction, equipment and maintenance. The distance is too great to walk in the hot sun of summer, or the mud, rain and cold of winter. Hundreds would patronize it daily. . . . The time has come . . . and we urge upon them to go to work *without delay*.[4]

Characteristically, Jones set to work with undivided attention and without fanfare. He ascertained the cost of the track, cars, stock, and labor; he determined the track's future route on Main Street—from the courthouse on the town square, to the Texas and Pacific depot; and he asked for, and was granted by the city, the necessary right-of-way. (Fort Worth officials reserved the right to allow other interested persons to build on adjacent streets if they wished.) With Van Zandt, J. P. Smith, W. A. Huffman, and George Noble, Jones organized the Fort Worth Street Railway Company. The company received its franchise on September 6, 1876, and awarded Jones the construction contract.[5] The following morning the *Fort Worth Democrat* expressed its pleasure that "the enterprise [was] in the hands of such energetic men."[6]

Pressure of time demanded immediate construction as the company wanted to discourage any other plans to begin a competing line near by. Despite his rapid preparations, Jones learned on November 16 that another group of local capitalists contemplated their own immediate construction.[7] That afternoon and evening he quietly called together his crew and, during the late hours of the night, began work on the roadbed. Local citizens found, when they awoke the next morning, that their first city transportation system was under construction. Again Jones won the race against time. During the next few weeks, progress on the line continued without delay—despite a near collapse, which Jones always suspected was a stroke, and a painful eye injury he suffered on the project. The rival group, discouraged by the swift progress, ad-

---

3 Interview with Mrs. Percy Jones (July 11, 1967).
4 *Fort Worth Democrat* (August 18, 1876), 4.
5 Paddock, *Fort Worth and The Texas Northwest*, 625.
6 *Fort Worth Democrat* (September 7, 1876), 2.
7 Interview with Mrs. Percy Jones (July 11, 1967).

mitted defeat. On Christmas Day men, women, and children celebrated the holiday by lining both sides of Main Street as W. A. Huffman conducted the first car over the line.[8] Jones, again the local hero, remained secluded at the Peers House, a boardinghouse near the depot.[9] Having so recently brought a railroad to Fort Worth, he had now provided the town with its first city transportation service.

The spectators watched the small mule-drawn car shake and jar its way slowly down the street. Editor Paddock, on hand as usual for any such occasion, suggested the mule's small size: "It is something larger than a West Texas jackrabbit."[10] The seven-foot-long car had windows which allowed the passengers to see, and to be seen by, the dusty pedestrians. They sat on seats running lengthwise down each side of the car.[11] On this initial run, at least, the mule did not bolt, the car did not jump its tracks, and there was no mud to slow or to stop the exhibition.

Jones owned slightly more than two-fifths of the company's stock, originally valued at $50,000.[12] After the first rush of business by those eager to ride "the mule car," the enterprise was not very profitable during the first year. In January, 1878, superintendent Dan Carey reported that two cars made 160 trips per day and averaged 440 passengers. At five cents a ride, the company's gross receipts averaged twenty-two dollars daily.[13] Through the years, however, business improved. Jones and Van Zandt continued their interest in the company[14] until 1900 when George T.

---

[8] Paddock, *Fort Worth and the Texas Northwest*, 625.

[9] Jones never owned a home. Throughout his life he was content to live in a rented room. His one "indestructible" trunk was never too small to carry his personal possessions. Restless and "incessantly energetic," work was all he ever knew. Though he never married, he admired and occasionally corresponded with several lady-friends. He kept in his trunk, for many years, a small batch of letters from Helen Gould, the daughter of Jay Gould, whom he sometimes visited in New York.

[10] Paddock, *Fort Worth and the Texas Northwest*, 625.

[11] Knight, *Fort Worth: Outpost on the Trinity*, 97.

[12] Morgan Jones Papers, Mrs. Percy Jones, *loc. cit.*; file 19, paper 1, and file 18, paper 1.

[13] Paddock, *Fort Worth and the Texas Northwest*, 625.

[14] Other members of the original group sold their shares earlier. General Dodge was one of the major stockholders in later years. Gross receipts in 1895 totaled $22,-197.50. (Morgan Jones Papers, Mrs. Percy Jones, *loc. cit.*, file 2, paper 18.)

Bishop, of Cleveland, and H. T. Goffinberry,[15] of Fort Worth, bought the property.

Morgan Jones found "nothing doing in Texas in 1877." He preferred to build railroads, but the country had not recovered from the panic of 1873. From that time, when the prices of railroad stock crashed to disastrous levels, railroad construction almost entirely stopped. The "high fever" mark of railroad building in that year, 5,217 miles, slumped in 1875 to only 1,606 miles. The following year, total mileage increased slightly to 2,575 miles of new track, including Jones's Texas and Pacific construction into Fort Worth; but in 1877 railroad building dragged even more sluggishly than during the preceding year.

The banquet honoring Texas and Pacific officials following Jones's completion of the line would have been less festive had the hosts and their guests known at the time that the western terminus of the railroad would remain at Fort Worth for nearly four years. During that time the town was "the clearing house between the legally constituted society of the East and the free and untrammeled life of the West."[16] The Texas and Pacific Railway Company completed and opened eighty-five additional miles of main track between Texarkana and Paris, Texas, on August 11, 1876, making a total of 111 miles for the year. President Scott informed the company stockholders in August, 1877, that little, if any, new track would be built during that year.[17] Operating expenses over the new rails increased sharply because of unusually heavy rains immediately following their completion. Costs listed under "maintenance of way," providing for repairs to motive power and rolling stock, greatly decreased net revenue for the year. Scott explained, also, that the older rails, neglected during the course of building into Fort Worth, needed much improvement. In the company's effort to complete the projects on time, its managers assigned men to the regular operating force to work on construction. Conse-

15 Crozier, *Dallas News*, 8.

16 Paddock, *Fort Worth and the Texas Northwest*, 614.

17 Sixth Annual Report of the Board of Directors of the Texas and Pacific Railway Company to the Stockholders, 8.

quently, a large number of old ties needed replacement, roadbeds needed improvements, and bridges needed new supports. The loss, along the north line, of a considerable part of the cotton crop to the boll weevil was another unexpected burden to the company.[18]

As he looked around for something to do, Jones considered another discouraging aspect of the railroad industry's plight. When he first arrived in the United States, direct government aid to the railroad builders was considered essential to the industry's success. The public approved of such assistance. Reacting to the public will, therefore, Congress during the fifties and sixties gave away the public domain with a lavish hand. By the early seventies, however, farmers in the trans-Mississippi West had not experienced that great bonanza which they expected in the wake of railroad construction. Even before the panic of 1873 depressed American industry, agrarians enjoyed no great prosperity. Rapidly, attitudes shifted against western railroads as the farmers, looking around them for the cause of their troubles, placed the blame on dishonest railroad practices. The "gift of God" quite suddenly became the "product of Satan." The iron horse, generally controlled by absentee owners, failed to create the expected utopia. In 1872, Liberal Republicans voiced agrarian discontent and objected to further land grants to the railroads. Other political groups supported similar sentiments. Eventually, this problem, grouped with various other agrarian complaints, developed into the "Granger Movement."

Agitation against the railroad industry was not widespread in Texas in 1877. It certainly was not typical of railroad attitudes in Fort Worth. It is a fact, nevertheless, that the new Texas Constitution of 1876 brought an end to all monetary aid to railroad construction in that state, although it still provided for land grants. Under these conditions Jones reluctantly turned his attention to other endeavors.

General Dodge suggested that he investigate the possibilities of developing a new stage line out of Fort Worth.[19] Correspondence

---

[18] *Ibid.*, 9.
[19] Dodge to Jones (December 17, 1877), Dodge Papers, *loc. cit.*, IX, 750.

between the two railroad builders tended to increase as each recognized the abilities of the other. During these early years the young Welshman often sought the General's advice. Jones's celebrated friend, whose correspondence was always in an almost illegible hand, seldom failed to respond. Jones respected and seriously considered every suggestion. He discovered, however, that Dodge, the famous Civil War leader, former member of Congress, and celebrated builder of the Union Pacific railroad, had few solutions for problems which Jones had not already considered.[20] Such was the case on this occasion.

The young immigrant observed during his first years in the United States that railroad construction in a new area altered, but did not destroy, the pattern of stagecoach and freight-wagon operations. When railroad lines supplanted stage and freight lines, the latter adjusted their routes and schedules and then served as feeder vehicles for the railroad. Usually this arrangement proved profitable to both enterprises. Aware of this, Jones knew that many of the stage and freight lines which formerly operated out of Dallas and served farmers and ranchers to the north, south, and west of that city would make Fort Worth their new eastern terminus. Based on these past observations, he knew, also, that new stage lines would be organized in Fort Worth to compete with the older firms.

During the long wait for the Texas and Pacific to reach Fort Worth, consequently, a number of groups made plans to operate new stage and freight lines. Shortly after Jones brought in the rails, these groups were ready for business. They sent stagecoaches and freight wagons out of Fort Worth to Weatherford, Cleburne, Decatur, and other regional points. One of the first local lines served a territory as far west as San Angelo—then known as Fort Concho. Older companies began service out of Fort Worth to

---

20 Overton, *Gulf to Rockies*, 66. Overton acknowledges their mutual respect and friendship but tends to overstate Dodge's influence on Jones's decisions. The General was indeed a natural leader of men and gave orders, issued directives, and made suggestions with or without solicitation from his associates. On the other hand, Jones, too, assumed responsibilities early in life and was exceedingly capable of making independent decisions.

Yuma, Arizona, El Paso, and Fort Griffin.[21] Many of the locally owned companies operated only briefly and succumbed to competition from their larger and more affluent rivals. By the time Dodge's letter arrived, therefore, Jones had already decided against operating another stage or freight-wagon line out of Fort Worth. Still looking around for something to do, he considered once again the opportunities in the mining industry. News from the Rocky Mountain regions, particularly from Colorado, was tremendously exciting.

Toward the end of 1877, word flashed around the country that rich silver deposits had been discovered at California Gulch, Colorado. It was a former gold mine, abandoned in the 1860's. Earlier prospectors had depleted its gold supply, but in the process they had completely overlooked its fabulous lodes of silver. Succeeding reports of its enormous wealth spurred Jones's interest. Within months California Gulch, renamed Leadville, mushroomed into the nation's silver-mining capital. Jones decided to go to Colorado. He left Fort Worth via the roundabout railroad route through St. Louis and Kansas City.

If Fort Worth were another "product of Satan," Leadville, in 1878, shared the same architect. Two miles above sea level, atop the Continental Divide, it resembled nothing Jones had ever seen amidst the Cambrian Mountains in Wales. As he entered the Lake County region, it reminded him even less of Fort Worth, Texas. The boom towns themselves nevertheless shared many of the same unsavory elements. Dozens of these "hell's half acres" spotted the trans-Mississippi West. Leadville was but an exaggeration of the Texas town Jones now called "home." There were more bawdy-houses, more professional gunmen, more swaggering drunks, more street fights, more senseless shootings, and more crowded hotels. There was, of course, more money in Leadville.

With two million dollars' worth of silver extracted from the mines that year and an apparently limitless supply for those who

---

21 Knight, *Fort Worth: Outpost on the Trinity*, 102–103; Spratt, *The Road to Spindletop: Economic Change in Texas, 1875–1901*, 20–22; Paddock, *Fort Worth and the Texas Northwest*, 264.

could get to it, the clang of prosperity was the raucous sound of Leadville. The booming mountain town could be heard almost before it could be seen. The roar of constant excitement filled State Street and its public places when the miners hit the town to celebrate the day's rewards or to drown their disappointments. Such chaos gave license for anyone to do anything. Irresponsibility was an accepted evil in the sprawling town which had not existed two years earlier. Lake County's population had exploded to 24,000 by the time of its first census in 1880. Colorado itself had gained statehood only one year before the town was born.

Morgan Jones, conditioned to the chaos of a boom town, calmly appraised Leadville, Colorado. He liked the energy and activity in the silver capital, he liked the opportunities available to any man able to take advantage of them, and he was mature enough to tolerate its crudeness if he could share its wealth. He knew, also, that a civilized way of life would eventually gain ascendency.

On his arrival from Fort Worth, Jones did not rush headlong into Leadville's business community. He carefully examined every phase of the town's development and learned what he could about mining and smelting from those who were experienced in the work. He was interested, as well, in other business opportunities—such as services and supplies—and almost immediately he recognized Leadville's acute lumber shortage. Before the end of the year Jones organized, in partnership with H. C. Moore, the Moore and Jones Lumber Company at 308 West 3rd Street, South.[22] Simultaneously, he and Dan Carey, an old Fort Worth friend, joined John E. Izzards, John Arkins, and D. Bauman in organizing the Lake County Railway and Tramway Company. Leadville needed a street railway, he observed, even more acutely than Fort Worth did in 1876. The company filed articles of incorporation with the Secretary of State on January 20, 1879. Jones planned to transport passengers and freight "from a point two miles west of Leadville and to a distance four miles east of the town, to Fryer Hill."[23] The company located its central office at Leadville. Its capital

22 *Leadville Directory*, 207, 267.
23 *Rocky Mountain News* (January 21, 1879), 4.

45

stock amounted to $30,000, at $100 a share. The five original stockholders planned to manage the company as its board of trustees.

Later that year Jones and one of his street railway associates, D. Bauman, joined George Partridge, Joseph E. Shoenberg, and Joseph Samuels and organized the Fryer Mining and Smelting Company. The owners listed its total capital stock as worth $100,000.[24] This venture into an unknown field proved to be one of the few enterprises in his long career in which Jones's remarkable sense of financial timing went awry. The company was hardly a year old when two incidents caused Jones to lose faith in all Leadville mining and smelting operations. In May, 1880, the Miners' Co-operative Union, led by Michael Mooney, went on strike and closed all mines in the area. The union demanded an eight-hour working day at four dollars a day. Almost simultaneously, a sharp decline in prices frightened Leadville's mine operators. Forty-dollar shares in the Little Pittsburg Company, for instance, suddenly dropped to six dollars, and other companies experienced a similar decline. Unfamiliar with the causes of these sudden crises in the industry, Jones sold his interests in the Fryer Mining and Smelting Company.[25] According to his own estimate, he lost about $80,000.[26] For one of the few times in his life Jones had acted too hastily. Within a few weeks the miners returned to work, and, under more conservative management, stock in the mining companies rose to higher levels. During that decade, more than $82,000,000 worth of silver was mined and sold from the Leadville mines.[27] Such men as H. A. W. Tabor, Samuel Newhouse, John L. Routt, and Meyer Guggenheim joined the ranks of the nation's wealthiest men through their mining and smelting operations at Leadville. According to Jones, his hasty action was

24 *Ibid.* (July 29, 1879), 8.

25 Crozier, *Dallas News*, 8.

26 It is difficult to determine whether Jones actually lost that much money. Sometimes, after having sold certain shares of stock, he commented on his losses. He did not mean that he sold for less than his purchase price but that he sold for less than the stock was worth at its most valuable period. (Interview with W. G. Swenson [November 9, 1967].) See also *Rocky Mountain News* (February 4, 1888), 4.

27 Carl Ubbelohde, *A Colorado History*, 157.

46

one of the biggest mistakes he ever made. He always referred to it as "my foolishly lost fortune."

There were other reasons, however, which prompted Jones's return to Texas. Rumors reached him through his railroad friends and through brief items in the *Rocky Mountain News* that various railroad construction projects were contemplated or already underway. First he learned that Thomas A. Scott, president of the Texas and Pacific Railway Company, had brought Jay Gould into that company. Jones had not met Gould, but he knew well Gould's reputation as a railroad promoter.

Gould was a native New Yorker, the son of a Roxbury farmer. After he attended Hobart College, Gould first worked as a surveyor, moved to the lumbering and tanning business for a brief time, tried his hand at banking for a few months, and then finally developed an interest in railroading. As a New York broker, he began to deal in Erie Railroad stocks and bonds, and in an amazingly brief time gained control of that railroad. Later, Gould invested so heavily in western railroads that newspapers referred to his empire as the "Gould system." In November, 1879, he succeeded Sidney Dillon as president of the Union Pacific, and the following month Thomas A. Scott brought Gould, Russell Sage, George Pullman, Charles F. Woerishoffer, and William T. Scott into the Texas and Pacific organization. Gould and Sage were elected to its board of directors. They moved swiftly with plans to renew T & P construction westward out of Fort Worth. On January 16, 1880, just before Jones returned to Texas, they entered into a contract with the Pacific Railway Improvement Company to construct the line to El Paso.

Jones assumed correctly that Gould and Scott planned also to connect the north branch of the Texas and Pacific to either Dallas or Fort Worth, on the main track.[28] The north branch, then called the Trans-Continental Division, extended from Texarkana to Sherman. Disillusioned with Colorado mining and eager to get back into railroad construction, Jones hurried to Texas. Shortly

[28] Shores, *From Ox-Teams to Eagles: A History of the Texas and Pacific Railway,* 26.

thereafter he signed a contract with Dodge, still the T & P's chief engineer, to build the connecting line from Fort Worth to Denton.[29] Meanwhile, another company was already at work to extend the road from Sherman to Denton via Whitesboro. While Jones's section connected the Trans-Continental Division to the main line, the Sherman-Whitesboro-Denton section successfully cut off the Missouri, Kansas and Texas Railway Company at Whitesboro. This forced the "Katy" line to switch to the T & P tracks in order to reach Fort Worth and points south.[30]

In addition to his railroad construction activities, Jones, within the next three years, expanded into coal mining, public utilities, and banking. Soon he was one of the Southwest's leading industrialists. While part of his construction crew built the Texas and Pacific extension, he put other crews to work on a short-rail line between Seligman, Missouri, and Eureka, Arkansas.[31] Simultaneously, he formed the Fort Worth Water Works Company and built Fort Worth's first public water works.[32] In rapid succession he invested in Major Van Zandt's Fort Worth National Bank; he helped to develop Colorado's "second largest coal mining property" at Trinidad;[33] and, with George W. Thompson, he organized the Raton Coking & Coal Company. Finally, Jones built an extension line from Saginaw (near Fort Worth) to the Red River for the Gulf, Colorado and Santa Fe Railway Company.[34] The former Welsh farmer, within a decade and a half after his arrival in the United States, had become an American capitalist of the first order.

Ironically, all of Jones's business ventures during the period of the early 1880's were highly profitable except his railroad construction projects. He made little profit from any of them and sometimes he lost money. The work also consumed most of his time and energy. Unexpected engineering difficulties on the

---

[29] Crozier, *Dallas News*, 8.
[30] Knight, *Fort Worth: Outpost on the Trinity*, 126.
[31] Crozier, *Dallas News*, 8.
[32] Knight, *Fort Worth: Outpost on the Trinity*, 152; Paddock, *Fort Worth and the Texas Northwest*, 624.
[33] Crozier, *Dallas News*, 8.
[34] *Ibid.*

48

Seligman-Eureka line, for example, absorbed most of his profit. Shortly thereafter, he lost money on the Gulf, Colorado and Santa Fe contract.

Jones was already plagued by his problems in railroad construction when officials of the Gulf, Colorado and Santa Fe asked him to build the Saginaw–Red River extension. He told them he was not interested. The company, aware of his reputation as a railroad builder, insisted—and finally prevailed. With his partner, Hugh Burns, Jones reluctantly signed a contract. Almost immediately serious problems developed. Burns, for reasons unknown, grew dissatisfied with the GC & SF. Jones had no other choice but to purchase his interest and complete the work. When the road reached its destination at Gainesville, however, the company again appealed to him to carry on the project to meet the Atchison, Topeka and Santa Fe tracks at Purcell, Indian Territory. Jones pleaded overwork and lack of time, but the company persisted and offered him a $100,000 bonus if he completed the work by a stated deadline. At length Jones agreed to continue the task.

He assigned Dan Carey to do the grading work. He made Al Haynes responsible for building the bridges. General M. F. Thomas, former commander of a Union brigade, directed the track-laying crew. The project started well enough, but eventually General Thomas became discouraged and said they could not meet the deadline. According to Jones, "things went to pot." Thomas resigned. His resignation forced Jones to take over his part of the track work. The Welshman faced another desperate situation reminiscent of the Fort Worth drama, as he again raced to beat the deadline. Once again he won the race, and the GC & SF's first locomotive pulled into Purcell two and one-half days ahead of schedule. Weary and sorry that he had allowed the railroad officials to talk him into the project, Jones decided to get out of the railroad construction business.

Unfortunately, his troubles with the Gulf, Colorado and Santa Fe did not end with completion of the line to Purcell. The company objected that some of the rock and masonry work was not satisfactory. Jones agreed that the project was unfinished and stated his

MORGAN JONES RAILROAD CONSTRUCTION IN TEXAS, 1870 TO 1911

1. *1870: Southern Trans-Continental Railroad Co. (Texarkana to Jefferson).*
2. *1872–74: Texas and Pacific Railroad Co. (Sulphur Creek area)*
3. *1876: Texas and Pacific Railroad Co. (Eagle Ford to Fort Worth)*
4. *1880: Texas and Pacific Railroad Co. (Fort Worth to Denton).*
5. *1882–83: Gulf, Colorado and Santa Fe Railway Co. (Saginaw to Purcell, Okla.*).*
6. *1885–88: Fort Worth and Denver City Railway Co. (Wichita Falls to Union Park, N.M.).*
7. *1888: Pan Handle Railway Co. (Washburn to Panhandle City).*
8. *1890: Wichita Valley Railway Co. (Wichita Falls to Seymour).*
9. *1903–1904: Wichita Falls and Oklahoma Railway Co. (Wichita Falls to Byers).*
10. *1905–1906: Wichita Valley Railroad Co. (Seymour to Stamford).*
11. *1906: Abilene and Northern Railway Co. (Stanford to Abilene).*
12. *1908–1909: Abilene and Southern Railway Co. (Abilene to Ballinger).*
13. *1911: Abilene and Southern Railway Co. (Anson to Hamlin).*
    *Modern Oklahoma boundary shown.

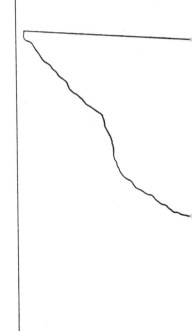

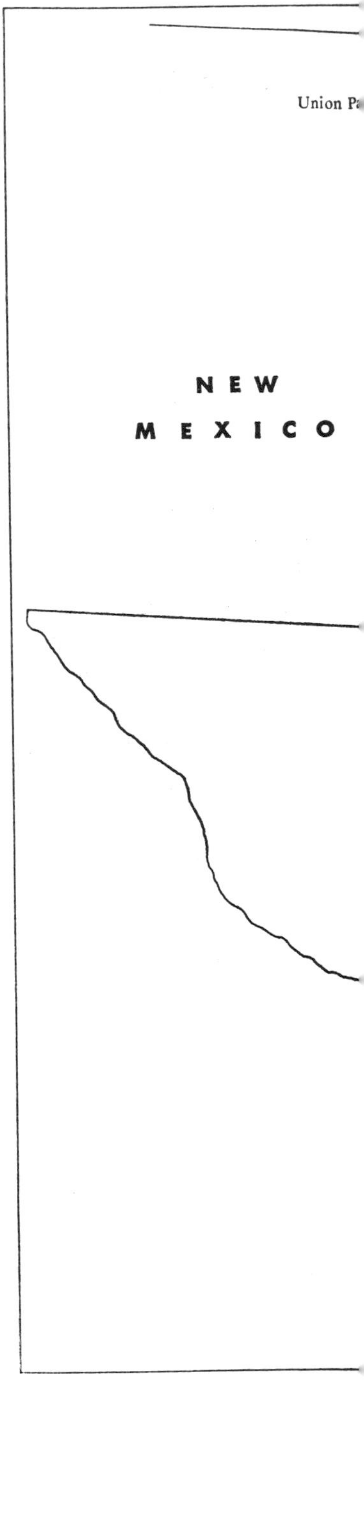

Union Pa

N E W

M E X I C O

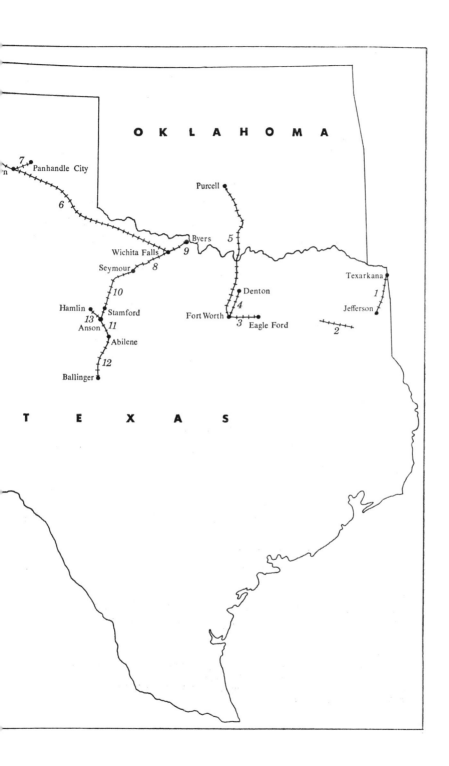

OKLAHOMA

7
Panhandle City

6

Purcell

Byers
5
Wichita Falls
9
Seymour
8
10
Denton
4
Texarkana
1
Hamlin
Stamford
Jefferson
13
Anson
11
Fort Worth
3
Eagle Ford
Abilene
2
12
Ballinger

T E X A S

willingness to complete the work according to company specifications. Meanwhile, he insisted that, since the road was in operation and was safe, he had met the company's deadline. The railroad officials disagreed. Convinced now that the GC & SF sought ways to release itself from the promised bonus, Jones employed Sawnie Robertson to represent him before a board of arbitration. For three weeks the board of arbitration held hearings in Dallas. Finally, it awarded Jones $60,000 for finishing the job on time, but since Jones, under the circumstances, refused to finish the rock and masonry work, the board of arbitration withheld the remaining $40,000.[35]

"It was the first quarrel I ever had and I quit business for good and all time,"[36] Jones said later. "I never would quarrel with those who worked for me, nor with those with whom I had dealings. Life is too short for quarrels."

Jones was indeed too busy to spend his time in the field on construction lines. During these busy years Jay Gould[37] and General Dodge, his chief engineer, pushed the Texas and Pacific's main line across Texas and met the Southern Pacific, coming eastward from California, at Sierra Blanca, Texas. At the same time, work had begun on a Gulf-to-Rockies railroad system between Fort Worth and Denver, Colorado. The Fort Worth and Denver City Railway Company planned to connect the ports on the Gulf of Mexico to the ranching and industrial areas of the Rocky Mountains. General Dodge, on April 29, 1881, contracted to build the Fort Worth and Denver City northwestward from Fort Worth. The line would meet the Denver and New Orleans road, out of Denver, at the Canadian River in the Texas Panhandle.[38] Morgan Jones, the budding American capitalist, was the largest Texas stockholder in the new company. By July, 1882, its rails reached Wichita Falls, Texas. This town remained the FW & DC's westernmost terminus for almost three years. In November of the following

35 *Ibid.*
36 Jones meant only that he would no longer build rails for a company in which he had no financial interest nor administrative control.
37 Gould bought out Scott's interest on April 12, 1881, for $3,500,000.
38 Overton, *Gulf to Rockies*, 89.

year, the company's directors asked Jones to serve as president of the Fort Worth and Denver City Railway Company.[39] Jones accepted the offer despite his many other pressing problems. He insisted, however, that he would serve, for the present time at least, without pay since he could not abandon his commitments to the Gulf, Colorado and Santa Fe at that time.[40]

Thus Jones, the railroad builder, assumed his first assignment as a railroad operator. His direction of the Fort Worth and Denver City as it pushed across northwest Texas developed into the most significant railroad accomplishment of his long career. He devoted unwavering loyalty to the company for the next sixteen years. During this period his honest and competent administration made him one of the most successful railroad leaders in the nation.

[39] Dodge to Jones (November 27, 1883), Dodge Papers, *loc. cit.*, X, 1081.
[40] Crozier, *Dallas News*, 8.

4. LIFTING NORTH TEXAS FROM THE MUD

THE Fort Worth and Denver City Railway Company[1] elected Morgan Jones president on December 11, 1883.[2] Elevation to that company's chief executive office made him, concurrently, chairman of its Board of Directors and chairman of the board's Executive Committee. Jones was one of the youngest railroad leaders in the nation. His twenty-five years in the industry, however, ranked him among the oldest in length of service. Within a quarter of a century he had advanced from common laborer to president.

The ambitious Welshman was not a man to reflect on past achievements, but he had accomplished goals for which he was justly proud. Uninterested in farming, he had spent seven years with the Cambrian Railway Company to learn the rudiments of railroad construction. Dissatisfied with the limited opportunities available to him in Wales, he had found those opportunities in America as a construction foreman with the Union Pacific Railway Company.

Having served his years as an apprentice and journeyman, he had organized his own construction company and had built sec-

---

1 The name was changed on August 7, 1951, to Fort Worth and Denver Railway Company, by an amendment to the original charter. (Fort Worth and Denver City files, A5–47.)

2 J. M. Eddy, Second Annual Report of the Board of Directors to the Stockholders of the Fort Worth & Denver City Railway Co., 2.

54

tions of rail for the Texas and Pacific and the Gulf, Colorado and Santa Fe railroads. Through wise investments he had become a relatively wealthy young man. His street railway companies, his utilities and lumbering companies, and his banking interests were financially successful. His railroad construction companies had had only limited monetary success, but he had become a master builder in the process. His failure in Leadville mining had taught him to exercise greater caution in investing large amounts of money in enterprises unfamiliar to him.

Now, at age forty-four, Jones decided to discontinue railroad construction and to concentrate on railroad administration. He turned to his new responsibilities as head of the Fort Worth and Denver City with characteristic energy and dedication. Predictably, the FW & DC was destined to prosper as long as Jones served as its commander.[3] He was a part of the fledgling company's history from the beginning, first as an interested observer of the initial attempts to organize.

The Fort Worth and Denver City's charter dated back to May 26, 1873. On that date the Texas legislature, by a special act, created the company.[4] Colonel W. H. H. Lawrence, a Fort Worth businessman, conceived the idea, drafted the charter, and procured its incorporation from the state.[5] He planned to build the line from Fort Worth to Denver, Colorado; to connect it with the Beaumont, Corsicana and Fort Worth Railroad; and to use it as a feeder line to the Texas and Pacific "transcontinental highway."[6] Thus he expected to turn the "wilderness of north-west Texas into a blooming garden . . . bring the Rocky Mountains to the head of salt water navigation at Sabine Pass . . . and [provide] another outlet for immense trade . . . to Texas."[7] The Lawrence Plan was part

3 Overton, *Gulf to Rockies*, 111.
4 "An Act to Incorporate the Fort Worth and Denver City Railway Company," FW & DC files, A5–47 (hereinafter referred to as "An Act to Incorporate").
5 Paddock, *Fort Worth and the Texas Northwest*, 510. Other charter members of the incorporation were J. M. Eddy, C. L. Frost, M. H. Gable, D. C. Adams, Daniel Stewart, John A. McCoy, Howard Schuyler, W. R. Shannon, W. A. Huffman, J. E. Ellis, J. P. Smith, E. M. Daggett, James Crutcher, Giles Boggess, John B. Bowman, M. B. Loyd, W. C. Nite, and J. H. Jones. ("An Act to Incorporate," 2.)
6 *Fort Worth Democrat* (September 13, 1873), 2.
7 *Ibid.*

of a larger program to make Fort Worth the major railroad center in Texas.

According to its original charter, the company's capital stock was set at $10,000,000, divided into shares of $100 each.[8] The FW & DC would receive a two-hundred-foot right-of-way through the state's public lands,[9] and sixteen sections of land for each mile of completed track,[10] and the company was authorized to issue its first mortgage bonds to the extent of $16,000 per mile of road within the state of Texas; in addition, the company officials would hypothecate their bonds, stocks, and lands for another $10,000.[11] By the end of summer, 1873, stock amounting to $250,000 was subscribed, an engineering corps had commenced its work, and a surveying party had driven the first stake.[12]

Within days the ambitious plan halted abruptly when Jay Cooke and Company's financial collapse spread panic throughout the nation. Fort Worth was not destined that year to send its tracks toward Denver nor to receive the Texas and Pacific's westward-bound rails. For eight full years, the FW & DC existed only on paper. Colonel Lawrence reluctantly shelved his records, but he never forgot or abandoned his dream.[13]

At that time, 1873, Jones was at work on the T & P's Trans-Continental Division. The Lawrence Plan intrigued him, but he was not financially able to participate in the initial organization. During his brief stay at Leadville, however, he recalled the Gulf-to-Rockies idea, and, impressed by Colorado's booming prosperity, was convinced that the Lawrence Plan was practical.[14] He mentioned its possibilities to General Dodge.[15]

---

8 "An Act to Incorporate," Sec. 2, 1.

9 *Ibid.*, Sec. 8, 2.

10 *Ibid.*, Sec. 10, 2.

11 *Ibid.*, Sec. 13, 3.

12 *Fort Worth Democrat* (September 13, 1873), 2.

13 Lawrence made another effort to revive the plan the following year. On March 28, 1874, the *Rocky Mountain News* editor received a copy of the Lawrence Plan and called it to the attention "of those interested in railway matters" (p. 2).

14 Credit for reviving the Lawrence Plan varies according to the source. Jones is most often cited, however. According to FW & DC files (1230A), Jones and Dodge were responsible. The *Amarillo Globe-News* (n.d.), under the heading "Early History of Denver Found," claimed that Frank E. Harrington, a retired FW & DC conductor, had located company records thought to have been destroyed by fire many years earlier. These recovered records were incomplete, but, according to the newspaper

There is no evidence that Jones presented the plan to former territorial Governor of Colorado, John Evans, although that is a strong possibility. The Welshman rarely engaged in social functions after a hard day's work, but preferred instead to return to his boardinghouse or hotel room to study railroad pamphlets or any other literature concerning that industry. It is entirely reasonable, therefore, that Jones knew, or knew about, Governor Evans, the state's leading railroad enthusiast.

After Evans resigned as territorial governor, he tried to bring the Union Pacific rails through Denver. When that effort failed, Evans built a line from Denver to Cheyenne to meet the Union Pacific. Later he built the South Park line into Denver from Leadville. Convinced that adequate railroad transportation was necessary to develop any inland state or city, and aware that such railroad towns as Cheyenne and Omaha would monopolize trade from eastern cities, Evans "joined enthusiastically in the move to build a direct line to the Gulf of Mexico and to give Denver the advantage of lower freight rates on imported goods."[16] He was, in fact, the "moving spirit" behind the enterprise.[17] On January 25, 1881, the Denver and New Orleans Railroad was incorporated. Jones probably was better informed about Fort Worth and the state of Texas than any other Texan then residing in Colorado. It is probable, therefore, that he spurred Evans' interest in the project back in 1879.

Down in Texas, General Dodge was interested in a road out of Fort Worth to meet the Denver and New Orleans. Fort Worth citizens were electrified by the news that Colorado planned to tie the Rockies to the Gulf of Mexico, and the Lawrence Plan quickly won many interested sponsors. Within three months General Dodge entered into a contract with Governor Evans to build the

article, Morgan Jones and General Dodge revived the Lawrence Plan. Finally, in 1923, Harry Benge Crozier interviewed Jones for more than two hours. It was, incidentally, the only formal interview Jones ever granted. Jones, who seemed to attach no significance to it, commented that he wrote and suggested to General Dodge the Lawrence Plan's possibilities. This occurred in the later 1870's while Jones was in Colorado. (Crozier, *Dallas News*, 8.)

15 Crozier, *Dallas News*, 8.
16 Harry E. Kelsey, Jr., "John Evans," 388.
17 Overton, *Gulf to Rockies*, 39.

Denver and New Orleans and the Fort Worth and Denver City to a junction point in the Texas Panhandle at the Canadian River. In addition, the Texas and Pacific, the Missouri Pacific, and the Missouri, Kansas, and Texas agreed to "operate their respective railroads as through lines in conjunction with the D & NO–FW & DC system."[18] Finally, during the spring of 1881, Dodge received the contract to build the Fort Worth and Denver City across northwest Texas.

Meanwhile, Jones returned to Texas from Leadville and proceeded to expand those interests which made him, suddenly, a wealthy man. While he took no active part in Dodge's new enterprise, Jones was a "leading spirit" in assisting him to organize the Texas and Colorado Improvement Company, which would build the road.[19] His eight hundred shares of FW & DC stock made him the company's major Texas stockholder.[20] Jones's shares ranked him second only to W. T. Walters of Baltimore.[21]

Such men as Jones, Dodge, and Evans invested more than money in the Gulf-to-Rockies system. Most of the Texans (particularly those in Fort Worth) who were willing to become stockholders in the companies did so only because of their faith in Jones's knowledge of the railroad industry. Easterners such as W. T. Walters were willing to support any railroad project General Dodge[22] promoted.

It seemed, even to those who invested in the new railroad, that the system's Texas section was designed to serve "an unpeopled immensity."[23] The entire area west of Fort Worth, in 1870, contained only 2,449 settlers.[24] Most of those, moreover, were farmers

18 *Ibid.*, 57–58.
19 Paddock, *Fort Worth and the Texas Northwest*, 510.
20 Overton, *Gulf to Rockies*, 103.
21 *Ibid.*, 103–104. Most of the stock was held by eastern capitalists, and only about one-tenth by Texans. It should be noted, also, that since the construction company was paid in stocks and bonds of the railroad company, the same persons exercised control over both companies.
22 Overton, *Gulf to Rockies*, 104.
23 John L. McCarty, "Background History of the Fort Worth and Denver City Railway," 1. (This is one of a collection of essays in the FW & DC files submitted during a contest to celebrate the company's seventy-fifth anniversary. All other essays are hereinafter referred to as FW & DC essays.)
24 "Summary History of Fort Worth and Denver Railway Company," 1, FW & DC file 1230.

in counties immediately adjacent to Tarrant County: Wise, Montague, and Clay. Beyond them, in 1881, only a scattering of ranchers dared to move beyond the frontier into the Texas Panhandle. General Ranald S. Mackenzie cleared the Blanco Canyon region in 1871, when he attacked and defeated Quanah Parker's Kwahadis tribe. By 1875, Mackenzie, with Generals A. R. Chaffee, Frank Baldwin, J. W. Davidson, and G. P. Buell, had frightened, defeated, and driven back the Comanche, Iowa, Arapaho, and Southern Cheyenne Indians who roamed the Panhandle from their reservations in the western part of the Indian Territory.[25]

Soon not even buffalo hunters crossed that part of the state. Between 1875 and 1879 the great buffalo herds were entirely wiped out. Without an Indian population, without buffalo and their hunters, and without permanent settlers of any type, the Texas Panhandle seemed indeed to be the "Great American Desert."

The Fort Worth and Denver City's promoters, however, were not impractical and foolhardy visionaries. They began with the reasonable assumption that they could develop a profitable trade between the Rocky Mountain towns and the Gulf of Mexico seaports. They reasoned, also, that any area which could provide sufficient grass to sustain enormous buffalo herds could now fatten equal numbers of cattle. They hoped that the Cross Timbers and lower western plains area could support certain grain crops—at least as far west as the eastern line of Panhandle counties—such as those already cultivated by a few farmers along the Red River. If this hope could become reality, the Fort Worth and Denver City might serve an agricultural population along approximately one-half of its line. The Panhandle region's vacant grasslands with twenty-inch annual rainfall could develop an open-range cattle industry. The Fort Worth and Denver City rails would cross three of the four major cattle trails leading from south Texas: the trail to Sedalia, Missouri, via Fort Worth; the Chisholm Trail to Abilene, Kansas; and the Dodge City Trail from the San Antonio–Austin country via Fort Griffin. Only the Goodnight-Loving Trail through

25 Rupert Norval Richardson, *Texas: The Lone Star State*, 244–45; R. C. Crane, "The Claims of West Texas to Recognition by Historians," *West Texas Historical Association Year Book*, Vol. XII (July, 1936), 20–21.

West Texas, eastern New Mexico, and eastern Colorado was farther west than the new railroad's proposed route.

The promoters shrewdly calculated the region's potential value. Their plan took courage, foresight, and unlimited faith in northwest Texas' destiny. Jones's relatively unrestrained investment proved his confidence in the project's future value. The country through which the road would be built was thoroughly familiar to him.

The eastern rails would parallel the upper reaches of the Trinity River and that part of the Red River which separated north-central Texas from the Indian Territory. Upon reaching the Panhandle, they would cross the Red River and turn slightly in a more northerly direction toward the Canadian River. From Fort Worth the route would cross four distinct geographical regions of the state: the Grand Prairies, the Cross Timbers, the rolling Western Plains, and the High Plains of the western Panhandle.

Annual rainfall dropped sharply between the eastern and western ends of the route. Fort Worth's annual precipitation averaged about forty inches, while the extreme northwestern corner of the Panhandle averaged no more than sixteen inches of rain a year. Natural vegetation ranged from Tarrant County's oak trees and tall prairie grasses to the Panhandle's treeless, short-grass country. Water levels varied in the Trinity, Red, and Canadian rivers, but none had sufficient depth to allow boat transportation.

In 1876, Texas legislators anticipated cattle industry development in the Panhandle region and created fifty-four new counties. From east to west, the area was approximately 180 miles wide. From north to south, the ten tiers of new counties measured a total of 300 miles. Shortly thereafter cattlemen brought their herds into the Panhandle and turned them loose. Charles Goodnight, in November, 1877, located a herd of 2,200 cattle at the head of the Red River, and by July, 1880, other open-range cattlemen had increased the number to 225,857.[26] The first cattle roamed the vast short-grass area at will, but, long before the Fort Worth and Denver City entered the Panhandle, the increased

26 S. S. McKay, "Economic Conditions in Texas in the 1870s," *loc. cit.*, 115.

cattle herds forced an end to the open range. By 1883 barbed-wire fences enclosed all large pasture lands.[27]

Jones and other local FW & DC promoters were familiar with the topographical features of northwest Texas and the recent developments there in the cattle industry. They were more familiar with the territory along the proposed route's first hundred miles. Small subsistence farms dotted the area immediately northwest of Fort Worth. Almost all farmers there had small cattle herds as well. Colonel W. H. H. Lawrence described Wise, Montague, Clay, and Wichita counties, following an inspection tour. His account, published in the local newspaper, provided valuable details. Although too liberally sprinkled with a promoter's flattering adjectives, his reports were relatively accurate:

> It is not only a good agricultural district, but is perhaps the best grazing portion of the State. For the first one hundred miles from Fort Worth . . . there may be found great numbers of small prairies, containing from fifty to five thousand acres completely surrounded by a beautiful growth of Post Oaks. The soil here is a rich, red loam . . . the very best order of wheat land.[28]

Directing his comments to those who would build the roadbed, bridge the streams, and lay the track, Lawrence assured them that the mesquite trees were large enough and numerous enough to provide the road's crossties. Lawrence reported coal in Wise County, and, at every point, native stone for bridges, masonry, and culverts. There were enough white oaks, post oaks, elms, and ashes to supply necessary timber for pilings and bridges.

The Texas and Colorado Improvement Company, under General Dodge's experienced direction, began construction work on November 27, 1881. The road commenced at Hodge, approximately five miles north of Fort Worth, at a station on the Missouri Pacific tracks. One day earlier, Southern Pacific and Texas and Pacific officials had agreed to join their rails ninety miles east of El Paso at Sierra Blanca. The agreement probably determined the

---

[27] R. D. Holt, "The Introduction of Barbed Wire into Texas and the Fence Cutting War," *West Texas Historical Association Year Book*, Vol. VI (June, 1930), 69; Walter Prescott Webb, *The Great Plains*, 312–17.

[28] *Fort Worth Democrat* (August 1, 1874), 2.

date that "dirt started to fly" on the Fort Worth and Denver City's roadbed.

Jay Gould originally intended to lay T & P rails into El Paso, but Collis P. Huntington's Southern Pacific crews reached that far West Texas town ahead of the T & P crews. Huntington gave orders to continue laying rails eastward. Tension mounted between the two rival companies as their rails approached from opposite directions. Each was anxious to receive its maximum land grants from the state. The agreement, therefore, to meet at Sierra Blanca averted possible violence.

General Dodge, chief engineer for the T & P as it crossed West Texas, was now ready to begin work on the Fort Worth and Denver City construction. According to a reasonably reliable source,[29] he intercepted T & P construction materials at Fort Worth and appropriated them for the initial section of FW & DC track. Dodge was part owner of both construction companies, but Gould had no interest in Dodge's Texas and Colorado Improvement Company. Gould claimed that Dodge's conscription of the T & P materials entitled Gould to part ownership of the new company. Dodge ignored him. The following year Gould came to Texas and restated his claims. Within minutes Dodge silenced the famous railroad manipulator's demands. During their first conference he reminded Gould that the Texas and Pacific Railway Company had paid Gould $2,000,000 for new equipment which the company never received. Instead, according to Dodge, Gould painted out "Missouri Pacific," substituted "Texas and Pacific" on the old rolling stock, and then sent it to the Texas and Pacific. Gould placed the new cars, Dodge continued, on the Missouri Pacific line.

The story seems credible for several reasons: first, Jay Gould's questionable ethics and unsavory railroad practices indicate a ready willingness to misappropriate T & P funds; second, it is a fact that the FW & DC's first rails were originally intended for the T & P's track from Sierra Blanca to El Paso. It is also a fact that Gould dropped his claim after Dodge's countercharge.

29 St. Clair Griffin Reed, *A History of the Texas Railroads*, 394; Overton, *Gulf to Rockies*, 93–94.

A second account gave support to the story, but altered Dodge's participation in it. That version credits Dodge's "hard-drinking, hard-working, fun-loving Irish track layers with appropriating the materials from the Texas and Pacific."[30] Dodge only entered the conspiracy to justify the crew's unruly enthusiasm to begin construction at Hodge.

Work commenced without the fanfare which usually accompanied such occasions. Fort Worth, by no less authority than the *New York Daily Chronicle*, was cosmopolitan in 1881. Its growing population was made up of various nationalities which combined "Broadway and the ranch brush."[31] Two major railroads already served the city, the Texas and Pacific and the Missouri, Kansas and Texas. The Santa Fe line was less than one week away as the construction crews approached the city from the south. Possibly Fort Worth citizens were too sophisticated to celebrate a new railroad's birth in the old-fashioned manner; possibly they conserved their energies to celebrate the Santa Fe's arrival, since, after all, a railroad into town meant its completion rather than its beginning; but, most assuredly, they were too accustomed to the "iron horse" to travel five miles over a dusty road to witness the mere shoveling of a few spades of dirt. They would reserve their praise for the completed task.

Farming folk along the proposed Fort Worth and Denver City route, however, displayed a different attitude. Itinerant preachers, as they traveled about their circuits, enjoyed larger attendance at their services. Whatever the weaknesses or strengths of their sermons—whatever the subject matter of the sermons—one could be sure to hear the latest news concerning the approaching railroad. The "Denver Road" was the "talk of the country" among settlers both young and old.[32] Word spread on one occasion that Morgan Jones was at the head of the line, talking with Dan Carey.[33] Their

---

30 McCarty, "Background History of the Fort Worth and Denver City Railway," 3–4, FW & DC essays.
31 Quoted in Knight, *Fort Worth: Outpost on the Trinity*, 124.
32 Mrs. A. W. Cottar, "A Bit of Reminiscence in the Story of the Ft. Worth & Denver R.R.," 2, FW & DC essays.
33 W. M. Mosier, "History of the Fort Worth and Denver City Railway in My Home County," 1, FW & DC essays.

names were familiar to every household, and although Jones was not at work on the project at that time, it is not unlikely that he visited the construction sites and talked with Carey, an old friend and business associate.

Farmers and their sons sought employment with the construction company as the work gangs built the roadbeds or laid the rails near their homes. Those with mules to spare contracted to work with the grading crews, and their young sons waited eagerly to apply for water-hauling jobs. When surveying crews arrived, settlers gathered around them, asked questions, listened earnestly, and then returned to their families to spread the delightful news that the road would run through or near their fields.

For many frustrating days and weeks the eager settlers awaited some sign that the construction crews would follow the route set out by the surveyors. Finally, a report circulated that wagons loaded with railroad equipment approached from the southeast. Overnight a tent city blossomed on the slopes of a near-by hill. Men, women, and children stared, entranced, as they watched a bustling, brawling, swearing civilization camp almost on their doorsteps. A large tent, centrally located, housed the mess hall and sheltered the single men's bunks. Many smaller tents for men and their families surrounded it.[34] Within hours the traveling community settled down; men climbed on wagons and rode back to the construction site; women hurried to and fro at their daily chores; children scampered about the hillside—and frequently lost their way in the tall sagegrass.[35]

Soon farmers' wives approached the noisy camp and offered buttermilk at five cents a gallon and sweet milk at double that price. Eggs and chickens from the same farms brought equally high prices. Young boys and girls, too small to carry water or perform other tasks for the working crew, fished in the streams and hunted wild turkeys for the railroad community. By the end of the first day at the camp's new location, several yearlings hung from trees ready to be cut into steaks.[36]

[34] Lillie Belle Garlington, "History of Fort Worth and Denver City Railway in Montague County," 4, FW & DC essays.
[35] *Ibid.*

Farmers and their sons who worked for the railroad crews earned $1.00 a day and rented a team of mules for $1.50. Thus every member in a family was gainfully employed during the brief time the roadbed and track-laying crews remained in their area.

Fort Worth and Denver City construction proceeded rapidly through Tarrant County's northwestern corner and across the light and sandy soil of the upper Cross Timbers region. They worked a "farmer's hours" schedule, from dawn to dusk, and pushed the roadbed past the Rhome Ranch, where Colonel B. C. Rhome experimented with a new breed of cattle. As early as 1879 this pioneer cattleman realized that the longhorn was "on its way out." His Herefords grazed in the fields two years before the first iron horse entered the area.[37]

The road crossed Wise County[38] from its southeast to its northwest corners and entered Montague County. Only the Red River's shallow waters separated Montague County's northern border from Indian Territory. Engineering difficulties increased as the construction crews reached the Cross Timbers. The elevation ascended more rapidly, and numerous hills in the area forced the men to build high-curved grades around them or to excavate passageways through them.

Sometimes residents of tiny communities, happy to have a railroad near by, tried to pressure engineers to build even nearer. At Queen's Peak, in Montague County, Engineer Tangley decided to blast a passageway through a mound. Residents in the little town realized that the rails would be nearer to them if Tangley circled the hill. Tangley's more practical plan prevailed. From that day residents jeeringly referred to the excavation as "Tangley's Gulch."[39]

In Montague County the Fort Worth and Denver City crossed the Chisholm Trail leading to Abilene, Kansas. One of the "tent

36 *Ibid.*, 5.

37 Edith Alderman Deen, *Fort Worth Press* (August 2, 1949), 6.

38 Named in honor of Henry A. Wise, governor of Virginia in the 1850's and a brigadier general during the Civil War. (Z. T. Fulmore, *The History and Geography of Texas as Told in County Names*, 225.)

39 Jeff S. Henderson, "History of the Fort Worth and Denver City Railway in My Home County," 2, FW & DC essays.

cities," started by the migratory workers at a point where the FW & DC rails crossed those of the Chicago and Rock Island, continued to exist after the laborers and their families departed. Within a year, Bowie, Texas, claimed a permanent population of 1,100 persons.[40] Thus a town which did not exist before the railroads arrived soon grew many times larger than Saint Jo—an old historic town east of the railroad route. According to legend, Saint Jo was once an old Spanish trading post.[41]

The roadbed stretched across Montague County's southwest corner and advanced toward Henrietta, in Clay County.[42] Through timber groves and across the deep red prairie lands the construction crews entered one of the most beautiful areas along the route. Early spring rains made it difficult to cross Little Wichita River. The roadbed crews, having advanced beyond the bridge-building crews, bound their equipment to wagon beds and pieces of timber and floated them across to the north bank. They repeated the difficult task when they entered Wichita County and arrived at Holliday Creek, near Wichita Falls.[43] The roadbed now stretched across 111 miles, and the first phase of the Fort Worth and Denver City was almost complete.

The rail-laying crews began the second phase on February 27, 1882, three months behind the grading crews.[44] As they advanced, engines and flatcars transported crews and materials to the railhead. Once again the settlers along the route worked with the construction crews. Rail transportation enabled the permanent workers to spread their "tent cities" farther apart. Often the temporary homes were unnecessary. Farm wives and children, consequently, no longer enjoyed the extra income earned by selling food

---

40 *Ibid.*

41 *Dallas News* (October 20, 1929), quoted in *Frontier Times*, Vol. VII (August, 1930), 516–18.

42 Named in memory of Henry Clay, speaker of the House of Representatives, secretary of state, senator, and Presidential candidate. (Fulmore, *History and Geography of Texas*, 53–55.)

43 Betty Illane Offutt, "The History of the Fort Worth and Denver City Railway in My Home County," 2, FW & DC essays.

44 "Memo Outline of History of Fort Worth and Denver City Railway Company," 1, FW & DC files, A5–47.

to the roadbed crews, but an event far more exciting than anything the roadbed gangs could offer overshadowed their disappointment. When the rails reached their area, the "iron horse" was not far behind.

Children climbed to the rooftops and to the highest tree branches, eager to sight the first great billow of black smoke. An excited shriek from one brought all of the others climbing and tumbling from their perches. Their elders, equally excited, ran to the doors. Together they raced to the tracks, the children hysterically leading the way, and then, before their very eyes, the "fantastic, thrilling drama" entranced the whole family.[45] The "swaying, rocking iron horse, teetering along on the two slim rails . . . [and] leaving behind a plume of black smoke" passed by them as it made its way to the construction site.[46] Sometimes the "impossible" happened and a friendly engineer stopped the great engine and offered the children a ride to the railhead. They had to "earn" their ride by sounding the whistle—"two short toots, timidly, then one long blast . . . reluctantly turned loose."[47]

On May 1, 1882, workmen completed the track to Decatur, located midway across Wise County. This little "cow town" was the county seat and the home of the Waggoner brothers, who started their cattle empire in the near-by prairie lands.[48] Settlers from miles around joined town residents as they awaited the first locomotive's arrival at the newly constructed depot. One of the awed spectators at the scene described the "auspicious occasion" many years later:

At the appointed hour the spewing and belching monster . . . moved up. The people stared, horses reared, family dogs . . . yelped and barked, children clung to the linsey woolen skirts of mothers . . . and brawney men of woods and pastures closed in and vented their feelings by emitting a wild Comanche whoop. Then they clasped the hands of

45 Mrs. Eugene McCluney, "History of Fort Worth and Denver City Railway in My Home County," 1, FW & DC essays.
46 Cottar, "A Bit of Reminiscence in the Story of the Ft. Worth & Denver R.R.," 1, FW & DC essays.
47 *Ibid.*
48 Henderson, "History of the Fort Worth and Denver City Railway in My Home County," 2, FW & DC essays.

67

the trainmen and visiting officials. . . . Of all days in Wise County before or since this was the prodigeous day.[49]

Decatur was only forty miles northwest of Fort Worth, but to the settlers who rode their wagons into town that day the distance would never again seem so far. The Fort Worth and Denver City rails had literally lifted North Texas from the mud.

Similar celebrations occurred later that summer at Henrietta, Clay County, and at Wichita Falls, Wichita County, when the first locomotives arrived and "pulled majestically to a stop." Their distances from Fort Worth were 91 and 111 miles, respectively. The Denver road's effect on tiny Wichita Falls was typical and was destined to be repeated on many occasions.

Citizens in the southeastern Wichita County area did not undertake to organize the county until they were sure the Fort Worth and Denver City would come their way. With county organization accomplished, they officially created a townsite.[50] High water from the Wichita River forced the settlers to move the townsite from its original location on the north banks of the river to its south side. Later R. E. Montgomery arrived and met with the citizens to make necessary arrangements to bring the railroad to them. Montgomery represented the Texas Townsite Company, owned by his father-in-law, General Dodge. Landowners agreed to grant the company 50 per cent of the property along the right-of-way.[51] With these problems solved, Wichita Falls citizens awaited the construction crews and that great day when the first locomotive would arrive.

On September 27, 1882, the first train—a construction car with one passenger coach—pulled into the new depot. That same day, according to a previously arranged schedule, the town-lot sale began. The choice lot, on Ohio Avenue, sold for $1,000.[52] Lots valued at $100 or less were paid for in cash at the time of the auction. Lots valued above $100 were sold for half in cash and the

[49] Cliff Cates, "History of the Fort Worth and Denver City Railway in My Home County," 1, FW & DC essays.

[50] John Gould, "City Got Its Long Pants in 1882," *Wichita Falls Chamber of Commerce Magazine* (Winter, 1951).

[51] Offutt, "The History of the Fort Worth and Denver City Railway in My Home County," 3, FW & DC essays.

[52] *Ibid.*

68

remainder to be paid within twelve months. Value of the average lots ranged from $200 to $500. New homes and business houses lined the town's main streets almost immediately. Many buyers were Fort Worth people who arrived via the first FW & DC train.

General Dodge's demands for liberal right-of-way and townsite lands were not unreasonable under conditions then existing. To those unfamiliar with the financial arrangements made to build the Fort Worth and Denver City, a law passed by the Texas legislature on April 22, 1882, seemed to strike a traumatic blow to any further construction.

On that date, just as the rail-laying crews approached Decatur, the state legislators nullified all earlier laws which granted land subsidies to railroads built in Texas. Overnight, the FW & DC lost more than four million acres along its proposed route.[53] If Dodge and his associates had financed construction in the usual manner, through the sale of land-grant bonds, the new law would have been disastrous. But Dodge, president of the construction company, and J. M. Eddy, president of the railroad company, both thoroughly familiar with railroad attitudes in Austin, had anticipated such a law. According to the agreement between the railroad company and the construction company, back on April 29, 1881, the construction company paid the road-building expenses while the railroad company paid operational expenses after its completion. Thus Dodge financed his construction by selling stock in the company.[54] W. T. Walters and Morgan Jones, it was pointed out earlier, were the two major stockholders.

The state legislators acted abruptly, but not arbitrarily. Except for the reconstruction years, 1869 to 1873, when land grants were illegal, the state had given liberally to railroad companies. In 1854 it granted sixteen sections of land for each mile constructed; two years later it loaned to the railroad companies $6,000 a mile from the school fund; and in 1871 the state authorized cities and coun-

---

53 Overton, *Gulf to Rockies*, 95; Reed, *A History of the Texas Railroads*, 152–55. According to FW & DC file 1230A, "Summary History of the Fort Worth and Denver City Railways," 2, the FW & DC, plus its branch lines, "would have come into possession of more than ten million acres of land."

54 Overton, *Gulf to Rockies*, 102–103.

ties to give bonuses. The Texas and Pacific, for example, received 5,167,360 acres as a result of these generous laws.

The Texas legislature in 1882 faced an unpleasant fact ignored by earlier sessions: the state had promised to railroads or given to Confederate veterans eight million acres more than it possessed.[55] The new law merely recognized and corrected a problem earlier solons chose to ignore.[56] The same 1882 legislators passed another railroad law, however, which suggested a growing desire to regulate that industry. They reduced railroad passenger rates from five to three cents a mile.

While the new laws did not stop Fort Worth and Denver City construction, they did add to the railroad officials' desire to operate the Fort Worth–Wichita Falls section as soon as possible. Hence, the construction crews worked at a feverish pace and completed the track to Decatur on May 1; to Bowie on July 1; and, finally, working on both ends of the line at once, completed the track to Henrietta and Wichita Falls on July 24.[57]

More than thirty months elapsed before President Morgan Jones, having replaced J. M. Eddy in that position, was able to move the Denver road west of Wichita Falls. Many sound reasons caused the delay. Not the least of these was the fact that hundreds of miles of track had to be built across that "unpeopled immensity" without benefit of the usual land grants from the state. In addition, company officials prudently decided to concentrate their efforts on the completed division—to make it financially stable—before they undertook the greater challenge across the Panhandle. Too many railroads, they knew, had collapsed as a result of overexpansion. The major cause for the delay, however, concerned Governor John Evans' troubles with the Denver and New Orleans Railroad.

Governor Evans, it should be recalled, incorporated the Denver and New Orleans on January 25, 1881. Its tracks were to link

55 Reuben McKitrick, *The Public Land System of Texas, 1823–1910*, 68.
56 Regulatory measures concerning the railroad industry in Texas cannot be considered "anti-railroad" until Attorney General James Stephen Hogg's administration, 1886–90. See Richardson, *Texas: The Lone Star State*, 265–69.
57 "Memo Outline of History of Fort Worth and Denver City Railway Company," 1, FW & DC files, A5–47.

with those of the FW & DC near the Canadian River. The combined roads proposed to connect the Rocky Mountain area, and more particularly Denver, to the seaports on the Gulf of Mexico. Denver, anxious to compete with the Middle West for eastern trade, would then be one thousand railroad miles nearer water transportation. Its freight rates, based on the land-water route, would therefore be cheaper than those based on the land routes via Chicago or St. Louis.

Evans was so convinced that the old Lawrence Plan could be profitable that he invested half a million dollars in the project.[58] He planned to build into New Mexico via Pueblo and Trinidad, but rival roads, hearing of the Evans Plan, formed the Tripartite Agreement[59] to block any new road in Colorado. When the D & NO opened for business on May 12, 1882, between Denver and Pueblo, the members of the Tripartite Agreement refused to exchange business with Evans. They issued warning pamphlets to other companies and cut their own freight rates between the two cities to five cents per hundred pounds.[60] At times they refused to transfer freight to the D & NO even when it was specifically assigned to it.[61]

To the Fort Worth and Denver City officials, Evans' Denver and New Orleans road seemed destined to progress no farther south than Pueblo. By 1883 the railroad war developed into an immovable stalemate.[62] There was certainly no reason to rush plans, consequently, to build the Texas end of the line to the Canadian River.

Meanwhile, traffic over the Fort Worth and Denver City line operated to the railhead at Wichita Falls. A *Fort Worth Gazette* reporter asked, after a trip over the route, "Is there anywhere in Texas . . . [with] more beautiful valleys and rolling land, timber and prairie?"[63] He reported that the trip between the two points on

58 Edgar Carlisle McMechen, *Life of Governor Evans: Second Territorial Governor of Colorado*, 189.
59 The three railroads were the Rio Grande, the Santa Fe, and the Union Pacific.
60 McMechen, *Life of Governor Evans*, 190.
61 Kelsey, "John Evans," 372.
62 Overton, *Gulf to Rockies*, 88.
63 *Fort Worth Gazette* (September 27, 1883). Clipping from the C. L. Frost Papers in the possession of Mrs. Robert Roy Duncan, Fort Worth, Texas.

71

the line was "a pleasant day's journey" and that he had seen great flocks of quail and doves and herds of antelope.

There were no air brakes or automatic couplers to make the journey more comfortable, but many local settlers made the trip to Fort Worth for no greater reason than to experience the ride.[64] The track was standard gauge—four feet, eight and one-half inches—and its embankments were twelve to fourteen feet wide. The company owned twelve eight-wheeler locomotives. It constructed its bridges of wood.[65] Within a short time it added freight and passenger cars to the regular trains.

By October, 1883, after the first full year's service to the settlers in North Texas, president Eddy presented an optimistic report to the company's stockholders. Local traffic steadily increased; towns along the line grew rapidly; the area farmers produced average crops, and prospects for increased yields looked encouraging; more families claimed farmlands along the way; and coal fields in Wise County promised to increase the following year's business by eight to fifteen thousand cars.[66]

Superintendent C. L. Frost reported that the company, within the past year, had built a station house at Alvord, in Wise County, and enlarged the one at Bowie. It built stockyards at Bowie and Alma and enlarged those at Wichita Falls. In April, May, and June, 1883, the company shipped more than 80,000 head of stock cattle from Fort Worth via the FW & DC to Henrietta and Wichita Falls. Equaling the president's optimism, Frost predicted that 150,000 cattle would be shipped on the line the following spring.[67]

Available records do not reveal why president J. M. Eddy resigned his position on December 11, 1883. The little road prospered, and the company still hoped to complete the tracks to the Canadian River at a later date. Eddy's final report to the stockholders expressed his faith in the company's future. Whatever his reason, he turned over the direction of the Fort Worth and Denver

[64] B. T. Hambright, "History of the Fort Worth and Denver City Railway in My Home County," 1, FW & DC essays.

[65] "Memorandum of Historical Data in Connection with Construction of Fort Worth and Denver City Railway," 1, FW & DC file 1230A.

[66] Annual Report, 1883, 4.

[67] *Ibid.*, 11–12.

City Railway Company to a most promising, if administratively inexperienced, successor. In spite of his other duties at the time, Morgan Jones accepted the assignment. The company's directors knew that Jones would devote all his talents and energies to his new responsibilities.

The company's Charter and By-Laws clearly defined the president's duties.[68] Jones would preside at all meetings of the Board of Directors; he would appoint all general officers or agents of the company, and could remove them for good cause; he would execute all contracts made with the company; and he would report semiannually the company's progress to the Board of Directors. As chairman of that board, he would report annually the company's general condition to its stockholders.

Jones's duties as chairman of the Executive Committee required him, with the other members of the committee, to provide for the "engineering, finances, construction and equipment of the road."[69]

The new president soon discovered another American custom which long ago had become a tradition, particularly in the southern and southwestern states: newspapermen were inclined to recognize one's business success by conferring the title "Colonel." Eventually others, who saw the title in print, adopted it. Thus, in the middle 1880's, the former Welsh farm boy became the American railroad industry's "Colonel Jones."

Colonel Jones was not by nature a "desk man." He preferred to work with his men on the line. With only a brief formal education, he did not like that part of his new duties which required him to make formal reports to the Fort Worth and Denver City's Board of Directors and the stockholders. Characteristically, however, he studied the unfamiliar duties associated with his position and was well prepared to perform them when the occasions arose.

He learned that annual reports must convey an accurate account of the company's condition, both physical and financial. The Colonel's reports, therefore, must review the company's earning

68 Charter and By-Laws of the Fort Worth and Denver City Railway, Sec. II, 11–12, FW & DC files A5–47.
69 *Ibid.*, 10.

power, its financial position, and its main physical characteristics. He must show its income and expenditures and, probably most important, prepare a financial statement or balance sheet. Finally, the company president was expected to itemize all physical statistics.

More specifically, Jones's reports must list gross earnings, operating expenses, net earnings from all sources, charges for interest, and dividends and surplus. The balance sheet must include a statement of capital liabilities and assets and current liabilities and assets. In addition, the directors and stockholders would expect the president to describe the length and physical characteristics of the road; the number, description, and performance of equipment; and volume and character of business done.[70] Colonel Jones soon mastered these and other details involved in his desk work.

He grew increasingly conscious, also, of the railroad industry's over-all importance to Texas and to the nation. For many years he kept a newspaper clipping which briefly summarized the railroads' influence:

They have furnished facilities for travel, and for transportation of merchandise, and of the products of farms and grazing land.
They have induced immigration, and attracted capital.
They have caused farms to be opened, and towns and cities to be built.
They have multiplied workshops and factories and stores and school-houses and churches.
They have given employment to labor, and rewarded industry, and furnished a large percentage of the money that has been the life current of commerce.
They have encouraged the education, increased the wealth and promoted the prosperity of the people.[71]

Jones kept this eulogy to the railroad industry in his black "indestructible" trunk along with the newspaper accounts of Victoria's coronation and Lincoln's assassination. If the latter two articles symbolized his loyalty to both Great Britain and the United

---

[70] For a detailed description of railroad annual reports around the end of the nineteenth century, see Thomas F. Woodlock, *The Anatomy of a Railroad Report and Ton-Mile Cost.*
[71] *Houston Age* (n.d.).

States, the former article must surely have been a guideline to Jones's dedication to his new administrative duties.

Colonel Jones during 1884 successfully released himself from various enterprises which had heretofore demanded so much personal attention and time and, as the months passed, devoted his talents more often to problems which confronted the Fort Worth and Denver City Railway Company. His major problem, as president of the company, was expansion. As the need to expand west of Wichita Falls grew more pressing, Jones informed the stockholders in October, 1884:

> At the time the road was completed [to Wichita Falls], the country was open, affording range for cattle shipped there, but since that time, by reason of the influx of settlers, it has been fenced so that cattle shipped there must be driven for several miles through lanes before reaching the open range. After having been carried for hundreds of miles, standing in cars, cattle are not in condition to be driven any distance before finding pasture and water, and therefore I believe this extension is necessary to enable us to hold our extensive cattle trade. . . . I also believe that this extension will draw to us business from the northern part of the Panhandle, which now tends toward the Kansas roads.[72]

Recognizing the company's need to expand, the Colonel was not one to wait long for General Dodge and his Texas and Colorado Improvement Company associates to decide whether or not they wanted to exercise their option to construct the road farther west.

On December 10, 1884, Jones issued a blunt ultimatum to his old friend to extend the line thirty-four miles into the open range before April, 1885. If the Improvement Company did not meet its commitment by that date, he declared, "it will be necessary for us to make some agreement to build it ourselves."[73] Obviously enough Dodge's former protégé was master of his own road. With Jones in control, "dirt would fly," in 1885, on the Fort Worth and Denver City route.

[72] Annual Report, 1884, 2, FW & DC file 1230A. (Several copies of the FW & DC annual reports, including that for the year 1884, are missing. Summaries of all reports from 1882 to 1901 are available, however, in the 1230A file.)

[73] Texas and Colorado Railway Improvement Company, Record Book, FW & DC files, Letter, Jones to Dodge, recorded in Minutes.

5. CLIMBING THE HIGH PLAINS

WICHITA FALLS remained the Fort Worth and Denver City's northwestern railhead from July 24, 1882, until February 3, 1885. The bustling little railroad center enjoyed the prosperity which flourished wherever the "steel ribbons" penetrated the cattle frontier. All along the route from Fort Worth, road stations and cattle pens hugged the rails and, around each little service point, shops and stores—mechanics and merchants—created a new village.

At the railhead there was even greater activity. Stockmen, cowboys, farmers, and railroad employees increased small-town enterprise. Following hurriedly conducted land auction sales, new public buildings of every sort expanded Main Street into a square. Usually, the lumber-yard owner reaped the first monetary rewards as the rail center developed into a boom town.

The railroad company created three businesses at once; consequently, it was the town's leading employer. The FW & DC's first trains brought in lumber to build a passenger depot, a freight house, and a stockyard fence. Thus from the beginning the railroad transported people, products, and livestock. Trade was brisk as station agents, Western Union clerks and messenger boys, baggage hustlers, warehousemen, and livery-stable hacks scurried about their duties.

Business and social life gravitated around the passenger depot.

When train time approached, excitement increased. Men, women, and children invented manifold excuses that "required" their presence at the station when drummers, cattlemen, immigrant families, and railroad personnel alighted from the coaches. Bus drivers, baggage hustlers, and hotel hawkers jockeyed for position around the more affluent-looking passengers. Pandemonium continued until every new arrival boarded one of the public-transportation vehicles. The "big, yellow coach-like busses" hauled the "aristocrats," while the "plain people," for twenty-five cents, rode the livery-stable wagons.[1]

The exuberant drivers then raced down the dusty main street, each eager to avoid the clouds of dust in the wake of later vehicles, each determined to be the first to deposit his passengers at their destination, and each proud to demonstrate his superior driving skill. The swaying, rattling coaches, heavily laden, challenged pedestrians, dogs, and all other moving objects for the right-of-way. It seemed, of course, the most dangerous part of the weary passengers' journey.

Meanwhile, brawny men unloaded the freight cars. Unfamiliar odors drifted across the station platform from barreled pickles and liquors—sometimes leaking their contents—salt pork, new lumber, tar, and all kinds of household goods.[2] These odors mingled with the peculiar fragrance of supplies destined for shipment to Fort Worth: bales of cotton, buffalo hides and tongues, enormous stacks of buffalo bones, and surplus grain products from near-by farms.

Season after season, grain products and cotton increased in volume as immigrants carved grazing lands into farms. By the mid-eighties earlier Texas pioneers had claimed the choice lands in East and South Texas, thus forcing later arrivals to push the farm belt farther and farther west. When railroads penetrated the sprawling open ranges, "nesters" inevitably moved in and broke the sod.

Wichita Falls intermixed cattlemen and farmers, cowboys and drummers, buffalo bones and lumber. The din of voices in the

1 Cates, "History of the Fort Worth and Denver City Railway in My Home County," 5–6, FW & DC essays.
2 *Ibid.*, 6.

77

saloons and hotel lobbies blended northern, southern, and western accents with those of Germany, Austria, and Russia.[3] The various voice inflections emphasized differences in experience, training, and education. Redeye whisky frequently converted differences into antagonisms and saloon brawls pitted cowboy against nester, northerner against southerner, and heaven against hell.

The historic conflicts among men on the Great Plains frontier collided at the railhead. Between 1868 and 1882, Plains Indians and United States soldiers fought more than four hundred battles from the Canadian border to the Río Grande. Slowly and sullenly the Indian retreated to his designated reservation. The cattleman moved in and, Spanish-style, turned his herds loose on the open ranges. This unique industry, brief as it was, "left an impact on the imagination of the American people not equalled by that of any other calling."[4] The West Texas open-range industry, fleeting and violent, yielded to persistent nesters' invasions following the 1883–84 fence-cutting wars. Cattlemen fenced their own lands or moved their herds to the more arid regions farther west.[5]

During the years that Wichita Falls remained the FW & DC's railhead, farmers gradually dislodged cattlemen.[6] Cotton production in particular made rapid strides.[7] The railroad permitted the farmer to abandon subsistence farming and to plant crops to sell at a distant market; hence North Texas developed into a crop- and stock-farming region.

Wichita Falls citizens knew that their thriving little city could not remain North Texas' westernmost trading center. Someday the rails would extend farther west and another town would distribute supplies to the distant pioneers. Wichita County's open-range cattle industry receded into neighboring Wilbarger County and, as this happened, pressures mounted to extend the rails beyond the barbed-wire fences. After the long journey from South Texas via

[3] Frank W. Johnson and Eugene C. Barker, *A History of Texas and Texans*, 811–12.
[4] Rupert Norval Richardson, *The Frontier of Northwest Texas, 1846 to 1876*, 302.
[5] R. D. Holt, "The Introduction of Barbed Wire into Texas and the Fence Cutting War," *loc. cit.*, 74–79.
[6] William Curry Holden, *Alkali Trails, or Social and Economic Movements of the Texas Frontier: 1846–1900*, 245.
[7] McKay, "Economic Conditions," *loc. cit.*, 1.

Fort Worth, cattle could no longer graze in Wichita County before continuing their journey to northern markets.

President Morgan Jones realized that the Fort Worth and Denver City must continue to penetrate the open-range regions. He rejected the argument that 1882 legislation, which repealed the Texas land-grant laws, prohibited railroad construction across the Panhandle. He knew that railroad construction in Texas virtually stopped after 1882; he agreed that the FW & DC promoters should pause long enough to appraise the new situation and to get the existing road on a paying basis; but he understood, also, that the Denver road must move cattle onto the open range. As grazing land moved westward, the FW & DC must move with it. In addition, no company official believed more firmly than Jones that the Texas rails must one day meet those out of Denver.[8]

Meanwhile, three Panhandle counties created by the Texas legislature in 1876—Wheeler, Oldham, and Donley—organized, designated county seats, and established local governments. Pioneers in other near-by counties indicated similar plans. Barbed-wire fences virtually eliminated the open range, and soon grazing lands for northern-bound cattle all but disappeared.

Jones grew increasingly impatient with men who continued to present reasons to delay new construction. His good friend General Dodge wrote from New York in January, 1884, "I am disposed to go very slowly until we see what the crop in Texas and our next summer's earnings are to be."[9] Dodge hoped, however, that they could construct fifty to seventy-five miles of additional track by the end of summer. When, in December, 1884, after a below-average crop yield in Texas, Dodge's Texas and Colorado Improvement Company still had not commenced construction, President Jones issued his blunt ultimatum: extend the track by April, 1885, or the railroad company would have to do it. General Dodge thereupon talked with Improvement Company stockholders

8 Jones's annual reports to FW & DC stockholders and his private letters to company officials almost always stressed the need to continue construction toward Denver. See Dodge Papers, *loc. cit.*, 1883–88, and Morgan Jones Papers, Mrs. Percy Jones, *loc. cit.*

9 Dodge Papers, *loc. cit.*, XI, 23, Dodge to Jones (January 23, 1884).

in New York and learned that they were not willing to finance further construction. The FW & DC Board of Directors, consequently, gave Dodge 360 first-mortgage bonds as payment for a thirty-four mile extension from Wichita Falls into Wilbarger County.[10]

Grading began less than three weeks later, on February 3, 1885, across Wichita County. It was a happy day for Morgan Jones, but "one of the darkest days in the town's history" for Wichita Falls citizens.[11] A new railhead meant a new town at that western point —a new distributing center—and businessmen anticipated a mass exodus from their town. The weather later that month did not lighten Wichita Falls' spirits nor the construction crew's labors. During February, 1885, North Texas suffered one of the worst blizzards in its history. Freezing temperatures and enormous snowdrifts killed thousands of cattle. Many stockmen in the area were wiped out of business.

The inclement weather soon improved, however, and the railroad construction crews progressed rapidly across Wichita County and northwesterly into Wilbarger County.[12] On May 5, 1885, they reached a point 33.5 miles from Wichita Falls. For a while, at least, the FW & DC railhead extended into good grazing lands, and again construction halted.

Wilbarger County, created on February 1, 1858, lay between the ninety-ninth and one-hundredth meridians. For two decades thereafter, only buffalo, antelope, prairie dogs, and wolves inhabited the former Indian hunting grounds. By 1878, John Young's 1,350 cattle shared Wilbarger County with the wild prairie animals, and later that year Bob Wiley and Tom Coggins brought in 8,000 additional cattle.[13]

The Western Cattle Trail from Bandera, Texas, due north to Dodge City, Kansas, passed through Wilbarger County. Stockmen

---

10 Overton, *Gulf to Rockies*, 115–16.

11 Gould, "City Got Its Long Pants in 1882," *loc. cit.*, 1.

12 Named in honor of Josiah and Mathias Wilbarger, who were the first surveyors in the area. (Fulmore, *History and Geography of Texas*, 283.)

13 Ruby L. Smith, "Early Development of Wilbarger County," *West Texas Historical Association Year Book*, Vol. XIV (October, 1938), 54.

and cowboys rested and watered their cattle along Pease River, Wanderer's Creek, St. Andrews Springs, and Beaver Creek. Abundant buffalograss in the area provided nourishment to the cattle herds. During the spring months, while the Fort Worth and Denver City rails advanced toward Wilbarger County, 300,000 head of cattle passed along the Western Cattle Trail.

Prior to the railroad's arrival, there were no permanent settlers in that county. After a brief stop, the cowboys continued their dusty journey to Dodge City. Such early ranchers as Young, Wiley, and Coggins stayed close to their herds and carved temporary homes—dugouts—into the sides of near-by slopes. They ate prairie animals, geese, and prairie chickens, and in season added wild grapes, currants, and persimmons to their diet.

Wilbarger County changed just as the FW & DC construction crews approached from the east. Thomas Boyle, an Irish immigrant via Australia and New Zealand, built a fence and established a sheep ranch along Lily Creek.[14] E. J. Randel, from Perry County, Tennessee, filed on a section of land in Wilbarger County under the 1883 State School Land Law. He agreed to pay two dollars an acre, one-fourth down, the balance in forty years, at 5 per cent interest. He agreed, also, to live on the land for three years. In the fall, 1883, he was the first to break the soil in "Farmer's Valley."[15]

In time other permanent settlers followed the sheep rancher and the farmer. They built homes with lumber brought to Harrold (the new railhead) from East Texas. Hauled by ox team, lumber at that distance cost sixty to seventy dollars per thousand feet.[16] Records do not reveal the price after the railroad arrived, but the volume of lumber brought to Harrold after 1885 suggests a considerable price reduction.

Harrold immediately developed into a major cattle center. It apparently enjoyed a brief period of glory before the rails continued westward and before the inevitable barbed-wire fence enclosed the lands. It soon boasted twenty-nine saloons and nineteen

14 *Ibid.*, 56.

15 Unidentified clipping, "A Sketch of Early Days in Wilbarger County and West Texas," FW & DC files, A5–47, 1.

16 Smith, "Wilbarger County," *loc. cit.*, 61.

gambling houses along with fifteen hundred inhabitants. For several years there were no schools and no churches.

Colonel Jones never failed to appreciate the cattle industry's importance to the FW & DC's financial success, but he was equally eager to encourage permanent settlement along the road. He kept a watchful eye on immigration into Wilbarger County and considered how the company could encourage more people to move there. As often as possible, he left his Fort Worth desk and made personal inspections along the line.

Jones's responsibilities as the Fort Worth and Denver City's president were varied and demanding. He wrote to Dodge about rumors (later proved to be false) that the Gulf, Colorado and Santa Fe Railway Company would attempt to gain control of the FW & DC at the next stockholders' meeting.[17] He watched carefully every effort by the Houston and Texas Central Railway Company to compete for FW & DC trade. He studied possible routes to extend the eastern railhead at Hodge into Fort Worth.[18] He made the long journey to El Paso to check the White Oaks coal fields' potential as a supply source for the FW & DC.[19] He sought ways to avoid the frequent grass fires caused by sparks from the engines. He sought ways also to cut down the number of cattle killed as they crossed the trains' path.[20] He fought for a company policy to pay damages to injured employees; and he wondered what he could do about unnecessary expenses incurred by his otherwise competent railroad superintendent, C. L. Frost.[21]

Most of the above-named problems, and many others, Jones omitted from his annual reports to the stockholders. It was his responsibility to check out rumors concerning the company's competitors, to determine safer ways to operate the road, and to cut unnecessary expenses. His reports did include, however, his recommendations concerning company policy. On October 31, 1885, he suggested that the FW & DC should "take proper steps to inform

17 *Ibid.*
18 Dodge Papers, *loc. cit.*, XI, 233, Jones to Dodge (October 29, 1885).
19 *Ibid.*, XI, 221, Jones to Dodge (October [n.d.], 1885).
20 *Ibid.*
21 *Ibid.*, XI, 233, Jones to Dodge (October 29, 1885).

immigrants of the great value for agriculture, stock, and mineral purposes" along the route. Above all else, he told the stockholders that the company should "continue its policy of extending the road as fast as the development of the country demands it."[22]

More than a year passed before Jones could move the rails beyond Harrold. In Colorado, the Tripartite group—Governor Evans' rivals who blocked efforts to construct the Denver, Texas and Gulf road south of Pueblo—refused to allow the Evans road to move southward.[23] In addition, Colorado, Nebraska, and Kansas suddenly applied a quarantine against Texas cattle because of an outbreak of Texas fever and hoof-and-mouth disease. The restrictions seriously hurt FW & DC movements of cattle in 1885, shortly after the road reached Harrold.[24] With the quarantine against Texas cattle and the reluctance of Texas and Colorado Improvement Company stockholders to go forward with new construction, Jones commissioned Dodge to extend the line to Vernon, 15.6 miles northwest across Wilbarger County. There were good reasons for Jones's determination to move the FW & DC toward the Panhandle. The Santa Fe, crossing Indian Territory, built rapidly toward the Panhandle, and the Rock Island system sought permission from Congress to build from Kansas to El Paso.[25] Jones must reach the Panhandle soon or lose trade in that area to rival roads. "Our present inactive policy is bad for us all around," he wrote to Dodge.[26]

Meanwhile, Vernon citizens, anxious to bring the rails into their town, offered a bonus to the company if the track reached them by October 15, 1886. The amount was small, only $5,000, but Jones never failed to respond to such inducements or to the challenge to meet a deadline. Dodge's construction crews, therefore, under Dan Carey's supervision and Colonel Jones's watchful eye, worked their way toward Vernon, Texas.

Vernon, Wilbarger County's seat of government since its earliest

22 Annual Report, 1884, 2, FW & DC file 1230A.
23 Overton, *Gulf to Rockies*, 145–46.
24 *Ibid.*, 121–22.
25 *Ibid.*, 124.
26 Dodge Papers, *loc. cit.*, XI, 311, Jones to Dodge (February 13, 1886).

days, typified cow towns throughout the West. It lay in the Pease River Valley among groves of trees and surrounded by bountiful grass. Good water was plentiful and every residence had its own water well.[27] Its pleasant natural surroundings belied its violent, if brief, history. During the early 1880's horse and cattle thieves roamed the countryside, men were shot down on its main street, and livery barns were burned. Vernon's permanent settlers sat on sidewalks armed with six-shooters and Winchester rifles, determined to enforce frontier justice. When the sheriff and other prominent citizens were arrested for their own lawlessness, Texas Rangers moved in to maintain peace.[28] Finally, the residents could keep their lamps burning at night without fear of having them shot out by drunken cowboys. They awaited anxiously the railroad's arrival, hoping it would bring settlers, prosperity, and a more civilized society. Pioneer Vernon citizens were determined to overcome their reputation for "more shooting to the square inch than any town in Texas."[29]

For a time it seemed that the construction crews could not meet the deadline. By mid-September, 1886, they completed the roadbed, but the slow shipment of rails from New York caused unexpected delays. Assured that the FW & DC would complete the project whatever the cost, Vernon citizens apparently saw an opportunity to gain the road without having to pay the bonus. "I am satisfied," Jones wrote to Dodge, "that they would like to get some excuse not to pay this subsidy."[30] Finally, however, the rails reached New Orleans and the company rushed them to the construction site. Toward the end of September the crews laid two miles of track a day. As they neared Vernon, its residents suddenly protested against Jones's plans to run the rails across two sections of public lands. Jones recognized it as a delaying maneuver and, undaunted, proceeded to push forward. On October 15, 1886, according to schedule and within the deadline, the first train

[27] Annual Report, 1884, 2.
[28] Smith, "Wilbarger County," *loc. cit.*, 68–69.
[29] *Ibid.*, 68.
[30] Dodge Papers, *loc. cit.*, XI, 513, Jones to Dodge (September 22, 1886).

84

reached Vernon.[31] The locomotive pulled behind it one combination baggage and express car and one passenger coach.

Despite their obligation to pay the promised bonus, Wilbarger pioneers welcomed the iron horse with the customary whoops and yells. Without a depot, the crowd gathered at the railhead in Tom Jones's pasture where the train pulled to a stop. Local Indians, their curiosity even greater than that of the cowboys and farmers, climbed over and under the coaches and engine for a better look.[32]

Under the influence of the railroad, Vernon, Texas, changed almost overnight its wayward characteristics. Until 1886, wandering Indians, exuberant cowboys, and cattle rustlers overwhelmed the permanent settlers, and only the Texas Rangers could keep the peace. Shortly after the railroad's arrival, however, new immigrants joined the earlier pioneers, incorporated the town, and passed ordinances to enforce the law. Local officials made it unlawful "for any person to ride or drive faster than a slow lope in any of the streets of the city."[33] Public-vehicle drivers who unduly harassed passengers alighting from trains were fined from one to ten dollars. Schools and churches replaced many of the saloons and gambling houses. Civilization accompanied the FW & DC's advance across the Texas frontier.[34]

President Jones's annual report to company stockholders on October 31, 1886, showed net earnings of $175,073.74 for the fiscal year. It was a masterful accomplishment, considering the disastrous drought throughout North Texas during that period. Jones's review of its effect on the FW & DC was characteristically blunt: the country along the route suffered its most protracted drought in memory, crops were a total failure, there was not

31 "Memo Outline" (A5–47), *loc. cit.*, 1.
32 Smith, "Wilbarger County," *loc. cit.*, 70.
33 *Ibid.*
34 The only recorded event of historical interest in Wilbarger County prior to the railroad occurred in 1860. Captain Sul Ross and his Texas Rangers fought a band of Comanche Indians along the Pease River and, after a three-day battle, killed Chief Nocona. Captain Ross discovered that the Chief's wife had blue eyes and a light complexion. She was Cynthia Ann Parker, captured by the Comanches at thirteen. For twenty-four years she had lived with her captors and was the mother of Chief Nocona's four children. Against her will, Ross returned her to her relatives and she died shortly thereafter. Her eldest son, Quanah, was the last chief of the Comanches. (Clyde L. Jackson and Grace Jackson, *Quanah Parker: Last Chief of the Comanches*, 38–45.)

enough grain produced to seed the land, grass and water on the pasture lands dried up, beef cattle did not fatten, and settlers ceased coming to the area. The FW & DC, consequently, lost its normal cattle and freight shipments and much of its passenger traffic.[35]

These calamities did not restrain Jones's efforts to convince the company that construction must progress. The road, in fact, continued past Vernon and reached Chillicothe, in Hardeman County, on the same day Jones presented his report. He insisted that the line must advance toward the Canadian River for very practical reasons:

> The building of the Atchison, Topeka and Santa Fe from Iowa [Kansas] southwest along the line of the Canadian River, crossing in the vicinity of Carson County [Texas], and of the Missouri Pacific through Kingman and Iuka, Kansas, thence southwesterly toward the Beaver [River], and connecting near our crossing of the Canadian River[;] the extension of the Rock Island to the southwest in the direction of Topeka and Hutchinson, indicating a crossing of our line near our crossing of the Canadian, *en route* to El Paso[;] and the development of the northern portion of the Panhandle due to the great influx of immigration, following the progress of the line from Kansas, has made it necessary for us to extend our line to the Canadian.[36]

Thus Jones's road faced continued adversity; its competitors threatened to seize the Panhandle's potential trade; cattlemen and farmers along the existing road contemplated disaster; and new settlements in the area almost entirely ceased. The Colonel acted swiftly to resolve each problem. He called his employees together in his Fort Worth offices, described the distress and suffering in certain counties caused by the drought, and asked for donations to buy seed for the farmers. The company, he explained, would transport the seed without charge. The employees unanimously contributed to the fund and bought thousands of bushels of seed wheat. In addition, Jones instructed his construction foremen to employ as many farmers as possible until the following planting season.[37]

Jones also intensified his efforts to advertise the North Texas

35 Annual Report, 1886, 3.
36 *Ibid.*, 4.
37 "Memorandum of Historical Data" (1230A), 2.

country to potential immigrants, and contracted with General Dodge's recently organized Panhandle Construction Company to build the Fort Worth and Denver City road to the Canadian River, where it would meet the Denver, Texas and Gulf Railway[38] from Denver. Jones was so determined to complete the project that, before he signed the contract with Dodge, he offered to resign as FW & DC president so that he could do the work himself.[39] The Dodge agreement provided, however, that the Panhandle Construction Company would take over the task as soon as the rails reached a point in Hardeman County two hundred miles west of Fort Worth.[40]

Jones and Dodge decided to build the road west across Hardeman County rather than to cut north across the Indian Territory's extreme southwestern corner (Greer County). They planned originally to determine the re-entry point after the rails crossed the Territory. Dodge preferred to re-enter Texas at Wheeler County, but Jones believed the route should follow a more westerly direction and re-enter at Collingsworth County.[41] They eventually agreed to keep the road entirely in Texas for two reasons: first, they were not sure that a later Congress would approve of the Indian Territory route, and, second, Jones decided that the road, after having reached Donley County in the Panhandle, could be more easily constructed to the Canadian.[42]

Meanwhile, Jones, Dodge, and Evans realized that construction must start once again from the Denver end. To accomplish this, Evans, after many frustrating delays caused by the Tripartite group in Colorado, signed an agreement to organize a third railroad company to connect the Denver, Texas and Gulf (then operating from Denver to Pueblo) and the FW & DC's proposed railhead at the Canadian River.[43] The new company was named the Denver, Texas and Fort Worth. Jones, as president of the FW & DC, Evans,

38 At that time, Evans' road was still stalled at Pueblo, Colorado.
39 Dodge Papers, *loc. cit.*, XI, 309, Jones to Dodge (February 11, 1886).
40 A point 8.7 miles west of Quanah, Hardeman County, Texas.
41 Dodge Papers, *loc. cit.*, XI, 239, Dodge to Jones (November 4, 1885); *ibid.*, XI, 303, Jones to Dodge (February 6, 1886).
42 *Ibid.*, 335, Jones to Dodge (March 18, 1886).
43 Overton, *Gulf to Rockies*, 148–49.

87

as president of the Denver, Texas and Gulf, and Sidney Dillon, as first president of the newly organized Denver, Texas and Fort Worth, officially signed the agreement on February 15, 1887.[44] The new railroad was incorporated on April 12, 1887, with Dillon as president, Evans as first vice-president, and Jones as second vice-president. Stockholders and company officials of the three railroad companies were so interchanged that the completed line could operate as a system.[45]

General Dodge then arranged with Governor Evans and Colonel Jones to organize the Colorado and Texas Construction Company to build the Denver, Texas and Fort Worth connecting line. Jones informed Dodge that he expected Dodge's construction companies to make the connection between Pueblo and Milepost 200 (two hundred miles from Fort Worth) within fifteen months.[46]

Before the Panhandle Construction Company's contract went into effect, the FW & DC tracks reached Quanah, a townsite located the previous year by an engineering corps, on February 1, 1887. Quanah was named for Quanah Parker, Cynthia Ann Parker's eldest son. It began as a cow town and shipping center, but nesters soon moved to the area. Shortly after the FW & DC reached the town, a car loaded with wheat left the track and overturned. Trainmen decided against reloading it, and President Jones directed that any local citizen who was willing to haul the wheat to his home and plant it could have it without charge. Several local men, consequently, planted the wheat. It produced an abundant crop at harvest time and, later, proved ideal for winter grazing. Quanah prospered as ranchers and farmers with children ready for school moved to the town and established permanent homes.[47]

44 *Ibid.*, 150.
45 Jones to stockholders, Annual Report, 1887, 5; Overton lists the four major purposes of the new company: "(1) to operate a railroad, along with certain branches, from Pueblo to the Texas-New Mexico border, and (2) to acquire control of both the Denver, Texas and Gulf and the Fort Worth and Denver City. At the same time, it was implicitly understood by the principals and their associates that (3) the Panhandle Construction Company would continue building the FW & DC . . . and finally, that (4) when all lines were completed, the three constituent railroad companies would be operated as a system." (Overton, *Gulf to Rockies*, 160.)
46 Dodge acknowledged Jones's request and agreed to try to fulfill it in a letter to Jones on March 31, 1887. (See Dodge Papers, *loc. cit.*, XI, 737.)
47 J. Paul Jones, "The History of Hardeman County, Texas," 65.

When the rails reached the two-hundredth milepost, 8.7 miles west of Quanah, the Panhandle Construction Company's contract to complete the road to the Canadian River went into effect. The remaining distance totaled approximately 170 miles. The *Fort Worth Gazette* congratulated Jones for successfully pushing the FW & DC 86 miles west of Wichita Falls under extremely adverse circumstances.[48]

During the late winter and early spring of 1887, the Panhandle Construction Company, with "boys whose chest stuck out and whose forehead stuck in"[49] built the line into Childress County.[50] The Fort Worth and Denver City, after six years' effort, finally reached the first Panhandle county. At a point 219.4 miles from Fort Worth, the railroad company built the Dwight Hotel. It was a frame building with eight bedrooms and a dining room and was soon the gathering place for ranchers, cowboys, and railroad men. Food was plentiful enough as wild turkeys and other prairie animals abounded near Horsehead Tank. The train hauled water to the hotel from a near-by creek.[51]

In addition to its location among the eastern line of Panhandle counties, Childress County was important to the FW & DC for other geographical reasons. It is divided roughly in half by the Prairie Dog Town Fork of the Red River, and thus became the most westerly point south of the Red River along the Denver road's route. Childress was the railroad center for all trade west and south of the Red River for many miles. It monopolized trade to the west until it reached the area served by the Atchison, Topeka and Santa Fe on the Río Grande in New Mexico. Childress also served an area approximately one hundred miles to the south. Beyond that range, most West Texas ranchers and farmers used the Texas and Pacific rail center at Colorado City in Mitchell County. For a while, the Fort Worth and Denver City's rail center in Childress

---

48 *Fort Worth Gazette* (March 1, 1887).

49 *Childress Index* (July 29, 1949), 4.

50 Named in honor of George Campbell Childress, author of the Declaration of Independence of the Republic of Texas. (Fulmore, *History and Geography of Texas*, 106.)

51 *Childress Index* (July 29, 1949), 4.

County served a greater area of frontier country than any other shipping point in the state.[52]

Childress County pioneers fought a typical political battle when they attempted to locate the county seat. The influential role played by officials of the railroad and construction companies was typical, also. Childress City was located upon a summit between Red River and Grosebeck Creek. Henry, another small town, was located four miles beyond, and on the FW & DC route. The railroad and construction company officials supported Henry's bid for the county seat. R. E. Montgomery, General Dodge's son-in-law, and general right-of-way and town lot agent for the Panhandle Construction Company, pointed out that there was no place to locate a railroad siding within two miles of Childress City and, therefore, Henry, with its railroad service, was the logical choice for county seat.[53]

Judge A. J. Fires represented the Childress City people who resented Montgomery's interference. Childress City won the first election, held in April, 1887, but the FW & DC officials steadfastly refused to build a depot there. They insisted that any train which stopped in the Childress City area could not build up enough speed to climb the steep grades just west of the town. The court thereupon announced that the first election was illegal, and sixty-five voters, most of them railroad employees, petitioned for a new election. The town lot agent, Montgomery, promised to give town lots in Henry to all Childress City people who owned similar property in the latter town. Finally, Henry citizens promised to change the name of their town to Childress if Henry won the second election. Henry's bid succeeded, and eventually the victors kept all their promises. Most business houses and many residences "were moved bodily from old Childress City to the new Childress."[54] The Childress Lumber Company enjoyed a second prosperous season, when county officials ordered lumber to build a new courthouse.

Fort Worth and Denver City officials had good reason to worry

52 T. A. Wilkinson, *The Panhandle Route.*
53 LeRoy Reeves, "The History of Childress County," 63–67; Johnson and Barker, *A History of Texas and Texans,* 972.
54 *Ibid.*

about the Panhandle's relatively sharp elevation as the track-laying crew advanced across the "unpeopled immensity." The Panhandle slopes southeastwardly from approximately 4,600 feet in the Canadian River area to 1,600 feet in the Childress County area. The surveyors constantly sought to follow a route which avoided sudden and steep inclines. Thus, when they reached the Prairie Dog Town Fork of the Red River, just inside the Hall County boundary line, the route turned sharply northward.

There were few people and no towns in Hall County until the railroad construction crews approached. When the surveyors determined the exact route, however, two towns—Salisbury and Memphis—sprang up. R. E. Montgomery established the railroad townsite (Salisbury) ten miles north and three miles east of the county lines. The area's generally smooth land surface influenced Montgomery's choice. Carpenters built a depot there before the rails arrived, and soon a thriving little town grew around the future railroad center. Predictably, its citizens planned to make their new home the county seat.[55]

Almost simultaneously, J. C. Montgomery (no relation to R. E. Montgomery) located a rival town along the railroad's route about six miles farther north. He named his town Memphis. Railroad officials, however, refused to stop the trains at Memphis. To do so, they claimed, would make it impossible to climb the steep grade just north of the town; Memphis citizens must therefore send wagons and coaches to Salisbury to pick up passengers and freight. Their argument almost prevailed, but local plotters secretly devised a plan to force the trains to stop at Memphis. Soon, northbound locomotives developed traction trouble as they attempted to race through the town. Engineers and conductors discovered, after they climbed down from their stalled trains, that their iron horses were the victims of the only available weapon at hand: homemade lye soap—heavily applied atop the tracks. The trainmen covered the slippery rails with sand, backed the trains downhill as far as Salisbury, steamed forward again, rattling and shaking under

---

[55] Inez Baker, "The History of the Fort Worth and Denver City Railway in My Home County (Hall)," 4, FW & DC essays.

maximum speed, but stalled once more at Memphis. FW & DC officials reluctantly admitted defeat and agreed to make the town a regular stop.[56] Soon thereafter Salisbury citizens accepted free townsite lots in Memphis, dismantled their houses, placed the lumber on railroad cars, and abandoned their old homes. Memphis had won the war against the railroad company and, with its victory, the county seat. Northbound trains provided the cunning pioneers additional entertainment not enjoyed by other communities along the route. After the curious crowds gathered periodically at the depot to welcome new arrivals, they moved to the edge of town to see whether or not the departing train could "pull Giles Hill." Frequently, the engineer had to haul the cars in relays to the top of the hill.[57]

When the trains reached the top of Giles Hill they crossed Donley County's[58] southern boundary. The county organized and had its county seat at Clarendon several years before the Fort Worth and Denver City arrived. This fact simplified some of the usual railroad problems and complicated others. The company employed many local citizens as laborers on the construction crews. Its permanent workers eagerly sought room and board in Clarendon homes built with lumber hauled by ox teams from Kansas City. They looked forward to home-cooked meals and feather beds—definitely an improvement over life in the company's tent cities. The crude, rough, uninhibited railroad builders did not know, however, that Clarendon already had established a reputation as "Saint's Roost" with every cowboy in the Texas Panhandle; that stockmen took their brides to honeymoon at Clarendon because it was the only safe place in the entire region to take a young woman; or that "Saint's Roost" was so completely domesticated that a Mr. Jessie Ring owned a turkey farm near by.[59]

Clarendon, Donley County, dated back to October, 1878. L. H. Carhart, a Methodist Episcopal minister, laid out the townsite at

[56] *Ibid.*
[57] *Ibid.*
[58] Named in honor of Stockton P. Donley, Civil War veteran and a member of the Texas Supreme Court. (Fulmore, *History and Geography of Texas*, 196.)
[59] ———— Harvey, "History of Fort Worth and Denver City Railway in My Home County," 2–12, FW & DC essays.

Carroll Creek, built a house, and named the "town" Clarendon— an honor to his wife, Clara. The enterprising young frontier preacher immediately began to advertise his "Christian Colony," describing it as "a city of culture and refinement" and predicting that great steamboats would soon dock along the banks of the Salt Fork of the Red River.[60]

Settlers from eastern states, including Carhart's brother-in-law, Alfred Sully from New York, rushed to the town. They bought lots and signed papers that they would never "sell liquor nor operate a gambling house."[61] Four additional Methodist ministers moved to the town, built a school, Allentown Academy, and made plans to build a college.[62] The frontier educational center was so peaceful that justices of the peace throughout North Texas threatened to sentence overintoxicated men to "a week in Clarendon."[63]

The welcoming committee which met the first FW & DC train into Clarendon was somewhat different from those which had gathered at earlier railheads along the route: Mrs. G. W. Antrobus' fourteen school children met the engine and caboose at the depot and, just south of town, at the Lelia switch, James Kilfeil awaited the first freight cars. For several weeks, Kilfeil guarded a huge stack of buffalo bones—forty feet long, fifteen feet wide, and ten feet high[64]—until the train arrived. Bone-stealing in the Texas Panhandle was almost as common as cattle-rustling, even at "Saint's Roost."

Jesse Ring, equally eager to see the first train arrive, waited with a more unique collection—fifteen thousand turkeys. A few years earlier, Ring had established a turkey ranch in a most unlikely area: just inside the Texas border and just outside the Indian Territory. While he awaited railroad transportation, his original flock multiplied almost beyond his ability to control. For years Claren-

---

60 *Ibid.*, 3.

61 Untitled Summary of the Fort Worth and Denver City Railway Company, FW & DC file A–47, 2 (hereinafter referred to as Untitled Summary).

62 Harvey, "History of Fort Worth and Denver City Railway in My Home County," *loc. cit.*, 3.

63 Untitled Summary (A5–47), 2.

64 Harvey, "History of Fort Worth and Denver City Railway in My Home County," *loc. cit.*, 11.

don's citizens—yearning for excitement—looked forward to Ring's turkey drive. Ring chose, however, to drive his turkeys to the Hedley station, a few miles southeast of Clarendon, where local cowboys were not as likely to do pistol-practice on his birds. Fifteen thousand turkeys finally began the twenty-mile drive. Ring's ordeal lasted for more than a week. When the turkeys tired, they settled down amidst clumps of shinnery, and neither Ring nor his horse could move them. When one turkey finally panicked and raced off, usually in the opposite direction, hundreds more followed. Exhausted, Ring's horse died before the turkeys reached the railroad station, and the exasperated turkey rancher made the last few miles on foot. The Panhandle's most spectacular turkey drive in history became legend among FW & DC trainmen.[65]

The Indian scare in Hall and Donley counties shortly after the Fort Worth and Denver City arrived at Clarendon provided that town with the excitement it missed during its quiet and orderly first decade. The railroad and telegraph offices at depots along the route played prominent parts in the incident. Explanations for its cause conflict, but pioneer settlers agreed upon essential details. The incident developed, they claimed, when W. L. Huddleston from Bell County bought a section of land in the southeastern Panhandle, just south of the Salt Fork of the Red River and, with his two young sons, rode the FW & DC from Fort Worth to Salisbury, Hall County. On the same train they shipped their livestock, household goods, tools, and wagon. At Salisbury, they loaded the wagon and drove off to L. H. Stall's farm to inquire about the two-room dugout Stall had contracted to build for the Huddleston family. Stall invited Huddleston and his sons to spend the night.

Just as the Huddlestons unharnessed the team, Will Johnson, Stall's neighbor, rode up and talked until sundown with the new arrivals. Suddenly, he realized that his wife was alone at home with their two small children and he hurried away. About half a mile down the road he saw a rider approach at high speed. It was Mrs. Johnson with their four-year-old son in front of her on the horse and their two-year-old son under one arm. Breathless with excite-

65 *Ibid.*, 12.

ment, she informed her husband that she had seen a band of Indians near the dugout on the Johnson farm. Together they raced back to the Stall farm and shouted that the country was full of Indians "on the warpath." Johnson and Stall hitched horses to wagons and with their families hurried toward Wellington. Meanwhile, the Huddlestons, unused to Indians on the warpath back in Bell County, raced away ahead of the other two families.

Johnson and Stall drove their families directly to the courthouse at Wellington, then spread the alarm through town, collected guns and ammunition, returned to the courthouse, and barred the doors. While the children slept, every man and woman sat—guns in hand—and awaited the first sounds of the rampaging Indians.

Huddleston and his boys, it developed, had not bothered with saddles. While Johnson and Stall had loaded their families on the wagons, Huddleston had jumped on his mule, his sons had jumped on their ponies, and together they had loped across the open country toward Salisbury. They warned every family along the route—the Jap Longs, the Ab Smiths, the Lowry Smiths—that wild Indians approached from their Indian Territory reservation. Each account added more tales of unbelievable cruelty and horror. As they neared Salisbury, one of the ponies fell. Not bothering to check whether its leg was broken, the boy climbed behind his father upon the winded mule's back. Father and sons continued their journey. At midnight the "lather-covered mule and pony," with their hysterical riders, reached Salisbury.

The terrified strangers spread the warning and families hurriedly crowded into the railroad depot. They barred the doors and stacked office furniture against them. The telegraph operator then sent frenzied messages up and down the FW & DC line. Fear intensified inside the depot. Up at the Clarendon station a startled operator received the message: "I see them coming. I am gone."

Clarendon was no longer peaceful and calm. Young men raced through the country to spread the alarm and soon thereafter wagons filled with frantic families rattled and bumped toward the town. Although it was impossible for anyone in Clarendon to know, someone yelled that cowboys held off painted savages only

95

half a mile from the Salisbury station. Business houses were closed when Jim Cain and other men at the depot decided they must hasten to Salisbury's rescue. They needed guns, ammunition, and transportation. While an FW & DC engineer readied an engine and caboose, the other men broke into Taylor's Store—there was no time to ask him to open the doors—and armed themselves. Jim Cain took four boxes of .38-caliber cartridges for his two .45-caliber pistols, and twelve-gauge shells for his ten-gauge shotgun. He confiscated two quarts of whisky to help him "keep calm" (Taylor had obviously violated his "Saint's Roost Pledge"). Other men in the rescue party similarly armed themselves and boarded the caboose.

Through the cold winter night the little train whistled its way toward Salisbury. Finally, at daybreak a little group of drunken farmers, cattlemen, and cowboys staggered toward the barricaded depot. Salisbury's "Indian victims" and Clarendon's "rescuers" stared at one another, completely bewildered. Joe Horn, inside the Salisbury depot when the train arrived from "Saint's Roost," said later, "There were enough drunks to have stopped all the Indians in the territory if they had been sober. It would have been a terrible slaughter if there had been Indians, because those volunteers were not able to take care of themselves, let alone fight."[66] Across the fallen snow, there was not a sign that Indians had visited the area during the night, nor at any time during the past twelve years. Clarendon, "the Chautauqua of the Texas Panhandle," now had a night to remember.[67]

President Morgan Jones apparently approved of the unscheduled midnight train to Salisbury. He encouraged every effort to establish good public relations along the route. The Colonel particularly appreciated Clarendon's voluminous trade with the FW & DC. He and his general superintendent, C. L. Frost, visited

[66] Quoted in Harley True Burton, "History of the JA Ranch," *The Southwestern Historical Quarterly*, Vol. XXI (April, 1928), 328.

[67] The best account of the Indian scare is Harvey, "History of the Fort Worth and Denver City Railway in My Home County," 13–19, FW & DC essays. Other sources for the story are Jimmie Gillentine, *Donley County Leader* (June 25, 1936); Harley True Burton, "History of the JA Ranch," *loc. cit.*, 327–28; and J. W. Casaway, *Clarendon News* (July 4, 1935).

96

"Saint's Roost" shortly after the Indian scare. He predicted a prosperous future for Clarendon's civic-minded populace but, diplomatically, did not mention the midnight ride to Salisbury.[68]

The Fort Worth and Denver City route beyond Clarendon continued its northwesterly course into Armstrong County. By August, 1887, the track-laying crews reached Washburn, located on the county's northern boundary and 319.9 miles from Fort Worth. In Armstrong County, the rails passed the sprawling JA Ranch. Colonel Charles Goodnight and Mrs. John Adair jointly owned "probably the finest and best-managed ranch in the Great Plains region."[69] When the FW & DC reached Donley and Armstrong counties, the road passed within twenty-five miles of the ranch headquarters. The FW & DC thus brought within easy reach for the first time huge quantities of needed supplies.[70]

During its early history, Fort Elliott in Wheeler County was the nearest settlement to the JA Ranch. According to Goodnight, Fort Elliott had "one store, outlaws, thieves, cutthroats, and buffalo hunters, and a large per cent of prostitutes."[71] Dodge City, Kansas, a small government post without railroad connections at the time, was the next nearest settlement. Tascosa, in Oldham County, was "just a good place to cross the Canadian River with cattle."[72] It was the third nearest settlement to the JA Ranch.

Supplies to the JA were ox-freighted from Trinidad, Colorado, some four hundred miles away. Goodnight paid one cent per hundred pounds, per mile, for goods sent from Trinidad. He paid $7.00 for a one-hundred-pound sack of flour, $225.00 for one thousand feet of lumber, and ten cents for twenty-five matches.[73]

Goodnight transferred most of his trade to Dodge City, Kansas, when the Atchison, Topeka and Santa Fe Railroad reached that town. In 1881, when the Texas and Pacific extended its line to

68 *Fort Worth Gazette* (November, 1887), in the C. L. Frost Papers, *loc. cit.*

69 J. Evetts Haley, *Charles Goodnight: Cowman and Plainsman*, 328.

70 Other large ranches in the Panhandle at that time were the Bugbee Ranch (Quarter Circle J brand), the Creswell Ranch (CC brand), the Henderson Ranch (Scissors brand), the Butes and Deal Ranch (LX brand), and the Littlefield Ranch (LIT brand).

71 Burton, "History of the JA Ranch," *loc. cit.*, 336.

72 *Ibid.*, 337.

73 *Ibid.*

97

Colorado City, Mitchell County, Goodnight traded at that railroad center.[74] The journey, by wagon, was still more than two hundred miles from headquarters.

Ten or twelve yoke of oxen pulled four or five freight wagons. Ranch hands tied the wagons together and worked the oxen as one team. Whenever a wagon train stalled at a steep grade, in a creek, or in sand, they separated the wagons and hauled them one by one across the difficult course. It was indeed a slow and expensive journey. It is not surprising, therefore, that Goodnight and other Panhandle ranchers welcomed the FW & DC despite the fact that a railroad's entrance into ranching territory brought many "nesters" in its wake.

As the FW & DC rails extended across Armstrong County, farmers and ranchers clustered around the designated water and freight stations to make their permanent homes. Often, tents and dugouts dotted either side of the roadbed before the rail crew arrived. Almost as often, a "tent city" formed a welcoming committee to greet the first train before the citizens could agree upon a name for their community.

At one station, Claude Ayres, the engineer, asked the little group what they had named their town.

"We haven't named it yet," replied a cowboy.

"Call it Ayres," the engineer suggested.

"No, sir-ee," the cowboy said. "We have too much air out here now."

"Then call it Claude," Claude Ayres answered. Thus Claude, Armstrong County, in the heart of the Texas Panhandle, honored the first railroad men[75] who entered the town. Later, the little community challenged Washburn for county seat. After a typical frontier battle, Claude won the contest by a narrow vote. The FW & DC served both communities and therefore had no reason to attempt to influence the election.

74 *Ibid.*, 337–38.
75 Posey, "The History of the Fort Worth and Denver City Railway in My Home County," 1, FW & DC essays. Many years later Claude Ayres died in California and, according to his request, his body was brought back to Claude, Texas, and buried in the local cemetery. The above account, therefore, of the origin of the town's name is apparently true.

By late August, 1897, the roadbed extended to the Canadian River and the rail crew approached the Potter County[76] line. Simultaneously, the bridge-building crew spanned the rivers and creeks in the area.[77] The grading crew hesitated briefly when a spirited contest—to determine a townsite location—developed between Henry B. Sanborn, a cattleman, and Colonel Bill Plemmons, a frontier lawyer. Tempers flared and violence threatened. Only one mile separated the two proposed locations. Diplomatically, the Panhandle Construction Company officials directed their men to grade between the two proposed townsites. The FW & DC directors and stockholders recently had agreed to extend the line beyond the Canadian River, and would not tolerate any unnecessary delay. President Jones recommended the extension beyond Potter County for several practical reasons:

The overflow of emigration into the Panhandle is very large, going in advance of the roads now building in that direction.

The agricultural possibilities of the Panhandle of Texas . . . are only just beginning to be appreciated and known. It has hitherto been considered entirely a cattle country. . . .

In the northwest corner of Texas . . . from fifty to one hundred miles north of the Canadian River, are immense deposits of coal . . . [which will] add very largely to the traffic of the road. If by any possibility the line from Denver should fail to reach the Canadian and connect with us, it would be policy for this Company to extend its line across the river and northward until it reached this coal measure.

. . . The pioneer road into the Panhandle cannot fail to secure advantages over succeeding roads by establishing towns and business centers, and furnishing the first avenue of travel into a new country.[78]

By the time the FW & DC reached Potter County in September, 1887, Jones had agreed to meet the Denver, Texas and Fort Worth at the Texas–New Mexico state line. He hoped to connect the two roads in February, 1888.[79]

Whenever possible President Jones made inspection tours. The

---

[76] Named in honor of Robert Potter, one of the signers of the Texas Declaration of Independence. (Fulmore, *History and Geography of Texas*, 116.)

[77] Letter, J. H. Barwise (early FW & DC employee) to General John A. Hulen (vice-president of FW & DC), (July 13, 1938), FW & DC file 1230A, 2.

[78] Annual Report, 1886 (1230A), 6.

[79] *Ibid.*, 7.

reserved Welshman never made speeches, but he talked freely with town leaders and newspapermen along the route when he believed the pioneers needed encouragement. Neither droughts, flash-floods, blizzards, nor disastrous fires caused him to lose faith in the Panhandle's ultimate prosperity.[80]

The Colonel particularly enjoyed riding the rails between Fort Worth and Amarillo—the Potter County town which eventually emerged from the Sanborn-Plemmons townsite war—accompanied by a stranger to the area. On such trips he explained to his companion why the railroad company created certain towns and why it bypassed others, why the company entered some and avoided other county-seat controversies.

Probably no town in North Texas was more determined than Tascosa to bring the railroad to its people. Apparently for reasons the railroad company could not avoid, the rails missed the town by the narrow width of the Canadian River. Quicksand in the riverbed prevented a crossing at the desired location. Tascosa consequently became "the outstanding ghost town of the Panhandle."[81]

Tascosa was located on the Canadian River's northern bank in northeastern Oldham County. The county was one of the first in the Panhandle to organize. In December, 1880, Tascosa was made the county seat.[82] Earlier, the area was, in succession, a Comanchero trading center and a notorious "nest" for western cattle thieves. As Tascosa gained more permanent settlers—and a certain degree of respectability—C. F. Rudolph, editor of the *Tascosa Pioneer* and the town's "greatest asset," presented numerous reasons why the Fort Worth and Denver City should build through Tascosa:

There are two ways for a railroad from the Southeast to build down

80 Jones was a familiar celebrity in every town along the FW & DC route. City and county newspapers from Fort Worth to the Canadian River apparently quoted almost every statement he made. It was typical of the Welshman that every quoted statement concerned the railroad, the country along the route, or the relationship between the two. Always, he was the optimistic promoter.

81 R. C. Crane, "Ghost Towns of West Texas," *West Texas Historical Association Year Book*, Vol. XVII (October, 1941), 7.

82 Johnson and Barker, *A History of Texas and Texans*, 986.

to the river to a crossing here, either of which is as simple and easy a descent from the Plains as could be found anywhere; and either of them leads directly into and through Tascosa. More than this, after the town is passed the route up Tascosa Creek leads to the Plains in the direction of Denver by a more gradual ascent.[83]

In Rudolph's imagination, the FW & DC would do no less for Tascosa than editor B. B. Paddock's "tarantula" railroad network did for Fort Worth. Jones's line would attract "other railroads, multiply business and population, national banks, slaughtering yards and refrigerating establishments, union depots, round houses, manufactories and foundries, colleges and churches . . . water works, street cars, opera houses, a tremendous boom in real estate and a morning *Pioneer*."[84] Tascosa, he believed, was destined to become the "Chicago of the Panhandle."[85]

Unfortunately, Rudolph's prognostications proved far less accurate than those made in the 1870's by the Fort Worth editor. Area ranchers, particularly Abner Taylor and John Farwell, owners of the XIT lands, and W. M. D. Lee of the LS Ranch, were determined to locate the townsite more convenient to their own interests. Together they declared war against Rudolph's ambitious plans. Lee offered to donate a townsite to the railroad three miles west of Tascosa. Taylor and Farwell reminded company officials that they could block the FW & DC's proposed route across more than fifty miles of their XIT lands if the company continued its plans to make Tascosa a major rail center.

[83] *Tascosa Pioneer* (January 26, 1887), quoted in John L. McCarty, *Maverick Town: The Story of Old Tascosa*, 210. This excellent study of a Texas Panhandle frontier town includes a thorough and accurate account of the FW & DC influence on panhandle development. Overton, *Gulf to Rockies*, 171, includes a first-rate summary of McCarty's Tascosa: "Tascosa on the Canadian, offspring of the Borregos Plaza of the Mexican *pastores*; turbulent crossroads of Indians, cowboys, nesters, Scottish and Irish noblemen, Yankee and Confederate veterans, businessmen, gamblers, and their women of diverse virtue; way point for Billy the Kid, Pat Garrett, and even General Dodge; outpost of the XIT, LS, and LIT ranch empires." It should be noted, however, that General Dodge's visit to Tascosa, if indeed he was there at all, must have been very brief. During the months the FW & DC crews worked between Amarillo and Union Park, New Mexico, President Jones and General Dodge corresponded frequently. Jones's letters contained lengthy descriptions of construction progress. All of the letters were addressed to New York City. They suggest that Dodge arrived at the construction site shortly before the connection at Union Park.

[84] McCarty, "Background History of the Fort Worth and Denver City Railway," FW & DC essays.

[85] *Ibid.*, 202.

Jones, Dodge, and Montgomery could hardly ignore the ranchers' objections to Rudolph's designs. They wanted to accept Lee's townsite offer and dared not offend the XIT owners in Hartley and Dallam counties. The report, which was apparently true,[86] that boiling quicksands lay in the Canadian River opposite Tascosa solved their dilemma. The FW & DC tracks remained along the river's south bank and missed Tascosa by less than a mile. The company, however, tried to pacify disappointed Tascosans. It built a frame, two-room station, directly across the river from the town. The town fathers, for their part, tried desperately to tie their community to the road. Hoping to make the station as accessible as possible, they built a wagon bridge across the dry river and organized a taxi and dray line.[87] But the "Chicago of the Panhandle"— so near the rails, yet so far away—was doomed. Moreover, its ambitious dreams had created competitive interest in other Panhandle towns along the route. Construction boomed down the line at Rag Town (soon renamed Amarillo). Other men initiated plans to build a city named Cheyenne a few miles north of Tascosa, and rumors persisted that A. G. Boyce and the XIT wanted a city in Hartley County conveniently near ranch headquarters. Tascosans sought their fortunes at these and other points along the FW & DC route.[88]

The railroad, therefore, having created many towns, and having brought prosperity to many others, brought eventual oblivion to Tascosa merely by failing to cross a river at the proper place.

On Christmas Day, 1887, the rails reached a point in southeastern Hartley County[89] near Channing, within the XIT boundaries. Morgan Jones continued to make frequent trips to the Panhandle to inspect the line, to Trinidad, Colorado, to inquire about coal mines in the area, and to Denver to confer with C. F. Meek,[90] newly appointed general manager of the entire Gulf-to-

[86] Hoyt, "Summary History" (FW & DC file 1230), 3; *Dalhart Texan* (Jubilee Edition), (May 25, 1951), 7.

[87] McCarty, "Background History of the Fort Worth and Denver City Railway," 219–20, FW & DC files.

[88] *Ibid.*, 223.

[89] Named in honor of Oliver Cromwell Hartley, one of a commission of three to codify Texas laws in 1854. (Fulmore, *History and Geography of Texas*, 199.)

[90] Dodge Papers, *loc. cit.*, XII, 59, Dodge to Jones (February 8, 1888).

Rockies system.[91] The *Fort Worth Gazette* reported that it was "next to an absolute certainty" that the Fort Worth and Denver and the Denver, Texas and Fort Worth would join their rails by March 15, 1888.[92]

The *Rocky Mountain News*, equally anxious to report the road's progress, informed its readers that the construction crews moved two and one-half miles closer together each day and that the FW & DC rails should reach the Texas line in Dallam County[93] by January 10.[94]

Newspaper reports concerning Texas and the railroads increased week by week in the *Rocky Mountain News*. New buildings erected in Fort Worth suddenly became news items in Denver. A struggle between Galveston and New Orleans for precedence in future commercial relations with the "metropolis of the mountains" obviously pleased the Colorado editor. He supported Fort Worth's bid for the Texas State Democratic Convention, and he sent a reporter to Fort Worth for more news items and to tell Texans about Colorado's summer resorts.

Rocky Mountain News subscribers learned to appreciate "the splendid rains" in West Texas and to look upon Fort Worth as truly "the Denver of Texas."[95] They read that Fort Worth was in every respect a western town: "It is too wide awake and orderly to be Southern, too quiet and orderly to be Southwestern."[96] Determined to create cordial relations between the two cities—whatever the cost to his integrity—a *News* reporter told his Colorado readers that Fort Worth never had "a drunken or disorderly man on the streets."[97]

The Colorado editor enthusiastically welcomed "the Honorable Morgan Jones" to Denver early in February, 1888. Several days

---

91 Meek's position, of course, was still below those of the three railroad presidents, Jones, Evans, and Dillon.

92 *Fort Worth Gazette* (December 27, 1887).

93 Named in honor of James W. Dallam, author of *Dallam's Digest*, based on Supreme Court decisions during the years of the Texas Republic. (Fulmore, *History and Geography of Texas*, 196.)

94 *Rocky Mountain News* (January 6, 1888), 1.

95 *Ibid.* (March 6, 1888), 9.

96 *Ibid.*

97 *Ibid.*

later, he reported in detail the visitor's statements at an "important meeting of railroad representatives."[98] Optimistic as usual, the Texan with the Welsh accent flattered the city of Denver, predicted a great rush of settlers to the Panhandle–southern Colorado area, promised a prosperous future for Colorado's rich coal fields, and guaranteed to furnish Denverites huge supplies of lumber from east Texas.

Meanwhile, the Fort Worth and Denver City construction crews progressed across Dallam County along the Mustang Creek Fork of the Canadian River; on January 26, 1888, they reached the state line. Determined to close the remaining gap between the two lines as rapidly as possible, Jones directed the construction company to extend the rails into New Mexico. En route to Fort Worth from his Denver visit in early February, he stopped briefly at the railhead and encouraged the men to try to complete the project by March 15. Four hundred and fifty teams thereupon kicked up an even greater cloud of dust among the rolling hills and conelike mountains in northeastern New Mexico.

At the end of the working day, March 13, 1888, Dan Carey informed General Dodge (who had recently arrived from New York to watch the final days' work), that the rails—at that moment less than four miles apart—should meet the following day.[99] With good weather and an early start, he hoped to beat the March 15 deadline by a full day.

Before sunrise the next morning, every man arose and had breakfast. Excitedly, they milled around and awaited enough daylight to start their work. Finally, at 4:30 A.M. Dan Carey, "standing cool and collected," fired a pistol to signal the last working day. The men rushed to their tasks, war-whooping and whistling their eagerness to begin. Dan Carey walked along the road and "watched every movement," while General Dodge, in a light, one-horse wagon, allowed "nothing [to] escape his notice."[100]

By noon the rails were two and one-half miles closer together,

---

98 *Ibid.* (February 3, 1888), 2.
99 *Ibid.* (March 15, 1888), 1.
100 *Ibid.*

104

and just before four o'clock the two construction crews met. Hurriedly, they cut two rails to make a proper connection. Then they adjusted the joints. General Dodge drove the first spike, Dan Carey the second, and newspaper reporters completed the connection.[101] They christened the historic spot "Union Park."

President Jones and general manager Meek awaited the news at the Fort Worth depot, 528 miles away. Governor Evans, 280 miles to the north of Union Park, at Denver, also awaited the message. Finally, the word from Dodge arrived:

We connected track at four p.m. twenty-five miles north of Cimarron, laying four miles of track up to four p.m. road is open for business Denver to Gulf.[102]

It was, said General Dodge, who a few years before had built the nation's first transcontinental railroad, "the most important connection I ever made."[103]

President Jones gave orders to send out a special train to Denver that same evening, and Fort Worth and Denver newspapers continued to inform their readers of each new development.

---

101 *Ibid.*
102 Grenville M. Dodge Letters, *loc. cit.*, Box 2, Letter No. 506.
103 *Rocky Mountain News* (March 15, 1888), 1.

6. SNOW-CLAD PEAKS AND ORANGE GROVES

THE *Denver Republican*'s morning edition announced that "the ceremony of driving the silver spike" would take place the following day, March 15, 1888. The announcement stated that, among other notable railroad men, President Morgan Jones and General Grenville Dodge would participate in that "most important event."[1] Eager to print the news before it happened, the editor erred on two points: first, the Fort Worth and Denver City's rails linked with those of the Denver, Texas and Fort Worth at four o'clock in the afternoon, March 14, and the ceremony occurred immediately thereafter; and, second, President Jones was not present when General Dodge drove the first silver spike.

The three railroad companies which comprised the Gulf-to-Rockies system prepared formal announcements—identical to those used to herald matrimonial events:

United
Mr. Snow-Clad Peaks,
of Colorado,
and
Miss Orange Groves,
of the South[2]

---

[1] (March 14, 1888), 8.

106

The enterprising Colorado newspaperman naturally assumed that President Jones, master of the "Miss Orange Groves" organization —the Fort Worth and Denver City Railway Company—would attend the auspicious union. Jones had almost literally forced the "bride" to march across North Texas and the Panhandle during the preceding three years. Having accomplished that goal, however, the Welsh bachelor, always the master at avoiding pomp and ceremony, arranged that other members of the official railroad family witness the fact. He stayed far away.

While General Grenville M. Dodge, Dan Carey, and R. E. Montgomery drove silver spikes and made appropriate speeches to representatives of the press, President Jones was back at the Fort Worth offices arranging to inaugurate the first freight and passenger train service. By the time Dodge's message arrived from Union Park, a special train stood ready to depart from the Fort Worth terminal to transport to Denver general manager C. F. Meek, general passenger agent George Ady, superintendent of trains John McCormick, and advertising manager Thomas F. Nelson. Jones avoided even this part of the ceremony.

Before his departure, Meek announced that another special train, with twelve Pullman sleepers, would leave Fort Worth on March 26 to take a group of Texas delegates to the first Denver meeting of the International Range Association. Those who wished to attend the cattlemen's convention and Gulf-to-Rockies railroad jubilee could purchase special-rate round-trip Pullman tickets for twenty dollars.

President Jones still remained in Fort Worth. He wanted to receive the company's first coal shipment from Trinidad, Colorado, which was due in Fort Worth the following day. He remained in Texas also, to help make arrangements for the March 26 Denver excursion train. General manager Meek handled similar tasks at the Colorado end of the road.

Ten days later Meek returned to Fort Worth accompanied by Dodge, Montgomery, and chief engineer Frank Bissell. The fa-

2 Pamphlet 385, Railroad Pamphlet File, Library, State Historical Society of Colorado, State Museum Building, Denver, Colorado.

107

mous General Dodge made another speech to the reporters and welcoming party, he complimented the city on its "magnificent terminal facilities," and he predicted that Fort Worth would become an immense railroad distribution center. General manager Meek announced final plans to dispatch the "great excursion" to Denver the following morning.

So many Texas cattlemen, their families, and friends bought tickets for the 807-mile journey to the Rocky Mountains that Meek decided to divide the group and to transport them on four separate trains. The first train would depart Fort Worth at 7:30 A.M., Monday, March 26, and each of the other trains would follow at half-hour intervals.[3]

Meanwhile, Denver's city fathers worked diligently to welcome and to entertain the huge Texas delegation. Donald Fletcher, president of the Denver Chamber of Commerce, was general chairman of the arrangements committees. He called for, and received, donations of more than $16,000—including $1,000 from city funds—to finance the jubilee.[4] Fletcher appropriated $1,500 for identification badges, $2,000 for use of the Opera House, $1,500 for a "Grand Ball," $1,000 for a parade, $800 for local advertising and printing, $450 for a cowboy band (plus $500 for "outside music"), and, finally, $3,500 to "electrically illuminate the city."[5]

Throughout the day on Sunday, March 25, trains brought into Fort Worth delegates from South and East Texas. They crowded into hotel rooms, jammed the lobbies, and talked only of Denver. Assistant passenger agent M. V. Newlin, assisted by several clerks, spent all day preparing, stamping, and issuing tickets.

Before sunrise on Monday morning, March 26, 500 Texas excursionists jammed the Union depot at Fort Worth and awaited assignment to one of the four trains. They came from every section of the state, and others planned to join them en route across North and West Texas. One of the largest delegations at the depot represented South Texas. Six weeks earlier the *Corpus Christi Caller*

3 *Fort Worth Gazette* (March 15, 1888); *Rocky Mountain News* (March 25, 1888), 1.

4 *Rocky Mountain News* (March 3, 1888), 6; (March 22, 1888), 6.

5 *Ibid.* (March 17, 1888), 6.

108

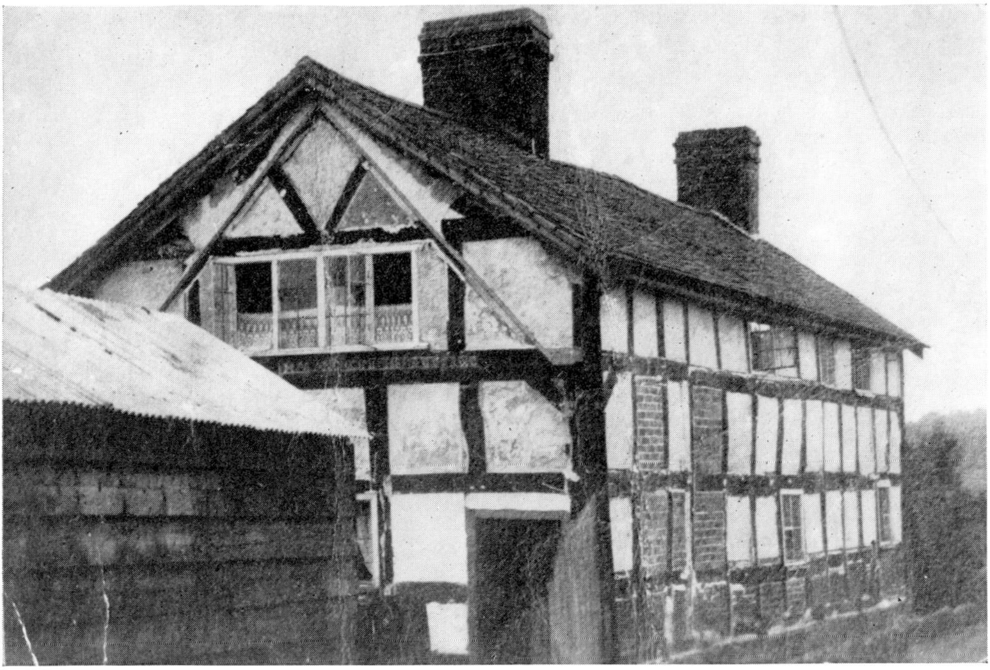

Vachwen, the estate where Morgan Jones was born on October 7, 1839. The farm is located near Tregynon, County of Montgomery, Wales.

COURTESY MRS. EDITH LONGSTAFF, SURREY, ENGLAND

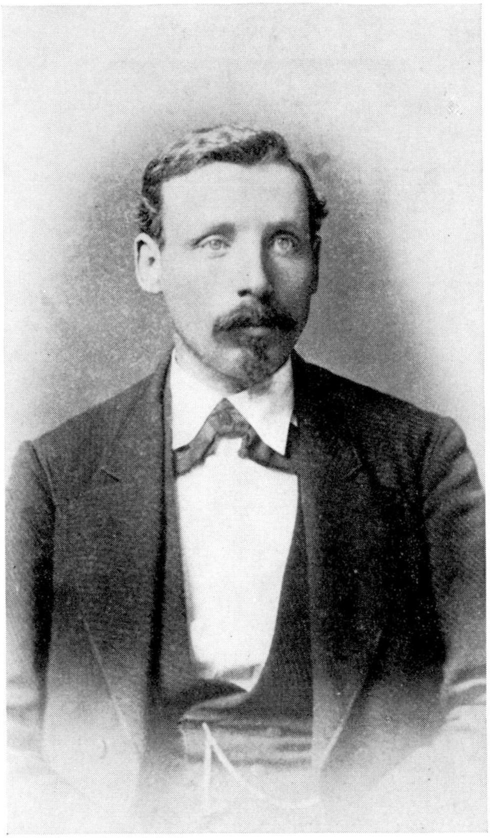

This picture of Morgan Jones was made about 1870, soon after his arrival in Texas. At this time he was a construction foreman for the Southern Trans-Continental Railroad Company. His assignment was the Jefferson Branch between Texarkana and Jefferson.

COURTESY MRS. EDITH LONGSTAFF, SURREY, ENGLAND

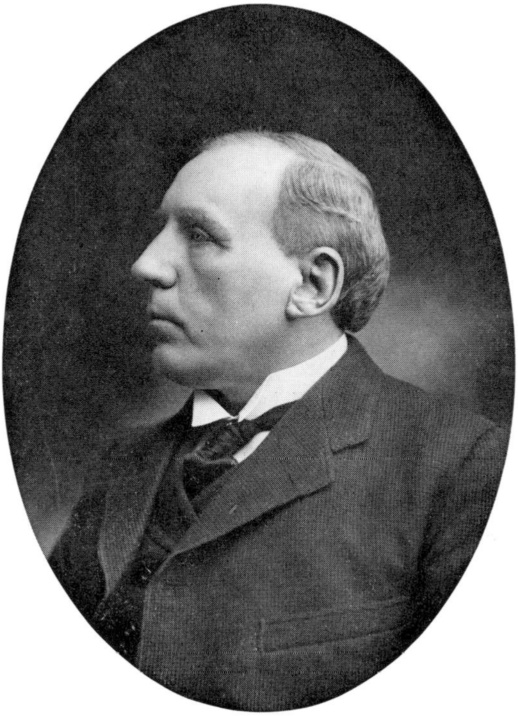

Colonel Morgan Jones, about 1880.

COURTESY MORGAN JONES, JR.

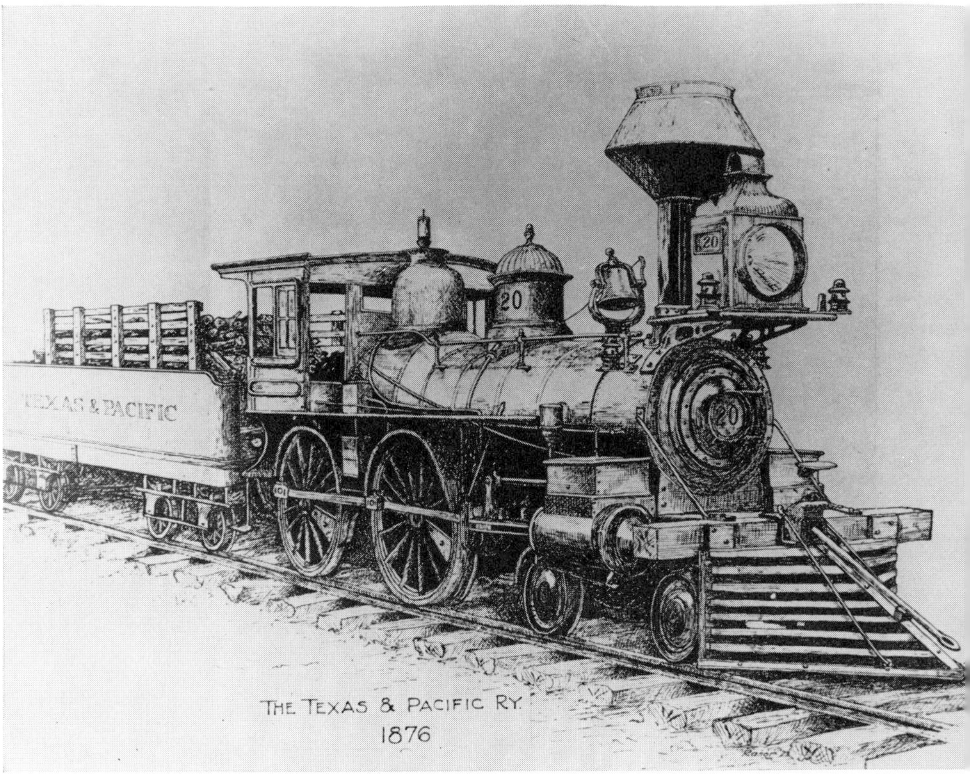
TEXAS & PACIFIC
20
THE TEXAS & PACIFIC RY.
1876

Texas and Pacific Steam Locomotive No. 20, which pulled the first train into Fort Worth, Texas, in 1876.

COURTESY WILLIAM C. SCHULTZ, TEXAS AND PACIFIC RAILWAY COMPANY

Bridge construction across the Brazos River as the Wichita Valley Railway Company rails approached Seymour, Texas, about 1890.

COURTESY MORGAN JONES, JR.

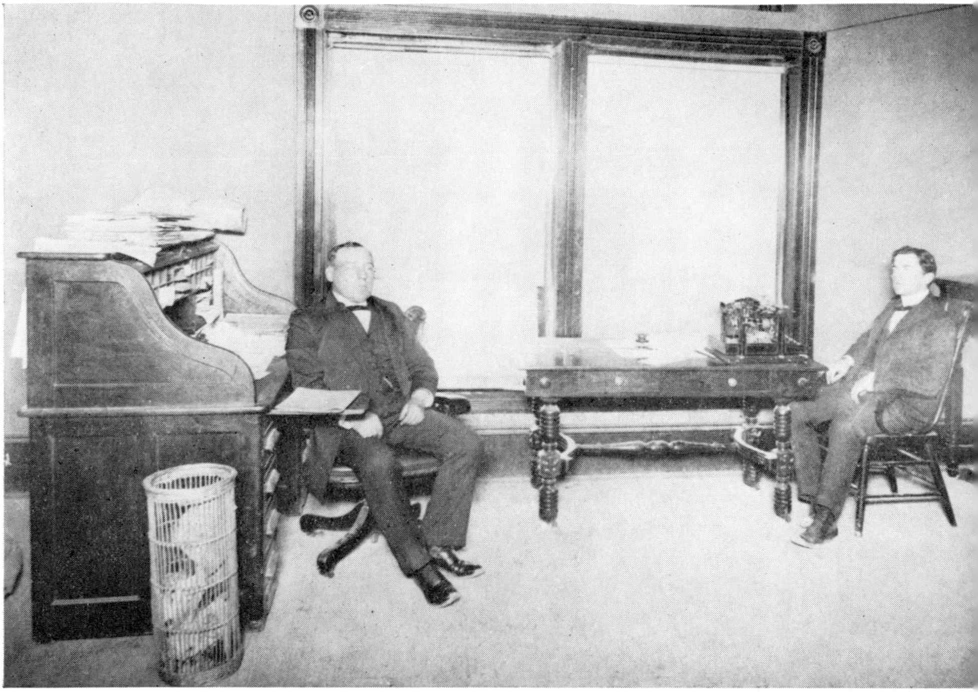

Colonel Morgan Jones (left) *and William Ernest Kaufman* (right) *are pictured about 1895 in their Fort Worth and Denver City Railway Company office, Fort Worth, Texas.*

COURTESY MRS. PERCY JONES

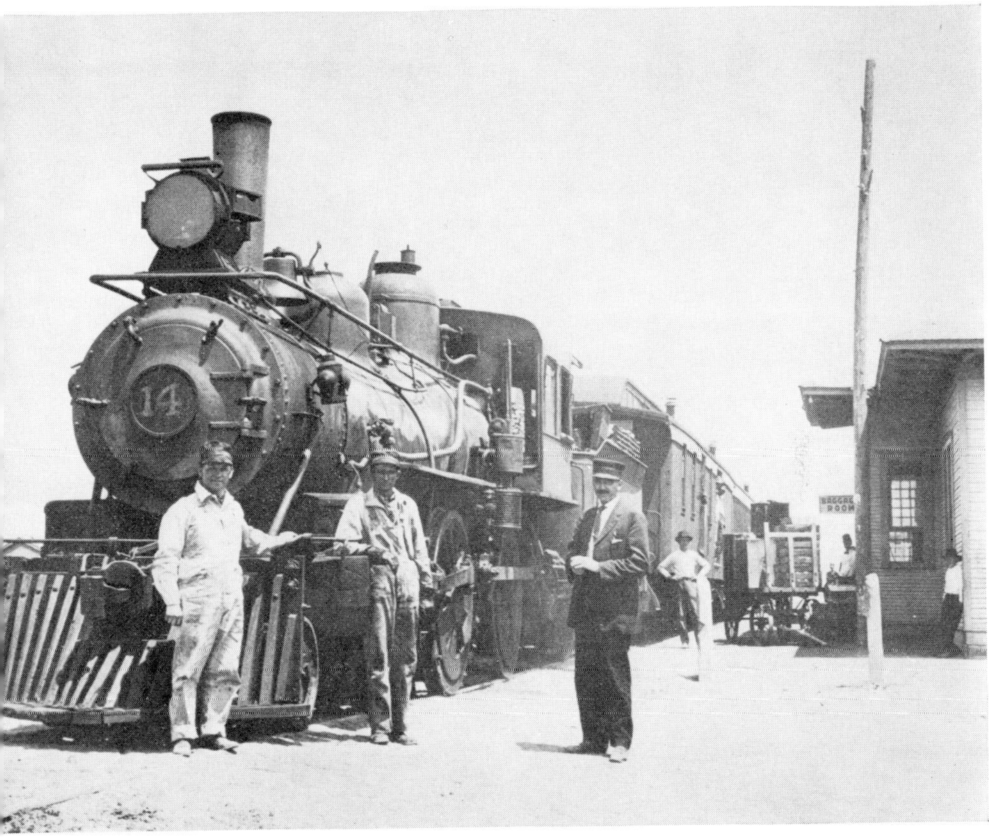
14

Shown here about 1900 as the conductor of the train, Morgan C. Jones was also superintendent of the Wichita Valley Railway Company.

COURTESY MORGAN JONES, JR.

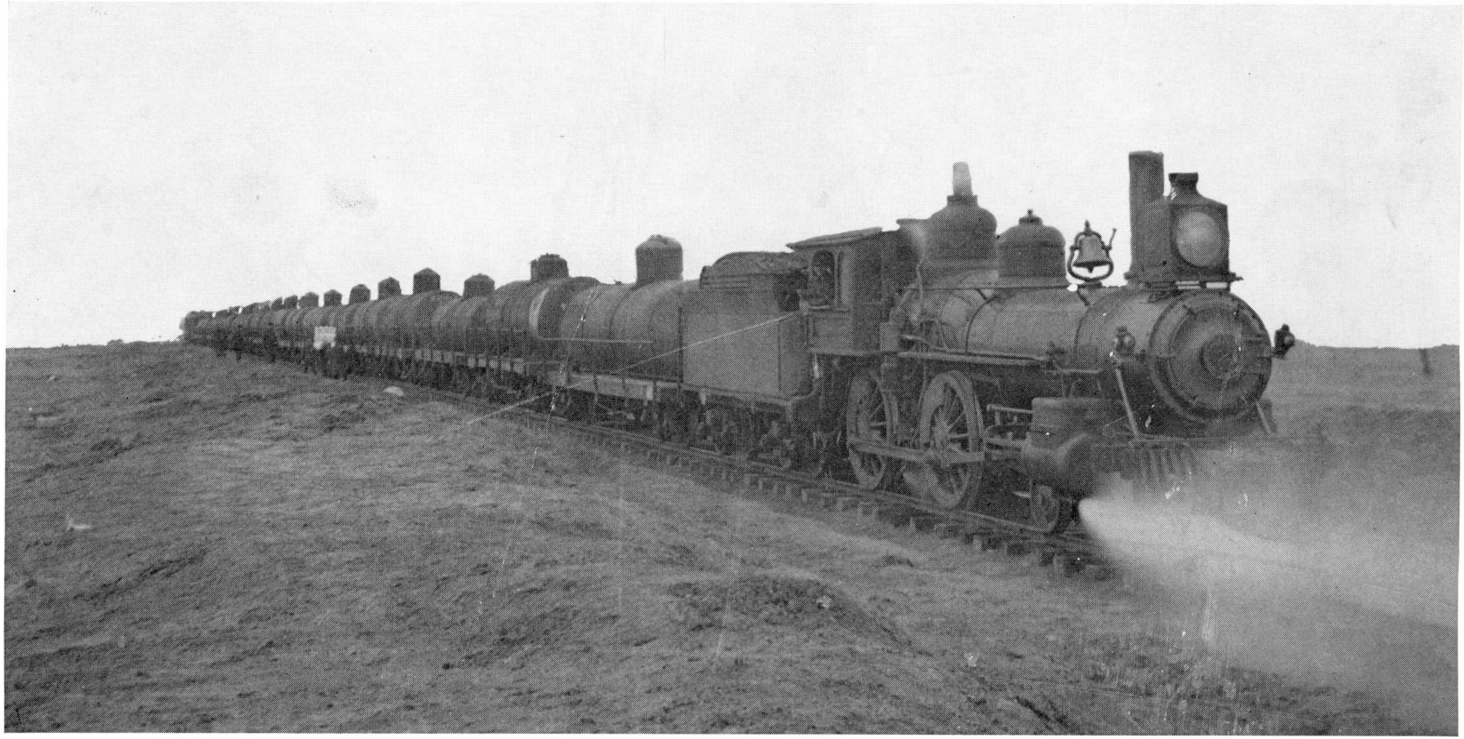

This Wichita Falls and Oklahoma Railway Company train was hauling oil from Petrolia to Wichita Falls, about 1904.

COURTESY MORGAN JONES, JR.

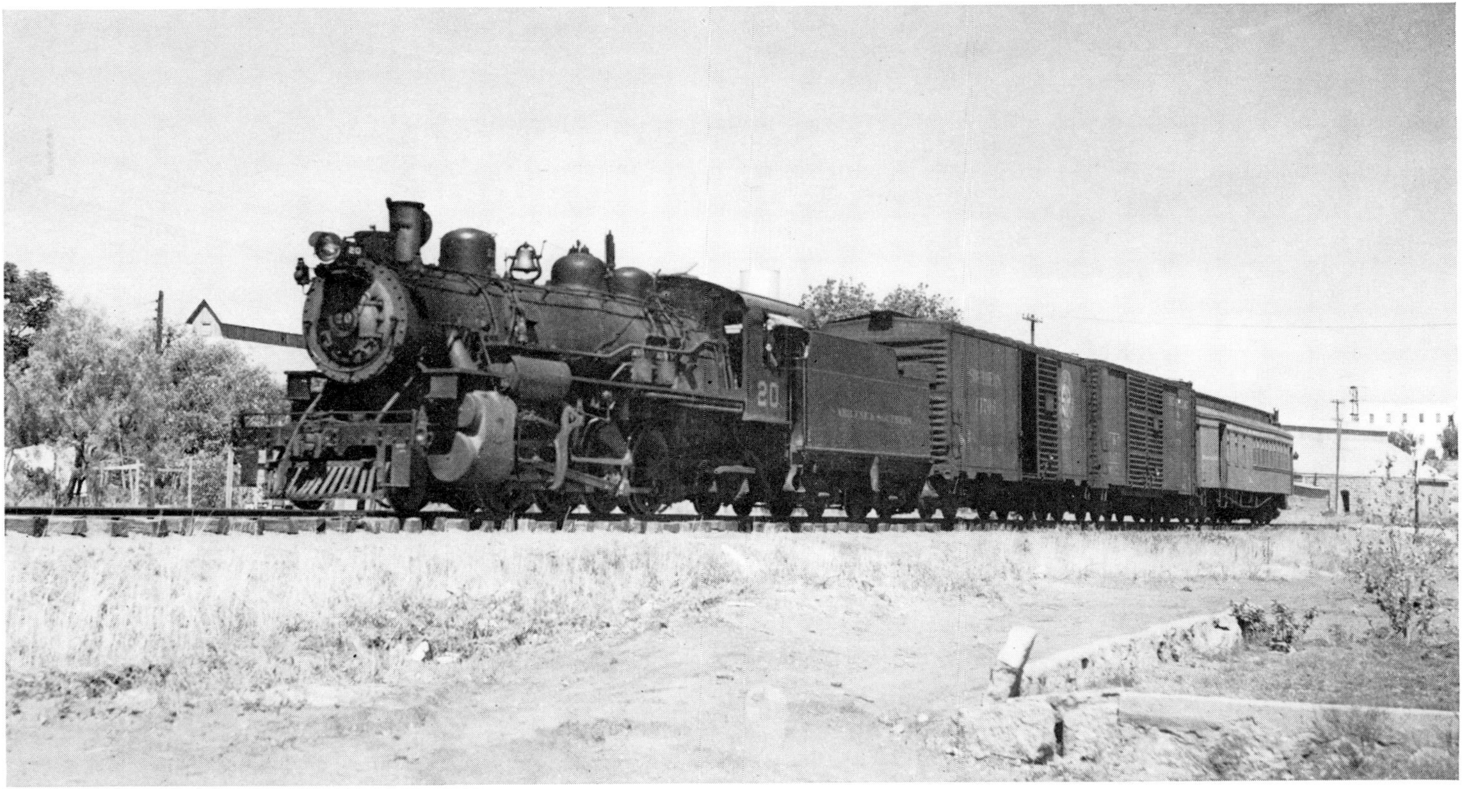
20

Mixed train, Abilene and Southern Railway Company, 1946.

COURTESY EVERETT L. DEGOLYER, JR. COLLECTION, DALLAS, TEXAS

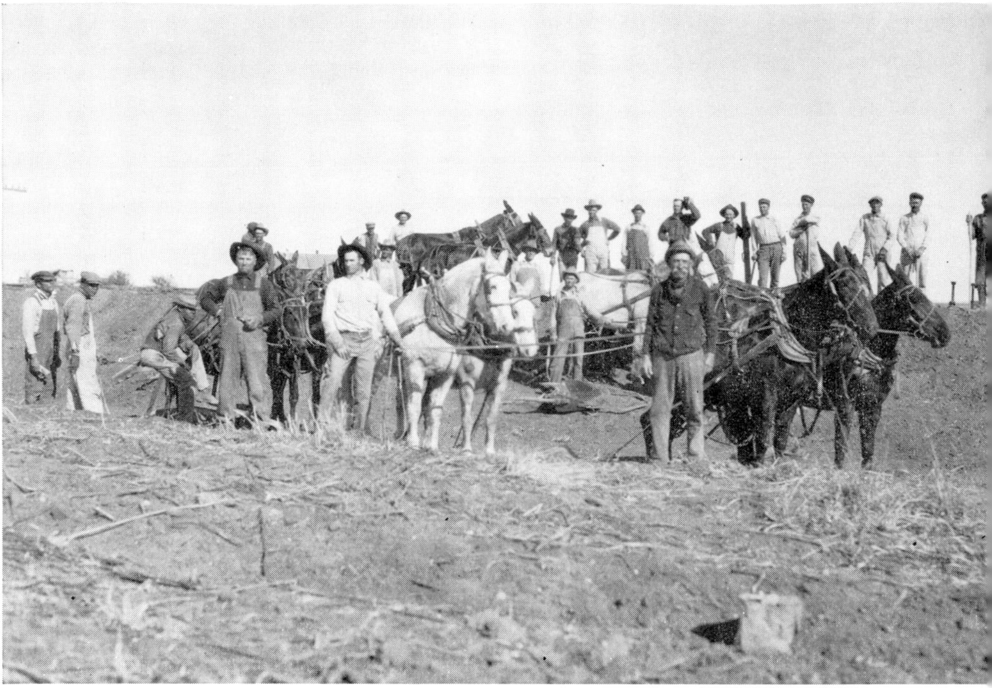

A grading crew for Abilene and Southern Railway Company as they approached Winters, Texas, in 1909.

COURTESY MORGAN JONES, JR.

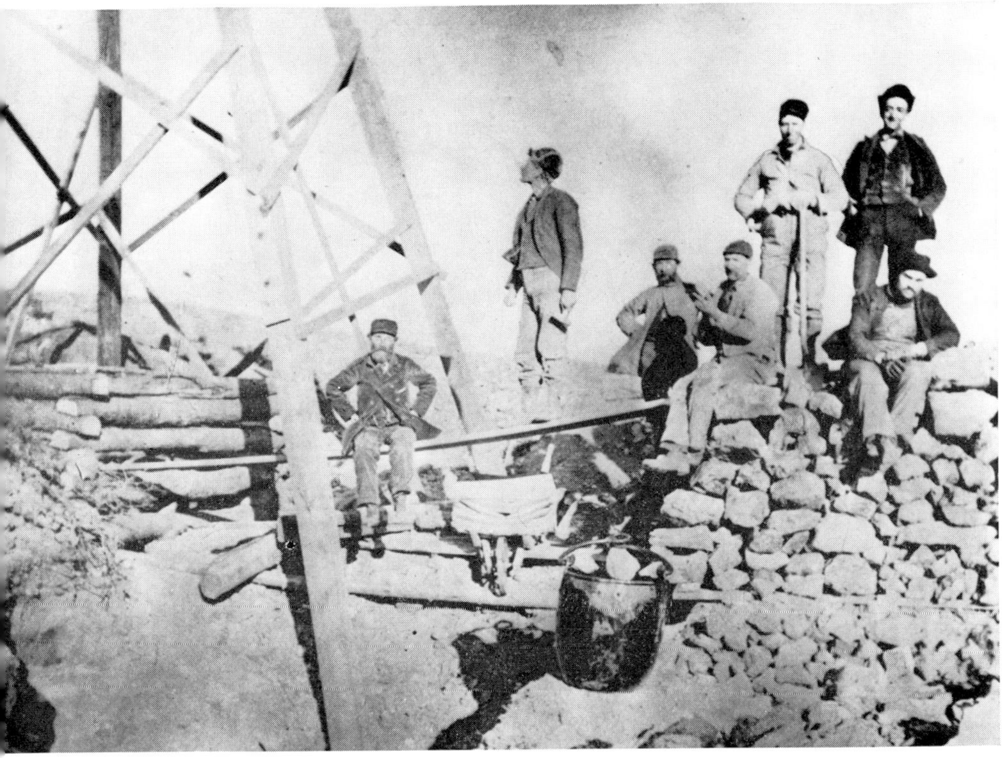

This picture of an unidentified railroad crew was found among Colonel Morgan Jones's papers.

COURTESY MRS. PERCY JONES

Engine No. 38, Fort Worth and Denver City Railway Company, photographed in June, 1940. The engine was last used on the Wichita Valley Railroad Company line.

COURTESY EVERETT L. DEGOLYER, JR. COLLECTION, DALLAS, TEXAS

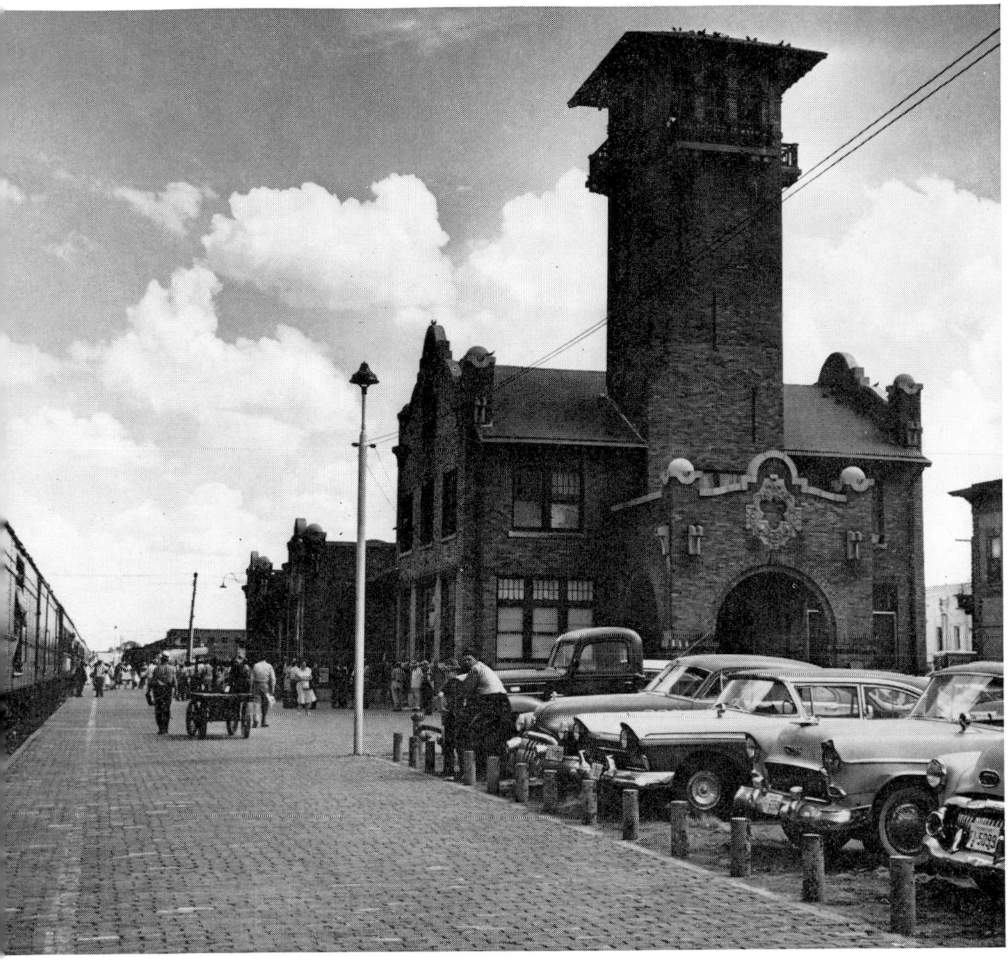

Fort Worth and Denver City Railway Company train at Union Station, Wichita Falls, Texas. The station has been demolished.

COURTESY EVERETT L. DEGOLYER, JR. COLLECTION, DALLAS, TEXAS

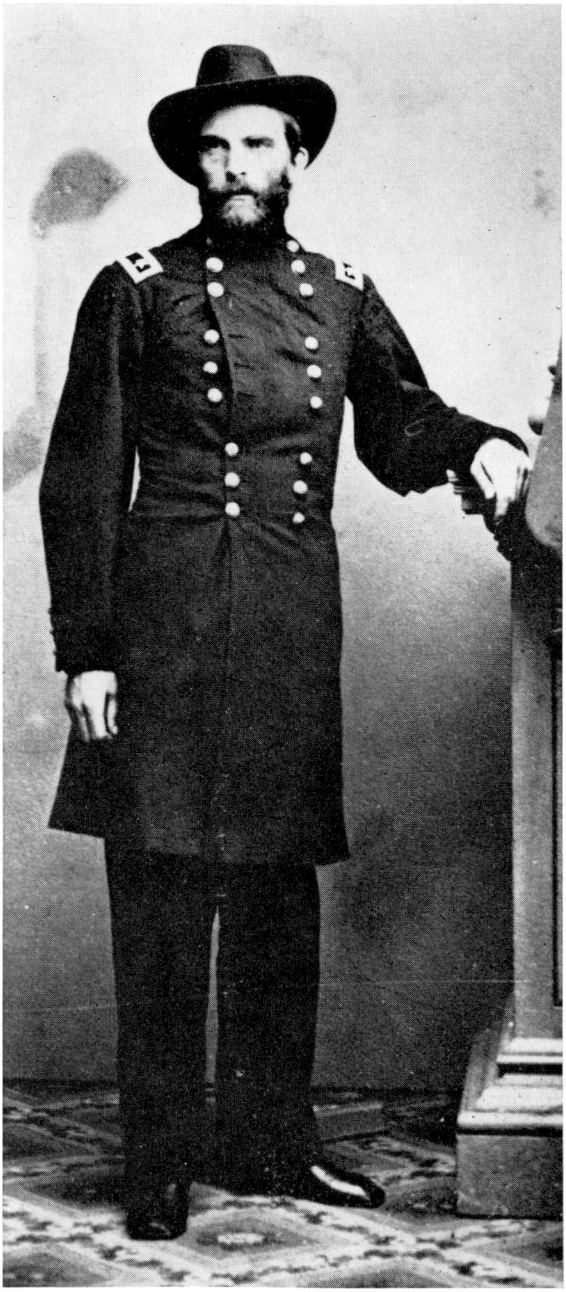

General Grenville M. Dodge in Civil War uniform. Another great railroad builder, he gave Morgan Jones his first job in the United States. The two men remained business associates and close friends until Dodge's death in 1916.

COURTESY UNION PACIFIC

a.

b.

a. *Morgan C. Jones*
COURTESY MORGAN JONES, JR.

b. *Percy Jones*
COURTESY MRS. PERCY JONES

c. *Roland Jones*
COURTESY ROLAND JONES

c.

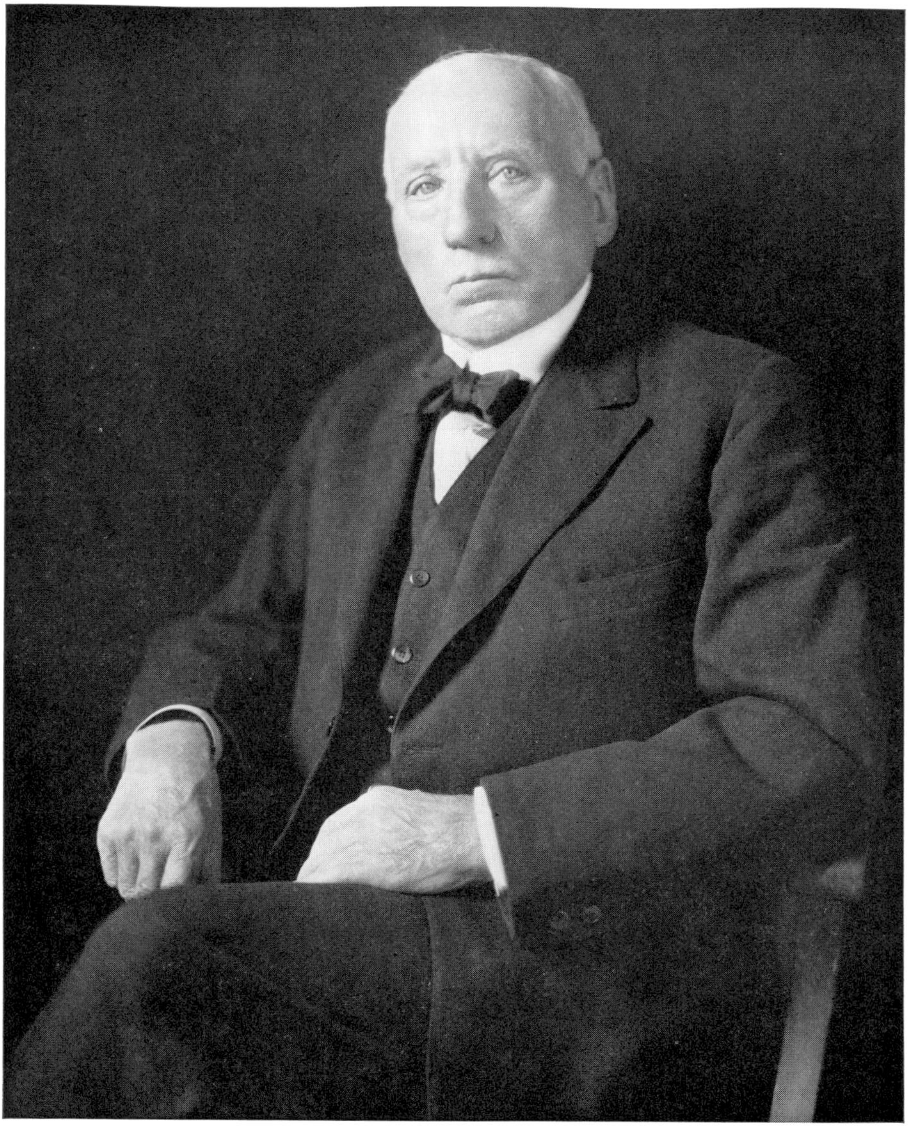

This photograph of Colonel Morgan Jones was made about 1920, when the railroad builder was eighty years old.

COURTESY MORGAN JONES, JR.

had suggested that "every stockman of Texas [should] attend the Denver convention."[6] At Gainesville, the Northwest Texas Live Stock Association had appointed its entire membership to the Denver delegation.[7] Many stockmen from that association accepted their appointments and, with their families, mingled at the depot with those from South Texas.

At daybreak it was "Fort Worth weather, the sky clear, the air pure and bracing, the sun shining, the birds singing in the trees."[8] President Jones assigned more than one hundred employees to temporary duties at the depot yard to insure the trains' prompt departure. One reporter described their frantic pace: "It was hurry, hurry, hurry, boom, boom, boom."[9] General Manager C. F. Meek directed their work "like a general," and had all four trains ready according to Jones's schedule.

The first train pulled away from the depot at precisely 7:30 A.M. It carried, in addition to approximately 250 passengers, a carload of bananas "picked in the tropics yesterday to be eaten in the Rocky Mountains tomorrow."[10] At half-hour intervals the three remaining trains followed, each sent on its way by a great shout from those on the platform who did not make the trip. Along the route, at farmhouses and at other rail stations, people clustered together to wave to the Denver-bound adventurers. One passenger asked a conductor to estimate the population of Lelia Lake, a town in Donley County. The conductor replied, "You can estimate them when we get there, for they will all be at the depot to put the train through."[11]

The "trail blazers" arrived at Wichita Falls between two and three-thirty that afternoon. They remained there long enough to eat dinner and to take on twenty-five additional excursionists and again headed toward Denver. At nine o'clock that evening they passed, and attempted to count, Lelia Lake's population. A few

6 (February 17, 1888).
7 *Gainesville News,* reported in the *Rocky Mountain News* (March 15, 1888), 4.
8 *Fort Worth Weekly Gazette* (March 30, 1888), 1.
9 *Ibid.*
10 *Pueblo Chieftan* (September 12, 1954).
11 Robert Gerner, "History of the Fort Worth and Denver City Railroad in Donley County," 3, FW & DC essays.

minutes later they arrived at Clarendon, where, according to schedule, they had supper. The excursionists, who traveled 277.2 miles in approximately fourteen hours, were in "good spirits and eager to get on to Denver."[12]

The following morning the trains pulled into the Trinidad, Colorado, station, where a welcoming throng waited to escort passengers to breakfast at the Grand Union Hotel. The Trinidad arrival was somewhat later than scheduled, somewhat later, too, than a normal breakfast hour. Frequent stops to take on additional passengers, delayed departures after several excessively long welcoming addresses, and the unwillingness of cautious engineers to speed along new tracks made it necessary to cut short some of the scheduled stops—this one included. Trinidad's disgruntled city fathers complained. They "wanted to march [the excursionists] through [the city's] . . . avenues while their appetites for the novel and wonderful are keen and fresh."[13]

The Texans had appetites for nothing more than food, and much of it, having arrived at 1:15 P.M. for breakfast. Main Street, "deep in mud," discouraged any desire to walk the "black diamond avenues." Despite the late breakfast hour, however, the visitors, in good humor, walked across the hastily laid planks from the station platform to the carriages and omnibuses which carried them to the feast. Within an hour after its arrival at Trinidad, train number one pulled away and headed once again toward Denver.

At Pueblo, the trains stopped for ten minutes, the passengers listened to city fathers deliver brief welcoming statements, accepted gifts ("supplies to keep [the visitors] from getting dry"),[14] and finally continued the last leg of their journey.

At 2:40 A.M. on March 28, forty-four hours after they departed Fort Worth, the first trainload of Texas adventurers arrived in Denver. As the train passed the Exposition Building, the welcoming committee, ignoring the early hour, fired a fifteen-round salute to the sleepy passengers. Since the railroad officials traveling on the fourth train had not arrived, the Denver hosts allowed their

12 *Fort Worth Weekly Gazette* (March 30, 1888), 2.
13 *Rocky Mountain News* (March 28, 1888), 1.
14 *Ibid.*, 4.

visitors to relapse into "refreshing slumber" until all trains reached the Denver depot.

Through the night cannon fire welcomed the second and third trains. Finally, at 6:30, "just as the morning sun began gilding the snow-capped mountain tops," the last train rolled into the depot yard. Immediately, the welcoming committees boarded the trains. General manager Meek, weary after more than forty-eight hours without sleep, cheerfully turned over to the Denver hosts his bois-terous Texas delegation.

The Denver jubilee began at once. As the Lone Star State's rep-resentatives made their way to the city's hotels, Denver displayed evidences of their welcome to the "Queen City of the Plains": celebrants overflowed the streets, flags waved from every public building, bunting and mottoes decorated the entire downtown area. Men, women, and children from every western state joined Denver's 95,901 official population. They packed hotel lobbies, business houses, and restaurants. The dense crowd overflowed into the streets, climbed upon streetcars, and blocked the tracks.[15]

Cornforth and Company's Holladay Street store resembled one huge Texas state flag, and the *Rocky Mountain News* proclaimed:

> They come to our land—our hats off
>   to greet you;
> Lone Star of Texas, we're all pleased
>   To meet you.[16]

Throughout the day bands played and the crowds, "wild with excitement," divided their time between the International Range Association meeting and sight-seeing tours through the city.

Miss Kate Castleton, "the idol of the fun loving public," con-sented to cancel her Wednesday night appearance in "For Good-ness Sake Don't Say I Told You" at the Tabor Grand Opera House. The city needed the building for the Cattle Convention Grand Ball.

Of the five thousand who had been invited to the gala affair, more than four thousand persons attended. "A greater crush was

15 *Ibid.* (March 29, 1888), 1.
16 *Ibid.* (March 27, 1888), 4.

111

never seen in Denver," reported the *Rocky Mountain News* the following morning. A promenade concert commenced the night's activities at eight o'clock. The cowboy band and Koenigsberg's "famous" orchestra alternated polkas, square dances, and waltzes. A larger platform, laid from the stage to the dress circle above the parquet, provided "four square inches of space" to each dancing couple.

The proscenium arch above the stage supported a cluster of lamps which spelled out the words "Denver's Greetings." Texas, New Mexico, and Colorado coats of arms decorated either side of the arch. Huge buntings draped from every wall. "Southern girls and northern boys kept good step together" to Waldmefels and Strauss waltzes.

Prominent Coloradans and their Texas guests viewed the scene from fashion boxes: Governor and Mrs. Alva Adams, Governor Routt, Governor and Mrs. O. C. Hadley, former Governor and Mrs. Eaton, and former Governor John Evans. General manager and Mrs. C. F. Meek shared the first box with Governor and Mrs. Adams.

Mrs. Mabel Day, "the Texas cattle queen" from Coleman, was "the most conspicuous figure on the floor." Obviously enjoying the special attention she received,[17] she insisted, nevertheless, that she did not deserve the title; all she owned, she protested demurely, was "a big bunch of cows."[18]

Frank Davis, sheriff of Wichita Falls, Texas, commented, "I ain't much on big towns, but Denver knocked me as flat as a gang of Panhandle cowboys."[19]

One local reporter described Mrs. Charles Goodnight: "A $500,000 wife . . . a charming lady . . . the envy of all the ladies in the state."[20] He did not make clear whether the envious ladies were Texans or Coloradans.

The following day 2,982 persons, 1,386 horses, and 802 ve-

---

17 *Ibid.* (April 9, 1888), 4. The following week Mrs. Day bought "a handsome residence" in Denver.

18 *Rocky Mountain News* (March 29, 1888), 4.

19 *Ibid.*

20 *Ibid.*

hicles participated in a seven-mile-long parade. Frank B. Houston, of Abilene, Texas, nephew of "the glorious patron saint" Sam Houston, led the parade.[21]

Two of Denver's leading newspapers, the *Rocky Mountain News* and the *Denver Republican*, vied for the most voluminous coverage of Denver's "greatest triumph." Each paper printed pencil sketches and biographies of almost every known railroad official and employee. The *Rocky Mountain News*, for example, devoted 190 column-lines to General Dodge, 198 lines to general manager C. F. Meek, 29 lines to contractor Dan Carey, and 23 lines to M. V. Newlin, the assistant freight and passenger agent.

Morgan Jones, president of the Fort Worth and Denver City Railway Company, indomitable promoter of the road's extension across "the unpeopled immensity," the second largest stockholder, and a railroad builder for a third of a century, was unknown to Denver reporters. His biographical sketch in the *News* totaled eight lines. The brief statement noted only that President Jones was "one of the wealthy men of Fort Worth" and that the railroad company's financial success was due "almost entirely to his admirable management."[22] The *Denver Republican* knew even less about the publicity-shy man. Its frustrated reporter merely stated that Morgan Jones was "President of the Fort Worth and Denver City."[23]

The Texas "Colonel," at once a celebrity and an anonym in Denver, was, nevertheless, predominantly mentioned in every congratulatory editorial. He was one of those railroad men who had "overcome all obstacles, with a courage and determination and zeal almost unparalleled in the history of railway construction."[24]

The visitors prepared to return to the Lone Star State on Sunday morning, April 1. Sheriff Frank Davis remarked, "We've had a good time ever since we left home." Among all their visitors from every part of the nation, and from every state west of the Missis-

21 *Ibid.* (March 30, 1888), 10.
22 *Ibid.* (March 28, 1888), 3.
23 (March 28, 1888), 10.
24 *Rocky Mountain News* (March 28, 1888), 12.

113

sippi River, Denverites paid particular attention to, and flattered, the Texans:

They are a broad-shouldered, tall, athletic, manly-appearing body of men. . . . An air of easy self-confidence and self-poise lingers around each one, that suggests manly independence and dauntless courage.[25]

The unknowing reporter accurately described the modest Welshman if not the average Texas excursionist.

President Jones did not attend Denver's jubilee. Characteristically, he had made a hurried trip to Denver for business purposes a few weeks prior to the great celebration and had then returned to his Texas offices. When the excursionists departed Fort Worth, preparations for opening regular freight and passenger traffic provided sufficient excuse for the dedicated administrator to avoid the Colorado celebration.

On March 17, only three days after the rail connection at Union Park, a Quanah newspaperman reported that a twelve-car train, loaded with Colorado coal and bound for Fort Worth, passed through the town.[26] Shortly thereafter, five cars of lumber, one car of rice, and one car of bananas left Fort Worth, all destined for Denver. Many orders for Colorado coal soon reached Jones from such Texas points as Paris and Abilene. Simultaneously, Colorado's demand for East Texas lumber was so great that Jones ordered 159 Texas and Pacific cars to transport the shipment to Rocky Mountain markets.[27]

Orders for FW & DC service, therefore, claimed Jones's attention long before he made formal arrangements to open the road. On Saturday, April 7, two days before the official opening, a full trainload of merchandise from New York, via the Atlantic Ocean, the Gulf of Mexico, and the Gulf-to-Rockies system, arrived in Denver. The twelve-day journey was slightly less than the average transcontinental journey via Chicago or St. Louis, and the transportation rate along the new route was considerably lower.[28]

25 *Ibid.* (March 29, 1888), 1.
26 *Ibid.* (March 18, 1888), 1. Many local citizens rushed to the depot to take pieces of coal as souvenirs of the first interstate trade between Colorado and Texas on the FW & DC.
27 *Ibid.* (March 18, 1888), 1.

The Gulf-to-Rockies system inaugurated a new epoch for Fort Worth, Denver, and all intermediate points. The *News* proclaimed: "The star of empire has changed its course. From East to West is no longer the sole orbit of its movement. . . . The blazing of a new trail is recognized from the South to the North."[29]

The Denver road reduced rates approximately 35 per cent below those of the Union Pacific, Burlington, and Santa Fe.[30] This meant, for example, that the tariff on southern lumber was thirty-five cents a thousand feet while a similar amount from the Missouri River, over the old routes, was fifty cents.[31] General Manager Meek assured the Colorado and Texas public that the lower Gulf-to-Rockies rates were not a temporary gimmick for advertising purposes—not "cut-rates"—but were possible simply because the new route to Denver was shorter and more direct.[32] When older lines sought to convince Denverites that the new rates were detrimental and that they would injure Denver business, the *Rocky Mountain News* chided railroad men who took "the anomalous position that cheap rates are not desirable and that exorbitant tariffs are a blessing."[33]

The *Chicago Times* attempted to assume a casual attitude toward the threatened competition from Denver. It referred on April 5, 1888, to "the usual slashing of rates so that the new road may get itself well-advertised."[34] A Chicago reporter did not expect a "rate war." Only a day later, nevertheless, the Colorado Traffic Association, meeting at Kansas City, announced lower rates on through traffic from New York, Chicago, St. Louis, and Missouri River points. Obviously the association's action was a deliberate challenge to the Gulf-to-Rockies system.[35]

Anticipating the move, more than one hundred interested individuals and groups sent messages from Denver, Pueblo, Trinidad, Fort Worth, Galveston, New Orleans, and Dallas asking Meek not

28 *Ibid.* (April 7, 1888), 6.
29 *Ibid.* (March 28, 1888), 12.
30 *Fort Worth Mail*, quoted in the *Rocky Mountain News* (April 10, 1888), 2.
31 *Rocky Mountain News* (April 5, 1888), 5.
32 *Ibid.* (March 29, 1888), 4; *Denver Republican* (March 28, 1888), 4.
33 *Rocky Mountain News* (April 5, 1888), 5; *Denver Republican* (April 2, 1888), 4.
34 Quoted in *Rocky Mountain News* (April 15, 1888), 1.
35 Overton, *Gulf to Rockies*, 195.

to compromise with his competitors.[36] The *Rocky Mountain News* editor, however, surprisingly adopted a conciliatory attitude toward the Union Pacific, a major competitor. Apparently apprehensive that a prolonged rate war would adversely affect Denver, he reasoned with the UP officials that their road need not be unfavorably affected by the Gulf-to-Rockies system. Since the Union Pacific's trackage was almost entirely west and north of Denver, that road should not worry about competition to the south and east of that city. Instead, the larger company should agree to receive at Denver the Gulf system's freight from the east and distribute it to points north and west of the Rockies. The arrangement would benefit the Union Pacific—which its officials eventually realized— and Denver as well, since it would make that city a major distribution point for merchandise designated for the Far West.[37]

Such practical reasoning prevailed by early summer, 1888. The Gulf-to-Rockies system and the major railroads in Texas and Colorado agreed to compromises at least temporarily satisfactory to everyone. The three companies which comprised the Gulf-to-Rockies system agreed upon a program, in both organization and operation, which was mutually beneficial to each company.[38]

A sharp increase in the value of Denver and Fort Worth stock, from twenty-five and one-fourth cents in 1887, to forty-six and three-eighths cents in 1888, seemed to prove that eastern financiers recognized the company's potential worth.[39]

The *Rocky Mountain News* editor considered the Gulf-to-Rockies system a major milestone in Denver's history. It ended the city's "pioneer period" and made possible its development as the "Great Inland Empire."[40] He predicted that Denver's population would double within the next five years. With obvious pleasure he reproduced an editorial from the New Orleans *Item* which encouraged Louisiana's citizens to discontinue their annual trips to Maine's seacoast resorts and Virginia's mountains. They should

36 *Rocky Mountain News* (April 5, 1888), 5.
37 *Ibid.* (April 11, 1888), 4.
38 See Overton, *Gulf to Rockies*, chap. 9, for the detailed program.
39 *Rocky Mountain News* (January 10, 1888), 4.
40 *Ibid.* (March 28, 1888), 12.

visit, instead, the spectacular Rocky Mountain regions. "Why not turn the tide of summer travel to the regions from which we expect a tide of trade?" the Louisiana editor asked.[41]

While Denverites anticipated uninterrupted prosperity as a major railroad distributing center, Texans were no less optimistic. Already they had witnessed revolutionary changes since the "ribbons of steel" crossed the "unpeopled immensity." The Texas Panhandle was "as inaccessible as Alaska"[42] until the Fort Worth and Denver City made possible permanent settlement. This region's transformation from an unpopulated, barren stretch of prairies, valleys, and hills, to a thriving country of fenced-in cattle ranches, farmlands, and railroad communities, was "one of the most astonishing developments of American history in the nineteenth century."[43]

Along the FW & DC route, community newspapers reported increasing immigration into their counties. The immigrants bought land, built homes and barns, and plowed virgin soil. A. T. Bogue was a typical North Texas farmer, according to the *Denver Republican*. In 1882 he moved with his family to Wilbarger County. He possessed a wagon, two mules, and $150 in cash. Bogue, his wife, and two small children made their home in a one-room dugout. Six years later, in 1888, the Bogue family owned a five-room house, a barn, several outbuildings, a water well, eight hundred fenced-in acres, and a fruit orchard. The farmer was debt free.[44] Throughout the area other pioneer families experienced similar success. The Texas North Plains, with railroad facilities, developed into an agricultural region more than two decades ahead of a similar development in the Texas South Plains.[45]

The population in Wichita County, where the FW & DC first provided transportation in 1883, increased from 443 in 1880 to 1,250 in 1887. Hardeman County's total population in 1880

41 New Orleans *Item*, quoted in the *Rocky Mountain News* (April 6, 1888), 4.

42 James Wilson, *Agricultural Resources of the Texas Pan Handle*, 22.

43 Carl Coke Rister, *The Southwestern Frontier*, 301.

44 *Denver Republican* (March 30, 1888), 10.

45 W. C. Holden, "Immigration and Settlement in West Texas," *West Texas Historical Association Year Book*, Vol. V (June, 1929), 75.

numbered only 50, but in 1887, one year after FW & DC tracks reached Chillicothe, the county claimed 1,236 permanent settlers. Potter County, located in the Panhandle's geographic center, had 28 permanent settlers in 1880 and 207 by 1887 after the railroad arrived.[46] Buffalo herds, roving Indian tribes, and open-range cattlemen fell victims to the iron horse's civilizing influences.

The Fort Worth and Denver City revolutionized livestock operations and shipments in North Texas, and assured the industry's later success; while it disrupted free grazing and colossal ranching, it enabled cattlemen to send fattened cattle directly from Texas grazing lands to northern markets. The railroad also encouraged West Texas cattlemen to breed better beef cattle and dairy stock. Hard experience taught them that it did not pay to send inferior animals to Chicago, Kansas City, St. Louis, or Omaha.[47]

Lack of transportation forced earlier cattlemen to make the long drives to Kansas railheads. Nature endowed open-range cattle with physical characteristics which enabled them to withstand their environment. Their long bodies and long, sharp horns protected them from other prairie animals. Eventually, such physical endowments enabled them to withstand the long drive to market. They brought increasingly lower prices, however, to Texas cattlemen. The short-legged, heavy-bodied Herefords, on the other hand, could not survive the long trail, but at distant markets one carload of Herefords brought a better price than a large herd of rangy cattle.[48] The railroad, therefore, made possible, in West Texas as well as elsewhere, a more productive cattle industry.

President Morgan Jones, fully aware of West and North Texas livestock interests, directed rail employees to stop the cattle trains whenever necessary and to water, feed, and rest their valuable cargo. He believed, also, that the Fort Worth and Denver City should continually improve its stock cars. Jones's constant atten-

46 L. L. Foster (Commissioner), *First Annual Report of the Department of Agriculture, Insurance, Statistics, and History, 1887–1888,* 94, 181, 234.

47 James Cox, "The Influence of the Railroads on the Cattle Industry," *Historical and Biographical Record of the Cattle Industry and the Cattlemen of Texas and Adjacent Territory,* 694–95.

48 Baker, "The History of the Fort Worth and Denver City Railway in My Home County," 8, FW & DC essays; Webb, *The Great Plains,* 233–40.

tion to such details enabled FW & DC trains to transport many thousands of cattle to northern markets.[49]

The FW & DC altered, also, but did not destroy, the North and West Texas stagecoach and freighting industry. These commercial transportation companies thrived, like the railroad, wherever population was great enough to support them. Before the Fort Worth and Denver City penetrated the area, commercial stage and freight lines hardly existed. During the open-range period, ranching interests owned and operated most freight lines.

The commercial freighter could not compete with the railroad where his route paralleled the steel rails. When such a situation developed, the freighter invariably altered his service. Usually he made the railhead his own supply center and from that point supplied those settlers who located several leagues west, north, and south of the railroad. Amarillo, for example, developed into the Texas Panhandle's wholesale trading center.[50] Before the railroad company built branch lines south of that Potter County town, more than four hundred private and commercial freighters served the area.

Through trains on the FW & DC route made only a few stops between Fort Worth and Denver except at connecting points with other railroad companies. At Washburn, Armstrong County, for instance, the FW & DC built a branch to Panhandle, Carson County, to meet the Atchison, Topeka, and Santa Fe. Most merchandise from Fort Worth or Denver that was destined for distribution between those cities was placed on local trains. During the early years locals stopped at any point on the road where freighters arranged to meet them. They usually met at a railroad siding, but sometimes freighters merely flagged down the local at any convenient place along the route. The merchandise normally included such items as lumber, coal, household furnishings, and food. Sometimes other pioneer settlers took advantage of the railroad company's special services and flagged down trains merely to purchase newspapers, magazines, candy, or fresh fruit from the train's "news

49 Untitled paper, Morgan Jones Papers, Mrs. Percy Jones, *loc. cit.*, file 3, paper 19.
50 Billy N. Pope, "The Freighter and Railroader in the Economic Pattern of Panhandle History," 79.

butch."[51] Gradually, as the region through which the Fort Worth and Denver City traveled gained more permanent settlers, company officials insisted that the freighters meet the trains at specially designated stops.

The stage lines provided mail and passenger service. From the FW & DC main line, stages connected Decatur (Wise County) to Jacksboro (Jack County); Wichita Falls to Seymour (Baylor County); Childress (Childress County) to Matador (Motley County); and Amarillo to Plainview (Hall County). The fare from Amarillo to Plainview, approximately eighty miles apart, was eighteen dollars.[52] Thus the stage and freight lines performed valuable services to pioneer settlers and to railroads. They enabled permanent settlers to occupy areas otherwise too far removed from the roads' main lines.

President Jones's report on October 31, 1888, to the company's stockholders reflected his optimism. North and West Texas settlers prospered, grain crops flourished, good will existed between the railroad organization and the people it served. He observed that "thrifty farmers" placed great confidence in wheat production, that new immigrants responded encouragingly to the company's advertising program,[53] and that cattle shipments continued to increase. On a comparative basis, Jones reported, the company handled 67,000 more cattle in 1888 than during the preceding year.[54] The completed road shipped 192,318 cattle during the first year. Between May 1, 1882, and November 1, 1888, 989,957 cattle traveled over the Fort Worth and Denver City rails.[55]

The company operated 511.03 miles of single track within Texas, including 469.03 miles of main track and 42 miles of sidings. This included, also, the 16-mile connection (between Washburn and Panhandle City) with the Atchison, Topeka and Santa Fe, which gave the FW & DC an outlet to Kansas City and other northern points.

51 *Ibid.*, 84.
52 *Dalhart Texan* (Jubilee Edition), (May 25, 1951), 57.
53 Annual Report, 1888, 6.
54 *Ibid.*, 15.
55 *Ibid.*, 16.

120

The tireless railroad builder did not intend, however, to allow directors and stockholders to rest on their company's recent accomplishments. Jones urged them to build the Fort Worth and Denver City tracks from Hodge into Fort Worth, a distance of approximately five miles. He explained that the company's joint use of the existing track into Fort Worth with other railroad lines caused unnecessary delays and, therefore, poorer service.[56]

Finally, Jones knew that immigrant families rapidly filled the country south and west of the main line. He wanted to build a branch line into the Wichita Falls area and worried that other railroad companies might soon get a similar idea. The FW & DC must make its move or surrender that territory to competitors.

[56] *Ibid.*

7. DROUGHT, DEPRESSION, AND DETAIL

COLONEL Morgan Jones was, first and last, a railroad man. More specifically, he was a railroad builder. Contemporary records do not reveal a single instance in which the Welsh Texan willingly engaged in trivial polemics with other railroad leaders. He stood on principle; he insisted on fair play, and he expected straightforward honesty from his associates. For these tenets he was a tough, aggressive, and persistent fighter. It was his nature to anticipate and to prepare for the unexpected. "He seemed to make sudden, lightning-quick decisions. Not so. He considered important problems for a long time. Once he made a decision, however, he acted incredibly swiftly."[1]

The Colonel enjoyed, above all, visible accomplishments: a new locomotive, steel rails projecting into a frontier land, prosperous farms along a completed railroad, a staked-off townsite at the railhead. "He was interested all day and all night in new projects."[2] He enjoyed nothing more than to journey into an agricultural frontier, to study its economic potential, to consider its transportation needs, to offer its pioneer settlers a solution to their marketing problems, to chart a new route, to supervise its construction, and to

[1] Interview with Mrs. Percy Jones (July 11, 1967).
[2] Interview with Roland Jones (November 8, 1967).

122

administer its initial services until the railroad, and the people it served, grew prosperous.

The Welshman was not, like his friend Grenville M. Dodge, a railroad "promoter"; he was not, like his friend Jay Gould, a railroad "manipulator"; he was not, like his friend Governor John Evans of Colorado, a railroad "politician." Such men valued his friendship, sought his advice, and respected his abilities, but, in essence, Morgan Jones was cut from a different cloth.[3] He resented every effort to draw him into petty conflicts, whether private or public. He detested trivial inter-railroad rivalries, petty jealousies, and political manipulation. He disapproved the tendency of some of his associates to seek public acclaim, just as he abhorred their "womanish panic" whenever federal or state officials called for certain railroad regulations.[4]

Jones liked orderliness, regularity, harmony, and privacy. He was inherently a practical man. Hence, according to his own explanation, he remained a bachelor since "women are too impractical to marry."[5] He was an honest man who, nevertheless, practiced the confidential methods of a diplomat. He labeled almost every letter he wrote "Private." When his business correspondents neglected to mark their letters similarly, he tersely reproached them in his next letter. When, as he awaited an eastbound train, a newspaper reporter inquired about his destination, he replied succinctly, "points East."

While Grenville M. Dodge engaged in state and national political affairs, while John Evans made speeches to Denver's city fathers, and while Jay Gould manipulated western railroads as if he were playing chess, Morgan Jones laid the foundations of a financial empire built on frontier enterprises. The former Welsh farm boy liked to make money. His intense faith in frontier devel-

---

[3] Letters between Grenville Dodge, Nathan Dodge, W. T. Walters, and Henry Walters amply demonstrate their admiration for Jones's railroad abilities.

[4] One fact seems sufficient to prove that Jones did not assume that all railroad regulation was bad. Jones was a major stockholder of the *Fort Worth Gazette* when Texas' Attorney General James Stephen Hogg entered the 1890 gubernatorial race. Hogg had won statewide acclaim for his vigorous fight for a powerful state railroad commission. The *Gazette*, nevertheless, supported him. See *Addresses and State Papers of James Stephen Hogg* (ed. by Robert C. Cotner), 17.

[5] Interview with Roland Jones (November 8, 1967).

opment made him a wealthy man, but, more significantly, his faith opened up unsuspected bounties to thousands of pioneer settlers. Their prosperity was his prosperity. He needed no other goals. With a single purpose and great success, Morgan Jones devoted almost every day to frontier development.

Prolonged administrative and executive routine bored Jones. It was his responsibility as the Fort Worth and Denver City's president, nevertheless, to direct most of his attention, in 1889, to administrative problems. The Gulf-to-Rockies system was the most important railroad built in the Southwest during the late 1880's[6] and, within that system, the Fort Worth and Denver City was the most prosperous of the three companies. The mighty transcontinentals, consequently, looked with disfavor upon the entire road. They impeded construction of the Gulf system's northern sections and, after its completion, they opposed its lower freight rates. The Union Pacific in particular feared the new road's competition for eastern business.

The Union Pacific, after 1869, briefly monopolized the nation's transcontinental trade. Within a decade and a half, however, other major lines joined the race for ocean-to-ocean trade. By 1883 the Northern Pacific, the Santa Fe–Southern Pacific, and the Rio Grande–Central Pacific reduced the Union Pacific's through trade to less than 10 per cent of its total traffic.[7] To compensate for that loss, the Union Pacific branched out toward the Pacific Northwest. It extended its rails, for example, from the main line at Granger, Wyoming, to Huntington, Idaho. From Huntington the Union Pacific secured rail rights over, and later bought, the Oregon Railway and Navigation Company's tracks to Portland, Oregon. Concurrently, the Union Pacific either built or bought other subsidiary lines to increase its carrying trade north and west of Denver, Colorado.

Union Pacific officials, and those of other western railroad companies, grew increasingly concerned as freight rates declined even before the Gulf-to-Rockies was completed. When the Gulf

---

6 *Poor's Manual of Railroads, 1868–1924*, xv.
7 Overton, *Gulf to Rockies*, 220.

system introduced still lower rates, such action added to an already worrisome situation. At the same time, competition rapidly developed between western railroad companies which desired to extend their rails to other points in the Southwest. As rates along existing routes declined, these officials felt compelled to build branch lines southwesterly into sparsely populated territory which could not possibly make the new extensions immediately self-supporting. Unbridled rivalry between western railroads was the natural result. It was not possible, therefore, that a major new line in the Southwest, such as the Gulf system, could avoid involvement in the struggle for the carrying business.

General Dodge, who helped to construct both the Union Pacific and the Gulf-to-Rockies railroads, rejected the idea that those two systems were natural competitors. He insisted that they should in fact complement one another. The Union Pacific, said Dodge, should encourage eastern merchandise to flow over the Gulf system's rails and, in return, the UP should receive that merchandise in Denver and distribute it over the UP's northwestern subsidiary lines. Governor Evans looked with suspicion upon Dodge's dual alliance. Evans distrusted Union Pacific motives wherever Denver's interests were concerned. Colonel Jones, who was a closer friend and confidant to both men than they were to each other, considered Dodge's suggestions with little more than polite toleration. Evans suspected that Dodge wanted to sell the Gulf system to the Union Pacific. "If we sell out we are gone," he wrote to Jones in February, 1889.[8]

Jones's railroad interests at that time pointed in another direction. New construction, he believed, would solve some of the Fort Worth and Denver City's problems and prevent others. His annual report to the company's stockholders in October, 1889, stressed the need to extend the company's rails five miles—from Hodge into Fort Worth—and, later, he recommended "one or more branches to the southwest in order to draw the business of that section to [the] main line, as there [was] . . . indication of other parties build-

[8] John Evans Collection, Evans to Jones (February 4, 1889), Letter Book No. 2, quoted in Kelsey, "John Evans," 383.

125

ing into that country."[9] In December, 1889, Jones suggested to Dodge that the company needed to build at once a branch line from Henrietta (Clay County) to Seymour (Baylor County). He was convinced that the Missouri, Kansas and Texas would connect these two towns unless the FW & DC moved quickly. He presented other compelling reasons why that branch line was necessary. He considered Clay and Baylor counties among the richest agricultural areas in Texas; he believed that a Henrietta–Seymour, or a Wichita Falls–Seymour branch line would prevent a Henrietta Western Railroad extension into that region; and finally, he believed his plan would discourage a Rock Island proposal to build southward from Indian Territory into Wichita Falls.[10] Convinced that his proposal was sound, Jones offered to furnish one-third of the funds for the fifty-mile project.[11]

Just before Jones's proposal reached Dodge in New York, Dodge informed his brother, Nathan Dodge, that the directors of the Gulf system's two northern sections—the Denver, Texas and Gulf and the Denver, Texas and Fort Worth—had agreed to a combination with the Union Pacific. The new organization, Dodge wrote, would be known as the Union Pacific, Denver and Gulf.[12] The combination, Dodge believed, was not only desirable but necessary. The two northern sections, from their inception, experienced financial difficulties. Poor crops along the route during 1889 aggravated the situation. Dodge was convinced, therefore, that Union Pacific support would protect the smaller companies' stocks and bonds.[13] On the other hand, after the Union Pacific purchased the Oregon Railway and Navigation Company, Dodge had convinced Charles Francis Adams, the Union Pacific president, that the Gulf-to-Rockies system could become a valuable feeder line to the UP's Oregon branch.[14]

9 Summary of Annual Reports, 1889, 11.
10 Morgan Jones Papers, Mrs. Percy Jones, *loc. cit.*, Jones to Dodge (December 5, 1889), file 18, paper 42.
11 *Ibid.* Jones did not specify the exact amount.
12 Dodge Letters, *loc. cit.*, Grenville M. Dodge to Nathan Dodge (December 3, 1889), Box No. 2, Letter 505.
13 *Ibid.*
14 Overton, *Gulf to Rockies*, 237.

On November 13, 1889, Adams and Dodge (who represented the Gulf lines) had signed a provisional agreement to consolidate the two northern sections of the Gulf system with seven Union Pacific branch lines (including the Oregon road) into the Union Pacific, Denver and Gulf Railway Company.[15] The new corporation did not include the Fort Worth and Denver City. For this reason, Jones apparently went along with the arrangement although he did not approve of it. The agreement finally went into effect on April 1, 1890. Significantly, the new company's directors (Morgan Jones included) owned controlling stock in the Fort Worth and Denver City.[16]

Governor Evans was unaware of the impending consolidation until the Dodge-Adams provisional agreement was announced. He argued strenuously that the Union Pacific would use the Gulf system only to the Union Pacific's advantage. Adams and Dodge denied Evans' accusation. Unable to prevent the inevitable, Evans managed, nevertheless, to insert into the final agreement a definite understanding that the Union Pacific, Denver and Gulf would "at all times be operated in its own interests,"[17] a point with which Jones, undoubtedly, was in full accord. Whatever the technicalities, the Union Pacific, Denver and Gulf was thereafter a part of the Union Pacific system. Moreover, the Fort Worth and Denver City's through traffic, to a larger degree, was dependent upon Union Pacific policy.

Jones fully expected, however, to direct the Fort Worth and Denver City according to its earlier policies. In local or Texas matters, he and the FW & DC Board of Directors often acted independently of the other companies within the system. For example, they had separately incorporated and built, in 1888, the Pan Handle Railway Company. That little line served a fifteen-mile area from Washburn, on the FW & DC main line, to Panhandle City. At this point it met the Southern Kansas road which extended across Indian Territory into the Texas Panhandle.

15 *Ibid.*
16 Union Pacific Annual Report, 1890, 10, 36.
17 Overton, *Gulf to Rockies*, 249.

127

Similarly, Jones and the FW & DC directors decided independently —and according to Jones's recommendation—to extend the line from Hodge into Fort Worth and, later, to build the Wichita Falls–Seymour branch.

The Fort Worth and Denver City's original charter, dated 1873, did not authorize the company to build branch lines anywhere in the state. When Jones and Dodge, therefore, agreed to build the Wichita Falls–Seymour branch, they separately incorporated the Wichita Valley Railway Company. While Dodge completed arrangements to consolidate the UPD & G, Jones decided that Wichita Falls, rather than Henrietta, was a more suitable location for the proposed line's eastern railhead. He explained to Dodge that the Wichita Falls route was several miles shorter and would discourage, just as effectively, any competing road into that territory. Thus the new company received its charter on February 8, 1890, and Jones, Dodge, and their associates financed its construction.

The new charter included permission to build a 400-mile road in a southwesterly direction from Wichita Falls.[18] Jones obviously envisioned more than a 50-mile branch to Seymour. He hoped to extend the line, eventually, to Abilene (Taylor County),[19] approximately 150 miles from Wichita Falls. The remaining 250-mile stretch allowed by the charter would, presumably, allow Jones to build beyond Abilene—still in a southwesterly direction—to a point on the Río Grande along the Texas-Mexico border.[20]

The Wichita Valley Railway Company's directors were Morgan Jones, Grenville M. Dodge, E. W. Taylor, W. F. Somerville, G. P. Meade, J. P. Smith, J. G. Jones, J. T. Granger, and L. Tillman.[21] The directors elected Morgan Jones president of the company, and he supervised the road's construction. He issued fifty-year bonds at

18 Hoyt, "Summary History" (FW & DC file 1230), 4.

19 Jones mentioned the "rich country" around Abilene in his letter to Dodge on December 5, 1889 (see above, n. 10), although his immediate aim at that time was to interest Dodge in the Wichita Falls–Seymour extension.

20 Jones dreamed about building a railroad across Texas and Mexico to the Pacific Coast while he traveled through Chihuahua during the mid-1870's. The dream persisted throughout the remainder of his life, and probably accounts for the "four hundred mile" clause in the Wichita Valley's charter. Overton holds to the opinion, however, that Jones's ultimate goal was to build to the Southern Pacific's main line along the Rio Grande.

21 Paddock, *Fort Worth and the Texas Northwest*, 515.

5 per cent interest, and at $15,000 per mile, and stock at $20,000 per mile. He personally invested $212,000 in first-mortgage bonds and $281,000 in the company's stock.[22]

Seymour's citizens quickly raised a $30,000 bonus and presented it to the company.[23] For years they had offered various inducements to FW & DC and other railroad officials to build a railroad to their town.[24] Their enthusiasm to make their tiny Baylor County community a "second St. Louis"[25] was typical of almost all frontier settlers. Hence, they had tried to entice the Missouri, Kansas and Texas and the Rock Island railroad companies to provide railroad service necessary to fulfill their ambitions. Their persistent efforts resulted in Jones's agreement to build to Seymour from Wichita Falls. The agreement also enabled Jones to begin the first step of his own dream to build into southwestern Texas.

Construction commenced during the spring of 1890, and the rails reached Seymour by September 1. The Wichita Valley Railway Company inaugurated its service with two locomotives, three passenger cars, and one freight caboose. The company later rented stock cars and additional engines from the Fort Worth and Denver City to haul large shipments of stock or farm produce. Oats, corn, and seed wheat grew abundantly, and, as Jones predicted, Baylor County proved to be one of the state's richest agricultural areas. Seymour developed into a thriving trade center for farmers in neighboring Haskell, Knox, King, and Young counties, and those in other counties between the Brazos and Wichita rivers. New settlers rapidly moved into the region via the Wichita Valley rails. The regular train included two passenger coaches, one freight car, and a caboose. It made a daily round trip from Wichita Falls to Seymour. The Wichita Valley Railway Company was a small enterprise, but it developed into an important feeder line for the Fort Worth and Denver City.

Jones shrewdly anticipated swift immigration into the area.

22 Morgan Jones Papers, Mrs. Percy Jones, *loc. cit.*, file 4, papers 17 A–C.
23 Mrs. George S. Plants, "History of the Wichita Valley Railway in My Home County," 1, FW & DC essays.
24 Mrs. W. T. Britton, "Wichita Valley Rail Road," 1, FW & DC essays.
25 Plants, "History of the Wichita Valley Railway in My Home County," 1, FW & DC essays.

With General Dodge, G. P. Meade, W. F. Somerville, and John Grant Jones (a distant cousin who settled near Wichita Falls), he organized the Western Industrial Company and secured for immediate sale 150,000 acres in Archer and Baylor counties. This group located the land company offices at Dundee, Archer County, and offered lands at three to ten dollars an acre according to the fertility of the soil and proximity of a site to the railroad.[26] Jones, with six–thirty-seconds interest in both the railroad company and the land company, was the largest stockholder in the joint enterprises.[27]

In addition to the Hodge–Fort Worth extension and the Wichita Valley branch to Seymour, Jones announced to the FW & DC stockholders on October 31, 1890, that company officials incorporated the Fort Worth and Denver Terminal Railway Company. The Terminal Company built seven miles of yard tracks in Fort Worth, a freight depot and transfer sheds in Fort Worth, five miles of side track along the main line between Hodge and Fort Worth, and, near Hodge, a roundhouse and company shop.[28] These were projects which President Jones most enjoyed reporting to the company's stockholders. His Annual Report informed them, also, that, in spite of a summer drought which reduced wheat, corn, and oat production per acre, the total crop was above that of the preceding year since new settlers had increased the area's total acreage. Cotton farmers expected an average yield for the year. Altogether, farm production, plus a sharp increase in passenger service, enabled Jones to report a net increase of $208,000 over the preceding year's business.[29]

Texas stockholders, therefore, were not overly concerned by the Union Pacific, Denver and Gulf's influence over Fort Worth and Denver City operations. The *Fort Worth Gazette* reported optimistically that, with Union Pacific support, the Gulf system might extend its rails from Fort Worth to the Gulf of Mexico.[30] It was an obvious effort to see the brighter side of the recent consolidation.

26 Morgan Jones Papers, Mrs. Percy Jones, *loc. cit.*, file 4, paper 21.
27 *Ibid.*, "Contract of Partnership," file 2, paper 13.
28 Summary of Annual Reports, 1890, 12.
29 *Ibid.*   30 (April 8, 1890), 4.

130

The *Gazette*'s hopeful prediction, unfortunately, was premature. Despite that paper's support for Attorney General Hogg's gubernatorial candidacy, other railroad men looked warily at Hogg's demands for a railroad commission with power to control railroad activities within the state. Under present conditions, it was not likely that the Union Pacific would financially support an extension from Fort Worth to the Gulf.

The Union Pacific had problems enough of its own in 1890. While competition increased from other western railroads, many western political leaders echoed the public's demands for railroad reform.[31] The Gulf system's problems multiplied, also, when, on November 26, Jay Gould forced out Charles Francis Adams as president of the Union Pacific and placed Sidney Dillon again at the head of that transcontinental line. Obviously, Gould planned to dictate company policy and to dictate it entirely for the Union Pacific's benefit. Company officials of the Union Pacific, Denver and Gulf and of the Fort Worth and Denver City braced themselves for further complications. Dodge warned Jones that "the general policy of the new management is in direct opposition to the old in so far as the treatment of the [subsidiary] lines is concerned."[32]

Gould's leadership brought immediate changes. R. J. Duncan replaced general manager Meek on the UPD & G, and S. H. H. Clark replaced W. H. Holcomb as vice-president of the Fort Worth and Denver City. Apparently, Governor Evans' predictions a year earlier would come true: the Union Pacific would concentrate its control over the entire Gulf system. Whether real or imaginary, Evans and Jones claimed that Gould's policies adversely affected the Gulf system. Evans charged that the Union Pacific took trade which rightfully belonged to the Gulf system, and Jones complained that the UP billed the FW & DC for equipment which his railroad did not receive.[33] During the succeeding months, Gould's policies made Jones and Evans increasingly suspicious.

---

31 Robert Edgar Riegel, *The Story of the Western Railroads*, 222–26.
32 Morgan Jones Papers, Mrs. Percy Jones, *loc. cit.*, Dodge to Jones (January 7, 1891), file 18, paper 55.
33 Overton, *Gulf to Rockies*, 275.

Presumably to consult with Jones and to reassure the frustrated Welshman, Gould sent vice-president Clark of the UPD & G, and other newly appointed officials, to Texas in November, 1891. Jones met the delegation at Childress. Whatever Gould's purpose, the meeting failed to win Jones's support for Gould's leadership. Clark was not the man to send on such a diplomatic mission. Somewhat pompously, he questioned the Fort Worth and Denver City's potential earning power. This was unwarranted criticism indeed from an official whose own company that year showed a deficit of more than $26,000 while Jones's company showed a net gain of $65,000.[34] "I think I convinced him," Jones wrote to Dodge, "that I knew about as much as he did about the property."[35] Two weeks later, the usually composed Welshman was still out of temper. "I can only stand a certain amount of this kind of business and if it gets too bad I shall kick and resign. . . . Life is too short to fight for the sake of fighting. If they have the controll [sic] my fighting the company will only injure the interests of all concerned."[36]

Dodge knew that Jones never made idle threats. Convinced that Jones would resign the presidency of the FW & DC if he could not retain local control, Dodge sent a telegram to Oliver Mink, the Union Pacific comptroller, and informed him that Jones must be placated. This, said Dodge, could only be accomplished if Mink would see to it that at the next stockholders' meeting a majority of the FW & DC Board of Directors were Texans.[37] As a consequence, Jones, J. P. Smith, J. M. Brown, E. W. Taylor, and K. M. Van Zandt, all of Fort Worth, eventually constituted a majority of the Board. Dodge and Henry Walters, also members of the Board, were Jones's close friends and could be expected to support his policies. Only S. H. H. Clark and Oliver Ames were Gould men.[38]

While Jones thus strengthened his control over FW & DC local policy, he could not modify all policies governing the system's through traffic. In April, 1892, John Evans again claimed that

---

34 Union Pacific Annual Report, 1891, 46.
35 Dodge Papers, *loc. cit.*, XIII, 186, Jones to Dodge (November 26, 1891).
36 *Ibid.*, XIII, 711, Jones to Dodge (December 7, 1891).
37 Overton, *Gulf to Rockies*, 282.
38 FW & DC Annual Report, 1895, 2.

Union Pacific management worked only for its own interests. Whatever the cause, the year ended disastrously for the Union Pacific, Denver and Gulf. The company failed to meet its fixed charges for the year ending December 31, 1892, by $379,454.90.[39] The year proved little better for the Fort Worth and Denver City, and Jones managed to report a net income of $3,380.41.[40] It marked a decrease from the preceding year of $61,355.07 and resulted, at least in part, from a prolonged drought along the entire Fort Worth and Denver City route.

The depressed state of western railroading in 1892 was but a preview of the cataclysmic year which followed. For a decade American industry, and particularly the railroad industry, had overextended itself. Ostensibly to create a higher standard of living for all, the nation's industries expanded beyond reason or need. Powerful industrialists such as Jay Gould were better known and more admired than Washington's political leaders. Competitive enterprise went unrestrained as long as its participants managed to appear within the law. Political leaders seemed powerless, if not unwilling, to curb the nation's plunge toward financial disaster. Predictably enough, a major eastern railroad's collapse provided the spark which ignited widespread panic. Just before President Benjamin Harrison left office in 1893, the Philadelphia and Reading Railroad went bankrupt. As a consequence, the New York Stock Exchange experienced the greatest selling spree in its history, and, as Grover Cleveland assumed office, the stock market collapsed. Banks withdrew credit and called in loans.

Union Pacific traffic, as well as that of the Erie, the Northern Pacific, and the Santa Fe, dropped sharply. At this critical time, the Union Pacific's old foe, Governor John Evans, renewed his attack. On August 13, 1893, he filed a bill in equity at Denver's United States Circuit Court and asked the court to appoint a separate receiver for the Union Pacific, Denver and Gulf. His petition, in effect, requested the court to appoint someone independent of the Union Pacific organization, to hold the UPD & G in trust while it

39 Union Pacific Annual Report, 1892, 114.
40 *Ibid.*, 118.

133

underwent a complete financial reorganization. He sought, of course, to regain for the Gulf-to-Rockies system a complete separation from the Union Pacific system.[41]

Evans charged that all UPD & G directors—except himself and Morgan Jones—worked against that company's interests and according to Union Pacific directives.[42] While Judge Moses Hallett considered his charges and wrestled with the problem of selecting a Union Pacific, Denver and Gulf receiver who would satisfy both Evans and Union Pacific factions, the panic continued to depress the railroad industry. Within a year, 118 railroads went into receivership. Then, in early October, 1893, the Union Pacific, unable to meet its financial commitments but bitterly determined to hold every mile of its subsidiary lines,[43] asked for a receiver for itself and for its subsidiaries. The petition to the court did not include the Fort Worth and Denver City.

The Gulf system's southern section was involved, nevertheless, in its own financial trauma. President Jones, for the first time, was unable in 1893 to meet the Fort Worth and Denver City's interest charges. The panic and an unusually severe drought in Texas

[41] Kelsey, "John Evans," 387.

[42] Overton, *Gulf to Rockies*, 291. Overton states that Evans' charge that General Dodge was a party to the "conspiracy" was a mistake. Overton demonstrates convincingly enough that the General worked diligently to protect the UPD & G from Union Pacific domination. He presents, also, a valid explanation for Evans' false accusation against Dodge; there was, unfortunately, a total lack of communication between the two railroad men. On the other hand, Overton expresses bewilderment concerning Evans' specific reference to Jones's "innocence." On this point, Overton falls victim to his own exaggerated interpretation of the Jones-Dodge friendship. His statement (p. 293) that "no one on the entire Gulf system was closer to Dodge or more disposed to follow his lead" is certainly misleading. Jones was indeed Dodge's closest friend, but it was a friendship based upon mutual respect and almost absolute candor between equals. Overton, in fact, records several instances of Jones's independent actions. For example, in 1885, when Dodge's Texas and Colorado Improvement Company hesitated to renew construction of the FW & DC out of Wichita Falls, Jones threatened to take over the project himself. In 1891, Jones, who was fully aware of Dodge's influential role in making the northern sections of the Gulf system a part of the Union Pacific system, warned Dodge that the UP managers must cease interfering in FW & DC affairs or he would resign from the company. Contemporary records do not reveal a single instance in which Jones, whom Overton frequently refers to as "that independent Welshman," followed blindly another man's lead. Jones, unlike Dodge, corresponded frequently with Governor Evans (see Kelsey, "John Evans," *passim*) and consequently Evans was aware that, as far as Union Pacific policy was concerned, Jones shared his misgivings. It would seem logical, therefore, that Evans had every reason to exempt Jones from his charges against the UPD & G directors.

[43] Overton, *Gulf to Rockies*, 298.

134

during that summer contributed primarily to Jones's dilemma. Only one week after the court appointed a receiver for the Union Pacific's main line,[44] Jones asked the federal court in Texas to appoint a receiver for the Fort Worth and Denver City. In view of the impending default, the court entered an order on October 24, 1893, to make Jones and John D. Moore, of Fort Worth, receivers for the company.[45]

Meanwhile, Judge Hallett continued to seek an acceptable receiver for the Union Pacific, Denver and Gulf. For four months he listened to recommendations from interested parties. He knew that he could not appoint either of the two leading antagonists. The Evans group would never accept Dodge, nor would the Dodge group accept Evans. Dodge headed a committee of UPD & G first-mortgage bondholders which compiled a list of acceptable candidates. Morgan Jones's name headed the list and the committee specifically urged his appointment.[46] The committee's petition to Judge Hallett emphasized that Jones was "thoroughly familiar with the entire road and would maintain it properly and run it as one independent system."[47] Significantly, Dodge also underscored the fact that Jones "enjoyed friendly relations with all connections."[48] It was an obvious reference to the close personal friendship between Jones and Evans.

Representatives of the federal government, which held a contingent interest in the Union Pacific, Denver and Gulf, also favored Jones's appointment.[49] Their recommendation in turn was supported by Drexel, Morgan and Company, trustees of the UPD & G bonds and stock.[50] Surprisingly enough, S. H. H. Clark, with whom

44 The original receivers appointed were S. H. H. Clark, E. Ellery Anderson, and Oliver Mink. In November the court added John W. Doane and Frederic Coudert to the group.

45 Union Pacific Annual Report, 1893, 16. See also Roy Sylvan Dunn, "Drought in West Texas, 1890–1894," *West Texas Historical Association Year Book*, Vol. XXXVII (October, 1961), 121–36.

46 Morgan Jones Papers, Mrs. Percy Jones, *loc. cit.*, Dodge to Jones (December 12, 1893), file 18, paper 64.

47 Dodge Papers, *loc. cit.*, XV, 366, Dodge to Hallett (December 5, 1893). Quoted in Overton, *Gulf to Rockies*, 304.

48 *Ibid.*

49 Morgan Jones Papers, Mrs. Percy Jones, *loc. cit.*, Dodge to Jones (December 12, 1893), file 18, paper 64.

50 *Ibid.*

Jones had exchanged bitter words at the Childress meeting only a year before, supported Jones's appointment.[51] Jones's support obviously was widespread, if not unanimous, and, in view of the fact that he was intimately acquainted with everyone who urged his appointment, his reputation for honesty and integrity was unchallenged.

Unfortunately, Jones did not want the assignment. Dodge wrote to him on December 12 that Clark was "unwilling that you should withdraw."[52] According to Dodge, "all of the other security holders" implored Jones to allow Judge Hallett to consider his appointment as receiver. General Dodge, hopeful that he had won Jones's consent, ended his letter with an urgent plea to "accept as gracefully as you can" if Hallett appointed Jones to the Union Pacific, Denver and Gulf receivership.[53] Neither the Jones papers nor the Dodge papers reveal Jones's response to such pressure, but many years later he indicated that he had ultimately refused to accept the assignment. In 1923 the modest old Welshman granted, for the first time, a formal interview to the press. He told the newspaper reporter that he "refused to accept the receivership of the road" because he did not believe that the Fort Worth and Denver City and the UPD & G receiverships should be combined.[54] Jones, who was always an unpretentious man, must have informed Judge Hallett, therefore, that he would not accept the receivership. At any rate, the Judge finally announced, on December 12, 1893, the appointment of Frank Trumbull, a former railroad man and a socially prominent Denverite who owned a wholesale coal business in Denver.

It is likely, also, that Jones's own manifold business interests influenced his decision to reject additional responsibilities with the UPD & G. He had long ignored the inevitable fact that he needed an assistant to handle his multifarious business transactions. Finally, in May, 1891, when he was fifty-two years old, he employed

51 *Ibid.*
52 *Ibid.*
53 *Ibid.*
54 Crozier, *Dallas News*, 8.

William Ernest Kaufman as his private secretary.[55] Jones had met Kaufman in July of the preceding year when Kaufman worked with an engineering corps on the Wichita Valley railroad. At that time, Jones had gone to Kaufman's tent, had introduced himself, and then had spent the rest of the day asking Kaufman "a million questions."[56]

Jones learned that Kaufman was born at Beckenham, England, on May 12, 1866; that he had been a clerk for a wholesale paper manufacturing company in London; that he had served as a French and German correspondent in the London office of a south Australian wholesale house; that he had hunted and fished in Canada; and that he had been a clerk in the Texas and Pacific offices at Fort Worth. Just prior to his work on the Wichita Valley railroad, Kaufman was with an engineering corps when the Fort Worth and Denver City built its extension from Hodge to Fort Worth.[57]

Jones listened attentively as the Englishman related his life story. At sunset the Welshman departed. Kaufman, Jones decided, was an alert, intelligent young man whose obvious self-confidence left a lasting impression. The following year, when Kaufman was working on another railroad construction project in Mississippi, Dan Carey informed him that Jones wanted Kaufman to join him in Fort Worth. Shortly thereafter, Kaufman accepted a job as Jones's private secretary at seventy-five dollars a month. For the next thirty-five years Kaufman was Jones's secretary, constant companion, and business associate.

After Colonel Jones opened the door wide enough to admit W. E. Kaufman to the solitary confines of his private life in 1891 and to the increasingly complex management of his business transactions, he opened the door once again to add a third member to his tight inner circle. His eldest nephew, also named Morgan Jones, arrived from England and joined him at Fort Worth. The young man, only sixteen years old but already six feet tall, immediately

---

55 Morgan Jones Papers, Mrs. Percy Jones, *loc. cit.*, "W. E. Kaufman Autobiographical Sketch," written on November 6, 1936, file 3, paper 6.

56 *Ibid.*

57 *Ibid.*

added a middle initial "C" to his name to avoid possible confusion with his widely known uncle.[58]

Young Morgan was born June 4, 1876, at Fence Houses, near Newcastle, in Durham County, England, to Thomas Charles Jones and Jane Elizabeth Goodwin Jones.[59] Upon his arrival at Fort Worth, his uncle decided that the youth should continue his formal education at the University of Virginia. He was too young to labor in Colorado's coal mines or with a Texas railroad construction crew. Furthermore, the Colonel revered college-educated men such as his friends Grenville Dodge and Henry Walters. Although he believed firmly that any man, particularly one in his own family, should "start at the bottom,"[60] he believed, also, that formal education enabled a businessman to "reach the top rungs of the ladder" more rapidly. Young Morgan, therefore, soon departed for Charlottesville, Virginia. He arrived at the university embracing a personal guideline which his uncle probably suggested to him: "To lend my ear to many, but my voice to few."[61] It was, at any rate, a maxim which the Colonel practiced throughout his lifetime.

Meanwhile, Jones dedicated himself to his responsibilities as receiver for the Fort Worth and Denver City Railway Company, while other industrialists and railroad men struggled desperately to survive the nation's most severe business depression. His primary goals were interlocking: to gain for the FW & DC net earnings large enough to enable the company to reorganize without foreclosure, to place control back in the hands of its owners, and thus to avoid new ownership by absentee strangers. Nature's forces and the nation's panic plagued his efforts throughout 1894. The drought persisted, farmers along the route lost another wheat crop,

[58] Interview with Morgan Jones, Jr. (November 7, 1967). The youth, like his uncle, was the first son of a new family generation, and therefore was given the traditional family name. Mr. Jones believes that the young man probably selected the initial "C" to represent his father's middle name, Charles.

[59] Morgan Jones Papers, Collection of Mrs. Morgan Jones, Jr., 3435 South 9th Street, Abilene, Texas, "Jones Pedigree from 1680," file 17, paper 1.

[60] Interview with Mrs. Morgan Jones, Sr. (November 28, 1967). This belief is readily accredited to the Welshman by all who knew him. See also *Abilene Reporter-News* (September 28, 1964), Sec. A, 15.

[61] Morgan Jones Papers, Mrs. Morgan Jones, Jr., *loc. cit.*, Morgan C. Jones to his mother (December 1, 1894), file 17, paper 10.

138

and the FW & DC's tonnage and earnings steadily declined. Jones worked diligently to keep the company from falling apart.

Fort Worth and Denver City owners appreciated his efforts and expressed their support. During the late spring, General Dodge headed a committee which inspected the property. The committee included George M. Pullman, William T. Walters, Franklin B. Lord, and Sidell Tilghman. It later reported to the company's bondholders that Jones had operated the property "closely and economically," and it expressed its confidence that the road would prosper as soon as the drought ended.[62]

The drought did not end, and later that year it seemed certain that the company would collapse. In December, 1894, the Mercantile Trust Company of New York (the trustee under the first mortgage) filed a bill of foreclosure against the Fort Worth and Denver City Railway Company. Consequently, the United States District Court at Fort Worth, as a further move to tighten control over the company's direction, terminated Moore's assignment and appointed Morgan Jones sole receiver for the property.[63] The situation, desperate at best and, to some, apparently hopeless, did not cause Jones to despair:

This has been the worst of the last four years of drought and short crops, the wheat and oat crops having been an entire failure, many counties not even raising seed; farmers became discouraged and it was necessary for the Road to furnish seed wheat for this season. . . . We distributed sixteen thousand bushels of wheat in small lots to the farmers along the line of our Road. . . .

The failure of crops has been far-reaching in its effect, it has caused a large number of small farmers to leave the country and has so impoverished those that have remained, that the falling off in shipments of the supplies in the country and also the great decrease in passenger travel has curtailed our income very seriously.

The cotton crop this season, as far as we can now judge, will be about 45% of that of last year, this, with the entire failure of the wheat and oat crops speaks plainer than any words of mine as to the cause of the reduced earning power of the property.[64]

62 Overton, *Gulf to Rockies*, 334.
63 FW & DC Annual Report, 1895, 5.
64 *Ibid.*, 7.

Jones's report to the stockholders and to the court ended, as always, with confidence that a better year would follow. Fall rains promised "more abundant crops," and the prospects for the wheat crop in particular "looked better than at any time since 1890."[65] Significantly, he noted a continuing trend toward crop rotation. "The farmers are following wheat with oats and cotton, and later . . . with forage crops."[66]

It was typical also of Jones's administrative policies that excruciating depression was not a reason to allow the physical property to deteriorate. He informed the court that he had spent $54,566.09 during 1895 for "general improvements." The following improvements were charged to the company's operating expenses:

Grade, 1½ miles of track changed, cribs built and bank rip-rapped 4 miles S. of Tascosa on the Canadian River	$ 6,702.97
New Stock Yard Side Track constructed at Southard, Texas	1,270.20
Two New Side Tracks laid in Texline Yards	1,880.15
New Stock Yards at Memphis, Texas	355.98
New Stock Yards and Side Track at Vernon, Texas	1,773.72
Enlarging Stock Pens at Rhome, Texas	195.38
Cast Colum Clinker Pit and Side Track at Wichita Falls	1,397.00
Forty New Cattle Guards	631.14
New Pump Houses at Giles and Brushey Tanks	619.73
Section Houses at Magenta rebuilt	333.81
Mail Crane erected at Wheatland, Texas	39.00
Depot at Henrietta rebuilt	650.75
Erecting Cotton Platform at Henrietta	114.72
New Side Track at Decatur, and between Decatur and Alvord	1,820.70
Enlarging Paint Shop at Fort Worth, Texas	897.00
1,000 Tons of New Steel Rails laid	33,407.84
3 Locomotives equipped with Steam Heat Apparatus	155.00
2 Combination Cars equipped with Steam Heat Apparatus	357.00
3 Coaches equipped with Steam Heat Apparatus	564.00
Pneumatic Lift built in Fort Worth Shops	200.00
17 Unserviceable Stock Cars converted into Coal Cars at	

140

an average cost of $70.00 each, being equipped with
M.C.B. Automatic Couplers with Yoke Attachments   1,190.00
Total _____ $54,356.09[67]

Jones's policy accomplished considerably more than the report could elucidate. Not only did Jones repair roadbeds, rolling stock, fences, and terminal facilities; his improvements, just as importantly, presented a prosperous image to the public and provided temporary employment for hundreds of destitute farmers from Fort Worth to Texline. In Clarendon, for example, the Fort Worth and Denver City's November, 1895, payroll included fifty-three employees. Eleven of them were permanently employed, while the remaining forty-two were local farmers who sought temporary work during the drought.[68]

The fall rains, which encouraged Jones in October, gradually diminished and, as the winter months passed, searing, scorching sand-storms again ravaged North and West Texas farms. Hundreds of farmers who had endured the preceding dry years reluctantly loaded families and personal belongings on their wagons and abandoned the land. Morgan Jones could no longer hope for improved conditions in 1897. He must find another way to solve the company's financial puzzle in 1896 or allow the Fort Worth and Denver City to fall into new hands. In October he would have served three years as receiver which, according to Texas law, was the maximum time a railroad company could remain in receivership. Unless Jones, Dodge, and their associates could reorganize the FW & DC before the receivership ended, the company would be sold at foreclosure.

Almost frantically these railroad men worked to piece together a reorganization program which would satisfy both the company's bondholders and the courts. Throughout the spring and summer months and into the fall, they strove diligently to uncover additional funds. In Fort Worth, in Baltimore, and in New York they

[65] *Ibid.*
[66] *Ibid.*
[67] *Ibid.*, 10–11.
[68] Morgan Jones Papers, Mrs. Percy Jones, *loc. cit.*, "Extract from November, 1895 Pay Rolls: Clarendon," file 4, paper 41d.

141

raced against the October deadline. Finally, on October 31, Jones managed to present a complicated, yet acceptable, reorganization plan to Judge S. P. Greene of the Forty-Eighth Judicial District at Fort Worth.

Jones gave to the UP $100,000 in FW & DC bonds and $17,000 in Union Pacific collateral trust notes to settle the $140,892.15 account held against the FW & DC by the Union Pacific Railway Company. The Union Pacific, in turn, gave up its additional collateral which it held as security against the Fort Worth and Denver City. Jones thereupon turned over to the Union Pacific $200,000 in 5 per cent bonds and $200,000 in Fort Worth and Denver Terminal Railway Company[69] stock, plus $100,000 in FW & DC stock and $13,000 in FW & DC bonds.[70]

Jones, as receiver, then turned over $165,000 in cash to the Fort Worth and Denver City which the company used to pay the interest on coupons due in 1896. Finally, he paid $20,035.70 to Henry C. Coke, counsel for the Mercantile Trust Company, and $1,000.00 to Henry W. Hobson, counsel for the American Loan and Trust Company.[71] The arrangement thus enabled the Fort Worth and Denver City Railway Company to meet all of its financial obligations, and on October 31, 1896, the court returned control to the company's own directors.

Throughout Jones's receivership, General Dodge served, officially at least, as president of the FW & DC and, for reasons unexplained, he remained in that position after 1896.[72] He continued to reside in New York, however, and Jones, as vice-president and general manager, administered the company as he did before its receivership. He returned also to its Board of Directors, where Texans still constituted a majority of the membership.[73]

---

[69] The company which was separately organized in 1890 to construct side tracks between Hodge and Fort Worth, and terminal facilities at both locations.

[70] FW & DC Annual Report, 1896, 8.

[71] *Ibid.*

[72] A fire in March, 1898, totally destroyed the FW & DC offices at Fort Worth and most of the records. The explanation for Dodge's continuance as president was probably destroyed at that time. Jones still prepared the annual reports to company stockholders, and Dodge noted that fact in each report. See, for example, the FW & DC Annual Report, 1898, 4, in which Dodge stated that Jones "had entire charge of the operations of the Road."

[73] FW & DC Annual Report, 1898, 2.

Jones's report to the stockholders in 1896 described another year of disastrous drought: forage crops totally failed and, as a result, farmers and ranchers moved cattle and hogs into Kansas and Indian Territory. He sought again, with greater difficulty than ever before, to include some words of encouragement. Somewhat lamely he reported that the rails, equipment, and rolling stock were "in good shape and condition."[74] Nevertheless, he still had faith in the Southwest's future prosperity. In December, 1896, he wrote to Jay Gould's only daughter, Helen, that "the cycle of depression has nearly run its course, and more favorable conditions will change the disposition of our average western citizens."[75]

His perpetual optimism was justified at last. Net earnings by the FW & DC increased during 1897 to $453,998.60. More general rains partially broke the drought, many farmers who remained in the area produced a normal grain yield, others produced a good cotton crop, and the company's through traffic increased substantially.[76] The following year, 1898, proved even more encouraging. Gross earnings increased $159,603.73 over the preceding year as passenger and freight traffic enabled Jones to report "improved conditions [in] the country tributary to our line."[77] He emphasized the point that the FW & DC prospered whenever Texas farmers received sufficient rainfall.

The road's physical condition, Jones proudly reported in 1898, did not betray the company's depressed years. Stockcars and engines were "in good condition" and the roadbed was "well-tied." He had added 150 miles of fencing during the year, there were no serious derailments, and the company's department heads and general superintendent had worked "efficiently and vigilantly." Excellent rains during the winter promised abundant crops during the next season.[78] After six austere years, it seemed that the Fort

[74] FW & DC Annual Report, 1896, 8.
[75] Morgan Jones Papers, Mrs. Percy Jones, *loc. cit.*, Jones to Helen Gould (December, 1896), file 17, paper 15.
[76] FW & DC Annual Report, 1898, 4–5. After the reorganization, stockholders' meetings convened in March. Hence, the next meeting after October 31, 1896, was March 1, 1898. The reports thereafter were based on operations for each calendar year.
[77] *Ibid.*, 5.
[78] *Ibid.*, 6–7.

143

Worth and Denver City would indeed enjoy a more prosperous future.

At the same Board of Directors' meeting, however, Morgan Jones resigned from the company. He had wanted for some time to free himself from "desk work," which to him was "mere detail." Only the financial distresses experienced by the company, the Texas farmers, and the nation in general, had kept him at his desk during the 1890's.[79] Since Jones liked to *build* railroads, and since the FW & DC had no immediate plans to extend its rails, he was eager to investigate other building possibilities.

During the fall of 1898, Jones decided to resign. While his FW & DC worries lessened during the year, he grew increasingly concerned about plans to reorganize the Union Pacific, Denver and Gulf. He strenuously objected to a plan to add the Denver, South Park and Pacific line, between Leadville, Colorado, and Denver, to the new organization. While the South Park was the shortest route between the two locations, it had consistently failed to pay its way. In addition, there was very little farming along the route, and Jones believed firmly that a railroad, no matter how short, needed local as well as through traffic in order to prosper.[80]

Another part of the reorganization plan bothered Jones. It seemed likely that Frank Trumbull would become the UPD & G's new president, and Jones questioned Trumbull's abilities. The Welshman observed that Trumbull, during his years as the UPD & G's receiver, was an excellent detail and office man,[81] "but outside of this he . . . [was] entirely at the mercy of his assistants."[82] Jones meant, in effect, that Trumbull was not a man who would leave his desk and get out on the road to learn, firsthand, the company's operations. Trumbull, according to Jones, had never shown a willingness to get "his hands dirty in the strenuous work of railroading."[83]

[79] Dodge Papers, *loc. cit.*, XVI, 865, Jones to Dodge (September 7, 1898).
[80] Crozier, *Dallas News*, 8.
[81] *Ibid.*
[82] Morgan Jones Papers, Mrs. Percy Jones, *loc. cit.*, File 18, paper 73, Jones to Dodge (March 15, 1898).
[83] Overton, *Gulf to Rockies*, 359. Dodge soon learned that Jones's evaluation of Trumbull was valid. Within months after Trumbull assumed his new duties, Dodge

144

Whatever his reservations, however, Jones would not block Trumbull's appointment. It provided, after all, an opportunity to relinquish his own position. Whoever assumed control over the Union Pacific, Denver and Gulf—which, after its reorganization late in 1898, became the Colorado and Southern Railway—would need to work closely with, and exercise certain influences over, the Fort Worth and Denver City. In September, Jones decided to go to Denver and to have a "general talk" with Trumbull. At that time he informed Trumbull that he planned to resign from the Fort Worth and Denver City at the next annual meeting in March, 1899.[84]

Thus, on March 7, 1899, the company's stockholders accepted Jones's resignation and passed the following resolution:

Whereas Morgan Jones has for many years rendered conspicuous services to this company as its President, its Vice President, and General Manager, and much of whatever success that has come to this company has been due to his wise, conservative and faithful attention to his duties while acting in such official capacity.

Therefore Be It Resolved that the thanks of the stockholders of this company are hereby extended to Mr. Jones for these services and for his long devotion to the interests of this company, and the Secretary of this company is directed to formally notify him of the passage of this Resolution, carried unanimously.[85]

At the same meeting, Trumbull replaced General Dodge as president of the Fort Worth and Denver City Railway Company. For the first time in its history, the entire Gulf system was under one president. D. B. Keeler was made vice-president, and Morgan

complained bitterly that Trumbull was extravagant and wanted to place "motive power" on the rails which were too heavy. Jones, said Dodge, would know better than to do that. "We cannot expect to get the economies in the management of the road now that we did when Jones was there with his eye on everything." (See Dodge Papers, *loc. cit.*, XII, 723–24, Dodge to H. Walters [August 2, 1899].) Two years later, when Trumbull informed Dodge that plans were underway to move certain company shops to Childress, Dodge wrote to Trumbull: "You had better take Jones's experience on these matters rather than anyone else. He has better knowledge on the subject than all of them combined, and his information is based on actual practical experience." (See *ibid.*, XVI, 935–37, Dodge to Trumbull, [July 3, 1901].)

84 Morgan Jones Papers, Mrs. Percy Jones, *loc. cit.*, file 18, paper 75, Jones to Dodge (September 7, 1898).

85 FW & DC files, Record Book, 1898, Annual Meeting of Stockholders (March 7, 1899), 8.

Jones remained on the Board of Directors. Most of the other members of the Board were Texans, and, with Dodge and Henry Walters always ready to support him, there was little likelihood that Jones would fail to retain a significant influence over the FW & DC's operating policies.

His resignation did not diminish his interest in the Gulf system, nor his faith in that or other southwestern railroads. On December 28, 1898, he subscribed $30,000 in new securities in the Gulf road,[86] and on March 19, 1899, he arranged with Kountz Brothers —New York investment bankers—to purchase six hundred shares of Texas and Pacific stock, six hundred shares of Missouri, Kansas and Texas stock, and three hundred shares of stock in the Southern Pacific.[87]

Shortly after his resignation, in 1899, Jones visited his relatives in Wales and England. It was a brief visit, however, as there was much in America he wanted to do, and many of his enterprises required his constant attention. He held major interests in the Wichita Mill and Elevator Company, the Western Industrial Company, and the Totallus Mining and Investment Company of Colorado. Also, he owned thousands of acres of coal, farm, and ranch lands in Texas and Colorado which he could not long neglect. The sixty-year-old American industrialist and railroad builder hurried back to his adopted country before the end of the year. He wanted to investigate railroad-building possibilities at Wichita Falls, in the Indian Territory, in Utah, and in California.

[86] Morgan Jones Papers, Mrs. Percy Jones, *loc. cit.*, file 2, paper 12–B.
[87] *Ibid.*, file 2, paper 27, Jones to Kountz Brothers (March 19, 1899).

146

8. SOUTHWEST TO ABILENE

COLONEL Morgan Jones returned to the United States in September, 1899, eager to build another railroad. All potentially prosperous western areas without railroad transportation interested him, but he preferred to build in Texas, his adopted state. At the turn of the century, Texas ranked second only to Illinois in railroad construction and would, in fact, surpass that perennial leader within half a decade.

Since 1869, when the young Welshman had arrived in the Lone Star State, railroad mileage in Texas had increased from 583 to 9,702 miles. Jones had helped to build more than one-tenth of that total. First as a construction foreman and later as the head of his own construction companies, he built sections of the Southern Transcontinental, the Texas and Pacific, and the Gulf, Colorado and Santa Fe. For sixteen years he served as president of the Fort Worth and Denver City Railway Company—North Texas' longest railroad—during its construction and its critical first decade. Throughout that period he argued persistently that the FW & DC should build branch lines to serve territories adjacent to the main line. During his presidency, therefore, the company constructed the Pan Handle Railway from Washburn to Panhandle City, and the Wichita Valley Railway from Wichita Falls to Seymour.

In spite of drought and depression, the indomitable builder ad-

147

vocated more feeder roads. A natural optimist, he was not fool-hardy. Economic distress in a virgin land, whether from natural or man-made causes, was only temporary. Droughts, he believed, could be local phenomena; a dry season in the Texas Panhandle was not necessarily a dry season in the Wichita Valley. Jones reasoned, apparently with greater conviction than many of his rail-road friends, that a branch line's abundant agricultural traffic during a productive year could counteract losses suffered elsewhere along the main line.[1]

While he waited, somewhat impatiently, for an opportunity to free himself from FW & DC administrative details, he took frequent reconnaissance trips into Greer County, Indian Territory, north and east of the main line, and into the Wichita Valley to the south and west. After each preliminary survey, Jones wrote voluminous letters to his good friend Grenville Dodge. He described the country, shrewdly evaluated its potential worth, suggested possible branch lines, and always offered to invest abundantly in any construction project.[2] In 1898 he traveled along the North, Elm, and Salt forks of the Red River and then wrote to Dodge that they should build from the main line at Vernon (Wilbarger County) or Quanah (Hardeman County) north across the Red River, upon the condition, of course, that Congress would open the Comanche reservation to settlement.[3]

Later that year, after another trip into Indian Territory east of Greer County, Jones was even more impressed. "It is the finest part of the Indian Territory that I have been in yet," he wrote.[4] He believed that a railroad from Wichita Falls to Fort Sill would prove more valuable than at any other area in the territory. As usual, he warned Dodge that, if they did not lay first claim to the railroad rights there, "some other road will be sure to build down

---

1 This encouraging hypothesis, so often presented in his annual reports to FW & DC stockholders, was more frequently expressed in personal correspondence to Jones's business associates.

2 See particularly Jones's letters to Dodge, Dodge Papers, *loc. cit.*, XV, Nos. 741, 879, 885, and 891 (May 28, 1898; September 3, 1898; September 25, 1898; and October 3, 1898).

3 *Ibid.*, XV, 741, Jones to Dodge (May 28, 1898).

4 *Ibid.*, XV, 879, Jones to Dodge (September 13, 1898).

Cash [Cache] Creek and to the Wichita Valley."⁵ The area so excited Jones that he began to ponder possible names for his proposed railroad. "How would it do to call it the Wichita Northern or the Wichita and St. Louis Railway?"⁶ he asked Dodge. The question, obviously, was designed to instill greater interest and support for the plan. Dodge, who was in New York and who had many friends in Congress, doubted that Congress would soon open the Indian Territory. He informed his Texas friend that Senator Matthew Stanley Quay, of Pennsylvania, strongly opposed the bill and would probably delay its passage.

The disappointing news forced Jones to consider another discouraging fact: even if the bill should pass, it would take two years to allot the land and prepare its sale.⁷ Depressed, Jones nevertheless determined to build a new road as soon as he could resign from his FW & DC duties. The persistent Welshman decided to limit construction to the Red River until Congress opened the Comanche lands. He ordered another preliminary survey in the area north of Wichita Falls; and, as a result, he reluctantly admitted that he must postpone all plans until a later day. Again his practicality overcame his builder's enthusiasm. The survey showed that the Red River at Charlie, Texas—the point at which the rails eventually would cross into Indian Territory—was 4,100 feet wide and would require such expensive trestles that it was impractical to build a bridge at that location.⁸ He discovered, also, that most of the area was cultivated between Wichita Falls and Charlie; therefore, it would take longer to gain the necessary right-of-way than he originally anticipated.⁹ Arrangements to resign from the Fort Worth and Denver City occupied much of his time and prevented surveys of other possible crossings at the Red River. Somewhat dispirited, the railroad builder temporarily shelved all construction plans.

After his resignation from the FW & DC, and following his brief

---

5 *Ibid.*
6 *Ibid.*
7 *Ibid.*, XV, 885, Jones to Dodge (September 25, 1898).
8 *Ibid.*, XV, 891, Jones to Dodge (October 3, 1898).
9 *Ibid.*

sojourn in Wales and England, Jones visited Dodge in New York. They talked at length about western railroad construction. Their conversations led to a decision to extend the Union Pacific's Salt Lake City branch, the Utah Central—which at that time extended into southwestern Utah—to Los Angeles.[10] This was a project eagerly sought and talked about by Mormon settlers. Dodge accompanied Jones to Fort Worth. Each still had certain duties in connection with the Fort Worth and Denver City's reorganization. Jones needed, also, to consult with Kaufman, his secretary, about other Fort Worth business matters.

In November, the two railroad men departed for Utah. Upon their arrival at Salt Lake City, they personally inspected that Union Pacific branch line to its railhead near the Utah-Nevada boundary line in southwestern Utah. Dodge had surveyed the route into Los Angeles some years earlier and was, therefore, familiar with the territory. They agreed to complete the line along the original route if Union Pacific and Southern Pacific officials agreed to their plan. Their joint consent was necessary, Dodge explained, since both companies "were in an agreement as to the occupation of that territory."[11]

Back at Salt Lake City, they met the Union Pacific's general manager who enthusiastically supported their plan. He explained, however, that the Union Pacific could not make a traffic agreement with them without the Southern Pacific's approval.[12] Jones and Dodge went to California to see Collis P. Huntington, who, years before, had built the Central Pacific and Southern Pacific lines. The old man "absolutely refused" to discuss a traffic agreement with them; and, moreover, he threatened to fight them if they attempted to complete the road.[13] Under the circumstances, Jones and Dodge concluded that it was not "good policy" to build into Los Angeles.

The two old friends enjoyed their rare opportunity to travel to-

10 *Ibid.*, XVI, 321, Dodge notes. Unlike Jones, Dodge was always conscious of his role in history. In addition to a rather detailed diary, Dodge frequently summarized his activities in essay form after an extended trip.

11 *Ibid.*, XVI, 321, Dodge notes.

12 *Ibid.*, No. 322.

13 *Ibid.*

gether and decided to extend their western tour. From California they briefly revisited Salt Lake City and witnessed a football game between Ogden and Salt Lake City—undoubtedly Dodge's idea—which involved "much rough play and quarreling."[14] Before they returned to Denver, they met Amerlia Fulsom Young, one of Brigham Young's wives. After a few days at Denver, they went to Leadville to inspect their mining interests; to Cripple Creek where they were caught in a snow blizzard; to El Paso where the sixty-eight-year-old Dodge had a brief but painful attack of gout; to the San Pedro mines, at the foot of the Sierra Madres, where Jones spent a day in the mines, tested the ore, and estimated its value at $50 to $150 a ton; and finally to Lazarus, where there were six lumber mills and where lumber, to Jones's great interest, was worth $16 a thousand feet.[15]

In mid-December they boarded a Southern Pacific–Texas and Pacific train at El Paso and returned to Fort Worth. Two observations during the western tour strongly impressed Jones: first, Mexico needed more rail transportation; second, everyone in the West seemed to need lumber. The perceptive Welshman reflected upon both observations. His old dream to build a Texas-Chihuahua railroad to the Pacific Coast quickly re-emerged and, since he could not build into the Indian Territory nor into the Wichita Valley nor into California, he decided, once again, to go back into Mexico. He left Fort Worth on January 12, 1900, and remained south of the border about six weeks. He was unable to find anyone who was willing to share his dream. The Mexican government at that time only wanted to extend the Isthmian Railway along the Pacific Coast to Guatemala.[16]

Since he could not build railroads, Jones turned his attention to the lumber business. After brief business trips back to Fort Worth and Denver, he went to the Pacific Northwest—an unfamiliar part of the country—with letters of introduction and a copy of Edward

14 *Ibid.*, No. 325.

15 *Ibid.*, Nos. 325–27.

16 Morgan Jones Papers, Mrs. Percy Jones, *loc. cit.*, file 18, paper 87, Jones to Nathan Dodge (February 28, 1900); Jones did not reveal in this letter any additional details concerning his trip to Mexico.

E. Eitel's *County Atlas of Oregon and Washington* to study en route.[17] Contemporary records do not reveal Jones's exact timberland transactions during the year 1900. For several months he traveled extensively through the Northwest and bought approximately 3,000 acres of redwood timberlands in Polk County, Oregon, and Lewis County, Washington.[18] From the Northwest he journeyed next to Illinois, where he purchased 1,040 acres in Perry County.[19] He continued his trip eastward as far as the Cumberland Mountains in Kentucky and Virginia and added 5,034 more acres to his timberland collection. En route home, Jones stopped again in Louisiana; on Honey Island, between the two Pearl rivers, he procured another "block" of land and established two lumber mills. Finally, back in Fort Worth, Jones invested $22,871.36 in more timberland in East Texas. During the year 1900 the railroad builder purchased between 15,000 and 20,000 acres of land. The desire to build railroads, however, remained uppermost in his mind.

Jones returned to Wichita Falls—the town from which he seemed determined to lay new rails—and renewed his correspondence to Dodge and Henry Walters: he wanted to extend the Wichita Valley Railway. The two friends seemed reluctant to join him, but they gave him no specific reason. Jones's plans were simply too ambitious "for these times," Dodge lamely explained.[20] Undaunted, he resumed his reconnaissance trips west and south of Seymour, and his detailed evaluations of that country literally overwhelmed his eastern friends.

The Welshman described "a new and growing town called Munday" in Knox County where settlers ginned more than one thousand acres of cotton during the preceding year.[21] Another town near by, Goree, was equally prosperous, he claimed. "This part of Knox County has great attractions for the small farmer. The

17Morgan Jones Papers, Mrs. Percy Jones, *loc. cit.*, file 1, paper 17.

18 *Ibid.*, file 2, paper 8; Crozier, *Dallas News*, 8. Years later Jones said that he bought approximately the same amount of land in northern California, but there is no record of his holdings in that state.

19 Morgan Jones Papers, Mrs. Percy Jones, *loc. cit.*, file 2, paper 8.

20 Dodge Papers, *loc. cit.*, XVI, 859, Dodge to Jones (April 5, 1901).

21 *Ibid.*, XVI, 907, Jones to Dodge (April 29, 1901).

soil is a sandy loam and holds the moisture better than the mesquite lands north of the river [Brazos]."[22] It was no coincidence that he described prosperous little communities directly southwest of the Wichita Valley railhead. It was precisely the area into which he wanted to build. "Some road," he warned, "will build to these settlements," and probably all the way south to that "fine country" around Abilene, in Taylor County.[23]

From Munday and Goree, Jones traveled southwest into Haskell and Jones counties[24] and talked with settlers in two other communities—Haskell and Stamford. They informed him that St. Louis and San Francisco Railway officials wanted to build down to their area from the Red River. The Texans were interested, but preferred instead a connection with the Fort Worth and Denver City via the Wichita Valley rails. He promptly relayed the information to Dodge. The Haskell men told him that they could raise a $40,000 bonus, and they assured him that Stamford and Abilene could raise equal amounts. "They would prefer to get our road," Jones emphasized, "if we will build and . . . they want to give us the opportunity before they close with other parties."[25]

The Welshman's crafty stratagem failed to win his friend's complete support, and consequently he returned to his lesser goal to build north from Wichita Falls to the Red River. Congress still refused to open a 480,000-acre area in Indian Territory, but Jones resumed his contention that a short line north of Wichita Falls would get "considerable business."[26] Finally, Dodge expressed greater interest. Jones's persistent letters, increased prosperity along the Fort Worth and Denver City route, and a new rumor that the Missouri, Kansas and Texas railroad officials planned to build down into Wichita Falls apparently convinced Dodge that Jones's plan was, after all, basically sound. In October, 1902,

---

22 *Ibid.*
23 *Ibid.*
24 Haskell County was named in honor of Charles Ready Haskell, who died at age nineteen, at Goliad, on March 27, 1836 (Fulmore, *History and Geography of Texas*, 146.) Jones County was named in honor of Dr. Anson Jones, the last president of the Republic of Texas (*ibid.*, 188).
25 Dodge Papers, *loc. cit.*, VII, 137, Jones to Dodge (April 9, 1902).
26 *Ibid.*, XVII, 321, Jones to Dodge (June 20, 1902).

153

Dodge wrote to Frank Trumbull, president of the Colorado and Southern, that he would like to "take the Wichita Valley and extend it," and that he had a plan which was comprehensive enough to allow an extension either north or south of Wichita Falls.[27] The following month Dodge told Trumbull that he was "very anxious to extend the Wichita Valley up to the Red River."[28] Meanwhile, Dodge asked Jones to write to him in more detail "about the condition of matters" around Wichita Falls.[29]

Jones promptly responded. A series of letters from Wichita Falls to New York City during the next few weeks testified to his earnest desire to "throw the dirt." A road to a point on the Red River from Wichita Falls, he explained, would stretch about eighteen miles; he was sure that he could secure the right-of-way from the settlers in that area; rails, ties, and bridge materials would cost about $100,000; grading and all other work would cost about $50,000; and, finally, he believed it was easier to form a new company to do the work than to amend the old Wichita Valley Railway Company charter, which did not include permission to extend that road to the north. When he suspected, during the course of their correspondence, that Dodge was again cooling toward the project, Jones decided it was time to play his trump card: he offered to invest $75,000 in the new company if Dodge and Walters would invest $37,500 each.[30]

Jones's suspicions were well founded. The General, who in the 1860's helped to build the nation's first transcontinental line, still hesitated to help his wealthy Texas friend build an eighteen-mile railroad. At that point Dodge, unaccountably, developed an interest in an extension northwest, rather than southwest, of Seymour. Jones thoroughly surveyed the northwestern route. He found it inferior to the country south of the Brazos; and although he informed Dodge to that effect, the General still wanted a second look. Dodge wrote to Trumbull that a road across Knox, King,

27 *Ibid.*, XVII, 489, Dodge to Trumbull (October 23, 1902). Dodge presented the plan to Trumbull as if it were his own idea. Jones's long campaign to interest others in a Wichita Valley extension was not mentioned.

28 *Ibid.*, XVII, 519, Dodge to Trumbull (November 6, 1902).

29 *Ibid.*, XVII, 499, Dodge to Jones (October 27, 1902).

30 *Ibid.*, XVII, 591, Jones to Dodge (December 22, 1902).

154

Dickens, and Crosby counties should attract trade to the Fort Worth and Denver City, which, at that time, went principally to the Texas and Pacific station at Big Spring.

Jones refused, however, to allow Dodge to sidetrack his Red River project. When Dodge emphasized the potentially large cattle shipments along the northwestern route, Jones countered that that area almost totally lacked good farm land.[31] The former Welsh farmer thus held that a railroad should serve a country with a diversified economy. He would build the Red River–Wichita Falls road, he said, with or without support from Dodge and Walters. He thereupon told Dodge that he had selected a route approximately ten miles east of the original course. The new route would touch the Red River near Byers, Texas. It was five miles longer than the original route, but the river at that point was somewhat narrower. In addition, the Byers route would allow Jones to build near a new oil field at Petrolia, in Clay County. Owners of the Byers ranch provided a third incentive to relocate the proposed road. They offered Jones a $15,000 bonus and a fifteen-mile right-of-way across their Clay County lands. Wichita Falls citizens, meanwhile, donated an eight-mile right-of-way across Wichita County.[32]

On October 26, 1903, Jones secured a charter and named his little railroad the Wichita Falls and Oklahoma Railway Company.[33] He contributed three-fourths of the necessary funds, and Dodge and Walters each contributed one-eighth.[34] The builder, happy to be back on the rails, supervised all construction and completed the project on June 24, 1904.[35] Later he built new depots at each end of the road, and stock pens and a water tank at Byers. The company's rolling stock included one 17x24-cylinder Schenectady engine, one combination passenger and baggage car, six boxcars, six flatcars, three handcars, and three push cars. On July 1, 1904, Jones leased the railroad to the Wichita Valley Railway Com-

---

31 *Ibid.*, XVI, 907, Jones to Dodge (April 29, 1901).

32 Morgan Jones Papers, Mrs. Percy Jones, *loc. cit.*, file 4, paper 10–D.

33 Jonnie R. Morgan, *The History of Wichita Falls*, 67; Hoyt, "Summary History," (FW & DC file 1230), 4.

34 Hoyt, "Summary History" (FW & DC file 1230). Actual construction costs were $148,666.47.

35 Morgan Jones Papers, Mrs. Percy Jones, *loc. cit.*, file 4, paper 10–A.

pany,[36] which, in turn, was a Fort Worth and Denver City branch line.[37]

One of the Colonel's rail hands with the Wichita Falls and Oklahoma construction crew was another young nephew, Percy Jones. The energetic and robust eighteen-year-old had joined his uncle at Wichita Falls in September, 1903.[38] Percy was born at Fence Houses, Durham County, England, on January 23, 1885. He attended Barnard Castle, a technical school in England, where he studied marine engineering, until he decided to join his uncle and eldest brother, Morgan C., in the United States.[39] He, too, was approximately six feet tall and bore a strong physical resemblance to his uncle. The young man set to work at once to adapt his marine engineering training to civil engineering with the Wichita Falls and Oklahoma railroad.

Shortly after Colonel Jones completed the new road, he sailed from New York aboard the *S.S. Astoria* to visit once again his brothers in Wales and England. He returned to the United States in September, spent some time in New York with General Dodge, and returned to Texas in October. During the Colonel's absence Morgan C. Jones married Miss Jessie Kenan Wilder, a young music teacher from Weatherford, Texas, who taught piano at Seymour.[40]

Colonel Jones remained in the Seymour, Wichita Falls, and Fort Worth areas for several months during the winter of 1904–1905. His secretary, W. E. Kaufman, resided at Wichita Falls where he was auditor of the Wichita Valley railroad. They decided that

36 Jones still served as president of the Wichita Valley Railway Company. His nephew, Morgan C., was superintendent of the same road. After one year at the University of Virginia, where he distinguished himself as Queen Victoria's staunchest defender, he worked in Leadville, Colorado, mines. Sometime later he returned to Texas, worked diligently in various positions for the Wichita Valley railroad, and eventually convinced his exacting uncle that he was qualified to serve the company as its superintendent. (Interview with Mrs. Morgan Jones, Sr. [November 28, 1967].)

37 In 1923 the line was extended across the Red River to Waurika, Oklahoma. (Hoyt, "Summary History," [FW & DC file 1230], 4.)

38 Interview with Mrs. Percy Jones (April 30, 1968).

39 *Ibid.*

40 Morgan C. Jones and Miss Wilder, daughter of Mr. and Mrs. George Wilder, were married at Weatherford on October 4, 1904. Miss Wilder was a graduate of Weatherford College and her father, a local merchant, allowed her to accept a teaching position at Seymour following her graduation, since she had an aunt and uncle who resided there. She and her husband made their home at Seymour until 1908. (Interview with Mrs. Morgan Jones, Sr. [Mrs. Morgan C. Jones], [November 28, 1967].)

Kaufman should move, with his family, to Fort Worth, where he could perform his secretarial duties more conveniently. At the same time, he could continue to work for the Wichita Valley and to serve as secretary and treasurer of Jones's Citizens Light and Power Company.[41] Since prospects to extend the Wichita Valley road had not changed materially, Jones decided to go to the Pacific Northwest to investigate the need for short-line railroads in that area where he owned extensive timberlands.

He reached Astoria, Oregon, in July, 1905, and visited an old friend, John McGuire, who was superintendent of the Astoria and Columbia River Railway Company. During that visit Lewis Garlinger, of Portland, telegraphed the Colonel that Garlinger held a letter for him, marked "Personal," from Grenville Dodge. In the letter Dodge expressed a changed attitude toward Jones's earlier proposal and implored Jones to return to Texas and to build, with all possible speed, an extension to the Wichita Valley railroad from Seymour to Stamford. Dodge explained that "outside parties" were trying to move into the Stamford area, that the country was filling up rapidly with settlers, and that the Wichita Valley Railway Company needed to move quickly to provide good rail service.[42] Dodge, in effect, stated precisely the same reasons to build the road that Jones had enumerated to Dodge dozens of times before.[43]

Jones accepted the assignment and telegraphed Dodge that he would return to Texas by September 1 "to take charge of matters."[44] In later correspondence addressed to Jones at Fort Worth, Dodge explained to Jones that Colorado and Southern officials wanted to finance the extension but were unable to do so at that time; the company could not issue additional bonds until 1908. Jones, Dodge, and Walters, and possibly three or four other interested parties financed all new construction until the Colorado and Southern was ready to relieve them of that responsibility.[45]

41 Morgan Jones Papers, Mrs. Percy Jones, *loc. cit.*, "Autobiographical Sketch" by W. E. Kaufman, file 3, paper 6–S.
42 Dodge Papers, *loc. cit.*, XVIII, 939, Dodge to Walters (August 18, 1905).
43 In his letter to Jones, Dodge probably acknowledged Jones's earlier desire to extend the road. His letter to Walters, however, left a strong impression that Dodge originated the whole idea.
44 Dodge Papers, *loc. cit.*, XVIII, 939, Dodge to Walters (August 18, 1905).
45 *Ibid.*, XVIII, 997, Dodge to Jones (October 19, 1905).

Jones agreed to that temporary arrangement and, eager to begin, agreed also to finance all preliminary expenditures until Dodge and Walters brought other members into the syndicate.

Under Jones's leadership, the Wichita Valley Railway Company prospered.[46] Farmers and ranchers along the route were equally prosperous, and Seymour, the seat of government for Baylor County, was in 1905 a thriving little town. The county was created in 1858, but for two decades it remained primarily a ranching area. The land was generally level except near the rough edges of the Brazos and Big Wichita rivers and their tributaries. The soil varied from loam to sand, and annual rainfall averaged approximately twenty-seven inches. The only trees were sparsely scattered mesquites. During frontier days, buffalo herds roamed the county and watered at the shallow rivers and creeks.

In 1876 immigrants from Oregon settled near the center of the county at a point where the Old Western Trail crossed the route to California. The settlers named their community Oregon City, but in 1878 they changed it to Seymour to honor Seymour Munday, a cowboy whose line camp was near by. In spite of that friendly gesture, Baylor County's ranchers and cowhands did not want Oregon's "nesters" in their midst. When, in 1879, the "nesters" planted a corn crop, the cowhands turned loose their cattle and trampled the plowed land. The feuders repeated the incident in 1880 and again in 1881. Finally, a typical frontier battle ensued, during which the county judge, G. R. Morris, was killed. The ranchers won the battle but eventually lost the war. Although the Oregon settlers moved away, many more settlers replaced them. By 1884, Seymour had a two-story hotel and a courthouse.[47]

The Wichita Valley railroad brought more settlers during the 1890's. Freighting and stagecoach companies established their headquarters at Seymour. Soon farmers began to plant cotton and to ship their bales via the Wichita Valley to distant markets. They plowed other acres and planted grain sorghums, oats, and wheat,

---

[46] *Ibid.*, XVIII, 939, Dodge to Walters (August 18, 1905).
[47] Walter Prescott Webb and H. Bailey Carroll (eds.), *The Handbook of Texas*, I, 124.

and sometimes produced such bountiful harvests that they also shipped their surplus grains to other markets.

Baylor County farmers and ranchers learned to appreciate Colonel Morgan Jones's "personal and neighborly service."[48] It was not unusual for "the old Colonel" to work sixteen to eighteen hours each day, and he expected nothing less from his nephews. There was only one regularly scheduled train between Seymour and Wichita Falls. Each morning, superintendent Morgan C. Jones, who served also as the train's conductor, left Seymour and returned late that afternoon. Often, however, it was necessary to run an extra train to Wichita Falls when large herds overflowed the cattle pens or when bales of cotton overran the depot platform. At such times, young conductor-superintendent Jones frequently made the regular run during the day and an extra run at night. The double schedule allowed little, if any, time to sleep.

On one occasion, while the regular train was at the Wichita Falls station, and while hired hands loaded the cars for the return trip to Seymour, Morgan C. dashed across the street to a local barbershop. He had not shaved for two days. As soon as he sat in the barber's chair he fell sound asleep. The barber, aware of Jones's arduous schedule, did not try to awaken him until a few minutes before the train's scheduled departure. By that time, however, the young man had fallen into such a deep sleep that the barber could not arouse him. Departure time arrived, and still the exhausted conductor resisted every effort to help him from the chair. The frantic barber, who knew that every Wichita Valley train must depart according to the Colonel's exacting schedule, rushed across the street to the station, explained his problem to Tom Smith, the brakeman, and to Myron Barwise, the assistant engineer. The two railroad employees, meanwhile, had decided to take the train back to Seymour without the missing conductor. Somewhat relieved to learn why young Jones had disappeared, they ran back to the barbershop, lifted the sleepy six-foot Englishman by his arms and legs, and carried him to the train.[49] Fortunately for young Morgan

48 *Vernon Times* (February 1, 1951).
49 Plants, "History of the Wichita Valley Railway in My Home County," 3, FW & DC essays.

159

C., Colonel Jones was in Fort Worth. It is not likely that anyone related the incident to him.

On September 23, 1905, the Colonel arrived in Wichita Falls from Fort Worth and immediately boarded the Wichita Valley for Seymour. He informed a newspaper reporter that he had completed all preliminary arrangements for laying the bridge foundation across the Brazos River, and he hoped to make an early connection at Stamford with the Texas Central railroad.[50] Within a month he contracted the road grading for a price which was, in Dodge's opinion, "very low." On October 22, J. P. Nelson, a railroad contractor from San Antonio, arrived at Seymour. Jones met him at the station, and together they announced that Nelson's crew would "break dirt" on November 1 and would complete the project not later than June 1, 1906.[51]

According to a suggestion Jones had made earlier to Dodge, the Seymour-Stamford extension, separately incorporated, was named the Wichita Valley Railroad Company (not to be confused with the Wichita Valley *Railway* Company, whose lines reached from Wichita Falls to Seymour). Meanwhile, the Colorado and Southern's executive committee met in New York and made final plans to purchase the entire road between Byers, Texas, and Stamford. First they agreed to furnish rails, rolling stock, and other equipment for the new Seymour-Stamford extension. Then they agreed to purchase, on or before January 2, 1908, the Jones-Dodge-Walters syndicate's interest in the new road. The Colorado and Southern planned to raise the money through the sale of securities based upon the extension itself.[52]

Finally, according to the November 4, 1905, agreement, Jones, Dodge, and Walters agreed to sell their interest in the Wichita Falls and Oklahoma Railway Company, of which they were sole owners, for $243,375 in cash, or its equivalent in Colorado and Southern Gold Bonds.[53] Jones and his associates agreed, also, to

50 *Abilene Daily Reporter* (September 23, 1905), 3.
51 *Seymour Banner* (October 23, 1905), 1.
52 Dodge Papers, *loc. cit.*, XVII, 1000, Dodge to Jones (October 27, 1905).
53 "Agreement: Grenville M. Dodge, Henry Walters, and Morgan Jones with The Colorado and Southern Railway Company," November 14, 1905, Morgan Jones Papers, Mrs. Percy Jones, *loc. cit.*, file 4, paper 47, 6–7; Annual Report, 1906, The Colorado

sell their two-thirds interest in the Wichita Falls–Seymour branch for $692,100, payable in cash or in Colorado and Southern Gold Bonds.[54]

Once again Jones tried to interest Colorado and Southern officials in his old plan to extend the Wichita Valley railroad to Abilene—about thirty-eight miles south of Stamford. Dodge supported the plan, but he told Jones that the Colorado and Southern directors were afraid to go into Abilene "for fear of antagonizing the Texas and Pacific people," whose rails already served that town.[55] "However, you know more about that than we do," Dodge wrote, and implied that Jones should not abandon his plan since the Colorado and Southern might agree to the extension at a later date.[56]

The *Haskell Free Press* announced to its readers on November 21, 1905, that "the Wichita Valley Railroad is coming, coming as fast as men and money can build it."[57] The enthusiastic editor summoned local citizens to prepare for the railroad's economic impact on the town: "Cotton seed oil mills and a flouring mill are of the first importance to meet the demand," he admonished the grain, wheat, and cotton farmers. Haskell County men quickly rallied to the call, and every farmer and rancher pledged—like frontier pioneers everywhere—to make their little county seat another great metropolis.

Haskell County was created in 1858 and until 1876 remained nothing more than a watering place for buffalo hunters. Before the hunters arrived, Comanche, Kiowa, and Kickapoo tribes camped around the small creeks and draws. The first settlers entered the county in 1883; they built the first grocery and liquor store in 1884; and, in 1885, they organized Haskell County. There was no dispute over the county seat's location since Haskell was the only

and Southern Railway Company, Morgan Jones Papers, Mrs. Percy Jones, *loc. cit.*, file 10, paper 16, 5.
54 "Agreement," Morgan Jones Papers, Mrs. Percy Jones, *loc. cit.*, 3–4; Annual Report, 1906, 5.
55 Dodge Papers, *loc. cit.*, XVIII, 997, Dodge to Jones (October 19, 1905).
56 *Ibid.*, XVIII, 971, Dodge to Jones (September 28, 1905).
57 *Haskell Free Press* (November 21, 1905), 1.

settlement. Soon the town had a courthouse and shortly thereafter a saloon named "The Road to Ruin." For a time there was no church, so every Sunday morning Haskell County citizens dutifully attended services at "The Road to Ruin."[58]

The construction crews rapidly worked their way across Haskell County's gently rolling surface. Jones supervised every portion of the project from Seymour to Stamford. He directed his surveyors to follow a route which roughly paralleled the dividing line between the Cross Timbers area of north-central Texas and the lower western plains; he personally requested and received the necessary right-of-way; he met with local citizens and accepted their promised bonuses; he inspected roadbeds and tested bridges; and he governed the rail-laying crew. As the men completed each section, Jones rode a handcar along the new rails, frequently stopped to note needed adjustments, and invariably handed construction foremen long lists of suggested improvements. It was, above all, the type of work he enjoyed most.

Just across Haskell County's southern boundary, the construction crews approached Stamford, in Jones County. Stamford was a relatively new community. When the Texas Central railroad entered Jones County in 1899[59] it was divided into city blocks from a section of S. M. Swenson's ranch land. Within two years after the first Texas Central train arrived on February 14, 1900, from the southeast, the railhead grew phenomenally into a model little city with schools, churches, a cotton gin, two hotels, and electric lights.[60] The Wichita Valley Railroad's arrival insured the town's continued prosperity.

Down in Taylor County, which bordered Jones County to the south, Abilene city fathers envied the fact that Stamford was a two-railroad town. Abilene was a Texas and Pacific town, and in 1906 had approximately six thousand residents. The city fathers were determined to make it the "Key City of West Texas." A "Key City," they reasoned, should have not less than twenty-five thou-

58 Webb and Carroll, *The Handbook of Texas*, I, 783.
59 *Ibid.*, II, 657.
60 Mrs. C. C. Ferrell, "Early Days in Stamford," *West Texas Historical Association Year Book*, Vol. III (June, 1927), 41–42.

162

sand permanent residents. They concluded, therefore, that a city with twenty-five thousand citizens needed at least two railroads. When they heard that plans were underway to extend the Wichita Valley road in a southwesterly direction from Seymour, they first assumed that Abilene was the Wichita Valley's ultimate goal. They refused to accept the later announcement that the line would end, instead, at Stamford.

Early in 1906, Abilene's "25,000 Club" set to work to bring the Wichita Valley into the "Key City." They discovered that Colonel Morgan Jones was their most influential ally, but they discovered, also, that Colorado and Southern officials (the Wichita Valley's parent organization) feared to invade Texas and Pacific territory. W. G. Swenson and Ed S. Hughes, who headed the "25,000 Club's" railroad committee, scoffed at the Colorado and Southern's timorous excuse. Morgan Jones worked diligently to promote an agreement between the railroad representatives and the Abilene railroad committee. A Colorado and Southern official, finally convinced that Abilene people would support the new road, whispered in Swenson's ear, "If you people in Abilene will build the road, we will agree to operate it."[61]

Within a few weeks, consequently, an Abilene group organized the Abilene and Northern Railway Company. They were granted a charter on February 8, 1906.[62] Swenson, who did most of the "walking and talking"[63] to make the Abilene and Northern a reality, was the company's first president. He obtained the necessary right-of-way, contracted with Morgan Jones to build the road, and offered Jones a $40,000 bonus if he completed the road by December 31, 1906. Jones accepted the challenge, kept his surveyors and construction crews together after they reached Stamford, and directed them to continue due south toward Abilene.

As he raced against time, unusually heavy rains delayed his progress. One local newspaper editor commented, "It doesn't rain

---

61 Interview with W. G. Swenson (November 9, 1967).

62 Gracie May Philley, "Wichita Valley Railway in My Home County," 2, FW & DC essays.

63 Katharyn Duff, *Abilene Reporter-News* (December 12, 1965), Sec. B, 1.

much in west Texas, but when it does, it rains like a damn fool!"[64] Week after week the project fell dangerously behind schedule. Jones sent an urgent request to his Fort Worth and Denver City friends to send to him as many laborers as needed work. Shortly thereafter, two hundred Greek immigrants arrived at the railhead. They toiled in rain and mud for several weeks, complained to him that they did not like to work in such wet country, refused to believe that West Texas was normally dry country and soon would become that way again, and ultimately demanded transportation back to Fort Worth.[65]

"That was the only time I ever attempted to bully laborers into working, and it failed," Jones later recalled. "We were short-handed . . . pressed for time . . . and none of them could talk English. It was raining all the time, and they wouldn't work. I threatened and expostulated to no avail. Finally, they hired carriages and left me."[66]

The rains ceased soon after the Greek laborers departed, and Jones's regular crews worked extra hours to accelerate their journey toward Jones County's southern border. As they approached the Clear Fork of the Brazos River, another crisis loomed. The chief engineer refused to use available sand on the masonry work. The Welshman conceded that Jones County sand was not the best in the world, but he insisted that it was acceptable for the task at hand and that there was no time to await another shipment from Kansas City. The engineer was adamant and, like the Greek laborers, abandoned the project.[67]

Again the harried builder telegraphed a Fort Worth and Denver City friend to locate, wherever he could, an engineer to complete the task. To his astonishment, he sent "that boy Percy Jones."[68] Percy was twenty-one years old at that time, and, after his brief employment with a Wichita Falls and Oklahoma construction crew, he had secured similar work with a Fort Worth and Denver

64 Quoted by Robert Nail, "Albany's Fandangle" (May 10, 1968), from *Albany News*.
65 Crozier, *Dallas News*, 8.
66 *Ibid*.
67 *Ibid*.
68 *Ibid*.

City repair crew. His agitated uncle wired back to Fort Worth: "I wanted a man, not a boy." The following morning he received the telegraphed reply: "You asked for the best man . . . for the job and we sent him to you."[69] Within days the "old man" grudgingly acknowledged that the "boy" was a capable railroad engineer.

Relentlessly, they pushed the project toward the Taylor County line. It seemed impossible, however, to recover lost time. Jones, ready to admit defeat, sent his attorney, D. T. Bomar, to Abilene to request a thirty-day time extension. In return, Jones promised to reduce the $40,000 bonus by 10 per cent. When the "25,000 Club's" railroad committee refused the request—they hoped that they could save all of the bonus money—Bomar told them: "You don't know Morgan Jones or you would assure me of this extension, for, if you don't Morgan Jones will pull trains into Abilene before the limit expires."[70]

Bomar's warning was not an idle threat. The old Welshman and his young English nephew devised an ingenious time-saving plan. They directed the track-laying crew to leave out one spike at every rail tie. The maneuver succeeded. Three days before the deadline, the first Abilene and Northern locomotive rolled into the Taylor County town. As soon as the train reached the depot—a boxcar just inside Abilene's city limits[71]—the rail crew began to add the missing spikes. Thus Abilene's "25,000 Club" paid four thousand additional dollars to learn, the hard way, that Morgan Jones could always beat a deadline.

The sixty-seven-year-old railroad builder was particularly proud of his line of Wichita Valley roads. He had personally supervised their construction from the Red River, along Texas' northern border, to Abilene in west-central Texas. The combined roads extended 173 miles in a southwesterly direction. They were well constructed, economically operated, and provided uncommonly good service. On May 23, 1907, the Colorado and Southern's president, Frank Trumbull, wrote to General Dodge, after an inspection tour, "The Wichita Valley lines look good, particularly west

69 *Ibid.*
70 *Ibid.*
71 Philley, "Wichita Valley Railway in My Home County," 3, FW & DC essays.

of Seymour, and there is good feeling toward our lines all the way to Abilene."[72]

The prosperous farmers, ranchers, and townsmen had every reason to appreciate their new railroad service. Whatever the cost to themselves, the Jones nephews practiced that "personal and neighborly service" which their unsparing uncle always preached. Farmers and cowhands learned that they could flag down a Wichita Valley train and order a plug of Star Navy chewing tobacco or perhaps a supply of snuff for their wives. Superintendent-conductor Morgan C. Jones or the young engineer Percy Jones dutifully delivered the order to the isolated settlers on their return trip.[73]

On one occasion, the Jones nephews delivered a grain binder to a prosperous farmer and deposited it on the right-of-way which adjoined the farmer's fields. The following day, the farmer and his son flagged down the train. "This binder business is new to us," the frustrated man explained to Percy, "and we can't make the danged thing work. We thought you might show us how to get it going."[74] The engineer, the conductor, other crewmen, and all male passengers on the train thereupon gathered around the binder, taught the puzzled farmer and his son the "binder business," and then continued their journey to Wichita Falls.

During the busy season, the regular train frequently stopped at loading pens to attach cattle cars. The cow hands expected the train crew and able-bodied passengers to give a helping hand. When the cars were loaded and attached, the men, "with coats off and collars open," would climb back into the passenger coach to join their irritated wives who, meanwhile, had emptied the water cooler and had chased unruly children from one end of the coach to the other.[75]

During prolonged droughts, the Jones brothers stopped to fight prairie fires and to allow sun-browned farmers to fill their cans,

[72] Dodge Papers, *loc. cit.*, XIX, 643, Trumbull to Dodge (May 23, 1907). Colorado and Southern officials, true to their earlier promise to Abilene's railroad committee, purchased the Abilene and Northern Railway Company shortly after its completion. (C & S Annual Report, 1906, 5.)

[73] *Vernon Times* (February 1, 1951).

[74] *Ibid.*

[75] *Ibid.*

166

buckets, and water barrels with water from the trains' tank cars.[76] Colonel Jones insisted upon such service, but, at the same time, he never failed to insist that the trains "keep to the schedule."[77]

The Colonel liked Abilene and its city fathers' enterprising spirit. He particularly liked W. G. Swenson, the energetic young member of Abilene's railroad committee. There was, however, no further work for Jones to do in Abilene. He remained there a few days to tour the Taylor County area and then departed for New Orleans to inspect his Louisiana Land and Lumber Company. Through the year 1907 and part of 1908, he visited his lumber mills at Honey Island and Lewisburg, Louisiana; he traveled to Oklahoma, where, with Thomas Self, he organized the Frederick Cotton Oil and Manufacturing Company; he remained for a while at Mineral Wells, Texas, where, with Sidney Webb, he operated several cotton oil mills; and, at his Baylor County and Archer County ranches, he added 4,828 cattle which he purchased from W. T. Waggoner for $75,609.50.[78]

His other duties included those as chairman of the board at Fort Worth's Continental Bank and Trust Company and as a member of the boards at the Citizens Light and Power Company, the Consumers Light and Heating Company, and the Fidelity Trust Company, all in Fort Worth. Those responsibilities kept him busy but not contented. He wanted to build more railroads. When he heard that a little community named Ballinger, about fifty miles southwest of Abilene, in Runnels County, wanted another road, Jones decided to investigate.

76 Plants, "History of the Wichita Valley Railway in My Home County," 2, FW & DC essays.

77 *Ibid.*

78 Morgan Jones Papers, Mrs. Percy Jones, *loc. cit.*, "Bill of Exchange," file 4, paper 16.

9. "THE BEST LITTLE ROAD I EVER BUILT"

"TEXAS has 12,500 miles of railroad and only one-fifth of her land developed," lamented the editor of the *El Paso Herald* in 1908.[1] The frustrated promoter of that landlocked, far West Texas town believed that his sprawling state needed fifty thousand miles of railroads. Economic and political conditions at that time, in both state and nation, provided little encouragement that Texas' transportation problems would soon end. The financial crisis that panicked eastern bankers and industrialists in the autumn of 1907 quickly spread westward; eventually, it created a currency shortage and closed banks in the Lone Star State. In addition to that catastrophe, Texas had a governor whose attitude toward the railroad industry was uncertain. In 1906 the voters had elected Thomas M. Campbell, whose platform promised tax reform and more effective regulation of business. Governor Campbell, moreover, emphasized his belief that railroad companies should pay higher taxes. When, in his bid for re-election in 1908, Campbell soundly defeated R. R. Williams, who called for "justice to corporations," the El Paso editor had good reason to expect even less railroad construction in the immediate future.

Railroad construction soon confirmed the editor's fears. New rails in 1907 totaled little more than half of that for the preceding

[1] Quoted in the *Abilene Daily Reporter* (September 17, 1908), 2.

168

year.[2] In 1908 only 340 miles of new track stretched across the enormous state.[3] It was indeed an infinitesimal quantity and "not a hundredth part"[4] of the pressing need. West Texas did not have a single navigable river to alleviate its burdensome transportation problems; only the narrow rails of the Fort Worth and Denver City, the Texas and Pacific, and the Southern Pacific bound that "unpeopled immensity" to Texas' more populous eastern regions. Unless railroad men, such as Morgan Jones, kept their faith, invested their money, and built branch lines between those larger trans-Texas lines, western Texas would remain a huge pasture land for a few cattle kings.

The old Welshman kept his faith. He continued to assume that "cycles of depression" were temporary and inevitable; he wanted to assume, also, that state politicians would never destroy the "railroad intellectuality." He never doubted West Texas' potential wealth. Its mineral resources, its vast ranch lands, and its millions of acres of rich farmland needed men with strong backs and a means to transport the products of their efforts to distant markets. In West Texas, only railroads could adequately supply both needs. Jones helped to supply that need in East Texas, he watched that region's amazing economic growth, and he benefited from it.

Prosperous Fort Worth served as a prime example to those who wished to measure East Texas progress. The little town whose citizens in 1876 looked upon the Welshman as their own local hero had developed by 1908 into a bustling city of more than fifty thousand inhabitants. The city of Fort Worth had paved streets, automobiles, electric lights, motion pictures, and a coliseum which could seat five thousand persons.[5] That East Texas city, however, no longer challenged Morgan Jones's pioneer spirit. It was a good place to build one's financial empire, but its half-dozen railroad lines left little room to build more roads.

Abilene in 1908 reminded Jones of Fort Worth in those challenging days during the 1870's and 1880's when editor B. B. Pad-

---

2 In 1906, Texas added 810 miles; in 1907, only 461. (*Texas Almanac, 1910*, 116.)
3 *Ibid.*
4 *Ibid.*, 117.
5 Knight, *Fort Worth: Outpost on the Trinity*, 167–94.

169

dock produced, overnight, nine Fort Worth railroads—on his "tarantula map." Fort Worth's example proved to every railroad town along Texas' main lines that more railroads, in more directions, assured rapid growth and great prosperity. The Welshman had recently discovered that Abilene's 25,000 Club was, undoubtedly, one of the most railroad-conscious organizations in the entire state. When, therefore, on May 22, 1907, the *Abilene Daily Reporter* announced that the 25,000 Club wanted another railroad to reach into South Taylor County and that Ballinger citizens in neighboring Runnels County wanted that road to extend to their community, Jones was ready to offer his services.

Taylor and Runnels counties were created, with twenty-one other West Texas counties, by an act of the Seventh Legislature on February 1, 1858.[6] On that date Taylor County had no permanent settlers, no cattle, and no timberland other than a few scattered post oaks along Elm Creek.[7] It was indeed "just a spot for travelers to hurry through" as they made their way to California under the protecting eyes of near-by Fort Belknap and Fort Chadbourne.[8] The Butterfield Mail road cut across the county's northwestern corner. The Callahan Divide, a topographic boundary line between the Brazos and Colorado river basins, crossed the county from east to west. That part of the county contains some conspicuous hills: Church Mountain, Castle Peak, Bald Eagle, and East Peak.

[6] The act required that the counties' names should honor eminent deceased persons in Texas history. Runnels County, consequently, honored Hiram G. Runnels, an early Brazos River planter, who represented Brazoria County in the Convention of 1845. (Webb and Carroll, *The Handbook of Texas*, II, 515.) For many years the *Texas Almanac* stated that Taylor County's name honored three members of the Texas state legislature at the time the act was passed. Since all three Representatives Taylor were still living when the act went into effect, the *Texas Almanac* was obviously incorrect. Primarily through the efforts of Mrs. Dallas Scarborough, chapter historian for the United States Daughters of 1812, the Texas legislature, on March 30, 1954, officially designated Edward Taylor, James Taylor, and George Taylor, all brothers who died in the Alamo, as those for whom the county was named. (Jewel Davis Scarborough, "Taylor County and Its Name," *West Texas Historical Association Year Book*, Vol. XXX [October, 1954], 73–82.)

[7] William E. Cureton's unpublished memoirs, Sarah Hardy Collection, 1730 South 12th Street, Abilene, Texas. Mr. Cureton, who, as a young man, accompanied his father on a cattle drive in the Abilene area in 1863, stated, "you could see a jack rabbit run for half a mile, where now grow thick forests of mesquite trees."

[8] Katharyn Duff, *Abilene Reporter-News* (April 8, 1956), Sec. E, 2.

170

Buffalo hunters and, later, bone collectors were the first white men to earn their livelihood in the area. As early as 1863, however, cattlemen began to take their herds to the excellent ranges and grassy valleys. They built pens along the creeks and held annual roundups. By 1874 ranchers had established a few scattered homes in Taylor County: Sam Gholson had a herd of cattle on Jim Ned Creek; William C. Dunn succeeded him and established the Dunn Ranch; John H. Simpson's Hashknife Ranch bordered Cedar Creek; G. H. Connell and Brooks Lee herded their cattle in the mountain range's buffalo gap;[9] and other cattlemen settled in Cedar Gap and Mulberry Canyon.[10] In 1877, Abe Hunter stocked a dugout with supplies of groceries for near-by settlers in the buffalo gap. Shortly thereafter "Hog" Jackson established a tent store which was, in turn, succeeded by the Wylie and Davis general store. As more settlers moved in, Wylie and Davis put in a stock of lumber hauled from Fort Worth.[11] The community of Buffalo Gap thus became Taylor County's first trading center.

The year 1878 marked more changes: the last buffalo herd in Mulberry Canyon was killed; the last band of "wild Indians" peacefully left the area; on July 23, Taylor County was organized and held its first elections; and on August 8, Governor R. B. Hubbard proclaimed that Buffalo Gap was Taylor County's seat of local government.[12] Within two years ranchers, cow hands, gunmen, gamblers, salesmen, lawyers, and merchants boosted Buffalo Gap's population to twelve hundred. Tens of thousands of Longhorn cattle followed the Western Trail through Buffalo Gap to Kansas markets.

Meanwhile, Texas and Pacific construction crews rapidly worked their way toward Taylor County. Pioneer settlers tried to purchase all unclaimed lands along the railroad's anticipated route. In many instances ownership was difficult and sometimes impossible to determine since titles were not recorded and no taxes were

---

9 *Ibid.*
10 Sam L. Chalk, "Early Experiences in the Abilene Country," *West Texas Historical Association Year Book*, Vol. IV (June, 1928), 95.
11 *Ibid.*
12 Scarborough, "Taylor County and Its Name," *loc. cit.*, 74–75.

paid. The exact route was still undetermined when the Texas and Pacific was less than one hundred miles east of Taylor County. The company considered and then discarded its original plan to build through Fort Phantom Hill, twelve miles north of the county line.[13] That decision meant, to Buffalo Gap residents at least, that the railroad company planned to extend the rails to their community.

They were overly optimistic. A meeting at the Hashknife Ranch headquarters, in September, 1880, proved Buffalo Gap's undoing. Among those at the meeting were John H. Simpson, of the Hashknife Ranch; S. L. Chalk, a surveyor; J. D. and C. W. Merchant, West Texas cattlemen; H. C. Withers, track and townsite locator for the Texas and Pacific; J. T. Berry, a merchant; and J. Stoddard Johnston, a land promoter from Kentucky. These men met to determine, once and for all time, the railroad's route through Taylor County. Upon their decision rested the future location of a major cattle shipping center. The majority of the group decided, not surprisingly, to direct the route across land recently purchased by Simpson, Berry, and the Merchant brothers. On December 18, 1880, Texas and Pacific representatives signed a contract with the landowners, and the latter, shortly thereafter, laid out a townsite. J. D. Merchant named the future shipping center "Abilene," a familiar name to all cattlemen who had made the long drive to Kansas.[14]

Rail-laying crews reached the new townsite during the week of January 9–15, 1881, and two months later, on March 15, town-lot sales began. Within twenty-four hours, 178 lots sold for a total of $27,550. Abilene, Texas, a "tent city" until the town-lot sale, was by 1885 a bustling cattle center and boasted such prosperous businesses as the Burton-Lingo Lumber Company, C. E. Fulwiler's livery stable, J. M. Radford's grocery store, and Ed S. Hughes's hardware store. Equally important, Abilenians—many of whom were former Buffalo Gap residents—voted to make their town Taylor County's new county seat. A typical frontier battle between

13 Naomi Kincaid, "The Founding of Abilene, the 'Future Great' of the Texas and Pacific Railway," *West Texas Historical Association Year Book*, Vol. XXII (October, 1946), 16.
14 *Ibid.*, 18–19.

172

the rival towns resulted, but on October 3, 1883, the railroad center's victory was declared official.[15]

Through the 1880's and 1890's Abilene developed into one of the most important cattle-shipping centers in Texas. During its early years, shipments of wool, buffalo hides, and buffalo bones almost equaled those of cattle. In the year 1887, for example, R. K. Wylie marketed 65,000 pounds of wool at Abilene, where Theo Heyck owned one of the largest wool warehouses in the state.

Gradually the Abilene country changed from large-scale ranching to agriculture and stock-farming. Later immigrants discovered that the area's 25.17 inches of annual rainfall and its fertile soils could produce abundant grain and cotton crops. Ranchers and cow hands scorned the pioneer farmers. Gardening was women's work, they said, and in West Texas, "planting anything was an indication of ignorance."[16] The agriculturalists generally ignored the taunts. By 1900 the "gardeners" planted 27,907 acres in cotton, 9,690 acres in corn, 7,487 acres in coarse forage, 2,000 acres in oats, and 800 acres in wheat.[17] After 1900, Taylor County farmers turned increasingly to cotton production, and by the time Colonel Morgan Jones returned to Abilene to offer the railroad committee a new road toward the south, more than 100,000 acres of Taylor County land produced abundant cotton crops.[18] Local hardware firms, grown prosperous from their harvesting machinery sales, helped to convince Morgan Jones that the city could support another railroad project.

In May and June, 1908, Jones presented his new railroad plan to Taylor and Runnels citizens. He talked first with Abilene's railroad committeemen, who assured him that Abilenians were ready to offer a bonus and the right-of-way to Taylor County's southern boundary line. The Colonel, in turn, promised to build the line if Winters and Ballinger folks displayed similar interest. On June 1, 1908, he arrived quietly in Winters, where, known only by repu-

---

15 Hugh E. Cosby (ed.), *History of Abilene*, 19.

16 Emmett M. Landers, "From Range Cattle to Blooded Stock Farming in the Abilene Country," *West Texas Historical Association Year Book*, Vol. IX (October, 1933), 76.

17 *Ibid.*, 78.

18 *Ibid.*

tation, he was not recognized.[19] He conferred immediately with five members of the town's railroad committee, proposed to build the road from Abilene for a cash bonus of $50,000, a fifteen-mile right-of-way, and adequate ground on which to build a depot.

The astonished committeemen promptly told the railroad builder that his figures were too high. Jones was not an experienced promoter, he was not a salesman, but he knew that the Winters men wanted a railroad as much as he wanted to build one for them. He had learned before his arrival that the Winters railroad committeemen had been "afflicted with railroad talk" for two years; he knew that they were fearful that someone would build a road through Runnels County and bypass their town; and he knew that many Winters folk purchased only "half a load of wood" at one time for fear that a railroad would bypass them and necessitate a move to the rails before they could burn a full load of wood.[20]

Since Jones had these facts, he was willing to counsel the committeemen, to give them more details concerning costs and difficulties of railroad construction, and to explain a railroad's value to such an isolated community as theirs. Jones then presented his strongest bargaining point: Winters citizens could wait until the road was constructed before they had to pay the bonus. The committee members, obviously inspired by Jones's promotional speech, promised to present his offer to Winters' citizens. Finally, Jones applied a touch of psychology to his sales method; without warning, he departed for another visit to his Welsh and English relatives. Somewhat disconcerted by that maneuver, the Abilene, Winters, and Ballinger railroad committees assumed that they would not see the railroad builder again unless they met his demands. They were not aware that the Welshman's visits to "the old country" were an almost annual affair.

Late in August, 1908, Jones returned to Fort Worth. Among his accumulated mail was a telegram from the Winters committee. It informed him that Winters was ready to "close up the railroad contract."[21] Jones telegraphed the committee that he would return

19 *Winters Enterprise* (September 28, 1908), 1.
20 *Ibid.*
21 *Ibid.* (August 31, 1908), 1.

to Winters within a few days, and, at ten o'clock on the morning of August 28, 1908, he arrived. The townsmen immediately recognized him, honored him at a luncheon, and informed him that the community had "heartily responded" to his earlier proposal. The local editor reported: "Mr. Jones's trip has cleared up all doubt in the mind of any who were skeptical as to his intentions. Many questions . . . have been explained, and all agree that Winters will get the road."[22]

During the luncheon several farmers began to discuss the area's recent lack of rain. Someone suggested that the town should hire a rain maker.[23] A lengthy discussion ensued which concerned, primarily, the costs for such services. The chairman then turned to Jones and asked whether or not a rain maker would come to Winters for the amount they were willing to pay. The wealthy visitor replied, "I was just wondering if I should, for that kind of money, make you the proposition myself!"[24]

When the news reached Ballinger, in south Runnels County, that the Winters railroad committee and Jones had signed preliminary agreements, more than a score of Ballinger farmers and businessmen called an emergency meeting. They met at the C. A. Doose and Company offices "to get a definite, cooperative unison of effort to the securing of a railway outlet to the north."[25] The *Ballinger Ledger* reported that "much confidence is generally expressed in the ability and desire of Mr. Jones to construct the proposed road."[26] When Jones arrived the following day, the railroad committee assured him that Ballinger would "enthusiastically support the movement with their money."[27]

Two days later Jones returned to Abilene and met with the 25,000 Club. They decided to call a public hearing and to present the following question:

22 *Ibid.*
23 It was a popular idea that explosives could produce rain. As early as 1871, Edward Powers, a civil engineer, claimed that heavy rains often followed military battles and Fourth of July celebrations. For these and other rain-making theories, see Webb, *The Great Plains*, 375–82.
24 Interview with Roland Jones (November 8, 1967).
25 *Ballinger Ledger* (August 31, 1908), 1.
26 *Ibid.*
27 *Ibid.*

Shall the Abilene 25,000 Club railroad committee proceed to endeavor to raise the necessary funds to secure the railroad from Abilene to Ballinger via Winters, with the location of the machine shops, round house, and general offices in this city as is proposed by Morgan Jones?[28]

On Friday night, August 31, 1908, more than two hundred citizens met at a local skating rink to consider the question. A standing vote revealed that all present except "probably a half-dozen" supported the new road.[29] Will Stith, chairman of the railroad committee, then warned those who attended the meeting that Jones was "a man who does things right now" and that they should lose no time.

Stith asked Jones to outline his requests. Accordingly, Jones asked Abilene to contribute $75,000 dollars, the right-of-way from an intersection with the Texas and Pacific tracks to the Runnels County line, sufficient grounds to build a depot, and five acres of land for machine shops and general offices. Stith then estimated that $30,000 to $40,000 would secure the city property, which, added to the bonus money, would total approximately $110,000. C. W. Merchant, T. A. Bledsoe, Henry Sayles, Sr., and A. H. Kirby made brief speeches to support the project.

Morgan Weaver, a local merchant, spoke against the plan. He arose reluctantly and only after everyone present assured him that they wanted to hear his views. He explained that, from a business standpoint, branch lines always curtailed a railroad center's retail trade territory, and that he personally expected to lose about $50,000 annually. The newspaperman present later reported that "in a good natured manner, every speaker following, jumped on Mr. Weaver."[30] At the conclusion of the meeting a second standing vote authorized the railroad committee to proceed at once to secure the new railroad.

By September 17 the Winters committee secured the required bonus pledges, drew up a final contract, and requested Jones to meet them at his convenience to close the contract. Jones arrived from Denver on September 22, 1908, signed the contract, and praised their "enterprising spirit." The *Winters Enterprise* claimed

28 *Abilene Daily Reporter* (September 1, 1908), 1.
29 *Ibid.*
30 *Ibid.*

that "all this was accomplished without any threats and bluffs on the part of Mr. Jones or our committee, but everything was done fairly and openly."[31]

Meanwhile, the *Abilene Daily Reporter*'s editor cautioned local businessmen that they must not delay their pledged support:

> Other line towns that appreciate Mr. Jones' ability to carry to a successful completion any railroad building proposition that he undertakes, have their eyes on Abilene, hoping that she will one time fall down.[32]

Concurrently, Ballinger's editor warned his readers that "Morgan Jones has offered the opportunity; he is not a man to fool with."[33]

Their efforts succeeded. By October 18, both towns had sufficient pledges to allow their railroad committees to sign contracts with Jones. The indenture required Jones to build a standard-gauge railroad from the Texas and Pacific tracks at Abilene to some point on the Gulf, Colorado and Santa Fe road at Ballinger. Everyone concerned seemed eager to begin. A newspaperman stated that "Mr. Jones is more than anxious to throw the dirt." The Abilene city council, in its enthusiasm, suspended the rules which required reading of an ordinance at three separate meetings before its passage. It immediately granted Jones a franchise to build the road "over and upon certain streets and alleys within the corporate limits of Abilene."[34]

Jones was indeed ready to begin. With assistance from his two nephews, Morgan C. and Percy, he managed to have grading crews at work by October 30, 1908. They commenced five miles north of Winters, just below the Runnels County line. Separate crews worked north and south of that point. Jones promised that "active grading will not cease until the track is actually laid."[35] He decided to locate the depot on South Third Street directly opposite the Abilene and Northern passenger and freight depot. The two tracks would run parallel to Cherry Street, at which point the new rails

31 *Winters Enterprise* (September 28, 1908), 1.
32 *Abilene Daily Reporter* (September 10, 1908), 1.
33 *Ballinger Ledger* (September 25, 1908), 1.
34 *Abilene Daily Reporter* (October 18, 1908), 1.
35 *Ibid.* (October 30, 1908), 1.

177

would veer sharply to the south. Local citizens marveled that Abilene, a Texas and Pacific town, with connections via the Wichita Valley to the Fort Worth and Denver City, would soon tie its steel ribbons to the Gulf, Colorado and Santa Fe railroad at Ballinger.

For this project, Jones did not seek Dodge's nor Walters' financial support, but he offered to "bring them into the company" if they were interested. Each of his old friends was well aware that the Wichita Valley and Abilene and Northern roads had proved profitable. Neither needed assurance that Jones knew precisely what he was doing. In a letter to Dodge on November 2, 1908, Walters wrote: "I note what you think about Jones and his road. I have not the least idea where the road is going . . . but I told him I would take an interest with him."[36]

The Jones men supervised every part of the construction and, without unseasonable rains, work progressed rapidly at each end of the line. By the beginning of the new year much of the grading was complete and the rail crews prepared to begin. Consequently, on January 6, 1909, at seven o'clock in the morning, a rail crew laid the first track.[37] The local newspaper gave the event a six-column headline: "THIS IS A MOST AUSPICIOUS DAY FOR ABILENE."[38] Only a few spectators, however, witnessed the event and the baffled reporter complained that "the demonstrations which usually accompanies [sic] such events were entirely missing." He rebuked the mayor who, "although famed for [his] addresses on such occasions, was soundly sleeping." The only witnesses, other than the workers, were Morgan Jones, Morgan C. Jones, Percy Jones, "and a lonely newspaper reporter."[39] The quiet, businesslike occasion undoubtedly pleased Jones as much as it disappointed the newspaperman.

The irked reporter, nevertheless, resolved to generate greater interest in the project. His daily accounts described the construc-

36 Dodge Papers, *loc. cit.*, XX, 239, Walters to Dodge (November 2, 1908).
37 *Abilene Daily Reporter* (January 6, 1909), 1.
38 This was only the second six-column headline in the newspaper's history. The first such headline announced William Howard Taft's election victory over William Jennings Bryan.
39 *Abilene Daily Reporter* (January 6, 1909), 1.

tion crew's progress and recorded the new tracks' total length. The rail crew, he explained, spent only half of each day laying track. They spent the remaining hours "surfacing up" and preparing the next morning's work. Six mornings every week the construction train left Abilene heavily laden with laborers, road ties, and steel rails. Each afternoon the train returned with approximately half of the laborers, whose duty it was to load the cars for the next morning's early departure. The other laborers remained at their various duties at the railhead. On alternate afternoons they took their turn to spend the night at their Abilene homes.

Jones hired local farmers to assist his regular laborers. It was his theory that such temporary employment—whether or not he needed them—increased local loyalty and pride in a new railroad. The newspaper reporter witnessed several instances when the old Colonel and his nephews assisted the laborers and were "at all times on hand to see that the workers made every blow count."[40] As the project neared completion, the newspaperman, obviously proud that his one-man publicity campaign brought results, announced that "large numbers" of people all along the route manifested much interest "and come daily to watch the progress of the track-laying."[41] He continued:

When one stops to consider that this road gives Abilene direct connection with the Gulf, Colorado and Santa Fe at Ballinger leading to South Texas and to points north by way of the Abilene and Northern, it will be plainly seen that Abilene's ultimate greatness is not far off.[42]

Meanwhile, several days after the rail crews commenced their work, Jones secured the Abilene and Southern Railway Company's charter. He and nine Fort Worth associates incorporated the company under the General Laws of the State of Texas.[43] The charter included the Abilene-Winters-Ballinger branch and an extension

---

[40] *Ibid.* (May 5, 1909), 6.
[41] *Ibid.*
[42] *Ibid.*
[43] Morgan Jones Papers, Mrs. Percy Jones, *loc. cit.*, file 1, paper 31, "Charter of Abilene and Southern Railway Company," January 7, 1909. Other members of the corporation were J. F. Britton, D. T. Bomar, E. H. Holcomb, Ed P. Williams, C. W. Clarkson, William P. Bomar, T. L. Fryer, Ben W. Fouts, and H. Ross, all of Fort Worth. (Article I.)

beyond Ballinger to "a point at or near the town of Sonoro [*sic*] in Sutton County, a distance of about One Hundred Sixty miles . . . with a branch . . . running thence in a Northwesterly direction to the town of San Angelo in Tom Green County, Texas, a distance of about Forty miles, making a total of Two Hundred miles."[44] Jones was president of the company and his private secretary, W. E. Kaufman, was secretary, auditor, and treasurer. The Board of Directors included General Grenville Dodge and seven additional members from Fort Worth, Abilene, and Ballinger.[45]

On May 19, 1909, the Abilene and Southern rail crews reached a point in south Taylor County a few hundred yards away from a tiny little community named Ovalo. Immediately its residents pulled up stakes and moved their few belongings near the rails.[46] The following day Colonel Jones dispatched the first regular train to the new town. The locomotive, one passenger coach, and one freight car, with Morgan C. in charge as conductor and brakeman, left Abilene early in the morning and returned at noon.[47]

By August 29 the rail crew at the line's southern end had reached the new bridge at Elm Creek, just north of Ballinger. The Colonel prepared to commence through service from Abilene to Ballinger within two weeks. Throughout the summer the passenger and freight traffic between Abilene and Winters was greater than Jones had anticipated. During its first season, the little line hauled between forty and fifty thousand bales of cotton to local markets.[48] Except for a brief trip to Colorado, Jones stayed busy at his Abilene offices and at the construction sites.

Finally, on September 9, 1909, at eight-thirty in the morning,

44 *Ibid.*, Article II, 10.
45 *Ibid.*, Article VII, 11. Other board members were D. T. Bomar, John W. Broad, and E. H. Holcomb, of Fort Worth; J. M. Radford and Ed S. Hughes, of Abilene; and C. A. Doose and C. S. Miller, of Ballinger.
46 A. C. Greene, *Abilene Reporter-News* (May 8, 1949), 12. The Abilene and Southern Railway Company owned fifty per cent of the Ovalo townsite property; Colonel Jones, Percy Jones, D. T. Bomar, and John W. Broad each owned one per cent. The new town, nestled against Bald Eagle Mountain, had streets and avenues which ran north and south, east and west. Like those in Abilene, the east-west streets were numbered, and the avenues had names familiar to every Abilenian: Bois D'Arc, Locust, Cedar, Chestnut, and Mesquite. (Taylor County Records, Plat Book No. 1, 64.)
47 *Abilene Daily Reporter* (May 19, 1909), 5.
48 Morgan Jones Papers, Mrs. Percy Jones, *loc. cit.*, file 18, paper 17, 7, Jones to H. Walters (September 1, 1909).

180

the first through train departed Abilene for Ballinger. It was a single 2–8–2 engine, No. 20, which pulled a long red combine car, No. 52. The combine was a combination caboose, passenger, express, and freight car. Its special features included screened doors and windows, coal-oil lamps, and a coal stove. Cast in iron on the stove's lid were the words: "If I am good please tell others about it."[49] The colorful little train arrived at Ballinger at twelve-thirty in the afternoon. Records do not describe its reception at Ballinger, in Runnels County. It was, however, a significant event. Colonel Morgan Jones had connected successfully the rails of the Fort Worth and Denver City, the Texas and Pacific, and the Gulf, Colorado, and Santa Fe. It connected Abilene to Runnels County's prosperous farmers and ranchers. Total costs amounted to $668,536.52.[50]

Ballinger was located on the Colorado River, which crossed Runnels County from northwest to southeast. Farmers in the area raised cotton, grain, sorghum, oats, wheat, and barley. The county's first permanent settler was William Guest, who moved his family to a dugout in 1862. The Rich Coffee family joined them the following year, and by the 1870's other ranchers claimed lands throughout the county. In the 1880's the Gulf, Colorado and Santa Fe built across the county, and on June 29, 1886, Runnels County settlers made Ballinger, originally named Hutchins City, county seat.[51] Soon thereafter, the few residents of tiny Runnels City moved to the new railroad town. The Abilene and Southern's arrival made the town a thriving railroad junction.

Within six weeks after the Abilene and Southern's initial through service to Ballinger, the *Abilene Daily Reporter* stated that passengers and freight loaded every train "to the extent of its capacity." Jones initially scheduled a daily round-trip to Ballinger, but within weeks so many farmers, ranchers, and their families traveled to Abilene that Jones added a round-trip evening train to the schedule.

Many passengers were immigrant farmers who purchased

49 Greene, *Abilene Reporter-News*, 12.
50 Morgan Jones Papers, Mrs. Percy Jones, *loc. cit.*, file 2, paper 44.
51 Webb and Carroll, *The Handbook of Texas*, II, 515–16.

acreage and carved farms from former ranch lands. Eventually, the Abilene and Southern developed, as Jones planned it, into a road used almost exclusively by farming families. "Yes, sir, it's a farmers' road. Built for them to use," boasted one local farmer many years later.[52]

Colonel Jones soon informed General Dodge that the little company's passenger earnings alone averaged better than two hundred dollars a day and that its freight cars hauled more than one-third of the Abilene-Ballinger cotton to local markets. With obvious pride, Jones claimed that the Abilene and Southern "competed successfully" with the Wichita Valley, Texas and Pacific, and Santa Fe railroads for the area's trade.[53]

When he was not at his Abilene offices, the Colonel often made inspection trips on the regularly scheduled trains. His weary nephews—Percy, the engineer, and Morgan C., the conductor— always dreaded to see "the Old Mahn" climb aboard. They learned to expect a lecture at the end of the line. If they drove too swiftly, he said, they could not see the farmers along the right-of-way who wanted to stop the train to order tobacco or snuff. If they drove too slowly, the "Old Mahn" claimed that his nephews tried to camouflage the road's "rough places."[54] As always, the old Welshman insisted upon "personal and neighborly service" over a smooth-running track. Whatever his railroad company's size, he never forgot that its purpose was public service. As he told Frank Trumbull, the Abilene and Southern was indeed "the best little road I ever built."[55]

Long before the rails reached Ballinger, rumors circulated that Morgan Jones planned to extend the Abilene and Southern beyond Ballinger. The secretive railroad builder, although he did, in fact, have numerous plans to extend the road into deep South Texas, refused to confirm or deny the rumors. A frustrated newspaperman

52 Greene, *Abilene Reporter-News*, 12.

53 Morgan Jones Papers, Mrs. Percy Jones, *loc. cit.*, file 18, paper 17, 12, Jones to Dodge (October 3, 1909).

54 Interview with Morgan Jones, Jr., (November 7, 1967).

55 Morgan Jones Papers, Mrs. Percy Jones, *loc. cit.*, file 18, paper 17, 15, Jones to Frank Trumbull (October 16, 1909).

182

could only report that "President Morgan Jones of the road is a very busy man, and seldom has anything to say for print and his plans are at present known only to himself."[56]

[56] *Abilene Daily Reporter* (September 8, 1909), 1.

10. "THEY HAVE HEADED US OFF"

MORGAN Jones never intended to end the Abilene and Southern rails at Ballinger. The company's charter granted permission to extend the line approximately 160 miles south of Abilene into Sutton County. Jones's ultimate destination, however, was San Antonio.[1] Between Runnels County and San Antonio lay the Edwards Plateau, a high, dry region which was six counties wide across the route Jones hoped to follow. Edwards Plateau included broad areas of steep slopes and rocky soil, but Jones knew that it included, also, thousands of acres of rich, rolling grasslands. The eastern plateau's thirty to thirty-two inches of annual rainfall made farming possible, while the drier western region already had proved valuable as a cattle- and sheep-grazing land. To the inexperienced eye, however, it was not a particularly promising region for a railroad. To Jones, the Edwards Plateau's climate and soil promised a type of diversified economy essential to successful railroading.

In May, 1909, the old Welshman and his nephew Percy made an automobile[2] journey across the Edwards Plateau while Morgan C. supervised construction details at the Abilene-Ballinger rail-

[1] *Abilene Daily Reporter* (May 13, 1909), 8.
[2] Jones owned nine automobiles during his lifetime but never learned to drive one. He was, however, a constant "back-seat driver." Invariably he berated his nephews when they allowed another car to pass them. "Never let a man get ahead of you that way," he would exhort. (Interview with Roland Jones [November 8, 1967].)

184

heads.[3] Jones and his nephew planned a branch line southwestward to San Angelo, but the main line, they decided, should bear southeastward through the agricultural region. During their reconnaissance, they met delegations from Millerview and Paint Rock, in Concho County, who wanted Jones to map a route through their towns. A week later he informed the Concho County men that he could see "no reason why the Abilene and Southern road should not be extended south to connect with San Antonio."[4]

Upon his return to Abilene, the Colonel learned that his old friend General Dodge was ill at Glenwood Springs, Colorado. Despite his busy schedule, Jones decided to visit the General. The two aging railroad builders—Jones was approaching his seventieth birthday, and Dodge his eightieth—discussed the plans to build into South Texas. Dodge, visibly improved after Jones's arrival, gave his enthusiastic support.[5]

When Jones returned to Abilene, where he had made his permanent home since December, 1908, he wrote numerous letters explaining his plans to interested parties. On August 9 he notified E. P. Ripley, president of the Atchison, Topeka and Santa Fe, that he wanted to extend the line in a direction "the least objectionable to your interests."[6] On the same date he wrote to C. A. Broome, chairman of San Angelo's railroad committee, requesting a meeting at Ballinger to discuss the Abilene and Southern's proposed branch to that town.[7] Later that month Jones alerted W. B. Switzer, vice-president of the Switzer Lumber Company in Shreveport, Louisiana, to expect a large order of railroad ties "for a planned road south of Ballinger."[8]

3 *Abilene Daily Reporter* (May 13, 1909), 8.
4 *Ibid.* (May 16, 1909), 1.
5 Morgan Jones Papers, Mrs. Percy Jones, *loc. cit.*, file 18, paper 17, 1, Jones to E. P. Ripley (August 9, 1909).
6 *Ibid.*
7 *Ibid.*, 2. At their conference Jones displayed an interest in building a line northwest of San Angelo to Sterling City. This was, apparently, a diversionary action on Jones's part, since it is not likely that Jones really wanted to build in an area unsuited to agriculture. A road to Sterling City would deprive San Angelo retailers of a great deal of trade in a triangular area marked by Sterling City, Colorado City, and Big Spring. It is likely, therefore, that Jones merely wanted to gain the San Angelo retailers' support for his proposed road to the south. (See *ibid.*, file 4, paper 15–A, T. J. Clegg to Jones [May 26, 1908].)
8 *Ibid.*, file 18, paper 17, 4, Jones to W. B. Switzer (August 30, 1909).

185

Jones waited impatiently for a response to his letter of August 9 to President Ripley. After three weeks the agitated Welshman wrote to Dodge: "The Santa Fe are trying to ignore us, they want *all* the territory south of us."[9] Ripley's silence, however, did not affect Jones's determination to carry through his plans. On September 1 he asked Henry Walters to inquire among his eastern friends about surplus rails they might want to sell to the Abilene and Southern.[10] The company, Jones explained, would soon need approximately forty miles of new or used rails.[11] The following day Ripley's letter arrived. "I hardly know how to answer your letter because our own plans are not quite matured. . . . We have had plans for building into the territory South of San Angelo . . . but have not yet fully decided,"[12] he told Jones. Ripley obviously attempted to stall the Abilene and Southern without committing the Santa Fe to a definite building project in that area.

His maneuver did not succeed. The Colonel and Percy Jones soon left Abilene and made a third preliminary survey through Sutton and Edwards counties, along the southern portion of the Edwards Plateau. It was precisely that area in which the Santa Fe professed interest. Back at Abilene, Jones wrote to S. D. Scudder, a New York friend, that he planned to "extend to San Angelo and from there South, say, a distance of 120 miles."[13] He informed Scudder also that he could build at least a one-hundred-mile railroad without having to borrow money. In its context, Jones's letter to Scudder attempted, through a third party, to convince Ripley that the Santa Fe could not intimidate him.

At that point, Jones undoubtedly planned to build into Santa Fe territory. On September 8 he informed Dodge that Eldorado's railroad committee offered him a $60,000 bonus to build to that Schleicher County community forty-eight miles south of San Angelo. "If you and Walters will put up ¼ of the cash," he said,

9 *Ibid.*, 3, Jones to Dodge (August 29, 1909).
10 *Ibid.*, 7, Jones to Walters (September 1, 1909).
11 That amount of tracks would reach from Ballinger southwest to San Angelo, or from Ballinger southeast to Paint Rock or Millersview.
12 Morgan Jones Papers, Mrs. Percy Jones, *loc. cit.*, file 18, paper 17, 5, Ripley to Jones (August 27, 1909).
13 *Ibid.*, 8, Jones to S. D. Scudder (September 7, 1909).

"I will put up ¾, say $750,000. . . . With this and the subsidies, I think we can build 120 miles, besides the 55 already built."[14] Three days later Jones notified the Illinois Steel Company at New Orleans that he would soon request bids on forty-five miles of rails "for an extension s.w. of Ballinger."[15]

Such actions convinced Santa Fe officials that their first stratagem had failed to discourage Jones. President Ripley thereupon wrote to the Welshman again and offered to purchase the Abilene and Southern. Jones promptly replied, "I do not want to sell this road."[16] Having failed to intimidate Jones or to force him to sell out, the Santa Fe president telegraphed the intractable Welshman: "We will start south of San Angelo as soon as you do."[17] That open threat again failed to frighten Jones. He told Dodge, "I do not propose to go back on the San Angelo proposition unless they [San Angelo's railroad committee] do."[18]

Jones had proposed earlier to the San Angelo group to build from their town to San Antonio for a $75,000 bonus plus the necessary right-of-way. He had promised, in addition, to complete the project not later than January 1, 1911.[19] The proposed road would provide Abilene, concurrently, a direct connection to the Alamo city. Abilenians immediately supported the exciting prospect.

On September 10, the *Abilene Daily Reporter* editorialized: "Abilene recommends Morgan Jones to San Angelo as a mighty good man to tie onto if that place really wants a direct communication with the metropolis of West Texas. . . . Colonel Jones builds railroads while others get ready to talk about the matter." The next day Jones arrived at San Angelo amid many rumors about his proposed railroad. Jones characteristically refused to confirm or deny them. The *San Angelo Standard* reported that the reticent railroad celebrity "had nothing to give out at all and then pleasantly looked

14 *Ibid.*, 9, Jones to Dodge (September 8, 1909). Eldorado lay approximately halfway between the headwaters of the San Saba and the South Concho rivers, a distance of about five miles from each.
15 *Ibid.*, file 18, paper 17, 10, Jones to James R. Mills (September 11, 1909).
16 Quoted by Jones in a letter to Dodge, *ibid.*, 11 (September 28, 1909).
17 *Ibid.*, file 18, paper 17, 11.
18 *Ibid.*
19 *Abilene Daily Reporter* (September 8, 1909), 5.

187

the other way and remarked that it was hot."[20] The obviously impressed newspaperman continued, "It is a proverbial fact that Mr. Jones is not given to talking, and this fact coupled with several others in the way of railroad building convinces most people that Morgan Jones is a man who does things and says little. Jones is as mum as the proverbial clam, and of that there is not the least possibility of a doubt."

Jones's railroad-building reputation had spread throughout the Lone Star State. For example, Weatherford, a Texas and Pacific town in Parker County, discussed for many years possible ways to build a north-south railroad from their community. Despite their efforts, no practical plan materialized until the *Weatherford Herald*'s editor suggested on September 12, 1909: "Why not organize a strong committee of business men and lay a plan before Colonel Morgan Jones . . . who is the greatest railroad builder in Texas, and get him to take hold of the matter?"[21] Jones's railroad activities in West Texas had attracted at least one newspaper editor's attention. He certainly attracted, as well, the Santa Fe railroad's attention.

Late in September, 1909, the company made its next move to block Jones's proposed road across the Edwards Plateau. On September 25 several Santa Fe officials arrived unannounced at San Angelo. "What does it mean?" asked the local editor, who proceeded then to answer his own question: "The prospects of raising the Morgan Jones bonus alarmed the Santa Fe officials. . . . The construction of a road south of San Angelo by Morgan Jones would cut into the Santa Fe's freight production territory."[22] The officials made no immediate announcement, but when, during the following week, the railroad committee successfully raised Jones's bonus and then asked him to come to San Angelo to sign a contract,[23] the Santa Fe announced plans to build at once south of San Angelo.[24]

[20] (September 11, 1909), 6.
[21] *Weatherford Herald*, quoted in *Abilene Daily Reporter* (September 12, 1909), 3. There is no record that the editor's suggestion reached Colonel Jones.
[22] *San Angelo Standard* (September 25, 1909), 5.
[23] *Abilene Daily Reporter* (September 27, 1909), 5.

The Santa Fe's latest threat, no longer a mere bluff, forced Jones to reconsider his own plans. The Santa Fe route, he learned, would parallel the South Concho River, almost due south from San Angelo. The only route left to Jones therefore was along a somewhat limited region southeast from Ballinger into Concho County, where, he observed earlier, there was "nothing except cattle, horses, and sheep."[25] Dodge and Walters, moreover, began to indicate that they did not want to get into a fight with the Santa Fe.

On September 22, for example, Dodge asked Jones to consider a compromise with the Santa Fe: Jones, he said, might build the road *for* rather than as a competitor to the Santa Fe.[26] Walters, on the other hand, warned that Ripley knew "so well how to fight"[27] that it was not worth the effort to contest him. By October 11, consequently, Jones admitted that he probably could not challenge successfully the entire Santa Fe organization. On that date he wrote to C. R. Mower, "it looks now that I may have to stop [the] extension at Ballinger."[28] Then, on October 16, he wrote to Frank Trumbull, "I had arranged to build 120 miles south-west but the Santa Fe has headed us off."[29] On October 22 he finally admitted defeat. He wrote to E. P. Alsbury, of Houston: "They have headed us off and we have stopped construction in that direction."[30]

On October 23, 1909, the *San Angelo Standard* announced that the "Morgan Jones road" was indefinitely postponed:

Owing to the uncertainty as to the purchaser of the Concho, San Saba and Llano Valley Railroad,[31] Morgan Jones, the railroad builder . . . has decided that he is not justified in building to Angelo from Ballinger at present.

Mr. Jones stated expressly that this decision did not mean that he

24 Morgan Jones Papers, Mrs. Percy Jones, *loc. cit.*, file 18, paper 17, 12, Jones to Dodge (October 3, 1909).
25 *Ibid.*
26 *Ibid.*, paper 115, Dodge to Jones (September 22, 1909).
27 Dodge Papers, *loc. cit.*, XX, 599, Walters to Dodge (September 24, 1909).
28 Morgan Jones Papers, Mrs. Percy Jones, *loc. cit.*, file 18, paper 17, 14, Jones to C. R. Mower (otherwise unidentified), (October 11, 1909).
29 *Ibid.*, 15, Jones to Frank Trumbull (October 16, 1909).
30 *Ibid.*, 17, Jones to E. P. Alsbury (October 22, 1909).
31 The Santa Fe, as Jones suspected, had bought the road. Its route, westward from Temple, projected into the area near the only route left open to Jones southeast of Ballinger. (*Texas Almanac, 1966–67*, 493.)

would never build into San Angelo; on the contrary, he hoped that future events would justify his return to this city.

"Mr. Jones is not to be blamed," declared a member of the committee Wednesday night. . . . He is to be congratulated on the admirable business sagacity in holding the matter in abeyance.

He has acted honorably and justly towards the city and has been the cause of many railroads taking a pot-shot at building a road here.

Morgan Jones has certainly been a good Samaritan to San Angelo. Slow moving railroads that otherwise may not have been induced to build in and around San Angelo have been aroused from their lethargy to action, and San Angelo has been the benefactor thereby.

In case Morgan Jones should ever return to this city to build, the citizenship will welcome him as a benefactor, a city builder, an honest man, true to the spirit, as well as the letter, of his word.[32]

The old Welshman returned to his Abilene offices, checked the Abilene-Ballinger line's progress, discovered that business was better than he anticipated, and learned that the Abilene and Southern depot was near completion. He learned also that local rumor claimed that he planned to sell the Abilene and Southern to the Colorado and Southern organization, and that the Colorado and Southern would, in turn, extend the road from Ballinger to San Antonio.[33] As tempted as he surely was to bring up stronger forces to challenge the Santa Fe's monopolistic practices, Jones denied that he planned to sell his prosperous little road. "There isn't a thing in it," he insisted. "I have never spoken to anybody regarding the sale of the Abilene and Southern road . . . and, furthermore, do not want to sell and will not sell!"[34]

When a third rumor circulated that Jones would sell, instead, to the Santa Fe, he denied, once again, that he had any such intention. He did not deny or confirm a fourth rumor that he planned to build a road from Cisco, in Eastland County, south to Brownwood, in Brown County. The fourth rumor, at least, was partially correct. Shortly after his plans collapsed to build south from Ballinger and San Angelo, Abilene's railroad committee asked Jones to consider a new line from Abilene southeast to Rising Star, in Eastland

32 *San Angelo Standard* (October 23, 1909), 1.
33 *Abilene Daily Reporter* (October 29, 1909), 1.
34 *Ibid.*, 2.

190

County.[35] The *Abilene Daily Reporter* immediately encouraged the idea and stated that, if Jones signed a contract, "that would be enough in itself to insure the project's success."[36]

Jones had, in fact, entered into a preliminary agreement on November 6 to organize the Abilene and Central Railway Company and to supply a major portion of the necessary funds. The local editor, awed by Abilene's only nationally known resident, and by his readiness to invest vast sums in Abilene projects, bestowed lavish praise upon the modest man. "Mr. Jones has been a prominent factor in the development of Texas for many years, and done as much good for the state of Texas as any other man in it. . . . He is a man known in the railroad world, and has never made a failure in any railroad he ever undertook to build."[37]

The preliminary agreement stipulated that the new road would follow a route southeast to Rising Star or to Brownwood, in Brown County; that Jones would invest $1,000,000 in the new project; and that other Abilene citizens would invest $100,000.[38] Several citizens, the local newspaper reported, "assumed burdens [stocks and bonds] in this railroad matter running as high as $15,000 to the individual."[39]

By January 5, 1910, preliminary surveys to Rising Star were complete, and new construction materials piled up at the Abilene depots. Jones recorded each shipment in a ledger prepared by a local printing company and inscribed "Construction Journal: Abilene and Central Railway Company."[40] Jones announced that "as soon as some minor matters, right-of-way, etc., are disposed of, grading will immediately begin."[41] Meanwhile, Abilene representatives traveled to Comanche County and discussed, with the Comanche railroad committee, various ways to extend the road to that town.[42] As the proposed project attracted wider attention, the

35 *Ibid.* (November 7, 1909), 1.
36 *Ibid.*
37 *Ibid.*
38 *Ibid.* (January 31, 1910), 8.
39 *Ibid.* (November 10, 1909), 1.
40 Morgan Jones Papers, Mrs. Percy Jones, *loc. cit.*, miscellaneous file.
41 *Abilene Daily Reporter* (January 5, 1910), 8.
42 *Ibid.* (January 13, 1910), 1.

191

Waco Business Men's Club offered $50,000 to extend the rails beyond Comanche southeast to their city.[43] While Abilene enthusiasm mounted, Jones grew increasingly detached. Local zeal was so spirited, however, that few, if any, railroad committee members noticed Jones's uncharacteristic placidity.

Suddenly, on January 30, 1910, just as plans to construct the Abilene and Central seemed complete, Jones announced that he had decided not to build to Rising Star. He gave no explanation and made no effort to defend his shocking announcement. He had not signed a binding contract and, technically at least, was free to abandon his plan. Bewildered Abilene citizens turned to the railroad committee for information, but its members were equally unable to explain Jones's action. When Jones refused to clarify his position, the railroad committee entered suit against him in the District Court.[44] The suit did not claim damages in a specific sum of money, but instead asked the court to force Jones to fulfill his part of the agreement. The local editor questioned the secretive Welshman—so recently a local hero—but reported that Jones "betrayed no surprise and made no comment [about the railroad committee's suit] and was apparently unshaken in his determination to pursue his new course."[45] The *Abilene Daily Reporter* did not reflect the public's ill humor. Jones always "dealt squarely with the town and its people," the editor insisted, and he chose to assume that Jones's recent "peculiarity" was "for good cause."[46]

The old Welshman had indeed sacrificed his local popularity for "a good cause." His proposed railroad, in this case, projected into territory which the Texas Central railroad authorities claimed as their own. When the report had reached the Texas Central that Jones proposed to build a line within fifteen miles of the Texas Central rails at De Leon in northeastern Comanche County, they were determined to stop him. The later report that Waco wanted Jones to build to that town frightened still more the Texas Central directors. An Abilene-Waco road would closely parallel for more

43 *Ibid.* (January 17, 1910), 1.
44 *Ibid.* (January 30, 1910), 1.
45 *Ibid.*
46 *Ibid.* (January 31, 1910), 1.

192

than 150 miles the Texas Central route. Texas Central officials, therefore, informed Jones that, if he built to Rising Star, they would extend a Texas Central branch from De Leon to Cross Plains. Jones ignored their first threat. He reasoned that no responsible company would build a branch line thirty to forty miles long, only three to five miles away from another road.

When his surveyors later reported that they worked within sight of Texas Central surveyors, he admitted that their threats were genuine. Jones decided again to abandon his newest construction project. Before he made public his decision, a Cross Plains delegation implored Jones to keep his secret until Texas Central construction was underway. As a favor to the Cross Plains people, therefore, and at great cost to his own local popularity, Jones agreed to say nothing.[47] The scheme worked. The Texas Central hurriedly began construction and by January 12, 1911, the branch line to Cross Plains was complete.

Meanwhile, the Abilene railroad committee's suit against Colonel Jones remained unresolved in District Court. A compromise offer, he decided, might placate the disappointed Abilenians. He remained during the spring months of 1910 in the Abilene area. A year earlier, he recalled, while Abilene and Southern construction progressed toward Ballinger, the 25,000 Club had announced that it next wanted to connect Abilene with that area to the northwest. Their first project, they said, was to build a road from Abilene to Hamlin, in northwestern Jones County, via Anson. A road to that town would connect Abilene to the Kansas City, Mexico and Orient railroad.[48] Jones studied the Hamlin route, evaluated its merits, and finally decided to revive the plan. Hamlin, he reasoned, would gain a near-by market and distribution center at Abilene;

47 S. F. Bond, as told to Jack Scott, publisher of the *Cross Plains Review* (May 24, 1968). Jones never revealed this secret to the public nor to the Abilene railroad committee. W. G. Swenson, a member of the committee, in an interview with the author, could not recall the incident. S. F. Bond, who still resides at Cross Plains, was a member of the Cross Plains delegation which asked for Jones's co-operation, and in his interview with Mr. Scott, clearly remembered every detail. The Texas Central, including the branch line from De Leon to Cross Plains, is now a part of the Gulf, Colorado and Santa Fe system.

48 *Abilene Daily Reporter* (May 25, 1909), 1. The Kansas City, Mexico and Orient railroad reached from Wichita, Kansas, to Alpine, Texas.

Anson would gain a connection to the Orient; and Abilene would project its business connections and influence in still another direction.

He first presented the new project to Hamlin and Anson citizens. On May 2, 1910, at two o'clock in the afternoon, the Jones County folk met Colonel Jones at Anson's opera house. The Colonel's proposal so excited his attentive audience that a "virtual revival meeting" resulted. They promised to "lay themselves upon the altar of sacrifice"[49] and thereupon pledged to raise a $45,000 bonus. Their enthusiasm mounted to excited frenzy as "two widow ladies who work for a living" each contributed $50. Johnny Purifoy, a small child, donated his entire bank account—five dollars—to the cause.[50]

Later, Jones returned to Abilene, presented his plan to the railroad committee, reported Jones County's wholehearted support, and offered to build the road. In exchange, he requested only a $20,000 bonus, due after he completed the project, and withdrawal of the railroad committee's suit against him. The committee promptly agreed to both requests and signed a contract subject to public approval. On June 20, 1910, J. M. Wagstaff, chairman of the committee, called a public meeting at the 25,000 Club's conference room.[51] Approximately fifty local citizens responded. Jones again presented his proposal and promised to complete the new road—an extension to the Abilene and Southern Railway Company—by October 15, 1911.

A large majority supported the plan, but two influential citizens vigorously opposed it. Mayor E. N. Kirby and Morgan Weaver, president of the 25,000 Club, spoke against all compromise measures and insisted that the committee should continue its suit against Jones. Other speakers arose to remind Kirby and Weaver that Jones had built every railroad into Abilene since the Texas and Pacific created the town. Jones, they continued, was the only man still willing to build more railroads into Abilene.[52] They con-

49 *Anson Reporter* (May 3, 1910), 1.
50 *Ibid.*
51 *Abilene Daily Reporter* (June 21, 1910), 1.
52 *Ibid.*

cluded that, since Colonel Jones was "a very wealthy man," since he had no "personal reason" to build another road, and since he asked for no bonus until he completed the project, those present should ratify the agreement. A standing vote showed that twenty-seven men supported Jones's proposal, seven supported the Kirby-Weaver objections, and approximately fifteen chose not to express an opinion.

Chairman Wagstaff decided not to proceed further until more Abilenians expressed themselves on the issue. The following day he wrote "An Open Letter to the Public" which the local editor placed in the center of the *Abilene Daily Reporter*'s front page. Wagstaff's letter explained that Jones's terms were "liberal towards Abilene," and that "this proposed road would give us a connection with the Orient Railway . . . and to any other point on the new line beyond Hamlin, if it should build beyond Hamlin."[53]

The next edition of the paper contained a long front page, double-spaced, editorial outlined by a heavy black border, and entitled "What is Abilene Going to Do?"

The Reporter is firmly converted to the conclusion that there has never been a period in the history of this city fraught with interest so vital to her future welfare as the matter upon which the citizenship must act within the next few days. . . .

Very few cities have been built without the assistance of railroads; usually it is the industries and enterprises which follow after the railroads as naturally as water flows down hill that materially assist in the making of a metropolis, but the great majority of these come in the trails blazed by railroads.

The promoter and proposed builder of the Abilene and Hamlin railroad is recognized as one of the most successful individual railroad builders in the South. His ability to foresee practical routes and construct feasible transportation structures has certainly been satisfactorily demonstrated right here in Abilene. If Mr. Jones is willing to put his money in a proposition which, with his extensive railroad knowledge, appears good, there is nothing for us, in our ignorance, to fear.

It is a fact that there is some truth in the contention of a few of our merchants that the building of additional railroads curtails their retail trade territory. But is it not better to lose this territory and gain a railroad, than to lose both railroad and territory?

53 *Ibid.*

195

Let's build more railroads, if for no other reason, because as they cut down the limits of the territory we have, they will bring inhabitants to the extensive unoccupied area right at our doors. . . .

Mr. Jones stands ready to demonstrate that a railroad from Abilene to Hamlin via Anson is a good proposition, giving all the emphasis that could be demanded, by putting up dollars against our cents, and *The Reporter* believes he knows what he is about. From Anson to Hamlin the road will permeate a rich and unoccupied territory and give this city a desirable connection with the Orient Road.[54]

The editorial accurately portrayed the significance of railroads to geographic regions without water transportation, Jones's railroad reputation and abilities, and the Hamlin extension's practical advantages to Abilene.

More than one hundred Abilene citizens responded to the editorial and to Wagstaff's letter. They convened at the courthouse on June 24, 1910.[55] Jones, meanwhile, left town to visit his Welsh and English relatives. His Fort Worth attorney, D. T. Bomar, represented him at the second public meeting. He reported that Jones was prepared to build a railroad from Abilene toward the northwest, and to pay damages incurred by his withdrawal from the Abilene and Central project. Bomar again asked the railroad committee to withdraw its suit against Jones. Since no one chose to discuss the matter further, Chairman Wagstaff requested another standing vote. Everyone present voted to drop the suit against the absent Welshman and to accept his offer to build a railroad to Hamlin. Before chairman Wagstaff adjourned the meeting, S. P. Hardwicke "rose to his feet laughing and said he was sure it was going to rain in a few days."[56]

Jones returned to Abilene toward the end of the summer, 1910, and kept his promise to complete the Abilene and Southern's northern extension to Hamlin by October 15, 1911—in time, he explained, to handle that season's crops. Soon after construction commenced, rumors circulated that Jones planned to extend the line beyond Hamlin. Called upon to deny or confirm the rumor,

54 *Ibid.* (June 22, 1910), 1.
55 *Ibid.* (June 25, 1910), 1.
56 *Ibid.*

196

Jones admitted that he had filed an amended charter with the Secretary of State at Austin to extend his road "to a number of points north and northwest."[57] He volunteered the information, also, that he had abandoned his old plan to build a branch line out of San Angelo.

Unknown to himself or to anyone else at the time, however, Jones would never build or extend another railroad. Despite his continued energies and interests, the Hamlin branch concluded his railroad construction career. Although West Texas sorely needed thousands of miles of additional railroad tracks, state and national legislators discouraged that industry. Increasingly the solons responded to public demands to fix railroad rates and to curtail the railroad companies' power to borrow money for new construction. Ironically, West Texans did not share the nation's anti-railroad attitudes. At a time when their region desperately needed to double its railroad mileage, West Texans fought vigorously against those whose policies discouraged new construction. Their sparse population could not afford to join the national trend toward surfaced highways for motor traffic. Only railroads could tie their isolated communities together.

It is not surprising, therefore, that a special delegation from West Texas traveled to the state capital to represent farmers and ranchers who demanded not more but fewer restrictions against railroad companies. An Abilene attorney, K. K. Legett, headed the group that arrived at Austin on January 28, 1911. For several days they mingled with legislators, pleaded with them to "let the railroads alone," and declared that Texas had "enough anti-railroad laws to serve a dozen states."[58]

One Texas railroad law, for example, that particularly restricted new construction, required that extensions and improvements to existing roads must be paid for with money earned by those roads. The result for the fiscal year that ended June 30, 1911, was that thirty-two of the largest railroad companies in Texas earned but 1.59 per cent on the value of these roads after im-

57 *Ibid.* (September 30, 1910), 1.
58 *Ibid.* (January 29, 1911), 6.

provement expenses were deducted.[59] Further analysis reveals that, after those thirty-two roads paid interest on outstanding bonds, their surplus totaled only $544,296.98 from a gross income of $103,822,873.63.[60] After those same roads spent $9,181,-193.03 to improve and extend their lines, they reported to the Texas Railroad Commission and the Interstate Commerce Commission a net deficit of $8,636,896.05.[61]

Under such conditions, no railroad builder, including Colonel Morgan Jones, dared to construct extensive railroads across that vast territory called West Texas. Texas, in 1911, had more railroad mileage than any other state in the nation—enough, in fact, to reach across continental United States five times. Its fifteen thousand railroad miles comprised one-fortieth of the world's total,[62] but the Lone Star State's railroad builders would ultimately add only two thousand miles more.[63] As the fabulous railroad construction era declined in Texas and across the nation, Colonel Jones gradually lost that driving desire to "get out on the line" with a construction gang. In 1911, as he approached his seventy-second birthday, he was still an energetic, alert businessman, who, while he listened to any reasonable offer to build, to improve, or to purchase a good railroad line, was broadening and diversifying his financial empire.

[59] State Tax Board, "Statistical Report," quoted in *Abilene Daily Reporter* (October 8, 1911), 11.
[60] *Ibid.*
[61] *Ibid.*
[62] *Texas Railroad Commission Report, 1913,* quoted in *Abilene Daily Reporter* (May 18, 1914), 6.
[63] *Texas Almanac, 1966–1967,* 493.

11. KNITTING TEXAS CLOSER TOGETHER

IT is not likely that Lyman Abbott, the American Congregation-alist clergyman and editor, knew Morgan Jones. It is even less probable that the Welshman read Abbott's literary works. Both men died in their eighty-sixth year after having witnessed America's phenomenal growth during the last half of the nineteenth century and the first quarter of the twentieth. If, in spite of their divergent interests, their paths had crossed, Abbott probably would have been the more impressed. Jones, the Welshman, personified as nearly as anyone else an American way of life which—the famous churchman and editor believed—explained America's greatness. Abbott wrote:

A nation is made great, not by its fruitful acres, but by the men who cultivate them; not by its mines, but by the men who work in them; not by its railways, but by the men who build and run them.[1]

Jones met these figurative specifications literally. He cultivated and owned fruitful acres in Wales and in the United States; he toiled in and owned Colorado mines; and, above all, he constructed and operated—with a singleness of purpose probably unparalleled in American history—many railroads, both large and small.

Morgan Jones came to the United States on the eve of the

[1] *Problems of Life,* quoted in Jacob M. Braude (ed.), *Speaker's Encyclopedia of Stories, Quotations, and Anecdotes,* 30.

nation's second railroad revolution, totally immersed himself in railroad construction, and finally emerged as the most successful individual builder in the leading railroad state. Others in Texas owned or operated more railroads, but Morgan Jones was "out on the line" during a longer period and over a greater distance than anyone else in the Lone Star State. His dedication to his work left no time or interest for marriage; it left no time to build or to own a home; it left no time for membership in civic organizations; it left no time even to learn to drive an automobile. He owned houses, which others made into homes; he owned buildings, which others managed; he owned farms, which others cultivated; he owned mines and ranches, which others operated; and he owned railroads —but railroads he built and operated himself.

When Texas railroad construction declined, as it inevitably did throughout the nation, Jones tried desperately to ignore the trend. He surveyed new routes incessantly; he sought encouragement— if not financial support—from his friends, and he fought stubbornly against everyone who tried to block his way. In his single, third-floor room at Abilene's Hotel Grace, he wrote voluminous letters to railroad committees in other towns, to railroad officials throughout the nation, and to his own close friends. Always, he wrote about railroad matters.

Morgan Jones moved in 1909 to the Hotel Grace, located at the corner of North First and Cypress streets, and selected a third-floor room on the hotel's west side. There he could observe every train's arrival and departure. The hotel, according to chauvinistic Abilenians, was "just as stylish, convenient, and comfortable as the Waldorf-Astoria," but its proximity to the railroad tracks was more important to the frugal Welshman.[2]

Whether or not Jones had another railroad construction project in mind, on the planning board, or in progress, he kept constantly in motion. Many of his business interests centered around the

[2] Whenever Jones left town, even for a single night, he packed his belongings in the same little "indestructible" trunk—his only real home since he had first arrived in America in 1866—and had it delivered to his Abilene and Southern offices across the street. It was an unnecessary waste, he insisted, to pay one dollar a night for an unoccupied room.

Dallas–Fort Worth area, but, since Abilene was nearer the "railroad frontier," he grew to look upon Abilene as his home town. His frequent arrivals and departures never failed to interest local newspaper reporters. Jones was, after all, the town's most renowned public figure. The reticent "Old Mahn" never provided "good copy" for a newspaper story. The frustrated reporters, nevertheless, considered it their duty to record Jones's activities even if they could not define them. Their news items, consequently, were brief and unrevealing, more of a log than a chronicle:

October 22, 1912:—Col. Morgan Jones went West last night.
October 29, 1912:—Col. Morgan Jones is back from a business trip East.
November 17, 1912:—Colonel Morgan Jones arrived in the city.
December 13, 1912:—President Morgan Jones of the Abilene and Southern returned to Abilene Wednesday morning after an absence of some time to state and out-of-state points, where he looked after his extensive interests.
January 10, 1913:—Col. Morgan Jones left Tuesday morning for a business trip to eastern points.[3]

The hapless newspapermen, unable to interview the busy man, obviously observed from a distance the direction in which the train pointed as Jones climbed aboard. Most often, the local celebrity's out-of-town trips concerned railroad matters.

As Jones completed the Abilene and Southern's northwestern branch to Hamlin, he sought to extend the line beyond that town. His thwarted attempts to build south from San Angelo, southeast from Ballinger, or southeast from Abilene left him no choice but to look north or west. In November, 1911, therefore, he left Abilene via the Wichita Valley railroad, transferred to the Fort Worth and Denver City line at Wichita Falls, and traveled on that road to Memphis, Hall County, in the Panhandle's southeastern corner. Memphis was approximately 150 miles north-northwest of Abilene. He rented an automobile, hired a driver, and, over dusty roads and wagon paths, Jones and his chauffeur scouted south and southwest through Hall, Briscoe, Floyd, and Motley counties. He dis-

3 *Abilene Daily Reporter* (1908–26), *passim.*

201

covered that the country south and east of the Panhandle's Cap Rock escarpment had richer soil and more water than the Llano Estacado (Staked Plains)[4] to the north. He thought that the four counties might develop, with proper cultivation and adequate railroad transportation, into a productive agricultural area.

The Colonel returned to Abilene and approached the same South Plains area from the south. His second reconnaissance disappointed and discouraged him. The area between Abilene and Briscoe, Floyd, and Motley counties, he decided, was too rugged and dry to cultivate. "I had in mind," he wrote to General Dodge, "an extension of the Abilene and Southern into that country, but there is 60 to 70 miles of country on which there is no business."[5] A line as small as the Abilene and Southern could not afford to cross such an unproductive region, although Jones was convinced that a major company would someday "occupy that country."

The indomitable railroad builder refused to believe that his construction days had ended. He considered next a less ambitious route. Southwest, from the Abilene and Southern railhead at Hamlin, lay a small community named Roby, in Fisher County. Roby residents wanted, like any other West Texas community, however small, a railroad within easy reach of some larger market. They were ready to pay a bonus for a railroad and asked Jones to consider their proposal. Jones reconnoitered the route between Hamlin and Roby, but had to tell the Fisher County folk that their town was "hemmed in" by larger companies. "I believe Roby would make a pretty fair little town if it had a railroad, but it is only six or seven miles from the Orient on one side and five miles from the Texas Central on the other,"[6] he explained to Dodge. "It hasn't got much territory and I do not believe it would pay to fool with it," he concluded.

It is not likely, moreover, that any other railroad builder in the state would have seriously considered the proposal. It was evident

---

[4] So called, according to most Texas historians, because there were so few trees on the Panhandle's High Plains that early travelers had to stake their horses at night.

[5] Morgan Jones Papers, Mrs. Percy Jones, *loc. cit.*, file 18, paper 118, Jones to Dodge (November 17, 1911).

[6] *Ibid.*, paper 120, Jones to Dodge (May 19, 1912).

to everyone but the seventy-two-year-old Welshman that the entire Abilene country was "hemmed in" by the Texas and Pacific, the Orient, the Santa Fe, and the Texas Central. To build another railroad, he needed to move into far West Texas, and, although he never admitted it, he was too old to blaze new trails. His only other railroad venture at that time was in the opposite geographical direction. Early in 1911 he purchased a one-half interest in the Texas Short Line Railway Company in East Texas.[7] He paid T. B. Meeks and W. P. Allen $50,000 for his share of the nine-and-one-half-mile road. The rails commenced at Grand Saline, in Van Zandt County, and ended at the near-by salt mines. Records indicate that Jones bought into the little company only to help his two old friends avoid bankruptcy.[8]

Since circumstances restricted Jones's railroad operations to the Abilene and Southern, his constant attention made the little company amazingly successful. Plentiful rains and increased settlement along the route augmented its normal prosperity. Heavy traffic on the Hamlin branch enabled him to pay, by April 1, 1912, all debts incurred during its construction. As early as May of that year, farmers expected to reap such abundant harvests, Jones reported to General Dodge, that the "road would have all it could do" to transport the crops to market.[9] Superintendent H. S. Phillips rushed the round-house and machine-shop construction so that all rolling stock could be used to handle the anticipated business.

The *Abilene Daily Reporter* proudly announced that "the Abilene country is just now coming into her own." Many local advantages attracted new settlers to the area, said the editor:

Northern homeseekers . . . happily found good land, a superb climate, excellent people, and a really great city. Satisfied and knowing the old conditions in the North, they dispatched letters teeming with Abilene facts to their friends, with the result that individual advertising did great work and brought splendid results in the upbuilding of the unadvertised Abilene country. . . . The fertile Abilene country will

7 *Ibid.*, "Memorandum of Agreement," file 1, paper 2 (January 21, 1911).
8 *Ibid.*
9 *Ibid.*, paper 120, Jones to Dodge (May 19, 1912).

immediately feel the great and natural results from the intensified farmings that only northern farmers really know.[10]

No one in the area believed more sincerely than the former Welsh farm boy that agriculture was a nation's backbone. Whenever he surveyed a new railroad route, he sought first to determine its agricultural potential; whenever he built a new road, he sought first to persuade farmers to settle along the route; and whenever farmers arrived, he sought first to encourage proper cultivation. When, on February 18, 1912, Colonel Henry Exall, president of the Industrial Congress and "the farmers' best friend in Texas," addressed the Abilene Chamber of Commerce (successor to the 25,000 Club) concerning improved farming methods, Jones contributed $1,000 to Exall's education program. The newspaper editor reported Jones's sizable gift and explained:

Colonel Jones has attended all the meetings of the state and government farm representatives and is imbued with the possibilities of this country if their educational campaign is carried out, especially as it effects [*sic*] this part of the state where agriculture is in its infancy.[11]

The editor understood, moreover, the relationship between the community's prosperity and the railroad's successful operation. He listed the Abilene and Southern's contributions to the diverse economic elements within the area: its "great interest in the agricultural development of the state"; its development of Winters as "one of the largest shipping points in the West for grain and cotton"; its assistance to local wholesale houses by "providing better shipping facilities"; its service to retail merchants in Abilene "by bringing to them new business from the surrounding territory."[12] Broad economic prosperity, the editor continued in a later issue, "made opportunities greater for other enterprises to locate"[13] in Abilene and the surrounding area. "Abilene," said the enthusiastic local promoter, "must remain not only the first on the [alphabetical] roll

---

10 (July 1, 1912), 4.
11 *Ibid.* (February 18, 1912), 2.
12 *Ibid.*, Anniversary Edition (June 28, 1914), Sec. 2, 2.
13 *Ibid.*

call of cities in Texas, but must advance first into all the fields of progress and development."[14]

The "Key City of West Texas" indeed faced a promising future. Its soil was fertile; smaller farms replaced early-day cattle ranches, and tenant farming was practically nonexistent. Farmers made cotton the staple crop, but many who regularly attended farm institutes applied new crop-rotation methods and planted thousands of acres of wheat, oats, milo maize, and alfalfa. Where rainfall was insufficient, many farmers irrigated their land from the shallow waters of the Clear Fork of the Brazos River. Other local settlers made Abilene country "one of the best poultry sections in the state" and shipped "eggs by the car loads" to eastern markets.

Agricultural prosperity and Abilene's excellent transportation facilities changed the "Key City's" frontier image within two decades. The *Abilene Daily Reporter* reviewed an earlier day when "pioneer settlers bought Navy Plug and squirted ambeer [*sic*] from their licorice quids while discussing Grover Cleveland . . . as they sat on rudely-carved box-board benches in front of the store building."[15] The newspaperman recalled the days when "groceries and dry goods were brought in prairie schooners from points to the east, over torturous roads of pristine roughness . . . and cheese that left the embarkation point with the fullness of the silvery moon, arrived in early Abilene much air-logged." Within twenty years, downtown Abilene had changed from "the little rickety, square-front, bench-flanked country stores to modern, attractive and show-windowed business houses, facing paved streets."[16]

Colonel Morgan Jones, having witnessed the same economic growth at Fort Worth during the 1880's and 1890's, watched Abilene develop during the first two decades of the twentieth century into west-central Texas' leading wholesale, retail, and distribution center. During the earlier period Jones invested substantially in various Fort Worth enterprises and, similarly, his West Texas investments equaled or surpassed those of any other investor. In May, 1911, for example, he purchased one-half of the stock in the

14 *Ibid.*
15 *Ibid.*, Sec. 3, 4.
16 *Ibid.*

Abilene Light and Water Company and the Abilene Gas Company.[17] During the next four years the wealthy Welshman purchased or established, usually with his old railroad friend W. G. Swenson, other public utility companies in Childress, Memphis, Haskell, Rule, Knox City, Munday, Goree, and Roby. At Haskell, Jones and Swenson installed the first intercity power line ever constructed in West Texas—a 6,600-volt power line from Haskell to Rule.[18]

While new farmers in west-central Texas turned increasingly to cotton production, Jones and Sidney Webb, of Mineral Wells, developed one of the largest cotton-milling industries in the state. Jones's investments in West Texas banking interests and his purchase of municipal bonds in area towns demonstrate his absolute faith that the Abilene country would prosper. He owned major shares of bank stock at Ballinger, Sweetwater, Abilene, Stamford, Winters, and Hamlin. He purchased municipal bonds for street improvements at Big Spring, Abilene, and Seymour. Thus the Colonel's interests and influence in the twentieth century expanded through West Texas as his late nineteenth-century interests and influence had spread through East Texas.

Concurrently, the Welsh bachelor's close family circle expanded and, as a consequence, tied him more firmly to his adopted state. In September, 1913, a third young nephew, Roland, joined his aging uncle and his two elder brothers in Abilene;[19] and, on Christmas Day, 1915, Percy married Miss Ruth Legett, a young

17 Morgan Jones Papers, Mrs. Percy Jones, *loc. cit.*, file 4, paper 33 (May 5, 1911). Jones paid $65,000 in cash and certain property in Seymour, Ballinger, and Iberis, for the Abilene businesses.

18 Interview with W. G. Swenson (November 9, 1967).

19 Interview with Roland Jones (November 8, 1967). Roland Jones was born at Fence Houses, Newcastle, Durham County, England, on April 19, 1895. Upon his arrival in Texas, his uncle employed him at the Abilene and Southern's Ballinger depot. At the outbreak of World War I in Europe, Roland returned to his native land and performed various military services. When the war ended, Colonel Jones wrote directly to Lloyd George, England's prime minister during the latter half of the war, asked for, and secured, Roland's release from military service. Roland returned to the United States and worked for his uncle at various positions in his Honey Island, Louisiana, lumber mills and at Weatherford, Texas. Roland Jones later married Christine Moore, daughter of a Van Alstyne physician. Mr. and Mrs. Jones now reside at the Circle 13 Ranch, Carrollton, Texas.

Abilene belle, former student at Virginia's Randolph Macon College, and a recent Simmons College graduate.[20]

Almost immediately following that festive occasion, however, Jones received a message from Council Bluffs, Iowa, that greatly distressed him: his closest friend and business associate for half a century, General Grenville M. Dodge, died at his Council Bluffs home on January 3, 1916. The bereaved old Welshman, unable to attend the funeral services, telegraphed the General's family: "[There is] nothing so sad to me as the loss of a true friend. The whole country has lost one of its greatest citizens."[21]

The General's death closed another chapter in Jones's railroad history. Although Dodge was in poor health several years prior to his death and although Jones needed neither advice nor financial assistance from his old friend, the loyal Welshman frequently wrote to the General, described his railroad activities, asked for the General's opinion's, and offered to sell part interest in any new construction project. Dodge's diminished wealth during his later years prevented large financial investments, but, to the end, he gave advice and offered suggestions whenever Jones requested them.

Jones's railroad interests never faltered in spite of his friend's death. His constant attention to Abilene and Southern matters continually improved the prosperous little company's services and profits. Its railroad tonnage in 1915 increased 100 per cent over that of the preceding year.[22] He read incessantly all available literature that concerned improved transportation techniques and vehicles. As more and more counties and cities voted bonds for hard-top highways and streets and as motor vehicles constantly improved their performances, Jones seriously considered "auto truck line" service to towns several miles removed from the Abilene and Southern. In April, 1915, he went to Winters, checked dis-

20 *Abilene Daily Reporter* (December 26, 1915), 1. Miss Legett was the daughter of retired Judge K. K. Legett, who led the West Texas delegation to the state capital to plead for less restrictive railroad legislation. His daughter's wedding to Percy Jones was performed at 602 Meander Street, the family home.

21 Dodge Papers, *loc. cit.*, XXII, 767, Jones to Mrs. R. M. Montgomery (January 4, 1916).

22 *Abilene Daily Reporter* (December 16, 1915), 7.

tances from that town to Crews, Norton, Wilmeth, Wingate, and Hylton, and explained his plan to interested settlers. Truck lines, rather than railroad branch lines, Jones explained, could make Winters a new type of railhead and distribution center. The *Winters Enterprise*, always willing to support a Morgan Jones promotion, presented the plan to its readers, but, its editor cautioned, "before this is realized, some work must needs be done on our roads."[23]

World War I forced Colonel Jones into almost virtual retirement and kept him closer to his Abilene nephews and their families. On December 28, 1917, the federal government, as a wartime emergency measure, took control of the nation's railroads. On June 15, 1918, therefore, it transferred Abilene and Southern's headquarters to the Fort Worth and Denver City offices at Fort Worth. The government located the company's machine shops at the Wichita Valley's Stamford repair station, and moved the Abilene freight and passenger center to the local Texas and Pacific depot.

Temporarily relieved of his railroad responsibilities, Morgan Jones vigorously promoted war bond drives. He freely purchased Liberty Loan subscriptions and challenged other area men to follow his example. On June 13, 1917, he purchased, for example, a $25,000 subscription and asked specifically that C. M. Largent, of Merkel, subscribe to a similar amount.[24] Abilene and Southern employees also followed his lead and pledged $21,000 to the war effort. Their pledge surpassed more than tenfold that of any other Abilene business firm.

The federal government returned the Abilene and Southern to Jones's control late in 1919 and, on March 1, 1920, the eighty-year-old railroad president moved the company headquarters back to its original Abilene location. Business was brisk even before the transfer as Abilene's railroad traffic totaled more than 26,000,000 pounds of freight in the month of November, 1919. Jones placed

---

23 *Winters Enterprise* (April 29, 1915), 1. Jones never established the auto truck service. Local failure to improve the roads before World War I, and wartime shortage of necessary equipment, probably forced Jones to abandon these plans.

24 *Abilene Daily Reporter* (June 14, 1917), 1. C. M. Largent was one of the first major west Texas ranchers to become interested in registry of Hereford cattle to upgrade the quality of range cattle.

an additional daily freight train on the Ballinger line, and a few weeks later Abilene's record-breaking freight traffic necessitated an extra train on the Hamlin branch. Soon the Abilene and Southern's administrative procedures returned to their prewar routine, and, although the "Old Mahn" spent much of each day at his office, Percy and Morgan C. assumed most of the responsibilities.

After the war, the elderly Welshman's wartime civic interests continued as he found fewer and fewer reasons to travel about the country.[25] He joined other Abilene businessmen who sought to make those improvements to the city that were neglected during the war. In 1920 he was a major investor in Abilene's street railway system. In 1922, when the city lacked funds to complete three new public school buildings, he loaned school superintendent R. D. Green $25,000 to complete the projects, stipulating that the city need not repay the loan until it received its promised school-building allocation from the State Department of Education. The following year, when Abilene's city fathers expressed a desire to build a new city hall on three vacant downtown lots, Jones, who owned two of the lots, agreed to sell. He required no money down, reduced the interest rate to 5 per cent (the other property holder asked 7 per cent), and allowed the city thirty years in which to pay.

Jones was a legendary figure during his own lifetime. Many local stories about Abilene's wealthiest citizen concerned his personal thriftiness. Some of them undoubtedly were true, since the old Welshman abhorred extravagance in any form. Jones's private secretary, W. E. Kaufman, liked to tell the following story: At the turn of the century, most restaurants offered two standard dinners,

25 Jones retired from the Fort Worth and Denver City Board of Directors at its annual meeting in Fort Worth on May 12, 1921. (FW & DC file A5–47, "Minutes of the Annual Meeting.") At the meeting the Directors unanimously adopted the following resolution:

"BE IT RESOLVED, That the members of the Board of Directors of the Fort Worth and Denver City Railway Company regret greatly that other business obligations of Mr. Morgan Jones have made necessary his resignation as a Director of this Company; they acknowledge gratefully his wise and valued counsel as such Director during the long period of Mr. Jones' business relations with this Company, beginning with the original building of the railroad, in which he took so important a part, including the time he was the President of the Company, as well as the Receiver of its property by court appointment, his acts in these capacities and all transactions were uniformly faithful to the best interest of the Company, they reflected a broad and sound business judgment and at all times conformed to the highest principles of integrity."

209

the fifty-cent plate and the one-dollar plate. When the two men traveled together, the Welshman always insisted that the only difference in the two dinners was the price. He liked to compare his own fifty-cent plate to the dollar plate at the next table. Unknown to Jones, however, Kaufman had for many years instructed the waitresses, prior to Jones's arrival, to serve the more expensive plate, which Kaufman paid for in advance. On another occasion, at the Hotel Grace, Jones complained to Kaufman that a certain waitress always ignored his request for dry toast. Upon investigation Kaufman discovered that the waitress, who did not know Jones, spread butter on his toasted bread because she "felt sorry for that poor man." Many other railroad employees delighted to tell about the times they shared their sack lunch with the "Old Mahn" because "he didn't bring enough to eat."

Records prove, however, that Jones secretly helped many worthy individuals. A typical example, one that was repeated in various ways many times over, related to Mrs. L. L. Gore, a Seymour widow. Mrs. Gore owned a farm near Seymour, but Jones owned the mineral rights. When the widow tried to sell her land so that she could send her son and a niece to college, she discovered that no one was willing to purchase the farm without mineral rights. Mrs. Gore wrote to Colonel Jones, whom she had never met, explained her problem, asked him to release his mineral rights, and promised to pay the Colonel's share after the sale.[26] Jones in turn wrote to his friend G. S. Plants, president of Seymour's First National Bank, to verify Mrs. Gore's story. Plants assured him that the widow's account was accurate. Jones thereupon sent Mrs. Gore a deed to the mineral rights, requested a one-dollar token payment, and praised her loyalty and concern for her "boy and girl."[27] On many other occasions Jones loaned money to personal friends who later were unable to repay him according to the original agreements. Whenever the debtors convinced Jones that their difficulties were unavoidable, he instructed his attorneys to extend the notes.[28]

26 Morgan Jones Papers, Mrs. Percy Jones, *loc. cit.*, file 4, paper 43–A, B (February 16, 1926).

27 *Ibid.*, paper 43–D (February 28, 1926).

210

While Jones's interests centered increasingly around Anson affairs, his interest in railroading never diminished. He kept informed on all railroad transportation innovations and adopted those that might improve the Abilene and Southern's service. During Abilene's postwar railroad boom, passenger traffic increased to such an extent that many passengers had to stand during their journey. After one brief trip to Winters, Jones returned to Abilene determined to relieve the crowded conditions. In 1923, therefore, he purchased a Brill No. 55 gasoline motor car. It was a single passenger coach, forty-five feet long, and included a nine-foot baggage and mail compartment. The new car was "modern throughout," with electric lights, leather upholstery, steel roller bearings, air brakes, and hot water heat. It accommodated forty-six passengers and was West Texas' first "interurban train."[29] Jones added the car to the Abilene and Southern's regular service between Abilene and Ballinger on November 1, 1923. On the initial run, Percy Jones escorted a small party of Abilene guests, and other guests boarded the new car at Winters and Ovalo. Despite a driving rainstorm throughout the journey, the gasoline motor car averaged twenty-five miles an hour and completed the trip in two and one-half hours. The proud host reminded his guests that the regular trains required four hours to travel the same distance.

Early in the 1920's, Jones seriously considered an opportunity to re-enter the railroad business on a large scale. The directors of the debt-ridden Kansas City, Mexico and Orient Railway Company offered to sell the controlling stock in the company.[30] At that time, the Orient's rails originated at Wichita and ended at Fort Stockton in deep southwest Texas. It revived, of course, the Colonel's old dream of building a railroad to Topolobampo on Mexico's Pacific Coast. The Orient's original owners planned to build the road to the same coastal area, but construction ended at Fort Stockton when the company exhausted its resources and subsequently went bankrupt. Jones liked to emphasize the fact, however,

[28] Interview with Walter W. Ford, Abilene, Texas (July 24, 1967).
[29] *Abilene Daily Reporter* (July 25, 1923), 1.
[30] Interview with W. G. Swenson (November 9, 1967); interview with Roland Jones (November 8, 1967); Crozier, *Dallas News*, 8.

211

that Kansas City was nearer the Pacific Coast via Topolobampo than San Francisco. He believed that the incomplete Orient line was still a wise investment, and he presented his plan to his old Abilene friend, W. G. Swenson. Jones offered to supply the money if Swenson would accept the company presidency. Swenson, a much younger man, tried to discourage the eighty-three-year-old railroad adventurer, but the old man persisted and added, jokingly, that he wanted to "keep the boys [his nephews] busy and give them something to worry about after I am dead."[31] Jones, with his nephew Roland, inspected the line's Texas section, carefully checked the roadbed and rails, examined every depot, and talked with the Orient railroad employees. Throughout the tour he revealed no indication of his impressions, but immediately upon his arrival at Fort Stockton, he announced his decision not to buy into the company: "I'm pretty old as far as years go and I am already a busy man," he declared. "I'm too busy to tackle that proposition."[32]

Typically, the Colonel emphasized his work rather than his age. Although he was in his eighty-third year, he remained in vigorous health. He was at that time president of the Abilene and Southern, and continued to serve as a director of the Continental Bank and Trust Company at Fort Worth, the Dallas Oil and Refining Company at Dallas, and the Memphis Cotton Oil Company at Memphis, Texas. He still walked briskly, spoke quickly, and "jabbed repeatedly with a pencil on a newspaper"[33] as he issued directives or attempted to clarify a point.

Early in 1924, however, he painfully injured his wrist and suffered multiple bruises when he fell down a flight of steps. On the morning of January 12, he was at his Weatherford Ice Company offices awaiting a train to Abilene. The train arrived early and, as the old Colonel rushed to leave the second-floor office, he fell. Despite his injuries he walked a quarter of a mile to the depot and boarded the train. A month later he fell ill with a severe cold and was confined for ten days to his room at the Hotel Grace. Concurrently, he suffered severe rheumatic attacks. During his con-

31 Interview with Roland Jones (November 8, 1967).
32 Crozier, *Dallas News*, 8.
33 *Ibid.*

valescence he took daily "needle baths" and relatively strenuous physical exercises,[34] but by midsummer he was still too feeble to leave Abilene. Reluctantly, he wrote the Roserio Mining and Milling Company's secretary at Fort Worth that he could not attend the annual stockholders' meeting. "I am not able to walk much," he admitted.[35]

When he recovered sufficiently to leave the hotel, he seemed more determined than ever to attend to his duties at the Abilene and Southern offices. He could not walk unaided, but each morning at nine o'clock his secretary or one of his nephews helped him to an automobile and drove him to his office. He remained there until noon, returned to the hotel, ate lunch, rested until three o'clock, and then returned to his office until dusk. On Sundays he inspected his other Abilene properties or rode "into the country." He particularly liked to ride out to the little railroad towns—such as Ovalo and Tuscola—which, he liked to say, were his "Abilene and Southern babies."[36] Both little Jim Ned Valley communities, he noted proudly, had doubled their populations every year since they were created. He was especially pleased when he saw a brick building under construction, and, when he learned that Ovalo had a First State Bank, he was sure that the town would never die.[37]

The "Old Mahn" gradually weakened during the winter of 1925–26, but late in January he insisted upon going to a business meeting at Dallas—much against his nephews' wishes. Shortly after his arrival at the Dallas station, he collapsed.[38] Upon his return to Abilene he spent most of his time at his nephews' homes and accompanied them each morning to the Abilene and Southern offices. In early April, Colonel Jones was delighted to learn that his old friend Henry Walters was in Fort Worth and planned to visit him in Abilene.

On Friday, April 9, 1926, however, the old Welshman collapsed at his desk. His nephew Percy took him to his home, where a local

34 Morgan Jones Papers, Mrs. Percy Jones, *loc. cit.*, file 4, paper 26.
35 *Ibid.*, paper 46, Jones to Myra Peacock (July 11, 1924).
36 *Abilene Daily Reporter* (November 16, 1924), 10.
37 *Ibid.*
38 *Fort Worth Record-Telegram* (April 12, 1926), 1.

213

physician and a nurse remained constantly at his bedside. At 7:45, on the following Sunday morning, April 11, Colonel Morgan Jones lapsed into a coma and died. He was eighty-six years old.

The Reverend Willis P. Gerhart, rector of the Church of the Heavenly Rest, Episcopal, which the Colonel attended, conducted the simple funeral rites at the Percy Jones home at three o'clock in the afternoon on Monday, April 12, 1926. A special Texas and Pacific train took railroad men and other business associates to the private service. Among the group were Henry Walters; J. L. Lancaster, president of the Texas and Pacific Railway Company; and F. E. Clarity, vice-president of the Fort Worth and Denver City Railway Company.[39]

Just three years prior to his death and only a few months before his health began to fail, Morgan Jones granted his first and final formal interview to the press. A reporter, Harry Benge Crozier, who represented the *Dallas News*, requested the interview, and Jones promptly invited the young newspaperman to his Abilene office. The Colonel's unexpected readiness to talk about his life surprised the reporter.[40] Incredible as it seemed, Crozier was convinced that Jones had arranged the meeting, possibly through the *Dallas News* publisher. This was a Jones characteristic which was unknown to the newsman: "He seemed to make sudden, lightning-quick decisions. Not so. He considered important problems for a long time. Once he made a decision, however, he acted incredibly swiftly."

One is justified in assuming, therefore, that Jones, in his eighty-third year and for the first time in his long life, reflected upon his multifarious experiences, gradually developed an awareness of his influence upon Texas' railroad history, and finally decided to

---

39 Pallbearers were W. G. Swenson, J. H. Shackelford, Henry James, Lee Signor, C. G. Whitten, and Charles Motz, Jr., all Abilene friends and business associates.

Honorary pallbearers were Henry Walters, K. M. Van Zandt, J. G. Wilkinson, F. E. Clarity, George Boggs, William Bomar, R. E. Hardin, E. H. Holcomb, K. K. Legett, Ed S. Hughes, H. O. Wooten, J. M. Radford, J. M. Wagstaff, John Guitar, Frank Kell, Sam Bellah, Sidney Webb, F. N. Foxhall, J. S. LeClercq, and George N. Aldredge.

In addition to his three Texas nephews, Colonel Jones was survived by a brother, Thomas Charles Jones; a niece, Mrs. Edith Longstaff, and two other nephews, Edward Jones and Charles H. Jones, all of Durham County, England.

40 Interview with Harry Benge Crozier, Austin, Texas (July 17, 1967).

214

record his personal recollections. Unlike his friend General Dodge, who preserved every letter, kept copious diaries, and wrote lengthy reports about every event in which he participated, Jones's private papers survived him probably through negligence and certainly not by design. His secretary, W. E. Kaufman, kept and preserved the "Old Mahn's" business records and correspondence, and his nephew Percy faithfully collected and stored his personal belongings. There is no evidence whatever that Jones considered any of these things worth a historian's research.

His characteristic modesty is the most obvious revelation in the Crozier article that appeared in the *Dallas News* on March 25, 1923. "Getting the right man to help is the biggest secret of business success," he said. He explained that the two "cardinal tenets" in his railroad builder's creed were: "I never got left; [and] I avoided quarrels and lawsuits." Throughout the interview Jones made no attempt to exaggerate or to glamorize his role in Texas railroading. He never mentioned the fact that Texas had more railroad mileage than any other state in the nation, nor did he appear aware that he had constructed or supervised, as an individual, more railroad lines than any other person.

The Welshman's railroads, nevertheless, helped to populate and to develop broad expanses of the sprawling Lone Star State where, without deep rivers or navigable streams, humanity could not otherwise permanently exist. The Texas cattle industry, for example, seemed destined to extinction until railroad transportation enabled Texas cattlemen to improve their stock and to abandon their dependence upon the Longhorn—the only brand of cattle able to withstand the long drive to northern railheads. Concurrently, as the quality of Texas cattle improved to supply a more selective market, the railroad industry helped to develop the vast interior of the state into one of the most productive and prosperous agricultural regions in the nation.

Morgan Jones played a prominent role in opening millions of acres of Texas soil to the farmer. From southeast Texas to the far corner of the Panhandle, and from northeast Texas to west-central Texas, he helped to construct the Southern Transcontinental (predecessor to the Southern Pacific), the Texas and Pacific, the Gulf, Colorado and Santa Fe, and the Fort Worth and Denver City. When the trans-Texas lines successfully tied together the state's divergent economic interests, Jones's branch lines tied together at strategic points these major railroads. As a consequence, Fort Worth, Dallas, Wichita Falls, Amarillo, and Abilene developed into the most significant distribution centers in their regions.

The Welsh railroad builder's unerring ability to select potentially prosperous areas in which to build feeder lines won respect and admiration throughout the Southwest. The Wichita Falls and Oklahoma, the Wichita Valley, the Abilene and Northern, and the Abilene and Southern railroads attracted farmers into areas that could never have proved their agricultural potential. The little "Morgan Jones roads" always prospered, and their prosperity symbolized the thriving farm and ranch lands they served.

There were other factors that played important roles in the Lone Star State's extensive development in wealth and population, but the railroads undoubtedly were the prime and moving cause. Contemporary writers gave scant praise to Morgan Jones's significant contributions to Texas' economic growth during his lifetime —indeed, he would not have spared the time to read it. But at his death, newspaper editors throughout the state paid homage to his contribution to Texas economic development. The *Dallas Morning News* headlined its front-page announcement of the prominent Texan's demise: "Morgan Jones, Denver Road Builder, Dies."[41] The following issue, on April 13, presented a three-column pictorial sketch centered on page one. The artist drew a single gravestone inscribed: "Morgan Jones, Empire Builder." Propped against the gravestone, a wreath bore a ribboned inscription from the donor: "The Southwest."[42] There was no other comment or identification mark on page one or the following pages. On April 14, however, the *Dallas Morning News* memorialized the deceased railroad builder in a lengthy editorial:

. . . Colonel Jones was a man of faith, since he saw fruitful fields and peopled towns where others saw only semi-arid plains. . . .

[41] (April 12, 1926), 1. [42] *Ibid.* (April 13, 1926), 1.

216

He was reckoned a rich man, among the wealthiest in this section of the nation. But he became so by opening up the unsuspected bounties of the land to those that were his neighbors of a later day. Vision and energy and diligence piled up provision for his own wants and more. But first of all they were bent upon the task of knitting Texas closer together and making it a better, happier, more prosperous place in which to live.[43]

Another noted American, Luther Burbank, died on April 11, 1926. Reports of the famed horticulturalist's death shared Texas newspapers' front pages with those about Morgan Jones. On April 14, the *Fort Worth Record-Telegram* honored in a single editorial the two men:

... In widely divergent fields of activity those two men contributed much to the happiness and welfare of peoples and communities. Their efforts made dollars for thousands of people and gave them homes, foodstuffs and fragrance of the blossom. Each in his line was directly responsible for concrete prosperity and contentment.
One was a builder of railroads. He gave North and West Texas the one thing necessary to make it an empire of homes. . . . Fort Worth and West Texas will never be able to estimate its obligation to Morgan Jones, the man who erected the framework for that which has been named the most prosperous and energetic collection of farming communities and towns in the world. With it all, men who knew him through most of his many years say he was a just man and an honest one. . . . The nation gives tribute to Luther Burbank, the botanical genius. . . . As variant as were their fields of endeavor the same finale may be written for both of them. They gave civilization much more than they kept for themselves.[44]

Although it was said that Morgan Jones was better known on Wall Street than in his own home town,[45] West Texans respected and honored the old Welshman who came to live among them during most of his final eighteen years. It was they who realized in 1926 even more acutely than East Texans that Morgan Jones's railroading genius was "one of the greatest factors in the upbuilding of a semi-desert."[46] The *Abilene Daily Reporter's* editor, less

43 *Ibid.* (April 14, 1926), 6.
44 Page 4.
45 Crozier, *Dallas News*, 8.
46 *Abilene Daily Reporter* (April 12, 1926), 3.

philosophical than his counterparts in Dallas and Fort Worth, nevertheless went straight to the practical point of the "Old Mahn's" greatest gift to West Texas pioneers:

Of the thousands who toiled and wrought in the building of Texas railroads, none achieved greater things than Morgan Jones. . . .

He built more than a thousand miles of Texas railway lines. He built the Fort Worth and Denver throughout its length [*sic*],[47] and served as its first [*sic*][48] president. He built long stretches of the Texas and Pacific. He built the Santa Fe from Saginaw, Texas, to Purcell, Oklahoma. He built the Wichita Valley from Abilene to Seymour [*sic*].[49] He built the Abilene and Southern.

In between times, Morgan Jones found silver and coal mines, engaged in the timber industry, in banking, in street railway construction, in public utility operation.

If ever anyone deserved the title of "empire builder" that man was Morgan Jones.

Over a span of more than sixty years, he was in the midst of the huge task of breaking trails into the virgin frontier country.[50]

Morgan Jones's greatest achievement—the one that made him a national figure—was his successful attempt to unite "the orange groves of Texas" to the "snow-clad peaks of Colorado." Many years later, the Gulf-to-Rockies system's official historian readily agreed that the Welshman's administrative leadership over the Fort Worth and Denver City "played a vital and distinguished role in its development. His superb financial management and rugged independence had a great deal to do with putting the railroad on a firm basis."[51]

Railroad administration, nevertheless, was not Jones's greatest pleasure. He liked to *build* railroads, and he seemed totally content only when he was "out on the line." When, in 1950, Fort Worth and Denver City officials asked G. K. Harrington—the last surviving member of that company's original construction crew—to

---

[47] Jones did not supervise the Fort Worth and Denver City's construction between Fort Worth and Wichita Falls.

[48] J. M. Eddy served briefly as the first FW & DC president.

[49] Jones built the Wichita Valley throughout its length, from Abilene to Wichita Falls.

[50] *Abilene Daily Reporter* (April 12, 1926), 4.

[51] Morgan Jones Papers, Mrs. Percy Jones, *loc. cit.*, file 9, paper 15, R. C. Overton to Roland Jones (October 27, 1952).

write the history of the Denver road as he remembered it, Harrington protested that he was "unworthy."[52] "Morgan Jones would have been the one to write that history," the old railroader explained. Colonel Morgan Jones, whose name rarely appeared in print, who never allowed his picture to appear in any newspaper, and who, until his eighty-third year, never reflected upon his role in history, would have refused to accept the assignment.

[52] FW & DC file, A5–47, G. K. Harrington to Robert L. Hoyt (January 20, 1950).

BIBLIOGRAPHY

I. *Unpublished Materials*

1. Private Collections

Abilene and Southern Railway Company. Papers. Mrs. Percy Jones, First National Ely Building, Abilene, Texas.

Cureton, William E. Papers. Sarah Hardy, 1730 South 12th Street, Abilene, Texas.

Fort Worth and Denver City Railway Company. Papers. Executive Department, Fort Worth Club Building, Fort Worth, Texas.

Frost, C. L. Papers. Mrs. Robert Roy Duncan, 1022 South Lake Street, Fort Worth, Texas.

Jones, Morgan. Papers. Mrs. Percy Jones, First National Ely Building, Abilene, Texas.

———. Papers. Mrs. Morgan Jones, Jr., 3435 South 9th Street, Abilene, Texas.

———. Papers. Roland Jones, Circle 13 Ranch, Carrollton, Texas.

Jones, Thomas Charles. Papers. Mrs. Curry Longstaff, "Little Court," 173 Old Woking Road, Pyrford, Surrey County, England.

Texas and Pacific Railway Company. Papers. 505 North Industrial Boulevard, Dallas, Texas.

2. Public Depositories

Dodge, Grenville M. Letters. Western History Department, Denver Public Library, Denver, Colorado.

———. Papers. Iowa State Department of History and Archives, Des Moines, Iowa.

Railroad Pamphlet Files. Library, State Historical Society of Colorado, State Museum Building, Denver, Colorado.

Taylor County Records. Plat Book No. 1, Taylor County Court House, Abilene, Texas.

3. Railroad Reports and Records

Abilene and Southern Railway Company. Charter. 1909.

Colorado and Southern Railway Company. Annual Report. 1906.

Fort Worth and Denver City Railway Company. Act to Incorporate. 1873.

———. Annual Reports 1882–99.

———. Charter and By-Laws. 1873, 1881.

———. Record Book. 1898.

Texas and Colorado Railway Improvement Company. Record Book. 1885.

Texas and Pacific Railway Company. Annual Reports. 1873–77.

Union Pacific Railway Company. Annual Reports. 1890–93.

4. Public Records: Vital Statistics

Great Britain. Certified Copy of an Entry of Birth. CF 759622. No. 225. Registration District of Newtown, Sub-district of Tregynon, County of Montgomery, Wales.

United States. Statement of Citizenship. Letter from John P. Creveling, prothonotary of Lehigh County, Allentown, Pennsylvania. January 2, 1968.

5. Interviews

Bond, S. F. Cross Plains Railroad Committee. Cross Plains, Texas. May 24, 1968.

Crozier, Harry Benge. Long News Service. Austin, Texas. July 17, 1967.

Duff, Katharyn. Assistant editor, *The Abilene Reporter-News*. Abilene, Texas. June 10, 1967.

Ford, Walter W. Percy Jones Estate. Abilene, Texas. July 24, 1967.

Gerhart, Willis P. Rector (ret.), Church of the Heavenly Rest, Episcopal. Abilene, Texas. July 25, 1967.

Jones, Grant. Abilene, Texas. November 7, 1967.

Jones, Mrs. Morgan, Sr. Abilene, Texas. November 28, 1967.

Jones, Morgan, Jr. Abilene, Texas. November 7, 1967.

Jones, Mrs. Morgan, Jr. Abilene, Texas. November 7, 1967.

Jones, Mrs. Percy. Abilene, Texas. July 11, 1967; April 30, 1968.

Jones, Roland. Carrollton, Texas. November 8, 1967.

Malone, R. A. Texas and Pacific Railway Company. Dallas, Texas. November 8, 1967.

Morris, C. Lee. Fort Worth and Denver City Railway Company. Fort Worth, Texas. October 23, 1967.

Newman, Vernie E. Professor of history, McMurry College. Abilene, Texas. September 27, 1967.

Pope, Walter S. Attorney at law (ret.). Abilene, Texas. May 31, 1968.

Richardson, Rupert N. Professor of history, Hardin-Simmons University. Abilene, Texas. June 13, 1967.

Swenson, W. G. Abilene 25,000 Club. Abilene, Texas. November 9, 1967.

6. Personal Reminiscences

Each reference below is located in the Fort Worth and Denver City Files. Executive Department, Fort Worth Club Building, Fort Worth, Texas.

Baker, Inez. "The History of the Fort Worth and Denver City Railway in My Home County (Hall)."

Britton, Mrs. W. T. "Wichita Valley Rail Road."

Cates, Cliff. "History of the Fort Worth and Denver City Railway in My Home County."

Cottar, Mrs. A. W. "A Bit of Reminiscence in the Story of the Ft. Worth and Denver R.R."

Garlington, Lillie Belle. "History of the Fort Worth and Denver City Railway in Montague County."

Gerner, Robert. "History of the Fort Worth and Denver City Railroad in Donley County."

Green, Lola Beth. "History of the Fort Worth and Denver City Railway in My Home County."

Hambright, B. T. "History of the Fort Worth and Denver City Railway in My Home County."

Harvey, ———. "History of the Fort Worth and Denver City in My Home County."

222

Henderson, Jeff S. "History of the Fort Worth and Denver City Railway in My Home County."

Hoyt, Robert L. "Summary History of the Fort Worth and Denver City Railway Company."

Lanning, Bea. "The History of the Fort Worth and Denver City Railway in My Home County (Carson County, Texas)."

McCarty, John L. "Background History of the Fort Worth and Denver City Railway."

McCluney, Mrs. Eugene. "History of Fort Worth and Denver City Railway in My Home County."

Mosier, W. M. "History of the Fort Worth and Denver City Railway in My Home County."

Offutt, Betty Illane. "The History of the Fort Worth and Denver City Railway in My Home County."

Philley, Gracie May. "Wichita Valley Railway in My Home County."

Plants, Mrs. George S. "History of the Wichita Valley Railway in My Home County."

Posey, Mrs. Aubrey. "The History of the Fort Worth and Denver City Railway in My Home County."

7. Dissertations and Theses

Jones, J. Paul. "The History of Hardeman County, Texas." Unpublished master's thesis, North Texas State College, 1949.

Kelsey, Harry E., Jr. "John Evans." Unpublished doctoral dissertation, University of Denver, 1965.

Lowe, Ida Marie Williams. "The Role of the Railroads in the Settlement of the Texas Panhandle." Unpublished master's thesis, West Texas State College, 1962.

Pope, Billy N. "The Freighter and Railroader in the Economic Pattern of Panhandle History." Unpublished master's thesis, West Texas State College, 1956.

Reeves, LeRoy. "The History of Childress County." Unpublished master's thesis, West Texas State College, 1951.

II. *Published Materials*

1. Books

Association of American Railroads. "A Chronology of American Railroads," *Railway Information Series*. Washington, D.C., Association of American Railroads, 1951.

223

Billington, Ray Allen. *The Westward Movement in the United States.* New York, D. Van Nostrand Co., Inc., 1959.

Braude, Jacob M. (ed.). *Speaker's Encyclopedia of Stories, Quotations, and Anecdotes.* Englewood Cliffs, New Jersey, Prentice-Hall, 1955.

Buck, Solon. *The Granger Movement.* Cambridge, Harvard University Press, 1913.

Collections of the Archive and History Department of the Texas State Library: Governors' Messages: Coke to Ross, 1874–1891. Austin, Texas State Library, 1916.

Cosby, Hugh E. (ed.). *History of Abilene.* Abilene, Texas, Cosby Publishing Company, 1955.

Cox, James. *Historical and Biographical Record of the Cattle Industry and the Cattlemen of Texas and Adjacent Territory.* St. Louis, Woodward and Tiernan Printing Co., 1895.

Daniels, Winthrop M. *American Railroads: Four Phases of Their History.* Princeton, Princeton University Press, 1932.

Farber, James. *Fort Worth in the Civil War.* Belton, Texas, Peter Hansbrough Bell Press, 1960.

Farrington, S. Kip, Jr. *Railroading from the Head End.* Garden City, New Jersey, Doubleday, Doran and Co., Inc., 1943.

Foster, L. L. (Commissioner). *First Annual Report of the Department of Agriculture, Insurance, Statistics, and History, 1887–1888.* Austin, Texas, State Printing Office, 1889.

Fulmore, Z. T. *The History and Geography of Texas as Told in County Names.* Austin, Texas, E. L. Steck Co., 1915.

Hafen, LeRoy R. *Western America: The Exploration, Settlement, and Development of the Region Beyond the Mississippi.* 2d ed. New York, Prentice-Hall, Inc., 1950.

Haley, J. Evetts. *Charles Goodnight: Cowman and Plainsman.* Norman, University of Oklahoma Press, 1949.

Hirshson, Stanley P. *Grenville M. Dodge: Soldier, Politician, Railroad Pioneer.* Bloomington, Indiana University Press, 1967.

Hogg, James Stephen. *Addresses and State Papers of James Stephen Hogg.* Ed. by Robert C. Cotner. Austin, University of Texas Press, 1951.

Holbrook, Stewart Hall. *The Story of American Railroads.* New York, Crown Publishers, 1947.

Holden, William Curry. *Alkali Trails, or Social and Economic Move-*

ments of the Texas Frontier: 1846–1900. Dallas, The Southwest Press, 1930.

Jackson, Clyde L., and Grace Jackson. *Quanah Parker: Last Chief of the Comanches*. New York, Exposition Press, 1963.

Johnson, Frank W., and Eugene C. Barker. *A History of Texas and Texans*. Chicago, The American Historical Society, 1914.

Knight, Oliver. *Fort Worth: Outpost on the Trinity*. Norman, University of Oklahoma Press, 1953.

Leadville Directory. Leadville, Colorado, Corbett, Hoye and Co., 1880.

McCarty, John L. *Maverick Town: The Story of Old Tascosa*. Norman, University of Oklahoma Press, 1946.

McKay, Seth Shepard. *Seven Decades of the Texas Constitution of 1876*. [N.p., n.d.].

McKitrick, Reuben. *The Public Land System of Texas, 1823–1910*. Bulletin of the University of Wisconsin, No. 905. *Economics and Political Science Series*, Vol. IX, No. 1, 1918.

McMechen, Edgar Carlisle. *Life of Governor Evans: Second Territorial Governor of Colorado*. Denver, Wahlgreen Publishing Co., 1924.

Moody, John. *The Railroad Builders: A Chronicle of the Welding of the States*. Vol. XXXVIII of *The Chronicles of America Series*, ed. by Allen Johnson. New Haven, Yale University Press, 1919.

Morgan, Jonnie R. *The History of Wichita Falls*. Wichita Falls, by the author, 1931.

Overton, Richard C. *Gulf to Rockies: The Heritage of the Fort Worth and Denver–Colorado and Southern Railways, 1861–1898*. Austin, University of Texas Press, 1953.

————. *Milepost 100: The Story of the Development of the Burlington Lines, 1849–1949*. Chicago, 1949.

Paddock, B. B. (ed.). *History of Texas*. Vol. II: *Fort Worth and the Texas Northwest*. Chicago, The Lewis Publishing Company, 1922.

Perkins, Jacob Randolph. *Trails, Rails and War: The Life of General G. M. Dodge*. Indianapolis, The Bobbs-Merrill Company, 1929.

Pollock, Norman. *The Populist Response to Industrial America: Midwestern Populist Thought*. New York, W. W. Norton and Co., Inc., 1962.

Poor's Manual of Railroads, 1868–1924. New York, H. V. and H. W. Poor, 1868–1924.

Potts, Frances E., and John W. Lewis. *The New Geography of Texas*. Dallas, Noble and Noble, Publishers, Inc., 1963.

Reed, St. Clair Griffin. *A History of the Texas Railroads and of Transportation Conditions Under Spain and Mexico and the Republic and the State.* Houston, The St. Clair Publishing Company, 1941.

Richardson, Rupert Norval. *The Frontier of Northwest Texas, 1846 to 1876.* Glendale, California, The Arthur H. Clark Co., 1963.

———. *Texas: The Lone Star State.* 2d ed. rev. Englewood Cliffs, New Jersey, Prentice-Hall, Inc., 1958.

Riegel, Robert Edgar. *The Story of the Western Railroads.* New York, The Macmillan Co., 1926.

———, and Robert G. Athearn. *America Moves West.* 4th ed. rev. Chicago, Holt, Rinehart and Winston, Inc., 1964.

Rister, Carl Coke. *The Southwestern Frontier.* Cleveland, The Arthur H. Clark Co., 1928.

Shores, J. B. *From Ox-Teams to Eagles: A History of the Texas and Pacific Railway.* [N.p., n.d.].

Spratt, John S. *The Road to Spindletop: Economic Change in Texas, 1875–1901.* Dallas, Southern Methodist University Press, 1955.

Starr, John W. *One Hundred Years of American Railroading.* New York, Dodd, Mead and Co., 1928.

Taylor, Virginia H. *The Franco-Texan Land Company.* Austin, University of Texas Press, 1969.

Texas Almanac for 1871. Galveston, Richardson, Belo and Co., 1871.

Texas Almanac for 1872. Galveston, Richardson, Belo and Co., 1872.

Texas Rural Almanac for 1873. Galveston, Richardson, Belo and Co., 1873.

Texas Rural Almanac and Immigrants' Hand Book for 1876. Houston, Burke and Vasmer, 1876.

Texas Almanac and State Industrial Guide for 1904. Galveston, Clarke and Courts, 1904.

Texas Almanac and State Industrial Guide for 1910. Galveston, A. H. Belo Corporation, 1910.

Texas Almanac and State Industrial Guide for 1966–1967. Anniversary edition. Dallas, A. H. Belo Corporation, 1965.

Ubbelohde, Carl. *A Colorado History.* Boulder, Colorado, Pruett Press, Inc., 1965.

Wallace, Ernest. *Texas in Turmoil, 1849–1875.* Vol. IV in *The Saga of Texas Series,* ed. by Seymour V. Conner. Austin, Texas, Steck-Vaughn Company, 1965.

Warner, H. T., *et al. Texans and Their State.* Houston, The Texas Biographical Association, 1918.

Webb, Walter Prescott. *The Great Plains.* Dallas, Texas, Ginn and Company, 1931.

————, and H. Bailey Carroll (eds.). *The Handbook of Texas.* 2 vols. Austin, The Texas State Historical Association, 1952.

Wilkinson, T. A. *The Panhandle Route.* Denver, By the author [1888?].

Wilson, James. *Agricultural Resources of the Texas Pan Handle.* Denver, By the author, 1888.

Winther, Oscar Osburn. *The Transportation Frontier, Trans-Mississippi West: 1865–1890.* Vol. V of *Histories of the American Frontier,* ed. by Ray Allen Billington. Chicago, Holt, Rinehart and Winston, 1964.

Woodlock, Thomas F. *The Anatomy of a Railroad Report and Ton-Mile Cost.* New York, S. A. Nelson, 1900.

Wright, John A. *A Paper on the Character and Promise of the Country on the Southern Border.* Philadelphia, Review Printing House, 1876.

2. Periodicals

Briscoe, P. "The First Texas Railroad," *The Quarterly of The Texas State Historical Association,* Vol. VII (April, 1904), 279–85.

Brookes, N. N. "Pen Pictures of the Pan-Handle Route," *Official Time-Table and Gazetteer,* Vol. I (December, 1888), 1–33.

Burton, Harley True. "History of the JA Ranch," *The Southwestern Historical Quarterly,* Vol. XXI (April, 1928), 327–54.

Chalk, Sam L. "Early Experiences in the Abilene Country," *West Texas Historical Association Year Book,* Vol. IV (June, 1928), 93–99.

Churchill, Frances M. "Notes on the Native Grasslands of West Central Texas Since 1854," *West Texas Historical Association Year Book,* Vol. XXXI (October, 1955), 54–64.

Cotten, J. B. "Securing Land from the State in West Texas," *West Texas Historical Association Year Book,* Vol. XXXV (October, 1959), 125–31.

Crane, R. C. "The Claims of West Texas to Recognition by Historians," *West Texas Historical Association Year Book,* Vol. XII (July, 1936), 11–33.

————. "Ghost Towns of West Texas," *West Texas Historical Association Year Book*, Vol. XVII (October, 1941), 3–10.

————. "The Press in the Development of West Texas," *West Texas Historical Association Year Book*, Vol. XXIV (October, 1948), 64–70.

————. "Railroads and Community Rivalries; Chapters from the Inside Story of the Orient and Santa Fe in West Texas," *West Texas Historical Association Year Book*, Vol. XIX (October, 1943), 3–35.

————. "When West Texas Was in the Making," *West Texas Historical Association Year Book*, Vol. XXIII (October, 1947), 46–61.

Douthit, Ellis. "Some Experiences of a West Texas Lawyer," *West Texas Historical Association Year Book*, Vol. XVIII (October, 1942), 33–46.

Duncan, John Thomas. "The Settlement of Hall County," *West Texas Historical Association Year Book*, Vol. XVIII (October, 1942), 72–76.

Dunn, Roy Sylvan. "Drought in West Texas, 1890–1894," *West Texas Historical Association Year Book*, Vol. XXXVII (October, 1961), 121–36.

"Early Settlement of Northeast Texas," *Frontier Times*, Vol. V (November, 1927), 1–57.

Ewing, Floyd E., Jr. "Copper Mining in West Texas: Early Interest and Development," *West Texas Historical Association Year Book*, Vol. XXX (October, 1954), 17–29.

Ferrell, Mrs. C. C. "Early Days in Stamford," *West Texas Historical Association Year Book*, Vol. III (June, 1927), 41–42.

"Fort Worth, 1849–1949," *Fort Worth Chamber of Commerce Magazine*, Vol. XXIII (June, 1949), 1–25.

"Fort Worth, July 19, 1876," *Fort Worth Chamber of Commerce Magazine*, Vol. XXIII (July, 1949), 1–8.

Gould, John. "City Got Its Long Pants in 1882," *Wichita Falls Chamber of Commerce Magazine* (Winter, 1951).

Grimes, Frank. "Pioneers Laid to Rest," *West Texas Historical Association Year Book*, Vol. II (June, 1926), 85–90.

Hammond, C. M. "How the Railroads Peopled Texas," *Frontier Times*, Vol. X (October, 1932), 378–81.

Harper, Carl. "Building the Santa Fe Railroad Through the South Plains," *West Texas Historical Association Year Book*, Vol. XI (November, 1935), 73–92.

Holden, W. C. "Immigration and Settlement in West Texas," *West Texas Historical Association Year Book*, Vol. V (June, 1929), 66–86.

Holt, R. D. "The Introduction of Barbed Wire into Texas and the Fence Cutting War," *West Texas Historical Association Year Book*, Vol. VI (June, 1930), 65–79.

Hutto, John R. "Pioneering of the Texas and Pacific," *West Texas Historical Association Year Book*, Vol. XII (July, 1936), 124–33.

Kincaid, Naomi. "The Founding of Abilene, the 'Future Great' of the Texas and Pacific Railway," *West Texas Historical Association Year Book*, Vol. XXII (October, 1946), 15–26.

Landers, Emmett M. "From Range Cattle to Blooded Stock Farming in the Abilene Country," *West Texas Historical Association Year Book*, Vol. IX (October, 1933), 69–81.

"Livestock and Agriculture in the Fort Worth Area," *Fort Worth Chamber of Commerce Magazine*, Vol. XXII (September, 1948), 1–14.

McAllister, S. B. "Building the Texas and Pacific Railroad West of Fort Worth," *West Texas Historical Association Year Book*, Vol. IV (June, 1928), 50–57.

McCall, Kenneth. "Railroad Nurtured West Texas Growth," *West Texas Today*, Vol. XXXII (July, 1951), 5.

McKay, S. S. "Economic Conditions in Texas in the 1870s," *West Texas Historical Association Year Book*, Vol. XV (October, 1939), 81–127.

———. "Social Conditions in Texas in the Eighteen Seventies," *West Texas Historical Association Year Book*, Vol. XIV (October, 1938), 32–51.

Mauldin, W. D. "The Coming of Agriculture to Dallam County," *West Texas Historical Association Year Book*, Vol. XIII (October, 1937), 105–11.

Pearce, William M. "The Establishment and Early Development of the Matador Ranch, 1882–1890," *West Texas Historical Association Year Book*, Vol. XXVII (October, 1951), 3–31.

Potts, Charles S. "Railroad Transportation in Texas," *Bulletin of the University of Texas*, No. 119 of the Humanistic Series, No. 7 (1909), 1–207.

Scarborough, Jewel Davis. "Taylor County and Its Name," *West*

Texas Historical Association Year Book, Vol. XXX (October, 1954), 73–82.

Sherrill, R. E. "Early Days in Haskell County," *West Texas Historical Association Year Book*, Vol. III (June, 1927), 20–29.

Smith, Ruby L. "Early Development of Wilbarger County," *West Texas Historical Association Year Book*, Vol. XIV (October, 1938), 52–71.

3. Newspapers

Abilene (Texas) *Daily Reporter*, 1905–26.
Abilene (Texas) *Morning Reporter*, 1919.
Abilene (Texas) *Reporter-News*, 1949–65.
Abilene (Texas) *Weekly Reporter*, 1918.
Albany (Texas) *News* [n.d.].
Amarillo (Texas) *Globe-News* [n.d.].
Anson (Texas) *Reporter*, 1910.
Ballinger (Texas) *Ledger*, 1908.
Buffalo Gap (Texas) *News* [n.d.].
Childress (Texas) *Index*, 1949.
Clarendon (Texas) *News*, 1935.
Corpus Christi (Texas) *Caller*, 1888.
Dalhart (Texas) *Texan* (Jubilee Edition), 1951.
Dallas (Texas) *Commercial*, 1875.
Dallas (Texas) *News*, 1923–36.
Denver (Colorado) *Republican*, 1888.
Donley (Texas) *County Leader*, 1936.
Fort Worth (Texas) *Democrat*, 1873–76.
Fort Worth (Texas) *Gazette*, 1883–90.
Fort Worth (Texas) *Mail*, 1888.
Fort Worth (Texas) *Press,* 1949.
Fort Worth (Texas) *Record*, 1926.
Fort Worth (Texas) *Record-Telegram*, 1912.
Fort Worth (Texas) *Star*, 1906.
Fort Worth (Texas) *Star-Telegram*, 1931.
Fort Worth (Texas) *Weekly Gazette*, 1888.
Gainesville (Texas) *News*, 1888.
Haskell (Texas) *Free Press*, 1905.
Houston (Texas) *Age* [n.d.].
New Orleans (Louisiana) *Item*, 1888.

New York (New York) *Tribune*, 1872.

Pueblo (Colorado) *Chieftain*, 1954.

Rocky Mountain News (Denver, Colorado), 1874–88.

San Angelo (Texas) *Standard*, 1909.

Seymour (Texas) *Banner*, 1905.

Tascosa (Texas) *Pioneer*, 1887.

Vernon (Texas) *Daily Record*, 1949.

Vernon (Texas) *Times*, 1951.

Weatherford (Texas) *Herald*, 1909.

Wichita (Wichita Falls, Texas) *Daily Times*, 1947.

Wichita Falls (Texas) *Record News*, 1950.

Winters (Texas) *Enterprise*, 1908–15.

INDEX

232

237